OXFORD HISTORY OF
MODERN EUROPE

General Editors
ALAN BULLOCK *and* F. W. D. DEAKIN

Oxford History of Modern Europe

THE STRUGGLE FOR MASTERY
IN EUROPE 1845–1918

By A. J. P. TAYLOR

SPAIN 1808–1939

By RAYMOND CARR

THE RUSSIAN EMPIRE 1801–1917

By HUGH SETON-WATSON

FRANCE

1848 — 1945

BY

THEODORE ZELDIN

DEAN AND SENIOR TUTOR OF
ST. ANTONY'S COLLEGE
OXFORD

Volume One

AMBITION, LOVE AND
POLITICS

OXFORD
AT THE CLARENDON PRESS
1973

Oxford University Press, Ely House, London W.1

GLASGOW NEW YORK TORONTO MELBOURNE WELLINGTON
CAPE TOWN IBADAN NAIROBI DAR ES SALAAM LUSAKA ADDIS ABABA
DELHI BOMBAY CALCUTTA MADRAS KARACHI LAHORE DACCA
KUALA LUMPUR SINGAPORE HONG KONG TOKYO

ISBN 0 19 822104 5

© *Oxford University Press 1973*

*Printed in Great Britain
at the University Press, Oxford
by Vivian Ridler
Printer to the University*

CONTENTS

LISTS OF MAPS AND FIGURES   vi

ACKNOWLEDGEMENTS   vii

INTRODUCTION   1

PART I

1. The Pretensions of the Bourgeoisie   11
2. Doctors   23
3. Notaries   43
4. The Rich   53
5. Industrialists   63
6. Bankers   77
7. The Ambitions of Ordinary Men   87
8. Bureaucrats   113
9. Peasants   131
10. Workers   198

PART II

11. Marriage and Morals   285
12. Children   315
13. Women   343

PART III

14. The Place of Politics in Life   365
15. Kings and Aristocrats   393
16. The Genius in Politics   428
17. Republicanism   467
18. Bonapartism   504
19. The Politicians of the Third Republic   570
20. Opportunism   605
21. Solidarism   640
22. Radicalism   683
23. Socialism   725

INDEX   789

LIST OF MAPS

1. The Contrast of Village and Isolated Peasants (1950s)   137
2. Tenants and Sharecroppers in 1892   161
3. The Growth of Industry, 1906–1931   211
4. 'The Mountain' in the Election of 1849   367
5. The Right in 1885   368
6. The Right in 1936   369
7. The Canton of Talmont (Vendée)   370
8. Chouannerie in Sarthe   375
9. Votes for 'the Mountain': Sarthe 1849   375
10. Election of 1956: Sarthe   375
11. Sarthe Property, 1909–1912   375
12. Rural Weavers in Sarthe   375
13. Noble Mayors in the 1950s   411

LIST OF FIGURES

1. Agricultural Production, 1815–1938   182
2. Wheat Productivity   182
3. Social Composition of the Municipal Councils of Bordeaux, 1871–1935   621

ACKNOWLEDGEMENTS

I N the eighteen years during which I have been doing research on this period of French history, I have received assistance from so many people that I cannot hope to acknowledge it all in a brief note. St. Antony's College has provided me with an almost ideal atmosphere and exceptional facilities for my work: my debt to my colleagues in it is incalculable. Christ Church has been extremely kind to me in many ways. A large number of friends and colleagues in Britain, France and the U.S.A. have given me help. I am no less grateful to them because I cannot list them all; but I should particularly like to mention Dr. John Campbell, Mr. Raymond Carr, Professor James Joll, Dr. Angus Macintyre and Miss Deirdre Wilson. My footnotes indicate all too briefly how much I owe to the work of other historians. I should like to thank also Miss Anne Abley, librarian of St. Antony's College, Mr. Giles Barber, librarian of the Taylor Institution, the staff of the British Museum, the Bibliothèque Nationale, the Widener Library, the Bodleian Library, the Musée Social, the French Archives in Paris and the departments, and many smaller libraries mentioned in the notes, Miss Deanne Nickalls, who typed my manuscript, and Miss Rose Barugh, who helped with the proof-reading and the making of the index. I owe a great deal to the kindness of my parents and my brother Dr. David Zeldin. Finally, I should like to add my thanks to the editors of this series and its publishers.

INTRODUCTION

ACCORDING to a public opinion poll, the French think of themselves as being, above all else, intelligent. All nations—as the same poll, carried further on an international scale, revealed—also consider themselves to be intelligent, but France was the country which placed intelligence highest, as the virtue it admired most. One of the aims of this book is to investigate this image, to assess the place that intelligence, or reason, or ideas have in French life, to explain how intellectuals came to be held in such exceptionally high esteem, and to show the consequences this has had. I hope this may serve to throw some light on the question of how the French differed from other nations in this period. But I believe the role of the intellectuals is something that particularly needs to be studied in France, as a basis for getting beyond the confusing and interminable conflicts of which its history seems to be composed. For not only have the intellectuals played a leading part in these conflicts, but they have also interpreted and labelled them in such a way as to influence all subsequent thought about them. It was they who formulated the issues which they claimed divided the country and defined the principles which were at stake. Their generalisations became accepted truths, to the extent that they shaped events, for new controversies were fitted into categories they had devised. They have bequeathed to historians a framework into which the events of the past can be conveniently slotted, but this inherited framework is not necessarily the only one that can be used. The reasons why it was evolved need to be examined more closely, and there seems to be room, at any rate, for another perspective.

Modern French history is usually interpreted in one of two ways. The more traditional approach is to show it as the unfolding of a struggle between revolution and reaction. In this view, France appears as fundamentally torn politically, religiously and ideologically. Instability, violence and unrelenting polemic are the result. An alternative approach is to regard these struggles as the superficial covering of social divisions and to show that power was concentrated, despite the victory of democracy, in the bourgeoisie, or even in a small section of it, composed of no more than a few hundred families. The triumph of this class is seen as the outcome of the Revolution and subsequent history consists in its efforts to consolidate its hold and in attempts by the masses to overthrow it. Both these interpretations involve stress, above all, on the factors which divided Frenchmen. In the former case, it is principles that are studied, and the different political ideas the country produced are judged to be crucial in explaining what happened. In the latter case, the inequalities of economic privilege, and their social consequences, are brought out to reveal the incompleteness of the Revolution and to show how far its principles were from being implemented in practice. A history which studies these conflicts can portray the past as some people of the time saw it. But it seems useful to ask also whether partisanship and prejudice did not distort the vision these people had, whether their parties were as disagreed as their leaders claimed, whether the reformers, while damning the past, did not silently cling to other parts of their heritage, and whether the animosities between social classes were as total as they sometimes appeared. The common beliefs, attitudes and values of Frenchmen, which often cut across ideological and class lines, are difficult to formulate, because little was said about them in the turmoil of political strife, but unspoken assumptions need to be taken into account if the divisions are to be seen in perspective, and if their limits and significance are to be assessed. It is helpful to know not only what Frenchmen quarrelled about, but also what place their quarrels had in their lives, beside those aspects of their existence on which they were agreed. The family is one example of a common institution which was largely unquestioned and which may have lain at the root of certain forms of behaviour which have been considered peculiarly French. At the same time, tensions within the family were probably as divisive as any political disagreements. This is a subject about which comparatively little has been written and on which new light is badly needed. My own contribution to it here must be regarded as tentative and exploratory. There seems to be scope for further investigation of the more permanent features of French society, to counterbalance the study of events, change, develop-

ment, movements and fashions which have attracted rather
more attention.[1]

I do not mean by this that I am seeking to define the immut-
able French soul, mind or character. But this is something
many people talked about and I have tried to investigate why
they came to believe that there was such a thing. The forces
that lay behind the attempt to create it deserve study. To understand it, however, one must first get away from the nationalist
perspective, which still unconsciously dominates much writing:
one should not unquestioningly assume that France was one
nation in this period, simply because the French Revolution
proclaimed it to be so. French history is too often told from the
point of view of the country's rulers and their preoccupation
with their own power. France in this period was composed of
a large variety of groups which had lives of their own. I have
tried to describe the problems, ambitions, feuds and frustrations of some of these. They form an important part of this book.

It is true there was a strong movement to master this variety
and to render it uniform. This created a struggle which was in
many ways more fundamental than the better-known debates
about monarchy and republic. Centralisation survived the
Revolution as is well known, but so too did the resistance to it,
which was far more vigorous than is often realised. The
struggle was not only political, but also intellectual, cultural
and social. One needs to examine not only the activities of the
state in order to understand it, but also the spread of myths
surrounding the state and the development of attitudes towards
it. The makers of the myths—the intellectuals—deserve special
attention, as much as the politicians.

It is customary nowadays to begin a history book with a preface of apology for its defects. This is not the result of modesty,
and it is no mere convention. Historical writing is in a state of
difficulty and uncertainty. History used to occupy a high place
in the hierarchy of the moral sciences. Revolutionary youth
used to flock enthusiastically to attend historical lectures, which
were sometimes landmarks in national agitation. Historical

---

[1] This stress on *change* can be seen in the titles of some of the standard works in
this period: *The Development of Modern France* by Sir Denis Brogan (1940); *L'Évolution de la troisième république* (1921) by Charles Seignobos; *Gloires et tragédies de la
troisième république* by Maurice Baumont (1956).

study was a part of political life. This is no longer so. Though still cultivated by some as a 'liberal education', history, following philosophy, has become largely an intellectual exercise or—when it is readable—even just an entertainment. It is the social sciences which have taken over its task of offering broad generalisations and universal explanations. Historians on the whole no longer claim to impart great truths of wide application, or to be on the point of discovering them. Even the lively small groups pioneering new approaches or tapping new sources have strictly limited expectations.

This situation is perhaps the inevitable result of the ever-growing ambition of the subject. There is no aspect of life which it does not attempt to investigate. The movement to extend its scope is not a new one. Voltaire, Macaulay and Michelet, for example, all in turn protested against the concentration on kings and parliaments. But the movement is today still something of a crusade, which shows how difficult it has been to achieve its aims. Inadequate sources hold up progress, new interests push back the horizon into an ever greater distance. The variety of human activity cannot be compressed into a single volume, and no individual can comprehend its totality. No one writing a general history can hope to attain the goal he sets himself.

However, there are now more historians than there have ever been before; but paradoxically this has made it even more difficult for anyone to form a full picture of the past. There is now too much to be read. In order to write a general history of France from 1848 to 1945, one should presumably be acquainted with the books published in those years. I calculate that there are about one million of them (roughly 10,000 appearing each year). If one reads one book every day, for ten years, one can sample only 3,650, and it would be an arbitrary sample. But there are also periodicals and newspapers, of which at least 2,000 were in existence in 1865, nearly 8,000 in 1938, and 15,000 in the 1950s. The manuscript material, distributed between national, provincial, ecclesiastical, business and private archives, is, despite the ravages of time and neglect, even more bulky. In addition to what the age itself produced, one needs to read what modern historians have written about it. The Annual Bibliography of the History of France lists 9,246 books and

articles as having been published in 1970 alone. A count made
in 1969 revealed that there were 1,380 doctoral theses being
written in French universities on history since 1789; 640 of them
were about France. This says nothing of the considerably more
numerous masters' theses, nor of the research in progress on
French history in the universities of other countries. As higher
education expands, their output is assuming alarming proportions. The number of doctorates in history awarded by the
universities of the U.S.A. increased fourfold in the twenty
years after 1945. No historian, however, can confine himself
to reading simply about his own period or country; nor can he
neglect new ideas being put forth in cognate subjects like
sociology, economics, psychology, political science, literature,
and their bibliography, in several languages, is even more
daunting. No one can ever feel fully qualified or ready to write
a general book.[1]

Research is being conducted in an increasingly thorough
way but on ever narrower subjects. This specialisation is
creating barriers of incomprehension between the different
branches of history. New techniques, for example in economic
history and historical demography, which are in some respects
becoming branches of mathematics, demand a completely
different training. This kind of detailed research, and these new
methods, often yield highly original results, but the problem
of communicating them is becoming difficult. The confusion
is exacerbated by the fact that historical research seldom
follows straight lines, with accumulative effects, towards clear
objectives, as, say, in medicine it is possible to aim at curing a
particular disease. The interests of every generation shift the
focus and grand projects peter out inconclusively. New discoveries enter the textbooks very slowly, and are usually fitted
into a traditional framework somehow, rather than radically
altering it. It is very difficult for an individual to obtain an
independent perspective over a really broad expanse of history.
So old generalisations survive tenaciously even though the
specialists have shown them to be false.

These are some of the reasons why historians apologise, as I

[1] List of French theses in progress, compiled by Professor J. B. Duroselle (unpublished, typewritten 1969); Boyd C. Shafer, *Historical Study in the West* (New
York, 1968), 204.

do. But it seems to me that there is also another side to these difficulties. History today is more vigorous, ingenious and skilful than it has ever been. The vast new mass of material available calls not for despair but for a new approach, different from that which seemed suitable when historians expected to have in their own libraries all the books they proposed to consider. Lord Acton, lecturing on the French Revolution, said that 'in a few years, all will be known that ever can be known'. He was mistaken, and history now appears as a subject in which the full truth will never be known. The attempt to make history a science was highly fruitful, but the benefits can be retained without making this nineteenth-century ideal a shackle. Natural scientists have in any case abandoned the illusions about methodology which that ideal contained. History can continue to learn from the natural and social sciences, but it does not increase its prestige by claiming to be a branch of whatever is currently most fashionable.

It has attractions and virtues of its own. It can turn its handicaps to good account. In an age of increasing specialisation, it remains, despite its own internal difficulties, the least limited of subjects. There is no aspect of life it cannot study. It produces no final synthesis, but it does allow its students to make their own. It leaves the fullest scope for each individual to develop it in his own way. The contributors to Acton's *Cambridge Modern History* were required to make sure that no one should know where one had laid down his pen and another had taken it up. This was acceptable when it was believed that the truth was there to be discovered and summarised, but it is no longer so. Historians admit that, however scrupulous they are, their selection of the facts and their use of them are coloured by their own personality. What they see in the past is partly the result of their particular kind of eyesight, of the education and upbringing they have had, and of their personal interests and prejudices. Except in certain statistical problems, it is unlikely that any two people will see quite the same thing, or express what they see in the same way. History is a subject which requires them to use all the resources of their individuality, imagination and sympathy in the appreciation of character and events. To urge them to repress themselves into faceless and mechanical anonymity is to make their task impossible. Technical competence is something they can acquire quite easily, but, unlike some scientists who apparently do their best work straight away in their twenties, historians benefit from wider experience and human qualities. One of their aims in being historians is indeed to broaden their contact with the world, however vicariously.

Historical study is a personal experience, and the subjective elements in it deserve to be valued, when so many other branches of knowledge are becoming largely technical. To admit that historians solve their problems of colour and light, that they create their compositions for reasons which are ultimately subjective, because these seem to them to be coherent and true, is not to admit a fault, but to assert that each individual historian can express himself in his work. Of course, the more careful and controlled his detail, the more likely he is to be convincing, but, since he uses literary style as his medium, he has the opportunity not only to prove a point, but to evoke the atmosphere of an age—to reconstitute it with a meaning and character which contemporaries might not have seen. Far from preaching that this or that brand of history—social, ideological, or statistical—is the right one, which all young men anxious to move with the times should pursue, I believe that the extremely varied way in which history is studied is the very source of its strength and will be of its continued popularity.

But I do not regard history as designed simply to give pleasure or to satisfy antiquarian curiosity. It is capable of being more than art or gossip. It is not a luxury, but an essential part of the constant process of re-assessment that every generation makes of itself, of the constant debate about what is worth keeping of the past and what is not. Detachment from present concerns is not in my view a necessary preliminary to the writing of 'scholarly' history. On the contrary, I believe historians can make a contribution to clearer thinking about present ideals, habits and institutions, in which the inherited element is always large.

I have, therefore, not written a chronological history of events, of which there are already several able ones. My method has been, rather, analytical, in the sense that I have tried to disentangle the different elements and aspects of French life, and to study each independently and in its inter-relationships.

I hope that in this way the generalisations traditionally made about France will as it were come loose, that it will be possible to see how they were invented, and by whom, and what they represent and what they conceal. My emphasis has been on understanding values, ambitions, human relationships and the forces which influenced thinking. This particular approach means I have left a lot out: my book has no pretensions to being comprehensive.

Volume two will look at the history of psychology and of fashions in behaviour to see how the individual and his emotional problems were viewed and how they were dealt with at different periods. It will examine the history of the provinces, to discover how far independent cultures survived the influence of Paris—which will help to clarify the significance of that influence. It will analyse relations with other countries, including the colonies, not from the point of view of diplomacy or governments,[1] but asking what Frenchmen knew about foreigners, how they treated them and how they evolved their sense of national identity in the process. I shall study the role of intellectuals, men of letters, teachers, the clergy and the army, analyse the influence they exerted and the kinds of outlook they propagated. I shall then try to show how these different forces interacted in the crisis which the First World War produced, how new solutions were unsuccessfully sought in the years that followed and how Vichy emerged as the tragic denouement of this civilisation. A general conclusion will summarise the argument of the book, in the light of the new perspectives created by developments since 1945. The footnotes are designed to indicate some of my sources; a fuller bibliography will be placed at the end of volume two.[2]

[1] This is studied in other volumes in this series; A. J. P. Taylor's *Struggle for Mastery in Europe 1848–1918* (Oxford 1954) has already been published.

[2] In the notes, place of publication is London for books in English and Paris for books in French, unless otherwise indicated. French money may be converted into British currency, up to 1914, at the rate of twenty-five francs to the pound: one franc equalled a little less than one shilling. After 1914 the exchange rate fluctuated between 40 and 70 francs 1919–23, collapsing in 1925 and 1926 to 87–245, steady at around 123 from 1927 to 1930, up to 80–90 in 1931–3, and 70–75 in 1935, then down to 74–106 in 1936, 105–52 in 1937 and 174–7 in 1939.

Part I

1. The Pretensions of the Bourgeoisie

THE bourgeois is a central figure in every modern history. In France more than anywhere else, because aristocracy and monarchy were defeated in the great Revolution, the bourgeois appeared manifestly supreme for a century and a half after it, to the extent that the two words have been combined into a single idea: *la France bourgeoise*. It is argued that it was in this period that the bourgeois attained self-confidence, ceased to aspire to enter the old hierarchy, and sought rather to replace it. He developed his own moral and economic doctrine and formed an original class with a spiritual unity.[1] At the same time he became an object of attack, satire and animosity, far more concerted than ever before. The Age of the Bourgeoisie is the setting in which the history of these years is usually placed. The notion has bred a large number of generalisations. The first stage in any study of France must be a clarification of its meaning and an assessment of its value as an instrument of explanation.

There are two ways of understanding the phrase *la France bourgeoise*. It means first of all the domination of bourgeois attitudes of mind. In this definition, the rise of the bourgeoisie can be traced, from the sixteenth century or earlier, not from the point of view of political or economic power, but in terms of the development of rules of conduct and ways of thought which gradually won increasing acceptance, in opposition to the ideals vaunted by the monarchy, the aristocracy and the Church. In this view what distinguished France after the Revolution was the prevalence of the bourgeois mentality, not just among the rich, but equally among artisans, shopkeepers and even peasants. The longevity of bourgeois domination—that

---

[1] Charles Morazé, *La France bourgeoise* (1946), 65. See also Régine Pernoud, *Histoire de la bourgeoisie en France* (1960–2); Elinor G. Barber, *The Bourgeoisie in 18th Century France* (Princeton, N.J., 1955); B. Groethüysen, *Les Origines de l'esprit bourgeois en France* (1927).

is to say, the rule of those who exemplified, practised or advocated bourgeois virtues most successfully—is explained by the masses' adhesion to and approval of those virtues. There were hard-fought struggles for success, but these disputes did not involve fundamental differences, and that is why regimes succeeded each other without transforming the structure of society. Only when the very rich tried to copy the old aristocracy and ceased to be the common man's ideal, did they meet with opposition and resistance. An attempt will be made here to define the bourgeoisie's values, to investigate how far these formed the basis of a consensus which held France together, and to analyse more closely the whole notion of consensus.

The second meaning of *la France bourgeoise* involves political analysis and economic determinism. After the monarchical and aristocratic *ancien régime*, it is argued, the Revolution gave political power to the bourgeoisie. The Declaration of the Rights of Man was only a pretence of democracy and equality. Though the seigneurial privileges were abolished, those of money were not. The bourgeoisie took the place of the aristocracy. They bought the confiscated national lands. They filled the parliamentary assemblies, even when universal suffrage nominally gave sovereignty to the masses. The equality of opportunity they preached was false since only the well-to-do could afford secondary education, which was the key to success. They devoted much of their energy to fighting the Church, which they claimed was imprisoning the people in mysticism and superstition, but there were those who said that this was only a way of consolidating their own leadership and distracting the masses from their social grievances. This theory has been refined by those who distinguish between the types of bourgeoisie which dominated in different periods. It is argued that each political regime based itself on a new 'rising class'. Thus Louis-Philippe was 'managed by the *grands bourgeois* for the profit of their class'. Napoleon III's reign was that of big business. The Third Republic was sustained by the middle bourgeoisie, the graduates of the scientific schools and universities.[1] However, the Marxists maintain that this apparent gradual democratisation is an illusion and that France has ultimately been controlled not by the bourgeoisie in general

---

[1] Charles Morazé, *La France bourgeoise* (1946), 149.

but by the financial magnates who held the purse strings in all the major activities and achievements of the country. Building on this, France has been exposed as dominated by 200 families. The royalists, incited by their hate of the Orleanists, provided more social documentation for this phenomenon, by showing how the families which came to the fore at the Revolution of 1789, clung to office through every subsequent regime, changing their party labels to suit the prevailing fashions but always accumulating new power by intermarriage, so that they became veritable dynasties, successfully preventing the growth of real democracy.[1] This view became particularly widespread at the time of the Popular Front. Léon Blum held this group responsible for his failure. Using the word bourgeoisie rather loosely, he wrote: 'Despite all appearances to the contrary, it is the bourgeoisie which has ruled France for the past century and a half.' Even when the masses made their will felt in parliament, the bourgeoisie was able to resist. It controlled the local assemblies, the upper ranks of the civil service, the press, finance, the business world, and, under the Third Republic, the Senate. 'The French bourgeoisie held power for all this time, refusing to resign it or share it.' In 1940 the disastrous results of their blindness and conservatism were revealed. They were shown up as degenerate, incompetent, out of date, wedded to traditions of routine, and with no reserves of energy or imagination to meet the crisis of that year.[2]

The succeeding chapters will investigate this interpretation and review the facts which give it its strength. But before studying the financial oligarchy, it is desirable to see how it related to other sections of the bourgeoisie, and how much cohesion this class had. It will be argued that the reason why the people put up with the accumulation of so much power in such few hands for so long, is to be found in the deep fragmentation of the bourgeoisie. It was the ability of these different small worlds to coexist, preserving a great deal of mutual independence, that made the abuses of each one acceptable to the many who were only marginally affected by them.

Nothing is more difficult to define than bourgeois, and it must be accepted at the outset that the notion is necessarily a vague

[1] E. Beau de Loménie, *Les Responsabilités des dynasties bourgeoises* (1943).
[2] L. Blum, *A l'échelle humaine* (1945).

one. In 1950, when polls were held in France and the U.S.A. asking people what classes they belonged to, 5·4 per cent of the Americans said upper, 45·2 per cent said middle, 10·6 per cent working, 0·8 per cent farming, 4 per cent lower, 6·5 per cent other and 27·5 per cent gave no answer. But in France 7·9 per cent said they were bourgeois, 22·5 per cent middle, 27·1 per cent working, 13·7 per cent peasants, 7·5 per cent poor, 2·3 per cent other and 19 per cent no answer. As with their political parties, so with their social status, the French give more complicated answers. 32·3 per cent of the professional, business and higher administrative people questioned called themselves bourgeois, but 57·6 per cent claimed to be middle class and 5·3 per cent working class. Likewise, 5 per cent of the artisans and skilled workers thought they were bourgeois, 36·4 per cent middle class and 52·9 per cent working class.[1] The bourgeoisie is a peculiarly French category—as is the peasantry, for few American or British farmers deny membership of the larger working world simply because they live by agriculture. It is impossible to say how many people one is talking about when one discusses the bourgeoisie. Does one mean the electors of Louis-Philippe's 'bourgeois monarchy'—200,000 males? But one knows, from the way he was overthrown, how arbitrary this distinction was and how it excluded at least as many of comparable social rank. Does one mean those who had servants? There were about a million servants in 1900, but would the fall in their number paradoxically mean that the size of the bourgeoisie diminished in the twentieth century? Does one mean those who had some inherited capital or income? That gives about 15 per cent of the population, but one should bear in mind that the average value of inheritances was about sixteen times higher in Paris than in the Ariège in 1900 (but falling to three times in 1934) so that the significance of private income varied enormously in different regions and that its distribution changed rapidly in the twentieth century. Does one mean those who had enough capital to pay for their funerals? The figure in Paris in the 1840s was 17 per cent.

---

[1] Natalie Rogoff, 'Social Stratification in France and in the U.S.', *American Journal of Sociology*, 58 (1953), 347–57. Cf. N. Xydias, 'Classes sociales et conscience de classe à Vienne-en-France (Isère)' in *Trans. Second World Congress of Sociology* (London, 1954), 2. 246–51.

Perhaps the best-known attempt to explain the significance of the word was made in 1925 by Edmond Goblot, a professor of philosophy at Lyon. His analysis fits in with what four-fifths of the Frenchmen questioned in 1950 stated was the principal criterion which determined class: style of life. Goblot insists that it is not wealth that makes a man a bourgeois, but the way the wealth is acquired and the way it is spent. There are rich people who are not bourgeois, and there are poor ones who are accepted as belonging to the bourgeoisie. A bourgeois must spend his money to maintain a certain decorum in his clothes, his accommodation and his food. This does not require large sums. The bourgeois spent less money than the worker on food. What distinguished him was that he served his food differently, with a tablecloth laid symmetrically, and placed in a special room, not in the kitchen. He had to have a *salon*, furnished with a piano, paintings, candelabras, clocks and bibelots, in which to receive visitors and to show that he possessed a surplus of wealth, dedicated to cultured living, beyond the basic necessities. The rest of his house could be of Spartan simplicity and often was, because he had to spend his money on other things, to keep up his status. He had to pay for his children to go to secondary school, to enable them to take up professions to keep them bourgeois. If they became artisans, he would lose his self-respect. A bourgeois had to be able to perform his job in bourgeois costume, so that manual or dirty physical work was unacceptable. That is why there was such a sharp social distinction between the shopkeeper, who served customers himself, and the wholesaler, who by giving orders and never touching his goods could therefore claim to be a bourgeois. There were indeed wholesalers who refused to receive retailers in their homes.[1] All this implied that the bourgeois gave much effort to distinguishing himself from the masses. He cultivated *distinction*, which involved a special kind of politeness, laying stress on giving a good impression. He had to show taste, which meant knowing what was *correct*, and inclining therefore to conservatism and understatement. That is why for so long the bourgeois wore a black uniform, pointing out his precise rank only with details of cut and cloth. He did not aim to outdo other bourgeois but to keep up with them: moderation and the

---

[1] Cf. Hugues Le Roux, *Nos Fils* (1898), on his grandfather, 65–82.

traditional virtues were his guide. Do as others do: that was the level he worked up to. Do not be common: that was the barrier he had to maintain.

Education and the family were two of the principal concerns of the bourgeois and he spent a lot of his money on them. He had to equip his sons with the *baccalauréat* and his daughters with a dowry. He laid stress on the acquisition of *culture générale*, which distinguished him from mechanics and artisans; by the twentieth century he may have quickly forgotten his Latin but at least he could speak classical French.[1] He did not allow his wife to work, until 1914 at least, but used her to cultivate the domestic virtues of which he made himself the champion. He linked morality with chastity, fidelity and duty. Even when he asserted his independence against the Church, his quarrel with it was about politics, not about ethics.[2]

However, there are difficulties about this kind of definition of the bourgeoisie. One could buy oneself in or out of the class within a couple of generations. The distinction between bourgeois and noble was not absolutely clear. Those who had been bourgeois long enough, and were rich enough, married into the nobility, which gladly welcomed their hefty dowries. The richest industrialists and financiers—like Schneider, whose four daughters all married noblemen and whose grandson married an Orleans—were rapidly absorbed into the nobility. Those who could not wait made themselves noble by a do-it-yourself process: they just assumed titles, a process which became much easier once the republic was proclaimed. The number of nobles paradoxically rose after 1789. There were about three times as many people falsely parading titles in the twentieth century as there were genuine nobles. Two thousand claimed to have papal titles, but between 1831 and 1906 the pope granted only 300 titles. And it should be remembered that many of the genuine nobles had legally bought their titles before the Revolution, by purchasing state offices.[3] The bourgeoisie and

---

[1] Raoul de La Grasserie, *Des Parlers des différentes classes sociales. Études de psychologie et de sociologie linguistiques* (1909), distinguishes between bourgeois speech, *parler familier* which the bourgeois might speak at home, *parler populaire* of the masses, and criminal slang. Cf. my forthcoming study of this author.

[2] Edmond Goblot, *La Barrière et le niveau. Étude sociologique sur la bourgeoisie française* (1925).

[3] Vicomte de Marsay, *Du temps des privilèges* (1946), chapter 27; Jean de Belle-

the aristocracy had much in common; what differed now was that movement between the classes was easier and more rapid. The distinctions were less firm and therefore there was more room for snobbish rejection. Noble exclusiveness was a matter of show. It strongly resembled the *distinction* the bourgeoisie cultivated. And the bourgeoisie adopted many of the ideals associated with the aristocracy. Though they praised work, their ideal was also to live off a private income, to have a house in the country, and divide their time between it and the town in exactly the same way as the aristocracy. Though they began as revolutionaries—like the eighteenth-century nobility—many of them, by the end of the nineteenth, had accepted Catholicism as a mark of respectability. Their attitude to commerce was aristocratic. They adopted aristocratic attitudes towards social status. The aristocracy for its part did not disdain to work in the bourgeois civil service: the departments of finance and justice and the army were particularly smart. The aristocracy joined the bourgeoisie in business and industry, particularly banks, insurance, railways, mines and steel, where the boards of directors often contained between a third and a quarter of noblemen.[1] The nobles went into agriculture in a massive way after 1830, but many bourgeois also had farms. Possibly the nobles claimed a peculiar quality and had as their special ideal *prowess*—as opposed to bourgeois moderation. They claimed this could not be acquired but could only be inherited; but the bourgeoisie also laid great stress on family qualities. Both were obsessed by making marriages of the right kind, and their politeness differed no more than their clothes. The argument therefore that the nineteenth-century bourgeois cultivated ideals radically different from the aristocracy needs to be qualified. The nobles were former bourgeois and the bourgeoisie were moving up. They may have differed before they reached the top, when they were climbing, but they adopted many of the nobles' values when they could.

fond, *La Ménagerie du Vatican* (1906); *Le Crapouillot* (1937), issue on 'Vraie et fausse noblesse'; Woelmont de Brumagne, *La Noblesse française subsistante* (1928). See below pp. 393 ff. for a discussion of the nobility.

[1] Jesse R. Pitts, 'The Bourgeois Family and French Economic Retardation' (Ph.D. Harvard, unpublished thesis, 1957), 235 n.

In the same way the values of the bourgeoisie were shared by many of those beneath them in the social scale. The gradations were equally blurred here. The bourgeois was supposedly distinguished from the worker by his education, but this was a distinction made more definitely by the academic members of it: there were many members of the provincial bourgeoisie who managed their properties and held influential positions in business without having a *baccalauréat*. Likewise there were *bacheliers*, especially in towns, who were the sons of workers and small shopkeepers, but the possession of the supposedly distinctive bourgeois education did not make them bourgeois: many entered business or the civil service, but married into the class they came from and remained in it. The son of the *instituteur* often climbed up in the social hierarchy, but the relation of class and education was complex and not automatic. The *lycée* was not an exclusively bourgeois institution, and indeed some bourgeois refused to send their daughters to it because they would be contaminated by lower-class girls. The masses did not distinguish as clearly between secondary and primary education as did the professors, and among the illiterate, any sign of learning made a man a bourgeois. Supposedly, the bourgeoisie represented the triumph of merit but they were quick to entrench their privileges in their families with the same determination as the aristocracy. The passion for thrift and for property was shared by the peasants and the artisans. Only the factory worker refused this ideal, from despair, and he could be classified by the amount he drank, showing the degree of his despair.[1] The taste for culture was not a bourgeois prerogative: indeed it was precisely for his false interest and conservative philistinism that the bourgeois was attacked. Though the bourgeois went to the theatre, so did artisans, clerks and even some workers, and it was they who probably in even greater numbers flocked to the painting Salons. The bourgeois kept his wife at home and gave her a servant to do the housework; but the worker called his wife *la bourgeoise* precisely because she was often not a wage earner either. The dowry was a universal institution with all but paupers, until it was whittled away, from the bottom of the social scale upwards, by inflation and depression between the wars. After 1900 the dowry was no longer required of women

[1] D. Poulot, *Le Sublime* (1870).

who married officers. Officers used to have all sorts of compulsory aids to maintaining their status as an élite—they were forbidden to go to cheap cafés and restaurants, to take cheap seats in theatres or railways, their wives were forbidden to work. (A *lycée* headmistress who married a captain had to resign.) But as men from the ranks were increasingly given commissions (and after 1904 there were more of these than there were graduates of St. Cyr) the differences between the bourgeois officer and the ordinary soldier were more like the difference between a foreman and a worker. Many merchants with a working-class way of life had servants, though there was still the difference perhaps that the bourgeois's servant never took her meals at the same table. The workers began going on holiday to the country, some had houses in their place of origin, even if the seaside resorts divided themselves on a class basis. While at the top end the bourgeoisie aped the aristocracy, at the bottom end, and in certain circles, they imitated some working-class practices. Even before 1914, some began travelling third class, while prosperous shopkeepers with no pretence to gentility and who were not even parvenus travelled second or even first. Bourgeois students took on manual work when they could not afford their fees.[1]

Bourgeois values were thus not just bourgeois. Other classes could also claim at least some of them as their own. Had the aristocracy and the workers believed in radically different ways of life, there would have been far more conflict between the classes. But the bourgeoisie's moderation meant that they consciously or unconsciously represented the common denominator of the ambitions of their time. The phrase *la France bourgeoise* was thus a tautology in that to be a bourgeois meant to subscribe to the most general national aspirations. The worker was far from being always the enemy of these. The difficulties arose when in response to economic frictions, some of the bourgeoisie claimed to represent not the good life but the ruling class.

In the middle of the nineteenth century strong objections were voiced to the suggestion that France was divided into classes.[2] The Revolution, it was said, had abolished these. Gambetta refused to use the word class and spoke of *couches*

---

[1] There is a good critique of Goblot in M. L. Ferré, *Les Classes sociales dans la France contemporaine* (1936), published by the author.
[2] A. Vavasseur, *Qu'est-ce que la bourgeoisie?* (1897).

sociales.[1] Increasingly, bourgeois became a dirty word, used by different people to categorise their enemies: it meant the exploiter for the socialist, the master for the servant, the civilian for the soldier, the man of vulgar taste for the artist, the capitalist for the penniless.[2] The grandson of Henri Germain of the Crédit Lyonnais published his memoirs under the title *Bourgeoisie on Fire*. Maurice Boudet wrote a book in 1953 called *Appeal by the Bourgeoisie*, as though it had already been condemned.[3] In a reaction, leagues and societies were formed to defend the bourgeoisie as a class, menaced in particular by inflation.[4] Some urged that the communist menace could only be met if the bourgeoisie put aside its selfish preoccupations and resumed the leadership it had enjoyed in the Revolution.[5] Bishop Ancel of Lyon defended the bourgeoisie as a ruling class, anxious, and equipped by its culture and abilities, to rule. They were, he said, heirs to the victors of the Revolution but also to the *noblesse de robe*, they were distinguished by their ability to place the general good above their individual interests: 'it is magnificent', he wrote, 'to be a true bourgeois'.[6] There were protests against the accusation that the bourgeoisie had ruined the country, couched, for example, in these terms: 'We, the honest bourgeois, formed by solid traditions and nourished by knowledge and experience, we alone carry in our solid heads the salvation of civilisation, but we shall impose our law only by force of intellectual vigour and moral rectitude.' Such men rejected the definitions of the bourgeois as he who had a salon, or he who had capital, and argued that his most important quality was that he was accepted as one, and showed it by his *distinction*. They quoted a Gallup poll finding that 70 per cent of Frenchmen would prefer to live in the *belle époque* of the Third Republic as proof of the triumph of the bourgeois ideal and the continued desire of the French to be bourgeois.[7]

[1] For the meaning of this see below, chapter 20.

[2] Pierre Sanbert, *Notre Bourgeoisie* (Nancy, 1931); and cf. Jean V. Altier, *Les Origines de la satire antibourgeoise en France* (Geneva, 1966).

[3] André Germain, *La Bourgeoisie qui brûle* (1951); Maurice Boudet, *Bourgeoisie en appel* (1953); cf. Pierre Lucius, *Déchéances des bourgeoisies d'argent* (1936).

[4] R. Aron, *Inventaires III: classes moyennes* (1939), 287–340.

[5] Just Haristoy, *L'Heure de la bourgeoisie* (1937), 229.

[6] Alfred Ancel, *La Mentalité bourgeoise* (1950), 70.

[7] Felix Colmet Daâge, *La Classe bourgeoise. Ses origines, ses lois d'existence, son rôle social* (1959). Cf. Georges Hourdin, *Pour les valeurs bourgeoises* (1968).

A great deal of research is still needed to trace the changes that have occurred in the bourgeoisie and to throw light on its professional and regional variations. In some regions, for example, the bourgeoisie was keen on buying land, in others it was not. In some it isolated itself from the masses more than in others; in some there was more rapid social renewal than in others.[1] In primitive and poor districts the word had a special significance. Jules Simon recounts how in Brittany in the 1820s a retired naval foreman had married a peasant girl. She and her daughters, all dressed as peasants, worked manually on his farm, but nevertheless he was considered a bourgeois, because he always wore a bowler hat and frock-coat and never clogs. He read his newspaper, an occupation which took him all day. He was called *Monsieur* Frélaut. He kept the books of the *mairie* for a small salary (there was no schoolmaster then at Larmor) and he played his game of *boules* every afternoon with the other bourgeois of Larmor. His son was a bourgeois like him, destined for the priesthood. At noon dinner was served to M. Frélaut, in which his son participated during the holidays: a bourgeois dinner—meat or fish and vegetables. The messieurs were waited on by the mother and sisters, who sat down only when the men had finished, to eat pancakes, milk and sometimes a piece of pork fat. The father was an atheist, though all his family went to church and his son was studying for the priesthood. Here the Church was the best way to rise out of the peasantry and the seminaries were full of boys who gave up after a few years and took jobs as notaries, clerks or tutors with scarcely enough to live on but allowed to wear top hats and tattered frock coats and to be called 'monsieur'. A family that succeeded in getting a son into the priesthood considered itself almost ennobled and took on new airs. The priests and the bourgeois were the only ones in these remote areas who could speak French, even though the former often spoke it in a stilted and correct way like a foreign language.[2]

Because of the vagueness of the notion, the supremacy of bourgeois ideals cannot serve as a key to understanding the

[1] *La Bourgeoisie alsacienne* (Strasbourg, 1954, published by the Société savante d'Alsace). Abel Chatelian, *Les Horizons d'une géohistoire de la bourgeoisie lyonnaise* (Lyon, 1950, extract from the *Revue de Géographie de Lyon*).
[2] Jules Simon, *Premières Années* (1901), 39, 91, 319.

forces at work in French society, at least until a much more careful analysis of these ideals is undertaken. This will be attempted over the whole course of this book, by examining in turn different aspects of life and the values manifested in them. Meanwhile, the second problem posed at the beginning of this chapter, as to how far the bourgeoisie dominated France, in terms of economic, political and social activities, can perhaps best be approached by a few detailed case studies. Six occupations will now be investigated, to show how difficult it is to attribute influence or cohesion to them in any simple sense. The conflicts within each group, and the isolation of each group within society, meant that many separate worlds could coexist side by side. How they interacted and how they related to the rest of the country is a complex affair.

2. Doctors

THE care a nation takes of its health always reveals a lot about its attitudes to life. In France, the medical profession is particularly interesting, for there is a political dimension to its influence. Its rise to power in the state is one of the striking features of this century. There were 15 doctors in the Assembly of 1789, 26 in that of 1791, 40 in the Convention. About a dozen served in the smaller Restoration Chamber of Deputies and 28 in that of July. In 1848, 49 of the constituents were doctors, and in 1849, 34 of the legislators. There were 11 in Napoleon III's Corps Législatif of 251 members, 33 in the National Assembly of 1871, but by 1898 their number had risen to 72.[1] It may be argued from these figures that doctors gradually replaced the old landowning class and in some cases the clergy as leaders of public opinion and that in the Third Republic they reached the zenith of their prestige and influence. But to say this is to beg many questions: it is to assume that doctors were not also landowners, that their influence was an alternative and opposed to the old notable class, that the profession meant the same thing over 150 years, that the opportunities open to doctors were unchanging, and that their appearance in parliament always represented an acknowledgement of their influence, rather than that the doctors were seeking new fields in which to act, to compensate for difficulties they were experiencing in the exercise of their profession.

Medicine in France in this period was in fact in a state of confusion and division as total as that which afflicted politics. It is impossible to paint a picture of doctors as the products of a new science whose capacity and skill were gradually established, recognised and accepted. There was no one medical science, and the rivalry between the different theories was as merciless and disruptive as the cut-throat competition of commerce. In 1850 the medicine of cure by bleeding, purging and the administration of enemas was still in existence, for all the

---

[1] P. Trisca, *Les Médecins sociologues et hommes d'état* (1923).

discoveries of the capital cities, whose doctrines were slow to penetrate the countryside. The efforts of Voltaire's doctor Tronchin (1709–81) and his school to replace this by the use of fresh air, exercise, vegetarianism, water-drinking, breast-feeding and vaccination were slow to win acceptance. The enlightenment even saw a regression to the doctrine of vitalism— the belief that a mysterious vital element regulates the organs and fights death. This doctrine was taken up by the faculty of medicine of Montpellier and taught by it till the twentieth century—so that Paris and Montpellier taught medicine in radically different ways.[1] The training which the doctors practising between 1850 and 1900 received preserved the strangest errors taught by men highly esteemed in the first half of the century. One of these, to take an example, was Broussais (1772–1838), a man of great eloquence, imposing presence, and unrelenting combativeness, who wielded great power in the medical world. He imagined that the cause of all diseases was inflammation, particularly in the intestines. He prescribed abundant blood-letting, leeches and severe diets. His starving patients, bled white, died like flies, but he was nevertheless made a professor at the faculty of Paris (1831). When towards the end of his career his star waned and his students turned elsewhere, he took up phrenology and his very popular lectures on this gave him a second lease of life. Equally influential but at a more popular level was F. V. Raspail (1794–1878), whose *Natural History of Health and Illness* (1843) and annual encyclopedias (1846–64) became best sellers as manuals of self-medication: he advocated camphor as the cure for all diseases.

Possibly the single most successful doctor of the nineteenth century was Philippe Ricord (1800–89), personal physician to Napoleon III and the national expert on syphilis. Born in Baltimore, the son of a bankrupt French shipowner, he rose to become Paris's busiest and possibly richest doctor. His house in the rue de Tournon contained five large salons for his patients to wait in: one for ordinary people, always crammed full and each given a number, one for women, who entered by a separate staircase, one for people with letters of recommendation, and a fourth for friends and doctors. All were decorated magnificently with paintings and sculptures, for he was a great collector.

[1] F. Berard, *Doctrine médicale de Montpellier* (1819).

An enormous fifth reception salon had two Rubens, a Van Dyke, Géricaults, etc. His office contained on three walls a large library surmounted by a gallery of busts of the great physicians of all time, underneath it glass cases with Paris's best collection of surgical instruments and on the fourth wall portraits of his masters Dupuytren and Orfila, and one of himself by Couture. He was France's most decorated celebrity after Alexandre Dumas, with seventeen medals: he was popular not least for being a man of the world, indulgent to his patients and famous for his witticisms.[1] His *Treatise on Venereal Diseases* (1838) did rightly distinguish between gonorrhoea and syphilis, but he insisted that the latter was not contagious through secondary lesions: he continued to administer his incorrect doctrine to all the rich of Europe, despite the discoveries of the more obscure Joseph Rollet of Lyon (1856).

The visitor to Paris in 1848 would have found some 1,550 doctors there, 300 of them decorated with the legion of honour, offering every variety of cure. At least 50 per cent of them had published books to advocate their theories and many of them advertised in every available medium. Dr. Bachoni offered electro-physico-chemical treatments with no payment if no result. Dr. Barras offered a modification of the Broussais doctrine, replacing gastritis by gastralgia as the cause of all ills. Dr. Becquerel offered cures for stammering in conflict with those of Dr. Jourdan with whom he conducted public disputes. Dr. Belliol's name covered the walls of Paris and the small advertisement columns in the papers offering a 'new vegetal method'. Dr. Leuret, author of *The Moral Treatment of Madness* (1840), though refuted by Dr. Blanche and voted against by the Academy of Medicine, persisted in tying his mad patients to planks of wood and throwing cold water over them. Dr. Brièrre de Boismont wrote that the number of madmen was bound to increase with the progress of civilisation and profited from this by running an asylum for the middle class, at fees ranging from 8,000 to 12,000 francs a year.[2] Dr. Piorry invented 'plessimetrism', known alternatively as 'organographism', which used percussion to discover about internal organs, and wrote a book on *Common Sense Medicine* (1864), advocating less use of dangerous

---

[1] Paul Labarthe, *Nos Médecins contemporains* (1868), 44.
[2] See his article in *Annales d'Hygiène* (1839).

drugs, more curing by deep breathing and by spitting.[1] Dr. Jean Giraudeau de Saint Gervais did not just cover the walls of Paris with his name, but paid newspapers to praise him and hacks to write books for him, and he had a permanent column of advertisements in several papers. His *Manual of Health, and Advice on the Art of Healing Oneself* was sold by the thousand in grocer's shops.[2] All manner of healers adopted scientific jargon and competed successfully against the teaching of the faculties, but it was not a struggle of unqualified quacks against learned professors. Phrenology (and also physiognomy and cranioscopy), for example, had academicians and professors teaching it, and applying it to education, jurisprudence and medicine. The Academy of Medicine treated old wives' tales with respect: in 1846 a Breton girl, Angélique Cottin, was reported to give electric shocks to those who touched her. The Academy appointed a commission under Arago to report on the case. In 1837 a member of the Academy established a prize to encourage investigations of magnetic healing. The 'microscopists', 'pharmaco-chemists' and 'numerists' (applying statistics to the study of disease) met with vigorous opposition. The Academy did not disdain to discuss theoretical questions. The doctors, far from ignoring the quacks and the theorists, engaged in constant polemic with them, and the medical press attacked and ridiculed every idea, new and old, and every personality in the same slanderous and uninhibited way as the political papers.[3] In the country, doctors had to fight the even more powerful resistance of superstition and traditional remedies. A whole army of rival practitioners offered cheaper and sometimes more acceptable treatment: the urine healer (who prescribed medicines after examining the urine of the patient), the *orviétan* merchant (the itinerant seller of drugs), the sorcerers, the nuns, the priests, the old women, the midwives, the pharmacists. The peasants in any case had their own views about diseases. They preferred annual purges to vaccination; they had a firm belief in the hereditary nature of illnesses and thought they could not catch (they would not have used that word in the

---

[1] Dr. Piorry, *La Médecine du bon sens* (1864).

[2] C. Sachaille de la Barre, *Les Médecins de Paris jugés par leurs œuvres ou statistique scientifique et morale des médecins de Paris* (1845).

[3] Louis Peisse, *La Médecine et les médecins. Philosophie, doctrines, institutions, mœurs et biographies médicales* (1857), 2 vols.

pre-microbe age) diseases their parents had not had; and they long persisted in calling in the doctor as a last resort—often too late—when all else had failed.[1]

In 1911 a doctor describing popular medicine in the Vendée reported that the doctrines of Broussais still had many fervent followers. Bone-setters still made a good living and died well-to-do, bequeathing their secrets to a chosen disciple on their deathbed. Magical and herbal cures, distributed by clairvoyantes, were much used; special trains were organised to take large crowds to holy places, where every disease was cured by miracles. Babies were given wine and eau-de-vie to make them strong. Madmen were considered to be the victims of curses and the Devil.[2] In 1953 an inquiry revealed that the competition of charlatans, especially in the countryside, remained very powerful.[3] The law made it very difficult to stop charlatans. If, for example, a doctor prescribed a remedy and the chemist who dispensed it decided to make it a speciality of his own, advertising it as 'recommended by Dr. X', nothing could be done to prevent him. Often these advertisements quoted recommendations from fictitious doctors, but the law again upheld their freedom. Thus in 1884 a doctor advertised artificial insemination saying that 'this operation which at first may seem immoral has not only been approved by the Academy of Medicine but has been the object of its felicitations and encouragement'— which was totally untrue. Another who sold 'uterine vacuum cleaners' claimed to have received medals for inventing it, but he was convicted for procuring abortions. At the turn of the century there were still doctors who prescribed superstitious remedies, like curing cancer by living on a boat on the Rhone and playing music during meals. The *Petit Méridional* of Montpellier contained advertisements by a doctor offering consultations by correspondence. This was fairly common: questionnaires were distributed for the prospective patient to fill in; when he had sent this in with a fee, he got back a prescription, often a very expensive one. It is true that Dr. Rey de Jougla, who, during the Second Empire, offered cures for all incurable diseases at

[1] Dr. Munaret, *Du Médecin des villes et du médecin de campagne. Mœurs et science* (1840, second edition).

[2] Dr. Boismoreau, *Coutumes médicales et superstitions populaires du bocage vendéen* (1911).

[3] Jean Éparvier, *Médecins de campagne: enquête* (1953), 23, 49, 64.

a flat rate of 16 francs was convicted for fraud, but it took a very long time to diminish the rivalry of the magnetisers and somnambulists, of whom in 1890 there were about 500 fully occupied in Paris alone. The faculty of medicine then voted to condemn them, but the government nevertheless allowed the foundation of a school to train them. In the 1890s, the courts were divided about them, some convicting them of illegal practice of medicine, but some (notably Angers) acquitting them. By a law of 1805 nuns and priests were allowed to give medical care, provided they signed no prescriptions and gave their advice free—but many women's orders did in fact distribute medicine and in Morbihan the success of their 150 illegal pharmacies was such that in the last twenty-five years of the century the number of doctors practising diminished by a third, driven out by their cheaper competition.

It is a mistake to think that science improved the health of the nation in gradual stages. The adoption of antiseptics by the French army was so slow that there was an actual regression in the efficiency of amputations: in the Napoleonic wars only about 2 per cent died after these operations but in the 1870 war the mortality was far higher, on occasions reaching 100 per cent.[1] The association of typhoid with impure water was established in 1854 but it was only in 1886 when the secretary of the Academy of Sciences lost three daughters from it that the idea was accepted, and in the 1890s deaths from typhoid were halved. There were, however, always areas of the country which resisted new remedies: smallpox continued to flourish because of objections to vaccination, especially in Brittany. The doctors were often their own worst enemies: it was not simply that they were unable to defend themselves against charlatans. The commission appointed by the ministry of justice in 1895 to find means to combat morphinomania 'which was invading all classes of society' blamed the spread of the addiction on the example set by doctors and pharmacists.[2]

Just as in politics the Action Française revealed reaction towards traditionalism in the period between the two world wars, so at the same time there was a similar return to the past

    [1] P. M. M. Laignel-Lavastine, *Histoire générale de la médecine* (1949), 3. 9.
    [2] Dr. P. Brouardel, *L'Exercice de la médecine et le charlatanisme* (1899), 106, 155, 249, 465–82.

in medical doctrines. Neo-Hippocratism was taken up by many distinguished doctors, professors and deans of faculty, culminating in the National Congress of Neo-Hippocratic Medicine in 1937, which was widely supported and reported. This doctrine stressed that the causes of many diseases remained unknown, that chemistry had its limits, that there should be a return to the clinical approach and to an appreciation of the individual temperament of each patient. Writing in 1945 on *Official and Heretical Medicine*, Alexis Carrel, the Nobel Prize winning biologist, described the differences which divided French medicine as inevitable reflections of differing conceptions of man and life. On the one hand there was official medicine, approved by the faculties and the state, but against it was independent medicine, often favoured by younger doctors starting their careers. It was not just the failure of the faculties to reform their educational methods. (The efforts of the powerful Charles Bouchard, professor at Paris from 1879 to 1912, co-operating with his friend Louis Liard, vice-rector of the Sorbonne, were defeated by the conservatism of the profession.) The variety of medical approaches in the nineteenth century crystallised in the twentieth into better-argued rival systems, often metaphysically based, and partially representing a reaction against physical-chemical science—not dissimilar to the reaction seen also in literature. Distinguished practitioners wrote in favour of reviving the study of 'humours'. Acupuncture was introduced in the 1920s and Soulié de Morant's book (1934) popularised it. Even medical astrology became respectable, rechristened cosmobiology. The first French Congress of Therapeutics in 1933 showed a new stress on nature cures. Above all, homoeopathy, which had first come to France with its inventor Samuel Hahnemann in 1835 and had won over about 150 doctors by 1914, increased its following to 567 doctors with orthodox qualifications by 1938, plus over 1,500 unqualified practitioners.[1] The homoeopaths were, it is true, bitterly divided themselves on the exact application of their doctrine: a modernising sect under Frotier-Bernoville modified the traditional teaching to make it fit with that of the Neo-Hippocratics. While Freud made some converts in the treatment of mental illness there were numerous alternatives to

[1] Laignel-Lavastine, 3. 576.

psycho-analysis. Desoille and Guillerey each developed different cures using dreams, the former basing his theories on those of his master Caslan the occultist. There was a long tradition of experiment with hypnosis. Miraculous cures were seriously defended. Whereas in 1904 and 1912 doctors who tried to write theses about the religious cures of Lourdes were failed, in 1930 Dr. Monnier successfully got a thesis on this subject accepted. As early as 1879 doctors had formed a medical authentication bureau at Lourdes, which Dr. Boissarie had run very successfully from 1891 to 1917, opening their findings to all the profession. Between the wars, scientifically inexplicable phenomena, far from being discredited, became respectable. In 1936 Dr. Delore called for the creation of a 'national institute for the authentication and scientific study of traditional and empiric practices'.[1]

Doctors thus remained controversial figures throughout these hundred years and did not automatically benefit from the respect for men of science to which—rather theoretically—it is assumed they must have been increasingly entitled. In 1833 Balzac did indeed write: 'Today the peasant prefers to listen to the doctor who gives him a prescription to save his body than to the priest who sermonises him about the salvation of his soul.' But he also made the doctor say: 'I was a bourgeois and for them [the peasants] a bourgeois is an enemy.'[2] A century later a doctor writing his memoirs said the worker preferred the schoolmaster to the doctor because the former was 'a man of learning and only half a bourgeois, whereas the doctor is a complete bourgeois and often a clerical too'.[3] The position of the doctors remained ambivalent. The question to ask about them is not how they rose in the social scale, how they won status and respect, for they were always a group of great diversity and attitudes to them varied according to region and circumstance almost as much as they changed with time. The important point to realise is that for long the doctor's profession was not

[1] P. Delore, médecin des hôpitaux de Lyon, *Tendances de la médecine contemporaine. La Médecine à la croisée des chemins* (1936), 164–89; Alexis Carrel (ed.), *Médecine officielle et médecines hérétiques* (1945); A. L. J. Rouot, *Essai sur l'information médicale du public* (Bordeaux, 1959) is a brief introduction to a subject that deserves further investigation.

[2] H. de Balzac, *Le Médecin de campagne* (1832).

[3] Dr. Ch. Fiessinger, *Souvenirs d'un médecin de campagne* (1933), 96.

really a career. Only to a very limited extent was it a way of rising in the world, partly because those who entered it needed a lot of capital to obtain the education, and partly because it seldom yielded high rewards. Charton's *Guide to Careers* of 1842 stressed the heavy expenses involved and the poor rewards: 'Some can obtain an honest living (from the exercise of medicine) but most will attain a mediocrity of position which is really hardly encouraging.'[1] He thought 3,000 francs a year was as much as the majority could expect to make. What he recommended the profession for was its independence. It allowed a man to be his own master. This was one of its great attractions when independence was a widespread ideal. The man who invested a similar amount of money in setting up a business or shop wanted to be his own master too, but very often he planned to make more money quickly so as to buy state bonds and retire to real independence on the interest. The doctor could not usually expect to make money; he seldom retired; his training was to a certain extent a sort of liberal education which enabled him to give dignity and influence to a modest inherited wealth. The doctors of humble origin—like Emile Combes—usually needed to marry money and ideally to marry the daughter of a doctor in practice. In the mid nineteenth century doctors could not live off fees from the masses: they were kept in practice by the fees of the rich, who as it were subsidised the influence doctors obtained by giving free or almost free treatment to the poor. This is one of the reasons why the doctor appeared so obviously as a bourgeois. But by no means all had the qualities to attract rich patients. To succeed in the upper ranks of the profession needed more than brains: 'nepotism, favoritism, camaraderie are carried to the highest degree'.[2] This explains why so many were forced to advertise, to offer cut prices and quack, but attractive and guaranteed, cures. But the real way to success became to find a part-time official appointment, giving a prestige which attracted more clients and yielding a small but fixed supplementary income (they were called 'fixes'). The plum appointments were of course physician to the bishop, consultant at the local hospital, but prison doctor, police surgeon, director of a thermal establishment were all valuable. Above all the less successful became official doctors treating the

[1] Charton, 394.   [2] Charton, 387.

poor of the commune, for which they often got a third or less of
their very lowest normal fee, but at least the guarantee of some
regular business. The development of these subsidiary occupations, the increase in the number of state and local authority
bodies which employed doctors, the growth of mutual benefit
societies which insured against illness, and the beginnings of
a social security system gradually transformed the situation of
many doctors, making them almost civil servants or officials—
but of a somewhat *ancien régime* type—paid in small amounts
from various sources.

It is difficult to discover how much the doctors earned at
different times. There are certainly ample complaints about the
inadequacies of their rewards, laments that there were too many
of them chasing too few patients, who did not pay their bills,
regrets that doctors did not have a uniform like the priest and
the magistrate to improve their status, and descriptions of some
who 'spoke Greek and Latin to men who hardly understood
French' and lined their consulting rooms with books to heighten
the impression of a mystic craft.[1] A doctor wrote a book in 1889
protesting against the ridiculous fee of one franc a head p.a.
paid for working in the medical service for the indigent, objecting to doctors being pushed to the very bottom of the social
ladder and ironically declaiming: 'We do not dispute the first
rank to the magistrature, clergy or army. Nor do we wish to
place ourselves on the same level as engineers, actors, painters,
architects and sculptors. We ask only that we may occupy
a middle rank, more or less: we would like for example to be
classed between the solicitor and the photographer'—not so
much for the respect as for financial reward.[2] It is interesting
that he felt the magistrates and clergy looked upon him as a
rival 'who penetrates the innermost secrets of families'.[3] In

---

[1] Dr. Munaret, *Du Médecin des villes et du médecin de campagne. Mœurs et science*
(2nd edition 1840)—a curious collection of social information, interestingly in
praise of the petty bourgeoisie.

[2] Dr. Victor Macrobius, *Malades, médecins et pharmaciens* (1889), 36.

[3] Dr. P. Brouardel, *Le Secret médical* (1887), 87. Certainly doctors were not
insignificant intermediaries in the marriage market and they worried about how
their oath of professional secrecy should affect their attitude in inquiries made to
them in arranged marriages: should they reveal that their patients were afflicted
with syphilis? Such was the atmosphere of secrecy among them that some even
refused to issue certificates giving the cause of death—some even to issue death
certificates at all.

1901 in an impressionistic but instructive survey of 'the intellectual proletariat', it was estimated that half a dozen doctors
earned between two and three hundred thousand francs a year,
about a hundred over 40,000, but about 80 per cent less than
8,000 francs. The majority of doctors, therefore, were 'proletariat' if they did not have private means. Many doctors in Paris
tried to supplement their income by acting as 'beaters' for more
famous colleagues, working for pharmacists to help sell expensive drugs, doing abortions etc. In the provinces half the doctors
could not earn a decent living—but 'the inquisitorial habits of
the countryside' did not allow interlopers to establish themselves easily. The less successful relied on making a good
marriage, and so becoming farmers, industrialists or *rentiers*,
according to the size of the dowry they obtained. 'The least
favoured went into politics.'[1]

Le Concours Médical, a professional journal, estimated in 1881
that 12,000 francs was the minimum a doctor needed to live in
the wealthier parts of France and asserted that the majority
were far from earning this. 'They spend their patrimony. For-
tunately sometimes a dowry re-establishes some sort of balance
and allows them to educate their children.' One should not take
their complaints too literally, for one Alsatian country doctor
admitted to earning a modest income but added that it was as
much as the combined salaries of the priest, the pastor and the
rabbi.[2] A doctor writing to the paper at this time reported
earning 11,000 a year, except that 35 to 40 per cent of his fees
were never paid, so he got only some 7,000. This was a common
complaint. There was an enormous amount of haggling over
fees and the doctors contributed to it by varying their fees
according to what they thought they could extract from their
patients. Dr. Récamier, physician to Mme de Boigne, said in
1828 that the fee for a visit used to be 3 francs but he felt he
must ask for 6. However, for her, he would reduce it to 4.
Nevertheless, in the middle of the 1860s provincial doctors were
still asking for only 1½ or 2 francs, and most of the consultations in their offices were free. The General Association of
Doctors of France, founded in 1858, was opposed to uniformity
or any central control, claiming that doctors could not be

[1] Henry Bérenger *et al.*, *Les Prolétaires intellectuels en France* (1901), 7–9.
[2] Dr. Georges Laffitte, *Le Médecin* (1936), xx.

expected to keep accounts and that they had no need for pensions. It argued that a doctor would lose prestige if he surrendered 'that arbitrary power which allows him, depending on the time, the place, the nature and the degree of the services rendered and a thousand other circumstances, to raise or to lower the price of his treatment'. In 1879 a more radical association, the Concours Médical, was founded to press for higher and more uniform fees: in 1897 it publicised Dr. Jeanne's tariff, as a model for adoption by local associations. But even this divided patients into three classes by wealth, and recommended flexibility between 1 and 10 francs a visit, depending on the patient's income; moreover it allowed many additions for extra time and care, and suggested the figures should be multiplied by ten for the 'highest masters of medicine'. In the same year the doctors of the Haute-Saône adopted a minimum tariff—on this same three-class basis—and the practice spread to other departments. The main benefit was to extract considerably more money from public authorities and insurance companies.[1] To get private patients to pay their bills, however, remained difficult: both the ethical code and the law made it almost impossible to force them. In some parts of France, e.g. Allier, doctors were customarily paid only after their patient's death, as a share in his inheritance, and it was normal everywhere to wait a long time for payment.

The elimination of competition by the unqualified and by charlatans was slow and never fully successful. For the first three-quarters of the nineteenth century, the main demand of the doctors was the abolition of the 'officers of health'. Until 1838 these were men, usually of humble origin, glorified medical orderlies, who obtained diplomas to practise medicine from specially instituted departmental committees with very low standards. After this date the faculties issued the diplomas and in 1854 the departmental commissions were abolished, so that the standard of education gradually rose. In the last decade of the July Monarchy almost as many diplomas were issued (2,850) as doctorates in medicine (3,045) but by 1869–78 the ratio fell to 1,014 officers against 5,344 doctors and by 1889–97 to 627 officers against 6,658 doctors. The idea had

[1] J. L. Cariage, *L'Exercice de la médecine en France à la fin du 19e siècle et au début du 20e siècle* (1965, privately printed).

been that in the poorer regions which had no fully qualified doctor, the officers of health would provide some medical services. In fact the officers found more lucrative employment in the richer areas, and large sections of the country continued to be underprivileged. In 1891 the poor department of Lozère had 24 doctors and only one officer; the Somme had 83 doctors and 141 officers, the Nord 353 doctors and 201 officers. The problem of the officers gradually died out: whereas in 1848 there were about 7,500 of them, in 1900 there were only 2,000 left. Instead foreign doctors became the new bogey: there were 541 in 1911, 750 in 1929, but even more threatening was the number of foreign medical students, who were particularly noticeable because they tended to concentrate in a few towns. In 1931 for example 76 per cent of the students at the Rouen medical school were foreign, at Tours 41 per cent.[1] Charlatans bought doctorates abroad, especially from the university of Philadelphia, which advertised them for sale at 500 francs.

In the country doctors often dealt with teeth as well, but in towns increasing competition came from a growing number of dentists. Dentistry required no qualifications: some practitioners were former mechanics and locksmiths. In 1890 France had only some 2,000 dentists (600 of them in Paris) as opposed to 4,000 in England and 15,000 in the U.S.A. The Americans' recognised superiority resulted in many of these coming to practise in France: Evans, dentist to Napoleon III, was one of the first and most famous. Many young Englishmen also found it useful to serve an apprenticeship in France, where there were no examinations: the enormous Dental Clinic of the Louvre was entirely manned by Englishmen. In 1892 a law was passed requiring qualifications for dentists and penalising the illegal practice of medicine in general. Hitherto the law had only allowed individuals to sue charlatans and they had to show that they had personally suffered damage. Now trade unions were allowed to bring charlatans to court. But their efforts seemed only to make the latter more famous. The herborists were spared by the new law (there were 300 of them in Paris, 50 in Marseille, and 50 more in other towns). Napoleon had established examinations for them, as a kind of junior health officer;

[1] Dr. Georges Laffitte, *Le Médecin. Sa Formation, son rôle dans la société moderne* (Bordeaux, 1936), 70.

a decree of 1854 had divided them into two classes, so confirming their status; and in 1892 the pressure from the doctors
to abolish them was unsuccessful because it would have been
extremely expensive to buy them out, their shops being worth
over 100,000 francs each when put up for sale.

As a result of all this competition and confusion, the nineteenth century did not see the rise in the number of doctors that
is often assumed to have occurred. On the contrary between
1847 and 1896 the number of doctors fell by some 3,500 and
the number of officers of health by nearly 5,000—though if one
counts all those who actually practised, the figures show
smaller diminution. The increase occurred only in the twentieth century, after the supposed zenith of medical influence.
The idea of medical influence needs to be analysed more carefully. The opportunities open to the upper ranks of the profession did gradually widen. At first it was men at the very top,
members of the Academy of Medicine, founded in 1820, who
were consulted by the government. Then in the Second Empire
onwards, specialised national and local committees were
officially established to deal with public hygiene, hospitals,
schools, etc., which gave some doctors a chance to become a
cross between notables and official advisers. Finally in 1930
the creation of the ministry of public health made it possible
for doctors to become senior civil servants and administrators
using public money. Meanwhile at the level of the mass of
doctors, important transformations were also occurring. It
became increasingly difficult to survive as a family doctor,
particularly if one tried to maintain a bourgeois standard of
living comparable with that of the more successful in the profession. More and more doctors took on part or full-time work
on a salaried basis and became workers in the sanitary industry
instead of independent professional men. They then began
forming trade unions, bargaining to improve their conditions
like other workers. Inevitably they could not unite completely.
Only in 1928 was a fusion achieved between the Union of
Medical Trade Unions and the Federation of Medical Trade
Unions. The Vichy regime organised the doctors into a corporation run by a state-controlled Order of Doctors, against which
organisations have developed to oppose its dictatorship. A
Federation of Salaried Doctors has also been founded, and

separate unions for general practitioners and specialists. The latter represent an important new rift. In 1958 there were no fewer than 14,680 specialists, i.e. one for every two general practitioners: specialisation was institutionalised in 1930 when the Social Insurance took the decision to reimburse specialist treatment at higher rates. The divisions did not prevent the doctors from looking more like a pressure group, fighting for public funds, pursuing selfish interests. The myth of the doctors as a solid phalanx of anticlericals and atheists also needs to be exploded. In 1936 a book was published entitled *The Freemason Doctors*, but the authors were able to produce few names to support their accusation. Doctors have stood for parliament as

	Doctors in practice	Total doctors	Officers of health
1847		18,099	7,456
1866	11,254	16,822	5,568
1876		14,326	3,633
1886	11,995		2,794
1896	13,412	14,538	2,114
1906	18,211		
1911	20,113		
1921	20,364		
1931	25,410		200
1958	30,318	47,000	

members of almost every party. There were certainly not more doctors in France than elsewhere. The impression visitors to Paris got that there must be was fair enough, because (in 1931) Paris did indeed have more doctors than any other city in Europe. But France as a whole came seventeenth in the world for the density of doctors, having one for every 1,578 inhabitants, compared to 1,183 in Great Britain, 1,280 in Germany, 1,326 in the U.S.A., and 788 in Austria. Proportionate to the population, there were over three times fewer doctors in Mayenne than in Seine.[1]

The problems facing doctors, the way they made careers for themselves, and the nature of their influence can be illuminated by taking a few examples. Dr. Gabriel Maurange, born in

[1] Jacqueline Pincemin and Alain Laugier, 'Les Médecins', in *Revue Française des Sciences Politiques* (Dec. 1959), 881–900; G. Laffitte, *Le Médecin* (Bordeaux, 1936), 31.

Bordeaux in 1865, had a clog maker as a grandfather and a railway clerk as a father; and his brother trained as a barrister,
though marriage turned him into a wine merchant. He failed
his *baccalauréat* in philosophy and so tried the one in science
instead, which he passed; he decided to enter medical school
rather than the Polytechnique partly because his mother had
died owing to neglect by her doctor. Bordeaux was still pretty
backward in medicine in the 1880s: sterilisation was adopted
only by accident, because the professor happened to see it used
on a visit to Paris for the *concours d'agrégation*. The system of
patronage, of the professor having a select band of disciples,
was in full vigour. When Maurange tried to write a thesis on a
mistaken diagnosis by his professor and to suggest a new cure for
peritonitis, the latter was furious and Maurange left for Paris.
It was easy enough qualifying but without a protector it was
almost impossible to establish oneself. The favourite students—
the *internes*—were given public posts to start them off; but the
vast majority barely knew their professors more than by sight
and as the number of students increased (they doubled between 1900 and 1935) they were lucky if they got that far.
Maurange was penniless but he knew that if he was to succeed
he must pretend that he was successful. He borrowed 500 francs.
He got smart bourgeois clothes on credit from a Jewish tailor. He
took a flat in the rue Littré for 650 francs and employed a *femme
de ménage*. He hired a carriage for 300 francs a month—a cheap
rate, because he used it only in the mornings; in the afternoons
it was let to rich old ladies. He spent his evenings talking to
young men in his own position: the eternal subject was how to
succeed. He was saved by the 'flu epidemic of 1889–90—he
helped the physician to the senate and earned 600 francs. The
south-west network assisted him: provincials nearly always
kept together in the capital and the successful among them
passed on patronage to the beginners. He asked his protector
to get him the *palmes académiques* from the senate: thus decorated,
he grew his beard, looked solemn, and ventured on a debt of
6,000 francs to set up consulting rooms. He made 5,000 francs
in his first year, but he also got to know some aristocratic
families. His name was passed round, and by his third year he
was up to 12,000 and in his fourth he had doubled that. He
found incredible ignorance among these aristocratic clients of

the most elementary principles of hygiene, limitless credulity in every kind of healer, absolute faith in all remedies which had the picture of a priest or nun on the label or simply the statement that they were manufactured in a convent or monastery. The aristocracy all had family doctors, but ignored their advice and kept them rather as a kind of retainer. The rich liked to call in second opinions. Maurange in the 1890s inaugurated the practice of seeing clients only by appointment and he did well. His father in Bordeaux, who from timidity had opposed his move to Paris, was now dazzled by his success and they were reconciled. Maurange's income increased as the social level of his clientele went up. He augmented it by starting a nurses' school but he made the mistake of having it undenominational: the religious issue brought discord: the protestants captured dominance, and he left, but rich enough now to give up all his part-time jobs. In 1908 he moved to a more fashionable address near the Madeleine. The war brought many foreign patients, particularly English and American ones, and he increasingly developed this lucrative side of his work. He obtained the title of Chevalier of the Legion of Honour, thanks to the actor Monnet-Sully of the Comédie Française, whose doctor he was and who was a friend of Clemenceau. The decoration brought a great increase in the demand for his services and the famous specialists began calling him *cher ami*.[1]

In the provinces success was achieved more gradually; several generations were often needed to build up influence, clientele and income. In Mende, capital of the Lozère (population about 6,000), the majority of medical practitioners in the eighteenth century were not doctors: the town had twenty-five surgeons, nine apothecaries and seventeen doctors—the surgeons receiving their education from privately owned schools. But after the Revolution surgeons were compelled to take degrees in medicine and faculties were opened for pharmacists. There was thus an upgrading and equalisation of the different categories. But there was not room in a small town for so many qualified people expecting to live at a fairly high standard: the number of doctors fell to eight or nine. The amount of money spent on medicine was concentrated into few channels and the 'notable' doctors of the nineteenth century

[1] Dr. Gabriel Maurange, *Livre de raison d'un médecin parisien 1815–1938* (1938).

were the result. Even then only one or two rose to this 'notable'
level at any one time. The history of the unsuccessful doctors
and those who dealt with the poor is undocumented: but their
poverty was almost inevitable, since the 'notables' were shameless pluralists, monopolising so many of the official appointments
open to doctors and then handing them down from father to son,
that there were few pickings left for the majority. One such
notable family was established during the Revolution by J. P.
Barbut. He was the son of a peasant, but because he was sickly
and had a malformed arm, he was sent to school. He was
patronised by a doctor who helped him to qualify. He became a
deputy, a justice of the peace, director of the Bagnols thermal
waters, took up farming, wrote a book on the agriculture of the
Lozère and became a member of the Superior Council of
Agriculture—while continuing to minister to all classes. Medicine was thus only a part of a wider social activity. After his
death, his practice was taken over by his son-in-law, Aristide
Barbot, born in 1800, who practised from 1827 to 1861. This
man, the son of a banker-barrister, had enough capital to spend
6,319 francs modernising his equipment in 1829–30; and he was
able to have his sons educated in Paris. He lived comfortably,
at the rate of about 2,500 francs a year. He subscribed to the
Journal de Médecine to keep himself up to date; he improved
his standing in the town by introducing Lennec's methods of
auscultation and Morton and Jackson's anaesthesia with little
delay. He accumulated the posts of prison doctor, member of
the sanitary council, surgeon to the National Guard, member
of the commission for public education and the *école normale*,
and was elected municipal councillor. He hunted, played
whist in a new club of which he was a founder member, went
to the theatre, and gave dinners, above all, great family
dinners: he had four brothers and sisters and sixteen cousins-
german and his wife had fourteen cousins. He was a liberal; he
kept all his jobs through every revolution. He married his
elder daughter to a notary, his younger son became a notary,
and his eldest succeeded him in his own practice (1857–98).
This son married the daughter of a manufacturer, became mayor
of the town, inherited his father's appointments, and collected
even more, outdoing him also in the sumptuousness of his
dinners—rivalry in which was one of the pastimes of the

bourgeoisie. And he was succeeded by his son. The nineteenth century was a golden age for the pharmacists too—the number in Mende fell to one or two—and monopoly brought them great prosperity. Even so, one family after having produced five generations of pharmacists, brought up the next son to be a doctor—the inevitable social progression.[1]

Success in medicine was, to many doctors, only a means to an end. Their ideal of the good life, while including service to the community, also often involved activity in other spheres, and in particular the arts. French doctors were famous for their dedication to hobbies, and one can see the place these had in their lives if one looks at some of the leading luminaries. Hippolyte Hérard (1819–1913), president of the Academy of Medicine, gave as much effort to his piano playing to the point of almost having two careers: 'was not Aesculapius the son of Apollo?' Albert Robin (1847–1928), who became a member of the Academy of Medicine at forty, also ran the metallurgical factory he inherited from his father and was a reviewer for the *New York Herald* for many years, which did not stop him publishing over 400 articles in medical journals and being a consultant to the Tsar of Russia. He, by the way, had been cut off by his father when he originally refused to enter the family business, and he had worked his way through medical school on his own. Louis Brocq (1856–1928) was another who was cut off for refusing to be a barrister like his father and his brother, both of them *bâtonniers* of Agen. When he became famous as a doctor the father relented, reconciliation took place, and he spent his annual holidays at home in Agen. But Brocq's passion was collecting: he had paintings by Monet, Pissarro, Sisley, Renoir and Degas. Jean Hallé (1868–1951) came of a long line of painters going back to the seventeenth century, though some members of his family turned to medicine in the nineteenth. He was a family doctor in the Faubourg Saint Germain where his family had lived for 300 years. He painted, exhibited, travelled abroad and between his two country houses.[2] French doctors have long had a very flourishing painting society, with large

---

[1] Dr. Marcel Barbot, 'Médecins, chirurgiens, et apothicaires mendois des origines au 20ᵉ siècle' (1952, unpublished typescript).

[2] Édouard Rist, *Vingt-cinq portraits de médecins français 1900–50* (1955), lives of members of the Academy of Medicine.

exhibitions; they have been critics and patrons of the arts.[1] An extraordinarily large number of writers have been trained as doctors, and not a few of them have then used their knowledge to attack the profession they forsook or could not find a place in, for its powerlessness and credulity.[2]

Two tentative conclusions may be suggested. The prestige of science and the conquests of medicine placed the doctors in key positions in society, but, like the clergy, their knowledge and their medicine was challenged. Their exclusiveness produced a hostility or jealousy against them which was the counterpart to the anticlericalism which the clergy aroused. This is a factor which needs to be weighed in any discussion of the domination of the bourgeoisie. Each section of this class raised itself up by a monopoly which gave them power and enemies at the same time. Bourgeois society was riddled with a vast number of different anticlericalisms. In these many-sided conflicts, not everybody knew who was his worst enemy. Secondly, the doctors demonstrate, as the other occupations to be discussed will also, that the prestige of technical knowledge in any one subject was seldom accepted as being, by itself, an adequate mark of success. The ideal of general culture remained the final crowning of life. Hence the preoccupation with the arts and letters which was so common. It will be argued in due course that perhaps one ought to talk not of the domination of France by the bourgeoisie, nor even by money, but of the unacknowledged rule of the intellectuals.

A later chapter, dealing with psychology,[3] will discuss in greater detail the relationship of the doctors with the intellectuals. Doctors, and particularly those concerned with mental health, offered explanations of human behaviour and motivation which were not necessarily the same as those proposed by philosophers, or biographers, or novelists. This question, of the way different groups viewed emotion, nervousness, melancholy and other similar troubles, can yield important clues about both the compartmentalisation of French society and about the ideas that were generally accepted in it.

[1] Dr. Paul Labarthe, *Le Carnet du docteur au salon de peinture de 1874* (1874).
[2] Dr. François Salières, *Écrivains contre médecins* (1948); René Cruchet, *La Médecine et les médecins dans la littérature française* (Louisiana and Bordeaux, 1933).
[3] See volume two.

3. Notaries

ANOTHER occupation which was regarded as having a key
position in social, political and economic life was that of
notary. The traditional picture of the notary is of a stable,
respectable, conservative and well-to-do man exercising a profound and acknowledged influence on the masses. It is true that
the notaries were often mayors of their villages. Even today 200
of them still are. The notaries published many books and articles
in praise of their profession and stressing their responsibilities
as notables.[1] One from Besançon, for example, writing in
Napoleon III's reign, ascribed their importance to their being
not only public functionaries but also independent men who
held their posts for life, and had paid for them. Their duties, he
said, placed them on a par with the clergy, for they were present
'at the origin and end of all things in civil life, as the priest
is in the religious order. It is the notary who in the marriage
contract establishes the first bases and first links of the family;
it is he whom the dying man summons to his bedside to confide
his final wishes. As a guardian of every kind of interest, as a con-
fidant of the most secret thoughts, as arbiter in most business
deals, as an almost necessary intermediary in the movement of
property and capital, he becomes the friend, the judge, the
protector of families. The good he can do in these tasks can be
readily understood: he can prevent divisions between relatives,
he can diminish the demands of a greedy or discontented creditor, save an unfortunate debtor from complete ruin; protect
minors, women and absentees in the inventory, accounting and
division of bequests; in short, everywhere he represents law and
justice.'[2]

There were about 40,000 notaries in the late eighteenth century, 13,900 in 1803, 10,300 in 1834, 9,765 in 1855, 8,910 in
1894, 8,164 in 1912, and 6,323, in 1969. These figures at once

[1] Good bibliography in Albert Amiaud, *Recherches bibliographiques sur le notariat
français* (1881).
[2] Édouard Clerc, président de la chambre des notaires de Besançon, *Théorie du
notariat pour servir aux examens de capacité* (3rd edition 1861), xxii.

reveal one of the main and constant problems of the profession: that it was overcrowded and that a large proportion was unable to get a decent living out of it. In the *ancien régime* there was an immense variety of notaries, royal and seigniorial, so that every little town had one and often more than one, and sometimes even villages had them.[1] Inevitably a lot were on the level of impecunious artisans; it was not unusual for their wives to be shopkeepers. An author writing in 1891 had personally known a Breton notary whose wife kept an inn next to her husband's office, to which his clients went for a drink before and after their business.[2] Until the eighteenth century, the notary's office was called a *boutique*; the first occasion the word *étude* was used was in 1736. In this period, the value of these practices was often low, since they were increasingly burdened by many kinds of taxation—even if they were exempt from many other taxes—and their profits were diminished by the creation of many new offices by the king. The top echelons had acquired compatibility of their profession with nobility, but the lowest were struggling for a bare living. In the cahiers of 1789, they demanded above all a reduction in their numbers, the prevention of competition between themselves and the suppression of rival professions. Napoleon met their wishes in part. He kept only the state notaries, and he divided these into three classes, the first with the right to practise within the jurisdiction of a court of appeal (about 4 per cent of them), the second within an *arrondissement* (about 13 per cent), and the third within a canton (the vast majority). They retained the ownership of their offices, with the right to sell them. They were civil servants but received no salary, relying entirely on fees. They thus kept a great deal of independence, but their plutocratic recruitment kept them in constant fear that their offices might be nationalised. There was frequent talk of buying them out and opening the profession to competition by examination —but it was calculated in the 1850s that this would require at least 800 million francs—as much as it cost to build a whole railway system.[3]

---

[1] Ludovic Langlois, *La Communauté des notaires de Tours de 1512 à 1791* (1911), 472.

[2] Jules Rouxel, *La Crise notariale. Étude économique et psychologique du notariat moderne* (1891), 20.

[3] A. Jeannest St. Hilaire, *Du Notariat et des offices* (1857), 115.

In order to become a notary one needed no diploma and even today the majority of notaries do not have a school leaving certificate (*baccalauréat*).[1] One usually served an apprenticeship[2] —but the 30,000 to 40,000 notaries' clerks very rarely became notaries, because the main qualification was the possession of 15,000 to 20,000 francs at the very least, in the mid nineteenth century, to buy the cheapest *étude*, and 40,000 francs upwards for most others, 100,000 francs for one in a departmental capital, 300,000 francs in a Paris suburb and up to 700,000 francs for the most lucrative of all in the centre of Paris.[3] In addition the purchaser had to give the state caution money varying according to the area he served, 1,800 to 5,200 francs for third-class notaries, 3,000 to 12,000 francs for second-class ones and 40,000 to 50,000 francs for the first class. The size of the town did not count in this reckoning of caution money: Roubaix with a population of 100,000 in the 1890s still required only 5,200 francs, because it was only the capital of a canton, but Nantes, with the same population, being a departmental capital, required 25,000 francs.[4] A notary's office was to some extent an investment. In 1870 it could be bought at ten years' purchase—but by 1890 it was down to seven or eight years.[5] Competition and crises made the returns less certain than might at first appear. After investing these large sums, notaries not infrequently went bankrupt. Since there was no serious control of their suitability or of their integrity, many absconded with their clients' funds. Until 1870 there was each year an average of a dozen scandals followed by loss of office. In 1875 there were 28 such scandals, in 1882 there were 31, in 1883 41, in 1884 55, in 1886 71, and in 1889 103. In the years 1880–6 62 million francs were embezzled or lost by notaries. In one canton in the Nord, in 1888, all five notaries took flight together, and in the same year four notaries in Nantes were simultaneously prosecuted. In the second half of the century, there was thus practically no canton in France which had not experienced a bankrupt or criminal notary. Hostile articles were written

---

[1] Paul Lefèvre, *Les Notaires* (1969).

[2] Lucien Genty, *La Basoche notariale. Origines et histoire du XIVe siècle à nos jours de la cléricature notariale* (1888).

[3] E. Charton, *Guide pour le choix d'un état* (1842), 464.

[4] Rouxel, 52.

[5] Cf. Charton with P. Jacquemart, *Professions et métiers* (1892), 708–10.

(following the lead of the President of the Court of Cassation
in 1854) saying the notaries had a crime rate three times higher
than the inhabitants of Paris, dangerous city though that
was. More recently only in Paris have bankruptcies been successfully avoided: there have been none there for the past fifty
years. It is the notaries of the south who are most prone to
default. The two worst periods were the 1840s and 1880s—
and each was followed by a campaign and legislation against
them.[1]

The crises were the result of vicious circles: the attraction of
the office put up the price beyond what it was worth and the
bankruptcies brought discredit on the whole profession. Many
towns, however agreeable physically, could not afford a notary.
The prospect of an easy and prosperous existence was a mirage,
produced by the few who had large inherited incomes. The
average net earnings of a notary in the 1850s were estimated
at between 2,000 and 3,000 francs.[2] The notaries pressed for
the abolition of the least productive *études* and, as occasion
offered, many were abolished—no fewer than 429 between
1895 and 1909. But in 1913—by which time prices and wages
had risen considerably, there were still some offices yielding
less than 2,000 francs a year gross, 1,572 yielding less than 5,000
francs gross, 2,760 5,000 to 10,000 francs, 2,880 10,000 to
30,000, and only about a thousand over 30,000—many of the
Paris offices of course reaching far higher figures, over 100,000
francs.[3] The variation in the income of notaries was thus so
great that some earned fifty times as much as others—which
no doubt helped to confuse popular conceptions of the office.
Some notaries were barely distinguishable from peasants—just
capable of reading and writing and having no education beyond
the primary school.[4] In 1970 this problem of the varied nature
of the notaries had still not been solved. Though on average
Paris notaries employed twenty-five clerks each, there were
still 593 notaries who worked alone without any clerk at all,
'like veritable artisans', and there were several hundred offices
up for sale unable to find purchasers. Though in 1934 a central

---

[1] Rouxel, 2–3.
[2] Jeannest, 155.
[3] Émile Bender, *La Réforme notariale* (1913), 143.
[4] Raoul de La Grasserie, *L'État actuel et la réforme du notariat en France* (1898),
159–60.

fund was at last established, on the basis of subscriptions from notaries, to guarantee the public against defaulters, and though in 1945 a slightly more vigorous system of education was introduced, the bankruptcies and embezzlements continue (in 1968 there were fourteen). The profession has set up a scheme to enable those without capital to borrow 50 per cent of the cost of their office—but the profession is still not demo-cratised. The Armand-Rueff commission of 1959–60 was the latest in the long line of inquiries set up to see how change could be effected. This commission was somewhat more effec-tive than that of 1909, before which the notaries refused to appear.

Balzac painted the notary as the model of respectability and reliability. 'When a notary has not got the immobile and gently rounded face you can recognise, if he does not offer to society the unlimited guarantee of his mediocrity, if he is not the polished steel cog that he ought to be, if there is left in him any suggestion that he is in the least bit an artist, capricious, passionate or a lover, he is lost.'[1] But it is very difficult to describe such a varied collection of people briefly with any accuracy; and in any case the role the notary played in the life of the country varied not only with his personal characteristics, but also with the region where he practised. Different provinces made use of his services in a far from uniform way. In the legal province of Grenoble (the area over which the court of appeal of Grenoble had jurisdiction) the notary was used in the 1850s to draw up only one legal document for every eleven inhabitants, but in Agen he made one for every six inhabitants. The notaries were like-wise used almost twice as often, proportionately to the popula-tion, in Caen as in Orléans. This was not strictly related to the litigiousness of the different regions. Grenoble and Caen used their notaries about the same, but the former went to court almost twice as often as the latter, four times as often as Orléans, and five times as often as Angers. The geography of legal influence deserves its map beside that of the Church's influence.[2] It is not easy to explain it until much detailed research is done. But a factor of importance is the cost of the notarial act. At first there was no uniformity at all in the fees

[1] Raymond Herment, *Sous la poussière des panonceaux* (Nice, 1955), 275.
[2] A. Jeannest St. Hilaire, *Du Notariat et des offices* (1857), 346–7.

notaries charged; vigorous competition and undercutting were
the rule. For long they resisted attempts to impose a uniform
tariff: but gradually different provinces drew up minimum
rates and it was only in 1945 that a national rate was agreed.
Even so the way fees were calculated was very complicated and
a notary had no trouble at all in juggling with the nomencla-
ture of the services he had rendered to vary his bill. The
drawing up of a power of attorney could cost (in 1900) either
9 francs or 26 francs, depending on how it was done.[1] The result
was that a host of unqualified competitors mushroomed to offer
alternatives. Every town began to see agencies set up in it—
information bureaux, estate agents, debt collectors, legal
advisory services, sometimes run in a hired room of an inn
by a retired sergeant-major, a barrister or a land surveyor.
Notaries' clerks wrote books advising people how to draw up
legal documents without the intervention of notaries. The saving
in money could certainly be enormous, even though the notaries
argued that the subsequent lawsuits, due to ignorance of the
law, cancelled these out, and that these amateur fees, being
uncontrolled, often turned out to be expensive swindles. But
a peasant dying in 1865 leaving a small field and a hovel
worth 900 francs might pay as much as 458 francs in fees to the
notary and other officials. He had strong temptations to go
elsewhere—all the more so because in addition the state had
a right to 208 francs in tax, and the notary was bound to levy it,
while the amateurs were not.[2]

For the notaries were tax collectors as well as lawyers and
indeed the variety of their functions was such that they exerted
an influence—both moral and financial—which could justly be
compared with that of the priests. In the country they worked
on Sundays, doing much business with peasants coming in to
church from the surrounding hamlets. Some even opened stalls
in the market-place and were so busy they got the peasants to
sign blank sheets of paper which they filled in later. Their textbooks enjoined them to use their skills to moralise and reconcile
their clients, bolster paternal authority and filial piety, urge
the unmarried to marry, but then to attend the wedding feasts
with 'an imposing gravity' designed to extirpate the indecency

[1] E. Breton, *Les Coulisses du notariat* (1904), 60.
[2] A. Granveau, *Analyse philosophique des usages en France* (1865), 46.

that so frequently marred these celebrations.[1] As will be seen later, the notaries played a major role in altering the financial aspects of family life through the way they drew up marriage contracts—thus contributing to establishing new relations between husbands, wives, children and relatives. They modernised the law—in keeping with pressure from public opinion—while in these matters parliament usually set up committees which never reported. It is strange their legislative activities have been so little studied. The way they have modified parliamentary laws, and found means to soften or get round them altogether, has probably been even more significant than the jurisprudence of the courts, essential though knowledge of this is to understanding what really happened in France, as opposed to what the politicians said ought to happen. The notaries had a decisive influence on the economic development of the country, through their control of the small man's investments. It was to them that people traditionally took their savings—when they ventured to go beyond the stage of keeping their money under the mattress—for a return, it seems, of between $3\frac{1}{2}$ to 5 per cent. They were the intermediaries when people wished to borrow and they found lenders, usually on mortgage security. It has been estimated that in 1912 they arranged loans to the tune of 748 million francs, whereas the Crédit Foncier de France lent only 124 million.[2] Now the principle which guided them was not the object of the loan, but the reliability of security which could be obtained for it. It is known that they channelled the majority of small savings into mortgages and state bonds. Their education and training were usually inadequate to enable them to cope with the problems of industrialisation. Because companies tended to avoid using them as far as possible, so as to spare themselves the high cost of official notarial acts, they had fewer relations with industry than was desirable from the point of view of economic expansion.[3] In this they seem to have kept up with the times less than in family relations—but again this is a subject on which more research needs to be done.

[1] R..., notaire, *Le Notariat considéré dans ses rapports intimes et journaliers avec la morale* (1847), 104; A. J. Massé, *Le Parfait Notaire* (1807).

[2] Fernand Dubas, *Du Rôle actuel économique et social du notariat français* (Caen thesis, Mesnil, Eure, 1918), 60.

[3] André Desmazières, *L'Évolution du rôle du notaire dans la constitution des sociétés par actions* (1948).

Now every act the notary drew up involved the payment of dues to the state as well as fees to himself. On average he collected eight times as much money in taxes as in fees. He therefore stood in the ambiguous position of being partly a tax collector and partly an adviser to individuals on how to avoid paying taxes. The notary has to pay the taxes on the deeds he executes, whether the client pays them to him or not, but he gets no personal commission from the taxes. His interest is to multiply the number of deeds, rather than to increase the tax yield. Until 1918 he made free use of deposit safes in banks to defraud the treasury of death-duties. (A law of 1923 required a representative of the ministry of finance to be present at the opening of these safes after a death.) Because of his fiscal responsibilities, he has to use a language in the drawing up of deeds which meets with the approval of the stamp duty administration, so he does not readily find new solutions for new situations: the old formulae protected him best. It is only very recently that he has been working towards the use of clearer language—though conversely he is also losing his role of adviser and confessor and becoming more of a technician.[1] To prevent him running off with the money deposited with him, or using it for speculation, laws have been passed requiring him to deposit it with the Bank of France: this was worth 1,400 million to the state in 1935 but it is not clear that the laws were always followed. More successful were the voluntary agreements by which he drew up the mortgages for loans made by the Crédit Agricole, in return for which employment he deposited large sums from his clients with it.

The simple view of the notary as a representative of bourgeois law, order and domination is clearly a myth of wishful thinking created by the conservatives themselves. No doubt he did influence the peasants' lives. No doubt being 'less superior, less isolated than the magistrature, more independent than administrative civil servants', he could more easily communicate with the masses. His parish was small enough—each dealt on average with around 3,000 people. But as one notary said, 'The subtle cunning of the peasant, cleverly disguised under the pretence of

---

[1] Marcel Brisse, *Essai sur le rôle fiscal du notaire* (1937), 214–17; Charles Collet and André Oudard, *L'Évolution du notariat parisien au cours de l'époque contemporaine 1900–1960* (1961).

ingenuous ignorance and an attractive *bonhomie*, give him undoubted advantages in [his] incessant struggle against the
notary.'[1] The scenes that took place in his office were often
ritual pantomimes or market bargaining rather than confessions,
with the peasants lying and the notary using his experience to
discern the truth that honour or slyness refused to reveal.
Economically, each was often trying to make a profit out of the
other. The town notary, shielded behind his clerks, was a
dangerous official. The truly rural one was a force in local
rivalries whom the peasant might try to play off against the
mayor and the irate officials. It was no accident that the
notaries were persecuted at the Revolution more than any
other profession, some say more than the aristocracy—for they
were usurers.

The notaries moreover were at war not just with their clients
but with the magistracy too. Poor though some of them were,
they were nearly always richer than the ill-paid judges, and
they had invested their inheritances to make money out of the
law. They had an active business life, while the magistrates,
brought up on the classics and condemned to a retiring and
modest existence, compensated for their poverty by a pretence
of social superiority. But the magistrates had in theory certain
supervisory functions over them—in disputes they could fix
their fees—and they used their powers with an acrimony
inspired by a fierce and notorious jealousy. Thus, for example,
in cases of compulsory seizures or sales, the courts had the
option of ordering the sale to be held officially by the justice
of the peace or privately by a notary, and they consistently
deprived the notaries of business. The latter replied by inventing
a procedure during the Restoration inserting clauses in contracts
they drew up that, in the event of a sale being necessary, this
should be done privately by the notary. But the courts declared
these clauses invalid. And so the quarrel continued under
different guises. Finally the notaries were ill at ease with
the government. Their privileges were under constant threat
and the question of the reform of the notariat recurred again
and again in parliament. Because of their image as solid
conservatives, they had a reputation of being Orleanist—
but this seems to be another over-simple generalisation.

[1] Jeannest, 168.

It was said that many were Bonapartist because Napoleon reconstituted their order after the Revolution and enhanced their prestige by ordering voting registers to be kept in their *études*. Under Louis-Philippe they did not oppose the government, but were constantly attacked by it. In 1844 they were required to pay the *patente* like petty shopkeepers even though an *ordonnance* of 1843 forbade them to take part in business or industry. In 1841 a tax of 2 per cent was imposed in the transmission of their offices, but they were given no guarantee to the ownership of them and plans to reform them were discussed. The Court of Cassation in 1841 made an exception of notaries and allowed the state to sue them for arrears of taxation for thirty years. It also declared null and void any notary's act not made in the real presence of two notaries (when it was an accepted practice that the second one added his signature afterwards). But then the government of Napoleon III harassed them with interference in the pricing of their offices: the Third Republic tried repeatedly to control their activities more closely.

The role of notaries in society has thus varied considerably in different regions and at different times. Most recently the notaries have emerged as a pressure group, organised at last in a trade union. In 1934 a series of *conférences générales des notaires* were established as a 'melting-pot of ideas and a centre of intellectual activity'. These have urged notaries to take a larger part in the social, economic and political life of the nation.[1] This may mean that, at the ebb of their influence, the notaries are seeking to revive their power by turning themselves into some kind of intellectuals. But perhaps it shows also how the sources of influence change with time: perhaps their activities hold a less important place in daily life today, or perhaps the other forms of power they sometimes combined with their notarial profession—leadership in local affairs—are now more exposed to attack and questioning.

[1] Herment, 333.

4. The Rich

A COMMON generalisation about France is that it was controlled for most of this period by 200 families who held most of its wealth, ran its major industries, and bribed its politicians to do their bidding. Behind the façade of democracy stood a discreet oligarchy, most of whose names the public did not even know. This idea was particularly current in the 1930s. Daladier made it a political slogan. 'Two hundred families', he declared to the Radical Congress of 1934, 'are master of the French economy and in fact of French politics. The influence of two hundred families weighs on the fiscal system, on transport, on credit. The two hundred families place their delegates in political office. They interfere with public opinion, because they control the press.' The precise number of families and the precise date at which they acquired their influence varied in the accusations of different people. Daladier called it 'a new feudalism'. A contemporary of his, the Senator Lesaché, who went into greater detail in unveiling the oligarchy, claimed it had grown up only in the 1920s, and he put the figure variously at between 150 and 300.[1] But already in 1869 Georges Duchêne, a friend of Proudhon, had inveighed against the monopoly of power in the hands of '200 nabobs', adding that 'Antiquity does not contain any examples of an oligarchy so concentrated.'[2] The figure of 200 was always rather theoretical. It was suggested probably by the annual meeting of the shareholders of the Bank of France. Though the Bank had over 40,000 shareholders, under its Napoleonic statutes only the 200 with the largest number of shares could attend the meeting. They had subscribed only a small fraction of the Bank's capital, but they had complete control of it. They elected its fifteen regents, usually from among their own number. Members of the same few families were regents for generation after generation, accentuating the oligarchical nature of the control. Even the Governor of the Bank, though appointed

---

[1] Henry Coston, *Le Retour des 200 familles* (1960), 10–12.
[2] Georges Duchêne, *L'Empire industriel* (1869), 299.

by the state, had to own 100 shares. The state's nominees to
the board of regents could be outvoted by the industrialists and
financiers who formed the majority.

This arrangement epitomised, in the eyes of the radicals and
socialists in particular, what went on in most large firms. Their
boards of directors were composed of men who held only a
small number of shares but enough to get themselves elected.
The great mass of shareholders did not have the leisure to
attend the company meetings, or else were specifically excluded
by the statutes, or by the issue of non-voting shares. The banks
offered to collect dividends for those of them who deposited
their shares with them and in return obtained the voting rights
of those shares. They were thus able to obtain a disproportionate
number of directorships for their own nominees, and all the
more so since they frequently demanded a seat on the board in
return for relatively small loans. The directorships of the large
firms in France thus came to be held by a narrow circle of men
who usually did nothing else for their livings, and could afford
not to, because they kept dividends down to a minimum but
paid themselves enormous fees. Already under Napoleon III,
Émile Péreire held nineteen directorships, his brother Isaac
twelve, and his nephew Eugène nine. Together with other relatives the Péreire clan thus controlled fifty companies with a
capital of five milliard francs.[1] Duchêne claimed that 183 individuals in this way controlled two-thirds of the share capital on
the market in 1869. In the 1930s, Lederlin was a director of 63
companies, Ernest Cuvelette of 47, Ernest Mercier of 46; there
were in all about 144 people, each of whom was a director of at
least ten companies.[2] Since many of these were intermarried,
family exclusiveness placed a further barrier between them and
the masses. Baron Georges Brincard, for example, President of
the Crédit Lyonnais, was the son-in-law of the founder of that
leading bank, Henri Germain. He was related to the Gramont,
Rothschild, Fabre-Luce, and Voguë families, all of whom had
numerous representatives on many other boards. Then the
Rothschilds were in turn related to the Fould, Heine and
Lazard banking families. Schneider the metallurgist was
related to Lebaudy the sugar refiner, Mame the Catholic

---

[1] G. Duchêne, *Études sur la féodalité française* (1867), 37.
[2] *Le Crapouillot* (Mar. 1936) issue on 'Les Deux Cent familles', 21–2.

publishers, Wendel the other great metallurgist, Cossè Brissac and Citroen. And so it went on. The opposition to these clans was inevitably exacerbated when they used their wealth to subsidise political causes (which was particularly noticeable in the inter-war period), when they bought up newspapers and gave directorships or shares to politicians they hoped to influence. Three presidents of the republic in the inter-war years —Doumer, Doumergue and Lebrun—had all been directors of leading companies.[1]

Another attack on the 200 families was made in 1910 by Francis Delaisi. He argued that only one-quarter of the national budget was spent on civil servants. About another quarter was paid in interest to the *rentiers*. The rest went to the state's contractors and suppliers of armaments and public works. Three-quarters of taxation was thus fed back to the rich. The oligarchy in charge of the Bank of France used the national wealth to support another clique, the republican party, as its tool in politics. The Crédit Foncier, which dispensed credit to farmers and had mortgages on one-fifth of the land of France, was also ruled by its 200 largest shareholders, paying $2\frac{1}{2}$ per cent to its petty-bourgeois investors but charging $4\frac{1}{2}$ per cent to its borrowers. The four large deposit banks paid $\frac{1}{2}$ per cent or 1 per cent to their 1,500,000 depositors, but charged 3 or 4 per cent to its most favoured borrowers; they diverted French savings into foreign stocks, for their private profit but with disastrous results for the French economy. The oligarchs were not anti-democratic, because they knew how to manipulate democracy. They spent money freely at elections, supporting radicals and independent socialists when it suited them. Briand's *Lanterne* was said to have been subsidised by Eugène Péreire and the Compagnie Transatlantique. When they did not put a deputy under an obligation to them at the time of his election, they were quick to offer him lucrative posts as 'legal adviser' to their companies. Thus Waldeck-Rousseau was paid (so said Delaisi) 100,000 francs a year by American insurance companies, in return for which they were allowed to drain France quietly of its savings. The Rente Foncière Company employed Mille-rand as its legal counsel, the Crédit Foncier and St. Gobain

[1] Jean Baumier, *Les Grandes Affaires françaises. Des 200 familles aux 200 managers* (1967).

employed Poincaré: and the latter after successfully defending St. Gobain in a lawsuit which might have sent to prison two of its directors, the Marquis de Voguë and Thureau-Dangin (permanent secretary of the Académie Française), was elected to the Academy. The pettiest provincial lawyer-deputy could now count on jobs from two or three companies, to earn 40,000 francs a year: former ministers could expect ten times that sum. The financial oligarchy safeguarded itself by quickly adding to its boards any budding politician likely to hold or to return to office. With all these precautions it was able to ensure that the *rapporteurs* of all bills concerned with contracts would be favourable to them. The Senator Humbert, *rapporteur* of the war budget, received 12,000 francs a year from the firm of Darracq, which manufactured lorries for the army, and it even gave him a percentage commission on every order he obtained for it. Humbert confessed all this, to prove his honesty, when brought to trial on another matter. He produced his accounts which showed, he said, that he behaved as all other politicians did—and no one contradicted him. His expenses were 64,200 francs a year, and his parliamentary salary 15,000. He bridged the gap by being 'agent général' of the Darracq lorry factory, at 12,000 a year plus commission; and by earning a further 18,000 for running *Le Matin*, a newspaper where he could beat the patriotic drum, which would stimulate military contracts.

Of course the oligarchs also went into parliament themselves, but they discreetly formed an independent group, which though small, was able to throw its weight to the left or the right in a decisive manner. Aynard the banker, regent of the Bank of France, on the boards of the Aciéries de St. Étienne, the PLM railway and the Compagnie Générale de Navigation, and Joseph Reinach, Rothschild's nominee, were pointed out as the men who controlled this group and so the destinies of ministries. The permanence of their domination came from the fact that the rich subsidised both left and right. The Crédit Lyonnais and the large industrialists subsidised the Catholics, the Société Générale, the Jewish bankers and the Comité Mascuraud of smaller businessmen paid the freemasons. In so far as parties depended on newspapers, and newspapers could not survive without financial advertisements (since other forms of advertisement took a long time to develop), the press was in the pay of the oligarchs. Censorship might have been legally abolished, but there were things which the bankers forbade the press to mention. Thus Jean Dupuy, owner of the best-selling *Petit Parisien*, is said to have made a deal with Waldeck-Rousseau to drop his opposition to Dreyfus, in return for a seat in the cabinet. Bunau-Varilla, owner of *Le Matin*, is said to have obtained confiscated monastic property for his son-in-law at a ludicrously low price, in return for showing favourable neutrality to Combes. Clemenceau was thrown out of parliament for having incurred the wrath of the *Petit Journal*, until the Jewish bankers behind *L'Aurore* decided to bring him back. So democracy in France was a façade. There were, said Delaisi, about fifty-five people who, by their control of big business, were omnipotent over the country's life.[1]

The theory of the 200 families draws attention to relationships of great importance—on which more will be said later—but it was never based on an impartial scrutiny of history. Thus the number of people in the oligarchy was probably very much larger than 200. In 1922, for example, a list of the main companies in France contained 434 firms (covering mines, metal, transport, banks, public utilities, insurance and property) with about 4,000 directors. Of these about 520 were directors of three companies or more.[2] By 1953 there were 22,753 limited liability companies, but even if one puts aside all those with assets of less than three milliard francs, one is still left with almost 2,000 directors.[3] Industry was not sufficiently concentrated to give even this group of people a dominant role in the economy. In 1906 there were 215 industrial firms with over 1,000 workers; in 1931 there were 421; in 1936 296. There were also, at these three dates 412, 713, and 615 firms with between 500 and 1,000 workers.[4] In 1906 51 per cent of the industrial working class were employed by firms with less than fifty workers.[5] A study still needs to be made of the proportion

[1] Francis Delaisi, *La Démocratie et les financiers* (1910).
[2] Based on Annuaire Chaix, *Les Principales Sociétés par action* (1932).
[3] Nicole Delfortrie-Soubeyroux, *Les Dirigeants de l'industrie française* (1961), is an analysis of these 1964 directors.
[4] J. M. Jeanneney, *Forces et faiblesses de l'économie française* (1956), 259. The statistics do not give information about ownership and these firms may have been owned by a smaller number.
[5] A. Fontaine *et al.*, *La Concentration des entreprises* (1913), 59.

of the national product for which the large firms were responsible.

Some idea of just how many rich men there were in France
can be obtained—very roughly—from the statistics of inheritances. In 1933 53·6 per cent of the people who died (354,147
out of 661,082) left nothing. Of those who did leave something,
52 per cent (185,473) left less than 10,000 francs. Another
119,774 left less than 50,000 francs. 25,808 left between 50,000
and 100,000 francs, and 14,838 left between 100,000 and
250,000. Now all those leaving between 10,000 and 250,000
francs together left only 6,606 million. But 1,512 people left over
one million each, 4,203 million together, i.e. 30 per cent of all
wealth left at death, and of these 1,512 162 account for 1,718
million. There were thus indeed 162 people dying in one year
owning about 10 per cent of the wealth left in that year. This
means that there was a very small minority of very rich people,
but this minority must be numbered in several or many thousands (multiply 1,512 or even 162 by 20, if wealth changes
hands every twenty years).[1] One may, to take it another way,
look at the wealth left by people dying in 1900, before death-
duties arrived to encourage fraudulent declarations. At that
date, a mere 2 per cent of those who left any money accounted
for over half of the total amount of money left. But in this year
about two-thirds of all those dying left something, and 2 per cent
of deaths produces well over 10,000 people a year.[2] 30 per cent
of the total value of inheritances were left by 15 per cent of those
leaving anything, so there was indeed a sizeable middle class.
It may be that as the total value of property left increased in the
course of this period—the value of successions rose from 2,700
million in 1850 to 7,200 in 1901—so the distance between the
penniless and the rich increased. But there seems to be some
disagreement about this. What a man leaves at his death does
not give a full picture of his prosperity. Statistics have been
brought forward to show that the distance between rich and
poor has decreased because the poor are less poor than they
used to be and there are fewer poor people. Colbert had an
income 500 times that of a labourer, but few could claim
the same today. The ratio between the income of a *conseiller*

[1] Augustin Hamon, *Les Maîtres de la France* (1936), 1. 21.
[2] P. Sorlin, *La Société française* (1969), 1. 131.

d'état and a labourer has fallen from 55 : 1 in 1800 to 18 : 1 in
1900 and 7 : 1 in 1960. Moreover, in 1800 75 per cent of the
population was at the level of the labourer but in 1960 less than
10 per cent were. In terms of purchasing power, the rich have
not got richer. The real purchasing power of a labourer has
tripled or even quadrupled since 1830 but that of a middle-
grade civil servant has barely changed. Men without qualifications have had their incomes raised to 80 per cent of those of
qualified workers, as opposed to 50 per cent in 1800. Women are
now only 20 per cent behind men.[1] In this period there was a
radical transformation of the status of the poor. Until the early
nineteenth century famine still descended on them whenever there
was a bad harvest. Their standard of living was directly dependent on the weather, and the price of bread could fluctuate
threefold in different years. But in 1850, for the first time, the
price of a quintal of wheat fell to less than 100 hours of labourer's
work, and 1856 was the last year in which it exceeded 200.
1891 was the last year in which it exceeded 100. By 1935 it
had fallen to 50, by 1955 to 25, and by 1958 to 20.[2] Differences
in wealth therefore meant different things at the two extremes
of our period.

Altogether in 1900 the idle rich might have consisted of as
many as half a million people. At any rate that number of
adults declared themselves to be *rentiers* pursuing no other
occupation; though of course a large proportion of these were
probably more idle than rich. It should be remembered that
in 1848 Louis-Philippe's electorate of the well-to-do had grown
to nearly a quarter of a million. But a very significant change in
the character of the rich took place in these fifty years, at least
so far as the source of their income was concerned. In 1848
only about 5 per cent of money left at death was in shares,
while 58 per cent was in land or houses. By 1900 31 per cent was
in shares and only 45 per cent in land or houses. At the beginning of this period therefore the rich were above all landlords,
drawing rent from houses or farms. These were considered the
safest form of investment, assuring the greatest social prestige.
As a result, the weight of the exploitation of the rich was felt
by the masses in a very different way at these two dates. The

---

[1] Jean Fourastié, *Machinisme et bien être. Niveau de vie et genre de vie en France de 1700
à nos jours* (1962), 52.   [2] Ibid., 65.

investor under Louis-Philippe liked to know personally exactly where he was putting his money. So he would buy a farm he could see, and a house whose tenants he would choose. He would lend substantial amounts of cash to individuals whose value he could assess. His money would extend his influence among a definite body of people: if he was rich enough he would build up a whole clan of dependants. This can be seen by looking at the distribution of wealth of men calling themselves 'proprietors' in the Paris of Louis-Philippe. They invested about 43 per cent of their wealth in land or houses (two-thirds of it in Paris, one-third in the provinces), they placed about 18 per cent in state bonds, safest after houses, and then they lent 15 per cent to individuals. They put only 3·7 per cent in company shares, and 4·5 per cent in the shares of the Bank of France. Retired members of the liberal professions, on average, lent 25 per cent of their wealth to individuals and put 53 per cent in land and houses. Those who were pure *rentiers* with no immovable property at all, lent 44 per cent of their wealth to individuals, put 33 per cent in state bonds but only 5 per cent in company shares. When, in the third quarter of the nineteenth century, the price of land began to fall, houses became even more popular as an alternative. Rents tripled in value between 1850 and 1913, as house building took on enormous proportions in the cities.

However, as prosperity increased under Napoleon III the rich began to have difficulty in knowing what to do with their money. That is why the speculation for which that reign is notorious could become so feverish. Not all the French were as frightened of taking risks as has been made out. A great many poured a lot of money into highly imaginative and even romantic industrial and financial schemes. Financial newspapers telling those with money to spare what to do with it sprang up on every side. In 1881 there were at least 228 of these (as against 95 political papers: who will dare conclude that the French must therefore have been more interested in money than politics?). In 1857 the largest circulation of a financial newspaper was 7,000; in 1880 there were several with nearly 100,000 readers each.[1] That is why Proudhon could castigate the

[1] Michael Palmer, 'The Press in the early Third Republic', D.Phil. thesis in preparation at St. Antony's College, Oxford.

plutocrats as speculators.[1] Nevertheless, though this press, for mercenary reasons, tried to sell every kind of share, it was only partly successful in turning the plutocrats into shareholders. The change did occur, as has been seen, but to a limited extent. The most respectable of the financial journalists counselled extreme caution. Paul Leroy-Beaulieu may be taken as the most influential of these: his work on *The Art of Investing and Managing One's Fortune* sold 33,000 copies in its first two years and was also serialised in the *Économiste Français*. He stressed forcefully that land had lost a quarter of its value between 1880 and 1900, and that its purchase could involve taxes of up to 10 per cent of the price. He thought that investment in houses was equally outdated, and should be left to experts. But he also vigorously dissuaded his readers from investing directly in industry. Industrial shares he classified as speculative. 'Recent disasters', he said menacingly, quoting the collapse of the Paris Omnibus Co. and the Say Sugar Refineries as examples, 'prove that industrial firms which are perfectly sound can in a few weeks or months and with no one suspecting it, be gravely compromised and sometimes even destroyed by the mistakes, optimism or fraud of their directors who appeared to merit every confidence.' Such shares, commendable though they were because they were often the instruments of the most recent progress, should be left to the great capitalists who could afford to take risks, though even they should confine themselves to industries of which they had some technical knowledge. To *pères de famille* Leroy-Beaulieu recommended state bonds and railways (French and foreign).[2] The figures do not all agree on exactly how far the French followed this advice, but it is certain in any case that by the turn of the century they were investing noticeably less in houses and lands. The anonymous shareholder replaced the personal usurer. It was this which encouraged the socialist outcry against the faceless plutocracy.

However, in the course of the inter-war period the French investor was changing once again. Bounding inflation forced a revision of traditional views. The collapse of many of the foreign countries into which they had poured so much money,

---

[1] P. J. Proudhon, *Manuel du spéculateur* (1856).
[2] P. Leroy-Beaulieu, *L'Art de placer et gérer sa fortune* (1908 edition), 83, 86, 203, etc.

most notably Russia and Austria, showed that state bonds were
far from being safest. So there was a return to land and houses
once more, slowly at first, but greatly speeded up by the
Second World War. According to one calculation, investment
in these rose from 37 per cent in 1908 to 43 per cent in 1934 to
54 per cent in 1949 and 60 per cent in 1953.[1] This change did
not entirely follow the rules of logic, for rent control introduced
after the First World War made houses less profitable, and
agriculture slumped. But after repeated disasters playing for
safety became the principal aim. This is shown for example by
the growing popularity of hoarding gold, even though, again,
this was not financially speaking the most profitable way of
using one's money. Such was the popularity of the gold louis
(far easier to hoard than the bulky ingot), that it carried a
premium of 40 per cent. But it did have the important attraction that it could most easily escape death-duties. The be-
wilderment of the French investor in the middle of the twentieth
century may be seen from an inquiry carried out into savings
habits in 1953. 24 per cent of Frenchmen thought that gold was
the safest investment (but only 3 per cent of Belgians, who in
general gave very different answers). The habit of saving had
not quite been destroyed by inflation. 58 per cent of the
bourgeois questioned and 34 per cent of the workers said they
believed in saving. However, by now they were equally
disillusioned with state bonds, and the Belgians proved to be
three times more willing to subscribe to them than the French.
72 per cent believed that investment in land, houses, gold,
jewelry and pictures was the most secure: only 16 per cent
stood up for shares. A mere 8 per cent followed the stock
market. Only 11 per cent had inherited shares. But this does
show roughly the considerable number of people involved in
the global category of the faceless plutocracy.[2] It had clearly
become a plutocracy on the defensive, which is perhaps why
it became so aggressive politically in the inter-war years. It
is not surprising that a guide to investment published in
1935 should be entitled *The Art of Managing and Protecting one's
Fortune.*[3]

1   Paul Cornut, *Répartition de la fortune privée en France* (1963), chapter 29.
2   Roger Truptil, *L'Art de gérer sa fortune* (1957), 50–93.
3   Constantin Piron, *L'Art de gérer et de défendre sa fortune* (1935).

5. Industrialists

THE reality behind the myth of the 200 families is complicated. It deserves to be looked at in greater detail. It would be useful also to study it in the light of another general accusation made about French industrialists, which in many ways contradicts it. This is the family firm theory of David Landes. He has argued that the average French entrepreneur was a small businessman acting for himself or at most on behalf of a handful of partners, and that this was not only true in 1875 but, despite some exceptions, was still so at the end of the century. These small businessmen were essentially conservatives, disliking the new and the unknown, slow to modernise their equipment, doggedly self-sufficient financially. With rare exceptions, firms were organised on a family basis, obtaining finance from family or close friends only and very seldom on the open market. They were seen not as a method of producing goods with a view to obtaining indefinite wealth and power, but as 'a sort of fief that maintained and enhanced the position of the family, just as the produce of the manor and the men at arms it could muster were the material basis of medieval status'. Business was thus seen only as a means, not as an end in itself, engaged in for the preservation more than the creation of riches. Caution therefore had to be its watchword, and rapid expansion was never sought. Such firms could exist side by side with the few modern companies which were established because their ethos was partially accepted by the latter also, who preferred to raise their prices rather than eliminate these inefficient competitors.[1] This picture of France as a country of small firms is of course supported by the global statistics, though the statistics conceal almost as much as they reveal.

Landes has been mainly concerned with explaining the weakness of the French economy, the slow rate of its industrial

[1] D. Landes, 'French Entrepreneurship and Industrial Growth in the Nineteenth Century', *Journal of Economic History*, 9 (1949), 45–61. See also his masterly general economic history, *The Unbound Prometheus* (1969), which gives further references.

growth in the nineteenth century, and its loss of the hegemony it held under Napoleon I. This is a debate which has proved somewhat inconclusive. Those who have attacked Landes have not produced any generally accepted alternative explanation. Perhaps a simple explanation is not to be looked for. There is even doubt as to whether there is anything to explain, in that, now that France has resumed its industrial expansion, some are arguing that the backwardness was only a temporary lull, or even that there never was any backwardness. If production figures are studied on a *per capita* basis, France does not lag much behind its rivals. What happened was simply that the populations of different countries increased at different times.[1] Besides, Germany was also a country of small family firms and the statistics of the size of its firms are almost identical with those of France. In Russia, as in France, business and industry were looked down upon as contemptible, but that did not prevent an annual rate of industrial growth in the 1890s of about 9 per cent.[2] Others are now claiming that the decisive factor in French economic development was the backwardness of agriculture, rather than of industry. Shortage of factory labour and a static home market are said to have held up industrialisation more than lack of capital, natural resources or ambition on the part of entrepreneurs. The economists are still disagreed, pending the publication of a giant quantitative analysis of all the available statistics being undertaken by a team under Jan Marczewski. It might be most profitable at this stage therefore to examine the different sectors of the economy to see who did run them and what little can be said about their methods and their mentalities.[3]

The industry which fits David Landes's description most easily is that of textiles, which, in the mid nineteenth century, was of course France's largest industry and at the end of this period was the fourth largest in the world, after Britain, U.S.A.,

[1] Rondo Cameron, 'L'Économie française, passé, présent, avenir', *Annales* (Sept.–Oct. 1970), 1418–33; id., 'Profit, croissance et stagnation en France au XIXe siècle', *Économie appliquée* (1957), 409–44; id., 'Economic Growth and Stagnation in France 1815–1914', *Journal of Modern History* (1958), 1–13.

[2] Alexander Gerschenkron, *Economic Backwardness in Historical Perspective* (Cambridge, Mass., 1962), 62.

[3] C. Kindleberger, *Economic Growth in France and Britain 1851–1950* (1964), is an excellent guide to the controversies. See the *Cahiers de l'Institut de Science Économique appliquée* for J. Marczewski's *Histoire quantitative de l'économie française* (in progress).

and India. Concentration made little progress. In 1950 only 9·5 per cent of the weaving factories had over 500 looms, 35 per cent had less than 100, 22 per cent had between 101 and 300. In spinning, the five largest firms had only 17 per cent of the spindles, seventeen other firms had 25 per cent of them, but 55 per cent were shared by no fewer than 138 firms. Family control of small units was the rule, but there was great variety among them. In the Second Empire, several different types of manufacturer could be distinguished. The most famous names in the industry were those of Alsace and the Nord, like Dolfuss in Mulhouse and Motte in Roubaix, which had built up a network of firms, related by marriage, and surviving throughout this century in the same families. Their members dominated the politics or social welfare of their towns, and sometimes won seats in parliament. But they were of course far from controlling anything like even a third of the total production of the country; and they did not present a united front, or exhibit a uniform conduct, in the face of either crisis or prosperity. The large firms of the Nord came to be the archetype of the conservative family business. Their practice was not to expand the size of their units, but rather to endow each new generation with its own small units. Thus a younger son would be married off to the daughter of a rival, and the two parents would combine to set them up with a factory of their own, to which they gave both their surnames, hyphened. The ideal seemed to be to give each member of the family economic independence, perhaps as an unconscious counterpoise to the closeness of their family ties. No member would be allowed to go bankrupt, the family would always rescue him and set him up again; but industrially they worked separately. Cut-throat competition obviously had no place in such an arrangement. These manufacturers concentrated on maximising profits, not production. Borrowing from outside the family was avoided. The ploughing back of profits (*autofinance*) was the normal way to expand, though of course expansion was limited by the need to set up younger sons on their own and pay dowries to daughters. What expanded therefore was the family rather than the firm. These leading families tended to have many children (which does not make them typical of France). Thus when in 1940 Mme Pollet-Motte died, she left 1,257 descendants, nephews and

nieces. But her particular (hyphened) firm was not especially
large. If there was not enough money to set up all the children,
then some went into the Church. Pious Catholicism, active
social work and a conscientious paternalism characterised these
textile families.

The memoirs left by some of the northern textile manufacturers are much more about their families than about their
firms. They stress the activity of their women in their businesses,
and not only by the introduction of a proportion of the initial
capital and by joining the name of their father's to that of their
husband's firm. 'One should not fail to recognise', wrote one of
them, 'the important role the women [of the nineteenth century]
played in the home which they animated with their permanent
presence. They had absolute control—that goes without saying
—of the running of the house, but at a time when the business
or the workshop and the home were built as one, they participated in the professional duties of their husbands at the same
time as they gave a great deal of attention to the education of
their children. It was on this close collaboration of the head of
the firm and his wife that the astonishingly rapid rise of industry
in Roubaix-Tourcoing in the early nineteenth century was
built.' The historian of the Motte-Clarisse family (of whom there
were 1,622 alive in this single branch in 1952) finds 'the family
spirit' evident from the very first extant letter in its archives.
Parents expected and obtained obedience. 'Believe in my affection', wrote a father to his daughter in 1869, 'as I believe in
your submission and your assiduity in your duties.' Children
were asked to pray for the dead members of their dynasty, as
for the living. All were required to attend weekly family dinners
which were raised almost to the status of religious ceremonies
or as one Motte called them 'compulsory festivals'. Madame
Motte-Bredart's Sunday lunches began with a sung grace and
the litanies of the Virgin were recited before the dessert. Mutual
aid among members of this family was the practical consequence
of their close-knit life. It was the closeness, the secrecy and the
exclusiveness that stimulated accusations of oligarchy. But
these families were not entirely self-sufficient. Though they
nearly always went into the business, lack of ability or inclination sometimes meant that they could not run them on their
own. They often delegated a great deal of power to managers,

who, in many cases, were then married into the families. There are not infrequent cases of new firms being set up for young men in association with foremen who had proved their worth.

Prudence characterised their economic policy. One Motte went on a pilgrimage in 1836 'to obtain illumination from the Holy Ghost so that we should never undertake anything in business above our strength, lest we should be troubled by hazardous speculations'. His wife's favourite saying was 'Economy is the first profit'. The rule against borrowing was sometimes written into their articles of association. They carried this into their private lives, where simplicity and austerity were severely practised and sentimentality rigorously excluded. One twentieth-century magnate, who was brought up in this textile world, recalls the bedroom of his parents furnished 'worse than a hotel for commercial travellers'. They rose early, worked hours as long as those they imposed on their employees, and very often thought of little besides their work. On the whole, they avoided higher education and they were stauncher patrons of the Church than of the arts.[1]

However, these generalisations about the notables in textiles ignore many exceptions. From time to time these families threw up individuals who were innovators, who broke with tradition (within limits), and who brought about expansion and modernisation. Alfred Motte, for example, born in 1852, and set up in business by his relatives, proceeded to establish at least four other firms. He was a veritable industrial impresario, but he concealed his work behind the traditional façade of family firms. Each of his new companies was set up in association with a manager, who was in charge of its daily running while Motte gave general supervision. Motte broke with the habit of specialising in only one branch of textiles; he was a great believer in industrial enterprise and in the legitimacy of competition and natural selection between firms. Family firms, that is to say, could be vigorous as well as defensive. The well-known textile firms of Alsace, in contrast to those of the north, often were. Their Protestantism set them even further apart from the

---

[1] Fernand Motte, *Souvenirs personnels d'un demi-siècle de vie et de pensée 1886–1942* (Lille, 1943, privately printed); Gaston Motte, *Les Motte, étude de la descendance Motte-Clarisse 1750–1950* (Roubaix, 1952, privately printed); Gérard Hannezo, 'Histoire d'une famille du Nord: les Barrois' (stencilled, about 1964).

rest of society. They were among the few supporters of free trade. This was not simply because they were optimistic but because as specialists in printing cloth they worked much more for the export market. Jules Siegfried, father of the famous writer, was among the most colourful and enterprising of these Alsatians. He became a millionaire at twenty-nine by seeing that the American Civil War would cut off France's supply of cotton: he went to India and imported from there. His activity as a cotton merchant took on an international scale. He travelled widely and sent his sons on world tours. He admired the U.S.A. and Britain as exponents of industrial initiative and he despised civil servants who were content with fixed salaries, engineers whom he thought of as pure theorists, and professors, for he had no use for books or culture. When his son André showed academic inclinations, he urged him to become Director of the School of Political Sciences, not simply its employee, for he understood only the success that brought power. His motto was 'to live is to act'—and he had it engraved even on his cuff-links. But it is interesting to see why he did not become a Rockefeller. He confined himself to cotton, a branch of industry where he felt he knew what he was doing. There were limits to his ambition. At forty-four he retired from business, giving his firm to his younger brother and devoting himself to politics and social work. He refused to marry 'well' and preferred the daughter of a Protestant pastor who turned him further in the direction of public service. He left his children to make their own way in the world, as he had done.[1]

However, these textile dynasties formed only a small proportion of the employers in this industry. The bulk, in the middle of the nineteenth century, were merchant-manufacturers still using artisan labour and just beginning to turn to mechanised weaving in factories. Such men had yet to establish themselves: they had often begun as dyers, or cloth merchants in small towns. Few rose very fast, for the self-made man was an exception in textiles. They did not set the pace: their humble origins made them continue to see their future in small, regional, if not purely local, terms. They preserved the mentality of the retailer. It is true that there were a few manufacturers, found in particular in Normandy, who did not look on textiles as an end

[1] A. Siegfried, *Jules Siegfried 1836–1922* (1946).

in itself, nor as a profession, but simply as a means of making money and rising in the social scale. Pouyer-Quertier, who became minister of finance under Thiers, was such a man. Born in 1820, the son of a small manufacturer and farmer, he had early seen the possibilities opened up by new machinery. He visited England and brought back ideas on modernisation. In 1859 he bought a bankrupt firm on the outskirts of Rouen, and made it the largest cotton-spinning factory in Normandy. His income reached 1,800,000 francs a year. But he used his wealth to go into parliament and become a politician. The textile dynasties by contrast never placed politics before their traditional family activity.

The variety of the textile employers was strikingly revealed in the 1860s when a severe crisis coincided with the shock produced by the free trade treaty with England. The well-established firms of the east, which had adequate capital, proved perfectly capable of withstanding competition. Some rising and enterprising firms in Roubaix, Armentières and Reims seized the opportunity to mechanise their factories and to form larger units. It was Normandy, which was the largest cotton-weaving area in France, but also the most backward, with artisan organisation and little capital, that was hit most severely. The effect of the crisis of the 1860s was to complete the transformation of the textile industry and to destroy hand weaving. Vigorous expansion coincided with catastrophic collapses. The expansion did not cease even after protection was re-established. The consumption of cotton textiles increased by 270 per cent between 1869 and 1913 and exports increased more than sixfold between 1867 and 1896, even if it was, to a considerable extent, to the protected colonial markets.[1] Concentration continued in the industry, so that whereas there were eighteen cotton firms in Alsace in 1861 there were only eight in 1910.[2] But these changes did not exceed certain limits. There was a levelling off in the twentieth century. Between 1900 and 1950 textile production fell by 10 per cent, as compared with an increase of 51 per cent in the rest of Europe. In the 1950s 240 plants were withdrawn from production but there were still nearly 2,000 left and only 255 had more than 200 employees.

[1] H. Sée, *Histoire économique* (1951), 2. 302.
[2] Kindleberger, 174 n.

The concentration affected ownership much more than production units. But even new-style magnates like Marcel Boussac (b. 1891), who by 1950 had sixty-five factories employing over 10,000 workers in all branches of textiles, from the import of raw cotton to the retail sale of his own products, with the firm of Christian Dior as one of his satellites, was still only responsible for 10 per cent of French cotton production.[1] The textile industry could not be labelled as congenitally backward. In the economic renaissance of the Fifth Republic, the disadvantages of price compared to other Common Market countries (30 per cent higher than the U.S.) were wiped out by a 50 per cent increase in productivity. But the family structure of the industry survived.[2]

The textile industrialists seemed a threat to democracy largely because their family organisation let very few facts about their firms escape to the public. Secrecy in business reached its maximum here. But it is clear from the statistics that this impenetrable world was a fragmented one. It is clear also from the history of employers' organisations that the textile owners were poor recruits and disliked regimentation by a union. They formed only ineffective alliances and gave little support to the employers' movement in general. The only exceptions were the woollen manufacturers—a small minority —who between the wars developed a keenness for corporatism.

The situation was very different in iron and steel. It is from this industry that the most numerous examples of concentrated control by the 200 families were given. Concentration indeed started early here. Under the July Monarchy there were about 1,000 iron foundries, but by the end of the century that number had been reduced by three-quarters. (In 1960 it was down to 140.) However already in 1828 the ten largest accounted for 39 per cent of the capital and were responsible for 22 per cent of production. By 1869 they had doubled their share of production to 55 per cent with de Wendel's firms alone producing 11·2 per cent of the total.[3] This was as concentrated as any industry became in France. Moreover, these iron

[1] Jacques Boudet, Le Monde des affaires (1952), 644–6.
[2] John Sheahan, Promotion and Control of Industry in Post-War France (Cambridge, Mass., 1963), 139. C. Fohlen, L'Industrie textile au temps du second empire (1956).
[3] Six articles by B. Gille (some of them under the pseudonym of J. B. Silly) on concentration in Revue d'Histoire de la Sidérurgie (1962, 1963, and 1965).

masters got together very early to form a pressure group. After various attempts under Louis-Philippe, they formed the Comité des Forges in 1864, which has been the most stable and powerful employers' organisation ever since. The secrecy with which it conducted its affairs gave rise to many legends. No serious history of its activities has been written. There can be no doubt, however, that it busied itself pressing for customs protection and for industrial clauses to be added to French loans to foreign countries, so that these would buy their equipment from France. It organised an employers' boycott of Millerand's *Conseils du Travail* and an insurance fund to enable them to resist strikes. In the 1914–18 war its power received official sanction and stimulus when the government virtually surrendered its control of the distribution of war contracts involving iron and steel to it and made it the official organ for the purchase of iron and steel abroad. Immediately vigorous attacks were launched on it for alleged profiteering, favouritism in the distribution process, and above all for a supposed deal with the government for its factories in German occupied territories to be spared from bombing. A parliamentary commission under Viollette's presidency was set up after the peace to investigate, but never reported. Instead, the members of the Comité des Forges were enriched by having the newly acquired mines and factories of Lorraine, once more French, distributed among them. Now the marketing agreements by the iron masters, begun as early as 1876 in the Comptoir de Longwy and multiplied since then, were accused of being dangerous cartels. In the 1930s the drastic drop in demand for iron and steel at a time when French output had reached record levels produced a tightening of unity among the firms and their ability to hold prices at higher levels, relative to other commodities, was taken as proof of their acting contrary to the public interest. Their open association with the political parties of the right and their public admission of financial participation in the elections of 1924, made their destruction an essential aim of the left. Iron and steel was scheduled for nationalisation, and would have been taken over but for the chaos of the early years of the Fourth Republic and the withdrawal of the Communists from the government in 1947. They used their escape to participate whole-heartedly in the Monnet plan and to combine into larger units, with enormous new plants. As a result the French iron and steel industry has a greater degree of concentration than either England or Germany. The four leading companies by 1960 accounted for 57 per cent of total output, with each one being responsible for between 12 and 14 per cent.

The power of the iron masters should not be exaggerated, important though it was. Their escape from nationalisation was due to luck, not to any resistance they put up. Though they controlled a crucial sector of the economy, in terms of their contribution to the national product, or of their capital, they were not as dominant as they seemed. In 1847 iron and steel were responsible for a contribution to the national product of 1·1 per cent (as against the textile industry's 17·9 per cent) and in 1910 2·2 per cent (as against textiles' 16·5 per cent). Even together with all the metallurgical industries it added up to less than one-third of the textiles industry.[1] The capital of Le Creusot in 1881 was about one-twelfth of that of the PLM railway and less than that of Paris's water and bus companies. Even in 1964 the largest iron and steel firm came only eighth among the top firms in France, in terms of capital.[2] The members of the Comité des Forges, moreover, were not as united as they might have appeared. This body experienced difficulties immediately after it was founded, with a rival Comité des Forges de Champagne being founded against it.[3] Its disputes were so severe that in 1877 it decided to stop discussing questions of manufacture, commerce and protection, with the result that it became little more than a social club. It was reactivated after 1890 and in 1904 appointed an energetic full-time secretary, Robert Pinot, who held the office for twenty-two years. Pinot was a disciple of Le Play. He had written admiring articles on the mutual benefit societies of Swiss watch-makers: he had been private secretary to the Bonapartist-royalist politician, Baron Mackau, and also deputy director of the Musée Social, until sacked by its founder the comte de Chambrun (who believed that study could solve the social question) for being too authoritarian. Pinot made the voice of

[1] M. Pinson, 'La Sidérurgie française' in *Cahiers de l'I.S.E.A.* (Feb. 1965), 11–12.
[2] B. Gille, 'Esquisse d'une histoire du syndicalisme patronal dans l'industrie sidérurgique française', *Revue d'Histoire de la Sidérurgie*, 5 (1964), 209–49.
[3] J. B. Silly, 'Les plus grands sociétés métallurgiques en 1881', *Revue d'Histoire de la Sidérurgie*, 6 (1965), 255–72. Cf. *Entreprise*, 31 Oct. 1964.

the Comité des Forges heard loudly; he appeared before every parliamentary commission; he set up a Society for Economic Study and Information in 1920, with fifteen full-time researchers, as a nominally independent publicity office. However, he had his difficulties. It was a dissident group among the employers who started the attack on the Comité des Forges which led to the Viollette investigation. The relations between the makers of iron products and their major consumers, like the railways, were far from uniformly cordial, and on several occasions led to the formation of splinter organisations. Pinot himself gave only lukewarm support to the Confederation of French Employers, fearing that if the decisions were reached by a majority, his own industries would easily be outvoted, as he put it, by quarries, leather goods and hotels.[1] The iron masters' cartels were never as powerful as the German ones. Their agreements were often broken, there were no penalties imposed on members, and they had only small staffs compared to their German counterparts. The concentration in the iron industry, though impressive by French standards, was, before the 1950s, below German levels. Thus in 1913 there were in the principal iron-smelting areas of Lorraine, Nord and Pas de Calais, nine firms producing 15 per cent of output, seven producing 38 per cent, four producing 33 per cent, and one (Wendel) producing 9 per cent; that is to say, twelve firms producing 80 per cent. By contrast Germany had seven firms responsible for 88 per cent of its production.[2] There was much controversy as to whether the iron masters used their power in a Malthusian way to limit production and keep up prices. The evidence is far from complete. It is clear that the large producers of the centre had increasing difficulties with raw materials in the nineteenth century. So as to be able to import these at minimal cost, they began building works on the coast. Le Creusot, founded in Saône-et-Loire originally because of its proximity to both ore- and coal-mines, found itself obliged to import from Algeria. However, the discovery of the Thomas process, and of the immensely rich iron deposits of the Briey region in the 1880s, led to a rise in production from 2·5 million metric tons in 1873–7 and 4·99 million in 1898–1902 to 14·4 million in

[1] André François-Poncet, *La Vie et l'œuvre de Robert Pinot* (1927).
[2] N. J. G. Pounds and W. N. Parker, *Coal and Steel in Western Europe* (1957), 309.

1910–12.[1] In the inter-war years the industry's performance compared favourably with the rest of Europe. But two features seem to distinguish it. First, competition within it was not ruthless enough to eliminate inefficient equipment or to stimulate technological improvements. French units of production were considerably smaller than Germany's. Whereas the U.S.A. had in 1927 demonstrated the vast increase in productivity possible through the adoption of wide strip mills and had by 1939 installed twenty-eight of these, with Britain then having two and Germany one, France got round to installing one only in the late 1940s. Secondly, the French iron and steel firms avoided distributing more than a fraction of their profits to their shareholders, and instead built up enormous reserves. Thus the Société de Commentry, Fourchambault and Decazeville never distributed a dividend greater than 60 francs per share between 1854 and 1914, when its net profits were over 200 francs per share in twenty-four of these years and over 300 in seven years. Similarly the Société des Forges de St. Étienne distributed on average 90 francs per share in dividends between 1869 and 1914, when its profits were 300 francs. The Aciéries de Longwy had a capital of 30 million francs in 1914 but had built up reserves of 35 million, after providing for depreciation. The iron industry, because of the connections of its directors, was in a particularly favourable position to raise money from the public, but it preferred to pay for a great deal of its equipment by *autofinance*. The complaints that it also kept prices unnecessarily high have been investigated in only one instance and proved unjustified. The price of rails fell from 3,200 (on an hours-of-work index) in 1828 to 2,100 in 1838 to 800 in 1882 and 250 in 1960.[2]

However, the iron masters' strength came also from the fact that they were not simply that. They had a stake in many other branches of the economy. In the nineteenth century the majority of iron masters were nobles. Iron was the one respectable industry. The bourgeoisie did own foundries particularly in the north and east but seldom worked them personally and rather used them as investments. The nobles were active

[1] Comité des Forges, *La Sidérurgie française (1864–1914)* (about 1920), 64.

[2] J. P. Courthéoux, 'Les Pouvoirs économiques et sociaux dans un secteur industriel: la sidérurgie', *Revue d'Histoire Économique et Sociale* (1960), 339–76.

themselves, however; Helvetius, Lamartine's father and many presidents of *parlements* were among the varied types who managed their own factories.[1] This tradition of part-time supervision never quite vanished. After the Revolution the iron masters went into politics in surprisingly large numbers. Under the July Monarchy the richest men in fourteen departments were iron masters and they enjoyed proportionate political influence. The large firms all had their representatives in parliament. Eugène Schneider, under the Second Empire, while building up his family firm's fortunes at a fast rate, did not grudge the time to be president of the legislature (1865–70), an almost full-time occupation for three or four months of the year at least. His son-in-law became a minister of MacMahon and his grandsons followed him in parliament. It is curious that some of the Wendels do not seem to have derived adequate satisfaction from their iron making, however brilliantly successful they were. Thus Ignace de Wendel (1741–95), founder (with William Wilkinson) of Le Creusot, committed suicide, expressing the hope that his children would not be as unhappy as he had been. His son François (1778–1825) had no interest in iron, and wanted to be a sailor, but both his career and his firm were ruined by the Revolution and he decided to revive the firm in order to 'establish my fortune on a solid basis and to leave a good reputation to my children, as the best of all inheritances.' But he also went into politics and desperately wanted a peerage as a reward from it. His will began 'I, the undersigned, François de Wendel, former pupil of the royal navy, officer in the regiment of hussars and cavalry, and today, *against my will*, iron master and owner of several firms which have prospered despite and against all . . .'He left four million francs, but considered himself a failure because he had not been a sailor, had shown only mediocre talent as a deputy in parliament, and had not solved all his industrial problems. His eldest son preferred to be a farmer. But his younger son went to the Polytechnic and with the help of another polytechnician, who married his daughter, the scientific progress of the firm was assured. In the next generation a nephew François de Curel, despite his literary tastes, was sent to the École Centrale. He joined the firm but wrote plays and novels and became a member of the French Academy. Another

[1] B. Gille, *Les Origines de la grande industrie métallurgique en France* (1947), 161.

François (1874–1949) while running the firm was also an active parliamentarian in the inter-war years, and vice-president of the Fédération républicaine. He was one of those who bought the newspaper *Le Temps* as a political instrument.[1] The iron masters were successful in obtaining influential office on several occasions. For example, Guillain, president of the Comité des Forges was a minister in Dupuy's cabinet of 1898. In 1957 it was calculated that fifteen of the directors of metallurgical companies had been or were ministers and fifty-four had been or were members of parliament.[2]

There were thus striking differences between textile manufacturers and ironmasters, and, in addition, neither were homogeneous groups. Other branches of industry would reveal still further variety. The secretiveness of these men has made it difficult to get to know them, but almost every new piece of research is bringing out their diversity, complexity, and, more often than hostile novelists have been willing to allow, considerable stores of individuality.

[1] René Sédillot, *La Maison de Wendel de 1704 à nos jours* (1958, privately printed), 122, 164, 247, 274; B. Gille, 'La Psychologie d'un maître de forges', *Revue d'Histoire de la Sidérurgie*, 6 (1965), 61–72.

[2] See further J. Vial, *L'Industrialisation de la sidérurgie française 1814–64* (1967), i. 170–85, 199. For an interesting biography of a nineteenth-century iron master, see G. Thuillier, *Georges Dufaud et les débuts du grand capitalisme dans la métallurgie en Nivernais au 19e siecle* (1959). Carol Kent's thesis on Camille Cavallier and Pont-à-Mousson (Oxford D. Phil. 1972), based on the firm's archives, is a valuable critique of David Landes's Theory.

6. Bankers

MORE than any other group, the bankers were accused of being the ultimate repository of power, the decisive oligarchy. 'The bankers', wrote Stendhal, 'are at the heart of the state. The bourgeoisie has replaced the faubourg St Germain and the bankers are the nobility of the bourgeois class.' Marx, in claiming that the monarchy of July was the instrument of the rich, made the qualification that it was the financial aristocracy, rather than the industrialists, who ran the country. Since then a large number of books have been written on the Rule of Money, backed, on occasion, by anti-Semitic attacks as in Toussenel's book on *The Jews, Kings of our Time*.[1] The sense of a small and closed circle controlling vast wealth was heightened by the notion of La Haute Banque—a term first used under the Restoration. The Rothschilds were the most famous of this group, but they became important only in the course of the first half of the century, when they rapidly outstripped a large number of rivals. The Haute Banque was not the united body it appeared to be. It consisted first of all of a number of Protestant banks originating for the most part in the eighteenth century, founded by Swiss Huguenots returning to their country of origin. Mallet Frères, founded in about 1713, is the oldest Paris bank surviving under its original name. Members of it have sat as regents of the Bank of France, which they helped to found, uninterruptedly from 1800 to 1936. It had interests in the PLM Railway, of which Charles Mallet was president, the Ottoman Bank, the Bank of Syria and Lebanon, the Banque Franco-Serbe, the Phoenix and National insurance companies, the Havre Docks, the Ateliers de la Loire, the Wolfram mines of Tonkin and Lesieur-Afrique. The Hottinguer Bank had a similar spread, though specialising in mines and metallurgy; the Mirabaud Bank in mines and food (Nicolas wine, Glacières de Paris); the Vernes and Neuflize Banks in a wide variety. The Jews joined this select circle in the nineteenth

---

[1] A. Toussenel, *Histoire de la féodalité financière* (1847).

century. Adolphe d'Eichtal was the first Jew to become a regent
of the Bank of France 1839–49; Alphonse de Rothschild
followed in 1855; Fould became finance minister of Napoleon
III and left a powerful political and industrial dynasty; his
bank amalgamated with another Jewish one, Heine.[1] There
was a great deal of intermarriage in these families, though their
members were also eagerly sought as husbands or wives by the
old aristocracy; but their community of interest should not
be exaggerated. Under Louis-Philippe there was a distinct
division between the older firms, who lived in the rue faubourg
St. Honoré and tended to be centre conservatives, and the new
ones, who inclined more to the left and lived in the rue de la
Chaussée d'Antin. Their wealth likewise was not as enormous
as people believed. The Mallet bank in 1823 had only one
million francs capital: André and Lottier (the predecessors of
Neuflize) only four million in 1848. It was probably Rothschild's phenomenally rapid rise, from the enormous profits he
made from state loans after Waterloo, that created the Midas
legend.

The magnates of finance must however be seen in a fuller
context. The magnates did not eliminate the lesser bankers and
money-lenders whose hold on people was often more direct. In
1866 there were 8,080 people in banking of whom 2,649 were
employers; and in addition there were 2,556 employers and
3,674 employed in 'credit establishments'. In these vague
statistics, it is not possible to distinguish the exact nature of the
services they performed. But the notable fact is that, as in so
many other branches of French life, the small man continued
to coexist with those of national importance. In 1896 there
were no fewer than 7,931 *patrons* and 30,484 employees in
banking (one-quarter of whom worked in firms of over 500
employees and one-quarter in firms of 50 to 500). In 1921 the
employees rose to 120,673 and in 1931 to 160,139. But even
after the increased concentration and the rise of monster institutions with several hundred branches, and even after the
elimination of simple money-lenders, there were in 1936 no
fewer than 2,100 banks. It was calculated that in 1936 there
were probably over 10,000 bank branches, which meant one for

---

[1] The Fould family, though originally Jewish, was converted to Protestantism in
the early nineteenth century.

every 1,000 households and one for every 200 traders and firms (*patentés*). Another calculation, made in 1954 and eliminating minor bankers more drastically, arrived at 268 deposit banks (6 large national firms, 82 Paris banks, 22 regional banks and 158 local banks), 38 investment banks, 19 specialised finance institutions, 27 foreign banks and 22 miscellaneous banks.[1] Now in 1937 the four largest banks received only 46 per cent of bank deposits, though if one added the eleven next largest, together they received 73 per cent of deposits. This left a quarter of deposits in the 184 other banks—and these calculations take into account only banks publishing their accounts.

The history of this mass of small banks is even more obscure than that of the large ones, but they clearly had an important place in provincial life. They survived because they provided a personal service and because they could assess their risks more accurately through personal knowledge of their clients. They frequently remained in the same family for many generations. The bank of Tardeaux Frères, founded in Limoges in 1809, has been handed down from father to son ever since. It has built up a faithful clientele in the local porcelain and shoe industries, and also among the farmers of the four surrounding departments, where it has built up thirteen branches and sixty-five part-time offices. The large provincial towns all had numerous well-established banks—Marseille as many as thirty. Alsace was another region with many strong local banks. The Crédit du Nord was so successful in the northern departments that it became larger than two of the six national banks.[2] At the very time when they might have been ruined by the competition of the large deposit banks, they were given a new lease of life by some of the Paris investment banks. The Banque de Paris et des Pays Bas, for example, which had no network of branches, used to collaborate with the Crédit Lyonnais for the sale of new shares in the provinces, but, being anxious not to be too dependent on one firm, it began using regional banks to place these investments for it instead. The regional banks were also able to perform services which the Parisian ones neglected. Thus the Charpenay Bank, established in Grenoble in 1864, worked in

---

[1] J. S. E. Wilson, *French Banking Structure and Credit* (1957).
[2] 1954 balance-sheet totals, in milliard francs: Crédit Lyonnais 493, Société Générale 415, B.N.C.I. 359, Caisse nationale d'escompte 359.

close touch with local industry. The son of the founder was trained at the School of Waters and Forests and his son-in-law as an engineer. These men could understand the new hydro-electric industry. They increased their capital in the early twentieth century with contributions from a score of local industrialists. By 1931 they had 1,957 shareholders, 9,135 current accounts, and seventeen branches. In that year they went bankrupt. But in the course of its existence the bank had lent 66 million francs to electricity firms, 83 to electro-metallurgical ones, 180 to papermakers and 63 to glovemakers—the major local industries.[1] This kind of industrial financing meant that the control of the economy continued in many aspects to be decentralised. Of course it involved risks, and in the catastrophic years 1929–37 670 small banks collapsed. However, French businessmen have continued the practice of using several banks simultaneously (which is not normal in England) and this has kept the latter's numbers up.

These small banks should not be looked at as valiant survivors of a better world, in the way the artisans were. It was due to very clear deficiencies in the traditional banking facilities that the large deposit banks won their mass support. Though in due course these large institutions were seen as a menace to freedom, they at first presented themselves as liberating the country from the stranglehold of the small money-lender. Louis Reybaud in his best-selling novel *Jérôme Paturot in Search of a Social Position* (1843) described his hero's attempts to get a loan from one of these men. The banker sent him to a subordinate, who received him with 'the contempt, the calculated coldness, the arrogance and the mistrust of a man who has a lot of money: all usurers are alike'. After some discussion, the loan was granted but on severe terms: interest 5 per cent, commission 0·5 per cent, renewable quarterly, i.e. 2 per cent p.a., fees and commission for the notary drawing up the security documents 2 per cent, stamp duties 2 per cent, which made a total of 11 per cent. The tyranny of usurers is seldom written about in histories of the nineteenth century, but it was certainly more severe, in many respects, than the taxation and controls of governments and the oppression of nobles or churchmen. Interest rates were high. Some nascent industries are known to

[1] G. Charpenay, *Les Banques régionalistes* (1939).

have paid between 10 and 15 per cent and even over 20 per
cent, which was why *autofinance* became so widespread.

Most bankers were, to begin with, traders as well. The
Seillière Bank (founded in 1800) which financed Le Creusot,
and which has remained, under its changed title Veuve
Demachy et Cie, bankers to the Wendels, was only part of a
wider economic activity by its founder, who was also a draper
in the Vosges, an iron master in the Ardennes and supplier
of military equipment to the Algiers expedition of 1830. The
Hottinguer Bank was for long also the principal importer of
cotton into France; Rothschilds had a virtual monopoly of the
importation of tea. Conversely Worms et Cie were for long
France's principal coal merchants before adding an investment
bank which is most probably the largest in Paris. The Haute
Banque tended to confine itself to a small number of clients, and
to live off the profits of a few large firms: the Seillière Bank
(which had only thirty clients) off Le Creusot and the Wendels,
the Périer Bank off Anzin. On a humbler level, the dozen
bankers of Nevers were nearly all products of the local pottery industry. Those of Lyon—more numerous still—were silk
merchants; those of Nantes shipowners. At an even more rudimentary stage, the money-lenders of the countryside included
notaries and *trésoriers généraux*—state officials who did more
private than public business. These small men had a massive
amount of business, because they specialised in mortgages on
land, long considered the safest of investments, and involving
some 500 million francs each year in the 1840s, at a time when
the Bank of France was discounting only about 150 million
francs of commercial paper. These two figures are not truly
comparable, since the Bank of France refused to give credit
beyond three months, and it required three signatures on the
paper it discounted.

The great problem of industry therefore was to get long-term
credit. But there was strong prejudice against the very notion
of this. Thiers in 1840, giving vent, as he so often did, to the
common opinion of the ordinary middle-class man, declaimed
against industry being given credit too easily or over too long
a period: that would be to 'make it possible for all sorts of
incapable men, men with neither ability nor money, to start up
businesses; they would spin cotton and weave cloth blindly,

without measure; they would burden the markets with a mass of products and would compete against old-established traders and these mushroom men would thus ruin men who have been in business for forty or fifty years'.[1] The Chamber of Commerce of Amiens wrote in the same way in 1836: 'To offer industry too much capital would be an inducement to it to give its production a dangerous expansion. . . . Our own capital can suffice for our needs.'[2] Since the days of Law, bank was almost a dirty word—banks were the cause of economic crises—and many banks preferred to call themselves *caisses*. Before 1848, France's banking structure was characterised by dispersion of resources, narrowness of activity, and ignorance of financial methods and the rules of credit. These features have been held responsible for the slow rate of industrialisation in the nineteenth century, and the explosion in economic activity which occurred under Napoleon III may be related to the discovery of new methods of utilising savings.

The real pioneer in these was Jacques Laffitte, the self-made notary's clerk who rose to be Louis-Philippe's banker and prime minister. In 1837 he succeeded in persuading the leading financiers, industrialists and merchants to subscribe 50 million francs to found a giant company designed to stimulate industry by offering to buy shares in new and promising ventures. Under the Second Empire two Jews from Bordeaux, Émile and Isaac Péreire, cousins of Olinde Rodrigues, who had been Saint-Simon's secretary, developed this idea on a larger scale. Their Crédit Mobilier, founded with the support of the Fould Bank and of Napoleon III's special patronage, played an important part in financing the rapid railway building of this reign, in founding the Compagnie Générale Transatlantique, the Paris Omnibus Co., insurance companies, and in fusing the six competing gas works of Paris. It handled the finances of sixteen firms with a combined capital of one billion francs, equal to one-fifth of the value of all stocks quoted on the Paris bourse. It set up an active branch in Madrid and negotiated to expand into several other countries. It helped to found, with a government subsidy, the Crédit Foncier. But it was faced with the

---

[1] Quoted by G. Palmade, *Capitalisme et capitalistes français au 19ᵉ siècle* (1961), 71.

[2] B. Gille, *La Banque et le crédit en France de 1815 à 1848* (1959), 371.

implacable hostility and rivalry of the Rothschilds, so that when it got into difficulties in the late 1860s, it was destroyed.

The Péreires were the most brilliant of a large number of financiers who rose to shake the traditional world of banking, which looked on them as speculators. National deposit banks were another innovation in the Second Empire. The Crédit Lyonnais was founded in 1863 by Henri Germain (1824–1905), the son of a Lyon silk manufacturer. He personally had only 100,000 francs capital, plus an income of 16,160 francs; he married the daughter of another silk merchant who brought him a dowry of 760,000 francs. However, he subscribed only 2,150 out of the 40,000 shares of his company: over 300 bankers and leaders of the silk and metal industries provided the rest. In the space of eighteen years he increased the capital twentyfold and had 109 branches. He managed the firm himself for over forty years. This was indeed the case of a financier enjoying control of millions in excess of his personal wealth. The bank carefully concealed the fact that in its first eighteen years it made annual profits of 24 per cent. It gave away only 9.52 per cent in dividends. 14.7 per cent went to reserves or to the directors, so that the latter got about 20 per cent a year return on their money. Still Germain had spotted that there was a vast amount of money lying idle in Lyon. He offered free current accounts to businessmen, and deposit accounts at 3 per cent. At first he lent almost one-third of his available capital to industry, but these turned out to be disastrous investments and the *Krach* of 1882 convinced him that industry was too risky. Henceforth he confined himself to dealing in insurance, property, public utilities and foreign state loans. 'Industrial enterprises', Germain told his shareholders, 'even those which are most carefully studied and even those which are administered most wisely, involve risks which we consider incompatible with the security indispensable to the employment of the funds of a deposit bank.'[1] The attraction of state loans was overwhelming, for, in the years 1871–4 alone, the Crédit Lyonnais made a profit of no less than 25 million francs simply from selling French government *rentes*.[2] It took over only one local

[1] G. Piron and M. Byé, *Traité d'économie politique*, vol. 4, *Le Crédit* (n.d.), 131.
[2] Jean Bouvier, *Le Crédit Lyonnais de 1863 à 1882* (1961).

bank in the course of its rise to be the largest deposit bank in France: it preferred to set up branches in its systematic search for new business. Its most rapid expansion took place between 1921 and 1931 when about a 1,000 new offices—all over the country—were opened.

Other banks soon followed, though they pursued slightly different paths. The Société Générale was originally started in 1864 as a ripost by the established banks against the upstart Crédit Mobilier: nineteen French firms and thirteen English ones subscribed over 80 per cent of its shares. It was thus at first an investment bank as well as a deposit bank, and it made profits several times those of the Crédit Lyonnais, but it took risks which caused it heavy losses, and after 1900 it concentrated simply on deposit banking and began opening up local branches on as massive a scale as the Crédit Lyonnais. The Crédit Industriel et Commercial, founded in 1859 on the model of an English joint stock bank, has by contrast avoided expanding into the provinces in the same way, but at an early stage took the decision to co-operate with local people to set up regional banks in which it invested, for example, Lyon (1865), Bordeaux (1880), etc., the Banque Dupont (established 1819 and powerful in the north), and in the 1930s the smaller banks which were in difficulties. The Comptoir National d'Escompte goes back to as early as 1848, and in 1870 it was the leading bank in France, but it was soon outdistanced by the Crédit Lyonnais and the Société Générale, and then suffered a severe blow when it backed the Société des Métaux with whom it shared several directors. The collapse of this speculation in 1889 caused the director of the bank to commit suicide—after which it became even more conservative than the Crédit Lyonnais. The Banque Nationale pour le Commerce et l'Industrie, on the other hand, dates only from 1931, when it was formed to replace another bank founded in 1913 forced into liquidation, but an immediate rapid expansion of branches brought it quickly into the big four. Though the banks have been unusually cautious in their attitude towards industry, it would be wrong to regard them as being uniformly timid. It has been claimed, for example, that after the era of Henri Germain, when caution was the rule, the early twentieth century showed a new outlook, dominated by Louis Dorizon,

who in 1896 became director general of the Société Générale
and who was much more interested in industrial development.
He co-operated with Noetzlin, head of the Banque de Paris et
des Pays Bas, in a programme of active investment. But in 1913
he was voted out of office by his frightened directors.[1]

By the time of the Popular Front, the presence of these large
banks, with their mushrooming branches, was being increasingly felt. Paradoxically, however, just when public opinion
became most hostile to their power, they were in fact suffering
a rapid decline. Government and semi-public institutions were
expanding very fast a good while before nationalisation. The
Caisse des Dépôts was founded in 1816 for limited purposes,
chiefly to look after moneys involved in legal disputes. Then,
however, it was used to manage various other state funds—
particularly the national savings bank and after 1930 the
national insurance scheme. As a result it controlled deposits in
1939 considerably larger than all the private credit banks put
together. The state savings bank (Caisse d'Épargne) expanded
enormously in the inter-war years, after the abolition of a limit
on the amount that could be deposited. Since it paid interest
of between $2\frac{3}{4}$ and $3\frac{1}{4}$ per cent (in contrast to the $\frac{1}{2}$ per cent or
$\frac{3}{4}$ per cent paid by the deposit banks), and the savings were
withdrawable on demand (in Paris, and with a couple of
days' notice in the provinces), there was a massive transfer of
funds to it, and in 1938 its deposits amounted to 63 milliard
francs, against 67 milliard in the main 132 banks publishing
accounts. The state achieved these results partly by refusing to
pay salaries to its civil servants (except senior ones) direct into
banks, and insisting on using *chèques postales* instead. These
state services did not appeal to a new class. In 1937 50 per cent
of accounts in the Caisse d'Epargne were held by 'proprietors,
rentiers and persons exercising no profession', another 15 per
cent were civil servants and employees, and a further 9 per cent
soldiers and sailors. Only 2·77 per cent were industrial workers.
Investment in the inter-war period also became state sponsored
on an enormous scale. Various national institutions were
established to give loans to different sectors of the economy: the
Crédit agricole (1920), Crédit national (1919), Crédit popu-

[1] R. Girault, 'Pour un portrait nouveau de l'homme d'affaires français vers
1914', *Revue d'Histoire Moderne et Contemporaine*, 16 (1969), 329–49.

laire (1917), and the H.B.M.[1] (cheap housing subsidies, dating back to 1894 but made active only after the war). The vast resources coming in to the Caisse des Dépôts were used for large public works programmes. Between 1913 and 1936 the banks increased their deposits by only 26 per cent, while prices rose fivefold. The rush away from the banks can be seen in the figures for one year in the great depression: in 1931 they lost 16 milliards of deposits, but deposits in the Caisse d'Épargne increased by ten milliards. The nationalisation of the banks thus followed a massive withdrawal of confidence.[2]

The relationship of the rich, the industrialists and the bankers to the rest of the population has been excessively simplified in the theories holding that it was a relationship of domination. Many detailed studies will be needed on individual firms and magnates before conclusions on this subject can be attempted. The state of knowledge on them is still rather rudimentary; serious company histories have only just begun to be published.[3] But modern research seems to be moving towards a view of the economy as far more fragmented and with far more autonomous pockets than the old generalisations suggest.

[1] Habitations à bon marché.

[2] Henry Laufenberger, *Les Banques françaises* (1940), 43, 77–80, 168; Robert Bigo, *Les Banques françaises au cours du 19ᵉ siècle* (1947); J. J. Laurendon, *Psychoanalyse des banques* (n.d., about 1963).

[3] Maurice Lévy-Leboyer's forthcoming publications will throw important new light on this; see his *Les Banques européennes et l'industrialisation* (1964).

7. The Ambitions of Ordinary Men

THE ambitions of people who never became very rich, who founded no dynasty or long-lasting company, and who lived in the middle and lower ranks of the business world, are difficult to write about, because they are seldom recorded. But the character of a society is greatly influenced by the form the ambitions of such men take, and by the extent to which they are satisfied or frustrated. Discussions of France's economic development have tended to move rather above this humbler level. Large industries and family concerns have attracted attention, and they can obviously be identified and investigated most readily. The firm which mushrooms from the invention of a clever man and is then sold to either a stranger with a different name, or, as seems to have happened very often, to a foreman or other associate within the firm, may be equally prosperous but its fortunes are far harder to follow. In the family firm, expansion is said to have been subordinated to the interests of the family. Persistence in producing the same things, at a moderate level, for a traditional market, and the setting up of small firms for younger sons and other relatives, was one way of interpreting this family interest. But it seems that there was an alternative which was possibly more frequently followed and that was to sell up as soon as one had made a reasonable amount of money—just as one had reached prosperity—and to retire on the proceeds, give oneself up to horticultural or literary hobbies, and finance the rise in the world of one's children by educating them for the liberal professions. Smaller firms, which were neither family firms nor joint stock companies, were by far the most numerous.

The discussion so far has been about how industrialists behaved. Another problem is why more people did not go into industry. It is well known that in France there were strong traditions which led parents to send their children into the civil service, or alternatively the liberal professions, and that these careers, once embarked on, were frequently passed on from father to son. Why did more people not become engineers and scientists? The answer is to be found partly in how people viewed ambition. If one examines the guides to careers, one can get some insight—however limited—into how contemporaries saw the job market at any one time. The advice of these books is of course biased and it may be argued that, in so far as they are sometimes concerned to urge people to enter certain careers, their advice has the weakness of all exhortations by moralists. There is no way of telling whether people actually listened to them. However, it is possible to compare what they said with what other sections of the community thought about the same problems from other angles. The exhortations of psychologists and doctors who were not concerned with economic growth are particularly instructive. It is possible that people were more willing to follow advice when they thought it would also benefit their health, so it is interesting to see how the doctors reinforced current economic prejudices. For all its inevitable limitations the history of attitudes to success is an important subject.

The guide to the choice of a career by Edouard Charton, published in 1842, is a good way of understanding contemporary opinion on the subject. Charton was a remarkable man with experience and contacts in many walks of life. Trained as a barrister, he was one of the most successful editors of the century, with an uncanny ability for spotting what the public wanted. He founded and ran the *Magasin Pittoresque* (1833), *L'Illustration* (1843), *Le Tour du Monde* (1860), three of the best-selling journals of popularized knowledge of this period. He was a Saint-Simonian in his youth, attaché at the ministry of justice 1840–8 (where he wrote the biographies of criminals condemned to death in these years, for the edification of Louis-Philippe), secretary-general at the ministry of education in 1848, prefect in 1870, deputy in 1871, senator in 1876, and president of the *Gauche républicaine* in the senate. His career makes him an enlightened, indeed advanced, bourgeois with an exceptional concern for the education of the masses, so that his opinions may be taken as being even a little ahead of his time.

Charton contrasts the situation during the July Monarchy with that prevailing during the *ancien régime*. In the latter people were kept out of a large number of activities by the accident of birth, and it was less easy to rise or fall in one's status. In addition *esprit de famille* opposed a barrier to individual desires and ambitions. 'A son looked upon it as a matter of honour, more than he would today, to uphold the reputation that his ancestors had acquired in their employment or trade.' Birth, law, custom and paternal authority combined to limit people's horizons and left little scope for uncertainty about their careers. But by the mid nineteenth century freedom of choice was, theoretically, unlimited. *Esprit de famille* had weakened. 'Parents and children were often separated by differences in education, opinion or beliefs and physically by the results of centralisation, which draws all young ambition to the large cities.' However, even a Saint-Simonian like Charton thinks that there were still a great number of advantages to be obtained from following in one's father's profession, so that 'one cannot be too perturbed to see them so often ignored or disdained'. The son who follows this 'most simple and most natural course' is spared a painful and long uncertainty; he can be taught his trade by his father and inherit his clients and relations, confidence and esteem. Charton recommends a break with this tradition only in special circumstances, as when the profession requires special gifts which are totally lacking in the son, or when it is dying out, or when there are too many brothers. That is, only negative reasons and insurmountable obstacles should make men move out of traditional occupations. Charton insists that if this has to be done, the alternative chosen should be one where the son will find help from relatives or other protectors. Clearly patronage was still a factor of the utmost importance. But perhaps the most interesting of Charton's recommendations is that people should not set their targets too high. They should seek jobs which 'lead to *l'aisance*, comfort rather than riches, to esteem more than to admiration, to a normal development of the faculties, to an increase of intelligence and morality rather than the satisfaction of the passions'. The jobs which can bring riches may quite likely prove disastrous and lead to poverty, just as those for which admiration and glory is the highest reward for a few, can bring shame and ridicule on the many who fail. If one pushes oneself too hard one will use oneself up rapidly. 'The best way to make one's life a happy one is to make it useful, modest, simple and not too busy (*peu affairée*). This is a truth that the sages and poets have repeated since the beginning of time.' The ideal for a young man who had a little money should be to aim not to compromise it, rather than to try to double it, to find an honourable and peaceful position in the world which occupies and develops his intelligence, and which leads him by a slow but sure path to public esteem.

It is true this had to be reconciled with the practice of most parents who sought for their sons 'a profession which seems to be placed in public esteem a little above that which they themselves exercise. In this they only yield to the sentiment which leads us to give our children a higher and higher position, in accordance with the supposition that happiness is proportionate to the elevation of social rank.' Charton thus recognises that upward social mobility had increasingly replaced acceptance of one's inherited station, but he saw these aspirations as fraught with dangers and urged moderation and prudence. Drive and ambition were not for him the way to success, and money should not be the goal. He constantly lays stress on 'public esteem' as the most rewarding aim and no profession which was either not respectable in itself or which had unrespectable practitioners should be considered, however much money might be earned. Thus a solicitor usually made more money than a barrister, except in the very top ranks, but his job was definitely 'less tempting'. Dentists and some pharmacists were highly prosperous but 'vain pride' kept people away from these professions. Financial middlemen had the reputation of being gamblers and the danger of being polluted by their 'immorality' was held against working with them. To win public esteem one must be prudent: the respected banker was the circumspect one, who lent money very timidly. The architect could only expect work if he 'won the confidence of the well-to-do and kept it by a severe morality'. Some concession, it is true, had to be made to those who thirsted for glory. Glory was a noble ambition, but parents were right to be hesitant to allow their children to become, for example, artists, whose reward was glory. Though artists had 'never been so honoured, encouraged and highly paid', quite exceptional talents were required, and besides the admiration of the crowds was a mixed blessing. 'The respected man is happier than he who is admired and the most desirable life is the most simple one.'

What the doctors had to say about ambition from the point of view of health was enough to put anyone off it. Descuret, in his work on *The Medicine of the Passions* (1842), was clear that excessive ambition revealed itself in immediate and dangerous clinical symptoms. The ambitious man 'becomes pale, his brow grows furrowed, his eyes withdraw into their sockets, his glance becomes unsteady and worried, his cheek-bones become prominent, his temples hollow, and his hair falls out or grows white with time. He is nearly always out of breath, he suffers from palpitations of the heart and from cruel insomnia. His pulse is normally feverish, his breath burning, and his digestion imperfect, with acute or chronic inflammation of the bowels. He is frequently killed by cancer of the stomach or the liver, by apoplexy, or by an organic affection of the heart. But the most usual end of this passion [of ambition] is melancholy and above all ambitious monomania.' The madhouses were full of unsuccessful ambitious people who imagined they were generals, popes or God. Every political revolution produced an overcrowding of the asylums: the middle-class ones were particularly full. The trouble with ambition was that it offended the basic rule of hygiene of the day: prudence. Dr. Descuret, basing himself on twenty-three years of practice in Paris, commented that ambition was 'much more common than one thinks; it is creeping into all ranks, all conditions, and even affecting children'. It was particularly common among bilious, bilious-sanguine and melancholic people, who sought jobs above their talents, going beyond the boundaries of emulation, which was the acceptable desire to distinguish oneself among one's equals. The cure for ambition was a country life, with long walks, hunting, light food to re-establish the digestion, massage, warm baths and varied but not tiring reading. The patient's pride should be humiliated, obstacles raised against his desires; he should be removed from large towns, especially the court and the company of parvenus, he should be given friends who were happy with their lot, 'undesirous either by modesty or circumspection, of raising themselves to a higher state. By their habitual company (for all is contagious among men) he will end up by being convinced that glory and happiness cannot be allied on earth and that most ambitious people are simply unhappy slaves who have painfully ascended the difficult path of life to arrive at death with more noise but also with more misfortunes than other men.' Dr. Descuret is firm: 'An ambitious man is a sick man.' The illness is most difficult to cure when it affects a statesman brutally disgraced without any recompense which might salve his vanity. Death or consumptive fever frequently follows. The physician, in the latter case, 'can only console and suggest religion as the best remedy'. Dr. Descuret is a good representative of the middle class, but his recommendations usefully remind one that a good half of this class at the very least was conservative and viewed social mobility with alarm. Ambition, he said, was inevitably stimulated by constitutional and representative government, which based itself on the 'pride of the middle classes' and he was worried that this 'pride had since been communicated to the lower ranks'.[1] The notion that doctors were usually radical is of course a myth.

Another doctor, Bergeret, writing in 1878 on *The Passions and Their Dangers and Inconveniences for Individuals, the Family and Society*, begins with 150 pages against the passion for wealth (before going on to the passion for debauchery). This passion, he says, caused men to work too hard, and it killed them 'by an excessive tension of the brain'. It led them to embark on all sorts of hazardous enterprises and all sorts of jobs: few succeeded and most became ill from overwork, starvation or infection. It was reasonable for brilliant boys to go to the city, but it was blind vanity to try to rise above one's station without exceptional gifts. 'Ambition is the ruin of man.'[2] As late as 1914, Dr. A. Culerre, curiously combining traditional prejudices and modern ideas in his study of *Nervous Children*, said that, though no job necessarily produced nervous troubles, it was wise to avoid those which require excessively hard work. So business, politics, journalism and art were all to be avoided because of the worries and disappointments they brought. The liberal professions were much more desirable. They allowed a regular and ordered life which 'favoured the equilibrium of physiological functions', and left plenty of time to relax. And for those who

---

[1] Dr. J. B. F. Descuret, *La Médecine des passions ou les passions considérées dans leurs rapports avec les maladies, les lois et la religion* (1841), 9, 572–91.
[2] L. F. L. Bergeret, *Les Passions, dangers et inconvénients pour les individus, la famille et la société. Hygiène morale et sociale* (1878), 25–9.

were predisposed to nervous disorders, the military life was best, because of the discipline it imposed.[1]

By 1908 a best-selling writer on how to succeed in life was saying that the French must modify their habits of stagnation and follow the lead of the U.S.A. if they were to keep their rank in the world, for supremacy which was formerly won by arms was now to be obtained by business, commerce and industry as much as, if not more than, arts and letters. He quotes Carnegie and a new magazine *Commerce et Industrie* which had been established to adapt for France the advice of the American *Selling Magazine*. Ambition is no longer condemned, action and energy are what is needed. 'To work to earn money', the reader is assured, 'cannot dishonour you, if you use honest means.' However, even he does not propose that the American example should be followed completely. The millionaire is not the ideal. 'In recommending my reader to make money, I do not urge him to amass enormous sums. On the contrary, I want to tell him that while he should as quickly as possible free himself from the servitude engendered by poverty, it should not be just to fall into another servitude, that of money, which is as tyrannic.' His aim should be absolute independence, well-being and comfort. He should simply free himself from the need to worry about survival, so as to be able to use his time as he pleases, to go on holiday, to surround himself with fine art, good furniture and books. In other words, the old French ideal really survived beneath the new phraseology. In France, he says, there was no need to make money with the same un-flagging dedication as there was in America. 'A Frenchman has a right to some pleasures, to vacations, to the charms of restful conversation and it is in this way, in this manner more conforming to our traditions, our tastes and our education, that I want to envisage the successful man.' He quotes doctors who have written books against *Haste* and against *Overwork*;[2] and he ends up recommending too much prudence in preference to temerity.[3]

In the light of these common prejudices, it is easier to

[1] Dr. A. Culerre, *Les Enfants nerveux* (1914), 291–2.

[2] Dr. Toulouse, *Comment conserver la santé* (1914); Dr. Pierrot, *Travail et surménage* (1911).

[3] Silvain Rondès, *L'Homme qui réussit. Sa Mentalité. Ses Méthodes* (1908), 70–85, 183–94.

understand why more able people did not go into industry. Charton pays the usual lip-service to industry's importance and even predicts that it would in the future hold out good career prospects, but it is clear that these were prospects at a humble level. 'The career of science', he says, 'as a profession is open only to a small number of people and it needs the unison of fortunate circumstances to rise in it with success.' By that he means there were a few openings in the university: he looked on science as an academic subject. He felt he could unconditionally advise only the sons of scientists to become scientists. They might hope to get their fathers' jobs 'almost by right, provided they are more or less worthy. To maintain a name is easier than to make one.' Unless one was in this category, 'it would not be prudent for a young man without fortune to try and earn a living by studying natural history, unless he has extraordinary gifts. He is unlikely to get even one of the jobs yielding a modest comfort and he will probably never emerge from a state close to poverty.' Applied scientists were not much sought after either. 'Disastrous examples would not be difficult to cite to prove how one must be on guard against modifications which experience has not sufficiently sanctioned. So the sort of aversion felt by many industrialists for men of science is not a complete error.' The rewards in industry were not high: one would start at only 1,500 or 2,000 francs and rise to only 6,000. All industries were risky. The best advice one could give to a man who took it into his head to go into industry was at least to beware of mushroom firms, basing themselves on the caprice of a fashion or on hazardous speculation. It would be wiser to seek a job with lower pay but more security. Charton says that it was 'quite rare for families having wealth or even a competency to destine their children for the vague functions and the chancy career of civil engineer'. There was the École Centrale which trained young people who could aspire to a modest existence; and it was a good thing for producing educated industrialists and able foremen. 'But for the big projects being planned or executed the country possesses a sufficient number of engineers and it will be rare for private industry to choose, for the management of these works, men who have only too easily assumed the title of civil engineer.' The right course for one who wanted to supervise great engineering feats was to go to the Polytechnic, serve the state in the Ponts et Chaussées for a few years, and then leave for private industry, which would pay him three or four times his state salary. The engineers were thus a small élite, controlled by the state.

Charton's advice to a man determined to make money quickly, despite all the moral pressures against such a course, was to enter retail trade. 'There are few jobs ensuring the highest profits which are more certain, more regular and, let us admit it, more considerable. It is not rare to see grocers, bakers and other merchants of this type retire after fifteen years at it, if not with a fortune, at least comfortably off.' Early retirement is assumed to be the aim, to enable people to live the good life—which money-making was not. Commerce, said Charton, was difficult to engage in with dignity—but esteem for it was growing, particularly in the upper ranks of 'high commerce', which required economic and geographic know-ledge. (The esteem was for the knowledge.) Of course, the higher one went, the riskier it became. It was only the modest shop that Charton advised. One can see therefore that this work by an influential publicist, summarising contemporary opinion, positively turned young people away from economic expansion, and almost from economic activities; at best he found in small commerce the most advisable way of making money, but he was careful not to lead anyone astray into wanting too much money.[1]

Charton had a son, born in 1840, just two years before his book was published. It is interesting to discover that he became an engineer, after graduating from the École Centrale des Arts et Métiers. Was he just asserting his independence of his father? In 1880 this son produced a third edition of his father's careers guide and it contains the answer. He thought that an engineer enjoyed great respect because of the magnitude of the achieve-ments of his profession in the nineteenth century, in railway building and public works, but even he recommended the pro-fession with reservations. First of all, he thought one was born an engineer, as one was born an artist. It required exceptional gifts. His article on the profession contains a long digression on

[1] E. Charton, *Guide pour le choix d'un état ou dictionnaire des professions* (1842). For confirmation of Charton's views see J. H. Donnard, *Balzac, les réalités économiques et sociales dans la comédie humaine* (1961), 277, quoting Chaptal, and the press of the July Monarchy.

Leonardo da Vinci, showing how art and science were one, and he ends by recommending James Watt as an 'extremely erudite man of letters'. Jules Charton obviously thought of himself as something of an artist or writer: he was defending his choice of profession not in terms of its own standards but more as a branch of the traditionally admired arts. Secondly, he warns that, though a graduate of the Polytechnic had an assured future if he became an engineer, others graduating from less smart technical schools had to start in inferior manual jobs and had to spend ten or fifteen years before they obtained the rank of engineer. Though an engineer, he agrees with his father that commerce is preferable as a career to industry. In commerce he says the risks are limited, a merchant can lose only the goods he has; but in industry the risks are unlimited, a manufacturer may lose all his capital. 'Every progress inevitably brings risk': machines are suddenly put out of date, so the manufacturer needs not just capital to start his factory but at least as much again in reserve. Only large companies have any real chance in metallurgy, which is subject to constant crises. Mining is made perilous by the frequency of accidents. Openings in the textile industry he does not consider even worth discussing.[1]

In 1892 another voluminous guide to careers appeared, edited by an Inspector-General of Technical Education, Paul Jacquemart. His job almost required him to urge people away from the classical liberal professions, but it is highly significant that he too does not push them into industry, but, rather, into commerce. Again he pays lip-service to the engineers 'whose name has baptized the century', but he does not advise anyone to try to establish great industrial complexes. The aim is still to 'establish oneself on one's own account'. He discourages men away from metallurgy where this ideal is almost unattainable. He points out that industrial chemists normally earned considerably less than foremen; and that an engineer who went into the railways would have to start at the bottom, driving engines. There was clearly an important obstacle to industrial expansion so long as management and technologists were isolated and very differently rewarded. There also appeared to

[1] E. Charton, *Dictionnaire des professions* (3rd edition 1880 in collaboration with Paul Laffitte and Jules Charton), 152, 286, 328–30.

be some discrediting of the engineering profession by the recurrence of economic crises, in the same way as politicians were discredited by scandals and ministerial crises. The engineer's profession was a noble one, he said, but only when properly understood. 'The engineer must impose a brake (*frein*) on the exaggerations of the time. He must resist the mad crazes, he must refuse to work in hazardous projects and speculative developments.' Jacquemart gives very little space to engineering, three and a half pages out of over 1,000. By contrast he is enthusiastic about commerce. Most of the lavishly rewarded directors of the great department stores of Paris, he says, started with no money at all. Such was the pressure to get into commerce that in many shops young people worked without pay (as they once had in the civil service, but no longer). People were realising that the liberal professions were overcrowded, that commerce, while being 'less brilliant in appearance', was much more remunerative. So the old aristocratic contempt for it was disappearing and it was now recognised as one of the vital forces of the country. So many people wanted to be bank clerks that the job could only be obtained through patronage and only a very modest salary could be hoped for. The tables were turned, and Jacquemart was writing now about commerce as people had previously written about the traditionally respectable occupations. He quotes the large sums men were now willing to pay to set up as bakers—25,000 to 40,000 francs and over 100,000 in Paris, and even more as keepers of cafés and restaurants: some cafés in Paris were sold at over one million francs. Travelling salesmen were no longer the contemptible starvelings described by Balzac: their moral level had gone up a lot and they behaved as though they were well brought up. It was the exception now, noted Jacquemart, for sons to follow their fathers' professions. 'Everybody is impatient to move out of his sphere and has pretensions to rising.'[1]

The preference for commerce rather than industry was strengthened by the closed nature of the large and the family firm. 'Since large firms are the thing of the future', wrote another career guide, 'young men, even if they are rich, will risk a lot if they establish themselves as entrepreneurs or manufacturers.

[1] Paul Jacquemart, *Professions et métiers. Guide pratique pour le choix d'une carrière à l'usage des familles et de la jeunesse* (1892), 326, 524–7, 776.

Of factories and firms of middle or small size, none can succeed except those which are passed on from father to son, or which are maintained by money and an old clientele. Young men will do better therefore to enter as partners into already large businesses. If they have the means, they ought not to start on their own before they are forty, after having ensured by their experience and relations and the confidence they have inspired in their work, the nucleus of a clientele willing to support a new business. It is not an easy thing.' There was thus little encouragement to the young to make their fortunes quickly in industry, to stake all on manufacturing a new product.[1]

By the end of the century, with the expansion of education, it was becoming clear that the direction of ambitions would have to be altered, since the mass production of *bacheliers* was assuming excessive proportions. The suggestions of the politicians were mainly negative and not persuasive since they were hardly following the advice they were giving and since they appealed as much to patriotism as to self-interest. Méline preached a return to the land, an abandonment of the towns and large-scale industry, and a revival of farming and artisan activities.[2] Gabriel Hanotaux thought that though everybody should have the opportunity to go to school till they were fifteen, they should be stopped from staying on unless they were likely to be Pico de la Mirandolas and urged to go, not into the over-crowded civil service, but into anything else—the colonies, agriculture, industry, commerce.[3] There was an accentuation of propaganda in favour of the colonies.[4] Even professors of literature began to think there was need for more practical activities, but it is interesting that one of them, who wrote on *Prejudices of Yesterday and Careers of Today* (1908), suggested only horizontal movement into other jobs of the same social level rather than trying to use the less crowded and new professions to raise oneself to a higher class. The job a man took should depend on his family and friendships. 'The humble live and develop with the aid of the humble and the rich live and develop through the rich.' Though boys should seek jobs

[1] Paul Bastien, *Les Carrières commerciales, industrielles et agricoles* (1906), 203.
[2] J. Méline, *Le Retour à la terre* (1905).
[3] Gabriel Hanotaux, *Du Choix d'une carrière* (1904).
[4] Lt. Col. Péroz, *Hors des chemins battus* (1908).

different from their fathers', the peasant's son should naturally try only to become a mechanic, the middle-class child to fill the middle grades in industry, and it was the aristocracy which would provide its leaders. This professor's realism may well have been justified to a large extent. He certainly made no attempt to change old prejudices by advancing totally new criteria. He hoped the new careers would acquire respectability by assuming the values of the old ones. It is generally thought, he said, that the liberal professions are not pursued for individual profit but from concern for the social interest and that is why they are rewarded with honoraria rather than wages, whereas economic careers are supposed to aim only at personal interest. This distinction, he said, should be ended. Industry did have social aims and the boys he urged to enter it should stress them by limiting their profits, by acquiring culture and by practising *mœurs* which would make them similar to the liberal professions.[1] The transitions were very gradual. When Andrew Carnegie's *World of Business* was translated, it was used to bridge the gap between the old morality of duty and the pursuit of riches.[2]

A work on *The Best Professions to Make a Fortune In After the War* (1916) is another vigorous attack on going into the civil service and liberal professions. It recommends commerce and industry as the careers of the future, 'even if they seem more modest'. But there are reservations. The author stresses that most of these desirable jobs have to be obtained through influence and patronage. Thus of engineers he says that the engineering schools find jobs for their graduates in the firms of their older alumni but that these did not have enough vacancies. 'To get a job oneself as an engineer, one needs relations, patronage and luck. It is an excellent profession for those who manage to find a nook in it.' It was the same with chemists: jobs were obtained through influence. It is interesting also that though industry is now acceptable (but still limited by the old-boy network), the financial professions—which were essential to the expansion of industry—were decried as dangerous and to be avoided. The

[1] Gaston Valran, *Préjugés d'autrefois et carrières d'aujourd'hui* (Toulouse and Paris, 1908), 135, 356.
[2] A. Berlan, *Du Choix d'une carrière par Gabriel Hanotaux et l'empire des affaires par Andrew Carnegie* (Saint-Quentin, 1904)—by a journalist.

prospect of many vacancies after the war 'which had ravaged the élite of the nation' was the only real source of optimism for the young man with no friends in high places.[1]

The compendious *Guide Carus* on careers for young people, published in the 1930s, still showed that entry into industry was difficult. The war had greatly increased the number of engineers and the crisis after it meant that there was little hope of high salaries. Things were improving and jobs could be obtained by engineers without great difficulty though they were seldom advertised. But the graduate still had to start at the bottom, as an engine driver or as a draughtsman or even in purely manual work; he would get a salary below that of a skilled worker. Chemists could not be confident about rising very high. Until recently, it says, it was very rare to see a man who had no capital, but only a degree from the School of Chemistry, become a director. 'Formerly and sometimes even today people say there are too many chemists being produced by the schools. It is true that the chemists are barely beginning to win a place in the sun; they have had many prejudices to conquer; and they will need to triumph over many others, apart from the mistrust and jealousies to be surmounted.' There was no career structure for them: the chief chemist in a factory would be assisted by subordinates with only an elementary education. The jobs which were presented as being most attractive in this period, and which were reported to be most sought after, were ones in commerce. Careers in commerce could more easily be reconciled with traditional values and the style of life they allowed was more like that of the old bureaucrats. People were interested in commerce now because it was 'a clean profession, exercised in a distinguished and elegant milieu. Men of taste appreciate the careful grooming, the distinguished manners, work in the company of colleagues from good society, courteous relations with a selected clientele, a pleasant atmophere in a shop arranged and decorated with art. The life was hard and busy, but enlivened by a reflection of grace and distinction.' The qualities required were good taste, love of order, elegance in elocution, that is, the qualities of a gentleman with discretion and moderate culture. It offered security, a fixed

[1] Jean Liévin, *Les Meilleures Professions pour faire fortune après la guerre* (1916), 19, 25.

salary with bonuses, and good prospects of reaching high rewards. The uncertainties of business in the mid nineteenth century were no longer frightening in the service of great department stores. Accountants were becoming valued professional people. In the large industrial firms, it was the commercial jobs which were most sought after. The commercial and administrative sections nearly all worked only a five day week, while the factories continued all day Saturday and some involved night work. There was little attraction in being exiled as an engineer to some bleak industrial area, isolated from the society and pleasures which even medium towns could provide.[1]

All this suggests that there was an additional reason for the special form France's industrial expansion took, which has not hitherto been studied, and which is to be found in the history of ambition and prestige. The civil service and the liberal professions had an attraction which survived tenaciously. When the pressure for public office and clients became too severe and the rewards too limited by comparison with other careers, it was to commerce if not to industry that the new generation's interests were channelled. There was a gap in the career structure of industry which prevented it from recruiting able men with high ambitions, unless they happened to be in that world already, or to stumble on some invention or fortuitous opportunity. It was difficult for a man to move from the middle to the upper ranks of industry; there were few openings for graduates in the middle ranks, where instead industrialists preferred to employ workers who had proved themselves, but who would not expect to rise to the top. The large family firms kept their opportunities open mainly to those who married into them. It was not just that the bankers would not finance new ventures: it was also that people hesitated to ask them for loans, because they did not believe in the idea of a new venture.

The career books were right in what they said about the opportunities open to engineers.[2] In 1955 it was calculated that industry offered proportionately to the number of people it

[1] *Guide général pour la jeunesse Carus* (1934), 213, 478–81, 503–4, 521–3, 527, 571, 667.

[2] There is no history of the engineering profession. M. Thepot is writing one for the period 1815–48. Cf. J. Petot, *Histoire de l'administration des ponts et chaussées 1599–1815* (1958). Mr. John Weiss's Harvard thesis promises to throw light on the educational background.

employed the lowest number of managerial posts. Only 2·85 per cent of its employees came in this upper category. In the older industries the figure was lower still—1 per cent in the coal-mines, 2·1 per cent in textiles, and it was only in a few new industries that the proportion was noticeably higher: 4·7 per cent in chemicals and 6·8 per cent in petrol. But commerce was more attractive even than this. It had 7·5 per cent as managers, banking and insurance together had 9·2 per cent (certain branches of insurance had as much as 20 per cent). Significantly the most attractive of all was still the civil service with 14 per cent (16 per cent in the state administration). An engineer who went into the service of the state would therefore do well, and it is not surprising that the graduates of the Polytechnic who went into private business were mainly the ones who came out bottom of their class. Taking as a sample the graduates of the Polytechnic who graduated in 1929, 1938, and 1950, one sees that only 4 per cent of the top twenty but 80 per cent of the bottom twenty went straight into private industry. The path increasingly followed by the brightest graduates was to work for a while in the civil service and then to use the double prestige of their school and their government connections to move straight into top posts in the private sector. The view that France was moving towards a technocracy is misleading. There was no real break from the rule of the civil service: the most powerful technocrats were still civil servants, except that they took over private business also. The very top managerial posts were reserved for such men.

A survey of upper management in the metallurgical and mining industry undertaken in 1956 showed that 46 per cent of the Polytechnic graduates were in this rank, but only 31 per cent of the graduates of the less prestigious École Centrale were in it. The graduates of Arts et Métiers and of the local engineering schools could seldom rise above the lower management ranks, in much the same way as it was difficult for workers to rise above the rank of foremen. The engineers thus had a very different future before them, depending on their origins. The upper-class ones tended to move from firm to firm and to end up in Paris. The lower ones often stayed all their lives in the same firm working their way up to the rank of department head. The man without an engineering degree who wanted to make his way in industry very seldom got to the very top of large firms. The idea of management by amateurs was not accepted by them. The non-scientist could become head of sales, finance, administration or personnel, but in France these never became top management posts, having far less power and prestige than in the U.S.A.: they were the dead end of a career, representing the upper level a middle manager could reach. It was the production managers who got the most promotion: the Polytechnic engineer after a spell in the provincial factories of the firm could expect to make a jump straight into a controlling position in Paris, above the other departmental heads with longer service. Prospects in family firms were less bright. Really able engineers could hardly be attracted to them since the ceiling of promotion was limited by the directing posts being reserved for members of the family. Only occasionally was a Polytechnic or a Centrale graduate imported to boost such a firm—and it was sometimes done by marrying him into the family. More often however there was a prejudice in family firms, particularly in the nineteenth century, against employing anyone with a formal and advanced scientific education. The more highly qualified an engineer, the more theoretical his training was. The Polytechnic graduate spent 75 per cent of his time in theoretical work. There were too few of them to manage anything more than a small number of large firms in a few industries. In the remaining ones, it was customary for the self-made or family-firm industrialist to disparage the *esprit ingénieur*, by which was meant the neglect of the commercial and practical side of things.[1] These firms preferred to employ the humbler product of the local arts and crafts school, who had spent 60 per cent of his training on practical work, and who was only a glorified mechanic with no pretensions to rising very high. Even this graduate had to fight hard to win a position of minor influence, because his degree gave him little advantage over the self-taught. It was estimated in 1962 that half the occupants of managerial positions in industry as a whole had no higher education at all, and many considerations—of experience, influence and family—were involved in their recruitment.

The ambition to become a captain of industry from humble beginnings was therefore not a realistic one in this period. The

[1] Hugues Le Roux, *Nos Fils: que feront-ils?* (1898), 127.

man who stood the best chance was the Polytechnic graduate, but, as is known, he usually came from good middle- or upper-class stock and he needed to make himself acceptable to the financial giants who controlled the large companies. This sort of person seldom attempted to establish his own empire. Many certainly did found their own firms, but very few seem to have reached any size. The obituaries of the Society of Civil Engineers are highly suggestive in this respect. They show that the engineers with no special family connections very often used their talents in two ways, neither of which contributed much to economic expansion in France. A certain number seem to have deserved the accusations of impracticality. Their education gave them a taste for pure science and they became part-time professors and writers. Others went abroad. It is striking to see the number of French engineers considerable parts of whose careers were spent in South America, Spain, Egypt, Indo-China, etc. French talent, like French capital, was exported to assist the industrialisation of other countries. The decorations they received and listed in their annuals included many from colonial and foreign governments and more of them appear to have been decorated by the ministry of education than by the Legion of Honour.[1] The career of Octave de Rochefort, son of the pamphleteer Henry Rochefort, can illustrate this. After graduating as an engineer from the École Centrale in 1884, he went off to manage a forest in Algeria for two years, was an engineer in Argentina, 1887 to 1880, and then entered the coal-mining industry in the U.S.A. There he became interested in typewriters: he returned to found a factory of these in 1896, producing also calculating machines, Braille machines and transformers—but all, it seems, without any great fortune resulting.[2] In the

[1] François Jacquin, *Les Cadres de l'industrie et du commerce* (1955), particularly interesting for a survey of the Renault factory managers; David Granick, *The European Executive* (1962), an illuminating comparative study of Britain, France, Germany, Belgium, and the U.S.A. The individual lives of engineers deserve study.

Statistics are not easy to acquire, and further research is needed. For obituaries see *Mémoires et compte rendu des travaux de la Société des ingénieurs civils de France* (1898), 418–28; (Nov. 1910), 501–19; (Jan. 1912), 17; (May 1912), 634 etc. For the engineers' literary activities see F. Divisia, *Exposés d'économique: Vol. 1: L'Apport des ingénieurs français aux sciences économiques* (1951).

[2] Henry Junger, *Dictionnaire biographique des grands négociants et industriels* (1895), vol. 9 of Henry Carnoy's series of dictionaries, 101.

twentieth century, the engineers found a third and different outlet for their frustrations: they saw themselves as social conciliators, intermediaries between employers and workers. Many tended towards social catholicism.[1]

One of the explanations of the rush into commerce is probably that until the Revolution commerce was regulated. To be a merchant was almost as privileged as to be a noble or a state official. The merchants had long fought vigorously to keep poachers out of their domain. The small shopkeeper of the twentieth century who tried to make as much profit as he could, who considered his clientele to belong to him and to owe him a living, was heir to the mentality of the *ancien régime* merchants who regarded their monopoly as a kind of *rente* paid by the public. The doctrine of the Church, that the needs of the seller should determine the price of his goods, that he ought to charge as much as was necessary to enable him to live decently, contributed to this attitude. It is true merchants were not esteemed by other classes but within their own they were certainly envied by those beneath them.

It is frequent in developing countries for the tertiary (commercial and administrative) sector of the economy to expand only after the primary (agricultural) sector has declined and the secondary (industrial) sector has grown. In France, the most rapidly expanding sector of the economy in the nineteenth century was however the tertiary one:

	1856	1876	1896	1906	1926	1931	1936	1946
Primary	51·7	48·8	44·8	42·7	38·3	35·6	35·5	36·0
Secondary	26·8	27·3	28·6	29·2	32·8	33·3	30·5	29·5
Tertiary	21·4	23·9	26·3	28·1	28·9	31·1	33·9	34·5

The table shows that it increased, in the forty years 1856–96, twice as much as the industrial sector. Another calculation, dividing the total population according to the occupation of the head of the family, gets the following even more striking results, in millions (though the 1856 figures seem very doubtful):

[1] Georges Lamirand, *Le Rôle social de l'ingénieur* (1923, new edition 1937); see also Marcel Barbier, *Le Problème français de la formation des ingénieurs, d'après quelques écrits récents* (1955).

	Total population	Agriculture	Industry	Commerce and transport	Liberal professions and civil service	Proprietors and *rentiers*	Without profession or profession unknown
1856	36·178	19	10·47	1·732	1·67	1·758	1·484
1876	36·9	18·969	9·275	3·89	1·96	2·153	0·704
1891	38·13	17·436	9·532	5·161	2·530	2·170	1·304

It is probable that the number drawing their income from commerce doubled, while those dependent on industry rose by only 50 per cent. However, in the twentieth century the commercial population increased by only a very moderate amount (from 1·88 million active population to 2·16 in 1946). It was only after the Second World War that the rapid rise was resumed, producing an increase as much as 34 per cent in eight years, but then the increase was related to an industrial explosion, whereas in the nineteenth century it was not. Commercial opportunities in the nineteenth century were multiplied by increasing prosperity in all forms of activity, added to the continued dispersion of the population, so that far more retail outlets were preserved than would have been normal in other industrialising nations. In 1954 37 per cent of the French population still lived in communes of under 2,000 inhabitants (compared with 18·5 per cent in Germany and 7 per cent in Italy). 40 per cent of the German population lived in towns of over 50,000, 30 per cent of Italians, but only 23 per cent of Frenchmen.[1] The way commercial activity increased may be judged best on a local scale. In the Forez, which contained the industrial town of St. Étienne, but also covered a large agricultural area, the number of fairs doubled in the nineteenth century, from 307 in 1809 to 713 in 1909, and this increase came mainly after 1870. In addition to these fairs, as against the 21 weekly markets in 1818, there were 90 in 1909. The number of wine shops doubled likewise, rising from 4,051 in 1857 to 8,738 in 1908.[2]

[1] Jean Fourastié, *Migrations professionnelles 1900–1955* (Institut National d'Études démographiques, travaux et documents, cahier no. 31, 1957), 157; Claude Quin, *Physionomie et perspectives d'évolution de l'appareil commercial français 1950–1970* (1964), 47. J. C. Toutain, *La Population de la France de 1700 à 1959* (1963), 146.

[2] L. J. Gras, *Histoire du commerce local et des industries qui s'y rattachent dans la région stéphanoise et forézienne* (St. Étienne, 1910), 398–400, 407, 423.

In Paris, the number of retail grocers probably doubled almost exactly in the short space of twenty-five years, 1856–79.[1]

Now a certain amount of the commercial expansion did take place in the form of more modern and larger units. By 1940 the co-operatives had 9,000 shops and 2·75 million members and had between 13 and 14 per cent of the commercial turnover; but 60 per cent of these co-op shops were to the north of a line from Cherbourg to Geneva. Chain stores are said to have begun in 1866 when four wholesalers of Reims began selling directly to the public; in the 1880s chain stores selling shoes appeared, then wine, milk, clothes and books. By 1940 there were 23,000 chain stores dealing in food alone—accounting for a quarter of the national turnover, but having grown almost entirely through self-financing and without any assistance from the banks. The large department stores were born under the Second Empire, again self-financed. The single-price shop, so successful in the U.S.A. well before the First World War, reached France in 1927 (or 1929). But in 1931 there were still only some 100 retail shops with over 500 employees, whereas there were approximately half a million tiny shops: 91 per cent of retail outlets employed three or fewer assistants. In addition there were those who ministered to the 200,000 fairs and markets in the country.[2]

These small merchants occupied a distinctive role in French society. Gabriel Hanotaux praised them as representing the most democratic of French careers, where it was easiest to start with a little and make a fortune, where there was the greatest independence, and where every man had a good chance of succeeding.[3] Parliament seemed to support this view when it repeatedly imposed heavy discriminatory taxes on chain and department stores, in an attempt to halt their progress. Any shop with over 200 employees had to pay a tax equivalent to about a fifth of the wages it paid to any employee above that number.[4] Special taxes were imposed on retail shops with turnovers

[1] Firmin Didot, *Annuaire Almanach du commerce* (1856 and 1879), lists of *épiciers en détail*.

[2] Centre d'Information inter-professionnelles, *Le Commerce: documents* (1943).

[3] Victor Ray, *Pour faire fortune, par un ancien commerçant* (Moulins, 1922), 8; A. Demonceaux, *Le Choix d'une carrière commerciale, industrielle ou financière. Guide pratique des parents et de la jeunesse* (3rd edition, n.d., about 1920).

[4] Law of 28 Apr. 1893. See Yves Guyot, *Le Commerce et les commerçants* (1909), 203.

above a million francs (and 91·9 per cent of retailers had turnovers below half a million), and double *patente* was imposed on
chain stores. In 1935 expansion of retail trade by travelling
vans was forbidden (*camions bazars*); in 1936 the creation of new
prix unique shops and of new shoe shops was forbidden.[1] It
should not be thought that parliament was simply yielding to
a pressure group. French society would have been far less
mobile without these small shopkeepers, however much the
cost of living might have been reduced by their disappearance.
It was not dynasties of shopkeepers that they established. A
retailer who had made a fortune, said the Chartons in 1880,
would make his son follow after him only very unwillingly and
as a last resort: he would do his best to make him enter the
liberal professions.[2] The visitor to Paris who absented himself
for twenty years would find very few of the same shops, owned
by the same people, still active. The ideal was to make money
quickly—which partly explains the high prices charged—and
then to retire to live off one's capital. The idea that retailers
did make a great deal of money was of course partly a myth.[3]
Some 40 per cent of small businesses normally went bankrupt
(at the end of the nineteenth century) but it will never be
possible to discover much about the finances of the retailer. Of
those who did go bankrupt 90 per cent kept no accounts. One
of the great attractions of retail trade resulted from precisely
this. It was easier to avoid taxation. It has been officially
calculated by the French government in 1955 that the joint-
stock companies were concealing 19–25 per cent of their net
profits, smaller individual enterprises and partnerships between
42 and 48 per cent, but that artisans and shopkeepers far outdistanced them.[4] The large store had to open its books to the
tax inspector: the small shopkeeper simply made a declaration.
Being a shopkeeper was to a certain extent a tax dodge, a way
of making money at the expense of the state. The history of
shopkeeping is indeed a history of a struggle to escape state
control. The controls of the *ancien régime*—though partially
abolished by the ending of the corporations—nevertheless

[1] Gaston Defossé, *Le Commerce intérieur* (1944), 175.
[2] E. Charton, 3rd edition, 152.
[3] Marcel Porte, *Entrepreneurs et profits industriels* (1901), 183.
[4] *Les Informations industrielles et commerciales*, no. 546 (7 Oct. 1955).

continued in a multitude of other restrictions. One of the lesser-known achievements of Napoleon III was to introduce greater liberty for shopkeepers, and in particular to end the limitations on bakers' and butchers' shops. However, every town had its own regulations and taxes and the shopkeeper had to be an adept at circumventing the law. That is why the radicals liked him. He incarnated resistance to authority, individualism and the right to better oneself. Commerce provided a means of rising in the world as important as education, though it has been less talked about by politicians and historians, because it was not institutionalised by legislation. It was as it were the back-stairs way up, for the civil code enshrined secrecy in commercial activities as a legal principle. The passion for secrecy made trade all the more hazardous. It restricted the rise of credit-checking firms and agencies supplying commercial information.[1] Commerce had some of the elements of guerrilla warfare. It was warfare, one should add, against the wholesaler as well as against the state, so that the shopkeeper was doubly the *small man*.[2] Far from diminishing with the rise of the large stores, the number of people setting up as shopkeepers on their own continued to increase.

The heroes of commerce were more democratic figures than those of industry. The ones who particularly caught the popular imagination—because the extent of their activities raised them out of this normally secretive world—were the founders of the large department stores of Paris. They came from humble origins: Boucicaut (1810–77), the founder of the *Bon Marché*, was the son of a hatter; he began as a pedlar before coming to Paris. Chauchard (1821–1909), the founder of the *Louvre*, was the son of a restaurant keeper; he worked his way up from being an assistant at a small shop, the *Pauvre Diable*. Cognacq (1839–1928) of the *Samaritaine* was a shop assistant from the age of twelve. All spent their early years in poverty. Boucicaut was the real pioneer in introducing new methods: fixed prices, low profit margins, commissions on sales for the staff, clearance sales at regular intervals and an elaborate social security system for all the employees. Chauchard was more of a social climber

---

[1] Maurice Mayer, *Le Secret des affaires commerciales* (1900), 276.
[2] Roger Picard, *Distribution et consommation, les cahiers du redressement français*, no. 11 (1927).

and political dealer: he appears to have got help from the financier Périer to found his shop in 1855, which catered for the rich with sumptuous salons and luxurious décor. His relations with the radical politicians remain obscure, except that he secured from them the exceptionally high decoration of Grand Officer of the Legion of Honour in 1906 and he left a lot of money to Georges Leygues. Cognacq started his first shop with his own savings of 5,000 francs and lost all. He took up peddling on the Pont Neuf, saved up another 5,000, and rented a small boutique nearby, the original site of the Samaritaine, in 1870. Two years later he married Louise Jay, a chief assistant in the dress department of the Bon Marché, who had saved up 20,000. This shows how quickly capital could be accumulated in commerce. The couple never borrowed a *sou* all their lives, and confined their advertising to sending out catalogues. The values and methods of shopkeepers were incarnated in this store. Each of the ninety sections was a separate shop, with the seller getting only a nominal retaining salary (300–1,200 francs a year in 1933), and relying on his 3 per cent commission, which could produce an income comparing favourably with any profession. Both Boucicaut and Cognacq introduced participation in profits for the staff (rising with rank). They and Chauchard all gave vast sums to charity and became leading philanthropists. In the case of Cognacq, it was said that his motive was a violent hate of the state and a determination to pay nothing in death-duties. None of them had children. Boucicaut and Cognacq both had very active wives, making their firms very much the husband-and-wife teams so common in retail trade. Mme Boucicaut ran the Bon Marché on her own as a widow with great success. After they had made their fortunes, Cognacq and Chauchard went in for collecting paintings, which they bequeathed respectively to the city of Paris and the Louvre Museum. Their collections were enormous and very valuable, but it is not clear that either of them was really interested in painting. Cognacq really loved the theatre, where declamation recalled to him his own successes as pedlar on the Pont Neuf. Louise Cognacq reconciled herself to his expenditure on art by saying she preferred 'for the sake of his health' that the money should go to art dealers rather than a mistress. Cognacq was in any case too short-sighted really to enjoy his pictures.[1] He was totally uninterested in politics but religiously read all the commercial advertisements in the papers. He occasionally travelled, because he found it improved his appetite. He sometimes went to the Opéra Comique, because music put him into a particularly relaxing sleep. But though the principles on which he built his fortune were commercial, and though he hated the state, in the organisation of his shop he followed the bureaucratic and hierarchic methods of the state with almost identical over-staffing and elaborate form filling. The Samaritaine was no anarchist federation of communes. Regulations governed every detail of behaviour, from prohibiting the wearing of silk stockings and *décolleté* dresses by the assistants, to the requirement that each of the 8,000 employees should always sit in the same place at the free lunch. 'Conformism was his law. Any initiative frightened him; his strength came from his inertia, systematically opposed to all audacity.'[2]

The world of commerce was infinitely varied not only because of the enormous differences in wealth between the extremes, but also because, particularly at the humbler levels, different practices and mentalities survived in different regions. Educational qualifications, at least until 1914, counted for little. The École Supérieure de Commerce de Paris founded in 1820 by some wholesalers to raise the level of 'citizens so contemptuously called merchants', bought in 1830 by Adolphe Blanqui, brother of the revolutionary, run by him as a profit-making concern, taken over eventually by the Chamber of Commerce, was principally patronised by well-to-do pupils, with families already in business.[3] Between the wars a few schools for salesmen (one of them modelled on Mrs. Prince's establishment in Boston, which trained people for Filene's Store and which was subsequently absorbed into Simmons College) and a few courses using Harvard Business School graduates were introduced, but they had little impact. Correspondence courses to obtain minimal qualifications were more popular.[4]

[1] Francis Jourdain, *Né en '76* (1951), 255–69, describes the relations of his father, the painter, with Cognacq, who was his best client.

[2] Fernand Laudet, *La Samaritaine* (1933); and Jourdain, 267.

[3] Alfred Renouard, *Histoire de l'école supérieure de commerce de Paris* (1898, 3rd edition, expanded, 1920).

[4] Daniel Briod, *La Science de la vente et sa place dans l'enseignement commercial* (1929).

Whether these modernised merchants made more money than the old-fashioned ones is not clear. What is known is that in the country as a whole commercial properties increased in value in the first half of the twentieth century more than any other form of investment, and they were the only form of investment which did not suffer from two world wars. The regional variations in profitability were, it is true, very great but they have not yet been analysed. They do not seem to be immediately related to local agricultural or industrial growth, and the enormous prosperity of the shopkeepers of the Aude and Vaucluse, for example, far in excess of neighbouring departments like the Var and Hérault and of rich ones like the Nord, has still to be explained.[1] But it may be that this accumulation of commercial wealth provided the same sort of basis for the economic expansion of the 1950s as the similar merchant prosperity in eighteenth-century England did for the Industrial Revolution which, partly for that reason, occurred so much earlier here.

[1] Paul Cornut, *Répartition de la fortune privée en France* (1963), 247–75. In Paris between 1900 and 1924, the value of retail businesses increased eightfold in money terms, or nearly twice in real terms. Restaurants and hotels went up in value fifteen times, grocery shops and *crémeries* ten times, butchers' shops eight times, bakeries six times and fruiterers four times. In the country as a whole, the number of retail businesses rose from 198,000 to 226,000 in the period 1901 to 1912; in these years, between 5 and 6 per cent of businesses changed hands every year. A. Bonnefoy, *L'Achat et la vente des fonds de commerce dans l'économie moderne* (1924); *Recherches statistiques sur la Ville de Paris* (1860), vol. 6, 630–1; E. Clementel and M. de Toro, *Larousse commercial* (1930), 607; Diane de Luppé, *Le Commerce de vin dans le département de la Seine de 1851 a 1860 d'après le fonds des faillites du tribunal de commerce de la Seine* (unpublished thesis in the library of the Paris faculty of law, 1968).

8. Bureaucrats

THE civil service is another of the professions where expansion is usually equated with the increase in the power of the bourgeoisie. There is a great deal of truth in this. However, increase in numbers and functions did not automatically involve an increase in influence or status. On the contrary, if one examines why people went into the civil service and what exactly individuals were able to do when they were in it, one sees that membership of it gave an ambiguous position in society, which altered in the course of the century, which varied profoundly with one's place in the hierarchy, and which by 1940 was subject to much hostility.

France was one of the pioneers of bureaucracy in Europe. In the seventeenth and eighteenth centuries the number of civil service jobs exploded to enormous proportions. The reason was partly that the king needed money and rather than obtain it from parliament, as in England, he preserved his absolutism by selling offices. These offices gave some exemption from taxation, the higher ones even brought a debased nobility with them, and all acquired prestige. State jobs became an investment, in which moderate return on capital was compensated for by social advantages. The French acquired the habit of putting their money into state offices, and into land, rather than industry. Low but secure yields were accepted as the correct ambition for sensible men, and a modest style of living for those who rose in this way was consecrated as a social norm. The Revolution ended the sale of offices—except in a few cases—but it did not alter the investment habits of the country, or the social status attached to public employment. A certain amount of merit was now needed to enter the civil service, but education, which was the principal proof of merit, still had to be bought. The myth of equality of opportunity heightened the status of those who rose in the hierarchy. The Revolution made the civil service more than an investment; it turned it into something of a lottery into which everybody in theory had the right to enter; and the hunger for its prizes became all the more frantic.

In 1842, in his Guide to the Professions, Charton gave some interesting reasons to explain, as he put it, why 'a career in the public service is very much sought after by those whom birth or education places in the upper and middle classes'. It was an alternative preferable to industry and the liberal professions, where the chance of failure or disaster was considerable. It was a safe career, but it also led to high stakes because the salaries of senior posts were large by any standards. However, it required only moderate amounts of capital to be laid out, smaller than were required in other professions.[1] The civil service was thus approached by men with much the same attitude as if they were thinking of buying property. The problem is to discover just what kind of advantages went with the investment and how attitudes to it developed. Certainly its attractions made themselves felt in all classes during the nineteenth century. Parliamentary government meant that the patronage necessary to obtain an introduction into it was much more widely available to anyone willing to make a bargain with a deputy in return for his vote. The spread of education gave more and more people a chance to obtain the basic qualifications.

France had the reputation of having the highest number of civil service posts in Europe at the beginning of our period and it maintained that reputation by quadrupling the number in the hundred years covered by this book. When in 1848 the government was asked to publish a list of all its employees it refused, saying the task would be too great and it would require fifty volumes. Accurate statistics were never a strong point before 1945 and the exact number of civil servants is not definitely established. But roughly speaking it seems that in 1848 there were about a quarter of a million, in 1914 half a million, and in 1945 one million. The real distinction between France and comparable countries is not in the number of public servants but in the number employed by the central government. Britain in 1950 had 687,000 civil servants, but it had in addition 1,500,000 local government employees, whereas France had only 370,000 of these. The U.S.A. seems to have more public servants of various kinds than France. Between the wars it was calculated

---

[1] E. Charton, *Guide pour le choix d'un état* (1842), 261.

that a city like Bordeaux had one public servant to every eighty-two inhabitants, but this was not much different from Newark, N.J., with 1:86 and was an average between Seattle's 1:52 and Dayton's 1:157.[1]

What was an even more radical difference was the place that the civil service had in French life. The civil service fulfilled two important functions, apparently contradictory. On the one hand it continued to serve as a major avenue for social mobility, but on the other hand the families it helped to raise in the social scale very often did not move out to make their way at a higher level in the world of business or industry, but stayed on in the service. Thus the bureaucracy as it expanded its activities became, to a certain extent, an enormous, constantly growing clan of families. While the test of merit was still increasingly applied, the civil servants almost formed a hereditary class, with considerable cohesion of outlook and values. They were not quite a corporation, but they had a lot in common with the rivals they were displacing, the clergy.

Detailed studies of the state's employees are still in progress—the sociology of bureaucracy is now a budding subject in France. There is one statistical analysis which, though it deals with the post-1945 period, is very illuminating and its conclusions will probably be found to be true of the pre-war years with due modifications to allow for the increased democratisation of education. The administrative grades of the civil service were in the 1960s filled for the most part by men of upper-class origin. Thus only 15.2 per cent of civil servants of humble birth reached this grade, 19.3 per cent of those of middle birth, but 65 per cent of those from the upper class. Only 12 per cent of all civil servants were born in Paris but 39.1 per cent of the administrative grade were. Only 23.3 per cent of this upper grade had no other member of their family in the civil service. In cases where they had a father who had been a civil servant, 87.3 per cent of these also had other relatives who were civil servants and 47.6 per cent had not only a father but also a grandfather or father-in-law plus other collaterals who were civil servants too. What is particularly striking is the limited movement in the upper class of French society between

[1] W. R. Sharp, *The French Civil Service, Bureaucracy in Transition* (New York, 1931), 418; F. Ridley and J. Blondel, *Public Administration in France* (2nd edition 1969), 29.

those who serve the state and those who do not. Thus only 9 per cent of sons of upper-class fathers went into the civil service when their fathers were employed in the private sector, but 57 per cent went in when their fathers were in public employment. There is an even stronger dynastic tradition in the lower ranks: 44 per cent of sons of private *employés* (clerks) go into the civil service but 82 per cent of sons of public ones. The closed nature of the recruitment of the state becomes all the more pronounced when it is seen that certain parts of the country are far more involved than others. Broadly, the south of France sends far more of its children to the civil service than the north. Over 5 per cent of the natives of Corsica obtain state employment, over 3 per cent of those of departments like Hérault, Aude, Ariège, Hautes-Pyrénées, Pyrénées-Orientales, Haute-Garonne, Lot-et-Garonne, Lot, Corrèze, Lozère, and the three Alpine departments.[1] Moreover, men born in small towns of 10,000 to 20,000 inhabitants—which often owe their importance mainly to their administrative function and which have proportionately a far larger number of civil servants, occupying the most prestigious roles in the towns—enter the civil service almost twice as much as those born in large cities (where the attractions of commerce and industry are overwhelming) or isolated rural villages.[2] It would be an exaggeration to say that one part of the country makes money while another part governs, but public opinion polls about the civil service reveal far less hostility to it in the south than in the north.[3]

The nature of the civil service has changed since the Revolution so that few generalisations apply equally to the whole period. In many cases, however, the changes were deceptive, and the traditions of the past were maintained under the new forms. But what did not happen was simply the opening of the careers to the talents.

One radical transformation in this period was the disappearance of large salaries. At the end of the July Monarchy, the rewards for those who reached the top were outstanding and placed

[1] Michel Crozier, *Petits Fonctionnaires au travail* (1955), shows that in a survey of 3,500 clerical workers, 33 per cent were daughters of civil servants and 40 per cent came from the south-west.
[2] A. Darbel and D. Schnapper, *Les Agents du système administratif* (1969), 22, 61, 70, 75, 91, 95.
[3] Bernard Gournay, *L'Administration* (1964), 83–4.

them among the richest men in the country. Four ambassadors were paid over 150,000 francs a year, 102 civil servants earned over 20,000 francs, and 1,009 over 10,000 francs. At the other end, junior officials earned derisory sums for what was very similar work; but work was not what they were really paid for. This was still a spoils system. There were 277 prefects and sub-prefects: two of them got over 60,000 but 228 got around 3,000 francs. Salaries varied greatly between the different ministries. The finances paid best: the director in charge of indirect taxation in a department got between 7,200 and 12,000 francs. The learned careers were paid worst. The engineer-in-chief, controlling the roads and bridges of a department, got only 4,500 to 5,000 and the rector of an academy, with several departments under him, got only 6,000 to 7,200 francs. Accordingly France's financial administration was the largest item in its budget: 89 million went to pay the salaries of financial officials, as against only 62 million for the army, 26 for the navy, 30 for religion, 15 for justice, 7·6 for the ministry of the interior, about 5 each for the foreign office, public works and education, 1·7 for agriculture and commerce, plus 11 million for central administration. This gives some idea of the distribution of the spoils available. But salaries were not the only rewards to be had. Some jobs were still paid in medieval fashion entirely from fees levied from the public—not just the notaries, but also the conservators of mortgages and the clerks of courts. Some obtained fees as supplements to their salaries: professors of faculties got a share of enrolment, examination and certificate fees; employees of the financial administration got bonuses for increasing revenue collected; those capturing contraband or discovering tax frauds got a share of seizures, fines and confiscations. The salaries of some, e.g. those working in the chancellories of consulates and in some financial jobs, were variable. The chief tax-collectors had the privilege of delegating their duties, so that a *receveur particulier des finances*, earning between 15,000 and 20,000 francs (side by side with and covering the same area as a sub-prefect earning 3,000 to 4,000), would often appoint a substitute at 1,800 or 2,000.[1] By the end of our period these variations had been largely ironed out and in 1946, when a uniform salary structure was worked out, the discrepancy

[1] Pierre Legendre, *L'Administration du 18ᵉ siècle à nos jours* (1968), 179.

between the best paid and the worst paid was no longer in a ratio of 150 to one but had been reduced to eleven to one (or eight to one after taxation). Mediocrity replaced splendour and economy took the place of largesse as the hallmarks of the public servant. The civil service ceased to be a path to riches.

On the other hand it had also been a part-time occupation for gentlemen who bought themselves in, and whose income came only in part from their salaries. Equally drastic therefore was the disappearance of private incomes as a necessary adjunct to many state jobs. Almost all the better jobs in the state service had required the young entrant to spend one or two years, and sometimes longer, working unpaid, learning his duties and winning favour. In some branches, e.g. the inspection of finance, candidates wishing to be deputy inspectors had to have a guarantee from their parents of a private income of 2,000 francs to last so long as they held that rank. In other posts parents had to promise to maintain their sons for at least two years while, e.g. they held the post of supernumerary in the department of direct taxation. When the son finally obtained a paid post, many jobs in the financial service required the deposit of caution money—equal to three times the salary received as a *percepteur* and, when promoted to be *receveur particulier*, equal to five times the salary. In the foreign service, until 1894, candidates had to have a private income of 6,000 francs. The civil service could hardly be said to be open to all the talents until, at the very least, it paid its young recruits a living wage. In the judicial service, the rank of entry, *juge suppléant*, ceased to be unpaid only in 1910. However, even after this, the cost of education necessary to enter the civil service remained an obstacle to democratic recruitment. For the best jobs, the École Libre des Sciences politiques held a virtual monopoly in the preparation of candidates for the ministries of finance and foreign affairs, and as it was a fee-paying institution, recruits to these ministries remained well-to-do. When therefore the peasant stared at a poster announcing a competition for admission to the civil service, with the democratic phrase 'The emperor (or the republic) invites all to apply', he was not taken in. The civil service still retained strong elements of a caste.

The introduction of impartial examinations as a method of entry was slow to take effect. The supposedly democratic competitions (*concours*) set up by the Revolution were generally decided by criteria of patronage and nepotism. When candidates were actually tested, the examinations were usually so perfunctory as to be purely symbolic. It was only in 1872–4 that an attempt was made to introduce serious examinations and they were regularly used after that for many jobs, but it seems that it was only at the turn of the century that they were fully established as normal. However, it should not be thought that this ended the matter and brought about impartial admission on merit. The civil service took the sort of recruits its conservative heads thought it needed. The *concours* often continued to test only a restricted range of qualities; success was sometimes determined by the relation of the candidate with a *patron*, whose teaching he was required to regurgitate. Recruitment to the colonial service, for example, was for a time reactionary because it drew mainly from the École Coloniale which was run by the Comité de l'Afrique française, and which admitted only people with the same mentality as the financial oligarchy interested in the colonies. The patronage system was thus transformed or modified rather than completely abolished. The early years of the Third Republic, when the stress on merit was trumpeted most loudly, were also years in which the 'abuse of recommendations was pushed to unheard of extremes': Léon Say, when minister of finance, likened the pressures on him for jobs to those prevalent in the *ancien régime*.[1] Millerand said he received 150 letters a day asking for jobs and between the wars the under-secretary of the Post Office was still receiving 100,000 letters a year from politicians and other influential personages recommending people for employment, promotion or transfer. A magistrate seeking promotion got thirty-eight deputies and senators to write to the minister of justice to support him, as was made public in a particular case in 1930. A crisis occurred at the turn of the century, when the passions produced by anticlericalism caused Combes to defend favouritism publicly and somewhat tactlessly. As a result, in 1905 every civil servant was given the right to see his file if he was threatened with a disciplinary penalty, with transfer against his will or with the postponement of advancement due to him

---

[1] Quoted by Vicomte d'Avenel, 'L'Extension du fonctionnarisme depuis 1870', *Revue des Deux Mondes* (1 Mar. 1888), 95.

by seniority. This transformed the annual reports of superiors about their juniors which were once a mine of information about every aspect of the man's life, into a purely formal and meaningless routine, and it made promotion by seniority an almost inflexibly applied rule.

Judges and university and secondary teachers had won their security in the 1880s, primary teachers were protected by laws of 1880 and 1919, but some departments were slower to win legislation, and for them the Conseil d'État served as an appeal court. Every year after 1919 about 1,500 cases of wrongful dismissal or failure to get promotion were brought before it— but a case often took four years to decide and if the government refused to implement the Conseil's decision, another four years would be necessary to force it. By the 1930s the trade unions were satisfied that they had eliminated favouritism, in so far as was possible. Deputies still continued to write to ministers recommending their constituents, and the ministers replied that they would submit their letters to the appropriate authorities who would see that justice was done. The deputies could send this reply to the constituent and in this way everybody was more or less satisfied.[1] However, examinations did not make the civil service into a coherent institution, all of whose branches recruited from the same source. Admission inevitably remained something of a mystery, affected by the accidents of social connections, when not only each university organised its competitions separately, but within each, different departments worked at recruitment totally independently. In 1927, for example, ten different bodies within the ministry of finance were offering jobs without any co-operation and there were 1,200 different competitions annually. Even if favouritism was eliminated, the individual eccentricities and traditions of each department could more easily survive in this fragmentary system.

A subtle change came about when civil servants who had been political nominees attempted to turn their jobs into life-time careers. For long politics played a significant part in many appointments. Until 1870 civil servants were required to take an oath of loyalty to the regime in power. Each revolution therefore produced sweeping dismissals and the introduction of

[1] Sharp, 73.

partisans of the new government. This situation altered for two reasons. On the one hand governments found it difficult to find tens of thousands of suitable civil servants in the aftermath of each revolution; inevitably many experienced men had to be allowed to stay on. With time the political complexion of their offices became diluted, and political appointments tended to be confined to a smaller number of posts. However, more important was the pressure from the civil servants themselves to obtain security. Once in office, even the political ones adopted the airs of disinterested public service: even Napoleon III's prefects, the principal instruments of his repressive policies, tried to cultivate detachment and to look on themselves as professional administrators.[1] They began protesting against senior positions of command being allocated arbitrarily to men with no experience. The political opposition in every regime found the centralisation of the civil service a good way of reducing the government's power. The obsession with pensions completed the transformation. It was only gradually that the prospect of a pension became a major attraction of public employment. Originally only the army had a satisfactory retirement scheme, giving pensions of a respectable size (4,000 francs for a lieutenant-general, 1,200 for a captain) after thirty years' service (twenty-five in the navy). The clergy never got any pensions at all, and the *percepteurs des contributions indirectes*, whose posts were considered not so much salaried jobs as purchased contracts, got nothing either. Others were paid under the law of 1790, which aimed to produce half pay after thirty years of service, though it is not clear that it always reached that figure. The law had in fact provided for the state to pay only one sixth of the top salary earned after thirty years of service to a selected and small number of civil servants. It also allowed 5 per cent of salaries to be paid into a fund to supplement this, but the fund proved inadequate. The state began subsidising it, but the arrangements of the fund remained complicated and different for each ministry.[2] Only in 1853 did the state unify the pension system and start paying pensions to civil servants directly itself, as it did to the army, except that it still retained the 5 per cent

---

[1] See Vincent Wright's forthcoming work on the Prefects of the Second Empire.
[2] Vivien, 'Études administratives: Les fonctionnaires publics', *Revue des Deux Mondes* (15 Oct. 1845), 215–70.

employee's contribution.[1] Inevitably once this happened it became much more difficult to dismiss anybody and deprive him
of his accumulating investment. In this way the civil servants
won back something of the *ancien régime* character of their
occupations, when they enjoyed a right to their salaries irrespective of whether they were performing a useful function. The
state in fact encouraged them to maintain the ancient obsession
with status and hierarchy, by developing a system of promotion
with so many different grades and sub-categories, that ambitions could both be satisfied by tiny increases in salary and
controlled by a rigid scale through which every career had to
proceed. The centralising doctrine, that salaries had to be linked
with a hierarchy of towns, so that promotions usually involved
transfers, meant that internal jealousies, rivalries and frustrations played a major role in the life of the civil servant, and made
his world more and more a private one.[2]

These changes inevitably affected the prestige of the civil
service. The more comfortable and secure the civil servants
made themselves, the more they cut themselves off from the
world of politics, the more they shut out merit and opted for
seniority, the more they lost their place of leadership in society.
The functions of the majority of them were in any case ceasing
to be administrative and supervisory. The great increase in their
numbers in the period 1850–1900 was due above all to the
recruitment of 80,000 new primary-school teachers and 50,000
new postmen, both inferior and poorly paid grades, so that the
average level of the civil service sank accordingly. Most civil
servants were not grand. Their salaries ceased to be impressive
and in 1901 articles were published lamenting their fate as a
new proletariat. The average salary in 1900 was only 1,490
francs, hardly equal to that of a good labourer.[3] At this period
only a thousand civil servants were earning over 15,000 francs
a year, and the highest salary was only 35,000. But the department stores of Paris by themselves were paying over 250 of their
employees salaries of 20,000 to 25,000, equal to that of most
prefects, and in business many could hope to earn 50,000,

---

[1] H. Blerzy, 'Le Fonctionnarisme dans l'état', *Revue des Deux Mondes* (15 Sept.
1871), 444–59.
[2] Cf. A. Granveau, *Analyse philosophique des usages* (1865), 25–7.
[3] Bérenger, *Le Prolétariat intellectuel* (1901), 63.

100,000, or more.[1] After the Great War, the situation of the civil servants grew drastically worse, as their salaries totally failed to keep up with inflation. In 1927, when the cost of living had risen five fold since 1914, the salaries of most of them had gone up between only two and three times in the upper ranks and between four and five times in the lower ranks. The senior men thus received yet another blow. Their humiliation was likened to that of the half-pay officers of the Napoleonic armies dashed down from their glory after 1815. Resignations flowed in at unprecedented levels. In 1920–6, out of a total of ninety inspectors of finance, seventy-four resigned; there were eighty resignations a year in the senior grades of the department of direct taxation, as opposed to twenty a year before the war. The number of candidates for admission fell so that it became difficult to recruit at all, even though standards were noticeably lowered. Thus before 1914 48 per cent of the candidates for the *enregistrement* were successful, in 1920–6 64 per cent were. There used to be about four candidates for every post of inspector in this department, there were now barely enough to fill the vacancies. The ministry of labour used to get 150 candidates for each examination to fill four or five posts, in 1927 it got thirty. Those who had maintained their status by supplementing honorific but poorly paid posts with their private incomes found their investments had lost most of their value. Magistrates were reported travelling in third-class railway carriages. Schoolmasters were compelled to take on second jobs. Engineers, who could double their salaries before the war by going into private industry, now had little choice, when the real value of their state salaries fell by half.[2] It remained possible to fill the lowest ranks, but men from poorer social and educational backgrounds had to be accepted higher up. Many jobs were now reserved for victims of the war and for their widows— 100 per cent of all concierge and copyist jobs, 75 per cent of mail carriers, 100 per cent of customs officials. This was one way of employing these people usefully instead of paying them pensions, but it conflicted with the principle of merit and it

[1] Vicomte d'Avenel, 'Fonctionnaires de l'état et des administrations privées', *Revue des Deux Mondes* (15 July 1906), 391–413.
[2] 'La Crise des cadres de la nation', *L'Europe Nouvelle* (26 Mar. 1927), special issue.

accentuated the image of shabbiness and mediocrity that the civil service increasingly assumed.

In 1927 a member of the Institute wrote: 'Today the élite no longer wants to serve the state.' This was a situation which had already begun at the end of the nineteenth century, he said. Till then, the civil service gave great honour and social rank. 'Thirty years ago, in provincial towns, social rank did not depend on wealth or personal value but on the job a man had and the family background to which he was linked by birth or marriage.' These considerations put men in 'good society'. Service in the state not only gave social rank but it also had a matrimonial value. But now this was no longer the case. Security of tenure meant officials no longer had power; they could not hire and fire as private industrialists could; automatic promotion meant there were no sanctions against the inefficient and no proofs of merit or even of influence.[1]

There was another reason why there were fewer applicants for each job. By 1945 there were twice as many jobs as there had been in 1914. Most of these were inevitably in the lower grades. The image of the civil servant changed, to become more drab and depressed. The old distinction between the highly paid and the men on starvation salaries was replaced by another, since hardly any were highly paid any more. There were now those who spent all their lives in the service and those who used it for their own purposes before they moved on. Because much of this increase in numbers occurred at a time of economic depression, the status of the civil service was doubly damaged. Those who entered it appeared to be taking refuge from the world, to be seeking security above all else, sacrificing income and hope. The isolation of these lower grades from the rest of the country was accentuated. On the other hand, in the upper echelons more and more graduates of the *grandes écoles* abandoned public service to go into industry and business. Young men of good family became inspectors of finance only as a preparation for careers with large companies. A low job in the civil service led nowhere. One at the top—provided one had the right family background or political connections— opened the doors of high finance. The links between business

[1] H. Truchy, 'L'Élite et la fonction publique', *Revue Politique et Parlementaire* (10 Dec. 1927), 339–48.

and the upper civil service grew much stronger, as more of the latter were drawn into the former, and as the leaders of both were increasingly graduates of the *grandes écoles*. The old dividing lines now became blurred. The idea of serving the state lost its quasi-military character when the mass of civil servants joined trade unions and argued their rights against the state, just like ordinary workers fighting capitalism. The distinction between private and public service became less important in the top ranks when both were monopolised by the same people. Success had to be redefined by new criteria. A peasant could still get his son to become an *instituteur*, who could in turn get his son to become a secondary-school master, and his son might well rise to be a university professor and even a member of the Institute. This was a frequent path of social promotion. But after his hard climb the professor would find himself confronted by financiers and businessmen who moved in and out of the best-paid posts with a facility he had never known. He would then realise that the holding of high office by itself gave only a limited status. When the state lost its arbitrary powers, a fact which had always been true became more obvious, that the great civil servants of the past owed their status to several different factors which they had succeeded in combining—money, family, unpaid local office, learning, membership of influential society, landownership. Without these, the new self-made civil servant, with only a pension between himself and the world, felt himself surrounded by forces almost as powerful as the state, but much more elusive: and there was a strong temptation to make his peace with them.

In the late nineteenth century, civil servants were supposed to be loyal adherents of republicanism, freemasons and laic opponents of clericalism. They were not as loyal as the myth required them to be, but they had at least to be discreet about their conservative family traditions. By the mid twentieth century this had changed. The upper ranks of the civil service contained a larger proportion of practising Catholics than was normal in the social class from which they came—in the 1960s as many as 40 per cent attended church regularly.[1] The *instituteurs* were perhaps the most steadfastly loyal anticlericals, but the secondary teachers always included many believers, and

[1] Darbel and Schnapper, 94.

even the Sorbonne, for long a citadel of the left wing, has in the last decade fallen too. In less political ministries conservatism was always respectable, partly because civil servants, when appointed by a revolutionary regime, usually tried to reconquer the social prestige their predecessors had enjoyed, but which they as new-comers did not immediately obtain, and this meant gaining acceptance in the salons of the upper class. The Bonapartists succeeded to some extent in this social climbing, and to a certain extent the opportunist republicans too, though often the civil servants had to form social circles of their own. This isolation, which diminished in the inter-war period at the top levels, persisted longer at lower levels. It was noticeable that civil servants rising in the hierarchy, and coming from poorer social backgrounds, tended to adopt the conservative habits of their superiors—e.g. religious practice—to make themselves acceptable, even though men of upper class origin could get by easily enough without religion.

As the rewards of the civil service became less certain, so some of its members exaggerated their pretensions and tried to bolster their role with the help of ideology and formalism. Bureaucracy was increasingly seen as anti-democratic and opposed as a survival of the *ancien régime*. The complaints grew louder just when the civil servants became increasingly insecure: against the magistrates who made up for their absurdly low salaries by wearing fancy dress, treating those who appeared before them with authoritarian aloofness, and living a withdrawn social life; against the resurrection of the feudal mentality in which the world was divided into 'administrators' and the public, who were called 'the administered', or even 'subjects'. There were attacks against the superiority complex of the civil servants who looked upon themselves as heirs of the nobles of the *robe* keeping the public at a distance, rather than being there to serve them. As taxation increased and the matters in which the state interfered widened, so these complaints became more bitter.[1] The new tensions can be illustrated from the way the civil servants defended themselves: 'The civil servants', wrote one of them in 1911, 'are objects of rancour but whether they know it or not, they do not care. They are conscious of their strength. They are aware that three-quarters of

[1] B. Gournay, *L'Administration* (1964), 82–5.

the French look upon them with envy and this certitude of superiority is the balm that heals the wounds inflicted on their pride. A civil servant is responsible only to his chiefs. Therefore, what distinguishes him at the outset is a perfect tranquillity of mind, due to the absence of all worries other than the very legitimate ones of promotion.'[1] Another author, writing in 1901, rationalised the civil servant's immobility into a virtue, making him an indispensable arbiter in a disorganised society. 'All the time, the civil servant is opposing to the passing and thought-less caprices of the elected powers the obstacle of his traditions and his sage delays.' He is unlike the businessman, whose fortune is built on the unstable foundations of speculative capital, 'too often lacking a scientific patrimony or a moral culture, without hereditary cohesion, without a common fund of ideas or beliefs'. The business world could be called an aristocracy only through 'poverty of language': the true aristoc-racy of modern France was supplied by the civil service, recruited from all classes, and so in close contact with them, endowed with a 'uniformity of preparatory education and then of work and intellectual development, which give it a solid and rich common basis'.[2]

The irony of the situation was that it was becoming increas-ingly difficult for the civil servant to make decisions. It is often maintained that since the ministers of the Third Republic stayed in office for so short a time, real power was exercised by the civil servants. The conquest of the French empire, for example, does indeed seem to a considerable extent to have been organised by them; until 1946 parliament had limited power over the colonies. In the foreign office men like Philippe Berthelot, its secretary general, exercised great influence over successive ministers.[3] The senior civil servant's power was prob-ably smaller in internal departments. The education ministry placed distinguished scholars at the head of its various sections. Octave Gréard and Louis Liard, for example, exercised enor-mous and still unchronicled influence on the educational system.[4] But in some technical ministries power was not given

[1] Anon., *Les Fonctionnaires* (3rd edition 1911), 19.
[2] René Favarielle, 'Le Fonctionnarisme', *Revue de Paris* (15 Sept. 1901), 405–7. On the bureaucratic mentality, see André Moufflet, *M. Le Bureau et son âme* (1933).
[3] Auguste Bréal, *Philippe Berthelot* (1937).
[4] W. Bruneau is writing a doctoral thesis on Louis Liard.

to the technical experts. Thus in the ministry of public works, the central administration was staffed by some 230 people most of whom had no technical knowledge: they had reached their position by slow promotion from the rank of *expéditionnaire*, for which only a primary education was required. These superior clerks ruled the engineers. What was worse, the ministry was rigidly divided into *directions* with no real co-ordination between them, so that if anyone succeeded in getting a policy adopted, he might find it negated by the work of another *direction*. This was particularly true in transport: railways, roads, and canals were constructed independently (after 1876) so that each built up artificial traffic, distributing subsidies to enable it to compete with the other forms of communication. Each territorial department had an engineer in charge—an area determined irrespective of the amount of work available, and sometimes far too big—but the engineer was subordinate to the prefect and was unable to make contracts himself. The national roads were under his jurisdiction but the departmental and local ones under the prefect's. Fishing in canals was under the control of the ministry of justice, but under the ministry of agriculture in other waters, while the ministry of public works had to ensure the upkeep of waterways. The decision to rebuild a little bridge could take years of negotiation and correspondence. It is true that the ministry of public works could point to the building of France's railway network as its great achievement, but the great financial scandals involved should not be forgotten. Certainly the engineers felt they were fettered by clerks and politicians, that their talents were not properly used, decisions were never made by those most competent, with the result that there was no real responsibility, since no one knew who had taken the decision.[1]

In those areas of state activity where civil servants were principally employed in routine tasks, which did not necessarily call for initiative or the formulation of new policies—for example, in its industrial activities or in tax collection—the power of the senior civil servants was drastically reduced when security of tenure and promotion by seniority were established. The director of a state factory was transformed into a kind of

[1] Henri Chardon, *Les Travaux publics. Essai sur le fonctionnement de nos administrations* (1904), 27, 357.

judge. Every act was foreseen in regulations, so that the director's function was only to keep peace and order, to proclaim the law. Since he no longer had an outlet for proving himself, he very often engaged in secondary activities such as teaching or consultancy and he made up for the prosaic nature of his duties by being an artist or a writer. He sought his identity therefore outside the service. In it, his task was to keep himself from being submerged: he had to ensure that the new and young technical experts should not challenge his own prestige by being given too much freedom to change things. As an alternative to withdrawing into the world of culture, the director could play out a theatrical role of being a busy and important man, constantly making weighty decisions, even though the decisions were always the same one. But one factor for effective decision making was totally lacking. The hierarchical structure made communication between different grades almost impossible. Some civil servants were befogged by being called 'collaborators' and 'dear colleagues' by their superiors, but the different grades (on the whole) came from different worlds, with independent recruiting systems; every man knew how far he could go. To protect his own small freedom of action, he had to hedge himself with impenetrable barriers of regulations which made genuine co-operation or exchange of ideas very difficult.[1]

Still, for all the ambiguities and insecurities in the position of the civil servant, the goodwill, if not the assistance, of the state was needed for the accomplishment of a great number of things, and the civil servant remained powerful, if only from his nuisance value, as an intermediary. He had perhaps ceased to be the master of the country, as he once may have appeared to be, but he made a significant contribution to the formation of those who were its masters. He was, however, too much on the defensive to use his prestige effectively. As Viollet Le Duc noted in 1863: 'If a project appears from which new ideas might emerge, it is submitted for examination to persons who are by conviction or rather by lack of conviction enemies of all innovation.'[2] It is not a simple matter to define the relation

---

[1] Michel Crozier, Le Phénomène bureaucratique (1963).
[2] Quoted in Pierre Legendre, Histoire de l'administration de 1750 à nos jours (1968), 526. Cf. Jules Ferry's attacks on the Eaux et Forêts in Pierre Soudet, L'Administration vue par les siens et par d'autres (1960), 42.

between the civil service and change in this century. The civil service had become a sort of Frankenstein.

The picture which these chapters on the bourgeoisie have been attempting to build up is one which does not support the view of this class as unified, coherent or self-conscious. The internal conflicts and contradictory interests within it appear as a major characteristic of it. These were conflicts of which Marx himself was very much aware, though he believed that they were 'intermediate and transitional', doomed to disappear. It is unfortunate that he never wrote the fifty-second chapter of *Capital*, which breaks off just when he was about to discuss this subject, because as a result rather simplified versions of his theory of class have been applied to this century, ignoring the fact that his theory was heuristic rather than descriptive of conditions in his day. If the bourgeoisie did have the means of material production in its control—a proposition which needs qualification—it was by no means clear that it also controlled the means of intellectual production. The subtle relationship between these two will need more detailed analysis. Meanwhile, the next two chapters will investigate further the question of how far the development of new forms of production was creating a polarised confrontation of classes.

9. Peasants

The Myth of the Peasant Democracy

THE peasants could theoretically have been masters of France. When universal manhood suffrage was proclaimed in 1848, they constituted well over half the population and in 1939 they were still by far the largest single class. However, they did not make use of their power. It is important to understand why. The history of the peasantry cannot be written simply in terms of the issues which parliaments debated or of the parties into which these were divided. These bourgeois preoccupations certainly affected the peasants, but the main reason why the peasants did not throw their weight more decisively was that they were fighting other battles, largely unchronicled by the literate classes, but far more important to them. It is with these battles that this chapter will be concerned.

In 1850 the economist Adolphe Blanqui, brother of the revolutionary, went on a tour of the French countryside and came back astounded by it. 'The economic fact', he wrote, 'which is today most worthy of attention in France, and which stands out in the most striking way, is the difference in the condition and well-being which distinguishes the inhabitants of the towns from those of the countryside . . . One would think one was seeing two different peoples, living, though on the same soil, lives so distinct that they seem foreigners to each other, even though they are united by the links of the most domineering centralisation that has ever existed.'[1] Blanqui was far from being the only man to write about the peasants almost as though they were a different species. Karl Marx, at the same time, compared the peasants of France to a sack of potatoes, each with individual characteristics but all of the same kind: he made no attempt to investigate them further. The peasants are not studied in Balzac's universal portrait of French society.

[1] A. Blanqui, 'Tableau des populations rurales de la France en 1850', *Journal des Économistes*, 28 (1851), 9.

Though he called one of his novels *Les Paysans* and devoted several volumes ostensibly to painting scenes of rural life, Balzac could not describe the peasants, because he was full of contempt for them. They were savages, like Fenimore Cooper's Red Indians, and he was concerned with them only as subjects for his schemes to improve them. The peasants indeed were the objects of denigration, far more sweeping than the artists ever bestowed on the bourgeois. Léon Cladel, himself just escaped from a remote village in Tarn-et-Garonne, enamoured of the sophistication of Paris but guilty and uneasy in its literary world, hurled insults back at them, as 'quadrupeds on two feet . . . Greedy, envious, hypocritical, crafty, cynical, cowardly and brutal, the peasant is the same everywhere, north and south.' He exclaimed with horror that these ignorant rustics should have so much power 'to order new dragonnades, to re-establish the inquisition', to back a new *coup d'état*.

People risen from their ranks often attacked them most vigorously, seeing education and peasantry as extreme opposites representing respectively civilisation and barbarism. The peasants did after all speak not only a different dialect, but sometimes even a different language. The peasants' silences were always a mystery to those who did not share their preoccupations. A country priest, in a book about them published in 1885, confessed: 'I would love the peasants, if the peasant did not disgust me . . . [The peasant] is the least romantic, the least idealistic of men. Plunged into reality, he is the opposite of the dilettante and will never give thirty *sous* for even the most magnificent landscape painting . . . He is original sin, surviving and visible in all its brutal *naïveté* . . . The peasant loves nothing nor anybody but for the use he can make of it.' He never gives presents. He never goes for an idle stroll. He gives his arm to his wife the day of their marriage for the first and last time. He is as uperstitious animal, believing in witches like the Romans and the Gauls. Nothing will move him from his opinions. But the minute he reaches market, he ceases to be a Christian or a man: he is at war with everybody and will spare nothing, however sacred, to get the highest price he can for his goods.[1] This was more or less the picture that Zola painted in his *Earth*, perhaps the first novel to have a peasant as its central character. For

[1] Joseph Roux, *Pensées* (1885).

Zola, the peasant was above all concerned with the acquisition
of land, to which he was attached with an animal passion: he
represented simplicity and ferocity, greed and conservatism.
Jules Renard entitled his novel of the peasantry *Our Savage
Brothers* and it was much praised for its accuracy.[1]

While some saw the peasant either as the raw clay from
which civilisation had to be fashioned, or as an obstacle to the
spread of enlightenment, others, who wished to change society
as it had developed, saw in him the repository of unsullied
virtues. The romantics, the Catholic revivalists, the believers in
a conservative and hierarchic order, all held him up as a model
of a human unspoilt by progress. George Sand wrote books
about him or rather books about how she would have liked
him to be, inaugurating a whole genre of rustic novels. She,
however, did more than just idealise him, even if she did admit
that she believed that 'in the rural life there are fewer causes of
corruption than elsewhere'. She really wanted to understand
the peasant, but she honestly confessed that she had failed:
'I cannot form a clear idea of his emotions,' she wrote, 'and
it is this that torments me.' Two painters of her generation
attempted the same thing: Millet (the son of a peasant and
himself a former shepherd) and Courbet showed them weighed
down by their labours.[2] Napoleon III inaugurated his reign
with an inquiry into popular poetry forgotten 'because of a
thoughtless contempt by our rather too worldly literature'.[3]
Folklore societies were formed. Vincent d'Indy (a church
organist) incorporated peasant tunes into his music for the
bourgeoisie. The revivers of regional literature made dialect
respectable. Eugène Le Roy wrote powerful novels about the
peasants of his native Périgord, suggesting that the spark of
revolution lay hidden among them. His *Jacquou le Croquant* (1904)
described a *jacquerie* led by an orphaned agricultural labourer
(based, for its details, on the sacking of Marshal Bugeaud's
château, not all that long before).[4] But Le Roy, the son of a
farm manager and a washerwoman, had climbed out of the
peasant ranks to become a tax collector. Émile Guillaumin is

---

[1] E. Zola, *La Terre* (1887); Jules Renard, *Nos Frères farouches* (1908).

[2] Millet, *Paysanne assise, Paysan greffant un arbre, Femme faisant paître sa vache*;
G. Courbet, *Casseurs de pierre*.

[3] See J. Antran, *La Vie rurale* (1856).

[4] Cf. M. Ballot, *Eugène Le Roy, écrivain rustique* (1949).

perhaps more significant because he always remained a peasant, never had more than a primary education, and wrote his books after a full day's work as a sharecropper. His *Life of a Simple Man* is the first genuine autobiography of a peasant. He decided to write it after reading *Jacquou le Croquant*. Two publishers rejected it and he only got it printed eventually on a shared cost basis. Guillaumin was the first defender of the peasants who did not idealise them or try to put heroic qualities into them. He consciously attempted to explain them to the townsmen who wondered whether they had brains or hearts. He admitted that the peasants were indifferent to the charms of nature, but thought that they gave the impression of lacking sensibility because they suffered from a punctilious modesty which prevented them from saying what they thought or complaining about their troubles. He wanted the peasants to get rid of their inferiority complex, their submissive attitude, their mistrust of novelty, their self-sufficiency, their envy, their *naïveté* and rapacity, their absorption with buying land, and so their inability to live in better domestic conditions and to enjoy leisure. He deplored submission to authority and the blind acceptance of traditions inherited from one's father. His book might therefore have been almost as much an indictment of his class as Zola's imaginative exercise, had it not inspired sympathy and interest instead of the horror that Zola produced. Though it made peasants human, they were still a separate world.[1]

All these points of view, favourable and derogatory, come together in one generalisation which is too often taken, rather naïvely, as the explanation of why the peasant made so little use of his political power. This is that the peasant was basically conservative, or at least resigned to his lot. Innovation, it is argued, has no place in the countryside. All creativity comes from the towns. The peasant will accept change only when it ceases to be new, when he can do so without causing a scandal in the village. There must be scandal if he gives the impression that he thinks he is cleverer than his father, for in his kind of society, prestige is to a great extent obtained from conformity

[1] R. Mathé, *Émile Guillaumin* (1966), a good biography. For more emotional, conservative portrayals of peasants, see R. Bazin, *La Terre qui meurt* (1899). For a good analysis of the literature, P. Vernois, *Le Roman rustique (1860–1925)* (1962).

with traditions (so that the son of a nonconformist would be expected to be one too). A peasant's prestige comes also from the reputation his family has acquired over several generations: therefore he cannot take a step without involving them; the whole weight of grandparents and female pressure is on him. Likewise the peasant will prefer to own eight thin cows, giving little milk, to five good ones, because prestige counts as much in his eyes as purely economic considerations. He often prefers to eke out a miserable living from an arid plot he owns himself, to the comfort and high wages he might earn working on an efficient farm. The peasant will thus always rouse the despair of agronomists who cannot get him to adopt their scientific methods. The peasant, for example, may not consider himself a true peasant if he does not produce his own bread, whatever his soil is best suited for. Self-sufficiency is his ideal, which may also imply independence of the wider world intellectually as well as materially.[1]

These generalisations about the innate conservatism of the peasant need to be interpreted carefully in the context of French history. The observance of traditional routines, agricultural and social, should not obscure the fact that conflict was part of those routines, and that the pressures involved in preserving them add up to a situation which is far from being one of stagnation. The peasants were neither satisfied nor contented. They were constantly trying to improve their lot, to enlarge their farms, to raise their status. Their world was torn by deep divisions, and by animosities both of interest and of pride. Their lives were absorbed as much by these as by the business of earning their living. It seems more accurate to see their world held together by tension than by a pastoral sleepiness. If that is so, their conservatism may be seen as more the product of insecurity than of innate sluggishness. The constant attempt to anchor themselves more firmly to their own plot of soil was a result of the same feeling, for the peasants of France were, despite the outward impression, perhaps the most insecure part of the nation. They had freed themselves from feudal ties but they had not succeeded in winning true independence. How

[1] Henri Mendras, *Les Transformations du métier d'agriculteur dans la France contemporaine* (1967), is an interesting study of the problems of change since the Second World War.

many of them could call themselves their own masters in the full sense? Debt was their great scourge; but they had to get into debt to round off their farms; and the sharecroppers and tenants likewise were nearly always in debt to their masters. In other countries this sometimes institutionalised into 'debt peonage' which was one remove from slavery. In France it could survive hidden under the mask of liberal rhetoric, because these peasants were no longer dependent simply on one noble class. They were indebted to one another, which made their relationships more complicated and more strained. Lucien Fabre, in a vigorous novel about them written between the wars, talked of 'the implacable subjection resulting from the fear the peasant is in, of not being able to pay his rent, his tax, his debts incurred for the purchase of machines, the ironwork for his cattle, his stock of seeds and of plants, the visits of the veterinary, the renewal of his farmyard livestock, the stud fees, and so many other things . . . He saw the bailiff at his heels whenever a hailstorm threatened or when the frosts of May killed the fruits in flower . . .' He owed money to the tax collector, the notary, the shopkeepers, the usurers, the landlord and a host more.[1] In such conditions the peasant could not afford to experiment. The real change in peasant attitudes could begin only after the First World War—when inflation cancelled their debts—and after the Second, when social security and tenants' rights came to compensate for the permanent uncertainties of the climate.

The supposed general conservatism of the peasant must also be reconciled with the readiness of a sizeable section of the peasantry to vote left wing, to engage in strikes, riots and revolutions, to leave the land, to emigrate seasonally or permanently to the towns. These various forms of protest occurred in different degrees in different parts of the country. Their regional distribution is explained by the immense diversity of economic and social conditions prevalent in France. Though the peasants may have appeared to townsmen uniformly as barbarians, there were enormous variations in their organisation and relationships. Indeed it has been claimed that France contained more than one 'agrarian civilisation', with varying social organisation and farming methods, but there has been

[1] Lucien Fabre, *Le Tarramagnou* (1925), 61.

some dispute as to just how many of these civilisations there were. The basic distinction is between regions of open-field farming common in the north and regions of enclosure in the

MAP. 1. The contrast of village and isolated peasants (1950s). Based on Fauvet and Mendras: *Les Paysans et la Politique* (1958), 29

west and south. The former involved communal control of agriculture, and was often accompanied by the agglomeration of the peasants in large villages, while the latter allowed their dispersal in hamlets and farms. Patterns of settlement are very distinct in Artois and Picardy where in about 90 per cent of the communes, the majority of the peasants live in villages, while in Brittany or the Massif Central only 30 or 40 per cent do. However, one needs to distinguish again between different forms of enclosure: that of the south, where it represented individualism and produced an irregular variety of crops, and that in the west, where it was the result of a collective attempt to add some grain to a system based principally on cattle raising. It was once argued that racial characteristics, Roman or German, survived in this way; then it was thought that it was the physical nature of the soil, and the distribution of water, which determined these variations. But increasingly historical investigation of the way the rural landscape has been formed has stressed different traditions in the way the land has been won for agriculture from waste and woodland, and has shown the different degrees of collectivism and co-operation shown by the peasantry. No simple division emerges, however, for the same sort of villages did not always produce the same kind of agricultural development: the large rural agglomerations of the south were individualistic while those of the north were collectivist. The collectivist traditions moreover decayed at different speeds in different areas: in the Caux and Thiérache for example there was enclosure in the seventeenth and eighteenth centuries, but for different reasons from those affecting the Vendée. The liberty of the south inevitably produced even more variations. But the different ways the peasants had acquired the land and conquered the soil in each particular area meant that they had traditions, problems and enemies of great variety. The north and the south of France were shown to be profoundly different, though further study revealed that this simple division required numerous qualifications.[1] However, it was made clear that peasants living in villages had very different attitudes to those living in lonely farms or hamlets. In the scattered type of settlement, the farmers were separated from the rest of the population. They lived on isolated farms, at best in hamlets with other farmers. The local artisans, the doctor, the shop, the church

---

[1] M. Bloch, *Les Caractères originaux de l'histoire rurale française* (1931), but see the modifications to his ideas in vol. 2 published in 1956; R. Dion, *Essai sur la formation du paysage rural français* (Tours, 1934); and E. Juillard *et al.*, *Structures agraires et paysages ruraux: un quart de siècle de recherches françaises* (Nancy, 1957).

would be situated largely apart from them in villages, to which the elderly and the widowed would also retire. Agriculture and its services were thus, to a considerable extent, separated and sometimes at war.

The sense of community depended also on the way the land was worked. The common generalisation that the peasants were innately individualistic and independent is another bourgeois myth. It is important to remember that though individual peasant property had developed before the Revolution, ownership did not imply complete liberty to work the land as one pleased. When the strips and plots were tiny, it was essential to co-operate in sowing and reaping. No man could reach his plot without going through those of his neighbours. After the harvest all had a right to pasture their animals freely in the fields.[1] The Revolution gave the rural population total independence, just as it allowed all men to practise whatever trade they pleased, but this legal right sometimes remained rather theoretical. The position in the nineteenth century was that the old community spirit was breaking up but it was not dead.[2] This was the source of one of the most bitter—though again largely unchronicled—fights which absorbed the peasants. A study of the Vendée plains has shown the survival of collective harvests, collective fruit picking, common pasture, gleaning and raking, well into the nineteenth century. Owners could not go into their own fields until a public proclamation allowed them, nor could they remove their wheat-sheaves till the opening of the paths was announced. The mayor and the municipal council went out into the vineyards to decide when the vine should be picked. One by one, villages abandoned these controls. In this region the collapse finally occurred only in the period 1870–1900, though one isolated commune, Petosse, kept its common pasture traditions till 1957. As the records of the commune of Le Langon put it in 1898, 'owners are anxious to enjoy full property of their lands'. The problem of how to acquire this full property was an important and absorbing one. And since there was often much dispute about who had the right to what, and cases of the rich usurping or

[1] O. Leclerc-Thouin, *L'Agriculture de l'ouest de la France* (1843), 43.
[2] On this, see A. Soboul, 'La Communauté rurale', *Revue de Synthèse* (1957), 283–307.

buying these rights, to the detriment of the poor, one of the first things the poor peasants did in 1848, when authority broke down, was to rush into formerly common lands, to reclaim their ancient rights. There were powerful pressures, working both ways, for and against their preservation.[1]

At the beginning of this period nearly five million hectares, i.e. about 9 per cent of French soil, was common land, owned and managed collectively by the communes; by the end of it, the figure was still as much as 8 per cent. There were about 1,700,000 hectares of forests and 2,800,000 of pasture and waste; only 150,000 were arable. The mountainous regions had a far higher proportion of their land in common. In 1863 Hautes-Alpes had 51 per cent of its territory in common, Hautes-Pyrénées 43 per cent, and Savoie 42 per cent. Nine departments had between 21 and 30 per cent of their territory in common and another 21 departments between 10 and 19 per cent.[2] Corsica in the 1950s still had 28 per cent of its territory in common: the area had declined only 10 per cent in the course of the twentieth century and only 7 per cent in the nineteenth. Some Corsican villages have as much as 67 per cent of their land in common.[3] In such regions the inhabitants depended for some of their livelihood, and sometimes almost completely, on the right to use the commons. The attitude of revolutions and governments to these commons had been ambivalent. In 1792 a law had ordered the division of these lands among the inhabitants but in 1793 another law repealed this. The agronomists thought common ownership was an obstacle to progress.

[1] Jacqueline Moguelet, 'Les Pratiques communautaires dans la plaine ven-déenne au 19e siècle', Annales (July–Aug. 1963), 666–76. On forest rights, see Henri Evrard, Notes historiques sur les biens communaux du canton de Varennes-en-Argonne (Paris thesis, Bar-le-Duc, 1912), and Michel Duval, La Révolution et les droits d'usage dans les forêts de l'ancienne Bretagne (Rennes, 1954). In general, A. Soboul, 'Survivance féodales dans la société rurale au 19e siècle, Annales (Sept.–Oct. 1968), 965–86; and for the situation in the east of France at the turn of the century, G. Eugène Simon, 'Les Biens communaux', La Nouvelle Revue, 88 (1894), 699–719, with graphic details about individual villages.

[2] J. de Crisenoy, 'Statistique des biens communaux et des sections de communes', Revue Générale d'Administration (1887), 257–75; R. Graffin, Les Biens communaux (1899); Edmond Cleray, De la mise en valeur des biens communaux (1900), appendix. 4,855,000 hectares in 1863, 4,316,000 hectares in 1877.

[3] Janine Pomponi, 'La Vie rurale de deux communes corses: Serra di Scopamene et Sotta' (Aix, Travaux et mémoires de la faculté de lettres, vol. 26, 1962, stencilled), 60, 100.

The rich wanted to buy and enclose. The poor were generally
opposed to division because paradoxically they had most to lose
by it. Even if the land was distributed equally and freely among
the inhabitants of the village, each would get a plot so small or
of such poor quality that it would be of little value to him; it
was usually more advantageous to the poor to have the right to
pasture their few animals on the wastelands: this could make
all the difference to their survival. A struggle was thus set up
between the rich and the poor, the individualists and the conservatives, over these commons, quite apart from the quarrels
which went on as to how the commons should be managed or
farmed. In many cases, the individualists won, even if by a
roundabout route, and a fully capitalist economy would be
introduced into the village. Thus, for example, in 1851 the
village of Caire du Cheylade in Cantal sold off two mountains
it owned in common and with the proceeds bought state bonds.
In the 1930s every family was still drawing a share of the interest from these bonds, but by then worth only the derisory
sum of 45 francs. This village, situated in a mountainous
region, had exceptionally vast commons, so it also decided to
divide another part of them equally among the inhabitants,
giving each a small plot. Many of the plots of course were
situated in highly inconvenient positions. A rich man came
along, bought these tiny bits up, and created enormous private
grazings for himself. Within a few years the village found itself
noticeably poorer than it had been.[1] In parts of Alsace there
were very sizeable commons; some villages had no local taxes,
because their income from the forests they owned sufficed to
pay their expenses. Financial crises might lead them to sell,
which could upset their whole economy and bring about
general ruin. Alternatively, when there were influential 'village
cocks' able to get their way, the commons would be leased out,
nothing would remain of the community organisation except
the notional rent. In other parts, however, villages distributed
commons to the inhabitants in plots which could not be sublet.
If they were badly worked, they reverted to the village. If there
were not enough plots, a waiting list was established. Living
in such a village thus carried with it the right to enjoy an

[1] A. Durand, *La Vie rurale dans les massifs volcaniques des Dores, du Cézallier, du Cantal et de l'Aubrac* (Aurillac, 1946), 146.

allotment. Some sense of community spirit could thus survive, but it could also be eroded as these rights became more like private property.[1]

It is possible to study the effect of these common possessions in the mountains of the southern Jura. This area lies at the junction of the northern *langue d'œil*, with its open-field villages and larger farms, and the south, with its smallholders, combining pasture and vine. One cannot simply contrast one with the other. Quite small areas have developed in different ways. In the poor communes, with no commons or forests, the peasants, with their excessively small and dispersed plots, and their low milk yields, have found no means of escaping from their stagnation. They have supplemented their bare livelihoods by taking orphaned and abandoned children from the Assistance Publique, which means they have more than their fair share of idiots and subnormal people. By contrast, in other areas the habit of managing the commons together has stimulated the growth of milk co-operatives, which are the basis of the Gruyère industry. But not all peasants have accepted co-operation with equal enthusiasm. Those who sold their milk to intermediaries have remained isolated from the consequences of the greatly expanded markets and they have been co-operators only from necessity. The most dynamic peasants in fact have been those whose vines were destroyed by phylloxera, who were forced into modern milking methods, and who have supplemented their earnings by polyculture. It would be far too simplistic to link the various traditions of common ownership and common agriculture with the willingness which some modernising peasants showed, in the second half of the twentieth century, to abandon their individualism. On the contrary, those who had common rights were often highly conservative. But co-operation was far from being alien to the traditions of the peasantry.[2]

The notion that a man could do as he pleased with his property, though proclaimed by parliament, was not accepted by the courts. The Civil Code had introduced a strong element of Roman law into its provisions on private property but this was gradually reversed. The first breach occurred in 1855, in a

[1] E. Julliard, *La Vie rurale dans la plaine de Basse-Alsace* (1953), 224–9.
[2] R. Lebeau, *La Vie rurale dans les montagnes du Jura méridional* (Lyon, 1955).

celebrated case which came before the court of Colmar. An owner had built a false chimney solely to spoil the view of his neighbour. The court ordered him to destroy the chimney. Lawyers protested that this decision was contrary to the Civil Code, but in 1887 the Court of Cassation expanded it into the general principle that owners must not cause a nuisance to their neighbours: it decided in favour of people protesting against the smoke emitted by railway engines passing by their land. The great enemy of the rights of the individual proprietor was Duguit, who wrote many books, and influenced a whole group of pupils, in favour of the new idea that property was not a right but a social function, that society allowed men to enjoy property provided this was subordinated to the social interest.[1] He claimed that the individualism of the Civil Code was based on an unreal, abstract view of man, who was naturally good, whereas law ought to be concerned with protecting the weak. At the same time therefore as the old community of the country-side was collapsing, the law courts and the legislators under solidarist influence bolstered it up in new ways.[2]

The republicans like to claim that it was the Revolution of 1789 which had brought equality to France, by expropriating the nobility and Church and creating a nation of small peasant proprietors. The Civil Code's prescription that land must be divided equally between children is supposed to have given every man a birthright. Michelet contrasted aristocratic England, owned by 32,000 rich men who got others to work for them, with democratic France, where the land was shared out between 15 or 20 million peasants who cultivated it themselves.[3] These figures were quite mythical and were made no truer by the fact that a Republican League of Small Property, presided over by Paul Deschanel, existed to propagate the myth.

The equal division of property among children was by no

[1] L. Duguit, *Les Transformations générales du droit privé depuis le code Napoléon* (1912); G. Pirou, 'Duguit et l'économie politique', *Revue d'Économie Politique* (1933).

[2] Gaston Morin, *La Révolte du droit contre le code* (1945). Outside agriculture, this movement revealed itself in restrictions on employment of women and children, provisions for confiscation of land for public utility schemes, leasehold reform, and the protection of tenants (1926, 1927, and 1933). During the First and Second World Wars farmers were obliged to work their lands, which could be leased to someone else if they were abandoned.

[3] J. Michelet, *Le Peuple* (1844; ed. L. Refort, 1946), 32.

means a universal demand of the peasantry. There were, it is true, some who said that the arbitrary whims of tyrannical fathers should be restrained, but others pointed out the much more keenly felt difficulty, that division could not work satisfactorily on poor lands and small estates. Equal division might destroy the nobility but it would also ruin smallholders, by fragmenting their lands into plots too tiny to provide a living and so it would turn proprietors into labourers. In Roman law, a father could dispose freely of two-thirds of his property if he had four children or fewer. This law prevailed in eight southern provinces, and in restricted form in seven others. But already before the Revolution considerable areas of France, ruled by customary law, had division of property among children as a normal practice. The Civil Code thus did not introduce a radically new system of inheritance. Its main effect was to limit the rights of fathers in the south. The Civil Code was in fact a compromise. It gave fathers with one child the right to dispose freely of half their property, to those with two children the right to dispose freely of one third and to those with three the right to dispose freely of one quarter. From the legal point of view, it did not change matters much in the north, and not that drastically in the south. In actual practice, in the way the Civil Code was worked, it made even less difference, because it was frequently not applied, and traditional customs survived despite it. The agricultural inquiry of 1866, which, among other things, investigated inheritance, revealed that the bourgeoisie on the whole accepted the Civil Code's principle of equal division but that the peasants did not. The latter were keen to leave the father with a larger share of his property to dispose of as he saw fit. Groups of small owners even got together to petition the senate for this reform.

By the time of the Second Empire, equal division was almost universal in the north-east of France, where custom favoured it, but even here this did not mean that the agricultural holdings were always split up. The larger and richer holdings allowed arrangements to be made among the heirs so that the profitability of the farms should not be damaged. One son would run the farm, and pay his brothers and sisters their share in money, from his profits, or he could rent their share from them. On the Breton coast, where alternative employment at sea or in market gardening meant that land did not have to provide a whole living, property was divided equally, and the little plots served as subsidiary allotments; but in the interior of Finistère and Morbihan, the poor isolated farmers could not allow this and farms were passed on whole to one son only. In the Côtes du Nord, uneconomic division was avoided by the heirs living together as a community, and the girls being prevented from marrying. Despite the Revolution and the Code, there were farms in Mayenne, of 20–40 hectares (50–100 acres) which had never been divided from time immemorial. The Bretons, like the Irish, had large families but postponed marriage as late as possible. The Normans sometimes solved the same problem by having fewer legitimate children but more illegitimate ones. In the centre of France the custom of migrating to large towns until retirement similarly encouraged the maintenance of the family farm as a working unit. The demand for greater testamentary freedom was particularly strong here. In the Nièvre, girls sometimes renounced their share of their inheritance on getting married, and various schemes were used to favour the eldest son. Notaries often helped by getting the children to accept a low valuation of the parents' estate. Of course, such stratagems did not always work, or not for long. Frequently they were disputed by the next generation and lawsuits dragged on for many years. Certain areas were notorious for the mercilessness with which heirs demanded their fair share against such ploys. In the eastern Pyrénées even the houses were divided up among them. In the Haute-Saône there was particularly active litigation.

The sociologist Le Play drew attention to the conflict between custom and law in his monograph of a Pyrenean family, which had owned 18 hectares for four centuries, passed on from father to eldest son. After the Revolution the property was nominally divided, but the eldest son received the *quotité disponible* (the share the father could bequeath freely) and took over the farm. He gradually paid off his brothers and sisters, though some helped by not marrying, living with him, and bequeathing their share to his eldest son. In 1836 the owner died leaving eight children and a farm worth 17,368 francs. The eldest was a girl. Her husband, in keeping with tradition, took her name and the farm. She got 4,342 francs as her free share (*préciput*), plus a one-eighth share in the remainder. Two siblings did not marry and bequeathed their shares back to her eldest; the others were bought out. But when she died in 1864, an uncle challenged the original settlement and, though he lost, the legal costs were heavy. His lawsuit encouraged the idea that the traditional system existed at the expense of younger children. Not the Civil Code, but this kind of local experience, is what brought about change. Only in the next generation did the husbands [of two sisters demand the payment of their share immediately. This forced the sale of part of the farm, which ceased to be a viable unit and in 1882 it was all finally sold.

An interesting study of the decline of the family spirit could be made from the records of inheritance. Ideally, it was agreed in the father's old age that one son (in some regions this son would be called the eldest, whatever he was in fact) should have the *quotité disponible* and the farm; in return he looked after the parents, who now retired, and he paid the other children a fixed sum over many years (which was often less than their true share). The division parents made could easily be disputed by rebellious children. The value of the property at the time of death, rather than at the time of the division, was what counted, so the whole settlement could be called into question if the decision was made before death. No generalisation is possible, in the present state of knowledge, about the progress of fragmentation of property as a result of the Code. It is certain that the number of parcels of land increased. In 1826 10·29 million parcels were counted, in 1881 14·29 million. In the process the average size of each parcel fell from 4·48 to 3·5 hectares, and by 1884 74 per cent of these parcels were of 2 hectares or less, but it cannot be said with what uniformity over the country as a whole. It was not a gradual and progressive movement. Property was certainly divided and subdivided in inheritance and France was notorious for the tiny plots into which the land was fragmented. But it was not inheritance alone that was responsible. The consequence of the Civil Code's provisions about inheritance was not to liberate the peasants in any simple way. They did increase equality of inheritance, but they also burdened the peasantry with a tyranny possibly as oppressive as that of the patriarchal father.

Mortgages were frequently necessary to carry out the division, to pay some heirs in land and some in money. Mortgages were often necessary to make farms fragmented by division into viable units. A large proportion of the spare cash of the peasantry was absorbed in healing the wounds of inheritance. A whole army of speculators, usurers and agents grew up to profit from the increasing freedom. In the mid nineteenth century they were known as 'the black bands'; these specialised in buying up large farms and selling them off in small bits. The peasantry bought on mortgage as much as it could. So its savings went into land purchase, rather than into modernisation. Legal fees and taxation on inheritance and sale were one of its major expenses.[1]

The paralysing effects of the struggle for the land were strikingly seen in the great Revolution. The bourgeoisie, much more than the peasantry, were the victors of this Revolution and it is important to understand why. The Constituent Assembly, controlled by the bourgeoisie, carefully distinguished between feudal dues classified as unjust and those which represented land rent. It abolished only the former, and decreed that the latter should be bought out with compensation. It was only in 1793 that all feudal rights were abolished. That was because the peasants refused to buy them out and simply ceased to pay these dues. But why did the peasants not also divide up the lands of the nobility and clergy, indeed all land, among themselves, by taking the law into their hands in the same way? The answer is that on this point their interests varied and they were not united. Already in 1789 about 30 to 40 per cent of France was owned by peasants, so there was a first division between those peasants who owned land and those who did not. Equal partition was not so attractive to those who already enjoyed a privileged position. Moreover, most of the land owned by the wealthier classes was rented out, under various forms of tenure, to peasants. These (tenant farmers and sharecroppers) were fighting their way up the social scale by acquiring these tenancies. They would lose if all the land was divided equally between all peasants, including the vast multitude of landless labourers. This conflict between the

[1] Alexandre de Brandt, *Droit et coutumes des populations rurales de la France en matière successionale* (1901).

various categories of peasants made it impossible for the whole body to act with unison.[1]

The French Revolution therefore did not create a peasant democracy. Nevertheless, a myth persisted that the land of France was owned (as Michelet said) by 20 million peasants. Michelet got this figure from out of his own head. He could not have got it from anywhere else, because the number of land-owners was unknown in his day, and remained unknown throughout this period. The statistics the government collected were incapable of revealing the facts, because they were compiled from taxation returns made for other purposes.[2] All that was known was that the land was divided into an enormous number of separate plots paying separate tax. In 1826, as has been seen, there were about 10 million of them; and by 1875 there were 14 million. It did not follow that there were as many landowners, and certainly not that there were as many peasants working their own fields. For (taking the figures for the year 1882, at the zenith of agricultural prosperity) 38·2 per cent of these plots were under 1 hectare (2½ acres) in extent. Another 32·9 per cent were between 1 and 5 hectares. Together these small plots covered only 13·5 per cent of the 45 million hectares in private ownership. About a quarter of the plots (26·4 per cent) were between 5 and 40 hectares in extent, but they covered only 31·5 per cent of the land. A mere 2·5 per cent of the plots, however (those over 40 hectares), covered 45 per cent of the land. It could be argued therefore that almost half of France was owned by large owners. Though France was nothing like England, where in the 1870s about 2,184 landowners with over 5,000 acres each owned half the land of the United Kingdom, there were at any rate some 49,243 plots in France of over 100 hectares (250 acres) covering one quarter of the country. These large farms were concentrated in certain regions: three departments had over 50 per cent of their territory covered by them,[3] and another eleven 40 to 50 per

---

[1] G. Lefebvre, 'La Place de la révolution dans l'histoire agraire de la France', *Annales d'Histoire economique et sociale*, 1 (1929), 506–23.

[2] The only way to establish the proportion of property owners is to study the question commune by commune, using the *cadastre* and the population census at this level, where every name is given. This is now beginning to be done by regional historians.

[3] Hautes-Alpes, Cher, Bouches du Rhône.

cent of their territory.[1] By contrast there were four departments where large farms covered under 6 per cent of the territory,[2] another eleven with 6 to 10 per cent, and a further twenty-six with 10 to 20 per cent. These large estates, however, were not necessarily the most prosperous, because almost half their extent was uncultivated. The large landowners had only 40 per cent of arable land, and only 31 per cent of vineland, but 68 per cent of forests.[3] Many of France's *richest* farmers did not fall into this category, with its wide expanses of deserted land. In dealing with large property in France, it is necessary to be clear what one is talking about, and to take into consideration not just acreage, but the income derived from it and the way it was farmed.

Some of the most illuminating work on this subject has been done by Philippe Vigier, who studied the landownership of some 600 communes in six departments of the south-east as it existed in the mid nineteenth century. Vigier showed that statistics on a departmental level—let alone a national one—are highly unreliable as guides to the real nature of land-ownership. The south-east is, by and large, a region of small peasant proprietorship. But if one looks at this at the level of the commune one sees at least six different types of such proprietorship. Thus the commune of Aiguilles in the Hautes-Alpes had in 1851 745 inhabitants of whom 458 were owner-cultivators. On the face of it this looks like a peasant democracy. But over three-quarters of the commune consisted of wood and pasture owned by the commune, so that each proprietor had private ownership on average of less than 2 hectares. This was quite inadequate for them to live off. Only a dozen or so could in fact get a full living from the land. The vast majority got a little from using the commons, but they had to absent themselves in seasonal migration to keep themselves. Another commune Saint-Julien-en-Quint (Drôme) was of the same size. Its lands were also divided between many proprietors—302. But two-thirds of the land was owned by about sixty-six people and there were in particular four landowners with substantially

---

[1] Alpes-Maritimes, Landes, Hautes-Pyrénées, Nièvre, Pyrénées-Orientales, Corse, Allier, Basses-Alpes, Loir-et-Cher, Indre, Var.
[2] Charente-Inférieure, Rhône, Seine, Tarn-et-Garonne.
[3] Flour de Saint-Genis, *La Propriété rurale en France* (1902), 83.

more land than the average. The majority of the peasant proprietors, here as at Aiguilles, depended on seasonal migration
and artisan activities; but the unequal distribution of the land
created a different social hierarchy, which was all the more
significant in that these small owners had bought their plots
over several centuries, in a silent struggle which gradually
deprived the nobles of their once dominant holdings. By contrast, the larger farms of Donzère (Drôme) had been created
over the years by rich men, employing sharecroppers, who had
reclaimed the river banks previously flooded. These farms
yielded a much higher income than others in the region. In
purely numerical terms, there were 438 small owners in this
commune. But they owned only 27 per cent of the land, while
eleven rich ones owned 39 per cent. Ostensibly this was a village
of small owners, but in reality these were dependent on the
rich for employment and it was with their labour that the rich
made their high incomes. The different relationships created by
landownership are shown again by La Frette (Isère) where
there were forty-six middle-sized owners with between 5 and 30
hectares, one rich man with 113 hectares, but 570 smallholders
with 56 per cent of the land. But the land was poor, unirrigated
and worth very little. The middle owners ran their farms with
little outside labour and so had little influence. The bourgeoisie did not consider it worth buying land here. So the small
owners were able to run the village themselves, and their
dependence was on each other. But they could hardly be said
to be living off the land; they had to engage in numerous
activities to survive. Valensole (Basses-Alpes) again had 442
smallholders, but they were concentrated in the *bourg* and the
surrounding area, which was divided into tiny plots, worked
very intensely. Beyond this, however, twenty-seven large owners
held 41 per cent of the land and employed 667 labourers and
servants so that two distinct societies coexisted, one in the *bourg*
and a different one in the countryside around it. Bourdeaux
(Drôme) provides a further variation: its larger farms yielded less
than half the income of those of Donzère but even so they were
worth over twice as much as the smallholdings.[1] Thus a small
proprietor was not necessarily a peasant and could be prin-

---

[1] P. Vigier, *Essai sur la répartition de la propriété foncière dans la région alpine. Son
évolution des origines du cadastre à la fin du second empire* (1963).

cipally an artisan, or subsidiarily a labourer; and his property in a great number of cases was far from giving him independence. Conversely one did not need an enormous acreage to enjoy dominant influence in a village.

The statistics of 1862 conveniently break up the agricultural population to show tenurial relationships. At that date there were 57,639 proprietors who cultivated their land through a farm manager. There were 1,754,934 proprietors who cultivated their land themselves and cultivated nothing but their own land. But there were even more landowners who could not survive simply on their own lands. 648,836 proprietors also cultivated other people's land as tenant farmers; 203,860 cultivated other people's lands as sharecroppers, and 1,134,490 worked for others as labourers. All these categories add up to 3,799,759 proprietors. There were, however, almost as many people on the land who were not proprietors: 3,553,091 in all. Of these, 386,533 were tenant farmers, 201,527 were share-croppers, 869,254 labourers, and 2,095,777 farm employees of different kinds (638,129 female servants, 584,320 male servants, 353,184 general farm workers, 219,753 shepherds, 122,803 cowherds, 110,801 carters, 66,787 foremen). This means that about half the population on the land owned some land, but only half of these (i.e. a quarter of the total agricultural population) had enough land to live off.[1] Moreover, though the people farming their own land were in a majority (to the extent of three-quarters), the acreage they covered was only half that of the country. Almost one-half of the land was worked by tenant and share farmers, who on average had farms two and a half times as large as the owner-occupiers (11 hectares, as against 4·37 hectares). Moreover, these tenants were particularly concentrated in the north of France, so that in some regions tenants predominated.[2] Sharecroppers likewise occupied large areas of the south-west and centre. The conclusion is that France was not a country of small peasant proprietors, but of small, middle and large owners, each covering about one-third of the country in total acreage, but distributed unevenly over the different regions, so that the land was worked in an enormous variety of ways. France had no

[1] A. de Foville, *Le Morcellement* (1885), 77–8.
[2] See map, p. 161.

latifundia to compare with Spain or with the Duke of Suther-
land's 50,000 hectares, but it had nearly everything else.

This varied agricultural world was split up by an exceptionally fragmented social structure. Political equality was
balanced by an elaborate hierarchy. Any one of these three
million odd proprietors could not expect to marry the daughter
of any other. Elaborate investigations of his precise standing
would first be necessary and when it came to detail, any one
man would find that there were not all that many girls who
would acknowledge him as a suitable match. The limits of
equality were revealed very forcefully in the marriage market.
Thus proprietors were distinguished not just by an infinite
variation of wealth, but by the kind of land they owned, how
long their family had owned it, the type of house they had, how
many animals they possessed, how much cash they had, and
how much, given the size of their family, they could afford
to spend on a dowry. A proprietor would consider himself
superior to a sharecropper, and even labourers distinguished
themselves according to their parentage. A brief survey of these
various gradations may be helpful.

In the most fertile regions of France, the richest and most
successful farmers were not landowners, but tenant farmers.
The land here was bought up to a considerable extent—around
Paris to the extent of 30 to 40 per cent—by city dwellers, as
investments.[1] The ownership of the land was still very much
fragmented. In Seine-et-Marne there were in 1942 no fewer
than 150,000 properties. But tenants rented them and farmed
them in large units. In this department there were only 7,930
farms. 50 per cent of the cultivated area was in farms of over
100 hectares. The trend here has been the opposite of that in
other regions, where direct owner-farming has increased. In
Seine-et-Marne tenants farmed 24 per cent of the farms in
1892, but 57 per cent in 1946. The size of farms increased
accordingly: in 1892 only 35 per cent were over 100 hectares,
in 1929 50 per cent were, in 1946 53 per cent. When workers
talk of the 'patron' here, they mean the tenant farmer, not the
landlord. The tenants indeed developed into a group of some
originality. In the first half of the century, an ordinary peasant

[1] For city investment in land see Henri Elhai, *Recherches sur la propriété foncière des
citadins en Haute-Normandie* (C.N.R.S., 1965).

could still hope to become one of them by gradually increasing the acreage he rented. A case is recorded of a farmer who began in 1880 with a mere 20 hectares rented and only 2,000 francs of equipment. Three years later he had made enough to rent a farm of 60 hectares, obtaining a loan of 7,000 francs for his equipment from the landowner. In 1887 he moved again into a farm of 100 hectares. In 1890 he bought his farmhouse for 4,000 francs, and over the next twenty years also acquired 120 hectares around it, as well as an additional farm of 80 hectares. By 1910 therefore he owned 200 hectares and rented 260.[1] However, the amount of capital required for the intensive, market-oriented farming that flourished here increased rapidly. If 1840 is taken as a base line, the capitalisation is estimated to have doubled by 1870, trebled by 1900, and quadrupled by 1940. Profits of course were much higher than in the subsistence farming regions: they were as high as 20 per cent in the first half of the nineteenth century, and around 15 per cent after 1860—enough to make possible the tripling of capital in a generation. After the crisis of 1880, they fell to 10 per cent, and 8 to 10 per cent has been the level they have remained at since then—except for the really bad years of 1928–41. The result of this high profitability has been that dynasties of tenant farmers have grown up, not dissimilar to those of the textile industrialists of the north. In the Soissonnais, the Ferté family had, by the 1950s, acquired no less than 5,300 hectares in seventeen farms, or, if their sons-in-law are included, 7,800 hectares in twenty-five farms. The Leroux family had 2,700 hectares in ten farms, and there were many more. In 1839 the Agricultural Society of Senlis, composed of landowners, opposed the admission of tenant farmers to its membership. But in 1859 the Bonapartist prefect of Seine-et-Marne talked of the tenant farmers as a 'caste', with 2,350 members 'of the first order, to whom the salons of the prefecture are open'. In 1840 the amount of capital represented by ownership was about six times that of the capital normally invested in running a farm. By 1870 the ratio was often down to 1:4 and by 1900 to 1:3 or even 1:2. The tenants became more and more men of considerable substance. Around 1850 they began to stop feeding

[1] Eugène Creveaux, 'Les Cultivateurs du Laonnais', *La Science Sociale*, 87 (Nov. 1911), 33–5.

their workers. By the turn of the century they had turned into
gentleman farmers, on a par with industrialists, no longer
educated simply at primary school, but sending their children
to the *lycée* or the church school and then to agricultural
colleges and to travel abroad. They lived in increasingly comfortable houses. In the 1930s they had tennis-courts and powerful cars and some even private aeroplanes. Jules Benard, of an
old and increasingly wealthy family of this kind, president of
the Agricultural Society of Meaux, even rose to become a regent
of the Bank of France, though he was quite exceptional. Some
of these families were old, like the Ferté, who had been in the
same farm at Terny since 1580. But there were also professional
farmers from other regions—notably the Flemish—who immi-
grated with capital accumulated elsewhere to seize the opportunities here—like the Cuypers who in under fifty years (over
three generations) accumulated six farms of over 300 hectares
each. 11 per cent of farms of over 400 hectares in the region
south of Paris, between the Seine and the Oise, were run by
people from Flanders. The new men were more vigorous in
their methods, and not much different from city speculators;
it was they who were the pioneers of new ideas. They took
pride in their achievements—as the older families took pride
in their ancestors. One, who tripled the size of his farm in
forty years, put up an obelisk in his courtyard to commemorate
the fact.

The tenant farmers became mayors of their communes in
many cases and after 1850 their influence was certainly more
widely felt than that of the aristocracy. The landowners in
these areas included some of the richest people in France.
Jewish and Protestant bankers liked to invest here. Half a
dozen Rothschilds owned between them over 10,000 hectares
near Armainvilliers and Chantilly, Péreire owned 3,000 hectares. Baron Hottinguer owned the Château de Guermantes.
Three branches of the aristocratic Grammont family owned
1,700 hectares and noble names were sprinkled over the
countryside: Mackau, Moustier, Ségur, Bertier de Sauvigny.
But to the local inhabitants by the turn of the century these
were frequently just names and their estates were concealed
and isolated behind high walls. These landowners were usually
barely a part of the local economy. The tenant farmers, being

too busy with agriculture, seldom ventured into national politics, so landlords like Broglie, Haussonville and Lafayette were able to enjoy the parliamentary seats. The power of the tenants penetrated instead into the local sugar industry—the indispensable adjunct of the beet farming which was one of the pillars of their prosperity. The profits from sugar refining were a valuable complement to those of agriculture: in the Second Empire the refineries often paid dividends of 50 to 60 per cent; that of Puisieux, near Laon, founded in 1865, paid a 100 per cent dividend in its first year. The tenants widened their influence by allowing some relatives to become notaries, judges and civil servants locally, but they were proud that their wealth allowed them to set up nearly all their children with farms of their own. They acquired even greater stability as a class by a tacit code which forbade competition between them: they refused to rent land which had formerly been let to a neighbour of equal status, they did not compete in the wages they paid, and would not employ labourers sacked by their neighbours. Such ties made it possible for them to form cooperatives, though it took them a long time to get round to this, and it was the pressure of the crisis of the 1930s and the organisation of the wheat market in 1936 that drove them into it. But once they discovered the benefits of co-operatives, they put them to good use, and so distinguished themselves still further from the small proprietors who toyed with co-operatives so timidly, though they needed them even more. By then of course these tenant farmers were living a different kind of life, in a different class, from the rest of the peasantry and from the traditional owner of middle-sized farms. The latter still worked with their labourers, and often ate with them; it was not impossible for a good worker to marry one of their daughters and to succeed to her family's farm. The large tenant farmers by contrast treated their labourers in much the same way as industrial employers did, and all the more so since the labourers were migrants, and (particularly after 1919) foreigners. However, the exclusiveness of tenant farmers should not be exaggerated. 'His physical appearance', wrote an observer as late as 1953, 'without being that of a peasant is nevertheless definitely of a man of the land. Among his workers and neighbours, it would often be impossible to pick him out, except perhaps by his more austere mien . . . He is capable of discussing general ideas, but he is still prudent, mistrustful and not really interested in other people's point of view.'[1]

In other regions, the accumulation of wealth by a peasant did not usually involve the same change of status. At the turn of the century in Lot-et-Garonne, for example, there were, within a radius of 20 kilometres, over a hundred farms yielding good profits, but none of them over 35 hectares. The owners possessed between 50,000 and 200,000 francs in capital; some were reputed to be millionaires; but they worked in the fields themselves, wore the same clothes and sat at the same tables as the men they employed. Less than a tenth of them had been landowners for more than four generations. Their grandfathers or great-grandfathers had been farmhands or sharecroppers. They had saved up say a thousand francs by the time they were twenty-five, had married wives who brought them half as much again in dowry, and within seven or eight years had collected three or four thousand francs, enough to buy land, on mortgage, for 5,000 francs. They went on working as labourers so as to pay off their debt and to buy cattle. They grew rich by constant hard work, by spending only the very minimum and turning practically all their earnings into capital, by marrying into families of the same origin and with the same ambitions, by being careful to use only well-tried agricultural methods, and by limiting the size of their families.[2]

Next in the social hierarchy was the peasant who succeeded in keeping his farm at the same size, providing for his children with his profits. Le Play made famous a particularly remarkable example of this kind in Béarn in the mid nineteenth century, remarkable because this peasant had maintained the patriarchal structure of his family. It was in the commune of Lavedan (Hautes-Pyrénées), in mountains covered by snow for half the year and intensely hot in the summer. There were 1,376 inhabitants, 473 of them artisans or merchant families, 172 wood-

---

[1] Philippe Bernard, *Économie et sociologie de la Seine-et-Marne 1850–1950* (1953); Pierre Brunet, *Structure agraire et économie rurale des plateaux tertiaires entre la Seine et l'Oise* (Caen, 1960); Michel Philipponneau, *La Vie rurale de la banlieu parisienne* (1956); J. P. Moreau, *La Vie rurale dans le sud-est du bassin parisien* (1958).

[2] G. Maydieu, 'Notes pour servir à une monographie du paysan proprietaire du Lot-et-Garonne', *Revue d'économie politique*, 9 (1895), 159–64.

cutters, 173 living mainly from renting their houses to tourists, 102 following liberal professions (it is not clear which), 372 peasants working exclusively on lands they owned themselves, and 84 working partly for themselves and partly for others. The family of Melouga owned 8 cows and 3 to 5 heifers, who provided them with two-thirds of their income, and 90 goats and 55 sheep who provided the rest of it. They had little land, and their animals got about 40 per cent of their food from pasturing on the village commons. The family made their own clothes and clogs, grew their own food, had their own honey. In winter they made objects in wood which they sold to outsiders. The cash from their milk and cheese they used to accumulate savings to pay dowries and constitute trousseaux; this meant they had to save on average 600 francs a year, since they usually had between eight and ten children. Their way of life seemed exactly proportioned to earning this surplus, which made it possible for the main family house and farm to remain intact through the generations.

The way a peasant had to resort to industry in order to buy land, and the way he was thus able to reach a very decent standard of living, can be seen from the biography of the peasant-soapmaker of Basse-Provence, written in 1859. This man was then aged 51. He lived in a village between Aix and Marseille, one-third of which was owned by a nobleman, with the doctor and the notary having the only other sizeable farms. No peasant owned more than 20 hectares here; the soil was arid and unirrigated and most people had to have subsidiary occupations. The subject of the biography had as a result of inheritance and a lifetime of saving built up a fortune worth nearly 25,000 francs (£1,000), invested in a house and 6 hectares. However, he still could not quite afford to live on his land. He spent most of his time in Marseille, in a soap factory, where he was lodged free and where he had risen to be a charge hand. Only two-thirds of his land was worked to provide food for the family. His wife ran the farm and some of his eight children helped but the work was mainly done by a labourer they employed. It was the man's intention to retire soon and work the land himself. (His father had also been a soapmaker-peasant like him, who had saved enough to go back to the land

¹ F. Le Play, *Les Ouvriers européens* (2nd edition 1877–9), 4. 445 ff.

at the age of 39; sixteen years later, at the age of 55 he had decided to retire from farming and to divide his land among his four children, on condition that they each paid him a pension.) Our man had thus begun with one and a half hectares, plus a quarter of a house. While he lived in the soap factory, he sent his wife back to the village, to live in this quarter of a house and to work as a dressmaker (which their daughter did too, as soon as she was old enough). With their combined savings they were able to buy up the whole of the house and farm from his three siblings, for between them they had a cash annual income of some 2,000 francs (£80). In addition the daughter had saved up a trousseau worth 900 francs (including ten dresses and twenty pairs of stockings). They had a dressmaker's workshop, a kitchen of 20 square metres, and two bedrooms, five beds (for ten persons), twenty-five chairs, a variety of tables and dresses, three religious statues, four pious pictures, three prayer books, two books of French grammar, one book of old pious legends, one catechism. He had two Sunday suits, three pairs of work trousers, four coloured flannel waistcoats and one woollen one, six calico shirts, three ties, three pairs of stockings, three pairs of shoes, two pairs of underpants, two aprons, two grey felt hats and one cap. His wife's clothing included three cotton dresses, eighteen blouses, three jackets, six skirts, six kerchiefs, six pairs of stockings, two pairs of shoes, two corsets, three aprons, eight bonnets and one large brimmed black felt hat. He and his wife spoke Provençal for they knew little French, though their children knew it well. They were all piously Catholic.[1]

That there was often no clear distinction between a peasant and a worker can be seen from the history of a certain Victor living at Blaumont (Marne) between Reims and Chalons. Born of poor parents in the Vosges, he started life by emigrating to the Champagne, as a pedlar of haberdashery, but falling ill, he lost the little he possessed, and so for ten years he was a wandering labourer, seldom staying in the same job for more than a few months, and developing habits which led to frequent dismissals. He seduced a girl of 16, who had served an apprenticeship as a dressmaker and who came from a rather better

---

[1] A. Focillon, Monograph (Feb. 1859), in Le Play, *Les Ouvriers européens* (2nd edition 1877), 4. 390 ff.

family, of proprietors and gardeners. When a child was born, they married against her father's wishes, but he was unable to support her, so she went back with her child to her parents, while he continued to wander about in search of work. He was heavily in debt and nearly always drunk. His wife persuaded her father to help him settle. At this time, in the early 1840s, a canal was being built in the district. They decided to set up a hostel for the navvies. Her father lent them some money to get a house. The prospect of being able to buy the house stimulated Victor to hard work: they soon repaid the loan, became owners of the house, and by 1854 had also bought a garden and a field. This land required only a few days to till, so he continued to be a labourer, in agriculture in the autumn, and in road mending in the spring; having established a reputation as a good worker, he could find employment easily, despite his insolence when drunk. Access to common rights played a great part in his ascent. The village wasteland could be used only by sheep, so only the rich could profit from it. But the highways were open to all, and from the ditches beside them his wife collected grass for her rabbits. Their ultimate ambition was to buy a cow, which could be brought here to pasture or scavenge more profitably. Meanwhile they built their fortune on the collection of manure from the highway. The wife got up early in the morning to get the dung left by the carthorses on the main road from Chalons to Reims and by hard work she could collect a cubic metre in a week, which could be sold for $5\frac{1}{2}$ francs. In 1847, in the economic crisis, when the canal building stopped and the family had no other resource, it lived off this manure collecting. Even when they were better off, they still collected a cubic metre each month, but they used it on the garden and field: the younger daughter, aged 13, was in charge of this task. When the biography was written this family owned 360 ares (36,000 square metres) worth 1,220 francs. They had fifteen rabbits (eight of which they sold each year, and ate five themselves), one pig, which they bought in the spring and killed off in December. Their house had an earthen floor, and all their furniture and clothes were valued at only 779 francs. This Victor nevertheless knew how to take life philosophically. His two recreations were tobacco and the cabaret, on which he spent 36 francs and 26 francs respectively a year, out of a total

expenditure of a thousand francs. This enabled him sometimes
to spend whole days playing cards and drinking, though his
increasing pride in his house and garden was now keeping him
at home more. The narrow margin of his pleasures, however,
can be seen from the fact that he had decided to destroy his dog
when the law of 1855 imposed a tax of a few francs on dogs.[1] He
could not recall this loss without deep emotion.[2]

Before the Revolution the most common form of tenancy was
sharecropping, *métayage*. In 1760 it was estimated that four-
sevenths of France was cultivated by sharecroppers; and in the
1830s still the proportion was believed to be between a half and
a third. However, rent tenancy quickly replaced it in the course
of the nineteenth century. In 1862 there were only about
400,000 sharecroppers (as against a million tenant farmers); in
1882 they were down to 320,000 and in 1929 to 200,000.
Nevertheless their presence continued to be felt more than these
figures suggest because they were concentrated in certain
regions, notably the centre and south-west. The poverty to
be found there was thus accentuated by a particularly old-
fashioned, and frequently oppressive, form of tenure. The
department of Gers had thirteen times more sharecroppers
than tenant farmers, and twenty-one other departments had
more of the former than the latter (in 1892): there were virtually
none in the north and east. No generalisation is possible about
what sharecropping implied in detail, because it differed so
much from place to place, being based on ancient local customs.
In 1913 the average size of a *métairie* was 50 to 60 hectares, but
it varied from 2 hectares in the Var to over 100 on average in
the Cher. The status of a sharecropper varied according to many
criteria. Basically, sharecropping involved a division of the
produce of a farm between owner and *métayer*—very frequently
on a fifty-fifty basis, but sometimes, as in the Landes, with the
métayer getting two-thirds or three-quarters. The *métayer* provided the labour; the owner provided the land, and nearly
always also the working capital, the cattle, machines and
fertilisers, because a *métayer* was essentially poor: if he had

[1] The law of 2 May 1855 required communes to raise a tax of between one and
ten francs on dogs in order to pay for their public works. Every dog-owner was
required to make a declaration stating the number of dogs he had and 'the purpose
for which they are kept'.

[2] F. Le Play, *Les Ouvriers européens* (1877), 5. 323 ff.

capital he would buy land or be a tenant farmer. But in some
richer areas, the *métayer* provided the machines and the other

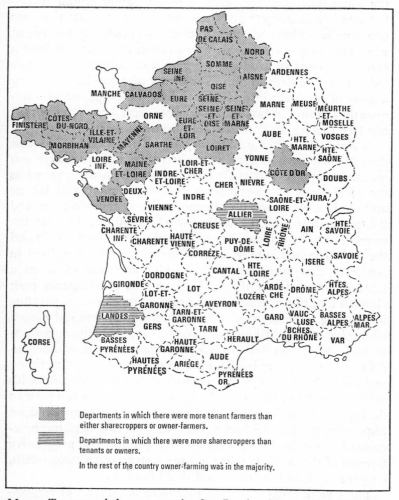

MAP 2. Tenants and sharecroppers in 1892. Based on Flour de Saint-Genis: *La
Propriéte rurale en France* (1902), 192

capital was supplied equally by both parties. The really important difference between cash tenancy and sharecropping was
that in the direction of the farming the sharecropper had to
follow the detailed instructions of the landowner—though in the

twentieth century this control diminished in some areas. In 1940 in the Limousin, there were still *métayers* who had worked the same land for three centuries—an almost feudal relic— but another characteristic of sharecropping was that the lease was usually verbal and short, so that it was virtually tenancy at will. The owner was in this way assured of getting at least a certain amount of produce, whereas a cash tenant was more liable to fall in debt to him. The owner also had in the *métayer* a kind of retainer: in addition to half the crops, he also frequently required quasi-feudal services (still known as *corvées*) like free carting, or domestic help from the wife.

A *Practical Treatise on Sharecropping* of 1882 said: 'The first duty of a *métayer* is to obey.'[1] Between 1880 and 1914 there was an aristocratic revival of sharecropping, which was praised as the ideal form of co-operation between capital and labour and the best way to ensure the moralising of the peasantry and the preservation of the authority of the upper classes: the number of *métayers* increased significantly between the 1882 and the 1892 censuses. Quite a lot of books have been written in praise of sharecropping, urging wider adoption of it, as a solution for social conflicts. The agronomist Gasparin even claimed that the egalitarian spirit of the French was in part due to the long existence of sharecropping. The system did indeed often give an industrious but penniless labourer the opportunity to have his own farm, to enjoy a certain amount of independence in his working habits, even to employ others sometimes, and conceivably also to save enough to buy a small plot of his own. In practice, however, the *métayer* was usually too poor to do justice to the land, and the owner too mean to spend on improving it, since he had to bear the whole cost of improvements but received back only half the profits. The progressive farmers of the north condemned the system as an 'association, on poor land, of slow work and timid capital'.

There were areas where *métayers* were submissive or respectful, though more recently the paternalism has increasingly died out. But in other areas sharecropping was the source of fierce antagonism which in 1908 even erupted into a revolt in the Bourbonnais, where the system was exacerbated by the owners using hated intermediaries—*fermiers-généraux*—to manage their

[1] A. de Tourdonnet, *Traité pratique du métayage* (1882), 207.

estates for them. The tensions and the human side of the system were poignantly described by a *métayer* of this region, Emile Guillaumin, in his *Life of a Simple Man* (1904). This masterpiece of peasant literature tells the story, clearly based on personal experience, of a sharecropper born in 1823, and the son of a sharecropper too. He had begun life as a goatherd at seven years of age, when he was punished if he came back with his charges earlier than eight or nine in the evening. At nine years he was promoted to look after the pigs; on fair days he would have the privilege of accompanying his father to the local town to sell them, but he would have to wait in the cold with them while his father went to a tavern to get drunk. Until the age of seventeen, he never possessed even the smallest coin of money. His first real contact with the outside world was military service. Every mother tried to save the 500 francs which could insure her child against call up (the insurer providing a substitute, as was still possible then). The mother of Tiennon (the hero of this book) managed to do this for her two eldest sons, but she had seven children and could not for him. Feeling that his parents had let him down, he left home and became a labourer. To go into the service of others, rather than helping one's father, was something of a betrayal, a rebellion, when it was not forced by need. Still, he went to the local fair with an ear of corn in his hat, and he was hired for a wage of 90 francs a year. But he was a labourer by his own free will, and he felt he could not marry an ordinary servant girl; he preferred to be bold and propose to a girl who had a dowry of 300 francs, and he was accepted when he obtained the same sum from his own father to balance it. After a few years more as a labourer, his father-in-law found him a *métairie* and he was able to enjoy the independence of his own farm, though on hard terms. He had to go straight into debt to his landlord to the extent of 1,000 francs, to buy his half share of the cattle, and he was charged 5 per cent interest on this: so he got considerably less than 50 per cent of the produce. He had to be very subservient to his landowner, who could never remember his name, who called him 'Thing', and who said to him 'Obey and work: I ask nothing else of you. And never bother me with requests for repairs: I do none, on principle.' In compensation, the landlord sometimes summoned him to the château and gave him a vast

chunk of pork to eat in the kitchen, as a special treat. But
Tiennon also had to be subservient to the landlord's manager
and the latter's mistress, who pestered his wife with requests for
menial services. Pathetic scenes took place which made him
exclaim: 'We are still slaves.' He had to work very hard to get
a living, sleeping only five or six hours a day, rising at four in the
morning. Nevertheless, as 'head of a farm, I felt myself to be
something of a king. Responsibility often weighed heavily on
me, but I was proud to sit at the head of the table, near the
loaf from which I cut large pieces at the beginning of every
meal; and proud also to have, in the winter evenings, the chair
by the fire, the place of honour.' After twenty years, he was able
to repay the 1,000 francs and save 4,000 francs, including what
he had inherited from his father-in-law. But he invested it at
5 per cent with a banker, who defaulted. He was back where
he had started. Then, when he was fifty-five, his landowner
demanded an increase of rent (for he paid a small rent—the
impôt colonique—as well as sharing his produce). He refused and
was given notice. All the effort he had put into improving his
farm was wasted. His brother, who had played for higher stakes,
and had used his 8,000 francs savings to buy a small farm
of his own costing 15,000 francs, had been unable to make his
mortgage payments and had also lost all. Old age held out only
the prospect of failing health and tense relations with the
children who had to support them.

The Revolution and the Civil Code had done very little for
the *métayers*. A law of 1889 which purported at last to give them
some protection in effect simply perpetuated 'local usages'. Bills
to improve their lot were introduced in vain. The Popular
Front's efforts (in a bill of 7 July 1937) to produce collective
bargaining and a codification of customs were abortive. Their
final emancipation came only in 1945 and 1946 when they
were given the option of converting their contracts on demand
into cash tenancies, so that in 1955 there were only 72,000
métayers left.[1] At the same time cash tenants were given first
option to buy their farms if the landlord wished to sell; in

[1] L. Durousseau-Dugontier, *L'Évolution du métayage en France* (Poitiers thesis,
Tulle, 1905), Pierre Laborderie-Boulou, *Le Métayage, particulièrement en Périgord*
(Bordeaux thesis, 1905); P. Rouveroux, *Le Métayage* (1934); J. Dudez, *Le Métayage*
(Bordeaux thesis, 1938), G. Pirou, *Traité d'économie politique*, vol. 1, part 2 (1941),
104–12.

any case they could not be evicted, since they were also given the right to renew their tenancies. A new age therefore started in 1945, when it was no longer the man who owned the land, but he who cultivated it, who became its effective master.

The wine-growing peasants were a very special case, economically and socially distinct, and with a reputation for having a different kind of mentality. Their history may help to explain this. Before the eighteenth century wine drinking was not a popular activity; and the wine produced till then was of a different kind. Until the sixteenth century indeed inns were forbidden to sell wine to locals: they provided it only to travellers. Peasants seldom drank wine, which was reserved for the bourgeoisie; at most they could hope for *piquette* (produced by running water over the residue left after the wine is made). Wine was generally produced by the upper classes for their own consumption, and that is why so many of the vineyards belonged to the nobility, to the Church and increasingly to the manufacturers and merchants of Bordeaux, Lyon and Dijon, and why the major wine areas are near important towns. The Parisian region was once a major wine-producing region; only around 1850–60 were the remnants of the vines there finally replaced by vegetables. However, in the course of the eighteenth century, the workers in the growing towns began demanding wine, and so a new kind of production developed to cater for their tastes. This was cheap wine, known as *gamay* as opposed to the fine *pinot*; its characteristic was that its yield was high, even if its quality was poor; and the people who produced it were the peasants who were gradually buying up the land in tiny bits from the upper classes. The first conflict of the wine-growing peasants was with the bourgeoisie and with the Church, whose lands they coveted and who, because of their resources, were able to produce a superior kind of wine, selling at a much higher price. Later, at the end of the nineteenth century, the peasants' main enemy were the mass-producing capitalists of the south, who beat the peasants at their own game by churning out vast quantities of *vin ordinaire* far more cheaply than any small peasant could. The winegrowers therefore had good grounds for being at war with the rich.

But, secondly, they also had a long tradition of conflict with the state and the municipal authorities, because these had replied to this new kind of catering for the poor drinker of the towns by imposing increasingly heavy taxes on wines. Cheap wine sometimes had to pay twice its value in tax by the end of the *ancien régime*. This became a burning issue between the masses and the government. So in 1791 the duties paid on wine entering the towns were abolished; but the loss of revenue was such that they were re-established in 1798 under the name of *octroi*. Town workers used to go to the suburbs outside Paris to escape it, and incredibly large numbers of wine shops sprouted in this desolate area. In the nineteenth century, the winegrower therefore continued to feel himself victimised by government taxation; he was at war with the civil service which collected it; and in very many cases he became a smuggler. Of course, different regions produced different situations: the Beaujolais region for example could afford to expand its production of cheap wine because it had the right to send its wines to Lyon cheaply; Mâcon by contrast had to pay tariffs four times higher and so found it necessary to specialise in fine wines; and again Orléans produced vinegar rather than fine wines not because of the nature of its soil but because the latter were destroyed by government policy. The result of this heavy taxation was that cheap wine did not cost very much less than good wine: the peasants who produced it therefore concentrated on quantity rather than quality, often harvesting three times as many grapes from their land, and selling these at half the price of the high-class vineyards. It was on this basis that they prospered, and it was under this pressure that skilled wine making suffered in the nineteenth century. By 1875, good wine was thus in a state of crisis. Fraud and competition made public sales difficult and the best wine production came to be concentrated in the private bourgeois châteaux.

The area devoted to wine growing continued to increase throughout the Second Empire. The railways opened up wide markets; the 1860 treaty facilitated exports. Wine became one of the major speculations of the period (indeed one of its major industries, for it came second only to textiles): all classes invested in it, from the small peasant to the stockbroker (like, e.g., Gaston Bazille, father of the impressionist); industrialists even closed their factories and bought vineyards instead. Then, at the height of this prosperity the phylloxera disease struck, with catastrophic results. Nearly all the vineyards had to be up-rooted. It required vast capital, as much as 5,000 francs a hectare, to replant with American roots and then a good deal of experiment, since the earliest grafts produced a wine with a 'foxy' smell (the English word was used, *vins foxés*). The distribution of wine growing was altered: several northern areas almost gave it up; but the south on the other hand greatly expanded its acreage. It planted new vines with high yields, suitable for mass production; and it also transformed the pattern of ownership, for here large capitalists moved in. While production was low, prices remained high, so the induce-ment to replant was strong. However, no sooner had the re-establishment of the vines been effected, than over-production occurred, and this has remained the chronic problem of the winegrowers ever since. It is true that the consumption of wine in France increased from 51 litres a head in 1848 to 77 litres in 1872 to 103 litres in 1904 and 136 litres in 1926. But during the phylloxera crisis the government had en-couraged Algeria to plant vines, and it had allowed Spanish and Italian imports. In addition fraudulent wine had flooded the market to the extent of about 40 per cent of the genuine product, as was revealed by the tripling of the amount of sugar used by the winemakers. It was in these years too that the vine-yards of California and South America expanded. Between 1870 and 1900, also, beet-alcohol production rose threefold. The winemakers emerged from their crisis into a very competitive world. There was so much wine, it hardly ever paid. Five disastrous years out of seven in 1900–7 brought the south not only to near bankruptcy, but actually to revolt. Parliament hastily passed ineffective laws, but the situation was finally saved by higher prices after 1912, and then by enormous pro-fiteering during the war. The peasants used their new-found wealth to pay off their debts, and favourable harvests from 1920 to 1929 restored their prosperity. But then once again over-production brought prices tumbling down and the 1930s were among the worst years the winegrowers had experienced. The Algerians, expecting a law to be passed to limit their produc-tion, increased their vineyards from 221,000 hectares in 1928 to 400,000 in 1935. There followed a remarkable revolution of

a new kind. In 1907 the winegrowers had simply demanded
that the government should find some solution to their problem:
they themselves had none to offer; but in the 1930s they har-
nessed the power of the government to enforce a unique state
control on their industry. Law after law was introduced to
limit production, to forbid new planting, to offer tax abate-
ments to those who destroyed their vineyards and to arrange for
the buying up of surplus crops and their transformation into
alcohol. The winegrowers made the nation subsidise them. The
peculiarity of these laws was that they were a triumph for
the small peasant: the controls were directed above all at the
capitalist mass-producers. However, they were not effective in
the long term. The 1939–45 war again brought profits; it was
followed by a further period of overproduction, and in 1953
there was further legislation. But because of the vast electoral
power of the peasant winegrowers, no fundamental transformation of land use was possible. From the rational economic point
of view, what was needed was not a freezing of productivity, but
the allocation of the land to those crops best suited to it and most
in demand. Wine should be sent back to the hills where nothing
else would grow, but where it flourished, and the plains should
be used for the production of meat and milk. But there were too
many emotional satisfactions and too many interests involved.

The world of wine was torn between the producers of quality
and the producers of quantity, between the capitalists who
treated their investment as they would any industry, and the
peasants for whom winegrowing was a way of life, between
the specialised small owner, the polycultural amateur, and
the labourer who worked on someone else's large farm. The
struggles between them had an element of tragedy, because the
mass of small winegrowers were essentially gamblers, who lost
much more often than they won. Some studies of individual
budgets have shown how their lives were a series of hopes
deceived and of accumulated debts, but with the occasional
marvellous harvest which cancelled it all out and allowed them
to start again. The small peasant seldom made a good living
from his vines. This is partly why he had a reputation as a Red.
The winegrowers certainly often voted left wing. But their
opposition to the state, the tax official, the capitalist, the
favoured owners of the fine brands, the wholesale merchant

and the usurers, did not take them beyond radicalism: their ideal was very definitely property and independence, by individual effort. The workers might vote socialist or communist on the large estates, but the small owners had reservations. When they surrendered part of their independence to form co-operatives, as they had to, it was in the spirit of solidarity and mutuality, not of co-operative labour. Each still tilled his own plot, though the co-operative could exercise great influence on the kind of grapes that were grown and when they were harvested. The radicalism of these small winegrowers involved independence in another way too. They were not genuine peasants. They lived almost in an urban culture, in villages of a thousand or more. They had very little to do in the early summer; they could almost have holidays in July, August and October too. They frequently visited the near-by towns which the wine merchants made prosperous and whose entertainment and shopping they enjoyed. They dressed differently from the peasant immediately after work, particularly the young ones, who habitually went out in the village in the evenings. Except in winter, the men, both young and old, met in the village square to chat while waiting for their evening meal, playing different versions of bowls, or sitting on the terraces of the cafés. The married women and spinsters spent long hours sitting on chairs outside their houses, gossiping interminably. On Sunday afternoons, there were balls for the young. This active social life put a premium on discussion. These men developed a taste for general ideas. They were seldom pious, but they loved the feasts of the Church and celebrated baptisms and communions with vigour. But they were far from prosperous. Their standard of living was below the average for their class. Not only socially, but economically also, wine growing stood between agriculture and industry. In the south, it was often an alternative to industry. Until the 1930s, wine growing had as important an influence on density of population as industry. Apart from Brittany, all areas with over seventy inhabitants per square kilometre were either industrial or winegrowing: the vineyards of the Bordelais and Languedoc could compare with the textile regions of the Vosges and Caux. Textiles and viticulture had in fact been alternative supplements for rural areas which agriculture did not keep fully busy. That part of France which did not produce wine had domestic looms instead. When the peasants on the borderline found it unprofitable to make wine, they turned to lace making, which as it were marked the frontier.[1]

At the bottom of the peasants' social scale were the labourers: nearly 3 million of them in 1848, $2\frac{1}{2}$ million in 1892, $1\frac{1}{2}$ million in 1929, 1 million in 1946. This was the group on which the socialists and particularly the communists placed great hopes for new recruits, but with little success. Their wages, it is true, were probably even lower than those of town workers, particularly when seasonal unemployment is taken into consideration. They might find lodgings more cheaply, but these again were often worse in quality than the town slums about which the pious reformers were so indignant. They frequently had to supplement their earnings with domestic industries, which were among the worst paid in the country. However, there was little possibility of organising them nationally. Many of them worked isolated on farms where they might be the only labourer employed. Their standard of living was low, but in some areas not much lower than that of their employers. For a good many, being a labourer was only a stage in life, from which they hoped to escape, either to proprietorship or to the towns. Even this class was highly varied. Just before the Second World War, those in the Vienne, Cher, Saône-et-Loire were receiving wages almost twice as high as those in Dordogne and Lot-et-Garonne, for example. Their conditions of employment and lodging varied enormously. In the 1950s, when sociologists interrogated them about their ambitions, it emerged that they very often did not consider themselves part of the working class even when they migrated to the towns; for many their ultimate goal was to set themselves up independently on their own.[2]

[1] Roger Dion, *Histoire de la vigne et du vin en France des origines au 19e siècle* (1959), a massive, masterly study; Armand Perrin, *La Civilisation de la vigne* (1938); Robert Laurent, *Les Vignerons de la Côte d'Or au 19e siècle* (1957), an excellent thesis; Gaston Galtier, *Le Vignoble du Languedoc méditerranéen et du Roussillon. Étude comparative d'un vignoble de masse* (Montepellier, 1960, 3 vols.), full of interesting information; C. K. Warner, *The Winegrowers of France and the Government since 1875* (New York, 1960), valuable for the legislative side; for a comprehensive early survey, Dr. J. Guyot, *Études des vignobles de France* (1868, 3 vols.); for biographical monographs, Paul Descamps, *La Science sociale* (June 1907), and *Les Ouvriers des deux mondes*, 2nd series, vol. 3, no. 166.

[2] Françoise Langlois, *Les Salariés agricoles en France* (1962), 9, and annexe XI;

The Duping of the Peasants

Thus the peasants cannot be regarded as the solid ballast that kept France stable over these hundred years. They were, as has been seen, too much in a state of turmoil and internal rivalry. Their conflicts were no less absorbing to them because they did not fit simply into a clash of capitalist–worker, and because the peasants' ambitions, in seeking land, were seldom to rise into the bourgeoisie. But the conflicts were all the more frantic because they took place at a time when the society they knew was collapsing. It was shaken and indeed transformed by what was the peasant counterpart to the industrial strike, but without leaders and without dramatic incidents. It manifested itself silently, in millions of individual peasants leaving the land and migrating to the towns. This could have enriched the peasants who remained; it could have transformed agriculture into an efficient industry unburdened by an excessive, tradition-bound labour force; but in effect, in these years, it only served to reveal that agriculture was no longer the backbone of the country. Those who remained were deserted, not liberated. Rural depopulation became a neurotic worry instead of a sign of increasing opportunity.

During the Second Empire the countryside was inhabited more densely than it had ever been, and in certain regions to a degree which was unequalled in Western Europe. When the population fell, this fact was ignored; the abnormality of the position in 1850 was forgotten and only the vast number leaving the land was noticed. At the same time, the total population of France ceased to increase so that the losses from the land were not made good by a higher birth-rate. The proportion of the nation engaged in agriculture fell from 61 per cent in 1851 to 53 per cent in 1861 to 45 per cent in 1891 and 32·5 per cent in 1931–46. This drastic drop still left France with far more peasants than most other western countries: in 1939 Britain had only 5·7 per cent, Belgium 17 per cent, Germany 29 per cent.[1] The rural depopulation continued rapidly after the Second

A. Souchon, *La Crise de la main d' œuvre agricole en France* (1914); Alain Touraine, 'Les Ouvriers d'origine agricole', in *Sociologie du travail* (July–Sept. 1960), 230–45.

[1] These international statistics, not always fully comparable, are quoted in P. L. Yates, *Food Production in Western Europe* (1940), 19.

World War: the agricultural population fell between 1946 and
1960 from 32·5 per cent to 20 per cent.[1]

The emigration was of different kinds. In the nineteenth
century it appears to have taken place with particular rapidity
at certain periods: in 1861–5, when about 650,000 people left
the land, in 1875–81, when the most intense emigration ever
recorded took place with 840,000 people leaving, and in 1896–
1901 when another 650,000 left. Each of these waves was a
response to a particular crisis, but they were all largely migrations of poverty, of people who were marginal to rural society,
or for whom the countryside could find no room. Previously some
of those who could not earn a living off the land became rural
artisans, or labourers, but these jobs were vanishing under
pressure from industry, from the crisis in agriculture, and because the leasing or partition of commons made it more difficult
to survive in the traditional ways. In the twentieth century this
kind of massive departure occurred only once again, in 1936–8
when perhaps a third of a million people left the land after the
urban workers won their important advantages under the Popular Front. However, for the rest of this century the emigration
seems to have been steadier, with roughly the same numbers
leaving each year in a regular trickle. Now, moreover, the depar-
tures were less of the poorest inhabitants as of the young and
the adventurous, positively seeking a better life. Whereas before
1914 migrants usually went to the local small towns and
reached the cities only over several generations, now they
moved directly to the cities. After 1945 there were again new
forms of migration, so it is not possible to describe this movement
with blanket generalisations. Individual villages responded to
the challenges with extraordinary variety; some showed great
adaptability while others collapsed with traumatic rapidity.[2]
There is need for more investigation of these unspoken disputes
and ambitions, asking the sort of questions that modern social
psychologists can pose. In one study of Brittany in the 1950s,
it was found that 42 per cent of those who migrated in that

[1] P. Barral, *Les Agrariens français de Méline à Pisani* (1968), 19, 217, has useful
tables.
[2] P. Clement and P. Vieille, 'L'Exode rurale', in *Études de comptabilité nationale*
published by the Ministry of Finance (Apr. 1960), 57–130, which includes a full
bibliography on this subject; P. Pinchemel, *Structures agraires et dépopulation rurale
dans les campagnes picardes de 1836 à 1936* (1957).

period had made their decision to do so, or at least had considered it, before the age of 14, and another 35 per cent between the ages of 14 and 17. This suggests, for migration of this particular kind, a class of peasants who knew from an early age that there was no room for them on the land. It was not necessarily frustrated or unsuccessful people who went to the towns; perhaps often the middle ranks did so most, because the ablest children, if they were not drawn away by scholarships, could generally find a place in their local society and the most stupid could not move.[1]

The landless naturally had most inducement to leave. The land was drained of labourers, with catastrophic results particularly for the small bourgeois farmers so prevalent, for example, in the south-west. They could retaliate by importing Spaniards, Italians, Poles or other foreigners, which transformed rural society in one way. Or they might be forced to abandon farming, letting out their land and using their houses as summer holiday houses, while seeking careers in the cities; and rural society was transformed in another way.[2] The social structure of the countryside was simplified. Though modern communications did bring the peasant closer to the towns in some respects, they also had the effect of isolating him from them even more in other respects, by drawing the non-agricultural professions to the towns. The nation was thus divided more sharply into those who tilled the soil and those who drew their incomes from the city. The decline of domestic industries meant that the peasant became more of a specialist. He was no longer additionally an artisan in winter, or a building worker in slack periods.

The peasant world was almost constantly in crisis throughout these hundred years and in some very fundamental ways. It should not be forgotten that the trials of 1846–50 were among the most severe that European agriculture had ever experienced. The prosperity of the Second Empire attracted even more people into landownership but increased production was not matched by increased efficiency. Prosperity did not mean that agriculture increased its share of the national income: on the contrary in 1890 the 45 per cent of the population which was in

[1] André Levesque, *Le Problème psychologique des migrations rurales* (1958), 186.
[2] Dr. A. Labat, *L' Âme paysanne* (1939).

it drew only between 30 and 35 per cent of the national income.[1]
Improved communications opened new markets but also made
possible the competition of American, Balkan and Russian
wheat; they stimulated production but they also brought about
catastrophic falls in prices. The price of wheat fell by one-third
in the 1880s and 1890s, as compared with the Second Empire.
The price of land, which, taking 1821 as 100, had risen to 255
in 1851, 366 in 1879, fell to 279 in 1894. The phylloxera crisis
wiped out another of the cash crops on which many farmers
depended: in 1875 a record 84 million hectolitres of wine were
produced, but in 1879 only 25 million, and it was fifteen years
before production exceeded even half the high figure of 1875.
Prices rose because of the shortage, but the total income from
wine was still less than half that earned under the Second
Empire. Moreover, it required enormous capital to replant with
new roots.[2]

The answer of the government was to introduce protection,
as early as 1881, which was gradually widened and finally
consolidated in Meline's tariff law of 1892. This had three
results. First, 'agriculture was saved', as the supporters of protection put it. That is to say, agriculture was able to go on much
as before, to preserve subsistence and unspecialised methods
and to keep a higher proportion of labour on the land than
would otherwise have been possible. France was able to remain
a land of peasants. Agricultural prices did fall, but not as much
as in other countries, England for example. By the turn of the
century they were back to remunerative levels, the crisis was
over, and in the years just before the 1914 war they even
reached new peaks. So protection appeared to be justified; and
it was preserved as a basic creed of the republic. The level of
tariffs on foodstuffs in France was the highest in Western Europe,
about 29 per cent, equalled only by Austria–Hungary, compared to 22 per cent in Italy and Germany, 15 per cent in
Switzerland and 24 per cent in Sweden.[3]

A second effect of protection, however, was to save the
peasants from the need to modernise. A crucial sixty years were

[1] Cf. M. Latil, *L'Évolution du revenu agricole* (1954), 10–40.
[2] Cf. P. Caziot, *La Valeur de la terre en France* (1914), 7–9; D. Zolla, *La Crise agricole* (1904).
[3] M. Tracy, *Agriculture in Western Europe, Crisis and Adaptation since 1880* (1964), 31; H. Liepmann, *Tariff Levels* (1938), 413.

allowed to pass in which the problem of adapting them to industrial society was purposely neglected. That is why, when the issue was at last faced after 1950, it produced such violent reactions and why a 'peasant revolution' took place in the 1960s. As Méline saw it, protection should be part of a more general agricultural programme, in which increased capital investment and improved technical education should increase profitability. He passed laws to encourage agricultural credit societies, on mutualist lines, and in 1897 gave them state backing; but these remained small and never developed into a significant factor in the economy. As late as 1883, an inquiry revealed that a sizeable minority of members of agricultural societies believed that 'borrowing at whatever interest is disastrous for the farmer and the small peasant: in 80 per cent of cases, it leads to ruin . . . It is less important to give loans than to show how to do without them.'[1] Technical education was likewise spurned, as being too theoretical. Colleges were established but were allowed to wallow in penury. The National Agronomic Institute, founded in 1848, abolished by Napoleon III, was re-established by the Third Republic, but it produced only 26 graduates in 1876 and 87 in 1913. About 80 other colleges of a lower level were founded, and some 250 peripatetic professors were sent out to teach new methods. But this was a tiny force with which to tackle the problem of peasant ignorance, and it reached about 1 per cent of the agricultural population. The primary schools were the only places where the peasants did receive education, but these were generally run by schoolmasters who believed that the aim of the bright boy should be to escape from the land. What was missing was an intermediate college, where practical training could be provided, and this gap was not filled in these years.[2]

Instead, and this was the third consequence of protection, the peasants were encouraged to believe that it was to the state that they should turn to improve their lot. They were not unique in this, but they were perhaps unique in the way they got the state to believe also that they were particularly deserving of state aid. They succeeded in obtaining very significant

[1] Société Nationale d'Agriculture de France, *Enquête sur le crédit agricole* (1884), I. 315, 319, quoted by P. Barral, 90.
[2] R. Chatelain, *L'Agriculture française et la formation professionnelle* (1953).

exemptions from taxation. In the 1890s a remarkable campaign for lower taxes on peasants, which a newspaper, *La Démocratie rurale*, organised and for which it collected a million signatures, was successful in winning important concessions. The peasants grew used to the idea that they should be subsidised by the rest of the nation. By 1963, seven-eighths of them paid no income tax; the state was devoting about 10 per cent of its budget to subsidising them; and the whole of Europe indeed contributed financially to maintaining their inefficiency.[1] But they were of course duped. The state got its own back by skimping on the services it provided for them, as will be seen. The peasants thought they were succeeding in preserving their independence, in being left alone, but they were in fact left behind. The paradox of the peasants' position in France is that they were idealised, subsidised and even feared as a great electoral force, but all the same they were unable to use their power, and they remained among the poorest people in the country.[2]

There were areas, however, where the peasants did seize the opportunities presented by the changing demands on agriculture. Farming in different areas developed very differently in the course of these hundred years. One can see this most strikingly if one compares Brittany with the region of the Garonne.[3] Around 1848, the Garonne was a reasonably prosperous agricultural region while Brittany was one of the poorest. The Garonne cultivated 68 per cent of its land, while Brittany cultivated only 57 per cent and allowed almost a third to lie waste. The Garonne derived its prosperity from its highly marketable wheat (to which it devoted twice as much land as Brittany), from its good quality wine and from its maize, with which it could feed a vast flock of poultry. Brittany by contrast was backward, isolated, its land lacking in lime and phosphate, so that enormous areas had to be left fallow for 40 to 60 years to enable them to recover from agriculture. Its inhabitants lived in primitive squalor, while those of the Garonne enjoyed a high standard of living, with white bread and wine. However,

[1] Daniel Chabanol, *Le Paysan, prolétaire ou P.G.D.* (1969), 11.

[2] M. Augé-Laribé, *La Politique agricole de la France de 1880 à 1940* (1950).

[3] Brittany: Côtes-du-Nord, Finistère, Ille-et-Vilaine, Morbihan, Loire-Inférieure. Garonne: Haute-Garonne, Gers, Lot, Tarn-et-Garonne, Lot-et-Garonne, Dordogne.

the changes of these hundred years completely altered this picture. By 1939 their positions were almost reversed. Production fell in the Garonne and rose dramatically in Brittany. The area of cultivated land in the Garonne fell to 65 per cent, while that of Brittany rose to 74 per cent. The wastelands of Brittany were brought under the plough and fertilised; its agricultural territory increased by one third, half of which was added to arable but half to pasture, for Brittany turned to the production of meat and milk for which there was an increasingly profitable market. The Garonne's concentration on wheat was disastrous, both because it exhausted the land and because the great depression hit hardest in the south-west. Wheat ceased to be profitable in small-scale farming. In addition the vineyards, destroyed by phylloxera, were reconstituted in great haste with plants of a quality inferior to that previously used but with much higher yields, for these new plants flourished particularly well in the liberally irrigated plains of the Garonne. The acreage devoted to vines fell by almost a half, but the total production was kept constant. However, in this production of *vin ordinaire* the south was able to beat it with even higher yields. In 1882 the Garonne produced 16 per cent of France's wine, and the south 28 per cent. By 1930–9, however, it was producing only 9 per cent and the south 51 per cent, for southern wine was always cheap, whereas Garonne wine was neither particularly cheap nor, any longer, good, and its yield was only 24 hectolitres per hectare compared with the south's 50 hectolitres per hectare. The Garonne made the mistake, that is, of not following the Loire valley, which reconstituted its vineyards with the distinctive Muscadet, capable of finding a good market. Brittany's wine production meanwhile doubled, its cider production tripled. In the production of food for the towns, Brittany's pastures were well placed, but the Garonne's vegetables and fruit had to compete with the climatically more favoured south and Algeria. Another of the traditional occupations of the Garonne, sheep farming, likewise ceased to be profitable with cheaper importation from abroad, and of its flock of over 2 million sheep in 1840 only 600,000 remained in 1939. The Garonne had naturally good communications but in addition it had early been favoured with roads and canals, of which it had twice as much as Brittany. By 1939, however, Brittany was no longer impenetrable: it had three times as much railway as the Garonne and five-sixths as much road. As a result, the population of the Garonne fell by 24 per cent, while that of Brittany rose by 14 per cent (1841–1936).[1]

The British or American tourist, disembarking at Cherbourg, nowadays sees a region totally different in appearance from what it was a hundred years ago. He may see the ruins of great barns, relics of the days when wheat was grown, and of cottages for labourers, who have likewise vanished. The region is now devoted to pasture, to the extent of as much as 95 per cent in the Cotentin, but there was practically no pasture in the time of Napoleon I. The land was then given over to buckwheat (the principal food of the people), wheat (their principal market product), rye, oats, barley and fallow. But between 1830 and 1930 the price of a cow increased sixfold, that of milk threefold. Wheat on the other hand became a little cheaper. Formerly the porous lands which were easy to cultivate, and on which roads could be built, were the really valuable ones. Now it is the heavy lands, turned over to pasture, and penetrated by the railways, which are most sought after. What was once a poor region is now one of the most profitable in France.[2]

The transformations which have occurred can be seen in more intimate detail by looking at the history of the village of Morette, in the Dauphiné, which happens to have been written by one of its inhabitants. After escaping to get higher education, the author decided to go back to the land. He shows how in 1806 his village had 398 inhabitants (in 81 families). In 1851 it had 528 and this was the highest ever. By 1901 the figure was down again to 402, by 1911 it was 326, by 1922, 232. It remained around this figure for the inter-war years; in 1946 it was down to 204. This decline was due principally to emigration, but also to a fall in the birthrate due to the ageing of the population. It is manifested physically in the ruins of abandoned farmhouses, undulating fields which had clearly once grown vines, and dis-

[1] Jean Chombart de Lauwe, *Bretagne et pays de la Garonne: évolution agricole comparée depuis un siècle* (1946). A. Armengaud, 'De quelques idées fausses concernant le pays de la Garonne vers 1840', *Revue d'histoire moderne et contemporaine* (Jan.–Mar. 1960), shows that the sharper contrast presented by Chombart de Lauwe needs to be toned down.

[2] Cf. Charles Vezin, *L'Évolution de l'agriculture de la Manche en un siècle, 1830–1930* (Paris thesis, printed at Saint-Lô, 1931).

used reservoirs in which hemp had once been steeped. The 113
hectares of arable land in 1827 were increased to 132 by 1862,
but by 1935 they were down to 45. The vines which covered
220 hectares in 1827 and 205 in 1862 were down to 65 hectares
in 1935. Undistinguished, they could not compete with the
cheaper products of the south, but a specialised crop like wal-
nuts had become highly profitable and 61 hectares were now
planted with it: and the return on this was four or five times
greater than that on wine or wheat. The pasture had risen from
35 hectares in 1862 to 216 in 1935; the 96 oxen of 1862 had
almost completely vanished, and had been replaced by cows.
Not only was the face of the countryside transformed, but also
the type of inhabitant. In 1851 the village had 1 lace maker,
2 wheelwrights, 2 tailors, 2 farriers, 1 clog maker, 1 hemp
comber, 3 weavers and 9 other textile workers, 7 carpenters,
1 mason, 6 sawyers, 3 drapers and 1 pork butcher. By 1896,
however, there were only 5 artisans left: a cobbler, a wheel-
wright, a dressmaker, a carpenter and a mason. After 1914 this
number was reduced to simply the mason and the carpenter
and they were absent from the village all day, since they found
their work largely outside it. The few small grocery shops fared
better; they survived because they were often part-time
occupations, run by wives, and now the motor car allowed
them to deliver over a larger area.

The old isolation was over. In 1848 the village had been
almost completely self-sufficient. The peasants built their
houses themselves out of wattle and daub, from local clay and
timber brought from the local woods. They clothed themselves
without spending any money: the weaver made them cloth from
hemp which they gave him and they wore clogs. They fed themselves on their own rye or black bread, cheese, chestnuts,
potatoes, beans and cabbages, pork but hardly ever beef or
lamb. They made their own oil and vinegar, and lit their homes
at night with a special oil they manufactured from nuts. Their
agricultural tools were nearly all wooden. When in 1849 the
municipal council attempted to break out from this isolation and
decided to subscribe to a newspaper for the mayor, the prefect
refused them permission to do it. These physical aspects of the
peasant's life changed soon after. A study of the possessions
of villagers, carried out by the Museum of Popular Arts and

Traditions, on the basis of notaries' inventories drawn up after death, showed that the break came around 1850–60. The furniture of the peasant of 1850 was hardly any different from what it had been in the eighteenth century.[1] By 1914, however, the houses in this village had stone or brick bases and window frames, they had concrete instead of earthen floors, they had plaster on their walls and manufactured tiles on their roofs. They were more spacious, with more furniture; chairs replaced benches. Shoes replaced clogs, clothes were made from varying materials, by tailors. Coffee arrived around 1860, though at first it was taken only on New Year's Day, but in time replaced bread dipped in eau-de-vie as the normal breakfast. In 1860 butcher's meat was not eaten, but it was gradually introduced together with such things as rice, macaroni and sugar. In 1908 the first telephone arrived—a public one, installed at the request of the municipal council; in 1910 the first bicycle was bought and quickly became a popular form of transport. In 1903 the primary-school master got a grant of 25 francs to open a library. His role in the village became increasingly important. He gained ground over the *curé* as people went to church less; an insolent answer by a girl who was refused absolution for refusing to give up dancing became famous and a sort of anticlerical warcry; and after 1914 the village had no *curé* at all. By 1914 the peasants lived no longer in their village but in a whole region, drawing more and more of their services from outside. The travelling *charcutier* got himself a telephone (the only private person to have one). The peasants met together in 1897 to form a mutual insurance society; in 1914 they affiliated themselves to a trade union specialising in supplying fertilisers at wholesale prices; in 1929 they combined to raise a loan to buy a threshing machine; after 1936 they sold their milk to a firm that came round in a lorry to collect it; the nut growers formed a co-operative to sell their produce at higher prices. The young women followed the Parisian fashions. Newspapers were everywhere, though almost no one in 1939 had yet seen a cinema. The effect of all these changes was to produce peasants who in some ways were more peasant than they had ever been

---

[1] Suzanne Tardieu, 'L'Équipement de la maison', *Revue de synthèse* (July–Sept. 1957), 347–63. This article draws attention to 14,000 monographic descriptions compiled between 1941 and 1946, still awaiting analysis.

before—working the land and owning more of it, since there were fewer of them to share it—but they were in other ways peasants of a new kind. One might try to assess in what ways their attitudes became really different.[1]

One way to investigate this question is to see what the peasants did with their savings. A study of their wills and post-mortem inventories in the Vaucluse shows that by 1938 6 per cent of them had bank accounts, 13 per cent were members of co-operatives. In 1900 21 per cent had put some money into the national savings banks, by 1938 37 per cent of them had; and this was the most popular kind of investment. Most interesting of all, however, is that in 1900 already 7 per cent of their wealth was in shares and by 1938 29 per cent of it. Even the very poorest peasants, who never invested in shares before 1914, put money into them after the war. The increasingly commercial character of Vaucluse agriculture had drawn the peasants into the capitalist system.[1]

The degree to which this took place is difficult to measure. There have been those who have argued that by 1939 the peasants were split into two groups, those who had adopted modern methods and produced their goods for the market, and those who had remained faithful to subsistence farming. This is a useful half-truth. There is no doubt that the farming of the northern plains bore little resemblance to the traditional poly-culture of the Massif Central. It is useful to be reminded that, from whatever angle one looks at the peasants, one never sees a homogeneous group. However, the facts about their attitude to modernisation require more careful scrutiny. The enormous variation in the wealth of peasants in different regions in 1848 is well known. Now in the course of the second half of the century these variations were to a certain extent equalised. The example given, of Brittany and the Garonne, shows how one formerly desolate province improved dramatically. But though

[1] Joseph Garavel, *Les Paysans de la Morette: un siècle de vie rurale dans une commune du Dauphiné* (1948). For another interesting village study, see Patrick Higonnet, *Pont-de-Montvert: Social Structure and Politics in a French Village* (Cambridge, Mass., 1971), which contains many stimulating ideas.

[2] Claude Mesliand, 'La Fortune paysanne dans le Vaucluse, 1900–1938', *Annales* (1967), 88–136. It should be stressed that this region was exceptionally commercial, and peasant investments would probably be different in the Centre of France for example.

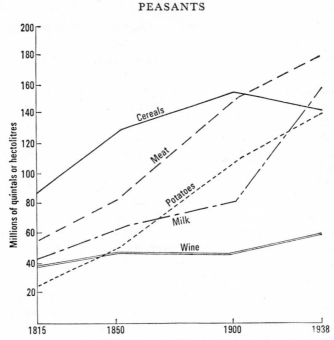

FIG. 1. Agricultural production 1815–1938. Based on P. Viau:
L'Agriculture dans l'économie (1967), 29

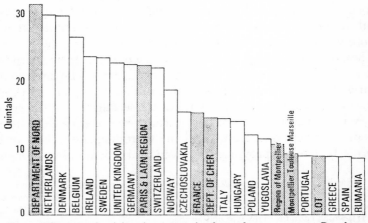

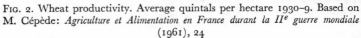

FIG. 2. Wheat productivity. Average quintals per hectare 1930–9. Based on
M. Cépède: *Agriculture et Alimentation en France durant la IIᵉ guerre mondiale*
(1961), 24

the crisis in agriculture presented opportunities, as for example for the Charentes, which changed from mediocre wine to good dairy, it also took a toll of victims unable to meet the challenges. In the course of the twentieth century, the regional disparities increased once again. Thus between 1892 and 1939 the yield of wheat per hectare over the whole of France rose from 12·6 to 15·4 quintals, but in fourteen departments it fell, and in another eight it remained static. The result was that in some cases modernisation widened the gap between the regions. Thus in 1954–5, the productivity of agriculture in the department of Aisne was 820,000 francs per worker, but in Creuse it was only between 300,000 and 350,000. In Aisne 36 kilograms of ferti- lisers were used, in Creuse 2·1. Figures of national averages are highly misleading. The graph opposite shows that agricultural production rose until 1892, remained static till 1939, and then rose again after the war. But if one looks at the statistics by department, one sees that while between 1852 and 1892 the national increase was from 100 to 185, in some departments it rose very much more, e.g. in Ille-et-Vilaine to 294, Mayenne 296, Creuse 320, and in some appreciably less, e.g. Nord 113 and Var 105. Again over the period 1892–1955, the figure for France as a whole was 98, but it was 46 in Saône-et-Loire, 48 in Vosges, and 260 in Pyrénées-Orientales. The Paris and nor- thern plains developed most rapidly in the first half of the nine- teenth century; in the second half of the century less favoured regions follow suit, eliminating fallow and waste. Mechanisation started in the north in the 1860s, but elsewhere only after the 1890s. The static market after 1892, however, meant that the differences between regions increased once more after that date and became almost as great in 1939 as they had been in 1848.[1]

Nor should it be thought that the traditional peasant was necessarily less well off than the modernising one. Laurence Wylie, in his highly instructive study of the village of Chan- zeaux, showed that the traditionalist probably did produce only half of what he could do by more modern methods, and he may have spent two months cutting down a hedge which a bulldozer would have dealt with in a day, but nevertheless he could end up with more money than the moderniser, if he had

[1] Jean Pantard, *Les Disparités régionales dans la croissance de l'agriculture française* (1965), 20, 43, 60.

a farm of the right size. He had no real inducement to modernise, because he earned an adequate living, obtained satisfaction
from his slower pace of work and from the freedom it gave him
to pause and waste time talking to passing friends. His young
neighbour, who had gone in for modernisation, was by contrast always on the run, and yet he was not making all that much
money out of it, because his farm was not really large enough.[1]
The structure of property and of farm areas did not develop
enough to make modernisation possible, except in certain regions.
It has been calculated that 15 hectares is the very minimum
necessary for a farm to yield any profit at all, and those under
this size survived because they used cheap family labour.[2]
Nevertheless such small farms did survive in great numbers as
this table shows:

Percentage of farms in *1892*, in *1929* and in *1955* having

1 hectare or less	39	25	6
1–5 hectares	32	29	29
5–10　　,,	14	18	21
10–20　　,, ⎫		15	24
20–50　　,, ⎬	15	10	16
50–100　,, ⎭		2	3
Over 100 ,,		1	1

The tiny plots have almost vanished. There were fewer small
farms, but not very many fewer: in 1892 three-quarters of farms
were under 10 hectares, in 1929 68 per cent were of this size
and in 1955 56 per cent. In 1929 only 29 per cent and in 1955
only 26 per cent of French agricultural land was in farms of over
50 hectares.[3]

The extent of the modernisation of agriculture should not be
exaggerated. In 1948–9 an able agronomist, René Dumont,
toured the country making detailed investigations into just
how far progress had gone, and his *Travels in France*, not unworthy of comparison with Arthur Young's, revealed very
forcefully how strong the obstacles to change were. For example, he went to the village of Saint-Chaffrey (Hautes-Alpes)

[1] L. Wylie, *Chanzeaux. A Village in Anjou* (Cambridge, Mass., 1966), 130–1. See
also another excellent book by him, *Village in the Vaucluse* (1961).
[2] J. Chombard de Lauwe, *Les Possibilités de la petite entreprise dans l'agriculture*
(1954).
[3] Barral, 224, 303.

and compared the reports on it made by an inquiry of 1857 with what he saw himself. The village was still divided into the same tiny plots. Agriculture was still mainly the concern of the women and children, for the men sought employment in various occupations in the surrounding region, as they had done a hundred years before. Yet the number of hours spent on extracting food from the soil was very high. This was genuinely primitive agriculture; barley and fallow alternated in some parts, as they had done in the middle ages. In the Queyras valley there was no additional employment to be had, so agriculture was the main activity, but it produced only just enough to feed the farmers and their animals; this was pure subsistence farming, with the surplus grain of good years never being sold, but hoarded to meet the deficits of bad years. North of Carcassonne he found perfectly ordinary vines being cultivated on terraces which required ten times more labour than vines planted in the plains. He witnessed the valiant efforts of the Nantes region to grow fruit and vegetables for export, in which they had long experience from the time of Louis-Philippe when they first planted William pears to sell in England. These had been ruined by American competition; peaches, melons and strawberries had replaced them, only to be ruined in turn by the cheaper produce of the Midi. They had then changed to tomatoes and celery, but they were less efficient, because less artificial, than the Dutch. Modern methods had not been adopted whole-heartedly enough for them to be successful on the international market. In Cavaillon (Vaucluse) he did find some very go-ahead market gardeners, climatically more favoured, constantly and successfully adapting their produce to the needs of the towns, but next door to them there were still peasants who maintained subsistence ideals and planted their market produce only as a side line. Near Wassy (Haute-Marne), the agricultural revolution had not taken place in 1929, when three-quarters of the soil was still left to fallow. The inhabitants survived only through incredibly hard work: the mortality and rapid ageing of peasants in this situation was a grim reminder of what was once common to most of the country. In Saint-Hilaire-des-Landes he found a family proud of having built its own house, as peasants regularly did in Eastern Europe, but particularly proud because theirs had two storeys, a feat formerly considered unattainable by any except the inhabitants of châteaux and cities: they felt they had, by this construction, raised themselves on the social ladder. Nearby, a *métayer* had refused to take advantage of the law of 1946 allowing him to transform his sharecropping contract into a cash tenancy, 'for fear of displeasing his landlord'. The provisions of other laws for the improvement of rented farm dwellings were similarly ignored: 'Social progress here', commented Dumont, 'almost needs to be *imposed* on those who would benefit from it.' In Elven (Morbihan), the changes which had occurred elsewhere in the eighteenth and nineteenth centuries were still continuing. The population had continued to grow until 1926, and to make room, the wastelands had been nibbled at steadily till then, but the soil was poor, and did not repay the enormous trouble taken over it. Subsistence farming was practised, but it fed the population only in good years. Most of the village was owned by a nobleman, so there was practically no land to buy. Prices were so high, because of the competition, that the bourgeoisie did not try to invest in land here. In 1938, when the rich plains of the Soissonnais cost less than 6,000 francs a hectare, the land at Elven, among the poorest in France, was selling at between 8,000 and 9,000 francs. Even in more prosperous Normandy, Dumont saw how the change to meat and milk production was carried out unscientifically. The French lagged way behind Denmark and Holland in productivity, for on the whole they preferred to go only half-way to modernisation, adopting extensive pasture, rather than intensive fodder. In Normandy this system simply used more labour than was necessary (and it was adopted perhaps in order to leave enough employment for the surviving peasants); but in the south pasture was disastrous, because it was often unusable in winter and dried out in summer.[1]

The inferiority of French agriculture, by comparison with other western countries, thus continued throughout these hundred years. In the 1850s, Léonce de Lavergne had pointed out how far it was behind England. At that period, he wrote, the 'most striking feature in English agriculture, as compared to ours, consists in the number and quality of its sheep'. England had about the same total number as France but living on one

[1] René Dumont, *Voyages en France d'un agronome* (2nd edition 1956).

third of the acreage; they were far larger, because meat was their primary aim, whereas wool was what they were kept for in France. Nevertheless the two countries produced roughly the same amount of wool, while England produced almost three times as much meat. France was inferior not only to England, but also to Scotland, and was judged just equal with Ireland. Again, France had 10 million cattle and the U.K. 8 million, which proportionately to the acreage gave England a considerable lead. France still used its cattle a great deal for labour, while England was interested mainly in milk and meat. Even cheese, said Lavergne, was superior in England (the cult of French cheese is more recent).[1] England produced twice as much milk as France. 'The art of rearing cattle for butcher-meat only is scarcely known in France.' England also had more horses and pigs. France was superior only in poultry, producing about eight times in value as much as England; this partly made up for what France lacked in butcher-meat. France of course was the largest producer of wheat in Western Europe, but the concentration on this was exhausting its soil and its yields were appreciably below England's.[2]

In 1939, French prices for wheat were 45 per cent higher than England's, because of low yields, small-scale farming and inadequate use of fertilisers. Where machinery was used, it was largely in harvesting, rather than in cultivation, and in the south ploughing by oxen, or even cows, still continued. The milk yield in France was the lowest in Western Europe, largely because of inadequate feeding: France used less oil cake than

[1] France imported more cheese than it exported: in 1909–13 49 million lbs. as against 32 million exported. But the French (in the 1920s) were consuming three times as much cheese as the Americans, who, however, ate almost twice as much butter. See T. R. Pirtle, *History of the Dairy Industry* (Chicago, Ill., 1926). For the growth of industrialised cheese making, under the control of the cheese merchants, see G. Tellier, *L'Industrie fromagère de Roquefort* (Albi, 1926). But, at least in the 1950s, Roquefort was a small industry. Out of a total production of 375,000 tons of cheese in 1951, Gruyère and Emmenthal accounted for 90,000 tons, Camembert for 85,000 tons, but no other one kind produced more than 20,000. O.E.C.D., *Organisation and Structure of the Milk Markets in O.E.C.D. Member Countries* (1963), 274. Margarine, invented by a Frenchman in 1869, was used in France before 1939 mainly to adulterate butter. J. H. van Stuyvenberg, *Margarine: An Economic, Social and Scientific History 1869–1969* (Liverpool, 1969), 319.

[2] Léonce de Lavergne, *The Rural Economy of England, Scotland and Ireland* (English translation, 1855). Cf. W. King, Earl of Lovelace, *Review of the Agricultural Statistics of France* (1848).

Denmark, although it had five times as many cows. Most of
its milk was produced in very small herds; only 0·4 per cent
of cows had their milk yield recorded, even though state subsidies were available for recording societies. About one-fifth of
the dairy herd was believed to suffer from tuberculosis; some
claimed the proportion was much larger. Breeding was difficult
because of the enormous variety of breeds, so that in the
Pyrenees there was almost a different breed in every valley.
Much progress had been made in Normandy and the Charentes,
but these areas were still backward by European standards.
Poultry keeping was still where it had been a hundred years
before: in the Côte-d'Or the yield per hen was estimated at
only 60 eggs per annum, of which about half were laid in the
three months of February, March and April. France was the
only country in Western Europe (except Italy, not included
in these comparisons) whose livestock still provided less than
half of its total agricultural output. France had maintained
a balance between its agricultural activities, but at the expense
of being unable to compete in the world markets. Its backwardness should not, however, be exaggerated. The standard
of living of the German peasant was roughly the same; in the
large areas of poor soil he had to work longer hours to achieve
it; his diet was less varied; he seldom had a car; though on the
other hand his housing was definitely better than his French
counterpart's: there was no sleeping in cowsheds.[1]

Peasants in all industrialising countries had cause for complaint. The share of the national revenue which they received
fell everywhere in the twentieth century. Thus in the U.S.A.
it fell from 20 to 7½ per cent between 1900 and 1960. In France,
over the same period, it fell from 35 to 12 per cent, but it was no
consolation that this was an international phenomenon. In
France, the peasants felt the losses more, because their numbers had fallen less than elsewhere. The peasants were conscious that they had to produce more and more goods in order
to buy the same amount of industrial goods; their efforts to be
like other men, to enjoy the same standard of living, were constantly thwarted. Thus in 1955 agricultural products had only
two-thirds of the purchasing power they had had in 1914 and
half of that of 1865–75. Between 1945 and 1958 production

[1] P. L. Yates, *Food Production in Western Europe* (1940).

increased by 25 per cent, but the peasant's income rose only 4 per cent, while the income of the rest of the country rose by 46 per cent. This agricultural income was moreover very unequally distributed, because 56 per cent of farms enjoyed less than 20 per cent of it, while a mere 8 per cent had a third of it. In 1956 the annual average expenditure of all French households was 253,800 francs, but that of agricultural households was only 194,000 francs while rural households not in agriculture spent 216,000 and urban households 283,800. In the centre and west of France agricultural expenditure was as low as 182,000. The peasants were thus forced to spend 10 per cent less on food, 28 per cent less on clothes and 50 per cent less on culture and leisure than their urban counterparts. In 1960 only 16 per cent of secondary-school pupils had peasants as parents, as against 21 per cent who had workers. Only 55 per cent of rural communes had running water (in some departments only 20 to 30 per cent); only 2 per cent had baths or showers, as against 15 per cent in the towns. The peasants suffered more from tuberculosis, but they had only half the doctors the towns had.[1]

It can now be asked whether these diminishing returns, this record of failure in the economic rat race, and the awareness of falling status produced a sense of unity or class consciousness among the peasants. The answer seems to be definitely that it did not. All students of rural conditions are agreed that the divisions among the peasantry not only remained but even multiplied; and indeed they have proposed a large number of different classifications. At the time of the Second World War the peasants were certainly still very much differentiated by the way they lived, by the kind of houses they occupied, and by their patterns of settlement in hamlets, villages or *bourgs*. They had different attitudes according to the type of their economy: the polycultural peasant of the Garonne, the cattle farmer of Normandy, the winegrower of the Hérault, the market gardener of Roussillon, the mountain peasant of the Pyrenees or the Cantal, the wheat farmer of the Beauce were different types with different problems. Some were still subsistence farmers, others were not. A map has been produced, showing the extent of 'autoconsumption' of wheat, which gives some indication of the

[1] Jean Maynaud, *La Révolte paysanne* (1963), 17–37, 88.

survival of the former class. No one has properly discovered just how much of this autoconsumption there was, though an economist has produced a figure of about 23 per cent of total production for 1938.[1] Maps can also show the striking regional variations in the use of credit, fertilisers and machinery. Again owners, tenant farmers, sharecroppers and labourers were not easy to unite; and each of these, moreover, had different relations with other classes. In the west they often accepted nobles as mayors (but not always). In some regions the peasants were democratic, in others they combined this with acceptance of the Church, in some they were divided by the religious issue; in some areas they accepted traditional hierarchies, in others they were dominated by the rivalries of clans and clienteles, and in still others the capitalist invasion placed them in situations not unlike those of industrial workers. The peasants have never all voted for the same political party.[2] When the scientific analysis of voting behaviour made possible detailed study of their politics, it was found, in 1956, that about 20 per cent of them voted moderate, 17 per cent communist, 14 per cent socialist, 12 per cent M.R.P. and 14 per cent Poujadist—which was not very different from the way the towns voted. The claim, which Halbwachs made in 1939, that the peasants found their unity in one thing, their hostility to the towns, cannot be accepted, at least in this simple form.[3]

The peasants were particularly slow in finding a voice to express their grievances. The people who spoke in the name of agriculture in the nineteenth century were not peasants. Méline was from an industrial region; and the vast majority of ministers of agriculture were barristers and doctors. The Society of French Farmers, founded in 1868 by a professor of the National Agronomic Institute was presided over in turn by Drouyn de Lhuys, formerly Napoleon III's foreign minister, by the marquis Élie de Dampierre, who had large estates in the south-west, and by the marquis de Voguë, who combined this task with the presidency of the Suez Canal Company, St. Gobain and the French Red Cross. It was a powerful pressure group but it

[1] André de Cambiaire, *L'Autoconsommation agricole en France* (1952), 178.
[2] For further details see chapter 14.
[3] Cf. H. Mendras, 'Diversité des sociétés rurales françaises' in J. Fauvet and H. Mendras, *Les Paysans et la politique dans la France contemporaine* (1958), 23–35.

PEASANTS   191

acted above all in the interests of the large farmers. It encouraged the formation of trade unions among the peasants, but
it successfully kept these absorbed in purely commercial activities, notably the purchase of fertilisers. It did a good deal to
prolong the influence of the nobles in the provinces, particularly
where the nobles decided to opt out of politics and try this new
approach. This was one reason why the agricultural trade
union movement flourished in Finistère, but not in the neighbouring Côtes-du-Nord, for in the latter the nobles continued
to pursue the parliamentary seats. The Society of Farmers was
powerful enough to incite Gambetta to found a rival National
Society for the Encouragement of Agriculture, designed to unite
the smaller farmers and to be an instrument for the spread of
republican doctrine. Thus the animosities of politics were
exacerbated by new frictions at the professional level. When
other unions, co-operatives and mutual insurance societies were
established, under a variety of stimuli, they were immediately
infiltrated if not taken over by the government or the politicians.
Laws were passed, amid much rhetoric, instituting subsidies
and credit banks to assist the peasants, but these benefits were
distributed on strict principles of favouritism. Local politicians,
particularly senators, became secretaries of the co-operatives
and mutual organisations in their constituencies so as to bolster
their electoral hold. The peasants, of course, were not keen on
paying their subscriptions, and in any case the law made it
difficult for their organisations to build up funds. None of these
groups therefore became a real danger to the state.[1]

However, they were important in laying the foundations
for some forms of common action. The peasants had long
traditions of mutual assistance, and in some regions even of
organised co-operation in farming. The nineteenth century was
in some ways a gap, a period in which these traditions were
suppressed while the peasants struggled for ownership of the
land; but towards the end of it there was some revival of the
co-operation. By 1941, 57 per cent of fertilisers used in France
were bought through peasant co-operatives. This did not mean
all that much, since so little fertiliser was used. The new dairy
industry was perhaps the most ready to adopt co-operation. In
Charente-Inférieure, 80 per cent of dairymen belonged to some

[1] Comte de Rocquigny, *Les Syndicats agricoles et leur œuvre* (1900).

form of marketing organisation in 1937. But by 1952, over the country as a whole, only 20 per cent of milk producers were co-operators. At the same time, 12 per cent of winegrowers were co-operators.[1] In 1910 there were about 110 co-operatives for the sharing of agricultural equipment, by 1920 500, by 1939 2,090 and 13,000 in 1967. The statistics, of doubtful reliability, which the leaders of these organisations proudly quoted, are not particularly impressive. Co-operation was definitely a minority movement, affecting mainly specialised growers and certain regions. Moreover, closer scrutiny of the way the co-operatives worked reveals that the idealism of the leaders was not very widely shared. It was a common practice to sell to the co-operatives products of inferior quality and reserve the best and most profitable part of the harvest for the merchants. The amount of co-operation in some cases was fairly limited: in the manufacture of Gruyère cheese, for example, some co-operatives were simply formed to buy equipment, which they then rented out to an individual who did all the cheese making and selling for his own profit; others manufactured collectively, but allowed each member to sell his own share; only some both manufactured and sold for the common benefit. Since many of these peasant organisations were led by conservatives, their aim was seldom to be revolutionary, to abolish the normal channels of commerce: rather they acted as watchdogs on the merchants and stepped in only when these failed. In sparsely populated regions co-operatives were often more expensive to run than private enterprise, because they continued to maintain numerous small uneconomic depots. In most cases the peasants were unwilling to assume the leadership of these co-operatives, because they had no leisure, or did not think it worth while to spare the time. The organisation was therefore in the hands of bureaucrats, nobles or clergymen; the central staff ran the services; and the peasants rejected any collective discipline. For example, they refused to stagger their sales of grain, preferring to make the best bargains they could. The return to collective agriculture was very slight indeed.[2]

[1] Producing 22 per cent of all *vin ordinaire* in France, 42 per cent of *qualité supérieure*, and 25 per cent of *appellation contrôlée*.

[2] André Hirschfeld, *La Coopération agricole en France* (1957); Jacob Baker *et al.*, *Report of the Inquiry on Cooperative Enterprise in Europe* (Washington D.C., 1937), 144–7; P. Boisseau, *Les Agriculteurs et l'entraide* (1968), 35; *André Cramois, Coopératives*

There were occasions when the peasants expressed their wrath or their resentments in spontaneous outbursts. The recapturing in 1848 of pastures and forests once held in common, the demonstrations and refusals to pay tax by the wine-growers in 1907 are examples. But there were also, after 1890, instances of protest with a certain amount of organisation. The impoverished woodcutters of the Centre formed 170 trade unions by the First World War and waged several strikes with some success, against the merchants who kept them on the very margin of survival.[1] The gardeners and labourers of the Paris region and the workers of the vineyards in the south formed unions which had much in common with industrial ones. The sharecroppers of Bourbonnais sprouted a few remarkable leaders of their own, organised themselves in protest against the more vexatious aspects of their leases, and even elected a deputy to parliament, though he was a primary-school master.[2] These were all, however, limited and local efforts, mainly affecting marginal groups. More significant was the penetration into the leadership of the general agricultural trade union movement, between the wars, of a 'new bourgeois peasantry', farmers with secondary education. The Church also played an important part in the democratisation of peasant organisations. Abbé Trochu, though frowned on by the hierarchy, founded and ran a highly successful newspaper in Rennes, L'Ouest-Éclair, between 1899 and 1930, in the name of Christian Democracy. This paper became the daily with the largest circulation in the west, and was backed up by half a dozen weeklies. Assisted by three other priests, Mancel, Geffriaud and Crublet, he stimulated the formation of some 200 unions, at the village level, with subsidiary youth groups, which effectively challenged the older unions run by the aristocrats. Brittany, partly as a result of

agricoles. Pourquoi et comment le paysan français est devenu coopérateur (n.d., about 1948); International Cooperative Alliance, Cooperation in the European Market Economies (1967), for comparative statistics see appendix; Susanne D. Berger, Peasants against Politics. Rural Organisation in Finistère (Harvard Ph.D. thesis, 1966), a stimulating, critical investigation based on fieldwork.

[1] M. Roblin, Les Bûcherons de la Nièvre (Paris thesis, 1903); R. Braque, 'Aux origines du syndicalisme dans les milieux ruraux de centre', in Le Mouvement social (Jan.–Mar. 1963), 79–116; and René Bazin, Le Blé qui lève (1907).

[2] L. Lamoureux, Les Syndicats agricoles (1914); A. Hodée, Les Jardiniers (1928); G. Rister, Le Travailleur agricole français (1923); Y. Tavernier, Le Syndicalisme paysan (1969).

this, was to become one of the strongest bastions of peasant agitation. On a national level, the Catholic Agricultural Youth movement (J.A.C.), founded in 1929, did a great deal to transform the attitudes of the new generation. René Colson, a peasant from the Haute-Marne who was its secretary general from 1942 to 1948, created a new style of forward-looking organisation, which was to bear fruit in the 1960s: his influence has been likened to that which Pelloutier had on the urban workers at the turn of the century.[1]

It was not the peasants themselves who formed the first peasant party. The *Parti agraire et paysan français* (so called to show that it stood both for the proprietors and the labourers) was founded in 1928 by a colourful schoolmaster, Fleurant, who preferred to call himself Agricola, assisted by two barristers. They were said to have obtained financial support from the richest wheat merchant in France, Louis-Dreyfus. They certainly had the backing of advertisers, whose announcements, incorporated into the film shows they held at the end of their public meetings, were a profitable source of revenue. They did not rival the traditional agricultural unions, even though they quarrelled with them about tactics. In the elections of 1936 they won eight seats, but then withered away in internal dissensions. They showed what could be done if the peasant flag was raised, but were too conservative and compromising to make a real impact on the peasant world. More significant was the *Défense Paysanne*. This was not the creation of a peasant either. Henri d'Halluin, who preferred to call himself Dorgères, was a journalist and the son of a butcher. As editor of a small farmers' newspaper at Rennes, he had specialised in discovering mistakes in the *cadastre* and obtaining tax reductions for his readers. He began holding public meetings to protest against more general grievances, at first on Sundays and then more frequently, until in 1936 he and his associates were organising as many as 400 a month. His enormous vitality—he was in his early thirties— and his gift for attracting publicity won him a sizeable following. He claimed that by 1939 his various newspapers had 410,000 subscribers, mainly in the west and north. He organised these

---

[1] Gordon Wright, *Rural Revolution in France* (1964), is an excellent history of peasant movements since 1930. Cf. Paul Delourme, *Trente-Cinq Ans de politique religieuse* (1936).

followers in an unusually effective way. He knew how to use
large crowds of peasants to put pressure on the state. He told
them to bring their pitchforks with them and to distinguish
themselves with green shirts; and he was not afraid of violence.
He came to employ no less than sixty people to help him in his
organisation, and most of these were genuine peasants, like, for
example, François Coire, who had been an agricultural labourer,
but who had the prestige of having won the Military Medal
during the war, when he was twice promoted sergeant and
twice demoted for his *mauvaise tête*. In 1936 Dorgères united
with Agricola to form the Peasant Front, which waged battles
against the strikers of the towns. The achievement Dorgères
claimed for himself, and with which he explained his success,
was that he created a new peasant pride, destroying the
inferiority complex that had been almost universal among
the peasantry; but in any case he certainly contributed to the
formation of a belief among some of the peasants that they
had the ability to get their complaints listened to by agitation,
demonstration and on occasion violent pressure. It cannot be
conceded that he made them feel really integrated in the state,
because the state was the great enemy for him, together with
the large capitalist trusts. He had no sophisticated programme,
though he wrote able books expounding his doctrine. Pétain,
whom he hailed as the 'Peasant Marshal', astutely appointed
him director of peasant propaganda. Dorgères was disappointed
with Vichy, but was nevertheless convicted of collaboration
after the war. He then founded an advertising agency, whose
profits enabled him, at the age of 55, to buy a newspaper and
start a new movement. He ended up in alliance with Poujade.[1]

The Vichy regime made it possible for the peasants to take
the really decisive step. The corporatist theory, which several
peasant leaders, and notably Louis Salleron, had taken up as
the cure for their troubles, was now officially adopted and a
law was passed setting up a Peasant Corporation to institution-
alise peasant unity. Every village was required to form a single
syndicate, and to elect representatives to regional and national

[1] Henri Dorgères, *Au XXᵉ siècle, dix ans de Jacquerie* (1959), interesting memoirs,
id., *Haut les fourches* (1935), and *Révolution paysanne* (1943); J. M. Royer, 'De
Dorgères à Poujade', in J. Fauvet and H. Mendras, *Les Paysans et la politique*
(1958), 149–206.

committees. This had a very important effect on peasant politics. 'Peasants of France', said Caziot, the farmer and expert on land values whom Pétain chose as his minister of agriculture, 'you used to be masters of your land, but your power too often stopped at the boundaries of your farms. You will now have control over your own profession and you will be able to act over a much vaster area, in a position of equality with the other professions. So the inferiority complex, which you always feel, and which placed agriculture below other occupations, will disappear.'[1] How far this was achieved is debatable. But the compulsory merger of the rival unions which had divided villages was in many cases permanent. Though animosities were not ended, the possibility of united action was at last appreciated. The peasants were also forced to elect 30,000 syndics, and these were to provide much of the leadership which was active after the war. The idea that the peasants themselves must carry out their own revolution came to have real meaning. Vichy's Peasant Corporation was unsuccessful in many ways, but it was more successful than its other corporations because it was the most democratic. It has a significant place in peasant history.[2]

In 1945, however, power still eluded the peasants, as it had done in 1848. National politics, indeed, was still foreign to many of them. They were often passionately interested in municipal affairs, but party labels did not always mean the same thing to them as to the rest of the nation. To look at election results to discover what they thought is to beg the question. The peasants had not discovered how to implement their demands, partly because they were still so divided and unclear about them, and partly also because their practical concerns could only with difficulty be inserted into the party programmes overladen with ideological commitments. Few of them got elected to parliament. In 1889, out of a chamber of 576 deputies, there was not a single working peasant, though 131 large landowners, 10 medium-sized owners, 3 veterinaries, 1 agronomist and some thirty barristers and businessmen with

---

[1] P. Caziot in *La Vie de la France sous l'occupation 1940–4* (1957), 1, 264.

[2] L. Salleron, *La Corporation paysanne* (1943) and *Naissance de l'état corporatif* (1942); Michel Cépède, *Agriculture et alimentation en France durant la deuxième guerre mondiale* (1961).

sizeable rural properties meant that the agricultural interest had about 30 per cent of the seats. By 1910 that figure had fallen to 18 per cent, and after 1924 it was as low as 11 to 13 per cent. By then the number of large landowners in parliament declined but they were replaced mainly by well-to-do medium ones.[1] The peasants did not step into the nobles' shoes. Their world was still a separate one.

[1] J. Fauvet and H. Mendras, 215.

10. Workers

The Worker and the Law

THE proletariat, in this period, were frequently talked of as outcasts of society, 'the dangerous classes', the pariahs. The limits on their freedom were very considerable. Investigators of their conditions were still saying in the early twentieth century that, 'without exaggeration', the rights of employers over them were 'heavier than those the feudal lords had over their serfs in the Middle Ages'.[1] Their legal position deserves to be examined, before one looks at how they themselves coped with their situation.

The French Revolution had done little for the worker.[2] He was given the right to practise any trade he pleased—the corporations were abolished—but subject to important and humiliating restrictions. He had to possess a *livret*—a certificate bearing his name, description and place of employment. He was forbidden to change his job until his master certified he was free of debt and obligations to him. Since it was very common for workers to receive loans in hard times from their employers, they could be effectively prevented from changing jobs by unscrupulous masters. If the employer agreed to the worker leaving, he could inscribe the amount owed to him in the *livret*, and the next employer was required to refund that sum to him in instalments, by withholding a proportion of the man's wages. The *livret* had to be held only by industrial workers, not by self-employed artisans nor by peasants, and was thus doubly discriminatory. It had its origins in the *ancien régime*, which had used something similar, as the decree of 1781 stated, 'to maintain subordination among workers in manufacturing districts'. Napoleon had required every worker, on leaving his job, to have his *livret* signed by the employer and

---

[1] D. Poulot, *Le Sublime* (1870); Léon and Maurice Bonneff, *La Vie tragique des travailleurs. Enquêtes sur la condition économique et morale des ouvriers et ouvrières d'industrie* (n.d., about 1908), 29.

[2] Roger Picard, *Les Cahiers de 1789 au point de vue industriel et commercial* (Paris thesis, 1910).

also by the mayor, who would insert in it the town to which
the worker stated he was moving. It thus served as a sort of
passport and a worker found that without one he would be
liable to imprisonment as a vagabond. But Napoleon failed to
match these sanctions on recalcitrant workers by penalties for
employers who ignored the law and in practice many employers
did not bother. (Some on the other hand took it upon themselves to inscribe comments about the worker in the *livret*,
which could damage his chances of future employment.)

In 1845 a bill was introduced to impose sanctions and make
it really effective, and in 1854 a law was finally passed to
reinvigorate the institution. Employers were instructed to
insist on *livrets*; all industrial workers, working in factories or at
home for an employer, and for the first time women too, were
required to have them. In Paris a police ordinance in addition
required employers to have the *livret* of every worker they took
on stamped with a visa by the police within twenty-four hours.
Nevertheless once again the law was only partially enforced—
mainly in large factories employing itinerant labour—but the
politically conscious workers protested violently against it,
as a *loi d'exception*. The mason-deputy Nadaud said they had
one foot chained to the police, and the other to the capitalist.
The liberal empire in 1870 proposed to abolish the whole
system, but fell before it could do so. It was only in 1890 that
the law finally ceased to look upon the industrial worker as a
dangerous person, needing careful surveillance.[1]

The workers were not deceived by the myth propagated by
the bourgeoisie that the Civil Code was egalitarian. Thiers
declared that the Civil Code was impossible to improve—at
most he could suggest only a few stylistic changes. Troplong,
First President of the Cour de Cassation, and author of the
leading commentary on the Civil Code (in 28 volumes, 1833–
58) 'justly named Troplong', revealingly declared himself
satisfied with it because he considered that democracy existed
when men have an equal right to the protection of the law 'in

[1] Alexandre Plantier, *Le Livret des ouvriers* (Paris thesis, 1900). The Second
Republic in 1851 limited the master's privileged position as creditor to 30 francs, and
the instalments repayable to 10 per cent of the wage. Despite its abolition in 1890,
the *livret* was reported to have survived in certain parts of the Nord nearly
twenty years later. L. and M. Bonneff, *La Vie tragique des travailleurs* (n.d., about
1908), 23–8.

conditions of inequality which they have created for themselves by the legitimate exercise of their natural powers'. The Civil Code certainly confirmed these inequalities. It had a narrow view of citizenship, which it confused with the possession of property, and so it made the penniless worker almost an outlaw. It was principally concerned not with making men equal but with protecting property. It contained numerous articles about contracts of sale, exchange and lease; it had as many as thirty-one articles about the legal position of rented livestock, but only two articles on the worker and his relations with his employers; and both of these were taken over from the *ancien régime*. The first stated that the services of a worker or servant could be engaged only for a definite period or task—a banal repetition of the abolition of serfdom. The second (article 1781) stated that in a dispute about wages, the word of the master was to be preferred to that of the worker in the absence of written records—just as article 1716 stated that in a dispute about rent, the word of the landlord was to be preferred to that of the tenant. The republican Garnier-Pagès might expostulate in 1847 against Guizot's 'detestable theory that there are different classes, the bourgeoisie and the poor class' and he might insist that 'there are no longer any classes . . . in France, there are only French citizens'. This was not true, even after 1848 when the masses were officially made citizens. Article 1781, as a result of repeated protests by the workers, was repealed in 1868. The workers, however, continued to complain that not only were they treated as inferiors on the few occasions they were mentioned in the Civil Code, but that even worse they were ignored by it. The law protected the bourgeoisie's property against thieves, but it did not protect workers against exploiters of their labour. 'We wish to cease to be helots in a nation of sybarites.'[1]

The Conseils de Prud'hommes, established by Napoleon to

---

[1] E. Glasson, 'Le Code Civil et la question ouvrière' in *Séances et Travaux de l'Académie des Sciences morales et politiques*, 25 (1886), 843–95; Albert Tissier, 'Le Code Civil et les classes ouvrières' in *Le Code Civil, Livre du Centenaire* published by the Société d'Études législatives (1904), i. 73 ff.; Pierre Lavigne, *Le Travail dans les constitutions françaises 1789–1945* (1948); G. and H. Bourgin, *Les Patrons, les ouvriers et l'état: le régime de l'industrie en France de 1814 à 1830* (1912–41). Cf. Daphne Simon, 'Master and Servant' in John Saville, *Democracy and the Labour Movement* (1954).

reconcile minor disputes between master and man, were likewise for long weighted against the worker. The members of
these conciliation tribunals were elected, partly by the employers and partly by workers of the town in which they functioned; but the employers were given a majority of seats, and
the only workers who had the vote were the *patentés*, a small
minority. The dissatisfied worker who appealed to them was
thus appealing to his superiors, not his equals. Even so these
courts were popular, because they were extremely cheap (a
case could cost between 30 centimes and 1 franc 75) and no
lawyers were involved. Founded originally in 1806 to settle
small day-to-day disputes in the Lyon silk industry about the
quality of work done and the rates of payment—matters which
required technical knowledge not possessed by ordinary judges
—they were gradually extended to some other industries,
mainly textiles and metals, and to other towns:

	Number of Conseils de Prud'hommes	Number of cases dealt with by them
1830	53	11,000
1848	71	18,000
1852	83	40,000
1870	109	30,000
1892	146	52,000

During the Second Republic they had been very busy because
for a few years the workers obtained the majority of the seats.
A law of 27 May 1848 gave the vote to all workers, not just
patentés, and allocated to their representatives the same number
of seats as to the employers. This was an obviously necessary
reform. But the law carried the workers' victory too far, for it
classified foremen and *chefs d'atelier* (artisans employing a few
others) as employers and so greatly reduced the representation
of the larger factory owner. Napoleon III reclassified these men
as workers in 1853 and angered the workers even more by
arrogating to the administration the right to appoint the president and vice-president of the councils—who were in effect
invariably chosen from among the wealthiest employers. When
the Third Republic in 1880 gave up this right and allowed the
councils to elect their own presidents, the employers frequently

lost their office when they did not all attend to vote. In protest they took to boycotting the whole institution. In Lille in particular the councils ceased to function for several years. The trade unions took to organising the elections to them, demanding a promise from those they supported always to decide in favour of the worker. The employers argued that the councils had ceased to be fair, and were out of date besides, for they no longer dealt with technical matters but with disputes which ordinary judges could well decide, if only their procedure were less cumbersome: three-quarters of the councils' cases in 1892 concerned wages. Many workers, however, considered this institution as potentially very valuable, as a first step to greater equality between master and man. Numerous bills were introduced into parliament to reform and extend it. A few got passed by the deputies but were rejected by the senate.

In 1905 finally a law allowed appeals from them to go to the ordinary law courts (*tribunal civil*): previously appeals were to the *tribunaux de commerce*, composed exclusively of employers. A law of 1907 restored the procedure of the Second Republic, that employers and workers were to take it in turn to be president—so ending the bitterness caused by the system of free election established in 1880. Women workers were given the vote but, in the face of the senate's opposition, were not eligible to serve as councillors, even though a great number of cases concerned women. The law allowed the establishment of councils for other industries—notably mines, transport and commerce—but (again owing to the senate's opposition) not agriculture. The workers had long clamoured for this, and for more councillors, so that each trade could have its representatives on the councils. Councils were henceforth to be established not at the government's pleasure but in every town which wanted one. Foremen were to vote as employers or as workers depending on whether they were principally engaged in surveillance or in the physical execution of the work—a compromise reached after the deputies had classified them as employers and the senate as workers. The reforms were rounded off by the issue of medals to all councillors as insignia of office and the promise of further decorations as rewards for long service. It thus took almost exactly a century of argument to establish equality between master and man in these conciliation tribunals.[1]

Again, workers were treated differently from their employers when they combined. They were liable to much higher penalties than them—a maximum of five years' imprisonment as against only one month's imprisonment or a fine for employers. Once the convicted workers had served their sentence they were in addition liable to a further two to five years of police surveillance. Moreover, employers were guilty of the offence of combination only when they tried to reduce wages 'unjustly and abusively', whereas the workers committed a crime however just their demands. The inequality in penalties was ended in 1849 (law of 15 November–1 December) but in practice the discrimination against the worker continued. The prohibition of all trade associations had been made in 1791 in the name of liberty. Rousseau taught that intermediary bodies between the individual and the state were undesirable, and the theory of *laissez-faire* opposed any combination which might hinder the free working of the economy. Though these theories and this justification might have been new, successive governments after the Revolution were merely continuing the practice of the *ancien régime*, of consistently suppressing workers' unions. By contrast, intermediary associations of employers were tolerated and even recognised. Chambres de Commerce had over the years been established in 70 or 80 towns; elected by merchants, they represented them in dealings with the state, giving their views on legislation and organising works and services of common interest. Industrial towns had similar bodies known as chambres consultatives des arts et métiers. These bodies were represented on the national conseil général du commerce and the conseil général des manufactures—partly elected and partly appointed by the government. The workers, by contrast, were allowed no similar organisations and they frequently complained that they were not consulted by the government.

Unions of employers were not recognised by the state, but they were tolerated and the reigns of Louis-Philippe and

---

[1] Robert Baffos, 'La Prud'homie, son évolution' (Paris thesis, 1908); Émile Mallard, *Des Conseils de Prud'hommes. Étude de la loi du 27 mars 1907* (Poitiers thesis, 1912); E. Cleiftie, *Les conseils de Prud'hommes. Leur organisation et leur fonctionnement au point de vue économique et social* (Paris thesis, 1898).

Napoleon III were remarkable for the rise of numerous private employers' organisations. Already under the Restoration local associations of iron masters and of silk merchants had been formed; in 1832 the sugar manufacturers established a committee to safeguard their beet sugar against colonial imports; in 1835 the Committee of Industrialists of the east of France was formed to maintain the protection of the textile industry; in 1840 three committees appeared, of metallurgical interests, machine constructors and colliery owners. In 1846 these various industries were successfully brought together into one Association pour la Défense du Travail National, to counter the activities of the free traders. Its president was Odier, peer of France, a textile manufacturer of the Vosges; its vice-president and principal organiser was Auguste Mimerel, president of the official conseil général des manufacturers; its secretary was Joseph Lebœuf, porcelain and pottery manufacturer and regent of the Bank of France; its treasurer was Joseph Périer (brother of Casimir) of the Anzin mines. It published a newspaper, *Le Moniteur Industriel*, which flourished thanks to plentiful advertising revenue. It was an acknowledged pressure group throughout the Second Empire and was particularly active in organising opposition to Napoleon III's free trade policy. The best-known organisation, the Comité des Forges, which discreetly traced its history back to only 1864, was in existence for some time before this and was only one of a number of employers' associations.

The smaller employers had their unions too. In 1873 it was estimated that there were a hundred of these unions in Paris and between 140 and 160 in the provinces. There were also federations of small employers' unions. In Paris in 1858 Pascal Bonnin, a lawyer, had founded a Union Nationale des Chambres Syndicales, which by 1874 grouped 70 employers' unions in the capital. It published a profitable newspaper, organised insurance schemes, information services, petitions to the government on taxation and legislation. It won control of the elections to the Tribunal de Commerce and this official court recognised it even if the government did not. The Tribunal de Commerce referred many commercial disputes to it for arbitration and settlement. The employers' unions were, however, divided and a second federation, called the Comité Central, was organised as a rival by F. Lévy; there was apparently a third minor federation too. The employers thus set the pattern for the workers in their organisations and in their divisions. To a certain extent they even stimulated the workers to unite by their example: this is specifically stated by several workers in the International Exhibition Report of 1862.[1]

The prohibition on workers' unions was abolished in several stages, with hesitations, delays and reservations which repeatedly deprived the government of any credit among the working classes for its concessions. In 1848 the Provisional Government published a declaration that workers had not only a right to unite but a duty to do so, 'to enjoy the legitimate benefit of their work'; but no sooner was their appetite whetted than the old restrictions on clubs, societies and meetings were restored and savagely enforced. Matters were back to where they had started, except that all combinations by employers or workers were to be equally penalised, whether they were 'unjust' or not (27 November 1849). Later Napoleon III, disliking the harsh sentences of imprisonment passed on workers, and particularly the compositors, for striking in a perfectly peaceful manner, issued numerous reprieves and then ordered new legislation on strikes. By the law of 25 May 1864 the offence of combination ceased to be known to the law. But though strikes now became legal, trade unions remained illegal, and the right to strike, moreover, was limited in two ways. First the use of violence, threats or fraudulent manœuvres in the organisation of a strike was severely punished, more severely than, e.g., in elections. The intention of the main author of this law, Émile Ollivier, was not to allow strikes of the traditional kind, but somehow to transform strikes into a peaceful parley, in preparation for their gradual disappearance from the ideal harmonious society of which he dreamt. Secondly strikers who impinged on the liberties of blacklegs, who interfered, that is, with the 'right to work', were likewise to be severely punished. This law had a didactic, moralising character which made it both impracticable and unpopular. It displeased both employers and workers; and prosecutions for infringing the liberty to work were henceforth almost as numerous as the old prosecutions for combining. But the law was a great step forward none the less and a remarkable achievement for its author, whose

[1] Roger Prioret, *Origines du patronat français* (1963).

idealistic infatuation alone carried it through, for Napoleon had begun to waver in the face of the mounting opposition to it.[1]

In 1868 the imperial government publicly promised to tolerate workers' unions in the same way as it did those of employers—but the reactionary governments which followed the Commune put an end to this temporary suspension of the law. It was only in 1884, after some eight years of intermittent debate, that trade unions were finally legalised. The men who carried this law wished to free the workers, but they also, like Ollivier, had hopes of changing their habits. This law therefore contained restrictions, complications and omissions. But many of its results were unexpected.[2]

Trade unions could henceforth be formed without any special government authorisation provided a copy of the statutes and a list of its officials were deposited at the town hall. This at once made many workers suspicious of the whole law, declaring it to be a police measure, though in fact it ended the police's right to attend every meeting. A good number of unions refused to register and remained technically illegal: some were in consequence dissolved when they came in contact with the courts. The trade union must consist only of men exercising similar professions or professions working together to produce the same goods: this excluded union leaders as soon as they became full-time paid officials—another pretext the courts could use to dissolve them. Thirdly, the unions must limit their activities to the study and defence of economic, industrial, commercial and agricultural interests. This meant they could not engage in politics. In practice of course the prohibition was seldom enforced, but it was resented as yet another threat suspended over the unions. There were occasional prosecutions, as for example when the president of the union of waiters and restaurateurs of Meurthe-et-Moselle was fined 50 francs for urging his

[1] T. Zeldin, *Émile Ollivier and the Liberal Empire of Napoleon III* (Oxford, 1963), 79–85; F. D. Longe, 'The Law of Trade Combinations in France' in *Fortnightly Review* (1867), 220–5 and 296–309; H. Ferrette, *Manuel de législation industrielle* (1909); Émile Ollivier, *Commentaire de la loi du 25 mai 1864 sur les coalitions* (1864); P. L. Fournier, *Le Second Empire et la législation ouvrière* (Paris thesis, 1911).

[2] Isidore Finance, *Les Syndicats professionnels devant les tribunaux et le parlement depuis 1884* (1911); J. Beslier, *Les Syndicats professionnels, leur capacité d'après la loi du 21 mars 1884* (Caen Thesis, 1911); Aimé Chevron, *Les Syndicats professionnels devant la justice* (Bordeaux thesis, Barbezieux, 1909); Pierre Aubry, *Des Syndicats professionnels. Étude historique, juridique et économique de la loi du 21 mars 1884* (Nancy thesis, 1899).

members to vote in a certain way at a municipal council election. But more frequently this limitation was used against religious propaganda—as when the *curé* of Fermel, finding it impossible to get permission to found a Catholic club, organised an agricultural trade union as a cover instead (1892). In the same year a union was dissolved for allowing religious lectures on its premises. The courts gradually established it as a rule that unions could participate in the election of prud'hommes but not of deputies. Civil servants were forbidden to form unions and the courts even held (1903) that the labourers of the Paris sewage system counted as civil servants. The limitation to 'the study and defence' of economic interests forbade unions to engage directly in commercial or industrial activities. This hit the agricultural unions. It had not at first been intended to allow peasant unions at all, and the word 'agricole' had only been inserted as an amendment at a late stage in the discussion of the bill. Rather surprisingly, agricultural unions were precisely the ones which were most stimulated by the law. The courts decided that these unions could buy fertilisers for resale to their members, and provided they made no profit, this would not be classed as an illegal commercial activity. Encouraged by this, the unions began dealing in seeds, machines and finally in all kinds of goods, openly establishing shops. Rival shopkeepers, disgruntled by the loss of custom, sued them and in 1908 the Cour de Cassation ruled—or rather reaffirmed, for it was well known—that trade for profit by unions was illegal. The very existence of agricultural unions, built up to their enormous size almost entirely by their practical use as co-operatives, was placed in jeopardy.

Unions were given the right to sue and to be sued, but they could not own land or buildings beyond what was strictly necessary for their meetings, libraries and professional courses. Their right to receive gifts was uncertain—though the courts soon allowed this. These restrictions reflected an outdated fear of mortmain. It was argued that their consequences were of great importance, because they prevented the unions becoming rich like the English ones, and so conservative like them. In fact the unions did not become rich because they could not collect subscriptions: they never had any money to save. They had the right to own other forms of property—i.e. money or shares—in unlimited amounts. More important perhaps was the provision that though they could offer friendly society benefits, the funds for these should be kept entirely separate and not used to subsidise strikes. This was an attempt to safeguard the savings of the worker for pensions and medical insurance, but in practice it served to discourage trade unions from offering these benefits in any substantial way. The suspicion of the working-class movement could be seen finally in the provision, passed after much resistance by the senate, allowing federations of unions, but withholding from them the right to own land or houses, or the right to sue.

The law was so frequently ignored in France, and so increasingly spurned by the revolutionaries, that, unlike in England, it was not so vital to the unions to seek amendments to it. The courts moreover interpreted the law in a somewhat inconsistent manner: few cases were taken to the highest court and even it sometimes avoided the issue. Unions preferred to dissolve and reconstitute themselves when faced with penalties, rather than fight their cases to appeal. From their point of view the major defect in the law was that employers continued to victimise members of unions. A bill to stop this, passed by the Chamber of Deputies in 1889, 1890 and 1895, was consistently rejected by the senate. A law of 27 December 1890 did indeed allow workers to demand damages from employers who dismissed them for belonging to a union, but it was seldom easy to prove that the dismissal was entirely due to this reason. The right to sue for damages was in fact more effectively used by the employers. Cases in the courts soon revealed that the right to strike was seriously limited by the law on breach of contract. The Cour de Cassation ruled (18 March 1902) that a strike involved a breach of contract unless due notice was given. In the test case of Loichot, a locksmith of Montbéliard who went on strike, his employer was awarded damages because Loichot had not given notice that he would stop working. Several other cases showed that the law of 1864 did not give the right to strike but only removed the criminal (but not civil) penalties to which strikers had been liable. Secondly, the right to strike was limited also by the means employed. The use of threats could make a strike illegal. Despite the abolition of article 416 guaranteeing the liberty of work, picketing was not fully allowed. 'Fraudulent manœuvres' by the strikers could give rise to damages being awarded to an employer. Thus Rességuier successfully sued Jaurès for seducing his workers during the Carmaux strike by his injurious and defamatory articles and speeches. A third restriction on the right to strike could arise from the aims of the strike. Thus in 1896 the Cour de Cassation held that a strike was legal if its object was the defence of professional interests but not if by 'pure malevolence' it sought to force the employer to dismiss a worker against whom there was no 'serious complaint', nor if it sought simply to force a worker to join the union, nor if it sought to defend private as opposed to general interests. Damages were awarded against a union, for example, in favour of a worker who could not get a job because the unions had blacklisted him and the employers feared to employ him. Likewise damages were awarded against another union for blacklisting an employer after a strike: vengeance was forbidden. This meant that the courts kept the right to investigate each strike, before they could determine whether it was legal or not. Even when the law of 1884 was completed by that of 1901 on associations, which allowed any group of people to join together whether they were members of the same trade or not, there were still many obstacles to the growth of unionism. But it would be a mistake to argue, as is too frequently done, that the law seriously hindered the rise of powerful trade unions. That these did not develop faster was due to more fundamental reasons, connected with the very nature of French society.[1]

Traditions

The size of the proletariat is something no one was or is quite sure about. The industrial sector, as has been seen, occupied between a quarter and a third of the active population. Excluding employers from these totals, one gets 2,700,000 workers under Napoleon III, 3 million in 1876 and 1886, 3,300,000 in 1891, a peak of 4,800,000 in 1931 but only 3,700,000 in 1936. One should then perhaps add a quarter of a million clerks in industry during the nineteenth century and half a million after the war. Of course, not all workers were male, nor were wage earners exclusively in industry. In 1906,

[1] Henri Pouget, *La Grève au point de vue juridique* (Bordeaux thesis, 1907); V. Diligent, *L'Action syndicale ouvrière* (Caen thesis, Roubaix, 1908).

when the total active population was 20 million, 11,700,000 were classified as wage earners, and of these 4,100,000 were women. But 2,090,000 of this supposed proletariat were in fact artisans working on their own—not strictly wage earners—who could barely be distinguished from 2,080,000 other artisans classified as *petits patrons*, though they employed no one. In 1906, only 742,000 people worked in industrial firms having over 500 employees. The statistics must be taken as approximate: detailed research frequently contradicts them. Thus in the Second Empire, despite all one reads about rapid industrialisation, it is by no means certain that the number of workers did rise: what may have happened was that there was an increase in factory workers at the expense of artisans, but little rise in the total of both together. The survival of the artisans can be illustrated by these figures of 1872:

Mining: 14,000 employers and 164,000 workers;
Factories: 183,000 employers and 1,112,000 workers;
Small industry: 596,000 employers and 1,060,000 workers.

The industrial population was then still divided almost equally between small workshops and factories, and it was only in the 1890s that the predominance of the latter became marked. The transformation proceeded at very different rates: the concentration in textiles and metallurgy was rapid during the Second Empire, but in 1914 the building trade (the third largest in manpower) was still almost entirely artisan. Concentration was restricted to a few regions (see Map 3 opposite). Much of the country felt the consequences indirectly. In the 1920s, a new complication was added by the contrast of the mass-producing factories, which created a large class of semi-skilled workers, noticeably distinct from those in more traditional firms.

It is impossible therefore to talk about the proletariat as a homogeneous class, because it was changing all the time, and because the variations within it were very considerable. In the Second Empire some workers were earning five or seven times as much as others. The porcelain makers of Limoges for example, or the glass blowers of the Loire, earning around 10 francs a day were veritable aristocrats to their junior labourers, and they had still less in common with, say, the weavers of Mulhouse earning a mere 1 fr. 65. The average metal worker earned 3 fr. 50 or 4 francs a day, but some working in teams at Le Creusot

made 10 to 11 francs, while inferior workers in the same trade
got only $1\frac{1}{2}$ or 2 francs.[1] Many artisans were not only manual

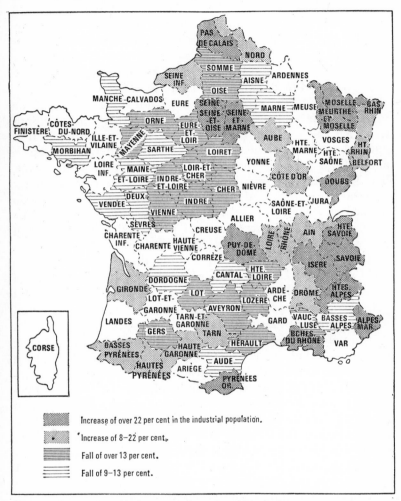

Increase of over 22 per cent in the industrial population.

Increase of 8–22 per cent.

Fall of over 13 per cent.

Fall of 9–13 per cent.

MAP 3. The growth of industry, 1906–31. Based on A. Sauvy: *Histoire économique
de la France entre les deux guerres* (1961), I. 274

workers but also merchants who sold their own products and
were proprietors of their tools and their shops. It is impossible
to classify them as necessarily enemies of the bourgeois order.

[1] G. Duveau, *La Vie ouvrière en France sous le second empire* (1946), 302–13.

The inquiry of 1872[1] into working-class conditions revealed that 80 per cent of employers were former workers and a further 15 per cent were sons of workers. The internal divisions among the workers were even more profound than those of the bourgeoisie. The fragmentation of the ruling classes into numerous parties riddled by individualism was more than matched by the workers. This tradition is one of the fundamental causes of the slow growth of trade unionism before the First World War.

The guilds of the *ancien régime* were not the ancestors of the modern trade unions but they reveal the traditional divisions to which the working class was for centuries subjected. It is often thought that these guilds contained all the merchants and artisans of a given region. This was not so. Some towns, like Lyon, had no guilds; some trades did not form them; some artisans abstained from joining, particularly those who worked on their own; and most rural ones were left out of the system. The guilds were really a privileged aristocracy with many working-class enemies. They were not organised on a uniform pattern and allowed varying degrees of equality to their members. Different trades were normally in a state of dispute with each other, just as guilds in different towns and guilds with overlapping skills engaged in perpetual warfare and vicious litigation. The idea of federating was quite inconceivable.

The union of workers against their masters goes back to the organisation known as the Compagnonnage, which deserves more detailed description because it was still a highly influential force in 1848. Just as the middle classes had found in freemasonry an institution from which they would evolve a united attack against the old order, the monarchists and the Church, so the working class, or rather the artisans, had a similar body in the Compagnonnage, with mystic rites as elaborate and secrecy as well guarded. In the case of the artisans, however, this served not to unite but to divide them and it explains why they remained so long absorbed in their own private world, fighting battles against each other much more than against their masters.

The Compagnonnage was an organisation of apprentices and journeymen. Its formation was stimulated by the frequent degeneration of the medieval guilds into oligarchies dominated by the masters, with high admission fees, so that it became

[1] G. Duveau, op. cit., 415; *Journal Officiel* (19 Nov. 1875), 9466.

increasingly difficult to be recognised and admitted as a master. Guilds sometimes decided to admit no more masters for ten or twenty years, or to confine admission to the sons of masters. The journeymen therefore formed their own societies, which had to be secret, and hence the complicated rites of initiation, the passwords and the mysticism. These societies enrolled their members from young beginners aged eighteen to twenty-five, and they became solidly established because they assisted young artisans in their professional training and in finding employment during their *tour de France*. It had become customary for many artisans to spend a few years of their early manhood travelling round France, improving their skill by observing different methods of work, and widening their horizon beyond what they could learn from their fathers. By joining the Compagnonnage, they would find in each town they visited members of their society ready to offer them lodging *chez la Mère* (the inn which had a standing arrangement to give them credit until they found work) and a local official, *le rôleur* or *rouleur*, who would obtain employment for them. As they prospered, the Compagnonnages were frequently able to hold a monopoly of this vagrant labour; by acting as intermediaries they were able to compel employers to pay minimum wages and to prevent journeymen accepting a lower wage with which, as strangers, they might feel obliged to content themselves. They could boycott recalcitrant employers and even organise strikes. In addition they provided useful assistance in case of illness or imprisonment.

However, the Compagnonnage did not produce a united artisan youth but the very contrary. About thirty trades were members but they were divided into three different factions. The *Enfants de Salomon* claimed their order had been established by King Solomon to recompense the artisans who built his temple. The *Enfants de Maître Jacques* claimed a French stonemason from Saint-Romili, who had distinguished himself in the building of the temple, as their founder. The *Enfants du Père Soubise* went back to a carpenter who was Jacques' colleague but who then quarrelled with him and whose followers eventually assassinated Jacques. According to another version Père Soubise was a thirteenth-century Benedictine carpenter and his order dates from a division among the *Enfants de Maître Jacques* during the building of Orléans cathedral. These different allegiances meant that the notion of class solidarity was somewhat obscured. Artisans of different orders refused to work together. In Paris the river was a strict dividing line, and rival orders of carpenters, for example, each held a monopoly of employment on the left and right banks. Membership of an order was shown by a different uniform. Each trade in each order wore a bunch of coloured ribbons, in varied combinations and lengths, in their buttonholes or hats; some wore ear-rings with different symbols on them, denoting their trade; nail makers wore their hair long in plaits; all carried canes, the more warlike trades having them long and strengthened with iron or copper. Each order had its own songs or ballads, many of which extolled one order and insulted the others. A number of trades were famous for their *hurlements*, a sort of chanting, with the words so pronounced that only their own order could understand them. Hence some earned the names of Dogs, Wolves, Werewolves, and they rejoiced in these titles.

The three orders were started by masons and carpenters, who gradually admitted other trades and revealed the rites to them. Much disagreement resulted because there were nearly always some trades which considered other trades to be so inferior as to be unworthy of the privilege of belonging to the Compagnonnage. The farriers for example refused to acknowledge the harness makers. The blacksmiths admitted the wheelwrights on condition that they wore their ribbons in their lower bottonhole, but the wheelwrights failed to keep their undertaking and took to wearing their ribbons as high as the blacksmiths—hence their implacable enmity. The bakers were unable to obtain admission at all, though the carpenters said they would sponsor them in return for the payment of a tribute and a promise to abstain from carrying a cane for seven years. Weavers and cobblers were likewise pariahs, the latter being held in particular enmity because they had discovered the secrets of the Compagnonnage without sponsorship, through the indiscretion of an initiate. It is possible that the well-known radicalism of cobblers in the nineteenth century was due to this contempt shown to them by other workers; for the Compagnonnage in general certainly appears rather to have stimulated conservatism and great pride in sectional traditions.

The result of these antagonisms was a great deal of physical violence. When two Compagnons met on the high road they would carry out the ritual of *topage*. 'Tope!' one would shout. 'Tope!' the other would reply. They would ask each other's trade and order. If they were of the same order they would drink from each other's gourds or retire to the nearest inn to celebrate; but if one considered his trade or order superior to the other's, he would raise his cane menacingly and demand that the other should get out of his way. A fight usually ensued, which in due course required revenge. In the towns pitched battles would be held: the judicial newspapers of the Restoration are full of reports of bloody and sometimes fatal conflicts between large groups of opposing *Devoirs*. To tear off a companion's ribbons was the worst outrage one could perpetrate upon him; to capture his cane was a sign of great prowess. Occasionally disputes would be fought out more peacefully by holding a competition, to see which order could produce the better piece of work: a representative of each would be locked up, sometimes for several months, to produce a 'masterpiece': the losing order would then be chased out of town in shame.

The Compagnonnage was an institution for young men who, when they completed their *tour de France*, normally retired from it 'thanking the society'. In many towns the retired frequently formed friendly societies—to provide for old age or unemployment—from which the later trade unions in part developed. Altogether it was estimated that in the reign of Louis-Philippe every three years 100,000 artisans passed through the Compagnonnage.[1] It was clearly an important influence on the working class; but it was then already in a state of decay. It had reached the zenith of its activity under the Restoration, but at the same time it had developed certain characteristics which stimulated future divisions. The aspirants (or novices) increasingly complained of the excessive brutality of the initiation ceremonies, of the high fees which the *rouleur* extracted from them for finding them employment, and of the privileges which the older members tried to arrogate to themselves. Under the July monarchy, as a counterpart to the revolution of 1830 (though as early as 1823 in Bordeaux according to some), many aspirants rebelled, seceded and formed a new order, the

[1] A. Perdiguier, *Le Livre du Compagnonnage* (1841), 1. 68; cf. his *Mémoires d'un compagnon* (1914, ed. D. Halévy), and J. Briquet, *Agricol Perdiguier* (1955).

Société de l'Union alias the Indépendants or the Révoltés, in which all were equal, and in which the initiation rites and mysteries were either abolished or made much more humane. In practice, however, these new Indépendants only exacerbated the conflicts, for they engaged in battles against their rivals in the traditional manner.

It is against this background that one must view the movement for fraternity which reached its climax in 1848. The reformers who preached the union of the working class were not typical of the majority but on the contrary were reacting against the cliquishness that was almost universal. Agricol Perdiguier, a joiner from Avignon, was almost alone in attempting to transform the whole spirit of the Compagnonnage by rewriting the warlike songs of the Compagnons to express more loving sentiments: he stimulated a lot of new ballads which deserve to be studied as genuine working-class literature. In 1839 he published these songs together with a description of the violent practices of the Compagnons and an exhortation to reform. 'We are accused of being barbarians, brigands, assassins . . .', he wrote in a passage which is very revealing about class relationships under Louis-Philippe and about the limited aspirations and mutual antagonisms of the workers. 'The rich and powerful form a poor opinion of our capacity and, perhaps not without some reason, contest our civil and political rights. Most people reiterate the severe judgement passed upon us. If we wish to reduce the just dissatisfaction of our brothers at work, if we wish to merit the respect and esteem of those who possess the public fortune and power, if we wish to approach them and to be really considered as their equals, let us not reject each other, for if we do this, they will have the right to reject us.' Perdiguier won some support, but was also bitterly attacked by many of his fellow artisans, who thought a book about them should have glorified their skill and extolled the virtues of their own particular societies. He roused great enthusiasm mainly among the romantics, and George Sand wrote a sugary novel in praise of the highly idealised *Compagnon du Tour de France* (1841) of the future. In 1848 for a time it seemed as though these hopes for the reconciliation of the artisans would be fulfilled. Perdiguier was elected to the Constituent Assembly by Paris (with more votes, significantly, than

Lamennais). A committee was established to effect a federation
of all the Compagnon orders. On 21 March 1848 between
8,000 and 10,000 Compagnons paraded through the streets of
Paris in witness of their reconciliation. Several trades, hitherto
spurned, were admitted into the movement. Even the cobblers,
who in 1847 had won some recognition in Lyon, were, in
November 1850, accepted by nine corporations. But the plan
for a general unification of all the orders and rites of the
Compagnons was thoroughly defeated. New schisms and disputes quickly broke out.

This failure came when the movement was already in decay
and it sealed its fate. The Compagnons' narrow exclusivism,
their outmoded dress, their cruel rites and their tyrannic
treatment of the apprentices made them increasingly unpopular
with the younger generation. The railways made travel less of
an adventure and destroyed the practice of the *tour de France*.
Increased industrial activity disrupted the old routines. The
Compagnonnage decayed rapidly during the Second Empire
and by 1870 it had lost its importance.[1]

It did not disappear entirely, for in 1900 there were still some
10,000 Compagnons. About a quarter of these belonged to a
new Fédération Compagnonique, founded in 1874 (later re-
named l'Union) which sought to modernise the institution and
to combine all the orders. This, however, was largely an artificial creation: it started new Compagnonnages in trades which
had never known it, like the mechanics, and it even claimed an
outpost in Buenos Aires, founded by an emigrant. Its self-
important congresses revealed it as a collection of archaic,
esoteric clubs. The real Compagnonnage survived mainly
among the farriers, wheelwrights, blacksmiths, thatchers, tilers
and locksmiths, genuine relics of pre-industrial France—
but not necessarily of rural France only, for in 1900 there were
still over 800 carpenter Compagnons in Paris.

Trade Unions

The way the ambitions of the proletariat developed can be
seen, from one point of view, by the way they formed trade

---

[1] W. H. Sewell, 'La Clause ouvrière de Marseille sous la seconde république',
Le Mouvement Social (July–Sept. 1971), 27–63, makes an outstanding contribution
to detailed study of the various types of workers in this period.

unions. The printers were among the first to organise themselves
effectively. As early as 1830 the compositors of Paris already
had forty friendly societies; by 1833 they had founded an
Association libre typographique with most of the aims of a trade
union: to obtain a uniform scale of wages from all employers,
to provide unemployment benefit and other forms of assistance,
and to improve the moral, material and intellectual condition
of all workers, with a particular emphasis on the development
of the spirit of association.[1] By 1842 they had won their wages
scale—the first ever negotiated by a union with their employers.
They made no efforts to subvert the social or political order:
they quickly made their peace, though reluctantly, with the
Second Empire and accepted a president nominated by
Napoleon III, in order to survive as a legal friendly society.
This even held its banquet in 1861 to the accompaniment of
the music of the thirty-third regiment of the line, placed at
its disposal, as a mark of official benevolence, by the marshal
commanding the army in Paris. It was thus able to negotiate
a new wage agreement in 1862; and when some employers
resisted it and got the strikers arrested and convicted, Napoleon
III gave the strikers a free pardon. With the consent of the
government, the friendly society turned itself officially into a
trade union in 1867. It did not join the International, even
though one of the founders of this body, Limousin, was a printing worker; but though it thus kept on the conservative side of
the working-class movement of this period, it gave generous
donations to revolutionary workers, including 2,000 francs to
the International and 500 francs to the weavers of Elbeuf when
they went on strike.[1]

The printers in the early years of the Third Republic were
in fact almost equally divided politically into three groups: the
Parisians, led by Alary, were mainly interested in establishing
co-operative printing works, i.e. buying out the employers. The
socialists, led by Allemane, derived their support much more
from the provinces and were keen on the federal and international aspects of the workers' movement.[3] Both these were
in due course defeated by the man who was to become the

[1] Paul Chauvet, *Les ouvriers du livre en France* (1956), 213.
[2] Ibid., 310.
[3] *Les Associations professionnelles ouvrières* (1899–1904), 1. 846–7, 860.

leader of the moderate wing of the French trade unionists, Auguste Keufer. This remarkable man became secretary of the book workers' union in 1884 and remained in that post till he retired in 1920. Born in Alsace in 1851, the orphan son of a factory worker, he emigrated to Lons-le-Saulnier after the German annexation, and here he was initiated into the doctrines of positivism which became his lifelong and openly professed creed. He was confirmed in his belief in the religion of humanity by the lectures of Pierre Laffitte which he attended when he moved to Paris.[1] Keufer remained rather unusual, from the point of view of his political inspiration, in the working-class movement. However, his opinions suited his own union perfectly. He was opposed to a class struggle and to violence. He believed that a better society could not be achieved by revolution, but only by a modification of mentality, by the substitution of altruism for egoism. Meanwhile trade unions should work to improve conditions, which was a necessary preliminary: and he favoured negotiating with the employers, through mixed commissions, using strikes as a very last resort.[2]

A critical year in the history of the printers was 1878 when a strike to force up wages not only greatly impoverished the union but also caused a number of important employers and notably Mame (the chief producer of Catholic books) to migrate to the provinces where wages were lower. This stimulated the Parisians to found a National Federation in 1881. It was Keufer who built this up into an exceptionally powerful and wealthy organisation. Unlike other federations, this one kept central control of funds and of strikes, only the details of administration being left decentralised. Its subscription was among the highest in the country: Keufer raised it gradually from 35 centimes to 2 francs a month between 1881 and 1904, and so his union was able to offer and pay substantial benefits. Far from breaking away from bourgeois society, he maintained close relations with both employers and government. In 1895 the master printers and the book workers held their congresses at the same time in the same city (Marseille): they exchanged

[1] Jean Montreuil, *Histoire du mouvement ouvrier en France* (1946), 200–1; Société Positiviste Internationale, *Auguste Keufer* (1925).
[2] Auguste Keufer, *L'Éducation syndicale: exposé de la méthode organique* (1910), 14–15, 43–4; id., *Rapport sur l'organisation des relations entre patrons et ouvriers* (1920).

friendly messages and Keufer accepted an invitation to lunch
with the master printers. Mixed commissions were instituted on
a national scale in 1898. Keufer was frequently to be seen in the
ministries: Fontaine, in charge of the *Office du Travail*, and
Finance, one of its officials, were both positivists, as was Fagnot,
a former typographer who became an official of the ministry
of public works. Keufer served for long on the Conseil supérieur
du Travail, of which the minister of commerce was president
and he vice-president. He was thus able to get employment
for his men in the Imprimerie Nationale (the largest printing
works in the country), as well as other jobs and decorations
in the government's gift. His treasurer Gaule was given the
Legion of Honour, though he himself refused it.[1] Keufer's independence was shown in 1906, during the movement for the
eight-hour day. He got his union to declare openly that they
considered this an impossible ideal to achieve immediately,
that they would seek at first only a nine-hour day and that they
would not join the national strikes of May 1906 until they had
exhausted all possibilities of negotiation. He met the national
organisation of employers in Paris, who decided by 232 to 179
against granting the nine-hour day. He tried then to get agreements at a local level with smaller groups of employers and
only when these failed did he allow a strike. It was generally
successful, for he was able to spend over half a million francs
on the campaign. But the struggle was very hard in the Nord,
where there was almost no contact between employer and
worker.[2] This regional variation is significant. It is impossible
to generalise in simple terms from the experience of the book
workers and to argue that, had other unions followed the same
policy, the embitterment of the working class might have been
avoided.

The miners were slow to organise themselves and even when
they began to do so they remained somewhat isolated from the
rest of the working class. They placed great faith in the state
and looked to it to improve their lot. Having won a privileged

[1] Maurice Harmel, 'Keufer', in *Les Hommes du jour* (27 Aug. 1910), no. 136
(this includes a portrait of him).
[2] A. Keufer, 'Les Grèves de mai dans l'industrie du Livre', *La Revue syndicaliste*
(July–Sept. 1906), 51–5, 83–9, 109–15.

position through special legislation, they took care to be moderate in order not to lose it. They showed little sense of solidarity, refusing to make common cause with other workers, and even with miners of other provinces. For long their organisation was self-contained—though torn by numerous and varied disagreements. They could have been a major force in the emancipation of the working class and theirs was a trade capable of a really mass movement: but they were paradoxically hostile to the general strike. So the revolutionary agitation remained largely the monopoly of trades quite incapable of implementing their threats.

Already under Louis-Philippe bloody strikes had broken out in the coalfields of both the Nord and the Loire but they were spontaneous outbursts of anger, and not the work of trade unions. In the Loire, the rudiments of a union existed but their programme and organisation were very elementary. In contrast to the politically conscious artisans of this region, the miners were generally peasant immigrants from the backward mountains around (Haute-Loire, Creuse, Puy-de-Dôme).[1] They were stimulated to unite largely by the union of their employers, who merged their companies into one, the Compagnie de la Loire. In 1852 the miners' vigorous and effervescent leader Garon went to Paris and obtained an interview with the Prince-President of the Republic. As a result the miners were given some concessions and the employers were forced to split up into four companies. The miners were clearly backward looking, yearning nostalgically for the days of the small unmechanised mines, run not by distant engineers but by gang leaders chosen by the men themselves.[2] The appeal to the state was revived a dozen years later by the next leader to rise up, Michel Rondet. He, however, unlike Garon, did not expect the state to emerge as the protector of the workers of its own accord. His plan was to force it to act by seeking out issues on which it would be hard for it to abstain. He showed that the employers were acting illegally in their handling of the miners' provident fund. He successfully sued them, using Jules Favre as barrister; and as

[1] Pétrus Faure, *Histoire du mouvement ouvrier dans le département de la Loire* (St. Étienne, 1956), 39.
[2] P. Guillaume, 'Grèves et organisations ouvrières chez les mineurs de la Loire au milieu du 19ᵉ siècle', *Le Mouvement social* (Apr.–June 1963), 5–18.

a result the government allowed him to create an independent fund, run by the miners themselves (*La Société Fraternelle*). This turned out in fact to be half-way to a trade union, but it could not control the miners, and their spontaneous and disastrous strike of 1869 destroyed all Rondet's work. Rondet himself was sentenced to seven months' imprisonment and the flirtation with the empire was over. On 5 September 1870, proclaiming the republic at Ricamarie, he shattered the statue of Napoleon III to the applause of the crowd; he took part in the St. Étienne Commune and was sentenced to five years' imprisonment. These clashes with authority did not, however, turn him into a revolutionary, and indeed with time he became increasingly moderate and conciliatory. He concentrated on a practical programme: the eight-hour day, pensions, miners' delegates for accident prevention and a *conseil de prud'hommes*. In 1882 he went to Paris to canvass the deputies, seeing among them Waldeck-Rousseau, who promised his help. Soon the first bills were introduced: Rondet became nationally known, always as an advocate of gradual improvements by legislative means. Even his ultimate ideal was to be achieved peacefully: 'The government', he said, 'should purely and simply withdraw the coal concessions from the companies and the state should *buy* up the equipment of the mines and exploit them itself to the profit of all.'[1] Rondet toured the mining areas of France and engaged in active propaganda to encourage the formation of unions. He organised the first Miners' Federation in 1883, of which he was secretary until 1896. For all his energy, however, he made little headway in his own department. At the end of 1897 there were still only 3,497 miners organised in unions in the Loire, out of 17,663. They were moreover divided into ten different unions, and Rondet's, the largest, had only 1,127 members. He had sought to stimulate interest by founding a library and a friendly society, but the latter was joined by only sixty miners. The small rival unions waged a bitter campaign against Rondet in the Departmental Federation, which he had himself started but of which he lost control—as he soon lost control of the National Federation.[2]

---

[1] Office du Travail, *Les Associations ouvrières professionnelles* (1904), 1. 344.
[2] C. Bartnel, 'Un Oublié, Michel Rondet', *La Vie ouvrière* (5 Jan. 1913), 15–24; cf. André Philippe, *Michel Rondet* (1948).

The power of the federation for long remained slight and the initiative passed to the miners of the Nord and Pas-de-Calais, who were suddenly becoming by far the most numerous group in the country.[1] Though they had had sporadic strikes in the 1870s all attempts to found a union had failed and it was only through the encouragement of Rondet that one was established at Denain in 1883. The secretary of this, Basly,[2] was to be the leading figure among the miners till 1914. He followed the same policy of moderation as Rondet, with two differences: he entered parliament himself (deputy for Paris 1885, defeated by a Boulangist 1889, deputy for Lens 1891–1928) and so worked for legislation discreetly, and he had none of Rondet's views on solidarity. He did not seek to spread unionism beyond his region and he kept the welfare of his own union uppermost in his mind. Within a year he had enrolled half the 7,000 members, but in 1884 a strike at Anzin, unsuccessful after fifty-six days and followed by a thousand dismissals, shattered the whole movement in the north. No union arose again in Anzin for fourteen years. The Anzin Company, which had been able to resist the strike largely because of the slack demand for coal, developed a very careful policy of recruitment, engaging new workers only from among the sort of men it knew it could rely on. It established a near monopoly of shopping facilities, becoming the principal baker, grocer and clothes merchant of its workers, so that these had no alternative source of supply or credit should they strike. Whenever there was a strike elsewhere, it told them that they would receive the same advantages as might be won by the strikers.[3] The strikes of 1884 had been supported by the small tradesmen who were hostile to the Anzin Company's co-operative and the Company wished to

[1]   Miners in Pas-de-Calais—1886: 10,000, 1890: 36,000;
          „   „   the Nord—1886: 15,000, 1890: 19,000.

E. Lozé, *La Grève de 1891 dans les bassins homillers du Nord et du Pas-de-Calais* (Arras, 1891), 36. The two departments produced 32 per cent of France's coal in 1869 and 63·3 per cent in 1903. E. Levasseur, *Questions ouvrières et industrielles en France* (1907), 35.
    [2] Émile Joseph Basly, 1854–1928. He was also mayor of Lens 1900–28. His heroism during the German occupation, and his organisation of the reconstruction of the town afterwards prolonged his popularity.
    [3] C. Lespilette, *La Vérité sur la grève des mineurs du Nord et du Pas-de-Calais en 1893* (Lille, 1894), 83–6.

destroy them too. Paradoxically, small shopkeepers were for long to be the principal financiers of workers' strikes, by giving credit for purchases, whereas the co-operatives were often instruments of capitalism. This is not surprising, however, for the shopkeepers were frequently former miners who had made good. Basly, who had started work in a mine at the age of ten, was dismissed for his union activities: he then earned his livelihood as a café owner.[1]

In 1889 improved economic conditions stimulated a revival of unionism in the north (except at Anzin) and a series of strikes won wage increases of 20 per cent. Membership soared but at the same time the union leaders showed less and less combativeness and vigour. They preached caution and moderation lest the gains of their negotiated agreement (the 'Convention d'Arras') be lost. Their regional victory increased their isolation from the miners in other parts of the country, and from the union movement as a whole. In moments of crisis they invited the socialist deputies, not the leaders of other trade unions, to come down to help them. The government's threat to withdraw its troops had helped to compel the employers to yield in 1891, and the miners were encouraged to look to it even more for aid against the companies. The companies for their part were driven to unite more effectively among themselves.[2] In 1893 they were able to obtain their revenge, when an unofficial strike, which the leaders had tried to avoid, revealed how precarious the miners' organisation was. Basly quickly made peace, to save the union's funds. Rondet on his side refused to bring out the Loire miners in sympathy. The intervention on this occasion of a quite extraordinary number of troops (thirty-five companies of infantry, ten squadrons of cavalry and 220 gendarmes) and the march of some of the strikers to liberate Anzin, the 'Bastille of the Nord', gave the impression of a veritable insurrection. The revolutionary elements were, however, a very small minority (there were only

---

[1] Basly was somewhat ashamed of this, however: the café was only in his name, he was never there, he said. See his evidence in *Procès-verbaux de la commission chargée de faire une enquête sur la situation des ouvriers de l'industrie et de l'agriculture en France* (1884), 225–6.

[2] Marcel Gillet, 'L'Affrontement des syndicalismes ouvriers et nationales dans le bassin homiller du Nord et du Pas-de-Calais de 1884 à 1891', *Bulletin de la Société d'histoire moderne* (Mar.–Apr. 1957), 7–10.

500 marchers in fact) and, as in most revolutions, there were paralysing divisions among them.[1]

The revolutionary minority urged a general strike but Basly repeatedly foiled them. He at length agreed to a referendum being held to decide the issue when 1,800 Montceau miners were dismissed in 1901 after an unsuccessful strike. The vote was in favour of a general strike (though more than half the miners abstained). Basly ignored the vote and negotiated with the government. Twice again referenda were held, producing increasing approval of a general strike—but still Basly refused to accept it. When a general strike was at last held in 1902, he effectively sabotaged it by regionalising it. The general strike was seen to be far less disastrous for the national economy than the bourgeoisie feared or the miners threatened. The miners in fact did not hold anything like the important position their English counterparts did.[2] The miners of Montceau, together with some other small unions, now withdrew in protest from the National Federation and formed their own Union Fédérale. Again, following a strike at Commentry which Basly likewise refused to assist—accepting government arbitration instead— a breakaway union was formed against him in the Pas-de-Calais by the anarchist Broutchoux.[3] These divisions postponed still further the admission of the miners into the C.G.T. Basly had no sympathy for its revolutionary aims. It feared to admit a moderate union of such enormous size which would inevitably be a drag on its forward policy. Only in 1908, in a moment of emotion caused by the arrest of leading unionists, did the miners join—but the divisions were not therefore diminished.[4] Broutchoux's young union failed to make the majority of the northern miners revolutionary: Basly's hold there remained. In June 1913 Basly indeed withdrew his union from the Fédération du Sous-Sol and established a separate miners' federation

---

[1] C. Lespilette, *La Vérité sur la grève des mineurs du Nord et du Pas-de-Calais en 1893* (Lille, 1894) is full of interesting detail.

[2] Comité Central des Homillères de France, *Documents relatifs à la grève des mineurs de 1902* (1903), 23, 94, 231.

[3] J. Julliard, 'Jeunes et vieux syndicats chez les mineurs du Pas-de-Calais (à travers les papiers de Pierre Monatte)', *Le Mouvement social* (Apr.–June 1964), 7–30.

[4] G. Dumoulin, 'La Fédération des Mineurs et la C.G.T.', *Le Mouvement socialiste* (Nov. 1908), 321–38.

of more moderate character. Violent polemics were exchanged between the opposing groups.[1]

The railway workers also had it in their power to organise a really influential trade union. There were 44,000 of them in 1854, 240,000 by 1883 and 310,000 by 1914. Their employers—half a dozen major companies—were a clear target. They were subjected to fairly uniform conditions of work, so that unity should have been possible. Their conditions stimulated many grievances. The companies consciously worked their men to the limit. A driver threatened with dismissal in the 1860s for failing to stop at three stations, replied that he had been driving for thirty-eight consecutive hours, and had simply fallen asleep. A petition to the National Assembly in 1871 revealed that drivers frequently worked forty hours without rest and often went for twelve hours without food.[2] It was only in 1891, after numerous vain exhortations by the government, that their working day was limited to twelve hours. However, the companies long continued to subject their men to a rigorous discipline: an elaborate system of fines penalised unpunctuality, insubordination, drunkenness and a whole list of carefully foreseen professional mistakes. There were plenty of mistakes made. For example, on the Nord Railway in the years 1900–10, there was on average one accident a day. 43 per cent of a sample of retired railwaymen at the turn of the century had suffered at least one injury during their employment. The companies did indeed pioneer a pension scheme, which was at first a great attraction, but with time the workers complained that this was an instrument of bondage, since they forfeited their contributions if they were dismissed. In the early years railwaymen had to some extent been privileged members of the working class, but after 1900 their wages failed to keep up with the rising cost of living. The drivers themselves, once an élite, now earned very little more than well-paid Paris artisans; the permanent way men were getting considerably less than navvies.[3]

[1] G. Dumoulin, 'La Fédération des mineurs', Le Mouvement socialiste (Oct. 1908), 241–57 (an informative history). E. Merzet, 'L'Unité minière', Le Mouvement socialiste (Jan. 1907), 75–83; G. Dumoulin, 'Le Dernier Congrès des mineurs', La Vie ouvrière (5 June 1911), 671–80; G. Dumoulin, 'Avec le bureau fédéral des mineurs contre Basly', La Vie ouvrière (20 Jan. 1913), 65–79.
[2] Cf. C. A. de Janzé, Les Serfs de la voie ferrée (1881).
[3] Guy Chaumel, Histoire des cheminots et de leurs syndicats (1948), 19–23, 87–99;

However, before 1914 a mere fifth of the railwaymen had joined a trade union. The history of their efforts to combine is particularly revealing. The first union was a *Société Fraternelle des Mécaniciens Français* founded in February 1848, whose main purpose was to press the companies to employ French rather than English drivers: at that time one-third of the drivers on the Nord lines and all those on the Paris–Havre railway were English. Haphazard strikes to compel the expulsion of the English failed completely and the society disappeared by the end of June 1848. The *Association des Travailleurs des Chemins de Fer Français*, likewise founded after the revolution of February, had as its vice-president a representative of the employers, whose donations alone kept it going for a couple of years. It had no revolutionary ambitions, any more than did the *Société de l'Union Fraternelle* (1871). This latter hoped to save its subscriptions to build a small local railway of its own—to safeguard its members against unemployment and to enable them to become independent. In 1880 Gambetta and Carnot helped to found another union, which was likewise devoted to self-help, providing pensions, sickness benefits and mortgages. Some members wished to use it to agitate for legislation to improve railwaymen's conditions, but the engineers and directors of the company infiltrated it as honorary members and kept it virtually a friendly society. Again the *Syndicat Professionnel (Association Amicale)* was founded in 1884 by well-intentioned but bourgeois deputies. Under their influence, it sought to solve its members' problems by a long-term plan of buying shares in the railway companies: it proclaimed itself an organisation devoted to conciliation and it opposed the use of strikes. It attracted little more than 3,500 members by 1890 and 12,000 by 1906.

A really large and independent railwaymen's union, the *Syndicat National*, appeared only in 1890. It prospered rapidly, claiming within ten years 45,000 members (much exaggerated, no doubt). It found in Guérard, who at the age of thirty-four became its secretary and remained so for eighteen years (1891–1909), an organiser of unusual talent. He believed that the

F. Caron, 'Essai d'analyse historique d'une psychologie du travail: les mécaniciens et chauffeurs de locomotives du réseau du Nord de 1850 à 1910', *Le Mouvement social* (Jan.–Mar. 1965), 3–40.

great problem was to unite the workers into powerful federations and he devoted himself unremittingly to this task of
building up numbers. He preached the general strike and
organised two, in 1891 and 1898, both woefully unsuccessful,
because only a tiny minority of his members stopped work.
Though Guérard was outstanding in the C.G.T. as one of the
principal advocates of the general strike, he became more
moderate in course of time. In the nineties he had secured
the passage of a bill (loi Berteaux, December 1897) giving
pensions to all railwaymen but the senate postponed passing
it into law till 1909. This failure of parliamentary methods, and
the refusal of the employers to negotiate with him, stimulated
him to organise the general strike of 1898; but its pitiful failure
caused him to modify his revolutionary ideals. He was soon
accused of having excessive relations with bourgeois parliamentarians, of attending a dinner given by Millerand and
indeed of preaching doctrines very much akin to those of the
moderate Keufer. The limitations imposed by the senate on the
Railways Pensions Law of 1909 produced so much dissatisfaction that the upper hand was won by the revolutionaries.
Guérard resigned and a strike was declared in 1910. It failed,
not surprisingly, and the revolutionaries were once more
voted into a minority. This is enough to show how the revolutionary unions were far from being irreconcilably hostile to the
regime. Their alienation was in large measure due to the in-
transigence of the capitalists and the government. But the
politics of the railwaymen should not be seen in terms of seizure
of power by clear-cut rival groups with antagonistic views. There
was much gradual evolution of attitudes in opposing directions. Thus while on the one hand Guérard gave up revolutionary for parliamentary agitation, the once conservative
engine drivers of the North, who had remained in a separate
union so as to avoid joining any revolutionary movement, who
had epitomised responsibility and loyalty to their employers,
and who had largely accepted the benefits of paternalism,
surprisingly came out on strike in 1910, in greater numbers
than any other group—70 per cent of them. Of those of them
who were dismissed as a result 38 per cent were aged over
40 (not far from the retiring age of 50), which shows that
some older men had changed their minds about strikes. The

employers on their side were on the one hand increasingly conciliatory after 1900 and, without avowing it, began negotiating
with the unions (which is why Guérard could change his
tactics); but on the other hand they felt they could not make
more concessions, because receipts were diminishing (and the
law imposed a ceiling for fares), while their expenses were
rising inexorably with costs.[1] However, for all the new currents
at work among the railwaymen, traditional attitudes clearly
continued to prevail. Only about 20 per cent of them were
members of a union as late as 1914. This figure, moreover,
included many moderates, as, for example, the *Est* Railwaymen's Union, which had refused to join in the movement of
1910, the majority in it being hostile to strikes altogether.[2]

In 1900 it was estimated that there were about 100,000
workers in the building industry. Only some 30,000 of these
were members of unions, and they were divided between no
fewer than 357 organisations. The Compagnonnage had been
extremely powerful in this industry, with old-established and
deep-rooted loyalties, and it kept the building workers separated not only by craft but in groups within each craft. The trade
unions rose up as a challenge to it, stimulated by a desire to
end the privileges or monopoly enjoyed by the Compagnons
in obtaining employment. However, the unions were themselves
distracted from the task of unification by their interest in establishing co-operative associations, for which the building trade
was particularly suitable. The exclusiveness of these co-
operatives, and the fact that they frequently paid their members
even less than the exploiting employers, in turn produced a reaction against them. However, repeated attempts to organise
a national federation (1882, 1892, 1902) had only limited and
very temporary success. The craft unions, led by the powerful
masons and carpenters, preferred to build up their own
independent national federations, until the strikes of 1906
revealed their weakness and the dangers of these traditional
divisions. It was only then that the *Fédération Nationale des
Travailleurs de l'industrie du bâtiment* came to be widely accepted.

[1] Caron, 34–40.
[2] Anon., 'Le Congrès des cheminots de l'Est', *La Vie ouvrière* (20 Jan. 1911),
120–2.

Its membership rose from 9,000 in 1905 to 30,000 in 1908, but the union frittered away its funds: in 1911 it gave away no less than 60,000 francs to the C.G.T., to help pay for its journal, *La Bataille Syndicaliste*; so when the strike of 1912 broke out, it had no money to support its men. Membership at once fell drastically and even more so when the federation raised its subscriptions in 1912. It was feared as a revolutionary monster, which periodically expanded and deflated, but it was less menacing than it seemed.[1] For example, despite its nominally uncompromising demand for an eight-hour day, on a national scale, it was in practice content to accept considerably longer hours, for in some regions builders worked as much as twelve hours a day, and they realised an immediate adoption of short hours was impracticable. The varied social conditions of France compelled them to be opportunists in practice.

The extremes to which craft particularism could go are illustrated by the trade unions of cooks. Under Louis-Philippe there existed in Paris two groups of cooks: *La Laurentine*, which was a social club, and the *Société des Pieds Humides*, so called because its members used to meet in the mornings at Les Halles in search of employment. In 1840 these two united to form the *Société des Cuisiniers de Paris*, whose sole object at first was to serve as a labour exchange. At the Revolution of 1848 they changed their title to *Société Centrale des Artistes Culinaires*, and in 1853 again to *Société de secours mutuels et de prévoyance des cuisiniers de Paris*, for this was the only kind of organisation the Second Empire would tolerate. It continued to concern itself with employment but at the same time it gradually developed a pensions fund, which by the end of the century was one of the most successful of its kind. The concentration on pensions was not surprising, for the cooks opposed the introduction of notice before dismissal into their craft; they wished to be free, as temperamental artists, to leave an employer without notice at any time. The concentration of this union on pensions, however, started a certain amount of dissatisfaction. A separate *Cercle*

---

[1] Raymond Joran, *L'Organisation syndicale dans l'industrie du bâtiment* (Paris thesis, 1914), 81, 90, 104, 232; Albert Thomas, 'Chez les travailleurs du bâtiment: deux ans d'organisation et de lutte', *La Revue syndicaliste* (May 1908), 1–6; *Les Associations professionnelles ouvrières* (1899–1904), 4. 1–56, 446–64.

d'etudes sociales et professionnelles des Cuisiniers de Paris was founded in April 1899, borrowing its statutes from the *Cercle d'études sociales des proletaires positivistes de Paris*: about fifty Comtist cooks joined this. A demand for more attention to professional education gave birth in 1882 to a *Union universelle pour le progrès de l'art culinaire*, which a year later obtained the prefect's authority to call itself instead the *Académie de Cuisine*. It purposely allowed itself only thirty full members, though an unlimited number of associate members. Candidates for full membership had to present a written thesis, which was read before the Academy. In 1884 the cooks of Paris were divided into seven different organisations. There were three friendly societies (serving also as employment exchanges) and four unions each with a slightly different emphasis: a *Chambre syndicale*, a *Cercle de la Fraternité*, a *Société des Cuisiniers français*, and the *Académie de Cuisine*. When in 1898 the *Fédération ouvrière des cuisiniers* (founded 1887) joined the C.G.T., it brought with it only a minority.[1]

Syndicalism

The impression left by traditional descriptions of the rise of the trade union movement is one of an increasingly revolutionary force, openly threatening to overthrow the whole social order, and refusing all compromise with it. The proceedings of the workers' congresses may perhaps have justified the terror of the bourgeoisie. The first of these congresses, held in 1876, revealed, it is true, no wish for revolution. It resolved that the emancipation of the worker would be achieved by the formation of co-operative associations; it condemned strikes; it said nothing about property, except that the worker should own his tools, and that interest on capital should be abolished. Some thought that it was idle to expect reform from the bourgeoisie, but their remedy was that the workers should elect their own representatives to parliament. Gradually, however, principally under the influence of Guesde, socialist views and the theory of the class struggle were introduced. The third congress of 1879, held

---

[1] *Les Associations professionnelles ouvrières*, I (1889), 515–49. P. Hubert-Valleroux, 'Les Syndicats professionnels en France', in *Revue sociale et politique* (Brussels, 1892), 431.

at Marseille, decided on the formation of the Party of Socialist Workers. Had this survived, the unions might have become the backbone of a French version of the Labour Party; but two factors prevented this. First, the socialist leaders (as will be seen in another chapter) were deeply divided and the party quickly split into several factions. Guesde's triumph was brief, and he had in fact never really captured the workers' movement. The Marseille congress was packed with his supporters and widespread indifference among unions allowed him to pass his resolutions in their absence. When they later began to attend congresses more conscientiously, they had relatively little difficulty in evicting him. For, secondly, there now became manifest among them a desire for direct action, as opposed to agitation through parliament. They wished to avoid entanglement in bourgeois politics, or in politics at all, for that served only to divide them. In 1892 they adopted the general strike as their method of action—against the policy of Guesde. Three years later Guesde had seceded and his Federation of Unions quickly faded out of existence. The workers' movement became completely independent, with anarcho-syndicalism as its creed.

This suggests the adoption of a thoroughly revolutionary attitude. The workers proclaimed themselves enemies not only of the capitalists but also of the state and of democracy. They openly preached violence as the only possible means of winning their objectives: the strike, boycott, expropriation. They had no intention of postponing the day of victory till all the workers were behind them. They believed in the rights of minorities. They joined, that is to say, to the socialist criticism of the capitalist order, and its belief in the class struggle as the method of emancipation for the working class, the anarchist horror of the state as an inevitable source of tyranny, and the desire to abolish it as a centralised organisation. They were less optimistic than the socialists, however, in that they did not believe that capitalism was bound to collapse from its internal contradictions. They insisted that the revolution would be achieved only through the efforts of the workers themselves. This, together with the belief that once the revolution was successful, the new order should be run by the workers themselves, organised in unions, is the real essence of syndicalism. But syndicalism was for many only a new form of the old working-class ideas of independence and dignity on the one hand and production associations as a means of achieving this on the other. In proclaiming themselves syndicalists the workers were often reiterating an old belief more than they were innovating.[1] Pelloutier's description of the new order they would establish is not all that different from Proudhon's.

It is true that syndicalism now no longer meant simply mutual help but was anarchist and revolutionary. The workers claimed to reject the bourgeois order rather than attempt to find a niche for themselves in it. They believed that strikes were their best instrument, instead of rejecting them as they had once done; indeed they even looked upon them as good things in themselves, a method of education in class consciousness. However, more careful examination of their attitudes, and even of their actions, reveals that they were far less uncompromising than all this talk of revolution suggests. Though they dismissed the Millerandists as traitors, though they contemptuously denounced partial reforms conceded by the bourgeois state as worthless, and though they considered the mutual benefits offered by the moderate unionists as diversions from the class struggle, in practice there were very few trade union leaders who did not work for the immediate improvement of the workers' lot by gradual reforms. They called it 'revolutionary reformism'—but whatever may have been their ultimate goal, it was reformism in practice. Their problem was to prevent the government reaping the reward of its social legislation and winning the workers away from the revolutionary struggle. They sought, that is, to satisfy the workers' immediate complaints but to keep them dissatisfied, to distinguish the short term from the long term.

The C.G.T. as a body was revolutionary but the majority of its members and of the unions in it were not revolutionary. This paradox is explained by the voting system. Every union had a vote, irrespective of its size. The small unions, which tended to be revolutionary because their small membership gave them no hope of ever achieving anything by peaceful

[1] For a good analysis of revolutionary syndicalism see Félicien Challaye, *Syndicalisme révolutionnaire et syndicalisme réformiste* (1909). This contains valuable references to articles by workers on this subject, which he unfortunately does not differentiate from the works of intellectuals from outside the movement. See also F. Ridley, *Revolutionary Syndicalism in France* (1970).

means, thus dominated the C.G.T. The six smallest unions, with a total membership of only twenty-seven, had as many votes as the six largest, which had some 90,000 members.[1] A minority of 45,000 unionists had enough votes, because they belonged to so many different small unions, to decide every issue.[2] The executive committee held about one-third of the votes by proxy, from small unions unable to afford sending their own representatives to congress. The C.G.T. was in fact almost run on the basis of rotten boroughs.[3] It justified its unrepresentative character in the name of the rights of minorities, but in its own proceedings it was ruled by majority votes.

The leaders of the C.G.T. were far from being the slaves of anarcho-syndicalism or indeed any theory at all. Griffuelhes, who was its secretary general from 1902 to 1909, not only made a point of emphasising this, but even went so far as to say he had not even read the theorists. 'I read Alexandre Dumas', he used to say contemptuously. The working-class movement, he repeated, was the product not of principles but of day-to-day events. Some of the members argued about the kind of society it would one day establish, but he did not consider that very profitable. 'It is always easy to formulate theories, it is harder to put them into practice.' Griffuelhes (1874–1923) was a cobbler, who specialised in making shoes for the luxury market in Paris, working for a wage under a humble master who was little more than an artisan himself. He had a hard life and joined his union 'to fight against the employers, who were the direct instrument of my enslavement, and against the state, which was the natural defender, because it was the beneficiary, of the employers. It is from the union that I drew all my strength for action, and it is there that my ideas began to grow precise.' He was essentially a trade union man, who worked consistently for the independence of the movement, for its interests, and not for the service of any party or theory. In his youth he was for a few years a follower of Blanqui, but his entry into the trade union movement quickly caused him to abandon political action. He considered it his task as a union

---

[1] Mermeix, *Le Syndicalisme contre le socialisme, origine et développement de la C.G.T.* (1907), 200.

[2] Guérard in *Humanité* (31 May 1907), quoted by F. Challaye, *Syndicalisme révolutionnaire* (1909), 132 n.

[3] Victor Diligent, *Les Orientations syndicales* (1910), 170.

leader to reflect the ambitions of the members of his union, without worrying about consistency of principle. 'The workers' movement', he wrote, 'has been a series of daily efforts linked to efforts of the previous day, not by any rigorous continuity but uniquely by the attitude and state of mind ruling the working class. The action of the working class has not been, I say it again, ordered by formulae or by any theoretical affirmations; nor has it been a demonstration following a plan foreseen in advance by us.'[1]

Griffuelhes was above all an organiser and an administrator. He had neither a brilliant mind nor any particular oratorical gifts; but he was able, efficient, disinterested and by nature a man who could command obedience. His great achievement was to give coherence to his thoroughly divided movement. Though he worked to maintain the supremacy of the revolutionary wing, he always kept his polemic against the reformists within reasonable bounds and took care not to force them out of the C.G.T. by any inordinate extremism. His essentially practical common sense should have been adequate guarantee that he would never have supported any premature revolution.

Griffuelhes's deputy at the C.G.T., Émile Pouget (1860–1931), was no demagogue either, with even less gift for public speaking. Pouget was a journalist, of *déclassé* bourgeois origin. His father had been a notary but died young, so compelling Pouget to earn his own living. He began as an assistant at a Paris department store (the Bon Marché), read *La Révolution sociale*, was converted to anarchism, spent three years in prison for taking part in one of its demonstrations, and then started a remarkable periodical called the *Le Père Peinard*, reminiscent in style of the *Père Duchesne* of the Revolution. He wrote this entirely himself. It at once attracted attention because it was written for workers in their own slang and with great verve. He claimed their language was entirely different from that of the bourgeoisie whom they could barely understand. When in 1900 the C.G.T. founded its own (weekly) paper, *La Voix du Peuple*, Pouget was made its editor. He always longed to run a daily, but his efforts to found one repeatedly failed. He wrote novels of working-class life (not very genuine ones). He was a friend of many of the impressionist painters—Pissarro and Paul Signac

[1] V. Griffuelhes, *L'Action syndicaliste* (1908), 8.

illustrated some of his writings—and he accumulated a sizeable collection of their paintings, given to him as presents. He ended his days as a salesman of catalogues which he arranged to have printed for art galleries. He was thus, like Pelloutier, something of an outsider in the movement. However, he played a very important part, by his leading position in the C.G.T.'s propaganda, in increasing the numbers of revolutionary syndicalists. He preached the class war as essential to all progress, but he did not reject partial reforms as worthless. If reforms came as gifts from the government, they must be received with caution, because they would inevitably contain a bias towards the employer, but they were acceptable if they were won from the government by force. The workers should organise so as to force reform by direct action, instead of waiting for the government to make presents to them.[1]

Yvetot, the secretary of the Bourses section of the C.G.T., was a vigorous antimilitarist (author of the celebrated *Manuel du soldat*, written in prison and published partly with funds from the government subsidy to the Bourses). His father had been in the *garde impériale* and the *gendarmerie*. He himself was educated by the Frères de la Doctrine Chrétienne, and never became an anticlerical. Merrheim, secretary of the metallurgists and in charge of the C.G.T.'s relations with the provincial federations, was a puritan from Roubaix who was horrified by the demagogy and immorality he found in Paris. Intellectual curiosity and a remarkable seriousness of purpose alone kept him from giving it all up and returning home. He insisted that it was impossible to defeat the capitalists by blind attacks. The workers needed to study their enemy. He undertook careful and thorough surveys of the organisation of the employers; his favourite reading was company reports. Pataud of the electricians on the other hand was the very opposite of Merrheim. He was an exhibitionist who loved nothing better than to be photographed and interviewed by journalists, but who took care to exchange his habitual bowler hat for a more democratic beret before he allowed the cameras to get to work. He plunged Paris into darkness by a strike in 1908, with a marvellous sense of publicity. Only the Bourse du Travail was allowed any

---

[1] Christian Demay de Goustine, 'Emile Pouget' (unpublished thesis in the Library of the Faculty of Law, Paris, 1961).

electricity and there Pataud received the journalists to show
them his power. On another occasion he got the electricians of
the Opéra to go on strike in the middle of a gala performance
given for a foreign sovereign: they got their wage increase after
a few minutes of negotiation in the darkness.[1]

The threat of revolution from the C.G.T. is seen to be even
more superficial when one realises that between a third and
a half of its members were not revolutionary syndicalists but
reformist syndicalists. As such, they hoped, no doubt, for the
same ultimate goal as the revolutionaries. They wanted, as one
of them said (in language which has an interesting antique
flavour) the complete emancipation of labour by the suppression
of wage earning and the replacement of bourgeois capitalism by
the association of workers. But their programme, as opposed
to their ideal, was one of immediate practical reforms.[2] They
did not believe in revolution by minorities but, admiring the
wealth and numbers of the British and German unions, they
wished to draw the majority of the French workers into unions.
They believed that only a mass rising could ever be successful,
or rather that when all the workers were union members, they
could one day simply say to the capitalists: 'We have had
enough.' The way to attract the workers into the unions was
first to respect their different opinions and beliefs, avoiding
politics, whether socialist or anarchist. Their neutrality was
expressed as aparliamentarianism, not as antiparliamentarianism. They rejected the idea of forming a Labour Party.

Secondly, as Niel of the book workers' union wrote, 'Syndicalism will be passionately loved by all the proletariat the day
it proves that it wants and is capable of bringing the working
class immediate alleviation and consolation, which numerous
naïve persons still hope from religion, from the employers or
from the politicians.' They demanded revolutionary reforms
rather than revolution. They continued to call themselves
revolutionaries, but explained this as meaning simply that
'every reform which snatches a piece of capital or a piece of
authority from the employer, to give it to the worker, is a

[1] M. Leclercq and E. Girod de Fléaux, Ces Messieurs de la C.G.T., profils révolutionnaires (1908); J. Julliard, Clemenceau, briseur de grèves (1965), 115.
[2] Maurice Claverie (of the Paris gas workers' union), 'Révolutionnaires soit,
mais réformistes d'abord', in Action ouvrière, 1 Dec. 1909, quoted by Pierre A.
Carcanagues, Sur le mouvement syndicaliste réformiste (Paris thesis, 1912), 36.

revolutionary reform . . . We are revolutionaries because we have proved that historically the Revolution is destined to take place [la Révolution est fatale].'[1] Keufer said the workers were just not ready to take over the means of production, in their existing state of ignorance. The total failure of the general strikes organised in the early years of the twentieth century produced a disillusionment with the idea of the general strike and even with the ordinary strike itself as a method of advancing the cause. Eight reformist trade union leaders, questioned about their attitude to the general strike, dismissed it as an illusion, a bluff or a decoy; three others approved of it only provided the workers were first educated, three were not certain whether it would be the method they would use, one thought it a useful sword of Damocles.[2] 'A new attitude is spreading among the unionists', wrote P. M. André of the railwaymen. 'The workers, led astray by the mirages of the theories of creative violence, have finally come to see that we [the reformists] have been right, that these theories were entirely childish. Unionists are considering themselves less and less as "revolutionary pioneers". They have never gone on strike in order to learn the art of revolution, but always to further their professional interests.'[3] The reformists now said that strikes should be used only as a very last resort; they insisted a referendum should be held among the workers involved before any strike was actually declared.[4] Increasing use of collective bargaining was urged, with the idea that ultimately the unions could tender for work from the employers and so gradually run the economy themselves.[5] *Action* was the revolutionaries' demand: '*useful action is our motto.*'[6]

The principal reformists were Keufer of the book workers,

[1] L. Niel, 'Les Réformes révolutionnaires', *Bulletin de la Bourse du Travail de Reims* (15 June 1909), and id., 'Évolution ou révolution', *Travailleur syndiqué de Montpellier* (Dec. 1901), quoted op. cit., 36, 39.
[2] Carcanagues, 21 and appendix.
[3] P. M. André, 'La Débâcle du socialisme anarchisant', *Le Socialisme* (9 Nov. 1909), quoted op. cit., 43.
[4] F. Challaye, *Syndicalisme révolutionnaire et syndicalisme réformiste* (1909), 120 n. 3.
[5] Carcanagues, 68.
[6] Challaye, 127. Cf. A. Keufer, 'Le Syndicalisme réformiste', *Mouvement socialiste* (Jan. 1905), 18. The main reformist organ was *La Revue syndicaliste* (1905–10), later *La Revue socialiste* (1910–14), which contains informative articles on union life as well.

Compat of the mechanics, Renard of the textile workers and Guérard of the railwaymen.[1] The builders and the metal-workers were the most prominent revolutionaries. But it is once again impossible to divide the unions neatly in this way. Moderate leaders, among the miners for example, had to contend with growing revolutionary minorities within their ranks. Able leaders with a strong hold over unions gave them a political complexion which was not truly representative of their followers. The moderate Guérard was in due course evicted from his leadership of the railwaymen, but in the 1911 strike the East railwaymen refused to take part, and their secretary, Le Leuch, was hostile to any strikes at all.[2]

The C.G.T. was particularly weak financially. In 1910 its income was only about 20,000 francs (£800). To support the general strike of 1 May 1906 it had appealed for funds—and received the ludicrous total of 5,000 francs (£250). The national federations likewise were very poor, but they kept what money they could collect largely to themselves, so that they retained a considerable measure of independence as against the C.G.T. The National Federation of Printers was actually ten times wealthier than the C.G.T. Its annual income was 220,000 francs (£8,800). The strikes of 1906 for the eight-hour day had totally absorbed its reserves, for it paid 3 francs 50 a day strike-pay to its members and 2 francs a day to non-unionists who made common cause with the strikers. It had been able to spend 628,000 francs (£25,120) on the strike, helped by gifts of 163,000 francs from foreign unions and the International Printers' Federation and by an equal sum raised by a 5 per cent tax on its members not on strike. In June 1906 it had a deficit of 14,000 francs. Three years later it had already paid this off and accumulated savings of 212,000 francs. These figures are those of the richest union in France, outdistancing all others by far; but though the French printers had the third largest membership in the International Printers' Federation, it was only the eighth in wealth. The London and Provincial Compositors, with an equal membership to it, had an income

[1] J. B. Séverac, *Le Mouvement syndical* (1913), 74 n. and 75 n.
[2] 'Le Congrès des cheminots de l'Est' (anon.), *La Vie ouvrière* (20 Jan. 1911), 120–2); cf. A. Picart, 'Le Troisième Congrès du bâtiment', *La Vie ouvrière* (5 May 1910) 547–58, 552.

five times as large. The next richest trade, but far behind the
printers, was the miners'. Their federation, it has been seen,
existed mainly on paper, and so though it had 30,000 members,
its subscription was only 5 centimes a month per member; its
total income was under 10,000 francs (£400) a year. The
regional unions were the bodies which kept the real power
among the workers, and by far the largest of these was that of
Pas-de-Calais; but even they had great difficulty in accumulating any reserves at all. It was only after the bloody strike of
1906 that the need for funds was accepted. The subscription
was raised from 50 centimes to 2 francs a month; but of this
2 francs, only 50 centimes went to the union—as before. The
rest was placed to the credit of each unionist, remaining his
individual property, to be used in case of strike or long unemployment. It was only by this subterfuge, that is by opening
a sort of savings bank, that the Pas-de-Calais federation was
able to accumulate 779,000 francs by 1909, from its 24,000
members; and no other union at that time could compare with
this. But it is interesting that this was achieved at the expense
of all the socialist principles. In the event of a strike, each member would draw a different amount of pay, in proportion to the
savings he had made. In the textile industry the national
federation had an income of only 26,000 francs (£1,040) from
20,000 to 25,000 members. The textile union of Roubaix, with
6,000 members, was five times richer. Frequently, as with the
metallurgical or building workers, rival craft federations split up
what little income was collected. All in all, it was estimated that
in 1910 French trade unionists paid 1,353,000 francs a year,
which came to about 2½ francs a head—viz. 2 shillings a year
each. Low though subscriptions were, the workers seemed to find
them not worth their while; it was seldom that, of the subscriptions promised, more than a small proportion was ever paid.
The federations could not offer attractive benefits: only the
printers had a fund for funeral and sickness benefits and only
they and the mechanics offered unemployment pay. Travelling
money was more frequent. Many federations promised strike
pay, few of them ever paid it. There were enormous regional
differences in the willingness of workers to pay subscriptions.
The glove makers of Chaumont paid 5 francs a month, those of
Milhaud and Grenoble only 60 centimes. In such circumstances

effective federation was impossible. The worker continued to trust only the small local union where he was individually known. The notion of national solidarity, though sometimes strikingly shown by union leaders in generous donations to other unions, was rarer among the mass of their followers, among whom peasant thrift and individualism had not always been extinguished.[1]

The best account of trade unionism before 1914 was written by Griffuelhes himself.[2] His tour of France in 1911 revealed how fragmentary was its organisation, how unequal its provincial foundation, how dependent its strength on personal factors. The majority of strikes were still entered into without any preliminary union organisation.[3] The strikes of the miners themselves in 1902 and 1906 had been the work of minorities opposing the union leaders. There were still numerous regions where unionism had hardly even won a foothold, and these sometimes included highly industrialised parts of France. 'The Vosges are full of weavers whom syndicalist propaganda has been unable to galvanise so as to produce any profound or vigorous movement. Protected by [the obsessive] hate for Germany, there has been established a bourgeoisie whose power is colossal. Against it a weak trade union movement can be seen showing itself by a few revolts, after which a deep calm reappears.' In Franche-Comté likewise there was little unionism despite the very considerable industrialisation. Apart from the watchmakers of Besançon, there had been no conflict in this region since 1899.[4] Rural areas, like the Cher, by contrast had been deeply penetrated by the movement. In Grenoble a period of revolutionary activity had been ended by the secession of the deputies, who had become independent socialists, and so more favourable to the government. Lyon was torn by personal and electoral competition. In Marseille the union movement was superficial; the dispersion and heterogeneity of the city's

[1] Charles Rist, 'La Situation financière des syndicats ouvriers français', *Revue économique internationale* (Brussels, Jan. 1911), off-print in Musée Social.
[2] Victor Griffuelhes, *Voyage révolutionnaire* (1911); cf. also his *L'Action syndicaliste* (1908).
[3] *Statistiques des grèves.*
[4] Cf. Jean Charles, *Les Débuts du mouvement syndical à Besançon: la fédération ouvrière 1891–1914* (1962).

inhabitants appeared as grave obstacles. The dockers, suffering
from unemployment in the last decade of the century, were
powerless: improved conditions after 1899 made possible a
sudden organisation, and a succession of strikes, culminating in
success; but after 1904, a lock-out shattered the movement and
largely re-established the dominance of the employers.[1]

The situation in the Vosges was exceptionally interesting.
Another observer wrote in 1906: 'The sentiments of the workers
towards their employers were for long ones of submission
and respect, not to say servility and subservience. Their only
political opinion was patriotism, acute chauvinism, which made
them rally behind Boulanger or against the Jews. This has
changed since the formation of the unions. The socialist spirit
is penetrating little by little into their heads. But, despite the
strikes and the agitation, its progress is still very slow.' There
were no unions at all before 1884. A few were then founded but
the only really successful one was that of the book workers—
which was of course very moderate. Then the cotton crisis of
the early years of the century, causing the wages of the textile
workers to be reduced, led to an outbreak of strikes. Four
textile unions were founded—but, very significantly, not by the
textile workers themselves but by Pernot, the leader of the
Vosges Book Workers' Union. He also founded a federation of
the unions in the department and started a newspaper for it.
It was only then that the central trade union leaders, Renard
of the textile workers and Keufer of the book workers, came on
a tour of the Vosges and stimulated the formation of other
unions. It was always to Pernot, however, that workers in
distress in the department appealed. It was he, for example,
who organised the paper workers at Étival and brought them
out on strike. In due course his federation had 18,000 members.
His leadership of it was at first very moderate indeed: he
belonged to the *Alliance Républicaine* which had employers
among its members and he accepted government subsidies
for an anti-alcoholic campaign in his paper. Under the influence of the general trend in France, however, he was driven
to adopt a more socialist line and the moderate radical editor
of his paper was forced to resign. Significantly, it was prin-

---

[1] M. Lartigue (*née* Vecchie), 'Les Grèves des dockers à Marseille de 1890 à
1903', *Provence historique*, 10 (1960), 146–79.

cipally the refusal of the employers to deal with him that made Pernot abandon his hopes of agreement with them by conciliation and mixed unions. They preferred to set up their own 'yellow unions'. It was in this way that a potentially moderate department became revolutionary.[1]

The Bourses du Travail

The growth of national federations was considerably delayed by the rise of a rival form of federation of unions, the local Bourse du Travail. It was under this name that the unions in any one town grouped themselves, sharing the same building for their offices. The Bourses have some resemblance to the English local trades councils (e.g. a union could be a member of both the trades council and a national federation) but they differed from them in many respects and the name is best left untranslated. First of all, the Bourses du Travail owed their origin, unlike the trades councils, to official action. They were given free buildings by the municipality and substantial subsidies to meet their administrative expenses. The Bourses were expected to perform a number of public functions—the most important of which was that of labour exchange. The demand for labour exchanges was an old one. It was first canvassed by a Catholic social economist, Molinari, in the 1840s.[2] The provisional government of the republic of 1848 decreed that every town hall should have one—a dead letter like so many of its decrees. The idea then spread that some shelter should be provided where the unemployed could gather; for traditionally they congregated in certain streets, or wine shops, where employers seeking workers met them. (The Place de Grèves, now the Place de l'Hôtel de Ville, was one of the principal meeting-places, and it is from this that the word grève came to be used to mean strike.) The initiative was finally taken by the city of Paris in the 1880s under the stimulus of the new attitude towards the workers symbolised by the law of 1884. The employment exchange, it was now considered, should be run by the workers

[1] G. Airelle, 'Le Mouvement ouvrier dans les Vosges', in *Le Mouvement socialiste* (Feb.–Apr. 1906), 218–31, 333–63, 455–75.
[2] See G. de Molinari, *Les Bourses du Travail* (1893), 121–5. His proposal was first published in the legitimist newspaper *La Gazette de France*.

themselves. and be one of the services which the trade unions—
in which there was then unbounded optimism—would render
to the community. The Bourse indeed became a means of
encouraging the growth of trade unions. In 1887 the city of
Paris opened one in the rue J.-J. Rousseau and in 1892
donated a sizeable new building to it. The Bourse was essential,
said the municipal council, to prevent trade unions leading a
precarious existence, because the subscriptions they levied to
meet their expenses kept away the majority of the workers. The
Bourse would provide a free meeting-place and offices, so that
all could come without fear of incurring financial obligations
beyond their means. 'The free and permanent use of meeting
rooms will allow the workers to discuss with greater maturity
and precision the many questions which interest their industry
and which influence their wages. They will have there to guide
them all the information, news and statistics they need, an
economic, industrial and commercial library, facts about trends
of production in each industry not only in France but throughout the world.' The Bourse was thus intended at once to
encourage the formation of unions, to keep their expenses down,
to diminish their isolation from each other, and to enable them
to work together for their common interests and education.
Though the president of the municipal council inaugurated
the Bourse in the name of 'solidarity and social peace', he also
declared that its purpose was 'to enable the workers to fight
capital with equal and legal arms . . . By permitting the demands of the workers to manifest themselves freely, scientifically
and legally, the Bourse du Travail will give the republican
government the means not to snuff out these demands but to
understand them and to work for a social order more conforming to justice.'[1] Paris was quickly copied by other towns
and by 1908 there were no fewer that 157 Bourses all over
France.

In this way there grew up an original form of workers' association. The Bourses became not so much employment exchanges
as societies of trade unions, grouped on a local basis. Though
subsidised by the authorities, nearly all of them were run by

[1] F. Pelloutier, *Histoire des Bourses du Travail* (1902), 63–4, 74; L. Le Theuff,
Histoire de la Bourse du Travail de Paris (Paris thesis, 1902), 35; E. Briat, 'La Bourse
du Travail de Paris', *Le Mouvement socialiste* (1899), 52–6.

revolutionaries, who frequently used these subsidies to attack the government. They managed to do this partly because many municipalities at this time were captured by socialists and public money could thus be voted to attack the bourgeois state. (Socialist municipalities used to vote money even to support strikes.) But even where the Bourses were subsidised as a form of charity, the financial dependence did not turn them into hirelings of the bourgeoisie. The fortunes of the Paris Bourse illustrate this interestingly. At first the subsidy was used by the workers in part to agitate for socialism, but even more to line the pockets of the organisers. An inquiry in 1891 revealed considerable peculation, large travelling expenses, grants to friends for imaginary duties.[1] This was soon remedied, but the propaganda continued. Governments reacted differently according to their political complexion and optimism.

Dupuy in 1893 closed down the Paris Bourse completely, on the grounds that nearly half the 270 unions which used the Bourse (a small minority of those in Paris, it should be noted) had not registered themselves in accordance with the law of 1884—because they were too revolutionary to accept that law. He used troops to occupy the Bourse: some unions talked of an armed rising to expel them. In 1896 the radical Bourgeois reopened the Bourse but with a new constitution which compelled the workers to share their control with representatives of the government and municipality. This arrangement met with considerable hostility among the workers, whose state of mind can be seen in their refusal of a subsidy to establish a statistical department, because they preferred not to give information to the prefect of police or the government. Millerand and Waldeck-Rousseau in 1900 restored full control to the workers. The municipality, controlled after 1900 by nationalists, opposed this, and replied by ending its subsidy— which it offered instead to individual unions (of appropriate political views). The Bourse was split and two rival ones coexisted. In 1905 official tutelage was reimposed.[2] The dependence on subsidies raised many problems and kept the Bourses absorbed by their relations with the authorities. The vicissitudes

---

[1] Charles Franck, *Les Bourses du Travail et la C.G.T.* (Paris thesis, 1910), 36–7.
[2] L. Le Theuff, 59–89; A. Boivin, *Les Bourses du Travail en France* (Lille thesis, 1905), gives a useful summary of relations with the government.

of the Paris Bourse were reproduced in different ways else-where, though with a time lag. Provincial Bourses generally started as a result of a petition from a number of unions to the municipalities, which would benevolently grant a building and a subsidy. The members quickly revealed that they were divided in their attitude to the authorities. Some thought they could accept the republic—and in the 1890s the republic was young enough for it to be reasonable to expect social legislation from it—but others wished to turn the Bourses into instruments of the class struggle. These latter on the whole rapidly prevailed, for the Bourses were nearly always run by minorities among the unionists, who were themselves a minority of the workers.[1]

Three factors gave the movement its particular character. First, it became a haven for anarchists. Secondly, the Paris Bourse, jealous of the National Federation of Unions which had been captured by Guesde, set up a rival federation of B.D.T. in 1892, from the dozen then existing, mainly in southern France, in a bid to keep its hegemony over the workers move-ment. Thirdly, in 1895 Fernand Pelloutier became secretary of this Federation of B.D.T. and by 1901, when he died, he had made it an extremely vigorous and active body.

Pelloutier inhabits the pantheon of working-class mythology. He died while still only thirty-three and so, like Gambetta, he had no time to fall into discredit before a younger generation. The information about him is all one-sided and must be received with some caution. Gambetta's career, on investigation, justi-fies the high opinion spread about him by his many friends. That of Pelloutier has still to be investigated.[2] The only bio-graphy of him is written by his brother. Pelloutier was not a worker but the son of a civil servant. The family was clerical and legitimist; his grand-uncle was made a baron by Charles X and Pelloutier himself was educated in a church school. How-ever, his grandfather, as an exception, had been a republican journalist and Pelloutier quickly followed in his steps. He was expelled from his *petit séminaire* for writing an anticlerical novel-At the Collège de St. Nazaire he started a school newspaper and

---

[1] Maurice Poperen, 'La Création des Bourses du Travail en Anjou 1892-4', *Le Mouvement social*, 42 (1962), 39–55.

[2] Jacques Julliard, *Fernand Pelloutier* (1971), an excellent study, appeared after this book was sent to press.

failed his *baccalauréat* (because of 'an inadequate English essay').
He was an idle, erratic boy, and he had already contracted the
tuberculosis which was to kill him and which soon manifested
itself in a frightful facial lupus; but he had a *personnalité rayon-
nante* which won him friends everywhere, and a feverish energy in
pursuit of what he really cared about—though it took him a
long time to discover what this was. He founded a number of
ephemeral reviews, and contributed to the *Démocrate de l'Ouest*,
Briand's radical journal. In 1899 he was briefly editor of a paper
founded to support Briand's candidature in Saint-Nazaire. But
then he had to take eighteen months' rest on medical grounds,
and he emerged from this transformed, disabused by politics and
believing that salvation lay in economic action. After a brief
period as a deputy secretary of the committee for the establishment of a workers' glass factory (a co-operative) and as a dissident member of Guesde's Parti Ouvrier Français, preaching
the general strike with Briand, he obtained the post of Secretary
of the Federation of B.D.T. in 1895. Here he laboured to exclude
all politics, to ignore such problems as anticlericalism, militarism, patriotism, parliamentarism, and to concentrate on the
organisation and education of the proletariat.

Pelloutier is an interesting man, because he consciously
devoted himself to separating the working class from the bourgeoisie and to developing institutions to enable them to live as
separate a life as possible. The cleavage of classes in French
society owes something to him. Of course, the idea that the
workers should rely only on themselves had been propagated
long ago by Proudhon and Tolain in the 1860s, but their ambition had been to turn the workers into petty proprietors, and
Tolain had quickly compromised with the bourgeois state. In
a society in which Tolain represented the general pattern
which careers followed, Pelloutier is original in that he voluntarily turned against the bourgeoisie, moved into the working
class and succeeded in becoming one of the very few bourgeois leaders of an exclusively working-class movement (which
the Bourses du Travail, unlike the Socialist Party, were).

Pelloutier was a bourgeois disillusioned by his own class,
a *déclassé*, a sceptic, a pessimist, an invalid who knew he was
dying and who imagined that the society around him, for
which he felt only disgust, was dying too. He claimed to despise

all bourgeois values. He declared himself to be the irreconcilable enemy of all its moral and material despotisms, a rebel against everything, 'without God, without master, without country'. The one gleam of light in his world came from the working class. He was fascinated 'as a student of social pyschology' by its sudden rise in a movement which was threatening to overthrow, as he believed, the whole political and economic order. At once he made common cause with it, and sought to guide it towards the creation of a truly free society. The workers alone could regenerate the world, destroy the hierarchic organisation of the bourgeois state and replace it by a free association of anarchist producers. In the Bourses du Travail he found his ideal instrument, for these would not only prepare the revolution but form the embryo from which the new order would spring. They would be 'within the bourgeois state a veritable socialist (economic and anarchist) state'.

Pelloutier deeply influenced the working-class movement in three ways. First, as an anarchist, he helped to detach it from co-operation with the bourgeois state, to spread scepticism about the parliamentary system, disillusionment with its social legislation and contempt for its ideas of the conciliation of classes. Secondly, as the organiser of the Bourses du Travail, he did a great deal to diminish the rivalries between trades which the unions and federations tended to preserve or strengthen, to introduce solidarity among the workers (which the politicians were trying to establish between classes in the nation as a whole). Thirdly, he popularised the idea of association among the workers by making the Bourses du Travail of immediate and practical use to their members, instead of simply being organisations which fomented strikes or which served as springboards for the ambitions of traitor politicians. He drew up a plan of work which gave the Bourses a uniform goal, with detailed advice on how best to use their meagre financial resources. This was taken up as a model by the numerous Bourses whose creation he stimulated. It gave them four objects to pursue: first to provide mutual benefits, unemployment pay, accident insurance, journey money for those travelling in search of work, and above all an employment exchange. Secondly, they should offer education to the workers since this alone could fit them for their new role: they should open libraries, social museums, information offices, classes of professional and general instruction. They should, thirdly, engage in propaganda among the uninitiated, spreading the word among the peasantry and sailors, and organising unions of them as well as of industrial workers. Fourthly, and it is significant he put this object last, they should have a section dealing with strikes, and with agitation against undesirable legislation.

Pelloutier gave himself up to his task as secretary with the almost superhuman energy of a man who knows he cannot have long. When he could no longer afford to have his journal printed, he set it up in type himself, after having written most of it on his own as well. He called it *L'Ouvrier des Deux Mondes* (was this title only accidentally reminiscent of Le Play?) and set great store by it, for he insisted that 'what the worker lacks above all is knowledge of his misery'. He undertook to inform him particularly in a series of articles which were later printed as a sizeable book entitled *La Vie ouvrière*—a great jumble of sombre facts, made to look more sombre still. His energy was rewarded, for by 1901 there were 74 Bourses in France and they were among the most vigorous elements in working-class life.[1]

However, while Pelloutier lived, no effective union between his federation and the national federations could be achieved. The Federation of B.D.T. had of course originally been formed in 1892 as a rival to the National Federation of Unions which was dominated by the Guesdistes; but even when the Guesdistes were ousted by the partisans of the general strike (of whom Briand, prompted by Pelloutier, was the leader), and the Confédération Générale du Travail was formed, devoted like the Bourses exclusively to economic action, Pelloutier remained jealous of his independence. Though he talked of the need for union, he was not willing to have it at any price. Personalities played some part in bringing this about: Pelloutier despised the secretary of the C.G.T., Lagailse, who was indeed a mediocrity, and apparently a traitor too (he was said to have given the government advance warning of a plan for a general strike). But Pelloutier claimed that the C.G.T.'s constitution in fact stimulated division under the banner of a false union. By accepting any union, whether local, departmental, national, craft or industrial, it did not force unions to organise themselves

---

[1] Jean Montreuil, *Histoire du mouvement ouvrier en France* (1947), 157.

into large federations. He claimed that politics played too great a role in the C.G.T. and he wanted a confederation on the same lines as that achieved by the Bourses, where adherents of different types of socialism put aside their political differences and concentrated on industrial activities. The C.G.T. moreover expected a revolution to take place very soon indeed and therefore ignored the long-term education of the workers. This was still the romantic age of strikes: any small workshop on strike appeared as the harbinger of the millennium and filled the C.G.T. with a fever of excitement. Pelloutier on the other hand was becoming increasingly practical in his outlook.

He grew disillusioned. In 1900 he sadly admitted that for every disinterested militant in the unions, there were nine egoists. His optimism about the transformation which education would effect was modified. Before his death, he even ceased to believe in the general strike.[1] It has been suggested that had he lived longer he might have evolved on the lines of Briand, his former associate, and become increasingly willing to co-operate with the state. His early ideas had certainly been confused and he had not always succeeded in clarifying them. For example, he had said that universal suffrage could not be used to solve the social question, because the law of supply an demand meant that no one man could become richer without another becoming poorer.[2] Later, writing on the possibilities of partial reform, he admitted that the state need not necessarily be evil in itself if the men who ran it were improved. He willingly accepted subsidies from the government and the municipalities. He agreed that co-operatives need not necessarily be egoistic. He abandoned his antimilitarism to the point of saying he would fight in a defensive war.[3] These modifications in attitude did not necessarily spread to all his movement; but some members certainly did become reformists. The Bourses should not be seen too clearly as one type. Pelloutier himself should not be regarded as their only leader. It just happens that more is known about him but there were many others, some of them of outstanding ability. Pelloutier's importance tends to be exaggerated, owing to the inadequacy of the sources. He did

[1] V. Dave's preface to Pelloutier's *Histoire des Bourses du Travail* (1906), vi.
[2] Maurice Pelloutier, *Fernand Pelloutier, sa vie, son œuvre 1867–1901* (1911), 76.
[3] Montreuil, 168–70.

not create the Bourses, of which there were already fifteen when he joined them, and their federation was formed before him, with Cordier as the first secretary. He was not an isolated leader, but an exceptional example of a rich crop of organisers who flourished in the last years of the century.[1]

Though the Bourses were full of life in this period, their achievements should not be exaggerated either. Their employment exchanges, one of their main attractions, were not very successful and provided jobs for only a small minority of workers, for employers not surprisingly disliked dealing with them. Their war against the commercial employment exchanges was crowned by a victory in the law (9 March 1904) allowing municipalities to abolish these, but the municipalities which did so then tended to set up their own free exchanges at the town hall. The Bourses now had to fight these instead because they were rivals and because they feared the municipalities would decide that they made the Bourses superfluous. The Bourses had the advantage that they had a national organisation, and so could theoretically give information about jobs all over the country. Attempts to organise this in practice, however, failed dismally. The viaticum (journey money for unemployed workers) was used as an inducement to win recruits. Angers Bourse, for example, gave 1 fr. 50 to unionists and 1 fr. 25 to others travelling in search of a job, and in addition offered coupons for free meals and lodging—but in 1896 only 186 coupons were issued. Some Bourses like Nantes did not send men to hotels but transformed their offices at night into dormitories with hammocks, where they harangued their guests with suitable propaganda. But gradually as these benefits, available to anyone, became known, a new race of idle tramps arose who travelled round the country parasitically making use of them. Pelloutier's great efforts to produce a national viaticum scheme (one was already effectively in operation among the book workers) failed because of local particularism, and because the large Bourses claimed the small ones could not offer truly reciprocal benefits. The question was canvassed and debated without issue for many years. Pelloutier's statistical office, to

---

[1] E. Dolléans, 'Pelloutier et le réveil du syndicalisme', *Société d'histoire de la Troisième République* (May 1937), 36–40, especially the comments of Zévaès and Halévy.

collect information on unemployment, collapsed in 1906. The government subsidy dried up when his successors refused to give an account of how they spent it (in fact, on propaganda); it ceased to serve an impartial public purpose when it kept labour away from strike areas. Pelloutier's scheme for unemployment and accident funds remained a paper one. His libraries, designed to spread enlightenment and knowledge, were disappointing. That of the Paris Bourse, by far the largest, still had only 2,700 volumes in 1910, many of them novels. Professional classes made rather more headway, but again on a small scale. Pelloutier had interesting ideas about winning the peasants over, saying that they should not be forced into unions of the industrial type, but instead should be offered co-operative ones adapted to their needs and admitting small proprietors with under 25 acres (10 hectares). In 1910, however, there were still only 9,320 agricultural workers in the C.G.T. His seamen's hostels did not prove popular, since the individualist fishermen rebelled against the urban workers' propaganda that was served up there, just as much as they disliked the Catholic bourgeois hostels. Only among the dockers were advances successfully made. In general, therefore, the Bourses remained in a precarious state. Pelloutier, though pleased with the success of his recruitment, feared that many of the Bourses which were formed were very weak and bound to collapse if official aid was withdrawn. He came to feel that no more should be created until the existing ones had become stronger and more independent, and had spread into the surrounding countryside.[1]

The reliance on public subsidies not only put the Bourses in a delicate and dangerous position but fomented quarrels within the movement as to whether the subsidies should be accepted at all, or whether they were a source of corruption. After Pelloutier's death, Yvetot, his successor, changed the character of the Federation of Bourses considerably, using it more and more for revolutionary and antimilitarist propaganda, as opposed to the purely working-class purposes Pelloutier had favoured. Many Bourses either lost or renounced their subsidies. In 1912, however, they still received 369,915 francs from municipalities and 52,900 francs from departments.[2] On

[1] Charles Franck, *Les Bourses du Travail et la C.G.T.* (1910), 71–199.
[2] *Annuaire des syndicats professionnels* (1912), xliv–xlix.

the eve of the war, the Bourses had still not solved the question of their financial independence, and one of their leaders rightly described them as being in a state of crisis.[1]

The Yellow Unions

At the right wing of the working-class movement stood the Yellow Unions, who for a time were probably not much fewer in numbers than the revolutionaries, though their existence has now been rather forgotten. The Yellow Unions were so called after the badge they adopted, the yellow flower of the broom. Their origins go back to the independent trade unions founded by Catholics, principally in Paris and the Nord. In 1887 Brother Hieron had founded a union of shopworkers in Paris, membership of which involved religious obligations, though after 1900 this requirement was dropped in an effort to widen its appeal. In 1898 and 1899 similar unions were founded for the book, metal, building, furniture and clothing industries. All of them offered a large number of mutual benefits, insurance and co-operatives. In the Nord the Catholic unions were so successful that they combined in a federation and even published a newspaper. All members of this federation had to undertake never to go on strike until arbitration had failed.

These unions, however, remained relatively restricted because of their over-close links with the Church and the employers: the initiative in their formation always seems to have come from above. Some of their leaders argued that they should openly declare themselves Catholic and openly engage in right-wing politics, and one of them, Delcourt-Hoeillot, started a Catholic miners' federation, the *Union des syndicats Sainte-Barbe*.[2] There were few employers, however, who were sufficiently demagogic or astute to start trade unions, the very idea of which was too awful to contemplate. The yellow movement therefore did not follow on from these Catholic unions, but was started independently by workers or at least by men who were not employers.

[1] Paul Delesalle, 'Les Bourses du Travail et leurs difficultés actuelles', *Le Mouvement socialiste* (1908), 161–70; cf. F. Marie, secrétaire de l'Union des Syndicats de la Seine, 'Les Méfaits de la manne officielle: le subventionnisme et l'organisation ouvrière', *La Vie ouvrière* (Oct. and Nov. 1911), 507–26, 635–54.

[2] Maurice Gros, *Étude du mouvement syndical ouvrier en France: syndicats jaunes ou indépendants* (Dijon thesis, Paris, 1904), 319.

The first proper yellow union was founded at Le Creusot by the blacklegs in the strike of 1899. Its leader, Mangematin, was a young house painter of twenty-eight who had experienced several spells of unemployment and was tired of strikes.[1] His union flourished. A similar one was formed in the mines at Montceau, and others followed rapidly. An employee of the Orléans Railway Company, Lanoir, established an independent Bourse du Travail in Paris, uniting these various unions. Laroche-Joubert, the Bonapartist paper manufacturer of Angoulême, came to his aid. The new nationalist majority of the Paris municipal council voted him a subsidy, which the socialist minister Millerand promptly cancelled. Nevertheless the president of the republic Loubet received Lanoir at the Élysée in 1901 and assured him of his sympathy for his work. Méline's Republican Association declared their support for him, but at the same time some accused him of being the tool of Waldeck-Rousseau. It seems that several political parties hoped to profit from his aid in the elections of 1902. Lanoir claimed he had 200,000 members, in 317 unions affiliated to his Bourse. The true figure was perhaps one-third of that. The movement nevertheless seemed to be an important one. Lanoir, who had a gift for political intrigue and negotiation as well as an insinuating personality, won a reputation as an innovator in influential circles.

However, internal discord knocked down the whole edifice like a house of cards when Lanoir's deputy, Pierre Bietry, rebelled against his authority. Bietry was an incorrigible agitator, a vigorous orator and an able organiser of masses. Born obscurely of humble parents, he had spent an adventurous youth in Algeria in various jobs (selling watches in native clothing according to some). He had learnt to read and write only when he joined up to do his military service. He rose to be a corporal but was demoted for misbehaviour. He then worked for a time as a watch-maker, but quickly got involved in organising strikes and unions, among several professions in the Doubs. On one occasion in 1898 he organised a march of 10,000 strikers towards Paris. He was a delegate to socialist congresses, where he opposed the general strike. An article he published in Lanoir's paper led to his expulsion from

[1] Mangematin later became assistant station master of Lyon. Gros, 139-43.

the Socialist Party. After working for Lanoir, he was expelled
by him in turn, and founded his own Fédération des Jaunes,
which soon eclipsed its rival. (Lanoir retired to Juan-les-Pins,
with a pension—it is not stated from whom.) In January 1903
Bietry transformed his federation into a political party and
called it the National Socialist Party. The French may claim
to have invented even that. The party lasted for only one year
and little is known about it, but the Fédération des Jaunes was
soon revived.

It is uncertain at what stage the movement won the patronage
of Japy, who employed 7,000 watch-makers in the Doubs.
Bietry had once worked for him, attacked him, but they then
appear to have come to an agreement. Lanoir had been skilful
at obtaining subsidies from industrialists and politicians. Bietry
took some time to learn this art, so that for a while poverty
kept his activities to a minimum. His headquarters was a single
room, later only a share of a room (unlike Lanoir's Bourse of
no fewer than twenty-seven offices). Bietry's socialism was also
quickly changing. He had at first been simply a heretic among
the socialists. He now opposed not only strikes, but also the
class struggle and expropriation. He preached the need for
a piece of property for every man. He now found the means
of achieving this in Japy's creed of participation in profits.
Laroche-Joubert, the paper manufacturer, had long practised
this and he too became a patron of the federation. Half a dozen
other industrialists joined in and the federation flourished. In
1906 Bietry was elected to parliament for Brest, as a candidate
of the workers but against the extremism of the revolutionaries;
a supporter of his, Dupourqué, was also elected. They claimed
400,000 members in their federation at this period (obviously
exaggerated).

However, Bietry's position now grew difficult, because of
the danger of weakening his federation by introducing politics
into it, and because of the accusations which were levelled
against him, that his unions existed only to further his political
ambitions. He tried to resolve his dilemma by founding in 1908
a political party which would be separate from the unions: Le
Parti propriétiste anti-étatiste. Its object was the capture of
power by its members—which it thought would take ten years—
so as to facilitate the acquisition of property by the largest

possible number of people and to limit the role of the state. Bietry thus ended up where one would have thought he would have begun, a defender of property, but property for the small man. He remained hostile to 'speculating capitalists' and to the Jews. He proposed, when the Western Railway was nationalised in 1908, that it should be run by a company of its employees. He envisaged compulsory unions and regional parliaments representing industry and agriculture, to which relevant legislation would be referred. On the subject of co-operatives his movement was divided: some favoured them but others objected on the ground that they might ruin small shopkeepers. Bietry differed from the social Catholics in that he objected to charity: he wished the workers to have a share in running industry; and Japy declared himself to be 'unfortunately' a bad Catholic and no clerical. The Yellow Union movement had some resemblance to later fascism, but Bietry, for all his considerable qualities, did not have the makings of a dictator, or even of a party leader. He retired from politics—it is not clear why—in 1910 and went off to Indo-China, where he died in 1918. The phenomenon which he represented was to reappear after the war.[1]

To get a true picture of trade union life, one should not look only at the few large national federations, which contained only a minority of the unionists of the country. The more typical unit was the local provincial trade union, of which there were in 1912 over 5,000. On average, each of these had around a hundred members; some had as few as eight or twelve.[2] They were spread thinly over France and inevitably frequently led an isolated existence. If one looks not at Paris or the Nord, but at, say, a poor department like Ardèche, one can see these small unions in a rather different perspective. They appear more as clubs than as part of an organised movement. In the whole of the department of Ardèche, the only important industrial town which could possibly have unions of any size was Annonay, and this had a population of only 16,000. The old trades of leather dressing and paper making were its prin-

---

[1] Auguste Pawlowski, *Les Syndicats Jaunes* (1911); Pierre Bietry, *Le Socialisme et les Jaunes* (1906); J. Jolly, *Dictionnaire des parlementaires français*, 2 (1962), 599–600.
[2] *Annuaire des syndicats professionnels* (1912) gives a full list.

cipal occupations and in the 1850s it had only three factories
with more than 100 workers. The early unions were, therefore,
really only fraternities. In 1848 some 40 or 50 men formed
a union of leather dressers, but it was dissolved in 1851. Several
other small groups appeared briefly: *La Belle Étoile*, *Le Soleil*
(the president of this was an innkeeper), *L'Union des Travailleurs*
(the president was a commercial traveller): these names are
enough to show that they were friendly societies of the traditional, mutualist character. A strike in 1855 was thus held
without any union being involved at all. The first union of
leather workers to last was established only in 1880, with 400
members, rising quickly to 1,000. It won many concessions, but
it was mainly prized for its co-operative bakery (founded 1885,
which by 1907 had a turnover of 100,000 francs) and for its
pension scheme. Another union of *Ouvriers Mégissiers Palis-
soneurs* with 500 members in 1900, and 350 in 1912, showed
even more strikingly how much akin to the old restrictive
guilds these provincial unions often were: it concentrated on
protecting its members against rival competition, and on
limiting apprenticeships. In other words, the leather workers
of this town had only a small minority of unionists among them
and even these could not agree to form a single union. The
proliferation of small groups was the rule. There were in addition a large number of tiny unions for various trades round the
department. Not one of these unions belonged to the C.G.T.
The only revolutionary one, which was not just local and
corporatist, was not a working-class one at all, but that of the
Instituteurs. The largest union in the department was in fact
an agricultural one, founded by a priest in 1896. It had 1,223
members, who annually celebrated the feast of St. Vincent by
attending a special mass, drinking military and agricultural
toasts and listening to speeches on social concord from a deputy
who simultaneously defended the liberties of the Church and
the privileges of the alcohol makers.[1]

Proselytism by individuals and the accidents of personality
often explain the unequal spread of unionism in different parts
of the country and their varying political character. Thus
Limoges during the Second Empire was not industrialised but

[1] Élie Reynier, 'L'Organisation syndicale dans l'Ardèche', *La Vie ouvrière*
(July–Aug. 1913), 19–26, 93–6, 147–54.

it was an important centre for porcelain making and so had numerous highly paid artisans. Suddenly in 1870 (before the war) these formed a union. Why did they choose this particular moment? The stimulus came from outside. In fulfilment of the decisions of the International, two porcelain workers from Sèvres were sent by the Paris unions to Limoges and their public lectures started the movement. In the same way the more revolutionary activity of the Limoges porcelain workers was originated by the lecture given in that town in 1883 by Allemane.[1] The spread of the movement to the countryside was in turn due largely to the lithographer Noel who toured from village to village, establishing an agricultural union. It is interesting that Allemane's influence did not, however, survive, at least in its original form. The leader of the trade union movement in Limoges, Treich, a porcelain turner, soon abandoned Allemane's leadership and became a Possibilist, and then a Millerandist. When Millerand visited them in 1899 Treich declared: 'Now that you are minister, we have become free workers.' Treich ended up with a *bureau de tabac* given to him by the minister as a reward for his services. The effect of his long leadership was to make the federation and Bourse du Travail he established distinctly moderate, rejecting the general strike. This moderation reflected the dominance of the porcelain workers in Limoges. Here the union movement originated among the best-paid workers and was gradually spread by their propaganda to the less privileged. It is instructive to see the kind of strikes the movement produced. A large number seemed to have been reactions against competition—from machines, women or apprentices. There was a strike in 1895 by workers who resented the increasingly strict rules of discipline imposed in the factories: they claimed the right to go out when they pleased, and on this occasion struck because they were not allowed to attend *en masse* an exciting trial concerning the exhumation of a corpse. In the same year the first women's union in the region, that of the corset makers, went on strike

---

[1] Allemane was likewise a decisive influence in starting the union movement among the slaters of Trélazé: François Lebrun, 'Ludovic Menard et la naissance du syndicalisme ardoisier', *L'Actualité de l'histoire* (Oct.–Dec. 1959), 6–7. Menard is another example of a single individual creating a whole movement. The slaters later joined the miners' federation, reinforcing the revolutionary element in it. The proselytising work of Allemane deserves study.

to end the compulsory religious practices their employer
demanded. The Limoges unions became a radical centre for
the spread of socialism, but just as the type of artisan pre-
dominating in the city modified the nature of the socialism
that was received from Paris, so in turn the peculiar economic
characteristics of the surrounding countryside modified the
teaching as it was received there. The socialist deputy, appealing to the peasant electorate, came out firmly in favour of
private property (except that sharecroppers would become
proprietors). Antimilitarism in these unions meant no more
than that troops should not be used to suppress strikes.[1]

The case of André Lyonnais—totally unknown on a national
level—illustrates the way the movement could spread locally. The
son of a journeyman stone cutter, he had worked at Le Creusot
for seventeen years, since the age of thirteen, until he was
dismissed because the man who guided his youth, a doctor, had
asked him to bury him in a civil ceremony, which he did at the
time of Broglie's Ordre Moral. He moved to Le Havre as a
book-keeper, and there organised no fewer than fifteen unions.
'I am not an enemy of capitalism,' he said, 'because I am
a partisan of co-operation and therefore, as such, I wish to
become a capitalist. I am not a partisan [either] of the interference of the state in industrial affairs . . . I have studied England for ten years now; I am filled with English ideas, I admit
it, but not to the point of wishing to copy our friends across
the channel servilely. . . . We want to achieve our deliverance by
ourselves, and it is the law on trade unions [of 1884] which will
be the instrument of this emancipation . . . In two or three years
time the employers will negotiate with us and there will be no
more strikes . . . We have no hostility towards [them] . . . we
wish to increase the number of employers . . . and to equalise the
profits of capital and labour.'[2] The English influence of this
man was probably not typical, but due to contacts in Le
Havre; the influence of the radical doctor, however, is a fairly
frequent phenomenon. Lyonnais was clearly a unionist of the
first generation. His evidence raises the question of whether, or

[1] Pierre Cousteix, 'Le Mouvement ouvrier limousin de 1870 à 1939', *L'Actualité de l'histoire* (Dec. 1957).
[2] Evidence of Lyonnais to the *Commission chargée de faire une enquête sur la situation des ouvriers de l'industrie et de l'agriculture en France, Procès-Verbaux* (1884), 103–10.

to what extent, the workers in France were more irreconcilable
enemies of the employers and the state than in other countries.

Workers and Employers

In 1901 a well-known journalist, Jules Huret, went round
a number of employers, asking them their views on unions,
strikes and arbitration. The verbatim reports of his interviews
reveal a very striking conservatism. These employers are a
minute sample, but they are representative all the same. Rességuier, the head of the glass works of Carmaux, said: 'The
workers have no personal ideas, no initiative, they are like
sheep . . . [they] need to be led.' The arrival of trade unions
meant only that they 'had changed masters' and the trade
union leaders now terrorised them. He spoke with angry hatred
of these leaders and of the socialists. He was an example of the
employer who resisted any change in relationships within the
factory and there were clearly a vast number of others, who,
like him, could not see that the introduction of democracy in
the political field (which many regretted) could not but affect
the industrial and commercial world. Teste, vice-president
of the federation of employers' unions in Lyon, insisted that compulsory arbitration of disputes would destroy 'order and prosperity, because it would destroy the authority of the employer'.
This hierarchical view of society was shown likewise by an
employer of Lille who refused to recognise trade unions: 'In
my factory, I tell my workers that if they have any complaints,
they may send the two oldest employees and I will talk with
them, because I am sure they would be reasonable.' This refusal
to negotiate with elected representatives left violence as the only
resort of the workers. In the documents of strikes in this period
one meets again and again instances of employers who haughtily
ignore the unions and do not even answer their letters. 'The
principal obstacle to harmonious relations between employers
and workers', wrote an author who knew the industrial world
well, 'is most often to be found in . . . the fact that the employers
are sometimes, as happens to injured husbands, the last to know
the aspirations, extent and intensity of the real or imaginary
grievances of the workers'.[1] Many employers heard their

---

[1] E. Lozé, *Conciliation et arbitrage dans le bassin homiller du Nord et du Pas-de-Calais,
1889–1898* (Paris and Nancy, 1899), 53.

workers' grievances only through the foremen but these were
far from being considered the workers' friends. The disputes
about which side of the Conseil de Prud'hommes they should
serve on show their equivocal position; numerous strikes
against their behaviour reveal that it was often more the foremen than the employers who exasperated the workers. Foremen were notorious for their favouritism. They not infrequently
had grocery shops or cafés kept by their wives and they preferred
workers who were their customers. Their shops represented
a patronage system additional to that of the employers.

According to Ribot there had been a transformation among
employers in the course of the last thirty years of the century.
'One meets far less often today those absolutist employers who
do not even consent to discuss with those who receive wages
from them.'[1] An example of the new kind can be seen in Savon,
who employed several thousand dockers in Marseille. 'The days
of the employer's arbitrary power are past, unfortunately', he
said. 'Till these last few years we did what we pleased with the
worker, or almost. And things did not go any worse then. But,
well, it is finished . . . The worker has opened his eyes or at least
men have taken it upon themselves to open them for him. He
is conscious now of what he is, of his power, of his omnipotence.
We must reckon with him from now on. For long we could hope
to subdue these trade unions that rose against our authority.
We seduced their presidents, and won them over to our side.
That too is finished, over. Then we had the idea that it was the
fault of the government. We asked ourselves if a good despot,
a king, an emperor, a Boulanger, strong, tough, could not
quickly bring these men to reason and bring all the old things
back to their old condition. That was not true either. We see
around us monarchical governments more frightened than ours
before the workers' movement . . . Let us therefore be sensible
and philosophic. A wave threatens to submerge us; let us not
try to prevent it advancing, that is impossible. Let us analyse it,
let us build dams.'[2]

Examples of this kind of philosophic resignation are, however,
rare. Briand insisted that the French unions could never re-
semble the English ones because of a fundamental difference in
the mentality of the employers in the two countries. 'Between

[1] Jules Huret, *Les Grèves, enquête* (1901), 140.   [2] Ibid., 60–4.

English employers and workers, it is simply a question of money. .... If in the course of a strike the employer sees that his interests are threatened, he does not hesitate to capitulate.' But in France the workers had to obtain a victory not only over material interests but also over 'sentiments of pride, arrogance and the caste spirit of the employing class'—so intimidation and force were inevitable. The French employer was usually guided more by prejudices about his authority than by his industrial interest, which he was willing to sacrifice to maintain appearances, to be able to say: 'I wish to be master in my own house.'[1] The contrast with England is perhaps based on too elementary a view of the English problem, but there was some truth in Briand's idea.

Even Henri Japy, described as one of the most liberal employers in France, and noted for giving participation in profits and pensions schemes to his 7,000 watch-makers, exhibited an attitude which many workers could not but find equally intolerable. The workers, he said, were not sly cheats trying to outdo their masters, but warm-hearted and honest, 'However, they are children, big children who want only protection and who think about revolting only when they feel they have lost this protection or that it tries to turn into domination.' For all his philanthropy, his aim was to preserve his influence over the workers. He gave them a share of profits not because he was a socialist but to give them a share of the pleasures of capital.[2] In the same way the chocolate manufacturer Devinck in 1874 had said that the way to conciliate the classes was to 'moralise the worker', to give him, that is, bourgeois standards and aspirations. 46 per cent of the children born in the tenth *arrondissement* of Paris were illegitimate. 'We must re-establish morality, without which there will never be order.'[3]

The fact that many employers were former workers who had made good did not improve matters. Frédéric Lévy, who for twelve years, during the Second Empire as a mayor in Paris, tried to bring workers and employers together in mixed unions and then admitted his failure, said that 'it is the workers who have become employers who are always the most difficult and

[1] Huret, 166–7.
[2] Ibid., 117.
[3] Fernand Desportes, *Enquête sur les associations syndicales* (1874), 85.

the most recalcitrant.'[1] These new men were certainly conscious of the breach between them and their workers, though
they seem unable to explain it. The president of the carpet-
weavers employers union of Paris complained in 1884 that
when he became a master, he took with him some of his old
work-mates—'to me they were not workers but friends'. But
when a strike broke out, they joined it—which gave him great
pain.[2] A lithographic master printer likewise declared that in
his trade nine-tenths of the employers were former workers, but
'from the moment you are at the head of a firm, you are despite
everything and *de parti pris* their enemy'.[3]

The workers resented being looked down on by their employers and being pariahs in the social order. However, they
might perhaps have borne this if they had been more convinced of their masters' superiority, but few employers were
successful enough to command their respect. Mediocrity and
incompetence were so prevalent that the workers had good
reason to despise many employers. It is very interesting to see
workers in the 1880s criticising not so much the capitalist
system as the inability of its leaders to run it successfully. Tolain,
one of the pioneers of the union movement, considered that
the recurrent economic crises were due to the ignorance of the
employers. The employers stupidly thought that wages were the
only flexible item which should respond to competition. They
neglected transport, credit and sales methods. 'The majority of
our industrialists are men with rather limited outlook, who see
work as simply a necessity to which they must subject themselves
for a certain time, so as to be able as soon as possible not to play
a role in the world but to go and live on their savings in some
distant corner and, as is vulgarly said, grow cabbages. The
industrialist who is in this position, who looks upon retirement
as the dawn, lets his equipment rot. He does not keep up with
what goes on in foreign countries. As soon as he has acquired
enough money to be able to take a rest, he sells his firm or if
need be liquidates it and goes off.'[4] The president of the Paris
Chamber of Export Commerce and Jacques Siegfried, the self-
made business magnate, both admitted the truth of this picture:

[1] Ibid., 148.
[2] *Procès-verbaux de la commission . . . sur la situation des ouvriers* (1884), 279.
[3] Ibid., 89.   [4] Ibid., 127–31.

French manufacturers, they agreed, hardly tried to sell their goods, to adapt their production to the needs of the world markets.[1] Tolain claimed that the hostility between master and man was increasing not only because of the growth of factories but also because of the open profiteering which spread during the Second Empire, when speculators cynically devoted themselves to making money by any and every means, ignoring all moral considerations. The worker could not feel bound by duty in such conditions.[2]

It certainly became clear that the workers were not getting a fair share of the profits of increased prosperity. Between 1806 and 1891 the value of the shares of the Anzin Mine Company increased 23 times; those of the Courrières Mines were worth in 1891 over 150 times their value in 1851; those of Lens were 90 times their value and yielded annually in dividends 3 times their original cost. During the same period the miners' wages rose by only a fraction, remaining roughly at subsistence level and they were even reduced pitilessly whenever there was an economic setback.[3] The employers on the whole systematically fought against any change in the redistribution of wealth. In the majority of cases they systematically fought the growth of unionism. With time a few began to realise that this attitude had contributed to making the French union movement more threatening to their position than it need have been. An employer told the Congress of the Federation of Industrialists in 1907: 'Hitherto, the employers have done all in their power to prevent reasonable workers from forming unions; the result is that it is the unreasonable ones who are masters of them.' Japy added: 'If the employers had not ignored the unions, we should not be in the position in which we are.'[4]

Working-Class Culture

The trade union leaders, interesting though they are, tell one about only one relatively small section of the proletariat. They

---

[1] *Procès-verbaux de la commission . . . sur la situation des ouvriers* (1884), 272, 274.
[2] Ibid., 130.
[3] E. Lozé, *La Grève de 1891 dans les bassins homillers du Nord et du Pas-de-Calais* (Arras, 1891), 22–3, 41.
[4] G. Olphe-Gaillard, ancien inspecteur du travail, *L'Organisation des forces ouvrières* (1911), 295. Cf. Peter Stearns, 'Employer Policy towards Labour Agitation in France 1900–1914', *Journal of Modern History* (1968), 474–500.

were an élite, usually with above average qualifications and education. They were, increasingly, the sons of workers, rather than new recruits into industry. Among others in this same situation, they were untypical in that, though well qualified, they were unwilling to try to climb out of the working class; they rejected the ambition of setting themselves up independently in their own business, and they had low expectations of promotion.[1] Conflict soon broke out between these militants and those they sought to represent, and the next stage of trade union history was dominated, to a considerable extent, by this.

In the growing manufacturing industries, a large proportion of the workers were peasants, and very often peasants trying to better themselves. It is obviously difficult to discover or to generalise about the motives that led people to forsake the land for the factories, but one investigation, carried out by a doctor in the Tarn, found that the ambition of these migrants was, in descending order, higher wages, more regular work throughout the year, insurance against illness and accident, and the prospect of a pension.[2] These certainly were advantages which agriculture could not offer in this period. For long, the newly arrived peasants kept many of their traditional ideas. In the mines of Carmaux, for example, they often kept a piece of land on which they grew much of their food; they expected their wages as miners to provide them with cash for the extras they could not produce, and for savings with which to buy or build a house. Far from reducing their hours of work by going into the mines (where hours were limited by law), they now worked much longer, because before or after their shift underground they would carry out in addition about half a peasant's day of labour on their plots. Friction inevitably arose between them and those who had lost contact with the land, because they, growing a lot of food themselves, could afford to work for less. The full proletarianisation of these peasants was a slow process.

In Carmaux at the turn of the century, some 37 per cent of the miners owned their own houses, and 44 per cent owned allotments. They were not primarily seeking better housing

[1] Marc Maurice, 'Déterminants du militantisme et projet syndical des ouvriers et des techniciens', *Sociologie du travail* (July–Sept. 1965), 254–72.

[2] Dr. Valatx, *Monographie sur le mouvement de la population dans le département du Tarn de 1801 à 1911* (Albi, 1917), quoted by Rolande Trempé, *Les Mineurs de Carmaux 1848–1914* (1971), 1. 184–5.

conditions, because they preferred to own inferior shacks rather than live in the new model housing estates the employers put up. In Carmaux, the mining company built 91 bungalows (each with two rooms and an outhouse) for its workers in 1866, but it managed to let only 20, because the workers hated having their rent deducted from their wages, having to pay compensation for the damage they caused, and generally having the company interfere in their private lives. This was a phase some workers moved out of. In Pas-de-Calais, the six largest mining companies succeeded in getting 51 per cent of their employees into company housing, and in the Nord some companies housed as many as 85 per cent. The peasant-workers, however, even refused the loans offered to them by their employers, preferring to borrow privately, at a higher rate of interest. The cash they put down as a deposit for a house was accumulated in the traditional peasant way, with help from their fiancée's dowry, or from their own inheritance. The sums they had at their disposal were tiny, but they won their way into the status of proprietor, even though they had to content themselves with buying only half a house, or one room—but always with a fraction of a garden and of a pigsty too. A sociological study carried out in the 1950s showed that these workers of agricultural origin remained far more optimistic about the possibility of moving up in the world than unskilled workers of urban origin. They had smaller families, they complained less about the disagreeable physical conditions they encountered, because they saw the factory only as a stopping place. Their level of education was generally lower than that of their factory mates, but perhaps because they were more ignorant of the world, they had high hopes of a better job, at least for their children. They generally had no desire to remain factory workers. They talked politics far less than other workers; they did not see society as ruled by class antagonisms. The very fact that they themselves had escaped from the land showed, as they believed, that individual effort could overcome social obstacles.[1] The constant influx of these peasants regularly diluted the militancy of the revolutionaries.

Going into the factories, however, brought the peasants serious new problems. In the first place, regular employment was far from assured: they became victims now of economic

[1] Alain Touraine and O. Ragazzi, *Ouvriers d'origine agricole* (1961).

crises, which they could not predict, instead of the seasons, which they could. One can see this in the mines of Carmaux, on which Rolande Trempé has recently thrown such precise light, by the simultaneous use of workers', employers' and public archives. The company frequently laid off its workers when it could not sell its coal—for as much as fifty-six days in 1886 for example. It stopped recruiting altogether from time to time; the fear of being sacked dominated the town. The workers felt victims of obscure forces. A new tyranny also irked them. When they first came into the mines, if they retained their links with the land, they would seldom work the full six-day week. Absenteeism was practised on such a large scale—sometimes reaching 50 per cent—that workers were given prizes if they achieved a mere twenty-three days' presence a month—a rare feat. Mondays were used to recover from Sundays; fair days and festivals were seized upon as an excuse to lay down tools. One of the major battles the company waged was to instil discipline into these men, whose irregularity cost them a lot of money. By 1914, absenteeism was down to 4 per cent. The company used fines, dismissals, threats, but in the end evolved new methods of payment as the best solution. This was another major source of conflict. The Carmaux company survived because it pursued a rigorous policy of reducing costs and increasing productivity. This was achieved partly by technical improvements but also by making the men work harder. The increased agitation of the unions was a clear reply to this tightening pressure. By 1890, the company had most workers at its mercy, because the majority of them were by then proletariatised, dependent on their wages, and it pushed its advantages to the very limit. No understanding of each other's position was ever reached between employers and workers. The workers had no knowledge of economics, or of the trends in the national market, and so they blamed all reverses on the company, interpreting every effort at economy as a sign of ill will, or as an attempt at revenge to compensate for the workers' success in a strike. Merrheim was one of the first trade unionists to make any real study of company finances, but that was only after 1910.[1] The mine company for its part was guided by the

[1] Christian Gras, 'Merrheim et le capitalisme', Le Mouvement social, 63 (1968), 143–63.

problem of production costs, ignoring that of the cost of living which was what the trade unions were worried about. Wages rose, but so too did prices and, even more, the expectations and needs of the workers. The retailer, into whose debt the workers were constantly falling, paraded tempting new foods before them which they soon found indispensable. In the 1890s they began complaining not just about the cost of food but also about 'many other needs essential to our existence'. In particular they took a greater interest in their clothes. The company directors could not understand this change, condemned their demands as mere 'pretensions', and continued to consider their frugality as 'natural'. Inevitably, therefore, there was increasing hostility between the workers and the employers and endless bickering about the details of payment. Since there was a vast multiplicity of different tasks, each paid for differently, and each with different rates of unemployment, antagonisms continued between the workers, but by the 1890s a sense of solidarity appeared to have overcome these. For a time the trade unions were able to bring the workers together. The struggle took on a political character, and the whole capitalist system was called into question. But then the splits in the union movement greatly reduced its prestige. Animosities built up against their leaders, who had become a new power, exciting jealousy and mistrust. The vigorous resistance of the employers led many workers to follow the prudent course of abstention. Repeatedly unsuccessful strikes, combined with a reduced demand for labour, made even the unions more circumspect. The union movement thus came to a halt, and its problems with its own followers became almost as difficult as its relations with the employers.[1] It will be seen how co-operation with the state was to be the unions' way out of this impasse. Just as the republicans, in the end, made a deal with the state, so many of the unions ended up being a channel of communication between worker and the state, much more than a representative of the former. The history of the trade union movement after 1914 is largely the history of how this came about.

The more or less uniform programme of the union leaders could not reflect accurately the wide variety of attitudes among the rank and file. Alain Touraine's work has shown how the

[1] R. Trempé, *Les Mineurs de Carmaux* (1971), a first-rate, highly instructive thesis.

Paris workers, who have more relations with other classes, see the world in a unique way: they are far keener to have their children pursue their studies and they are more ambitious for them. Their optimism is partly based on the fact that they are better paid than workers in the rest of the country; but they also have a far wider view of the class to which they think they belong, and form their judgements in political more than professional terms. Their situation contrasts markedly with that of workers in purely industrial towns, and again with that of workers in medium-sized towns, which are dominated by the state bureaucracy, and where workers are three times as keen to have their children become civil servants. These regional variations—which are much emphasised by every local study—are cut across by important professional distinctions. Thus gas workers think they have twice as much chance of promotion as miners do and their attitudes vary accordingly. Building workers have little class consciousness and often aim to set themselves up independently. Metal workers, among the most combative of unionists, have been particularly insecure in their rapidly changing industry, and have been staunchest in their loyalty to the working class, defending it rather than trying to escape from it; but even within their ranks, there are considerable differences according to the kind of factory and speciality. Thus to the question posed by Touraine of whether there were any people whose interests were absolutely opposed to the general interest, 44 to 47 per cent of metal workers in factories employing over 500 answered that the capitalists were the enemies, but in factories of 10 to 50, only 12 to 15 per cent gave this answer. There is a further difference between qualified, partially skilled and unskilled workers. The first category stress professional advancement and economic gain as their main ambition, but the semi-skilled are less optimistic about their chances and they are content that their children should remain workers. However, because they are in the working class to stay, they are often more determined to defend it as a unit. Insecurity in employment also varies enormously; in some sectors and grades it was as high as 60 per cent, in others it fell as low as 6 per cent.[1] Mobility of labour—on which more

---

[1] A. Touraine, *La Conscience ouvrière* (1966), 55, 60, 106–7, 138, 173, 119–215, 242.

historical evidence is needed—was shown to be high in Chombart de Lauwe's investigation of working-class families in the 1950s, with 24 per cent of his sample having changed their place of work eleven times or more, and 42 per cent having changed their trade four times or more. 73 per cent of unskilled workers, 78 per cent of skilled workers and 59 per cent of highly qualified ones expressed a desire to change their trade. This mobility was the workers' answer to monotony, insecurity and repression, but it was barely compatible with tight union organisation. Again, the distinction between the different grades of workers was very strikingly revealed, as late as 1954, in the statistics of children who died under the age of one year. The rate was 61·7 per thousand for unskilled labourers' families, 51·9 for average workers, 42·5 for qualified workers, 34·5 for shopkeepers, 32·4 for master craftsmen, 30·5 for clerks, 23·9 for industrial employers and 19 for the liberal professions.[1]

The divisions between workers were often accentuated in their recreational pursuits. Thus in St. Étienne, the miners tended to join gymnastic clubs, while the armourers formed rifle clubs; the shopkeepers and artisans were keen on pigeon shooting, while pigeon breeding was a particular speciality of miners. The armourers were, however, of two kinds, depending on whether they worked for the state or in small artisan workshops: the latter were vigorously anticlerical, but also hostile to unionisation.[2] Even drinking, which was the principal recreation of many workers, was carried on in remarkably particularist groups. In the nineteenth century there was a vast increase in the number of cabarets, which the bourgeoisie condemned as dens of debauchery and clandestine agitation, but where the workers found warmth, comfort, sociability and a meeting-place for their clubs. Between 1856 and 1858 the number in Lille rose from 909 to 1303. In St. Étienne (which came second only to Paris) there was, in the early Third Republic, one cabaret for every 62 inhabitants, which meant one for every 15 electors or every 3 houses. These cabarets may have reinforced the network of relationships among neighbours and were an important social factor. The kind of particularism that

---

[1] P. Chombart de Lauwe, *La Vie quotidienne des familles ouvrières* (1956), 7 n., 25.

[2] Janet Jacobs, 'A Working Class Community: St. Étienne 1870–1914' (thesis in preparation at St. Antony's College, Oxford).

prevailed is illustrated in Lille, where friendly societies under
the Second Empire were known to have expelled members who
drank more than half a litre of beer in a cabaret other than that
where the society met. Lille during the Second Empire had
63 drinking and singing clubs, 37 clubs for card playing, 23 for
bowls, 13 for skittles, 10 for archery, 18 for cross-bow archery.
They had their presidents, deans, treasurers, and numerous
officials; they organised boisterous banquets and festivals, at
which they sometimes used up all their savings. So the worker
could have a very busy life, quite apart from the unions.[1]

It was not necessarily to the unions that he would look for
the solution of his private frustrations. One of the most striking
differences between the factory worker and the rest of the
population was that he often did not come home to lunch, as
they did. The amount of time he spent with his family was
far shorter—because of his long working hours—than was normal among the bourgeoisie, whose complaints that he did not
practise their own domestic virtues seem strangely hypocritical.
His housing conditions were often so appalling that there was
no room for him to do much but eat and sleep at home. Overcrowding was notorious in Lille, for example, where in 1864
there was a tenement building inhabited by 271 people, with
an average of 1·70 square metres of living space each. In the
1950s, the living space of unskilled Paris workers was 7 square
metres per person, and 11 square metres for highly qualified
workers. This does not mean there was a gradual improvement.
New suburbs were sometimes as bad as the slums they were
designed to replace. An inquiry into the leisure activities of
workers carried out in 1924 showed that patterns of behaviour
were often unaltered by changing conditions. Thus those who
worked ten hours a day did little else; but those who had their
hours reduced to eight often got part-time jobs, which raised
their total to twelve. More leisure stimulated a return to older
ideals. In St. Étienne, the eight-hour day increased the demand
for gardens tenfold. The life of the miners of the Moselle was
barely altered: they got up at 4 a.m. went to work at 6, finished
at 2 p.m., got home at 3.30, ate at 4 and went to bed at 6. The
greatest change of the twentieth century was the end of irregular
work: lazy Mondays and Tuesdays were no longer tolerated by

[1] Pierre Pierrard, *La Vie ouvrière à Lille sous le second empire* (1965), 302.

employers.[1] The self-made Denis Poulot, writing from personal experience, said that in 1870 a good worker who did 300 days a year was very rare; ordinary ones usually worked only 200 to 225, and changed their employment three to five times a year.[2] An English mechanic, Henry Steele, who spent twenty-three years working in France, wrote in 1904 that discipline in French factories was less tough than in England, more freedom was left to the worker, more respect accorded to him by foremen and masters. There are suggestions that, in the twentieth century, particularly in certain new and modernised industries, this laxity was tightened. It took some time for the transition to be accepted. Steele noted that French workers tended to enjoy themselves, as far as possible, without paying, unlike the English workers who spent vast sums on their bank holidays. This probably changed even later, perhaps not till after 1936.[3]

The possibilities open to the workers can be seen from the autobiography of one of them, Georges Navel. His father (whose thirteenth child he was) spent forty years working as a labourer in the Pont-à-Mousson factory. His work, his children and the republic had all proved disappointing to him. He was completely resigned. 'The earthen pot', he used to say of the C.G.T., 'will never break the iron pot.' His only consolation in distress was drink. Georges's eldest brother also spent his whole life in the same factory, but he accepted his lot more readily, because he found satisfaction in hobbies, gardening and a happy family life. Georges himself, however, was a rebel from childhood. He never learnt anything at school because he was usually sent outside the classroom as a punishment for misbehaviour. He could not bear the factory, and wandered off to every part of the country, in a large variety of jobs. He hated his status as a wage earner, which he considered undignified, a vestige of ancient slavery. He felt he belonged to a class looked on as animals, isolated in ghettos and despised. This was impossible to bear without faith in revolution or social progress: political activity, he said, was the only cure for *la tristesse ouvrière*. This family illustrates three distinct attitudes.

[1] Jean Beaudemoulin, *Enquête sur les loisirs de l'ouvrier français* (Paris thesis, 1924), 212–36.
[2] Denis Poulot, *Le Sublime, ou le travailleur comme il est en 1870 et ce qu'il peut être* (1872).
[3] Henry Steele, *The Working Classes in France: A Social Study* (1904), 17, 121.

All three raise the question of the isolation of the proletariat. Georges Navel said that the only things he knew about bourgeois life were what he saw at the cinema: as a young man they had appeared to him 'a superior race, which spoke and dressed better than us, and knew everything that was taught in the schools'.[1] Even his attitude towards the bourgeoisie was not one of simple hostility: there was also a hint of admiration or envy.

This can be seen more clearly in René Kaës's interviews with workers in the 1960s. Only 21 per cent of his subjects thought the workers ought to have their own culture. 70 per cent were against this, because they defined culture as communication. What they lamented in their condition was their isolation. What they admired the liberal professions for was that their members were able to meet many different types of people, be at ease with all of them, work when they liked. Only the most highly qualified workers dreamt of their children getting to such a status. But admiration for commercial travellers, shop assistants and state employees, common among the least educated workers, was for the same reason, that such people came in contact with the world, heard news, could read and write easily, and had dealings with the public. They welcomed education as an escape from their isolation, to help them achieve dignity. Far from rejecting the bourgeoisie's culture, and even their study of Latin, only 37 per cent were in favour of purely technical education, while 6 per cent were in favour of the traditional classical course and 50 per cent of both together. A carpenter defined 'culture' as the opposite of humiliation, which ignorance stamped on them. The primary-school master was much admired. The educational work of the Third Republic was thus appreciated, and the values it represented were at least partially shared by the workers. They believed that education was something acquired in the schools; only 10·5 per cent were dissatisfied with the schools and most regretted that they had not had more schooling. It was not just knowledge that they wanted, but even more the 'ability to live in society', to know how to conduct themselves in circles different from their own, to talk well and tactfully, to be at ease with people. The great divide came on the question of what chance a worker really had of reaching this ideal. 39 per cent thought he could, 31 per cent

[1] Georges Navel, *Travaux* (1945), 28, 66.

thought it impossible, 17 per cent thought it possible but very difficult.[1] This is what workers thought in a period of prosperity, and in a welfare state. It is impossible to argue back from these figures, even to guess about the division in a different situation. But more research in social mobility might, at any rate, reveal how the realities corresponded to the dream.

After 1914

1914 is a crucial date in the history of the trade union movement. The C.G.T. had repeatedly affirmed that it would reply to a declaration of war by a general strike, which would be tantamount to a revolution. But it did nothing of the sort. Jouhaux (its secretary 1909–47) turned a somersault and supported the war.[2] The propaganda of antimilitarism was suddenly replaced by patriotism. This has long been looked on as something of a mystery. To the bourgeoisie, threatened with civil war, it was a miraculous escape. The myth of the general strike was shattered. It was the end of revolutionary syndicalism as a threat that had to be taken seriously. The union leaders explained their volte-face by saying that if they had not supported the war, their members would have shot them as traitors: they claimed they were pushed from behind, but the evidence for this is rather slight. The episode raised the whole question of the relationship between the leaders and the masses. Jouhaux appears to have acted instinctively, without consulting his colleagues; and it is said that he was principally moved by a desire to prevent a violent repression of the working class which would occur if it did resist. This was not so much a collapse of the old syndicalism, as a revelation of what it was really like. The extremism had often been superficial, and it was not unanimous. Jouhaux may have been expressing what he felt was the profounder desire of the workers, to be integrated into the nation (in the way that Jaurès understood the nation). The C.G.T. had hitherto tried to raise a barrier between the workers and the rest of France, but 1914 suggested it was a barrier of hurt pride rather than of alienation. The attitude of the masses

---

[1] René Kaës, *Images de la culture chez les ouvriers français* (1968). On isolation, see also Maurice Halbwachs, *La Classe ouvrière et les niveaux de vie* (1913), 119–23.

[2] Bernard Georges and D. Tintant, *Léon Jouhaux* (1962), 102–58.

is difficult to discover. A recent study of the metal workers shows that there was never any enthusiasm for the war among them. They looked on the patriotic *union sacrée* as the work of their leaders. Their mood appears to have been one of indifference: neither integration, nor alienation. The force they were most conscious of was the presence of the police, and the threat of being sent to the front if they misbehaved in their factories. They felt their union leaders had made a deal with the state. Their reply was to disown them and find new leaders, nearer to their own preoccupations. Their sense of autonomy was not radically changed. The integration of the working class into the nation, which some have seen as the significance of 1914, is by no means proved.[1]

1914 marked a change in the position of the trade unions, much more than in the workers. They were transformed from opponents of the state into institutions which were increasingly almost part of it. During the war leaders of the C.G.T. served in government commissions, co-operating with members of all classes.[2] In trade disputes, they appealed to the government for support and intervention. After the war, they negotiated and obtained the eight-hour-day law of 1919.[3] This was largely a declaratory law of principle, requiring ministerial decrees to enforce it in individual industries: there was therefore need for further negotiation. (By 1926 probably about 5 million workers were affected by it, though all sorts of exemptions reduced the effect.) The trade unions before the war had sabotaged the 1910 insurance law, but in 1928 they co-operated to secure the passage of a new one. Their attitude was different now: they sought to defeat the employers, who set up paternalistic insurance schemes to woo their workers away from the unions, by enrolling the assistance of the state to do the same or better. The 1928 law, in which workers and employers each contributed 5 per cent of wages, was compulsory for all workers earning

[1] Jacques Julliard, 'La C.G.T. devant la guerre (1900–1914)', *Le Mouvement social*, 49 (Oct.–Dec. 1964), 47–62; A. Kriegel and J. J. Becker, *1914, la guerre et le mouvement ouvrier français* (1964); M. Gallo, 'Quelques aspects de la neutralité et du comportement ouvriers dans les usines de guerre 1914–18', *Le Mouvement social*, 56 July–Sept. 1966), 3–33.

[2] Roger Picard, *Le Syndicalisme durant la guerre* (1927) (Carnegie Endowment for International Peace; Economic and Social History of the World War: French Series); Alfred Rosmer, *Le Mouvement ouvrier pendant la guerre* (1936–59).

[3] Cf. Robert Veyssié, *Le Régime des huit heures en France* (1922).

under 18,000 francs a year, and was designed to give a 40 per cent pension after thirty years. The senate had held this up because it originally involved a state subsidy: as it was now established, it cost the state nothing, but the state emerged as the intermediary between worker and employer. The law required union co-operation in establishing insurance funds, and the unions henceforth gave much of their time to organising these. They met the employers increasingly in government offices. They participated in more and more official bodies, and most notably in the National Economic Council in 1924. They no longer hesitated to accept government subsidies for their unemployment funds, which even the communist C.G.T.U. received. The Bourses du Travail became simply state-financed employment exchanges. The C.G.T. even supported the bill of 1925 which would have required compulsory government inter- vention in all labour disputes. It used strikes sparingly now, and largely to draw the attention of the state to troubles it wished to cure, rather than to defeat the employers. This was known as the *politique de présence* which meant that the C.G.T., while rejecting actual participation in government, obtained a place for itself in every discussion concerning the working classes. In other words, the unions increasingly saw their role as one of lobbying and bargaining with the state.[1]

This relationship reached its climax in 1936, when the state imposed the Matignon Agreement on the employers. By this agreement the employers were forced to recognise the unions, and to negotiate collective bargains with them, but under state supervision. The unions, though they represented a minority, were, through government support, given the status of repre- sentatives of the whole labour force. The ministry of labour further decreed that the C.G.T. should normally be considered the 'most representative union' with which the employers should negotiate their collective agreements. Collective bargain- ing had been organised by a law of 1919, but by 1933 only 7·5 per cent of wage earners had been affected by it, mainly in mining and shipping: in the metal industry only 1·4 per cent of workers had been affected. The resistance of the employers

[1] Georges Lefranc, *Le Mouvement syndical sous la Troisième République* (1967), 283 ff. gives a useful description of this from the C.G.T. point of view. Lefranc was a leader of the teachers' union.

and their refusal to recognise the unions had kept France way
behind her neighbours in this matter. All this changed in 1936,
but one of the most significant features of the new order was
that in the event of unions and employers failing to agree, and
in the event of disputes arising about collective agreements, the
deadlock was to be resolved by government arbitration. As it
turned out, in the succeeding years, all but 4 per cent of disputes
were decided by the government. Labour relations and strikes
depended increasingly, therefore, on the state, and on public
opinion, rather than on the attitudes of the rival parties. The
strategy of social conflict was thus fundamentally altered. The
C.G.T. never faced up to this and never really discussed the new
problems which were created. Its 'Minimum Programme' of
1918 talked only of the nationalisation of key industries and
a greater share for the workers in economic decisions. Its plan
of 1934 showed it had no immediate desire to abolish private
enterprise beyond that, though it favoured national economic
planning with worker representation. In 1944–5, therefore, it
was the state, not the unions, which emerged as the principal
challenge to the employers, and which took over the battle to
reduce the latter's remaining independence.[1]

These developments can be partly explained by the peculiar
composition of the trade unions. The unions had extraordinarily
little success in winning recruits from private industry, and they
became instead representatives of the state workers and the
civil servants. For most of the inter-war period there were only
about one million unionists. Their number shot up enormously
in two periods of agitation and enthusiasm. In 1918–19 they
almost doubled; in 1936 they shot up from one to over five
million. However, in the textile, metal and building industries,
union membership in 1930 was lower than it had been in 1914.
The great permanent increase in unionisation was in the public
sector, or in related industries which were partly controlled
by the state, like mining, transport and the docks. The state

[1] There are some good American books on inter-war labour relations, notably
Val R. Lorwin, *The French Labor Movement* (Cambridge, Mass., 1954); Henry W.
Ehrmann, *French Labor from Popular Front to Liberation* (New York, 1931). See also
François Sellier, *Stratégie de la lutte sociale. France 1936–60* (1961); Pierre Laroque,
Les Rapports entre patrons et ouvriers (1938); Adolf Sturmthal, 'Nationalisation and
Workers' Control in Britain and France', *Journal of Political Economy*, 61 (Feb. 1953),
43–79.

encouraged this because it formed mixed commissions with them. In the civil service it was claimed in 1930 that unionisation was as high as 90 per cent, that it was 75 per cent among miners and 60 per cent in semi-public utilities, but (apart from the printers) below 20 per cent elsewhere. These figures are all much too high, but the variations appear to be in the right proportions. A recent author gives 6·3 as the percentage of workers in private industry who belonged to unions.[1] In 1935, at any rate, of the C.G.T.'s 775,000 members, 350,000 were civil servants or public employees and 165,000 were railwaymen (whose conditions were regulated by special statute).[2]

When the masses came into the unions, in periods of crisis, the old leadership could not cope with them. The new members, on the whole, represented a different kind of worker, usually the semi-skilled employees of industries in the process of being rationalised, with more recent peasant origins and no traditions of solidarity. In 1936 there were 1,063,000 industrial workers in firms with over 500 employees and another 1,393,000 in firms with between 100 and 500 employees. Mass production brought them together in larger numbers but these workers were trained in a week, instead of the old slow apprenticeship. This created a new atmosphere in factories. The strikes of these new recruits often almost completely by-passed the regular trade unions. Thus in May 1919 the C.G.T. organised a demonstration to mark its return to agitation after the war and this was followed by a succession of strikes all over the country, which suggested a massive onslaught on the capitalist system. But in fact there was very little connection between the different strikes, which confined themselves to winning concessions on a strictly local basis. In 1920 the railwaymen, who formed at that date the largest union in the country, went on strike and got the C.G.T. to declare a general strike to support them. The result was disastrous. Only about 40 per cent of the railwaymen came out. The vigorous resistance of both the state and the middle classes prevented the economic chaos that could have resulted. The C.G.T.'s timid policy, of launching its

---

[1] Saposs, 127; Ehrmann, 25. For detailed calculations of trade union numbers, see Annie Kriegel, *La Croissance de la C.G.T. 1918–21* (1966), and Antoine Prost, *La C.G.T. à l'époque du front populaire, 1934–39: essai de description numérique* (1964).
[2] For the civil servants, see Georges Mer, *Le Syndicalisme des fonctionnaires* (1929).

general strikes in successive waves proved totally ineffective. An extremist minority, led by Monmousseau, had captured the railwaymen's union, and forced the C.G.T.'s hand, so internal disagreements paralysed the movement. 12 per cent of the railway strikers were dismissed (about 18,000 men, or 5 per cent of all workers in the railway's employ). The victory of the employers was total, and profound discouragement almost immediately halved union membership. The C.G.T. had proved incapable of leading the working class. Important strikes had broken out without its consent, and within individual federations, local unions had likewise defied their leaders. This was particularly noticeable among the metal workers, who disowned their union's agreements with the employers on the eight-hour law. Then the workers repudiated their local unions.[1]

The union movement was further discredited by its split in 1921, when the anarchists and communists seceded to form a rival to the C.G.T., the Confédération Générale du Travail Unitaire. The Russian Revolution had a profoundly important effect on the working class. Its influence, and the rise of the communist party in France, are subjects which require separate treatment.[2] But from the trade union point of view, the result of this split was not only that the strength of the C.G.T. was gravely reduced (to 250,000, against 500,000 secessionists) but also that the C.G.T.U. created a new type of union. By 1924 the communists had captured the C.G.T.U. and expelled most of the anarcho-syndicalists. This reduced their strength to as little as 230,000 (the membership they claimed in 1935).[3] But they controlled this rump with an all-powerful, permanent body of leaders who took their orders from the communist party. They created a bureaucracy to run the unions, completely against the anarchist traditions of elected and rotating leadership. Their unions thus became a source of protection and security, rather than a meeting-place for free discussion.

[1] A. Kriegel, *Aux origines du communisme français* (1964), 1. 359–547, contains a thorough study of the railway strike, based on a wide range of new sources, including the employers' archives. E. L. Shorter and Charles Tilly, 'Le Déclin de la grève violente en France de 1890 à 1935', *Le Mouvement social* (July–Sept. 1971), 95–118, shows that after the 1914–18 war, violent strikes were six times less frequent than before it. They argue that this shows an increase of integration of the workers.

[2] See volume 2.

[3] The C.G.T. by then was three times as large, thanks mainly to the adhesion of the civil servants.

The communist view was that unions were simply one way of organising the workers, but what really mattered was membership of the party, for the workers by themselves were incapable of acquiring a revolutionary conscience. Discipline, for which the factories had prepared the workers, must be the keynote of union organisation. In 1936 the C.G.T.U. rejoined the C.G.T. By 1938 the communists had a majority in this reconstituted C.G.T. The position of the worker in his union was now considerably different.[1]

   The transformation was completed by the events of 1936, when the workers went through what was in many ways the most moving and important experience of the century for them. The change was remarkable and paradoxical. It has been seen how the Popular Front Government used these events to force the employers to negotiate with the C.G.T. and the unions. But while they had their status thus enhanced, and though their numbers increased in an unprecedented manner, they did not succeed in becoming the true representatives of the will of the workers. The fivefold increase in the number of unionists in the space of a single year totally changed the character of the unions. In the chemical industry, unionisation increased sixtyfold, in the glass industry twenty-three times, in metals eighteen times (whereas by contrast the civil servants and teachers, the backbone of the C.G.T. in the 1920s, rose by less than 50 per cent). There was now at last something approaching mass unionisation, at least by French standards, for the over-all level was just over 50 per cent. But this meant that the unions were swollen with semi-skilled workers with no experience of organisation, and the leadership was unable to deal with them. It is said that the organisers spent all their time just collecting dues. That is how the communists were able to move in and provide a bureaucracy to run and direct these masses into political channels. Belonging to a union, after 1936, was no longer an act of rebellion; it was rather the man who did not join who attracted attention. Membership of the communist party became a far more significant political gesture.

   In 1936 the C.G.T., with its reformist traditions, was anxious to maintain order and negotiate peacefully. Three-quarters of

---

[1] Maurice Labi, *La Grande Division des travailleurs, première scission de la C.G.T. 1914-21* (1964).

its members did not participate in the strikes of that year. These were spontaneous outbursts by unorganised workers, acting independently. The occupations of the factories have become a legend in revolutionary history, and they were revolutionary in that for a time the workers felt themselves to be freed from the disciplinary restrictions of their work. They brought the employers to their knees and the relations between the two looked as though they could never be the same again. But it is important to note that these strikes were united only in their method: the occupation of factories suddenly appeared as a new weapon, and it spread by spontaneous imitation, not under any central or union orders. The workers saw their action as signifying that it was no use relying on unions, or even on governments; they were taking matters into their own hands. They negotiated therefore each with their individual employers, for advantages for their own factories only. The occupations, at their peak in mid June, involved about one million workers but they were settled at a local level in different ways. Almost none seemed to have envisaged any destruction of the capitalist system: there were sit-ins, occupations, but not take-overs. Red flags were flown, but the public services were not affected, and no effort was made to rise against the bourgeoisie as a whole. The trade unions did increase their membership, but in the course of the strikes the workers rejected their direction. When they wanted help from outside, they called in the local deputy or mayor or municipal councillors. A director of Huntley and Palmers' biscuit factory at La Courneuve who was imprisoned by his workers—not as widespread a phenomenon as is believed —said that he could easily have reached agreement with the workers, but for the constant interference of the local communist deputy, who urged them not to give way.[1]

After 1936, the trade unions had more to do with the employers, but from the workers' point of view they were almost superfluous, since it was the government which decided in disputes. There were many who felt that the union leaders had taken over the role of the politicians, and become masters

[1] Salomon Schwarz, 'Les Occupations d'usines en France en mai et juin 1936', *International Review for Social History*, 2 (Amsterdam, 1937), 50–104; Alexander Werth, *The Destiny of France* (1936), 296–310, vivid journalistic reports for the *Manchester Guardian*.

8221045 K

rather than servants of their followers. By 1946 indeed the C.G.T. had between 5,000 and 6,000 permanent officials. Political action was nevertheless seen to be all-important now, and this is what the communists offered, in a new way. But again, it is rash to generalise too much about the significance of the unions before the war of 1939. Unions still meant different things in different regions. The well-organised mass unions of the north and north-east, based in large factories, were distinct from those of the centre and west, based in workshops, with more individualist militants, looser coherence, and loyalty to nineteenth-century revolutionary traditions. In the south political and temperamental considerations were predominant, with the individual rather than the party as the unit. In Paris, Lyon and Marseille, again, the mixture of classes in these towns meant that professional grievances were not in the forefront as much as elsewhere.

It is not possible to conclude simply therefore about class consciousness at the end of this period. At one level, the workers seemed to be segregated into a separate party, hostile to the whole capitalist order, but their successful participation in politics was also a sign that they had a recognised place in it. At the cultural level, their position was ambiguous, but far from irretrievably antagonistic. In the crisis of 1936 they had forced unity upon their leaders, but it was a fragile one. Many workers, moreover, stood completely outside the union movement, and a small section—soon to grow much larger—organised themselves separately in Christian trade unions. The traditions of the proletariat and the pressures upon them were too varied to make their behaviour predictable.[1]

[1] Michel Collinet, *L'Ouvrier français. Esprit de syndicalisme* (1951), and id., *Essai sur la condition ouvrière 1900–1950* (1951), are valuable and stimulating analyses. See also Jean Bruhat and Marc Piolot, *Esquisse d'une histoire de la C.G.T. 1895–1965* (1966). For subsequent developments, Richard F. Hamilton, *Affluence and the French Worker in the Fourth Republic* (Princeton, N.J., 1967).

Part II

11. Marriage and Morals

THE family, as organised in France in these years, had an effect on people's lives as profound as any political regime or any economic force. It was a powerful institution which resisted change with remarkable vitality—the counterpart, in private life, of the administrative centralisation of the *ancien régime* which, for all the attacks on it, survived into the mid twentieth century. It deserves attention as much as the changing governments and the industrial revolutions, but it seldom receives it because there are very great difficulties—many of them insuperable—in discovering the facts about it. Its activities were inevitably hardly ever recorded and research on it is still fragmentary. It has too often been described simply as one of the values to which the bourgeoisie paid greatest homage. Certainly in 1940 the Vichy government included *Famille* in the new motto it devised for France, with *Travail* and *Patrie*. Perhaps only in the Students' Revolution of 1968 was a real threat to its organisation widely noticed and the tensions concealed in it revealed publicly. The ambitions and frustrations the family produced have more than a private interest. But the historian cannot easily assign dates to developments in it. Rather than talk about changes and gradual evolution he is conscious of haphazard personal influences—of people reacting against their upbringing but of others perpetuating traditions, of different classes, professions, regions having their own peculiar customs. The history of domestic relations cannot be written in the same way as the history of international relations and any description of them must be tentative and incomplete.

In a work published in 1883, the marriages of the day were described as being of three kinds: those contracted for convenience, those produced by sympathy or love, and those entered into from duty.[1] Is it possible to discover what the proportions between these varieties were, and how they changed during this century? In public opinion polls held in 1947 men

[1] Alexandre Laya, *Causes célèbres du mariage ou les infortunes conjugales* (1883).

and women agreed, to the extent of 71 per cent and 78 per cent, that love marriages were the best kind. But it does not follow that this represents the triumph of the romantic ideal. Even the most calculating matchmakers of the nineteenth century hoped that if love did not precede a marriage—and it could hardly do so if the couple had barely met—it should result from it and be the basis of its strength: the girl married off for reasons of convenience had a duty to love her husband. Views about how to contract a marriage may have been different in the nineteenth century, but not necessarily the way the marriage functioned. When in this same opinion poll of 1947 people were further asked what they valued most in life, only 1 per cent of men and 5 per cent of women considered love as most important. 47 per cent of men and 38 per cent of women thought money was more important: health, peace, wealth, a nice family and hope were preferred in that order.[1] In an inquiry among 10,000 young people in 1966, both boys and girls placed fidelity as the first attribute they sought in their ideal spouse—before love, beauty or intelligence.[2] When in another inquiry, women who had, to the extent of 83 per cent, mentioned attachment to a man as necessary in order to be happy, were questioned further about what they hoped to get from this, only 22 per cent talked about love; 41 per cent wanted 'a good husband', variously described as faithful, understanding, courageous and kind, who stays with his wife and children; and 20 per cent wanted 'a good home', with mutual understanding, harmony and peace. 54 per cent of the women said they were definitely not romantic, and the figure was only a little lower for those still in their twenties: romanticism survived rather interestingly most strongly in rural areas and small towns, where the figure rose to up to 60 per cent; it was lowest in the cities (47 per cent). Only 44 per cent of women believed in the idea of the *grand amour*. Only 61 per cent of single women under twenty-five believed in it. Only 29 per cent of all women claimed to have experienced a *grand amour*: these came twice as often from professional and white collar families as from farming ones. Peasant girls might claim to be romantic, but few apparently had the opportunity to be

[1] Georges Rotvand, *L'Imprévisible Monsieur Durand* (1956), 131.
[2] Roberte Franck, *L'Infidélité conjugale* (1969), 86.

so. It is important to distinguish between what happened in real life and the ideals and fantasies obsessing the novelists. The changes that did occur were more subtle than a radical rejection of the values of the past.[1]

How should a man choose a wife, what should he expect of her and what could he expect their relations to be? The answers throughout the period were varied. So long as obedience was the principal virtue inculcated into children, so long as girls were brought up to be models of innocence, to be ignorant of the world, skilled in domestic arts, and destined for marriage, then the choice was made by the parents, using their own criteria. Parents seem to have been influenced by the position they held within their class. The marriage of their children was a public valuation placed on the parents' position, and it was also a method of improving that position. The great problem was to avoid a *mésalliance*, which was why love was the great enemy, the rebel against parental authority which could bring disaster on all their plans. The aristocracy laid greatest stress on the antiquity and nobility of the families they married, though if they were strong themselves in the matter of antiquity, they were willing to marry for money—provided the sums to be acquired were very large—and many did. In any case, it was generally accepted that property arrangements had to be satisfactory, to maintain both the couple immediately and their children after them. The bourgeoisie accepted these values. Marriage was for them the great means of social ascension. The larger the dowry they could obtain for their son, the better the situation he could buy and the more optimistic his prospects. In the lower commercial bourgeoisie, the combination of two fortunes was often used to start up or expand businesses. The peasantry had the same practice on a more modest scale, with the accumulation of land into larger units as the aim. Only the poorest industrial workers were the pariahs of this society. Quite often in the nineteenth century they did not marry at all, because they could not afford the expense of the ceremony. Rootless in the city, there was not the same family pressure. But when they rose to the artisan class and accumulated some property, they followed the same pattern.

[1] French Institute of Public Opinion, *Patterns of Love and Sex: A Study of the French Woman and her Morals* (1961), 133–49.

   This picture of a society basing its domestic arrangements on financial considerations is only part of the truth. It was certainly in this way that a large number of people described marriage throughout these years. As late as 1912 a justice of the peace of the tenth *arrondissement* in Paris issued a judgement which began: 'Whereas in antiquity marriage was based uniquely on the love of two people of different sex; whereas, since the advent of Christianity, the morals of marriage have undergone substantial changes; so that during the past century and more particularly nowadays the social system considers it as a veritable financial contract to hold in check possible trickery between the two parties and to reassure the silent distrust of the future spouses, because the true reason of modern marriage is money; the husband seeks a dowry and the woman buys at once a protector and a manager considered more experienced for the administration of her property . . .'[1] After the war of 1914 emancipated girls were complaining that men never mentioned marriage without talking about the size of the dowry. Men even advertised for dowries in newspapers and a notary would tell a young man that 'at the present time, given the high cost of living, a young man should not marry a girl who has less than 100,000 francs of dowry'.[2] The situation does not appear to have changed drastically since 1806, when Joseph Droz, of the French Academy, wrote his *Essay on the Art of Being Happy*—a book which reached its seventh edition in 1853 and which was placed on the open shelves in the Bibliothèque Nationale, presumably as an accepted guide. He said: 'Marriage is in general a means of increasing one's credit and one's fortune and of ensuring one's success in the world.'[3] France, it was pointed out, was the one country in Europe which did not have the custom of long engagements. Young people were unwilling to wait and to save before getting married. They expected to be able to keep up the style of life they were brought up in, and the dowry was therefore essential.[4] The dramatists of the Second Empire wrote innumerable plays on this subject, to resolve the question of what constituted a good marriage.

---

[1] Jules Thabaut, *L'Évolution de la législation sur la famille* (1913), 17 n.
[2] H. Bordeaux, *Le Mariage* (1921), 167.
[3] J. Droz, *Essai sur l'art d'être heureux* (1853), 189.
[4] Armand Hayem, *Le Mariage* (1872), 152.

They took it as an axiom that the financial question was of major importance. The safe moral, which men like Émile Augier preached, was that the most successful marriages were likely to be those in which the wealth of the two partners was equally balanced: the ideal marriage was the fair bargain. He showed the scrapes people got into when they broke this rule, which they obviously did. Merit could to a certain degree be translated into monetary terms; but the wife should not be much richer than the husband, or she might treat him the wrong way, nor should she be poorer, or she will be called a schemer. Alexandre Dumas fils, after thirty-five years of writing about marriage, concluded that though the love marriage might be the ideal, it was not a practical reality, and people must not expect too much from marriage: they must be thankful for whatever happiness they might find. The use of marriage for social climbing presented conflicts and difficulties. Marriage was, as Dumas said, 'not only the union of two people but the alliance of two families'. Relations were most likely to be satisfactory if the social climbing was gradual and the two families capable of talking to each other, and using each other for their mutual aggrandisement.[1] Thus marriage, like education, was a way of bettering oneself. It fitted in best with the prevailing mania for social advancement when conceived in this way. In so far as equal opportunity and the rule of merit failed to be fully introduced, this attitude to marriage survived.

However, the marriage dowry was not simply a method by which men acquired wealth. A marriage usually involved a marriage contract—not just among the rich, but even sometimes among servants and labourers with only a few hundred francs each. The way this contract was drawn up was crucial in determining the nature of the household which would result. For though the Napoleonic code made the husband the guardian and administrator of his wife's wealth, numerous obstacles could be placed in his path and the wife could retain powerful rights against him. The practice in the north and south of France was originally very different. In the areas where Roman law had prevailed the *régime dotal* gave the husband use of the

---

[1] C. E. Young, *The Marriage Question in the Modern French Drama (1850–1911)*, Ph.D. Wisconsin, in *Bulletin of the University of Wisconsin*, no. 771, Philology and literature series, vol. 5, no. 4 (Madison, Wis., 1915), 19, 44.

income from the dowry, but the capital was inalienable. It was conceived of as a guarantee against widowhood and could remain in the control of the wife's family. In the north, where customary law was followed, these restrictions did not apply and the husband could even sell the dowry to pay his debts. The position of wives was thus different in the south: but in the years 1835–60 the dotal system was largely abandoned in the south-west. The change can be precisely dated from the reports of the notaries who drew up the contracts. The reason given for this change was that the dotal system suggested both suspicion of the husband and doubts about the wife's capacity to look after herself, independently of her family. The system was best suited to a stable society; merchants and industrialists were the first to abandon it, and it lasted longest, well into the twentieth century, among rentiers, civil servants, the nobility and the very rich who were content to live off their capital. It made an active investment policy difficult; it made frequent recourse to loans necessary; and involved high legal costs. Not least, it deprived the wife of any share in the profits her husband might make by using her money.

The courts, for their part, attempted to maintain the strict inalienability of the dowry, claiming that it was in the public interest to strengthen the family, so that if, for example, the husband went bankrupt, the dowry, under this system, could not be seized and his wife and children were safeguarded. The notaries, at the request of their clients, attempted to foil this inalienability by introducing greater flexibility; but increasingly they encouraged its abandonment. The change in the south-west can be partly attributed to a generation of notaries educated at Bordeaux, who spread the practices of the merchants there to the surrounding countryside. Now instead marriages became joint partnerships, by the widespread adoption of the *régime d'acquêts*. By this both spouses shared equally in the profits of the marriage. It is interesting to find notaries reporting that couples came to them saying they wished to be associates and equals and to have a contract drawn up accordingly. The Civil Code prescribed that if no contract was made, property should be owned in common. Now this, paradoxically, gave a predominant power to the husband. Most of those who abandoned the dotal system therefore preferred the alternative of separation of property, by which what they brought in continued to belong to each separately, and only the common profits of the marriage were shared. With the reintroduction of divorce in 1884, there were even stronger reasons for adopting this latter course. Between 1900 and 1949 therefore the percentage of contracts adopting separation of property rose as follows:

	per cent		per cent
1900–9	9–15	1930–4	47
1910–14	14	1935–9	45·5
1915–19	21	1940–4	56
1920–4	22	1945–9	66·1
1925–9	40·7		

These are figures from one sample taken in Paris and must be interpreted with the appropriate reservations (they include marriage contracts by divorcees and widowers; if these are eliminated the rise is from 7 to 48·5 per cent). The survival of the dowry system has not been studied statistically. Only when the notarial archives for the late nineteenth and early twentieth century are opened will it be possible to appreciate accurately exactly what the role of money in people's marriages was. The complexity of the arrangements, however, reinforces the view of marriage as very much a business affair, whatever may have been the equality with which it was conducted. 'For the great majority of the bourgeoisie', wrote Paul Bureau in 1927, 'marriage is the greatest financial operation of their lives.'[1]

The history of the emotional relations between married couples is even more difficult to trace. The flowering of the romantic ideal did not of course necessarily mean an increase in domestic intimacy. On the contrary, the idealisation of women placed even greater distances between them and men. The cult of their purity made them inaccessible: pleasures in sexual intercourse could not in such circumstances be sought with them, who were dedicated to motherhood. Romanticism probably made the prostitute even more necessary. It has been argued that positivism had a not dissimilar effect. 'Materialism and the hate of all metaphysics destroyed enthusiasm and

[1] Albert Eyquem, *Le Régime dotal. Son histoire, son évolution et ses transformations au 19ᵉ siècle sous l'influence de la jurisprudence et du notariat* (1903); Jacques Lelièvre, *La Pratique des contrats de mariage chez les notaires au Châtelet de Paris de 1769 à 1804* (1959), 391; P. Bureau, *L'Indiscipline des mœurs* (1927), 60.

closed up the doors of the infinite. So, in literature, in art and in life, men threw themselves into physical love with a violence exacerbated by their intellectual refinement and their subconscious spiritual needs. From this resulted the brutalities, and the perversions, the sadism and hysteria which infect recent conceptions and paintings of love . . . [This has worsened] the war of the sexes.'[1]

Anticlericalism likewise divided the family. It was very common for husband and wife to be in fundamental disagreement about religion. In the prevailing atmosphere of polemic and strife over the power of the clergy, the wife appeared as the instrument of the domination of the *curés*, benighted by medieval prejudices, so that the inclination to regard women as an inferior species was strengthened rather than reduced in the nineteenth century. A *lycée* schoolmistress pointed out that in the eighteenth century girls were simply taught the catechism, but their minds were at least left empty, so that, thanks to early marriage, they were soon free to read and converse with men. In the revolutionary conflict of the following century, however, greater efforts were made to instil reactionary principles into girls. They entered marriage encumbered with theories which made it impossible for them to be friends with their husbands.[2] Men like Michelet complained that a liberal husband did not feel free in his own house: his wife spied on him on behalf of the priest, to whom she told all his secrets in the confession. The priest was the only man who claimed the right to talk to a wife alone, in private, whenever he pleased.[3] It was with a mistress or at a café therefore that the husband sang and laughed.[4]

The intellectuals, for all their liberalism, were incapable of solving this dilemma. Michelet wrote several books in praise of women's marvellous qualities, of the beauty of love, of the delights of a harmonious, cosy home. He urged that worship of theological abstractions should be replaced by the religion of the home. He demanded that women should become no longer

[1] Édouard Schuré, art critic, quoted by Ph. Pagnat, *Enquête sur l'amour* (1907), 60–2.

[2] Marie Dugard, *De l'éducation moderne des jeunes filles* (1900), 51.

[3] For the relation of the confession to sexual relations see Theodore Zeldin (ed.), *Conflicts in French Society* (1970), 13–50.

[4] Léon Richer, *Lettres d'un libre penseur à un curé de campagne* (1868), chapter 14, 'Ce qui se passe dans la famille'.

the slaves nor the enemies of men, but their associates and companions, and that couples should bring up their families together in touching unity. He found nothing so moving as seeing workers scurrying home in the evening to get back to their wives. Michelet is usually listed among the heroes of female emancipation. A criticism of his books by a woman, Adèle Esquiros, shows, however, how inadequate his proposals were from the point of view of women. Her book on love, much more than his, deserves to be ranked as a classic of women's liberation literature. She is appalled by Michelet's arrogance, which she regards as typical of middle-class men. Michelet says he wants men to stop shutting themselves up in their jobs and claiming superiority from their specialised knowledge; he claims that he wants men to share their lives with women, but in effect he only imposes a new tyranny upon women. His idea is that men should educate their wives, fashion them in their own mould, tell them what to think. He claims to liberate them but he only really wants them to acknowledge their husbands as their God. 'I do not believe', writes Madame Esquiros, 'in the homoeopathy of M. Michelet, who wants to cure the [old male] pride by an increase of pride.' She complains that marriage should be a source of happiness but so many men make it a pain. Women only went to the priest for confession because husbands did not perform the function themselves. Michelet says that wives got bored with their husbands and became frigid. 'I regret, monsieur, that you have neither found nor sought the cause of this frigidity which exists in almost all marriages.' The reason for it, she says, was that men were either 'brutal, gross and savage' or else they thought they were being respectful towards their wives by not being demonstrative. There was a common prejudice, in the middle classes particularly, that familiarity breeds contempt. The only result was that wives became dry and peevish prudes who said that they knew what their duty was, while their husbands were respectfully egoistic, shutting themselves up in the performance of duty with a similar sobriety and strictness. 'Strange respect and strange duty!' The husband ought to get his wife to know him, to become more truly familiar with him, and among people with feeling, familiarity will produce respect. Men should stop being concerned so much with themselves, they should not try to take more than they give, they should try to understand their wives. Women had their own ideas, caprices and sensitivities and men still had everything to learn from them. Dissimulation would then be replaced by confidence and freedom. She had no use for the poet who once told her: 'To love, is to admire oneself in another.' (Half a century later, Valéry could still write 'Love is the way to love oneself absolutely'; Proust discussed love as an illusion created by men in their own image.) Men had monopolised all the jobs, honours and pleasures of the world. They were consumed by pride, tobacco, spirits and evil passions. They had destroyed women by degrading them into nonentities. They would have happy homes only when they appreciated that women had much more to offer than men at present admitted.[1]

There certainly were advocates of intimacy and friendship between the sexes from an early date. In the debates about marriage during the first revolution, Oudot, deputy of the Côte-d'Or, had demanded the abolition of paternal consent after the age of twenty-one so that there should be no obstacles to 'two people uniting themselves, when they were really suited, as came about when there was conformity of character', even if considerations of ambition, avarice and pride opposed themselves.[2] There were the utopians, above all Fourier, who wanted relations between the sexes to be totally free. But it is more interesting to find pillars of respectability beginning to feel that men ought to have more fun in their married lives. Already in 1806 Joseph Droz (1773–1850), member of the French Academy, and descended from a long line of magistrates, in his manual on how to be happy, urged that marriage should cease to be simply a way of improving one's status and should become a means of being happy. Women should be given a chance in it to correct the pedantry, pride and severity of men. He rejected the idea that love would follow from an arranged marriage. 'I am of the opinion that one should not marry a woman except after one has won her love, for it is doubtful whether love will be inspired by a husband.' But he did not go anywhere as far as Mme Esquiros. He still thought

[1] Adèle Esquiros, *L'Amour* (1860).
[2] Dr. Louis Fiaux, *La Femme, le mariage et le divorce. Étude de physiologie et de sociologie* (1880), 27–8.

of the husband as being older than the wife, and educating her. To marry as heroes married in novels was dangerous: 'The dreams of lovers spoil the reality when they are married.' The man, he still thought, must exercise the authority in the household: the wife should only have influence over him. Joseph Droz marks a first stage, which does not go beyond Michelet.

Gustave Droz (no relation) trained at the École des Beaux Arts (the son of a successful sculptor, grandson of a director of the mint), a journalist and for long Buloz's assistant in the *Revue des Deux Mondes*, wrote a best seller in 1866 called *Monsieur, madame et bébé*. This went through 121 editions between 1866 and 1884. He said he proposed to do what no one else had done: write about love in marriage. People had made marriage sound so grim and frightening, overwhelmed by duty, but the men who propagated this notion were husbands exhausted by prostitutes and rheumatism, who wanted to make marriage an asylum of retirement, of which their young wives would be the angels. He felt he had to convert women from this role. 'It is nice being an angel, but, believe me, it is either too much or not enough . . . A husband who is stately and a little bald is all right, but a young husband who loves you and who drinks out of your glass without ceremony, is better. Let him, if he ruffles your dress a little and places a little kiss on your neck as he passes. Let him, if he undresses you after the ball, laughing like a fool. You have fine spiritual qualities, it is true, but your little body is not bad either and when one loves, one loves completely. Behind these follies lies happiness. Thank heaven if in marriage which is presented to you as a career you find a side that yields laughter and joy; if in your husband you find a loved reader of the nice novel you keep in your pocket; if in your husband you find a . . . But if I say the word you will cry Scandal!' A great battle would have to be fought, said Droz, before women overcame the inhibitions imposed on them by their education which made them so stuffy. He held up the ideal of the married couple who were lovers.[1]

The notion that women could obtain pleasure from sexual intercourse was no invention of the twentieth century and Marie Stopes has wrongly been credited with inventing the female right to orgasm. The works of the seventeenth-century

[1] Gustave Droz, *Monsieur, madame et bébé* (published by Hetzel, 1866), 112.

Dr. Nicolas Venette, frequently reprinted in the nineteenth, painted a picture of women as being naturally more lascivious than men, and offered advice on how to meet their sexual demands. A doctor who produced a revised edition of Venette's book on conjugal love in 1907, like Droz, urged married men to treat their wives sexually in the same way as they treated their mistresses.[1] Among the numerous guides to sex and marriage published in the nineteenth century, there were some moralistic ones, but quite a few stressed the importance of satisfying women emotionally. One particularly successful one, by a retired army medical officer, which went through 173 editions between 1848 and 1888, was quite specific about women enjoying intercourse as much as men. It advised men that whereas some women go into a delirium of pleasure at the least contact, others require frequently repeated caresses to reach orgasm. For extreme cases of inhibition he prescribed flagellation, but his main advice was to win women by tenderness and kindness. He said that doctors were agreed that a married man between twenty and thirty should only exercise his conjugal rights two to four times a week, but always with an interval of a day; twice a week till forty, once till fifty, once a fortnight till sixty, but never beyond that age. Over-activity—'five or six times a day as many young men do'—produced regrets later. Women were capable of indulging more often than men, but they should restrict themselves because it could lead to diseases and to cancer. 'The solitary masturbation practised by many women dissatisfied with their husbands' should be avoided for the same reason.[2]

Another doctor, who published *A Little Bible for Young Spouses* (1885), though writing with more discretion, stressed the need for husbands to give their wives sexual pleasure and to aim for simultaneous orgasm.[3] But all this advice had to work against firmly engrained prejudices in both sexes. There is a case recorded of a wife demanding a divorce because of the excessive zeal and 'unnatural caresses' of her husband: he pleaded that he was only trying to please her and increase her affection for him:

---

[1] Dr. Nicolas Venette, *Tableau de l'amour conjugale* (new edition by Dr. Caufeynon (pseudonym for Dr. Jean Fauconney) (1907)).

[2] A. Debay, *Hygiène et physiologie du mariage* (n.d., 54th edition).

[3] Dr. Charles Montalban, *La Petite Bible des jeunes époux* (1885), 36, 56.

the court found in his favour.[1] In 1887 a book advocated a reform of the art of love-making, on the ground that adultery was caused by husbands not satisfying their wives: women had a right to orgasm.[2] In the 1950s in a poll of married women, 68 per cent said sexual relations were an important part of marriage, 22 per cent said they were only for a minority, and 10 per cent would not answer. But only 46 per cent of these women considered that physical love in marriage proved satisfying; as their ages went up, an increasing number spoke of disappointment.[3]

The lady who asked for a divorce because her husband's love-making alarmed her was very likely the victim of the conflict produced by the hostility of many conservatives to the enjoyment or discussion of sex. The doctrine preached by the Catholic clergy was that the purpose of marriage was definitely not pleasure, but the constitution of families and the procreation of children. In 1920, Abbé Grimaud, in a work which was to go through at least 33 editions and which was crowned by the French Academy, summarised their attitude well when he said that 'God foresaw in his wisdom that couples would not accept the heavy obligations of paternity unless they were pushed by the charms of pleasure'. But sexual pleasure should not be an aim in itself. The clergy generally spoke of the husband as having sexual urges and the wife as submitting to them. Taking their own practice as an ideal, they urged the repression of sexual desire as the ultimate aim: Joseph and the Virgin Mary, who loved each other but never copulated, represented ultimate virtue. Few people could be expected to reach these heights, but, after procreation, continence by mutual consent in marriage was recommended as desirable, even though it would mean abstention from all touching, looks or words of affection, which might reinflame desire. The clergy were genuinely concerned with the dignity of women, but sometimes conceived it in a way which restricted women's intellectual aspirations. Thus Abbé Grimaud, in discussing what kind

---

[1] Georges Anquetil and Jane de Magny, *L'Amant légitime ou la bourgeoisie libertine* (1923), 518.

[2] J. P. Dartigues, *De l'amour expérimentale ou des causes d'adultère chez la femme au 19e siècle. Étude d'hygiène et d'économie sociale, résultant de l'ignorance du libertinage et des fraudes dans l'accomplissement des devoirs conjugaux* (Versailles, 1887), 124, 188.

[3] French Institute of Public Opinion, op. cit., 173.

of wife a man should choose, vigorously advises men to steer as completely clear of intellectuals and professional women (unless they were willing to give up their jobs) as of prostitutes. A woman must be primarily a mother devoted to bringing up her children as Christians. For all his belief in the equality of souls, he likewise urges men to marry only girls of their own class. If a man feels that he is about to fall in love (he likens it to being attacked by a microbe) his first thought should be to go to his parents and ask them to ascertain whether the girl was suitable. Then, when all the demands of reason were satisfied, he could allow his passion to capture him. Passion would of course pass rapidly and could not be the basis of marriage. That is why it was so deplorable that employers were putting 'young men and girls to work at the same tables. Go into a bank, for example, and in a flash, if you are just a bit of a psychologist, you will appreciate how much a young man, even though he would like to remain honourable, is menaced by the possibility of contracting an unhappy marriage. Next to boys—often very distinguished ones, who have studied, and come from a certain level of society—one sees typists, among whom are some of excellent education, but also many others less *sérieuses*. One can judge what the majority of these girls are like from the clothes they wear. One suspects that in this mixed company it will not be the good quiet girls, modest like nuns and reserved like mothers of families, who will attract the men's glances. They will be called boring and unattractive. The others on the contrary will not fail to please the young men rapidly, because they do not hesitate to surround them with the most provocative attention.'[1]

The Church's view of marriage laid stress on gravity, devotion to duty, the bringing up of children, resignation, acceptance of one's lot, and consolation from prayer and piety. It was vigorously opposed to contraception and, through the confession, some clergy even pressed women to resist their husband's embraces if they practised *coitus interruptus*, which was the commonest contraceptive method employed in this period. It sought to maintain morality by preaching self-control. It offered a great deal of emotional consolation, but it was God and prayer, not the husband, who were the consolers. The only

---

[1] Abbé Charles Grimaud, *Futurs Époux* (1920), 287–90, 301–15.

true and full love women could have, one author pointed out, was love of God. Bishop Dupanloup in the 1860s stressed that marriage brought dignity to the mother but it also gave authority to the father. In 1920 when General de Castelnau issued his Declaration of the Rights of the Family at the Estates General of the French Family (an anti-contraceptive organisation), he defined the family as being 'founded on marriage, hierarchically constituted under the authority of the father, having as its goal the transmission, support, development and perpetuation of human life'. The stress was on the family unit against the rights individuals claimed against it.[1] Sexual education was seen mainly as an exhortation to piety, chastity and repression. The Church opposed sexual education in schools and insisted that it should be left to the parents.[2] One author held up as a model on how the facts should be told the history of a pious father who, when his son reached the age of eighteen, summoned him to his study and told him: 'My son, I have some great truths to tell you. Let us kneel and say an Ave Maria.' Asking whether his son had understood the prayer he explained the divine mystery of the Incarnation, and from that moved on to show the less sublime origins of miserable humanity; then he pointed out our duties, the dangers that would be encountered and the precautions to be taken. The boy listened, hardly asking any questions, and understood the ideas which would transform him. 'I felt', he said, 'that I became a man.' The conversation ended with a prayer as it had begun.[3] Marriage was thus seen as a duty, second best to the complete dedication of the self made by the nun or the monk.

The moderate liberal tradition took a very similar view of marriage. Jules Simon founded a fortnightly *Revue de Famille*, which lasted for twenty years, aiming at the revival of the country's morals by the family spirit. Bishop Dupanloup had thought that hierarchy could not survive in politics or social life unless it was maintained in marriage. Simon, similarly, thought only family virtues could save France from communism. 'The more one is attached to one's home, the more one is ready to die for

---

[1] H. Bordeaux, 208–10.
[2] *L'Église et l'éducation sexuelle*. Proceedings of the seventh national congress of the Association du Mariage Chrétien (1929).
[3] Grimaud, 37–8.

one's country.' The liberals were as anxious to promote duty rather than pleasure as the Catholics, but they slightly moderated the latter's stringent austerity. They agreed it was legitimate to enjoy sex in marriage in moderation, though they were unwilling to discuss it and discouraged people from thinking too much about it. They saw women as performing clearly separate functions in the family. One doctor who wrote a guide to *The Health of Married People* gave this as his advice: 'Happiness in marriage is not possible unless each keeps perfectly within his role and confines himself to the virtues of his sex, without encroaching on the prerogatives of the opposite sex.' The husband, who provided the element of force and activity, had as his function 'to represent the family or to direct it in its relations with the external world and to ensure its preservation and its development. The wife, so well endowed with grace, intuition and a ready emotional sympathy, has as her mission to preside over the internal life of the house, whose well-being she ensures by her knowledge of domestic details.' The children were the result of this union, and were the reward or punishment of it, depending on how successful it was. He recommended marriage between persons of differing temperaments—the bilious should marry the lymphatic, the sanguine should unite with the nervous—because the children produced would be healthier mixtures in this way.[1] This is not to say that intellectual compatibility was regarded as a disadvantage. Many authors were keen to stimulate it, though they often seemed to think of it as coming after marriage. Paul Janet, a leading university moralist in the second half of the nineteenth century, thought the husband ought to be the head of the family because men had a superior power of reason, more suitable to command, having greater breadth, logic and impartiality. Women had reason too, but of a different kind, and their subordination was necessary only because it was best to have one person in charge. Otherwise there should be 'moral equality' between husband and wife.[2] A contemporary of his, Amédie de Margerie, in a strange work praising the virtues of the family but clearly uneasy that there was something wrong with it, urged men to spend their evenings talking with their

---

[1] Dr. Louis Seraine, *De la santé des gens mariés* (2nd edition 1865), 112–16.
[2] Paul Janet, *La Famille* (4th edition 1861).

wives and, when their conversations died out, to read together. This man was keen to increase the moral influence of the wife in marriage, because she was more often religious and her mission was to convert her husband. 'The times we live in need strong women.' Wives must save the family from the indifference of men. Indeed, he said, 'though their official position in it was subordinate, their influence in it is preponderant'.[1] The subject of the preponderant wife is one which will be discussed later in relation to its effect on children.

In 1920 there was an interesting debate in the press about what relations between husband and wife should be. It is one of the few occasions when, from the letters ordinary people wrote, one can obtain direct evidence of trends in common behaviour, and when one can see revealed widespread dissatisfaction with the traditional kind of marriage. One should not conclude that this was produced by the war, by the absence of men for several years and the increased responsibility women bore, though that certainly brought some tensions into the open. Adèle Esquiros's book had voiced complaints sixty years earlier. But the war broke routines and enabled people to see what habit had concealed from them. 'This unanimous explosion of independence among women, provoked by the absence of husbands,' wrote one letter writer, 'suffices to show what forces and aspirations were repressed in them even by the most loved of tyrants . . . Conjugal affection, the joys and worries of motherhood make them accept in silence many vexations.' The explosion was by no means unanimous, but quite a number of women now had a different view of marriage. They objected to men's expecting their wives to be domestic servants. They demanded that husbands should treat them as friends and companions. But the war had also increased the opportunities for men to develop new interests in life, which took them increasingly away from the home. A railwayman wrote that far from having a higher regard for women because they had done men's jobs in the war, he now saw women as economic rivals. 'Women no longer want to obey . . . We talk about marriage between men and women as people talk of peace between the Boches and the French.' And on the other side a judge refused a divorce to a

[1] Amédie de Margerie, *De la famille* (1878, first published 1860, five editions in all), i. xxxi, 209.

disgruntled husband, saying he must use gentleness not firmness to win back his wife.[1] In the 1950s the opinion polls said one-third of wives thought their husbands had changed for the worse since marriage, but almost exactly one-third also thought they themselves had deteriorated. This is the nearest one can get to any statistics about the extent of disillusionment with marriage.

An important factor in determining the nature of marriages was the age of the couple at their wedding. 'In general', wrote a member of the French Academy in 1917, 'a man does not consent to take a legitimate wife until the moment when life, of which he is a bit tired, begins to bore him.' It was natural therefore that he should expect submission and docility from his wife. The wife was usually much younger and could hardly challenge him. Léon Blum wrote a book in his youth suggesting that until there were identical codes of moral behaviour for girls and boys, inequalities of experience were bound to pro-duce friction. He made the bold proposal that both sexes—instead of just men—should marry only after they had sown their wild oats and were willing to accept monogamy volun-tarily.[2]

In the working class, inequalities of age and experience tended to be smaller and it was claimed by some that family life was accordingly friendlier, more one of equality and com-panionship. Possibly here women acquired more influence earlier, since they did not have to fight against the husband's technical prestige. For long the problem with the industrial workers was to get them to marry. Moralists saw marriage at this level as a means of shackling the men, of keeping them off the streets, of reducing crime and of instilling love of prop-erty in the poor.[3] It is by no means clear that love played a greater role in their marriages: in the country in particular local customs concerning courtship—which differed consider-ably—maintained the authority of parents and the haggling over dowries continued to the very humble levels. There were areas where marriages were generally fixed at Christmas time—provided the harvest had been a good one—by the parents. On

[1] H. Bordeaux, op. cit.
[2] Léon Blum, Le Mariage (1907).
[3] Institut de France, Statistique: mariage civil et religieux des pauvres (1846).

occasion it was the girls who proposed to the boys. Intermediaries were used to a considerable extent—travelling tailors seem to have been particularly active in this role.[1] In the towns of course marriage bureaux flourished. They offered their services, it should be noted, to parents more than to the parties concerned.[2] (After the Great War, they were supplemented by divorce agencies, with fees fixed in inverse proportion to the time they took to obtain the decree: 2,000 francs for one year's delay, 5,000 francs if it was completed in three months.) It was claimed by an author comparing France, England and the U.S.A. that French women had less freedom in choosing their husbands, but once they were married, they acquired more influence.[3] In many ways it will be seen that the marriage system oppressed children more than wives. Wives, after all, could look forward to increasing power as they became mothers, grandmothers and matriarchs.

Money played such a large part in marriage, sexual relations were subject to so many restrictions, wives were so keen to transform themselves from brides into matriarchs that inevitably adultery and prostitution were essential to the working of this system. An additional reason, not usually appreciated, is the slow elimination of women's gynaecological diseases. Too much attention is perhaps given to the diseases which killed, like smallpox and tuberculosis, and not enough to those which simply made life unpleasant. One such was leucorrhea. In 1865 a doctor estimated that, particularly in cities, as many as 80 per cent of women suffered from it.[4] Another doctor, writing in 1868, described the large number of other diseases, metritis, ulcerations, inflammations, tumours, haemorrhages, etc., many of which he attributed to irritations caused by amateur contraceptives.[5] A work commended by the Academy of Moral and Political Sciences in 1872 pointed out that because of these diseases it was very often impossible for husbands and wives to copulate, putting aside all the other illnesses which could

[1] Évariste Carrance, Le Mariage chez nos près (Bordeaux, 1872).
[2] Journal Matrimonial. Gazette des familles (1 May 1850).
[3] Auguste Carlier, Le Mariage aux États-Unis (1860), an interesting criticism of Tocqueville.
[4] Dr. Louis Seraine, De la santé des gens mariés (1865), 136.
[5] Dr. L. F. E. Bergeret, Des Fraudes dans l'accomplissement des fonctions génératrices. Dangers et inconvénients pour les individus, la famille et la société (1868).

nauseate like eczema, rheumatism, tumours, etc. The proportion of young people who were both healthy and attractive was comparatively small. No figures are available for women, but the facts revealed by conscription about boys are appalling. An analysis published in 1872 said that of the 325,000 young men of twenty called up, 18,106 were under 4 foot 10 inches tall. There were 30,524 of 'feeble constitution', i.e. suffering from rickets or consumption, etc. 15,988 were cripples, mutilated or sufferers from hernia, rheumatism, etc. 9,100 were hunchbacks, club-footed or flat-footed. 6,934 had defects of the ears, eyes or nose. 963 had speech defects and 4,108 were toothless. 'Precocious debauchery' had ruined 5,114. 2,529 were victims of skin diseases, 5,213 of goitre and scrofula, 2,158 were paralytics, convulsives or cretins, and 8,236 had miscellaneous troubles. In all therefore 109,000—that is, one-third—were infirm or deformed, and this was at the age of twenty.[1]

The great bogy the moralists used to keep people chaste was the danger of catching syphilis. It was indeed a major blight on the country. Flaubert, in his *Dictionary of Received Ideas*, defined it as being almost as common as the cold: 'More or less everybody is affected by it.' At the turn of the century insurance company records revealed that between 14 and 15 per cent of all deaths were from syphilis. Another source gave a figure of 17 per cent. Between the wars a third estimate suggested that probably one-tenth of the population suffered from it, i.e. four million people, and that 140,000 lives were lost annually from it. Over 40,000 still births a year were attributable to it. It was one of the principal causes of madness. Half of syphilitics caught the disease between the age of fourteen and twenty-one. In the bourgeoisie a tenth caught it at school. One could draw up a list of many distinguished figures in French history who are said to have had the disease, from Gambetta to Baudelaire.

The main reason why it survived so tenaciously was that every government ignored it in hypocritical silence. The Academy of Medicine appointed a commission to find means of checking it in 1887; a Society for Sanitary and Moral Prophylaxis was founded in 1901, but though parliament at last got round to discussing it in 1907, it did nothing. The war

[1] Armand Hayem, *Le Mariage* (1872), 243.

stimulated some governmental activity, particularly in the army; in 1924 a National League against the Venereal Peril was founded and there were many other societies. But there was nothing like the compulsory treatment established in the U.S.A. In the nineteenth century the treatment available was very inadequate. Few beds were allocated to it in hospitals and some hospital nurses refused to allow syphilitic patients to be admitted. Until 1871 the main hospital in Paris devoted to it, Lancine, had underground cells for the punishment of patients considered morally reprehensible. The fact that going to this hospital involved public admission of one's disease kept many away. A real change came only in 1880 when Alfred Fournier had the first chair of venereal diseases established for him. He opened a clinic at an ordinary hospital, with privacy assured, and in 1882 had 31,000 cases come to him, whereas only 4,800 went annually to Lancine. The whole question was confused by the myth that it was the prostitutes who were responsible and that the only need was to control them. Another great obstacle to a reduction of the disease was the vast number of charlatans offering bogus cures. Their advertisements covered the walls of public lavatories, and one of the main activities of the societies was to fight the charlatans. Syphilis was one of the major causes of misery and suffering in this period.[1]

Extramarital sexual relations were a normal feature of life throughout it. Moralists always look back to a golden age of purity. But already in 1865 a doctor wrote: 'Today people do not think they can get rid of the burden of chastity early enough.'[2] 'It is rare', wrote another, 'to find in the present state of our morals boys who are virgin after seventeen or eighteen.'[3] Flaubert makes one of his heroes say of a brothel: 'That is the only place where I have been happy.' Pierre Louÿs's *Aphrodite* was looked upon as a breviary in praise of prostitution. Published in 1896, it had by 1904 sold 125,000

---

[1] E. Jeanselme, *La Syphilis. Son aspect pathologique et social* (1925); *L'Église et l'éducation sexuelle* (1929), 156; Louis Fiaux, *Le Police des mœurs devant la commission extra-parlementaire du régime des mœurs* (1907–10), 1. cxxxix, cxlvi; A. Fournier, *Les Dangers sociaux de la syphilis* (1905); id., *Syphilis et mariage* (1880); id., *Traité de la syphilis* (1899–1906).

[2] Dr. Louis Seraine, 23.

[3] Dr. Louis Fiaux, *La Femme, le mariage et le divorce* (1880), 43.

copies and inspired three plays and four opera libretti, and since then it has been regularly reprinted.

Visits to prostitutes started at school. On holidays and the Thursday half-day the brothels swarmed with schoolboys.[1] This precocity was encouraged by the massive war that was waged against masturbation. The danger of masturbation was one of the prime obsessions of parents and schools. The efforts used to extirpate it were so enormous they can only be likened to a new version of the medieval witchhunts.[2] Manufacturers produced excruciating corsets for children to make it impossible. Books were filled with advice on diet, exercises and clothing best suited to prevent it. Priests fought against it in the confession, and teachers at school. They preached self-control, which they thought ought to last ideally until the age of twenty-five, for young fathers produced feeble children and young debauchees were ruined for life. Some church schools were said even to periodically bleed pupils who revealed excessive sexuality.[3] Prostitutes played an important role in the life of the adolescent. Even in an inquiry among practising Catholic married males, 60 per cent admitted to having had premarital sexual activity, and 47 per cent of these said they had been initiated by a prostitute. This is a radically different situation to that in Britain or the U.S.A. today.[4] Whether there is more premarital sexual activity today in France than there was a hundred years ago is impossible to say. In the 1950s, 30 per cent of a sample of married Frenchwomen interviewed admitted to intercourse with their husbands before marriage. The figure, however, was only 24 per cent when the husband was a farmer but 43 per cent when he was a worker and 34 per cent when he was an executive or professional man.[5] Male and female attitudes towards this remain contrasted. In the poll of 10,000 young people held in 1966, 60 per cent of the girls were against premarital sex, and 66 per cent of the boys were for it.[6]

[1] Abbé Timon-David, *Traité de la confession des enfants et des jeunes gens* (1865, 14th edition 1924); cf. C. Féré, *La Pathologie des émotions* (1892), 269–71.

[2] J. M. W. van Ussel, *Sociogenese en evolutie van het probleem der seksuele propaedeuse* (Amsterdam thesis, 1967).

[3] Dr. J. Agrippa, *La Première Flétrissure* (3rd edition 1877).

[4] Henriques, 259.

[5] French Institute of Public Opinion, op. cit., 121.

[6] Roberte Franck, 86.

After marriage, adultery was almost inevitable.[1] It has been seen how, in this same poll, all boys and girls placed fidelity first as the quality they sought in their future spouse, above love, beauty or intelligence. But 84 per cent of the boys thought that it was possible to deceive one's wife without ceasing to love her: only 18 per cent of the girls agreed. Only 52 per cent of the boys, as against 74 per cent of the girls, thought that adultery necessarily damaged married life. They were agreed (79 and 76 per cent), however, that divorce was not preferable to adultery. The institution of marriage was not threatened, because it was not interpreted in the way the Church demanded. A recent study of the sexual habits of the French married man reveals that adultery is maintained precisely by the survival of traditional moral doctrines. An industrialist of fifty who was interviewed said: 'I make love with my wife when I want a child. The rest of the time I make love with my mistresses. Wives are to produce heirs. For pleasure men seek other women.' The low divorce rate conceals many marriages in which sexual intercourse is totally absent and in which husbands normally seek their satisfaction elsewhere. This study shows the existence of a separate world, maintained more or less secret, sometimes with elaborate subterfuges, hidden behind the respectable façade of married life.[2]

In the 1850s it was estimated that London had about 24,000 prostitutes but Paris, with almost half the population, was said to have 34,000.[3] Until 1946 the state regulated their activities, on the principle that their existence was inevitable and that they should practise their trade in the least offensive manner possible. Public opinion was less outraged by their trade, than by their trade being carried on publicly and in a manner which constituted a nuisance for those who did not require their services. A *police des mœurs* was established and prostitutes were required to live in brothels (*maisons de tolérance*), subject to medical inspection. The number of these official brothels in Paris was 180 in 1810, 200 in 1840, but they gradually fell to 145 in 1870, 125 in 1881 and 59 in 1892. The reason was the growth in

---

[1] Pierre Veron, *Paris vicieux: le guide de l'adultère* (1883); T. Revel, *L'Adultère* (1861); E. Cademartori, *L'Adultère à Marseille* (1866).
[2] Jacques Baroche, *Le Comportement sexuel de l'homme marié en France* (1969).
[3] Henriques, 224.

clandestine brothels, which the police estimated contained some 15,000 prostitutes in 1888. In the years 1871–1903, some 155,000 women registered as prostitutes but the police arrested 725,000 others suspected of prostitution. In 1900 the prefect of police, Lépine, carried out a reform designed to take into account the new habits. He authorised *maisons de rendezvous*, that is to say, establishments in which prostitutes did not reside but merely came to work: provided the entrance fee was above 40 francs, the police did not make any demands of registration or inspection. The pleasures of the middle class were thus liberated from state control.[1] Lépine viewed prostitution as a perfectly normal activity, and not in itself offensive. His regulation included this sentence: 'Since brothels are considered as public places, any person committing, in an establishment of this kind, in the presence of other persons, an act of immorality constituting a public outrage to modesty (*pudeur*), will be prosecuted.' His aim was to abolish perversions, and to establish a new kind of clean brothel: 'No more peep-holes, no more turpitudes' was his motto, but in vain. Flexner, the American investigator into European prostitution during the war, was amazed by Paris's specialisation in every kind of perversion, and the way the brothels rivalled each other in inventiveness. In the 1960s the Paris police estimated that the brothels of the city—with about one million adult males in it—had 40,000 clients a day; and this suggests that perhaps a quarter of all Parisians had relations with prostitutes.

In the provinces the situation was slightly different. Each town made its own arrangements and regulations. The Second Empire practised a *laissez-faire* attitude, but in the 1880s the government attempted a revival of control. Of the 557 known regulations about prostitution, only 219 date from before 1880. The majority, which were made after this date, varied enormously from town to town. Compulsory medical visits varied from two a week to two a month. In Vichy every prostitute had to deposit three photographs at the police station. At St. Étienne they were forbidden to walk in the streets in clothes other than those of 'respectable women'. Autun and Melun imposed restrictions on their hairstyles. In southern towns and

---

[1] On part-time prostitution in all classes see L. Fiaux, *La Police des mœurs* (1907–10), I. 37; Roberte Franck, *L'Infidélité conjugale* (1969), 224.

in the ports—most famous of all, in Marseille—the medieval whores' quarter survived. Regulations had little effect because the public prosecutors in general abstained from bringing scandals into the open. When between the wars a number of cities, notably Strasbourg, Grenoble and Nancy, attempted to close down their brothels, there was little change in men's habits and publications immediately appeared to supply clandestine addresses. Every garrison provided a substantial clientele. Soldiers were officially forbidden to visit brothels but the army created them specially in the colonies. It was claimed that prostitutes had to work far harder in these military brothels than in any private establishment exploited by an unscrupulous ponce. It was this exploitation and the white slave traffic that led to the official ending of *maisons de tolérance* in 1946. The abuses were certainly very real, but there is also evidence that a liberalisation of conditions in brothels occurred in the late nineteenth century, with increasing numbers of them being non-residential.

In the nineteenth century the brothel was a place of relaxation as ordinary and as natural as any other. Maupassant in a story of a provincial town describes one where respectable businessmen and young men met regularly, just as in a café, and where the Madame was treated with respect. The streets of the cities were plagued with importunate prostitutes in the same way as with beggars. Around 1900 there were 115 *brasseries* in Paris, which were ordinary cafés, except that the girls employed there made themselves available and took clients to a hotel. These got their best custom from schoolboys and students. There were many other establishments, like perfume shops, baths and massage institutes which performed the same functions. An annual *Guide rose* provided a full directory to all the opportunities. In addition theatres and luxury stores were recognised as amateur haunts. The rumour that middle-class women sometimes worked part-time as prostitutes, to earn money to keep up with the neighbours, has been confirmed by a recent sociological survey. (One suffragette wrote a book to demand brothels for women.) Some students, before they took to sleeping with each other, lived with *grisettes*—working girls who wanted a lover rather than a client and who had ambitions to rise in the world. When one of these *grisettes*, wrote an observer in 1840, had a child, she would set him up as a printer, or, if a girl, send her into the theatre—anything to avoid their having to do needlework like their mother. The *grisette* 'whom the student loves a little better than his dog and a little less than his pipe, madly throws away the best years of her life to love, pleasure and temporary liaisons'. She wears a mask of jollity but underneath is generally sombre, with a great contempt for life. She is greedy, and will accept a dinner from anybody; she is easily picked up at balls. But she consoled the students in their depressions and nursed them in their illnesses.[1]

Brothels always existed to cater for every class, but with time some became more like department stores, offering mass-produced luxury at a popular price. Between the wars several old firms in Paris were expanded from grubby slums into palatial establishments with armies of girls always available, including Saturday and Sunday, and offering themselves at a low fixed price. These brothels changed hands for large sums. Some owners built up chains of them. More and more girls, however, set themselves up as luxury prostitutes operating more discreetly. It was estimated that whereas in 1789 only 10 or 20 per cent of prostitutes were luxury ones, about a half are today. Their total number, it is claimed, has risen considerably. At the Revolution Poncet de La Grave in his *Considerations on Celibacy* (1801) estimated that there were 100,000 of them in France. In the 1960s, by which time the population of the country had doubled, a figure of 400,000 was suggested. But in the 1960s the young appear to have begun to abandon using them and a new morality now coexists with the old.[2]

The position of different forms of relaxation in French life may be indicated by the comparative incomes of different institutions of culture and licentiousness in Paris in the 1920s. The receipts of the Opéra were 12 million francs, but the Folies Bergères came second with 10 million francs, more than either the Comédie Française or the Opéra Comique. In 1923

---

[1] Alphonse Esquiros, *Les Vierges folles* (1840, new edition 1873).
[2] Dr. Félix Regnault, *L'Évolution de la prostitution* (1906); Fiaux, op. cit., containing numerous documents. The best history is by two *agrégés*, J.-J. Servais and J. P. Laurend, *Histoire et dossier de la prostitution* (1967). See also Marcel Rogeat, *Mœurs et prostitution. Les Grandes Enquêtes sociales* (1935), and the pioneering work of Dr. Parent-Duchâtelet, *De la prostitution dans la ville de Paris* (1836), enlarged edition 1857).

already the Paris cinemas had receipts of 85 million, against 110 million for all the Paris theatres. From the reports of the antipornographic societies, it is not clear what could be classified as culture. They complained of the cinema's 'gross and brutal art, the scenes of crime and passion' exploited by profiteers without taste or scruples and the grave dangers of the medium for children and adolescents. But equally the theatre tried to titillate the bourgeoisie with plays about adultery, free love and divorce, on the pretext of portraying the times; the competition was who could 'push furthest scenes of the phases preparatory to love-making, beds included'. In 1914 *Le Temps* asked that copulation should take place on the stage so that at last the police could intervene. In the music halls and café concerts, there were certainly 'tableaux and scenes which went so far as to represent sexual intercourse'. No one has yet studied these or the vast outpouring of pornography, of books, magazines and photographs, for which colossal sales were reported and which constituted a not insignificant part of the country's entertainment.[1]

The history of modesty—of what was considered permissible and what was not—and the history of repression in the name of public morality are both complicated subjects. Littré defined licentiousness as what offends modesty and obscenity as what offends modesty openly. The law tolerated the former but not the latter; and it made the distinction that the licentious could be defended on the ground that it was 'artistic, excluding all idea of lucre and addressing itself to an élite', whereas the obscene had 'low and pecuniary aims'. As one court ruled in 1884, 'obscenity exists where . . . art does not intervene to raise up the ideal and where the appeal to the instincts and the gross appetites was not opposed or defeated by any superior sentiment'.[2] In the second half of the century it was gradually agreed that art could not be obscene, but new forms of it always took time to be recognised. Flaubert's *Madame Bovary* was adjudged obscene because, it was claimed, it did not hold up an ideal against adultery. In the same way, a totally boring

[1] Paul Bureau, *L'Indiscipline des mœurs* (1927); Paul Gremähling, *L'Immoralité péril pour la race* (Bordeaux n.d., about 1925, published by Le Relèvement Social and the Ligue pour le Relèvement de la Moralité Publique).
[2] Tribunal de la Seine (11th Chamber), 11 Feb. 1884.

book about the life of a woman of easy virtue, who moved from one man to another, but with nothing scatological at all in it beyond that, was condemned a few years later, for much the same reason.[1] At about the same time a merchant of chamber-pots, on the bottom of which was painted an eye, with the words 'I see you', was also convicted for obscenity. But a man who distributed cards announcing the opening of a brothel was acquitted. In 1902 a court ruled that the simple representation of the human form, however indiscreet, could not be condemned as obscene because that would place too great a burden on art, which, whatever it portrayed, 'aided morals within certain limits and purified thoughts by making them more elevated'.[2] At the same time as newspapers and cheap reprints of the classics began pouring from the presses, so the flow of porno-graphy increased, and the invention of photography added to it. Illustrated pornography made its appearance on the mass market. But the public prosecutors brought almost exactly the same number of cases for obscenity each year. Between 1876 and 1906, when this explosion took place, there were regularly around 55 cases a year, involving about 85 people. Very few cases were brought before juries (only 34 in the twenty years 1881–1902) because so many were acquitted (42 per cent). Parliament passed a law in 1898 increasing penalties and extend ing the definition of obscenity, and ministers of justice issued circulars urging the stricter enforcement of the law, but with little actual effect. Only Fallières in 1891 succeeded in doubling the number of prosecutions, but the situation quickly returned to normal. The main change was the multiplication of puritan societies: the first Congress against Pornography was held in 1905. The League for Public Morality, the Central Society against Licence in the Streets, the National Association for the Protection of Workers were a new way in which the middle classes defended order.[3]

[1] Claude Fougerol, *Scènes de la vie galante. Les Amours d'une ingénue* (1862).
[2] Tribunal de Vervins, 29 Nov. 1902.
[3] Albert Eyquem, *De la répression des outrages à la morale publique et aux bonnes mœurs ou de la pornographie au point de vue historique, juridique législatif et social* (1905); Jules Gay, *Bibliographie des ouvrages relatifs à l'amour, aux femmes, au mariage et des livres facétieux, pantagruéliques, scatologiques, satiriques etc.* (4th edition 1894); F. Drujon, *Catalogue des ouvrages, écrits et dessins de toute nature poursuivis, supprimés ou condamnés 1814–77* (1879).

There was one aspect of sexual behaviour, however, in which repression noticeably subsided. Homosexuality was universally condemned at the beginning of this period. 'With all its disgusting and ignominious horrors, how can it exist in an advanced civilisation like ours?' asked the *Encyclopédie Larousse* in the 1860s, which was otherwise liberal and was not too horrified by the ideas on heterosexuality of men like Fourier. There was a curious class consciousness in its condemnation. 'Unbridled debauchery, blasé sensuality can to a certain extent explain homosexuality but it is difficult in many cases not to admit a veritable mental derangement in the moral faculties. What can one say indeed of one of these men come down from a high position to the lowest degree of depravation, drawing into his home sordid children of the streets before whom he kneels, whose feet he kisses with a passionate submission before begging from them the most infamous pleasures?' This can only be 'the most shameless madness'. In the middle of the nineteenth century male prostitution and blackmail was said to have become 'an industry of almost unbelievable dimensions'. From time to time the police descended upon this world. In 1845 there were 47 accused in the *affaire de la rue du Rempart*; and in successive prosecutions after that numerous homosexuals were brought to trial. The Second Empire, in two swoops, arrested another 97 and 52 people. Several murders, including one of a certain Ward, brought public attention to the matter and one magistrate, Busserolles, showed particular energy in trying to repress homosexuality. Research has not revealed when or why the prosecutions ceased; it would be worth elucidating the context in which men like Montesquieu were able to flaunt their tastes, and in which Proust could write about it and Gide openly confess it. These men drew attention to the torments involved in it, and perhaps modified public opinion. In 1937 it was claimed that homosexuality was coming out into the open in all classes, and that there were at least a quarter of a million homosexuals in Paris, with the police keeping files on some 20,000 of them. The clubs, restaurants and baths they frequented made them into something of a separate world, to which theatrical and literary celebrities gave both notoriety and respectability. They claimed the protection of the Napoleonic Code, one of whose authors, Cambacères, was said to be a homosexual, but they were still subject to bullying from the police. In the state *lycées*—where it flourished much more than in the church schools—it was of course still vigorously and unsuccessfully repressed.[1] The notion that homosexuality was a symptom of the aberrations in family life was very slow to be accepted.

[1] Ambroise Tardieu, *Étude médico-légale sur les attentats aux mœurs* (7th edition 1878), 195–217; Michel du Coglay, *Chez les mauvais garçons* (1937); *Larousse du XIXe siècle*, 'Pédérastie'; *Le Crapouillot*, issue on 'Les Pédérastes' (1970).

12. Children

THE myths about marriage are paralleled by myths about children. A large proportion of France's children did not have a full family life. Around 1900 for every fifteen families which had both father and mother alive, there were six families incomplete (four of them having a father dead and two a mother dead). Only 54 per cent of marriages lasted longer than 15 years: 15·6 per cent were cut short by death within 4 years, and 29·7 per cent within between 5 and 14 years, and only 31·3 per cent lasted over 25 years. 45 per cent of children were orphans in their teens, and a very significant number were so before then.[1] The First World War perpetuated this situation: in 1931 a further 646,000 families existed who had lost their fathers in the war. There were then also 1,322,000 children with fathers who were mutilated or injured by the war.[2] Of the children born in the year 1875, 93,000 were abandoned by their parents. One out of every fourteen was illegitimate.[3] A considerable number were sent away by their mothers, immediately after birth, to be reared by professional wet-nurses in the country.

It is generally believed that the basic transformation of the family has been the rise of children to the position of central importance in the home, after centuries of neglect, and their being accorded the right to a life of a special kind, different from that of adults and with different expectations placed upon them—this again after centuries in which they were treated simply as adults of miniature size, but to be dressed and to work as adults. Philippe Ariès has argued that the change took place in the eighteenth century. Before that there was no social prestige to be derived from being a good parent, and none to be lost by being a bad one. The family was not primarily a sentimental unit. Conservatives like Villèle sought to maintain primogeniture because they believed that emotions were too fragile a basis

[1] *Statistique des familles* (1906 and 1936).
[2] André Scherrer, *La Condition juridique de l'orphelin de la guerre de 1914–1919* (Nancy, 1933), 11.   [3] Vicomte d'Haussonville, *L'Enfance à Paris* (1879).

for the family's existence; but the abolition of primogeniture is one sign of the end of the family as a unit which was almost a business firm. The increasing interest people took in their children, says Ariès, did not mean liberation from restraint. On the contrary, neglect was replaced by an obsessive love which greatly increased the demands made on children. Discipline and reason were forced on them with a new severity. Instead of being left to their own devices, they had the notion of guilt instilled into them. They were no longer allowed free sex play, as they were in the sixteenth century. The classics were expurgated for their benefit and it was claimed that their innocence had to be protected.

Ariès's pioneering work has been advanced and modified by that of David Hunt, who has studied the childhood of Louis XIII—on whom there is, by chance, a great deal of intimate information. Hunt has shown that it is difficult to distinguish different forms of child rearing into clear chronological periods. Adults did play publicly with Louis XIII's penis when he was a baby; he was allowed to masturbate, to satisfy his sexual curiosity and to read pornography, and he was subject to very little toilet training. But it is untrue that there was a total lack of repression in this period and that children enjoyed a freedom from the modern kind of problems. There was a conflict in society about sex even then: some believed in freedom and some preached continence. The child was still subject to anxieties; the details of sex were still a mystery to him; and his relations with his mother were not unrestrained. It was six months before Louis XIII's mother embraced him and his relations with her remained cold until his father died. Till then the mother belonged to the father. While their fathers were alive children could not get at their mothers. There is some doubt about whether paternal authority did in fact diminish in the *ancien régime*: there are those who claim that the authoritarian monarchy bolstered it up. In any case, the old order has not completely passed away: neglect of children still exists and children are not always the centre of families today. Hunt shows that generalisations about children are as difficult to make as generalisations about any other group of such enormous size.[1]

[1] P. Ariès, *Centuries of Childhood* (1962); D. Hunt, *The Psychology of Family Life in Early Modern France* (1970).

Disagreement about the rearing of children, and about their place in society was almost as great as disagreement about politics, and in the years covered by this book different attitudes coexisted. It is not enough to read the medical manuals in order to trace changes. There certainly were radical alterations in the advice these manuals gave, with a dramatic break in the eighteenth century. Till then the books advocated that new-born babies should be purged, that wet-nurses were preferable to the mother, that feeding should not be scheduled, that swaddling, cradles and cold baths were a good thing. After that, there was instead increasing stress on keeping babies warm, on the avoidance of sex play and masturbation, on the undesirability of thumbsucking (this last appears only in the mid nineteenth century). There was more mention of the need to show babies affection, but also increasing limitations were placed on ways of doing this, for fear of overstimulating them.[1] There was ambiguity, however, in some crucial aspects of this advice. Above all, the advice rather resembles the moralising of the Church. Breast feeding by mothers was advocated long before Rousseau, apparently in vain since the doctors repeatedly complained of the neglect of their advice. After him, it was still not totally accepted, and wet-nurses flourished till the end of the nineteenth century, to be ended not by the force of ideas, but by the new developments in medicine, which made animal milk safe for babies. Rousseau's views on breast feeding, though so famous, were in fact adopted by him almost as an afterthought, when it was pointed out to him that he had omitted any treatment of infancy in his *Émile*. He said he knew nothing about it; a friend gave him a contemporary work by Desessartz, from which he copied almost word for word.[2] Much more important about Rousseau is his giving a philosophic basis for a new treatment of the child. He publicised the view of the child as pure and innocent, who should be left free to develop his own individuality, who was neither a beast nor an adult, but possessed of peculiar ways of thought, with reason being acquired only at the age of fifteen and love even later.

[1] Alice Ryerson, 'Medical Advice on Child Rearing 1550–1900' (Harvard Ph.D. thesis, 1960, unpublished).

[2] Congrès international pour la protection de l'enfance: *L'Évolution de la puériculture* (1933), 114.

This conflicted of course with the Catholic view of the child as sinful, in whom obedience must be instilled, and with the empiricist view that the child was infinitely malleable, all of whose characteristics were the effect of experience. These varied traditions all survived in the nineteenth century and if any generalisation can be made—tentatively owing to the dearth of evidence about the behaviour of families—it is that perhaps Rousseau's notions of innocence did not gain anywhere near universal acceptance. Rousseau's thought was a major turning-point in the history of theory rather than of practice.[1]

Throughout this period, the majority of books published about children reflected not Rousseau's views but conservative and indeed reactionary Catholic opinion. It must be remembered that tradition, handed down from mother to daughter, played a decisive role in influencing conduct, that women were not subject to the same pressures from new educational ideas as men were and that differences in opinions and attitudes between men and women were a fundamental feature of society. One should not argue that these Catholic guides determined conduct, but rather that they reflected *ideals* which were current. It is unlikely that families were brought up in full conformity with any one ideal. Some of these Catholic ideals persisted in the doctrines of liberal and advanced thinkers, and equally some of the latter's views modified the teaching of some Catholics. The over-all picture in child rearing is a wide variety of positions, but also considerable hesitation and confusion, induced by the difficulties which the theories met in practice. This was not a period therefore when Frenchmen were brought up in one particular way, but a period of uncertainty. The conflicts experienced by successive generations were to a significant extent conflicts resulting from the unreconciled coexistence of varying aspirations and traditions in parents.

The conservatives believed that values should be transmitted to children through the exercise of authority and by the instillation of respect. The family was a reflection of the divine order; the father was the delegate of God and exercised power akin to God's. A work addressed to children on the subject of filial love, published in 1862 in Hachette's best-selling Bibliothèque Rose Illustrée, said: 'Your parents, in receiving from

[1] See Roger Mercier, *L'Enfant dans la société du 18ᵉ siècle (avant Émile)* (1961).

God the mission to educate you, receive at the same time what is necessary to fulfil it . . . It is the voice of God that you hear in their voice.'[1] In 1946, Robert Rochefort showed how such a relationship worked out in practice. In his memoirs, he talked of his childhood as having been spent 'in the Kingdom of Father'. 'I lived in his strength; in his will, in his presence, as a believer lives in God. There was no room for choice, for acceptance, refusal or doubt. But we were joined in every part so closely that we could not suspect that another world was possible. The face of Father was usually impenetrable. One hardly dared look him in the face at meals, so thoughtful was his face, so charged with clouds.'[2] Coldness and distance had been characteristic of relations between some fathers and sons in the eighteenth-century aristocracy. Mirabeau said of his father: 'I never had the honour to touch the cheek of that venerable man.' Talleyrand doubted whether he had slept two nights running under the same roof as his parents. Chateaubriand was transformed into a statue by the sight of his father. This coldness was sometimes copied by the bourgeoisie. Quinet so dreaded his father that even at the age of fifty he did not dare help himself to food at his father's table, and when once he did, he was given a sermon by his mother.[3]

One of the causes to which moralists attributed the decline in paternal authority was excessive familiarity. Joseph Droz thought that *tutoiement* was damaging to the relationship of subordination which ought to exist and it introduced a 'ridiculous equality'. A successful manual for *Well Brought Up Children* repeated in 1886 the importance of traditional formalities. It told children to stand up when their parents entered the room. 'When you have the honour to be admitted into the salons of your mothers, you must behave yourself in such a manner that they do not regret having accorded you this favour . . . You will, rightly, not dare present yourself in a salon without your gloves. Provincials are even more rigid observers of this etiquette than we.'[4] A study of *Badly Brought Up Children* (1890) insisted that the way to be successful with children was to be authoritarian.

[1] T. H. Barrau, *Amour filial. Récits à la jeunesse* (1862), 375.
[2] Robert Rochefort, *Dans le royaume du père* (1946), 1, 4.
[3] Hippolyte Durand, *Le Règne de l'enfant* (1889), 7.
[4] Comtesse de Ferry, *Les Enfants bien élevés* (Mame, Tours, 1886; reprinted eight times before 1913; 1924 edition), 45, 49.

'By the exercise of authority, one makes one's sons respectful and men of duty.' Children should not be treated as the equals of parents, but rather—the simile is the author's—'like dogs'. 'If a man has a dog, he tries to attach it to himself, to make it know and like his house; he does not let it wander according to its whim. He takes care to make it obey by employing threats sometimes and caresses at other times. Well, he ought to take at least the same amount of trouble with his child . . . At the least calculated resistance, punish with real severity, that is the great secret of authority. Obedience must be demanded without restriction.' Another way to obtain it was to make the child accept that he was not in this world to enjoy himself. From an early age he should be taught that the ideals of sacrifice and resignation should guide him, that life was a trial not a pleasure and that success was rare and ingratitude frequent, that his own egoistic desires were his principal enemy. This book argued that a child had only one basic instinct—a fear of suffering. Beyond that 'the child will appreciate people and events in accordance with the education he receives'. Filial gratitude and obedience were thus not natural and there was widespread agreement that it was far weaker than maternal love. So it devolved on parents to instil these feelings of gratitude, and people wrote books for children to recite, enumerating the benefits they owed to their parents.[1] Nevertheless there were some writers who rejected this view; they claimed filial affection was the natural consequence of shared blood and they attacked the psychologists for denigrating the relationship of mother and child.[2]

One of the features of this system of education was that it looked on life as a succession of dangers and temptations which had to be avoided. A book about what children should do on holidays, published in 1935 by a canon and recommended by a bishop, begins with a chapter on the dangers of holidays. Its opening sentence is: 'The first duty of parents is to understand the risks involved in holidays.' Children were left to themselves

[1] Fernand Nicolay, Les Enfants mal élevés. Étude psychologique, anecdotique et pratique (1890).
[2] Louis Doucy, Introduction à une connaissance de la famille (Éditions familiales de France, 1946); Abbé F.-M. L., Devoirs des enfants envers leurs parents (Librairie Catholique, Lyon, 1896); anon., Dieu et famille, l'enfant et la conception laïque de ses droits et des devoirs des parents (n.d., about 1925).

more, unwatched by their teachers, so that they unlearnt all
the moral lessons instilled into them at school and picked up
bad habits from the wider range of children and amusements
they might meet. 'People excuse this lack of surveillance by
quoting the example of America, but, apart from a difference
in temperament between the French and Americans, one can
assert that America is hardly a model of family life: little
intimacy, many divorces, few children.' The fear of the child's
friends was an obsession: better to invite one's cousins, about
whom one could be more sure. Guided visits to isolated mountains and nature study were safe, much safer than holidays by
the sea, which were a serious threat. In 1934 the accumulating
apprehensions of parents burst into a 'Fight against the Immorality of Beaches'. The semi-nudity was a sign of debauchery and
of an atrophy of the moral sense. 'Christians, remain Christians
on the beaches' was the cry. Avoid the 'manners, exhibitions,
and frolics reminiscent of pagan antiquity, the savage tribes of
central Africa and ancient Germany'. Doctors were found to
warn that sunbathing should be indulged in only under medical
supervision. 'Games are agreeable but they are extremely
dangerous.' Henry de Montherlant in his advice to his son,
wrote likewise: 'You are in a canoe, which is a new toy for you,
on an ocean of dung, which is the world. It will be a miracle if
you do not capsize.'[1]

In this school of thought the most serious danger facing
children was the awakening of sexual desire. The most serious
duty falling on parents was to postpone as long as possible its
manifestation and curiosity about reproduction. Repression
was advocated unanimously by the conservatives with as much
vigour as it was denounced by the Freudians. A work by Jean
Viollet, which sold widely in the inter-war period, may be
taken as an example of their views. He insisted that 'it is false
and dangerous to put the child brutally face to face' with the
facts of life. The child must be taught first to have a mystic
regard for parents, so that he looks on marriage more as
involving a moral responsibility of great dignity than carnal
relations. Then he must be habituated not to seek his physical
well-being and bodily satisfactions: love of food and comfort
should be repressed. His will-power should be developed by

[1] Henri Pradel, *Les Devoirs de vacances des parents* (1935), 5–8, 233–45.

giving him the habit of renouncing things he wants and being used to the sacrifice of personal pleasure. He must be isolated from friends who might lead him astray. That this policy sometimes worked is seen in the cases he quotes of the appalling ignorance of convent-educated girls about sex. One rushed to the confession after a man in a train had put his arm around her: she believed she was pregnant as a result. A curious analysis of letters in Italian popular women's magazines in the 1950s reveals similar instances and confirms that the facts of life and the most elementary notions of anatomy have successfully been kept from many girls well into adolescence.[1] But Viollet laments that this complete innocence was becoming increasingly rare. He was conscious of a rising tide of opposition to his views. 'The purity of the young', he wrote, 'appears to the majority to be an anomaly and a sign of inferiority.'[2]

The stress on authority was not preached blindly, even though in some extreme cases the impression is of a demand for total and constant repression. The works of Bishop Dupanloup, published in the 1860s but continuing to be read and quoted throughout this period, were inspired by a genuine and moving love of children, and written by a priest who began life as a highly successful teacher. Dupanloup was not ashamed to quote Rousseau, though more frequently he quoted Fénelon and at enormous length—showing how influences are perpetuated for centuries. Republican writers in their turn, like Janet, were not averse to quoting from Dupanloup. There was a lot of interpenetration of ideas between the parties. Dupanloup represented a middle view based on a great deal of experience. He warned parents that if they neglected their children, their children would neglect them when they grew up. He stressed, like most conservatives, the need for authority, respect, innocence, purity, obedience. He said the main reason why these virtues were found less and less (always assuming a golden age when they did exist) was that parents had been too lazy to accept their responsibilities, too vain to admit any defects in their children, and too uncertain about their own

[1] Gabriella Parca, *Italian Women Confess* (1963). Cf. also F. J. Kieffer, *L'Autorité dans la famille et à l'école* (1916, 14th edition 1924).
[2] Jean Viollet, *Éducation de la pureté et du sentiment* (1925, 32nd thousand, 1944), vi, 1, 33, 50, 69 n., 78–80.

ideas to know what exactly they ought to instil into their children. From Dupanloup's books—and he knew a lot of families intimately—one gets the impression that the control of the young in his period was fitful, sporadic and arbitrary. What he attacked more than anything else was the spoilt child. But it was by no means always in the interests of the children that parents yielded to the whims of their offspring and could find no wrong in them. They resented any criticisms of their children from teachers, they demanded academic success irrespective of the gifts of the child. Dupanloup wrote in praise of authority, but also in defence of the child. He attacked pride, sensuality and cupidity as the worst faults of children: he rigorously forbade boys at his school to adorn themselves with perfume or gold chains, or to give excessive attention to their hair and clothes. He fought against masturbation, homosexuality and all sexual interests in his school. He tried to extirpate indocility, independence (which he classified as a vice) and contradiction from them. But he also defended their rights against their parents, so that his book on *The Child* has been called a charter for children. The child had a right to respect of his individuality, of his intelligence and his vocation. 'I have a religious respect for children,' he wrote; 'I have even learned to fear them.' Each one needed different treatment. The first task of a parent was to study the child's nature to discover what he was capable of. The great enemy of the child was parental egoism, ambition and vanity, which too often sought to push the child into a job unsuited to it. The worst offenders of all were the parents who goaded their children hard to obtain academic success and then forced them into jobs they considered respectable.[1]

Lay psychologists and educationists for long took a view of children which was not all that different from these opinions based on an acceptance of original sin. Bernard Perez, who wrote one of the earliest books specifically devoted to *The Psychology of the Child* (1882), drew his inspiration from science and evolution, but he was far from championing the innocence of the child in the manner of Rousseau. He stressed the importance

---

[1] Bishop F. A. P. Dupanloup, *Le Mariage chrétien* (1869), *L'Enfant* (1869), and *L'Éducation des filles* (1873–4). Cf. the odd but significantly titled work by Angely Fentré, *Contre le mariage actuel. Tout en faveur des enfants* (1882).

of hereditary factors in determining the child's behaviour and the innate vices which were as powerful (though he did not say it) as original sin. Children were innately victims of fear, anger and jealousy. They lied naturally, for 'cunning was innate in every animal.' Their minds were similar to those of animals but inferior to adults and to experienced animals. Despite these innate qualities, like animals, one could 'with justice and kindness, make almost anything one wanted from a child'.[1] Gabriel Compayré, a leading republican educationist who wrote on the *Intellectual and Moral Evolution of the Child* in 1893, attacked original sin and exonerated the child of many of the evil qualities Dupanloup attributed to him. The child's cruelty, he said, was due to ignorance, his lying to fear or playful imagination, and defective education was to be held responsible for any faults he developed. Even so, Compayré did not go the whole way with Rousseau. The child he said, did have an evil base (*un fond mauvais*) which no indulgence could explain away. He was not only perverted by social factors: he was naturally perverse. He had innate antisocial instincts.[2]

The scientific study of children was slow to develop in France and foreign ideas penetrated with difficulty. In the 1860s Caron tried to give a course of lectures on the art of bringing up infants—to which he gave the name Puericulture—but though he was supported by Victor Duruy, the Empress Eugénie judged it indecent, and he had difficulty in finding an audience. In 1865 when he tried to speak on this subject at the meeting of the Provincial Learned Societies at the Sorbonne, the chairman refused permission on the ground that the subject would 'provoke hilarity'. It was only in 1919 that a School of Puericulture was founded, but at the instigation of the American Red Cross, as a souvenir of its work in the war.[3] Alfred Binet, France's great pioneer in intelligence testing, waged an almost lone campaign to modify the monolithic educational system to suit individual needs. Writing in 1910, he complained that very few people asked whether the child was anything other than a miniature man, and most assumed that there was a

[1] Bernard Perez, *La Psychologie de l'enfant: les trois premières années* (1882, 11th edition 1911), 70–90, 123–6, 329.

[2] G. Compayré, *L'Évolution intellectuelle et morale de l'enfant* (1893), 307, 315.

[3] Paul Tissot, *Notes pour servir à l'histoire de la puériculture* (Chambéry, 1959), 4; Dr. B. Weill-Hallé, *La Puériculture et son évolution* (1929), 9.

standard type of child, whom all resembled more or less. Teachers concentrated on the value of what they taught rather than on the aptitude of the child. But Binet was unable to advance knowledge of the emotional needs of the child. His work was essentially on the measurement of intelligence, memory, vision and hearing. Though he recognised the inadequacies of a relationship with the child based on reason, he could not get beyond the traditional ideals of authority, respect and altruism.[1]

In the inter-war period, the most ostensibly scientific books on children stressed the determining influence of physical factors, to the extent of appearing to regress to Zola's emphasis on heredity. Dr. Victor Pauchet (whose work was given a prize by the French Academy in 1929) attributed the characteristics of children to their physical constitution, to the extent of 90 per cent, and he thought the best way of curing their defects was to subject them to thyroid treatment. However, he too could not refrain from repeating the traditional statements about the need to exercise authority over infants, using the same example of the dog; and his remedy for timidity, which he called moral feebleness, was the old one of self-control, taught by rational argument. He welcomed Freud, and praised efficiency as a virtue, but the lip-service to new doctrines could not obliterate ingrained attitudes.[2] Another child psychologist, G. Collin, writing in 1943, was all in favour of the ideas of Montessori, Dewey, Decroly, etc. penetrating into kindergartens and the first forms of primary schools (but that was as far as he went) and he regretted that psychologists had studied the intelligence of children much more than their emotions. However, in discussing how infants could be cured of fear, he suggested two methods: improve their physical health, so that their strength will immunise them against fear, and 'appeal to their reason'—end their ignorance.[3] The intellectualist approach survived powerfully. And it had its effect on the children. It is precisely in the intellectualism of the French child that Laurence Wylie sees the principal difference between

---

[1] Alfred Binet, *Les Idées modernes sur les enfants* (1910); Edith J. Varon, *The Development of Alfred Binet's Psychology* (1935).
[2] Dr. Victor Pauchet, *L'Enfant* (1929), xv, 91, 227–8; id., *Le Chemin du bonheur* (1929).
[3] G. Collin, *Précis d'une psychologie de l'enfant* (1943), 49, 64–8.

him and the American child. The French child, as a result, learns to control his impulses, to see education as the memorising of categories established by others, to behave in each segment of life in the way deemed appropriate.[1] The weakness of French psychology in this period is partly to be explained also by the strength of *characterology*, a peculiarly French science. It was a development of the ancient doctrine of the four humours: sanguine, bilious, phlegmatic and melancholic. When the science of anatomy disproved the physical existence of these humours and showed instead the importance of the nerves, the system was modified and made psychological rather than physical but the classification into a definite number of types was retained. In the nineteenth century further subdivisions were added and the categories reorganised. Dr. Fourcault reduced it to three basic types, dominated by the nervous, sanguine or cellular systems, which could be combined to produce seven other types. In 1858 Dr. Eugène Bourdet, in his work on *Diseases of the Character*, produced 36 different types. Professor Azam in his work on *The Character in Health and in Sickness* (1887) produced 120 subdivisions. It would be tedious to enumerate the large number of variations of increasing complexity—and also of Platonic simplicity—in the many works written about this. This was no aberration limited to the nineteenth century. The popular versions of the same idea were physiognomy and graphology, and it should not be forgotten that the graphological test was used by employers as readily as Americans used the psychological ones.[2]

The liberals—those who were liberal in other spheres—did not offer a radically different method of upbringing. Jules Michelet—who described himself as a spoilt only child, who flew into a rage at the least contradiction and sought constant pretexts for disobedience, who lived isolated, with only one friend and a couple of favourite books, who was so maltreated

---

[1] Laurence Wylie, 'Youth in France and the U.S.', in E. Erikson, *Youth: Change and Challenge* (N.Y., 1963), 243–60.

[2] E. Bourdet, *Des maladies du caractère* (1858); Azam, *Le Caractère dans la santé et dans la maladie* (1887); B. Perez, *Le Caractère de l'enfant à l'homme* (1891); Ribot, 'Sur les diverses formes du caractères' in *Revue philosophique* (Nov. 1892); F. Paulhan, *Les Caractères* (1894); F. Queyrat, *Les Caractères et l'Éducation Morale: étude de psychologie appliquée* (1896); Abbé J. H. Michon, *Système de graphologie* (1878); J. Crépieux-Jamin, *L'Écriture et le caractère* (4th edition 1896; 7th edition 1921).

at the *lycée* that he felt he hated all men—proclaimed that children were born innocent, illuminating and purifying all by their innocence. He sung the praises of family life. But he was too astute to think that family upbringing was producing satisfactory results. By itself, he said, it was capable of suffocating children and making them wholly unfit for the world. Parents were ceasing to abandon children to the care of vicious domestic servants, but instead they spoilt them by making them participate in their own vices of drinking and obscenity. They allowed the awakening of the children's senses and so destroyed their ability to educate them. Michelet therefore urged not a closer intimacy in the family but on the contrary more formality. 'The child—for his own good—ought to be a little apart, watched and held lovingly, but always at a certain distance, and not mixed indiscriminately in the life of his parents, as is done today. He will be more modest, if he thinks that the family consists of only two people, and that he is an accessory. Its intimacy should be closed to him.' This interesting passage suggests that contrary developments were taking place at the top and the bottom of the social scale. The bourgeoisie were tiring of formality, but at the very same time the upper levels of the working class, rising into the petite bourgeoisie, were attempting to abandon their traditional easy-going approach.[1]

By contrast with Michelet, Paul Janet, writing about the bourgeois family in 1861, praised 'the intimacy, confidence and liberty that reigns today in families'. He insisted that this did not represent the decay of the institution. Parents spoilt their children more now, but they also looked after them better. Formerly they imposed respect on them but neglected them. Neglect had not disappeared: 'There are houses today where children see their mothers only at certain hours of the day.' But Janet applauded that parents were now seeking to win respect not by discipline but by love.[2] The apparently conflicting approaches of Michelet and Janet, however, conceal a basic similarity. In both cases the child remained an instrument for the gratification of parental aspirations—producing either higher social status, or affection. From this point of view the changes in methods of upbringing in this century were often

---

[1] J. Michelet, *Ma Jeunesse* (1884), *Nos Fils* (1869, reprinted 1903), 94–5.

[2] Paul Janet, *La Famille* (1856, 4th edition 1861), 145.

less important than contemporaries thought, and less a diver-
gence from the traditional avowed subjection of the child to
the interests of the family. That is why the rebellion of the young
was not diminished, as will be seen.

The longing for affection can be seen in that wildly successful
book *Monsieur, madame et bébé*, previously mentioned. After
urging men to be friends with their wives and to have fun with
them, Droz told them to do the same with their children. He
pitied fathers 'who do not know how to be *papas* as often as
possible, who do not know how to roll around on the carpet,
play at being a horse and a great wolf, undress their baby. These
are not simply agreeable forms of child's play that they neglect
but true pleasures, delicious enjoyments . . . How simple it is
to be happy.' But he went on to say that paternal love was
more calculating, less instinctive than a mother's love. The aim
of this frolicking was to win the child's affection. 'To be loved
all one's life by a being one loves, that is the problem to solve.'
Filial love did not grow naturally: it had to be won and
deserved, and so was done best of all by amusing the baby.
'Be his playmate a little, so as to have the right to remain his
friend.' Droz acknowledged it was no simple thing, for he said
that children had great acuteness of judgement and that those
who were subject to clumsy pressure became rebels. The
sentimentalism of this approach concealed a serious purpose.
Droz was important not because he was advocating a new
approach towards children—numerous instances could be
quoted from the seventeenth century onwards to show that this
kind of familiarity was not new—but because he saw the
difficult problem of communication and understanding between
generations. His jolly solution was almost one of bluff.[1]

In almost the same year as Droz published his book Ernest
Legouvé (a member of the French Academy) noted that the
change Droz was advocating had already taken place. 'Children today', he wrote in 1867, 'occupy a far larger place in the
family. Parents live more with them, and live more for them.
Either by an increase of prudence and affection, or from weakness and relaxation of authority, they think more about their
children's well-being, and listen more to their opinion.' But
the result of it was, he said, that 'these poor little creatures of

---

[1] Gustave Droz, *Monsieur, madame et bébé* (1866), 339–45.

three or four are enervated by this attention and indulgence; at seven they are egoistic, despotic, greedy masters of the house; at twelve they gravely go up the street to school with a cigar in their mouth; at seventeen they argue with their father and yield neither before age nor before superiority; at eighteen they discuss politics and art and are even atheists; at twenty they are idle and demand a share of their father's wealth to satisfy their private tastes.' Legouvé (and others) discussed the need for parents to learn from their children but avowed a kind of helplessness before the problem of how to avoid the tyranny of the child that resulted.[1] At the same time as people were praising the family as a source of bliss and morality, they were also lamenting that it would be this if only it did not go wrong so often. The tyranny of the child was the most frequent complaint. When he was paid attention to, he was seen to be uncontrollable. Gavarni's cartoons, *Les Enfants terribles*, showed the reverse side of the joys of intimate family relations.

Alain, the philosopher of republicanism, provided an acute analysis of the problems which were being created in this way, and showed how matriarchy was a corollary of the child being king. In discussing the married couple, he decided that the *real* couple was in fact the mother and child, not husband and wife. Marriage without children was only 'an idea, not a fact'. The love between mother and child was the only *real* love. The relations between the child and his father were necessarily difficult, particularly in the case of boys. The father was a stranger to his child, because he moved in the world where childhood and the laws of affection which governed it had to be forgotten, whereas the mother remained with the child in the other world ruled by affection where things could be obtained by asking and begging. The child wants to win the affection of his father but the father is too demanding; he expects the child to achieve what he himself has failed to achieve. The child copies the mother in obeying the father, but the father is severe and impatient, so the child cannot really admire the father. The child is often a humiliation to his father because he has not been freely chosen. The father is expected to love him independently of his merits, but this conflicts with the rules of

[1] Ernest Legouvé, *Les Pères et les enfants au 19ᵉ siècle (enfance et adolescence)* (1867), 1–3, 347–52.

reason which govern the father's world. The child in turn cannot consider the esteem of his parents adequate because they love him irrespective of his personal qualities. Family life thus involves conflict with society. The family fails to share the values of the world outside it: it does not judge the value of individuals and of actions impartially. In the outside world, things are weighed in the light of the criterion of real services rendered, but the family bases itself on favour and chance. If left to itself, the family is 'savage'. 'Because so much is expected in it, disappointment often takes the shape of hatred. It is thus that paternal love sometimes turns into unmeasured severity and, in return, a child can show signs of bitter hatred. And because each one knows that reconciliation is not far away, and is even already effected, the trouble is all the worse.' Pride forbids any total reparation for anger, and these crises in the home often lead to an injured silence, quite apart from boredom. The different system of rewards in the school and in the home complicates the child's life. But Alain insists that the school can remedy the defects of family education. The school must be the influence which 'civilises' the child, draws him into the real world, gives him universal ideals by its teaching of the humanities, and offers him the chance to make friends outside his narrow circle.[1]

Alain's brilliant essay deserves to be read as a supplement to the better-known but more conservative work of Durkheim on *Moral Education* (1938). Durkheim, like Alain, insisted that the family by itself was incapable of giving the child an adequate upbringing. He argued, in a rather abstract fashion, that it caused the birth of the child's first altruistic tendencies, but that these were of a limited kind, being based on affection rather than duty. The school was therefore an essential supplement to the family and only it could inculcate into the child wider perspectives and the spirit of discipline, which Durkheim prized as much as any Catholic did.[2] Durkheim, concentrating above all on the interests of society and the preservation of cohesion in it, had an approach which neglected the psychological reactions of individuals to the marvellous solidarity he

---

[1] Alain, 'Les Sentiments familiaux' in *Cahiers de la Quinzaine*, 18th series, no. 8 (1927).
[2] E. Durkheim, *L'Éducation morale* (1938), 168.

hoped to impose upon them. Since he thought that society made individuals what they were, he could see no justified conflict arising between them. His conclusion strongly resembles that of the Catholics. Alain is a useful reminder of the divisions that existed among republicans, as among Catholics, and of the survival of an unquenchable individualism.

It will be obvious by now that there was no Dr. Spock in France in this period: no one book dominated child rearing, but if anybody came anywhere near to Spock's position, it was perhaps Dr. Gilbert Robin. He was a doctor with a gift for incisive and down-to-earth prose and he published at least a dozen volumes in the inter-war period about children. His works mark a real advance, in that the subjects he treated showed that at last people were realising that ordinary children, as opposed to chronically sick ones, could have important psychological problems. He wrote a book called *Hate in the Family* which listed the many perfectly natural relationships which could produce tensions and animosities. He wrote about *Difficult Children, The Dramas and Anxieties of Youth* and *Nervous and Psychic Troubles of Children*. He had no radically new remedies to offer and most of what he said had been said before. He represented a moderate eclecticism, and quoted both Freud and Father de Buck (author of *Difficult Cases*). He was typical enough of his times to believe that comfort was mortally dangerous, because it weakened will-power, and he advised parents against using central heating, comfortable armchairs or 'pick-up' gramophones which saved the child the trouble of changing the record. But he was important for combating the myth that all would be well if children stayed meekly at home and obeyed their parents. He is interesting also for revealing how the individualism of Alain, and the whole tradition Alain represents, could be reconciled with conformity. The child, says Robin, is not more difficult to satisfy than the adult. He demands before all else to be free and like the adult, it is not liberty to do what pleases him that he is keenest about, but liberty of thought. 'In return for this liberty, you will obtain from the child, without effort, submission to habits and to rules of hygiene, punctuality, cleanliness, politeness. The hours devoted to study cease to be burdens. They are on the contrary the instruments indispensable to the installation of the child's kingdom. They serve as marks of respect to others and to win respect from them, to live in good accord with everybody, to give every man his due, so as to be repaid likewise. Thus, these habits are useful to ensure his liberty. The child has paid for his seat: he believes in the dream-show he gives himself.'[1] This fits in very well with what Laurence Wylie observed in his comparison of French and American children. Wylie stressed that the reason why the French child appeared to accept the formal requirements of his elders, was that he was skilled at withdrawing into his own private world where he was free.

Suspicions that maternal love could, in certain circumstances, have disastrous results took an increasingly positive form. Dupanloup had inveighed against the doting mother, very perceptively but perhaps in old-fashioned language. Marie Dugard, an interesting writer, pointed out in 1900 how spoiling and domination by mothers was a result of the transitional stage through which girls' education was passing. The conflict between what was taught to girls at school and what was taught at home produced internal tensions which manifested themselves when girls became mothers. On the one hand marriage was still regarded as being the aim of a girl's life, brains were considered an obstacle to marriage and the best marriage was one of convenience, to someone she barely knew. On the other hand germs of ambition were inculcated into girls. 'Incapable therefore of either the submissions of the past or the duties of the present', inadequately prepared to assume responsibility, taught in their convents 'to regard anyone who thought as suspect, and anyone who was independent as a rebel, guided by the instinct which pushes us to model our children on ourselves and by the passionate love Frenchwomen reserve for their children, they surround their sons and daughters with anxious surveillance, keep them jealously at home, and so as to be able to possess them longer, repress energy and all initiative in them.'[2] However, the sacrosanct image of the

---

[1] Dr. Gilbert Robin, *La Guérison des défauts et des vices chez l'enfant. Guide pratique d'éducation* (1948), 59. Cf. also his *Les Haines familiales* (1926); *L'Enfant sans défauts* (1930); *Les Drames et les angoisses de la jeunesse* (1934); *Les Troubles nerveux et psychiques de l'enfant* (1935); *Comment dépister les perturbations intellectuelles et psychiques des tout petits* (1936); *L'Éducation des enfants difficiles* (1942); *Enfances perverses* (1946), etc.

[2] Marie Dugard, *De l'éducation moderne des jeunes filles* (1900), 52–3.

mother, even if she did react against enforced femininity and against her indifference towards her husband, by overpossessive love of her children, was perhaps less an object of attack than the image of the authoritarian father, which invited denigration more readily.[1] The deposition of the father had wider implications. The great challenge to him came when the sons of the illiterate learnt to read and for the first time could judge their parents. This side of the campaign against illiteracy was still to be investigated. The one thing that Julien Sorel's illiterate father could not forgive him was his passion for books. Upward social mobility, to which families were so devoted, eroded the bases at the same time as it outwardly strengthened the structure of the institution. Freudian ideas entered France only very slowly but, by the end of this period, there were those who saw hate of the father as the initial conflict of perhaps the majority of men. Jean Lacroix, writing on the strengths and weaknesses of the family in 1948, pointed to the family as the crucial factor in most human resentments, and 'the principal obstacle to men's most profound desires and most essential demands. One could explain a large part of the present-day democratic movement by the desire for parricide . . . The death of the father was necessary to man's liberation.' Atheism was only another form of this same parricide.[2]

The idea of youth as the happiest time of one's life began to be challenged. As from around 1890 books about adolescence began to appear in increasing numbers: by 1930 at least 100 novels had been published on this theme. The peculiar problems of this period of life were recognised as unique, forming a separate category between infancy and adulthood. Psychologists and educationists wrote special studies of adolescence.[3] In the two years preceding the First World War, there were no fewer than five 'inquiries' by journals on the problems of youth, of which Agathon's was only the most famous.[4] In 1929 a whole

[1] On overprotective mothers see André Rouède, *Le Lycée impossible* (1967).
[2] Jean Lacroix, *Force et faiblesse de la famille* (1948), chapter 1. Cf. G. Mendel, *La Révolte contre le père* (1968).
[3] P. Mendousse, *L'Âme de l'adolescent* (1909); G. Compayré, *L'Adolescence* (1910); Auguste Lemaître, *La Vie mentale de l'adolescent et ses anomalies* (1910); Paul Gaultier, *L'Adolescent* (1914).
[4] Henri Mazel, 'Nos Enfants, à quoi rêvent-ils?', *La Revue des Français* (Jan.–Apr. 1912); F. Laudent, 'Enquête sur la jeunesse', *Revue hebdomadaire* (Mar.–June 1912); Agathon in *L'Opinion*, reprinted as *Les Jeunes Gens d'aujourd'hui* (1913);

issue of the review *L'Éducation* was devoted to 'the crisis of adolescence'.[1] A study of crime in 1905 revealed that the number of minors accused of homicide, arson, assault, vagabondage and theft was almost double that of adults accused of the same crimes.[2] Henry Bérenger declared adolescence, far from being a period of delightful innocence, was one of 'anxiety of the mind, of the emotions and of action'. Jules Laforgue entitled one of his poems *The Complaint of Difficult Puberties*. Romain Rolland, in *Jean Christophe*, depicted the adolescent in all his aspects. Formerly, education had been devoted to curing people of adolescence, to urging them to grow up. Between the wars a cult of adolescence developed in protest against adult values. In 1923 the first novel by an adolescent was published, written by Raymond Radiguet, aged seventeen. Five years later another one, by Jean Desbordes, made an even more powerful impression, because it substituted a technique of shock and impudence for Radiguet's sobriety. It was greeted as a manifesto by the young, as Barrès's work had been thirty-five years before, but it had a different significance. This represented more than a revolt against the opinions of the previous generation. There is a new social malaise, wrote Henry de Montherlant in 1926, *adolescentisme*, a new competitor against feminism. The cult of sports which became fashionable at the turn of the century was giving new prestige to youth.[3] After the war Abel Bonnard said that respect for the old was yielding to a cult of youth.[4] Edgar Quinet had been told on his seventh birthday that he had reached the age of reason, but now people were willing to take longer to grow up. André Gide wrote for adolescents and prided himself on keeping contact with them. Moreover, he told them to cultivate those very qualities which were not considered adult: he praised restlessness, anxiety and desire and hated everything the family stood for. 'Families, I hate you', he said; the phrase was to become a motto. His homosexuality was the

Émile Henriot, in *Le Temps*, reprinted as *A quoi rêvent les jeunes gens* (1913); Gaston Riou, *Aux écoutes de la France qui vient* (1913).

[1] *L'Éducation* (Oct. 1929).

[2] G. L. Duprat, *La Criminalité dans l'adolescence* (1905).

[3] Pierre de Courbertin, 'Le Sport et la société moderne', *Revue Hebdomadaire*, 6 (1914), 376–86.

[4] Abel Bonnard, 'Le Préjugé de la jeunesse', *La Revue de Paris* (1 Dec. 1922), 655–63.

decisive discovery of his life—he was interested in young men, not in relationships with women, which were the standard mark of adulthood—and he discussed his sexual problems openly, against the rules of adult society. Adults moreover read him too. The attentive interest in young people, and the serious curiosity about their emotions and thoughts, was a new phenomenon. It certainly increased the self-confidence and self-consciousness of the young. And the young emerged from this scrutiny, as an isolated group, shut off from adults, as Mauriac said, 'by a wall of timidity, shame, incomprehension and hurt feelings'.[1] Gide asserted that it was impossible for any member of his family to be a friend of his.[2] However, this was more than a confrontation of generations in the traditional sense. The extent of the conflict was not as great as some of the participants thought. Of the hundred novels on adolescence in the period 1890 to 1930, only fourteen deal with revolt against authority, and only five of these give this a large part. Far more frequent was the subject of sexual awakening and its problems.[3] The young were still only trying to understand themselves.

It is useful to examine the impression made by the novels protesting against the myth that parents always knew best. Jules Vallès's autobiographical novel of his childhood was one of the most powerful and moving.[4] It described a boy whose mother acted in accordance with the moral precepts enshrined by tradition. He was taught to read in a book which said he must obey his father and mother, but he felt no affection for either. He was ashamed of his father who was a poor, timid, ill-dressed teacher, the son of a peasant who had cringed his way up the ladder of social promotion. The mother was anxious that her son should continue this climbing. She forbade him to play with the cobbler's boy, because that was degrading; she wanted to make him *comme il faut*; she wanted to save him from the fate of being a peasant, as she had once been. She beat him every day because she thought he ought not to be spoilt. She refused him food he liked and gave him what he disliked, so as to develop his self-control. She promised him

---

[1] F. Mauriac, *Le Jeune Homme* (1926), 79.
[2] A. Gide, *Le Retour de l'enfant prodigue* (1922).
[3] Justin O'Brien, *The Novel of Adolescence in France* (New York, 1937), 187.
[4] Jules Vallès, *L'Enfant* (1879).

pennies if he was good, but then put them into a savings box which he could not touch. She was so keen for him to have some capital when he grew up that she never gave him any pocket money. 'To be clean and hold oneself straight, that summed up everything.' He was never conscious of any love in the house. He felt thoroughly guilty. The more his mother beat him, the more he was sure she was a good mother and he an evil boy for being so ungrateful to her. To the outside world he was just an ordinary boy, and this was an ordinary respectable family. Neither the world nor the family knew how he felt. The *coup d'état* of December 1851 gave Vallès a chance to escape. He participated in the republican opposition. His father replied (this happened in real life) by having him sent to a lunatic asylum. Vallès protested: '[My father] has the right to have me arrested, to treat me as though I were a thief; he is master of me as of a dog.' He went into socialist politics, and when the Commune was proclaimed he greeted it with deeply felt personal emotion. 'Here it is at last, the moment hoped for and waited for since the first cruelty of my father, since the first slap from the usher, since the first day spent without bread, since the first night passed without lodging. Here is the revenge against school, against poverty and against December.' In exile afterwards, Vallès attempted to found a league for the protection of the rights of children and he dedicated his novel 'To all those who died of boredom at school or who were made to cry at home, who during their childhood were tyrannised by their masters or thrashed by their parents'. His book was a protest also against another deeply ingrained prejudice of his time, that a child should follow in his father's profession, and should keep on climbing the social ladder. He did not want his father's job of a 'learned dog'. He longed to be an ordinary peasant, on whom there was—in his idealised view—no pressure. Though he escaped into revolutionary activity, he concluded 'it seems that there will always remain from my childhood gaps of melancholy and painful wounds in my heart.'

The reaction this book received from the critics (in 1879–86) was one of anger. Brunetière began his review: 'It is of an evil man that I am going to speak' and castigated Vallès as an example of exaggerated conceit. Brunetière characterised this as the illness of the century, so he was conscious of dealing with

an important phenomenon, whose right to existence he preferred to deny. 'This father and mother', he wrote, 'at bottom
committed no other wrong except to have brought up their
child perhaps severely, but we in our turn have the right to say
that they brought him up too gently, since he was to become
the man we have known.' He protests that Vallès is immoral,
because he questions the very existence of society. Another
reviewer remarked that what was unpardonable was that
Vallès should have written the book as a novel with the son
accusing the mother: the public should legitimately protest
against that.

Fifteen years later a curiously different reception greeted
Jules Renard's *Ginger*.[1] This again was an autobiographical
novel, protesting against the myth of family harmony. It
portrays a boy made vicious and miserable by lack of love,
ignored by his father, cruelly teased by his elder brother,
always criticised by his mother—again with the aim of instilling
moral principles into him and producing more conformist
behaviour from him. In this equally respectable family, the
boy feels himself an orphan. At school he sees a young master
kiss a boy. He reports him, and when the master is sacked, Poil
de Carotte shouts after him: Why did you not kiss me? Renard
offers a different explanation of his parents' behaviour. He sees
his taciturn father (an engineer, later mayor of his village)
being driven into silence, withdrawing from family life, seeking
consolation in unfaithfulness, by the fact that he had nothing
in common with his wife, whose domination exasperated and
frightened him. Renard attributed her alienation to her being
a pious Catholic, which the husband was not; but he makes the
father say that it is his own neglect of his wife which had driven
her to get her revenge by taking it out on her son. The boy
complains to his father: 'My mother does not love me and I do
not love her.' The father replies, 'And I, do you think I love
her?' But this did not bring the two together: the boy was never
admitted into the confidence of the father: harmony was totally
absent. Later, when Renard got married, his mother tried to
dominate his wife and it was this that spurred him on to write
his novel. The reception of the book was, however, strangely
favourable. What critics objected to most was the realistic

[1] Jules Renard, *Poil de carotte* (1894); dramatic version 1904.

portrayal of the child as an animal, so far removed from the idealised angel in favour. But the attack on the mother was now accepted as true, even as showing something typical, the neurotic mother. The play of the book was put into the repertoire of the Comédie Française and three films have been made of it. However, it should not be thought that the right to criticise the family was thereby won. In 1923 Victor Margueritte had his Legion of Honour withdrawn by President Millerand on the ground that his book *La Garçonne* had calumniated the French woman. It all depended on the way the criticism was made.[1]

In the 1950s, a sample of French people were asked which commandment they considered most important. The fifth, 'Honour your parents', won easily. Only 12 per cent thought the new generation represented progress over the old, and only 27 per cent thought it was more or less equal. 70 per cent considered that discipline was extremely important in bringing up children, and a majority wanted greater severity towards children. 52 per cent of parents were against sexual education for children at school.[2] It is clear that traditional values had survived in the majority, at least as ideals. What parents believed and what they did were not the same thing. An interesting study by a schoolmaster of the psychology of his pupils, published in 1913 on the basis of many years' observation and note taking in a varied selection of schools, stressed that the great majority of parents neglected their children. 'One cannot imagine', he wrote, 'the indifference of the great majority of parents for all that concerns the intellectual and moral advancement of their sons.' In one class, at the beginning of the year, only four fathers came to school to discuss their sons with the teacher—which was a respected custom—out of thirty-three. The peasant was particularly careless: 'Uniquely preoccupied with his land, he abandons his sons to their instincts.' The teacher thought the children he knew got little affection or even intimacy from their parents. 'They are not happy.'[3] The teacher's observations do not of course contradict the findings of the polls. The conflict between principles and

[1] I am indebted to Dr. Nicholas Hewitt for permission to use a paper on this subject which he wrote for my graduate seminar at Harvard in 1969.

[2] Georges Rotvand, *L'Imprévisible Monsieur Durand* (1956), 124, 131–4.

[3] J. Fontanel, *Psychologie de L'adolescence. Nos lycéens. Études documentaires* (1913), 56, 82, 262.

practice was another of the sources of tension, and this particular conflict was only one of several. It was not only in the family that children were subjected to opposing pressures.

One important instance of this emerged in children's peer groups. The inevitable reaction of children to the isolation imposed on them by their parents and the authoritarianism of their teachers was that they formed groups at school. It has been claimed that these had a vital and lasting influence upon all their subsequent behaviour. Jesse Pitts has described them as delinquent groups, meaning that what held them together was their hostility to the teacher. These groups provide an outlet for rebelliousness, while preserving loyalty to the family. Since the teachers are a challenge to the authority of the family, the parents do not disapprove of the petty warfare these groups engage in. The co-operation between families and peer groups is, however, tacit and unspoken. Families are not mentioned in the groups: the two are separate worlds, and members are not normally invited to each other's homes. The groups are societies for mutual defence. They are purely negative. Whereas the American peer group is recognised by both school and parents, gives prestige, prepares for distinction in sports and provides opportunities of importance to the whole of the child's social life, the French one has no adult values, it protects the children against the teacher, it involves co-operation only in forbidden pleasures, but perhaps its main function is to guarantee each member the enjoyment of his private interests. It seeks to destroy authority, to discredit the teacher, for example, by making him declare his political views. The teacher replies by trying to subvert the cohesion of the group. This is its test, for the group's solidarity covers a very limited range of behaviour. Distrust of one's fellows remains within it, and the child remains isolated. His isolation is concealed by such things as interest in politics, which appears to place the group on a more universal level. But in reality it only raises the delinquency into a more general rejection of the established political order. This is seen as a root of the ideological opposition of each generation; and also of the shallowness of the opposition. The group involves only an abstract and purely verbal rejection of the adult world. The member can then fall back safely into the comforts of dependence on his family. Jesse Pitts sees the survival of these peer groups—described in Jules Romains's *The Pals* (*Les Copains*), a perennial best seller with adolescents— in the cliques, salons and old-boy networks of adult life. These behave in the same delinquent way, stressing untramelled liberty of speech, violent hatreds against other cliques, with slander and denigration serving to produce blood bondage. When a member of one of these cliques comes into contact with a state official and wants a favour, the interview begins by trying to establish their group memberships, to see whether they can combine in a delinquent community against the state —in which case the favour is granted. In this way there is intense social and political activity, but the *status quo* is saved. The really powerful force, thinks Pitts, that survives beneath the agitation is the family, because only it is really relied upon. Respect for the public interest is thus undermined at the very earliest stage of life. Friendship itself, though paraded, is unreliable.[1] In the light of this theory, one can argue that not only is the emotional development of children stunted by the rigours of the family, but their social capacities are restricted by the nature of their peer groups. They are prepared more for a negative obstructionist and verbal role rather than for co-operation and action.

Indeed, school, family and peer groups each pulled in a different direction. The school nominally sought to develop sociability in the way Durkheim preached, but in fact it did its best to destroy the groups children formed of their own accord. Roger Cousinet, whose pioneering work on child sociology Pitts developed, showed how, for all its lip-service to solidarity, the school continued to be individualist in its influence. It gave very few opportunities for games, it sought to supervise the children as much as possible, it allowed them to play only in breaks, and stopped them when they were noisy. Above all it was one of the principal destroyers of young children's groups by its stress on intellectual achievement. It was the marking system which, thought Cousinet, did as much as anything to split the groups as the children grew up and marks became more important. The family, on its side, feared these school friendships and tried to limit their scope; but on the

[1] Jesse R. Pitts, 'The Bourgeois Family' (Harvard, unpublished Ph.D. thesis, 1957).

other hand it did not accord its co-operation to the school. It paid great attention to social inequalities, which became the other major obstacle to the continuation of young children's friendships.[1]

But while school, family and peer groups exerted contradictory pressures on children, they also maintained a conflict between the world of the child and the adult world. A French psycho-analyst, comparing the French and American child in 1953, pointed out how the French child thought of himself as being different from the adult, of whom he had a deep distrust. His life involved a coerced learning of adult behaviour but without the compensating reward of adult privileges. Whereas adults could be guided by pleasure, children were expected to be *sage*. Life therefore began only with the end of childhood. This is not to suggest that the more spontaneous American child, whose parents took so much pains to leave him free lest he be traumatised, in fact enjoyed greater real autonomy in childhood. He owed his independence to the privileged position accorded by Americans to their children, and he was much more influenced by social and psychological pressures. French parents did not worry about whether they traumatised their children. They made constant use of bogy men to frighten their children into conformity. Though corporal punishment was abolished in schools, the *martinet* whip continued to be widely used; and obliging policemen were employed by parents to threaten children who remained recalcitrant even then. It was an accepted procedure to frighten the child to make him obey—with force, the police, illness or God. The American child learnt about restraint in a noticeably different way from the French child. This analyst claimed that there was far more certainty among French parents about how to bring up their children, but this certainty derived essentially from their own family experience and the belief inculcated into them that the individual was first of all a member of a family. Those who consulted her always gave as their justification what 'in my family' was considered the right thing to do.[2]

[1] Roger Cousinet, *La Vie sociale des enfants. Essai de sociologie enfantine* (1950).

[2] Françoise Dolto, 'French and American Children as seen by a French Child Analyst' in Margaret Mead and Martha Wolfenstein, *Childhood in Contemporary Cultures* (1955), chapter 23.

The consequences of these differences were interestingly noted by Martha Wolfenstein in a comparison of how French and American children played in parks. Each French family kept its toys strictly separate; friendliness between children of different families was not encouraged; parents intervened frequently in games to scold those who broke the rules; the children were not expected to fight their own battles; physical aggression was kept in check and so instead verbal disputes were substituted. French children were content to spend long periods alone with their own families; they were much readier to play with children of all ages, unlike the Americans who divided into age groups cutting across families. The French would only watch children from other families, not join in with them. Though French parents intervened as umpires, on the whole they busied themselves with other tasks and left the children alone, again unlike the Americans who liked to be good sports. The adult world was a separate one, and the children's activities were subordinated to it. Liberation came only after childhood, and that is why Americans think the French had a greater capacity for enjoying adult life, instead of looking back on childhood, as Americans do, as the happiest time of their life, when everything was allowed.[1]

[1] M. Wolfenstein, 'French Parents take their Children to the Park', ibid. chapter 7.

13. Women

THE simultaneous idealisation and repression of women and children was one of the ways by which French society developed its peculiar characteristics. Repression was compensated for and mitigated by giving women considerable power in certain strictly limited fields. There was nevertheless resistance to that repression, which took two forms: psychological and political. The former was by far the most efficacious and widespread: withdrawal, peer groups, alliance with the Church and a variety of personal reactions served as stratagems to limit the rigour of male and adult rule. Children had no other recourse. Some women, however, organised themselves and agitated to protest in public. Their history is interesting, above all because their failure throws valuable light on the ambivalent and subtle nature of their position.

The legal situation of women was very definitely inferior to that of men. The French Revolution had done little for women beyond abolishing male primogeniture. The law still required the wife to obey the husband, in return for which the husband owed her 'protection'. She had to reside wherever he chose and he was entitled to use force to compel her to do so. If she committed adultery, she was liable to imprisonment for a period of between three and twenty-four months, but he could engage in it with impunity. He committed a crime only if he actually maintained a concubine in the conjugal home, and then he was punished only by a fine of 100 to 2,000 francs. If he chanced to discover her committing adultery and killed her, he would not be guilty of murder—but she was not allowed to attack him in similar circumstances. She could not go to law without his permission, even if she had her own business and she could not sell or buy without his approval. Indeed the law treated women as minors. Normally marriage involved community of property, but not community in the management of it. The husband had the sole right to administer the joint estate: he could alienate her personal property, though he could only enjoy the usufruct of her real estate. Even in marriages with separation of property the wife could not alienate her own real estate without her husband's consent. Even if the wife obtained a separation from her husband, she still needed her husband's signature for all her business affairs; all she gained was the right to live where she pleased, with whom she pleased, but she could not sell her property. He had full powers over his children, but when he died, she must act with the consent of his two nearest relatives. As a widow she had custody of her children, but if she re-married, the family council met to decide whether she could keep the children.[1]

Women at the beginning of this period were paid half the wages of men. Most professional careers were closed to them. They were offered far fewer educational opportunities. Guizot's law on primary education omitted to deal with girls. Only in 1850 were communes with a population of 800 required to have girls' schools, and only in 1867 those with 500—and even then the lack of properly trained teachers limited the value of the education. Girls' teacher-training colleges were established in every department only in 1879. Secondary education for girls took even longer to get started. Victor Duruy got some fifty *lycées* going by a law of 1867, but many of them did not survive long. Only in 1880 was a regular system of secondary education for girls established, thanks to the law of Camille Sée (a deputy aged thirty-three), but the girls were given only certificates issued by their own school at the end of their course, not the state *baccalauréat*. Their courses were different and more super-ficial than the boys'. The Sorbonne excluded women from attendance at lectures till 1880; the Paris faculty of medicine till 1868. The first woman to get the *baccalauréat* was a Paris primary-school teacher, aged thirty-seven, who, after being refused admission to the examination in Paris, was accepted by the dean of the faculty of Lyon on his own responsibility. The Paris faculty of law's first woman student, in 1884, was a woman 'of a certain age' who came accompanied by her husband and by the secretary of the faculty, frightened that there might be a scandal. In 1913 there were still only 4,254 women at univer-sities, compared to 37,783 men. Until 1876 five women or

[1] Léon Richer, *Le Code des femmes* (1883); Charles Lefebvre, *La Famille en France dans le droit et dans les mœurs* (1920); Frances I. Clark, *The Position of Women in Contemporary France* (1937).

fewer obtained the *licence* each year; in 1913 the number was still only sixty-nine.[1]

The inferiority of opportunities for women was backed by a long tradition of writing on the subject. Rousseau thought that women should be given only a domestic education. Joseph de Maistre said: 'Knowledge is what is most dangerous to women.' Proudhon could see only two possible roles for them, housekeepers or prostitutes, and rated their intellectual and moral value as one-third of that of men.[2] Michelet, as has been seen, wrote in praise of them, but only to extol them in their traditional domestic role. Comte firmly believed that they must stay at home, and that 'man must provide their food for them'. It is true that Montesquieu, Helvétius and Condorcet demanded an equal education for them, but in the nineteenth century feminism was principally supported by the socialists. Fourier invented the word, and argued that the extension of their rights would be the measure of general progress; he envisaged full educational equality for them; his advocacy of a radical marriage reform was far in advance of his time. The Saint-Simonians not only preached equality but practised it in their organisation—again causing general horror. In 1848 Victor Considérant demanded that women should be given the vote, and in 1851 Pierre Leroux introduced the first bill to this effect, though he limited it to municipal elections. It was these *men* who started the feminist movement and ultimately it was they who brought it success.

Unfortunately for the women, their cause was taken up by a minority party, acting on theoretical and disinterested grounds. The majority of the republicans, by contrast, believed that since women went to church much more than men, giving them the vote would mean the triumph of a clerical reaction. The radical party took this danger very seriously and, for all its support of educational reforms for women, it remained a principal obstacle to the granting of the vote. The conservatives, who stood to gain, were too attached to the traditional family system to imperil male supremacy in the home. The trouble was that the feminist cause could not be tacked on to any other. In

---

[1] Edmée Charrier, *L'Évolution intellectuelle féminine* (1931), a mine of statistics about female academic achievements.

[2] P. J. Proudhon, *La Pornocratie de la femme dans les temps modernes* (1875).

the U.S.A. it was linked to the emancipation of the slaves: if illiterate negro slaves could vote, so could women. But in France, though the socialists always coupled the liberation of the proletariat and of women, these two were in fact economic rivals. The proletariat having got the vote were by no means keen to share it with women. Women's lower wages perhaps needed to be raised to prevent undercutting, but their competition at work threatened unemployment. Thus, though the C.G.T. declared in favour of equal wages in 1898, it unanimously added that it accepted only work by spinsters and widows: in general 'man must feed woman'. Proudhon had clearly expressed a generally accepted view. Only in 1935 did the C.G.T. accept full equality.

Unlike England, where vigorous agitation by women won them the vote in 1918, in France there was comparatively little open pressure on the men, and what pressure there was, was for civil rather than political emancipation. There was no mass feminist movement. Mrs. Pankhurst's explanation of this was that France was run by the backstairs influence of women: Frenchwomen knew they had power and they did not think the vote would increase it.[1] 'Though legally women occupy a much inferior status to men,' wrote Violet Stuart Wortley in 1908, 'in practice they constitute the superior sex. They are the "power behind the throne" and both in the family and in business relations undoubtedly enjoy greater consideration than English women.'[2] Already at the end of the *ancien régime* Necker had said: 'Do you wish to get an opinion to prevail? Address yourself to the women. They will accept it because they are ignorant, they will spread it because they are talkative, they will support it because they are obstinate.'[3] Foreign observers seem unanimous in stressing the exceptional influence of Frenchwomen. 'In most French households, women reign with unchallenged sway.'[4]

The early women feminists were isolated individuals and their activity was at first purely literary or journalistic. Olympe de Gouges is usually credited with being the first woman

[1] L. Sauna, *Figures féminines 1909–1939* (1949), 42.
[2] Violet Stuart Wortley, 'Feminism in England and France', in *The National Review*, 51 (Mar.–Aug. 1908), 793–4.
[3] Amélie Gayrand, *Les Jeunes Filles d'aujourd'hui* (1914), 61.
[4] Miss Betham-Edwards, *Home Life in France* (1905), 89.

feminist, in honour of her Declaration of the Rights of Women of 1791 (which she had to dictate, for she was barely literate). The Saint-Simonians produced the first feminist review edited by women only, *La Femme Libre*—a title which they had to change, because of the unfortunate meaning placed upon it, to *La Femme de l'Avenir* and then *La Femme Nouvelle* (1832–4). Even though this did not demand the vote but only the right to education and to work, a *Journal des Femmes* (1832–7) was started to reply to its exaggerations, as an organ of Christian feminism. In 1836 Madame Herbinot de Mauchamps founded *La Gazette des Femmes*, run exclusively by women, to demand the vote, and the right to enter the professions and the civil service; but her interest was confined to the bourgeoisie. The revolution of 1848 produced a number of ephemeral feminist clubs and newspapers; Jeanne Deroin, on 23 March 1848, went to the Hôtel de Ville to ask for the vote; in 1849 she stood for parliament and obtained fifteen votes; she founded a paper, *La Politique des Femmes*, to attack Proudhon. Juliette Lamber in *Les Idées antiproudhoniennes* (1858) declared that family life was not enough to absorb women's energy. 'The role of the brooding hen is doubtless very respectable, but it does not suit all women and it is not as absorbing as is claimed.'

However, feminism as a continuous movement was really launched by a man, Léon Richer (1824–1911). He had been educated for the profession of notary but family reverses kept him employed for fifteen years as a notary's clerk at Choisy-le-Roi, at a wage of 1,200 francs. In his spare time he took to speaking at public meetings, and particularly at the Grand Orient, on women's rights; he wrote for Guéroult's *Opinion National*; some of his articles were reprinted as a successful book entitled *Lettres d'un libre penseur à un curé de village*. The alliance of freemasonry, anticlericalism and feminism had begun. In 1869 he founded his own paper, *Le Droit des Femmes*, and in 1871 the Association (later the League) for the Rights of Women. He organised an international congress on women's rights, held in Paris at the same time as the international exhibition of 1878, which created some stir and was the first important act of French feminism. He got Victor Hugo to become president of his society and so launched feminism as a significant movement. His aims were limited to legal equality: he did not ask for the vote, saying, 'The female mind is still too dominated by the yoke of the Church.' He was a journalist well connected in the political world, and able to obtain Victor Schoelcher and then René Viviani to succeed Hugo.[1] The first important woman ally he attracted was Maria Deraismes (1828–94), a lecturer like him at the Grand Orient, and a journalist, founder-editor of *Le Républicain de Seine-et-Oise* (1881–6), an active anticlerical, the first woman to be admitted as a freemason (1882), and later founder of a mixed lodge (1893). Like Richer she favoured gradual and limited reforms—no doubt because of her connections with opportunist republican politicians.[2]

The moderation of Richer and Deraismes soon led to a split in their society and the foundation of a rival one by Hubertine Auclert (1848–1914), France's first suffragette. She was not a *grande dame* like Deraismes, nor highly cultured like her, but an orphan with only a modest private income. She joined the cause soon after leaving her convent school but broke away in 1876 when Richer decided the demand for the vote was impossible. She put all her impetuous and uninhibited energies into agitating in the manner the English were to adopt. Her constant feuds with the authorities, her refusals to pay taxes, her insistence that she would yield only to force, compelled the press to take notice of her. She did indeed succeed in converting a few deputies and she helped win a vote for the political equality of the sexes from the *conseil général* of the Seine (1907). However, her extremism found few imitators and her career marks the failure and abandonment of activist methods at the very start of the feminist campaign.[3]

After her, the feminists behaved like all the innumerable moderate societies in favour of mild social causes. The main reason for this was that they were a definitely bourgeois and upper-class movement, led by the wives of the republican politicians, and they had no desire to threaten a regime to which they were basically attached. Thus the National Council of French Women, founded in 1901, was presided over by Sarah Monod, of a well-known family of academics and divines. In

---

[1] René Viviani et al., *Cinquante Ans de féminisme 1870–1920* (1921).

[2] See her very conservative moral opinions in Maria Deraismes, *Nos Principes et nos mœurs* (1868).

[3] File of her press cuttings and letters in the Bibliotheque Marguerite Durand, the main feminist library, located in the *mairie* of the fifth *arrondissement* of Paris.

WOMEN 349

1912 she was succeeded by Mme Jules Siegfried (1848–1922), another Protestant, daughter of a pastor, wife of a moderate millionaire politician, organiser of many good works for widows, women workers and unmarried girls. She in turn was succeeded by Avril de Sainte-Croix, who had specialised in the defence of prostitutes and who remained at the head of the council till she was nearly eighty.[1] After her came Marguerite Pichon-Landry, sister of a radical minister, aunt of another, wife of an industrialist member of the Comité des Forges; she continued the tradition of respectability and moderation, content to run her organisation 'as a sort of conservatory of feminist principles discreetly pursuing its little tasks in the shelter of the lugubrious walls of the Musée Social'.[2] The National Council was a federation of some 150 different bodies (300 in 1938), but it completely failed to unify the activities of its members. Numerous, often rival, organisations dispersed the efforts of well-meaning matriarchs. There was a National Union for the Women's Vote and a National Union for Woman's Suffrage. The former was presided over by Cécile Brunschwicg,[3] wife of a professor at the Sorbonne; she did a lot to improve the social conditions of the poor, and to help alcoholics and tuberculars, but the radicals were all personal friends of hers and she agreed with them that female suffrage was too dangerous so long as the republic was in difficulties, which it always was. The second Union was presided over by the duchesse de La Rochefoucauld,[4] a minor poetess and allied to the Catholic and moderate right-wing parties, so it too was unlikely to cause much trouble. Yvonne Netter, a successful barrister and a warm speaker at public meetings, presided over the League for the Emancipation and Well-being of Women: she demanded the vote but she became increasingly absorbed by her professional work and unwilling to fall foul of the law. After the war, two different associations of war widows were founded—one of remarried ones (anxious to keep their pensions after remarriage), and one of widows who had not remarried: they were rivals almost to the point of physical violence—but of violence against each

[1] Secretary general 1901–22, president 1922–32.
[2] Louise Weiss, *Ce que femme veut* (1946), 41.
[3] Succeeding Mme de Witt-Schlumberger, granddaughter of Guizot, in 1924.
[4] Succeeding its founder Mme Le Vert-Chotard, president 1920–31.

other, not the state. There was a communist league of women for peace and liberty (later 'against war and fascism'). The more numerous the associations, the smaller their individual membership. No reliable figures are available, though it is said that the largest female demonstration before the war, on 5 July 1914, was 6,000 strong.[1] The Conseil National des Femmes Françaises in 1929 claimed 150,000 members; the Union Française pour le Suffrage des Femmes, which had 300 members in 1909, and 9,000 in 1914 (in 45 departments), claimed 100,000 (in 200 groups) in 1929.[2]

The most successful woman's organisation was the Patriotic League of Frenchwomen, which claimed 250,000 members in 1906 and half a million in 1914 but it had nothing to do with the suffrage and scarcely anything with politics.[3] It, like nearly all the others, was run by ladies of leisure for middle-class women. There was no participation by the peasantry and virtually no attempt to interest it. After 1934 Louise Weiss, an energetic journalist, tried to bring new vigour into feminism by introducing the methods of modern propaganda, and standing at elections, drawing the uninitiated into public meetings (which hitherto had often been merely social gatherings of old friends). She was treated coldly by the established organisations and found insurmountable resistance among women outside their ranks. 'The peasants stood open-mouthed when I spoke to them about the vote, the workers laughed, the shopkeepers shrugged their shoulders and the *bourgeoises* repulsed me in horror.' No change in the law would be possible, she concluded, until women changed their opinion of themselves and of their interests.[4]

The war of 1914 did not produce any radical change in feminine attitudes, largely because it did not make all that much difference to the women. The legal difficulties created by the

---

[1] Li Dzeh-Djen, *La Presse féministe en France de 1809 à 1914* (1934), 208: well-informed and far broader in scope than the title suggests; cf. Evelyne Sullerot, *Histoire de la presse féminine en France des origines à 1848* (1966).

[2] André Leclerc, *Le Vote des femmes en France. Les causes de l'attitude particulière de notre pays* (1929).

[3] Yvonne Delatour, 'Les effets de la guerre sur la situation de la française d'après la presse féminine 1914–1918' (D.E.S. May 1965, unpublished, copy in M. Durand library), 23.

[4] L. Weiss, 24. These memoirs are most amusing and very informative on the bitchiness in the feminist movements.

absence of husbands were dealt with not by reform of the law,
but by temporary legal fictions—particularly the 'tacit consent' of those absent at the front.[1] The peculiar characteristic of
France was that already before the war it had a far higher
percentage of its women at work than most European countries.
In 1906 68·2 per cent of the male population of all ages worked,
and 38·9 per cent of the female population. These figures
remained almost constant for the next thirty years, rising by
3 per cent in 1921 for both men and women, but returning to
68 per cent and 37 per cent in 1931 and in the economic depression of 1936 still remaining at 65·39 and 34·2 per cent. France
first of all had an exceptionally large agricultural population,
which kept women at work. But 20·2 per cent of married
women had jobs outside agriculture in 1906 and the figures did
not increase after the war: 1921 (19·1 per cent), 1926 (16·4 per
cent), 1931 (19·4 per cent), 1936 (18·7 per cent). The only
significant change was the move out of the factories. In 1911
56·6 per cent of women working in non-agricultural jobs were
in industry, 18·6 per cent in commerce, 7·5 per cent in the
liberal professions and 17·3 per cent in domestic work. In 1921
the figures were 52·9, 21·7, 10·6 and 14·8. In 1936 they had
switched to 44, 27·1, 13·8 and 15·1. The change thus came well
after the war and not as an immediate result of the war.
Whereas before the war there were two men to every woman in
a factory, in 1939 there were three men to every woman. The
number of commercial employees rose threefold. Domestic
servants fell in number, but also the *petites patronnes*, the independent artisans, who were now replaced by the shop assistants
and the clerks. The basic fact, however, is that France had
twice as many married women at work as England.[2] The real
importance of the war, in this context, was its effect on the
bourgeoisie, more of whose daughters had to go to work to compensate for their vanishing private incomes. That is partly why
feminism was largely a middle-class affair, for the bourgeoisie
only now became properly aware of the problems of the working woman, to which the poorer classes had long ago adjusted.

[1] André Isoré, *La Guerre et la condition privée de la femme* (Paris thesis, 1919),
481–97.
[2] Jean Daric, *L'Activité professionnelle des femmes en France* (1947), an excellent
monograph, as are also Madeleine Guilbert, *Les Fonctions des femmes dans l'industrie*
(1966), and id., *Les Femmes et l'organisation syndicate avant 1914* (1966).

The *jeune fille moderne* appeared quite early. Already in 1864 the Goncourt brothers had written the first novel about her, *Renée Mauperin*, in which they had attempted a realistic portrait of 'the modern young girl, such as the artistic and boyish education of the last thirty years has made her'.[1] However, an important reason why feminism failed in France was that it came very early to that country, burnt itself out and produced a conservative reaction among women already by 1914. In the middle of the nineteenth century George Sand (1804–76) had not only raised the standard of revolt but had lived the life of an emancipated woman. She told her husband, 'I shall go where I please, without having to render account to anybody.' She left him for most of the year and lived a Bohemian life in Paris. She kept herself by writing novels, which, like her own life, were a protest against the repression of women, against the duty imposed upon them by society to love their husbands, irrespective of their merits.[2] She herself had ceased to respect her own husband, to whom she had been married before she knew her own mind, and she had had the courage to leave him. But George Sand was not a full feminist: her romantic temperament forbade her to be one. She believed in equal education for the sexes, in civil liberty and in 'sentimental equality'. She thought that the servitude in which man kept woman destroyed for her the prospect of happiness, which was impossible without freedom. 'Women', she said, 'are maltreated; they are reproached for the idiocy into which they are plunged; their ignorance is despised; their learning is mocked. In love they are treated as courtesans; in conjugal relations as servants. They are not loved but made use of, they are exploited and all this is designed to subject them to the law of fidelity.' The real crime, she argued, was not for a woman to leave a man for another whom she loved, but to give herself to a man whom she did not love, even if he was her husband. One explanation of George Sand's tormented promiscuity was that she never could obtain sexual satisfaction, and she sought out new lovers in the hope of finding it. She did not seek much more than the right to divorce. She did not want the vote, saying that woman's function was different from man's—'What she must save, in the midst of

[1] E. and J. de Goncourt, *Renée Mauperin*, preface to the edition of 1875.
[2] See G. Sand, *Indiana* (1831), Preface.

gross passions, is the spirit of charity.' She did not take up writing to make herself independent, but simply because she needed money. In her years of more serene maturity, she wrote with increasing respect of marriage, and in the end said, 'If I had to live my life again, I should be chaste.'[1]

The tradition of George Sand continued for many years and female rebels against convention are portrayed in numerous novels.[2] However, the rebels were confined to a small class, those who were left wing, or highly educated, or both. By 1914 they appeared out of date to most girls. The Catholic and conservative reaction of the 1900s may have been partly responsible for this. Certainly the Church maintained a traditional view of woman's role.[3] Bishops even fulminated against the 'scandal' of new styles in female clothing, and against 'indecent and provoking fashions'; the Archbishop of Paris joined in a protest to the *couturiers* of his city.[4] An inquiry among girls in 1914 revealed a situation very similar to that prevailing among young men, as shown in Agathon's *Les Jeunes Gens d'aujourd'hui* (1913). The girls were no longer moved by the poetesses in revolt against custom and restraints, who made an 'unbridled appeal to sensual pleasures'. They wanted discipline, order, reason. Alain said that the favourite philosopher of his female pupils was Comte, the advocate of the most rigorous discipline in family and society. 'The first feminists', they said, 'had sought to be friends with their husbands': for the new generation this was not enough: 'We do not wish to lose anything of our feminine prestige.' Coquetry, femininity quickly came back into fashion. The strong man became the ideal, instead of the 'pretty boy' who was admired by the previous generation. They rejected the violent methods of the English suffragettes. They were patriotic. They saw

[1] A. Maurois, *Lélia ou la vie de George Sand* (1952), 125, 147–9, 151, 165, 367–9, 423, 493.

[2] V. Margueritte, *La Garçonne* (1922); Colette Yver, *Les Cervelines* (1903) and *Princesses de sciences* (1907); Gabrielle Reval, *Les Sévriennes* (1900) and *Ruban de Vénus* (1906); Marcel Prévost, *Les Vierges fortes* (1900). Camille Marbo, *Hélène Barraux, celle qui défiait l'amour* (1926); Renée-Tony d'Ulmès, *Histoire de Sibylle* (1904–9); Marcelle Tinayre, *La Rebelle* (1905); cf. Jules Bertaut, *La Littérature féminine d'aujourd'hui* (1907).

[3] Semaines Sociales de France, Nancy, 19th session, 1927: *La Femme dans la société* (Lyon, 1928): 'La femme forte, c'est la mère de famille', 31–66.

[4] Delatour, 84.

motherhood as woman's supreme role. They wanted education as a means of safeguarding themselves against the compulsory marriage of the past; with a job, they could choose freely between a marriage that suited them and independence, but most were opposed to married women working or even voting. Only the woman who led a man's life had the right to his privileges.[1] One of the most popular women novelists of this period, Colette Yver, protrayed the lives of bluestockings as lonely and frustrated: 'Woman is made for love, before being made for knowledge.'[2] The correspondence columns of *Eve*, a best selling woman's magazine, read by all classes, show an overwhelming preoccupation with love and literature—and very little indeed with feminism: novels dealing with personal relations appealed to the imagination of girls far more than political programmes for their emancipation.[3] When a more modern American-style woman's paper, *Marie-Claire*, was started in 1937, and sold 800,000 copies, it in no way diminished the circulation of the traditional magazines.[4] Even Simone de Beauvoir, whose brilliant self-analysis in her autobiography and whose books on *The Second Sex* provide the best-known description of the attitudes of the emancipated woman of the inter-war period, was uninterested by the feminist movement. Her approach to life was existentialist; she was interested in herself as a person, rather than as a woman; and her message was: 'One is not born a woman, one becomes one.' Her books, however, are full of reservations about the possibility of a woman achieving an independence equal to man's. Though she lived with J.-P. Sartre unmarried, in a much discussed liaison, she also forcibly stressed the difficulties she had in liberating herself from tradition. The fact that she did not have children prevented her experiment from being a model for her contemporaries. She wrote of women in the context of a world dominated by men, but at a time when conditions were begin-

[1] Amélie Gayrand, *Les Jeunes Filles d'aujourd'hui* (1914).
[2] C. Yver, *Dans le jardin du féminisme* (1920), 111.
[3] Fernand Goland, *Les Féministes françaises* (1925), contains numerous extracts from the female press. Cf. Marcel Prévost, 'Les femmes lisent-elles?', in *La Revue de France* (15 Oct. 1922), 673–94 and id., 'Comment lisent les femmes', ibid. (15 Nov. 1922), 225–44.
[4] Geneviève Gennari, *Le Dossier de la femme* (1965), 266; Evelyne Sullerot, *La Presse féminine* (1963).

ning to change rapidly. She was widely read by the post-1945 generation, but she was also a reminder to the middle-aged of their struggles and failures.[1]

Female emancipation was faced with traditions which could not be easily overthrown. Taine had remarked on the strength of these: 'To postpone the awakening of ideas and of feelings, to keep the soul in primitive candour and ignorance, to teach obedience and silence, that is what education was reduced to, total repression.'[2] Edmond About explained this by saying: 'We want above all to keep women faithful to their husbands. So we hope that the girl will bring to the world an angelic provision of ignorance which will be immune to all temptations.' Thus a father might praise the academic successes of his son, but recommend his daughter for her innocence and for the purity with which she had left her convent school.[3] Scribe was accused of having only insignificant, stupid, timid girls in his plays, puppets who could say only 'papa' and 'maman', but Jules Lemaître defended him saying these were realistic portraits, to be explained by the fact that men had developed a taste for such girls. 'The impossibility of penetrating the secrets of the feminine soul at eighteen, the sentiment of a sort of inviolable mystery are part of the idea we have of the young woman.' The theatre of the Second Empire was full of girls who happily married the man selected by their fathers: Émile Augier and Dumas portrayed them because they existed but partly also to encourage them to behave like this. Madame E. Garnier, in her memoirs of *A Parisian University Family in the Nineteenth Century*, recalled: 'We had confidence in the wisdom of our parents, we did not think we demeaned ourselves by sharing their opinions.' Timidity was long considered a virtue. Guizot told his daughter: 'You have too much pride, that is to say, too much self-confidence. Think always about this defect.' The woman journalist Séverine recalled her youth as one of constant repression. 'Nature had to be conquered. According to my parents it was desirable that children should have no will of their own, that a strong discipline should from the beginning break their

[1] Simone de Beauvoir, *Mémoires d'une jeune fille rangée* (1958), *La Force de l'âge* (1960), *Le Deuxième Sexe* (1949).
[2] H. Taine, *Vie et opinions de Thomas Graindorge* (1867).
[3] E. About, *Le Progrès* (1864).

inclinations, their tastes, the awakening of the personality. Not only ought the child not to say I wish, but preferably it ought even to be ignorant of the possibility of desire.' Madeleine Danielou's successful *Livre de sagesse pour les filles de France* (1950) shows how the ideal of submission and purity survived, particularly in Catholic families.[1] Against those who believed in the spread of girls' education, there were others who insisted that this should be different from that which was given to boys. Xavier de Maistre wrote to his daughter: 'The great defect in a woman is to want to be a man and it is to want to be a man to want to be learned.' Barbey d'Aurevilly's attack on *Les Bas bleus* (1878) represented a view that continued to be strongly held. As parents, women appear to have largely supported this traditional method of bringing up girls and, in so doing, defected from the cause of their own liberation.

It is not surprising therefore that little real progress was made in improving women's legal position, and that when legislation was introduced, law and practice remained at variance in many sections of the community. Two laws of 1881 and 1895 allowed women to open post-office savings accounts in their own names and draw money out of them without their husbands' consent. A law of 1907 allowed a married working woman to keep full ownership and use of her wages. However, these measures were not easily enforceable, particularly since the husband still remained legally responsible for his wife's debts. In practice, most stockbrokers and bankers ignored the law and refused to buy stocks or open bank accounts for married women without the consent of the husband. A story is told of a schoolteacher of Marseille who received two different bills for her taxes, one in her maiden name and one in her married name. She protested in person; the tax-collector apologised for the mistake and asked her to send in a written objection. She did so at once, but he returned it to her saying though the tax was for money she herself had earned, only her husband could sign the letter of protest. 'You exist from the fiscal point of view, but you have no legal existence.'[2] The law only slowly got round to remedying this. One of 1893 gave separated women legal capacity; another

---

[1] M. A. Martin, *La Jeune Fille française dans la littérature et la société 1850–1914* (Rennes, n.d., c. 1930).
[2] L. Weiss, 115.

of 1917 allowed women to be guardians of children. In 1920 married women were allowed to join trade unions without their husbands' consent; after 1927 they could have a different nationality from their husbands. Finally the law of 1938 gave married women legal capacity. This was hailed as a great revolution and as a new 'Family Code'. A commission had been set up in 1904 to revise the Civil Code on the occasion of its centenary. When it had got to article 212 saying, 'The couple owe each other fidelity, help and assistance', Paul Hervieu had suggested that the word 'love' should be added, and this had been adopted. But the commission's proposals had never been turned into law. Now, after taking six years to get through the senate, the law of 1938 repealed article 213, which stated that the wife owed obedience to her husband. The husband's marital power was abolished, at least in name, in the sense that it ceased to be stated as such in the code. Secondly, the wife was granted full legal capacity. The wife could now appeal to the courts against her husband's choice of residence, and against opposition by him to her taking a job. The onus, however, rested on her. In reality, the apparent concessions on examination turned out to be largely illusory. The husband was no longer entitled to obedience, but he was called the 'chef de la famille', which seemed to be taking back with one hand what was being given with the other. The full civil capacity given to married women immediately raised many difficult problems and conflicts with other laws, so that it was virtually unworkable.[1] The law courts generally refused applications to override the husband's objection to the wife's working, since they laid it down that the husband had merely to say that this would be against the family's interest: they did not inquire whether his claim was justified.

Only in the matter of divorce was real change achieved—but then, of course, easy divorce was not a feminist demand. The law passed through several stages. In 1792 divorce was allowed on the grounds of incompatibility or by mutual consent. Napoleon made it more difficult, with adultery, cruelty or

---

[1] Jane Cérez, *La Condition sociale de la femme de 1804 à l'heure présente, étude de sociologie juridique* (1940), disappointing but not useless; Charles Vacheng, *L'Application pratique de la loi du 18 février 1938 sur la capacité de la femme mariée* (Aix thesis, 1941), solid; Thomas Kallai, *La Notion de chef de famille* (1950).

grave injury as the main grounds. Only about fifty divorces were granted a year in Paris as a result; very few indeed in the provinces. In 1816, however, divorce was abolished altogether and it remained so until 1884. An attempt by Crémieux in 1848 to re-establish it failed. Alfred Naquet (also a Jew) was the man whose tireless advocacy of the cause of divorce carried it through. He was a professor of chemistry, an ardent republican and free thinker, convicted for organising a secret society in 1867 and for publishing an attack on *Religion, Property and Family* in 1869. He at first proposed a return to the situation of 1792, then to that of 1815; he was successful only when he agreed to make divorce a punishment for a matrimonial offence and to exclude divorce by consent. His victory was, however, incomplete. Only in 1904 was the guilty partner allowed to marry the respondent with whom he or she had committed adultery. Adultery, though a ground for divorce, remained a crime and punishable. In practice, prosecutions became very rare, though occasionally token fines were imposed. The law of 1884 was harder than Napoleon's in that all possibility of divorce by consent was eliminated, but the courts made increasingly liberal use of the grounds of cruelty and injury. The mere refusal to return home allowed the deserted spouse to obtain a divorce. One wife obtained a divorce because her husband did nothing when she was insulted by their servant; another because her husband had sold her jewels without her permission; a third because she was allowed no initiative in the internal conduct of the household.[1] On the other hand, one husband sued for divorce because his wife attended lectures at the Collège de France without his permission, showing 'a dangerous spirit of insubordination and adventure'.[2] There were 7,363 divorces in 1900, 15,450 in 1913, 29,156 in 1920, 32,557 in 1921, but the figure was stable at around 20,000 between 1923 and 1939. 5·4 per cent of marriages thus broke down, though the figure in Paris was 11 per cent. By 1930, 450,000 families had been split up by divorce.[3]

In marriage women continued to have an important

---

[1] André Mollier, *La Question du divorce* (Dijon law thesis) (Besançon, 1930).
[2] Célia Bertin, *Le Temps des femmes* (1958), 39.
[3] Mollier, 90, 95. G. Le Bras and M. Ancel, *Divorce et séparation de corps dans le monde contemporain* (1952), vol. 1, is a useful summary, with a bibliography.

grievance. By the law of 31 July 1920, propaganda in favour of abortion and contraception was forbidden: not just the act or even the intention to abort was punished but its mere advocacy. This was designed to increase the birth rate about which politicians were becoming worried. But juries in fact refused to convict or even the law officers to prosecute. Between 1920 and 1939 only about 350 cases were judged every year, and even the Vichy government did not prosecute more than 2,000. The real effect of the law was to limit the use of contraceptives and to maintain the practice of abortion. Though accurate statistics are of course impossible, it was reasonably estimated that between the wars 400,000 to 1,200,000 abortions took place every year: they were, that is to say, as normal and almost as frequent as childbirth. A study carried out in 1947 showed 73 per cent of those obtaining abortions were married women acting with the consent of their husbands. In 1945, Paris had fourteen 'secret' maternity homes specialising in abortions, and each department at least one.[1]

Equal pay for women came officially in 1946. In 1848 women's wages in industry were around half of men's. In the 1914–18 war they rose greatly in the metallurgical industries: in 1913 they were 45 per cent lower, in 1917 only 18 per cent, but in 1921 they were 31 per cent lower. The collective bargaining agreement in 1936 fixed female wages at 13 to 15 per cent below male wages. In the teaching profession equal pay was accepted in 1927, and equal maxima in 1932. But the civil service as a whole continued to discriminate against women by fixing a limit on women entrants, so as to prevent male unemployment; the Vichy regime in 1940 severely limited the right of married women to work. Careers in the various liberal professions were opened up early enough, but in 1882, there were only 7 women doctors practising, in 1903 95, in 1921 300, in 1929 519. In 1914 there were only 12 women barristers, in 1928 96. In 1930 the universities had 6 women professors. Women certainly won individual distinctions very early on: in 1905 a woman came second in the male *agrégation de philosophie*; in 1913 Lili Boulanger won the grand prix de Rome for music and Odette Pauvert for painting in 1925. In 1936 Léon Blum appointed

[1] Andrée Michel and Geneviève Texier, *La Condition de la française d'aujourd'hui* (1964), I. 122–4.

three women under-secretaries of state in his government. But as a whole women were still far from sharing equally with men in professional life. In 1960 still only 14 per cent of the jobs in the liberal professions and only 3 per cent of administrative jobs were held by women.[1]

Women received the vote in 1944. The long delay was due to the obstinate opposition of the senate, representing radical, provincial prejudice. The arguments used by the senate reveal how little effect the passage of centuries, and the supposed spread of enlightenment, had had in some quarters. One senator made a very long speech consisting of quotations from ancient authors, whose authority he considered a sufficient refutation of women's claims. 'The woman of the Latin race does not think, does not feel, does not develop like the woman of Anglo-Saxon or Germanic race. Her position in the home is not the same.' The decisive argument to some was that if women were given the vote, then prostitutes would have it too. It would be indecent, said others, for men and women to mix freely in the polling booths. But the real objection was the fear that women, being more frequent church-goers than men, would vote for the clerical parties and so threaten the existence of the lay republic. Viviani had introduced a bill for the female vote in 1901; in 1910 163 deputies favoured female suffrage in local elections; an 1919 the chamber voted for full female suffrage by 344 to 97. The senate rejected it by 156 to 134 and renewed its opposition for the next twenty years on successive occasions. It was only the eclipse of the radical party during the war and the suspension of parliament that enabled General de Gaulle to introduce the female vote by decree in 1944—under the influence of the communists on the one hand, who had many women among their supporters, and of the M.R.P. who hoped to gain from the vote of the Catholic women. Subsequent research revealed that 85 per cent of women voted in the same way as their husbands, and it was largely aged widows and unmarried girls who voted differently from their male counterparts. It is not clear therefore that the vote by itself was all that important in changing the position of women in French society.[2]

---

[1] E. Charrier, *passim*, and Michel and Texier, 1. 143.

[2] Mattei Dogan and Jacques Narbonne, *Les Françaises face à la politique* (1955), 187–92; Joseph Barthélemy, *Le Vote des femmes* (1920).

Male supremacy was challenged in another way, by the limitation of paternal authority in the interests of children. By the Napoleonic code, article 375, a father had the right to apply to the courts to obtain the arrest and imprisonment of his child up to the age of 16, in the event of his seriously misbehaving; for children over 16, the courts had discretion as to whether they would agree or not. (A widowed mother needed the consent of the two nearest relatives of the father to apply for an arrest.) By article 148, parental consent was essential for men wanting to marry up to 25 and girls up to 21; but even up to the ages of 30 and 25 respectively, consent had to be asked, though it could be ignored after three refusals. Well after the mid nineteenth century, there were many men and women, aged 30, 40 or even 50, married and with children, who were as submissive to their parents as in their childhood. But a law of 1889 allowed the courts to declare the forfeiture of parental authority in the event of drunken or scandalous conduct or of ill treatment endangering the health, security or morality of their children. A law of 1898 allowed the courts to deprive criminals of the custody of their children. In the early nineteenth century, the paternal power had been upheld by the courts against grandparents: decisions of 1825 and 1853 confirmed a father's right to refuse to allow his children to visit their grandparents. But in 1857 the Cour de Cassation began the destruction of the father's absolute rule: it laid it down that others had rights apart from him.[1] The factory and education laws limited his rights further still. At the same time the mother's role may have changed when children were kept at home longer, and as the practice of sending babies out to wet-nurse in the country, first regulated by the law of 1874, gradually died out.[2] The roles of both women and children in

---

[1] Louis Delzons, *La Famille française et son évolution* (1913); Jules Thabaut, *L'Évolution de la législation sur la famille depuis 1804* (Toulouse thesis, 1913).

[2] See Zola's *Fécondité* for a description of the appalling conditions in which the *nourrissons* were brought up. E. Sorre, *Des modifications à apporter à la loi de protection des enfants en bas âge* (Loi Roussel) (Paris medicine thesis, 1903), 1, 49, confirms the accuracy of this description. Bertrand Dreyer-Dufer, *De la protection des enfants du premier âge* (Paris law thesis, 1900), is a good history of the question. In 1840–60 the death-rate of infants under one rose from 16 to 18 per cent, owing to the spread of the *nourrisson* system. The publication of detailed statistics by country doctors showing a death-rate of up to 70 per cent among these infants led to an official

these changing conditions were redefining themselves, but the situation in 1945 was still one of uncertainty and confusion.

The legislative changes effected in these years showed, on the one hand, that there was dissatisfaction with the system of family relations as it existed, but on the other hand that this system, though subject to tensions, was still immensely powerful. The division of the country into self-conscious family units complicated all other relationships. It gave people loyalties, ambitions and a sense of direction which were seldom talked about openly, but which were one of the deepest sources of motivation in this period. If all the private conversations which took place in it had been recorded, it might, in theory, have been possible to rewrite the political and economic history of the country in terms of clans and families. But this huge part of daily life is something of which historians have been left almost no records, and their account of the past must, for that reason, always be inaccurate.[1]

inquiry and the passing of the law of 1874. This reduced the death-rate drastically, but some departments ignored the law for many years, until the turn of the century.

[1] Elizabeth Glass of St. Antony's College is writing a thesis on women in 19th-century France, using notarial archives.

Part III

14. The Place of Politics in Life

THE history of French politics is usually presented as a record of failure. That is why French politics are confusing. But to present it as a failure is to misunderstand the significance of politics in French life.

France has the reputation of being a country tormented by repeated revolutions, ministerial crises and scandals. Political instability has long appeared to be its major problem. It has been unable to develop coherent parties and has seldom had anything but coalition governments, paralysed by internal dissensions. Success at the polls only occasionally leads to positive reform or real change, because laws take many years to get through the barrage of obstacles, first to their promulgation and then to their implementation. In any case, the country is said still to be in the grip of a powerful centralised bureaucracy. No escape is possible from this stalemate, because the nation is too divided. Disputes of the past accumulate, so that present issues are still debated in terms of historical precedents, and old allegiances produce permanent animosities. Religious, social, constitutional and regional divisions cut across politics in different ways, so that agreement is nearly always only partial. As though to compensate for the inevitable compromises, there is a constant appeal to principle. But this causes the compromises to be widely rejected. There seems little to show at the end of the strife.

To understand French politics, one must first get rid of the Anglo-Saxon model on which so much criticism of them is based, not least by Frenchmen. It is, often unconsciously, assumed that because France has adopted a form of constitutional government which has vaguely resembled, at different times, that of Britain or the U.S.A., that it has failed because it has not evolved the two-party system necessary to make it work on Anglo-Saxon lines. France has indeed borrowed ideas and labels from abroad but it has assimilated them very thoroughly into its own traditions, so that any resemblance to the original is largely nominal. Electoral practices and parliamentary usages in France have functions and a character which are substantially different from those in other countries. One must take into account, in assessing these practices and usages, the peculiar attitude towards power which surrounds their working. The legacy of France's troubled history, and of the rise of its monarchy to such heights among the nations was to discredit power, at least for internal consumption. The function of constitutions became to control and limit its exercise. Even Napoleon III, in resurrecting his uncle's dazzling empire, modified it to allow a large place to individual initiative; even General de Gaulle, while reviving France's prestige abroad, favoured mutual association, not state control, as the key to the country's renewal at home. All the more so, the Third Republic was devoted to preventing governments from becoming too powerful over their citizens. Nationalism was possibly the compensation for this. So though it was true that the political system which prevailed in France was not efficient in terms of passing laws and creating strong long-lasting ministries, that was not what it was intended to do. On the contrary, it was efficient in protecting the individual from excessive interference and allowing him to express his idiosyncracies with the minimum of constraint. The parliamentary constitutions check-mated the bureaucracy. Political and administrative power was on the whole used as a defensive mechanism. That is why the muddles into which it got were tolerated. Political skill revealed itself in *débrouillage*, more than in the manipulation of parties. Of course, there were reactions by minorities against this system, but it was the norm. To appreciate the role of politics, it is important to relate politics to the social conditions surrounding it. It is best to start not from a study of the central organs of the government but in the provinces, in the small towns and in the villages, to see what people wanted from the government, and how they adapted, as it were, the speech of Paris to their own dialects. Only then can one see the work of the politicians in its full context.

One of the most striking consistencies in France's political life has been the way certain regions have voted the same way over more than a hundred years. For example, very considerable areas of the west have been stalwart adherents of conservatism, from the days of the counter-revolution, through the long years of hopeless monarchism, to the modern independent right-wing parties. The extreme left by contrast has always found support in certain areas of the south and centre. It was

MAP 4. 'The Mountain' in the election of 1849

persecuted there in the White Terror of 1815, it triumphed there, as 'the Mountain', in 1849, and the communists still draw much of their strength from these same regions. The study of this phenomenon was pioneered by André Siegfried (1875–1959), who invented 'electoral geography', later known as electoral sociology. This has placed party divisions in a new perspective. Siegfried had the great advantage of both knowing France very well and of standing somewhat aloof in it. He was a Protestant; he was the son of a self-made, American-style

Departments in which over 37·5 per cent of the electorate voted Right.

MAP 5. The Right in 1885

millionaire; he had travelled round the world as a young man; he spoke in 'almost a foreign accent' and he wore check tweeds like a globe-trotting character out of Jules Verne. In four successive elections (1902–10) he tried to enter parliament; rejected, like Tocqueville, he turned to studying the mysteries of politics into which he could not fit.[1] His ingenious *Political Portrait of the West of France* (1913) made use of the detailed local knowledge he had acquired in his campaigns, to argue that

Departments in which over 37·5 per cent of the electorate voted Right.

MAP 6. The Right in 1936

political divisions could be closely related to regional 'temperaments'. 'Just as there are individual temperaments,' he wrote, 'so there are provincial temperaments and national temperaments.' In his book, he tried 'to translate into conscious terms

[1] F. Goguel, 'En mémoire d'André Siegfried', *Revue française de science politique* (June 1959), 333–9; *Hommage à André Siegfried* (1960). On Jules Siegfried see above, p. 68.

the profound unconscious of these psychologies'. He made, first, a geological study of his region, and classified it according to the type of soil and vegetation, distinguishing in particular between granite, woodlands, chalk plains, and quaternary marshlands. He made maps of the density and distribution of population, noting which areas had their population huddled in villages and which had them dispersed in isolated farms. He then compared these with maps of landed property, on which

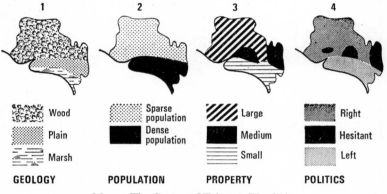

MAP 7. The Canton of Talmont (Vendée)

he had drawn the areas which had large, medium or small ownership. Finally he studied the political complexion of each commune, as revealed by their votes and the votes of the deputies they elected. He came up with a remarkable concordance. From this he concluded that it was possible to predict, more or less, how a particular village would vote by examining these factors. The decisive one was property. When the region was dominated by large resident landlords, when the peasants were dependent on them, directly for their tenancies and their livings, or indirectly on their goodwill, then they voted as the landlords did, that is to say right wing. Areas of small independent peasant proprietors, on the other hand, were the backbone of democracy. There was much more political life in regions of agglomerated population, which therefore tended to be more left wing, whereas scattered settlement reduced political discussion to a minimum and allowed the rural nobility to remain the principal influence.

An additional important factor was the power of the Church.

There were areas where the priest was all-powerful, even more so than the noble. The nobles had preserved their estates most successfully in Anjou, where they still lived in some splendour, but in Brittany they were often poor, at once pretentious and needy, frustrated and without initiative, their authority constantly challenged. In these latter areas, some priests enjoyed far higher incomes, like the curé of Folgoët, for example, who profited from a perpetual influx of pilgrims and whose living in 1913 was worth 50,000 francs a year. Such a man was king of his parish. His wealth, of course, was an exception: and it was not this wealth alone that made him influential. Much more important was that in areas like Léon, the clergy were the élite, of popular and local origin, and accepted as such. Though small property predominated here, the clergy were all-powerful. The Superior of the College of Lesneven, where the clergy were educated, was therefore the grand elector of the region and his orders were read from every pulpit.

In other regions, economically similar, the influence of the state was decisive. On the coast, the peculiar problems of naval conscription made the electorate keen to elect deputies who had the ear of the authorities. The large number of state jobs—in the customs, lighthouses and arsenals—made the government the dispenser of favours few men could ignore. More generally, many people considered it wise to be on the side of the government, since so many of the needs of daily life had to be approved or supported by it. When there were no strong religious convictions, the government, as in Normandy and Maine, could get its candidates elected without difficulty. In some regions, the power of the state was captured by a group, like the Catholics for example, and then these could offer a lot of local civil service jobs, in addition to posts in the world of insurance and railways which they controlled. But even when all these pressures were exerted, in other regions still the electorate seemed to be influenced by personal considerations, and an individual who knew how to please by his own personal charms, and by attuning his rhetoric and activities to those of his constituents, could succeed, with the vaguest of party affiliation. Finally there were regions which seemed to have no view of politics at all: to be totally indifferent doctrinally and to respond only to straightforward appeals to their material interest.

'According to a prevalent view,' concluded Siegfried, 'elections are the domain of nothing but incoherence and whim. By observing them at once closely and from afar, I have come to the opposite conclusion. If, as Goethe said, "hell itself has its laws", why should politics not have its own too?' His 'laws' were, at first sight, simple enough, that electoral results were the result of social relationships, modes of settlement, occupation, religious belief or finally mysterious ethnic characteristics. The great significance of this conclusion was that politics did not necessarily involve the expression of opinion, or a choice between different views of how the country should be run. Only in the towns, he thought, was there real political life. The majority of peasants followed leaders, noble, religious or governmental, who used their votes for their own purposes. What elections did therefore was to conceal the existence of a large variety of deep-seated 'temperaments' and to give France the appearance of unity, or at least of being divided into two basic parties, the left and the right.

The more carefully one reads Siegfried's work, the more one becomes conscious of his qualifications, reservations and subtle dependence on intuitive observation. He simplified French politics by showing the limitations of their ideological content. He showed that politics had a deeper psychological significance. Instead of preoccupying himself with the chaos of party labels and programmes he transferred attention to the problems of the attitude of the elector to his neighbours and to the world beyond. Siegfried made no claim to being a scientist and disclaimed the title of economist. He was proud to belong to the Moral section of the Academy of Moral and Political Sciences. 'It is perhaps as a moralist that I should be proudest to be regarded, on condition that a moralist is not one who makes morals, but one who discusses the conditions of conduct.' The value of his work, as he rightly realised, was in its suggestiveness. He abhorred simple explanations, which claimed to open all doors. 'I have a horror of standard questionnaires', wrote this father of psephology, 'of frameworks prepared in advance, of rigid structures which claim to organise the expressions of the human spirit but in doing so destroy it.' He believed in a constant renewal of the angle of approach in study, in intuition, in an understanding which based itself 'not on quantity but on curiosity and above all on affective curiosity, that is to say, a spontaneous sympathy for the varied forms of life.' He was the enemy of specialisation: he wrote books indiscriminately about the U.S.A., England, South America and New Zealand. He disliked over-elaborate techniques of research. But it was to his inspiration that a whole school of sophisticated electoral sociologists—a major branch of French political science after the war—proclaimed their allegiance. Their work, centred round the Fondation Nationale des Sciences Politiques, and published in numerous monographs, has moved the understanding of French politics on to a new plane.[1]

Siegfried's intuitions have remained fruitful, but it was quickly discovered that his generalisations were not based on really rigorous research. His statement, for example, that large property dominated in the Vendée was supported by figures for only three cantons out of twenty and he added vaguely that the same situation was found in the others. His assessment of the influence of the clergy is supported by maps of private girls' schools, with no statistics about religious practice. His electoral maps were too general, showing in the same way majorities of 51 and 90 per cent. Many problems are simply answered by new ones; right-wing voting is explained, for example, by religious conviction, but the reasons for this are only superficially examined. His rules were not capable of generalisation, and produced some strange anomalies. The new generation of electoral experts pushed his arguments to their extremes, and pointed out how, in simplified form, they did not work. Thus for example Lower Normandy—a region of small property, of few nobles, no religion, no royalist traditions—ought to have voted left wing, but it has on the contrary been stolidly conservative throughout the nineteenth and twentieth centuries. Likewise, Trégorrois in Brittany, a region of large property and a powerful nobility, suddenly in 1910 voted left. Why? Siegfried answered because they at last 'dared to'. But it was not clear why other people did not dare to vote against nobles and clergy who were supposed to be dominating

[1] *Hommage à André Siegfried 1875–1959* (1960); F. Goguel, 'En mémoire d'André Siegfried', *Revue française des sciences politiques* (June 1959), 333–9; A. Siegfried, *Tableau politique de la France de l'Ouest* (1913), and *Géographie électorale de l'Ardèche sous la Troisième République* (1949).

them; or how strong a domination could be if it could be over-thrown simply by courage. Once Siegfried's subtle psychological nuances are omitted, his edifice collapses. The advantage of this is that it has stimulated some excellent work, some of it of almost equal imaginative brilliance.

Siegfried studied fourteen departments. Paul Bois took one of these, Sarthe, which was more manageable, for a detailed study. It is particularly suitable because its western half was royalist in the Revolution, voted right in 1848 and has continued to do so in all elections since then, while its eastern half was republican, voted for the Mountain in 1849 and then became strongly communist. The dividing line goes through the canton of Ecommoy, small enough for really thorough investigation. Now this canton contains one commune, Laigné, which is reactionary, but it is an area of small peasant proprietorship. Another commune in it, Saint-Mars, is very republican, but it has not got much small property. Siegfried's equations seemed to be disproved. A study of property ownership throughout the department showed that both the conservative and republican sides have large and small property in them. Siegfried did not always get his facts on property right. Bois therefore discards the view that the size of property ownership is a significant factor, particularly when, in investigating how noble landlords could influence their peasants, he found that the amount of land the nobles owned was, in total, really quite small—under 25 per cent, and much of it was forest. Only one in fourteen peasants were dependent on the nobles and in forest areas that dependence was as likely to produce hostility as subjection. Moreover, if the leases of the nobles' tenants are examined, it is found that the harsh controls in them do not seem to have affected political behaviour—for after the agricultural crisis of the 1880s, the severe clauses disappear from the leases, but the peasants continue to vote the same way.

Is prosperity or poverty the explanation of the contrasting politics of the two halves of the department? Certainly there were differences between them in this respect. The west was more prosperous than the east, but only up to the depression of 1880, after which it declined far more severely than the east. Yet the west continued to vote conservative throughout, whether it was prosperous or not.

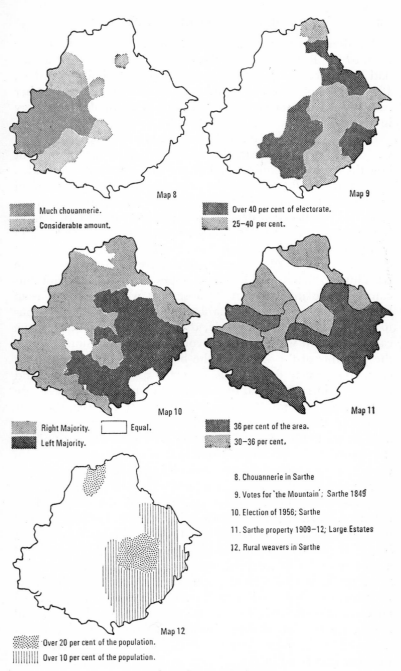

Map 8

Much chouannerie.
Considerable amount.

Map 9

Over 40 per cent of electorate.
25–40 per cent.

Map 10

Right Majority. Equal.
Left Majority.

Map 11

36 per cent of the area.
30–36 per cent.

Map 12

Over 20 per cent of the population.
Over 10 per cent of the population.

8. Chouannerie in Sarthe
9. Votes for 'the Mountain'; Sarthe 1849
10. Election of 1956; Sarthe
11. Sarthe property 1909–12; Large Estates
12. Rural weavers in Sarthe

MAPS 8–12. Paysans de l'Quest

An alternative explanation could be that the division goes back to the Revolution and the *ancien régime* and that the east had been more subject to oppression by the privileged orders. If the *cahiers* of 1789 are examined, however, it emerges rather surprisingly that the people were hostile to the nobles and clergy in the conservative west but not in the east.

Bois suggests that what is important is not whether the land was owned in large or small holdings as Siegfried thought, but how the land was acquired and what social situation surrounded it. Thus in this department the peasants owned $12\frac{1}{2}$ per cent of the land. The bourgeoisie owned $51\frac{1}{2}$ per cent, that is, more than the privileged orders. It is a well-known fact that most of the land sold at the Revolution went to the bourgeoisie and this was very much the case here. However, in the west of the department of Sarthe, the peasants were, at the time of the Revolution, richer, and they had hopes of buying the land that came on the market. But because this western land was of better quality and more valuable, the bourgeoisie were anxious to buy it, while, on the whole, they neglected the land in the east. The result was that the Revolution set up tension between the peasants of the west and the bourgeoisie. The Revolution came to represent for these peasants the thwarting of their land hunger by intruders, and that is why they made common cause with the nobles against a common enemy. In the east, the poor land, sold off in smaller plots, attracted few bourgeois buyers, and no such hostility was created. The different attitude to the bourgeoisie by the two halves of the department is also explained by another factor. Agriculture was the basic activity throughout Sarthe, but it did not everywhere provide the peasants with enough to live on. Those in the west had an income a third higher than those in the east, because the soil was so very much better. The east therefore had to supplement its agriculture by artisan activities and accordingly it contained a great number of weavers, who often accounted for as much as 20 per cent of the rural population. There were also some weavers in the west and north, but they lived in towns, and had no contact with or influence on the peasants. The west had almost no peasant-weavers: instead it grew hemp, which it exported to the east. In the east, by contrast, there were weavers who lived in the hamlets with the peasants. The conclusion is not that the growing of hemp produces royalism and that peasant-weavers are necessarily republican, but rather that artisan activity produces a special kind of interaction between town and country. The weaving areas have constant contact with the towns, because merchants come to them to supply raw materials and to collect the finished cloths, and they bring with them the ideas of the towns. The weavers prove to be ready recipients for revolutionary ideas, particularly because of their jealousy of the richer peasants of the west. In years of bad harvests, the rich peasants survive without difficulty, consuming their own produce and profiting from rocketing prices, while the weavers, who have to buy their food, cannot afford to. The weavers, moreover, are hostile to the government which hampers them with controls on their production and on quality, controls which inevitably reduce their earnings. The westerners know less of the towns, and to them the church serves the same function as the town does to the easterners. It is to church that they go to escape from their isolation; and it is to the church that they rally when the emissaries of the towns attempt to overthrow their priest. So, in this interpretation, the decisive division in France is produced not by property and not by landscape, but by the attitudes which different areas have towards innovations and to capitalism. The principal factors are therefore land hunger, and the strife of town and country, with revolutionary ideas infiltrating from the former to the latter through the artisans. It should not be forgotten that until the end of the nineteenth century no towns ever voted conservative.[1]

Placed on a wider sociological canvas, this interpretation can be developed to associate the progress of advanced ideas with urbanisation. These ideas are to be found not only in towns, but they also penetrate into rural areas affected by urbanisation, that is those which produce goods for the urban market, which are linked to it by roads and the frequent exchange of money. R. Arambourou, studying the *arrondissement* of La Réole (Gironde) showed how the left-wing vote started at the capital of the *arrondissement* at the beginning of the Third Republic and gradually spread outwards to the countryside—

[1] Paul Bois, *Paysans de l'Ouest, Des structures économiques et sociales aux options politiques depuis l'époque révolutionnaire dans la Sarthe* (Le Mans, 1960).

retracting, however, after 1914. In this way, electoral geography can escape from the accusation of presenting a static view of politics.[1] Charles Tilly, studying the Vendée of 1793, showed that the common opinion that economically backward areas, with no urban contacts, are necessarily reactionary, is too simple. In trying to explain why the counter-revolution was so powerful here, he puts forward the explanation that counter-revolution occurs not in totally backward areas, but in ones in which a certain amount of penetration of urban forces had occurred, but incompletely. The counter-revolution represents a conflict of balanced forces. The effect of urbanisation on a rural community is usually selective: only certain classes and certain activities are affected at first. A conflict is set up between those inhabitants who continue to be absorbed in local affairs and those whose outlook and interests have become bound up with outside, national concerns. Julian Pitt-Rivers, the social anthropologist, has shown in a study of a French village how there are two worlds of activity in it. Patois is used when discussing animals, farming, the weather and family matters. French is spoken when dealing with politics, fashion, learning, commerce and national affairs. Today, most French villagers have learnt to be bilingual and bicultural, but a century ago their patois culture was being faced with French culture as an intrusion and a challenge. If urban–rural conflict is due to mutual ignorance or incompatibility, then one would expect to find it strongest in areas where the two are most insulated from each other. But two groups who do not meet cannot fight. The conflict occurs as a result of the two cultures meeting and setting up tensions. The representatives of the towns introduce power into the village from new, outside sources, as officials or as merchants. They challenge the old ruling class and the established distribution of influence in the village. They re-form local rivalries along new lines, linking them with divisions having national significance. Thus the most serious struggles of the counter-revolution occurred not in the remotest woodlands of the Vendée, but near Cholet, where in the eighteenth century the textile industry developed rapidly, to create a sudden clash of new and old influences. The

[1] R. Arambourou, 'Réflexions sur la géographie électorale', *Revue française des sciences politiques* (July 1952), 521–42.

new bourgeoisie celebrated the Revolution by expelling the nobles and peasants from village offices. There was no conflict where the bourgeoisie was already in unchallenged control of the town. The trouble occurred where they were still on their way to the acquisition of influence. This is partly a social explanation, but also a personal one. The counter-revolution was often begun by men seeking to settle personal scores and to redress entirely local grievances. They seldom had plans beyond rectifying the balance of power in their village. They got their support from young men, often hired hands, anxious to avoid conscription, which was one of the most serious forms of national intrusion into the village. The clash between the parties was therefore not on simple class lines (any more than it was in the English Civil War). Though the revolutionary forces were led by bourgeois, there were also some on the opposite side, and there were many artisans in the counter-revolutionary armies. The generalisations have to be made with many reservations.[1]

The sociologists are only one group among the electoral analysts. The geographers, who could claim to have started it all, continue to make important contributions. Siegfried's conclusions seemed to suggest that granite produced right-wing votes and chalk left-wing ones. He was never as simple minded as this, but he did have a strong belief in geographical determinism. In his *Electoral Geography of Ardèche* (1949) he related the different 'climates of opinion' to the geological map, which, he said, gave the 'veritable explanation'. The right was dominant in the mountains, the left in the plain. There was one psychology in the heights, another in the valleys and a third on the slopes. 'It is as though barometric pressure can generate opinions.' It is true that he goes on to modify this by adding that religious factors are overriding, but he seems to regard religion as a 'disturbing influence' rather than a fundamental one. The geographers, particularly of Grenoble University, have continued the study of these interrelationships. They have argued that geographical factors used to be decisive, but that they have ceased to be so as modern developments have brought in more powerful new influences.[2]

[1] C. Tilly, *The Vendée* (1964).
[2] André Siegfried, *Géographie électorale de l'Ardèche sous la Troisième République*

Historians who have contributed to this debate have been unable to produce any simple generalisations about the effects of modern changes. The increasing number of local histories based on a thorough investigation of all possible sources and factors have on the contrary tended to stress the diversity and originality of small regions, and to show how complicated the play of forces has been. Most disconcerting of all, perhaps, has been a brilliant study of the Hérault by Gérard Cholvy, which attempted, among other things, to isolate the influence of the political battles of the nineteenth century on opinion, by studying the effects of the introduction of a revolutionary and Catholic press and of lay and ecclesiastical schools. The political parties have attributed great importance to the propagation of their ideas in newspapers and they have often tried to repress those of their enemies, as dangerous and disruptive influences. But when one looks at the villages and towns where these newspapers were bought, it becomes clear that this influence has in fact been very limited. Newspapers seem to have given heart to the faithful, rather than converted opponents. In the commune of Roqueredonde, to take a small but precise example, in 1907 ten daily newspapers were regularly bought: three Catholic and seven republican. But this was a largely religious parish and the anticlerical newspapers did nothing to destroy its faith. The peasants did not read the newspapers, whose influence, if any, was on a small élite. In many places the republican papers were simply what republican civil servants bought. With the progress of time, newspapers won a wider audience, though at the same time they lost much of their political content. The effects of the press in the nineteenth and the twentieth centuries were by no means of the same kind. The formation of public opinion, in historical perspective, is still something of a mystery.

Likewise, it is usually assumed that the lay schools and the *instituteurs* were important agents in converting the new generations to the republic. But here again it emerges in detailed local study that this is by no means proved, and that their influence has almost certainly been exaggerated. Only a minority of *instituteurs* seem to have been really vigorous in

(1949), 113; G. Veyret-Verner and others in *Revue de géographie alpine* (Jan.–Mar. 1954).

the campaign of laicisation; there were great differences in their personalities and attitudes and their action varied over the century. The Church thought it could win back ground by establishing its own schools, but these probably halted a tide rather than changed a situation, and they were not successful in regions which had already become detached from Christianity. The growth of towns is another factor which has been linked with an increase of hostility or indifference to the Church. Here detailed investigation of opinion in the town before it grew shows that there was often no change as a result of growth. Immigrants, arriving with a feeling of inferiority towards the older residents, may be quick to assimilate the accepted attitudes: the resulting city's attitudes will depend on a combination of the immigrants' past and the way they are treated when they arrive. The Spaniards who flooded into southern France, for example, came from an ostensibly Catholic country, but their conformity there had usually been purely social, and their move to France was a liberation and escape from the old pressures. One is repeatedly brought back to more and more distant historical factors.[1]

Another crucial historical problem is that of the changing composition of the ruling class in politics. Philippe Vigier (whose penetrating thesis—one of the most important since the war—on the Alpine region from 1848 to 1852, contains insights and ideas of far wider significance than his title might suggest) has illuminated the varying fortunes of the old notable class in the face of universal suffrage. In contrast to Siegfried, who dealt with an area where the nobility's influence survived in a rather special way, he has investigated a region with far less large property and few nobles. Here the emancipation of the people from the rule of the notables occurred at different speeds in different areas. In some places, particularly where the ruling class of Louis-Philippe had wasted itself in petty internal quarrels and coterie jealousies, the advent of universal suffrage revealed that they were discredited, and already in July 1848 the peasants were using the municipal elections to start a 'république paysanne'. Whereas in the west of France the poor continued to leave politics to their traditional rulers or to the educated classes for over half a century, here their participation

[1] Gérard Cholvy, *Géographie religieuse de l'Hérault contemporain* (1968).

was very quickly established. Their allegiances, however, did not all go the same way. A large number gave their support to the Reds, and engaged actively in politics in the numerous secret clubs that sprang up in many villages. In the Comtat, however, they preferred popular royalism under noble leaders. Elsewhere Bonapartism appeared as a means by which they could win their place in public affairs, against the old ruling cliques. Many factors determined the moment when the masses entered politics: historical traditions—the kind of leadership the notables had provided, the type of conflicts in which the peasants had been involved before they were given a voice; geographical forces—like the isolation of the mountain regions, where indifference prevailed; and economic influences—and here particularly the way the economic crisis of 1848 hit different classes and different areas. A comparison of Vigier's findings with those of some of the other important local studies recently undertaken shows that universal suffrage affected politics in a wide variety of ways and that one cannot talk simply of one class displacing another in power at any given date, certainly not on a national level.[1]

So far, this discussion has used the terms left and right. It is a traditional view of French politics that under the multiplicity of party labels the real struggle has been between two major tendencies, labelled according to the parts of the chamber the deputies of the First Republic occupied. The French invented the notion of left and right, and it has been adopted almost universally. This is the distinction, said Emmanuel Berl, which is by far the most living one for the mass of the French electorate. 'A sure instinct enables us to know if a person is left or right', said André Siegfried, though it was difficult to explain why we knew it. Generally speaking, to be left wing denoted acceptance of the enlightenment, of the idea that man was naturally good, capable of infinite progress, which would be achieved above all by the application of reason, that the world as it was required improvement, and that this 'improvement' should be sought in accordance with the wishes, and in the interests, of the majority

[1] Philippe Vigier, *La Seconde République dans la région alpine* (1963), 2 vols.; André Armengaud, *Les Populations de l'est aquitain 1845-1871* (1961); Pierre Barral, *Le Département de l'Isère sous la Troisième République* (1962); Georges Dupeux, *Aspects de l'histoire sociale et politique du Loir-et-Cher 1848-1914* (1962).

of the nation. To be right wing was generally to prefer to maintain the *status quo*, or even to bring back the good old days, to believe in hierarchies, the inequality of men, to doubt whether free discussion was the way to truth, to place great emphasis on the wisdom of the past and to look on the Catholic Church as the greatest repository of that wisdom.[1] Under Louis-Philippe, the left clarified its intentions by calling itself the party of movement and the right the party of resistance. The Dreyfus affair owes some of its fame to the fact that it re-divided the country clearly once more, when distinctions had been blurred, so that those who supported Dreyfus were left and those who condemned him were right. To intellectuals, this long remained the test case to determine a man's basic allegiance. However, though the great merit of this distinction was that it seemed to make politics more intelligible, in other ways it introduced as much confusion and ambiguity. In the course of the nineteenth century, the left was more successful than the right, and so more and more people thought it desirable to call themselves left, however limited their attachment to its principles. Also, more and more people of the left, when they attained power, found it hard to implement their plans of reform and spent more time resisting the attacks of new men who emerged to be more left than themselves. Thus the anomaly arose of conservative parties having 'left' as a prominent part of their name; appellations which had once suggested extreme revolutionary tendencies came to mean the very opposite. Thus radicals were once clearly left wing, their programme in 1869 was extreme, but by the end of the century they were sitting in the centre of the chamber, and they are now on the right. There have been groups, like the Republican left, which sat on the right, and were conservative in all but their memories. 'Progressist' in 1885 meant advanced, but in 1898 it meant moderate and by 1906 it was positively right wing and even clerical. In the south there have been 'anticollectivist socialists' who are in reality conservatives. There is no consistency in the content of the distinction either. A man calling himself right wing was often clerical, but this was not always the case and there are regions which have been moving steadily to the right in direct proportion to the increase in their religious indifference;

[1] Cf. E. Beau de Lomenie, *Qu'appelez-vous Droite et Gauche?* (1931).

and in the 1930s and 1940s the Catholics successfully detached themselves from conservatism. A man calling himself left wing might be thought to be liberal rather than authoritarian, but this could be an illusion and is by no means always or necessarily the case.[1]

It is not possible to associate the left wing simply with industrialisation and the rise of a working class. The east of France, after having been left wing for the first half of the Third Republic, became right wing for the second half. Now this is a region which includes some of the largest industrial agglomerations of the country, and yet there has been a peculiar absence of socialism and communism. Clearly the conservatism of the west, so graphically described by Siegfried, is quite different from that of the east. One cannot talk of the influence of the employers dominating the workers in the east, for they are often of a different religion and apart from some famous exceptions, they have been 'egotistic exploiters'. It seems that what has been the determining factor in the east is its position on the frontier, its fear of invasion, its nationalism precisely because its French character is somewhat uncertain. So when nationalism was represented by the left it voted left, but then moved right when nationalism became a creed of the right. It favoured strong and authoritarian government, so its republicanism was always of a special character, and it voted massively in favour of De Gaulle. Industrialisation has had a completely different result in the north, with its strong communist vote, and in the east, where it is tiny.[2]

There are so many differences within each of these two 'temperaments' as they have been called, that it has been suggested that the terms left and right should be used in the plural. The right should, in this view, be seen to be composed of basically three distinguishable varieties, which were originally called legitimism, Orleanism and Bonapartism. With time, the ideologies of these varieties and the support for them have changed, but the new forms of conservatism, like corporatism and nationalism, and movements like the M.R.P., Poujadism

---

[1] René Rémond, *La Droite en France* (new edition 1963), contains an excellent analysis. Cf. E. Weber and H. Rogger, *The European Right* (1965).

[2] *Recherches sur les forces politiques de la France de l'est depuis 1787* (Strasbourg, 1966), cahiers 8 and 9 of the Association Interuniversitaire de l'Est.

and Gaullism, can be linked with them.[1] The left wing should be divided at least into two, for its extreme wing, ending in communism, has clearly developed distinct functions. This modification of the left–right dichotomy certainly makes for greater clarity, though the danger in it is that it encourages an over-schematic attitude towards political phenomena, and a blurring of incongruities in the interests of simplicity. It can be of assistance in understanding new forces, particularly since historical traditions play such an important part in shaping these, but, unless carefully used, it can suggest that the ultimate aim is to be able to categorise them, and that ultimately there are only two possible solutions, two basic psychologies.

It should not prevent one from realising that the purpose of these labels is partly to conceal differences, to make common action possible, to rally support, and not just to enlighten the public. Some who adopt a label are mistaken in thinking that it represents what they would like it to represent. The labels perpetuate distinctions, feuds, enmities whose origin is almost forgotten and whose significance is largely historical. Their use keeps politics in a vicious circle, which makes it difficult to perceive and assimilate new forces and problems; it keeps the parties which adopt them at one remove from reality. There is much to be said for writing the history of Frenchmen not in terms of what divides them but of what unites them. Apparently radical reforms, when actually implemented, turn out to be much more moderate than their proponents made them out to be, and often to approximate to the common denominator of public opinion. The Revolution of 1789 is now seen to have been far less of a break with the past than was once believed. The separation of Church and state, fought for for so long by the anticlerical left wing, in the end strengthened the Church. The equilibrium that seems to be maintained despite the efforts of either side to tilt the balance in its favour is a useful pointer to the consensus which party strife obscures. The two sides have more in common than they are willing to admit. An understanding of this common factor in the mentality of political opponents is essential to a proper appreciation of just how much place politics has in the life of a nation. This common

[1] René Rémond, 261–92, has a discussion of the links. Cf. François Goguel, *La Politique des partis sous la Troisième République* (3rd edition 1958), 17–29.

mentality, precisely because it was accepted, was often a force of far greater power than anything a party could create. France did indeed appear to be moving leftwards throughout this century, but the cult of originality very often flourished in people who also had, in other ways, a deep hostility to it. The ambivalence of the radical party, which survived so long because it incarnated with such muddle and guile the feelings of the average man, illustrates this well, and Proudhon, who was so sympathetic to large sections of the working classes, was of course simultaneously revolutionary and conservative. It is important to accept these contradictions as real and not to attempt to clarify too much what was confused and hesitant. The political parties did not necessarily fight for the objects they thought they were fighting for. The radicals who tried so hard to destroy Catholic teaching and introduce a lay morality never quite caught up with the fact that the morality they preached was very little different from that of the Catholics. Were they fooling themselves or the electorate?[1]

The real issues about which people cared were not necessarily represented by the parties; and, in any case, it should not be forgotten that France had no parties, in the British or American sense, organised and with clear programmes, until the communists introduced one. To vote for a party therefore meant something different in France. The vocabulary is misleading. So it is not enough to count votes to discover the opinions of a constituency or a region. To assert the opposite is to imply that the whole nation was fully integrated, fully conscious of the options open to it, and that it saw them in the same terms as the politicians. This was clearly not the case in this period. In different regions, in different sections of society, and at the personal level, votes had many different meanings. Some opinions represented ambitions and attitudes which could not really be expressed in political terms. Only with the advent of public opinion polls has it become possible to come anywhere near a satisfactory analysis of the significance of political votes. When one poll in 1952 asked Frenchmen whether they thought France ought to remain neutral in a war, the vast majority answered yes. But when it asked further whether France could

[1] See Theodore Zeldin (ed.), *Conflicts in French Society* (1970).

remain neutral in a war, the vast majority answered no.[1] Much
subtlety is needed to distinguish between the theoretical and
the practical content of a vote. In France, the distinction is all
the more difficult to make because people have often been more
reticent in answering public opinion questionnaires than they
are in the U.S.A.; American sociological techniques do not
always produce comparable results in France. But the use of
these polls has suggested that there is more consensus than the
political system leads one to believe.

The violence of party strife has given France the reputation
abroad of being a nation in whose life politics play a very
important part. The number of Frenchmen who have actually
joined a political party is, however, infinitesimal, around 1·5 per
cent in the 1950s, and very much less before when there were
fewer parties which believed they could actually enrol members.
Only the communists have managed to get more than 100,000
party members. There is some justification for the view of those
who have claimed that the political nation in the twentieth
century is no larger than that of the days of Louis-Philippe,
when votes were limited to the rich. Charles Maurras was not
an impartial commentator but his suggestion that only about
20,000 to 30,000 people were really involved in politics may
contain some truth.[2] The vicomte d'Avenel, a social historian
and analyst of considerable merit, whose writings enjoyed
much esteem at the turn of the century and who has somewhat
unjustly been forgotten, began his book on *The French* thus:
'Politics does not at all have, in the lives of each one of us,
the place it holds in the newspapers, in conversation, in the
apparent life of the nation. The public life of a people is a very
small thing compared to its private life. So the modifications of
government do not have the influence on our well-being, on the
material or moral situation of each one of us, or on our un-
happiness, that is commonly believed. They are not matters of
indifference, but in the end they do not matter much. So people
as a whole do not bother a great deal about politics; and this
attitude is fortunate. If it was otherwise, nations would be

[1] P. Fougeyrollas, *La Conscience politique dans la France contemporaine* (1963), 144.
For the results of polls, see *Sondages*, periodical published by the Institut Français
de l'Opinion Publique.
[2] C. Maurras, *Enquête sur la monarchie* (1900), xcii.

ungovernable.'[1] D'Avenel's conclusion may be debatable, but his assertions are supported to some extent by electoral and poll statistics. Between 1815 and 1846 abstentions in elections, even though the vote was limited to a few, were occasionally as high as 30 per cent, and fell to 10 per cent only once, in 1830. After the Revolution of 1848, there were only 16 per cent abstentions in April, but by December, in the presidential election, they were up to 25 per cent, and reached 35 per cent in May 1849. Under Napoleon III they started at 37 per cent and fell gradually to 18 per cent in 1870. Under the Third Republic, abstentions were as high as 30 per cent in 1881, 29 per cent in 1893, 27·7 per cent in 1898, 27·5 per cent in 1910, but in hard-fought elections, when the clash of issues was stressed, they fell to 20 per cent, as in 1881, 1902 and 1906. On the whole, however, abstentions diminished, and in the 1930s they were down to between 15 and 16 per cent. Though some greeted these figures as showing that depolitisation (so noticeable in the content of newspapers) was a myth, the Fifth Republic saw the figures rise again to between 22 and 24 per cent and as high as 31 per cent in the election of 1962. These figures should probably be reduced by 5 per cent—to allow for mistakes in the electoral role, and those physically incapable of voting—to reveal those who voluntarily abstained; but they should also be compared with the abstentions in local elections, which in 1937 were as high as 40 per cent, in 1952 43 per cent, in 1955 38 per cent. These are national totals: in some cantons the majority, even 60 per cent, abstained.

Perhaps France's reputation for interest in politics came to it from the eighteenth century. It could be argued that after 1848 politics ceased to be a major preoccupation. 'People engaged in politics, they discussed them in conversations and newspapers; they published pamphlets and even a few important books. But what a contrast intellectually with the eighteenth century, when politics were a principal concern of the great minds, and when books about the state and its laws were best sellers.' In the nineteenth century, most of the great thinkers, like Saint-Simon and Proudhon, were enemies of politics, anxious to reduce government to the minimum. Demolins wrote a book entitled *Is it worth capturing power?* Until the 1930s,

[1] G. d'Avenel, *Les Français de mon temps* (1904), 1.

young intellectuals dreamed of writing poetry and novels rather than of emulating Aristotle or Tocqueville. The prestige of politics was well below that of literature or science. It was only after 1945 that French political science really established itself as an independent discipline.[1] In a poll held in 1959 only 9 per cent of those questioned said they were very interested in politics, 47 per cent said they were interested a little and 42·5 per cent said they were not interested at all. This 9 per cent of very interested people contained twice as many men as women (12 per cent men, 6·5 per cent women; 52 per cent of women as opposed to 32 per cent of men said they had no interest in politics at all). 35 per cent of men in the upper ranks of management and administration said they were very interested, 22·5 per cent of members of the liberal professions, 15 per cent of middle management, 14 per cent of people in agriculture, 13 per cent of junior employees in business, 12 per cent of artisans, 7 per cent of industrial workers and 6 per cent of agricultural labourers. Among the industrial workers, the figure for qualified ones was 9 per cent, but for labourers 3·5 per cent. In the same year (which was of course a crucial and exciting one in French history) 89 per cent of those interrogated said they had attended no electoral meeting of any kind, 54 per cent had not bothered to read any electoral posters, 35 per cent had not heard any political broadcasts. Only 19 per cent said they regularly read the political articles in newspapers, but 21 per cent said they never did. It seems unlikely that the interest in politics was higher in the nineteenth century, in a population with so much less leisure and far greater illiteracy.

Now, abstention from politics is in France often a political act in itself. Some conservatives in particular take up the attitude that parties are ruining the country and when they stand for parliament they say they are doing so unwillingly, simply to put right what the politicians have spoilt. They dislike the word party and prefer to organise 'movements', 'unions' and *rassemblements*. Napoleon III made the criticism of parties one of the main planks in his platform: parties, he claimed, paralysed reform and produced only agitation: against them he offered a return to order and union. Pétain in 1940 attacked

[1] *Revue internationale d'histoire politique et constitutionnelle*, 7 (1957), special issue on 'L'entrée de la science politique dans l'université française', 1–119.

the sterile quarrels of the parties of the Third Republic, which had encouraged the feverish unleashing of personal ambition and ideological passions, with permanent incitement to division. De Gaulle's prime minister, Michel Debré, in the same tradition, positively advocated depolitisation, arguing that the removal of vital problems from partisan discussion was essential in the national interest. The advocates of technocracy, from Saint-Simon and Comte downwards, have been the enemies of unbridled politics. The civil service, the army, certain business circles have all in varying degrees echoed this distaste for and discrediting of politics as something dishonest and futile. Not even the republic's hard-won moral-education classes themselves, which are supposed to instil patriotism into children, seem to encourage a different attitude. A sample of children were asked in the early 1960s who in history had done most good to France. 48 per cent said Pasteur, 20 per cent said St Louis, 12 per cent said Napoleon, 9 per cent De Gaulle, 4 per cent Colbert, 2 per cent Louis XIV, 1 per cent Gambetta and 1 per cent Robespierre. The most popular heroes are not politicians.[1]

Moreover, those people who are interested in politics are not always interested in political questions. At the village level, politics sometimes appears as simply a pastime in which people engage to save themselves from boredom, particularly when there is a rural middle class with a certain amount of leisure and pretension. In the south-west, politics could be ideological but also have an element of game playing in it, particularly when an autarchic economy meant that the election results and the outside world's policy had less material consequences than fluctuations of the weather. In the west, when the social structure was more rigidly hierarchical, the struggle to replace the old élite by a new one could assume a more bitter and angry complexion, as traditional supremacies and a whole view of life were simultaneously challenged. Some villages have their political alignment firmly settled by the rivalries of families, clans and clienteles, and the battles for influence and prestige

[1] Jean Meynaud and Alain Lancelot, *La Participation des Français à la politique* (1961); Georges Vedel, *La Dépolitisation. Mythe ou réalité* (1962); J.-P. Charnay, *Le Suffrage politique en France* (1965), 180; Charles Roig and Françoise Billon-Grand, *La Socialisation politique des enfants. Contribution à l'étude de la formation des attitudes politiques en France* (1968), 64.

between them are carried on, under sophisticated labels, with infinite subtlety.

When the results of an election are known, their significance is not easy to assess. Under the voting system adopted during most of the Third Republic, a majority of those who cast their votes were not represented in parliament. In 1881, for example, 4·5 million votes were cast for the deputies elected, but 5·6 million for others.[1] The inequalities of the constituencies accentuated the gap between public and parliamentary opinion.[2] 49 per cent of people questioned in 1963 did not consider that any of the political parties was suited to defend their interests.[3]

The study of political behaviour is, despite all the advances made, particularly over the last few decades, still in a rudimentary stage. The way people acquire their political ideas, the influence of parents, schools and peer groups and of the increasingly varied pressures to which people are subject, has not been satisfactorily unravelled. In the U.S.A., the choice of party is said to be made by children at a very early age. Parties do not have the same position in French society, but divisions on national issues appear to be established firmly in the schools. The interactions of politics and family organisation, and of the models of authority inculcated in childhood with subsequent behaviour, are worth investigating. Meanwhile French politics cannot be seen simply as the clash of two ideologies, or even a number of them. Indeed, judged by the amount politics meant to the masses, it might seem that they should not be accorded too much attention. But, if it is granted that the ideological clash symbolised or revealed other conflicts, the exceptional richness of the political material can yield insights not to be derived from any other source. There are definite limits to what the historian will ever find out about family life. The mass of political archives and newspapers is by contrast almost inexhaustible in its variety. Through a study of politics, this section will attempt to enable the reader to become acquainted with one of the ways in which Frenchmen

[1] Eugène d'Eichtal, *Souveraineté du peuple et gouvernement* (1895), 204. The figures for 1885, 1889 and 1893 were similar.

[2] J. M. Cotteret, *Lois électorales et inégalités de représentation en France 1936–1960* (1960).

[3] *Sondages*, 2 (1963), 69.

expressed their character, their ambition and their frustration. The ideas and the activities to which politics gave rise are fascinating in themselves, but a good deal of their significance and intelligibility depends on their being seen also as part of a wider whole. The links between the parts, between the different sides of life, are elusive, but it is in the search for them that history acquires its universal interest.

15. Kings and Aristocrats

THERE is a great deal of drama in the history of royalism after 1848—secret conspiracies, tense crises, prolonged rivalries. The leading protagonists included colourful extremists, vigorous, stoical and melancholy agitators, and men strangely out of touch with reality. The fate of royalism, at this personal level, is usually presented as the result of individual mistakes, mismanagement and lost opportunities. In 1873 it seemed that the monarchy was *almost* restored; in 1889 Boulanger *almost* staged a *coup d'état* in its favour. In this interpretation, France would have been a monarchy again but for the errors and divisions of the royalist leaders. This chapter will ask just how much part accident played in what was, for many people, the major tragedy of this period. It will attempt to analyse why the leaders acted the way they did, where and why they won support and why they lost it, and whether, if the monarchy had been restored, it could have lasted. One can, by the study of these questions, get a glimpse of a section of society whose preoccupations were considerably more complicated than a loyal devotion to hereditary monarchy.

For royalism was a movement aiming at much more than the restoration of the monarchy and it was backed by forces far more powerful than those of a corrupt court, or a decaying nobility regretting its lost prestige. Its history cannot be written off simply as one of failure. It is true that by the 1890s it had ceased to be a significant political force; that its resuscitation by the Action Française in the twentieth century was the work of a tiny if vocal minority and that today, for all practical purposes, it is dead. However, the men involved were not fighting simply about forms of government, or about ideology. Paradoxically, many of those who worked hardest to secure the king's restoration were, in fact, among his bitterest enemies. The nobles of Brittany were famous in the nineteenth century for the perseverance with which they supported the royalist cause. But in the eighteenth century they had been among the king's principal enemies. They were not inconsistent. In both centuries they stood above all for a view of the distribution of political and local influence, which involved the rule of the countryside by an élite. In the eighteenth century they saw the king as their enemy; after the Revolution they believed the republic was an even more dangerous threat. Royalism was part of this struggle about decentralisation, about the unification of the state, about the evolution of a ruling class within it, and about the way those interested in power balanced themselves between Paris and the provinces. The royalist cause was not entirely lost, if seen from this point of view. The republic, in the form in which it ultimately triumphed, did not secure an unadulterated victory over this movement against the state: on the contrary, the republic triumphed partly because it absorbed the movement. *La république des camarades* evolved its own way of diffusing power and of limiting central authority. It ended the rule of the aristocracy, but it replaced it with a new kind of élite, in which the hereditary element was not totally absent. So deep were the passions involved, that neither side could admit that they had anything in common. The struggle over the monarchy was not one in which the alliances were natural ones, or the enmities as inescapable as they may have appeared.

One of the basic and acknowledged divisions of royalism was between legitimism and Orleanism, between the partisans of the eldest line overthrown in 1830 on the one side and those of the younger branch of Louis-Philippe, overthrown in 1848, on the other. But, to begin with the first of these, it is not always appreciated that the legitimists were themselves divided into three different groups, each advocating different methods of securing a restoration. On the one hand there was the party of violence. These were the successors of the *chouans* of the first Revolution, of the men who had waged civil war against it and against Napoleon, and who believed that the king and his nobility could still raise an army of one or two hundred thousand men, principally in the west, which would be able to restore the fleur-de-lis once more to Paris. These advocates of conspiracy were led by the duc des Cars, 'a small, thickset, energetic, taciturn man, a visionary all the more attached to his chimeras in that he divulged them only to those he knew in advance would approve them ... Outwardly cold, but deep down ardent

to the point of temerity, he was impenetrably discreet, indefatig-
ably active, an enemy as much of the salons as of parliament. He
never went into fashionable society. His true friends received
his visits at five or six in the morning.'[1] His policy was tried out
in 1832, by the duchesse de Berri, but the planned rising of that
year was discovered before it had actually broken out, and the
policy, because it had never decisively been proved impossible,
was therefore able to survive. The opening up of Brittany and
the Vendée by new roads and then by railways, the establishment of garrisons in formerly impenetrable regions, the economic development which created a new prosperity, new classes
and new relationships between the nobility and the people,
soon created different conditions to those prevailing during the
counter-revolution, but for long there were royalists who continued that tradition. They were associated with absolutist
doctrines, but the exposition of doctrine was not their strong
point.

Secondly, there was the legitimist parliamentary party,
which believed that the monarchy could and should be restored
by parliamentary means, by fighting elections and winning a
majority for it. Its leader was Berryer, and he was not even
a nobleman. Indeed, he was barely a Frenchman. He came
from Lorraine if not from Germany, his father's name had been
Mittelberger. But just as the Tory party in England bought
the Irishman Burke an estate, so likewise the legitimists set up
Berryer as a country gentleman. For Berryer, though now
somewhat forgotten perhaps because he never held office, was
in his day regarded as probably the most powerful orator of the
century, in a century which prized oratory as one of the most
important political gifts. 'He who has never heard Berryer on
one of his good days does not know what eloquence is.'[2] For
thirty-eight years (1830–68) Berryer led the sizeable ranks of
legitimists who went into parliament despite the pretender's
orders to abstain. He stood for a constitutional monarchy,
though circumstances were never to reveal just how liberal he
intended that to be. One of his associates, the comte de Falloux,
wrote a book in praise of Louis XVI as a man who had really
understood his times, which suggested that the aim of this party

[1] Comte de Falloux, *Mémoires d'un royaliste* (1888), I. 222.
[2] E. Ollivier, *L'Empire libéral*, I (1895), 439.

was to restore the *ancien régime* but reformed on the lines envisaged by Turgot, another of their heroes. The legitimists were far from having clear aims.

Thirdly, there was left-wing or popular legitimism, which was in some ways a precursor of radical Toryism. Its tactic was to 'dish the Whigs', to steal the thunder of the left and to restore the monarchy by means of referendum, by legal but extra-parliamentary means. Their methods were similar to those of some radical republicans and they were willing to enter into alliance with these. They were among the first to demand an extension of the suffrage, and they directed their propaganda at the masses, hoping for an alliance of the nobility with them, against the bourgeoisie. They acted above all through the press, which they made into a vigorous instrument of agitation. Their leader, the Abbé de Genoude, was editor of the *Gazette de France*. This remarkable man, again, does not fit into the stereotype of the aristocrat. He had made a lot of money under the Restoration, and after 1830 he used it to finance his newspaper. When his wife died, he became a priest. Wearing neither tonsure nor cassock, he preached at the Chapelle du Temple, using as his sermons his leading articles, which he read out from the printed proofs before publishing them the next morning. His ally, the marquis de la Rochejacquelin, a nephew of the great *chouan*, once a cavalry officer, but an industrialist after 1830, even preached the sovereignty of the people and made his main demand a referendum on the question of republic or monarchy. Under Napoleon III, who adopted this appeal to the people, he agreed to serve as a senator, to cries that he was a traitor to his party. He illustrates well how the distinction between parties was not wholly clear cut.[1]

The division of the legitimists into three types is apparent mainly when one looks at the leaders; but if one goes a stage further to examine lesser-known men, a considerably greater variety emerges. Above all, there were profound differences in legitimism in the different regions, which the leaders only partly reflected. Thus in the west legitimism was essentially rural, drawing its strength from the close relations of the nobles

---

[1] Comte Alexandre d'Adhemar, *Du parti légitimiste en France et de sa crise actuelle* (1843); C. de Lacombe, *La Vie de Berryer* (1894–5); C. de Mazade, *L'Opposition royaliste* (1894); C. T. Muret, *French Royalist Doctrines since the Revolution* (1933).

and the peasants, cemented by the Church, but with little journalistic intervention. It showed its strength by a kind of passive resistance. In the south, by contrast, where there were few resignations from the civil service after 1830, the legitimists were most powerful in the towns. Toulouse was their principal stronghold, but they exerted little influence in the country around it, where a rich 'rural bourgeoisie' successfully rivalled it. Far from being abstentionist, the legitimists fought elections with demagogic fervour. In the Nîmes–Montpellier–Montauban region this vigorous attitude was envenomed and impassioned by the conflict against Protestantism. In Marseille, legitimism was different again, based not on traditionalism but on an alliance of a few nobles, but far more businessmen, with the masses: it was an opposition party, against Paris and against the holders of state offices. One of their leaders was Béchard, who was a leading theorist of decentralisation; and it was no accident that it was there that Berryer got himself regularly returned to parliament, to uphold a liberal interpretation of the royal cause. Southern legitimism as a whole could more properly be called reactionary or counter-revolutionary, perpetuating old animosities. In Lyon, by contrast, it was watered down to a respectable conservatism, so moderate as to be ready to ally with any government maintaining public order. In the Nord, it was closely connected with Catholicism and manifested itself as much in charitable work as in political organisation.[1]

To which of all these forms of legitimism did the pretenders adhere? The answer is, to none. This was one of the major sources of weakness for the monarchists, who wore themselves out in vain efforts to win the ear of the pretenders, only to be constantly resisted and discouraged. It is also a result of the paradox of legitimism, that the legitimist party was almost inevitably at loggerheads with the pretender. It wanted to give him power, but at the same time it opposed his exercise of that power, for it wanted decentralisation. This is not the only difficulty the party had with its leaders. Royal power and party organisation are not easily compatible. The pretender always felt the need to appeal beyond his own followers, to appear to

[1] A. J. Tudesq, *Les Grands Notables en France 1840–9* (1964), I. 130–236, is the best social study of legitimism, though it deals only with Louis-Philippe's reign.

be a national leader. He had to work hard to avoid being enslaved by party (as Queen Anne of England quickly realised when parties were first organised here). These difficulties were obscured by the mystical devotion legitimists bestowed on their pretender, existing side by side with their criticisms but for long triumphing over them. The devotion was essential, for the record of the pretenders was an appallingly unsuccessful one. It had been no easy thing to admire Louis XVIII, obese to the point of immobility, scrofulous, egoistic, conceited, concerned primarily with his own physical well-being, opportunistic when it served him but rigidly archaic in his obsession with ceremonial and court ritual. He had got his throne back and this gave him a reputation for sagacity, but it was hardly deserved. His moderation and balancing of the parties had been designed primarily to keep himself the supreme arbiter in politics. His ignorance of conditions in his kingdom and of changing opinions was astounding. Charles X had been more attractive, with far more grace, even if his genuine benevolence was somewhat ovine. Unlike his elder brother, he was not concerned with showing his own importance, and he always had a kind word to say to everyone. He could win real affection from those with whom he had dealings. But he too was ignorant and uneducated. His keen desire to perform his duties punctiliously proved his undoing, for he did not understand compromise. He believed that opposition must be met with frontal attack. For all his devotion to the public welfare, as he saw it, the result of his reign was catastrophic.

The comte de Chambord (born in 1820), pretender for forty-seven years (1836–83), was an equally difficult leader to follow. Educated by conservative noblemen of narrow outlook, it is said that he was instructed in political economy, cosmography, trigonometry and botany, and that he was therefore alive to the new ideas of his time, but his hagiographers also add what probably gives a truer picture of his interests—that he knew by heart the history of all the dynasties of Europe with their dates and his own genealogy right back to Roman times. His tutors had been told to teach him no history beyond 1788. In any case his main activity was hunting. In 1841 he broke his leg in a riding accident and limped for the rest of his life. He was not of a particularly prepossessing appearance. He grew to be almost as fat as Louis XVIII. He was exceedingly hairy (or, as the court sycophants put it, 'his pilose system was very developed'). He was lazy and not particularly intelligent. He could tie neither his own shoe-laces nor his cravat. He maintained the etiquette of the *ancien régime* with a scrupulous devotion, and preserved relics of Louis XVI and Marie Antoinette religiously in glass cases. But his court was sordid rather than grand. He furnished his residences in a drab style which his disappointed visitors found too bourgeois. He obtained relaxation from his hunting by playing cards for high stakes till the early hours; he enjoyed most of all bawdy stories about barrack rooms and Jews. He lacked generosity; he made donations to charity only when pressed for them. His marriage was a gloomy one. His bride, the twenty-seven-year-old daughter of the duke of Modena, was unequivocally ugly, with a face one half of which was larger than the other. She was passionately reactionary; she was ruled by a Jesuit, who, however, is said to have betrayed all her secrets; but then her principal topic of conversation was pilgrimages. The pretender's court was in Austria, at Frohsdorf, where a painful boredom kept a retinue of aristocrats busy with petty intrigues and with the reproduction of the etiquette of the court of Louis XIV. Nevertheless, seeing in the comte de Chambord not a man but the embodiment of a principle, these followers closed their eyes to his defects, his dullness and coarseness, and worshipped him. The ultimate power of decision was left with a man for whose personal qualities his abler followers had no respect.

Because he lived in Austria, Chambord was able to maintain more easily his independence of the legitimists in France, but also to ignore their advice. His policy was determined instead by his constant companions, the comte de Blacas, the comte de Vaussay and above all the duc de Levis. Levis's ideas could be summarised in the word prudence: his great aim was to prevent Chambord from committing himself, and indeed he got Chambord to declare repeatedly that he would make no decisions as pretender, that all controversial questions would be left until he returned to the throne. This attitude could be presented as the one which would make fewest enemies, but it was not one which could rally new support or win the popular imagination. Chambord, however, did not see his role as that of an agitator. He was waiting for the French to see the errors of their ways. His basic principle, reiterated in all his proclamations, was simply that hereditary monarchy was the 'unique port of salvation in which they would at last find peace'. He was asking for a return to a faith, for France to 'confide her destinies' to him. He was confident that no other form of government could take root in France because only monarchy was morally justified, and morality, for him, meant renunciation of personal desire in favour of a divinely preordained order. Republics involved social anarchy, and 'favoured all forms of greed and all forms of utopias'. He would wait till men abandoned their selfish aspirations. Monarchy, as he saw it, was almost identical with religion. There would clearly have had to be a very drastic transformation of French life, as it was in the nineteenth century, before such a restoration could be feasible. Occasionally, it is true, Chambord, under pressure, made some ostensible concessions to his times. He issued denials that he wanted 'power without limits'. 'Why do men still suspect me of wishing to be nothing but the king of a privileged caste, or to use a phrase they employ, the king of the *ancien régime*, of the old nobility and of the old court?' He did indeed hope to be leader of the whole nation. He promised 'the exclusion of all arbitrary rule, the reign and the respect of laws, honesty and justice everywhere, the country sincerely represented, voting taxes and co-operating in the making of laws, expenses really controlled, property, individual and religious liberty inviolable and sacred, communal and departmental administration judiciously and progressively decentralised, and free access for all to honours and social advantages'. But these promises were balanced by contradictions and reservations. Though he talked of 'submitting with confidence the acts of government to the serious control of freely elected representatives', he made it clear that government would remain in the hands of the king. He sometimes mentioned 'judicious liberty' but far more often emphasised the need for 'strong authority', for the first essentials were security, stability and order. Though he denied that he wished to go back to the *ancien régime*, 'no one', he declared, 'under any pretext, will obtain from me that I should become the legitimate king of the Revolution', for the revolutionary spirit was the great obstacle to the kind of liberty he envisaged. He promised decentralisation, but partly to prevent a repetition of 1830, when a Parisian coup had overthrown the dynasty overnight, and partly to 'create amongst us a natural hierarchy conforming to the spirit of equality'. This meant the creation of a new élite of local notables to strengthen the decaying aristocracy. He encouraged workers' associations, but with corporatist intentions; they would become 'important collective interests with the right to be represented and to be heard', but he assumed that they would use this right only to obtain 'efficacious protection' and that they would cease to be 'instruments of trouble and revolution'. He promised, in language which parodied Louis Napoleon's, 'to march at the head of the social movement', but only 'to give it a moderate and useful direction', and ultimately he placed his faith in a general return to religion. 'The Christian worker' was the basis of his dream of 'social resurrection'. He firmly supported the pope's temporal power, because 'the fall of the most august sovereignty in this world would bring down with it all other sovereignties'; but he was so anxious to keep the Church subordinate to him in France that he forbade his courtiers to address bishops as *monseigneur* and ordered that they be called *monsieur*. He alone was *Monseigneur*. It was not all that easy, therefore, for contemporaries to see exactly what Chambord stood for, and their suspicions of a return to the past were not without foundation. Chambord's policy was never clearly expressed: his declaration on agriculture, for example, stated that the sufferings of the peasants 'merited serious attention' but did not give any hint that he had any practical solutions. So when Chambord declared in 1871: 'I bring back only religion, concord and peace', that was, to a great many Frenchmen, probably both too little and too much.[1]

It is doubtful, however, whether legitimism was a political force because of the adherence of many people to this ideology. Those who advised Chambord to remain silent or vague did

---

[1] Pierre de Luz, *Henri V* (1931); comte de Chambord, *Correspondance de 1841 à 1879* (5th edition 1880), 377, 395, 159–60, 283, 357, 209, 267, 396, 155, 330; comte René Monti de Rezé, *Souvenirs sur le comte de Chambord* (1930); Marvin L. Brown, Jr., *The Comte de Chambord* (Durham, N.C., 1967); baron J. G. de Hyde de Neuville, *Mémoires et souvenirs* (1892); baron M. de Damas, *Mémoires 1785–1862* (1922); marquis René de Belleval, *Souvenirs de ma jeunesse* (1895).

so because they appreciated that legitimism was a web of personal and social relationships rather than a party with a programme. The nobility formed its backbone. It might be assumed, therefore, that this was another basic cause of the weakness of legitimism, for the nobility are supposed to have been a dying class in the nineteenth century. This was not quite the case. On the contrary, the nobility survived the Revolution, despite severe trials and heavy losses. In 1789 there were perhaps 12,000 families in the hereditary nobility, making some 60,000 individuals in all. In addition there were about 100,000 people with personal titles not transmissible to their heirs. In the mid twentieth century there were between 3,600 and 4,400 families—about 30,000 individuals—who were genuinely noble. But in addition there were about 15,000 families falsely claiming to be noble, and in most cases accepted as noble by society at large. That is to say, the demand for ennoblement did not cease with the Revolution. Before then the king had been able to obtain very substantial revenues by selling offices carrying ennoblement to a bourgeoisie eager for honorific distinction and for recognition by the state. In the eighteenth century the law courts and the financial civil service succeeded in obtaining recognition that tenure of their posts carried with it ennoblement. Even the regent doctors of universities claimed nobility by virtue of their degrees, but unsuccessfully, except for those of the papal university of Avignon, and there are today fifteen families enjoying nobility by virtue of descent from doctors of law of that institution. The nobility, for all its exclusiveness, had long been a class, membership of which could be bought or won. A large proportion of the real nobles surviving today obtained their titles by this kind of purchase. Only 20 per cent of them can trace their titles to the fifteenth century or earlier. Another 19 per cent go back to the sixteenth, and 17 per cent to the seventeenth century. That leaves 40 per cent who go back no further than the eighteenth century (20 per cent to the eighteenth century, 8 per cent to Napoleon, and 12 per cent to creations of 1814–70).[1] In 1848 titles were abolished and their public use forbidden, but

---

[1] H. Jougla de Morenas, *Noblesse 38* (1938), 101. These statistics should be regarded as very rough, in view of the numerous inaccuracies in the genealogical dictionaries.

Napoleon III allowed the use of those which could be proved to be genuine. His law of 1858, penalising false titles, has remained the basis of jurisprudence to this day. Numerous bills introduced into parliament to abolish titles have all failed. Napoleon III allowed people to obtain confirmation of their titles by having them scrutinised by a committee of the ministry of justice, in return for the payment of a substantial fee: 5,000 francs for a duke, 2,000 for a marquis or count. (These sums were levied when an *ancien régime* title was claimed. For imperial titles, a dukedom cost only 200 francs and a barony 65 francs.) This proved a useful if small source of revenue, for the Fourth Republic found it worth while in 1947 to increase the fee to a flat rate for all kinds and grades, 100,000 francs a time. In this way, people were able to resuscitate their nobility after the fall of the monarchy.

But in addition there were legal means by which they could give themselves the appearance of nobility. The law allowed the 'rectification' of birth certificates, and large numbers of people continued to appeal to the courts to insert the particule *de* into their names. The particule was not a legal sign of nobility, but it gave the impression of aristocratic descent. It was in this way that a bourgeois called Laurent Delatre in 1829 got the court of Poitiers to 'rectify' his name to de Lattre de Tassigny, supposedly to distinguish him from relatives, by adding the name of a piece of land he owned. It is from this para-ennoblement that the Marshal descended. It was in the same way that a certain Millon in 1864 was allowed to call himself Millon de Montherlant, which is how the writer obtained his name. The war of 1914–18 provided additional means for these changes, for the heirs of a soldier who had died on the field of battle were allowed to add his name to theirs. This is said to have ennobled more people than ever Louis XIV did. Thanks to it the future minister Felix Gaillard became Gaillard d'Aimé; the magnate of ready-made tailoring Thiery became Thiery de Bercegol du Moulin. A person who became famous under a pseudonym was allowed to make it part of his real name and thus Franz Wiener became in 1910 François Wiener de Croisset. Aristocratic lines on the point of becoming extinct were known to advertise for heirs, and it was thus that in 1864 M. Achille Lacroix was adopted by the last

Vimeur de Rochambeau and became Lacroix de Vimeur de Rochambeau. Modification of spelling was not difficult to obtain and it was such modification that allowed the Marshal Franchet d'Esperey to appear noble, though originally called Desperey. The Action Française leader Beau de Loménie obtained his particule only in 1923. The organiser of the employers' federation, the Comité des Forges, Robert Pinot, became in 1922 Pinot-Périgord de Villechenon. Ennoblement thus continued even though there was no monarchy. Since the republic did not enforce the legislation against the false use of titles, these multiplied more vigorously than ever. Many genuinely noble families adopted titles to which they had no legal claim. Different branches of the Chambrun family called themselves indiscriminately marquis, count and viscount, without, as the genealogists claimed, proper justification. But even more vast numbers of people with no claim to nobility of any kind, adopted the title of their choice to consecrate their social aspirations. The *Bottin Mondain* has been the directory in which more or less anyone who pays for an entry can include his name among the aristocracy, with the title of his choice, giving as his address whatever château he had bought or whatever house he cared to call a château.[1]

This survival and re-creation of nobility would not have been very significant if it had not been allied with a preservation, and in many cases a reinforcement, of the nobility's wealth. The nobles lost land at the Revolution but apparently far less than is popularly assumed. Hitherto studies of noble wealth have concentrated on the *ancien régime* and there is no proper account of it since then; but sample investigations suggest they remained a powerful economic force. Thus in the 1840s, there were 530 electors paying over 5,000 francs in tax; about 238 of these were noble and another 78 had noble pretensions. Of the 58 paying over 10,000 francs in tax, 39 were noble. Louis-Philippe's reign, which is considered as representing the triumph of the bourgeoisie, still had a very strong aristocratic element in it.[2] The fate of these noble fortunes over the nine-

---

[1] Henry Bellamy, 'Vraie et fausse noblesse', issue of *Le Crapouillot* for Mar. 1937; Philippe du Puy de Clinchamps, *La Noblesse* (1949); G. Chaix d'Est Ange, *Dictionnaire des familles françaises anciennes ou notables à la fin du 19ᵉ siècle* (Évreux, 1903–29), 20 vols. but reaching only as far as the letter G.

[2] A. J. Tudesq, *Les Grands Notables en France 1840–9* (1964), 1. 431.

teenth century has been studied in the department of Loir-et-Cher. Here between 1848 and 1914 the nobles lost only about 10 per cent of their land. Small property ownership progressed considerably, but at the expense of only a section of the nobility. A few noble families with large estates disappeared, but it was rather the families with small estates which succumbed. In individual communes noble property fell by between 10 and 50 per cent, but the most powerful families strengthened their position. Thus the largest estate in the department was still owned in 1914 by the family of the comte de Chambord— over 5,000 hectares. The comte de La Roche-Aymond inherited the estates of the prince de Chalais-Périgord and added 600 hectares more to them, so that he had 4,500 in all. The duc de La Rochefoucauld-Doudeauville added 1,100 hectares to the inheritance of 3,200 hectares he picked up from the duchesse de Montmorency. The marquis de Vibraye doubled his estate between 1848 and 1914. The prince de Broglie, a new-comer to the area, bought the property of the d'Etchegoyen family and added to it, so that by 1914 he had 2,079 hectares.[1]

Nor was it only in agriculture that the wealthy nobility prospered. Many of them went into industry and finance. 30 per cent of the directors of the railway companies in 1902 were noblemen, 23 per cent of those of the large steel and banking companies. In the insurance companies which survived nationalisation after the war of 1939–45, 20 per cent of the directors were noble.[2] Judicious marriages brought a considerable amount of new capital. The American heiress had already arrived in Paris in the mid nineteenth century. In 1887 Charles de Talleyrand-Périgord, duc de Dino, having divorced Elizabeth Beers Curtis, married Adele Sampson, widow of Levington Stevens, with a dowry, it was said, of 7 million dollars. In 1888 the duc Decazes married Miss Singer for 2 million dollars. Comte Boni de Castellane made news when his bride Anna Gould brought him 15 million dollars, though she then divorced him and married another Talleyrand, prince de Sagan. Rothschild heiresses were snapped up by the duc de Gramont, the prince de Ligne and the prince de Wagram.

---

[1] Georges Dupeux, *Aspects de l'histoire sociale et politique du Loir-et-Cher 1848–1914* (1962), 577.
[2] Jesse Pitts, *The Bourgeois Family* (Harvard Ph.D. thesis, 1957), 235 n.

Prince de Chalençon-Polignac married a Mirès, the duc de Richelieu a Heine, the marquis de Plancy an Oppenheim, the marquis de Breteuil a Fould.[1] These were only exceptional windfalls for a class which was constantly recombining its wealth. The family of Rocheouart-Mortemart, in the late nineteenth century, listed 124 noble families to which it was allied.[2] There was little prospect of a noble inheritance falling into a commoner's hands.

Marrying advantageously and judiciously was a major part of the art of being noble; and that is why the principal intellectual activity of the nobleman was often the study of genealogy and heraldry, of family titles and property deeds. A nobleman needed to understand these, since so much of his status and livelihood depended on them. A considerable amount of money was spent in proving nobility, hiring so-called experts to do research and publishing lavishly produced books illustrating obscure genealogies, in a manner reminiscent of the upstart English gentry of the seventeenth century. As a result, the nobles were considered to have an excessively selfish concern with their own family problems, but their concern was justified by their own criteria. Maintaining and adding lustre to their families was inevitable to a class drawing its principal distinction from heredity. Concern with their own style of life became increasingly important after they had lost the fiscal and feudal privileges which had differentiated them, particularly since this was the way they could keep control of their rebellious children. The nobles were associated with the cult of the family, but internal family disputes possibly reached the most bitter and violent levels among them. Under the *ancien régime*, they made enormous use of *lettres de cachet* to control their children. In the nineteenth century, they called in the Church and the schools to help them instil obedience, but these were only partially successful.

To explain the survival of legitimism by the fact that the nobles supported it is to beg many questions. The nobles were the hereditary enemies of the king, whose centralisation they

---

[1] Vicomte A. de Royer, *Y a-t-il une noblesse française?* (n.d., about 1899), 34–9.

[2] Vicomte A. de Royer, *Nous avons une noblesse française (1899–1901)*, 1. 188; comte Adrien de Louvencourt, *Notices sur les familles nobles existant actuellement dans le département de la Somme* (Abbeville, 1909).

abhorred, of the people, whom they had long oppressed with exactions, of the bourgeoisie, whose urban power they resented and whose enlightenment they feared. The alliance of classes behind legitimism in the nineteenth century was thus not a natural one nor a historical one, and this was an important weakness in legitimism. Even the clergy, who are inseparably linked with the nobles as supporters of the king, had a long history of rivalry with them. Under the *ancien régime*, there had been no spectacular conflicts but a great deal of petty wrangling in the inevitable struggle for dominance in the village, disputes about the tithes the nobles had usurped, hostility to the interference of bishops from outside. The alliance of Church and aristocracy in the nineteenth century was cemented by the latter's return to religion but it should perhaps be regarded as a tactical alliance, inspired by the terrors of the Revolution and a surviving belief that unity was the best way to preserve the authority of both over the masses. In due course the Church would see that there was nothing sacred in the alliance. The same was true of the nobles' alliance with the king. They were old enemies who believed they stood to gain from union against the republican enemy, but the nobles with time learnt how to extract what they really wanted from the republic. They learnt to become magnates of a new sort in a pseudo-egalitarian society. The strengthening of the economic position of the rich aristocracy in the nineteenth century inevitably led to apostasy from the royal cause, even though allegiance might be maintained at the verbal level. The petty nobility who, by the twentieth century, found it difficult to survive on their landed estates made their peace with the centralising state and accepted civil service jobs. Though the nobles had always stood basically for decentralisation, they had never been united about this. Younger sons, left without land, had gone off to join the royal ranks, and sometimes returned to their native provinces to implement state policy against their families. Whether state or aristocracy was dominant in such a situation in a particular area depended on the political situation, on the economic strength of the local nobility, and on how the rivals judged each other. If the state officials felt intimidated by the 'influence' of the local nobles, they would prefer to ally with them, and the civil servants would become part of local clienteles. That is what was meant when certain areas of France were said to be ruled by the aristocracy, but it was a rule preserved by timidity on the part of the state.

For in the age of universal suffrage, ultimately the power of the nobles rested on whether they could get the masses to vote for them. The poor had many good reasons for overthrowing the yoke of their former masters. The legitimists, particularly the backwoodsmen amongst them, feared progress and modernisation, education, luxury and the material benefits brought by the towns. 'Their leisure was haunted', as their own *Gazette de France* said, 'by the phantom of the terrible reactions of the proletariat.' La Rochefoucauld duc de Doudeauville wrote to Napoleon in 1852 urging him to reduce the number of scholarships offered by the state, so as to stop the ambitious from starting revolutions in their search for better jobs.[1] On the other hand the nobles in many regions for long succeeded in retaining their hold on the peasants by the links of patronage. Even if this was to a certain extent resented it was decisive so long as the nobles appeared to be, as members of the local community, safer protectors against the dangerous, unknown forces of the outside world. The liberation of the peasants from their control would come only when the peasants were either integrated into the general life of the nation, or developed institutions of their own to give them an independence which they could not have individually. Until then, the nobles could insist on deference being paid to them as leaders of the local community. The comte de Comminges has described his youth in a château in Haute-Garonne, where 'customs kept their feudal colours'. The peasants, he said, were very attached to his father 'even though he treated them like blacks'. Feudal services were demanded of them long after their legal abolition. 'When my father had need of stones, for example, he had the fact shouted out at the end of mass' and the peasants found it worth their while to help him.[2] The survival of this relationship depended on the efficiency of the nobles in giving the peasants reciprocal protection and help. Their return to the land after 1830 strengthened their bonds with the peasants, for there was much more in this patronage than the economic control the nobles could exert on their tenants.

[1] Halt, *Papiers sauvés des Tuileries* (1871), 7.   [2] Tudesq, I. 122.

The influence of the legitimists depended more than anything else on their activity. In the west their activity was agricultural, social, communal. In the south it was much more
conspiratorial. The nobles there specialised in forming secret
societies. These went under different names, but had in common a hierarchical organisation, elaborate ritual and a secrecy
which was often as fascinating as what any revolutionary group
could offer. The 'Grand Priory' of the south-west had a whole
network of 'Little Priories', run by the rich, but admitting the
poor without subscription, provided they took oaths to obey
orders and keep their secrets. Often arms were distributed.[1]
Occasionally the freemason lodges were captured and turned
into legitimist organisations. In the Vaucluse they called themselves the Association of the Friends of Order, organised in
legions, centuries and decuries, ready for armed revolt. These
clubs were most successful where they could fit into village
rivalries, family feuds and religious animosities. Many villages
welcomed them not for doctrinal reasons so much as because
the republican club called for a counterweight. The constitutional question, of whether France should be a monarchy or
a republic, became the label under which old animosities were
made respectable. The organisation of these clubs reveals as
much about the clan structure of the provinces as about
political opinions.[2] In the towns, the nobles had another
effective way of bringing together the great variety of people
whose personal interests could be organised to serve their
cause. Charitable and mutual benefit societies were frequently
given a political direction. The most powerful of all, the Society
of St. Vincent de Paul, had over 30,000 members by 1859 in
1,300 branches, becoming so powerful a weapon of the legitimist
revival that Napoleon III dissolved it. It recruited people like
shopkeepers, artisans, waiters, cab-drivers, employees of the
Church, clerks, servants and not a few factory workers. In
elections these would often act as a significant army of propagandists, particularly when the societies worked closely with
a politically passionate clergy. Members of the middle class

---

[1] Jeanne Lesparre, 'Les Partis politiques dans la Haute Garonne à la fin de la
monarchie de juillet', in J. Godechot, *La Révolution de 1848 à Toulouse* (1948), 31–5.
[2] Jack Barnouin, 'Le Parti légitimiste en Vaucluse 1830–1883' (unpublished
D.E.S. mémoire, n.d. (1950s) in Montpellier University Library).

could hope to be admitted into the salons of the aristocracy if they joined.[1] Legitimism could appeal to many forms of snobbishness and interest.

But its appeal was limited for two reasons. First, the legitimists could not always conceal their patronising contempt for the middle classes, contradicting their pretence that they were a national party open to all. Too many of them made it clear that true virtue could be found only among peasants, and that the towns were a source of vice and artificiality. Secondly, they were indecisive in their use of governmental influence to bolster their own. Chambord told them to resign *en masse* from all their jobs and elected offices. Some did. A few of them lost little by their withdrawal, but in most cases this gave their opponents the chance to dangle alternative patronage before the electorate. However, perhaps about a half of the legitimists decided to stay on as *conseillers généraux*. In 1852 there were about 450–500 of them elected out of 2,500.[2] After 1848 they stayed on in local politics with greatest perseverance in the west, and in the 1950s this was still the area where their descendants survived as mayors.

To a certain extent the collapse of legitimism was the result of abdication, of the nobles abandoning their traditional leadership. It was also the result of the state and other classes learning to do what they had done and offer an alternative leadership. The nobles were distributed very unequally over France. There were over thirty departments where there were so few of them that it was a simple matter for the state to monopolise the sources of influence or for professional politicians to emerge as intermediaries. This set up a pattern which spread to other areas. Where the nobles could be played off against other forces, or where they gave up the initiative in politics, they were soon supplanted. The process by which the masses came to look elsewhere for personal advantages was occasionally dramatically rapid—1848 witnessed some complete volte-faces

---

[1] See Austin Gough on Catholic Legitimism and liberal Bonapartism in Theodore Zeldin (ed.), *Conflicts in French Society* (1970), 107–17. On the working-class alliance see Denise Lefort, 'Le Parti légitimiste dans les Bouches du Rhône 1830–1848' (D.E.S. mémoire Aix-en-Provence, 1956, unpublished, kindly lent by M. Pierre Guiral).

[2] A. Gough, 'French Legitimism and Catholicism 1851–65' (Oxford, D.Phil. thesis, 1967, unpublished), 127–8.

—but more usually it was slow, as new customs were evolved to go with universal suffrage. In some areas the Bonapartists

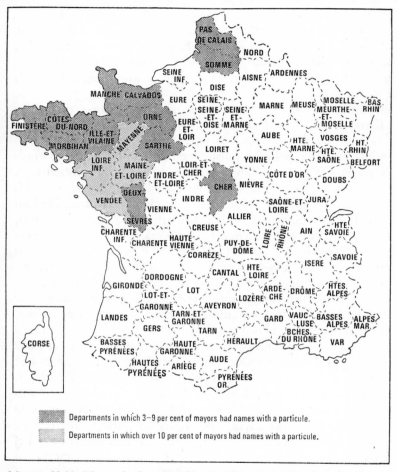

MAP 13. Noble Mayors in the 1950s. Based on Fauvet and Mendras: *Les Paysans et la politique* (1958), 35

played a crucial role in the destruction of noble influence, but even they did not always have the self-confidence to see how vulnerable that influence was. The Third Republic of course did not have national parties which put up candidates at elections in every single constituency. The electors therefore often did not have a choice put before them. That is why the decline of noble influence was both fitful and slow.[1]

Skilful leadership could probably have postponed this decline. The politically experienced legitimist nobles complained bitterly about Chambord's inability to provide any form of leadership at all. They criticised him for refusing to come out clearly in favour of any particular tactic, for ruling the party despotically, ignoring the advice of men with far more knowledge of French conditions than he possessed; for being a bad manager of men, incapable of putting to good use the great stores of loyalty offered to him; for disowning all his really active and zealous followers by his cautious, inactive prudence; for dealing so unimaginatively with his public relations, a field in which Louis Napoleon had shown how much could be accomplished with quite moderate effort. Chambord preferred to organise his forces so that they remained firmly under his control. He had a central committee of twelve, known as the Bureau du Roi, which met, at least in theory, once a week in Paris. Its members were selected by him, presided over by the duc de Lévis or in his absence, the duc des Cars or General de Saint Priest (a replica of des Cars, but rather more sociable and conciliatory). Far from considering this as an advisory body, he made it clear that its function was executive, to carry out his instructions, and to inform him about opinion in France.[2] Under the Third Republic the organisation was tightened up. France was divided into three regions, each placed under the control of one man. In 1877 these three sections were united and put under the marquis de Dreux-Brézé, through whom all communications to and from Chambord passed. Under him were departmental committees of twenty members, nominated directly by Chambord, meeting every two months in the chief town of the department to discuss the political situation, to organise elections, collect funds and stimulate the formation of a local royalist press. Their minutes were sent to Chambord. Wherever possible, similar sub-committees were set up in each *arrondissement*. The press was given a central party line to follow by the royalist newsagency. This had been founded in 1848

---

[1] The excellent thesis of Jean Meyer, *La Noblesse bretonne au 18ᵉ siècle* (1966), is the most comprehensive study of the nobility in the modern period.

[2] Membership in Noailles, *Le Bureau du roi* (1932), 96–9.

by a M. de St Chéron, who every evening sent out reports, in the form of letters, on the political news of the day, to provincial newspapers. By 1867 he had a consortium of seven royalist papers subscribing to his service. Some rich legitimists then combined to make it possible for this correspondence to be sent to all royalist papers in the country, which it continued to do till 1883. Between 1873 and 1883 the *Correspondance St. Chéron* was supplemented by a *Correspondance A–Z* (later known as *Les Nouvelles*) which was set up by the royalist deputies to supply the provincial press with summaries of parliamentary proceedings. To this was soon added a daily leading article, designed to be published throughout the country by papers without the resources to employ their own leader-writers. Equally important was the organisation of banquets, which enabled legitimists to meet and to win recruits. The acceptance of an invitation to one of these, at which a toast to the king was drunk, was one of the regular ways by which outsiders came into the royalist ranks. Funds for all these activities were always inadequate. Only in 1879 was a central party treasury organised, on an original basis particularly suited to French conditions, for it was well known that the regular payment of subscriptions was not a national characteristic. The legitimists were invited to lend Chambord money at 3 per cent interest. They would promise not to ask for their money back, until either Chambord died or became king. It was understood that meanwhile Chambord could do as he pleased with the money. Comte Arthur de Rougé was appointed to travel round France collecting for the fund. Thus did Chambord build up a national organisation completely at his command. Rebels could have no place in it.[1]

When the revolution of 1848 broke out, Chambord was presented with a real opportunity, for that revolution was a triumph for the legitimists as well as for the republicans. Lamartine offered Berryer a ministry in his provisional government. At least a hundred legitimists were elected to the constituent assembly. But by themselves they did not have a majority. They needed, at the very least, the support of the Orleanists, the supporters of Louis-Philippe who believed in monarchy, provided it was constitutional monarchy. Why was their alliance never obtained?

[1] Marquis de Dreux-Brézé, *Notes et souvenirs* (1899), 24–30, 43–4, 55–63.

The Orleanists in theory differed from the legitimists on four crucial points. They denied that the king ruled by divine right, as most of the legitimists claimed. It is true they did not go to the opposite extreme of claiming that sovereignty lay with the people—at least in 1830 they defeated a motion proclaiming this. They took some pains, like the English Whigs in 1688, to conceal the fact that Charles X had been evicted: they declared the throne vacant and put Louis-Philippe on it as his hereditary successor. If sovereignty lay anywhere, they would say it lay in parliament. Secondly, they did not wish the king himself to govern. They increased the power of parliament considerably, giving it the right to initiate laws, they abolished hereditary peerages, they deprived Louis-Philippe of the emergency powers Charles X had used in 1830. But they were divided amongst themselves as to exactly how much power the monarch should have. Louis-Philippe and Guizot thought that he should take an active part in government, while Thiers and his followers wanted him to reign but not rule. All were agreed, however, on some form of parliamentary government. Thirdly, the Orleanists declared in 1830 that the Catholic religion was no longer the state religion and that the king should no longer be instituted in a religious ceremony. They included many unbelievers and Protestants among their numbers—though after 1848 many of the former returned to the faith, or at least came to see the value of religion in maintaining order among the masses. But this new emphasis on religion came at a time when religion was losing its hold on the masses. Fourthly, the Orleanists accepted the French Revolution, while the legitimists on the whole did not. The Orleanists, despite their conservatism, were not a party of the *ancien régime*.

At the personal level, the Orleanists' leaders were ambitious men with whom compromise would not be easy, even if agreement could be reached in principle. There was great variety of character and opinion among them. Orleanism often seems to have some of the qualities of a mirage, or of a chameleon. It is difficult both to locate and to characterise.

Louis-Philippe, though he had served in the revolutionary army, was no radical. He had opposed the elder branch as much from personal rivalry as from principle. Though he loved to talk about his youth, he hardly ever mentioned the Revolution, because his memories of it filled him with horror. He had no wish to set Europe on fire; his dearest wish was to be accepted as a real king by the other sovereigns of Europe and a policy of conservatism at home and peace abroad was the way he hoped to obtain this. He greatly enjoyed being king: he had a passion for power and an immense conceit about his political abilities. He felt he must have power also because if he behaved as a constitutional king and left politics to the politicians, they would produce a terrible mess, revolution, war, and he would be overthrown. That is why he worked so hard to influence policy and why he was so absorbed in intrigues with the politicians, to the neglect of the masses. Since he thought the support of Europe was essential to his throne, he concentrated on foreign policy, and indeed read only foreign newspapers. So far from being content with being a constitutional monarch, he regretted bitterly that the rules of the game forbade him to make speeches in parliament. He cultivated his image as a bourgeois king in order to win popularity. 'I know the French. I know how to manage them,' he confided to an ambassador. His umbrella, his famous wig were publicity stunts. His walks through the streets of Paris, unaccompanied and unguarded, were not the sign of a bourgeois nature, but a deliberate policy by a very brave man, for he probably held the record for attempted royal assassinations. A real bourgeois would have stayed at home. He put on the façade of simplicity in order to conceal his intrigues and ambitions. He had a profound belief in the efficacy of flattery as a means of getting his own way, and he used it constantly on his ministers, and on the nation at large —by his bourgeois act. He had a special employee with card indexes to enable him to greet everybody he met with a friendly inquiry about their family. So far from being a bourgeois, he was one of the richest men in France, largely by inheritance from the duc de Bourbon-Penthièvre, Louis XIV's bastard who had been one of the richest men of his day. He devoted a great deal of time after the Revolution to reconstituting his estates, which he succeeded in doing after a lot of litigation. His principal relaxation was the restoration of the crumbling château of Versailles, where he recreated the ancient glory of his ancestors without the expense or danger of war. So far from being a believer in parliamentary government, he devoted his reign to preventing its establishment, systematically working to diminish the authority of the prime minister, playing off the politicians against each other, so that they were unable to impose the supremacy of parliament upon him.

Louis-Philippe's most distinguished minister, Guizot, who survived until 1874, was a Protestant of dour and pessimistic outlook. He was profoundly convinced of the weakness and inadequacy of human nature. He believed that the eighteenth century had been very wrong in thinking that man was naturally good and omnipotent. Guizot conceived of right government as the fulfilment of the will of God. This meant the rule of reason and justice—not of popular sovereignty, which Guizot execrated. The problem for him was not how to discover the popular will but how to discover what was reasonable; and he believed that there was an elect minority with the capacity to judge what was reasonable. The rule of the upper bourgeoisie was justified in his eyes because it was the rule of merit, of men who demand not what they want but only what they ought to want. They represented the rule of duty and of justice, rather than of will and of rights. Though Guizot won fame as the theorist of representative government, his use of that phrase was misleading. He envisaged not the voluntary delegation of rights but on the contrary the exclusion of individual wills from power and the prevention of universal suffrage and popular sovereignty. For him liberty meant what is just. He distinguished between political and personal rights. All men were equal to him in the sense that they had an equal right to be protected by the state and to behave as they pleased provided they did not interfere with the rights of others. But political decisions concern others besides oneself: therefore they should be exercised only by those who were properly qualified. Guizot confused legitimacy and liberty. For him, liberty was obedience to the will of God, not to that of man. The revolution of 1830 had therefore created no new rights: on the contrary, it had created the danger of anarchy, so that though Guizot accepted the revolutions of 1789 and 1830 he thought they had done enough and that a halt must be called to the revolutionary spirit. His famous exhortation, 'get rich', meant earn the leisure and the qualities needed to make you one of the elect who can see reason: it was the very opposite of the materialism it was often taken for. Guizot's major reform was in education, because this was the means to knowledge and reason. He did not however carry this to the point of wanting to turn the peasants into educated men but rather to moralise them, to teach them why they should be contented with their lot. It was not the business of the state to interfere in the social or economic order, but only to establish the free conditions in which God's will should be done. 'Real virtue in institutions consists in calling citizens to the duties which they are fit to carry out.' Guizot could not therefore be forced easily into compromise. His theories could be interpreted as being basically a rationalisation of the *status quo*. He was a doctrinaire, who turned accidents into principles, and who achieved his dominance by providing arguments for salving the conscience of the rich. He was possibly a blind politician, but it should not be concluded that he was wildly out of touch with his age. Rather his weakness was that he represented only one aspect of it. His comment on the revolution of 1848 which overthrew his system was, 'God has spoken.'[1]

There is a great difference between the way Orleanism worked and what it came to stand for. Under Louis-Philippe it was authoritarian, based on a narrow electorate of propertied men, with king, parliament and ministers struggling indecisively for supremacy, no party system in any organised sense and even greater ambiguities in its local manifestations. After 1848 it came to stand for liberalism, parliamentary government and the imitation of England.[2] Its opponents condemned it as egotistically middle class, materialist, timid in its foreign policy and blind in its social attitudes. All these descriptions have some truth in them. Orleanism certainly meant different things when it was in power and when it was not. If it could be summarised in the phrase the *juste milieu*, that meant that it stood for compromise, and so its character depended on circumstances. It was the party of the most vocal and fluent section of the community, which interpreted Orleanism in an infinite

[1] There is a valuable guide to the large bibliography on the Orléans monarchy, which falls outside the period covered by this book, in Douglas Johnson, *Guizot* (1963), 443–56.
[2] See in particular Pierre Guiral, *Prévost-Paradol* (1955), which is a rich source of information about liberal thought under Napoleon III in general, as well as an illuminating biography of an important thinker.

variety of ways. Its theorists—many of them men of exceptional distinction—had a more elevated notion of how it should work than the practical politicians and indeed than they themselves had when faced with the problems of power. It is perhaps better to talk therefore about Orleanists than about Orleanism. It will then at once become apparent how inevitably evanescent this party was.

Some members were monarchists. They were Orleanists because they had been dissatisfied with the way the Bourbons had interpreted monarchy. But by judging the personal merits and policy of the king, they made monarchy so fragile and so open to debate that it became very difficult to win really firm support from them. Some were liberals. But as a result they could not reject a liberal empire or a liberal republic and many of them indeed rallied to one or both of these, however reluctantly. Some were personally devoted to the Orléans family. But among these there were men who had also served Napoleon, and indeed many whose families had emerged into fame and wealth in the upheavals of the Revolution and empire: they had other loyalties too. 1830 had been a triumph for Napoleon's followers—exiled in opposition after 1815—as much as for anyone else. As one moves down the social scale, the Orleanists appear increasingly as notables keen to enjoy local influence but anxious for government backing. In one sense they could be allies of the legitimists, in that some of them favoured decentralisation, though they were of course rivals of the legitimists for local influence. But they also needed a more powerful consecration of their status than mere respect for their personal merits and their wealth, which they saw was increasingly challenged by what they called the forces of anarchy. Their complacency concealed a deeper insecurity. They needed a strong government to check the popular and revolutionary threats to their position. The Orléans monarchy had once seemed just right, but out of power it was of little use to them. These notables, who could be classified as the 'friends of government' would make friends with any government that was willing. With appropriate reservations, they supported empire and republic in turn. Men in business, men in industry, men of ambition, men with pretensions, could not for ever work against a centralised state which had so much to offer.

For all these reasons, the Orleanists were always uncertain allies.

They were also allies of diminishing influence. Orleanists were a corps of officers but it was never clear that they had much of an army. Under Louis-Philippe, they had no occasion to apply themselves to winning a mass following. After 1848 they adapted themselves to the new conditions of politics with varying degrees of success. In about 50 per cent of municipalities the mayors in office before the Revolution were re-elected in July 1848: the greatest change occurred in the south and south-west, but in the north and north-west they survived best. Universal suffrage did not at once destroy their rule. Those Orleanists who were expelled in 1848 often returned a year or two later, on the wave of conservatism or panic that swept the provinces. Conscious of the dangers of division, they often united with the legitimists and conservative republicans as part of a 'moderate' alliance, to fight the red menace. In certain regions, the socialists and the Bonapartists succeeded in putting up new leaders to the electorate and throwing the Orleanists out. The Orleanists survived where there was no such challenge to them, and they lasted so long as they knew how to play politics in these new conditions. In the process, they became less and less Orleanist, or at least their Orleanism became increasingly, as it were, a mere perfume that they could not get rid of, implying a certain family origin, a certain distinction and opinions which were once liberal. If Orleanists were men of substance or education, aspiring to consequence and respect in a mass age, there could not, by definition, be many of them.

The expectation of a monarchist restoration after 1848 was widespread, but it was based on a whole series of illusions. Orleanists and legitimists had more things dividing than uniting them. The leaders of both parties knew they could not work with each other. Thiers could never expect office from a monarchy he had done so much to overthrow. Broglie knew there was no chance of real constitutionalism from Chambord. Chambord for his part had enormous difficulty even in talking to the Orleanists, whom he considered to be rebels. When they sent emissaries to him to negotiate, he refused to discuss the basis for a treaty. Exasperated by Napoleon III's success, and relying on the fact that Chambord was childless, the Orleanists offered to help restore him to the throne, putting up with his deficiencies until their own pretender could succeed him on his death. In this way the breach of the royalists might be healed. But they always had reservations, as can be seen from a letter Louis-Philippe's son wrote to Chambord in 1857: 'In expressing to you our sincere desire to see France summon you one day to its throne, in speaking to you of our wish to devote all our efforts to obtain this result, I did not offer you a blind and indefinite support. A preliminary agreement would have been necessary to determine our conditions. Our conditions could be summarised in three points which our convictions and the respect we owe to our family's past, demand that we should never abandon. First, the maintenance of the tricolour flag, which is today in the eyes of France the symbol of the new state of society—the incarnation of the principles consecrated since 1789. Secondly, the re-establishment of constitutional government. Thirdly, the agreement of the national will to this re-establishment as well as to the restoration of the dynasty.'[1]

The longer the restoration was postponed, the slimmer were its chances. The plots for a legitimist military *coup* in 1849 and for an Orleanist one in 1851 never materialised. Once Napoleon III was in power there was no chance of success in such an enterprise, particularly since the emperor gave the royalists plenty of freedom to continue their agitation and refrained from driving them to desperate acts. In 1871 at last their chance came. The National Assembly had a royalist majority. But this was highly deceptive. The nation elected them because it wanted peace, because the Bonapartists were associated with defeat and the republicans wanted to carry on the war. Had the royalists then succeeded in bringing about a restoration, the nation might well have refused to accept their act. Civil war might well have followed. The failure to bring Chambord to the throne, which is so often explained in personal and parliamentary terms, was probably inevitable, given the way such large sections of society had assumed a new attitude to politics since 1830. The negotiations themselves were in any case conducted on a basis of mutual ignorance and equivocation, so that their collapse in 1873 was not surprising. The dramatic announcement at the last minute that Henry V (as Chambord

[1] Marquis de Noailles, *Le Bureau du roi 1848-73* (1932), 148.

was to be known) refused to abandon his ancestral white flag should not be interpreted as a sudden caprice which ended a movement on the verge of success. On the contrary, Chambord's attachment to his flag had long been known, but it had been concealed by his declaring that it was something he would decide upon after his return and by his seclusion which prevented people from realising just how much it meant to him. In 1871 Chambord had stated that he was determined not to accept the tricolour, but his entourage kept the fact secret to prevent the negotiations from coming to a halt. In reality the negotiations never had a chance, even before they had begun.

This insurmountable difficulty to a restoration—because it was symbolically very important—was matched by equal difficulties on the Orleanist side. The reconciliation which took place between Chambord and the Orleanist pretender, the comte de Paris, did not have the full support of the Orleanists. At least a quarter of the Orleanist deputies in the assembly of 1871 preferred a republic to a monarchy with Chambord as king, whatever guarantees he might give. The duc de Broglie, it is said, was so repelled by Chambord's authoritarianism that he hoped to make such impossible demands on Chambord as a condition of restoration, that the latter would abdicate in favour of the comte de Paris. The duc d'Aumale, fourth son of Louis-Philippe, a man of great personal distinction, sometime Governor-General of Algeria, and a man also of great personal wealth, intrigued against the restoration not only of Chambord but of Paris too, hoping that if it proved impossible to restore either, then the assembly would elect him president of the republic or lieutenant-general of the kingdom. His ambition was to be a stadtholder. He issued a declaration that if France preferred a republic, he was ready to serve it. He got himself elected to parliament in 1871 and mixed with all the deputies as an equal, in a proper republican manner. When he was elected to the French Academy in 1871, he asked to be addressed as monsieur, not monseigneur. He refused to visit Chambord and left most of his money to the nation, not to his family.

Finally, even the personal reconciliation between Chambord and Paris in August 1873 was not as complete as was thought. Chambord consented to see Paris on condition that the latter

made an agreed public statement to him, in which were to be
included the words that Paris came 'to resume his place in the
family'. Paris at the last moment omitted this phrase and substituted one that Chambord 'would have no competitor among
members of his family'. The political divisions, that is to say,
continued. At their meeting, not a word was uttered about
politics. Their reconciliation was superficial. It was perhaps just
as well that it all came to nothing. Chambord would have
caused far more confusion had he pretended to be what he was
not. His honesty spared France a second revolution of 1830. But
his failure in 1873 made him more suspicious than ever of co-
operating with people who did not share his attitudes and who
wished to change him. He ordered his followers to abstain from
all electoral alliances. Many of his followers on their side, dis-
heartened by his obstinacy, withdrew from politics, never to re-
emerge. When Chambord died in 1883, his party was a weak
relic of what it had been, particularly when compared to the
republicans, now firmly entrenched in power. His more die-
hard supporters proclaimed Don Juan of Spain, who had
married Chambord's sister, pretender, creating a new legitimist
religion, but one without practical significance. The great
majority of legitimists, however, acknowledged the comte de
Paris as the new leader. Legitimists and Orleanists were at last
united. This ought to have meant that the forces of royalism
were greatly strengthened, but the legitimists were not keen to
have much to do with Paris. Chambord's organisation was
wound up and the funds he had collected were paid back to the
subscribers. A new era was opened up.

The comte de Paris, who was pretender from 1883 till his
death in 1894, had far more vigour, intelligence and suppleness
in him. He was the son of Louis-Philippe's very promising son
the duc d'Orléans, who had been noted for his energy and
liberalism, and of a Protestant German princess, though he was
brought up as a pious Catholic. Born in 1838, he was, from the
age of ten, educated in England, for which he developed a great
affection and admiration: it was not without significance that
he spent most of his life there, whereas Chambord had preferred to live in Austria. He was a well-travelled man. He
visited the U.S.A. and served in General MacClellan's army

in the Civil War. He toured the cotton factories of Lancashire, which stimulated an interest in social problems. In 1869 he published a book on the trade unions of England, advocating participation in profits. He welcomed as 'one of the finest pieces of progress of our century . . . the raising of charity to the status of a social duty and a political right'. When allowed back to France in 1872, he toured the factories there too. He appeared to be one of the first socialist millionaires—socialist perhaps only in a rather loose sense, but very much a millionaire. He had an income, it was said, of 500,000 francs (£20,000) a year, which increased very considerably thanks to the legacies from royalist supporters, culminating in one bequest of 20 million francs from Madame de Galliera in 1888.[1]

The comte de Paris was the very opposite of Chambord also in that he was above all an opportunist who, far from adhering to his principles as Chambord had done, was determined to broaden his appeal as widely as possible. He cloaked his policy, which came near to being power at any price, beneath a grave and pious exterior and a family life of irreproachable chastity: he had all the appearances, someone said, of a scholarly German professor, but he was profoundly ambitious. To begin with, he converted himself from an Orleanist into a legitimist, in an attempt to make the fusion of the royalists into a reality. After having made his submission to Chambord in 1873, he became an intransigent upholder of heredity and rejected all attempts to put forward his candidature in place of Chambord's. On Chambord's death he assumed the title of Philippe VII instead of Louis-Philippe II. He attempted to unite under him the Catholics who suspected his anticlerical antecedents, the Protestants who expected him to remember his mother's religion, and the sceptics who wanted toleration; to win back the conservatives who had gone over to the republic with Thiers, and at the same time to keep legitimists and Orleanists loyal. It was perhaps an impossible task, but by February 1884 the fusion of the royalists had been successfully achieved in at least 24 departments. On the other hand, the legitimists remained aloof in at least 13 departments and in 13 others there was no

[1] Marquis de Flers, Le Comte de Paris (1888), 114; Marcel Barrière, Les Princes d'Orléans (1933), 182–3. Eugène Dufeuille (who was in charge of distributing the comte de Paris's subsidies to the royalist press), Réflexions d'un monarchiste (1900).

royalist organisation or activity at all. But he captured the royalist press: 130 royalist newspapers supported him, against only 13 hostile ones.[1]

Secondly, for Chambord's policy of abstention, Paris substituted one of vigorous action. He became an energetic, hard-working party leader. He realised that the majority of Frenchmen were not royalist. It was just possible that they were conservative. So in the elections of 1885 he ordered the monarchists to stand not as such, but as conservatives, to carry out a new fusion between monarchism and all the forces of the right, on the basis of the widespread dissatisfaction with the republic, its ineffectual parliamentarianism, its financial deficits, its expensive colonial policy, its menacing anticlericalism. In October 1885 his *Union conservatrice* obtained 177 seats against the 129 won by the republicans. This brilliant victory, however, was made possible by the dissension of the republicans who, rallying together in the second ballot, succeeded in winning the elections as a whole. Replying to his threat, they sent him into exile.

But, from Sheen House near Richmond, he pressed on with his policy of a programme which would offer something to as many people as possible. To those who were simply conservative, he promised to re-establish order and firm government, but to avoid reaction, to reconcile the principles of historic tradition with modern institutions, to bring in a monarchy which could be freely accepted by the nation but which would not be a slave to 'the sovereignty of numbers'. To the Catholics he offered liberty of education and the end of persecution. To please the Bonapartists he proposed to hold a plebiscite, or at least to summon a constituent assembly, to approve his restoration: indeed he borrowed large sections of their programme. Attempting to benefit from the disillusionment with parliamentary government (once so dear to the Orleanists, but taken over by the republicans), he said that universal suffrage made constitutional monarchy as it had existed between 1815 and 1848 out of date. Parliament would no longer be supreme: the king would govern with the co-operation of the chambers (a

[1] Samuel M. Osgood, *French Royalism under the Third and Fourth Republics* (The Hague, 1960), 36–7. In 1892, however, an anonymous article on 'Les Anciens Partis' talked of about 250 newspapers being royalist. *Le Figaro* (2 Apr. 1892), 59.

phrase to be found also in Bonapartist manifestos) and ministers would no longer be at the mercy of majorities. He kept quiet about divine right—and also about his economic and social policy.[1]

The comte de Paris did not wish, however, to return by means of a *coup d'état*. He was not made for conspiracy or violence. He was determined that if he got the throne he should be strong enough to keep it. His hope therefore was that the republic would collapse and that he would then be the man to whom France would look to end the ensuing chaos. In 1888 he played his last card to bring about this situation. Under the influence of two former Bonapartists who had become royalists, the president of the *Union conservatrice*, baron de Mackau, and the journalist Arthur Meyer, he decided to back General Boulanger. A leading royalist lady, the duchesse d'Uzès, put up a large sum of money to pay for the great adventure in which the general would throw the republicans out of office and end parliamentary government. At the last moment, of course, Boulanger lost his nerve. The collapse of his movement was the greatest blow the royalists had suffered since 1873. The prospect of a restoration, which had re-emerged as a possibility, ceased for ever to be a serious one. Not only was there a widespread desertion from the royalists as a defeated party, but there was a fatal split among the royalists themselves. The Orleanist wing, for whom parliamentary government was sacred, realised that the pretender no longer stood for the principles they cherished. They wanted constitutional monarchy and not just monarchy, and the republicans now appeared as the true defenders of parliaments. The Orleanists in any case could hardly continue to support a pretender who, infuriated by their refusal to obey his instructions to support Boulanger, publicly damned them with disgrace, abruptly ending many old personal friendships. Paris was at the same time equally enraged with those who had advised him to join the Boulangists, so that the relations in the royalist party became strained in the extreme. Paris had been an able pretender, but adversity revealed his limitations. He could not bear to take the blame for the disaster and did not know how to maintain hope in his defeated ranks. As one who knew him well wrote: 'He could not bear to be

[1] Text in Flers, 406–10.

contradicted; he enjoyed flattery; he could never admit that he was wrong. Even the superiority of certain scientists and great scholars offended him as though he was their rival.'[1] Perhaps in fairness to him it ought to be added that in this same fateful year of 1889 his doctors told him he had an incurable disease and could not last long.

Monarchism died finally in the *ralliement*, when the republicans dropped their attacks on the Church and offered the supporters of monarchy and empire union against socialism. Pope Leo XIII urged Catholics to accept the republic, which had proved its solidity. The comte de Paris himself, while resenting this papal interference, admitted that the royalist cause was hopeless and put his faith in religion: there was no chance, he thought, until France became Christian once more. After 1894, therefore, royalism ceased to be a major force in politics. It will be seen elsewhere how it was reincarnated in the Action Française, but that was in response to new conditions, which require separate examination.

The pretenders who succeeded the comte de Paris stood at the very fringes of political life. The duc d'Orléans (1869–1926) educated at Sandhurst, a specialist on hunting in Nepal and interested more in food and women than in politics, was so lazy, superstitious and indecisive that he could not be considered a serious pretender. His opinions were anachronistic to the point of dreaming of the absolute monarchy of the Merovingians, and being unable to bear the mention of democracy. His entourage, led by the comte Eugène de Lur-Saluces, the owner of the Château d'Yquem, was composed almost entirely of legitimists. He had followers who wished to link his name with the nationalist movement and present him in this refurbished guise, but with little success.[2] In 1896 the police estimated that there were royalist committees in only thirty departments. In 1908 an article on the royalist movement suggested that hardly one elector out of ten would know the name of the pretender. The activities of the duc d'Orléans became a matter mainly for the social columns of the *Gaulois*. Though he reluctantly came to accept Action Française in 1911, he was never its

[1] Barrière, 161–3.
[2] Eugène Godefroy, *Quelques années de politique royaliste: du ralliement à la haute Cour 1892–1899* (1900), xii–xiii, 213.

driving force.[1] The duc de Guise, who was the next pretender, 1926–40, led a retired life. His son the comte de Paris (born in 1908) for a time had hopes of reviving the royalist cause. He started a newspaper in 1934, *Le Courrier royal*, resuscitated the royalists' organisation, repudiated Action Française, had himself interviewed repeatedly by the press and published a book expounding his programme in detail. During the war, there was a plan to proclaim him head of a provisional government in Algiers, but Eisenhower scotched it. An opinion poll held on 1 January 1945 showed that only 6 per cent of the nation thought that the royalist party had an important role in France and about 75 per cent thought not.[2]

[1] E. Dimnet, 'The Neo-Royalist Movement in France', *Nineteenth Century* (Aug. 1908), 287–93. Georges Cerbeland Salagnac, *Quatre Règnes en exil* (1947). The Action Française will be dealt with in volume 2, but there is great deal of information relevant to the pretenders in the excellent standard work by Eugen Weber, *Action Française* (Stanford, Cal., 1962).

[2] Comte de Paris, *Essai sur le gouvernement de demain* (1936); Osgood, 137–81, has a good account of this later history.

16. The Genius in Politics

FRANCE in the nineteenth century cannot be understood without an appreciation of the role of the utopians, any more than the Revolution of 1789 can be without a knowledge of the *philosophes* of the Enlightenment. The utopians were historically important because they introduced the *genius* into politics. The genius became the nucleus of a new class, challenging the state, demanding power and threatening to dismember the traditional centralised authority, an élite like the nobles, and with similar pretensions. Genius, men generally believed in this period, could not be acquired; it was something that one was born with, but, as with nobility, one could associate with it and become assimilated to it. One of the marks of genius was that one was understood by other geniuses. So those who accepted their leadership could enter into this new class of *illuminés*. Against the nobles, who spoke as the representatives of local community life, the geniuses spoke in the name of a new community of the enlightened. The genius indeed was a new kind of individual ideal. Hitherto the chivalric hero, the saint, the courtier, the *honnête homme*, had been universal models, but only for private conduct. The attainment of that status brought self-gratification, honour and public respect, but no political power. The genius was much more dangerous. Until the eighteenth century *génie* had meant simply talent or skill. But with Diderot the genius was held up as an exceptional apparition, standing outside his time, almost outside his species, whose importance was that he could perceive truths others could not. He was therefore not subject to common standards, ethical rules or controls. He produced great ideas and 'every great idea', as Lamartine said, 'is a struggle against society, a revolution'.

The basis for this new role for the intellectuals had been laid in the eighteenth century. Around 1700 the 'man of letters' usually lived in a state of insecurity and constraint, shackled by an arbitrary censorship exercised simultaneously by the king, the *parlement* and the Sorbonne. He often had to use pseudonyms or conceal his identity altogether. Only in the second half of the century did a few of them manage to live by their pens. These successes did a good deal to raise the status of what was becoming almost a profession. The government began employing writers to influence public opinion, 'to prepare the way for legislation', as Moreau described his own function. But it was slow to accept advice from them. 'It is not up to an obscure writer,' said L'Averdy, 'who often has not a hundred écus to his name, to indoctrinate persons in office.' A book about L'Homme de lettres published in 1764, by one of them, admitted with regret that they were 'kept outside the state'.[1] The first stage in their ascent was for them to win honour, respect and security. They did not think of power yet. They solicited the subsidies, pensions and presents, of tiny amounts, which the government gave them—a mark at once of patronage, disdain and fear. They were for long treated essentially as entertainers. Voltaire complained of the 'excessive disparagement attached to this equivocal state' of the writer. Montesquieu was appalled when he learnt that his son was developing a taste for learning: 'He will never be anything', he exclaimed in horror, 'but a man of letters, an eccentric like me.' He had planned to buy him a state office, the mark of respectability (which he of course enjoyed also, as member of a parlement). However, as the censorship relaxed, books on politics gave the writers increasing authority. Foreign admirers in particular did much to raise their status. It was the philosophes, not the nobles, whom the visitors from abroad came to see. That was one reason why the writers assumed with such vigour the mission of French culture abroad. Frederick II invited Voltaire to his table, to the horror of the French king. On the eve of the Revolution in 1778, Mercier wrote, 'the influence of writers is such that they can today proclaim their power and no longer disguise the legitimate authority they have over men's minds'.[2]

The Revolution confirmed their power in a dramatic way, but not least because its enemies accused them of having been a principal cause of it. Of course historians no longer believe that the theories of the philosophes produced the collapse of the ancien régime. Much more emphasis is laid on the aristocratic revival and the attempt by the nobles to recapture power from

---

[1] 'En dehors de l'état': Garnier, L'Homme de lettres (1764), chapter 5.
[2] L. S. Mercier, De la littérature et des littérateurs (1778).

the king. After the catastrophe they brought about, the nobles
put the blame on the writers. However, even at this apparent
zenith of their influence, when the democratic ideas some of
them preached introduced immense new forces into the political
arena, the writers did not claim any direct power for themselves. They had seen themselves as advisers to those in power.
Voltaire had supported enlightened despotism. Montesquieu
had supported the *parlements* against the king. If they envisaged
power, it was only very indirectly. 'If opinion is queen of the
world,' wrote Voltaire, 'the *philosophes* govern that queen.'
This was the germ from which the pretensions of the nineteenth-
century utopians developed. Until then they had not entirely
emerged from their inferiority complex or from the antique
pretence that love of letters was incompatible with cupidity
or ambition.[1]

The literary romantics rationalised this complex into the
doctrine that the genius was inevitably doomed to be misunder-
stood. The genius was a prophet, but a prophet in the wilder-
ness. They accepted that he should be met by incomprehension,
that his lot should be suffering and even martyrdom, and that
he should obtain acknowledgement of his worth only from
posterity. Stendhal thought people would start reading him
only forty years after his death.[2] But Saint-Simon broke away
from this arrogant modesty by greatly expanding the idea of
genius. To the skills of the man of letters and the imagination
of the artist he added the new knowledge and new prestige
of the scientist. Combining these he produced what was in
effect the intellectual. He claimed for him the spiritual power
in the state. The romantics had thought principally of themselves as geniuses; it was a tiny group they placed at the
apex. Saint-Simon certainly thought he too was divinely
endowed, but he greatly broadened the class of those who
had the gifts and the wisdom to lead mankind. In effect, he
proposed the intellectuals as a new clergy, and not much
smaller in number. The amazing thing was that he won

---

[1] Peter Gay, *Voltaire's Politics* (Princeton, N.J., 1959), 34, 93; Maurice Pellisson,
Les Hommes de lettres au 18ᵉ siècle (1911), 41, 50, 239–40; C. P. Duclos, *Considérations
sur les mœurs de ce siècle* (1751), 263; Lucien Brunel, *Les Philosophes et l'Académie
française* (1884); D. T. Pottinger, *The French Book Trade in the Ancien Régime 1500–
1791* (Cambridge, Mass., 1958), 353.

[2] G. R. Besser, *Balzac's Concept of Genius* (Geneva, 1969).

disciples of this kind, who did constitute a visible élite and who succeeded in making their mark. His proposals for the rule of the intellectuals were not just a dream, they became almost a reality. The Saint-Simonians were, in some ways, a new aristocracy.

The utopians, more generally, effected the democratisation of genius. New schemes for the reorganisation of society pullulated in large numbers. The socialist utopians, of whom there are about a dozen major ones, are only the better known of a vast host of writers in similar vein, but with lesser talent. New religions, mysticisms, visions, prophecies—new ideas of all kinds and even more new mixtures of old ideas—acquired respectability, when established authority was no longer powerful enough to condemn them to ridicule or oblivion. The Revolution suggested that change was perfectly possible, that utopias need not be purely theoretical. It was now open to any man to have ideas and publish and propagate them. It is in this way that the intellectual in politics arrived. His self-consciousness was stimulated all the more by the fact that he won hostility as well as esteem. In his favour the phrenologists claimed that genius could be recognised in the conformation of the skull. The doctors, however, defending the superiority of their profession, replied that there was no physiological distinction between genius and madness. Dr. Lelut decried genius as a form of hallucination. Dr. Moreau de Tours called genius a neurosis: 'The constitution of many men of genius', he wrote, 'is really the same as that of idiots.' This was a battle, between the genius and the philistine, which was to continue unabated, and to be a permanent limitation on the power of the intellectuals.[1]

The utopians were important also because of their special relationship with public opinion—a relationship which could be compared again with the links of the nobility with the local community. The majority of utopians—and most notably Fourier and Proudhon—became popular because they tried to give expression to widely felt aspirations. There were some precedents for this in the eighteenth century. Rousseau in particular had obtained an immediate echo from a vast audience which recognised something of themselves in him or

[1] For further details, see vol. 2, chapter on psychology.

reflected his mood. But though most of the *philosophes* had seen themselves as leaders if not creators of public opinion, they had been primarily concerned with creating the conditions in which public opinion could express itself freely; they had on the whole sought to influence governments rather than to investigate the problems of the ordinary man. The latter was the second stage, and the utopians gave a great deal of attention to it. It is important to assess the extent to which the utopians were speaking for a public opinion which pre-existed, and the extent to which they created a new kind of consciousness. This is difficult to do. The utopian message was taken up like a popular song, whose tune one heard repeated everywhere, even if the words were often got wrong. The analogy with songs is not purely metaphorical. A lot of these new ideas were propagated in songs.[1] No one has yet made a proper study of these. They might well contain clues for the formulation of an archaeology of popular sentiment. The utopians were thus significant at two levels, that of the intellectuals and that of the masses. With them a new range of public opinion made itself felt in politics. The extent to which the ideas of the utopians were acceptable in 1848 can be seen from the way so many of them were spontaneously elected to the Constituent Assembly. Buchez was its first president. Louis Blanc and Hippolyte Carnot were members of its first provisional government. Pierre Leroux, Proudhon, the revolutionaries Barbès and Martin Bernard, the Fourierist Considérant were all deputies. It will be seen in due course just how widespread was the participation of their disciples in public life.

The intellectuals had a vital role to play in many of these utopias, because one of the characteristics of the utopias was that they were designed to unite mankind, in a moral harmony of which the intellectuals would inevitably be the priests. The utopians reacted against the eighteenth century's destructive criticism. They represented the longing for order and peace after the Revolution. Unlike the *philosophes* who saw the Church as their great enemy, the utopians were much more favourable towards religion, and they sought only to reform Catholicism. They hoped that this new religion—which they

---

[1] *La Chanson française* (3 vols., published by Éditions Sociales, Classiques du peuple), especially vol. 2, *Le Pamphlet du pauvre*, edited by Pierre Brochon (1957).

variously called the new Christianity or the Religion of Humanity—would provide the spiritual cement to hold the society of the future together. So whereas liberty had been the watchword of the previous century, fraternity was that of utopians. Fraternity was expressed in religious terms as association or co-operation, as opposed to capitalist exploitation. The utopians were concerned with the whole mass of the population and wanted to bring everybody in to share in the new era. But because they laid so much stress on the moral or spiritual basis of this unification, they—as formulators of the new creed—held a key position.

Saint-Simon (1760–1825) was not only a genius who sometimes resembled a madman; he actually spent a period in a sanatorium for mental diseases and received treatment from the celebrated Dr. Pinel. His political ideas represent only one part of a life filled with a large variety of hare-brained schemes. Having lost his mother at the age of seven, he spent his youth torn between rebellion against an aged and authoritarian father and guilt at not deserving affection but repeatedly pleading for it. His was first of all a philosophy for orphans. He had passionate relationships with a Prussian count and former ambassador, with whose money he became a speculator in national lands, and then with a succession of young men, whom he adopted as his pupils. His life was a constant search for patrons to back him and collaborators to assist him in the elaboration of his ideas. He was a man of great warmth, with an ardent longing for its reciprocation, never hesitating to beg for it, but always confident in his own genius and ever optimistic, except for an attempted suicide in a moment when he felt particularly abandoned. His character was reflected in his preaching of fraternity. The summary of his New Christianity was: 'Love one another and help one another.' This plea, which historians tend to interpret in political or religious terms, may have received such widespread adhesion because it was also an appeal against the coldness of contemporary family life, by a generation no longer ashamed of its emotions. 'To do great things', said Saint-Simon, 'it is necessary to be passionate.' He might have been the founder of modern sociology, as some now claim, or even a precursor of *Planification*[1]

[1] Pierre Ansart, *Sociologie de Saint-Simon* (1970); François Perroux and P. M.

but that is no excuse for assuming that his thinking was predominantly rational. His mysticism, illuminism and apocalyptic style were an essential part of him, as they were of so many of his contemporaries. The importance of Saint-Simon, indeed, is that he helped to shift thinking from the theoretical to the emotional.

He also turned away from the political interests of the eighteenth century, to a stress on social and economic forces. He was not interested in party politics, or in increasing the participation of people in government. Progress for him involved practical achievements: the building of roads, and massive investment for great public works. The aim of every institution should be 'the moral, intellectual and physical amelioration of the most numerous and poorest class'. The way to do this was to stimulate economic development and public education. The condition of the exercise of the rights of citizenship should be the passing of an examination on the 'national catechism'. Saint-Simon was not a democrat. He wished to deprive those who were idle of their leadership of society: the idle nobles, the 'metaphysicians and lawyers' were his great enemies. He proposed to give power to the *industriels*, i.e. to those who worked, which included all classes, but he expected policy to be formed by the 'most important' of these, the great manufacturers and leading financiers, merchants and agriculturalists. He never made it clear how they would be chosen, except that he thought that constitutions should reflect economic realities. He wished to abolish inheritance, but not property, nor inequality produced by merit. His slogan was: 'To each according to his capacities, and to each capacity according to his works.' This was meritocracy—and some say technocracy, the foreshadowing of a managerial revolution. But Saint-Simon in his last years moved away from this, since the rich were not appreciating him, and he turned increasingly to the working class. The ambiguities in his theories were never resolved, and that is why he won support from every class except the nobility, to whom alone he was constantly hostile. The ambiguity is partly explicable, however, because government was a matter of little importance to him. He looked forward to the virtual elimination of the

Schuhl, *Saint-simonisme et pari pour l'industrie XIX–XXe siècles* (*Économie et Sociétés*, Apr. 1970).

state, since a harmonious social order would deprive it of most of its usual functions. He was opposed to government regulation; his method of producing change was not revolution, nor violence, but persuasion, enlightenment, and a free rein to economic forces. His ideal was peace (whereas governments fought wars) and prosperity (and governments exacted taxes). This deep-rooted hostility to the state will be seen again and again throughout this period—balancing the fawning on it. Saint-Simon contained the contradiction within him: he begged the king to become 'the first of the industrialists'.

Though Saint-Simon stressed economics, and said that politics was 'the science of production', he also thought that no society could exist without 'common moral ideas'. He wanted scientists and artists to enjoy a power equal to that of industrialists, to provide the latter with inspiration, and to rouse the masses to greater exertions for the mutual good. Whereas the eighteenth-century *philosophes* had seen men as more or less the same, and therefore equal, Saint-Simon, following the doctors Cabanis and Bichat who wrote in the early nineteenth century, believed in their diversity and uniqueness. There were different types of men, suited to different occupations. That is why he distinguished between these three classes. In his view people were not concerned with equality but with the expression of their individuality. Society must therefore aim only for harmony among these inequalities. The equality of the eighteenth century had brought brutal competition and strife, which he wished to eliminate. His whole doctrine was a reaction against the destructiveness of the *philosophes*. The age of criticism was over: Saint-Simon wanted an age of harmony. Hence the importance of the intellectuals, whose duty it was to minister to the new spiritual unity, replacing the corrupt clergy but in some ways perpetuating their functions. The problem of conflict within this new order was never analysed by Saint-Simon, and this might be a justification for calling him a utopian. He blithely assumed employers were the natural leaders of the workers. But this was a problem other utopians tried to solve.[1]

[1] Saint-Simon's main works have recently been republished in 6 volumes (1969–70); there is also a good selection in his *Œuvres choisies* (3 vols., Brussels, 1859). An excellent biography is by Frank E. Manuel, *The New World of Henri Saint-Simon* (Cambridge, Mass., 1956). For a full guide see Jean Walch, *Bibliographie de Saint-Simon* (1967).

Just as Saint-Simon's thought passed through several phases, so the movement which developed his ideas was equally varied. Saint-Simonianism, as it flourished in the mid nineteenth century, laid stress on religion, financial investment, and the emancipation of both the proletariat and that class of whom so little had hitherto been heard in the writings of political theorists, women. But this programme failed to win a mass following. Though bits of it were absorbed into other mass movements, Saint-Simonianism remained the creed of an élite. It was a very remarkable and influential élite. It included about a hundred graduates of the École Polytechnique. Engineers, managers, financiers and writers adopted it with a fervid enthusiasm. As a result, one aspect of it was magnified and it has appeared ever since as a doctrine for technocrats. But some of these men also had emotional problems, and they gave Saint-Simonianism an even more esoteric slant. This was another reason why it did not become a mass movement. These particularly active disciples were men who had failed to enter the traditional ruling class; a good number of them were Jews. Olinde Rodrigues had wanted to go to the École Normale but had been prevented by his Jewish birth and had had to become a stockbroker instead. Gustave d'Eichtal—in turn a Jew, a Catholic and a Saint-Simonian—wrote in 1866 that 'there has perhaps not been a single person among the Saint-Simonians who was not urged to join by some family trouble'.[1] Bazard was illegitimate and had been maltreated as a consequence. Enfantin had been stopped from joining the King's Bodyguard by the bankruptcy of his father. Saint-Simonianism was financed by wealthy men who devoted their inheritances to preaching that inheritance should be abolished.

It was above all Enfantin (1796–1864) who turned Saint-Simonianism into a religion, and almost a monastic order. He was a man of great personal beauty and quite exceptional charm, able to exercise a magnetic fascination, so that highly intelligent men worshipped him and listened respectfully while he talked absolute nonsense. For in a prolonged phase of mystical enthusiasm, Enfantin introduced the strangest ideas into the doctrine. He got his disciples to proclaim him *Le Père*—

[1] G. Weill, *L'École saint-simonienne. Son histoire, son influence jusqu'à nos jours* (1896), 21, 47 n.

the 'industrial pope'—a title he had embroidered on his clothes. He got them to follow him first into monastic seclusion at Menilmontant, and then on a fantastic journey to the East in search of the ideal woman, *La Mère*. He got them to wear strange uniforms, which buttoned at the back, to remind them that people were interdependent. The managing director of Le Creusot, the giant ironworks, resigned his job to follow him, in company with distinguished officers, mining engineers, civil servants and a professor of medicine. Enfantin's gifts modified the nature of the movement. He was above all an unctuous confessor, and in no way made to be the leader of a rabble. He therefore objected to his supporters mixing too much with the unconverted world. He preferred a closed society, held together by ardent emotion. The life in this community was 'intense, the feelings of fraternity touching, the exaltation of hopes prodigious; the faithful tasted pure joy and knew unbridled enthusiasm'. Inevitably, however, this put into the background any idea of associating the workers in ending the exploitation of man by man, which represented the socialist side of Saint-Simon's original doctrine. A proposal by a few in 1839 to start a *Social Party* was rejected. Internal conflicts brought an end to this mystical phase. By 1848 Saint-Simonianism had no organisation.[1]

The importance of Saint-Simonianism in the future was to lie in the way of thinking it had imprinted in their youth on many subsequently important individuals. Its direct influence, however, has generally been exaggerated. It is true that in 1848 the ministry of education was run by three Saint-Simonians,[2] but it left no permanent achievements. Their short-lived National School of Administration to produce higher civil servants may look like a Saint-Simonian attempt to train a new ruling class based on merit, just as the lectures for women which they authorised at the Collège de France seemed to implement Saint-Simon's new deal for the female sex. However, when in March 1848 some sixty Saint-Simonians held a meeting to decide what concerted action they should take, they could

[1] Hippolyte Carnot, 'Sur le Saint-Simonisme', *Séances et travaux de l'Académie des sciences morales et politiques*, 28 (1887), 122–55; S. Charlety, *Histoire du saint-simonisme* (1931); Léon Brothier, *Du Parti social* (1839), quoted by Weill, 97 n.
[2] Hippolyte Carnot, assisted by Jean Reynaud and Édouard Charton.

reach no agreement. The master's doctrines had been too variously interpreted; there had been a complete failure to establish priorities. Gustave d'Eichtal thought the moment had come to found a religious democracy, but as a first step he urged the erection of a statue of Moses in the Place de la Concorde. Olinde Rodrigues drew up a constitution for the new republic, abolishing the right to make wills, limiting inheritance to the direct line only, proposing participation in profits for the workers and political rights for women, but at the same time he gave the directing role in the running of the country to the University and the Institut. Prosper Enfantin, for his part, suggested that the state should buy up all the railways, then the mines and then all the factories making products for the railways; and it should take over industrial planning. However, he also said the time had come to establish the Kingdom of God. Since this proved to be not immediately practicable, he founded a newspaper instead, *Le Crédit*. It lost him a great deal of money. He supported Cavaignac but, when he failed, rallied to Louis Napoleon, hoping that he would be strong enough to advance the cause of industrialism. Enfantin's notion that he was called by Providence to give a new place in the social order to the proletariat and to women therefore did not get very far. He ended up a relatively minor business man.

The Saint-Simonians never ran the new industry of the Second Empire, as is too often believed. They never achieved their objective of financing expansion by inflation. The railways they had a hand in were balanced by others in which they played no part. They influenced Napoleon III's Algerian policy perhaps, and also his Mexican adventure, but so did others. Napoleon III cannot really be called one of them. However, they had always used the press in a particularly vigorous manner: they were experts in public relations, and what they bequeathed was not an actual achievement but a myth. Their greatest triumph probably was that some of their doctrines ceased to bear the specific imprint of Saint-Simonianism because everybody came to believe in them.[1]

Charles Fourier (1772–1837) represented a different stratum

[1] Enfantin left enough money for the *Œuvres de Saint-Simon et d'Enfantin* to be published after his death in 47 volumes (1865–78). Cf. Crampon, *La France saint-simonienne à son déclin* (1867).

of society. He looked at the world from an entirely different viewpoint. He was a humble commercial traveller and clerk; his utopia was essentially one for the small man, the consumer, the petty bourgeois. He claimed his discoveries had been started, like Newton's, by an apple: when he saw apples being sold in Paris for a hundred times the price they fetched in the district where they were grown, 'I began to suspect that there must be something radically wrong in the industrial mechanism.' At the age of seven he was punished for telling the truth by his father, a draper, who declared he would never be any good in business; it was then that he swore a Hannibal's oath of eternal hate against commerce. This later hardened into a criticism of the whole social order for which he proposed a complete transformation. 'Harmony' must replace the antagonism of civilisation. Co-operation must replace blind and vicious competition. The parasites of commerce must be done away with. The toil of the peasant, both stupefying and inefficient, must be made a joy. Man was naturally good but society as at present organised corrupted him; it alone was responsible for the conflict between private and public interest, for the repressions and frustrations he suffered. Fourier's purpose was not to improve man, but to liberate him, to allow him to do what he pleased. Unlike his contemporary Robert Owen, who hoped to modify human nature by modifying its environment, Fourier wished to make the environment suit human nature, to satisfy human needs and passions. He denied that any of these passions were vicious and needed to be suppressed (in what was a remarkable foreshadowing of modern psychological theories); in the harmonious state he dreamed of, all of them could be expressed and reconciled. Men wanted principally to eat and drink well, to work in very moderate amounts, at tasks they enjoyed—and not necessarily in the same occupation all the time. They wanted independence and security.

Fourier invented a scheme to achieve all this, without strife, without leaving anyone out and without dispossessing the minority who were well-to-do in the existing order. The world should be organised in *phalanstères*. These would be communities of about 1,600 people, of every variety of age, wealth and character, for the more variety there is, the quicker would harmony be established between them. Ideally the number should be 1,620, for Fourier calculated there were no fewer than 405 different temperaments in each sex. These *phalanstères* would consist of a farm (which would make each one self-sufficient) surrounding a large building (rather like a large eighteenth-century country house or Oxford college in appearance). The building would contain dining-rooms, common rooms, studies and a library; one wing would house the workshops; the rest would be divided into living accommodation, of various types, from the humble room to the luxurious flat. All classes would live a separate family life, but there would be a communal kitchen; meals, available at different prices, would be taken either in the common restaurant, or in private rooms or in the individual apartments. The communal kitchen would not only effect enormous economies in fuel and food, but would also free women from domestic chores; only those who enjoyed cooking would cook; the rest would swell the labour force.

When everyone worked and the waste of competition was eliminated, production would increase fivefold. Only goods of the highest quality would be made, and the most delicious food grown; arduous agriculture would be diminished or mechanised and men would turn rather to horticulture and arboriculture. Far shorter working days would be needed; and men would work only because they enjoyed it. However, men liked to compete and intrigue against each other, so all work would be done in small teams of people who enjoyed being together. Every individual would be a member of different teams, each performing a different job; and he could move around from one to another in the course of the day. The monotony of labour would thus be ended. The team spirit, fostered by prizes, would ensure that work was highly productive. Class distinctions would disappear because no man would be tied to any one occupation. Disagreeable jobs would as far as possible be eliminated. The dirty jobs that were unavoidable would be done by children, who naturally love getting dirty. In civilised society, children were punished for getting dirty, but Fourier finds social use for every human characteristic, however undesirable it may superficially appear. He was a pioneer of education through activity, of the development of the child's natural inclinations; he proposed that children should learn not by playing useless games, but by helping in elementary industrial and agricultural pursuits. This would enable them to discover their vocations freely, since they would be introduced to a large number of different occupations at an early age. He urged useful professional education instead of formal classical courses, but always offered in response to interest expressed by the child. Fourier in other words sought to enable people to do what they pleased, women as well as men. He was bold enough to apply this to sexual relations: some people wished to live with the same partner for life, and they could do so in his *phalanstère* if they wished, but others wanted variety, as they did in their work, and he allows this too, by ingenious schemes which rule out social discrimination against the promiscuous. Crèches are provided, so children are no problem. He prefers indeed that children should all be educated in what is virtually a comprehensive school (of which again he was a pioneer advocate) so that class prejudices should be eliminated.[1]

Fourier wished these *phalanstères* to be voluntarily established by individuals, each subscribing a share of the capital needed. He offered subscribers 33 per cent interest on their capital. He did not wish to overthrow capitalism but to outdo it, to reconcile it with socialism. He believed that property was what all men longed for; he observed that men working on their own account produced twice as much as wage earners in factories in which they had no interest. In the *phalanstère* there would be no more wage earners: he would abolish the proletariat. All would be both capitalists and workers. Those who had no capital at first would receive a share in the *phalanstère* simply by offering their labour; later they would be able to buy shares. The profits of the community would be distributed between all its members, who would be associate owners of it, though in varying degrees. Capital, labour and talent would all draw dividends. There would not be financial equality, but there would be social equality. A minimum income would be guaranteed to all, and pensions for the sick and old. Competition would be replaced by association. The advantages of large-scale production would be combined with co-operative ownership.

Government would be virtually abolished. Positions of

---

[1] David Zeldin, *The Educational Ideas of Charles Fourier* (1969).

leadership in the commune would be by election. Fourier was not interested in politics and thought they could be dispensed with. He waited for the first *phalanstère* to be founded by some rich individual; he asked nothing from the state. When his schemes were universally adopted, he foresaw the establishment of industrial armies where the young would use up surplus energy in great public works instead of in war: among these, he foresaw the piercing of the Suez and Panama Canals and the irrigation of the Sahara Desert.[1]

Fourier's principal works are in six long volumes. They are written in a difficult style, with barely understandable neologisms and numerous eccentricities of presentation; the good sense and prophetic intuition in them is buried in a jungle of wild fantasy which sometimes borders on madness. He obtained few careful readers and was much misinterpreted. His ideas on the relation of the sexes caused scandal. His *phalanstère* was quite wrongly thought to involve common ownership and common living in quasi-military barracks. However, he also won much sympathy and considerably more disciples than Saint-Simon. The bibliography of books and pamphlets dealing with Fourierism is a hundred pages long.[2] The circulation of the Fourierist newspaper rose to 3,700 in 1848, and among its readers was Louis Napoleon. However, this paper did not minister to any closely knit society such as the Saint-Simonians formed.

The man who took over the leadership of Fourier's followers after his death, Victor Considérant (1808–93), adopted a policy which was precisely the opposite to that chosen by Enfantin. Considérant was a graduate of the Polytechnic who resigned his commission as a captain of artillery to devote his very considerable journalistic talents to the cause. He successfully defeated an attempt by one of Fourier's disciples, Just Muiron, to organise a Union des Phalanstériens, which would have meant the creation of something like another Saint-Simonian religious sect.[3] Considérant tried instead to spread knowledge of Fourier's ideas as widely as possible; and he was

[1] C. Fourier, *Œuvres Complètes* (1841); H. Bourgin, *Fourier* (1905).
[2] Giuseppe del Bo, *Charles Fourier e la scuola societaria 1801–1922, saggio bibliografico* (Milan, 1957).
[3] H. Bourgin, *Victor Considérant, son œuvre* (Lyon, 1909), 41, 81.

a vigorous and effective propagandist. He wrote books which clarified the doctrines of Fourier and presented them in a much more vivid and intelligible style. He founded a journal (with financial assistance from an English admirer, Arthur Young) and in 1843 successfully transformed it into a daily newspaper, *La Démocratie pacifique*. Considérant jettisoned the more ridiculous or inconvenient products of Fourier's imagination. He quietly dropped such ideas as that men would in 15,000 years time grow tails with an eye at the end of them and he explicitly abandoned Fourier's opinions on sex. He strengthened the appeal of his doctrines to the middle classes by making it clear that Fourierist socialism was not revolutionary, but essentially a search for the peaceful reconciliation of the antagonisms and class hatreds of present society. Association, he said, meant 'the organisation of all new rights [i.e. the rights of the masses] without hurting vested interests'. He warned the middle classes that if they continued the *laissez-faire* regime, they would soon lose their property and their small businesses, which would become concentrated in the hands of a very few magnates. 'The French bourgeoisie [must] not allow itself to be sheared and despoiled with impunity of its property and be thrown into the proletariat.'[1] At the same time Considérant made Fourierism more attractive to the lower classes. He rebelled against Fourier's apathy towards politics and he gradually became an advocate of democracy. At first he accepted the constitutional monarchy of Louis-Philippe, and merely held that though all had a right to participate in government, the rights of the masses should be adjourned until they had enough competence to understand the issues: they should be treated as minors.[2] However, on 25 February 1848 he came out in favour of the republic and he soon threw in his lot with the left wing. Socialist unity became his watchword: he was outstanding among the socialists for the generosity and modesty with which he treated the rival schools while still disagreeing with them—in sharp contrast to the vituperative bickering of the others.[3] In 1849 he formed a Democratic and Socialist Committee in Paris in collaboration

[1] Victor Considérant, *Principes du socialisme* (first published 1843, reprinted 1847), 13.   [2] Ibid., 77.
[3] Victor Considérant, *Le Socialisme devant le vieux monde* (1848), 31–110.

with Proudhon and Ledru-Rollin; and on 13 July 1849 he joined them in their call to insurrection, though this was in contradiction to his long preaching of pacific methods.[1]

The Fourierists now also relied less on private initiative and assigned a new role to the state. Considérant asked parliament to finance a phalansterian experiment. Victor Hennequin, who was a member of the legislative assembly in 1849, modified the master's doctrines much further. He argued that the desire to experiment in the commune was out of date. It had been understandable in the apparently secure atmosphere of the July Monarchy, but the chaos into which society had fallen after its collapse meant that a more general programme for total reconstruction was needed. He proposed therefore that the state should take over and itself run industries and commercial concerns in which abuses prevailed, rather than try to palliate their abuses by fixing wages and prices. Thus coal was too expensive, the miners were paid too little; the state should exploit the mines itself, though not necessarily all mines. The state should set an example of how to run an industry efficiently and fairly: it should be like the chief orchestra conductor of industry—'but the conductor must not play all the instruments in the orchestra', only give a lead. The state should also buy out the railways and canals which were the 'blood of society' and the insurance companies which created solidarity between the members of the body politic. For the communes he urged a form of municipal socialism: municipal crèches, old age hostels, butchers, bakeries, public gardens and town planning, rural banks and entrepôts for agricultural produce to eliminate the parasitic middlemen and retailers of commerce. While still believing that the regeneration of society would be achieved through a reorganisation of agriculture, in rural communes, Hennequin nevertheless gave consideration to the problems of industrial workers. He proposed pensions for all and favoured the encouragement of trade unions and mixed associations of workers and employers: these would encounter many difficulties but they would give some satisfaction to 'the moral need of the worker who aspires to the status of associate and who will soon be led, by the failure or by the success of

[1] Felix Armand, *Les Fouriéristes et les luttes révolutionnaires de 1848 à 1851* (1948), 41–2, 56–7.

these elementary forms of association, to seek the conditions for normal [or thorough] association in a regenerated commune'. He insisted that 'confiscation, abolition and destruction are not words in our vocabulary'.[1]

Hennequin concentrated on demanding the 'garantist' state, which was the half-way house Fourier had imagined before 'harmony' was established; but the trouble with both ideals was that they were very expensive to achieve. In France only a few attempts were made to set up Fourierist communes. These were disowned by the leaders of the movement because they were only partial experiments, making many compromises; they failed in any case, from want of capital or perseverance. The nearest approach was that of Godin (1817–88). Originally an ordinary metal worker, he was struck on his *tour de France* in 1834 by the poverty of his fellows and the inefficient way they organised their work. Determining to establish a factory on fairer principles, he set up on his own. He invented a new method of making stoves and of enamelling them, so that his business prospered, and grew into a factory. He read Saint-Simon, Owen, Cabet and finally decided that Fourier provided the best guidance on how to organise his factory. In 1859 he was at last wealthy enough to build a 'social palace' near his factory and to introduce solidarity amongst the workers by sharing the profits. He took 5 per cent for his capital, plus his wages as manager and a share of the profits as a worker. All workers received a share of profits likewise in addition to their wages. This was not quite Fourierist, since wages were not abolished, and there were four different grades of workers. However, Godin was sufficiently popular to be elected to parliament in 1871, and when he died in 1888 he left a large part of his fortune, some 2½ million francs, to the *familistière*. Henceforth the 1,200 workers largely owned the factory themselves.[2]

There were some other experiments which, in varying degrees borrowed ideas from Fourier, like 'Le Travail', an association of housepainters, which distributed profits more or less in accord with his principles; but they all soon foundered. There were never any really successful ones in France to serve as

---

[1] Victor Hennequin, *Programme de l'École phalanstérienne* (1848).
[2] Charles Gide, *Les Colonies communistes et coopératives* (1927–8), 131, 181–8; Bernardot, *Le Familistière de Guise et son fondateur* (1889).

models.[1] Fourierist experiments were far more numerous abroad: about thirty at least in the U.S.A., the most famous of which, Brook Farm, was described by one of the participants, Nathaniel Hawthorne, in his *Blithedale Romance* (1852).[2] Fourier was also influential in Russia, though it is interesting that the *phalanstère* built by Petrachevsky in 1848 was burnt down by his peasants, too attached to their traditional ways.[3]

Zola's novel *Le Travail* (1901) has an attractive account of a Fourierist commune, and Eugène Sue's *Les Misères des enfants trouvés* (1851) contains a detailed description of one actually established in Sologne. Fourierism thus passed into literature, into the common French inheritance; but it quickly disappeared as a party and only Charles Gide, the co-operative leader, acknowledged Fourier's influence. In 1895 Georges Sorel wrote, 'Nine out of every ten Frenchmen interested in social questions are partial or illogical Fourierists. No one reads Fourier or even Considérant, but the quintessence of their doctrines or rather of their solutions, has passed into the common domain.'[4] Fourier's ideas were shared out between the socialists and the radicals, blurring the dividing line between them. It is interesting how Considérant, who was a man of extraordinary adaptability, prepared the way for this. After spending most of the Second Empire trying unsuccessfully to found a community in Texas, he refused to stand for parliament during the Third Republic; he insisted that he had no wish to repeat his attempts to found the ideal *phalanstère* and that different efforts were now needed, on 'absolutely scientific bases'. He spent his old age instead attending lectures at the Sorbonne and the Collège de France, so as to be able to marry new knowledge and science with the old ideals. Dressed up in scientific garb, some of the principal elements of Fourierism were in fact revived in Solidarism. It was no accident that a statue of Fourier was erected in Paris only in 1900, when Solidarism reached the height of its influence.[5]

[1] C. Bouglé *Socialismes français* (1946), 130.

[2] A. J. Bestor, *Backwoods Utopias* (1950).

[3] Georges Sourine, *Le Fourierisme en Russie* (1936), 59.

[4] Quoted by Hubert Bourgin, *Fourier* (1905), 581.

[5] At the corner of boulevard de Clichy and rue Caulaincourt. Cf. Gaston Isambert, *Les Idées socialistes en France de 1815 à 1848. Le Socialisme fondé sur la fraternité et l'union des classes* (1905), 197.

Fourier's was a utopia for the petty bourgeoisie. Another, which particularly had in mind the problems of industrial workers and of unemployed artisans, was that of Louis Blanc (1811–82). He was considerably less original that his predecessors: he borrowed Fourier's ideas on association and combined them with Saint-Simon's on authority, to produce a state-sponsored socialism; but he is important for then attempting to reconcile their ideas with universal suffrage and the republic, producing the first democratic brand of socialism. Louis Blanc's father had been a civil servant, sacked after 1815; his mother was the daughter of a Corsican solicitor. He obtained his school education thanks to a scholarship; he was then tutor to the son of an iron master of Arras, from whose 600 workers he learnt something of the problems of industry. He entered into Paris journalism in 1834 and quickly rose to a leading position in the party of *La Réforme*. He was an extremely able writer, with a very vivid and vigorous style: his *Histoire de dix ans 1830–40* (1841–4), a solid work in five volumes, highly readable because of its lively detail, would by itself have made him permanently noteworthy. He achieved his popularity with the masses by his *Organisation du travail* (1839), a practical programme for the immediate introduction of socialism without revolution. His ideal was that state authority should ultimately become unnecessary, but meanwhile he saw it as the instrument of the emancipation of the working classes. He proposed to raise a gigantic loan, and with the proceeds establish 'social workshops', i.e. factories in which co-operative association would be practised. The profits would be shared equally by the workers, but a considerable amount would be set aside for pensions and assistance for the sick, and a further amount would be used to help other workers to buy their own tools, and to set up independently in the same way. Gradually the system of association would spread throughout industry. The social workshops would at first exist side by side with capitalist factories producing the same goods, but their superiority would soon drive the latter out of business. The state would only provide the initial impulse and appoint the first managers; after that it would leave all to the workers themselves, who would elect their own managers. Unlike Fourier, Blanc did not offer the capitalists a share of the profits, but only a fixed, though advantageous, interest on their loan; but like Fourier, he hoped to achieve his reorganisation with their help. He argued, like Fourier, that competition was ruining the bourgeoisie as well as impoverishing the workers; that continuance in it would mean 'war unto death' with England, unless France was willing to confine itself solely to agriculture. He was far from proposing the abolition of all private property: he considered it to be a natural right, though it must not be allowed to produce privilege.[1] However he criticised Saint-Simon's formula 'To each according to his merits' and replaced it by an egalitarian one, 'To each according to his needs'. He disliked the hierarchical and authoritarian aspects of Saint-Simonianism, for he believed that no progress could be achieved without universal suffrage—he defined justice as equality.[2] His political ideas had a curious resemblance to those of the seventeenth-century English levellers: he feared long parliaments, which only set up mistrust between people and government. He wanted annual elections, so that those who held power should be perpetually conscious of its popular origins—and he demanded that certain fundamental rights should always remain inviolable, outside their scope.[3]

Louis Blanc was one of the most talked-about men of 1848 because he had found a simple formula 'The Organisation of Labour,' which seemed to offer the solution for the major social problems all at once. However, a period of economic crisis was no time to raise capital for his industrial schemes. The modest workers' associations he set up went largely unnoticed and affected only a tiny fraction of artisans. Unfortunately for him the National Workshops (which had no connection with his theories, since they simply gave useless labour to the unemployed for a very small wage) got confused in the popular imagination with his 'social workshops', and thoroughly discredited him. He was unable to get a ministry of progress or of labour established, or any significant budget vote to enable him to achieve anything. However, he had time to draw up a bill 'to prepare the social revolution and to abolish the proletariat [i.e. wage earning]

1 L. Blanc, Le Socialisme: droit au travail, reprinted in his Questions d'aujourdhui et de demain (1873-84), 4. 317-25.
2 L. Blanc, Le Pouvoir, ce qu'il doit être (1841).
3 L. Blanc, Du suffrage universel (1850).

gradually, peacefully and without shock'. The state should buy up the railways, the mines, the Bank of France and the insurance companies and set up a national wholesale and retail commercial chain. With the profits of these, it should set up workers' co-operative associations, which would compete against private enterprise. Blanc's plans are important for distilling into a single document the common aims of most socialists in 1848.[1] However, when in 1870 he returned to France from more than twenty years of exile in England, he had completely ceased to hold this intermediary position, though he was still popular enough to be elected to parliament. He opposed the Commune, because he was still a believer in the centralised state. Though he had appealed to universal suffrage he had never given much thought to the organisation of the peasantry which comprised its principal part. He became obsessed with anticlericalism and placed more emphasis on it than on social reform.[2] He even quoted approvingly from Thiers's book on property.[3] Though he had been a pioneer democrat, he disliked the parliamentary democracy of the Third Republic, and the idea of party organisation was alien to him. He had always been hostile to the small constituency which could easily be led astray and he cherished the illusion that if only 'all France could meet in a single *place publique*', his ideas would be triumphantly acclaimed.[4] He now called himself a radical and he was no longer on the extreme left. He was a man marked by the failure of 1848, but on the other hand some of his ideas were becoming respectable and to that extent he could claim a lasting achievement.[5]

The most widely known socialist doctrine in 1848 was that of Étienne Cabet (1788–1856). His book, *Voyage en Icarie*, went through five editions between 1840 and 1848; even though it was a closely printed volume of 600 pages, it was much read by

---

[1] L. Blanc, *Histoire de la révolution de 1848* (1870), i. 161.
[2] L. Blanc, *A mes électeurs* (12 Feb. 1876), L. Blanc, *Discours politiques, 1847 à 1881* (1882), 208, 372.
[3] L. Blanc, *Le Parti radical, sa doctrine, sa conduite* (15 Oct. 1872).
[4] L. Blanc, *Du gouvernement direct, du peuple par lui-même* (1851), in *Questions d'aujourd'hui et de demain* (1873–84), i. 200.
[5] J. Vidalenc, *Louis Blanc* (1848); I. Tchernoff, *L. Blanc* (1904); L. A. Loubère, *Louis Blanc; His Life and his Contribution to the Rise of French Jacobin-Socialism* (Evanston, Ill., 1961).

the workers. Cabet was not a powerful thinker, but this did not make him any less interesting. His book attempted to reflect with exceptional directness the ordinary hopes of the common worker. For Cabet held out above all the prospect of prosperity. He sacrificed liberty entirely in order to have equality. He was himself of working-class origin. His father had been a cooper of Dijon, 'an honest and industrious artisan' Cabet called him. Thanks to scholarships, Cabet became a teacher and then a barrister, with the ultimate ambition of being appointed a professor of law. But the Restoration closed the avenues of promotion to him, for he preferred Napoleon to the Bourbons. He joined the Carbonari and was active in the liberal opposition before 1830; but when the July Monarchy was established, he could not find a settled place in it. He was made Prosecutor-General in Corsica but was quickly dismissed for his blind attacks on the powerful vested interests there. When elected a deputy for Dijon, he bitterly criticised Louis-Philippe for not breaking with aristocracy and privilege. He demanded a true republic, with votes, education and a decent living for the masses. His newspaper, *Le Populaire*, was distributed at a very low price to the working class.[1] 'We do not want to despoil the rich,' he wrote, 'but to enable the poor to acquire a competency and to enrich themselves by working.' The rich could build themselves as many palaces as they pleased, so long as all the poor had a cottage.[2] He was repeatedly prosecuted by the government and finally forced into exile.

It was in England that he became a communist. Some say this was due to the influence of Robert Owen; others claim Cabet owed more to Babeuf (whose communism represented the longing of poor peasants for the old common organisation of pre-capitalist open-field agriculture and for the traditional common rights of pasture and firewood).[3] Cabet decided that

[1] Sales in 1846 were 3,600 copies; but in the 1830s on some occasions 20,000 copies were sold. Cf. the entry by Proudhon in his diary for Sept. 1843: 'Getting on badly with everybody, what can I hope? The masses are still too ignorant; and besides Cabet has taken the lead in their esteem.' *Carnets de P. J. Proudhon* (1960), 1. 8.

[2] *Poursuites du gouvernement contre M. Cabet, député de la Côte-d'Or, directeur du Populaire* (1834), 2. 28, 45. A sort of autobiography by Cabet is to be found in the first thirty pages of this volume.

[3] Jules Proudhommeaux, *Icarie et son fondateur, Étienne Cabet. Contribution à*

the basic cause of human trouble was inequality and he deduced that only common ownership could end this. His ideal state he described in the form of a novel, a kind of science fiction for his time. Icaria, as he called it, will be above all a land of plenty. All the luxuries of Paris and London will be found in it in abundance, but no longer as the exclusive possession of a privileged few. All will be owned by the state and the state will feed, clothe, lodge and provide work for everybody. All jobs will be equally esteemed and all equally rewarded. Every man will contribute what he can and draw what he needs. Machines will not be abolished but on the contrary multiplied, for there will no longer be any danger of their depriving anyone of employment: they are designed in fact to lighten man's labour enormously. All homes will be identical, identically furnished in lavish style by the state: they will all have bathrooms and dressing-tables and carpets. Each will be inhabited by one family; larger families will have larger flats in proportion to their size. There will be no hint of Fourierist libertarianism. Strict morality will flourish universally; marriage and pro-creation will be encouraged; celibacy punished; the 'free unions' of the workers ended. Everybody will wear the same kind of clothes, all lovely because 'bizarre and tasteless designs' will be banished. Every profession, every age, however, will be distinguished by a different uniform, so there will be no lack of variety. Fashion, however, will never change any more, and ladies' hats will be so cunningly designed by the best brains that they can be worn by heads of every size and shape. Commerce will be abolished. Government will be based on democratic elections but the possibility of disagreements is barely envisaged. Truth is one, and so only official newspapers will be allowed; the liberty of the press is necessary only against kings and aristocracies, not in popular democracy. 'Nowhere is the police so numerous,' says one of the characters in the novel, 'because all our public servants and even all our citizens are obliged to survey the execution of the laws and to prosecute or to denounce crimes which they witness.'

Cabet was not a revolutionary. His experiences as a Carbonaro had filled him with hate of secret societies. The second

l'étude du socialisme expérimental (1907), 144; M. Dommanget et al., Babeuf et les problèmes du babouvisme (1963), 55 ff.

part of his book describes transitory measures, to extend over about fifty years, while society is gradually made ready to adopt communism. During this period, work would not be compulsory, and private property would continue, though it would be gradually reduced by taxation and by the formation of co-operative associations. Wages would meanwhile be regulated, poverty abolished through state action and the new generation prepared for equality by free education. The attraction of Cabet was that he offered a clear ideal without offending morals or religion; indeed he maintained his scheme was only a development of primitive Christianity. His brand of communism—reformist and deist—quickly became by far the most popular one, outstripping the tiny sect of revolutionary materialists, led by Theodore Dezamy in the tradition of Buonarotti. The government quite failed to distinguish between them. Lumped together, they appeared a terrifying menace. 'The Communists are about to rise', wrote the liberal *Journal des débats* on 20 January 1848. 'Thirty thousand of them are ready to take up arms to overthrow the government. Their chief has even been chosen who will doubtless be in charge of sharing out all property.' But Cabet in fact had surprisingly little influence during the Second Republic. The socialists, and notably Louis Blanc and Ledru-Rollin, vigorously dissociated themselves from him and would not support his candidature to parliament. He obtained only 20,000 votes in Paris in April 1848 and 68,000 the following June—never enough to get a seat.[1] Already before February he had summoned his followers to leave the old country and set up the utopia, as an experimental community, in the U.S.A. The first 69 settlers left France on 29 January 1848. He followed them in December. His authoritarian temperament, his contempt for individual independence, increased the practical difficulties that faced him. When he died at St. Louis in 1856 he was already a man of the past, from the point of view of French politics. But the ideal of which he dreamt was not therefore forgotten.[2]

Pierre Leroux (1797–1871) was another socialist who for

---

[1] Pierre Angrand, *Étienne Cabet et la république de 1848* (1948), 65, 70.
[2] Fernand Rude, *Voyage en Icarie, deux ouvriers viennois aux États-Unis en 1855* (1952), with a valuable introduction on Cabet.

a brief period enjoyed some popularity and then was almost completely discredited. He was very highly esteemed by the generation reaching manhood before 1848.[1] Lamartine prophesied that 'Pierre Leroux will one day be read as the *Social Contract* is read today'.[2] The *British and Foreign Review* for 1843 wrote: 'We think his works far more worthy of attention than those of almost any modern thinker.'[3] The son of a humble café keeper, he was educated at the Lycée Charlemagne, but his parents' poverty prevented him from going on to the École Polytechnique. He became a printer, and later a journalist: he founded and edited *Le Globe*, which was in turn Liberal and Saint-Simonian. In 1831 he broke with Enfantin and evolved his own theories. He was probably the first Frenchman to call himself socialist, though there was nothing sectarian about him at all. He had been a Carbonaro in his youth, but he had disliked its violent methods. He preferred to be, as he called himself, a 'pacific revolutionary'. He saw a growing conflict between proletariat and bourgeoisie but wished to avoid it: he prescribed the granting of special parliamentary representation to the working class as the answer. His aim was always to reconcile. He invented not only the word socialist but also solidarity—the new link between the classes to replace charity, since equality must replace hierarchy. He modestly called himself 'the fourth socialist', for he looked on Saint-Simon, Fourier and Robert Owen as the founders of socialism. For him they stood respectively for equality ('the improvement of the lot of the greatest number'), liberty and practical fraternity. His plan for a democratic and social constitution in 1848 placed even more emphasis than Louis Blanc's on the need for democracy: its sub-title was 'the infallible means of organising the nation's work without hurting liberty'.[4]

Pierre Leroux had at one stage appeared to be the man who best united the aspirations of his age. His Encyclopaedia, modelled on and designed to replace that of the eighteenth

---

[1] E. Renan, *Souvenirs d'enfance et de jeunesse* (1883), 249; Theodore Zeldin, *Émile Ollivier and the Liberal Empire of Napoleon III* (Oxford, 1963), 5–6, 9.

[2] Henri Mougin, *Pierre Leroux* (1938), 13.

[3] Quoted by D. O. Evans, 'Pierre Leroux and his philosophy in relation to literature', in *Publications of the Modern Language Association*, 44, no. 1 (Mar. 1929), 283.

[4] P. Leroux, *Projet d'une constitution démocratique et sociale* (1848).

century, raised great hopes that a new creed of action was about to be evolved. But Leroux took a turning into a blind alley. His Religion of Humanity, though in keeping with the prevalent view that Christianity needed to be regenerated and that society required a new moral basis, turned into an amalgam of mysticism and nonsense. He came to preach reincarnation (though breaking with his friend Jean Reynaud when the latter decided reincarnated spirits travelled from planet to planet) and a method of food production using human manure. The constitutional bill he introduced as a deputy in 1848 was *unanimously* defeated. Fat, round, puffed up, red faced, wrapped in a vast shaggy frock-coat, his head covered with bushy and unkempt hair, he appeared like a wild creature from the woods, and though he had more wit in his little finger than ten of his parliamentary colleagues put together, he was the victim and butt of perpetual jokes.[1] When he died, a subscription to raise a statue of him obtained almost no support; the Commune agreed to send two representatives to his funeral but made it clear it was doing homage to the defender of the people, not the mystic.[2]

Buchez (1796–1865) created another sect of socialists, which is principally interesting for the way it moved away from socialism. Buchez began as an atheist and a revolutionary, and it was in his room in Paris that the French Carbonaro movement was founded. He was then converted to Saint-Simonianism but in 1829 broke with Enfantin when the latter turned it into a religion and developed his unorthodox ideas on women. Buchez attempted instead to reconcile socialism with Catholicism. He believed in progress, the improvement of the lot of the masses and the end of their exploitation, but he stressed above all the need to produce a moral regeneration and he thought Catholicism could help in this. He never became a practising Catholic himself, rather like Maurras, though many of his disciples ended up as priests. Buchez argued that the practical application of Christianity would solve the social

---

[1] Jules Simon, *Premières Années* (n.d.), 386.
[2] P. Felix Thomas, 'Pierre Leroux' in *Entre camarades* (1901), 257–68; id., *Pierre Leroux, sa vie, son œuvre, sa doctrine* (1904); D. O. Evans, *Le Socialisme romantique* (1948); P. Leroux, *L'Égalité* (1838).

question; by this he meant that workers should pool their savings and borrow to found associations, in which they would all be equal, their own masters and drawing equal wages. By dint of economy and austerity they would soon repay their loans and would then swell the associations' capital, which, he insisted, should always be indivisible. These were in effect production co-operatives and Buchez in practice helped to found several, of which the most famous, the Gilt Jeweller Workers, lasted from 1834 till 1873, prospering so that it had no fewer than eight branches in Paris. The snag was that the workers remained in great poverty themselves while the association flourished and the indivisible capital increased. It was too much an association of saints to appeal very widely.

Buchez was highly esteemed by two different sets of people. The moderate republican newspaper *Le National* favoured his ideas, and particularly Garnier-Pagès, Jules Bastide and Recurt, who all became ministers in 1848. Buchez was accordingly appointed deputy mayor of Paris immediately after the Revolution, and in April he was elected president of the constituent assembly, with his disciple Corbon as vice-president. He owed his position, however, to the support of the moderate conservatives, not to any wide popularity among the workers. This patronage from the bourgeoisie only alienated him still further from the socialists.

There was, however, a small group of workers who were devoted to him and who are remarkable because they ran a journal uninterrupted for ten years propagating his ideas. *L'Atelier* (1840–50) was, as its sub-title stated, 'The Special Organ of the Working Class, edited exclusively by workers'. It defined socialism in a rather vague way as 'an instinct, a sentiment, a need . . . an energetic desire shown by the working classes to rise to a better social condition', meaning that none of the doctrines of the individual utopians could be taken as exclusive truth. In practice, however, it meant more by socialism, for it asserted the inevitability of a conflict of interests between workers and employers, and the need for solidarity among the workers themselves. But it did not wish them to fight the employers and it disapproved of trade unions. These could do nothing to end the cause of the trouble, which was twofold. First, workers had a right to the full product of their work (which was the formula it offered in contrast to Louis Blanc's right to work) and they believed employers and foremen were parasites depriving workers of this. Secondly, the division into master and man was an insult to the workers' dignity. The paper is extremely interesting on this subject. It complains bitterly of 'this stupid and humiliating phrase "inferior class" ' which is applied to the workers and of the insults that are thrown at him, unintentionally sometimes, simply by the way superiors act towards inferiors. When in 1846 some factory owners established a prize committee to recompense workers who distinguished themselves by their 'good conduct' and 'morality', it sarcastically proposed to set up a 'committee of encouragement' of its own, which would award prizes to factory owners whose conduct was exemplary in every respect. The status of master must be abolished: 'The worker must cease to be an instrument and become a man.' Since property was the necessary guarantee of liberty and dignity, all workers should possess property: it proposed common ownership of the instrument of production, in the form of workers' associations, but individual property of consumable wealth. Dignity required that the worker should achieve his emancipation by his own efforts; so it opposed equally Louis Blanc's faith in the state and the advocates of participation in profits, which left the hierarchical organisation untouched. As temporary measures till the establishment of associations, it demanded wage regulation, easy credit and far greater use of the *prud'hommes*.

The *Atelier* modified Buchez's doctrines considerably, away from Saint-Simonianism. Buchez had been socialist in the original sense of being anti-individualistic, and in placing emphasis on the needs of society. The *Atelier* had followed him at first but gradually, and particularly after 1848, it emphasised instead 'human values' and the need for individual liberty. It urged comparison between the Russian serf and the citizen of the United States.[1] Its Christian sympathies also got the better of its socialist ones. It thought that moral interests should be given greater weight than material ones. It sided therefore with the bourgeois *National*, with which it agreed about morals, rather than with the socialists, to whose ideas on economics and the organisation of labour it was

[1] Armand Cuvillier, *Un Journal d'ouvriers: L'Atelier* (1954), 73.

sympathetic. This was really its undoing. Its asceticism, its moderation, its awareness of the practical difficulties of emancipation, its Catholic tendencies, all repelled the workers. So paradoxically the readers of this workers' journal (never more than 1,500) were mainly middle class. Proudhon wrote of it that it lacked 'any real and sound popularity' among the workers because instead of making itself the echo of the people's feelings, it mistrusted them, 'in too learned a language, with excessively peremptory theories'. It enjoyed only indirect influence because in 1849 its editor, as president of the legislative assembly's committee on labour, was able to pack the council for the encouragement of workers' associations with his friends. This body was charged with distributing 3 million francs to workers seeking to establish production co-operatives. It imposed the Buchez principle of indivisible capital upon them and so perhaps helped to discredit the scheme. In 1848 Louis Blanc enjoyed a little power: in 1849 the followers of Buchez had their day.[1]

But they did not contribute to the development of later socialism. One of them, J. P. Gilland, a locksmith, declared 'I like my trade, I like my tools and even if I could live by my pen, I would not wish to cease to be a locksmith.' He published a collection of stories and poetry, to which George Sand wrote a preface, and he remained faithful to the democratic cause. Others among these worker-journalists evolved differently. Anthime Corbon (1808–91) was successively a weaver, sign writer, surveyor, compositor, sculptor in wood and marble. 'He has worked at all trades and succeeded in all', but though able, he was not friendly, and rather cold and peevish. A deputy in 1848 and again in 1871, he became a permanent senator in 1875, and eventually lived by journalism. He published a curious book called *The Secret of the People of Paris* (1863), with the object of revealing the real nature of the working class, but it is disappointing, and not very informative. By then he had really broken away from his class and abandoned both his socialism and his Catholicism. One of his colleagues in the editorship of *L'Atelier*, Quénot, a hatter, became an employer and by 1865 had one of the largest factories in Paris: he likewise forgot all his old beliefs and even started a paternalistic

---

[1] Armand Cuvillier, *P. J. B. Buchez et les origines du socialisme chrétien* (1948), 73; and the theses of F. A. Isambert.

friendly society to compete against the old-established and exclusively working-class Hatters' Society.[1] Buchez's school in effect proved to be a diversion of the workers' efforts from socialism: it offered them alternative experiments and it was a failure.

Proudhon (1809–65) was the most genuinely plebeian of the early socialist thinkers. He was the son of a rural artisan— cooper, innkeeper, small-scale brewer, smallholder. However, he did not follow in his father's footsteps, for reasons which show why traditions of resignation were breaking down. Proudhon's father lived on the borderline of subsistence: he was ruined by his lack of business sense: he too honestly sold his products for just enough to cover his costs and keep his family, leaving nothing in reserve for bad times. His plight made a profound impression on Proudhon, whose political philosophy was in consequence designed above all to make it possible for artisans like his father to survive, for honesty to pay, for fair prices to be charged. As a boy, his intelligence was spotted by a local *curé* who got him a place in the lycée of Besançon, but because of family misfortunes he had to leave before he could complete the course. He became a compositor. In this trade he was able to indulge his passion for books and to become a leading example of that new class of men, the autodidact artisan, self-confident, basically conservative but innocently open to all new ideas.

A school prize when he was fourteen, Fénelon's *Proof of the Existence of God*, had first sown some doubts about religion in Proudhon's mind. As a printer and proof-reader of mainly theological works, he learnt the art of disputation, as well as accumulating a mass of half-digested erudition, and a knowledge of Latin, Greek and Hebrew. He began questioning everything. He printed Fourier's *Nouveau Monde Industriel* and for a while was his enthusiastic supporter. 'There was no system, no heresy in which, as I discovered it, I did not believe.' When the crisis of 1830 threw him out of work, he went on a tour of France: his repeated difficulty in finding work exacerbated his hostility to the existing order. The printing firm he eventually succeeded in establishing soon collapsed when his

[1] A. Cuvillier, *L'Atelier* (1954), 61.

father committed suicide. He avoided bankruptcy by obtaining a scholarship to study in Paris, but the fruit of his study, a book entitled *What is Property?* lost him this support. It was in this unusual way that Proudhon became a polemicist and a journalist, but despite the enormous bulk of his writing, he was never able to support himself properly by it. It is possible, indeed, that he might never have become a rebel had his life not been so much of a struggle and had he not been so harshly rejected by bourgeois society. 'I hoped to find a refuge in some honourable commercial employment', he wrote, but 'I am repulsed everywhere as if I had the plague.' He would have been willing to compromise with Louis-Philippe or Napoleon III had they shown more sympathy for his economic ideas.[1] His failure as a practical politician in 1848 and again in 1863 intensified his attacks on the established order, even though, as will be shown, he was not as much its enemy as he appeared to be. The combination of radicalism and conservatism in Proudhon's thought is highly significant, for it helps to explain also the ambiguities of later French socialism.

There was no subject on which Proudhon did not have an opinion. He loved talking and he wrote with great facility: he had no inhibitions about making asides or digressions. He published 26 volumes in his lifetime, 12 more appeared posthumously, as well as 14 volumes of correspondence. It is not surprising that he was seldom original. His importance indeed derives partly from the very fact that he was not original. Proudhon was popular because he expressed the feelings of the masses, or at least a very considerable section of them. He freely admitted that he had no higher ambition. 'We are the monitors of the people, asking it to speak, interpreting its acts. To interrogate the people is our whole philosophy and all our politics.' The most he pretended to do was to 'widen the people's horizon and clear paths for them'. His mind was more analytical than constructive. He showed up the significance of received ideas, pushed home to their logical conclusions, seeking to create, as he said, 'a people's philosophy'. He pointed out the weaknesses of the society of his day far more than he offered

---

[1] Daniel Halévy, *La Vie de Proudhon 1809–1847* (1948), 412–21; but G. Gurvitch, *Pour le centenaire de la mort de P. J. Proudhon: Proudhon et Marx, une confrontation* (1964), 59 ff., disagrees with my view.

alternatives to it. In any case, the people, he claimed, had no wish for utopias. He epitomised the scepticism of the Paris *frondeur*, the eternal critic.[1] Proudhon was wrongly accused by Marx of misunderstanding and misapplying Hegelianism. Proudhon showed up the contradictions of the world but he had no hope of reconciling them into a synthesis. His world was a pluralistic one, in which truth had several faces, and in which the problem was to enable inevitable differences to co-exist side by side. The variety and ultimate paralysis of the Third Republic found a true prophet in him.

Proudhon considered the principal aim of the masses to be the attainment of independence, self-respect and a sense of their own dignity. His main concern was that society should be organised to make this possible. He believed that the qualities it needed were justice, equality and liberty. Justice he defined as mutual respect for other people's dignity, which meant that men should have dealings with each other only on a basis of strict reciprocity: in this way there would be no more oppression. His passion for equality distinguishes him from Saint-Simon, who believed in a hierarchical society, from Fourier, who reserved special rewards for both capitalists and men of ability and also from Cabet, who wanted complete uniformity in wealth. What Proudhon cared for most was social equality. He believed, it is true, that, given education and equal opportunity, men would become increasingly equal intellectually, but he did not demand equal pay, only that every man should receive the whole of what his labour was worth. Nor did he extend his demand for equality to women. Advanced ideas did not attract him as much and he said the masses were not really attracted by them either. Woman's place, he said, should be in the home. He was deeply influenced by biblical ideas, by the Napoleonic Code, by the scraps of Roman law he had picked up, and by the unemployed workers' fear of female competition. Women, he argued, were inferior to men on all counts; they must find their fulfilment in chaste marriage and their pleasure in obedience to their husbands. Proudhon was a puritan. Adultery he considered to be the greatest cause of the decay of modern society. Sexual intercourse should be reserved for procreation. The father's power should be 'almost unlimited' in

[1] P. J. Proudhon, *Correspondance* (1875), 7. 10, 10. 12, 14. 161.

his family. Family life he regarded as the basis of dignity and he never considered that it might be an obstacle to liberty.[1]

After a family, where he was complete master, a self-respecting man must have property. Proudhon made his name by proclaiming that 'Property is Theft',[2] but in fact he had no wish to abolish property. All he meant was that landlords who did no work themselves were guilty of stealing, because profit obtained without labour was theft. What he wanted was to give the land to the peasants who cultivated it and to establish more or less equality between them. He condemned absolute property but proposed something only slightly less absolute, 'possession' or usufruct—ideas he picked up again from Roman law. Full ownership should remain with society, to ensure fair distribution and to prevent profiteering by landlords at the expense of their tenants. At first he identified society with the state but later he proposed that the control of the land—its allotment and the levy of taxes on it—should be in the hands of the communes, so that neighbours could settle these questions freely and amicably amongst themselves. With time, however, he grew increasingly suspicious of the social controls on property he had originally favoured and he came to insist that 'possession' should be hereditary (so as to avoid destroying the family), and even that it should not be withdrawn if the land was neglected or left uncultivated. In the end his major proposal for real reform was the enfranchisement of tenants: after a tenant had paid the equivalent of the value of his land, plus 20 per cent, in rent, he should be considered to have bought out the landlord. By the time of his death, Proudhon had abandoned his early flirtation with the fief and declared the superiority of allodium. He calculated that a peasant family needed about twelve and a half acres of varied arable, pasture and vine land, with rights of common and forest and this— clearly derived from his memories of his native Franche-Comté, where this variety existed—was his ideal. He wanted a balanced society of small peasant proprietors. Communal ownership was anathema to him. 'The peasant', he wrote in

[1] P. J. Proudhon, *De la justice dans la Révolution et dans l'Église* (1858), 1.98, 175–6; on women 3. 181 ff.
[2] Proudhon was not the first to use this phrase. Brissot said something similar in the 1789 Revolution. But Proudhon was probably unaware of this when he wrote it.

a passage which says much about himself also, 'is the least romantic, the least idealistic of men. He loves nature as a child loves his wet-nurse, he is less concerned with its charms (though he is aware of these) than with its fertility. The peasant loves nature for its powerful breasts, for the life it disgorges.' Proudhon fully accepted the peasant's selfishness and he was never a utopian building a system on any hoped-for altruism.[1]

But for all his conservatism—and he called himself a conservative—he was also an enemy of many established values. The property he was attacking, it should be remembered, was that of the early nineteenth century, untramelled by any social restraints, with no possibility of compulsory purchase and no rent control. His contemporary Laboulaye called property a divine institution. The Convention had decreed the death penalty for any one proposing a law which endangered property. Proudhon's views on property were linked with his hostility to the Catholic Church: he criticised it for holding that poverty was inevitable, that property for all was not one of its aims, that charity was commendable—attitudes he considered incompatible with human dignity and equality.

However, the peasant and the worker, even when they owned property, were still far from free, because they lacked the capital to make use of it and were usually in debt. The first step to liberty was economic liberty, and for this cheap credit was needed. Proudhon claimed he had discovered a system which could provide it almost by a stroke of the pen. The tyranny of money should be ended simply by abolishing money. Instead, a system of exchange should be instituted: goods would be valued by the amount of labour put into them. A central bank would give credit to all who were able to produce anything. Interest would be abolished, or at least reduced to $\frac{1}{2}$ per cent. Public and private indebtedness would be extinguished. Virtually free credit would be available to all; tenants would gradually become owner-occupiers; workers would get the full value of their production. This was Proudhon's *mutuellisme* designed to bring justice into economic relationships.

[1] P. J. Proudhon, *Qu'est-ce que la propriété?* (1840); Aimé Berthod, *P. J. Proudhon et la propriété. Un socialisme pour les paysans* (1910).

The men he hoped to save by it, however, were the independent small peasants and artisans whom he considered to be the healthiest element of French society. His economic views were in many ways backward looking, hostile to expansion and industrialisation. For a long time he even opposed workers' production associations (which was one reason why Louis Blanc called him antisocialist). Proudhon's people's bank was designed to give individual workers independence: he feared the associations would restrict it. With time, however, he came to accept the general view, as he so often did: he agreed that the associations were a useful preparatory step towards the reciprocal system; he then even saw them as the ideal form of replacing large capitalist companies, like mines, where individuals were powerless on their own.[1] Proudhon, it is important to note, wished to destroy only the top section of rich idle capitalists; for the rest, he was very keen to conciliate the mass of the bourgeoisie and the proletariat. He hoped that an appreciation of the dignity and joy of work, made more varied and interesting by a wide education (on which he laid great stress) would, in a society where work never involved exploitation of others, lead to true social equality. He wanted not just the right to work but the emancipation of work.

This reorganisation of economic relationships would make governments of the traditional kind superfluous. He carried Saint-Simon's idea of the administration of things replacing the government of men to its logical conclusion, and it is in this sense that Proudhon is the father of French anarchism. He hated all authority, all control on his independence and believed this to be an innate characteristic of man (and it probably was of a great many Frenchmen). He wanted a loose federation of autonomous communes or cantons to replace the centralised state which he saw only as an oppressor, not as an instrument of progress. He was, therefore, hostile to the unification of Italy and Germany into centralised states. He advocated that all arrangements between individuals should be based on free contracts between equals. He attacked Rousseau's *Social Contract* because it involved the surrender of responsibility and power and the creation of a government over the individual.

[1] Aimé Berthod, introduction to P. J. Proudhon, *Idée générale de la révolution au 19ᵉ siècle* ([1851] 1923), 32–46.

He was a bitter critic of democracy, of universal suffrage, and of violence and revolution. Political action was never adequate for him. He was hostile likewise to the Church, which represented authority and oppression to him: he was one of the most vigorous pioneers of anticlericalism. He wished to deprive the Church of its control of education, but he wished to transfer this not to a state system but to the free enterprise of parents. State education would in any case, he thought, be too expensive. He longed to reduce taxation, not to institute a welfare state. In many ways, therefore, Proudhon differed fundamentally from contemporary socialists.

Proudhon had ambitions to be an active politician but no talent for it. After being defeated in the parliamentary election of April 1848, he won a seat in a by-election in June but he never became a party leader. His journalism won him numerous convictions, including repeated imprisonment and exile, which he devoted, perforce, to writing. The political line he adopted was erratic, and almost perversely paradoxical. He was unenthusiastic about the revolution of February 1848 (because it did not accept his ideas), but hopeful after the *coup d'état*. His flirting with the empire discredited him for a time. In the election of 1863, consciously opposing the policy of all other republicans, he changed his tactics and urged mass abstention from the polls. His call went unheeded: how few his contacts with the workers were was seen when he tried to find some to serve on his electoral committee. It was in fact only in his last book (unfinished and published shortly after his death) on the *Political Capacity of the Working Classes* that he finally succeeded in grafting his ideas on to a political movement. He changed his tune somewhat when he developed a philosophy out of the manifesto of sixty Paris workers (1863) demanding that the workers should stop voting for bourgeois candidates and elect only men of their own class to represent their interests. He announced the dawn of a new age, in which the working class was for the first time self-conscious, separated from the bourgeoisie and with ideas in complete contrast to theirs. Just as atheists did not go to church, so the workers should stop going to the church of bourgeois politics. They should concentrate on effecting economic change. They should try not to take over the power of the centralised state, but to abolish it.

Proudhon has apparently been highly influential since his death. He was frequently referred to as a source of inspiration in many quarters. He seemed to be to the second half of the nineteenth century what Rousseau had been fifty years before, and like Rousseau, he was interpreted very variously. The French section of the First International constantly quoted from his works and their mutualism was identical with his in most respects. The Commune of 1871 has been looked upon, in one interpretation, as the fulfilment of his thought. The revolutionary syndicalism of the Trade Union movement was considered to draw many of its precepts from him: both Pelloutier and Jouhaux talked reverentially of him. The Anarchist movement of course considered him, with Bakunin, as their founder. Gambetta acknowledged him as his master and he clearly had many links with the radicalism of the late nineteenth and early twentieth century. His name was then taken up by the Action Française and he was one of the patrons of the Vichy regime. A society, Les Amis de Proudhon, was founded to further the study of his works, which have been painstakingly reprinted over the last thirty years in a grand new edition. It is important, therefore, since his name is to be found in so many corners of French history, to be clear exactly how influential he was and to what extent his name has simply been taken as a cloak.

'The masses do not read me,' said Proudhon himself, 'but without reading they hear me.'[1] In the 1860s the cobbler Rouillier always carried a volume of Proudhon in his pocket: its pages were uncut, but he considered himself a Proudhonist all the same.[2] For Proudhon said what these artisans rather incoherently thought. If this is realised, it becomes clear that Proudhon's direct influence was far smaller than has hitherto been believed; and modern research is increasingly taking the view either that the events and ideas were moving in a Proudhonist direction in any case, or that, where he did have influence, it was far from complete. Thus the memoir of the Parisian workers to the Geneva Congress (1866) of the First International was full of Proudhon's views; but these workers did not slavishly follow them. Proudhon condemned strikes but

---

[1] *Correspondance*, 21 May 1858; M. Harmel, 'Proudhon et le mouvement ouvrier' in *Proudhon et notre temps* (1920), 33.

[2] Maxime Vuillaume, *Mes cahiers rouges au temps de la Commune* (1910), 313.

they, as practical union leaders, finding strikes necessary, used them; he condemned political action during most of his life, but they engaged in it when they saw opportunities. Soon they adopted attitudes which seemed to support an acceptance instead of the influence of Marx or Bakunin, but there was no real influence there: the practical problems of organisation led them to adopt new politics—which in turn led them to the adoption of modified or new ideologies.[1] The same will be seen in the Commune, the limited socialist and Proudhonist elements in which will be discussed below.

The effect of the utopians on political life was thus not to create a series of coherent new parties, but on the contrary to uproot tradition, to sow confusion, to stimulate hope, to construct dream-worlds which alienated Frenchmen from the present and consoled them for its shortcomings. The attitudes they encouraged were perhaps more important, from the long-term historical point of view, than the precise details of their schemes, because men mixed up and recombined their ideas in a large variety of ways. What they achieved was to give a high status to ideals and theories. They made people feel enlightened when they indulged in theorising, rather than when they belonged to a certain party. They thus helped to undermine the stability and prestige of ordinary political life. They placed themselves, as their intellectual successors increasingly did also, outside organised society, whose doom they predicted. But they also claimed a role of direction and influence in the society they condemned. The tradition they established became one of the most powerful forces in French life. Their idealism, even if it was seldom implemented in practice, reflected widespread aspirations, and playing with idealism, verbally or more deeply, was a constant feature of this century.

[1] J. Rougerie, 'Sur l'histoire de la Première Internationale', *Le Mouvement social* (Apr.–June 1963), 41–3. See also the forthcoming large-scale work on Proudhon by R. Bancal.

17. Republicanism

THE significance of republicanism is that it reflected changes in social relationships which gave a new dimension to politics. It was through republicanism that popular political organisation appeared as an alternative to the system of patronage and clientage on which the nobles and royalists had based their power. The republicans thus mobilised another force in French society. The nobles and the notables had dominated politics because of their wealth, their connections and their active search for power. The republicans counter-balanced their influence with that of the electoral committee, the political party and many kinds of societies in which ordinary men, by getting together, were able to stand up to the notables and challenge their monopoly of public office. They offered the masses an alternative they had not had before, because they united local resistance under a national banner.

However, republicanism was not a mass movement in a simple sense. There were several varieties of it and it produced contradictory results. While appealing to the masses, it also developed a new class of notables. Its ambiguities explain why it attracted so much support, and also why so many myths have been generated about it to cloud over its confusions. There was a mystique about republicanism which long discouraged impartial investigation. The subject has only recently emerged from the realm of partisanship and passion, now that the republic—after tottering in 1940—has established itself as a generally accepted form of government. There are thus many legends about it which need to be dispelled.

The first concerns the way the republic of 1848 was established. This poses the problem of how far the proclamation of the republic was the spontaneous expression of the popular will, in what ways that will was influenced by the economic crisis which struck the whole of Europe in those years, and why the monarchy collapsed. Now it is clear that the monarchy was weak long before the economic crisis. It is quite conceivable that even if there had been no economic crisis, Louis-Philippe might have abdicated all the same, in a row with his own supporters.[1] On the other hand, the events of 22–4 February 1848 suggest that it was by no means inevitable that Louis-Philippe should have been overthrown at that particular time. All the banquets of the opposition involved less than 17,000 people spread over 70 different meetings.[2] The demonstrations of 22 February were started by little over 1,000 students and workers, and the crowd swelled to only about 3,000 in the course of the day. Its slogans were directed against the police, not the monarchy. Its wrath was exacerbated when troops were called in, but a rapid withdrawal of these might have produced a very different turn of events.

The republicans were prepared to accept a regency,[3] for they were under no illusions about their strength: they were a small minority party. The victors in these events could have been the dynastic opposition. But they lost control. It was as a result of the withdrawal, rather than the overthrow of the old ruling class, that the republic was established. It was established in Paris, which had been lost to the government some years already, for most of its deputies were in the opposition. There were no fights in the rest of France. The old administration withdrew. This might be taken as an admission of their weakness, or alternatively as proof of the superficiality of the republican victory. In these three days of February, about 350 people were killed and 500 admitted injured into hospitals. It was the least bloody of French revolutions.[4]

Tocqueville had predicted the revolution but this should not be taken as a sign of extraordinary political perceptiveness. A large number of people had predicted it too—indeed the prediction was a commonplace of discussion. The king himself was worried by its imminence more than anyone. Nevertheless when it came many people were startled by it. Garnier-Pagès, a participant in it and a member of the provisional government

[1] Douglas Johnson, *Guizot* (1963), has an excellent and very fair chapter on 'Guizot and 1848'. Cf. Paul Thureau-Dangin, *Histoire de la monarchie de juillet* (1884–92); P. and T. Higonnet, 'Class Corruption and Politics in the French Chamber of Deputies 1846–8', *French Historical Studies*, 5 (1967), 204–24.

[2] J. J. Bingham, 'The French Banquet Campaign of 1847–8', *Journal of Modern History*, 21 (1959), 1–15; L. Girard, *La Deuxième République 1848–51* (1968), 34.

[3] L. A. Garnier-Pagès, *Histoire de la révolution de 1848* (1861–72), 5. 213.

[4] C. Seignobos, *La Révolution de 1848, le second empire* (1921), and P. de la Gorce, *Histoire de la seconde république française* (1887), contain detailed narratives.

of 1848, thought that if Louis-Philippe had yielded promptly, if he had withdrawn his troops from the capital, if he had been, in other words, willing to be a constitutional monarch, there would have been no revolution.[1] The royalist Falloux, another acute observer, thought the revolution was 'an effect out of all proportion to its cause'.[2] In England, Lord Brougham, fulfilling for this revolution the role Burke had performed for that of 1789, declared that it was 'the sudden work of a moment—a change prepared by no preceding plan—prompted by no felt inconvenience—announced by no complaint . . . Without ground, without pretext, without one circumstance to justify or even to account for it, except familiarity with change and . . . proneness to violence . . . It was the work of some half-dozen artisans, met in a printing office . . . a handful of armed ruffians headed by a shoemaker and a sub-editor.'[3]

The opinion of Guizot on his own fall was not quite so extreme but he found the explanation within the middle class. It had been divided and this division had ruined the monarchy. Granier de Cassagnac, a protégé of Guizot but later one of Napoleon III's supporters, agreed that the rivalry and ambition of the politicians had been disastrous, but he concluded from this that parliamentary government was unworkable: therefore Louis-Philippe was trying to do the impossible. No section of the country supported the regime of July with enthusiasm. That is why a riot was enough to topple it. Thiers, for his part, who had distinguished himself repressing similar riots earlier in the reign, argued that the revolution would have been avoided if the troops had been withdrawn from Paris and later taken the city by assault. This is what he successfully did in 1871 with the Commune.

But Louis-Philippe himself had no such optimism. In an interview with a journalist after his fall, he saw the revolutionary movement as being much stronger than these supporters allowed. He considered that his regime had been very weak, because freedom of the press had produced so many attacks on him (he was very sensitive to them) that the authority of the monarch, and indeed of monarchy, had been greatly diminished:

[1] Garnier-Pagès, 4. 368.
[2] Comte de Falloux, *Mémoires d'un royaliste* (1888), 1. 254.
[3] J. S. Mill, *Dissertations and Discussions* (1859), 2. 339.

it had therefore been easy to overthrow. In 1848, said Louis-Philippe, public opinion was no longer behind him, as it had been in 1830. He had spent his reign trying to repress the spirit of revolution, while securing the gradual development of the principles of 1789. To have allowed the reform movement to triumph would have been to allow the revolution to come to power and to plunge Europe in war; and he preferred to abdicate rather than be the king of the revolution. He would not use force, because he had as much horror of civil as of foreign wars. Louis-Philippe did not analyse why public opinion had abandoned him, for he had come to see all opposition as part of the revolution.[1]

In contrast with these interpretations, which concentrate on the disputes of the middle class, other historians have attempted to claim the republic as the result of far deeper causes. The comtesse d'Agoult, aristocrat turned republican, mistress of Franz Liszt, author under the pseudonym of Daniel Stern of one of the best contemporary histories of the revolution, hailed it as a product of the spontaneous union of the people and the bourgeoisie. It was not an accident but the natural result of several powerful forces. The eighteenth-century *philosophes* started it all with their movement for free thought. The masses became increasingly keen on winning political power after 1789. The industrial proletariat, rendered increasingly miserable by repeated economic crises and unemployment, stood out in sharp contrast as the prosperity of the other classes waxed. 'At first', she said, 'hardly anyone was aware of this conflict.' Fourier and Saint-Simon alone pointed out these injustices: but their views went unheeded: 'There was blindness everywhere.' However, that section of the bourgeoisie which had not yet become rich gave expression to the confused sentiments of the masses through its parliamentary opposition. The corruption of the government 'brought forward the hour of conflict . . . When the battle was joined, instinct triumphed over science, popular sentiment over political cleverness. Democratic France, in an outburst of indignation, overthrew the government of the French bourgeoisie and proclaimed itself free under a republican government.' This was a very subtle analysis. Madame d'Agoult introduced social and intel-

[1] E. Lemoine, *L'Abdication du roi Louis-Philippe racontée par lui-même* (1851).

lectual factors but very astutely limited their role as actual causes of revolution. She did not quite offer an explanation. On the one hand she said that public opinion demanded a republic, but on the other hand she concluded it soon became clear that the revolution had come too early. She did not explain why, as she put it, the people lost confidence in the republic and why in June 1848 the republic finally repressed the people. She contradicted herself by implying that the republic was not as popular as it had appeared in February, and that the people were not masters of it.[1]

Karl Marx, who wrote some brilliant journalism about the revolution, gave the proletariat only a very modest role in it. He argued that the monarchy of Louis-Philippe was dominated by the 'financial aristocracy'—bankers and large landed proprietors: it was 'nothing other than a joint stock company for the exploitation of France's national wealth, the dividends of which were shared among ministers, Chambers, 240,000 voters and their adherents'. The opposition to it came from what he calls the industrial aristocracy, and it is this group which captured power in 1848. The revolution for Marx was therefore not a proletarian one. The proletariat obtained no power from it and it was duped again, as it had been in 1830. February 1848 was nothing like as important as 1789. The real significance of the revolution, for Marx, derived from the June days when the bourgeoisie repressed the workers and by thus destroying the alliance of the two, prepared the ground for the genuine struggle of the proletriat against the bourgeoisie, which he predicted would come at the next economic crisis. Marx placed only limited emphasis on the crop failure, and the agricultural and commercial crisis of 1845–7, by which the revolution had only been 'accelerated and the mood of revolt ripened'. It is much more his disciples who have stressed this economic aspect and it is thanks to them that a great deal of research has been undertaken to reveal the extent of popular distress.[2]

The idea that the revolution was an accident was vigorously attacked by Albert Crémieux in 1912, in a detailed study of the

---

[1] Daniel Stern, *Histoire de la révolution de 1848* (1850–3).
[2] K. Marx, *Class Struggles in France 1848–50* (English trans., 1924); J. Dautry, *1848 et la deuxième république* (1957); G. Duveau, *1848* (1965); and the Sorbonne lectures of E. Labrousse. Good analysis in R. Price, *The Second French Republic* (1972).

four days 21 to 24 February 1848. He condemned previous historians who had concentrated on the role of ministers, deputies and political parties and pointed out that the barricades were put up not by their orders, but spontaneously by the people. 1848 was therefore essentially a popular revolution. He brought forward a mass of evidence from police reports of the agitation during these days and statements made by participants. He attributed the intervention of the masses in politics to the economic crisis, the spread of socialist doctrines and general dissatisfaction, but he did not discuss just how far these factors directly affected their behaviour on the crucial days.[1]

Recent research has shown that no single explanation of the revolution of 1848 will hold water. The agricultural crisis began after the harvest of 1845. By the spring of 1847 the price of bread was at about double its normal level—but there were large variations in different parts of the country. In May 1847 for example the price of a hectolitre of wheat was 34 francs in Var, but 49 francs 50 in Haut-Rhin. The harvest of 1847 was a very good one. By the time of the revolution, prices had tumbled everywhere to levels below the previous average and they remained so throughout the republic. The revolution was therefore not a revolution of hunger in the direct sense of there being a shortage of food. There had been some bread riots in 1847 but they had been very minor and had had no political consequences. Not all the population suffered equally. The large wheatgrowers were compensated for the bad harvests by high prices. Smaller producers who could not afford to hold back their wheat till prices were favourable suffered. Tenant farmers who had rented their farms at high rents during the years of prosperity found themselves in difficulties. It was the labourers who were hardest hit, particularly when they were not lodged and fed by their masters. Sacked by their impoverished employers and unable to obtain, because of the general crisis, the supplementary industrial employment which was essential to their survival, they experienced some of their worst years in the century. One of the great problems of 1848 was unemployment. Not only people on the borderline of starvation,

---

[1] Albert Crémieux, *La Révolution de février: étude critique sur les journées des 21, 22, 23 et 24 février 1848* (1912). Cf. Pierre Quentin-Banchart, *La Crise sociale de 1848: les origines de la révolution de février* (1920).

but large sections of the population were plunged into debt. So even when the harvests were normal' again, the difficulties were by no means over. When wheat prices did fall, they did so in a way the peasants could not recall the like of since 1787. The labourers now benefited but the producers got derisory returns. The crisis continued therefore for several years after 1848, with varying groups being affected. The winegrowers, for example, had done well in 1847, but then suffered four consecutive years of unprecedented severity, as this table of their income shows (for Loir-et-Cher):

1843	96	1849	66
1844	96	1850	41
1845	176	1851	59
1846	87	1852	136
1847	143	1853	143
1848	72	1854	87

It should not be thought that the crisis brought prosperity to a sudden halt. The farmers had had problems throughout the previous reign, some more than others. What made this crisis so catastrophic was its extension over the whole of the economy.

The textile industry had been reducing wages for some years and had been heading for disaster because of uncontrolled overproduction. Now demand collapsed. 35 per cent of textile workers are estimated to have been sacked, the same proportion of metal workers, 20 per cent of miners. Work stopped on the construction of railways; orders for house building dried up; and many small rural industries found their markets disappearing. Metal production fell by 50 per cent. The financial crisis was perhaps the most serious of all, because it made recovery impossible. The stock market collapsed. The 3 per cent *rente*, which was 75 francs in February 1848 remained at between 56 and 58 francs for three years. The volume of discounts at the Bank of France fell by 40 per cent and was still a third below normal in 1851. In desperation manufacturers dumped their goods on the market at knock-down prices, with disastrous results on the small shopkeepers. 'Hence', said Karl Marx, 'the innumerable bankruptcies among this section of the Paris bourgeoisie and hence their revolutionary action in February.'[1]

[1] K. Marx, *Works* (1950), I. 133.

The significance of the doubling of bankruptcies should not be exaggerated, however. In Paris in 1845, a normal year, there were 691 bankruptcies, between August 1846 and July 1847 there were 1,139. These were not a massive class. But together the agricultural, industrial, commercial and financial crises created not only a whole new mass of unemployed and hungry men, but also a middle class in severe distress, and an upper class conscious that the very basis of society was being shaken. In January 1847, the comte de Castellane noted at the ball of the duchesse de Galliera, wife of one of the richest of railway magnates, that people prophesied the pillaging of châteaux: 'We are threatened', he noted, 'by social upheaval.'[1]

It does not follow, however, that those men who suffered most, the starving unemployed, played an important part in the revolution. Research into the industrialised regions of France has revealed little subversive activity among them. In Lille, the number of poor in receipt of public assistance did increase from one in six in 1828 to one in 4·2 in 1846, but the attitude of the working class to this seems to have been not anger and sedition, but submission and resignation. The Church retained its hold here and successfully preached acceptance of misfortune by the poor. In 1848 the workers did not revolt. Their political activity—if it can be called that—was confined to demonstrations against foreign workers, particularly Belgians, who were serious competitors for work in periods of depression. The revolution seemed an opportunity, above all else, to expel the foreigners. The only political riot by the workers of the Nord occurred on 5 December 1851, after the *coup d'état*, and this was confined to some fifty miners of Anzin.[2] In Alsace, socialist ideas were confined almost exclusively to the bourgeoisie. The workers' material conditions were appalling but there was no evidence under Louis-Philippe of agitation by them. 'The population of Alsace', concluded Mme Kahan-Rebecque in her thorough study of the years 1830–48 in the province, 'did not feel very strongly the need for profound social reforms, first because the industrial employers themselves

---

[1] E. Labrousse, *Aspects de la crise et de la dépression de l'économie française au milieu du 19ᵉ siècle* (Bibliothèque de la révolution de 1848, no. 19, 1956).

[2] André Lasserre, *La Situation des ouvriers de l'industrie textile dans la région lilloise sous la monarchie de juillet* (Lausanne, 1952).

carried out some reforms, and secondly because the Alsatian was very respectful of the established order.' Even during the crisis of 1847, which hit the workers very hard, there was only one insurrection, in June, when some 300 or 400 workers demonstrated against the high price of bread.[1]

The workers in France as a whole were far from being incapable of protesting against their conditions. In the eighteen years of Louis-Philippe's reign 382 strikes have been counted (and there were probably more) occurring in 121 different places. But it was not the large industries which went on strike most often: building workers, followed by tailors and carpenters were the most militant. It was the privileged silk weavers of Lyon who provide the one case of workers taking up arms to further their demands. There certainly was much organisation and planning of industrial action, especially by miners and woolworkers. The government often used troops to repress these strikes and sentenced many workers to imprisonment for their participation. But the links between industrial and political action were still only embryonic. These strikes prepared some workers for active participation in the Second Republic, but they had not gone far enough to give the workers as a whole the initiative in politics. It was in any case the urban artisans, not the factory workers, who were most active; and it was precisely in areas where conditions were worst that protests by factory workers were almost non-existent. Likewise, the agrarian disturbances of 1846-7 produced by the high price of bread occurred mainly in the west, not in regions which voted socialist in 1849. The uniquely free conditions that prevailed during the republic made possible the manifestation of grievances which had remained concealed, and which were by no means always the same as those revealed before the revolution.[2]

The republic was thus established first because the monarchy lost its nerve, lost its self-confidence and its belief in its own mission. It did so under the influence of a demonstration of popular discontent of a very exceptional kind—not just a press

---

[1] Mme Kahan-Rebecque, *L'Alsace économique et sociale sous le règne de Louis-Philippe* (1928).
[2] R. Gossez, 'Carte des troubles en 1846-7' in E. Labrousse, *Aspects de la crise* (1956), 1-3; J. P. Aguet, *Les Grèves sous la monarchie de juillet* (Geneva, 1954); Peter N. Stearns, 'Patterns of Industrial Strike Activity in France during the July Monarchy', *American Historical Review*, 70 (Jan. 1965), 371-94.

campaign, nor party agitation, but unorganised, uncommitted, ordinary Parisians breaking the habits of routine and protesting in a way for which few comparisons can be found. It is this that needs to be explained, which can be done only by looking far more widely than simply at the economic distress or the immediate events of February. The character of the Second Republic cannot be understood just by examining the sparks which set it alight. Precisely because the revolution was so much an expression of anger, its significance was by no means clear. The nature of the republic still had to be worked out.

It was, moreover, a Parisian revolution. In the provinces there was no real struggle for power, and no similar mass demonstrations. The local authorities, the prefects, put up no resistance. In the north and west many towns accepted the republic without enthusiasm; the old monarchist officials proclaimed the new regime and continued to govern as before. In Bordeaux, where the opposition to Louis-Philippe was weak and where a prosperous upper class of Orleanist wine merchants and shipowners was firmly installed, the republic was not inaugurated until 29 February, and then only by the general of the garrison, acting under orders from Paris. In Lons-le-Saulnier, the national guard remained loyal to the king and for several days the monarchist prefect and a revolutionary committee coexisted as rival claimants to authority; it was only on 3 March that the republic was finally triumphant, when the colonel of the national guard accepted a compromise and reluctantly embraced the republican leader.[1]

There was a long tradition of republican thought before 1848 and of considerable agitation and organisation, but it was con-

---

[1] For the revolution in the provinces see Albert Charles, *La Révolution de 1848 et la seconde république à Bordeaux et dans le département de la Gironde* (Bordeaux, 1945); E. Dagnan, *Le Gers sous la seconde république* (Auch, 1928–9); A. Desannis, *La Révolution de 1848 dans le département du Jura* (1948); P. Muller, *La Révolution de 1848 en Alsace* (1912); G. Rougeron, *La Révolution de 1848 à Moulins et dans le département de l'Allier* (1950); Élie Reynier, *La Seconde République dans l'Ardèche* (1948); G. Rocal, *1848 en Dordogne* (1934); J. Godechot, *La Révolution de 1848 à Toulouse et dans la Haute Garonne* (1948); *La Révolution de 1848 dans le département de l'Isère* (Grenoble, 1949); F. Dutacq and A. Latreille, *Histoire de Lyon*, vol. 3 (1952), and the works of Tudesq, Vigier, Chevalier, Armengaud, and Dupeux already cited. There is a large amount of information in the publications of the Société de la Révolution de 1848, appearing under different titles since 1905.

fined to relatively small circles. The importance of 1848 is that the masses were drawn into politics, and won over to this movement. This did not occur uniformly over the whole country. The republicans succeeded in winning the peasants over only in some regions. They made least impression in the west, where many continued to accept the leadership of the nobles, and to ally with them against the cities. The south, by contrast, they managed to convert from a stronghold of royalism into a steadfastly republican region. The process by which this was done can best be illustrated by looking at a single department. In 1815 the department of the Var was a region where the White Terror raged with a passion that revealed the political leadership of an active nobility. In December 1848, however, it gave 12·2 per cent of its votes to the republicans, in May 1849 27·4 per cent, and in March 1850 31·5 per cent. It was the department in which the largest uprising against the *coup d'état* of 1851 took place. It remained for the next century in the vanguard of the republican movement. In 1936 it elected two communist deputies. Yet this was a rural department with no large-scale industry. Its conversion to republicanism can be explained by the development of different forms of independent popular action in the early nineteenth century. Until the 1830s villages had little hope of preventing the descendants of their feudal lords from usurping common rights in the woodlands around them, which meant so much to the poor; but after that date an increasing number of communes brought lawsuits against the rich and more often than not won them. A new sense of local power developed. Poor communes could not afford the legal fees—but the richer ones were able to carry on the struggle, not only against the lords but even to extend it against the state also, which tormented them with its Forestry Code and its endless taxation.

There were villages in this region with populations of between 1,500 and 5,000, often including small industries like tanneries, paper-mills, silk weaving, cork and oil manufacture. They had strong artisan elements, and so differed from the towns only slightly: the transition from one to the other was imperceptible, with no real change of type. These villages—if they can be called that—had ancient traditions of combination in religious fraternities. In the nineteenth century these developed into new forms of association and in particular friendly societies and drinking clubs. The latter, known as *chambrées* or *chambrettes*, were a peculiarly southern institution, men's clubs devoted to drinking, gambling and conversation. They acquired a political complexion because they quickly came into conflict with the government over their avoidance of wine duties and of the laws restricting gambling and public meetings. Precisely because they served an important social purpose, they grew in numbers despite all attempts to repress them. Under Louis-Philippe there were between one and seven in every commune.

The tradition of young men getting together in groups was an old one, but their clubs had usually been ephemeral. Now the *chambrées* became more permanent organisations, for men of all ages, modelled rather more on the bourgeois club, into which the upper classes had for rather longer organised themselves. This increasing imitation of the bourgeois was perhaps a natural outcome of the spread of education. The number of army recruits who could read and write in this department increased between 1831 and 1851 from 33 per cent to 60 per cent. The peasants were gradually acquiring the means of participating in national life. Knowledge of French was spreading. The village theatres began acting classical plays in addition to the old folkloric ones. Musical societies were founded, going beyond the ballad to perform choral works in French. Their musical activities were often combined with more practical ones, particularly mutual insurance, so that they were doubly social institutions, and some called themselves 'philanthropico-harmonic' societies. Thus in 1842 the single village of Cabris had five different clubs: the literary club (to which the professional men and largest landowners belonged—the notary and the doctor), one artisans' *chambrée*, and three peasants' *chambrées*, each catering for a different area. All these channels for southern sociability provided an excellent breeding-ground for popular political involvement.

However, the transition from the influence of the notables to the independence of the masses did not take place in one step. The societies were made political to a considerable extent by the intervention of dissident members of the bourgeoisie. One of the classical types of popular hero in the mid nineteenth century was the barrister who had represented the commune in its lawsuit against the descendants of the feudal lords. Another is the bourgeois philanthropist who was worshipped for the benefits he brought to his village, particularly if he was self-made. But it was above all the 'bohemians of the village, the failed graduates, the doctors without patients, all sons of peasants who had become rich and who, tired of emaciating work in the towns, retired and used up the income of their papas, who were stupidly proud of this strange progeny'. So wrote a mayor of Toulon in 1870, about the youth of the 1840s. The rise of this class of 'young petty bourgeois, idle and intellectual, libertine and sociable' was very important in spreading the ideas of Paris to the provinces. Important too were the bourgeois bachelors, ostracised from the society of their equals because of their liberal opinions or their moral conduct, because, unable to marry for fear of dispersing their families' wealth, they lived with concubines. Such men frequented the cafés and clubs and created links between the classes. Many of these peasant and artisan clubs had honorary bourgeois members who provided leadership or advice. Established manufacturers naturally supported the government under Louis-Philippe, but there were many cases of small ones, still almost artisans, who challenged their domination equally in business and in politics. The well-to-do, or those rising on the social scale, were not necessarily all on the same side. In particular the sons of manufacturers, educated beyond their fathers' station, often came back to their villages to side with the workers and provide a republican leadership. Once again family problems can be seen to have a significance for politics.

But republicanism can be connected with traditional forces too: the risings of 1851 had much in common with the old *jacquerie*. What changed now was the method of expressing it. Before 1848 the peasants acted through municipal channels. After 1851 they learnt to act through political parties. That was the achievement of the republicans; but it was not the doing of any party organisation. Often a village which emerged with a large vote for the Reds was converted by the isolated activity of a single enthusiast, who subscribed to a Paris newspaper and set himself up as a local sage. There was much accident in the way the seeds thrown to the wind sprouted over the country. The seeds did not all necessarily come from Paris.

One of the complications of republicanism was that local plants adopted national names, but did not lose their individuality because of that. 'The Paris revolution', Louis Chevalier has written, 'was only the occasion for these troubles' in the rural areas of France. 'It was not really their cause. It did not communicate to them either its rhythm, or its preoccupations, or its ideology. It only allowed a sudden reawakening, on a more violent scale, of that agrarian fever that goes back to the great revolution and before that, whose scarcely extinguished ardours Balzac, Tocqueville and Proudhon have described.'[1]

The role of young people and of students in the creation of republicanism was an important social development and it also had an interesting theoretical basis. Students entered politics long before 1968. The first *Political History of Students* in France was published in 1850.[2] Just as after the war of 1945 the number of university students doubled and trebled, creating new problems and a new class, so in the mid nineteenth century the *bacheliers* and *licenciés* more than doubled in a single generation. The number of men awarded the *baccalauréat* annually rose from 3,200 to 7,200 between the 1840s and the 1870s, and the number who got the *licence* rose from 338 in 1842 to 865 in 1876. This new intellectual élite was still small enough for personal relations to be possible within it. Each batch of graduates from Paris (and from every major town) could know one another. Common ideas and common action were possible. The ties of friendship or common experience gave these groups a unity. There thus grew *la jeunesse républicaine*, including past students even more than actual ones. Nor should one omit to include in this failed students, for about half the candidates at the *baccalauréat* were rejected. Paris also had many '*ex-jeunes gens*, known as students in their seventeenth year ... recognisable by their untrimmed beards, their unkempt clothing and their

[1] Louis Chevalier, 'Les Fondements économiques et sociaux de l'histoire politique de la région parisienne (1848–51)' (1950, unpublished, but very important thesis), 196; id., *La Formation de la population parisienne au 19ᵉ siècle* (1950); Maurice Agulhon, *La République au village: les populations du Var de la Révolution à la Seconde République* (1970) and id., *Pénitents et francs-maçons de l'ancienne Provence* (1968) both outstandingly original; Lucienne A. Roubin, *Chambrettes des Provençaux* (1970).

[2] Antonio Watripont, *Histoire politique des écoles et des étudiants* (1850). Only volume 1 was published. The manuscript of volume 2 was, however, seen and briefly summarised by the author of the interesting article on students in P. Larousse, *Grand Dictionnaire universel du XIXᵉ siècle*, 7 (1870), 1085.

eccentric hair-styles' who rarely went to lectures except those of political celebrities like Michelet and Quinet.[1] As students these men had been something of pioneers, the first of the meritocrats, but the state, which had brought them into being, alienated them by simultaneous neglect and repression. The students had high pretensions. They claimed that their presence made Paris 'the most powerful centre, the most active agent of civilisation . . . a home of discussion, a vast laboratory of ideas'.[2] The great artists, scientists and writers of France, and the great statesmen of the revolution, had risen from their ranks. Already in 1830 they had played a significant part in the revolution. Balzac had spotted that these young men, whom literature liked to portray as lazy, eccentric and devoted to pleasure, were a new force to be reckoned with. The monarchy of July, he said, had been brought into power by 'intelligence' and by 'youth', but it had then forgotten what it owed them, it had refused them the right to sit in parliament or even to vote. 'Youth', he prophesied, 'will explode like the boiler of a steam engine . . . The new barbarians are the intellectuals.'

The government could not provide enough openings for this increasing class. Its fiercely competitive system of recruitment, vitiated by nepotism and political bias, made frustrated ambition a common fate. It could not find docile teachers to indoctrinate the young. A great deal was demanded of the teachers, but they were rewarded with the most meagre salaries and the minimum of status and respect. In the secondary schools, 55 per cent of the teachers were of peasant, artisan or shopkeeper origin: and only 14 per cent of them married into the liberal professions.[3] The children of the bourgeoisie were thus taught in the *lycées* by the bright children of the working classes, an anomaly which inevitably created tension. At this stage, the teachers had not been absorbed into middle-class society: they lived on its fringes, often unmarried, insecure in their jobs as well as socially. They were in some ways interlopers, brought in by the state against the clergy, and they were thus a threat to the traditional order at the same time as they were supposed to

[1] Alphonse Lucas, *Les Clubs et les clubistes* (1851), 122–3.
[2] Larousse, loc. cit.
[3] P. Gerbod, *La Condition universitaire* (1965), 110, 629, 636.

bolster it. The paradox of the situation was that these poor teachers were most of them at bottom intellectually quite conservative, passionately attached to the classics, and with their horizons normally quite restricted. Because they were so conservative, they denounced the materialism and corruption of their times—much like the clergy. The state did not know how to handle them. It allowed this idealism, which reflected a sense of unease and isolation in the world, to develop into political opposition. The republicanism born among the teachers was savagely persecuted, which exacerbated its tone and made it appear more revolutionary than it really was. Once the persecution was over, republicanism revealed its true colours. Republican radicalism came to mean conservatism. This was not a betrayal, but a proof of an attachment to traditional values, which had always been there.

A distinguishing characteristic of student agitation in the early nineteenth century was that it was led by teachers. Persecuted professors were often the heroes of demonstrations. Guizot had begun life as a liberal professor, and one has only to read his lectures to see how they could be taken as political programmes. There were many others who used their position to preach doctrines the government in power disliked. Just before the revolution of 1848, the two Paris student newspapers, *La Lanterne du Quartier Latin* and *L'Avant-garde, Journal des Écoles*, had been organising demonstrations to protest against the closing of the lectures of Michelet, Quinet and Mickiewicz. It was not uncommon, during the Restoration and July Monarchy, to find crowds of students outside parliament, applauding the opposition deputies; nor for students to go on strike. It was not surprising that on 22 February 1848 they should have provided the nucleus of the demonstrators who started the revolution. Michelet's lectures to them in 1848, at the Collège de France, encouraged them to act, rather than to study. He told them that they had a mission to fulfil which no other class could. As young men, they had the time, the warmth of feelings, and the ability to mix freely with all classes. They alone could start the reign of fraternity, the moral union of the nation, by taking the ideas of the intellectuals to the people. They had not yet been limited and narrowed by the responsibilities and outlook of a specialist profession. They could still be interested in men for their own sakes. They should therefore be the intermediaries, the 'mediators of the city', for it was the young who could best bridge the great abyss between the masses and the bourgeoisie. The trouble with men of letters, said Michelet, was that they wrote for other men of letters, and even workers who wrote books wrote in the style of the men of letters, not for the people. The masses were still isolated, divided by a hundred different patois. The young should seek them out. They should translate for them the message of the geniuses.[1]

The persecution of professors like Michelet turned them into heroes. During the Second Republic and the Second Empire some outspoken professors, dismissed for their independence, or resigning from their chairs rather than take an oath of loyalty to the regime of Napoleon III, became martyrs of the young. Vacherot, who had acquired great influence as deputy director of the École Normale, and Jules Simon, who resigned from the Sorbonne, are only the most famous of them. A host of lesser-known ones retired from the state educational system to humbler posts in private schools. Sainte-Barbe, one of the best cramming establishments in Paris, became a haven for them. Some 700 secondary teachers were sacked or resigned during the Second Republic alone. In the primary schools, the *instituteurs*—who likewise began by being on the whole conservative—were regimented and victimised in the same way. This is the origin of the *république des professeurs*.

Republicanism also attracted many doctors and barristers, partly because theirs were professions in which political independence was possible. The problems of the doctors have already been discussed. Those of the lawyers were not dissimilar. A normal liberal education in the mid nineteenth century ended with the study of law. The legal profession was therefore vastly overcrowded. Young barristers without clients, living from hand to mouth by private tutoring or literary hack work, were a principal ingredient of the intellectual proletariat of most towns. They were the natural champions of the underdog. Rhetoric was the common language of the Bar and of politics. Barristers were another of the intermediaries between the

[1] J. Michelet, *L'Étudiant* (Lectures of 1848 not printed till 1877, reprinted 1970), 57, 67, 76.

centres of power and the masses. It was no accident that when the republic was at last established, they should have occupied so prominent a role in it. In 1881 41 per cent of the members of the chamber of deputies were lawyers, or 45 per cent if one includes those with a legal training who had not practised. In 1906 the figure was still 37 per cent (or 40 per cent). 52 per cent of all ministers between 1873 and 1920 had legal degrees. But a legal education, of course, was no stimulus to innovation or imagination. The skill of these lawyers was in effecting compromises, in acting as interpreters between classes and powers which could not understand each other, in administering and in bringing a semblance of order in anarchic situations. That is why they were so highly valued in the early years of the Third Republic. They helped to consolidate it. But by winning leadership of it, they also prevented it from becoming genuinely radical. It was no accident that the proportion of lawyers in parliament fell after 1920: they were of less use when new challenges demanded change. A republic of lawyers was even less of a threat to established values and traditional ways of thought than a republic of professors. But their oratory and their youth made it difficult to see just what they were aiming for.[1]

In 1848 and in the three succeeding years several different forms of republicanism manifested themselves. First, there was the utopian, fraternal republicanism over which Lamartine presided. This blossomed out in the first months of the revolution of 1848, in a situation of unprecedented anarchy. The disappearance of the monarchy created a totally new sense of freedom, because the government that replaced it was, at least in name, that of the whole people. There was suddenly the liberty to speak as one pleased, without fear of the police, to publish any book one liked, to issue newspapers without tax, caution money or censorship. Three hundred newspapers appeared in Paris. Seventeen new ones were founded in the department of Nord alone. By May, the circulation of papers produced in Paris simply for the working class was 400,000.[2]

[1] Statistics in Y. H. Gaudemet, *Les Juristes et la vie politique de la Troisième République* (1970), 15, 18.

[2] Claude Bellanger *et al.*, *Histoire générale de la presse française*, 2 (1969), 208; J. Godechot, *La Presse ouvrière 1819–1850* (Bibliothèque de la Révolution de 1848, no. 23, 1966), 185.

People could meet and form associations without restrictions. Within a month 145 clubs were established in Paris; and there were probably 300 three months later. In the provinces they multiplied rapidly. Those which had been informal or secret assumed a new importance, and often developed into electoral organisations or even went beyond discussion and became production associations—firms run by the people. The corporations of the artisans enjoyed a sudden revival, and at public ceremonies the different trades were solemnly represented. The juxtaposition of a powerful government and isolated individuals was replaced by groups of every size, who could believe that they held their destiny in their own hands. Social, professional and traditional animosities were swamped by a wave of fraternal good feeling, the 'solidarity' the utopians had called for. The proletariat, for a brief period, were no longer looked on as outcasts, but were idealised as heroes of the revolution. Some bourgeois ladies even thought it fashionable to wear clumsy workers' boots; men covered their fine linen with artisans' blouses, allowed their beards to grow and called each other citizen.

Lamartine, head of the provisional government and minister of foreign affairs, epitomised and represented this ecstatic atmosphere better than anyone else. The hope of this kind of republicanism was not the triumph of one class over another, but the fusion of classes and their abolition altogether. Lamartine was particularly suited to lead this movement because he stood above the clash of faction and even of the conflicts of class. He was an aristocrat, but a bankrupt one, who liked to say that he was simply a winegrower. He had nationwide popularity as a poet. He could hold out a hand to all parties, because he had served all and none. After having been a diplomat under Charles X, he had first accepted Louis-Philippe and then turned against him. He had proclaimed himself a democrat under the monarchy, but he had consistently kept outside the established parties. He claimed that his principal political gift was his instinctive sympathy for the masses, his ability to commune with them in some mystical way, so that he, better than anyone else, understood the 'fundamental idea of the time'—reconciliation. He had always believed that he had been picked out by Providence to give effect to the popular will: he had even 'longed for the storm, in order to be brilliant and heroic in the struggle'. He did not deny that for him politics was essentially a matter of sentiment, for he insisted that all the great achievements of history had been the product of a sentiment moving the hearts of the masses. He believed there was a popular yearning not so much for political or economical change as for the moral regeneration of mankind, a return to primeval virtue and innocence, and the solution of all problems by love, which had hitherto been shackled and frustrated by society. He had great faith in the power of oratory to bring this about. As a result he often believed that he had achieved his purpose simply because he had proclaimed it in fine language. But his naïve enthusiasm was echoed by a large mass of people. In the elections of 1848, a quarter of a million men voted for him in Paris, and one and a half million in the nine other departments where he was spontaneously put up. He was the first hero of universal suffrage: no one then could equal his popularity. Within a very short space of time, however, he was seen to be incapable of dealing with the realities and he lost power as suddenly as he acquired it. But the attitude he represented was tenacious. His brand of republicanism, even though it had proved so inadequate, did not die, because it was the reflection of a widespread idealism and generosity. Lamartine's search for popularity among the masses, rather than among the party politicians, his contempt for parliamentary government, his ideal of a mixed republic, popular at its base but heroic at its summit, led by a great man with a passion for the idea of his generation, using a strong centralised state to improve the lot of the poor, following a foreign policy at once glorious and disinterested, based on the principle of nationalities and aiming eventually at a federation of European states—this together formed a programme which has survived him. Napoleon III's policy echoed it in many ways. The Fifth Republic had much in common with it. Between these two periods, many politicians have admired Lamartine—Ollivier, Waldeck-Rousseau, Combes and Barthou for example—but, beyond individual cases, his tradition constitutes a not insignificant element in the subconscious of the republican party. Republicanism always harboured a penchant for bold humanitarian gestures and generous action which served no class or private interests. On occasion it could move very close to Bonapartism. These ambiguities often brought internal discord and sometimes catastrophe for the movement, but they were never exorcised, because they appealed to a temperament with deep roots. Republican politics continued to attract poets, orators and dreamers, even if, after 1848, they paid lip-service to science and realism.[1]

The republicanism of the democratic socialists, who made republicanism Red, was in some ways equally woolly and vague. It derived its inspiration partly from the Revolution of 1789 and partly from the utopians. The former was a confused memory and the latter, as has been seen, attracted relatively few adherents. However, Red republicanism went beyond utopianism. It turned it into a mass movement, by grafting it on to the traditional institutions of the workers and the peasants. It made it not just intellectually or emotionally attractive, nor simply a novelty—resistance to which was always strong—but part of the community life of ordinary people. In this form, republicanism brought the masses into politics, in a way which the mere proclamation of the republic and of universal suffrage did not. It organised them in such a way that they were able to overthrow—even if only temporarily—the notables who had hitherto ruled them.

The republic of 1848 was to begin with a largely urban phenomenon. Historians have concentrated on the events in Paris, but the permanent consequences of what happened there were limited. Before 1848 the workers of Paris had already developed many forms of organisation. They had artisan corporations which still had life in them. They had mutual benefit societies—262 in 1846 (60 per cent of them linked with trade associations, and counting 22,000 members). They had clubs for self-improvement and recreation, evening classes and choir singing. They had gone on strike under the July Monarchy five times more often than any other city. They had been touched by the writings of the utopians, and they even had

[1] There is a good selection of Lamartine's speeches and writings in *La Politique de Lamartine*, ed. L. de Ronchaud (1878); see also A. de Lamartine, *La France parlementaire* (1865); E. Harris, *Lamartine et le peuple* (1932); C. Latreille, *Les Dernières Années de Lamartine* (1925); Gordon Wright, 'A Poet in Politics: Lamartine and the Revolution of 1848', *History Today* (1958), 616–27; and G. Flaubert, *L'Éducation sentimentale* (1869).

their own newspapers. The republic of 1848 was to a considerable extent their creation.

They entered political life with enthusiasm. On some occasions their response to calls for united action was profoundly impressive—as in the demonstration of 17 March, when as many as 200,000 of them marched through the city. In the Luxembourg—where once the peers of France had met—they had a Government Commission for the Workers sitting, which between 150 and 200 representatives of different trades attended, with a view to evolving a new order for them. In the clubs and cafés also, they gave themselves up to interminable discussion, and some pretty effective organisation. Paris was alive in these days in a way which has only been repeated in two or three critical periods since then. But at first the majority of the workers lent their support to the lyrical republic of Lamartine. They did not foresee how difficult it would be to redress their grievances. The petitions they sent in to the government confused ephemeral and fundamental aims, and hesitated between nostalgia for the past and vague longings for change. Counterbalancing their humanitarianism, they were keen on expelling foreigners, on limiting work by women and by convents, on controlling apprentices—because all these were rivals and what they wanted above all else was employment. The Right to Work was their slogan. Somehow they thought the government could give it to them. Their other slogan was the Organisation of Work, which meant the participation of workers in running industry, but again they were not clear whether they intended this to be started or assisted by the state, and what the place of capital in it would be. In the immediate present, they negotiated for higher wages, improved methods of payment and minimum scales.[1] In the elections of April 1848, Lamartine came head of the poll in Paris by a wide margin, with 259,800 votes. The moderate republicans in his ministry got over 200,000 each. But Ledru-Rollin came twenty-fourth with 131,000, Louis Blanc got only 121,000, Barbès 64,000, and Cabet 20,000. The workers of Paris were not won over unanimously to an extreme form of republicanism. Paris was an active breeding-ground for revolutionary ideas and for advanced doctrines; it was so before and remained so

[1] R. Gossez, *Les Ouvriers de Paris*: Livre 1: *L'Organisation 1848–51* (1967).

after 1848. But once universal suffrage was proclaimed, it could no longer decide the fate of France. And it was too varied a city, with too many complicated relationships and traditions, for it to have a single will.

The rising of June 1848, which took place when 100,000 unemployed workers were told that society could do nothing more for them, was one of the most frightening episodes of the century, but it was not a class war in simple terms, with workers fighting the bourgeoisie. The researches of Remy Gossez in the files of those arrested after it have shown that there was no class war. There were workers on both sides of the barricades. The national guard which suppressed the rising contained a complete cross-section of the population, proprietors, shopkeepers, workers and intellectuals. At the barricades raised in the rue Soufflot, the partisans of order were led by the scientist Arago and the typographer Pascal (one of the writers for *L'Atelier*, the workers' paper) : their discussions with their opponents showed mistrust by the manual worker of the intellectual much more than envy by the poor of the rich. The intellectual could be more of a stranger to the worker than his employer, with whom he lived and worked. A leading role in the repression was played by young workers, especially those from the provinces. They were natural enemies of the older workers who held the jobs, and whom they, being bachelors, could undercut. Many of them had enrolled in the *garde mobile* simply because they needed work. The interests of young students and young workers did not always coincide. The rebels, moreover, were not, on the whole, Parisian workers at all. Only one-seventh of them, and only one-ninth of those arrested, were born in Paris. They were not necessarily underprivileged workers either, but often men who had come to Paris to complete their professional training, to rise in the world—and a good number of them had done so: there were foremen and even employers among the insurgents. It is true that there was more approximation to a class war in the large factories of the mechanical construction industry and the railway workshops, whose workers took a leading part in the insurrection, but here there were also cases of foremen, engineers and even directors leading their workers out to revolt. All sorts of unemployed, vagabonds, journalists, even *déclassé* aristocrats and bankrupt bankers were found on the rebel side. There were representatives of every class in both parties. The leaders were by no means predominantly proletarian. Women took a very important part in the rising: it was a rising as much of women as of men, but this side of it has been forgotten and cannot easily be investigated further because few of them were arrested or made depositions. If there was one single category which the insurgents were united in hating, it was their landlords. Most of them were behind with their rents: the revolution of February had given them an excuse to postpone paying. In the arrests which followed, denunciation by landlords was the principal source of information used by the police. The conflict of generations, the animosities between workers and shopkeepers, tensions between individuals and the frustrations of housewives all played their part in this holocaust. The workers certainly paid the price for it: 11,000 of them were imprisoned or deported and another 1,500 shot without trial. The aftermath of the repression was probably almost as damaging as the insurrection itself. The clubs, the right to strike, the freedom of speech were brought to an end. The exhilarating and enervating experience of freely organising themselves and planning their future could not be forgotten. The trade union and the republican movement were both deeply influenced by the experiences of 1848. Paris was confirmed as a centre of revolution. But not the whole of Paris, nor all the workers, were converts to democratic socialism. In December 1851 Paris rose again to protest against the *coup d'état*. It showed its republicanism with a massive vote of 80,000 against the plebiscite—but 133,000 voted for Louis Napoleon.[1]

The really dramatic gains which the Red republicans made in 1848–51 were among the peasants. In the election of May 1849, the democratic-socialists got 34·8 per cent of the votes cast, 2,357,900 votes in all. In 16 departments they won a majority, with a vote rising to as high as 67·6 per cent in Saône-et-Loire. In 27 other departments they got between 34·8 and 50 per cent of the votes. These victories were won above all in rural areas. Paris itself cast only 37·8 per cent of its votes for them.[2] What is so interesting about this rural protest is the way

---

[1] R. Gossez, 'Diversité des antagonismes sociaux vers le milieu du 19e siècle', *Revue Économique* (1956), 439–58.

[2] Jacques Bouillon, 'Les Démocrates socialistes aux élections de 1849', *Revue*

the peasants became conscious of the possibilities open to them only gradually, and then methodically and deliberately took advantage of them, producing a sense of an immense power being slowly unleashed. In the first days after the revolution, they were aware only that the government had gone. Their first reactions were not political. They invaded the commons and forests, claiming back the traditional rights they had lost to the rich: they sacked the houses of those who resisted them; they drove tax collectors and policemen into hiding; they refused to pay taxes and tolls. This was behaviour similar to that which took place in towns, where textile handloom weavers destroyed machines which were threatening their livelihoods and where carriage drivers and boatmen burnt railway stations and tore up the track of the new invention that was ruining them. But as a whole the peasants were slow to see the implications of universal suffrage. In the Constituent elections of April 1848 they took no independent initiative. The real change occurs in the local elections a few months later. Over half of the mayors and deputy mayors in office appointed by Louis-Philippe were re-elected by popular suffrage. The peasants in many areas accepted the traditional hierarchy. But in certain parts of France, mainly the south-east, the south and the Paris region, these local elections were an extraordinary revolt by the masses, who expelled the notables from office and took over themselves. In the election of the president in December 1848, this was turned into a public declaration of independence, when the peasants, ignoring the instructions of the notables, who were largely in favour of Cavaignac, voted Louis Napoleon in with a decisive majority.

It could be said that the republic of peasants dates from this, except that the peasants were divided as to what kind of republic they wanted. A majority made a deal with authority and accepted the Bonapartist version of the republic, and it was left to the next generation—that of Gambetta—to draw them away from this. A sizeable minority, however—about one third of the total—chose the democratic socialism of Ledru-Rollin. He obtained only 5 per cent of the votes in the

française de science politique, 6 (1956), 70–95, correcting the earlier calculations (still to be found in most textbooks) made by G. Génique, *L'Election de l'assemblée législative en 1849* (1921).

presidential election, as against Cavaignac's 19 per cent and Louis Napoleon's 74 per cent but he made enormous gains in the following year when the extent to which Napoleon was in league with the notables became clear. Ledru-Rollin's disciples toured the countryside, visited the *chambrées*, made converts in village after village. They resurrected the old Carbonaro traditions[1] but widened them beyond their élitist, exclusive character. Secret societies with a mass recruitment, with a full complement of passwords, secret signs and initiation rites, developed out of the drinking clubs and friendly societies, driven underground by government repression. The *Société des Montagnards*, the *Solidarité républicaine* and other regional associations, with remarkably active teams of propagandists, made these essentially local clubs into a force of national significance. Their strength came in part from the fact that they effectively combined peasant and artisan activity with intellectual leadership. Red deputies elected in 1849, who led this movement, included 127 'intellectuals' (76 lawyers, 25 doctors, 13 journalists, 13 teachers and men of letters) out of a total of 211 about whom details are available.[2]

The Reds believed they could win the election due to be held in 1852. They were probably over-optimistic, since their successes were confined to only certain parts of the country. But their judgement of their strength was vindicated in December 1851, when a veritable peasant rising, complementing that of the towns, followed immediately on the *coup d'état*. The departments in which the largest number of arrests were made were precisely those in the south and south-east where they had implanted themselves. These arrests deprived the Reds of their leadership for at least ten years. But during the Second Republic the Reds of these regions had effectively challenged the rule of the notables and they had introduced a new kind of politics, with genuine popular participation.[3]

They had, however, failed to capture power at the national

---

[1] On the Carbonari in France see Alan Spitzer, *Old Hatreds and Young Hopes* (Cambridge, Mass., 1971), which is a very thorough investigation of all that can be discovered about them, and, on secret societies in general, John Roberts's book (in the press).

[2] J. Bouillon, op. cit. A further 19 were in agriculture, 19 in commerce and industry, 11 were workers, 11 soldiers, 9 civil servants, 7 mayors, 8 miscellaneous.

[3] P. Vigier, op. cit., and A. J. Tudesq, op. cit.

level. The responsibility for this must be partly borne by their leaders. Ledru-Rollin was the son of a well-to-do physician; he inherited a very decent private income (30,000 francs a year); he could afford to buy one of the privileged barrister's practices at the court of appeal (for 300,000 francs). As soon as he had reached the age of eligibility, he had tried to enter politics under the patronage of Odilon Barrot, leader of the 'dynastic opposition' under Louis-Philippe (that is, of the opposition which accepted the monarchy). Eventually, however, he was adopted by the republicans of Sarthe as their candidate to succeed Garnier-Pagès, one of their leading figures who had died prematurely. He alone was rich enough to subsidise their local paper but also willing to issue a manifesto radical enough to suit them. Already in 1841 he could have made the famous statement with which he is always associated: 'I am their leader, I must follow them.' He used his wealth, augmented by the dowry of his half-English wife, to subsidise *La Réforme*, the principal democratic newspaper. He had a loud voice and an imposing presence; he was amiable, impetuous, easily given to declamation. His manifesto in his first election was considered so bold that he was prosecuted for it; but he was no innovator, for he owed at least some of his popularity to his sharing the prejudices and superstitions of the working class. He demanded universal suffrage, proportionate taxation, more equality in the army conscription system and the pursuit of glory in foreign policy. He saw the social problem principally in the industrial workers of the city. 'Thanks to the immortal revolution', he said, 'the workers on the land are in a comparatively tolerable material position, even though it is still very imperfect. They are less dependent than workers properly so called.' This real proletariat should be given the right to form trade unions and to strike, and higher wages; but ultimately it should be, as far as possible, abolished. Ledru-Rollin was hostile to large-scale industry, which he considered to be the product of cupidity. As England's experience of it showed, it caused too much suffering. France should remain essentially agricultural and industry should be relegated to a secondary role, in the same way as France considered herself militarily as a land power, and limited her navy to minor proportions. He advocated that industrial workers should be repatriated to the country and given smallholdings: this would revive agriculture, which was being ruined by emigration into corrupting towns. When all workers were made owners of property, they would be 'more tranquil and more moral'. He rejected communism, and vigorously dissociated himself from it. He was hostile to state interference: 'I do not wish to abolish liberty of industry. I do not wish to make the state either a producer or a manufacturer. I wish to make it only an intelligent protector.' He had little use for parliamentary government either: he wanted the direct rule of the people, in the tradition of 1793. His ideas were all those which could appeal to the small man, seeking a modest rural existence—radicalism was already a doctrine of the small man—but this was forgotten in the fury of his rhetoric and in his resurrection of memories of the Terror. He was one of the very few who took the republic's civil uniform seriously, and actually wore suits in the style of Robespierre. 'You are agents of a revolutionary government', he wrote to his prefects when he became minister of the interior, 'and you are revolutionaries too . . . You ask what your powers are: they are unlimited.' Ledru-Rollin had a genius for frightening the middle classes, without meaning to. His flamboyance concealed lack of subtlety and, some have even said, of intelligence or will-power. He was responsible to a considerable extent for making his party into bogy-men.[1]

At the popular level, republicanism contained elements which made it a form of permanent revolution. One of the great problems of the movement was to reconcile this with capturing and holding power. As soon as the republic was successful and became a government, it inevitably came into conflict with supporters whose temperaments made it difficult for them to be on the side of authority. Much of this popular basis was therefore lost in turn to the socialists and then the communists. This happened particularly because a new class of republican notables grew up, who developed (as opposed to the utopian and the popular types) the third variety of republicanism. Republicanism thus represented three contradictory things: a belief in an ideal government which could not exist, a popular

[1] A. A. Ledru-Rollin, Discours politiques et écrits divers (1879), 1. 4–5, 20, 46, 2. 99, 420–9; De la décadence de l'Angleterre (1850); R. Schultz, Ledru-Rollin et le suffrage universel (1948); A. R. Calman, Ledru-Rollin après 1848 (1921).

opposition to all government, and a new establishment party, accepting responsibility, honours and compromise. This latter willingness to compromise had deep roots. The word radical sometimes meant extreme or revolutionary, but under Louis-Philippe it also meant moderate republican, because the word was borrowed from the English and signified a democratic concern perfectly compatible with monarchy and parliamentary forms. One had to distinguish between the 'radicals' and the 'exclusive radicals'. Only the latter were total enemies of Louis-Philippe. In 1847 Carnot (of unimpeachable republican descent) published a pamphlet, which publicly offered the king support in carrying out democratic reforms, which, said Carnot, could perfectly well be achieved within the framework of the monarchical constitution. A good number of republicans would have accepted the monarchy if it had widened the franchise and turned its attention to improving the lot of the masses, just as, under the leadership of Émile Ollivier, a good number were to accept the empire of Napoleon III. This willingness to compromise has naturally always been played down by republican historians, because it has been seen as treachery.[1]

When invested with power, these republicans behaved in a manner which was not all that different from their monarchist predecessors. The rivalry for jobs and promotion, the expulsion of political opponents and their replacement by friends and relatives of the new masters of the country, were as pronounced among the republicans as they had been under Louis-Philippe, whom they had attacked so bitterly for corruption and nepotism. From the point of view of the masses, the new republican prefects, mayors and civil servants often represented simply one clique taking over from another, perhaps less wealthy and less experienced, but still usually bourgeois. This clique, once possessed of power, was as difficult to deal with, for the small man with no strings, as any other. Surrounded by friends and acolytes, it could become as exclusive as the aristocrats had been. It did not hesitate to use the very same pressure in elections, which it had denounced the authoritarian regimes for employing. It was even willing to use force in a very vigorous way to repress popular agitation. The question arises therefore why, if

[1] Cf. A. Bonnard, *Les Modérés* (1933); H. Carnot, *Les Radicaux et la charte* (1847).

there were republicans with this sense of reality and with an ability to use power, the republic failed to get established in 1848. These men would perhaps have created something like the republic of Washington or that of Thiers, respectable, solid and safe. They did not do so for several reasons.

First, they never won a majority in the country. The republicans were still a small group before 1848. They held office for a few months after February only while a vacuum of power existed. In the elections of April, contrary to general belief, they were not successful. It is usually said that the majority of the Constituent Assembly was republican, but one can make this calculation only if one considers as republican everybody who said he was one. Many conversions were purely superficial. Recent research has shown that only one third of the assembly consisted of men who had been republican before 1848—285 out of 851 deputies. Of these about 55 were extreme republicans or socialists, so the moderates, whom the influential historian Seignobos has made out to be the victors of the election, were in fact only 230. More than half the assembly were monarchists of one kind or another.[1] The moderate republicans held power under sufferance, because the monarchists were not ready to attempt to resume it: they were in disarray, divided and confused by universal suffrage. It would take a long time for these new notables to establish themselves, let alone permanently oust the old set.

Secondly, their great weakness was that they were unprepared for government office. They were not just an opposition party, but one which had not worked out an identity to deploy in these new circumstances. There were no men of outstanding ability or exceptional personality among them. Cavaignac was after all summoned to become chief of the executive not because of any particular merit—though he had been a decent general in Algeria and he was an upright and worthy man—but because he was the brother of Godefroy Cavaignac, one of the best-known republican journalists of the monarchy, who had died in 1845. This Godefroy, moreover, was a republican, as he

---

[1] Frederick A. de Luna, *The French Republic under Cavaignac: 1848* (Princeton, N.J., 1969), 110–13. This shows the errors of the essay on the elections of 1848 by a student of Seignobos, J. Tournan, on which Seignobos based his statement. It is also a well-argued reconsideration of this neglected period of the republic.

himself said, through filial loyalty: he was the son of the regicide member of the Convention. Carnot, minister of education, was in the same position. Republicanism had this element of family tradition which made it the perpetuation of family feuds, at the centre of government as at the village level. Garnier-Pagès, another member of the government, also owed his office to the fact that he was the brother of another dead hero, a Marseillais of humble origin, one of the republicans' most brilliant orators. These men had yet to win popularity for themselves, or to establish more widespread networks, to draw more people into their still restricted cliques. As a result, the policy they followed was cautious, exploratory, indecisive. They arrested vast numbers after the June riots, refused an amnesty, but in practice gradually released all but about 250, who were gaoled, and 450, who were transported to Algeria: they thus earned a reputation for being both repressive and weak. Their opinions about the social question were not all that different from those whom they repressed: they believed in workers' co-operatives and state aid for the unemployed. Even after the June days, they continued to spend money on both of these, and they developed advanced programmes for agricultural credit, education and representation, for free public and lay primary schools. The germs of the Third Republic legislation were all here.

The Cavaignac government (June–December 1848) is wrongly thought to have been a reaction against the provisional government of February. It continued its work, and retained many of its personnel. There were thus about eight months of office by which to judge the republicans. What they showed was that they had not learnt the art of government. They lost the opportunity of winning the loyalty of the peasantry by a dramatic gesture on taxation. They would have liked to have carried out reforms—they promised them—but ultimately they were too intimidated by orthodox financial theories. They had inherited a whole series of deficits from the monarchy. They refused to declare bankruptcy. On the contrary, instead of reducing taxation, and while simply talking about the merits of a progressive income tax, they levied an additional land tax, known as the 45 centimes. They refused to exempt the poor— as Ledru-Rollin demanded—and so one of their very first actions was to penalise the peasants, while the townsmen went scot-free. There was a great movement of discontent: many refused to pay: some departments paid about three-quarters of what they ought to have but others paid only 2 per cent: by mid July less than half had been collected. Other tax measures showed a similar lack of political skill. The salt tax was abolished but only as from 1 January 1849. The tax on alcoholic drinks was ended but was replaced by another levied in a different way, so transferring discontent from the wine merchants to the producers and consumers. The abolition of the tax on butcher's meat had almost no effect, because the slaughterers did not pass much of the benefit on to the retailers. The feeble attempt to tax the rich, by a 1 per cent duty on mortgages, could not be enforced: it would have involved borrowers denouncing their creditors to the tax collectors. The republicans would have achieved far more if they had instead done something to help the peasant free himself from his debts.[1]

Their attitude to press censorship was similarly equivocal. The freedom allowed in the first months was soon brought to an end. The caution money was reintroduced for newspapers— earning them the enmity of the press, even if the new tax was at a much lower level than that imposed by Louis-Philippe. Finally, they paved the way for their own doom, by helping to draw up a constitution which brought about most of the things they wished to avoid. This constitution proclaimed the sovereignty of the people, and naïvely assumed that this would guarantee their freedom. It declared that the separation of powers was the first condition of a free government, and so it established on the one hand an executive president and on the other a legislative assembly of 750, both elected by the people, but each independent of the other. Reacting against Louis-Philippe's supposedly English-style parliamentary government —which had brought only weak and corrupt coalitions—it made the president more powerful than the king with the ministers entirely dependent on him. The president could hold office for only four years and the constitution could be revised only with difficulty. Within a very short space of time, president and parliament were at loggerheads. Only force could decide between them and that was in the president's hands. Thus,

---

[1] Alfred Antony, *La Politique financière du gouvernement provisoire, février–mai 1848* (1910); M. Marion, *Histoire financière de la France depuis 1715*, vol. 5 (1928).

almost inexorably, the constitution produced a dictatorship. As a result of this, the Third Republic went to the other extreme and concentrated all powers in an assembly, but this had equally disastrous results.

No less important was the republicans' failure to deal with the problem of the Church. They were on the whole no enemies of religion. They believed in the need, if not for Catholicism, at least for a religion of some kind—the new Christianity of Saint-Simon, the religion of humanity of Leroux, the Christian socialism of Buchez. Many of them defined fraternity as the implementation of the ethics of primitive Christianity. Universal suffrage reinforced the political power of the Church, but the republicans hovered on the bounds of anticlericalism. The alliance of the clergy with Louis Napoleon was, in due course, to clinch this matter and make the republicans firmly hostile.[1]

These mistakes were made, thirdly, because moderate republicanism was the product of very diverse origins and had not been welded into a coherent ideology. The distinction textbooks usually make, between the followers of the *Réforme* and the *National* newspapers, is superficial. The differences between these papers were largely ones of personality. Far more important were the different sources from which they derived their republicanism. There were some who saw the republic as the rule of virtue and whose heroes were the ancient Greeks. For many republicanism meant patriotism, the revival of national glory, French leadership of the world. Such men, of whom perhaps Carrel was the most eminent and vocal, were often distinguishable only with difficulty from the Bonapartists. Until 1830 republicanism and Bonapartism were closely allied. Then vast numbers of the generals, civil servants and admirers of Napoleon I were given office by Louis-Philippe and partially absorbed into Orleanism—the distinction between the parties was by no means clear cut. Those who remained in opposition continued to flirt with the Bonapartists, and it was a republican paper which published the writings of Louis Napoleon when he was in prison. Carrel (whom Jules Simon in his memoirs was to

[1] Paul Bastid, *Doctrines et institutions politiques de la Seconde République* (1945); Jacques Cohen, *La Préparation de la constitution de 1848* (1935); Georges Cogniot, *La Question scolaire en 1848* (1948); O. Festy, *Les Associations ouvrières encouragées par la Deuxième République* (1915).

describe as 'all powerful over the minds of the youth' of the 1830s and 1840s) was the first man to call himself a 'conservative republican'. He was opposed to revolutionary methods and to violence. He declared that he would prefer a monarchy with a little liberty to a republic with none. The young Bonaparte was his hero and in his ideal constitution he would have had a first consul at the head of state, or a president modelled on the U.S.A., with strong powers.[1] The American revolution indeed was as much an ideal in France as the French one.[2] The First Republic was so bathed in unpleasant memories that people preferred to forget about it; ignorance about it was extraordinary, even if vague family feuds dating back to it continued to smoulder. Thiers—an Orleanist—began its rehabilitation under the Restoration, but it was only in the 1840s that histories of it became really numerous. Till then it was synonymous with the Terror. But now every writer stressed a different aspect of it, and division among its admirers was bitter.[3]

These internal enmities were linked with the increasingly numerous interpretations republicans formed of the Enlightenment. Voltaire was read avidly: 36 editions of his complete works were published between his death in 1784 and 1877, 22 of them under the Restoration. Some editions involved as many as 125 volumes, and these filled the bookshelves of men of intellectual pretensions who could afford them, but there were also available *The Cottage Voltaire* and *The Small Property Owner's Voltaire*, at more modest prices. The single work reprinted most often was his *History of Charles XII* (74 editions, 1815–80); his theatre was far more popular than his *Philosophic Dictionary* or even *Candide*. So it is by no means clear what people made of him. A Voltairian could be either an Orleanist or a republican. His tendency to sarcasm and rebelliousness, to doubt and

---

[1] *Œuvres politiques et littéraires d'Armand Carrel*, ed. Littré and Paulin (1857), 3. 58, 122, 176, 4. 137, 5. 366; Jules Simon, *Premières Années* (n.d.), 181; R. G. Nobecourt, *La Vie d'Armand Carrel* (1930); Angus MacLaren, *Armand Carrel* (Ph.D. thesis, Harvard, 1970).

[2] René Remond, *Les États-Unis devant l'opinion française 1815–52* (1962), 2. 640–1.

[3] Thiers's history appeared 1823–7 (10 vols.). Among other histories of the revolution were Félix de Conny, 1834–42 (8 vols.); E. Cabet, 1840 (4 vols.); L. Blanc, 1847–62 (12 vols.); J. Michelet, 1847–53 (7 vols.); Abbé de Genoude, 1845–8 (7 vols.); A. Esquiros, 1847 (2 vols.); A. Gabourd, 1846–51 (10 vols.); A. Laponneraye, 1845 (3 vols.); A. de Lamartine, 1847 (8 vols.); and the parliamentary history edited by P. Buchez, 1834–8 (40 vols.).

frivolity but also to strong definite opinions made it difficult for
him to be unreservedly on any one side.[1] It was even more the
case with the disciples of Rousseau that they could draw
divergent interpretations from his writings, and besides many
republicans, converted to positivism, turned altogether against
Rousseau in the second half of the century.[2] Dupont de Bussac
showed the complicated amalgams which could be formed
when he said that he thought of himself as continuing the tradition of Condorcet and Turgot, Price and Priestley.[3]

In their attitude to the common man, the republicans placed
varying emphasis on the improvement of his material lot and
on his education; but some tempered their democratic leanings
with a certain élitism. Vacherot, for example, argued that 'free
thought' was the ultimate goal which the human mind, in
perfect maturity, could reach, but only a rare élite had the
'philosophical spirit' necessary to achieving this, to freeing
itself completely from all prejudice, passion and self-interest.
Moderately intelligent people could only approximate to it if
they had a developed critical sense. But even they were pretty
rare: they were found mainly among male Aryans: there were
very few among the Chinese, negroes and women. Vacherot
distinguished between the doctrines fit for the élite and the
watered-down, simple proverbs which the masses were capable
of understanding, and he wrote rather contemptuously of the
prejudices of the bourgeoisie who had received no classical
education.[4] This élitism, again, was linked with the Protestantism
which, as will be seen later, was one of the constituent elements
in republicanism. Some republicans, even if they were not
Protestants, felt sympathy for its attack on Catholic dogmatism;

---

[1] Georges Benesco, *Voltaire: bibliographie de ses œuvres* (1890), 4. 163, 195; J. F.
Nourrisson, *Voltaire et le voltairianisme* (1896), 656–7; Abbé Berseux, *Le Voltairomanie*
(Lanenville, 1865); Pierre Guiral, in *Hommage au Doyen E. Gros* (Gap, 1959), 193–204.
[2] J. F. Nourrisson, *J.-J. Rousseau et le rousseauisme* (1903); J. R. Talmon, *The
Origins of Totalitarianism* (1952); J. Jaurès, 'Les Idées politiques et sociales de J.-J.
Rousseau', *Revue de métaphysique et de morale*, 20 (1912), 371–81; Harald Höffding,
'Rousseau et le 19ᵉ siècle', *Annales de la Société J. J. Rousseau*, 8 (Geneva, 1912),
69–98. For an example of a Rousseauist republican see Demosthenes Ollivier's
views in Theodore Zeldin, *Émile Ollivier* (Oxford, 1963), 3–4.
[3] G. Weill, *Histoire du parti républicain en France 1814–1870* (new edition, 1928), 111.
[4] E. Vacherot, *La Religion* (1869), 255, 267, 411–13; cf. his social doctrines in
La Démocratie (1860). For a life of this very interesting man, E. Boutroux, 'Notice
sur la vie et les œuvres de M. Étienne Vacherot', *Mémoires de l'Académie des
sciences morales et politiques*, 21 May 1904, 25 (1907), 83–114.

but there were also complex and tortured Calvinists who found in republicanism an outlet for their search for salvation. Religion, however, is so large a question in the making of republicanism, that it must be left for separate treatment.

The nature of the moderation of these republicans can be illustrated with the case of Alexandre-Thomas Marie, minister of public works in the provisional government and of justice under Cavaignac, and president of the Constituent Assembly in June 1848. Few people have heard of him now, but he was popular enough in 1848 to be elected to parliament by Paris, with more than twice as many votes as Lamennais received. He came of a family which had been lawyers for two centuries, but his father, a younger son, was an impoverished archivist who soon left him an orphan. Marie worked his own way up as a barrister, until in 1840 he became *bâtonnier* of Paris. He had had to wait a long time to earn the money to become an elector: he felt the insult, and he joined the republicans to demand universal suffrage. He did not differ profoundly from Guizot in his general views; he agreed that reason should be sovereign, but he thought that it manifested itself not through an élite but through the masses. He deplored the 'mad dreams' of the 'new aristocracy' of bourgeois. He argued that democracy was a 'social necessity' because the masses had, after many centuries, at last freed themselves from the powers which had dominated them and had learnt their strength: they now demanded respect, and it could not be denied to them. But Marie hated the agitation of the clubs and the revolutionaries. He was an enemy of violence. He had not pressed for the immediate proclamation of the republic, because he did not believe that a party had a right to impose a particular form of government on the nation. He agreed to join the provisional government because he wanted to help maintain order and to prevent anarchy, and he looked back with pride on its repression of successive popular risings. The people were children who had to be shown that their utopias would not work: he therefore approved trying out the National Workshops, and then ending them when they got out of hand. 'A lot of blood had to be shed', he wrote, 'to dethrone the false gods.' The masses, more than any other class, needed to be strongly governed. 'The despotism of a thousand heads is a thousand times more odious than the despotism of a single man.' Liberty had to be combined with order. He supported the freeing of the press, but then agreed that it had gone too far and needed to be controlled when it abused its liberty and attacked the very basis of society, 'insolently calling into question all the traditions of the past'. He was all in favour of democracy, whose function was to develop the moral and material interests not of some but of all, but he was also for realism. Universal fraternity was a 'sublime idea' but 'is man's heart large enough to contain so much charity, devotion and heroism?' He thought national groupings were probably more practical. The fatherland was like 'a great home' in which the citizen found all the protection and all the love that in his private capacity he found in the family home. One can see in Marie how the moderate republicans were still in the process of working out their relations with the masses.[1]

The republicans had a great deal to learn from the other parties before they could discover how to establish themselves. Their experience of defeat and their tribulations under Napoleon III, were to have a profound effect on their attitudes and thinking. In 1870 they emerged in many ways transformed.[2]

---

[1] Aimé Cherest, *La Vie et les œuvres de A. T. Marie* (1873).

[2] Compare I. Tchernoff, *Le Parti républicain sous la monarchie de juillet* (1901), and id., *Le Parti républicain au coup d'État et sous le Second Empire* (1900).

18. Bonapartism

FOR over a hundred years, Bonapartism has been the intellectual's nightmare. It has represented the silencing of free discussion, the domination of the military and the rule of a heavy-handed bureaucracy. It has implied the discrediting of the man of letters, in favour of the industrialist and even the peasant. So though Bonapartism has, at times, won more votes than any other party—whatever may be said about how it obtained these votes—it has been always vigorously and almost unanimously attacked by writers. There have been some able Bonapartist propagandists, but only of the kind who have addressed themselves to the masses. There have been— with few exceptions—no serious Bonapartist historians or theoreticians to create an intellectually respectable doctrine, or to defend the programme of the movement in universal terms. As a result, the Second Empire has been studied far less than other regimes—as a glance at the sparse entries in the annual bibliography shows—and there is still no full history of Bonapartism as a movement.[1]

The simplest definition of Bonapartism is that it is the perpetuation of the ideas of Napoleon I, the cult of his genius and the appeal to his methods for the solution of France's problems. Guizot summed up the secret of its strength in its ability simultaneously to represent national glory, to guarantee the maintenance of the achievements of the Revolution and to affirm the principles of authority and order. Bonapartism, that is, reconciled democracy and authority in a way which was neither reactionary on the one hand nor parliamentary on the other. It offered itself as the answer to the rule of anarchic and discredited parliaments. It provided a leader to appeal to the whole nation—against the parties and factions which monopo-

[1] The main histories are Pierre de La Gorce, *Histoire du Second Empire* (7 vols., 1894–1904); C. Seignobos, *La Révolution de 1848. Le Second Empire* (vol. 6 of E. Lavisse, *Histoire de la France contemporaine*) and *Le Déclin de l'empire et l'établissement de la Troisième République 1859–75* (vol. 7 of the same series), both 1921; Albert Thomas, *Le Second Empire* (1906, in Jaurès, *Histoire socialiste*) and Émile Ollivier, *L'Empire libéral* (18 vols., 1895–1918).

lised power for their own benefit—elected by the nation, and responsible to it. Unlike royalism, which claimed equally to be national, to maintain order and to provide security for property, Bonapartism aspired to preserve the work of the Revolution, by affirming the equality of men, careers open to talent, and the abolition of the privileges of castes and corporations.

However, it is a great mistake to assume that Bonapartism meant the same thing throughout the nineteenth century. The fact that its leaders paid homage to Napoleon I should not conceal the variety of their interpretations of his message, nor the changing circumstances in which they tried to apply it. Some political scientists and historians have attempted to find the essence of Bonapartism, to isolate its individuality, as though they are studying a disease, which erupts from time to time; and if they discover that it is not always identical, they dismiss any deviation as an aberration. Thus H. A. L. Fisher, in his eloquent and influential lectures on Bonapartism, asserted that the First and Second Napoleonic Empires were 'to a large extent inspired by the same principles, rested upon the support of the same intellectual and social forces, appealed to the same appetites, flattered the same vanities'. However, he did not investigate in detail exactly what these forces and appetites were, beyond quoting with apparent approval Tocqueville's summing up of the Second Empire as 'the paradise of the envious and the mediocre'. More recently, parallels have been drawn between Napoleon III and de Gaulle. Jacques Duclos, the Communist leader, has written a book placing them both in the same tradition, of authoritarianism, contempt for public opinion, thirst for power, pride and egocentricity. The use of plebiscites has been seen as the essential damning feature of Bonapartism. When de Gaulle achieved his sweeping triumph in 1962, L'Express recalled the words of Émile Ollivier in 1870: 'One is never weaker than when one appears to be supported by everybody.' André Siegfried, one of the ablest of commentators, distinguished between 'true' Bonapartism, which was that of Napoleon I, and Bonapartism as it evolved, 'and in my view became corrupted', under Napoleon III and Eugénie, for in this second phase it was clerical, aristocratic and reactionary. In his opinion, therefore, Bonapartism for most of the century was not proper Bonapartism at all. It ceased to be national and was a party like any other. When it tried to become liberal and parliamentary in 1870, it was contradicting itself and denying its 'true character'. It discovered in fact that if it allowed free discussion of its government, it would commit suicide, but if it did not, its repression deprived it of the support of many liberals and workers, so that it was forced into alliance with the reactionaries. It thus ceased to be democratic and left wing and became a prisoner of clericalism. It is difficult to see when Bonapartism was 'its true self'. One might indeed wonder whether there ever was such a thing as Bonapartism. Is not Napoleon III supposed to have said, 'The empress is legitimist, my cousin is republican, Morny is Orleanist, I am a socialist; the only Bonapartist is Persigny and he is mad'?[1]

One has only to glance at some maps of the regions of France from which Bonapartism derived its strength at different dates, to realise at once that its support was not constant. Under the Restoration Normandy was royalist but in the early Third Republic it was staunchly Bonapartist. Under the Restoration the east of France was Bonapartist, and it voted for Louis Napoleon in 1848, but after 1870 it was a bastion of republicanism. The west of France, which was always regarded as the stronghold of royalism, elected considerable numbers of Bonapartists in the Third Republic. The south was uniformly hostile throughout the century; but the south-west, which had virtually no Bonapartist party in 1848, became the fief of whole dynasties of Bonapartist deputies, until it was transformed once again into a major centre of republican radicalism. These variations need to be explained. They certainly show that one is not dealing with an unchanging clientele or a static doctrine; and they raise the question of whether Bonapartism meant different things in different parts of France.

When it is suggested that liberal Bonapartism was simply a corrupt form of Orleanism, it is assumed that Orleanism was distinct and different from Bonapartism. From the ideal, theoretical point of view it might have been, but in practice they were rather like estranged brothers, offspring of the same

---

[1] H. A. L. Fisher, *Bonapartism* (Oxford, 1908), 3, 87; André Siegfried, *Tableau politique de la France de l'ouest* (1913), 473–95; Jacques Duclos, *De Napoléon III à de Gaulle* (1964); *L'Express*, 5 Apr. 1962; M. Rubel, *Marx devant le bonapartisme* (1960).

father. For some time after 1815 the distinctions between the
opposition parties under the Restoration were not clear. Men
who were later labelled as Orleanist, Bonapartist and republicans all contributed to establishing the monarchy of Louis-
Philippe. Before 1830, the Bonapartists often called themselves
liberal, in the same way as their allies did.[1] The first consequence
of the revolution of that year was to bring back into power the
vast horde of Napoleonic generals and civil servants who had
been dismissed in 1815. Orleanism is one of Napoleon I's
unacknowledged legacies. It was Napoleon I who invented the
société censitaire, the rule of notables selected on the basis of
a property qualification. It was he who abolished universal
suffrage, who established the rule that only men with private
incomes should enter the higher ranks of the civil service.
Napoleon I gave his nobles no fiscal privileges, but when he
gave titles, he allowed them to become hereditary provided the
recipients were rich enough. He, perhaps even more than
Guizot, could have been credited with the injunction to 'get
rich'.[2] If Orleanism was liberal, so too were the Additional
Act of 1815 and the legend of a constitutional monarchy which
Napoleon created on St. Helena. What distinguished Louis-
Philippe's reign from Napoleon's was that the notables got the
upper hand after 1830. They obtained far more power from the
king whom they installed on the throne, than they had been
able to exercise under the shadow of the military conqueror.
But they became even more loyal to Napoleon's memory once
he was safely dead. It was under Louis-Philippe that they
brought back Napoleon's ashes to France and raised monu-
ments to his glory. However, they steadfastly refused to end the
exile imposed on Napoleon's family. The trial of Louis Napoleon
in 1840 was conducted by a court of 4 former ministers of
Napoleon I, 6 of his marshals, 56 of his generals, 14 of his
councillors of state, 19 of his prefects, 7 ambassadors and 21
chamberlains who were then members of Louis-Philippe's
chamber of peers. It was these men who created the Bonapartism of the future by their treatment of Louis Napoleon, who
might have been content with a modest share of the spoils

[1] Cf. Balzac, *Le Député d'Arcis*: *Œuvres*, ed. Bouteron and Lognon (1949), 283–4.
[2] See Jacques Godechot, *Les Institutions de la France sous la Révolution et l'Empire*
(1951), 496–7, 502–3.

which they refused to share with him.[1] Louis Napoleon had to transform the Napoleonic legend, to base himself on universal suffrage, in alliance with the republicans, in order to get back into France. Bonapartism could be called an Orleanist heresy.

Alternatively, it could be seen as a variety of republicanism. Militarism, the passion for glory and foreign adventures was, before 1848, essentially a characteristic of the republicans. The army was considered a dangerous hotbed of liberalism and revolution. It was only later that the republicans accused Bonapartism of militarism, when the army, like the notables, developed an independent *esprit de corps*, forgot its revolutionary origins, and became the defender of hierarchy and order. Louis Napoleon modified the interpretation of Bonapartism produced by the Orleanists, by grafting on to it two republican doctrines, universal suffrage and an active foreign policy.[2] The republican leaders had little use for him, but he was far from being looked on as an enemy by the lower ranks of their party.[3] His break with them came only after 1848, when he allied with their enemies, and after 1851, when he persecuted them with unprecedented severity. When he obtained power, both his doctrine and his support were altered. Bonapartism was continually evolving. It is important not to create stereotypes for it, any more than for Orleanism or republicanism. These became increasingly differentiated with time: what one needs to ascertain is why. In this way, one will see whether the divisions of French politics were inevitable, necessarily embedded, as commentators have argued, in irreconcilable 'temperaments', and inescapably following from incompatible

[1] J. Taschereau, *Revue rétrospective* (1848), 140–1; *Aux Mânes de l'Empereur, la patrie reconnaissante. Notice biographique des 192 pairs de France ayant reçu des faveurs de l'Empereur et qui aujourd'hui sont les juges du prince Napoléon* (1840), Bibliothèque Nationale shelf-mark Lb(51)3137.

[2] See the views of Thiers, a 'Napoleonist', on the republicanism of Louis Napoleon, *Moniteur universel* (1851), 185, and those of Crémieux, ibid. (1845), 884. Douglas Jerrold, *Life of Napoleon III* (1875–82), i. 250–1, letter of Louis Napoleon to Vieillard, 29 Jan. 1836; P. Thureau Dangin, *La Monarchie de juillet* (1897–1904), i. 594, Baron Gustave de Romand, *De l'état des partis en France* (1839), 23–5. Jean Vidalenc, *Les Demi-Soldes. Étude d'une catégorie sociale* (1955), shows that Bonapartism was not common among these former soldiers of Napoleon I. G. Perreux, *La Propagande républicaine au début de la monarchie de juillet* (1931), shows the inter-relationships of the parties.

[3] See Carnot's denunciation in *Moniteur universel* (1841), 1538.

principles. It is worth asking whether, on the contrary, the party's divisions were created gradually, and adopted principles to give respectability to animosities which often had personal or fortuitous causes; whether, that is to say, the politicians and the theorists helped to produce the divisions. It will be suggested that Bonapartism was the intermediary for the effecting of social changes which republicanism was unable to carry out on its own and that it contributed a considerable amount to the evolution of republicanism, which became its bitterest enemy. Polemic has obscured its work.

First, it is necessary to see how Napoleon III stood in relation to the masses, the notables, the parties and what effect his reign had on these. Napoleon III ruled France for twenty-one years, longer than anyone else in the country's modern history. The usual view is that he was a well-meaning visionary out of touch with reality, a confused charlatan, a feeble parody of his uncle, an adventurer whose bluff and gambles were doomed to a catastrophic end. He owes this reputation partly to the repeated fiascos of his foreign policy and partly to the fact that the majority of intellectuals of his day were opposed to his regime; he has never quite recovered from their witty and pungent attacks. In the twentieth century, there has been, almost inevitably, a reaction to this hostile interpretation. Some historians have instead painted him, not as aping the past, but as a man far ahead of his time, principally concerned with the economic development of his country, a precursor of technocracy and of the modern dictators. This is to go too far in the opposite direction. For Napoleon III cannot be classified accurately in any single category. One should not assume that he was a man with certain set ideas, which he described in his books and which he then put into practice when he became emperor. For if his books are read with care, it will be seen that they contain contradictions on nearly every subject. In his writings he was a republican, an opponent of nobility, a protectionist, a believer that colonies were unnecessary and that the Church should be kept out of education. Once in power he proclaimed the empire, created dukes, made the free trade treaties with England and many other nations, established an empire in the Far East and supported the clericalist Loi Falloux. There are those, nevertheless, who claim that Napoleon was basically a

Saint-Simonian: they point to his concern for the lot of the poor, his stimulation of industry, his interest in communications and in the Suez and Panama canals, his belief in a hierarchical society and his advocacy of agricultural colonies. They argue that he must have got his ideas from Louis Blanc and the *Atelier* newspaper he is known to have read, for he never actually mentions Saint-Simon; they think he may have read Enfantin's *Colonisation de l'Algérie*, because this contains ideas similar to his own; they suggest he may have been influenced by Vieillard who was a Saint-Simonian. There is no direct evidence for any of these suppositions and there is much that throws doubt upon them. For in his writings Napoleon was an enemy of the industrial revolution; his agricultural colonies were designed to send town workers back to the land; he himself later said that they were modelled on the example of experiments in foreign countries (presumably van der Bosch's in Holland and Belgium); his economic aim was not to produce as much as possible but to keep the masses in employment; he did not want the country to be ruled by industrialists; and as for his famous statement that the government was not a necessary ulcer but the beneficent motor of society, there were more numerous declarations by him praising individual initiative and holding England up as the ideal. The fact that many Saint-Simonians were successful industrialists in his reign does not necessarily mean that he belonged to their school. On the contrary he frequently criticised doctrinaires, party men and utopian theorists.[1]

Napoleon III's political ideas were essentially opportunistic. His most fervent belief consisted in a deep admiration for his uncle, but this was not an uncritical admiration, for he considered Napoleon I a great man because he gave the people what they wanted as well as what they ought to have. Likewise he admired William III of England for ending a century of revolution in that country by giving it the liberties and religion it sought. Politics for Napoleon III was not the slavish imitation or revival of the past but, as he himself said, the application of

[1] Napoleon III, *Œuvres* (1856), 2. 5, 31, 125, 367; 3. 27, 54, 59, 118, 148, 162, 182, 236; Douglas Jerrold, *Life of Napoleon III* (1875–82), 2. 280. The evidence on his familiarity with Enfantin's book suggests he was introduced to it by Urbain only in the late 1850s.

history to the present.[1] That is why the majority of his works were historical: studies of Napoleon I, William III, Julius Caesar, the history of artillery. History revealed why statesmen had succeeded or failed and it also showed that there were great irresistible currents, such as the movements for economic progress, liberty and nationality, which it was the function of great statesmen to assist. His romanticism produced in him enormous veneration for such men and his mysticism convinced him that he was destined to be one himself. 'I believe', he wrote from his prison in Ham, 'that there are certain men who are born to serve as a means for the march of the human race . . . I consider myself to be one of these . . .' He added: 'The history of England says clearly to kings: March at the head of the ideas of your century and these ideas will follow and support you; march behind them and they will drag you after them; march against them and they will overthrow you.' The mark of a great statesman is that he can discover the wishes of the people, identify himself with them and lead them to the attainment of their goal.[2]

This is not to say Napoleon had no programme of his own, or that he envisaged his role as that of a passive intermediary for that of the people. He insisted that the duty of a government was to lead only *right* ideas and the establishment of universal suffrage—the first plank in his platform—would not necessarily produce a mandate in favour of right ideas, for as Switzerland showed, the masses were really conservative, attached to old prejudices and rejecting every improvement.[3] Though he was always to watch public opinion closely and to pay great attention to it in formulating his policy,[4] he did not expect it to take the initiative in dictating policy to him. Liberty he defined as 'a chief ruling according to the will of all' and by *will* he understood something very like Rousseau's General Will.[5] He considered that democracy existed once the people were the source of power, even if they did not control its exercise. The popular election of the ruler was therefore the main requirement for good government. In this sense Napoleon's ideal was a

---

[1] *Œuvres*, 2. 243, and 1. 98. [2] Ibid. 1. 342; 1. 31–2.
[3] Ibid. 1. 398.
[4] See L. M. Case, *Public Opinion on War and Diplomacy during the Second Empire* (Philadelphia, Pa., 1954).
[5] Cf. *Œuvres*, 2. 83.

popular dictatorship, but it does not follow that he stood for absolutism as opposed to the liberalism of the republicans. Under Louis-Philippe very few people distinguished between liberty and democracy; universal suffrage, it was generally believed, would secure both. During this period Napoleon differed from the republicans only in preferring the government of one man to that of a party committee. However, he quoted his uncle as saying that constitutions should be flexible; it was impossible to leave too many chances open for modifying them. With time indeed the strong government of one man would develop respect for law and a public spirit such as existed in England; this would provide a basis and a demand for more liberty, the ultimate establishment of which had always been his uncle's aim.[1]

Napoleon's social aims naturally therefore incorporated the most commonplace ideas of his time: careers open to talent, the fusion of classes, the ending of all privileges except those based on merit, prosperity for all, but not at the expense of the rich, employment and social benefits for the working class, cheap credit and less taxation for the mortgaged peasantry, property ultimately for all men, great public works and improved communications which would be self-financing because they would increase the national wealth, peace but also glory. Napoleon's view of popular pyschology was that the masses would be content with nominal sovereignty, with political equality between classes, with opportunities to rise in the social hierarchy and to make a better living.

However, Napoleon was elected president in December 1848, confirmed in December 1851 and became emperor a year later not because his programme as a whole was approved by the electorate but because so many sections of the electorate placed their hopes in him. Napoleon was not simply the emperor of the peasants, against the industrial town workers and the bourgeoisie. Many peasants did vote for him but many also did not, particularly in the clerical west and the republican centre and south. Some town workers voted against him but a great many more voted for him. There was opposition to him from artisans, rural as well as urban, but again this was by no means the case everywhere. In 1848 many parliamentary leaders

[1] Œuvres, 1. 44, 52–5.

supported him for the presidency but a considerable section of the bourgeoisie seems to have preferred Cavaignac. In 1851 and 1852 these leaders went into opposition, but their rank and file, terrified by the threat of another revolution, largely accepted his dictatorship. Again many legitimists supported him in 1848, as a conservative against the republican Cavaignac, but later, when he seemed to be about to become emperor, abstained. Everywhere the vote was complicated by local issues, the vital significance of which will be explained in due course. Napoleon's success was due to spontaneous reactions much more than to the effect of propaganda. A. J. Tudesq has produced some very interesting maps showing on the one hand how the different regions voted in December 1848 and on the other whom the local newspapers supported. There is little correlation between the two.[1] Napoleon's election did not represent the triumph of a programme. The significance of Bonapartism still had to be worked out. It was to depend very much on interaction with events and opinion.

In any case, Napoleon III, as emperor, did not possess the power to do as he pleased. He inherited institutions, customs and legal practices from his predecessors, so that his was a modified rather than a completely reshaped version of previous governments. The three major constitutional changes were the reduced independence of ministers, the diminished powers of parliament and the increased vigour in censoring and suppressing opposition. But Napoleon had to act through individuals of widely different backgrounds and ideas. There was thus possibly even less coherence in his government than in the chaotic struggle for influence that prevailed under the July Monarchy. It is true that he commanded a great deal of personal allegiance from those who worked with him. He had a strange charm for those with whom he came into contact. He could flatter without seeming hypocritical; he was generous; he was a good listener. But there was always something opaque about him, so that it was no easy matter following his lead. His silent meditations and his mystical communion with public opinion made him—when he was successful—a kind of wizard.

[1] A. J. Tudesq, *L'Élection présidentielle de L. N. Bonaparte, 10 déc. 1848* (1965); R. Pimienta, *La Propagande bonapartiste en 1848* (1911); A. Ferrère, *Révélations sur la propagande napoléonienne faite en 1848 et 1849* (Turin, 1863).

In his old age, sick and racked by pain, his judgement, though often shrewd, was clouded even more by the languor which always interrupted his moments of energy. Communication between him, his government and the masses was never simple.

In 1852 Napoleon may have appeared to be the absolute master of France but the history of his reign cannot be summarised in his own biography. Certainly, he determined personally the general direction of government policy but he was not sufficiently assiduous in administration nor sufficiently attentive to detail to get his will regularly enforced in practice. It is true the constitution gave him complete control of the executive: the ministers were grand civil servants responsible to him alone and he insisted that they should do nothing important without his approval. He regularly presided over cabinet meetings, led their discussions and made the final decisions in them. He changed and moved his ministers around frequently. But that he had to do this indicated just how little they were pliable tools in his hands.

The duc de Persigny, for example, a bankrupt petty aristocrat and Napoleon's fellow conspirator in his early days, was fervently devoted to him but his zeal led him to adopt a policy more extreme than Napoleon desired. In 1852, as minister of the interior, he organised demonstrations demanding the proclamation of the empire and so made Napoleon move towards it faster than he had intended. In his conduct of the elections, particularly in 1863, his wild attacks on the clericals, his blatant use of administrative pressure was judged by Napoleon to be excessive and he was dismissed. Persigny worked to create a coherent Bonapartist party, to whom all power and all rewards should be confined; but the emperor wished also to make some sort of compromise with the notables, to win over Orleanists and legitimists, even if their loyalty was not as religious as Persigny's: most of his ministers were in fact of this kind.[1]

Morny could be called a typical Orleanist. He was a grandson of Talleyrand and Napoleon III's illegitimate half-brother. He had been a soldier and a sugar manufacturer under Louis-Philippe. He was a patron of the arts, a rake and a speculator but he was also a man with enormous ambition and sang-froid

[1] V. F. de Persigny, *Mémoires du duc de Persigny* (1896); H. Farat, *Persigny* (1957).

behind his languid exterior. He played a decisive role in ensuring the success of the *coup d'état*. He never obtained the leading position in the empire to which he aspired, but as president of the legislature (1854–65) he contributed a great deal to increasing that body's constitutional importance and powers, and to hastening the advent of the liberal empire of which he was a persistent advocate. Achille Fould (minister of state 1852– 60, minister of finance 1861–7), a Jewish-Protestant banker, had been an Orleanist too. He and Pierre Magne (minister of finance 1854–60, 1867–9), a barrister who had been a civil servant under Louis-Philippe, both influenced Napoleon's financial policy, though in different ways, and attacking each other.[1] Baron Haussmann (prefect of the Seine 1853–70) was in perpetual dispute with these two men because of the way he raised money for rebuilding Paris. In planning the new city Haussmann followed Napoleon's personal instructions for many details but the authoritarian methods of execution were his own.[2] The marquis de Chasseloup-Laubat (minister of Algeria and the colonies 1858–9, minister of the marine and colonies 1860–7, minister president of the Conseil d'État 1869) came of an old noble family, was the son of a general of the First Empire, a councillor of state and a deputy under Louis-Philippe and then a leader of the independents in Napoleon's first parliament of 1852–7. The principal achievement of his long ministry, the annexation of Cochin-China, was his own work, to which he converted Napoleon by means of a strongly argued memorandum. In 1869, when asked to prepare a constitution for the liberal empire, he followed Napoleon's instructions but also went beyond them, giving deputies the right to initiate legislation. Chasseloup so retained his independence while serving the empire, that he was one of the few Bonapartists to be elected to parliament in 1871, and he was then appointed *rapporteur* of the important Army Law of 1872.[3] Victor Duruy (minister of Education 1863–9), the anticlerical historian and

---

[1] A. Fould, *Journaux et discours* (1867); J. Durieux, *Le Ministre Pierre Magne* (2 vols., 1929); R. Pflaum, *The Life of the Duc de Morny* (N.Y. 1968).

[2] J. M. and B. Chapman, *The Life and Times of Baron Haussmann* (1957); G. Lameyre, *Haussmann* (1958); D. Pinkney, *Napoleon III and the Rebuilding of Paris* (Princeton, N. J., 1958).

[3] J. Delarbre, *Chasseloup-Laubat* (1873); memorandum on Cochin-China in his private papers, which his descendants have kindly allowed me to examine.

inspector of schools, served the emperor without abandoning his well-known republican ideals: he was another whose individuality was widely acknowledged.[1]

Baroche[2] and Rouher[3] were the two principal barristers in the government, and they were accused of advocating in turn every different policy that Napoleon adopted. Baroche was indeed a fairly docile instrument of Napoleon's will, who executed decisions rather than helped to make them; but then he had a great admiration for the emperor, whom he genuinely looked upon as the saviour of society against the socialist menace. Even so he did on occasion resist his sovereign: he spoke firmly against the Crimean War; in 1862 he offered his resignation as a protest against concessions to the clericals and by this means he was able to obtain their attenuation. Rouher's attitude was even more pronouncedly conservative, and though he continued to serve Napoleon after the liberal concessions of 1860 and 1867, he made no secret of his opposition to them. His vast capacity for work, his ability to master the details of the most complicated legal and economic questions, his vigour as a speaker, made him increasingly indispensable to Napoleon. People called him 'the vice-emperor'. Rouher entrenched himself in power with a veritable clientage of dependants distributed throughout parliament and the civil service: it was said that he suffered no job, no decoration, no favour to be given without his advice. When ultimately he had to retire in 1870, with the final advent of the liberal empire, he was still able to organise strong opposition to it. He did much to impress an authoritarian stamp upon the regime.

The legislation of the reign was prepared by the Conseil d'État. This body was nominated by the emperor, but he himself complained that it was very difficult to carry reforms through its conservative committees. That his laws were such pale reflections of his ideas was due in no small measure to it.[4]

---

[1] V. Duruy, *Notes et souvenirs 1811–1894* (1901); Jean Rohr, *Victor Duruy, ministre de Napoleon III* (1967). Cf. in general Roger L. Williams, *Gaslight and Shadow* (1957).

[2] Minister of interior 1850–1, vice-president of the Conseil d'État 1852, president 1853–63, minister of justice 1863–7, 1868–9. See J. Maurain, *Baroche* (1936).

[3] Minister of justice 1849–51, vice-president of the Conseil d'État 1852–5, minister of agriculture, commerce and public works 1855–63, president of the Conseil d'État 1863, minister of state 1863–9, president of the senate 1870. See R. Schnerb, *Rouher* (1949).

[4] Vincent Wright is writing a book on the Conseil d'État in this period.

The law on workers' combinations (1864) is a good example. Napoleon intended it to be a concession, the Conseil d'État hedged the concession with so many provisos as to render it worthless, and an intrigue between Napoleon, Morny and Ollivier was needed to give it some meaning. The conservatives soon discovered that the easiest way to obstruct change was to hold up technical legal objections, before which Napoleon nearly always yielded. Many parts of the civil service, apparently an instrument of the emperor's omnipotence, were of equally limited pliability.

The Second Empire has been called a police state, but its police force was little different in size or structure from that of preceding and succeeding regimes. An attempt was made in 1852 to create a ministry of police, but it collapsed within fifteen months, foiled by the resistance of the prefects who refused to submit to it; and in any case it was mainly a supervisory institution with only a small staff. What was significant was its creation, and the authoritarian character it gave to the early years of the empire. Apart from it, however, Napoleon kept the disorganised and complex variety of police forces he inherited, in the same way as the Third Republic kept most of what he bequeathed to it. The different police forces were responsible to different ministries and co-operated unwillingly. Until 1854 Paris was patrolled by only 450 men, and even after the reforms of that year, it still had no more policemen than London, about 4,000 in all. Marseille, with 300,000 unruly citizens, had only 213 policemen. Napoleon's most important change was to double the number of *commissaires de police*—who had hitherto existed only in towns of over 5,000 inhabitants— to 1,745, but they were still very unevenly distributed and some had to cover an area larger than a canton. They were poorly paid and enjoyed little prestige or respect. In the villages, the government relied on the *gardes champêtres*, who worked part-time (paid a couple of hundred francs a year), men without uniforms and usually stooges of the mayor or the local notable. Compared to modern totalitarian regimes, the Second Empire's police was amateur and muddled. The prefect of police from 1858 to 1866, Boittelle, conducted his operations from an office crammed full of paintings, mainly of beautiful women, with a studio behind where he amused himself restoring them. The police needed to be feared not for its efficiency but for the arbitrary and haphazard way it used its power. It could repress political opposition with grim violence, but it does not appear that it was particularly active in the control of petty crime. It incarcerated its political enemies, often without trial, but this was still an age when the enemies of the government could write books against it from prison: they were allowed to publish their attacks and usually punished afterwards, sometimes with prolonged trials which gave them valuable publicity. The police was supplemented by the *gendarmerie*, composed of former army non-commissioned officers, run by the ministry of war, and used mainly in the countryside. Louis-Philippe had about 14,000 of them, which he used, for example, to keep order in the royalist west. Napoleon III raised their number to about 25,000, and employed them unashamedly as electoral agents, to obstruct political agitation. They (and indeed the police too) thus became, in the popular imagination, one of the principal ingredients of Bonapartism. But in the really decisive crises—such as the mass arrests of political opponents in 1851 and 1858—Napoleon also needed the army.[1]

What was original about the Second Empire was not its police but the new place the army came to occupy in national life. This does not mean that it was a militarist regime, for the army did not run the country. However, until June 1848 public order had been maintained, in periods of crisis, by the national guard. Under Louis-Philippe this had the reputation of being a bourgeois force, but bourgeois should be understood in a very wide sense, for it recruited its members from all except the 'dangerous classes', the vagabonds who were the terror of peaceful citizens. The problem of personal security was a very real one until the mid nineteenth century; only when it was solved did the 'social question' replace it as the new scourge. The national guard was almost the nation in arms designed to keep peace at home, while the army had the task of defending

---

[1] Howard C. Payne, *The Police State of Louis Napoleon Bonaparte* (Seattle, Wash., 1966). For the repression in 1851 see Eugène Tenot, *Étude historique sur le coup d'état* (new ed. 1877–80) and for that in 1858 E. Tenot and A. Dubost, *Les Suspects en 1858* (1869). For the *gendarmerie*, A. Germond de Lavigne, *La Gendarmerie* (1857), H. Delattre, *Histoire de la gendarmerie française* (1879), 126, 144, 163, 165, baron Cochet de Savigny, *Gendarmerie: notice historique sur la révolution du mois de décembre 1851. Coopération de la gendarmerie dans la répression des troubles* (1852).

France on her frontiers. But in 1848 the national guard showed that it could not preserve order. It had decayed under Louis-Philippe; the middle classes had used all sorts of stratagems to avoid fulfilling the tiresome obligations it imposed. Instead it was the army which emerged as the guarantor of society, both in the June days and again in December 1851. The bourgeoisie seemed to prefer to allow professionals to deal with revolution, rather than do it themselves. That is how a militarist state became possible.

But it should be remembered that the first 'militarist' regime was that of the republic: General Cavaignac was the republic's saviour, assisted by General Lamoricière and by officers trained in military rule in Algeria. When Louis Napoleon became president, he had General Changarnier placed at his side by the *burgraves* in command of both the army and the national guard. The Second Empire was in fact an interim period. In due course universal military conscription, adopted by the Third Republic, put the nation in arms but in a new way, for now these soldiers were placed under military discipline, and they did not elect their officers, as the national guard had done. Previously the army had been liberal and revolutionary. In raising its prestige, Napoleon III was fulfilling the demands of the liberal patriots. But in the course of his reign, because the army became a pillar of his autocratic regime, for the first time it was denounced as reactionary. Participation in the repression of December 1851 was counted as one year of active service. Numerous favours were granted to the army, to win its allegiance to Bonapartism. In 1858 the colonels of the Paris garrison declared to their troops: 'The army is called upon . . . to play a political role in moments of crisis.' The Imperial Guard, with its splendid uniforms, appeared as a new pretorian bulwark of the regime.

But, paradoxically, the greatest defenders of the military system as it existed in this period were the Orleanist opposition. Napoleon, very conscious of the defects of his army, wanted to establish universal military service, copying the Prussians. Men like Thiers, however, protested that to do this would be to turn France into a huge barracks. The bourgeoisie valued its right to buy itself out and the peasants cherished the hope that they would draw a lucky number in the lottery which would exempt them altogether. Military service for all, it was said, would be the re-establishment of a new *corvée*. The most vigorous support for a professional army came not from the Bonapartists but from Thiers. The whole notion of militarism was changing its face in this period, but this is a large subject, which must be left for fuller treatment in the second volume. It will be seen also, in due course, that in Algeria, where the question of military rule was directly posed, Bonapartism did not mean a strengthening of army control so much as of capitalist dominance, with large companies being given incredible privileges to start off public works on a huge scale.[1]

Parliament under Napoleon III consisted of a senate of loyal dignitaries and a 'legislative corps' of only some 260 members (as against 750 under the republic). This lower house was indeed elected by universal suffrage, but its powers were considerably less than those of the legislative assembly created by the constitution of 1848. Its approval was necessary for the budget and all laws, but it was deprived of the power to initiate bills. It was allowed to suggest amendments, but the government was not required to accept these. It met for only three months every year. Its debates were—for the first eight years—published only in a colourless summary. Since press and public meetings were also severely restricted, its role was a very secondary one. Yet by 1870 it re-emerged as a major power in the state. This evolution is one of the central features in the development of Bonapartism, and it needs to be understood, for this did not represent simply the collapse of the system, as some have argued. The pressures which were exerted on Napoleon from within the parliament were very varied, and they illustrate just how many different interpretations there were of Bonapartism among the men who were either its adherents or agreed to collaborate with it. Some insisted that Bonapartism was essentially 'conservative', that politics was not a matter for the masses, who should delegate the affairs of state to responsible men and then get on with their work. They thought liberty was necessary, but by it they understood the abolition of privilege;

---

[1] L. Girard, *La Garde nationale 1814–71* (1964); R. Girardet, *La Société militaire 1815–1939* (1953); M. Howard, *The Franco-Prussian War* (1961); J. Bouillon, P. Chalmin, *et al.*, *L'Armée et la seconde république* (Bibliothèque de la Révolution de 1848, vol. 18, 1955).

they were in favour of reform but they thought that the first and overriding requirement was order. Many saw Bonapartism as a rejection of Louis-Philippe's timidity and caution, a national revival, a great patriotic movement for glory, in foreign affairs, and in the material sense too. This patriotic element was very strong, but not everybody accepted its social consequences. There were those who insisted that 'the present empire is not democracy incarnate, it is not the republican idea crowned . . . it is a real monarchy.' Some wanted this monarchy to be tempered by aristocracy, with decentralisation, sharing power with the notables who were supposed to bolster the 'moral force of society'. On the other hand there were men who claimed Bonapartism as being essentially democratic, the rule of the parvenus, destroying the influence of the old cliques, but saving universal suffrage from demagogy by leading the people towards material improvement and prosperity. Some thought a strong central power was essential to bring this prosperity, others believed in *laissez-faire*.[1]

Centralisation

If one concentrates on the parliamentary history, the foreign policy or the court intrigues of the Second Empire, one would be inclined to conclude that this was a reign so muddled in its objectives and so blundering in its actions that it has no permanent significance in French history, beyond showing once again the inability of an authoritarian monarchy to deal with the problems of the nation. The importance of the Second Empire lies elsewhere. It was a catalyst in the meeting of democracy and centralisation. Centralisation is well known as being one of the most distinctive features of French society. Tocqueville's famous book showing that its origins go back to the *ancien régime*, and that it was not a creation of Napoleon I, has led historians to investigate those origins, and some very interesting studies have been published about the increasing power of the old monarchy. There is no similar analysis of what happened to centralisation in the nineteenth century, when it was faced with a peculiarly interesting crisis, the proclamation of universal suffrage.

[1] T. Zeldin, *The Political System of Napoleon III* (1958), 46–51, gives quotations and references.

Bonapartism was in fact the means by which centralisation solved the problem, at least in part. It was able to do so because the newly enfranchised peasants—through Bonapartism—found in the centralised state the means of liberating themselves from the rule of the nobles and the notables. In the towns and the quasi-urban villages of the south, the liberation occurred, as has been seen, directly through republicanism. In the rural areas where the possibilities for popular union were more limited, the Bonapartist state provided a lever by which the old hierarchy could be overthrown. The price paid for this was that centralisation survived, side by side with the democracy which emerged. The Third Republic had to absorb the traditions of the old monarchy and the empire. That is why Bonapartism cannot be regarded as something radically different from republicanism: it remains encapsulated in it. That is why, also, neither it, nor republicanism, can be regarded as always signifying the same forces: the Second Empire effected social changes of a kind the First Empire did not, and likewise the Third Republic made compromises which did not tempt the more naïve and optimistic pioneers of 1848. The apparent enigma of why one of the leading republican advocates of universal suffrage under Louis-Philippe, Cormenin, author of the celebrated pamphlets of 'Timon', should also have defended centralisation and then become a senator under Napoleon III becomes clear if viewed in this light. Cormenin said that centralisation gave independence if not liberty. Independence seemed the necessary first stage.[1]

The key to the power of Bonapartism among the peasants was the poverty of the villages. The principle of centralisation was that all villages were equal, at least in their institutions. France was divided into 36,000 communes. The average size of each was about 1,000 inhabitants.[2] 8,000 of these communes, under Napoleon III, had fewer than 300 inhabitants. Only 1,300 had over 3,000 people in them. The possibility of the small ones having an independent civic life was negligible, particularly since they had very little money to carry on any independent activity. The amount of taxation a commune

[1] See L. de Cormenin, *Reliquiae* (1868), *Pamphlets anciens et nouveaux* (1870), and P. Bastid, *Cormenin* (1948).
[2] In Italy, by contrast, the average was 2,845.

could raise for its own use was strictly controlled by the prefects. The bulk of taxation paid by Frenchmen went to the state. A tiny fraction, known as *centimes*, was added to this taxation for the benefit of the communes. The larger towns could levy duties on consumption, known as *octrois* (only some 1,500 did). The villages for their part had another ancient tax in *prestations*, by which every inhabitant had to give three days' labour annually to road mending, or to pay a tax to enable the commune to find a substitute. Only in 1903 was a law passed to convert this tax in kind into a money one, but it remained optional, and in 1911 17,947 communes still had the old *prestation*. Together these formed the tax revenue of the communes. In addition they were variously favoured by income from communal property, which, for France as a whole, provided them (in this period) with 11 per cent of their total income (though some villages, as has been seen, were much luckier in their inherited wealth: private incomes produced inequalities among the supposedly equal communes as much as among the people). The final source—at the discretion of the government—was subsidies, which of course greatly reinforced the domination the state could exert.

The communes could not spend their money as they pleased. The state worked out for them what they ought to use it for. It decided that certain public services should be considered the responsibility of communes and the communes had to pay for them. Thus certain expenses involved in primary education, police, road building and the repair of public property were placed on the shoulders of the communes. The job of the prefects was to ensure that the communes paid. The more state legislation was introduced in the name of progress, the more burdened were the communes: but their power was not proportionately increased. It was the prefect who appointed the schoolmaster (whom, after 1833, every commune had to employ), the state paid him, but the commune had to find him lodgings and a school. Obviously a village of 500 could not afford to build a school, and it was therefore dependent on the state for subsidies. Its own tiny resources were increasingly absorbed in incidental expenses, each of them insignificantly small but together enough to be a heavy burden on the commune. While the power and activity of the state increased, an outdated and totally inadequate system of local taxation kept the communes in bondage. If a village wished to raise and spend money which it was not compelled to, it had to obtain the authorisation of the state to the levying of additional *centimes*—but the law placed strict limits on the number of these, as it did on its power to borrow.

The Council of State kept a watchful and jealous eye to make sure that the communes did not develop excessive ambitions, usurping functions reserved for the state. It long remained the enemy of municipal socialism. The result was that the communes did not borrow a great deal, compared with other countries. In 1890 the communes of France had a debt of 84 francs per inhabitant, compared to 180 francs owed by English local authorities. But most of this borrowing was by large towns: 84 per cent of the local debt was owed by 246 towns. If Paris is left out, the French communes owed only 37 francs a head. Paris owed 798 francs a head, Rouen 389, Marseille 285, compared with New York's 288, Boston's 650 and Rome's 398. In general the rural commune made its terms with the state for subsidies, while the cities got embogged with the capitalists. This goes far towards explaining their different histories.[1]

The financial problems of the villages may be illustrated by taking one individual case. Plibou in Deux-Sèvres (population 801 in 1846 and 522 in 1911) had a municipal life which centred around the provision of successive forms of progress, each involving frightening expenses. First there was the question of the priest. The village did not have one until 1840, when at last they got their own (instead of using the services of the *curé* in the next village), but this meant 100 francs a year to pay for his rent. Decency required that he should have a presbytery. For twenty years they argued about this. At last in 1851 the municipal council voted to buy him a house for 2,962 francs— but this was an enormous amount, equal to its whole annual budget. It did not think it could afford more than 1,500 francs itself, and it proposed to levy this through taxation, in additional *centimes*. All depended on the goodwill of the prefect—who provided first 1,000 francs as a state subsidy, and then 1,087 francs from departmental funds. After the purchase had been completed, it emerged that expensive repairs would be necessary and the business developed into a nightmare. Further appeals were made to the bishop, who persuaded the prefect to ask the state for 2,000 francs, but only 500 was granted. So further taxation was needed. Only in 1860 was the bill of about 7,500 francs finally paid. The commune had had to go through ten years of heavy financial strain. At times, when funds ran out, the mayor had to advance money to the workers and to the vendor (who happened to be his uncle) out of his own pocket. The key roles of the mayor and the prefect in this crisis were naturally full of political implications: they had led the villagers to civilisation, and had also saved them from the bankruptcy this would have entailed, but for their help. And the new luxury the villagers had acquired turned out to be as difficult as an expensive wife. When a new *curé* was appointed in 1859, he declared that the house was too small, or at least he wanted the commune to buy the one next door for him also, so that he would not have his conversations overheard by it and so that the danger of its one day being turned into an inn or a 'house of scandal' should be prevented. To have obtained this would indeed have shown the power of the priest to be at a high point. But the municipal council, overwhelmed by the expenses it had borne 'principally', as it said, 'under the inspiration of its priests', rejected the demand, adding that it did not know what a house of scandal was and that in any case it was not customary for other householders to buy up neighbouring properties to prevent a purely hypothetical possibility of contamination. Nevertheless the priest succeeded in getting, again after twenty-five years of debate and procrastination, a vote to repair the church in 1878. 2,300 francs were provided by state subsidies and a further 3,152 from voluntary subscriptions. The cost, as usual, trebled in the course of the work, reaching 9,852 francs, to which the commune contributed 2,217 francs. This shows once more how every major village improvement depended on state aid.

The great school-building programme of the Third Republic between 1878 and 1888 cost the communes about 300 million francs, to which the state added 216 millions in subsidies. Plibou drew up plans for its school in 1878, at an estimated cost of 35,800, the largest undertaking it had ever envisaged. The sub-prefect told them to start it off by getting a loan of 12,000 francs, which they could repay, at a cost of 18,000 francs, over thirty-one years, by levying 14 additional *centimes* on themselves. The municipal council with prudent thrift refused to bind itself for a whole generation, and voted to borrow only 6,200. It successfully obtained 10,000 francs subsidy from the department's *conseil général* and 20,000 from the state. By 1910 the loan was paid off. The school was like a palace in their midst. It is a good example of the way the state on the one hand encouraged the communes into extravagant expenditure, but also of the way the communes for their part were able to use the subsidy system to embark on projects far more grandiose than they would have ever dreamt of if they had been financially independent. Still, the building of the school raised the *instituteur* to the zenith of his importance. He now lived splendidly. In 1840, when the priest had been paid 100 francs a year to rent a house, the *instituteur* had been given a lodging allowance of only 40 francs, raised to 50 francs in 1855, 90 in 1856 and 120 in 1870. His salary, paid in equal shares by commune and state, was 200 francs in 1834 and 1,444 francs in 1872. He was, unlike the priest, partly a servant in the pay of the villagers, until the Third Republic turned him fully into a state functionary.

But they spent much less on him than they did on what was always the major item in their budget, the maintenance of roads. Between 1,000 and 1,400 francs were voted for this every year, but mostly this tax was paid in kind, for the villagers had plenty of leisure in winter, and they thus kept up their roads very cheaply. But they were quick to seize on government subsidies to build new ones. When they made roads for themselves, little money changed hands. When parliament voted a great road-building programme, with lavish credits (10 million francs a year for ten years in 1868, 80 million francs in 1880, etc.), the villages put in their claims, approved plans, raked in their subsidies (500 francs a year for Plibou after 1868) and took care to claim all possible compensation when the new roads went through their land—which they seldom did if it was a purely communal venture. Plibou got its roads for about 20 per cent of their cost, plus the individual benefits from increased property values. It should not be thought, however, that it was only these large grants that mattered to the villagers. A lot of effort was spent obtaining very small favours from the state, particularly for the benefit of the poor. Public assistance was another function of the commune, but here too it begged subsidies from the prefect. In 1855 it obtained 150 francs (i.e. £6), in 1865 and in 1869 as little as 50 francs. The commune itself voted 15 francs in 1884 to help one old man. The great bureaucratic system could reach out to and influence the humblest pauper.[1]

The municipality was the creation of the state and part of it, a geographical unit rather than a traditional organism. The idea of the unitary state meant that local government was not in the hands of autonomous bodies but was an outpost of the central administration, and that all authority was arranged in a hierarchy, with a clear chain of command. Thus though there was an elected municipal council in the village, its functions were limited, its agenda was prepared for it, it met only briefly (and not publicly) at fixed times or when summoned by the mayor, its deliberations could be annulled if it exceeded its attributions, and if it blocked the state's plans, it could be dissolved. The real power in the village was the mayor. He wore a tricolour sash (not the arms of the corporation as in England) to indicate that he was primarily the representative of the state, as well as being head of the commune. His function was to carry out the state's laws, as much as to defend the interests of the commune. He was originally appointed by the state. After 1831 he was chosen from inside the municipal council, so that an elective element was introduced during the July Monarchy. The Second Republic maintained this system for towns of over 6,000 inhabitants and for capitals of departments and *arrondissements*, but elsewhere allowed the free election of mayors. Under Napoleon III the appointment of all mayors was resumed by the state, so that the authoritarian character of the office was enhanced. Even when after 1871 the election of mayors was revived (Paris remaining a special case), the force of the centralising tradition maintained their supremacy over the municipality. The council now elected the mayor for the same period of six years as it itself sat, and it could not dismiss him. In the

[1] Marcel Denieul, *Histoire des finances d'une commune rurale* (Poitiers, 1912). Cf. R. Brun, *Le Budget de Montmarlon: étude d'une très petite commune* (Lyon thesis, 1919).

event of a quarrel, it was the council which usually lost. Every year there have always been many dissolutions of councils, ordered by the prefects, so as to resolve deadlocks between them and their mayors.

Under the Second Empire the mayors were more than ever conscious of their role as the government's representatives, and they were a major instrument in its control of the masses. They were always unpaid, but this gave them an even greater sense of their own importance. One of them, a doctor in a village in Lot, wrote a book in their praise, in which he described their function as 'a kind of priesthood, with which one cannot be invested without feeling oneself transformed, that is raised above oneself and having to win respect for something other then a mere individual . . . Either to meet general expectations, or because of the feelings which his position naturally gives him, the mayor sometimes takes on a certain grandeur.' This man, being possessed, as he put it, of a noble intelligence, allied to a great fortune, undertook 'to discipline the village', and he achieved a lot so long as he was supported by the favour and aid of the government. But it was no simple matter getting on with the prefect, who too often treated him as a mere office boy. Besides there were three powers in the village, the mayor, the *curé* and the teacher, and their rivalry complicated the mayor's task. The mayor had no difficulty with the municipal council: 'the government rightly allowed them to be ignored.' But when the mayor tried 'to make himself master of the terrain on every point', he inevitably aroused opposition. This particular mayor was dethroned following a battle with the *curé*. He rightly pointed out that the mayor was most successful when he was supported and consecrated by the priest, and when he could either act as the arbiter between priest or schoolmaster, or best of all when these two united and made the school an instrument of their joint supremacy. The mayor's aim should be to 'destroy factions, dominate the masses and make this domination loved through the good that it spread in the village'.[1]

The state gave the mayor a great deal of influence which, with skill, he could use so that the villagers saw in him their protector against the forces of the outside world and their

---

[1] Paul David, *La Commune rurale. Observations et études* (Toulouse, 1863), by the mayor of Saint-Matré (Lot).

representative in it. In a society with a large number of
illiterates, and when even many municipal councillors might
be illiterate, he had obvious advantages. He could make life
very difficult for anybody who refused to co-operate with him:
he could, for example, be obstructive in signing documents, or
he could prevent a man getting a road up to his farm. The sign
of his success was that the village voted as he asked it to. As one
Bonapartist sub-prefect said, 'A mayor who has not enough
influence to get his subjects (*administrés*, that is how mayors
referred to the inhabitants of their village) to vote for an official
government candidate should not remain mayor.'[1] The mayor
had to explain to them that only if they voted the right way
could they hope to get their subsidies. 'Mes chers administrés,'
wrote one mayor on a poster he placed outside his office, urging
the village to vote for the government candidate, 'I feel I can
give you this advice with the most profound conviction that it is
that which a wise father would give to his children.'[2] In a
rural situation, it was not difficult for a mayor to see every one
of the electors and show them exactly what material and local
issues were at stake in elections. To help him he had a small
army of officials—his deputy mayor, the village constable, the
road mender, the tax collector, the postman, the innkeeper who
depended on him for his licence, the tobacconist whose trade
was part of the state monopoly, and not least the schoolmaster,
who was often also mayor's secretary. Together they formed an
electoral machine which no opposition party could easily rival,
and which could reach every village. That is why so many
villages voted almost unanimously, in the way they were asked
to by the government, and the mayors took care to point out
that they did so in the expectation of material rewards, in the
form of subsidies and favours. If the post of mayor was given
not to the family which had ruled the village for generations
but to a new man, with tact and a gift for winning popularity,
then the balance of social forces in the village could be radically
altered. Bonapartism could then mean the building up of a
new kind of clientele system, challenging that of the nobles and
the notables.

[1] Archives Nationales, C. 1347, protest by Anatole Lemercier, Charente-
Inférieure.
[2] A.N., C. 1368, Loire-Inférieure file; cf. C. 1351, Ille-et-Vilaine file.

The patron of the clientele was the prefect. The Second Empire raised him to new heights of power and prestige. 'In the prefect's hands', wrote one of them, 'are concentrated all the powers of the state, all the moral force of the country, all the municipal liberties of the communes.' He represented the principles of unity and equality proclaimed by the Revolution. He was 'the guardian of the communes', maintaining their rights, but preventing their mistakes, treating them like minors. He had to approve all the budgets of the municipalities; he could impose taxes on them when they neglected to fulfil their compulsory obligations; he supervised all the printing, publications, bookshops, fairs and prisons in the department. It was through him that all projects on roads, railways and bridges, which the local engineers drew up, had to pass on their way to the ministry of public works, for though he took his orders from the minister of the interior, he was head of all the services in his department. He appointed the mayors, 'an immense right, which by itself gave him the widest sphere of action a man can exercise'. Napoleon rightly called the prefects 'little emperors'. Even when they lost their complete dominance over the mayors in 1871, they remained extremely powerful. The elected departmental *conseils généraux* with which they were then supposed to share their power were never to acquire great importance. Few were ever dissolved, because they were seldom able to be obstructive. The councillors tended to act privately, making individual deals with the prefect for the canton they represented. The standing committee the decentralisers of 1871 tried to establish, to keep the council alive as a watchdog outside its brief sessions, never became anything like a local government. In 1964, when the reforms of the whole system, promised for almost a century, at last became law, the prefect was not only confirmed as the head of the department, but his role as co-ordinator of all the other services in it was strengthened.[1]

Under the July Monarchy, the prefect's supremacy was challenged by the members of parliament, who in return for giving their votes to the government made a bid for its favours to be channelled through them. The same challenge was to occur under the Third Republic. Because the electoral element

---

[1] A. Romieu, ancien préfet, *De l'administration sous le régime républicain* (1849).

flourished in these two periods, the prefects' task became much more difficult, but during the Second Empire, the prefects were sometimes able to effect an important shift in the balance of social forces, so that after 1870 their problems were no longer quite the same. The deputies of Louis-Philippe's reign were powerful partly because they were notables, capable of exercising influence on others through their social position, independently of the government. When universal suffrage was proclaimed, there was some uncertainty as to whether the masses would remain subject to that influence in the same way. Napoleon III inevitably had to employ as prefects many men trained in the civil service under Louis-Philippe and they naturally tended to assume that the notables could not be ignored. Such prefects saw their task as the conciliation of the notables, rallying them to the empire, in the belief that the masses were still under the influence of the notables and that the government could get the votes of the masses only with their support. They helped former Orleanist and legitimist deputies to get elected under a Bonapartist label, simply because they thought they were bound to win, and it was better to have them at least nominally for the empire rather than against it. As a result of this timidity, dynasties of notables were assisted in establishing themselves even more firmly. In this way, the parliaments of the empire were infiltrated by men whose allegiance was very doubtful, so that it is not surprising that, as soon as the danger of revolution abated, they pressed the emperor for a more liberal constitution. There were some prefects, however, who had the ambition of destroying the influence of the notables and substituting their own. 'Until now', wrote the prefect of the Haute-Loire in 1852, 'the administration has been under the thumb of the factions, now of one, now of the other . . . The time is ripe to recapture the high position which the government ought never to have lost; it must control the passions of the masses and not follow them or elude them . . . The mediocrities who for forty years have exploited power will never forgive the prefect who will reduce them to impotence . . . but the confidence of our rough peasants can be won by an energetic authority which proves that it knows how to punish and to protect.'[1] Persigny, the minister

[1] A.N., F (1c) II 100, 14 Jan. 1852.

of the interior in 1852 and 1863, who, having long been an
exile, had not been contaminated by Orleanism, encouraged
such prefects to destroy the notables where they could. 'It is
the masses', he declared, 'who make elections today, and not
the old influences . . . What matters is that there should be no
canton where the hand of the government has not at least
sapped the foundations on which the old influences rested.'[1]

The effect of this kind of Bonapartism was that the peasants
were accustomed to ignoring the nobles and the wealthy men
of their village. When a prefect was able to find an able,
possibly self-made man to become mayor, in preference say to
the legitimist noble, after twenty years of such government, of
favours and public works being channelled through him, the
noble's status was seriously diminished. These prefects paid
little attention to ideological indoctrination. They interpreted
the aspirations of the peasants in largely materialistic terms,
and believed they were profoundly indifferent to politics. The
prefects could succeed in this kind of policy, indeed, precisely
in those areas where the peasants did feel like this, which is why
they did not make much impression in the south, where the
peasants had their own institutions for political argument and
agitation. But in the depressed regions of the west, they were
able to detach many peasants from their allegiance to the local
lords by assiduously holding out the bait of local improvements,
roads and railways, to open new and profitable markets,
education and jobs for those who wished to get on in the world,
cheaper credit for those who were in the clutches of the usurers.
A sub-prefect in the west wrote in 1853, 'The peasant who
sixty years ago owned nothing, is today everywhere a landowner.
Henceforth his interest prevails over old traditions. When the
wastelands were divided . . . he nearly always found the old
aristocracy as his antagonist, either because it revived old
claims, or because it exhumed old title deeds, or because it used
the fact of its possessing extensive properties to claim a proportionately larger share. The peasants have preserved the memory
and the grudge. They are happy to reach municipal office
which gives them some authority over the descendants of their
lords. The influence of the nobility in the countryside received
a first blow in this way. Every electoral defeat [of the legitimists]

[1] A.N., F (1c) II 58 and 98.

has reduced it further. Forced to live on their capital, obtaining no part of the profits of commerce or industry, or from the salaries of administrative offices, the nobility has gradually fallen into debt—the registry of mortgages tells how much. Finally, by refusing the oath [of allegiance to Napoleon III] and abdicating all participation in the deliberations of our councils and our assemblies, it has given itself the final blow. All these circumstances do not escape the perpetual attention of the peasant. . . . Placed between the promises which have for over twenty years announced an ever-postponed restoration, and the acts of the empire, at once energetic and benevolent, he is almost converted to new ideas which daily effect new progress and new benefits for him under his own eyes.'[1] In areas where the clergy did not have a powerful influence, the peasants, through the lever of the administration, often emancipated themselves from the control of the nobles. The way Bonapartism was sometimes a kind of half-way house to republicanism is seen in the winegrowing areas of the Nantes region, an enclave of small proprietors surrounded by large legitimist estates: some turned republican to assert their independence, but some, for the same reason, became Bonapartist. Likewise, in those areas of the Vendée where large and wealthy monasteries flourished as alternatives to noble land-lords, the fear of the revival of the tithe was an important cause of the peasants allying with the administration against royalism. These were often the descendants of the peasants who had opposed the royalist rebellions at the time of the Revolution, who had bought Church lands or made money out of state employment. The Bonapartists in the region of Sables warned the peasants that if they voted for the royalist comte de Falloux, they should expect the tithe to be re-established. These traditional fears were more important here than any simple correlation with small peasant landownership, for many small proprietors continued to vote Catholic and royalist; but once a breach had been effected with the old oligarchs, it was difficult for the peasants to go back.[2]

The south-west, likewise, was still dominated by legitimists

---

[1] Sub-prefect of Ancenis, 28 Feb. 1853, F (1c) III Loire Inf. 8.
[2] L. Girard, *Les Élections de 1869* (1960), 149–62, article by M. Faucheux on Vendée.

in 1848, with some influential Orleanists, but virtually no
Bonapartists and only a nucleus of republican middle-class
militants. This situation was transformed by the Second
Empire. Its prefects worked hard to destroy the power of the
notables. 'Our aim', wrote Pietri, prefect of the Haute-Garonne,
'is to remove all that can give importance to the party or
coterie leaders and to create a direct communion between
[Napoleon] and the people, which can admit of no intermediary.
Every attempt at oligarchy, at patronage, outside the administrative hierarchy, is an evil: if it appears a source of strength
now it will certainly be a danger later.' So he took great care
in the appointment of civil servants, down to the lowest ranks
of primary teachers, forest guards and village policemen. He
watched their actions closely, prevented them from being
arbitrary or vexatious, particularly with regard to taxation and
forest offences, insisted on their treating all equally and fairly,
protecting the humble, provided of course they repaid the
protection with respect for the prefect's authority. Every job,
every public enterprise was awarded with a view to the same
purpose.[1] As a result, the legitimist influence was gravely
weakened and in the 1870s this was a major area of Bonapartist
success. The republicans of course benefited also from the destruction of the influence of the old cliques. When they obtained
power after 1871, they in effect adopted in modified form some
of the techniques of these Bonapartist prefects. That is partly
why the south-west, after a period of allegiance to Bonapartism,
became in due course a stronghold of radicalism. The significance of these two doctrines was not all that different. The
Gascons in due course became such staunch radicals partly
because the Third Republic developed the policy of subsidies
to a peak of perfection far beyond anything the Second Empire
was able to achieve. It should not be assumed that the Second
Empire spent more *money* in indirect electoral corruption of this
kind: on the contrary the Second Empire's subsidies were
meagre indeed compared to those of the Third Republic,
which rose from 18 million francs in 1880 to 28,800 million in
1947, as the solidarist, welfare state made progress. Only
gradually were rules developed to apportion the subsidies

---

[1] André Armengaud, *Les Populations de l'Est-Aquitain au début de l'époque contemporaine 1845–71* (1961), 351, 398.

between local bodies on some fixed criterion, such as population, or territory, or wealth. It will be seen in due course how the republicans modified rather than completely rejected the methods of the Bonapartists.[1] During the Third Republic, the south-west was the region which supplied a larger share of the civil servants than any other. The government provided the peasant with the means to escape from his bondage to the soil. The great ambition of the peasant here was to get himself a horse and cart, to stop walking, to get away from the land, to set himself up as a pedlar, to get a job in the transport industry or in commerce. 'There were villages in which it was difficult to find an able-bodied man at certain times of the year':[2] peasants often left their women to work on the land while they travelled around in search of speculative gain. The jobs of the civil service and the railways inevitably made a great appeal here.

Reliance on government favours meant of course that once the Bonapartists lost power, their survival as a party became precarious. This can be seen in Corsica, which might be considered the most loyal home of the cause. And yet by 1881 it had abjured its allegiance and sent Gambettists to parliament. The explanation of this is that the decisive period in Corsican history was the First Empire. Napoleon I gave Corsica very important fiscal immunities which lasted throughout the century. In 1910 a commission appointed to inquire into them discovered that the island was saved a total of over three and a half million francs each year thanks to reduced succession and sale duties, lower indirect taxation and concessions on tobacco taxes and customs duties. The Corsicans had good grounds for avoiding trouble with the government in Paris. For long, indeed, they did not demand any large public works. The Second Empire did not grant them any special favours in the form of large public expenditure on roads or railways. Corsica remained appallingly poor and underdeveloped. What the inhabitants wanted was the chance to get out. Corsica exported large numbers of people to France—not to industry, commerce, or domestic service—but to the police, the army and the civil

---

[1] Jean Boulois, *Essai sur la politique des subventions administratives* (1951).

[2] Edmond Desmolins, *Les Français d'aujourd'hui: les types sociaux du midi* (about 1898), 157.

service, where the Corsican could enjoy a position of command and dignity which his warlike traditions caused him to hold in highest esteem. Bonapartism was attractive because it boosted the prestige of these official jobs. But then the Third Republic offered identical opportunities and the Corsicans could not afford to cut themselves off from them. Corsican Bonapartism was another variety of Bonapartism absorbed by the republic, whose police force continued to be filled by Corsicans perpetuating the authoritarian traditions of the Second Empire. As a political force, Bonapartism vanished from Corsica and turned simply into a kind of saint-worship. When the Bonapartist mayor of Ajaccio, Napoleon's birth-place and the last refuge of his cult, wanted to get into parliament in 1910, he had to transform himself into a republican. Corsica became such a safe radical seat that even Arthur Ranc, Gambetta's old friend, and Émile Combes were elected to be its senators.[1]

The theorist of centralisation as the instrument of the liberation of the masses was Dupont-White (1807-78), who wrote a number of closely argued works defending the intervention of the state in the life of the nation. He was also the man who translated J. S. Mill into French, and he argued that centralisation was compatible with liberty. Against Tocqueville, he maintained that local self-government did not necessarily prepare men to take a more responsible part in national affairs, because it fostered the 'spirit of locality' which made them incapable of seeing large issues. Against the admirers of the English constitution, he pointed out that England was moving increasingly towards centralisation. Against Lamennais, who described the French system as 'apoplexy at the centre and paralysis at the extremities', he defended centralisation as necessary to destroy privileges, castes and the evils of *laissez-faire*, and he argued that Paris could produce a political élite more suitable to lead a democracy than the rotten provincial aristocracies. He praised Paris as the source, the battle ground and the school of the parvenu.[2] Centralisation thus appeared

[1] Thadée Gabrielli, *La Corse: ses luttes pour l'indépendance, son annexion à la France, ses représentants 1770-1937* (1937); Marcelle Stromboni, 'Le Parti bonapartiste à Ajaccio de 1889 à 1914', *Corse Historique*, 34-5 (Ajaccio, 1969), 5-45.

[2] C. B. Dupont-White, *L'Individu et l'état* (1856), *La Centralisation* (1860), *La Liberté politique considérée dans ses rapports avec l'administration locale* (1864), *Du progrès politique* (1868).

to many people as the safest bulwark against the 'revival of feudalism' and the return of aristocracy. Centralisation, wrote Troplong, president of the Cour de Cassation, 'is the most important and most magnificent feature of our history. Rome produced an outline of it; only France has been able to realise it in its full power.' Centralisation has survived because too many people have feared that national unity would be endangered by its abolition, and that the forces of reaction would be the only ones who would profit from such a reversal of the distinctive characteristic of French history over many centuries. When a few republicans joined the leaders of the Orleanists and legitimists to demand decentralisation ('the programme of Nancy', 1865), they were attacked by several of the main republican newspapers as dupes of reaction. Alphonse Peyrat, who in 1871 became president of the *Union républicaine* in the National Assembly, denounced them on the ground that it was to centralisation that France owed 'the cachet of her incomparable nationality. It is through centralisation that those things, which make our nationality a unique type in history, have been achieved.' All the republican commissions, both in 1848 and after 1871, which were set up to promote decentralisation, produced minimal results. The second volume of this work will attempt to explain the deeper causes of this timidity.[1]

Paradoxically, the Second Empire, while on the one hand raising centralisation to new peaks, at the same time did almost as much as any regime to advance the cause of decentralisation. No one was taken in by its laws which simply transferred some powers from the central ministries to the prefects. But Napoleon III, it should not be forgotten, was a believer in *laissez-faire* as well as in strong government. 'Possibly the greatest danger of modern times', he had said, 'is this false opinion with which people have been indoctrinated that a government can do everything, and that any particular system must meet all needs and remedy all evils.' He had urged that 'the number of jobs in the gift of the government should be limited, for this often turned a free people into a nation of toadies. That disastrous tendency should be avoided which causes the state to do itself

---

[1] Odilon Barrot, *De la centralisation et de ses effets* (1861); Louis Blanc, *L'État et la commune* (1866); A. Simiot, *Centralisation et démocratie* (1861).

what individuals can do as well and better than it. The centralisation of interests and initiatives is in the nature of despotism.'
After the failure of the 1849 commission on decentralisation to
achieve anything, Napoleon III in 1863 asked his government
to revive the question. 'Our system of centralisation,' he
wrote in a public letter to Rouher, 'despite its advantages, has
the grave inconvenience of bringing with it an excess of regulations', so that a small commune wishing to perform a very
minor service to which no one raised any objection had to ask as
many as eleven authorities and wait two years for permission
to proceed. As a result two laws were promulgated extending
the power of both departmental and municipal councils. These
did not touch the political question of the method of nomination
of mayors and presidents of *conseils généraux* and have therefore
been forgotten; but they marked an important stage in the
financial emancipation of the communes. In 1802 the communes
had been allowed to vote additional *centimes* within narrow
limits and subject to the prefect's veto. The law of 1867 gave
them the right to spend their money more freely once they had
fulfilled their compulsory obligations. They were allowed to
borrow to finance schemes of their own invention, to buy
property without the prefect's approval, to embark on repairs
and maintenance, to grant leases—all within limits, but at
least limits fixed by law and not by the prefect's whim. In 1870
the liberal empire, while waiting for the report of a grand
commission on decentralisation, passed a law requiring mayors
to be chosen from among the municipal councillors. Decentralisation was a very live issue during the Second Empire: at
least seventy-seven books were published on it in the 1860s
alone, not counting pamphlets and articles.[1]

These hesitant half-measures reflect a fundamental ambivalence in Bonapartism. There were limits to the extent to which
it would go in destroying the provincial oligarchies. Some of
these limits were involuntary. Thus Bonapartism failed to make

---

[1] Napoleon III, *Œuvres* (1856), 3. 119; *Larousse du XIX siècle*, article on centralisation; Maurice Block, *Les Communes et la liberté. Étude d'administration comparée*
(1876); P. Molroguier, *Du régime municipal en France* (1849); Étienne de Toulza,
De l'administration des communes en France (1869); Jacques Droz, 'Le Problème de
la décentralisation sous le second empire', in *Festgabe für Max Braubach* (Münster,
1964), 783–94; Ferdinand Béchard, *Du projet de centralisation administrative annoncé
par l'empereur* (1864); A. Pougnet, *Hiérarchie et décentralisation* (1866).

much impression on the towns, though it tried hard. As soon as its mayors were faced not with a few hundred electors to manage, but several thousands, they were helpless. The empire never found a way of getting round the difficulty. The only alternative it could use was the press, but despite all its efforts to repress that of the opposition, it failed to win control of the city newspapers. Thus in 1861 in Paris, the five pro-government newspapers had a circulation of only 52,000, to which might perhaps be added the 17,000 copies of the *Journal Officiel*, which published mainly laws and parliamentary debates. Against this the 'progressive' newspapers of Paris sold 91,000 copies, the Orleanist ones 36,000 and the legitimist and clericals 38,000. This was a very different picture from that in the provinces where the government had 202 newspapers favourable to it, with 207,000 subscribers, while the republicans had only 13 with barely 23,000 subscribers, the Orleanists 13 also, with 20,000 subscribers, and the legitimists 34 with 31,000 subscribers. But when the press law of 1868 relaxed the censorship, 150 new newspapers were founded in the provinces within a year, 120 of which were hostile to the government.[1] How far newspapers were effective in converting people is doubtful, but they certainly acted as a focus for agitation and it was round them that the middle and lower ranks of the bourgeoisie, led by the barristers and the journalists, organised their opposition committees, with their newspaper sellers and bar keepers as their electoral agents.

The urban masses as a whole were not necessarily hostile to the empire. Industrialisation, by increasing the numbers of the proletariat, did not automatically reduce Bonapartism's clientele. On the contrary, in Paris, the new suburbs which contained the large factories were not hostile. The opposition in Paris was led by Belleville, where there were very few factories. The people who lived here were—far more than the factory workers—Parisian-born, exiles from the centre of the city, where the rents had become too high for them. Most of them went into the centre daily to work in small artisan establishments: their protest was that of men battling against modern transformations, from a slum quarter known as the

[1] A.N., F (18) 294 (for Paris), 294 (for the provinces' 1862 figures), 307 (for 1869).

Siberia of Paris.[1] The wave of strikes that swept France between
1869 and 1870 has sometimes been interpreted as revealing
an explosion of dissatisfaction by the workers with the empire,
particularly since some members of the Socialist International
were involved. The strikes, however, were only marginally
political, and were primarily a protest against the rising cost
of living. The magnitude of some of the strikes—as many as
15,000 came out in Alsace in July 1870—and the activity of the
press gave them unprecedented publicity, but, as a careful
historian of these events has shown, the workers were far from
all being republican, and they got little sympathy from the
republican deputies, who were as frightened by their activities
as everyone else. It was the government—particularly in
Alsace, and partly so in Le Creusot—which proved to be the
workers' best supporters: the prefects were cheered by the
workers when they went to negotiate with the employers, and
to such an extent that the Bonapartists were accused of using
the strikes as a tool against the industrial magnates, who were
often members of the liberal opposition. Napoleon III never
lost the reputation he derived from being the author of the
Extinction of Pauperism.[2] The causes which led the workers to
become republican were not simple, for though Marx identified
Bonapartism with speculative big business, the workers did
not always do so. Thus Marseille was a city in which Bonapartism never made any headway. But then it was a city with a
consistent record for abstention (35 per cent in 1969, 33 per cent
in 1958), an old tradition of legitimist hostility to centralisation,
a constant flow of immigration, very rapid growth, exceptional
problems in assimilating its heterogeneous population. Bonapartism could not mean much here, except to the Corsican
colony, quite apart from the class struggle.[3]

The Bonapartist system often failed in the villages also,
because its success depended on a formula which could rarely

[1] See J. Rougerie's brilliant article on Belleville in L. Girard, *Les Élections de
1869* (1960), 3–36.
[2] Fernand L'Huillier, *La Lutte ouvrière à la fin du second empire* (1957), 70, 78.
[3] L. Girard, *Les Élections de 1869* (1960), contains a detailed study by A. Olivesi
of Marseille in 1869, 77–123; P. Corticchiato, *Les Corses et le parti bonapartiste à
Marseille en 1870 et pendant les premières années de la république* (Marseille, 1921);
Chambre de Commerce et d'Industrie de Marseille, *Marseille sous le second empire*
(1961), 75–88, 143–64.

be carried out perfectly. The mayor had to be on good terms with the other officials of the village for it to work properly, but this was not easy to achieve. The *curé* and the schoolmaster often had pretensions of their own. Every debate in the village could produce disagreements and discontents, exacerbated by men who had personal jealousies or grudges to satisfy. A former mayor, evicted from office, often provided the focus for opposition. As political discussion revived in the 1860s, the whole system was liable to be challenged ideologically by men whose horizons extended beyond the village's boundaries. The prefects were by no means always tactful or judicious in their choice of the faction they supported, nor always consistent in their support. The unitary conception of village life therefore could not always be maintained. That conception, in any case, was not the only one the government adopted. For though Bonapartism, as Napoleon III defined it, aimed at satisfying the interests of the most numerous classes, it also sought to win the support of the upper classes.[1] Even Persigny, who said that the emperor had 'no friends except below' among the masses, wanted to bring 'the highest ranks of society' to his aid.[2] As a result, the policy of dethroning the notables was not always followed. It depended on the energies and ambitions of the prefect. So in many cases the mayor of the Second Empire was the same man who had held the office under the July Monarchy or the republic. Unfortunately, no one has yet undertaken the enormous task of analysing the changing politics and status of the mayors. No statistical statements can be made about the proportions in which the Bonapartists confirmed the notables in their influence or destroyed them.

The *conseillers généraux* of 1870, a more manageable number, have, however, recently been put on a computer, from which some very interesting facts have emerged. Of course, these people were not as significant as the mayors; they were not as powerful and formed as it were the upper house of the department, so that it was natural that eminent dignitaries should be chosen for it. Nevertheless, it is very striking that 27·6 per cent of the *conseillers généraux* in 1870 were nobles. In 1840 only 17

---

[1] E. d'Hauterive, *Napoléon III et le prince Napoléon* (1925), letter by Napoleon III, 58–9.

[2] G. Goyau, *Un Roman d'amitié* (1928), letter of Persigny to Falloux, 160.

per cent of them were noble, and after the revolution of 1848
21·5 per cent were noble. This stresses the fact, which has
already been suggested, that the nobles should not be thought
of as a class whose significance ended with the Revolution or
the Restoration. The rich ones among them survived with
remarkable success, and got richer still. There were some among
them who augmented their prestige by accepting jobs and
honours from the empire: 45 per cent of the generals in 1869
were (or claimed to be) noble, 32 per cent of the staff colonels
and lieutenant-colonels, 34 per cent of the officials of the
Conseil d'État, 34·5 per cent of the members of the legislative
body. In 1870 there were 317 noble *conseillers généraux* with
incomes of over 30,000 francs a year. Some 26 per cent of them
had residences in Paris, so that they could still appear to be a
national élite. They were on average far richer than the non-
noble members of the *conseils généraux*. One can interpret this fact
in two ways. Either it meant that the domination of the notables
survived and was acknowledged in the *conseils généraux*. Or it
meant that nobles had to be twice as rich as commoners to get
into these councils. Nevertheless, the Bonapartism of Napoleon
III, like that of Napoleon I, clearly involved an alliance with
that section of the old aristocracy which was willing. And there
were plenty of Bonapartists who were ready to turn themselves
into aristocrats. The domination of the National Assembly of
1871 by the nobles should not be regarded as an aberration,
and it should not be assumed that they lost power finally with
the end of the 'republic of dukes'. In 1882 they still survived
on the *conseils généraux* and by judiciously accepting the republic,
many survived very much longer. The Second Empire did not
effect any profound change in the social composition of these
bodies:

Conseillers généraux

	1840	1848	1852	1870
Businessmen	14·3	14·1	14·5	15·5
Liberal professions	23·7	35·8	30·4	29·95
Lawyers	38·2	36·5	33·2	30·5
Civil servants	28·2	17·5	19·2	20·95
Landowners	33·8	32·6	35·8	33·6

(The above percentages add up to over 100 because of multiple professions.)

It is remarkable that manufacturers and bankers did not gain more than 1·5 per cent. The 'couches nouvelles' of Gambetta thus did not enter these bodies before 1870, nor did the Second Empire represent a take-over by speculators. However, too many general conclusions should not be drawn from these statistics, for the *conseils généraux* were always the bodies which were slowest to reflect political or social change, but it is useful to be reminded just how slowly policies proclaimed in Paris took to alter the customs of the provinces.[1]

The problem of Bonapartism was the same as that of republicanism in 1848. It lacked leaders. The vast majority of the educated population had served other regimes and made their careers thanks to their favours. Thus the parliament of 1852, which has often been dismissed as a collection of puppets, contained less than a third of people who could in any way be called Bonapartist and besides, many of these had been Orleanist before 1848. The few who could claim to be unsullied in their cult of the emperor were either Napoleon III's personal followers, or men of modest social status whom the heirs of the marshals and prefects of Napoleon I had little use for. The Bonapartist committees which these petty agitators started under the Second Republic were dissolved by the duc de Morny, as minister of the interior, because they interfered with his policy of attracting the magnates. There were quite as many legitimists and Orleanists in this parliament as Bonapartists—rallied it is true, but altering the nature of the regime by supporting it. The new self-made men, merchants, industrialists, lawyers and others on whom the empire pinned some of its hopes comprised a mere sixth of the total. The flirtation of Bonapartism with legitimism is most significant. The legitimists were sometimes used by the Bonapartists to destroy their common enemy, the educated liberals, and sometimes as dupes, playing them off against each other, to undermine the traditional bases of royalism. Sometimes, however, both they and the Orleanists were left in place because the Bonapartists felt unable to dislodge them. The implantation of Bonapartists therefore varied very much from region to region; and under the Third

---

[1] L. Girard, A. Prost, R. Gossez, *Les Conseillers généraux en 1870* (1967), 47–8, 116–31 and *passim*. This (mainly the work of M. Prost) is a most remarkable and instructive example of computer techniques being applied to historical research.

Republic they never even tried to contest half the constituencies where they had never made much impression.[1]

Moreover, though in certain departments the prefects increased the authority of the administration and obtained political advantage from centralisation, the influence of the old notables did not always devolve to the government. The Bonapartists also created their own new class of notables. As the empire entered its more liberal phase, and as the government relaxed its control of the provinces, its supporters found that they had to fend more for themselves. The clienteles they built up became more independent, even personal. The allegiances they had built up became the nuclei of a new kind of fief. The Bonapartism which was entrenched firmly enough to survive into the Third Republic was often that in which personal contact with the electors had been assiduously cultivated over a long period. Some prefects in particular had exceptional gifts in contact with the masses, which rivalled those of both the nobles and Napoleon III. Janvier de la Motte, for example, gave huge banquets for the peasants, whom he enrolled as village firemen, in what was almost a private army, rivalling the religious societies of the legitimists and the clubs of the republicans. He had an extraordinary memory for names; he was always ready to do favours for anyone who would accept his leadership; he spent the fortunes of two wives and ran his prefecture into a large deficit so as, as he said, 'never to refuse anything'. He transformed his Norman department, which had once been subject to the Orléans, Passy and Broglie families, into a Bonapartist stronghold, which he then represented in parliament after 1876. In other regions, when the prefect was weak, members of the legislature subordinated him to their purposes, and used the power of the state in the same way. The Bonapartists thus added to the repertoire of methods by which notables could influence the electorate, at the same time as they helped to destroy the very notion of a notable.

The Liberal Empire

In republican histories, the Second Empire has been regarded as a gap in French history, an interruption in the development

[1] Theodore Zeldin, *The Political System of Napoleon III* (1958, paperback reprint, N.Y., 1971), 10–45, contains an analysis of the parliament of 1852.

of parliamentary government, and a period of reaction during which liberty was repressed for nearly twenty years. This view can no longer be maintained. The Second Empire, in the first place, was responsible for a number of gains in civil liberty which were no less important because they contradicted the restrictions on political liberty which were reinforced at the same time. France had, for most of its history, been a protectionist country. In 1860 Napoleon III made a commercial treaty with England, by which import duties on English goods were reduced to a maximum of 30 per cent, and in return French wine was admitted at lower rates into England. This was followed by free trade treaties with Belgium, the Zollverein of Germany, Italy, Switzerland, Spain, Holland, Austria and Portugal. The Third Republic rapidly restored protection: it is only in recent years that Napoleon has come to be seen as a precursor of the Common Market. His intentions were partly political—he wished to strengthen his alliance with England—but mainly economic, to stimulate agriculture and industry in France by competition and to benefit the masses through lower prices. However, this experiment in free trade was badly mismanaged, for totally inadequate measures were taken to prepare industry for this radical change or to derive political capital from it. As a result, the strains involved in adapting to it produced a vast and uncomprehending opposition. Exports of wine to England more than doubled as a result, but affected almost entirely wine of fine quality: the mass producers of ordinary wine derived little benefit. The silk industry also reaped great rewards, particularly because the closing of the American market during the Civil War and then its limitation by high tariffs made the English market more important than ever. The Cognac, Armagnac and Sauternes regions long remained Bonapartist under the Third Republic, but it is uncertain how much this should be attributed to the Second Empire's commercial policy, for Charente had voted enthusiastically in favour of Louis Napoleon in 1848, long before; and on the other hand, the Lyon silk workers remained steadfastly hostile to him.

French industry in general was in a state of transformation; the construction of railways was providing a great boost to the iron producers, and drastically reducing transport costs. After 1860, the efficient iron firms were able to hold their own against the British and even to export large quantities of iron goods, especially locomotives and other machinery, but there were loud protests against free trade from the firms which had been slower to modernise, or which were held back by high production costs, bad transport and mines nearing exhaustion. In the cotton industry, the issue was confused by the American Civil War, which stopped the supply of raw cotton, and required changes in machinery to take cotton from India. Many small firms did not have the capital to carry these out; rapid fluctuations in prices also put them at a disadvantage; and there were numerous bankruptcies, which were naturally blamed on the ending of protection. In the Rouen region, in the 1860s, 12 out of the 32 printing mills closed down, but this had little to do with competition from England, which had similar problems. Free trade stimulated the wool and worsted weaving firms to install power looms—the number in Roubaix increased tenfold from 1856 to 1867—and Roubaix, by specialising in particular cloths, was able almost to quadruple the value of its exports to England. But in Elbeuf more conservative manufacturers failed to adapt to the new conditions, and it was they who led the complaints against free trade. The free trade was only partial; it left enough protection to prevent the French market being flooded by English goods; but it was enough to discredit Napoleon with a large section of the business community. They, who were active in the liberal movement for political liberty, were not necessarily liberal in other respects.[1]

Napoleon followed the English lead in several other respects, but again failed to obtain credit for what he did. Thus in 1864 he passed a law allowing workers to combine and to strike to improve their conditions (which the first Napoleon had of course rigorously forbidden). The industrialists were horrified and were violent in their protests. The workers' leaders complained that it was damaging to trade unions, because (following the English Combination Act of 1825) it allowed the 'liberty to work' as well as to strike, i.e. it protected blacklegs, and because it included a phrase forbidding 'fraudulent manœuvres' in the organisation of strikes, which seemed to be a loop-hole. In fact, the main mistake Napoleon made was in the tactless way he

---

[1] A. L. Dunham, *The Anglo-French Treaty of Commerce of 1860 and the Progress of the Industrial Revolution in France* (1930).

passed this law: he chose a renegade member of the left, Émile Ollivier, to get it through parliament, and failed to bring in the workers and republican leaders by adequate consultation. In the circumstances of the reign this was almost impossible. Ollivier had even wanted to introduce compulsory arbitration but could not get his way. The limitations which the law of 1864 imposed on strikers were removed in 1884, but the economic historian Henri Sée was right to recognise it as 'a law of major importance in the social history of France'.[1] Equally important, from the economic point of view, was the law of 1867 which allowed limited liability companies to be formed freely, without need for government favouritism. A host of other minor measures 'freed industry from the restrictions in which preceding governments had entangled it', as for example the need to obtain state approval to install a steam engine in a factory, or to open a foundry. Butchers, bakers and taxi drivers were liberated from the complicated controls to which they had been subject.[2]

Bonapartism, as it developed under Napoleon III, deeply influenced the character of republicanism, which emerged considerably different after 1870. Before 1848, the republicans had been very divided as to the kind of constitution they wanted. There was a strong element among them, led by Blanqui and Comte, in favour of some kind of dictatorship. Ledru-Rollin advocated direct government by referendum, in the tradition of 1793. The constitution of 1848 had balanced the Legislative Assembly by a strong and independent president. England was regarded by the democrats as aristocratic and feudal, no model for France, and the parliamentary government of Louis-Philippe as chaotic. Napoleon III discredited the republican visionaries of 1848 and largely eliminated their influence from practical politics, by showing their *naïveté*. But he also, by bringing into being a constitution, in the latter part of his reign, which in many ways fulfilled these old republican dreams—for he too

---

[1] É. Ollivier, *Commentaire de la loi du 25 mai 1864 sur les coalitions* (1864); P. L. Fournier, *Le Second Empire et la législation ouvrière* (1911); J. Barberet, *Les Grèves et les coalitions* (1873); L. Barthou, 'Des atteintes à la liberté du travail', *Nouvelle Revue* (1 Feb. 1901), 321–34; H. Sée, *Histoire économique de la France* (new edition 1951), 2. 342.

[2] E. Levasseur, *Histoire des classes ouvrières et de l'industrie en France de 1789 à 1870* (1904), 2. 495.

was heir to the traditions of the Revolution and of the romantic age—made the republicans, in a process of reaction, give up their interest in strong presidents and plebiscites.

The liberal empire of 1870—far from being a belated triumph for Orleanism, as political scientists like Maurice Duverger have claimed—was a resurrection of the peculiar regime France had adopted in 1815, under the inspiration of Benjamin Constant. It sought to establish not parliamentary government, but representative government. This idea was that the cure for despotism was not to transfer power from a monarch to a parliament, which could be just as dangerous to individual liberty as an aristocracy, but to divide power. The executive should be kept independent, the legislature should be freely elected but confined to legislation, imposing 'principles but not ministers' on the executive.[1]

The gradual increase in political liberty which characterised the 1860s has usually been interpreted as a concession forced on Napoleon III by mounting hostility to his despotism. There can be no doubt that opposition to him, silenced in the crisis of 1851–2, when the threat of a socialist take-over was a source of real terror to a large section of the population, revived when the threat seemed less imminent, and that it was augmented by dissatisfaction with Napoleon III's methods of government. His conservative and clerical allies became disillusioned; his nationalist supporters were appalled by his foreign policy; every industry that suffered a depression blamed its troubles on him; the revived political activity of the working class and then the hostility of the press, which was gradually freed from censorship; the return to active politics of the old party leaders: all this combined to make Napoleon feel that his star was waning, that he was losing popularity, and that he had to do something very striking if he was to save his dynasty and indeed avoid a revolution overthrowing him. However, the forces working independently for a liberalisation of the empire, from within the regime itself, should not therefore be overlooked. Napoleon had always seen himself as not simply giving expression to public opinion, but sensing its development almost before it became self-conscious. He had always seen politics as the art of compromise and the relative. He had a belief in liberty as well

[1] B. Constant, *Principes de politique* (1815).

as a fear of it. He had always admired England for giving 'unrestricted liberty to the expression of all opinions [as well as] to the development of all interests', for maintaining 'perfect order in the midst of the vivacity of debates and the perils of competition', and for making possible, through private enterprise and individual initiative, its vast commercial and industrial prosperity.

The duc de Morny likewise believed that, just as the *coup d'état* had been necessary to save society from the radicals, so in the 1860s a liberal transformation was needed to dish them, to destroy them permanently and establish the dynasty on 'imperishable foundations'. He was convinced that obstinate refusal to change would inevitably lead to a repetition of the revolutions of 1830 and 1848, which had been brought about by just that, and each of which postponed stability for another generation. He was particularly keen on civil liberty, because he thought that in France the government was so powerful that the individual needed to be protected against it. He did not want a revival of Louis-Philippe's parliamentary government but simply an increase in the legislature's power, the easing of restrictions and the ending of abuses like nepotism. He dreamt of winning fame for himself as 'the Richelieu of liberty'.

He found an important ally in the leading journalist of the reign, Émile de Girardin, who invented the phrase 'the liberal empire' to mark the new ideal of Bonapartism, and who, after having supported the autocracy, now urged Napoleon, in the new circumstances of the 1860s, to transform himself into a constitutional monarch. The many supporters of Napoleon who had enjoyed considerable power as members of the parliaments of previous regimes, who had accepted the despotism as necessary in the crisis of 1852, increasingly felt that they could help by sharing some responsibility. In the 1869 elections, they rejected the title of official government candidate, which they had previously valued, and formed a new party, intermediate between the opposition and those led by the empress, who continued to resist change. Adolphe Thiers might have been the leader of these liberal Bonapartists. Had he not done as much as anyone to restore the glory of the first Napoleon? In 1840 Louis Napoleon had appointed Thiers prime minister when he had landed at Boulogne to claim his uncle's throne. Discussions took place, but Thiers's terms were too high—he wanted both a complete abandonment of Napoleon III's championship of nationalities and a total restoration of Louis-Philippe's parliamentary government, with a prime minister in command. Had his arrogance not been resented so much, more efforts might have been used to persuade him, and Thiers might have led the empire on a new path, just as later he emerged as the saviour of the republic, a regime he had long opposed.

Above all, the liberal empire was brought to fruition through the collaboration of Napoleon III with Émile Ollivier. Because Ollivier involved France in the war of 1870 and particularly because that war was lost, he has been treated severely by posterity. Because he abandoned the republicans to join the Bonapartists, he has been condemned as a traitor to the cause of liberty. Had the war not occurred, Ollivier might well be remembered now as the author of one of the most original political experiments of the century. As a young man, Gambetta had seen in Ollivier a combination of 'the passion of Fox with the political genius of Pitt'; later, he abandoned him as being unrealistic, the most striking representative, he said, together with Lamartine, of that execrable kind of politician, the brilliant orator with a fascinating command of language, but totally blind to the realities of the world. Ollivier was the son of a republican Carbonaro. In 1848, at the age of twenty-two, he was appointed prefect of Marseille. He showed himself to be one of the purest examples of the spirit of 1848, seeking the unity of all parties and the fusion of classes, preaching Christian fraternity and improving the lot of the workers, but he failed hopelessly, for old antagonisms could not be ended by rhetoric. In 1857 he was elected to parliament, as a member of the republican opposition, but he was more intent than ever to avoid purely partisan criticism of the regime. He was convinced that it was futile to work for a revolution to overthrow the empire, even though he hated its despotism, because revolutions inevitably led to reactions, and the cycle of instability which had plagued France would be resumed. Since the ultimate aim of republicans was liberty, he wished to advance its cause before all else, and he was willing to support any regime which worked for liberty. He would not place the capturing of power by his party as his first objective. His ideal was not Danton nor

Robespierre, but Washington. Intellectually, he was an eclectic. He knew Enfantin, the Saint-Simonians and Proudhon, but he also read Benjamin Constant, de Maistre and Montalembert; he had a horror of sectarianism. Culturally, he was a European: Italy, on whose painting he wrote several books, and which he toured with Édouard Manet, was his 'second fatherland'; he was one of the first to welcome Wagner's music to France; he married the daughter of Liszt. He deplored Napoleon III's foreign adventures. But he did believe in the need for a strong executive and he became convinced that Napoleon, if pressed by public opinion, could well become the founder of liberty in France. The two men met, got on well and after a series of hesitations, the liberal empire was inaugurated on 2 January 1870. For the first time under the empire the government was composed of ministers drawn from parliament, having a majority in it, and with Ollivier at its head. The *Revue des deux mondes*, normally sceptical, declared of this transformation of the despotism that 'if it is not the greatest of all revolutions, it is at least one of the most interesting, one of the most salutary and most opportune'.

The liberal empire initiated a vast programme for the reform of the country's institutions. Commissions were established, on the English model and with distinguished members from all parties, to prepare laws to end centralisation, to give self-government to Paris, to destroy the monopoly of the university, to set up a programme of technical education for the new industrial age, to improve communications, to revise the inquisitorial criminal code, and to establish institutions of 'social peace' to bring employers and workers together. The government introduced bills to abolish its own rights of arbitrary arrest, to repeal the stamp duty on newspapers, establish trial by jury for press offences and free the workers from the need to carry *livrets*. It created a new ministry of fine arts, to end the 'contempt for taste and intelligence' which had alienated so many writers and artists from the empire. The French Academy responded by electing Ollivier a member, with rare unanimity. In a plebiscite, 67·5 per cent of the electorate ratified the new constitution and transformed regime. The Napoleonic dynasty seemed to have been given a new lease of life, and a new image.

There were certainly limits to the liberalism, and ambiguities in the whole idea. The liberal empire was rejected by the republican leaders, and violent demonstrations were organised by the extreme left wing. The police was brutal in its repression. The arrest of all members of the Workers' International was ordered. The threat of a revolution by the left was used to create a sense of crisis, and to rally the support of reactionaries, who proved treacherous allies. Once the plebiscite was won, the reactionaries, led by the empress, set to work to undermine the new regime. The emperor himself could not completely abandon his old friends of his autocratic days. Ollivier's parliamentary majority became precarious. The constitution left the question of where ultimate power lay unclear. Ollivier in fact had intended this, for though his first principle was that government should be based on popular approval, he was anxious that absolute power should rest neither with parliament, nor with the emperor, nor even with the people. He believed in the division of power and the working of checks and balances to prevent despotism by any one force. His theories were too subtle, however, for most people, who feared that Napoleon, still declared to be 'responsible to the French people' might take all the concessions back. The Franco-Prussian War prevented this liberal version of Bonapartism from receiving more than seven months of trial.[1]

Bonapartism, in its most simple interpretation, meant prosperity. It has been claimed that basically this was what Napoleon's domestic policy was aimed at, and certainly it was as much for its prosperity as for anything else that the Second Empire was regretted after 1870. Whereas diplomacy, justice and police had been the principal activity of the state before the empire, the economic development of the country was a major preoccupation under Napoleon III, bringing dramatically visible results. 'The Napoleonic idea', he had written, 'is not an idea of war, but a social, industrial, commercial and humanitarian idea.' The economic side of the despotism was complete government control over public works and their financing, and government approval for the appointment of the directors of all large companies and for the formation of new businesses open to public subscription. In this way, there was

[1] T. Zeldin, *Émile Ollivier and the Liberal Empire of Napoleon III* (Oxford, 1963).

central economic planning and control. Financiers and industrialists acquired a new prestige, in what seemed like a realisation of Saint-Simon's dream of giving them the leading position in the state. The July Monarchy had wasted years in interminable discussions as to whether railways should be built by the state or by private enterprise (and some people—Thiers among them—were frightened of railways altogether). In 1848 only 1,931 kilometres had been completed; in 1852 only 3,000, and this by twenty-four different companies, each building independent, unconnected lines with inadequate finance and frequent bankruptcies. Napoleon III did not worry about great capitalists becoming too powerful. He grouped these numerous railways into six regional companies, gave them the backing of a state guarantee for their shares, and so made possible the systematic construction of the principal arteries covering the whole country. By 1870 almost 18,000 kilometres were in use, that is roughly half the lines ever to be built. Telegraph stations, of which there were only seventeen in 1852, with 2,133 kilometres of wire, were increased by the end of the reign to 1,500 stations with 37,000 kilometres. Thus not only were the communications of the country dramatically altered, and new possibilities opened up for commerce and industry, but a new prosperity and importance was brought to the towns the railways linked up. The reduced costs of transport were far more important for economic development than the protectionist tariffs, which, for example, might add 15 centimes to the price of a quintal of coal, whereas to transport it used to cost between 2 and 6 francs.

Paris was transformed under the direction of Haussmann. Large, straight tree-lined avenues, with classical perspectives were cut through the chaotic mass of small streets, so that rapid movement across it was made possible for the first time. New systems of water supply and drainage removed the foul odours which had pervaded it; parks on the English model were laid out both in the centre and at its fringes in Boulogne and Vincennes. Most of the private buildings on the Île de la Cité were demolished and the present official ones substituted; the Opéra and Les Halles were constructed; the Polytechnic, the Fine Arts and Mines schools, and the National Library were rebuilt. On a lesser scale similar reconstruction took place in the great cities, notably Lyon, Marseille and Le Havre. Nothing like this, as Taine observed, had been seen since Roman times. The unemployed masses were replaced by scurrying builders; it was a heyday for architects and engineers. At the peak of the activity, 20 per cent of Paris's labour force was engaged in the reconstruction. All this, however, brought Napoleon little reward in terms of support. Though a vast number of people made a lot of money—and some of them very large amounts of money—out of all the speculation, the compensation for expropriation and the business opportunities, the whirlwind of activity also brought havoc, jealousies and new problems. Property values in the cities were turned topsy-turvy, there was plenty of unfairness—dishonesty in allocating compensation, businesses were ruined as well as made by the new streets, taxation and rents rose. The workers were expelled from the centre of the cities to ghetto suburbs, and the vast influx of immigrants (Lyon's population for example rose from 258,000 to 350,000 between 1854 and 1865) increased the pressures and the competition. The rebuilding of Paris cost about 2,500 million francs, which was forty-four times the city's normal annual budget at the beginning of the reign. The money was raised, as far as possible, by bypassing the legislature, avoiding its control by all sorts of stratagems, some of them illegal, so that Haussmann's work came to be regarded as epitomising the irresponsibility and arbitrariness of the despotism. The work was completed only by mortgaging the city to an extent which was quite unprecedented. The orthodox financiers refused to accept the idea that this should be looked on not as a loan but as an investment, and that the interest could easily be repaid from the higher values and taxes which would follow. In 1855 Haussmann borrowed directly from the public; later he obtained aid from the renegade Crédit Mobilier, so that all the traditional powers of the financial world were against him. The cities benefited most, at least directly, from the Second Empire, but they were the source of the greatest opposition to it.

It was the same with the railways. The state did not and could not pay for them, but it lent its support to speculators and to corporations who were thus able to mobilise the savings of all classes, and rake in large profits in the process. All this roused hostility. The government could reply that the only works undertaken by traditional financial methods—the canals, ports and roads—made relatively little progress. Nevertheless the notables, after having opposed the railway building in the name of legality and economy, eventually captured control of it, and in its second stage after 1857 succeeded in getting the concessions of the lesser lines given no longer to the court favourites, but to themselves.[1]

The Second Empire was a period of prosperity in over-all terms. There have been calculations suggesting that the national income rose by more than half, that the income of French industry rose by 73 per cent and that of agriculture by 58 per cent. There is some disagreement among economists over the figures, which are inevitably extremely difficult to work out in view of the inadequacy of the material. There is disagreement over the question of when prosperity reached its peak, some placing it as early as 1857, others 1859 or even 1868. There seems no doubt, however, that, by contrast with the stagnant 1880s, the Second Empire was a period of boom. Different sectors benefited in unequal proportions. Proletarianisation had not yet gone very far. In 1865 about 70 to 75 per cent of the industrial labour force was still artisan. The value of the artisan's production increased by 22 per cent. That of large-scale industry doubled. In some industries the average annual increases in production were very high—6·1 per cent in coal, 8·2 per cent in printing, 11·8 per cent in gas, 12·5 per cent in rubber. The increase in all indutrial products was 2·3 per cent p.a. (These are figures for the first dozen years of the empire.)[2]

However, the upper classes seem to have benefited much more from this prosperity than the masses:[3]

	Profits	Wages	Real Wages
1850	100	100	100
1860	220	113	97·4
1870	386	145	128

[1] L. Girard, *La Politique des travaux publics du second empire* (1952); D. H. Pinkney, *Napoleon III and the Rebuilding of Paris* (Princeton, N.J., 1958); J. M. and B. Chapman, *The Life and Times of Baron Haussmann* (1957); G. E. Haussmann, *Mémoires* (1890–3); C. M. Leonard, *Lyon Transformed: Public Works of the Second Empire 1853–1864* (Berkeley, Cal., 1961).

[2] T. J. Markovitch, 'Salaires et profits industriels en France sous la monarchie de juillet et le second empire', *Économies et Sociétés* (Apr. 1967), 79–87.

[3] E. Labrousse, *Le Mouvement ouvrier et les idées sociales en France 1815–1900* (Cours

Thus, whereas the wage of a miner at Anzin rose by about 30 per cent during the Second Empire, the dividend paid by the Anzin Mines Co. tripled each year.[1] It is true that, just as under the First Empire the myth was that any soldier could hope to become a marshal, so under Napoleon III people believed that ordinary workers could still rise to independence. This was confirmed by the inquiry of 1872, already mentioned, which showed that 80 per cent of employers were former workers and 15 per cent were the sons of workers.[2] The number of men paying the *patente* tax rose by 16 per cent in the Second Empire, which meant that there were a quarter of a million more people with independent commercial or industrial establishments. However, the actual number of factories did not increase in this period, though the value of their buildings tripled, which suggests that the large firms did best, and that they were generally beyond acquisition by the rising worker. The number of savings accounts (some of them working class) rose from 742,000 to 2,079,000.[3] What made the Second Empire appear an age of prosperity was that some people prospered, and the rest could nurture the hope of prospering too. But it is not at all certain that the prosperity was all that widespread. In the towns 'the material situation of the worker rarely improved; it sometimes got worse but most often it remained stable'.[4] Men in skilled occupations and in new industries did well, but artisans were frequently in distress. In Paris, over half the working population was in debt and only a quarter managed to save. The city is said to have contained over a million people living in a state of poverty verging on starvation. However, by contrast with the crisis of the last years of Louis-Philippe and of the republic, the Second Empire was indeed a golden age. Although economic depressions did occur, in 1857 and after 1866, there was no repetition of that catastrophic unemployment which was the masses' most terrible scourge. It is in this sense that the Second Empire meant prosperity: it brought full employment and expanding markets.

---

de la Sorbonne, 1949); id., *Aspects de l'évolution économique et sociale de la France et du Royaume-Uni 1815–80* (1949), 99.

[1] G. Duveau, *La Vie ouvrière sous le second empire* (1946), 410–11.
[2] Ibid., 415.   [3] Levasseur, 2. 735, 688.   [4] Duveau, 410.

Paradoxically, the peasants who gave Napoleon more support than the town workers, did not necessarily always prosper more than they did. In the Ardèche, for example, the prefect reported in 1859 that the workers were doing well, but that the peasants had had bad harvests for six years and were in distress; in 1866 he was still reporting very mediocre conditions in agriculture. In the Charente-Inférieure, the peasants did enjoy great prosperity, cabarets opened up in large numbers for them to spend their money and their leisure in, but some of the most prosperous of these peasants were hostile to the government. It is unfortunate that no study has yet been made of the peasantry under Napoleon III, so that no general picture is really possible.[1] It is certain, however, that Napoleon failed to give the peasants the 'credit' he, and many others, had diagnosed as their main need. The *Crédit Foncier* put very little money into the land; it gave none at all to small men, and quite failed to replace the mortgage system controlled by the notaries. The railways did open up new markets for agricultural produce, but they also attracted the peasants away from the land. The support Napoleon got from different classes cannot be simply correlated with the material benefits they derived from his rule.

In the same way, the Second Empire did a great deal for the Church. It increased the salaries of priests (as it did those of soldiers); it allowed their numbers to increase from 48,000 to 52,000. It helped the Church multiply its schools and even gave it some authority over state education. The Second Empire, to begin with at any rate, was based on an alliance with the Church. The priests recovered their dominance, at the expense of the professors, now silenced and disciplined. It was, however, a very uneasy alliance, in which both sides soon ceased to feel the goodwill they had protested at the outset. Napoleon aided the new kingdom of Italy, which annexed the papal states, but did not dare go the whole way, and supported the pope's temporal power in Rome. In the 1860s he was in constant conflict with the clergy, whose ultramontanism, political ambition and reactionary tendencies, raised to new levels by the Syllabus of 1864 condemning liberalism, made co-operation impossible. Nevertheless Bonapartism remained ambivalent

[1] G. Kulnholtz-Lordat, *Napoléon III et la paysannerie* (Monte Carlo, 1962), is a brief though useful sketch.

and divided towards the Church. Its bitter, broken-down marriage with it was ultimately a serious source of weakness.[1]

Again, in its foreign policy, the Second Empire was unable to find a clear direction which could unite the nation or even win widespread approval. All sorts of explanations have been given of Napoleon III's diplomatic aims. Some have argued that he had a single deep-rooted objective, though there is disagreement as to what this was. The principle of nationalities is one theory. The desire to extend France to the Rhine is another. The ambition to unite Italy is a third.[2] It is impossible to be certain. Napoleon III carried on his foreign policy in a mysterious way, so that often his own ministers did not know what he was up to. He employed, to head the ministry of foreign affairs, people who do not seem to have shared his ideas. Drouyn de Lhuys was an Orleanist diplomat who believed in order and tradition and opposed the whole idea of a revolutionary policy. Walewski was a Catholic, favourable to the pope and hostile to the Italian kingdom Napoleon helped to create. Thouvenel was another career diplomat, who was willing to follow the emperor's instructions but he was not kept for long. Numerous influences battled round Napoleon urging him in different directions, from the empress who advocated national honour and respect for the pope, to Prince Jerome-Napoleon who was against the pope, to the businessmen who cared only for peace and commercial expansion. Napoleon seems to have used his gift for silent rumination and secret intrigue to resist all these pressures. His upbringing had impressed a number of deeply felt hopes and fears upon him. Thus, he hated war very sincerely. When, in typical paradox, he got involved in one in Italy, he hastened to end it very rapidly, and he surrendered in the Franco-Prussian war even more speedily. He differed profoundly from his uncle in this respect. He believed that the best way to settle international disputes was by conferences, and he was always calling them. He was not willing to be led here by public

[1] Jean Maritain, *La Politique ecclésiastique du second empire* (1930), is a full masterly treatment of the subject—one of the first detailed theses on the Second Empire.

[2] See, e.g., the review of theories by A. Pingaud, 'La Politique extérieure du second empire', *Revue historique* (1927), 41–68; P. Henry, *Napoléon III et les peuples* (Gap, 1943); H. Oncken, *Die Rheinpolitik Kaiser Napoleons III von 1863 bis 1870* (Stuttgart, 1926); Richard Millman, *British Foreign Policy and the Coming of the Franco-Prussian War* (1965).

opinion. Indeed, he repeatedly flouted it: the Italian and Mexican wars were not the result of popular pressure and were opposed by most of his entourage. Only after 1867 did he feel that patriotic pride compelled him to take a different line towards Prussia and he did so hesitantly. He was a European in a profounder way than most who shared this sympathy, for he was a cosmopolitan who had lived outside France between the ages of seven and forty. He declared that for European nations to fight was to engage in civil war. He was, however, also a patriotic Frenchman, with an expatriate's zeal, enhanced by what he felt he owed to his name. He was determined to erase the disgrace of 1815, to restore France to its old prestige, to end Louis-Philippe's timid policy. He combined these views in a vague hope of regenerating Europe on the basis of nationalities, with possibly an ultimate aim of a European federation of national states.

Napoleon was thus a supporter of French glory, but also opposed to a purely selfish national policy. He had grand ideas, but they were inadequately connected with the realities around him. If he had simply pursued his aims by normal methods, he would have failed, modestly. What led him to disaster was that he was carried away by the grandeur of his objectives, so that he was unable to see the obstacles. He had a sense of mission which made him refuse to stop in the face of difficulties. He had won his throne by this kind of fanaticism, against all odds, and as he said, he could not have done it had he not had the mentality of a martyr. He tried to ensure himself from the same fate as had befallen his uncle, by assiduously cultivating friendship with England, but he never overcame its suspicions of him. He was attracted by too many grand causes for his policy to be coherent. He wanted France to lead the world, in the Jacobin tradition, but also to protect Catholicism, in that of the monarchy of the *ancien régime*, and at the same time to bring material prosperity to Europe by economic development. There is no need here to analyse the complicated history of his foreign adventures, which has been treated in another volume of this series.[1] The confusion of aims and the very personal methods by which they were advanced meant that Napoleon

[1] See A. J. P. Taylor, *The Struggle for Mastery in Europe 1848–1914* (Oxford, 1954).

was brought to his downfall by what, ultimately, was in-competence.[1]

Bonapartism after 1870

Bonapartism was by no means a hopeless cause after 1870. It is not clear that its chances were all that poorer than those of the royalists; for despite the catastrophic way the Second Empire ended, there was still much loyalty to it. Twenty years of rule had created a strong Bonapartist clientele. The terror caused by the Commune and the political chaos resulting from the inability of the other parties to found an alternative regime, produced a nostalgia for order and strong government. The Bonapartists were quick to recover from their overthrow. Half a dozen successfully got into the National Assembly in 1871. A party organisation was speedily set up, under Rouher, with a house in the Champs Elysées, owned by the empress, as its headquarters. Though police spies disguised as street cleaners worked night and day sweeping the pavement in front of it, it was able to develop without molestation. Rouher was assisted by Pietri, the former prefect of police, and Chevreau, one of the empire's most vigorous prefects. All were men who had exerted enormous power in their day. In 1872 a regular party committee was formed, of former ministers, prefects, generals and deputies, meeting twice weekly. Correspondents were appointed in the provinces, at the level of the canton and *arrondissement*. Able men were selected to command whole regions, as for example Eschasseriaux, who was given the task of organising nine departments of the south-west. Napoleon was convinced the press had a vital role to play in his restoration and asked for the support of numerous papers to be obtained. Already in August 1871 the owner of one important daily, *Le*

[1] The bibliography on foreign affairs is enormous. A guide can be found in Taylor, op. cit. Some particularly useful recent works include L. M. Case, *Public Opinion on War and Diplomacy during the Second Empire* (Philadelphia, Pa., 1954); W. E. Mosse, *The European Powers and the German Question* (1958); Pierre Renouvin, *Histoire des relations internationales*, vol. 5 (1) (1954); L. M. Case and Warren F. Spencer, *The United States and France: Civil War Diplomacy* (Philadelphia, Pa., 1970). (Professor Spencer is now writing a biography of Drouyn de Lhuys.) N. N. Barker, *Distaff Diplomacy, The Empress Eugénie and the Foreign Policy of the Second Empire* (Austin, Texas, 1967); Harold Kurtz, *The Empress Eugénie* (1964), the best biography of her.

Gaulois, declared his conversion to Bonapartism. One hundred thousand francs were given to Clément Duvernois, who had been one of the most effective journalists in the emperor's pay, to start *L'Ordre* (significantly named), which became the official party organ. The provincial press was placed under the direction of Giraudeau (who had been head of the press service of the ministry of the interior) and then of Mansard, who started a *Correspondance Mansard*, providing articles, written by an able team of journalists, for local papers to reproduce. By 1874 there were over seventy Bonapartist newspapers, including twenty-seven dailies.

Various levels of the literate population were reached in this way, but even more effort was put into the simplest kind of propaganda—the distribution of portraits of Bonapartist heroes, and in particular of the prince imperial. In 1874, on the occasion of the prince's coming of age, 300,000 were authorised, and a lot more printed in England and Belgium and distributed freely to serve as a kind of religious relic.[1] Old soldiers, dismissed civil servants, and indeed civil servants still in office, worked as hawkers of these pictures and of the pamphlets which were also produced. The Bonapartists still had many sympathisers in the administration and in particular in the police. The famous story of Renaudet, the prefect of police, discovering a footman asleep, clutching a copy of the Bonapartist daily *Le Pays*, in the house of the royalist minister, the duc Decazes, simply illustrates how after 1870 it was as difficult to remove Bonapartists from government service, as the Bonapartists themselves had found it to get rid of Orleanists after 1848.[2] It was the same in the army, which the Bonapartists actively courted. Friendly societies were formed to bring sympathisers in it together; two colonels were given the task of creating clubs for retired officers; *L'Ordre* was sent free to serving officers; imperial eagles were distributed and signatures collected for letters to the prince imperial. The Paris working class was stirred up by Jules Amigues—a shady character who had previously moved on the fringes of opposition to the empire and support of the Commune, and who was accused of dishonesty and worse. He

[1] Article on 'Appel au peuple' in P. Larousse, *Grand Dictionnaire universel* (supplement), 16 (1877), 172–84.
[2] Pierre de Witt, *L'Épuration sous la troisième république* (1887).

organised Bonapartist committees in cabarets and cafés, with a
radical Bonapartist paper to back them, and a central committee to hold together what became an important propaganda
machine, even though the conservatives were horrified that
a man so near socialism should be employed. But that had
always been one of the faces of Bonapartism. Amigues was
successful, not so much with the native workers of the city, as
with the provincial immigrants 'who still believed in sorcery'.[1]

The petty bourgeoisie, likewise, was encouraged to cultivate
a nostalgia for the prosperity of the empire, as is revealed by
the memoirs of a lady cook of Grenoble who had, thanks to
the 'beaux jours' of the empire, been able to save enough
money to retire on. She worshipped Napoleon, the army and
'officers of a certain age'. In 1872 she visited England to
express to the exiled emperor her appreciation of his reign,
which had meant that poor people like herself could now wear
silk dresses. A fruit seller in Les Halles remarked: 'In those days
we used to complain out of habit, but now we do so from necessity.'[2] Every grievance was exploited with this expurgated
history of the good old days, which was a new version of the
soldiers' tales of Napoleon I's campaigns. The small savings of
pensioners, retailers, peasants and civil servants were solicited
by the Star Insurance Company, whose agents formed yet
another Bonapartist network.

This propaganda was very effective in certain regions. In
departments which Bonapartist prefects or deputies had mastered
under the Second Empire, they were often able to keep their
hold on those whom they had obliged. In Charente, Eschasseriaux had always been an expert in politics based on personal
relations. He had a card index of every voter in his constituency,
so that he knew exactly how to please each one.[3] The Bonapartists were pioneers in this kind of electioneering, applying
Orleanist techniques to universal suffrage. However, the weakness of their position was that there were many departments
in which, even at the height of their power, they had never
succeeded in creating a party or local notables of their own.

---

[1] Jules Amigues, *Les Aveux d'un conspirateur bonapartiste* (1874); Georges Lachaud,
Le Prince Napoléon et le parti bonapartiste (1880), 15.
[2] Rosalie Berruyer, *Les Mémoires d'une Bonapartiste, ou le souvenir de mes voyages
en Angleterre* (Grenoble, 1894), 33, 48, 51.
[3] John Rothney, *Bonapartism after Sedan* (Ithaca, N.Y., 1969).

Thus in 1876 they put up only 320 candidates for 525 seats, as against the 400 or so put up by the royalists and conservatives, and the 600 republicans. They thought they had a chance of success in only thirty-three departments. Though they collected money from wealthy supporters for propaganda purposes, they never had a great deal, and the sums they were able to distribute to candidates in elections were usually small.[1] Even more serious were their internal divisions. After the Second Empire, Bonapartism fell apart into its constituent elements and was unable any longer to hold together its contradictions. Napoleon III himself postponed acting until the German troops had withdrawn, so as to avoid foreign interference. He waited for the chaos, which he thought was bound to occur, to discredit the provisional regime. He had plans to go secretly into France through Switzerland, rally some regiments on the border which he knew to be loyal, and march on Versailles. But he could not ride a horse, owing to a stone in his bladder. That is why he had his operation, though he knew it to be risky. His death destroyed the Bonapartists' chances of a quick return from Elba, and ended the unity of their movement, which only a quixotic character like himself knew how to hold together. The new leadership made it far more conservative and indeed reactionary. Rouher's policy was to unite with the legitimists to destroy the republic, and then, when the legitimists found they were unable to restore their king, to get their support—and that of all conservatives frightened by the growing anarchy—for a proclamation of the empire. He hoped, that is, to repeat 1848. In 1873 it was the Bonapartists who, accordingly, provided the decisive votes (there were about thirty of them in the assembly by then) which enabled the royalists to get rid of Thiers and to install Marshal MacMahon who was probably a royalist but who had also served Napoleon and been made a duke by him.[2] The new prime minister Broglie gave the Bonapartists their reward in the form of three ministries.[3] After the failure of the Restoration, they conspired to overthrow Broglie, and were again rewarded with two posts.

[1] See private papers of Segris, letter of Berger to Segris, 16 Jan. 1875, showing the local newspaper being run on a budget of only 3,200 francs.

[2] J. Silvestre de Sacy, *Le Maréchal de MacMahon* (1960).

[3] Magne (Finance), Général du Barail (War), de Seilligny, nephew of Schneider (Agriculture and Commerce).

However, these successes, increasing victories at the polls, and the discovery of the strength of the Bonapartist organisation, through a police raid on their headquarters, created a scare and at the election of 1876 they had to fight hard against all sides. Nevertheless, they won about seventy-five seats, which made them larger than either royalist party. In 1877, profiting from a revival of the official candidate system and from alliances with royalists and conservatives, their number rose to 105 deputies, more than the Orleanists and legitimists put together. Though these tactics paid off in the short term, it is not at all certain that they were not ultimately disastrous, for, as a result, the Bonapartists lost the most important source of their strength, their ability to appeal to both left and right. They became the main minority group, but also condemned themselves to remaining a minority.

It is said that the alliance with the royalists went so far as a proposal that the childless comte de Chambord should adopt the prince imperial. It may be that the prince would have accepted such a deal, but it is very difficult to get at his real opinions. There are those who claim that he was a liberal but others who quote die-hard reactionary letters from him.[1] It is undisputed that he was a pious Catholic, though not necessarily a clerical. His education did not enable him to make friends outside the upper classes. As a boy, he did not go to school, but teachers from the leading Paris *lycées* came and taught him privately the very same syllabus they taught to their public pupils, they marked his work in competition with his absent classmates and gave him a secret, unofficial place in class. He was at first rather backward educationally, showing no particular talent except in drawing (and particularly caricaturing), but after the fall of the empire, as though stimulated by the tragedy, he suddenly blossomed out into an energetic, hard-working and ambitious youth. His father sent him to study physics at King's College, London, but he was not advanced enough to keep up and could not make friends there. So he went as a cadet to Woolwich, where he at last found his true vocation, got on well with the others and caught up on his studies by not playing games. He emerged a soldier above all else. 'The army'

---

[1] Comte d'Hérisson, *Le Prince Impérial* (1890); Fidus [E. Loudun], *Journal de dix ans: souvenirs d'un impérialiste* (1883), 2. 133.

he wrote, 'will be the keystone of the social edifice, the great school of the nation . . . I love the French army not merely because I am a soldier and a Frenchman to my very marrow, but because I consider that in it alone dwells the force that can first save French society and then restore its greatness.' He opposed parliamentary government but also absolute monarchy, because the inheritance of genius could not be guaranteed. Stability should be sought by basing government on 'the only social forces: religion, the army, the magistracy and property'. Reactionary commentators claim that he was for complete press censorship, for an Estates-General every seven years and provincial assemblies. Whatever truth there is in these statements, at any rate they show that some of his supporters were scarcely distinguishable from the most outdated of Chambord's followers.

The prince himself, however, had no illusions about what he could achieve by his own actions. He accepted that the majority of the nation was indifferent to politics and wanted only quiet. He thought that if he suddenly appeared in Paris, he would not have a popular rising in his support but would simply get arrested. He decided to wait till 'the government of Gambetta becomes detestable to the nation, which will then look round for a saviour . . . It is not our efforts that will overthrow the republic, but it lies with us to take advantage of its fall.' He was not afraid of waiting, for the masses did not forget the first Napoleon between 1815 and 1848: he could afford to wait ten years. After 1877, he said that the party could achieve nothing by its electoral activities. He was, in any case, not keen to be restored by a parliamentary intrigue, for it would make him 'the slave of certain men and of a whole party. I would never have accommodated myself to such a position and I dreaded rather than desired it . . .' All depended, therefore, on what he himself could do. If he could make himself popular, or great, 'the strength of the imperial party would increase tenfold'. He was tired of entertaining politicians and journalists and 'working with them to stir up social problems', which is what his advisers urged on him; he refused to tour Europe with his retinue 'like a fairy-tale prince, to view all the princesses and boast of my political elixir . . . I have not cared to let my wings be clipped by marriage and my dignity refused to stoop to the part of princely commercial traveller. When one belongs to a race of soldiers, it is only sword in hand that one gains recognition.'[1] So he went to fight in the Zulu war in South Africa. Had he survived, it is possible that he might have made the Bonapartists a much more effective challenge in the late 1890s, and enabled them to take advantage of the Boulangist crisis. As it was, after 1879, the Bonapartists ceased to be a significant political party.

The way Bonapartism bequeathed at least part of its inheritance to the radicals can be seen in the career of Jerome-Napoleon (known as Plon-Plon), son of King Jerome Bonaparte and cousin of Napoleon III. He was a man of considerable intelligence, deep ambition and impulsive energy, though all his gifts were thwarted by his lack of tact, moderation and self-control. He was the member of the family who interpreted its mission in the most democratic way. At the age of fifteen, when sent to a military school, he had rejected its discipline, 'thinking it silly, contrary to the rights of man and offensive to his democratic principles'. He was a rebel from earliest youth; he was a brilliant and sarcastic conversationalist, a merciless critic, excelling in pulling characters and actions to pieces, loving to entertain men of letters and artists, even if they opposed his dynasty. Though officially married to the daughter of the king of Italy, he lived openly with a mistress, after discovering, too late, that his wife's main ambition was to achieve beatification if not canonisation. He was a violent anticlerical, to the point of being called an atheist, though he was simply a spiritualist, a Gallican and an admirer of Napoleon I's Church settlement. He had a profound cult of the Napoleonic principle, but he constantly quarrelled with Napoleon III and even more with Eugénie, behaving with furious and undisguised jealousy when, by giving birth to a son, she deprived him of the succession. He was unpopular in the army, but he longed for military distinction. In 1848 he got himself elected to parliament and sat on the extreme left. He opposed Napoleon's policies almost consistently, receiving public rebukes in return; one of them was even inserted in the *Moniteur*. He represented the tradition of Bonaparte as first consul. He was quite happy that France should be a republic, provided it had strong

---

[1] A. Filon, *Memoirs of the Prince Imperial, 1856–1879* (1913), 187–8; cf. Alain Decaux, *Connaissez-vous le Prince Impérial?* (1958).

government, with a president elected by the people, having the right only to recommend a successor to them.

Jerome-Napoleon became the leader of the party in 1879, to the horror of the conservative wing. He made no attempt to keep their loyalty, or rather to win it, for he had never made his hate of them a secret. In 1880, in the crisis over the republic's educational policy, he publicly supported the anticlericals, and denounced the Bonapartist alliance with the conservatives. He founded a new paper, *Le Napoléon*, to preach a programme of a lay society, the abolition of the temporal power of the pope, the destruction of the tyranny of the great financiers, the improvement of the lot of the masses, democratic taxation, free trade and revision of the republican constitution so that both president and senate should be elected by the people. He accepted the republic, and, even worse for the conservatives, the anticlerical republic. There were only about ten Bonapartist deputies willing to follow Jerome-Napoleon in this path.

The majority of the party disowned him. Jolibois, deputy for Charente-Inférieure, formed a syndicate of Second Empire dignitaries which raised 40,000 francs a year as an income for Jerome-Napoleon's son, Victor, whom they proclaimed leader of the Bonapartists, against his father. Victor's opinions were precisely the opposite of those of his father. Through his mother he was descended from Louis XIV and Marie Thérèse of Austria and he was a cousin of the Emperor of Russia. The Bonapartists were thus split between Jeromists and Victoriens. In the election of 1881, they stood as opposing parties. The former, 'democratic Bonapartists', attempted to negotiate an alliance with Gambetta, on the basis of a division between those who accepted the Revolution and those who did not. Gambetta was too suspicious, but Jerome-Napoleon nevertheless asked his supporters to vote for the republican whenever there was no Bonapartist candidate. He adopted a programme which was virtually that of the radicals (divorce, a political amnesty, the abolition of compulsory Sunday closing) summarised thus: 'We want the Republic, Revision, Election of the president by the people: our candidate is Jerome-Napoleon.' However, he was poor; he had only one newspaper and he put up little more than thirty candidates. Only a dozen were elected, and none of them were his personal friends; Lenglé, who was to have been their leader in parliament, was defeated, and so they lost all significance. In 1885, Jerome-Napoleon did not put up any candidates at all, urging his supporters to become republicans. Several of his main supporters, indeed, had already joined them. When, in the following year, all pretenders were exiled, Jerome-Napoleon's parting cry at the Gare de Lyon was: 'Vive la république quand même.' He now demanded simply a revision of the republican constitution, not an empire. 'The incurable weakness of the republican party', he said, 'is its fear of executive power. It is perpetually haunted by memories of Brumaire and December . . . My aim is to reform the republic, not to abolish it. How can you think that an old democrat like myself should agree to exchange this glory for the outdated pomp of a restoration in which I do not believe?' He negotiated with Boulanger, but not for a restoration. He saw his mission as being to found the republic on a permanent basis, just as Napoleon I had consolidated the Revolution. He insisted that the republic was the logical consequence of universal suffrage. He did not even have any particular fetishism for plebiscites, saying that they were in many cases democratic only in name. How authoritarian his rule would have been it is impossible to guess.[1]

Jerome-Napoleon died in 1891: his remaining followers became republicans. After the prince imperial's death, one of the latter's closest friends, Tristan Lambert, had become a royalist and many had followed the example. Still, though Bonapartists now lost all importance, a rump continued to be active for another fifteen years. Prince Victor continued to hold meetings, to issue circulars and to receive reports from groups which organised lectures and celebrated anniversaries. It was claimed in 1886 that the party still had over forty newspapers; in 1891 it still had seven.[2] It had exceptionally vigorous propagandists in the Cassagnac family whose newspapers continued to be Bonapartist, in one way or another, till the war. The Cassagnacs, father and son, were violently anti-republican,

[1] F. Berthet-Leleux, *La Vrai Prince Napoléon* (1932); Jules Richard, *Le Bonapartisme sous la république* (1883); Paul Lenglé, *Le Neveu de Bonaparte, souvenirs de nos campagnes politiques avec le Prince [Jérôme] Napoléon Bonaparte 1879–1891* (1893); Émile Sauvage, *Le Clergé et le bonapartisme* (1886); Georges Lachaud, *Bonapartistes blancs et bonapartistes rouges* (1885); P. Cordier, *Boulangisme et bonapartisme* (1889).

[2] *Le Gaulois* (2 Apr. 1892), 56–7 and *Le Figaro* (7 May 1892), 77, contain interesting studies of Bonapartism at this period, of uncertain reliability. Mr. Keith Underbrink of St. Antony's College, Oxford, is engaged in research on this subject.

because they considered the republic inescapably demagogic; its anticlericalism made them more irreconcilable then ever because they were 'Catholic first of all'. 'My main aim', wrote Paul de Cassagnac, 'is the destruction of the abhorred republican regime.' He wished to replace it by authoritarian government, with 'only necessary liberties preserved', that is those which give the country material and physical prosperity (reduced taxes, improved roads, local railways). 'Luxury liberties' of the press, speech and public meetings concerned only a tiny minority and should be postponed till the masses had been satisfied. 'Liberty to live well must come before liberty to talk and to write.' But he was too independent himself to do as the pretender asked and in 1894 he declared that since he could not obtain a restoration of the empire of 1852, he would accept a monarchy. The empire was the modern form of monarchy, but 'in view of the pretender obstinately adhering to his contemplative attitude, passively waiting, like the Indian Buddhas, for the mountains to come to them', he had lost hope in him. 'The place of a pretender is not at the tail of his party but at its head.' Cassagnac called himself an imperialist rather than a Bonapartist. In 1917 he suddenly discovered the incarnation of the principle of authority in Clemenceau and accepted the republic.[1]

This was the final, deathbed marriage of Bonapartism and radicalism, though both were very altered with age. It is significant that even Émile Ollivier, who stood at the extreme liberal end of Bonapartism, had talked, when organising his electoral campaign in 1875, of rallying the conservatives against the 'reds'.[2] Now the radicals had come to feel the same about the socialists, and Clemenceau was repressing strikes just as the Bonapartists had done. The marriage between Bonapartists and conservatives was more than a marriage of convenience. They had more in common than they had known. Henceforth, the cult of the Bonapartes survived only in a spirit of antiquarianism. But Bonapartism left descendants, though under other family names.

[1] Paul de Cassagnac, *Articles du Pays et de l'Autorité* (1905, 8 vols.); André Martinet, *Le Prince Victor-Napoléon* (1895); Charles Faure-Biguet, *Paroles plebiscitaires 1906–1913* (1913); Paul de Cassagnac, *Faites une constitution, faites un chef* (1933); Dr. Flammarion, *Le Bonapartisme* (1950); K. Offen, *Paul de Cassagnac* (in the press).
[2] Ollivier to Segris, 28 Mar. 1876, Segris private papers.

19. The Politicians of the Third Republic

THE Third Republic was one of the most confusing and paradoxical of political regimes. It was supposed to mark the advent of democracy, but it produced disconcertingly little fundamental change in the structure of the state, which remained monarchical, or even *ancien régime*, in many ways. Its vision—as Allain-Targé, one of its founders, expressed it in 1867, and as many others continued to repeat with much rhetorical embellishment—was a free, egalitarian and fraternal society, in which constant discussion of common interests would lead all classes to a higher sense of solidarity and justice. But in practice it gave power to an oligarchy of discredited professional politicians, who maintained their dominance by placating the particularist interests of their more influential constituents and by closing their eyes to the corruption which surrounded them. The exceptional longevity of the regime is difficult to reconcile with its equally unprecedented instability. The endless succession of barely distinguishable ministries provides little clue to the evolution of policy or the implementation of reform. There was an extraordinary gap between the principles which were proclaimed as guiding the politicians and the legislation actually passed. Even when laws were at length enacted, as often as not they failed to be implemented. Lip-service to the glory of the fatherland was balanced by bitter criticism of it, more devastating in France than anywhere else. Confused and inconsistent programmes were advocated in the name of logic and rationality.

The chronicle of repeated crises and scandals, though often entertaining and sometimes dramatic, thus inevitably leaves the reader bewildered. It does not help matters that the right-wing parties call themselves left wing, and that the radicals turn out to be conservatives. It can be claimed that this is a purely nominal confusion, that basically France was divided into two clear groups—those for the Revolution and those against it—and that all that is needed is to decide who fits into which group: the struggle was always the same one. In this perspective, the triumph and development of the republic represents the progress of 'Movement' against 'Reaction', each successive generation advancing the same cause. However, there were so many ambiguities in this supposed progress, so much ambivalence in the attitudes of the progressives, that it soon becomes uncertain whether change and reform were the real issues in politics. The principles invoked in the battle between the two sides were too far divorced from the realities to be accepted as the guiding lines of action. They clearly had a more subtle purpose. In many ways it is more instructive to consider what politicians did not talk about than what they did. Indeed it is perhaps easier to see from these silences why the apparently chaotic system was tolerated and even popular. For it protected values which were deeply cherished, even if they were not publicly admitted.

The politics of the Third Republic were governed by a constitution which lasted far longer than any other French constitution. This longevity is explained by certain unusual features. The constitution lacked the qualities which most theorists had recommended and generations of statesmen had striven for: logic, clarity, order, completeness. But it achieved many of their aims, paradoxically, by not trying to. It was not designed as a permanent constitution at all. Its purpose was to temporise, to prepare, as some hoped, the way for a monarchy. It was the first constitution therefore not to require an oath of loyalty from all who served it, with the result that it excluded no one unnecessarily from the start. It was essentially a compromise; both monarchists and republicans gained something from it, and so it had few really implacable enemies. Since its authors came from different parties, it was unable to begin with a proclamation of principles or fundamental rights, on which they held diametrically opposed views.[1] It was thus a

---

[1] There was some debate, consequently, as to whether the Declaration of the Rights of Man remained part of the law of the land. After the triumph of the republicans, there was no serious doubt about this, but it might have been otherwise had the monarchists been victorious. The matter was only officially settled in 1911 when the Conseil d'État quashed, in the name of the principle of equality before the law, exceptions made in favour of individuals in some sanitary regulations. (Case of Roubeau, judgement of March 1911.)

constitution without a label—revolutionary or reactionary, and also it was the shortest of French constitutions. It consisted of only three laws—thirty-four articles[1]—making it one-third the length of the constitution of 1848, one-half those of 1814 and 1830, and one-tenth that of 1795. It was more a guide to procedure than a proper constitution and contained the minimum to quarrel about. The Third Republic was quite unique in coming near to having an unwritten constitution.[2]

The result of this state of affairs was that on the one hand the nature of the institutions which people thought ought to be created continued to be a major theoretical preoccupation, and politics continued, on the surface, to revolve around fundamental questions of principle. But on the other hand, the constitution allowed unprecedented free play to the prejudices, private interests and local customs which formed the basis of personal relations. Its fluidity enabled it to mould itself around these traditions. It based itself on *débrouillage*, the art of getting by somehow. It allowed people to find a corner where they could be more or less comfortable, and where, so as not to be disturbed, they took care not to disturb others. Naturally all this could be unreservedly condemned in the name of efficiency and so it was. The parliamentary machinery creaked and clogged. Vested interests were respected in a way which made the Third Republic almost medieval in its acceptance of the *status quo* and its respect of privilege. But the institutionalisation of inefficiency was so organised that more people stood to gain than to lose from it. It was sustained by the enormous strength of inertia; but because the rewards it yielded could not be respectably defended it compensated for its theoretical weaknesses by passionate attachment to grand principles, though little was ever done about these in practice. The turbulence and rhetoric of politics were necessary to draw a veil over the more sordid and humdrum reality, in which people agreed to live and let live. The relationship between the ideal and the reality

---

[1] Eight of these articles were repealed in 1884; one was added in 1926.

[2] Text and contemporary comment in F. A. Hélie, *Les Constitutions de la France* (1880), 1348–1456; amendments in L. Duguit, H. Monnier and R. Bonnard, *Les Constitutions et les principales lois politiques de la France depuis 1789* (7th ed. 1952), 286–319; cf. A. Esmein, *Éléments de droit constitutionnel français et comparé* (5th ed. 1909); M. Sibert, *Les Constitutions de la France, 1870–1940* (1946); J. Barthelemy and P. Duez, *Traité de droit constitutionnel* (new edition 1933).

THE POLITICIANS OF THE THIRD REPUBLIC 573

is in many ways much more revealing than the conflicts of ideology.

Liberty was the republic's first principle. There were indeed certain liberties which it both proclaimed and allowed. The Napoleonic Code had forbidden meetings of more than twenty people without police permission; but after 1881 a simple declaration of an intention to hold a meeting was adequate; and after 1907 even this was abolished. As a result of laws of 1884 and 1901 Frenchmen could form associations freely. The abolition of censorship in 1881 brought complete freedom of the press. But all this did not amount to full individual liberty. The methods of the police and the rights of the judiciary were not radically altered. Though the *lettre de cachet* was gone, it was still possible for men to be imprisoned without trial and without charge, to be beaten up, and to be subjected to endless interrogation. In 1899, for example, there was a case of seventy-five people being arrested in the middle of the night under the pretext that they were plotting a conspiracy. Most of them, after being detained for between three and six weeks, were released, without a charge being made. In the end, of those who were kept for several more months, only three were convicted. The police continued to confiscate letters in the post, to conduct searches and inquiries with their traditional brutality— and often ignoring the law. They systematically collected damaging information about everybody, paying informers and tolerating people on the fringe of the criminal world in return for their gossip. But they used their power with a fine sense of discretion, which prevented an effective protest against it. They seldom beat up people who could made a fuss, and they were indulgent to those with influence.

The free citizen of the Third Republic thus continued to live within the powerful and authoritarian state Napoleon had organised. In some ways he was even more exposed, because the formal abolition of censorship was not balanced by any control of libel. The freedom of the press gave journalists, or those who could buy them, immense power to slander reputations, with virtually no means of redress. A libel law introduced in 1894 proved virtually impossible to enforce. The Action Française was able to preach the murder of socialist politicians with impunity; and one minister was indeed driven to suicide by a press campaign. Though everybody was nominally equal under the law, some were better than others at knowing how to get round it, for the rule of law was established with a certain amount of flexibility. A host of moral and economic tyrannies survived. Wide toleration was balanced by a tradition of bitter and malicious polemic. The battle for freedom was far from having been won in the supposedly easy-going *belle époque*. But there was a little more freedom than the country had ever had before, and people *felt* a lot freer.[1]

It was the system of parliamentary democracy, incapsulated within the traditional centralised state, which spread this feeling. The people could consider themselves sovereign. It is uncertain whether they were right, because there was some legal debate as to whether it was not parliament which was sovereign. Still, there was universal suffrage, and it was used in a way which gave people a sense of their individual importance. In fact, not all men were quite equal. A certain amount depended on where they lived. The system of election used for most of the Third Republic was that of the *scrutin d'arrondissement*, by which each *arrondissement* was represented by one deputy. However, they differed widely in their population, and one constituency (such as Barcelonnette) might have only 3,000 electors. *Arrondissements* with over 100,000 inhabitants were given a second deputy, those with 200,000 a third and so on, but even so the sparsely populated regions were considerably over-represented. In these, 275 deputies were elected by 15,320,000 inhabitants, but the rest of the country had only 251 deputies to represent 20,782,000 people. Attempts were made to take into account demographical changes, and some 58 constituencies were abolished between 1889 and 1936, but despite some modifications in 1926, the old constituencies survived tenaciously, and in 1939 there were 347 constituencies (as opposed to 275 in 1875) which were over-represented. In 1931 the first *arrondissement* of Paris had one deputy for 42,166 people, but the sixteenth *arrondissement* (first constituency) had a deputy for 108,501 people, and Saint-Denis (1) one for 143,093. This was a system which gave the rural inhabitants a feeling of privilege, to counterbalance their poverty, and it also gave a sense of resentment to the suburban workers, so that there was

[1] Maurice Claudel, *Nos libertés politiques* (1910).

a constant agitation to abolish it all.[1] Between 1885 and 1889 the *scrutin de liste* was tried, whereby each department elected a number of candidates, and the parties presented lists of names for wholesale nomination by the electors. This turned out to be so advantageous to the enemies of the republic, who were thus able to unite their forces, that it was quickly abandoned. From 1919 to 1927 a modified form of the *scrutin de liste*, combined with proportional representation, was used. This was so complicated, and often so doubtfully fair—for candidates failed to be elected after winning more votes than others, because the average vote of their list was low—that it too was abolished. The majority parties had again lost by the reform.

An important feature of the single constituency system was that if no candidate obtained an absolute majority, a second ballot was held a week later, when a simple majority was all that was needed. Between the two ballots, the candidates bargained as to who should desist in whose favour. Sometimes parties made agreements to support whichever of them got the largest vote on the first ballot. This was the basis on which the republic survived, for the fragmentation of parties meant that the number of candidates was enormous. In 1928 there were 2,763, in 1936 4,815 (that is, between 5 and 8 for each seat). On the second ballot, the left could rally to defeat the monarchists. The main beneficiaries of this arrangement were the radicals, who, poised in the centre, could make deals with either side. They were the beneficiaries also of the electoral inequalities as a whole, for they tended to represent small rural constituencies. Thus it was calculated that, in 1932 for example, they got 42 more seats than they would have done under proportional representation, while the communists got 38 fewer. With time, the importance of the second ballots increased, for there were 227 of them in 1910, but they rose gradually till in 1936 there were 424: in that year only 3 departments elected all their deputies in the first ballot.[2] In the political sense, the deputies were thus far from faithfully reproducing the opinions of the electorate. Intrigues and compromises between the candidates frequently determined the issue.

[1] J. M. Cotteret, C. Emeri and P. Lalumière, *Lois électorales et inégalités de représentation en France 1936–1960* (1960).
[2] W. R. Sharp, *The Government of the French Republic* (New York, 1938), 60–3.

The republicans were thoroughly confused as to what they wanted from elections. Because the empire had had single member constituencies, the republicans turned against them and declared the *liste* to be the only proper system, emphasising principles rather than personalities, and discouraging improper pressure, which was more difficult in a large constituency. However, once the single-member constituency was established by the monarchists in 1871 and the republicans learned to manipulate it and obtained victory despite it, so most of them became attached to it. As a result, the republican system was not very different from the monarchical and imperial one; it preserved the influence of traditional forces, local considerations and personal pressures. The republicans had to stress the unity of the state because in practice they allowed sectional and village interests so much weight. The deputies were supposed to represent the nation, but they came to devote themselves above all to their own small constituencies. The emphasis on principle in their rhetoric was counterbalanced behind the scenes by constant attention to the individual complaints, demands and threats of each constituent. 'We are obliged', said Poincaré in 1926, 'to use the largest part of our efforts in petty errands and unrewarding solicitations. Under the pressure of local influences we find ourselves considering our daily meddling in administrative questions as vital to keeping our seats.'[1] The deputy maintained very close contact with his constituents. He prided himself on knowing their ambitions and needs. He asked for their votes on the basis as much of his personal qualities and his personal relations with them, as on his political opinions. As a result, they looked on him as being obliged to them for their votes and for his living. They pestered him shamelessly for favours. They asked him to use his influence with the authorities to obtain the favourable settlement of all their dealings with them. He had to spend most of his mornings running round the ministries to press their suits, to obtain subsidies for every village improvement. He had to devote a great deal of time simply to writing letters, replying to his constituents, forwarding their requests to the ministers, and reporting back on the results of his efforts. The deputy became the constituents' Paris agent. The stock joke was that he could even be asked to

[1] A. Tardieu, *La Profession parlementaire* (1937), 43.

buy an umbrella for them at a department store, to find a job
for their daughters as a servant in some wealthy household, to
trace the wills of relatives who might have bequeathed them
some money. For much of their time, deputies were concerned
not with large issues of policy but with the satisfaction of petty
particularist interests.[1]

It is not surprising therefore that being a deputy became a
profession. Parliament was not composed of a typical cross-
section of the population. In 1881 there was only one peasant
and one worker in it. 50 per cent of the deputies were members
of the upper bourgeoisie (108 proprietors, 85 former senior
civil servants, 44 bankers and industrialists). There were 120
barristers, 15 solicitors and notaries, 60 doctors, pharmacists
and veterinaries, 10 merchants, 10 engineers, 20 journalists.
The colourful Thivrier used to wear a worker's blouse over his
frock-coat but he was an innkeeper not a manual worker.
Twenty years later, in 1902, the working classes still had not
penetrated in any number: the rich bankers, company directors
and landowners still had 160 seats, the senior civil servants 52,
the middle classes and liberal professions 252.[2] The deputies
received a salary (9,000 francs in 1875), the equivalent of a
university professor, a colonel or an appeal court judge. After
thirty-two years they could retire on something almost equal
to their salary. Till 1914 their pension was paid by a friendly
society, but it was then turned into an official one, subsidised
by the state. A certain *esprit de corps* developed among them, so
that the variety of their opinions, which they exhibited in public,
was muted by a camaraderie which they shared after their
debates. It became customary for them to *tutoyer* each other. In
elections they gave the impression of being the irreconcilable
enemies of their opponents. In the chamber they got on well
enough. They formed groups of all sorts which cut across the
official party labels they gave themselves—they sometimes had
as much in common with other representatives of, for example,
the metal industry or colonial interests, or sardine manufacturers,
as with their co-religionists. They sometimes joined groups as a
result of personal relations they formed when they arrived in

[1] Max Bonnefous, *Le Scrutin d'arrondissement et la politique* (1926), gives a good
summary of arguments for and against the system.
[2] Roger Priouret, *La République des députés* (1959), 85, 180.

Paris, for the first time lonely and bewildered and were be-friended by ambitious colleagues anxious to build up a following. Some joined groups simply for the advantages this gave in appointment to commissions: there was even a 'group of deputies not members of any other group', and another of 'young deputies', who had only their age in common. The political labels a man used in order to get himself elected as deputy were therefore often no indication or guarantee of how he would behave in parliament.[1]

This *esprit de corps* made the deputies pretty indulgent towards each other in judging the way they voted. It was accepted that a man sometimes had to vote a certain way 'to satisfy his constituents'[2] and they often supported each other in defending their independence against party discipline. For long they turned a blind eye to corrupt practices in elections, out of deference to the peculiar difficulties of each constituency. The deputies judged the validity of the elections themselves, and began each parliament with protracted debates of validation, listening to petitions from aggrieved candidates. This washing of dirty linen in public, which served to dampen somewhat the idealism of the electoral months, revealed that many considera-tions apart from politics determined the results. Government pressure, so effective under Napoleon III, did not cease to be exerted. The most notorious example was in the elections of 1876 and 1877, when Broglie, who as a high-minded liberal had criticised the Second Empire for this very failing, reproduced its methods almost exactly and with almost equal vigour. The direct and open support of official candidates by the prefects was soon abandoned, but it survived in a modified and more moderate form, particularly in the more backward constituen-cies.[3] Since governments came and went, what the candidate had to show to his electors was that he knew how to obtain the official favours they coveted. The title of official candidate was dropped because the roles of prefect and deputy were reversed. The deputy now took the initiative in acting as the intermediary

---

[1] Robert de Jouvenel, *La République des camarades* (1914).
[2] See, e.g., Bernard Lavergne, *Les Deux Présidences de Jules Grévy 1879–1887* (1966), 31.
[3] L. Puech, *Essai sur la candidature officielle en France depuis 1851* (Montpellier, 1922); G. D. Weil, *Les Élections legislatives depuis 1789. Histoire de la législation et des mœurs* (1895).

between the government and the village, the individual and other interests. Thus in 1909, in an election in Saint-Affrique (Aveyron), in which the economist Paul Leroy-Beaulieu was trying to evict the radical Fournol, who had given excellent service as a distributor of government favours, the local newspaper published an article showing the achievements of the two candidates in this respect. In one column they recalled the favours won by Fournol: subsidies for school building, an increase in the number of new teachers, the establishment of a post office, benefits to the old people's home, the building of bridges, more books for the schools, and so on. In the other column, under the name of Leroy-Beaulieu, they wrote in large letters 'Nothing'. The article ended with the conclusion: 'Long live Étienne Fournol, the government's friend.' This article was read out in the chamber by the supporters of Leroy-Beaulieu, who were trying to get Fournol invalidated, but it aroused only laughter. Fournol's friends retorted by reading out one of Leroy-Beaulieu's own electoral circulars: 'M. Leroy-Beaulieu can render considerable services to his electors. Everybody knows that it is in Paris that all important business is decided, concerning schools, railways and indeed everything. Look then at the ministries in turn. First, the ministry of finances. Is not M. Léon Say, who has been minister of finances four times and who will doubtless be back as minister again soon, the colleague of M. Leroy-Beaulieu at the Institut, his collaborator at the *Journal des Débats* and an old friend of his? Next look at the ministry of education. The director of secondary education, M. Buisson, was his school-friend at the lycée Bonaparte. Go to the ministry of public works. One of the main directors, M. Cheysson, the engineer-in-chief, is a colleague of his at the School of Political Sciences. At the ministry of justice, one of the main directors is a close relative. At the ministry of the interior, one of the main directors, M. Herbette, was a friend at the lycée Bonaparte and at law school. In the Midi Railway Company, the president M. d'Eichtal is one of the oldest friends of the Leroy-Beaulieu family . . . This list could be continued endlessly. We ask our readers whether all these contacts, all this support, which cannot be denied, are not useful for the schools, roads, railways and all the personal services electors can hope to expect.'

Right-wing and opposition deputies worked in the same way as the left-wing ones, though a deputy in good standing with a government could arrange rather more dramatic use of Parisian influence. Thus he could get all the subsidies the constituency was waiting for to be announced immediately before the election, as for example Georges Leygues did in 1898, in Lot-et-Garonne, when over 80,000 francs were distributed to orphanages, churches and old people's homes in three months. 'A rain of decorations', 'kilometres of purple ribbon' could be poured into the constituency at the right time. Government favour could also be used to force the issue by less scrupulous means. In an election in 1889, the prefect was accused of defeating a candidate by fiddling the electoral registers, refusing to show them to him and getting all the mayors to ignore his complaints about the honesty of the vote.[1] Several other fraudulent registers were discovered: in Nîmes in 1902 they seem to have contained the names of over 2,000 electors who were dead or had left the town; in Lille in 1914 an enormously inflated register, involving many thousands of false names— almost a fifth of the total—was uncovered.

Money played an increasing role in elections. Jules Simon, writing in 1901, recalled how in 1848 the expenditure of 3,000 or 4,000 francs seemed enormous, but people were now spending 100,000.[2] There had been millionaires in politics under the Second Empire, and there were others under the Third Republic, who used much the same methods. The wealthy sugar manufacturer Lebaudy, for example, made arrangements with the mayors of his constituency in Seine-et-Oise by which they distributed bread and coal coupons to poor electors, who would remember the fact in their vote. He placed the mayors under an obligation to him by giving them private loans for urgent municipal needs, circumventing the delays of the state and as it were substituting himself for it. The electoral largesses of the Rothschilds in the 1920s were notorious. The village firemen were invited by one Rothschild to present themselves at the town halls of his constituency on polling day, to have their measurements taken for new uniforms to be made at his

[1] Paul Leroy-Beaulieu, *Un chapitre des mœurs électorales en France dans les années 1889 et 1890* (1890).
[2] Jules Simon, *Premières Années* (1901), 338.

expense. Every friendly society, hunting club, charity and good cause received a gift at the appropriate time. Those who did not have ready cash, as he did, promised it: one candidate had his election invalidated in 1928 because he had undertaken to distribute the whole of his parliamentary salary to his constituents. Free drinks were considered a perfectly proper part of electioneering, provided they were offered discreetly and individually. A great deal of wine was consumed, but the candidates who got into trouble were only those who tried to make too dramatic an impression of generosity. Thus in 1906 one sent the *garde champêtre* to announce, to the beat of his drum, that free drinks were being offered. Another placed barrels of wine in the polling station itself. In 1902 in Montreuil (Pas-de-Calais) it was calculated that each elector consumed 500 glasses of wine, over and above the normal intake, in the two months preceding the election. The chamber of deputies, in considering complaints about this, took the view that 'though they deplored intemperance, they did not consider it was their task to reform the customs' of regions which liked drinking; and even the Conseil d'État ruled that 'if libations did take place in the taverns . . . the complainants cannot prove that this affected the liberty or the sincerity of the vote'.

Votes could be bought for ready cash, particularly in the poor mountainous regions. They normally cost not less than 10 francs each, though the poor in the Doubs sold theirs for only 2. In 1890 there was a notorious case of a certain Bouttain who formed an association to collect together all men willing to sell their votes. He found 1,600 of them, and then made a contract with the banker Bischoffsheim to sell them to him for 20,000 francs. This was discovered after the election when Bouttain blackmailed Bischoffsheim by asking a further 8,000, and on being refused, denounced him to parliament. What was more, one could buy not only electors, but even candidates. There was a gentlemanly convention—it is not clear how long it lasted—that a candidate who desisted in the second ballot should have his election expenses refunded by the beneficiary. This practice could be extended so that rivals were paid to desist, or alternatively to stand as candidates, in order to take votes away from more serious rivals. Thus the respectable Leroy-Beaulieu paid an opponent in 1906 1,000 francs to desist in the second ballot, half to be given before the vote and the other after, and this was done literally with a 1,000 franc note cut into two.[1]

Elections were not generally invalidated for this kind of corruption and pressure, unless there were quite exceptional abuses. Invalidation was reserved as a political instrument by the republicans to expel notorious opponents of the regime: it was indeed one of the methods used to help establish the republic. In 1876–7 102 opponents were invalidated, 90 of them for being official candidates of the fallen regime of 'moral order'. Between 1881 and 1902 85 more were invalidated, nearly all of them royalists or clericals. Between 1906 and 1939, however, there were only 22 invalidations. The most notoriously corrupt of all elections, which were those of the colonies, were never even examined, because it was accepted that nothing could be done to change things. The respect of local custom was the rule. It is in this context that the famous scandals of the regime should be placed: they were simply the extension of common practices from a local to a national scale.[2]

It was only in 1914 that a law was passed to establish secrecy in the voting booths; and no limitations on financial expenditure or libel in elections were ever imposed. Money, however, never became the decisive factor in politics. Businessmen did occasionally spend very large sums (for example Coty against Blum, the banker Octave Homberg in Cannes, the industrialist Loucheur in Avesnes) but an American political scientist, investigating money in politics in different countries, came to the conclusion that, on average, French candidates spent considerably less than English or German ones. They spent very little indeed on nursing their constituencies, compared to their neighbours. Expenditure on printed propaganda was also far less. Very few of them maintained offices. Their meetings cost them virtually nothing since they held them in schools or cafés, and their most effective work was done in conversations over drinks. The state provided them with free advertising space for their posters. Their largest items of expenditure were for travel around the constituencies, and for the buying up of newspapers.

[1] A. Pilenco, *Les Mœurs du suffrage universel en France 1848–1928* (1930).

[2] J. P. Charnay, *Les Scrutins politiques en France de 1815 à 1962. Contestations et invalidations* (1964), 117–20.

Unlike American candidates who bought space to advertise themselves directly in newspapers, the French preferred to buy editorial support, or to set up their own newspapers, though they often distributed these free. Before 1914 posters played a major part in elections: General Boulanger is said to have put up 1,300,000 of them in 1889 in the seventh *arrondissement* of Paris, and his opponent could only afford to order half a million of his own—less to read, of course, than to cover up the other's. The law of 1914 put an end to this papering of whole cities. Newspapers then became the influence which candidates particularly valued. Parties, of course, never had much money, and gave only small sums to help their candidates. The radicals gave least of all (in 1928, they apparently assisted only 90 candidates). The contributions of big business still remain largely a mystery, though it seems that in that same year they might have involved some 10 million francs.[1]

The really important financial scandals occurred not in elections but afterwards. The deputies, conscious of their dignity as sovereign legislators, occasionally protested vehemently against accusations that they were in the pay of the rich; occasionally they uncovered scandals even though these brought great discredit upon them. Their links with the business world, their acceptance of directorships and consultancies, have already been described.[2] The deputies knew very well that even the puritan campaigns of Clemenceau against corruption and inefficiency were based on shady support from financiers like Cornelius Hertz. The public scandals erupted when the system, practised by most people, got out of control, through excessive zeal, righteousness or carelessness. The Wilson affair of 1887 did not involve anything new. Wilson was not the first man to sell decorations, but people had other grudges to settle against him. The Panama scandal of 1892, in which it was revealed that deputies sold their votes and accepted money in a dubious speculation, evoked the protestation from Rouvier, accused of dishonesty: 'What I have done all politicians worthy of the name have done before me.' No one could deny this. The list of

[1] J. K. Pollock, *Money and Politics Abroad* (New York, 1932), 279–319.

[2] Above, pp. 55–7. R. Mennevée, *Parlementaires et financiers, répertoire des senateurs et députés directeurs ou administrateurs des sociétés financières commerciales, industrielles et économiques* (2nd edition 1924), lists over 140 deputies and over 100 senators.

public scandals[1] was considerably shorter than the minor ones which continued privately, as a normal part of the political game: the scandals were, to a certain extent, a method of getting rid of rivals who were too successful in it. Parliamentary democracy did not rid France of the corruption and the pressures which its partisans had criticised in previous regimes.

What distinguished the Third Republic was the dominance of the deputies. Parliament was kept in almost constant session: it was required to meet for five months, but since it never completed its business on time, and indeed seldom got round even to passing the budget, extraordinary sessions prolonged it for a further three or four months so that it became as permanent as the government. It never quite accepted the idea of delegating its powers to the government or allowing the government a separate existence. The tradition that parliament was the enemy of the government, rather than the source of its strength, survived from the theories of the *philosophes*, and from the traditional struggle to win power for parliaments from the monarchical regime. 'Every legislator', Mably had written, 'must start with this principle, that the executive power has been, and will always be, the enemy of the legislature.' New traditions were quickly evolved after 1871 to subject governments to strict control, which is a partial explanation of the inability of the latter ever to achieve very much.[2] Questioning the government by means of *interpellations* became one of the principal activities of deputies. The question of confidence was frequently posed in these endless discussions which took up a great deal of time, whether they were on minor or on major topics. The practice halted business to such an extent that in 1909 a system of written *interpellations* was introduced, to save time. But the deputies used this to show their constituents how busy they were on their behalf (every question and answer was published in the *Journal officiel*). In the parliament of 1919–24, 20,000 such questions were asked, usually about matters of very limited interest, as, for example, why some policeman had not been

[1] Robert Arnitz, *Les Enquêtes parlementaires d'ordre politique* (Paris thesis, 1917), gives a full list, with references to the reports on them; A. Dansette, *L'Affaire Wilson* (1936); on the ineffectiveness of the inquiries see Louis Michon, *Des enquêtes parlementaires* (1890).

[2] Joseph Barthélemy, *Le Rôle du pouvoir exécutif dans les républiques modernes* (1906), 420.

promoted as he deserved.[1] A great deal of energy was expended in this way, safeguarding the rights and ambitions of the individual in his contact with the government, even if it meant that larger issues of policy had to be held up in the process.

A second method by which parliament exercised its power was through the right every deputy had to initiate legislation. Historically this had been a crucial demand in the struggle for parliamentary government and it was kept even though at last parliament had a government fully responsible to it. A deputy had the right to get up in the middle of any debate, ask to speak as a matter of urgency, and propose a bill on any subject he pleased. Thus in the parliament of 1889 to 1893 there were 546 sessions. 873 bills were proposed by deputies in these. There was obviously very little chance that they could even be considered. In the following parliament, 1893–8, with 633 sessions, the number of bills increased to 1,112: in addition the government presented 2,216 bills of its own, three-quarters of them of purely local interest. The effect of this appalling amount of legislation was that most bills were passed into law without debate or discussion. Every session began with the president mumbling the titles of bills no one cared about and pronouncing them carried, because no one opposed them. So though parliament was ostensibly in charge of legislation, the rapid drafting and inadequate scrutiny its laws received meant that their effect depended on the goodwill or interest of the civil servants who had to implement them. Laws were seldom passed in the way the legal experts of the Conseil d'État advised; and they tended to be couched in rather general terms, with the details being left to be worked out by administrative ordinance. It was in this second stage, which escaped both parliament and even ministers, that the civil service was able to exert its power. There is some doubt also whether parliament's control of the budget was really effective, so confused and slow did the processes become. In the first thirty years of the republic, on average two million francs were spent irregularly each year.[2] The passion for legislation was self-destructive. It was possibly at its mildest

---

[1] Joseph Barthélemy, *Le Gouvernement de la France* (1925), 110. René Bloch, *Le Régime parlementaire en France sous la Troisième République* (Paris, thesis, 1905), 79–83.
[2] Emmanuel Besson, *Le Contrôle des budgets en France et à l'étranger* (1899), 552–61; Désiré Ferry, *Le Contrôle financier du parlement* (Paris thesis, 1913).

in the amendments to the budget which the deputies constantly proposed. The budget of 1895 was subject to 371 amendments, that of 1898 to 547. Many of these involved extra expenditure, and contributed not inconsiderably to the deficits which were such a regular feature of the republic. In proposing a bill, therefore, a government knew that its chances of carrying it unchanged were negligible, and that even its chances of getting it heard or passed in any form were pretty poor. It was not surprising therefore that the proclamation of principles was often looked upon as all that was really necessary: it was not practical politics to try and do anything about implementing the principles.[1]

The third way in which governments were kept in subjection to the deputies was the system of parliamentary commissions. Every bill had to be discussed by a commission of deputies. The old tradition was that the commissions were appointed *ad hoc* for each bill. But then permanent commissions grew up, not to discuss a particular bill, but all bills in a particular field. The first was that on finance, started as far back as 1840; others, for foreign affairs, the army, etc., were added until by 1902 there were sixteen grand commissions.[2] The peculiarity of the system was that the commissions were permanent, so that they were in effect counter-ministries. The president and *rapporteur* were rivals of the minister, and not infrequently succeeded him when he fell. There were thus two conflicting sources of authority in the chambers. The commission of finance was particularly powerful. It was as president of it that Gambetta wielded his influence between 1877 and 1881. On several occasions this commission overthrew ministries. As Tardieu said, 'real power rests no longer with the minister, who frequently falls within a month, but with the *rapporteur* of the budget commission who often continues in office from one legislature into another.' In this way parliament, rather than the government, formulated policy. Because, after having been a *rapporteur*, a deputy inevitably considered himself experienced and capable enough to be a minister, this was a strong inducement to overthrow governments on the slightest pretext.[3]

---

[1] Louis Michon, *L'Initiative parlementaire* (1898); Émile Larcher, 'L'Initiative parlementaire pendant la sixième législative (1893–8)', *Revue politique et parlementaire* (Apr. 1898), 597–611.

[2] There were 6 in 1893, 11 in 1898; in 1920 the number was increased to 20.

[3] Joseph Barthélemy, *Essai sur le travail parlementaire et le système des commissions*

The chamber of deputies, which ruled France in this way, consisted of 533 members, rising to 602 by 1914. It was a relatively small body, compared with the 1,118 deputies of the Estates-General of 1789, or the 750 members of the assembly of 1849. Altogether 4,892 deputies sat in parliament between 1870 and 1940. Not quite half of these, 2,271, were members for only one legislature. Power was concentrated in those who continued to be re-elected time and again. There were 2,621 deputies who sat for more than one legislature. At any one time, about a quarter of the members of a parliament had served for 20 years, and 3 per cent had served for a third of a century. The stability in the membership of the parliaments was quite exceptional. Only 33 per cent of the total 4,892 deputies left politics because they were defeated in an election. 16 per cent did not stand for re-election. But 19 per cent moved on to be senators, and 13 per cent died while still holding their mandate. 12 per cent survived to be deposed by the Vichy regime. Only 2·5 per cent changed constituencies in the course of their careers. One gets a picture therefore of a long-lived almost permanent group of rulers, closely tied to their local origins, often unknown until they were sent to Paris. It was these men who controlled the fate of ministries, rather than the electorate directly, for three-quarters of ministerial changes occurred while parliament was sitting, and only a quarter from the vote of the masses.[1]

There were 108 ministries between 1870 and 1940. The average length of each was therefore about 8 months. This compares with the mere 44 ministries England had in almost twice the time, between 1801 and 1937, with an average tenure of 3 years and 1 month. France therefore had a reputation for instability, which, it might be added, was not exceptional. Belgium had forty-one cabinets from 1831 to 1937: until 1918 they lasted an average of 3 years and 9 months, but after the war only 1 year and 8 months. Italy's cabinets lasted 1 year and 2 months between 1918 and 1922. Germany's Weimar Republic had 21 cabinets lasting only an average of 8 months

(1934); H. Mauchant, *La Commission des finances de la chambre des députés* (Nancy thesis, 1927); R. K. Gooch, *The French Parliamentary Committee System* (1935).

[1] Mattei Dogan, 'La Stabilité du personnel parlementaire sous la troisième république', *Revue française des sciences politiques*, 3 (1953), 319–48.

each, as also did Austria's from 1918 to 1934. This kind of comparison can easily be misleading. The frequent changes of ministers conceal an underlying stability. First of all, the French electorate was exceptionally consistent in its loyalties: France did not, on the whole, suffer from swings of the pendulum. Secondly, these ministerial changes meant that power was kept in the hands of the deputies, who constituted the stable core of the regime. The deputies, being deeply suspicious of governments were not averse to overthrowing ministries frequently to maintain their supremacy. Whereas in England governments were overthrown not as a result of surprise votes, but on major issues of policy, the French deputies did not hesitate to topple a government on points of detail. They could do so because parliament lasted its full term whatever they did and they did not have to fear dissolution. When a ministry fell, it was frequently reconstituted with many of its old members, as will be seen, but with only a few new members, who quite often were the deputies who had organised the *interpellation* which had destroyed the old ministry.

Ministerial instability followed also from the fact that the office of prime minister was unknown to the law until 1934. Till then (except on six occasions, all of them after 1914) the prime minister held a portfolio which kept him busy, so that he had little time to be anything but the chairman of the government. He had no staff or patronage of his own, apart from that of his portfolio; only in 1934 did he get an independent office. Usually, he was not the elected leader of the majority of deputies, and often not even the leader of any party at all. He could not count on the definite allegiance of the deputies. He was overshadowed to a certain extent by the president of the republic, who, as will be seen, sometimes used his prerogative in choosing the prime minister in such a way as to prevent over-ambitious individuals from getting power. The deputies always kept the upper hand, for they could refuse to approve the president's choice.[1] If one wanted to be a minister it did not on the whole pay to be a party leader. Because parties were so fluid and unreliable as supports, ministers had to work hard to collect support from any source they could, outside their own

[1] As they did, e.g., in 1914 (Ribot) and 1920 (G. Leygues). Jacques Verdeaux, *Le Président du conseil des ministres en France* (Bordeaux thesis, 1940).

parties as well as within them. They stood a better chance if they abandoned partisanship altogether, and offered themselves as arbitrators between the parties, reconcilers of opposition. This meant, of course, that they seldom satisfied everybody, and holding office was like walking a tight-rope. Clear policies were thus difficult to pursue. Deputies who reached office often made their names as radicals, but almost necessarily became moderate once invested with power. In so doing, they lost the support of the extreme wings and often of their very own parties. Party leaders, aspiring to be national figures, thus often turned against the whole idea of party, which constant coalitions in any case diluted. The extremism and radicalism of new parties was a natural reaction to this regular evolution, and should not therefore be taken completely at its face value.

The most successful ministers were those who were most deferent to the wishes of parliament. He who wanted to come back into office most often resigned most often, for a clash with the deputies would ruin his career. Ambition thus encouraged instability still further. Briand carried the art of resignation to the peak of perfection: he even used to resign before a vote was taken; he perpetuated himself at the expense of frequent cabinet crises. So, if one looks at how long ministers, as opposed to ministries, lasted, one discovers that there was in fact a small group of politicians who remained in office for very long periods. There were 561 ministers in the Third Republic, of whom only 217 were minister once. 103 held office twice, 71 three times, 48 four times and 122 more than four times. Of the 94 governments between 1879 and 1940, 74 had at least one member of the previous government in it, and 40 kept over half of the ministers of the previous government. Thus Briand was a member of 25 different ministries and was in office for 16 years and 5 months. The record for the longest tenure was held by Sarraut, the radical, who was minister for 18 years and 2 months. Other notable figures were Barthou (14 years), Leygues (13 years), Delcassé (11), Queuille, Freycinet and Chéron (10), Millerand and Poincaré (9).

The Third Republic thus does not have to be divided into 108 different periods, each with a different set of men and a different programme, but falls naturally into much longer phases. Only 5 out of the 63 ministers who served between

1870 and 1879 continued to hold office after that date. The republic of dukes is a clearly defined era. The years 1879 to 1885 were dominated by Ferry, who was minister of education in 5 of the 8 ministries. There is only a brief break with Gambetta, who lasted 3 months in 1881–2. The continuity of the rule of the opportunists is seen in Freycinet, who was prime minister 9 other times: for 7 of these, he was minister of war and was able to carry out army reforms, just as Ferry was able to pursue his educational changes while riding repeated cabinet crises. Rouvier was minister of finance 4 times between 1889 and 1892 and later prime minister twice, Fallières was minister 7 times between 1882 and 1892. It is possible to understand this clique of opportunist politicians as a group; there is no need to despair in confusion at their constantly changing recombinations. In the middle period of the republic, ministries became longer: Waldeck-Rousseau was prime minister for 3 years (1899–1902), Combes for 2 years and 7 months (1902–5), Clemenceau for 3 years and 4 months (1906–9). Delcassé controlled foreign policy for 7 years, from 1898 to 1905. After that ministries appeared to fall faster than ever, but the same men dominated politics. Between 1920 and 1940 ministries lasted on average only 6 months each, but the continuity between them increased, so that frequently up to 80 per cent of one ministry survived into the next. The small group of the radical left, which had between 32 and 50 members, had a member in every one of the 29 ministries between 1924 and 1936. The radicals controlled the ministries of education and the interior for 12 of the inter-war years and the ministry of agriculture for 10. It became increasingly clear that from amongst themselves, the deputies selected a small group of people to fill the ministerial posts. One could say that the core of this group consisted of only 122 men, the ministers who held office more than four times. These were men, of course, who accepted the system, and the supremacy of the deputies. The rebels against it, however able, seldom lasted very long.[1]

It was the intention of the conservative makers of the constitution that the chamber of deputies should be held in check, at

---

[1] A. Soulier, *L'Instabilité ministerielle sous la Troisième République 1871–1938* (1939); Jacques Ollé-Laprune, *La Stabilité des ministres sous la Troisième République 1879–1940* (1962).

least partially, by the senate. This body of 300 was designed to give weight to the stable rural backbone of the country against the impetuousness of the towns. It was elected by representatives of the municipal councils. Originally every commune had one vote, whatever its size. In 1884 greater representation was given to the cities, but only to the extent of allowing one elector for every commune with under 500 inhabitants, rising to 24 electors for those with over 60,000. This new arrangement kept the favouritism towards the villages, but added a disproportionate influence for the medium-sized town of 5,000 to 10,000 in which the republican élites were to be found. The cities remained grossly under-represented. In the department of Bouches-du-Rhône, Marseille (with 900,000 inhabitants) had 24 electors, while all the other communes put together, with 250,000 inhabitants, had 313. In Seine, Paris had 147 electors, while its suburbs, with half its population, had 1,032. There were 370 rural communes, each with fewer than a hundred inhabitants, who were given 370 votes, while eleven cities, with an aggregate population of two and a half million, had 264 votes. The average senatorial constituency had 800 voters. 90 per cent of these were delegates from the communes: the local deputies and local councillors had a vote each in addition. Seventy-five of the senators were elected for life by the National Assembly, but this category was allowed to die out after 1884 and replaced by elected members.

The intentions of the founders of the regime were not fulfilled. The republicans at first denounced the senate as undemocratic and some continued for twenty years to demand its abolition. But in practice they quickly infiltrated it and it became one more bastion of the rule of the politicians, for it was a chamber which essentially represented them. The people elected were largely retired deputies and civil servants. After the war, indeed, politicians increasingly preferred its calm debates and the greater certainty of re-election it offered, to the rowdiness and risk of the lower house. It appeared to be a retreat, wrote an English journalist in 1900, 'for elderly men of education, whose faculties are undimmed and whose favourite pastime is to meet in a debating society to recite to one another essays on abstract legal or historical questions, with an occasional reference to topics of the hour. The president takes his seat in a leisurely fashion and gives a tone to the afternoon's proceedings by pronouncing in admirable language an obituary eulogy of one of their number snatched away since their last meeting.'[1] It was a reminder of the survival of the slower pace and gentler life of the provinces, for whom the agitation of Paris was a kind of theatre, to be watched and talked about. 'The senate', said Caillaux in 1938, 'is the assembly of the peasants of this country. This earns it some abuse, but, with the support of its electors, it opposes a perfect serenity to certain attacks from the press and the street, which do not rise to merit even its contempt.' The politics of the senate were accordingly considerably more conservative than those of the deputies—though staunchly republican. The senate was an obstacle much less to the power of the deputies as a group than to the political extremists among them, and to the masses as a whole.

While the republic was being consolidated, little importance was accorded to the senate. Ferry, on having his famous Article 7 rejected by it in 1880, simply turned his bill into a decree. In 1896, however, disapproving of the radical ministry of Bourgeois, the senate refused him credits and he resigned, though as a radical he might have interpreted the constitution in such a way as to allow him to ignore it. Its importance as a brake on advanced or socialist legislation increased considerably after that. It was due to its resistance that the income tax and female suffrage were so long delayed. It prevented the law of 1884 from formally allowing divorce by consent; it buried many proposals for social legislation by consideration so protracted that they were forgotten about. Its work was not just negative, however: though it contributed little to commercial or economic legislation, it was responsible for quite a number of unspectacular but influential measures, like the Nationality Law of 1889, the laws of 1885 and 1891 on the punishment and release of criminals, and it made significant additions to many other proposals. Between the wars it came to be the bastion of conservative republicanism against the demands for modernisation: it overthrew the ministries of Herriot, Tardieu, Laval and Blum. It was the other side of the republican coin, the prudent, hoarding, traditional counterpart to the declamatory oratory of the deputies. To a certain extent the deputies could be so

[1] J. E. C. Bodley, *France* (1899), 267–315.

extremist because they knew that their elders would stop any real change coming about.[1]

The deputies also had to contend with the president of the republic in the exercise of their power, but then he again was one of them. His position was dependent, to a considerable degree, on the character of the individual who filled the office. He was clearly not the most important person in the state (unlike in 1848). The republicans, reacting strongly to the experience of the Second Empire, were now hostile to the idea, which they once considered democratic, of a responsible president elected by the people. The president was purposely made weak: he was elected by parliament, so that he would have little authority against it; he was declared irresponsible, so that he should remain outside politics; and he was given a low salary, making him the poorest head of state in Europe.[2] However, in so far as he was, through the influence of the monarchists, given the powers of a constitutional king on the English or Orleanist model[3] he could play a very important role in politics. He appointed the prime minister. The fragmentation of parties meant that any one man was seldom the obvious or necessary choice and the president was thus able to exclude over-powerful figures whom he feared (like Gambetta and Clemenceau), weaken those he disliked by giving them office prematurely (e.g. the radicals under Bourgeois in 1895) or appoint minor politicians who were his friends (e.g. Carnot's friend Tirard). His choice was not confined to parliament but he had to be careful not to defy it. When Poincaré chose the right-wing Ribot to form a ministry in the left-wing parliament

[1] Gaston Coste, *Rôle législatif et politique du sénat sous la troisième république* (Montpellier thesis, 1913); François Goguel-Nyegaard, *Le Rôle financier du sénat français: essai d'histoire parlementaire* (Paris thesis, 1937); Yvan Barthomeuf, *Les Débuts du sénat républicain* (Paris thesis, 1939). For biographical information see the list of biographical dictionaries etc. in David Shapiro, *The Right in France* (St. Antony's Papers, no. 13, 1962).

[2] 600,000 francs, plus 300,000 francs household expenses and 300,000 francs travelling expenses (£48,000 in all). This was trebled between the wars, so the salary failed to keep up with the rising cost of living. No president was enriched by holding the office.

[3] It is sometimes said that the constitution was influenced by the ideas of Prévost-Paradol's *La France nouvelle* (1868) and V. de Broglie's *Vues sur le gouvernement de la France* (1861). These books expressed opinions held by many of those who took part in the drafting of the constitution, but direct influence cannot be proved. Cf. P. Guiral, *Prévost-Paradol* (1955).

of 1914, he was promptly censured by the deputies and had to give way. The president's influence depended to a great extent on his tact. He presided at meetings of the council of ministers, which were held at the Elysée. Though there were cabinet meetings also, at which ministers met without him (but frequently with junior ministers) these never replaced the formal meetings (as they did in England). The president kept a number of the prerogatives of the restoration monarchy. He could sign treaties of alliance, which, unlike treaties of commerce and of peace, needed no parliamentary ratification. In the history of French foreign policy of this period, the presidents of the republic played almost as important a role as the ministers.[1] Since they were elected for a seven-year term (and could be re-elected) they had a considerable advantage of experience and stability.

The republican parliamentarians therefore on the whole elected second-rate politicians to be president, for fear that they might be faced with too powerful a master or rival. Gambetta, Ferry, Waldeck-Rousseau, Clemenceau and Briand were all defeated, in favour of lesser men. On five occasions the president of the senate was promoted in the hope that an uncontroversial mediocrity would make the supreme office a sinecure for aged politicians. On three other occasions the president of the chamber of deputies—somewhat withdrawn from the struggle for power —was elected. Ambition, however, sometimes triumphed and even the mediocrities proved to have more individuality than had been bargained for. Jules Grévy (1879–87) had in 1848 proposed that the office of president should be abolished altogether, as being dangerous to a republic. When he was himself appointed to this post in 1879, he made a historic declaration which greatly diminished the role of the presidency. Marshal MacMahon (1873–9) in 1877 used for the first and last time the president's power to dissolve the chamber of deputies, of whose increasing radicalism he disapproved.[2] The republicans were returned triumphantly, MacMahon was soon forced to resign and Grévy declared on succeeding him, 'Sincerely accepting the

---

[1] 'Opinions de Paul Cambon sur le rôle, en politique étrangère, de quelques ministres et de divers Présidents de la République', *Revue d'Histoire Diplomatique* (1954), 202–7; L. Rogers, 'The French President and Foreign Affairs', *Political Science Quarterly* (Dec. 1925), 540–60.

[2] Y. Haikal, *La Dissolution de la chambre des députés* (Paris thesis, 1935), 55–61.

great principles of the parliamentary regime, I shall never oppose the national will as expressed by its constitutional organs.' After this the president's power of dissolution was never used again—a fact of momentous importance in making the chamber the predominant power in the country. But Grévy, while appearing to be a purely titular head of state, also took a very active interest in politics. 'He pretended', wrote Freycinet, 'that he did not wish to influence any of his ministers, so as not to shift responsibility from them. So he was careful when a proposal was made in the council, not to express an opinion either for or against it. He allowed the discussion to flow, maintaining an indolent reserve which might give the impression that he was not following it entirely. If he approved, he merely nodded or signed quickly, but he abstained from making any comment. If he did not approve, he appeared to awake from a light doze just before the vote: "You have no doubt, gentlemen, reflected carefully on the hostility this might rouse against you"; and then in a seemingly indifferent tone, he would point out the dangers which would arise and very gently in a quiet and masterly way described them like one who had not missed a word of the discussion. "But it is your business, gentlemen; it is you who are responsible. I only mention this to inform you, in case these objections have not occurred to you. Do as you please." It frequently happened that instead of doing as we pleased, we took the file away, rather abashed by the objections we had just perceived and that we altered the project and sometimes even abandoned it.'[1] Grévy certainly played a major part in causing the French to abandon Egypt, and also in avoiding war over the Schnaebele incident in 1887. Sadi Carnot, his successor (1887–94), in a different way, did much to bring about the Franco-Russian alliance, by choosing premiers, or insisting on his premiers choosing ministers of foreign affairs and of war, who favoured that alliance.[2] He intervened less in domestic politics, which had absorbed and fascinated Grévy, but whereas Grévy had devoted himself to a purely Parisian life of political intrigue, Carnot inaugurated the practice of touring the provinces: his travels during the Boulangist crisis were a significant contribution to republican propaganda.

[1] C. de Freycinet, *Souvenirs 1878–1893* (1913), 75–6.
[2] A. Dansette, *Histoire des présidents de la République* (1953), 77.

The president was shielded from political controversy by a custom that neither his name nor his opinions should be mentioned in parliament and by special protection in the press law.[1] Gambetta was sentenced to imprisonment for his speech urging MacMahon to accept republicanism or to resign; a newspaper was prosecuted for a cartoon showing MacMahon on a horse, with the legend: 'The horse looks intelligent.' Casimir Périer's term as president (1894–5) showed, however, that this protection was useless when it was not backed by public opinion. Gérault-Richard, prosecuted for a violent article against Casimir Périer, was sentenced to one year's imprisonment but Paris at once elevated him to parliament and so freed him. Jaurès, who defended him in court, was able with impunity to call the president's establishment a house of debauchery and worse. The foreign minister Hanotaux systematically refused to consult the president or to show him all dispatches. Within eight months Périer, declaring himself powerless, a prisoner, a mere master of ceremonies, open to blows but unable to return them, resigned. He had been elected after Carnot's assassination as a symbol of order, but as one of the wealthiest industrialists in the country, he was cut off from the people.[2]

After him, men of humbler origin, who could symbolise the triumph of merit, however modest, were chosen. Every man could dream of emulating them. Thus Félix Faure (1895–9) was the son of a chair maker of the rue Faubourg Saint-Denis who started life as an apprentice tanner, built up a sizeable business at Le Havre, importing leather from South America, and then became the city's deputy. But as president he behaved not just like a Napoleonic marshal, but like the emperor himself. He treated sovereigns as equals if not as inferiors; he devoted himself passionately to hunting; he made Rambouillet his summer residence; and acquired the nickname of Le Président Soleil. His pomp was popular, because he could always begin his speeches with the words, 'As the son of a working man, and as a working man myself . . .', even though in reality he was a bourgeois. His father had married the niece of a well-to-do wine merchant and property speculator. With a loan from this

---

[1] Article 26 of the law of 29 July 1881.
[2] P. Barral, *Les Périer dans l'Isère au XIXe siècle* (1964), 163–4.

uncle Faure Senior established a second factory at Beauvais. Faure served his apprenticeship in Amboise, but completed it by marrying the daughter of the town's mayor, who later became a senator.[1]

Loubet (1899–1906) was the son of a true peasant (though a well-to-do one); Fallières (1906–13) was the son of a legal clerk and *justice de paix* and grandson of a blacksmith. Both had become barristers, mayors of their small towns (Montélimar and Nérac respectively), entered politics and worked their way up by making a lot of friends, till they were president of the senate.[2] Faure, an old freemason (though to please his women-folk, he died within the Church), helped to stimulate the retrial of Dreyfus.[3] Loubet, a moderate, tried hard to hold Combes's anticlericalism in check during the separation of Church and state and steadfastly maintained Delcassé in office as foreign minister for seven years.[4]

However, during this period the president slipped increasingly into the background. Félix Faure said, 'I am criticised for doing nothing; but what do you expect? I am the equivalent of the Queen of England.'[5] Fallières, on taking office, assured the cabinet that he would never pursue a policy of his own and he tamely allowed giants like Clemenceau, Briand and Caillaux to become prime minister.[6]

This diminution of the presidential power began to appear regrettable as men became increasingly worried by the instability of ministries. The parliamentary regime was firmly established by now, the danger of a Boulangist dictator was passed, and so good republicans could safely consider making more use of the president, without fear of jeopardising democracy. Poincaré, clearly thinking that he could be more powerful as president than as prime minister, abandoned the latter office to go to the

---

[1] E. Maillard, *Le Président Félix Faure* (1897).

[2] Henri Avenel, *Le Président Émile Loubet et ses prédécesseurs* (1905), shows Loubet as a vigorous local administrator and as 'le premier mutualiste de France' because he favoured pension schemes. His origins too, were not quite as humble as was made out. His father was a mayor of Marsanne (Drôme) 1844–8, 1860–82; and Loubet inherited the Château de Grignan from Doctor Loubet (an uncle).

[3] Charles Braibant, *Félix Faure à l'Élysée*, souvenirs de Louis Le Grall, Directeur du Cabinet du Président de la République (1963), 22–3.

[4] Émile Combarieu, *Sept Ans à l'Élysée avec le Président Émile Loubet* (1932), 308.

[5] R. Poincaré, *Au Service de la France* (1826–33), 3. 34.

[6] H. Leyret, *Le Président de la république: son rôle, ses droits, ses devoirs* (1913), 37.

Elysée (1913–20). He had no desire for a revision of the constitution: 'Before revising the constitution,' he had said, 'we might perhaps try to apply it . . . We must first draw from the constitution of 1875 the unused resources concealed within it: henceforth the president of the republic must freely exercise the powers of which he has been deprived by custom.'[1] Poincaré's tenure of the office was inspired by the belief that a strong man could transform it, and for a time he did indeed transform it. 'I will see to it', he told the Austrian ambassador, 'that a man takes my place [as foreign minister] who will carry out my policy. It will be as though I were still at the Quai d'Orsay.'[2] The conduct of foreign policy did remain largely in his hands for several years. When he and the new prime minister Viviani visited St. Petersburg in 1914, it was Poincaré who took the lead in all the discussions, leaving Viviani very much in the background.[3] 'In the council of ministers, as neither Viviani nor Briand presided effectively, he [Poincaré] intervened constantly and with authority', for he worked hard and was better informed than his ministers. He summoned civil servants to brief him directly. To such an extent did he abandon the president's self-effacing role in the council that he engaged in violent argument to get his views accepted. On one occasion he shouted at the prime minister Briand, 'You lie, sir!' 'The latter threw down his portfolio on the table. Doumergue, between them, cried in a ridiculous voice: "There is France!" Finally they were brought together and embraced.'[4] This was very different from the cabinet meetings of Grévy, but Poincaré's dominance continued only so long as his premiers were weak or ineffective. The situation was completely transformed in November 1917, when Clemenceau, replacing Poincaré in the eyes of public opinion as the country's hope for a vigorous prosecution of the war, became prime minister. At once the president was relegated to his traditional obscurity. His advice and his letters were ignored by Clemenceau; the foreign

[1] Speeches of 1898 and 1902, quoted by Gordon Wright, *Raymond Poincaré and the French Presidency* (Stanford, Calif., 1942), 23. F. Poincaré, *Questions et figures politiques* (1907), 78–9, 197.
[2] Ibid., 62.
[3] S. V. Gallup, 'The Political Career of René Viviani' (Oxford unpublished thesis, 1965), chapter 5.
[4] Wright, 162 n., 164.

minister Pichon took his orders from the prime minister, not the president; and at the peace conference, despite the president's theoretical right to negotiate treaties, it was Clemenceau who represented France. Poincaré's experiment was thus a failure, in the sense that he was unable to make any permanent change in the president's role. But he had shown its possibilities enough for Clemenceau to seek election to the presidency in 1920—and for parliament to defeat him.

The elegant Deschanel, who was elected instead, had long prepared himself for the presidency of the republic. For twelve years he had served as an impartial president of the chamber of deputies. All his life he refused to join any parliamentary group (he advocated, but never actually created, a 'Tory' party) and he declined all offers of a ministry. He was another of the many politicians who wrote a book in praise of Lamartine, whose combination of literary and political glory he longed to emulate: politics was almost a branch of literature, or of rhetoric, to him. He aimed, like Poincaré, to revive the influence of the president. 'It is a constitutional heresy', he said, 'to consider the president of the republic an inert cog or similar to a constitutional king. An elected chief cannot be like a hereditary prince, the impassive arbiter between the parties.' He must give 'active advice' to the prime minister.[1] Owing to ill health Deschanel had to resign after only eight months (February to September 1920) but his successor Millerand (1920-4) continued his campaign and took it much further. He demanded not simply that the constitution should be enforced in the way that had been planned in 1877 but that it should be revised, to increase the president's powers by new legislation. Millerand, who like Poincaré was prime minister when he was raised to the presidency, tried to keep his own ministry in office, under the nominal leadership of Leygues, so as to be virtually prime minister and president in one. When that failed he continued to intervene actively in day-to-day politics and in the conduct of government, while making public speeches in favour of a revision of the constitution. In the election of 1924 he openly took sides—against the left. He opposed

[1] Louis Sonolet, *La Vie et l'œuvre de Paul Deschanel 1852–1922* (1926), 136-9, 276; P. Deschanel, *La République nouvelle* (1898), *La Décentralisation* (1895), and other collected speeches in many volumes each under different titles; René Malliavin, *La Politique nationale de Deschanel* (1925).

parliamentary rule itself, saying that sovereignty, which belonged to the people, had been usurped by the chamber; a strong president, and a supreme court of justice were needed to check it. He wished to make frequent use of the power of dissolution and to introduce referenda. The parliamentary leaders retaliated by refusing to form a ministry so long as he remained president. He was forced to resign.[1]

Even this crisis, however, did not diminish the standing of the president. Gaston Doumergue (1924–31) is said to have intervened in politics more than any other president since Grévy—which he was able to do because he had great tact as well as much experience of the parliamentary world. His humble origins and his southerner's geniality made him as popular with the masses as his political skill made him influential. When he was recalled from retirement to be prime minister in 1934, to save the republic after the Stavisky scandal, he proposed a revision of the constitution, to enable the president to dissolve without the senate's consent. His proposal, because it was made too late after the crisis, instead of as a condition of his accepting office, came to nothing.

In the last years of the republic the status of the president diminished again. Paul Doumer (1931–2) son of a railway worker, president of the senate, was elected to keep out Briand. He was industrious but too puritan and aloof to be influential; he was assassinated, in any case, within a year, by a Russian lunatic.[2] Albert Lebrun (1932–40), again a president of the senate, and of peasant origin, an efficient and conscientious Lorrainer, graduate of the *Polytechnique* and the *Ponts et Chaussées*, took his duties seriously. He prided himself on reading everything before he signed it and he frequently secured amendments to administrative decrees (which had become increasingly numerous).[3] He considered resigning after the elections of 1936, for he disapproved strongly of the Popular Front: he decided to stay so as to 'moderate its excesses' and to prevent the election of a socialist president, but in fact he exerted little influence. It was only in the crisis of 1940, when the ministries

---

[1] Jean Magnien, 'Alexandre Millerand' (D.E.S. unpublished mémoire, Paris, 1962).
[2] P. Bastid, 'Doumer', *Revue Politique et Parlementaire* (Dec. 1934).
[3] Daniel Brune, *Du pouvoir réglementaire du chef de l'État* (Bordeaux thesis, 1898), 98.

were vacillating and divided, that his role became crucial once more. His case illustrates well what was true throughout the republic, that the president's position in the government varied enormously, depending on his personality and on how the other parts of the constitution were functioning. The generalisation, frequently repeated, that he lost his importance after 1877, is very misleading.[1]

Another force the deputies had to contend with was the civil service. The extent to which they kept it in subordination again varied considerably. A powerful deputy, by assiduous canvassing, could get a favourable prefect, sub-prefect and civil servants appointed to his constituency, and if he was sufficiently active he could ensure that the strings of influence and promotion remained in his grasp. Inevitably, however, the civil service had an *esprit de corps* of its own. The prefects of the Third Republic are less famous than those of the Second Empire, partly because their activities were less dramatic, but partly also because they have been studied less. They were in fact of two kinds. There were some among them who accepted a relatively subordinate role in the political system, regarded themslves as administrators, and pressed for security of tenure, to make them like all other state employees. It is not usually realised, however, that many of them regretted the grand days of more unchallenged authority which they enjoyed under previous regimes. They formed an association to defend their interests in 1907, where the principal topic of discussion was their prestige. Every generation of prefects had its contingent of those who complained that their powers were diminishing, compared to the previous one. Some rejected security and insisted that their role was essentially political: the more risk there was in it, the more they could personally achieve. They maintained the paraphernalia which gave them status as charismatic representatives of national power: they kept up their palatial residences, with a social life surrounded by distance and respect. They insisted that they were unlike other bureaucrats, for their skill lay in their ability to handle men. There is no doubt that, although they could no longer manage elections single-handed, as some had once claimed to do, electoral activities continued to be one of their

[1] Albert Lebrun, *Témoignage* (1945), 223–57.

main preoccupations, and their success in them played an important part in their promotions. Brisson sacked ten prefects in 1898 because he thought they were unfavourable to his brand of politics; Combes sacked eight in 1904; Herriot sacked eight after the election of 1924 and moved one-third of the whole corps around. It is true Combes introduced a custom of treating dismissed prefects very gently and finding them profitable sinecures to retire to; his own son Edgar, who was a prefect and who as secretary general of the ministry of the interior supervised all these matters, ended up himself as director of the lunatic asylum of Villejuif.

There is an interesting book describing the equivocal position of the prefects by one of Gambetta's friends who had served as a prefect himself. He was keen that their status as 'the highest functionaries of the administration' should be restored; he was furious that, in the official order of precedence, he might find himself lagging behind bishops, admirals and judges. (The association of prefects indeed has ever since agitated for more decorations to be given, quasi-automatically, to prefects.) He resented that his right to travel free came from a pass issued by the railway company, not by the state. He lamented that his influence was so dependent on his personal popularity and tact, for he had lost his control of the mayors. (This was partly remedied by a system of *délégués*, whom the prefect appointed in villages whose mayors were hostile to him: he channelled all favours through them and so built up his own party.) He had to use much effort to win the co-operation of mayors by constant friendliness, but then if he became too popular, the local deputies got jealous. They would complain to the minister, who tended to play prefect and deputy off against each other. The prefect therefore had to be very careful what he wrote to Paris, lest it be shown to the deputy. When he moved departments, he usually took with him all personal and political files he had accumulated with the result that his successor had to start from scratch learning about the balance of local forces. Though he had lost control of the mayor, he still appointed the *instituteur*, who was frequently secretary of the municipal council and who could therefore be an invaluable tool. But he appointed him on the nomination of the inspector of the Academy; the whole academic administration was increasingly building up an independence of the prefectoral authority, and its Paris headquarters regularly supported them against the prefects. 'It is not going too far to say that the greatest embarrassments a prefect can experience come to him from the inspector of the Academy, supported by his rector, supported by the offices of the ministry.' The *instituteurs* knew their promotion came to them from their inspectors, and though most of them were republican, the ministry, keen to place the university outside politics, therefore appeared reactionary, because it pursued an independent line instead of backing the prefect's efforts to 'republicanise' his department systematically.

The idea of a united party getting control of the whole country is far too simple. The diversity of the civil service was considerable. Quite apart from the clergy, the prefect often had trouble with the numerous officials of the ministry of finance, who had the reputation of being particularly conservative. Its registrar's department (*l'enregistrement*) was especially regarded as 'the refuge of all that is most clerical and most Jesuit in the administration, and if a prefect known for his inflexible republican opinions denounces an official of this department as a reactionary, that official is almost bound to get immediate promotion'. The ministry of justice was more politically conscious, and prefects could influence the appointment of judges of the peace, but on the other hand magistrates were often conservative. The ambitions of the prefects in turn roused vigorous resistance in others. Liberals denounced them as relics of the *ancien régime* and the empire. 'Like their predecessors,' wrote Gaston Jèze in 1911, 'the prefects of the twentieth century are the natural enemies of political liberties.' The civil servants in the older branches of the administration, like justice and finance, were proud of the tradition of their services, and valued the prestige which they felt they inherited from the dignitaries of the old monarchy, who had bought their offices and who had acquired nobility through them. This, again, is another side of the republican regime that was put somewhat in the shade by the rhetorical declamation. The old authoritarian state survived, despite the Revolution. The deputies were representatives of liberty against it, but when they became ministers they were unhesitating in maintaining its power. The republic exhibited herself in public wearing liberal clothes, but one had grounds for suspecting that she was simply the old Napoleonic state disguised, not altered too fundamentally. What the deputies put into her mouth needs to be examined very closely. The great mistake in studying the Third Republic is to take its polemic at its face value and to believe that politicians who attacked each other were enemies for the reasons they gave, or sometimes indeed that they were enemies at all.[1]

[1] Edgar Monteil, *L'Administration de la République* (1893); Jeanne Siwek-Pouydesseau, *Le Corps préfectoral sous la troisième et la quatrième République* (1969); Henri Chardon, *Le Pouvoir administratif* (1910); Henri Joly, *De la corruption de nos institutions* (1903).

20. Opportunism

REPUBLICANISM is not easy to define, because it had different meanings in different contexts. No generalisation about it can escape being vague or confused if it fails to distinguish between at least four types. At the level of the masses, republicanism was closely linked with old traditions, prejudices, rivalries, some going back a long time, but many of them sharpened and embittered by the Revolution and the struggles it fomented. It reflected developments in social relationships whose origins had little to do with the doctrines which were preached in Paris, though these doctrines were sometimes used to rationalise and make respectable personal, family and local animosities. At a level above this, the professional politicians saw the republic as a defence of the individual against the state, as a means of social ascension, and as an instrument for the emancipation of local communities from traditional tyrannies. But making themselves the necessary intermediaries of this defence and liberation, they assumed the positions of merchants or retailers in the political system. They acquired an ascendancy which gave them some of the characteristics of a new ruling class, but also laid themselves open to jealousy and contempt as profiteers. Republicanism for them was thus both a panacea and a living, an ideal of equality and a source of supremacy. There was tension between them and the masses on the one hand and the government on the other. The republicanism of the ministers they raised to power was of a third kind. The ministers were more conscious of national than of local considerations. They inherited the command of an immensely powerful state. Republicanism for them meant not the defence of the individual but the creation of order, unity, glory, all of which required sacrifice from individuals for the attainment of higher principles. Finally, at the fourth level, republicanism had its philosophers, who provided these principles. These of course had no necessary relation with the realities. They often misled people as to what was going on; they often idealised the Revolution, so that its shortcomings were concealed and they stressed divisions which were more theoretical than real. It is from the interplay of these four elements that the total picture of republicanism must be built up. Previous chapters have discussed the popular origins of republicanism and the role of the deputies in it. This one will examine the ministers, with a view to discovering in what way and to what extent they attempted to reorganise the state or to modify economic and social relations. Their careers will help define the boundaries of republicanism, the limits beyond which it would not go, and the degree to which it was content to preserve the inheritance of the past. It will emerge that some of the most important elements of republicanism were those which sought to bolster traditional forces, values or myths. But it will be seen that its attempts in this direction were not all based on popular demand. When the republicans obtained power, they were so deeply imbued with prejudices instilled by many centuries of monarchical rule, that they often had no desire to break away from them. There was thus a fundamental contradiction within republicanism, between what it was in opposition and what it was in office. This can be explained less by the ambition and greed for power of particular individuals, than by the dominance of deeply ingrained intellectual traditions. Republicans wanted to demolish the state when they were in opposition, but to strengthen it when they became ministers. A study of the lives and ideas of some of the leading ministers will help to show how and why this came about, and why, though they saw themselves as the advocates of popular wishes, they so often proved, almost inevitably, impotent.

The man who did as much as anyone to establish the Third Republic was Adolphe Thiers (1797–1873), who had never been a republican at all. Thiers was one of the most astute masters of the French political game in the nineteenth century. He played a leading role in establishing the July Monarchy in 1830, in having Louis Napoleon elected president in 1848, in destroying the Commune, and in founding the regime of 1871. He gave the impression of unsurpassed clarity of mind. It was said of him that there was no subject, however complicated, which he could not understand. He could certainly give this impression, and since he had firm views on all subjects, he was one of the most persuasive speakers of his time. He had infinite

skill as a manager of men. His inexhaustible energy, his imper-
turbable self-confidence, his dogged determination made him
unsuppressible. He was only 33 when he raised Louis-Philippe
to the throne, he was minister of the interior at 35, member of
the French Academy at 36 and an all-powerful elder statesman
while still in his fifties. His influence came to him partly because
he was willing to accept only supreme power, so that he seldom
held office, but he became the *éminence grise* of several generations. He came of undistinguished origins; he was five feet two
inches in height; he had only his wits to live on. He made himself
one of the most striking examples of the self-made man. He
benefited from the prestige this status could give, but he assimilated rapidly into the ruling class. He became president of one
of the most profitable firms in France, the Anzin Mine Company.
He also enjoyed an independent position as one of the country's
most widely read historians, at a time when history was almost
a branch of political philosophy.

His significance, in the long term, was that he incarnated
certain important prejudices of the early nineteenth century,
and he used his dominant position in politics to preserve and
strengthen them against new currents. The republic he founded
was therefore a dyke against these as much as against anything
else. He reveals particularly clearly what was common to the
different regimes he supported in turn. He had served Louis-
Philippe but, even more, he had quarrelled with him. 'I do not
call myself an Orleanist', he said. 'The Orleanist family have
no claim on me; they have always persecuted me and I have
opposed them. By birth I belong to the people ... By education,
I am an aristocrat. I have no sympathy with the bourgeoisie
or with any system under which they rule.'[1] He shows how
difficult it was for any particular regime to win a permanent
loyalty, and how partisanship was often a label stuck on by
opponents rather than voluntarily adopted. He illustrates how
Orleanists, Bonapartists and republicans all tried to draw
strength, in different ways, from their popular origins, and how
they moved away from them towards aristocracy or oligarchy.
If he could have his way, he once said, he would distribute the
Coburg family on to the thrones of all Europe. His ideal was
constitutional monarchy, with power firmly in the hands of a

[1] N. Senior, *Conversations with Thiers, Guizot* ... (1878), i. 39.

prime minister. The nation was sovereign, but only theoretically, in the sense that it should not be expected to make decisions
on every issue, but should leave these to its delegates in parliament. He tried to abolish manhood suffrage in 1850. He had
only contempt for 'the vile multitude', a phrase that, significantly, made him permanently execrable only to a small
minority on the very fringes of politics. The establishment of
parliamentary government was his main aim. Coupled with
free elections and personal security for the citizens, it provided
all that the country needed.[1]

He had a profound hostility to every form of socialism. In
1848 he published an unflinchingly conservative defence of
property as the basis of French civilisation. Though he represented the triumph of merit, he was also proud of having been
admitted into the inner sanctum of the ruling class, and he had
no desire to diminish its power. He adopted its traditional
pessimism about the possibility of any drastic change and its
scepticism towards reform. He agreed that there were evils
governments should try to remedy, but there were also evils
'inherent in human nature which no imaginable perfection in
governments could spare men'. Railways, when they first
appeared, had roused only suspicion in him and he had thought
the best thing was to avoid them. Though he was an industrial
director or because he was one, he was very gloomy about the
chances of industrial success. 'Failures are much more numerous than successes, and if [industry in France] has created quite
a considerable number of middle-sized fortunes, it has established very few large ones, above all very few capable of in-
fallibly surviving serious crises.' Even if a firm did succeed, it
did so only after having ruined several competitors. Workers'
associations had not the slightest chance of being more successful than capitalist firms. His solution was prudent protection
from foreign competition.[2]

Thiers saw that this was not a programme to rouse enthusiasm among the masses. 'What we do in Paris,' he said, 'what
we say in the chambers, has no impact on the country. But

---

[1] See his speech on Necessary Liberties, *Annales du Corps Législatif*, 2 (1864).
305–16, and on the pre-eminence of political solutions, ibid. 2 (1865), 87–98,
and 1 (1866), 202–15.
[2] A. Thiers, *De la propriété* (1848), 192–204, 241, 363.

when the country learns that they are going to fight . . . and that they have been victorious, . . . children are moved and women cry. Is it too much to spend 60 millions to maintain what is left of moral sentiments and of disinterested passions, to prevent France from huddling over a footwarmer?' National glory was the essential counterpart to parliamentary government, and 'an article of faith' to him. Napoleon I was 'the man who has inspired France with the strongest emotions she has ever felt'. Thiers's books did as much as anyone's to glorify the emperor's genius, for whom he had a profound admiration. If he had a model, it was the first consul. The one thing he could not forgive Napoleon III for was that he had allowed Germany to outweigh and outshine France in Europe. Thiers was a Bonapartist also in his horror of disorder. The riots of 1848 had filled him, as he said, with rage, and in 1871 when 'mob rule', which he hated above all else, seemed to threaten, he showed how ruthless he could be in its suppression.[1]

It was no accident that Thiers should have been called in as the country's saviour in 1871, in the agony of national defeat. The effect of his tenure of power was to stamp an indelible conservatism on the institutions of the regime. First, Thiers repeated the repression of the working-class agitation which he had carried out in the 1830s and in 1848; indeed he saw the Commune as an opportunity to end this menace once and for all. He succeeded, but at the expense of a civil war. The consequence of this was almost to suggest the exclusion of a section of the community from full membership of the nation. Paris was defeated by the provinces but at the cost of making it permanently hostile to the regime. Centralisation was maintained. It no longer represented the dominance of the Parisians, but rather of provincials who had made good and crowned their triumph by capturing the state. The failure of the Commune meant that the methods of the old regime survived, defended and taken over by the provincials who had so long suffered from them. Thiers was one of the firmest supporters of centralisation. He tried his best to prevent the royalists from increasing the powers of the municipal and departmental councils, and he did succeed in retaining for the prefects the right to appoint mayors

[1] On his 'rage' see Bibliothèque Nationale, N.a.f. 20618, f. 597, copy of letter from Thiers to duc d'Aumale, 6 Jan. 1861.

in the larger towns. The republic Thiers founded was thus endowed with the institutions of Napoleon I, his hero.

This can be seen even more clearly in the military system which, after 1871, was immediately called into question. Thiers had very conservative views here too, preferring a professional army which he considered the necessary basis of French prestige. It was his insistence that prevented France following the German model and instituting a conscript army. He wanted soldiers to serve for seven years: the reformers wanted universal service for three years. A compromise of five years was agreed, which meant that not everyone was needed. The democratisation of the army was avoided; the army increasingly became a bastion of conservatism and resistance. Its 'republicanisation' remained a major problem for several decades.

Above all, it was Thiers who prevented the reform of the old system of taxation. He won wide acclaim for rapidly raising the money to pay off the indemnity exacted by the conquering Germans, but he staunchly refused to allow the introduction of the income tax to meet the increased costs of government. He preferred to raise existing taxes, however inequitably distributed they might be, than to introduce new ones. He had assisted the financier Baron Louis in 1830 and never changed the views he acquired then; he saw the experience of the Restoration as a vindication of Napoleon I's financial system. France, he thought, should maintain the institutions which had made it great. He objected to the Second Empire's desire to tax new forms of wealth. He believed governments should concentrate on reducing the national debt rather than raise new taxes. It was he who saved the *rentier* in the 1870s.[1]

The attitude of Gambetta towards the state and its institutions was not as radically different as might be supposed from a man who was held up as incarnating the popular will. Though one of the main founders of the republic, he held office for only three months. By the end of his career he was feared or mistrusted by the leaders of the regime he had done so much to create. He

---

[1] R. Schnerb, 'La Politique fiscale de Thiers', *Revue Historique*, 201 (1949), 186–212, and 202 (1950), 184–220. The fullest biography of Thiers is by H. Malo, *Thiers* (1932).

began his life as an apparently extreme radical and ended it as a mild opportunist, claiming that compromise was the essence of politics. A great deal of myth grew up around him and there is more hagiography about him than almost any other politician of his era. There has even been a *Société Gambetta*, founded in 1905, to cultivate his memory in a spirit of hero worship. He is difficult to evaluate because his popularity was due partly to personal qualities, to a distinctive, captivating charm, which an early death maintained as a pure memory among a host of friends, and to which future generations have paid a rather mystified homage.

Physically, Gambetta both repelled and attracted. He himself said he was ugly. He was coarse and untidy. He had a glass eye. He appears to have suffered from syphilis. His health was poor: in later years he grew fat and his complexion reddened. But he was the most approachable of men, with a gentle and ready smile, simple manners, a warm but soft voice, and he could talk as no one else could. His speeches lacked distinction, harmony or any of the classical perfection so carefully cultivated by his better-educated colleagues; they are full of repetition and banality; but they could captivate mass audiences by their overwhelming impression of sincerity and involvement. He did not measure his gestures, nor grow animated at appropriate and preordained moments, as trained barristers should; he prepared only the first and last phrases of his speeches, but in between allowed himself to be carried away by his emotions. He did not so much impress his audiences as move them. There was no haughtiness in him. He made friends almost with a kind of passion. He was particularly good at encouraging and welcoming young people making their first appearance in public life, with a friendliness and grace which won him dazzled admirers. He found time for all this social activity because he slept very little, staying up into the early hours chatting and playing cards, but getting up at seven in the morning. He combined a vast capacity for work with a deep-rooted laziness, so that he alternated between industriousness and sloth. He was a Bohemian, a bachelor, a foreigner, a parvenu, so that he was never restricted by the traditions of any particular class. His father was an Italian grocer who had settled in Cahors. He had had a hard struggle to get his education; he had been a mediocre student at school; he had some difficulty in passing his law degree; he never read much, though he had a good memory for some things and he could recite whole pages of Rabelais by heart. The friends he collected round him were of the same kind, most of them of obscure origin, who had suffered failures of various kinds and who found in politics a justification, a purpose and also an income. They were a new class of men, who lived by politics, and who had no private incomes to retire to. Gambetta himself lived with an old aunt in a mean apartment until he moved into the splendid residence of the president of the chamber of deputies; he acquired a small house only in 1878 and had no other property. Spuller, whom Gambetta called his faithful Achates, and whom he made his under-secretary at the ministry for foreign affairs, was the orphan son of peasants of German origin, who also had great trouble getting through his law course and who then scratched a poor living by his pen, in a shabby attic. Eugène Étienne was another orphan in the entourage, who started as a shop assistant and only later acquired a fortune in Algeria. Delcassé again was a parvenu and a man who kept failing his examinations, working as a junior teacher until politics raised him and a rich marriage enriched him. Challemel-Lacour came of a bourgeois family ruined by bankruptcy; he was one of the few who had academic success, through the École Normale, but the advent of Napoleon III threw him out of work. He nurtured a deep resentment against the class from which he issued but which had rejected him, and he consoled himself with the study of Schopenhauer. Several of the followers of Gambetta had tried to practise as barristers and had failed. Few of them had provincial ties, let alone properties: they were *déracinés* making their fortunes alone in Paris. They were bachelors for the most part, or were involved in irregular unions. Gambetta himself lived with Léonie Léon, of mixed black and Jewish origin, brought up in a convent, an orphan while still a girl, and the mistress of an inspector general of Napoleon III's police, before she met him. Challemel lived with a married woman, in a union which cast gloom over his whole life. It was no accident they supported the law on divorce. They had no family life to divert them, though Gambetta's passion for his mistress absorbed him increasingly just when power came to him. They needed each other's company and led a life of close friendship and constant discussion which perpetuated the intimacy of student cliques into middle age.

These men desperately needed hope, and they therefore tried to give it to others who were struggling against misfortune like themselves, who did not have their careers and their dowries laid out before them by their parents. Gambetta was their inspiration and their hero emotionally as well as intellectually. Paul Bert (to be his minister of education) wrote to him: 'You are the man I love most strongly and most completely.' Dionys Ordinaire (who was to run his newspaper for him) wrote to him after hearing him speak: 'You made me cry from love and admiration.' Spuller was said to have found in Gambetta's company the equivalent of mother's milk. 'When Gambetta spoke, he closed his eyes so as to impregnate himself better with his words. He had no thought which did not come from Gambetta, or which did not involve him.'[1]

Gambetta made himself the spokesman of these parvenus who had not quite made good, and interpreted the republic as the form of government which would open the doors of power and of society to them. The republic, he said, meant the advent of the *nouvelles couches sociales*.[2] He meant by that that a revolution must take place in the composition of the ruling class. The old aristocracy, and the wealthy bourgeoisie who had assimilated themselves to it, must make way for humbler men, who had gradually acquired self-confidence since the Revolution and were only slowly taking advantage of universal suffrage. These new men were beginning to make their way into the municipal councils and a few of them even to parliament. The republic must be a regime open to all classes. It must make democracy a reality. Gambetta did not preach class war. He was not asking the workers to replace the employers, for—except on a few occasions towards the end of his life—he denied that such things as classes existed in France, let alone an

---

[1] J. Chastenet, *Gambetta* (1969); G. Wormser, *Gambetta dans les tempêtes* (1964); P. Deschanel, *Gambetta* (1919); Joseph Reinach, *La Vie politique de Gambetta* (1919); H. Stannard, *Gambetta and the Foundation of the Third Republic* (1921); D. Halévy and E. Pillias, *Lettres de Gambetta* (1938); E. Pillias, *Léonie Léon, amie de Gambetta* (1935); P. B. Gheusi, *La Vie et la mort singulières de Gambetta* (1932); E. Krakowski, *Challemel-Lacour* (1932); P. Sorlin, *Waldeck-Rousseau* (1966); Juliette Adam, *Nos amitiés politiques* (1908); G. Hanotaux, *Mon temps*, vol. 2 (1938).
[2] *Discours et plaidoyers politiques de M. Gambetta* (1881–5), 3. 99, 113.

irreconcilable enmity between them. He considered all elements in society who contributed to its productivity, from the capitalist and the merchant to the peasant, to belong to the same category of men who were making their way in the world. He was their champion equally, because he saw France as composed of 'individuals in the process of rising' in the social order. He spoke with respect of the bourgeoisie as 'those who think, who work, who amass wealth, who know how to use this wealth judiciously, liberally and profitably to the country' and who formed 'the enlightened, active and generous part of the nation'. Though he threatened the rich with an income tax and the destruction of their monopolies, his great ambition was to smooth the path that could lead the poor to independence and leisure. Gambetta described the *nouvelles couches* as having been created, first, by universal suffrage, and secondly by economic development, which had brought into existence a new 'world of industry, commerce, science and art . . . imbued with a spirit of enterprise . . . the soul and nerves of democracy'. Their frontiers were thus vague, but they included both the bourgeoisie and the workers. What Gambetta wanted was their unification by the instrument of property. 'Property is, in our view,' he said, 'the superior, preparatory sign of the moral and material emancipation of the individual.' In some confusion (perpetuating the myth Michelet had spread), he imagined that 80 per cent of the country owned some property, so it was only a question of continuing a movement which was well under way. He saw small proprietors, small industrialists, small shopkeepers as the backbone of the *nouvelles couches sociales*. It was for such men that he wanted more active participation in public life.[1]

His ultimate aim, as one of his disciples explained, was that these new men should be accepted without rancour or contempt into the ruling class, which should not be allowed to remain closed, as it had been under the monarchy with its limited franchise. Having got to the top themselves, they should likewise accept that they would be superseded in turn by younger, abler men. That was life. A constant turnover would be accepted if men saw it as an inescapable, scientific law; and if social barriers were no longer raised to halt this inevitable evolution.

[1] *Discours*, 4. 155–6.

Ultimately 'the rich financier, who today lives withdrawn behind his formidable signature, will see his son acknowledge the grocer round the corner who has become a millionaire. People will get round to receiving their tradesmen socially as guests and the aristocrats will be lucky if one day their former valets do not inscribe themselves for the first dance with madame la marquise.' All France would then form one undifferentiated *couche*.[1] Gambetta appreciated that all this could not be achieved at once. In particular he saw that the peasants were ignorant and prejudiced, many of them hating all that came from the towns. He urged his followers to go to them as 'elder brothers', to win them away from their apathy, to teach them to enjoy 'independence of mind'.[2] He looked forward to 'the indissoluble union of those who work and those who possess . . . the alliance of the proletariat and the bourgeoisie'.[3]

Gambetta thus placed human dignity, social equality, national union as the most important objective of the republicans. This must be achieved not by sentimentalism, as in 1848, but by more effective and positive measures. A military reform must turn France into a nation in arms, with universal patriotism replacing the exclusiveness which had been the officer's hallmark. Education for all classes in the same schools must unite the country in the same way. 'It must teach [the pupil] what his dignity is, what solidarity links him to those around him; it must show him that he has a rank in the commune, in the department, in the nation; it must remind him above all that there is a moral being to whom all must be given, all must be sacrificed, life, future, family, and that this being is France.' Until this civic education has penetrated, 'you will always be in the presence of these two imminent perils, either the exploitation of the people by intriguers, adventurers, dictators, ruffians, or something even more grave, the unforeseen explosion of the inflamed masses, who suddenly obey their blind fury'.[4]

Gambetta's purpose was not revolutionary. But he felt he

---

[1] E. Monteil, *Les Couches sociales* (1880). This book, which no historian seems to have used hitherto, appears to be the only commentary on Gambetta's theory of classes, by a close colleague.

[2] *Discours*, 2. 27–30, 5. 117.

[3] Ernest Charles, *Théories sociales et politiciens 1870–1898* (1898), 52–3.

[4] *Discours*, 2. 254.

had to wage a war against one of the main pillars of society, the Church, because it stood in the way of this emancipation, it opposed the republic and it flouted its laws, because its monks acknowledged a foreign sovereign and educated their pupils to different allegiances. He was a free thinker, as he publicly admitted,[1] but his quarrel was not with religion as such. His war cry, 'Clericalism is the enemy', should be interpreted in the light of another slogan uttered by Paul Bert, also a free thinker: 'Peace to the *curé*: war against the monk.' This distinction was not maintained, because the secular clergy rallied to the defence of the regulars, and the Church emerged as a formidable obstacle to republicanism. Gambetta wanted the triumph of science over religion but he also preached liberty of conscience. Education was too important to be confided to obscurantist teachers. If properly organised, it would prevent social animosities, class hatreds and revolution, for 'no one is more confirmed in the anger and hatred that poverty necessarily breeds, than the disinherited man who suffers without knowledge or understanding'.[2] This could be interpreted to mean that Gambetta's aim was not all that different from that of the Church when it taught people to accept their lot. Gambetta never urged the people to rise against economic oppression. He vehemently denied that there was a 'social question'. There were only 'economic and industrial problems', and these did indeed inflame rivalry and envy, but they had to be solved one by one, individually, for they varied according to local conditions and local customs. 'Let us remain on guard against the utopias of those who, dupes of their imagination or backward in their ignorance, believe in a panacea, in a formula which has only to be found to bring about happiness in the world. There is no social remedy, because there is no social question.'[3] The republic's function was only to make the individual free and enlightened, to prepare him 'for the struggle and for triumph'. He believed in association, but also in competition. By association, he took care to point out, 'I do not understand those forms of it which confiscate the individual, suppress and absorb him, because I consider legitimate only those associations which leave the individual the plenitude of his free and active

[1] *Discours*, 2. 179.   [2] *Discours*, 9. 376.
[3] *Discours*, 9. 122–3, 2. 263.

individuality'.[1] But 'those who have arrived' should act as the 'elder brothers . . . the initiators, the patrons, the guides, the protectors of those who, placed beneath them, have not been able to receive the benefits of education and of fortune but who have their rights too'.[2]

There were limits to what he hoped to achieve. Human societies existed, he said, not to ensure happiness but to establish the reign of justice. It should be left to the next generation to seek 'the most extreme consequence of the principle of human solidarity'.[3] He even claimed to be a conservative, because he was safeguarding the work of the Revolution, which was already nearly a hundred years old.[4] He had no desire to dismantle the state, but on the contrary wanted to strengthen it, to make it, almost in the Napoleonic tradition, 'a motor of progress, protector of all legitimate rights and an initiator of all the energies which constitute the national genius'.[5]

Gambetta derived his national standing from his vigorous activity, as minister of the interior and of war in 1871, when he organised the military and popular resistance against Prussia. He acquired a reputation akin to that of Carnot in the first Revolution, though his dictatorship and his refusal to make peace also condemned him in many eyes as a dangerous fanatic. He was elected to the National Assembly by ten departments, but he had identified his party with war and it was soundly defeated. However, he learnt the lesson very rapidly, and changing his tactics, he secured victory for it within six years. He showed himself to possess exceptional skill as a political strategist. First, he worked hard to destroy the reputation republicanism had for bringing anarchy and revolution. He made compromise his watchword. He urged his followers to be *sage*. He pointed out that his party sought not the control of the country for a new clique, but the end of exclusiveness. He was willing to admit into the fold old Bonapartists and royalists who were ready to forget the past and to work for concord in the future. He admitted that the rich were bound to play a major part in a republican society, because they had so many advantages of education and wealth; he sought not to dispossess them but to win them over, to make them the guides

[1] *Discours*, 11. 9.   [2] *Discours*, 5. 117.   [3] *Discours*, 2. 262.
[4] *Discours*, 5. 44.   [5] Charles, 48–9, 77.

and liberators of the poor. He accepted Thiers, his former enemy, and allied willingly with hostile parties if it was to the advantage of his cause.

Gambetta, secondly, was one of the greatest of France's election managers. He probably invented the phrase 'electoral geography', for the study of which he had a passion: 'Universal suffrage', he said, 'is the most interesting thing in the social life of France.'[1] By 1874 he had enormous maps or tables showing at a glance the position of the republican party in every municipal council throughout the country, with the name and profession of every supporter. 'I am quite proud of my invention,' he wrote, 'for I believe that no government has yet realised or applied it.'[2] He insisted, however, that a party could only make headway with universal suffrage if it made personal contact with the electors. Universal suffrage, he said, 'will support only those who devote themselves to it without respite or rest; it needs to be visited, enlightened, informed'. He set new standards for party leaders: he toured the country making speeches everywhere and getting to know personally the local organisers and local conditions. Some people ridiculed this and called him the republic's commercial traveller, but the method was so successful that they soon began to worry that it was giving him a popularity that recalled Napoleon's. Gambetta organised the republican campaigns of 1876 and 1877, based on the policy of candidates on a national scale and the simplification of the issues, to make them elections for the expulsion of the royalists. He was a partisan of the *scrutin de liste*, because he believed that a two-party system was impossible if local considerations predominated. He founded newspapers to develop a doctrine and a policy for the republicans. *La République Française*, subsidised by sympathetic businessmen, became not only his official organ, but the instrument of a shadow cabinet. His principal followers were each given one speciality to write about,[3] with the injunction that they should treat it with gravity and responsibility, proposing policies they would

---

[1] *Discours*, 9. 276.

[2] D. Halévy and E. Pillias, *Lettres de Gambetta* (1938), letter 219.

[3] Challemel, Ranc and Spuller on internal affairs, Proust on foreign affairs, Allain-Targé on finance, Freycinet on war and public works, Paul Bert on education, Berthelot on science, Dr. Lannelongue on hygiene and medicine, Léon Clery on law.

be ready to implement. This was directed to the educated classes. For the masses he had *Le Voltaire* and *La Petite République*, in more popular vein, reproducing his provincial and parliamentary speeches for a wide audience.[1]

Gambetta, however, did not epitomise republicanism, which was too diverse to accept his leadership. The well-to-do members of the party, the rural notables and the successful professional men disliked his coarseness, despised his upstart Bohemian friends, and kept their distance. Grévy, president of the republic, could not abide him, and kept him out of office. The members of parliament feared his ambitions, and with reason. When he finally became prime minister, he attacked their power at once. He did not have a reliable majority behind him, he knew he would not last long and he was not unwilling therefore to martyr himself. There was a strange contrast between his tact in opposition and his blundering in office. He revealed his limitations as a politician when he became prime minister, and he allowed himself to be destroyed by his own creation. In an attempt to increase governmental power, as against that of the deputies, his minister of the interior required all the latter's applications for favours to be transmitted through the prefects, with their approval. Now that the prefects were republican, they ceased to be enemies and could be used to strengthen the republic's authority. Gambetta created new ministries without parliamentary consent. He gave jobs to former royalists, in defiance of the deputies' demands for the spoils of power. He declared war on the whole system on which the deputies based their influence, pressed for the adoption of the *scrutin de liste* and offered a deal to the senate, agreeing to abandon his plans for its reform, in return for their approval of the *liste*. He was accused of plotting a dictatorship for himself, which his popularity in the country seemed to support. In fact he was trying to turn the republicans into a party of government, whereas they were inescapably attached to their habits of opposition. It is significant that Gambetta took the portfolio of foreign affairs, placing the re-establishment of French glory as his prime aim.[2]

---

[1] C. de Freycinet, *Souvenirs 1848–1878* (1912), 281–2.

[2] J. Reinach, *Le Ministère Gambetta, histoire et doctrine, 14 novembre 1881–26 janvier 1882* (1884).

When Gambetta died at the age of forty, his disciples made out that he had been a deep thinker, one of the main philosophers of the republic. It is true that he had sometimes claimed to base his actions on the latest ideas of the time. He publicly called Comte the greatest thinker of the century; he described himself as an interpreter of Littré; he praised Proudhon and borrowed his dictum that democracy was *démopédie*. He paid tribute to positivism and science. One can also find him praising Montesquieu for advocating a balanced constitution, against the popular tyranny he saw in Rousseau, whose ideas he declared to be no longer valid. All this should not be taken too literally. Gambetta was no doctrinaire and not much influenced by books. He simply talked in the language of his day, adopting phrases from those around him.

Gambetta's *nouvelles couches sociales* were slow to win acceptance and even slower to win power. No one has yet made a thorough study of the municipal councils of France, to trace how and when they entered into them. One investigation, of the city of Bordeaux—which of course cannot be considered typical—suggests, however, that the petty bourgeoisie won a majority in its municipality only in 1925. In the 1870s the city was dominated by the rich old-established merchant families, the industrialists, and the large property owners. The very rich continued to occupy between a third and a quarter of the seats till 1925. By 1888 an equilibrium was established between the classes, the rich, the middle class and the petty bourgeoisie each holding a third. In 1896 the petty bourgeoisie (i.e. junior civil servants, artisans, shopkeepers) for the first time had more seats than the *moyenne bourgeoisie;* their numbers rose steadily after that, till they reached a peak in 1925. By then, however, those who took part in politics were no longer the same. The ordinary workers no longer stood and small contractors replaced them; the old dynasties of wholesalers were replaced by more aggressive *nouveaux riches* ones. It is not easy to draw a general conclusion from this example, but it appears that though the exclusiveness of politics diminished slowly, it was replaced by new forms Gambetta had not foreseen.[1] In any case, one should not exaggerate the effect of the intellectual

[1] Jacqueline Herpin, 'Les Milieux dirigeants à Bordeaux sous la Troisième République', *Revue Historique de Bordeaux*, 15 (Oct.–Dec. 1966), 145–65.

content of Gambetta's programme on the electorate. It is by no means certain that his peasant audiences took it all in. In the 1950s one of France's leading rural sociologists, Henri Mendras, asked the peasants of the Haut-Rhin: 'What *couches sociales* are there in French society?' The majority of those interviewed said they did not understand the question.[1]

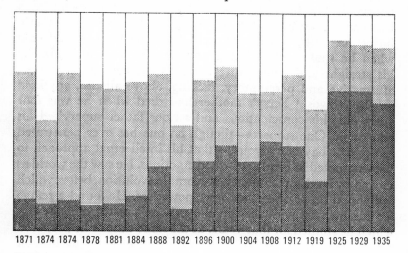

1871 1874 1874 1878 1881 1884 1888 1892 1896 1900 1904 1908 1912 1919 1925 1929 1935

☐ 1   ▨ 2   ▨ 3

FIG. 3. Social Composition of the Municipal Councils of Bordeaux, 1871–1935. Percentages of (1) upper bourgeoisie, (2) middle bourgeoisie and (3) petty bourgeoisie.

The republic, therefore, for men like Gambetta, meant fraternity, but fraternity took on a different appearance if it was approached from above rather than below. For Gambetta it meant the opening of doors and the breaking down of barriers. For Jules Ferry, fraternity was also the aim, but he interpreted it in a different way, seeing the problem from a different angle. He was not so much interested, as Gambetta was, in social mobility. He came of a family which had arrived, and was very solidly bourgeois. In the seventeenth century his forbears had been artisan bell founders, but his grandfather, a substantial tile manufacturer, rose to be mayor of his native town

[1] H. Mendras, *Les Paysans et la modernisation de l'agriculture* (1958), 84.

throughout the consulate and empire, while his father became its leading barrister and married the judge's daughter. Jules Ferry was a man of independent means. He married into the republicans' Alsatian industrial plutocracy. Hanotaux remembered him above all as a 'bourgeois, son of a bourgeois, brought up correctly in the bourgeois manner, wearing the bourgeois top hat and frock-coat, with a pale complexion between his mutton-chop whiskers, his fingers in his mouth, biting his nails, withdrawn, cold when he listened and cold when he spoke, intimidating anyone who addressed him by his straight and penetrating look, always certain of himself, affirmative and peremptory, lacking, above all else, any hold on the crowds'.[1] Ferry's mother had died when he was four years old; his conscientious and serious father supervised his education. One suspects—though no one has ever penetrated the psychology of his youth—that his intellectual approach to life was rooted in firmly repressed emotions. He saw the world as moved by large forces and an inexorable evolution, before which individual human passions were powerless. He found a refuge for his own individuality in the private pursuit of painting, which he studied for four years, at the same time as he prepared for the bar; at one stage he even thought of devoting himself completely to art. However, he was far too ambitious, determined, self-willed to be content with that. He had planned to enter the Conseil d'État, but he reached manhood just as the Second Empire was established and his family had no influence with it. He became a barrister instead, and was a moderately successful one, though he lacked any special gifts in this direction. His real talents, for clear, logical argument and vigorous exposition, emerged more forcefully in his work as a journalist. He joined Le Temps (a liberal–conservative paper), where he wrote commentaries on contemporary events, which showed exceptional powers of lucid analysis, penetration and detachment. He became famous for his articles attacking the financial irregularities in the rebuilding of Paris, which he republished under the clever title of Les Comptes fantastiques d'Haussmann; and in September 1870, when the Bonapartist regime fell, he was appointed to Haussmann's job.

Ferry was always intensely serious, and determined to be

[1] G. Hanotaux, Mon temps, 2 (1938), 178.

clear sighted. He considered the establishment of fraternity to
be the great need of the time because he was profoundly conscious of the tensions which were straining and paralysing
France. He saw the peasants 'avid for gain, isolated, mistrustful, spending their lives on the defensive', regarding everything
as dangerous to them—the weather, the neighbours, strangers,
and above all the police. He dismissed as a schoolboy dream
the notion of them 'loving the parliamentary regime, developing
a taste for the Paris press, following the details of diplomacy
and being ready to die for some charter. Politics for the men of
the fields will for long remain local, narrow, self-interested,
timid. It is for this reason that universal suffrage, which is
revolutionary only in the passport it carries, is at bottom
nothing but a conservative instrument.'[1] Things, however,
could not be left as they were. The problem of the relations
between rich and poor was becoming more acute with the
passing of time, because the separation of capital and labour
was increasing. Wealth was becoming more and more concentrated in the hands of a few, and a powerful class of entrepreneurs was emerging. It was no use trying to prevent these
developments: they were inevitable, and they could not be
fought. They had their good side to them, because they were
reducing the costs of production and so were contributing to a
necessary improvement in the lot of the masses, enabling the
workers to satisfy their just demands for increasing prosperity.
However, the power of the capitalists had to be held 'wisely in
check, with counterweights'. He saw two ways in which this
could be done. First by the use of 'opinion, as the agent of
social morality, upon the capitalists', and secondly by the collective organisation of the workers in trade unions—with increasing
education to make this possible. Ferry thus accepted capitalism
as 'a natural law' but condemned laissez-faire as 'immoral'.
Pure individualism was antisocial. It was valuable as a weapon
to fight against oppression, to secure independence, to destroy
the restrictions of the ancien régime, but it was powerless to create
anything; it led only to conflicts of egoism and was the negation
of social life. The great problem of this period, he considered,
was national unity, spiritual unity, harmony between the dispar-
ate elements in France, divided by alien traditions and torn by a

[1] Discours et opinions de Jules Ferry, ed. Paul Robiquet (1893–8), i. 50.

century of political strife. He saw France as faced with almost the same kind of problem as the U.S.A., which was likewise attempting to build up a national identity.[1] The Second Republic had attempted to achieve unity in a spontaneous emotional outburst of fellow feeling, led by poets, but Ferry dismissed this sentimentality of 1848 with contempt as a miserable failure. He preferred therefore to talk not of fraternity, but of sociability—a more scientific concept—as his aim. The two great enemies of modern free thought, he said, were mysticism and intellectual frivolity.[2] Religion could no longer perform the function it once had; it was 'irremediably decadent', and its 'theological illusions' could not stand up to criticism. Its morals 'rest on an egoistic calculation which places it in contradiction to the most imperious manifestations of modern life. Its preoccupation with personal salvation is, in itself, antisocial. It leads to the monastic ideal, that is to say, to the condemnation of liberty and the desire for prosperity . . . For the masses for whom life means liberty and who aspire to prosperity, it can now offer only vague counsels of resignation.' Religion had 'an incontestable social value' in the Middle Ages, for resignation was highly appropriate when slavery and oppression ruled—but it was no longer adequate.

Ferry's thinking was deeply influenced by that of Auguste Comte, far more decisively than Gambetta's. Ferry was one of the republican leaders who both read and absorbed Comte, being introduced to positivism by one of Comte's disciples, Deroisin. Ferry said he belonged 'to the religion of the Feasts of Humanity'. Comte came to be one of the main philosophers of the republican regime, compulsory studied in schools, but mediated by many different interpretations. Ferry was not a devotee of any one Comtist sect—neither that of Laffitte, to whom he gave a chair at the Collège de France, nor that of Littré, who set himself up as philosophical adviser to the republicans. He drew his inspiration from his own reading and understood Comte through the bias of his own personality.

The religion of humanity meant liberty for Ferry because it

[1] Article by Ferry, reprinted from *La Philosophie positive* (Sept.–Oct. 1867) in *Discours*, 1. 581–8; two unpublished articles by him on industrialism, written for the *Revue des Deux Mondes* in 1862, and published in *Discours*, 7. 447–535; cf. also *Discours*, 3. 69.
[2] *Discours*, 2. 194–5.

encouraged the development of 'sociability', which he saw as a growing force in modern society. He meant that the egoism he attributed to Christianity was being replaced by a new outlook with the right of the strongest giving way to the duty of the strongest. Humanity was now emerging as 'no longer a fallen race, doomed by original sin, dragging itself painfully in a valley of tears, but as a ceaseless cavalcade marching forward towards the light'. He felt himself 'an integral part of this great Being which cannot perish, of this Humanity which is ceaselessly improving' and he believed he 'had conquered his liberty completely, because he was free from the fear of death'. The next stage was to effect 'that fusion of classes which is the aim of democracy'. Ferry wanted to make men equal, not to the extent of 'the absolute levelling of social conditions which will suppress relations of command and obedience', but in their rights and in their dignity. Mutual respect must replace animosity and contempt. Contracts, which gave both sides rights and obligations, must replace the oppression of castes. He saw the change as a moral much more than as an economic one. Equality of this kind would not be possible so long as some people were educated and others were not. 'I defy you ever to make out of two such classes an egalitarian nation, a nation animated by that spirit of unity and that confraternity of ideas that makes the strength of true democracies, if, between these two classes, there has not been the first *rapprochement*, the first fusion which results from the mixing of the rich and the poor as children on the benches of a school.' He wanted education to be directed to creating a common morality. He wanted it placed therefore in the hands of a united body of teachers. The influence of the Church must be removed. The teachers must concern themselves with the inculcation of altruism, for human nature had two fundamental and contradictory dimensions— altruism and egoism—and education was the way to make the former preponderant. Women must be educated as well as men. Ferry read and quoted J. S. Mill on their emancipation. The two great prejudices that needed to be eradicated in order to achieve equality were, he said, class prejudice and sexual prejudice. Democracy was impossible so long as the Church kept women in subjection. 'He who controls women controls everything, first because he controls the child and secondly because he controls the husband.' Women must be given an education in harmony with that of men. The family must be united, so that society would be also. 'Modern anarchy' must be ended in the home as well as at work. He praised the plans of Condorcet, in the first Revolution, for a national educational system and in many ways implemented them, but whereas Condorcet aimed for happiness, Ferry more precisely wanted unity as the end product. When asked by Jaurès to summarise his ambitions, he replied decisively, 'My aim is to organise humanity without God and without King.' The word organise was significant.[1]

Whereas Gambetta concentrated on foreign affairs and electoral reform, Ferry preferred to be minister of education and he held that office for fifty months in all.[2] He inaugurated the regime's concentration on education and his work touched every branch of it. Primary education was made both free and compulsory; the teaching of the catechism in schools was abolished and replaced by 'civic and moral education', given by teachers, who were made lay state employees; every department was required to establish a training college for women primary teachers to replace the nuns; and state help was provided for the building of new schools. At the secondary level, state schools were established for girls, the classical syllabus was reformed to allow more individual thinking and less memorisation, gymnastics were made compulsory and military training introduced. The Catholic universities were suppressed. The details of these reforms and their social consequences will be discussed in separate chapters, devoted to the development of education. But from the political point of view, their effect was to introduce a great deal of confusion.

Far from establishing unity, the insistence on lay education, and the elimination of God from the civic manuals, divided the country profoundly, and exacerbated the clash of Church and republic. Ferry antagonised not only the Catholics, but the moderate republicans too, led by Jules Simon, and the radicals, led by Clemenceau, the former because they thought he was going too far, and the latter because he was not doing enough.

[1] Louis Legrand, *L'Influence du positivisme dans l'œuvre scolaire de Jules Ferry* (1961), 103–94.
[2] Feb. 1879–Nov. 1881, Jan.–Aug. 1882, Feb.–Nov. 1883.

Opinions were divided on this very delicate issue in infinite gradations. Ferry himself had no desire to destroy religion, because he believed it was going to die of its own accord; but the radicals were unwilling to wait patiently in this way; and Ferry, because of the balance of parliamentary forces, was obliged to use their support. His hopes of appeasement were dashed. The Catholics, for their part, could not conceive that a school could be neutral. Both sides in fact attributed far more influence to it than, in the long run, it proved to have. In the twentieth century it emerged that good Catholics could survive in the lay schools, obtaining their spiritual inspiration from their parents and priests; but it took a very long time for this to be seen and accepted. The battle was all the more misleading because Ferry, though he talked of a new moral code to be instilled into the young, meant by it nothing different from 'the good old morals of our fathers', and it was in effect barely distinguishable from the traditional one. What resulted, therefore, was a battle over principles much more that a real struggle of conflicting interests, but the subsequent history of the next fifty years was profoundly embittered as a result. The expulsion of the congregations was largely symbolic: it affected only some 5,000 men, who were soon allowed to return in any case; the establishment of free education (which some Catholics objected to, because they thought education should be a moral duty that fell on parents, rather than a right for children) was not a complete innovation, because primary education was largely free in most parts of the country; compulsory attendance was for long only partially implemented, and the physical training programmes—if they had any significance—were a farce in practice. The reforms of Ferry illustrate how ministers hovered, as it were, over the peaks of volcanoes, interpreting the omens and not infrequently spreading alarm. Several of the laws associated with him were in fact initiated by deputies, remodelled over and over again by the two houses, and often did more than the minister intended.

Just as Gambettism could be seen as the protest of the parvenus, so Ferryism has sometimes been described as the revenge of the Reformation, because a large number of the people around him were Protestants: Freycinet, Waddington, Léon Say, Le Royer, Jauréguiberry, Buisson, Pécaut, Cazot, Steeg,

Scheurer-Kestner, not to mention the fact that both he and Paul Bert married Protestants. It will be seen, in another chapter, how men like Renouvier, one of the philosophers of republicanism, preached Protestantism as the solution to France's problem —a way of combining modernity and religion, order and freedom—and how the anticlerical movement was influenced by Protestant thought. The Protestants in France as a whole were not predominantly republicans, but belonged to every party. The republican leaders who were Protestants were nearly all of them non-practising renegades, men who had despaired of the conservatism of their own sect and were seeking other solutions, keeping only the severe morals of their upbringing. This whole question of religion, anticlericalism and education is, however, a very large one, which cannot be understood simply in terms of the ideas of Ferry, of a few politicians or indeed of parliamentary legislation. One can offer many other clever explanations of anticlericalism, as a substitute, for example, for military revenge against Germany, as a method of holding the republicans together, as a way of diverting the attention of the workers from their grievances against their employers. But anticlericalism became intermeshed with so many aspects of life that its significance must be unravelled in a broader framework. The struggle of republic against the Church becomes more complicated, and less straightforward, the closer one looks at it.

Ferry need not have alarmed the traditionalists as much as he did. Polemic obscured his intentions, even though his exceptional clarity of exposition enabled him to formulate the guidelines of his actions far more precisely than Gambetta was able to do. He accepted the inheritance of the old monarchy, in that he believed in the maintenance of a strong centralised state. In his liberal days under the Second Empire, he had supported decentralisation, but he later retracted and said he had learnt better. He insisted that the republic's government should be one that really governed, denying that there was a contradiction between the ideas of authority and progress. He condemned the desire to diminish the government's power as being 'in complete opposition to the state of our civilisation and our customs, and all our traditions'. He considered that 'because of our historical antecedents, which cannot be suppressed with a stroke of the pen', because the people 'were accustomed to look above, through habits acquired over centuries, to seek supreme direction', a republican government, based on the popular will, had to provide leadership. The government must not be shackled by the chambers, but left free to carry out the demands of the people. The first of these, he claimed, was that order should be maintained: the people had no desire for radical transformations, and neither had he. He declared that he stood half-way between complacent fatalism on the one hand and irrational utopianism on the other. Progress was not achieved in quick changes nor by force: 'It is a slow development, an evolution, a phenomenon of social growth, of transformation, which starts first in men's ideas, and then descends into habits, and only finally passes into laws.' Governments had to provide protection and stability for this slow evolution to take place. The intransigent determination of the radicals to destroy the past, to refuse all compromise, was futile. The fact had to be accepted that democracy in France had to be based on the peasants. He considered it an achievement to have won them over to it. A peasant republic was 'not gay, not Athenian' but it was the only kind possible; and he was aware that, as he put it, the peasants had become republican because they were conservative.[2]

Ferry believed in a careful balance between state intervention and free enterprise. He accepted the capitalist system. 'Every legitimate profit,' he wrote, 'and in our system of unlimited free competition it is not possible to say that there are illegitimate profits—every profit corresponds either to an invention, or to an improvement or to better commercial or administrative organisation . . . To abolish the element of profit in the economic field is to suppress the essential stimulant of progress.' In his youth he had been a free trader, but he came to modify this view and helped to start the move back to protection. He thought that political liberty was one essential counterweight to the industrial oligarchy that capitalism produced, but he thought also that the government ought to encourage, and to a certain extent subsidise, mutual benefit societies, savings banks, insurance schemes with which the poor could improve their material lot. A government's duties, he said, 'certainly do not include finding immediate remedies' to social problems; but

[1] *Discours*, 7. 53–6.   [2] *Discours*, 6. 170–3, 280; 1. 284–8; 7. 40–2.

though its 'functions were not therapeutic', it did have duties of 'social hygiene'.[1] One of the most characteristic of his reforms was to make the new lay university a corporation run by the professors themselves, independent, to a certain degree, both of the state and also of other influences. This may recall Comte's 'spiritual power', but it was also a half-way house between two extremes.

Ferry was a nationalist, in the tradition of the old monarchs perhaps even more than of the Revolution. He insisted that France could not be simply free, like Belgium or Switzerland; it must also be great, 'exercising on the destinies of Europe all the influence that it has, it must spread this influence over the world and carry everywhere its language, its customs, its flag, its arms, its genius'.[2] Apart from his educational work, he is associated also with the development of the French colonial empire. He was not originally responsible for the colonial expansion which took place in these years. It was civil servants, explorers, soldiers and sailors, acting under their own initiative, who carried the French flag to new lands. But Ferry supported them, once they had involved themselves, in order to save its honour. It was Baron de Courcel, director of political affairs at the Quai d'Orsay, who persuaded Gambetta to take Tunis. Ferry had never been interested in colonies and was the last of the ministers to be converted to taking action in this case. He did not intend it to be a precedent, and he has with some justification been accused of playing the whole episode down in such a manner that French colonialism never recovered: as a result of his tergiversation, Tunis appeared to be another Mexico expedition and the French became as divided about their colonies as about so many other things. It was Brazza who gave France its opportunities in Central Africa, but Ferry supported his expeditions and then won European sanction for his annexations at the Berlin Conference. In Madagascar Ferry was persuaded to act by the colonists of near-by Réunion, who were seeking trading advantages and who misled Ferry on the difficulties and the issues. He rather recklessly moved into war in Indo-China in order to consolidate the gains his predecessors had made. Only afterwards did Ferry develop a neo-mercantilist doctrine to justify his actions and to argue that

[1] *Discours*, 6. 236.   [2] *Discours*, 5. 220.

France needed colonies for its economic growth and its political prestige. In fact just as Britain acquired much of its empire at the very time when colonies were considered to be useless, so France acquired its when its population was falling, its colonial trade minute and its people had no interest in over-seas expansion. Ferry argued that France needed markets. It was only twenty years later that the economists realised that France could really use its colonies, but as a source of raw materials, not as markets.[1]

It was Ferry's patriotism that turned him into an imperialist but at the same time his imperialism alienated French patriots and caused his downfall. He achieved what he did thanks to the encouragement of Bismarck, who was glad to turn France's energies away from Alsace, but Ferry's realism in seeing that revenge had to be postponed for the time being won him accusations of treachery. He became one of the most unpopular men in France. No politician had been reviled so mercilessly since Émile Ollivier (whom he had admired in his youth and whose first wife he worshipped) had been publicly declared worthy of lynching. Twice assassinations were attempted on him and the radical press regretfully attributed his escapes to the fact that he had no heart to shoot. A temporary setback in Tonkin was the immediate source of his downfall but only because hate of him had become a 'sort of paroxysm'. During the Commune when he had organised rationing, he had won the opprobrious title of Ferry Famine: he was then Ferry the persecutor of the Church and now he was Ferry Tonkin, Ferry the valet of Bismarck, who was ruining his country in foreign adventures. He was particularly unpopular in Paris, which harboured so many extremists, so that he could not show his face in the streets without being insulted. All his efforts to defend himself in newspapers, which he bought up with the help of an impressive collection of capitalists, but which he ran with incompetent journalists, were in vain.[2]

His failure was the product of his manner as much as of his policy. As the wilier Freycinet wrote: 'He was too confident in

[1] F. Pisani-Ferry, *Ferry et le partage du monde* (1962); C. A. Julien, 'Jules Ferry', in *Les Politiques d'expansion impérialiste* (1949), 11–72.
[2] René Bastien, '*L'Estafette*, le journal de Jules Ferry 1889–93' (unpublished D.E.S. mémoire, Nancy, 1963).

his own intelligence and wisdom, and had adopted an air of disdain towards the moderates which recalled Guizot. The parliamentary successes he had won brought about in him that phenomenon frequent in men who have been in power long— the evil of infallibility. The disciples of Gambetta around him who formed the most solid core of his majority suffered from this manner which was so little in harmony with their own tendencies. The anathemas he cast upon reforms made them uneasy. Several of them got into the habit of voting with the radicals.' The hostility to him was partly personal, partly the result of his very competence of which he was the victim just as Gambetta had been the victim of his own popularity. Ferry himself admitted that he could not be considered representative of the masses. He had long thought that once he had passed his reforms, he could then follow a policy of moderation. By 1885 he had concluded that he had no option at all. He regretted the sectarianism which had introduced such bitterness into politics. It was necessary to mark time, for at least four years. His reforms, he said, had not been 'digested' by the masses, there was a noticeable movement of reaction amongst them and it was not possible to pursue 'great innovations'.[1] This was not quite a confession of failure, but an acknowledgement of the barriers that separated the different levels of republicanism.[2]

The republican system required ambition to be kept in check. Ministers who threatened to become dictators were invariably eliminated, though they might be briefly rescued from retirement to deal with serious crises. The kind of minister who was most acceptable to parliament was a person like Freycinet, who made it his rule to serve it, and who had no ambition to dominate it. His long tenure of office shows how power rested ultimately with the deputies and the civil servants. Freycinet was prime minister four times, and a member of nine other ministries. He was senator for Paris for forty-three years. Originally he was a civil servant on whom Gambetta picked, simply on the grounds of ability, to assist him in technical and

[1] J. Ferry, Lettres, 1846–1893 (1914), 388.
[2] The fullest biography is by Maurice Reclus, Jules Ferry 1832–1893 (1947); cf. G. Froment–Guieysse, Jules Ferry (1937), the memorial volume, Jules Ferry (1894), and P. Sorlin, Waldeck-Rousseau (1966), which is the best guide to the politics of this period.

administrative matters; he had no oratorical gifts, no popular
appeal, no political standing or even allegiances but he became
one of the most powerful men of the republic because he carried
to perfection his role as an intermediary, a conciliator and a
manager. He was a Protestant engineer, and a graduate of the
Polytechnic. He managed the Midi Railway for several years
under the Second Empire, and was Gambetta's administrative
assistant at the ministry of war in 1871. His political views can
only be defined as 'moderate'. Though he published two
volumes of memoirs, they are written in such carefully guarded
style, with no offence given to anyone, and studied compli-
ments to everyone, that it is difficult to conclude anything
positive about him. Self-effacing modesty ensured that he made
no enemies: his aim, he said, was simply to be an organiser and
administrator of the great ideas which great men had, to be
a scientist in the service of the republic. The extraordinary
effect this had was seen on the occasion of his first election to
the senate. Gambetta put him up and vouched for him, against
the objections of those who doubted his republicanism. Victor
Hugo was considered the master of this election, as the leading
republican luminary of the senate, and his approval was
essential to every candidate. Freycinet cultivated him with
fawning flattery. But Hugo considered himself free to advocate
radical policies—like an amnesty for the Communards—
which was not to the taste of the staid local councillors who
formed the bulk of the electorate for the senatorial seats.
Hugo was elected last but one. Freycinet, though completely
unknown to them, was elected top of the list. They wanted a
man who had no dreams of grandeur, but would make the system
work in the way they wanted it to work. This is the explanation of the dominance of safe mediocrities in the republic.

   Gambetta admired Freycinet's skill at giving clear summaries
of technical questions: he called him 'un filtre'. Freycinet certainly excelled at producing formulae to solve difficult problems, which had the appearance of clarity or even firmness, but
he knew also how to skirt round difficult issues at the same time.
Until he established himself in politics, he remained in the
civil service, obtaining repeated periods of leave while he
carried out political or industrial jobs. He was an exceptional
example of the way business, bureaucracy and politics avoided

conflict by mutual penetration. The result of this was an approach to problems which Freycinet summarised in two words—opportunism and union. This was what guided his whole political career. Opportunism meant that though one should be bold in one's ideas, one should be prudent in executing them. He was too wily to make the mistake Ferry made, of pushing his reforms through quickly, because he thought they were right. He saw danger in the multiplicity of innovations and in excessive haste in bringing them forward. Priorities should be established and the more controversial measures postponed. For, correcting Ferry's other mistake, he saw the greatest danger of all to be the disintegration of the republican party. Controversy and haste would kill it. 'Concentration' was his watchword, which meant that the ideal government was a coalition of all factions. He devoted much of his career to trying to get the radicals—Ferry's great enemies—to join with the moderate republicans in holding office: together, they would have an impregnable monopoly. He advocated conciliation towards the enemies of the republic, but insisted that it should be offered from a position of strength. He was in favour of purging the administration of hostile elements, of building up a self-conscious republican party, and then of admitting outsiders who were willing to accept this system. Thus though Freycinet entered politics as a protégé of Gambetta, and always spoke of him with profound reverence, he soon developed an independent line. He refused to serve in Gambetta's great ministry, knowing that it would not last long, and he was careful not to join the right-wing republicans—with whom he had much in common—because they had only limited chances of getting power. The reward of this discretion was that he was the middle-of-the-road choice on whom everybody could agree. Freycinet's kind of government meant papering over divisions, excluding men of energy, and sacrificing all to stability. Freycinet believed that the divisions of France were superficial, that what it needed was conscientious and gradual reform, and that political stability was the essential basis for progress. He had above all a keen sense of material interests. These are what Freycinet represented. He reflected a vital part of the republican mentality, as opposed to its ideology.

The consequences of this kind of attitude were revealed in

Freycinet's public works programme. He drew this up in the late 1870s and obtained final parliamentary approval for it in 1883. It was an enormously expensive plan to extend the railway network of France on a scale even greater than Napoleon III had attempted. It was in due course carried out, and France's railways were doubled in length over the next twenty years. This steady transformation of the country was something that deserves as much attention as the Parisian political debates, because it was one of the most important local preoccupations, one of the most impressive economic achievements and one of the greatest financial scandals of the period. The contradiction or conjuring trick contained in the type of republicanism Freycinet represented was that it attempted to reform the country without any increase in taxation. Instead the republic promised and indeed gave reductions in taxations to various sectional interests, particularly the peasants, balancing equality and privilege with exceptional skill. This meant that within a few years of their gaining office, the republicans had plunged France into recurrent deficits. They nevertheless wanted to embark on this grandiose public works programme.

They did it by means of a remarkable deal with the railway companies. Out of office they had looked on these companies as a resurrection of feudalism, bastions of reaction run by monarchist directors, and they had preached the nationalisation of railways. France had since the very beginning been divided between those who had wanted the state to build the railways and those who had favoured private enterprise. Fear that the state would become too powerful if it entered this new industry, and fear of the heavy taxes which the vast capital expenditure necessary would involve, had resulted in a characteristic compromise solution evolved by the July Monarchy and the Second Empire and completed, without fundamental change, by the Third Republic. The accusations made against the first two of these regimes, of being run for the benefit of the speculators, seemed to become even truer under the last of them. The principle adopted was that the freehold property of the railways remained with the state, which gave concessions to private companies for up to ninety-nine years. Ultimately, the state expected to get all this property back, worth as much as the whole national debt. Meanwhile it was saved any large outlay of state funds. Under the Second Empire, when profits were considerable, the railway companies did well and the state did not lose anything. But in 1865 a new situation arose. The major intercity lines had been built, and the problem of dealing with less profitable local railways presented itself. The state refused to subsidise these, but offered a guarantee on the loans which the companies raised to build them with. In return the state was to receive a share of any profits. The local railways, of course, failed to make any profits, and quite a few of them were threatened with bankruptcy.

In 1871 the first thought of the republicans was to nationalise everything. But the six large companies were far too expensive to buy out. So attention was turned to the ailing local companies; and in 1878 the state bought up a number of them in the Charentes and the Centre. This was thought of as being a trial run, to see how state ownership could improve things; but since the lines bought had not been commercially viable in any case, it was not a successful experiment and greatly weakened the case of the partisans of nationalisation. The Second Empire had already started what the Third Republic took to greater extremes, the habit of yielding to local pressure to authorise railways in every constituency, for largely electoral reasons. The question then was, who would foot the bill? In the Charentes experiment, the state had tried to build railways itself, but it did not have enough engineers to pursue this policy, nor was it willing to borrow the capital necessary. When the era of deficits began in 1882, the conservative financiers of the republic, led by Léon Say, insisted that the state must stop borrowing. The republicans, after having threatened nationalisation, therefore capitulated to the companies.

A deal was made by which the six main companies would agree to build the vast new network of secondary railways. They would raise the money themselves, so that the national debt would not be burdened and taxation could remain steady. They agreed to pay the state two-thirds of any profits made. But in return they exacted very favourable conditions. The state would subsidise the construction of these lines to the extent of seven-eighths, from funds which the companies raised on its behalf, and which the state would then pay back to them in annuities. The state would guarantee the dividends and the interest on loans of the companies. The companies therefore could not lose. The politicians made out that the state would thus get a railway network built without endangering the credit of the state and without further taxation, and that it was unlikely that it would ever have to fulfil its promise in guaranteeing the companies' finances. This, however, proved too optimistic a forecast. All but one of the companies failed to make adequate profits. The deal of 1883 was made at the end of a period of boom and at the beginning of a long-drawn-out depression. Railway revenue failed to progress as fast as the state had calculated. So the bargain turned out to be all in favour of the companies. Thus in the eleven years following it, 7,016 kilometres of railway were built, at a cost to the companies of 1,200 million francs. But the state was called upon to pay out 926 million francs in guarantees on interests. The person who had actually signed the conventions with the railway companies was a Jewish merchant, Raynal, minister of public works at the appropriate time. In 1895 the radicals attempted to impeach him for damaging the interests of the state. The six-day debate in parliament brought out a lot of interesting information about this complicated negotiation. The radicals sought to unmask it as a gigantic hoax or swindle at the expense of the country. But nothing was done about it, because there were too many beneficiaries from it.

Thus railway shares had become a gilt-edged investment, even though the railways were not making a profit, and even though the state was having to bolster them, subsidising a small section of the community at the expense of the rest. Electoral pressures were successfully met. Freycinet's original estimate for the whole cost of his programme had been four milliard francs: parliament had doubled it, so that nearly every constituency got a share of the spoils. The railways, in any case, were built, so that whereas in 1870 there were 17,400 kilometres, by 1910 there were 39,000. Outwardly, there was consistent progress; chaotic competition was avoided. The state was able to keep a supervisory control over the railways and to enjoy the illusion that it was their ultimate proprietor: the principles of centralisation were safeguarded. But at the same time the railway companies increasingly became the great capitalist bogy-men of the republic, draining its blood. This was one of the legacies of opportunism. It will be seen in due course that when the radicals won power and dealt with the problem, their policy was just as equivocal.[1]

Another example of the way reform had to be dropped or postponed is national military service. Freycinet's experience in the Franco-Prussian war had convinced him of the serious inadequacy of his country's military organisation. He rejected the conservative complacency of Thiers. He believed universal short-term service was essential. However, the forces of inertia were so powerful, and his own system of pleasing everyone so irreconcilable with drastic reform, that he succeeded in obtaining a minor modification to the professional army's five-year service only in 1889. What he achieved then was only a feeble compromise (reducing the period of service to three years): it made little real difference, because the bulk of the conscripts served only one year, and were not to be used for front-line fighting. France still did not have a properly trained fighting force. Only in 1905 were the exemptions and inequalities ended. Freycinet's inability to do more is particularly significant because he placed great store on military reform and expected important political results from it. He thought that if everybody served in the army they would learn the need to obey in civil life also, 'to understand and to accept everywhere the principle of authority and the hierarchy without which there is no stable organisation. As a result, the military establishment, instead of being in opposition to civil society, will become its foundation and best support.' His failure to bring this about, like his failure to end the formalism of bureaucracy, which in his youth he had seen as a major evil, was, however, an inevitable consequence of the policy of conciliation he adopted.[2]

[1] Henry Peyret, *Histoire des chemins de fer* (1949), is the best brief general history; Richard de Kaufmann, *La Politique française en matière de chemins de fer* (1900), is a massive study with excellent summaries of the parliamentary debates; cf. C. Colson, *Les Chemins de fer et le budget* (1896); Henry Ferrette, *Étude historique sur l'intervention financière de l'État dans l'établissement des lignes de chemins de fer* (1896).

[2] C. de Freycinet, *Souvenirs* (1912), 1. 90, 96, 160, 254–5, 287; 2. 79–83 and *passim*; Noël de Clazan, 'M. de Freycinet', *Le Correspondant*, 291 (1923), 693–712; Hector Depasse, *De Freycinet* (1883); André Beauvier, *Visages d'hier et d'aujourd'hui* (1911), 241–7; Capt. W. Zaniewicki, 'L'Œuvre de Freycinet au ministère de la guerre 1888–1893', *Revue historique de l'armée*, 19, no. 2 (1963), 55–72; review of his scientific work in *Journal des savants* (Mar. 1896), 125–32.

One can thus see three different ways in which republicanism produced stalemate and immobility. First, the hostility shown to powerful ministers by the deputies meant that those who wanted to change things drastically were kept out of office. Secondly, the ministers who did get into power adopted in varying degrees the traditions of the ancient monarchy and upheld the rights of the state to a degree which was incompatible with the attainment of the reforms they had preached in opposition. Thirdly, those ministers whom the deputies allowed to hold office could survive only by making compromises to uphold unity and by respecting vested interests. The republic, which originally had been viewed as the instrument for a thorough transformation of the country, had become strangely conservative. This had become clear within a dozen years of its foundation. The problem now is why it could not be got out of its rut.

21. Solidarism

A FTER the establishment of the republic, its victory over
monarchism and its inauguration of a lay educational
system and a colonial empire, one is generally given the
impression that, by the 1890s, the regime represented a spent
force, with nothing new to offer. Jacques Chastenet, in his six-
volume history of the Third Republic, claimed each decade in it
had a special character. The 1870s were marked by a determination to recover from the humiliating defeat of the Franco-
Prussian war and the Paris exhibition of 1878 was a gesture to
show that France was itself again. Eleven years later, the
exhibition of 1889 demonstrated that the republic was securely
established, and preaching its dedication to science. But after
that the exhibition of 1900 'lacked a soul': France had no new
ideal. The Panama scandal (1892–3) and the Dreyfus affair
(1894–9) gave the impression that internal bickering, corruption and an ageing oligarchy had brought reform to a halt.
Stagnation appears to be the mark of the nineties. There is a
traditional view that only in 1905, when the clerical question was
more or less solved, did the republic at last free itself from its old
preoccupations and henceforth it was the social question which
dominated politics. The *fin de siècle* is thus an interlude.

This kind of generalisation is the result of regarding French
history as a chronicle, in which laws and crises follow each
other in blundering succession. To concentrate on the scandals
is to give excessive importance to symptoms and to lose sight of
continuities and breaks of deeper significance. It is wrong,
first of all, to imagine that interest in social questions became
predominant only after 1905. The opportunists are usually
criticised for not having a social policy, but the previous
chapter has shown that though they may not have passed
many laws on the subject, social questions were very much in the
forefront of their minds. They believed in political and educational solutions to them, and those which they offered did seem
to win much support. They were not blind to the threat of

socialism, even though that was then attracting only a tiny minority. And moreover, in the nineties a new social doctrine—solidarism—was virtually adopted by the republican government to meet the increasing challenges of industrialisation.

It is wrong, secondly, to assume that after 1905 religious disagreements ceased to be a major divisive force, even though Church and state were separated. The problems facing the French did not change drastically at the turn of the century: the unequal distribution of wealth, education and religious belief was a permanent feature, and successive regimes and governments had policies on each of them. These are the acknowledged continuities in French history. The question that remains unresolved is why so little headway was made in tackling them. The nineties are particularly illuminating in providing the answer, for they were a period when original efforts were made to adopt new approaches, in institutional, religious, social and diplomatic ways. This chapter will describe these efforts—some less well known than others—and will try to explain why they were largely unsuccessful. The failure is very important, because it meant that France could not get out of its rut. The purpose of this group of chapters is to indicate what this rut was, what ways of thinking and what inherited institutions were so firmly entrenched that they cast off reforms like water off a duck's back.

In politics, a situation of deadlock had been reached through the triangular conflict of state, ministers and parliament. This could only be ended by revolution or a *coup d'état*. That is what Boulangism attempted. Boulangism has a very colourful side to it, with the result that it is usually studied in a largely personal way. The vanity and ambition of General Boulanger with his blond beard, on his white horse, turning discipline in the army upside-down, trying to win popularity with the junior officers against his fellow generals, collecting votes in election after election, negotiating with every opposition party, accepting vast sums from the royalists, consorting with shady political adventurers, placing all his bets on being able to capture power, but lacking the nerve to be a new Saint-Arnaud or the character to be another Mahdi, so finally running away to Belgium and committing suicide on the grave of his mistress, provides an entertaining contrast to the boring speeches of the grey-beard politicians.[1] This comic-opera approach has led a recent historian of the Third Republic, Guy Chapman, to call Boulangism 'a trivial and tedious episode, which should never have happened and almost certainly never would have but for the absence of men of character and courage. It is surprising that after so much fret so little resulted from it.'[2] This judgement, however, is precisely the opposite of that which this chapter will put forward. The Boulangist crisis deserves to be compared with that of 1848 rather than with some adventurer's intrigue. It had a similar social background, and it was similarly a challenge to a whole system of government. For twenty years the politicians were absorbed in getting a sufficient measure of agreement in the country to consolidate the republic. They thought they had found it. Ferry was proud of having got the peasants behind him. 'We must seek nothing further beyond this for a long time to come,' he said. Boulangism questioned this. The country's judgement, as between Ferry and Boulanger, was a vital one, pregnant with implications.

By 1885 republicanism had shown its limitations as well as its merits. It could be accused of being, like the July Monarchy, a joint stock company to exploit the country for a small group of shareholders. The opportunists who held power ceased to command a majority in the country. Ferry was unable to hold his policy of marking time for a decade. Just as Louis-Philippe was abandoned by some of his supporters, so Ferry found radicalism undermining his system. The deputies discovered the electoral advantages of criticising the government. The policy of conciliation, preached by the ministers, was unworkable in the constituencies, which were seething with a new generation of ambition. In 1885 the opportunists lost almost half their seats, falling to about 200 and the radicals returned with 170. The conservatives, profiting from this division, doubled their numbers (from 90 to 180). Parliament was thus faced with a stalemate of three almost equal and irreconcilable parties. The reformers made a survey of the opinions of the deputies and found that there was not a single policy for which a majority could be found. Out of 543 deputies, the most who could be

[1] Saint-Arnaud, general in charge of the *coup d'état* of 1851; it was Ferry who made the comparison with the Mahdi.
[2] Guy Chapman, *The Third Republic: The First Phase* (1962), 291.

got to agree on anything were 240 who were in favour of a
reduction in the period of military service, 184 who wanted the
separation of Church and state, and 159 who favoured income
tax. The opportunists could not stand still, since alliance with
the right would mean abandoning their anticlericalism and
favouritism, and alliance with the left would lead them to
reforms they did not want.

The only way out of the impasse was a revision of the constitution. Different parties viewed this each in their own way,
but they were agreed on the destruction of the system Gambetta
and Ferry had established. Numerous grievances were ready to
hand to justify and support the agitation. The most important
was economic. Opportunism was failing to give prosperity.
The peasants were suffering from the import of foreign wheat
and from the phylloxera crisis; the fall in the value of their land
began ironically with the establishment of 'the republic of
peasants'. The building, metallurgic and mining industries
suffered a serious slump after 1885, with around a quarter of
a million workers being thrown out of work. The impact of
this was all the more noticeable in that it was concentrated in
certain areas and in Paris worst of all. Import duties were now
levied to save the peasant, so the price of bread rose in 1887,
and increased further because of the bad harvest of that year.
A general slackening of economic activity plunged the state's
budget into greater deficits: receipts from taxation between
1883 and 1887 were repeatedly inferior to the estimates. The
Wilson scandal (the president's son-in-law selling decorations)
revealed corruption in high places, barely concealed behind a
front of moral rectitude.[1]

The massive support that united behind General Boulanger
showed how powerful were the forces which rejected the opportunist republic. The royalists are said to have put between 6
and 8 million francs in the campaign in his favour. Even the
U.S.A. joined in, with the publisher of the *New York Herald* and
an American cable magnate contributing enormous cheques.[2]
Radicals and Bonapartists and socialists, Jews and anti-
Semites, nationalists, mobsters and intriguers, combined

[1] For the wider significance of the Wilson scandal, which was the climax of a
fascinating career as a press magnate, see vol. 2.
[2] Frederic H. Seager, *The Boulanger Affair* (Ithaca, New York, 1969), 258, 186.

strangely in the hope that he would overthrow the system. But the system survived, because it too had great strength behind it. First, it tried to meet the challenge by carrying out reforms, to dish the radicals. Floquet, a radical, but much mellowed as president of the chamber of deputies, was made prime minister. When he failed to stem the tide, force was used. Constans was appointed minister of the interior. This bankrupt manufacturer of lavatory cisterns who had then become a professor of law, deputy and governor-general of Indo-China, had survived accusations of corruption, and won fame as a master of election management. He threatened Boulanger with arrest, but cleverly allowed him time to escape, which Boulanger obligingly did. The agitation was quickly snuffed out. The radicals, terrified by the monster they had created, agreed to co-operate with the opportunists in the election of 1889. The republic was saved.[1]

The importance of Boulangism was twofold. On the one hand it showed the limits of opportunism. Ferry did not fully understand the Boulangist movement and dismissed it as the work of extremists manœuvred by monarchists. He failed to appreciate the social discontents which had given Boulanger much of his popular support. But so too did the radicals. The result was that the republic lost the chance of keeping the support of the industrial workers. These had rallied to Boulanger in the hope of getting a government which would do something to alleviate their distress. The crisis was a double disillusionment for them: not only the opportunists, but even the radicals revealed themselves as being incapable of really understanding the workers. As a result it was the socialists who became the backbone of Boulangism when the radicals deserted it. They defined it clearly as a movement for social reform, for action to meet the economic crisis, with constitutional revision as the means. Boulangism survived after the flight of the general, to become one of the elements in a reinvigorated socialism. It turned Jaurès, hitherto an opportunist, into a socialist. It was thus an important catalyst in the development of a new social conscience. But secondly the apparent defeat of Boulangism confirmed the conservative tendencies of the regime. Ferry failed

[1] The result was 363 united republicans, 167 conservatives, 38 Boulangists (18 of these being in Paris).

to become president of the republic, because too many people hated him, but he was elected president of the senate, and his system was thus entrenched in that bastion of moderation. The long-term significance of Boulangism is that it confirmed that, in a crisis, the republic would show itself to be conservative rather than attempt innovation, and that though its oratory was all about justice, its instincts rated stability more highly. The ultimate meaning of republicanism is to be found in the values which it thus tried to preserve, and from which it could not escape.[1]

By the 1890s, the time seemed to have come for a new classification of political divisions, on the basis of the changed realities of the time. Monarchy was no longer a practical possibility. The nobles and notables who had attached themselves to it needed to find a new outlet for their ambitions. The question was whether the republicans could be flexible enough to provide this, to give them some stake in the regime, democratically accepting the fact of their surviving influence and growing economic power. The position of the Church also had to be reconsidered. The battle against its influence had become somewhat confused, as was shown by the contradiction between the polemical rhetoric and the moderation of what was actually done. The republicans were not as totally at war with the Church as appeared, and, for their part, many Church leaders were conscious that the war had got out of hand and that they could not profit from its continuation. The problem of how to deal with industrialisation, with socialism and with increased expectations among the masses in general demanded new thinking. There were good reasons therefore for the 'new spirit', which Spuller, Gambetta's faithful disciple, demanded and for the *ralliement*, by which the former enemies of the republic were invited into its fold.

[1] Jacques Néré, 'La Crise industrielle de 1882 et le mouvement boulangiste' (Paris doctorat d'État, 1959, unpublished, in the Sorbonne library), is the fullest study of the social and economic basis of the movement; also his complementary thesis, 'Les Élections de Boulanger dans le département du Nord' (unpublished, 1959). A. Dansette, *Le Boulangisme* (1938), and F. H. Seager, *The Boulanger Affair* (New York, 1969), are also very able accounts, from different viewpoints. For contemporary views see Mermeix, *Les Coulisses du boulangisme* (1890), and Maurice Barrès, *L'Appel au soldat* (1900).

As early as 1880 the Church had tried to make a deal with Freycinet for mutual concessions. The very news of it had caused parliament to force his resignation, but in 1890–2 Freycinet was back in office as prime minister, and once more open to offers. Several attempts had already been made in the 1880s to reach some agreement. In 1886 Raoul Duval, an energetic Bonapartist industrialist, had attempted to start a conservative alliance against socialism and radicalism, which would have cut across the old alignments and created a *Droite républicaine*; his death a year later destroyed what small chances it had of success. In 1887 Baron Mackau, leader of the monarchists in parliament, had offered the opportunist Rouvier his support, to save the republic from the radicals, but Mackau then went on to back Boulanger, with the hope of overthrowing the republic, so it is not surprising that these monarchist overtures were treated with great suspicion. In 1888 Albert de Mun had tried to found a Catholic Party, free of dynastic attachments, modelled on the Centre Party in Germany, but his social ideas worried the conservatives and the pope, fearing that he would be unable to control it, ordered its dissolution. A basic difficulty of any *ralliement* was that in order to benefit from it, the Catholics needed to be united in a party; but their leaders, having royalist backgrounds, could never be trusted by the republicans and so could never obtain office, however many concessions they made. The more concessions they made to the republicans, the more they lost their royalist supporters.

This was the dilemma that ruined the efforts of Jacques Piou. In 1890 he founded another 'Constitutional Right', consisting of Catholic and royalist deputies who, after the Boulangist débâcle, were willing to make a deal. They would abandon their support of a royalist restoration in return for religious and economic concessions: that religious instruction should be allowed in primary schools which wished to give it, that the laws exiling the pretenders should be repealed, that public expenditure and taxation should be reduced, and that decentralisation, social legislation and tariff protection should be introduced. Piou's idea was to collect support on the right to enable opportunists (who now usually called themselves progressists) to do without radical votes and so to end the anticlerical campaign. In February 1893 he agreed to be satisfied if the government merely enforced the school laws in a 'neutral' way, abandoning the demand for their repeal. He declared that he accepted the republic *with its laws* and he changed the name of his party from 'Constitutional Right' to 'Republican Right'. But in the election of that year only thirty-six of his ninety-four candidates were elected. He himself, de Mun and Lamy, the three leaders, were defeated. The royalists as a whole refused to accept the bankruptcy of their movement and fifty-eight intransigent ones were elected as such. The dying cause of the monarchy refused to die. The confusion of the monarchist and clerical issues led to a stalemate.

It is true the advocates of a *ralliement* had mixed motives. A new pope, Leo XIII, brought a new willingness to negotiate and to compromise, based on a realism and an awareness of social change which marked an important modification in the Church's attitudes. But the republicans were, not surprisingly, suspicious of the fact that he hoped to widen the appeal of the Church by this modernisation, that his attack on Gallicanism would strengthen his own power, and that, from the diplomatic point of view, he sought in France an ally to help him recover the papal states from Italy. Cardinal Lavigerie, whose famous toast to the republic in 1890 publicly launched the idea of the *ralliement*, believed that a modification of the Church's attitude to the republic was essential, because the Church's very existence was at stake: he feared that the ending of the concordat would ruin its finances. He did not expect the republic to last very long, at least in its present anticlerical form; he urged co-operation with it simply to reduce its hostility to the Church, and to keep the Church going until the inevitable collapse. Nevertheless, Étienne Lamy, whom Leo commissioned to found a republican Catholic party, was one of 363 deputies who had followed Gambetta in 1876, and he was willing to accept that the majority of Frenchmen were not active Catholics. He wanted the Church to work not for a purely Catholic programme, but for the end of anticlericalism in the name of liberty, to unite, that is, liberals and Catholics. In the election of 1898, he put up Catholic candidates wherever they had some chance of success, and, when they were defeated on the first ballot, he arranged for them to desist in favour of the opportunist-progressists in return for promises of a relaxation of the anticlerical campaign. However, he could find few men who were both republican and Catholic, able and willing to stand as candidates. He was unable to impose a central control over local politics, and his plans for a united party collapsed. The pope's hope of a *ralliement* was sabotaged above all by the parish priests, who, since they were the people who suffered most from the republic's anticlericalism, had little sympathy for the idea of reconciliation. The Assumptionist Order, important for the newspapers it controlled, waged a vociferous campaign against the republic, oblivious of the papal commands.

On the other side, the republican government was halfhearted in welcoming these overtures from the Church. It paid lip-service to religion as a great moral and social force which, provided it was freed from the domination of the royalists, could be an invaluable weapon against socialism. It allowed unauthorised religious congregations—even the Jesuits—to go about their work unmolested. It took local circumstances into consideration in its enforcement of the laicisation programme, and did not force the clergy out of primary schools when there were no ready replacements. But it was worried by the accusation that it depended on the aid of the reactionary Right, on the obscurantist Catholics, for its survival, that it had sold out the traditions of the republic. The fear of progressing beyond these traditions paralysed it; and in any case it could not carry its supporters in a new policy. The local republican notables, even the prefects, could not abandon the habits of a generation, and continued their anticlerical struggles, just as the parish clergy did. The national leaders were powerless. They would not offer the Catholics any share of power. They were willing to accept Catholic votes only with reservations. They said their republic was an open one, but it was not to be handed over to the Catholics, *ouverte* but not *livrée*. The *ralliement* was a failure. The attempt to achieve it had shown that some people had a vision of politics organised on new lines. But the clerical obsession could not be exorcised.[1]

[1] Alexander Sedgwick, *The Ralliement in French Politics* (Cambridge, Mass., 1965), using the papers of Étienne Lamy; Maxime Lecomte, *Les Ralliés. Histoire d'un parti 1886–1898* (1898); Denys Cochin, *L'Esprit nouveau: origine et décadence* (n.d., about 1912); David Shapiro, 'The Ralliement in the Politics of the 1890s', in *The Right in France 1890–1919*, St. Antony's Papers, no. 13 (1962); Emmanuel Barbier, *Histoire du catholicisme libéral*, vol. 2 (1924); id., 'Du royalisme à la république ou

In the economic field, there was a similar inability to meet the challenge of international competition, or to adopt new attitudes in industrial planning. The failure can be illustrated in the career of Jules Méline, who as minister of agriculture under Ferry and who as prime minister in 1896–8, gave clearest expression to this policy of resistance to change. Méline is known to history as the principal creator of the far-reaching system of protection established in the 1880s and 1890s, and called the Méline tariff.[1] Some historians have tended to dismiss him as a mere tool in the hands of the industrialists; others have it the other way round and believe he represented the agricultural interest, using the industrialist for its benefit. His skill as a middleman is certainly revealed in this double reputation. He won fame as the saviour of both industry and agriculture.

He was himself neither a manufacturer nor a farmer and he knew very little about either occupation: his daughter said that he could never tell the difference between a sheaf of wheat and one of barley. He came of modest, lower middle-class stock. His father had owned some land but had also been *greffier de la justice de paix* of Remiremont, a very junior civil servant. His mother was the daughter of a provincial notary of peasant origin. Méline's ambitions always remained modest, circumscribed within his own small world. He dreamt of a career in the *Bureau de l'enregistrement* (which registered documents and levied stamp duties). He became a barrister, but did not achieve any particular success. He lived most of his life on his salary as a deputy, in the same humble apartment in the rue de Commaille.[2] He made no pretence of being other than what he was, though he was very proud of his wife who came of a family of small calico manufacturers, representing a marriage above his station and setting a seal on his rise in the social hierarchy, minimal though that was. He entered politics, moved neither by enthusiasm, nor by passion nor by a vivid imagination, but as an essentially practical, common-sensical,

le ralliement du marquis de Solages', *Annales du Midi* (Jan. 1959), 59–70. For provincial opinion see Gaston Routier, *La Question sociale et l'opinion du pays. Enquête du Figaro* (1894).

[1] E. O. Golob, *The Méline Tariff* (New York, 1944); cf. Marcel Dijol, *Situation économique de la France sous le régime protectioniste de 1892* (n.d., about 1910).

[2] No. 4, Paris 7e.

stubborn party worker, with a smiling and somewhat sly equanimity. Small, thin, with slight gestures and a discreet bearing, he gave the impression of being an obscure provincial notary. As a student in Paris he had been an admirer of Proudhon, whose ideal of a society of satisfied petty proprietors reflected his own exactly. He had joined the Freemasons in 1865 but by 1870 he had left them. He was too *sage* for their increasing bellicosity. He had reservations about Ferry's anticlerical programme. He believed in a lay state, but also in tolerance. He was a deist who thought that religion was inextinguishable. His wife was a fervent Catholic and he approved of his daughters being brought up to practise that religion. He had worked for Thiers in the electoral campaign of 1869 and he ever retained a genuine admiration for this incarnation of the self-made provincial. He spoke with reverence of Jules Ferry as a great statesman but he was never on intimate terms with him. Ferry was too aristocratic for him. His patron in politics was Claude, senator and president of the *conseil général* of Vosges, who had been a foreman in a textile factory, rose to be its director, and then its owner. 'I am only the pupil of M. Claude', he said, and if he had gone further than his master, 'it was only the force of circumstance.' Méline typified the petty bourgeois in a static society, whose mentality the Méline tariff helped to save and perpetuate.[1]

Méline was not an economist nor a theorist, nor had he studied the controversy between free trade and protection in any serious way. He had certain elementary beliefs. 'The best economic regime for a country', he said, 'is that which produces the greatest amount of employment.' He stated plainly that he was an opportunist not a doctrinaire, and 'if I were an Englishman, I should be a free trader'. But he had no wish that the French should become like the English. His tariffs have been criticised for slowing down the pace of industrial development, but then that was precisely what Méline wanted. He was against industrialisation, and here the continuity of attitudes between Proudhon, Thiers and himself is evident. He admitted industry had produced some material benefits, but on the other hand it was draining the countryside of labourers, it was

[1] A. M. Heber-Suffrin, 'Les Débuts politiques de Jules Méline 1870–1885' (unpublished D.E.S. mémoire, Nancy, 1963).

always having crises of overproduction, and in the future increased mechanisation would produce even more unemployment. The socialist remedy of reduced hours of work would only raise costs and prices. His own solution was the revival of agriculture, which should be made efficient and prosperous once more by protective legislation, modernisation, co-operative marketing, less taxation, more liberal credit, the revival of rural industries. He published a book entitled *The Return to the Land and Industrial Overproduction*.[1] He compared his ideas rather vaguely to those of Chamberlain in England and the Centre Party in Germany, but the parallels were misleading. The arguments he used to justify protection reveal a different attitude, distinctive of France in this period. He did not offer industry protection so that it could afford to modernise and produce more. He had a deep fear of producing too much. French taste, he thought, conflicted with mass production: it was suited to making varied but individual goods. France should therefore keep its 'multitude of small workshops' and from the moral and social point of view 'nothing is more desirable than a sensible distribution of work and of profits, to allow thousands of small employers to win a modest competence'. Protection was the only way to avoid a reduction of wages, which would be forced by foreign competition, since he ruled out the possibility of modernisation. He frankly admitted French employers were timid, inefficient and failed to use enough capital, but he accepted this as an inevitable counterpart of the pursuit of the golden mean and the virtue of moderation. He did not spurn the progress of science. He looked to it and to education to make agriculture profitable once more, but he always put aside any notion of structural change among the peasantry. Transport costs were a major cause of the uncompetitive price of both agricultural and industrial products in France, as well as high taxation. His remedy was not to remove these impediments, which with peasant resignation he accepted as inevitable, but to offer compensating protection. He believed that the duties he imposed, after elaborate calculations, were mathematically the exact compensation needed to offset these disadvantages.

It was the economic crisis of the 1880s which gave him the

[1] J. Méline, *Le Retour à la terre et la surproduction industrielle* (1905).

idea by which he reconciled protection of both industry and agriculture. The poverty of the peasants was making it impossible for them to buy the produce of the manufacturers. Since the republic was above all a government based on public opinion, it was only fair that the peasants should get some advantages from the state like everybody else. Steeped in the old centralising tradition, he did much to confirm the peasantry in their habit of looking to the state for their salvation. The widespread sympathy Méline won was recognised in his election as president of the chamber of deputies (in preference to Clemenceau). His assumption of Ferry's mantle was seen in his tenure, from 1893 to 1902, of the editorship of *La République française*, the paper which Gambetta had established as the principal organ of the republicans.

When Méline became prime minister in 1896, he made an attempt to reorganise the political parties on the basis of the issues which he considered were the real ones. He believed that there was an urgent need to end the meaningless republican coalitions, repeatedly abortive of legislation. Méline formed a cabinet composed entirely of moderates. He wanted to redefine the divisions in politics, to show that the major difference among politicians was over socialism. The republicans were no longer divided simply in degree, over questions of method. The socialists were no longer simply their left wing, just advanced reformers, as they might have been in Gambetta's day, for they wished to subvert the whole social order of which Méline was the champion. The groups of the right were no longer a threat to the republic, because they had virtually abandoned their royalism. They were obvious allies in the struggle against socialism. The radicals, on the other hand, needed to be split: they embraced too many incompatible tendencies. A section of the radical party had, under the leadership of Goblet, made common cause with the socialists. No alliance was possible with it. By contrast, there were only two questions on which the moderate republicans differed from the right—the army and the Church. On these Méline advocated the implementation of Walpole's famous maxim, 'Let sleeping dogs lie.' The army, he insisted, must not be provoked: the Dreyfus case must be silently buried. Attacks on the army by the left were only producing a reaction in the form of a dangerous nationalist movement. For the same reason, the progress of socialism must be halted or it would produce a demand for a new saviour of society, a new Napoleon. The monarchists should therefore be welcomed into the republic, instead of being forced into opposition by persecution. Anticlericalism should in the same way be abandoned, to cement this alliance with the right: and in any case it was a dead issue, which profited only the radicals. The republic had built up enough defences against the Church. It would be an enormous source of strength if, by a policy of appeasement, the Church could be induced to accept Ferry's legislation and a limited role in the new order. In this way there could be a genuine political confrontation of the defenders of private property against those who wished to abolish it, of those who believed in the conciliation of the classes against those who advocated the class struggle, between those who saw trade unions as instruments of a new co-operative society and those who regarded them as a revolutionary means of paralysing capitalism, between those who looked on taxation as a contribution to public expenses and those who hoped to use it to produce greater economic equality, between those who saw in the senate a rampart of order and those who wished to weaken or abolish it, between those who respected religion and would allow freedom to the Church provided it respected the concordat and abstained from politics, and those who, denying that this was possible, demanded the separation of Church and state.[1]

Méline's ministry lasted longer than any previous one under the republic, but he was unable to achieve the political reorganisation or religious appeasement with which he hoped to complete his economic work. It required more than the skill of an individual. Méline never succeeded in building up a party to present his ideas to the electorate; his followers were poor attenders in the chamber; they never dominated the parliamentary commissions; some of them objected to his hostility to the radicals.[2] But Méline deserves to be remembered not just as the author of protection, but also as the person who carried

---

[1] J. Méline, 'Les Partis dans la république', *Revue politique et parlementaire*, 23 (Jan. 1900), 5–16; see also Edmond Demolins, 'La Nécessité d'un programme social et d'un nouveau classement des partis', *La Science sociale* (Feb. 1895), 105–16.

[2] 'Le Parti progressiste, par un député', *Revue politique et parlementaire* (10 June 1897), 485–507.

through the law of 1898 on friendly societies (*sociétés de secours mutuel*). The significance of this has seldom been noticed. It was part of the solidarist movement which characterised the 1890s. The period cannot be understood without going further into this product of a philosophy, by which the Third Republic attempted, again unsuccessfully, to break away from the past.[1]

Solidarity was the most talked about ideal of the nineties and the first decade of the twentieth century. The president of the republic, Loubet, opening the great Exhibition of 1900, declared that all governments paid homage to 'this higher law', and acknowledged it as 'the great common inspiration' of the day. His socialist minister of commerce Millerand hailed solidarity as a new scientific revelation containing 'the secret for the material and moral grandeur of societies'. The monarchist comte d'Haussonville remarked, 'Today, anyone who wishes to receive a sympathetic hearing or even to obtain professional advancement must speak of solidarity.' It was claimed that solidarity was exciting people as passionately as Cartesianism had once done, and that its formula 'Every man his neighbour's debtor' caused as much stir as Proudhon's 'Property is theft.' People started writing theses about it, conferences were held, and the Academy of Moral and Political Sciences devoted four sessions to debating it.[2]

The first significant feature of solidarism was that it represented a new attitude to the French Revolution. Worship of the principles of the Revolution had always been an essential mark of a republican. Lip-service to these principles still continued to be paid, but now, coinciding almost exactly with the

[1] *L'Œuvre économique et sociale de M. Jules Méline* (pamphlet published by the Association nationale républicaine, 1902, copy in Remiremont Municipal Library); *L'Œuvre agricole de M. Jules Méline* (n.d., Assoc. nat. répub.); Georges Lachapelle, *Le Ministère Méline* (1928); Gabriel Hanotaux, 'Jules Méline', *Revue des Deux Mondes* (15 Jan. 1926), 440–53.

[2] The fullest account is in J. E. S. Hayward, 'The Idea of Solidarity in French Social and Political Thought in the Nineteenth and Early Twentieth Centuries' (unpublished Ph.D. thesis, London, 1958). See also his article, 'The Official Philosophy of the French Third Republic: Léon Bourgeois and Solidarism', *International Review of Social History*, 6 (1961), 22–5. John A. Scott, *Republican Ideas and the Liberal Tradition in France 1870–1914* (New York, 1951), 157–86; Charles Gide, *La Solidarité*, cours au Collège de France 1927–8 (1932); C. Bouglé, *Le Solidarisme* (1907); Louis Deuve, *Étude sur le solidarisme et ses applications économiques* (Paris thesis, 1906).

centenary of 1789, a more critical and even hostile reaction emerged among men with impeccable radical antecedents. There had been vague talk about implementing the promises of the Revolution more fully, but now people suggested that they were inadequate. Léon Bourgeois, leader of the radical ministry in 1895, said that the Declaration of the Rights of Man needed to be supplemented by a declaration of his duties. The individualism which the Revolution had consecrated was an evil and a delusion. The liberty it proclaimed was only force under another name, which allowed the rich to oppress the poor. The individual it tried to liberate was an abstraction, for men were not independent beings capable of being considered apart from their obligations and ties to other men. The sociologist Durkheim wrote that the Revolution must be studied in its historical context, and only when this had been done would it be possible to say whether it was a 'pathological phenomenon' or not. The Revolution was seen as the product of metaphysical confusion, which the new positivism rejected. It was described in the schoolbooks as the dawn of a new era, but it was becoming clearer all the time that it did not break with the past all that completely. Tocqueville's dictum was recalled, that the *ancien régime* was still alive, and that the repeated attempts to kill absolute power had only placed new heads of liberty on the same servile body. As the problems involved by implementation of the Revolution's ideas became increasingly complicated, protests were raised against persisting in 'a tradition that was exhausted, and a political method that was out of date and sterile'.[1]

Laissez-faire, which the Revolution had adopted as a principle, had in the course of the century been rejected by the republicans in varying degrees, but they had been equivocal about it when they gained power. Charles Gide's *Principles of Political Economy*, published in 1883, demanded that it should be openly and officially abandoned. He declared that orthodox liberal economics were discredited and 'a thaw' of its harsh doctrines had set in.[2] Henri Marion's thesis on *Moral Solidarity* ('an essay in applied psychology') argued that morality could no longer be considered simply a question of individual virtue,

---

[1] Th. Ferneuil, *Les Principes de 1789 et la science sociale* (1889); review of this by Durkheim in *Revue internationale de l'enseignement* (1890).

[2] C. Gide, *Principes d'économie politique* (1883).

that the ideal of the noble savage was a false one, that reliance on divine providence or exhortation were inadequate, because human character was deeply influenced by the environment in which it developed. Man's liberty was really very restricted, and moral progress therefore required active organisation: it could not be expected to happen naturally.[1]

The new discoveries of science were held to require new attitudes in politics. Hitherto Darwin's teachings about the struggle for life had been seen as justifying *laissez-faire*, for it led to evolutionary progress. But now Milne-Edwards (a French zoologist) argued that living organisms were made up of large numbers of cells working together. The 'law of nature' was therefore co-operation, not hostility, solidarity not individualism. Works on the *Fauna of the Normandy Coast* and *Comparative Physiology* were quoted by politicians to support the view that man should no longer be considered as being born perfect, invested with rights against his fellow citizens, but rather as part of a larger organic whole, from which he had much to gain and on which he was necessarily dependent. Durkheim's thesis on the *Division of Labour* (1896) condemned the society of the day as crumbling from 'anomie'. The weakening of the old bonds of religion and the family had created moral chaos, and economic specialisation had completed the disruption. The Revolution had believed in effecting reform by state action or by leaving it to the individual. Neither was adequate. Durkheim argued that a new morality was needed to hold the country together and a new social organisation, based on professional associations—precisely the bodies the Revolution had tried to destroy.[2] Every branch of knowledge was reinterpreted, to show man's interdependence and the need for co-operative action, rather than unrestricted liberty, to enable him to flourish.

It was Léon Bourgeois who brought together all these hints from the scientists to make solidarism a political doctrine. Born in 1851, the son of a watchmaker, he had made his own way out of the lower middle class, through the civil service, to become prefect of police at the age of thirty-six. He was a man of great

---

[1] Henri Marion, *De la solidarité morale. Essai de psychologie appliquée* (1880, 3rd edition revised 1890).

[2] E. Durkheim, *De la division du travail social* (1896).

charm, animated by a constant desire to please, but it was a sign of the new times that, though brought up as a servant of the state, he did not continue to worship it when he became a politician. Bourgeois's contribution was to give solidarism a theoretical basis, with his doctrine of the 'social debt' and the 'quasi-contract'. Men were not born free, he said. Even a child was a debtor to society, first to his mother for his food, then to his teachers for his education, then to a far wider group for his economic opportunities, and he incurred new debts all his life. This idea was not a new one, but Bourgeois transformed it from a moral one into a legal one. He claimed that men had not simply a moral duty to repay their debt, but a positive obligation, enforceable with sanctions, because they had made a 'quasi-contract' with society. He found an obscure section of the Civil Code which showed that individual agreement was not essential to create a binding contract. Rousseau's notion of the social contract for mutual benefit was overthrown. Rights were replaced by obligations. However much one contributed to society, one also had debts to repay. In this way the rich owed something to the poor, who were part of society. Charity, which was optional, should be replaced by solidarity, which was compulsory. The state could legitimately force people to pay their debts.

This gave a new justification for a programme of social welfare, founded on an income tax, but one poised carefully half-way between liberalism and socialism. On the one hand solidarism accepted that men were unequal in ability, and that they should continue to derive benefits from their different natural endowments; but justice required that these inequalities should not be increased by inequalities of social origin, like education and inherited wealth. All who enjoyed special advantages of this kind should be required to pay larger taxes to compensate. However, Bourgeois firmly rejected socialism. Its ideal, he said, was a collective one, whereas he started with collective obligations as a fact of life, and his aim was to free men from them, by getting them to pay their debts to society. His ideal was the free individual, and he believed that private property was the 'prolongation and guarantee of liberty'. 'My social ideal is one in which every man will have reached, within the limits of justice, individual proprietorship.'

Solidarism required men to co-operate not in production or in the division of wealth, but in insuring themselves against the risks of life. Equal wages were neither possible nor desirable, but a minimum wage was necessary, in the name of justice, and illness, accident and unemployment insurance were a social duty. Taxation should exist not for the purpose of levelling incomes but to support common services, though each should contribute in proportion to his income. Education should be free. The important thing was that the only limit to a man's ascent should be his natural abilities. Bourgeois thus saw society as a giant mutual insurance company, which helped the disadvantaged, but left each man free to make his own way once he had paid his premiums. There was no need to hope optimistically that men would behave altruistically. As Alfred Croiset, one of his supporters, said, 'Once the machine is set up, it works automatically, and the well-being of all is the necessary result of the operation, if it is conducted intelligently. This gives it a sort of scientific character which is pleasing to the spirit of our time.' Charity was condescending. Justice was too dry and narrow. Fraternity, as was seen in 1848, was too sentimental. Solidarity, based on biology, was scientific. It would transform the blind and unfair but inevitable interdependence of humans, which had created so many social evils, into a voluntary and rational relationship based on equal respect for the equal rights of all. It would socialise not property, but men's minds and give them a new conscience. France would then be, in Michelet's phrase, *une grande amitié*.[1]

Though solidarism was supported by arguments drawn from the natural and social sciences, which made it appear topical and new, its doctrines were of course composed of much older elements. The word itself had been invented by Pierre Leroux, as the opposite of individualism. Auguste Comte had written about it, though largely confining himself to solidarity between generations. Renouvier had attacked the ideals of the eighteenth century and had urged that solidarity should be added to liberty. The revolution of 1848 had expressed the same

[1] Léon Bourgeois, *La Solidarité* (1896); Maurice Hamburger, *Léon Bourgeois 1851–1925* (1932); Alfred Croiset and Léon Bourgeois, *Essai d'une philosophie de la solidarité* (1902); Léon Bourgeois, *La Politique de la prévoyance sociale* (1914–19, 2 vols.); Émile Ferré, *Un Ministère radical* (1897).

longings in a more emotional manner. Solidarism could not escape the accusation that it was fraternity dressed up in scientific clothes. However, it was popular because many aspirations—socialist, aesthetic and Christian—found some echo in its teachings. It was to the Third Republic what Cousin's eclecticism had been to the July Monarchy. It was, almost inevitably, equally confused, if not hypocritical. It had more than a suggestion of being designed to steal the thunder of the socialists. It was more or less contemporaneous with William II's new course in German politics, in which Christian socialism was aimed at winning the workers away from revolution: it could be called a lay version of it. Though the solidarists claimed that the peculiar feature of their movement was that it was totally French, this international context was not irrelevant. They were, to a certain extent, inspired by fear or remorse, as much as by a constructive idealism. Hanotaux said that the bourgeoisie 'has sinned by its laziness, its imprudence, its egoism'. It had treated the government as its enemy and it had therefore not used it to help the people. It had failed to bridge the gap between the classes. Poincaré, in a famous speech, asked in the same vein, that the bourgeoisie should make 'necessary concessions'. Renouvier—the profoundly religious inspirer of so many republican ideas—declared on his death-bed, 'The bourgeoisie has not kept its promises: it has worked only for itself.' Solidarism was a kind of retribution.

Its theoretical paraphernalia was probably more cumbersome than helpful. To suggest to those who possessed nothing that they were in fact debtors to society, and to add that they could never repay their debt because they were always contracting new ones, to inform them if they succeeded that their achievements were not their own, was hardly a way to win enthusiastic support. Though solidarism contained idealistic elements, it was also, in important ways, conservative. It appeared to be a new justification of unequal private property. Its sociological arguments took what existed as the norm and condemned forces that disrupted society as pathological. Durkheim's professional groups seemed too like the corporations of the *ancien régime*. Izoulet, professor of philosophy at the Lycée Condorcet, whose book on the modern state was quoted approvingly by the solidarists, defined the problem they were trying to solve as how to prevent the crowd from overthrowing the élite, while yet admitting the crowd 'loyally and cordially into the state'.[1] The solidarists were divided among themselves as to exactly what they meant, and as to what language they ought to use. Those with religious (usually Protestant) backgrounds disliked the word debt and wanted to talk of duty or sacrifice. Liberals objected to the use of sanctions, which, they said, made solidarism no different from socialism; but the socialists ridiculed it as a half-way house, which ignored the problem of the exploitation of labour. It was pointed out that though microbes might indeed be mutually dependent, there was no evidence that they loved one another. Gabriel Tarde, whose book on *Imitation* had argued that this was the main principle determining human conduct, claimed that solidarism was based on a contradiction and would therefore inevitably lead to socialism: it aimed at harmony, but the idea of debt was bound to lead to quarrels about the extent of each individual's debts and either the debtors or the creditors would seize power. This showed that the doctrine was not properly understood, and that was certainly one of its weaknesses.[2]

The solidarists placed their main hopes on the development of voluntary mutual benefit societies. They hoped that these would provide the whole range of social services—employment exchanges, loans, medical attention, pharmacies, pensions and insurance—all without much cost to the state. 'The French Republic', said Paul Deschanel, 'must become a vast mutual benefit society.'[3] Now mutualism already had a long history in France. Though forbidden by the Revolution, societies had started up soon after. They received encouragement from the July Monarchy, which in 1837 allowed their formation provided official permission was obtained. By 1845 there were 262 in Paris alone. The revolution of 1848 gave them a new stimulus, so that in 1852 there were 2,488 societies with 239,500 members. Then Napoleon III found a new use for them. Fearing that they

---

[1] J. Izoulet, *La Cité moderne: métaphysique de la sociologie* (1894).

[2] 'Étude sur la solidarité sociale comme principe des lois', *Séances et Travaux de l'Académie des sciences morales et politiques* (June 1903), 305–434. C. Bouglé, professeur de philosophie sociale à l'université de Toulouse, 'L'Évolution du solidarisme', *Revue politique et parlementaire*, 35 (10 Mar. 1903), 480–505.

[3] G. Weill, *Le Mouvement social en France* (1924), 452.

might develop into subversive organisations, he transformed their character. He exempted them from the general prohibition of clubs, provided they did not have members from more than one commune, and kept their numbers to a maximum of 500 (if 'approved' or 2,000 if declared of 'public utility'). He reserved to himself the right to appoint the president of every society, and to dissolve them with the minimum of formality. They had to admit as 'honorary members' the village notables who would preserve them from revolutionary tendencies; prefects, *curés* and mayors were required to help establish societies in as many communes as possible. Ten million francs, from the confiscated Orleanist estates, were set aside to provide encouraging subsidies. Napoleon thus made these societies the stimulants of thrift and prudence, nuclei for a new self-reliance, but also political and electoral organisations, disunited so that they could not develop any independence against him. By 1870 half a million people had been enrolled.

The solidarists gave this movement an enormous boost. A law of 1898 gave the societies the same freedom as the law of 1884 had given trade unions, but adding financial privileges and the promise of state subsidies on an elaborately calculated scale, proportionate to their achievements. By 1902 over a million more people had joined, to which should be added half a million school children enrolled in a junior branch.[1] In 1910 it was claimed that there were 15,832 societies with 3,170,000 active members and 400,000 honorary members.

Mutualism was the practical and popular aspect of solidarism. There was a National League of Mutuality (launched with a gift of 10,000 francs from the millionaire owner of the Magasins du Louvre, Chauchard, and the blessing of Sadi Carnot, president of the republic). Six national congresses were held by it, from 1883, and in 1900 the first international congress, in Paris, was an impressive affair. Newspapers and journals entitled *L'Avenir de l'Épargne*, *L'Écho de la mutualité*, *La France prévoyante*, *Le Mutualiste*, *La Mutualité*, *La Revue des institutions de prévoyance*, etc. appeared in large numbers. It is curious that no historian has ever done research on these papers

---

[1] This junior branch was known as the *petit Cavé* after its founder. The children paid very small subscriptions, but considerable insurance benefits were promised, down even to funeral expenses.

or these congresses, in contrast to the large number who have
investigated the activities of the far less numerous socialists.[1]

Being a member of a mutual society came to be looked on
almost as a public service. Organisers were rewarded with
medals. The Second Empire had instituted a special medal—
black ribbon with a blue selvage—for the most successful of
them, but it was a decoration which could not be worn on its
own and in any case only at society meetings. Between 1898
and 1903 the restrictions on its use were abolished, and the
holders of the gold medal were allowed to wear it publicly as a
rosette (instead of as a mere ribbon). In 1875 only 579 such
medals had been awarded. In 1895 no fewer than 3,281 were
given. In 1900 the figure rose to 8,175 and in 1907 no fewer
than 17,000. It was almost as though the societies were formed
to obtain medals, and it was asked what kind of medals these
were, which were awarded for extorting subsidies from the
state. If left to their own devices, the societies would have made
a loss of about 10 million francs a year. Subscriptions accounted
for only two-thirds of their income; the rest was obtained from
public subsidies and even more from honorary members. It was
not surprising therefore that many people looked askance at
the societies, as organisations for legalised begging, subject to
the domination of the rich. The presence of honorary members,
like the state subsidies, made these societies very different from
the English friendly societies (which had far more members—
over 5 million in 1898—and were three times as rich as the
French societies). They never had any of the *friendly* character
of the English ones. In England, social activities played as
important a part as the insurance, with the annual feast or
outing, the hearty drinking at the monthly meetings—the
expenses of which were put down as 'room rent'—the initiation
ceremonies and mystic rituals of such bodies as the Oddfellows
and the Free Foresters. The English, by excluding the upper
classes, made it possible for these societies to form a part of
working-class culture. The French societies, by contrast, were
absorbed into the tradition of state intervention, employers'
paternalism and political manœuvring.

[1] *Premier Congrès international de la mutualité 1900*, (president M. V. Lourtiès,
sénateur), report ed. Jules Arboux (1901), contains a lot of information. Cf. the
criticism of the national organisation by Eugène Joly, president of a society in St.
Étienne, *Le Passé, le présent, l'avenir de la mutualité* (St. Étienne, 1893).

Subscriptions were very low—on average 13 francs a year (about 50 pence). The benefits were therefore equally low. The average pension paid at the turn of the century was less than 71 francs (£3) per annum. The societies sought to offer as many benefits as possible, in order to qualify for the maximum number of subsidies which each kind of service attracted. They therefore performed none satisfactorily. Running expenses absorbed on average 27 per cent of their income. The societies were far too small to provide a proper insurance service. In 1902 71 per cent had fewer than 100 members and 39 per cent had fewer than 50. Ignorance of the principles governing insurance was common, methods of administration amateur in the extreme. The government did not really help, even though innumerable guides on how to practise mutualism were issued. The most serious omission was that the whole movement was never established on a proper actuarial basis. The tables of sickness and mortality promised in a decree of 1852, promised again in the law of 1898, were still unpublished in 1907, when the minister of labour, Viviani, declared that they were so difficult to prepare that they could not be expected for some time. France was in this respect over fifty years behind England, where more or less reliable tables had been produced in 1845.

Unlike Napoleon III, the solidarist politicians urged the mutual societies to unite. They had visions of a great moral upsurge, in which the egoism of the small societies would be replaced by a solidarity spread throughout the land: the union of friendly societies would be the basis of a new reconciliation of all Frenchmen. But the old habits were too firmly ingrained. A national council was formed, but it had no authority over the societies and merely acted as an organ of propaganda. It was accused of being unrepresentative and its policies were disputed. Some federations were established on the departmental level, and these were sometimes effective: they were able to provide, between them, pharmacies, clinics and baths. The contrast between the idealism and what was achieved can be seen in the matter of baths. Baths, it was said, were extremely important. Fernand Faure declared: 'When Frenchmen come to have two baths a week, the moral, intellectual and political condition of our country will be transformed.'[1] The researches of Russian and Japanese professors on the value of baths were carefully studied. The number of microbes removed by baths of various kinds were counted, from which it emerged that all baths increased the microbes, while showers reduced them. This was fortunate, for showers were much cheaper to build and used less water, and the hygienists had intended to build showers in any case. But then came the question of money, and far less was done than was promised. Similar frustrations arose in the medical services provided by the societies, which moreover were often used more by the well-to-do than by the poor. Relations with the doctors and pharmacists always remained difficult. So the effect of mutualism was to create a great new vested interest, which did not provide the social services demanded of it, but stoutly resisted their development by the state. In 1900 only 30,000 peasants had joined and only half a million manual workers out of 11 million.[2] The politicians inflated the membership figures (just as the trade unions did theirs) and talked of a 'mutualist élite', comprising one-fifth of the working class, infused with a respect for the established order, and a pillar against 'the rising champions of collectivism and anarchy'.[3]

Mutualism made far more rapid progress than the co-operative movement. A bill to encourage the latter was discussed and amended for eight years, only to be finally rejected by the senate. This was largely due to the opposition of the small shopkeepers. Only about half a million people showed an interest in co-operation before the war. The movement was split in 1890 between socialists and independents, with the result that small local societies tended to avoid joining either federation. Reunion was finally negotiated in 1912, with victory going to the independents under Professor Charles Gide, one of the earliest solidarists, but he admitted that its progress was halted by more than these doctrinal divisions: 'Frenchmen', he said, 'and especially French workers, do not like to be governed by their equals.' The movement for profit sharing, on which a

[1] Michel Heim, *Contribution à l'étude de quelques services supérieurs de la mutualité dans le département de l'Hérault* (Montpellier thesis, 1913), 99.

[2] Léon Bourgeois's figures in *La Politique de la prévoyance sociale* (1914-19), i. 149.

[3] A. Weber, *A Travers la mutualité: étude critique sur les sociétés de secours mutuels* (1908), 262; Armand Alavoine, *L'Action économique et sociale des sociétés de secours mutuels* (Paris thesis 1914); Georges Assanis, *La Mutualité pratique: guide . . .* (1914).

great deal was also written, and which also held national and international congresses, converted only a tiny minority and involved only about 500 firms. The appeal to private enterprise was not successful.[1]

One of the common misconceptions about the Third Republic, before the 1914 war, is that it passed very little social legislation. On the contrary, there was a great deal of it. It is worth examining because it shows, on the one hand the solidarist ideas being put into practice, and on the other the limitations, inadequacies and failures of the doctrine. To supplement the work of the mutual societies, several important social services were set up. The largest problem that needed to be tackled was that of the poor. If private charity was to be replaced by solidarist assistance, a major redeployment of resources would be needed. There was already an institution for dealing with the poor in the *bureaux de bienfaisance*, which in theory were supposed to distribute aid in each commune, under the direction of the mayor; but in 1871 only 13,367 out of France's 35,989 communes had one, catering for only 60 per cent of the population; and on average they distributed only 28·6 francs in a whole year to each person they helped in Paris and 14·9 francs in the provinces. The commission appointed to inquire into them in 1872 made no recommendations for any radical change, since it accepted the traditional attitude to charity.[2]

However, in 1886 a special office to deal with public assistance was set up at the ministry of the interior and Henri Monod, a Protestant solidarist, took charge of it until 1905. He soon realised that the implementation of the solidarist ideals could not be achieved in one general reform. Opposition to helping able-bodied men out of work was strong. So he started by agitating for help for the sick, the infirm, children and the aged. Several societies were started and five national congresses were held between 1894 and 1911. In 1893, 'in the name of the great principle of solidarity', a law was passed by which 'every Frenchman without financial resources should receive without charge . . . medical aid at home, or, if he cannot be effectively

[1] J. Gaumont, *Histoire générale de la coopération en France* (1924); Albert Trombert, *Charles Robert, sa vie, son œuvre* (1927–31), and the publications of the *Société pour l'étude pratique de la participation du personnel aux bénéfices*, founded 1879.

[2] Ministry of Interior, *Enquête sur les bureaux de bienfaisance* (1874), report by Paul Bucquet.

cared for there, in a hospital'. Every commune was required to establish a *bureau d'assistance*, to draw up lists of those entitled to such aid and the state promised 80 per cent subsidies. At that date the communes were aiding less than half a million people. By 1897 the list of those entitled to aid contained 1·9 million persons and 13 million francs were in fact distributed to 701,000 people in medical aid. This, however, represented only 19·5 francs a head per year. The incurable, moreover, were excluded from this law, so though a hospital would take in a poor man free of charge, it would send him home as soon as it declared him incurable. An attempt was made in 1897 to remedy this serious defect by offering a state subsidy to local authorities, to enable them to pay pensions to the incurable old; but again this failed because local authorities refused to spend money for this purpose: five-sixths of the sum voted by parliament was never used. The situation therefore was that in order to get an old man free medical treatment it was necessary to prosecute and convict him for begging. Even so free hospital treatment did not carry with it payments to compensate for loss of wages, or to care for dependants. A bill was therefore moved to create in the words of its title 'a public service of social solidarity', in the form of obligatory assistance to the old, infirm and incurable and in 1905 it finally became law. It provided for the relief of the sick aged over seventy. In its implementation it revealed widespread distress. Over half a million people were to benefit from it each year: the state's subsidy was 49 million francs in 1907 and by 1914 it had been increased to 100 million.[1] But the poor still received on average only 34·9 francs each annually, compared to 180 francs (£7·20) distributed to almost twice as many in England. In 1914 there were still 8·6 million Frenchmen living in communes without *bureaux d'assistance*. The bureaucracy created to manage all this became filled with political nominees, so the standard of efficiency was exceptionally low.

In 1901 the government introduced, as 'an act of solidarity', a bill to give about 10 million workers the right to a pension,

[1] C. W. Pipkin, *Social Politics and Modern Democracies* (1931), 2. 190. This is a good study of the social legislation of this period: volume 2 deals with France. L. Mirman, 'Une Loi de solidarité sociale', *Revue politique et parlementaire* (July 1903), 49–73; J. H. Weiss, 'The Third Republic's War on Poverty' (unpublished paper, Harvard, 1966); Henry Joly, *De la corruption de nos institutions* (1903), 196–7.

but it was only in 1910, after much protestation by the senate at the expense involved, that it became law, in modified form. The delay was encouraged by the opposition of employers and workers alike. An inquiry into the opinion of trade unions in 1901 revealed that a great number of them were hostile to all contributory pension schemes because they believed it would diminish what they had to offer and would make the collection of their own subscriptions more difficult. The chambers of commerce declared they preferred mutuality to a compulsory state scheme. But mutuality had clearly not been successful, for in 1900 only 10 per cent of the working class were insured for their old age.[1] Under this new law, some 10 million workers were to receive pensions at the age of sixty-five, from a fund of which half was to be subscribed equally by employers and workers and half by the state. Some 6 million independent workers and peasant proprietors were given the chance to insure voluntarily. In 1912 the pensionable age was reduced to sixty. France took a long time to reach this result, and appeared all the more dilatory because the principle of compulsory insurance against illness and old age had been admitted as far back as 1894 in a law confined to miners.

A law of 1898 provided that workers who sustained accidents would be compensated on a generous scale, whoever was to blame. (Previously the victim had to prove that the employer had been negligent.) Three further laws had to be quickly passed between 1898 and 1902 to remedy serious defects produced by excessive caution. Employees were encouraged but still not compelled to insure themselves against accidents. The insurance companies, over-anxious to profit from the new business, began forming a consortium to raise their premiums. The state therefore offered an alternative official insurance scheme (1899) but most of the insurance continued to be done by the companies. Mutual schemes were disappointingly inactive. In any case, the laws applied only to industries using machines, and they excluded illnesses contracted at work.

The *prud'hommes* had long provided a court of arbitration for the settlement of disputes between masters and individual men.

[1] Maurice Bellom, 'Les Retraites ouvrières en France, Le Referendum de 1901', *Revue politique et parlementaire* (Jan. 1902), 119–39; M. Duboin, *La Législation sociale à la fin du dix-neuvième siècle* (1900).

The new solidarist hopes of social peace, together with the emotion caused by the great miners' strike at Carmaux, gave birth to the law of 27 December 1892, setting up similar machinery for arbitration in collective disputes. Appeal to arbitration, however, remained entirely voluntary and little use was made of it. In November 1900 Millerand moved a bill to make arbitration compulsory, but this received such opposition from both employers and trade unions that it was never even discussed by parliament. Instead masters and men were brought together in a series of consultative institutions. In 1891 a *Conseil supérieur du travail* was created to advise the minister on social problems; at first it was nominated by the minister, but after 1899 one-third of the members were elected by trade unions and one-third by employers' organisations. It was an important body, for all its tribulations, because it did a lot of work on most laws proposed in this period, virtually taking over the functions of the legislative section of the Conseil d'État, as far as labour questions were concerned. In 1891, likewise, an *Office du travail* was set up in the ministry of commerce, with the function of collecting information on labour conditions. It issued some fifty volumes in its first ten years of more or less imaginary statistics, for it had no power or staff to undertake direct inquiry, and it had to rely on others for its sources. Local *conseils du travail* were set up in theory by a decree in 1901, elected by employers' and workers' organisations, but this meant that the majority of French workers, not being members of unions, had no vote: the idea was to encourage them to join. In practice only five were set up in the main cities.

The first law controlling the employment and working hours of children in factories had been passed in 1841 (eight years after the English Factory Act of 1833), but in the absence of governmental interest or any effective inspectorate, it had been ignored.[1] The census of 1851 showed that half of the employees in factories were women and children, but only in 1874 was a new law passed providing for the appointment of fifteen inspectors and forbidding factory work under the age of twelve (or, with government permission, ten). This law again was only partly effective, so in 1881 and in 1885 the chamber of deputies passed further bills, which were, however, rejected by

[1] A decree of 1813 had forbidden the employment of children under ten in mines.

the senate. Only in 1892 had the spirit of solidarity spread sufficiently for a law to get through, limiting women and children aged sixteen to eighteen to eleven hours a day, children of thirteen to sixteen to ten hours, and forbidding children under thirteen to work at all, unless they had a certificate of primary studies, in which case they could work at twelve. This law also required one day's rest a week. There were thus several different legal working days. The result was that enforcement proved to be almost impossible, and the government closed its eyes to the flouting of the law. A new law of 1900 limited all factories in which women and children were employed to a uniform ten hours a day (including men). The employers again ignored this, or else paid the small fines for breaking it; some dismissed the children in order to be free from inspection. Exceptions were moreover officially sanctioned by a law of 28 March 1902 and a decree of 30 April 1909. Nevertheless the importance of the law of 1900 was that, in certain cases, i.e. in model factories, the hours of adult men were limited and this was the thin end of the wedge that led to the eight-hour day. But workers in shops and in the food trade remained unprotected. In 1905 the eight-hour day was introduced for miners—but only in 1919 was it extended to all workers.

The fixing of a minimum wage, though promised, was postponed. Millerand in 1899 asked state public works to pay the 'normal wages in the region', but this requirement was not binding on local authorities who (except for a few large ones) ignored it. A truck bill introduced in 1892 was held up by the senate. A wages law, passed in 1895, protected workers against creditors receiving over one-tenth of their wages, but the main beneficiaries seem to have been the legal officials who drew large fees from the complicated machinery established to enforce it. The *livret*, which every worker, like a suspect criminal, had to carry since Napoleon instituted it, and whose abolition had been promised as far back as 1870, was finally abolished in 1890, at last making employer and worker equals in law. That was as far as the solidarists could get.[1]

If carried to its logical conclusion, solidarism would have

[1] E. Levasseur, *Questions ouvrières et industrielles en France sous la Troisième République* (1907); Astier, Godart et al., *L'Œuvre sociale de la Troisième République*, leçons professés au collège libre des sciences sociales (1912).

involved a very drastic transformation not only of social relations but also of the state. Some of its advocates adopted an entirely fresh outlook on the traditional character of the state. Until the end of the nineteenth century, French jurists had been content to comment on laws and decrees, to describe the judicial system as it worked, but they did not attempt to explain or to question its bases. The cult of the law was too powerful and jurists considered themselves as its priests. This attitude was shown by the publication in 1886 of a version of the Civil Code in verse: it had become a classic. Sieyès had said: 'The end of every public institution is individual liberty', and Esmein, a leading law professor at the turn of the century, approved this in his standard work on public law. Now, however, the question of where the state derived its authority, and what it could use it for, was reconsidered by a new school of legal theorists, led by Léon Duguit. Because the purpose of the state was considered to be the safeguarding of liberty, and because after the establishment of universal suffrage it was held to derive its authority from the people, the conclusion had been drawn that—apart from administrative errors—the state could do no wrong. Duguit protested against this, pointing out that in effect this meant that the *ancien régime* state had been preserved in a new guise. He argued that the rule of law and justice was independent of the state and of the government, which should be subject to it as much as the individual. The civil servants should be regarded as performing a public service, not as exercising sovereignty, 'a myth whose efficacy is exhausted'; and power should be considered as legitimate only when properly used. Governments had obligations, more than rights; they were not the embodiment of the nation, as they claimed; and the individual should be able to sue them if they did not carry out their duties. The Conseil d'État went some way to accepting this new doctrine and to allowing appeals by individuals against official mismanagement. A new kind of jurisprudence developed. But the courts could not force the civil service to act, they could only issue injunctions to them. The omnipotence of the state was therefore not undermined.[1] Solidarism did not produce the radical change it could have

---

[1] Michel Halbecq, *L'État, son autorité, son pouvoir 1880–1962* (1965), discusses the new legal theories; Léon Duguit, *Law in the Modern State* (1919).

done. This, rather than the lack of social legislation, was the great failure of the nineties.

One explanation of the stability which underlay the polemic can be found in the career of Waldeck-Rousseau. It spans two generations: he was minister under Gambetta (1881) and also prime minister at the time of the Dreyfus Affair twenty years later (1898–1901). His career is particularly instructive because he was associated with some striking, though unsuccessful, attempts to bring about change. In it one can see why the grand paper reforms were so often less than what they appeared to be, and one can get a clearer understanding of the limitations both of the politicians and of the environment in which they worked.

Waldeck-Rousseau was the son of a barrister of moderate means (with an income of 5,000 to 6,000 francs—£200 to £240—rising to 12,000 in the best years). His origins were thus distinctly modest; he inherited little; he was brought up to economise; and he had to support his father in his old age. By the end of his life, however, he was one of France's most successful barristers, able to save 136,000 francs in the three years 1885–8. He married at the age of forty-two the widow of an even richer colleague and lived in great style in a grand house filled with impressive *objets d'art*.[1] He kept a yacht and mixed with the rich. His friends, he said proudly, were 'great industrialists'. He was set on his feet by the Société Dreyfus, exporters, whose legal consultant he became and who paid him a retainer during most of his career. He specialised as a barrister in commercial cases bringing in large fees. His admiration was increasingly for the rich. He criticised the men of 1848 for being too emotional about the lot of the poor. He once asked himself why he was so little moved by their misery, and he never seems to have had any particular sympathy for them.

Like so many of the followers of Gambetta, he had been an unsuccessful student; he had failed his *licence* at the first try, he had abandoned his doctorate, and at the age of twenty-two he was already filled with a profound bitterness towards life which never left him. He concealed his timidity and disillusionment with a coldness and a reserve which made everyone compare

[1] 35 rue de l'Université, Paris 7ᵉ.

him to a fish. Success turned his brusqueness only into arrogance. He never had a personal following. His best friends were
his animals—dogs, cats and birds. As a student he had not
mixed with his contemporaries; he had lived on the right bank
in Paris. As a barrister establishing himself in a town where he
had no ties, he had shunned society and could be seen daily at
the same café, alone: he was famous for his public silences. He
was barely influenced by the intellectual movements of his day.
He knew virtually nothing of positivism; he read little; he
despised politicians, theoreticians and doctrinaires. When he
did go into politics—which he never looked on as a career but
to which a strong ambition drove him—his disappointments
exacerbated his animosity and added a hate of parliaments and
deputies, whom he called 'pygmies' and 'larvae'. As an adolescent he had been a practising Catholic, a fervent defender of
the pope's temporal power and even a member of the Society of
St. Vincent de Paul. In 1868 he lost his faith not from conversion to science, but in a revulsion produced by a sense of having
wasted his youth, and possibly as a result of separation from
and disagreement with his father. He never dreamt of replacing
faith by science. He did not share the republicans' passionate
interest in education; he never asked for a school for his
constituency. He had been educated in a church school in
Nantes and had no complaints about its teachers: it had taught
him, he said, that Catholicism need not necessarily be militant.
He was uninterested by Gambetta's anticlericalism, as he was
by his patriotic fervour: he hated the nationalism of Deroulède.
He travelled all over Europe in his holidays, but went mainly to
beaches and museums. One month by the English seaside was
enough to make him conclude that the English were a nation
of hypocrites. He appears to have had little knowledge of
foreign affairs and to have taken little interest in them. He was
almost blind in one eye. His main hobby was painting. Hunting,
riding, canoeing, gymnastics, boxing, 'all sports, even violent
ones, attracted him'. He accepted with resignation that life
was inevitably boring and happiness impossible to achieve.
'Puisqu'il faut s'ennuyer, ennuyons nous.'[1] Waldeck-Rousseau
is worth studying because he was so different from the standard

---

[1] Henry Leyret, *Waldeck-Rousseau et la Troisième République (1869–89)*, 54, 56. See
the excellent, stimulating biography by Pierre Sorlin, *Waldeck-Rousseau* (1966).

image of the optimistic republican militant, an idealised mythical creation if there ever was one.

It was this man, however, who was chosen by Gambetta to be his expert on the social question. Waldeck's ideas on the subject were pretty vague. His principal interest hitherto had been the reform of the magistracy, which he believed to be crucial to the development of the republic: this was something barristers (and even more republican ones who had been fined or imprisoned by judges) felt strongly. The social programme he developed was one aimed at establishing social peace. He considered that industrialisation had given the capitalists an excessive and therefore dangerous preponderance. The workers would not put up with this indefinitely. They had to be given greater equality, and this could be achieved through association: united they could face their employers on a fair basis. 'I consider', he said, 'association as the regulator of social forces and the way to bring about equilibrium in them.' They would enable the educated and moderate workers to teach the ignorant and impulsive ones, and the responsibility of managing these organisations would show them that strikes were not the answer to their problems. Improved moral and material conditions would make the workers bastions of order. Waldeck preached to them what he had done himself—that they should rise in the world, save, make money, and lead a sober bourgeois existence—and he did so sincerely, for he had no prejudice against the lower classes. He harboured something of the fraternal utopianism of 1848, inherited from his father. It should not be forgotten that before becoming a republican, he had been an admirer of the naïve romantic Émile Ollivier (whom he had described in 1869 as the only statesman who had studied politics 'scientifically') and that his favourite in literature was Lamartine. Waldeck's ideal was a fraternal society, without any of the paternalism or hierarchy of the Christian socialists. Bills he introduced into parliament in 1882 included many of the proposals the solidarists were to adopt on pensions, insurance, *prud'hommes* and *sociétés de secours mutuels*. The trade union law of 1884, with which his name is linked, was not his own, and he only helped it pass its final stages. He wanted a much broader treatment of the question of associations, and thought unions—which were only one form—should not receive special treatment.

This reveals how much his proposals were developed in isolation from the working-class movement. The socialist Malon said his ideas were admirable but utopian, out of touch with reality. Waldeck in fact met only moderate worker's leaders, and mainly artisan ones; he seems not to have appreciated what the miners told him, that in the mines workers' associations would never be strong or rich enough to free them from capitalist domination. He saw a minority of extremists as misleading the large mass of sober, honest workers. This meant that his social policy, when he became prime minister, was one of hostility to the vigorous, organised, politically oriented unions, while he tried to raise a new kind of workers' association against them. His bills on pensions and compulsory arbitration were opposed by the unions. In social questions, he hovered between two positions. On the one hand he felt uncomfortable in crowds, he did not wish to be led by the masses and thought that men like him had a duty to establish a new order of justice, to help transform the wage earner into a property-owning partner, even if the masses in their ignorance could not properly understand what he was doing. But on the other hand he believed that, in his resistance to extremism and socialism, he represented the silent majority, 'the true country, the hard-working country, which is not heard often enough because it does not speak enough, and whose opinion needs to be found in its very intimate manifestations'. Increasingly he looked to the provinces against Paris, to the peasants against the extremist towns. He saw the radicals as the great menace. His situation in 1900 was thus not all that different from Louis Napoleon's in 1848. He continued to preach the ideals of that revolution. He wished to win the workers away from their leaders. He appointed a renegade socialist, Millerand, to his ministry: he looked on left-wing politicians as simply men with strong ambitions. But he was also firm with the employers, whose paternalistic attitudes he criticised as being equally serious obstacles to social peace. Arbitrating in a strike at Le Creusot, he laid it down as a principle that employers must not discriminate against trade unionists and must not oppose the election of shop stewards.[1]

[1] R. Waldeck-Rousseau, *Questions sociales* (1900), contains his main speeches on this subject; cf. Henry Leyret, *De Waldeck-Rousseau à la C.G.T.* (1921).

Waldeck had a reputation for firmness, which he established with his authoritarian, antiparliamentary attitudes as Gambetta's minister of the interior. He was opposed to decentralisation. He opposed the granting of more freedom to the city of Paris, and its emancipation from the control of the prefect of police. He condemned the city councillors as unrepresentative and he urged businessmen to replace the professional politicians among them, so that the 'economic élite' could run its administration in the most efficient manner. He had temporarily retired from politics in 1889 'in disgust' with the parliamentary system. He returned as a senator, but seldom attended debates, and never spoke much in parliament even when he held office. His most interesting political experiment was an attempt in the 1890s to start a new kind of party. He wanted to 'close the era of politicians'. 'Purely speculative politics has lost its importance and its interest.' Practical questions should replace it. Businessmen and industrialists should get elected to parliament instead of the lawyers, doctors and journalists.[1] He wanted to introduce his image of English parliamentary government into France: to unite the scattered moderate groups in the chambers and what political associations existed into a cohesive party, to hold elections on issues, and to reduce the power of the individual deputy to obstruct government by interpellation. He had, as minister of the interior, been interpellated about dustbins and his government could have fallen on this issue. The country needed strong and long-lasting ministries. He attributed the slowing down of the economy to political instability: the important effect of his reforms would be to stimulate prosperity, and so make it unnecessary to introduce an income tax, for the old taxes would, if properly reorganised, yield enough revenue once more. He looked upon income tax as subverting the principle of the French Revolution that there should be equality of rights and burdens. The tax would, he claimed, create a new privileged class, dividing the nation between those who paid taxes and those who did not. His great aim therefore was to split the radicals, to win over the moderate antisocialists among them, and so create a great centre party. This would, he hoped, not be simply a new coalition, and certainly

[1] Speech of 3 July 1896 to the Société d'économie industrielle et commerciale, quoted Sorlin, 382.

not the old 'concentration'. It would be based on a common programme, not on a compromise. He dreamt of putting up 500 candidates with one platform.

In June 1897 Waldeck-Rousseau launched the *Grand Cercle républicain*, modelled on the English Carlton and Reform Clubs, and a sort of counterpart to the aristocratic Jockey Club. The subscription was high: 200 francs for Parisians and 100 for provincials. He sent young men out to canvass the rich businessmen and industrialists throughout the country. His club would be quite different from the other similar associations (and to some of which he himself belonged). The *Association nationale républicaine* (presided over by Audiffred), the *Association gambettiste* (whose president was Cazot) were primarily concerned with spreading republican propaganda from Paris into the provinces. Waldeck-Rousseau's new organisation was designed to recruit a new kind of leadership for the nation. But by March 1898 he had managed to persuade only about 1,000 people to join. His club never really got under way. The politicians had no wish to destroy the system they were running or to submit to Waldeck's yoke. He got the support only of a few fence-sitters like Poincaré and Deschanel, who were without any personal following. The local notables were unwilling to sacrifice their independence. The defeat of Méline gave the club a serious set-back: the Dreyfus case completed its disintegration. Waldeck-Rousseau himself destroyed his own creation when he took office with a socialist in his government, and accepted socialist and radical votes, abjuring the very policy for which he had founded his club. In any case he lacked the demagogic talents necessary to create a popular party. The *Revue politique et parlementaire*, founded in 1894 to further Mélinisme, and which became the principal organ of the new club, was the only relic that survived of Waldeck-Rousseau's plans; but it was too serious, running to 240 pages each month, with only a narrow intellectual appeal. The businessmen refused to stand for parliament, though a few, including a regent of the Bank of France, gave him sizeable donations. The *Comité républicain du commerce et de l'industrie*, which he helped to found and of which Mascuraud, a jewellery manufacturer, became president, preferred to work behind the scenes, representing the interests of employers, trafficking in decorations—and discreetly subsidising the professional politicians. Waldeck thus failed to change the system. It is not clear that he would have got much further even if he had had more suppleness and guile.[1]

Waldeck-Rousseau sought not the separation of Church and state but the very opposite, the strengthening of governmental control over the clergy and particularly over the religious orders. These latter had not been mentioned in the concordat of 1801 and so by implication they continued to be excluded from France, but they gradually infiltrated back and they enjoyed a freedom from state supervision quite unknown to the secular priests. Waldeck-Rousseau wished to remedy this lacuna in the law, to be 'the Bonaparte of the monks', to bring the concordat into line with the realities of the new situation, to republicanise (not to abolish) the Church. In 1900 there were about 162,000 regulars, almost 60 per cent more than in 1789; they appeared to be the richest single group within the state; it was estimated (rather wildly) that they had doubled their wealth in the last fifty years and that they now possessed at least a milliard francs (£40 million). They had openly taken a part in politics, culminating with their violent campaign in the elections of 1898; the Assumptionists in particular had developed an antirepublican organisation to rival the state. They had refused to pay the admittedly heavy taxes imposed upon them and had been an obstacle to the *ralliement*. With the years the republic had succeeded in filling the bishoprics perhaps not with docile prelates but at least with conciliatory ones, and Waldeck-Rousseau revelled in the power to treat them in the same way as he treated his prefects, to send them stern letters of rebuke when they made the wrong political pronouncements and to withhold their salaries if they were obstinate. Waldeck-Rousseau believed (too optimistically) that the rivalry which had developed between bishops and regulars would enable him to win assistance from the former in making the latter submit to them. For the regulars had usurped many secular

[1] Léopold Marcellin, 'Waldeck-Rousseau et le Waldeckisme', *Revue universelle* (1 Aug. 1923), 306–29; Boris Blick, 'Waldeck-Rousseau 1894–1904' (Ph.D. Wisconsin, unpublished, 1958); *Revue politique et parlementaire* (1894 ff.), and in particular the issue of Apr. 1900 (vol. 24) which contains a history of the journal and the club; Victor Meric, 'Mascuraud', in *Les Hommes du Jour* (12 Mar. 1910), no. 112; Paul Reynaud, *Waldeck-Rousseau* (1913), for his authoritarian reputation.

functions: in Paris alone they had 511 chapels as against 76 parish churches; in France they ran 49 of the 87 grand seminaries which were training the new parochial clergy.[1] Waldeck-Rousseau's aim then was not to abolish all congregations, but to bring them as far as possible within the fold of the episcopal hierarchy, virtually to secularise them. Waldeck-Rousseau brought forward a bill on associations requiring congregations to be authorised by the Conseil d'État, and laying it down as a condition that they should accept the jurisdiction of the bishop. Certain orders would of course never do this, and Waldeck-Rousseau definitely intended to evict the particularly intransigent ones, like the Assumptionists and the Jesuits with whom no compromise was possible. (One of his first acts indeed had been to prosecute the Assumptionists as an illegal association and the courts had declared them dissolved in January 1900.) Altogether 215 congregations, out of 830, preferred not to seek authorisation and formally dissolved themselves in order to escape the law. Waldeck-Rousseau, persevering as ever, issued instructions that secularisations would not be recognised unless the former monks placed themselves under the authority of their bishops.

Nothing worked out as Waldeck-Rousseau planned. The deputies added a clause to his bill forbidding members of unauthorised congregations to teach at all. This attack on the Catholic schools precipitated matters and made quite impossible any compromise with the bishops. Another addition required the congregations to be authorised by parliament, not by the Conseil d'État, and so Waldeck-Rousseau lost control over his schemes.

Waldeck-Rousseau had come to power at the head of a government of republican defence but he never succeeded in turning it into one of republican union. The republican leaders refused to join it, in the same way as they had refused to join Gambetta's great ministry of 1881: Waldeck-Rousseau's ambition to be a 'real' prime minister was incompatible with his having over-powerful colleagues. In consequence two of his ministers (Caillaux, finances, and Baudin, public works) had been deputies for only one year; another (Decrais, colonies) was a former prefect and ambassador of Orleanist origins, who had only been elected to parliament in 1897. His main adviser was the minister of war, General de Gallifet, famous for his repression of the Commune.

So, far from uniting all moderates, Waldeck-Rousseau split them. When voted into office in 1899 he was opposed by the right, the nationalists, most of the progressists and some 30 radicals. He had the support of only 61 moderates, and survived thanks to 173 radicals and 21 socialist votes. Waldeck-Rousseau had little skill in the management of men, and for all his dominating personality, found himself carried away by the left, whom he disliked but on whom he depended. It was he, not the left, who was duped. He virtually admitted as much when he resigned after increasing his majority in 1902, saying it was too large. He advised the formation of a radical government. Perhaps he hoped to give the radicals a chance of discrediting themselves, in the expectation that he might then return to power at the head of a moderate party of which he could be the real leader. He suggested that Combes should succeed him. Combes at once proceeded to destroy his work. Waldeck-Rousseau died in 1904 protesting against the consequences of his own political career.[1]

It is against this background of deadlock and stalemate that one should judge the significance of the Dreyfus Affair. It is frequently said that the case of the obscure Jewish army staff captain who was wrongly convicted of handing military secrets to the Germans, and who, because of the opposition of the army, the nationalists and the clericals, was never able to get the verdict reversed, split the country into two. On the one hand, the Dreyfusards are seen as standing for justice and for the individual, demanding his acquittal whatever reasons of state or military prestige stood in the way. They appear as heirs of the eighteenth-century movement of individualism and liberty. Against them were the army, devoted to order, hierarchy, obedience, possessing a different set of values from the republicans, with Catholic officers perpetuating the ideals of the *ancien régime*. Against them also were the anti-Semites, who

---

[1] Sorlin, op. cit., gives a full bibliography. For a more laudatory view of Waldeck see Henry Leyret, *Waldeck-Rousseau et la Troisième République 1869–1889* (1908).

saw in the Dreyfus case an enormous Jewish conspiracy, backed by Protestants—for the Dreyfusards included a lot of both— undermining the integrity of the nation. The clergy took up this cry and the hierarchy refrained from condemning them. However, the matter is far more complicated. The truth about this case has not been fully established, and almost every year a new theory is produced to explain its mysteries. Dreyfus was not guilty but it is not known who was, and the discovery that a forgery to help convict him was concocted by an over-zealous officer, who later committed suicide, does not solve the question of who the traitor was. The suggestion that the government and the army tried to suppress further investigations, in the name of the national interest, is only partly true: repeated inquiries and new trials were ordered, but the truth was so complicated that no obvious course of action emerged. The refusal to release Dreyfus, even when it became clear that his conviction was debatable, to say the least, shows not a reactionary conspiracy, for those in power were far from united, but rather two more fundamental factors.

It was difficult to be rational when all the facts were not known and nearly everybody knew only some of the facts; the conviction was upheld on the general circumstances of the case, and people were variously affected by these. Once they had formed their opinion, they found it difficult to change it, because the proofs were never conclusive; passions and prejudices repeatedly clouded the issues. It was thus a human, psychological failure more than a political one. Secondly, it was a legal failure. The case showed the limitations of the French legal system, in which the odds are loaded against the accused, and Dreyfus, who was a poor witness, could never refute the circumstantial evidence which made him a more or less plausible culprit, particularly in the atmosphere of the time, when spies were seen on every side.

The defence of Dreyfus was taken up by a number of distinguished intellectuals, who presented his case as the same one for which the French Revolution had been fought, and themselves as defenders of truth against expediency. Certainly, it was due to their insistence and sometimes courageous agitation that an innocent man was released. But one cannot accept completely their version of the matter. The Dreyfusards were

not all inspired simply by a passion for justice. There were
a large number, Boulangists among them, happy to seize this
new occasion to fight the established system. They, for their
part, made accusations almost as wild as their opponents did,
without adequate proof, even if they did present them in the
name of 'science'. Their *esprit de corps* was probably stronger
than that in the army they attacked, which was much more
socially diverse than they imagined. As experts trying to
identify the criminal through examination of different hand-
writings, they showed the limitations and divisions of science.
The battle for Dreyfus was part of a battle against clericalism
for many people, as much if not more than for individual liberty;
the claim of the Dreyfusards that they were the representatives
of liberalism was hardly borne out by their willingness to
persecute Catholics.

The Dreyfus affair was important, perhaps above all else,
in giving the intellectuals a sense of their mission, and in
confirming their importance. The politics of the nineties, as
has been seen, were dominated by a desire to escape from the
traditions and divisions of the past. The intellectuals claimed
that they were clarifying issues when they insisted that the
French could not escape, that they were inexorably divided by
the Revolution, between those who accepted and those who
rejected its principles. It may be claimed that they set France
back thirty years by this, refusing to let it go forward to the
solution of the problems of the day. One result of the Dreyfus
case was the resurrection of the question of Church and state
and the persecution of the congregations. It is curious that
socialist historians have continued to accept and transmit so
much of the mythology of this period. The mass of the people
were not interested by Dreyfus.[1] He was hardly mentioned at
all in the election of 1898, which was fought, if anything, on
the issue of the price of bread, which had just rocketed because
of a bad harvest, despite the temporary duty-free importation
of wheat allowed by 'Méline Pain-cher'. The case did indeed
serve the purpose of freeing the socialists of their anti-Semitism,
and turning this into an exclusively right-wing phenomenon;

[1] On the election of 1902, see Claude Levy, 'La Presse de province et les
élections de 1902: l'exemple de la Haute-Saône', *Revue d'histoire moderne et contemporaine* (1961), 169–98.

but it also exacerbated anti-Semitism and chauvinism into far larger proportions. It was one of the great failures of the republic, precisely because it impeded advance beyond the disputes of the nineteenth century.[1]

[1] Joseph Reinach, *Histoire de l'affaire Dreyfus* (1901, 7 vols), the fullest Dreyfusard account; Douglas Johnson, *France and the Dreyfus case* (1966), the most judicious and perceptive study; Roderick Kedward, *The Dreyfus Affair* (1965), contains selected documents, which very effectively bring the passions back to life, with penetrating comments by the editor. The bibliography on this subject is enormous: good guides will be found in these last two books and in L. Lipschutz, *Une Bibliothèque Dreyfusienne* (1970). For general deflation, see Georges Sorel, *La Révolution Dreyfusienne* (1911, 2nd edition); for the intellectual view, the lively account by Léon Blum, *Souvenirs sur l'Affaire* (1935). Modern French studies include M. Baumont, *Aux sources de l'Affaire* (1959), F. Miquel, *L'Affaire Dreyfus* (1961), M. Thomas, *L'Affaire sans Dreyfus* (1961).

22. Radicalism

RADICALISM was one of the main pillars of the Third Republic. It was, however, an extremely contradictory, many-sided and complicated force. Its partisans preached doctrines they did not implement. They claimed to speak in the name of reason, logic and principle; they divided the country clearly into those who stood for progress and those who were against it, but they were constantly allying with their supposed enemies, temporising, compromising and muddling through. They incarnated so many of the ambivalences to be found in French society that they are exceptionally difficult to characterise precisely. It might be best, therefore, to examine them not through their vague political programmes but through two of their leaders—Combes and Clemenceau. This will make possible an investigation, in concrete terms, of two essential aspects of their work: the separation of Church and state and their treatment of the social problem.

Émile Combes (1835–1921), radical prime minister from 1902 to 1905, described himself as 'short in stature, with a common face and a common appearance. I looked a perfectly ordinary man and indeed I was a perfectly ordinary man for the crowds.' His father had been a peasant who had also engaged in tailoring and kept a small wine shop. Through the patronage of an ecclesiastical relation, he was admitted into the local church seminary. His Superior decided that he did not have the vocation to be a monk, so he was instead appointed a teacher in a Church secondary school. In later years, when he became a leading enemy of the Catholics, and was denounced for turning against his benefactors, he replied that as the son of a poor man, he had had to obtain his education where he could find it. He had worked without salary for his first year as a teacher and so, he said, he had paid his debt—a common enough attitude towards Church education, perhaps, for the majority of the Church's pupils never took holy orders. This early background certainly made Combes cynical about why

men of his own class entered the Church. Most religious vocations, he claimed, resulted from a very practical view of life:
young peasants saw in the congregations an easier, more agreeable life than any to be found in their own world. He had no
fear that in attacking their privileges he was attacking anything
holy. But though he was a renegade, the imprint of his early
education was firmly stamped upon his political work. His
doctoral thesis on Thomas Aquinas had attacked the saint for
his liberalism; his Latin thesis on St. Bernard and Abelard had
severely criticised modernistic ideas. Both revealed him as a
firm ultramontane, a militant, it was even said, who would not
hesitate to re-establish the Inquisition. He was equally extreme
when he changed sides. He was always intolerant and saw
issues in clear-cut terms. He transferred to politics something of
that obsessive passion first kindled by the Albigensian heretics
of his native Tarn and not totally extinct.

He was also determined to get on in life. While a teacher in
the Catholic school at Pons (Charente), receiving a salary of
3,000 francs (£120) per annum, he made a judicious marriage
with the daughter of the local novelty merchant, who brought
him a dowry of 70,000 francs (£2,800). Her mother insisted,
however, that as a teacher he was not quite worthy of his bride.
He therefore went to Paris and, keeping his family by giving
private lessons, he studied medicine. Six years later, having
qualified as a doctor, he returned to Pons. For his first ten years
he earned much the same as he had done as a schoolmaster,
but as rivals died off and he built up his practice, his income
rose to £400–480 per annum.

Combes quickly entered republican politics in Pons. He
became a municipal councillor in 1869 and mayor in 1874,
retaining this office (apart from a temporary dismissal by the
conservative government of 1876) till his death. He acquired
considerable popularity for the improvements he carried out in
the town and he developed electioneering skills to rival the
Bonapartist Jolibois, the Grand Elector of Charente. He knew
every one of his electors in Pons and memorised a great deal of
personal details about the inhabitants of the whole parliamentary
constituency. Twenty years later he could still recite, without
hesitation, the exact numerical results of every local contest in
the region. In 1885 he was elected a senator. He organised

a group, the *gauche démocratique*. In recognition of his acumen at political manœuvring and his zeal in the service of the radical cause, he was elected a vice-president of the senate; and in 1895 he was briefly minister of education under Bourgeois. He was the senate's *rapporteur* of Waldeck-Rousseau's law on associations and this suggested that he might be a suitable successor to carry out Waldeck's unfinished work. He was expected to be a docile tool, but he carried out the ideas of those who prudently remained behind the scenes with such fanatical zeal that he became the symbol of the anticlerical movement, wildly popular and bitterly hated.

He was not quite what he appeared to be. He was a spiritualist and believed in immortality, but he was far more old-fashioned than Ferry who had also been a spiritualist, for Combes had no faith in the positivism with which Ferry had sought to replace Christianity. He dismissed the teaching of the state primary schools as superficial and narrow and insisted on the continued need for the Church's moral doctrines. Though he rejected the hierarchy and many of the dogmas of Catholicism, he still felt a need for its consolations. The abstract principles and uncertain conclusions of positivism left him uncomfortable and dissatisfied; and he could not do without faith. He found one in a muddled mystical belief in progress as a great force ruling the world according to settled laws, not far different from Voltaire's Great Watchmaker: the legacy of his past revealed itself when he quoted Bossuet to make the point that in such a scheme of things, there was no room for chance. He saw himself, a poor man raised to the heights of power, as the instrument of Progress, chosen to destroy the menace of the congregation. He was not the leader of new forces or of new ideas. He picked up his principal beliefs from Michelet, whom he worshipped as the prophet who had 'lifted a corner of the veil' covering 'the great Secret'. He vaguely hoped science would one day complete the revelation. His great hero in politics was Lamartine, whose speech on taking office on 24 February 1848 he used to declaim repeatedly for the edification of his friends.[1]

He was a model of bourgeois domestic virtue. He adored his family and wrote poems to celebrate its anniversaries. He handed

---

[1] Émile Combes, *Mon Ministère: mémoires 1902–5* (1956), 33–5; cf. Léopold Marcellin, 'Émile Combes et le combisme', *Revue universelle* (1 Oct. 1923), 65.

over his earnings to his wife, who paid all the bills and gave him 35 francs a month (£1·40) as pocket money, which he would partly use to buy books on the stalls on the *quais*. Before setting out on a journey, he would arm himself with small coins to enable him to avoid giving excessive tips. He liked to economise on paper, and wrote so small as to get 3,600 words on to a single page. He seldom entertained, and never went to the theatre or the café, saying he had not been able to afford these as a young man and was too old to learn to enjoy them. He was a teetotaller, though at public banquets he drank reddened water so as to offend no one. In the evening he studied languages; having got through Spanish, Italian, English and German, he was learning Russian when he was prime minister. At sixty he learned to ride a bicycle, regretting that he had not done so earlier, and so been spared the expense of a carriage. His son, however, did not inherit these characteristics: he married an American heiress, Miss Cutler, and lived in great style.[1]

Combes began as a figure-head prime minister. In 1902 it was in fact the *Délégation des Gauches* which took power. His name was only used to characterise the new situation. 'Combisme' came to mean political partisanship carried to extremes, but it was the rise of new organisations that made this possible. In 1901 an Action Committee for Republican Reform had been created, to fight the coming election. The republican, radical and radical-socialist groups, while keeping their individual labels, agreed to co-operate in the elections, and so between them won thirty-five more seats. Whereas Waldeck-Rousseau could never be certain of getting a majority, Combes, after 1902, could, and this majority was held together for him by hidden party managers. The origin of the *Délégation des Gauches* goes back to 1893, when it had begun as a loose combination of groups, but now it took over the leadership of parliament, and it organised the majority for Combes, so that, freed from the need to bargain for votes, he could concentrate on carrying out its legislative programme. Each member of the *Délégation* represented about ten deputies: seven were moderates, eight radicals, six radical-socialists, and five socialists. The astute, if somewhat pompous, radical Sarrien was its president, but the

[1] Yvon Lapaguellerie, *Émile Combes* (1929).

real direction came from that master of compromise, the socialist leader Jaurès, who time and again saved the majority from disintegration and the ministry from collapse. The function of the *Délégation* was to find acceptable formulae on which all four groups could agree—no easy task, in view of the diametrically opposed views of moderates and socialists. Anticlericalism was one thing they could agree on. The socialists realised they could not hope to achieve their reforms until the Church question had been got out of the way. Just as Waldeck-Rousseau was a moderate carrying out a radical programme, so Combes was a radical egged on by the socialists. Jaurès, significantly elected one of the vice-presidents of the chamber, became in fact the secret 'leader of the house'. He frequently drafted motions to satisfy all sides, and then had them recopied by someone else, lest his writing should be recognised and his too frequent direction resented. Combes, however, readily accepted the leadership of the *Délégation*. He tried even to establish one in the senate, but Waldeck-Rousseau, with his fondness for authoritarian rule, defeated him, denouncing it as a 'dangerous method, which tends to place government not in the hands of ministries but in that of political groups.'[1]

Combes's aim was to 'republicanise' the administration, the army and the Church. He issued a circular urging the prefects to reserve 'the favours of the republic' for the friends of the parliamentary majority. A 'delegate' was appointed for each canton to watch over the distribution of these favours. The partisanship of the civil service was accentuated. Combes's son Edgar, as secretary-general of the ministry of the interior, declared that he was determined to expel the reactionary prefects and that he would reserve decorations for political services. Combes surrounded himself with the largest retinue of political acolytes any ministry had seen: fifteen *chefs de bureau* and eighteen *attachés*.[2] The Freemasons supplied the ministry of war with information about the political and religious beliefs of officers, to ensure that only republican ones should be promoted.

Combism has been called 'Bonapartism, minus the glory'. The foundations for such extremism did not exist. Combism

[1] R. A. Winnacker, 'The Délégation des Gauches', *Journal of Modern History* (1937), 449–70.
[2] Abel Combarieu, *Sept Ans à l'Élysée avec le président Émile Loubet* (1932), 206–7.

was based on compromises, and these could not survive the strain. Combes's increasing popularity among the anticlericals in the country, his unrealistic sense of mission, and his increasing lack of tact, alienated more and more of the political leaders. The moderates became worried at the excessive influence of the socialists in the framing of policy; the *affaire des fiches* (the revelation of the army's use of Freemasons' notes on the political and religious views of officers) gave them the opportunity to break away. In 1905 the decision of the International at Amsterdam to forbid socialist participation in bourgeois governments compelled Jaurès to withdraw from the *Délégation* and thus the temporary union of the centre and left was ended. It lasted long enough, however, to make possible the carrying out of the separation of the Church and state.

The separation is remarkable for the very great difference between what it was intended to do and what it in fact achieved. Most republicans—from the time when Gambetta issued his Belleville programme in 1869—had demanded the separation but they had never found it convenient to carry this out when they won power, because they found they could exert more control over the Church through the concordat. The separation was now passed in something like a fit of temper after the Dreyfus Case, in retaliation against the Catholics' violence.[1]

Whereas Waldeck-Rousseau had planned to bring the religious congregations under state control, Combes transformed his 1901 law on associations so as to effect the complete dissolution of the monasteries. He spared only five orders, politically useful because they engaged in missionary work in the colonies, or harmless like the silent Trappists. All the others were declared illegal. Their property, estimated to be worth 1,071 million francs, was confiscated, to be used to finance the workers' pensions scheme. Their numerous chapels were ordered to be closed, on the ground that the 38,000 secular churches in the country were enough for their needs. Above all, an attempt was made to shut down all their schools, and to forbid them to teach in other schools: their threat to the moral unity of the

---

[1] Dr. M. J. M. Larkin is writing a book on the separation. See meanwhile his articles in the *Journal of Modern History*, 36 (1964), 298–317, *Historical Journal*, 4 (1961), 97–103, *English Historical Review*, 81 (1966), 717–40.

nation would thus be ended. Jules Ferry's Article Seven rejected in 1879 was at last passed by Combes.

In practice the dissolution was far less effective than was intended. Though a large number of the regulars went abroad, particularly to Belgium, most of them simply turned themselves into secular priests and continued their old work in a new costume. The Church secondary schools were closed down easily enough but the primary ones frequently could not be, because in a great many villages there was no alternative school. Enormous funds and vast numbers of new state teachers would have been needed to replace them. The state therefore decided to close them only gradually over a period of ten years; so in practice the majority survived. Again, the congregations' 'milliard' somehow evaporated. This sum was probably a gross overestimate, because it ignored debts and mortgages: the congregations were not all as prosperous as was believed; but in any case the state obtained little of whatever wealth they did possess. In order to make the liquidation appear impartial, it was carried out by the courts, instead of by the administration. The result was that much of the money was swallowed up in lawyers' fees and expenses. (Millerand is said to have made a lot as legal representative of various congregations.) The sale of their property was inefficiently and frequently dishonestly carried out. The Chartreuse, the source of the well-known liqueur, valued at 10 million francs, for tax purposes, and paying 270,000 francs a year in taxes, was sold for 629,100 to Cusenier, a rival maker of liqueur, who had, it was said, bribed the liquidator. One of these liquidators, Duez, was arrested and condemned, confessing to having extracted at least 6 million francs from the congregations. Whereas in the first Revolution the property of the Church was bought by people with money, the dissolution in 1902–5 seems to have benefited people who could make friends in the right places. The whole operation is shrouded in obscurity. The dissolution has had many books written about it, but all from the political and legal point of view. Its economic history and its practical consequences have still to be studied.[1]

The same is true, to a lesser extent, of the separation of

[1] A. Latreille, J. R. Palanque, E. Delaruelle and R. Remond, *Histoire du catholicisme en France* (1962), Book 4, contains a good summary of research to that date; J. M. Mayeur, *La Séparation de l'Église et de l'État* (1965), for extracts from the debates.

Church and state. Here again Combes did not achieve all he set out to do. His main work was to start a quarrel with the papacy, break off diplomatic relations and start legislation for ending the concordat. However, he fell from power before this was carried out and the separation as finally arranged was far more liberal than he had intended. Combes's own bill—which was not passed—would not have effected a real separation at all. The Church would have lost its privileges, but the state would have kept the right to interfere in its affairs; it would have leased the churches to each parish on renewable ten-year leases, 'according to its needs'. Combes would also have used the separation to destroy the unity of the Church, for he would have forbidden parishes to form unions extending beyond one department. Supporting Combes there were some men of Protestant origin who saw in the separation an opportunity to effect a second reformation, to encourage the growth of schismatic sects, so that the power of popes and bishops would disintegrate. Méjan, the permanent head of the *ministère des cultes*, was the son and brother of Protestant pastors and hoped that the separation would produce an internal spiritual revival or reformation of the churches. But he wanted a liberal law allowing freedom to worship, for he believed the French nation was, like himself, a nation of believers.[1] The extremists who wanted to destroy religion as such were a minority. The radical Allard declared: 'We are fighting religion and all religions, religious feeling and all religious dogmas . . . Offspring of Judaism, the Christian religion is a scourge which has wrought such havoc on humanity that it can be compared only to alcoholism.' But the men with views like his never won power. Ferdinand Buisson, president of the chamber's commission on separation, and one of the radical leaders, made it clear that he was in favour of liberty for the Church.[2]

A settlement designed to be widely acceptable was provided by Aristide Briand, a young socialist who had only just entered parliament. After having advocated revolution and the general

---

[1] L. V. Méjan, *La Séparation des églises et de l'État* (1959), an important thesis based on Méjan's private papers. On the Protestants, see the attacks by Ernest Renauld, *Le Péril protestant* (1899), and *La Conquête protestante* (1900), which gives names.

[2] F. Buisson, 'La Crise de l'anticléricalisme', *Revue politique et parlementaire*, 38 (Oct. 1903), 5–32. Louis Capéran, *Histoire contemporaine de la laïcité française* (1957–61), and *L'Invasion laïque* (1935).

strike, he now suddenly emerged as the apostle of conciliation towards the Church. It needed a man from outside to sense the changing atmosphere. The radical majority which had only recently applauded the violence of Combes, now approved of Briand's moderation. One of the characteristics of radicalism was that it seldom implemented its doctrines, when it came to deeds rather than words. Clemenceau had already led the way when he had supported the dissolution of the monasteries but had opposed the persecution of the monks and the prohibition against their continuing as teachers. The violence of the polemic was producing a reaction. An interesting inquiry into the 'social, political and religious tendencies of French youth', carried out in June 1901, concluded that a new tolerance was entering French life. This was made up partly of indifference to religion and partly of exhaustion at the perpetual struggles in France. The negative animosities of the anticlericals were ceasing to arouse enthusiasm among many of the young, who were seeking more generous emotional outlets for their energies. They felt they were being burdened with out-of-date quarrels, too old to be of interest or to be capable of solution, and still fomented only by ambitious politicians for whom they felt no respect. A more constructive approach was needed to deal with the divisions of the country, since the moral unity Ferry had sought to establish had so clearly failed.[1]

Combes was thus not representative of the country in 1905 (nor even of his own party for that matter, as his 1848 spiritualism shows). The clash with the Church was brought to a head ten whole years after Dreyfus's conviction, when the paroxysms had already begun to die down. They had not died down enough, however, to allow negotiations with the Church, still less with the papacy. This produced the great snag in Briand's bill, that it was unilateral, was rejected by the pope, and could not be carried out as planned. The interest of the separation is thus twofold: how Briand modified the idea of separation and secondly how Briand's law was, because of the Church's refusal to accept it, itself modified by the force of circumstances in the course of its execution.[2]

[1] Eugène Montfort, 'Les Tendances sociales, politiques et religieuses de la jeunesse française au vingtième siècle', *La Revue*, 37 (15 June 1901), 581–609.
[2] For Briand, see A. Briand, *La Séparation* (1904–5), and *La Séparation, application*

The law of separation ended the state's support of the Church and the 40 million odd francs it had been paying annually to it. Church buildings (which since the Revolution belonged by law to the nation) would continue to be available to the faithful, but provided that in each parish a religious association was formed, consisting of at least seven resident adults, to take over the responsibilities of their upkeep. This was a key provision in the law. Its effect would have been to give laymen a majority in the running of the local churches, for small communes had only one *curé*. It would have been fatal to the hierarchic Catholic organisation. Briand publicly admitted that in freeing the Catholics from the control of the state, he did not wish to 'leave them bound by the discipline of Rome'. The democratic transformation of the Church was his ultimate aim. The associations were forbidden to receive bequests, on the ground that 'religion must not be maintained by the heritage of the dead, but by the voluntary liberalities of the living'. The accumulation of mortmain was forbidden, and the amount of capital each parish association could possess was limited to five times its annual budget. Property left to the Church for purposes not strictly religious—particularly for charitable purposes—was given to the communes to assist the poor in the state's institutions. Priests were forbidden to attack the government or the civil service on pain of fine or imprisonment. The Church was thus disarmed politically. Otherwise, however, every effort was made for the actual act of worship and the administration of the sacraments to continue without difficulty. Pensions would be paid to priests for four years— starting at full salary and gradually falling to half—to enable the faithful to worship in the transitional period until they could finance their priests from their own contributions. In small rural communes, where this would be more difficult, the pensions were extended over eight years. Though the church buildings remained state property, they could be leased to the associations at nominal rents where the municipal council was well disposed. For the first ten years the rent payable for the

du nouveau régime (1909); also L. Crouzil, *Quarante ans de séparation* (Toulouse, 1946).

buildings was in any case limited so as to save Catholicism from immediate extinction in hostile villages.[1]

The liberalism of the Briand law was offered at a price. Most of the bishops of France (and many leading laymen) were willing to pay some of that price, for they had had long experience of making compromises with the state. They argued that the Catholics in Germany had managed to turn an even more rigorous system of associations to their advantage. They accordingly devised a form of association which was inoffensive from the hierarchic point of view, but acceptable to the state and able to benefit from the Separation Law. It would simply manage the property but would not involve lay interference in church government. Pope Pius X, however, embittered by the government's unilateral actions, wished to put an end to the tradition of Gallican compromise and indeed to the independence of the Gallican Church. He believed that firm resistance could destroy the law and that ultimately a restoration similar to that of 1815 would follow these persecutions in the style of 1793. In two encyclicals he condemned both the government's associations and those devised by the bishops. The Catholics, though many of them did so reluctantly, accepted his decision. The law was thus effectively checked at the very outset.

Briand, however, as minister for religions from 1906 to 1910, was able to save much of his policy by preventing the Church from being martyred. 'If the adepts of a religion, whether clergy or laymen, do not wish to form religious associations' he announced, 'they are not, because of that, deprived of the right to practise their religion.' He passed a law (2 January 1907) giving Catholic priests the right to use the churches, and a circular (1 December 1906) pointing out that services could be held in accordance with the law of 1881, which permitted meetings of all kinds, provided only the police were given notice in advance. Briand specially exempted churches from the rule that meetings could not be held after 11 p.m. (so as to allow midnight masses) and he dispensed them from the requirement that the 'meeting' should begin with the election of a chairman and secretary. When the Catholics refused to give notice of their

---

[1] Gustave de Lamarzelle and Henry Taudière, *La Séparation de l'Église et de l'État. Commentaire théorique et pratique de la loi du 9 décembre 1905* (1906); Charles Gide, *La Séparation des églises et de l'État* (Toulouse, 1905).

services to the police, Briand passed another law (28 March 1907) abolishing this requirement. It was this careful avoidance of persecution, this consistent refusal to make matters intolerable to the Catholics, that ensured the relative success for the separation.

The obscure complications of Briand's law, however, required the Catholics to wait and see what would happen, since they could not know how things would change. The law needed interpretation by the courts for its detailed application, and the courts, in a long series of judgements, consistently interpreted it in the Church's favour. They extended the definition of 'place of worship' so widely as even to include the building of a gymnastic society sponsored by the Church. Instead of being narrowly confined to their altars, the priests were enabled to enjoy possession of all the buildings they needed for a full religious life. Indeed, they soon obtained more than just possession. Briand had declared that the *curés* had the right to occupy churches but 'without legal title' (for only associations could have a title). The courts, however, ruled that their right to use churches was a legal one, for it involved legal responsibilities and therefore legal rights. Whereas at first Catholics appeared to have the right to go to church only in the same way as they had the right to go to market, now they were able to sue others for disturbing their use of the churches. The courts even forced recalcitrant mayors to assist the churches. The law of 1905 left the upkeep of the church buildings to the associations, but since these were not founded, the law of 1908 allowed the state, departments and the communes (which legally owned these buildings) to repair them, though it did not compel them to do so. The Conseil d'État in its decisions extended this law so as to allow partial rebuilding, and in 1914 it even compelled a commune whose church had been burnt down to use the insurance money to rebuild it. Communes which granted their churches hidden subsidies, part-time jobs or cheap accommodation for the *curé*, were supported by the courts, and those which tried to interfere in the celebration of services, by requiring the churches to be open or shut at certain hours, had their decrees annulled. The *curé* emerged master of his church, free to organise its worship and access to its services as he pleased. All idea of fomenting schism disappeared: the courts supported only the *curé* approved by the bishop. This attitude of the courts was partly an implementation of the spirit of the separation laws of 1905 and 1907, but it needs some further explanation, for the Conseil d'État under Combes had been violently radical in its treatment of the congregations. The variation in the opinions of the judiciary needs further study. The new moderation, however, was not universal, and men like Doumergue and Viviani protested against it. Anticlericalism was far from dead. In 1912 Chaumié, as minister of education, decreed that priests could not compete in the *agrégation*. Only in 1939 did the Conseil d'État lay it down that a woman could not be refused a job as a primary school teacher on the ground that she had been educated in a religious school.[1]

These legal decisions were made to settle particular disputes. They indicate the triumph of the spirit of conciliation, but they also show the survival of the traditional feud of the mayor and the *curé*. There were very many villages where persistent attempts were made to obstruct and annoy the clergy. Ingenious mayors prosecuted *curés* for habitual mendicancy when they sought gifts from the faithful, for obstruction when they processed through the streets, for disturbing public tranquillity when they rang church bells, and they played innumerable tricks with the keys to the church. But though the feud continued, the law now repeatedly came in to protect the clergy and not the mayor. Such was the paradoxical consequence of the separation. The only real danger that threatened the Catholics was the law that if a church was not used for six months, it could be turned by the village to other purposes. Though the Catholics were able to continue to worship, their refusal to form associations meant that they had no legal method of inheriting the property of the Concordat Church, which was instead 'resumed' by the state. Some 30 to 35 million francs were involved—but once again unknown profiteers must have been the principal beneficiaries. As soon as the state obtained possession, it began

---

[1] Gabriel Le Bras, 'Trente Ans de séparation' in *Chiesa e Stato*, 2 (Milan, 1939), 435–62; René Fontenelle, *L'Échec pratique de la loi du 9 décembre 1905 au regard du culte catholique et les efforts d'adaptation au fait cultuel* (Lille thesis, 1921); Pierre Prugnard, *Les Églises publiques depuis la Séparation* (Paris thesis, 1923); Paul Bureau, 'La Séparation de l'Église et de l'État devant le parlement et les tribunaux', *La Science sociale* (Jan. and Feb. 1912), fascicules 89 and 90.

selling, but it seldom sold at the full value and it seems to have realised only some 10 million francs. It is interesting that there was no property at all to sell in nineteen departments and virtually none in twenty others.[1]

The Church after 1905 reflected this unequal distribution of piety and its clergy became much more unequal when they lost their uniform salaries. The priests in the large towns were frequently better off as a result of the separation. Mgr Delamaire was given two palaces by benefactors, one at Cambrai and one at Lille. The Archbishop of Toulouse built himself a very sumptuous one. On the other hand, the Bishop of Tarentaise moved into a very humble cottage. The rich clergy became richer, the poor ones poorer. Paris, Lyon and Lille soon found they could collect adequate incomes from their parishioners. Twenty-four new churches were built in Paris between 1906 and 1914. The diocese of Le Puy, however, could raise only one-third of the sums it needed for current expenditure. Much depended on the financial acumen of each bishop, for they were left to their own devices. Many placed their funds in Russian bonds, fearing a second confiscation if they bought French ones. Cardinal Richard in Paris abolished luxurious funerals and marriages, urging those who would have paid the high charges to donate these savings instead directly to the Church. This proved to be based on a misjudgement of human nature; the order was soon rescinded and the Church began encouraging elaborate ceremonies, so as to profit from the increased fees. The state's salaries were replaced by the 'denier du culte', a form of ecclesiastical taxation backed by religious sanctions, sanctions which were used also to urge parents to send their children to church schools. Little information, however, is available about the new Church's finances.[2]

One important consequence of the separation was the increase in the power of the pope and the destruction of the independence of the Gallican Church. The pope could now choose his bishops freely and he chose them for some time afterwards—as the French government had long done—for their docility. He forbade them to meet, just as Napoleon had done. While

---

[1] Joseph Filatre, *Étude du droit de retour crée par la loi du 9 décembre 1905. Les biens repris par l'État dans le département du Pas-de-Calais* (Lille thesis, Arras, 1914), 132.

[2] J. de Narfon, *La Séparation des églises et de l'État* (1912), 218–97.

strengthening his hold over them, he reduced their omnipotence over their clergy: after 1910, the ordinary *curé* ceased to
be liable to be dismissed at will by his bishop. The lower clergy
certainly needed to have their position improved, for the separation produced an accentuation in the fall in recruitment.
The Church could no longer offer an assured salary and a pension. On the other hand, the clergy gained greatly in vitality
when they ceased to be part of the state and associated with
its bureaucratic complacency. Catholicism was certainly not
annihilated.

The separation was completed in 1921 when diplomatic
relations between France and the Holy See were resumed from
obvious political convenience. Rome now accepted a new form
of association, diocesan in form, controlled by the bishops, with
power and legal right to own property, collect subscriptions
and donations (but unable, until 1940, to receive bequests). The
roundabout subterfuges of forming private companies to build
new churches could thus be abandoned. The clergy were allowed
to form ecclesiastical unions to manage the religious affairs
of the Church, and the education and pensions of priests. The
agreement between the pope and the government was reached
despite vigorous opposition from the rank and file, radicals and
priests alike, for whom compromise was anathema. A new
place for the Church in society now became possible. But the
anticlerical war did not therefore end. There were still grievances: in particular the Church demanded state subsidies for
its schools, resented the limitations on its wealth and regretted
the considerable sums it had forfeited in 1905. The battles of the
past could thus continue, even though most of the issues had
been settled. Men could not change their habits so quickly. It
would take some years for the pope to bring in bishops with
a new outlook; and even longer for a new generation of radicals
to emerge.[1]

The separation of Church and state is usually regarded as
marking the victory of the anticlerical, lay republic, but an
analysis of the way it was carried out, and the results which
followed from it suggest that this is too simple a view. On the

---

[1] A very good guide to this period is Harry W. Paul, *The Second Ralliement: The
Rapprochement between Church and State in France in the Twentieth Century* (Washington,
D.C., 1967).

surface, the struggle of radicals against clericals was the dominant theme, and that struggle continued in party programmes.
But beneath the surface, it was conciliation which triumphed.
The relation between these two levels of consciousness is what
provides the key to the apparent contradictions. French politics
can become clearer if one investigates not simply what the
parties demanded, but also the seemingly incoherent, colourless,
compromising realities which followed from their demands,
and which won general approval even though they were universally attacked. Politics in many ways was a protest against the
facts of life. Historians need to study not just the protests but
also the acceptance of them and how people got by while protesting. In volume 2, an attempt will be made to investigate
further the origins and functions of the activity of protesting.

Clemenceau

The elections of 1906 were a triumph for the radicals who won
247 seats—42 per cent of the total—and who were thus easily
the majority party. The radicals had a long programme of
social legislation which held out the promise of a new era. But
in the next few years it became clear that they had no intention
of implementing it. They proclaimed their belief in progress,
but no longer represented it. They appeared increasingly to
look on reform now as a concession, not as a conquest. Justice
began to interest them less than power; and foreign policy—
revenge for 1870—increasingly preoccupied them. Already
before 1914 radicalism had the makings of an ageing valetu-
dinarian who knew how to look after himself. The interesting
question is why it remained alive till 1940.

Clemenceau's ministry (1906–9) can be taken as a turning-
point. He came to power with a programme of no fewer than
seventeen reforms which suggested that at last, now that the
monarchist and clerical obstacles had been eliminated,
Gambetta's radical administrative and social reforms, proclaimed at Belleville in 1869, would be implemented. But
though his ministry lasted two and three-quarters years,
Clemenceau achieved virtually nothing, and on the contrary
distinguished himself for the violence of his repression of all
opposition. The reasons for this are all the more worth dis-

covering because Clemenceau had for long been the principal advocate of radical reform, against opportunism. What made him change? He took good care to see that posterity should not know. During his retirement, he systematically destroyed his papers. No full biography of him exists and it will never be possible to write one. Enough is known, however, to make one guess that there was no real change in him in 1906. His ministry revealed the latent sterility of his life, as it did that of the radicals; it showed up the contradictions in both.

Georges Clemenceau (1841–1929), who for so long had made himself the partisan of justice for the people, was of noble stock. His father was the Chevalier Clemenceau de la Clemencière and lived in a moated medieval château in the Vendée. But the family were rebels against their class and were leaders of the small minority which opposed the royalists for which the west was famous. One of them voted in the Convention for Louis XVI's death. For at least three generations they practised as doctors as well as being country gentlemen: this marked their link with the bourgeoisie and the people, but they remained at war with their own society. There seems to have been some deep resentment in the family, which suggests that part of Clemenceau's hostility to the world has a hereditary explanation. His father, at any rate, is known to have been a dour misanthrope with vigorous hatreds and a mocking, revengeful irony, who led a lone and brooding existence among the Vendée woods;[1] he too was a republican (a friend of Michelet and Blanqui) and arrested as such by Napoleon III. The violent hatreds of his father and the romantic destructiveness of Blanqui— whom Clemenceau also greatly admired—were the principal inheritance of his youth.[2] His own training as a doctor—he never practised—gave him an interest in science and particularly in the theory of evolution which provided a doctrinal basis for this bitter view of life. The struggle for survival, violence, carnage was the law of nature, applicable equally to man as to all living things. Wisdom consisted in accepting this and realising that peace was unlikely. Whereas Léon Bourgeois

[1] Gustave Geffroy, *Clemenceau* (1918), 27–9. This book is by one of Clemenceau's best friends—the biographer and friend of Blanqui too.

[2] Fernand Neuray, *Entretiens avec Clemenceau* (1930), 43–4; General H. Mordacq, *Clemenceau* (1939), an interesting study of his character by an admiring but not uncritical subordinate.

and the solidarists drew an optimistic conclusion from the
discoveries of science, Clemenceau declared that he, as a
pessimist, saw in nature not co-operation but conflict.[1] He did
not therefore reject solidarism. Selfishness produced in men 'the
need to be called and later the need to feel good, generous,
helpful'. Altruism thus develops, but in perpetual conflict with
egoism; from this conflict comes all progress. The function of
politicians was to stimulate this altruism and develop justice
from it, but politics was essentially a struggle against the laws
of nature, to light up an ideal in 'the sombre cosmos where
everything is linked by an iron law'. 'To contain conquering
[nature], to raise up the conquered, appears to be the first duty
of him who understands the supreme law. Let us preach peace,
since there is only battle; justice, since iniquity surrounds us;
goodness, since hate flourishes. Above all, let us act, for merit
lies in protesting by action against the fatal law of the fall of the
weak.'[2]

Clemenceau felt alone in the world. An unhappy marriage—
significantly with an American—soon ended in separation.
He gave himself up entirely to politics, which enabled him to
fight the world. He made a virtue out of his loneliness. He became a champion of radical individualism, but with this difference, that he sought to protect his independence by a vigorous
aggressiveness. His unhappy experience of the Commune, when
as mayor of the eighteenth *arrondissement* he had in vain sought
to avert the conflict, left terrible memories and the consciousness
that he had a greater gift for making enemies than friends.[3] He
devoted his long parliamentary career (he was first elected a
deputy in 1871) to attacking the republicans for their inadequacies: he broke with Gambetta and became the leading
figure in the radical opposition. He carried radicalism to
extremes, into radical socialism. In a vague way he claimed he
was a socialist, though he believed neither in revolution, nor
in general nationalisation nor in Marxism. When asked by
Jaurès what his programme was, he replied; 'You have it in
your pocket: you stole it from me.' The only difference was,
he claimed, that he wished to achieve it more gradually. His

---

[1] G. Clemenceau, 'Sur la démocratie', *Neuf Conférences rapportées par Maurice
Ségard* (1930) [Lectures given in 1910], 128.

[2] Id., *La Mêlée sociale* (1895), preface, xlii, and *passim*.

[3] Id., *Sur la démocratie* (1930), 17.

programme can be summarised more accurately in the words
justice and *patrie*. It was in their name that he demanded social
reform, that he opposed colonial expeditions which frittered
away the national resources, that he attacked Ferry so bitterly
and that he prevented him from being elected president of the
republic. But if examined with care, his ideas are seen to be
full of contradictions, for he could not resist attacking even
them. Though he claimed to be the great defender of the
French Revolution, he despised the Convention as 'an assembly
of cowards who killed each other from fear'.[1] Though he
championed democracy, he spoke contemptuously of the
masses and insisted on the importance of élites (open ones, it is
true) to lead them.[2] He argued that parties were essential, but
he devoted himself to attacking their corruption and bankruptcy.[3] He was the most passionate partisan of a single
chamber, but he ended up a satisfied senator. His view of himself as the representative of modernity contrasted strangely
with his belief that political problems had not changed much
since the Greeks. Demosthenes, if anybody, was his hero.[4] The
real key to his career is to be found in his temperament rather
than in a doctrine. He was essentially a fighter. He took up the
case of Dreyfus, partly, it is true, because he believed in his
innocence but much more because it was just the kind of battle
that he loved, against everybody. When he urged Anatole
France to join him in 1897 in support of Dreyfus he said, 'We
shall be alone. We shall have all the world against us', and he
complacently enumerated all the forces which were hostile
to Dreyfus. 'But we shall win', and he repeated the phrase with
pleasure, 'we shall be alone, but we shall win.' 'How many
intellectuals', commented Anatole France, 'has Clemenceau
won by filling them for an instant with his frenzy of courage
and pride?'[5] Clemenceau admitted that he enjoyed fighting;
peace, he said, would never exist among men. Men were inevitably selfish, biased, unfaithful, ambitious, passionate.[6] His
only novel, called *The Strongest*, about the struggle for power and

---

[1] Georges Wormser, *La République de Clemenceau* (1961), 84.
[2] Georges Clemenceau, *Sur la démocratie* (1930), 60–2.
[3] Id., *Dans les champs du pouvoir* (1913), 400.
[4] Id., *Démosthène* (1926).   [5] J. Caillaux, *Mes Mémoires*, 1 (1942), 301.
[6] A. G. Gola, préfet honoraire, *Clemenceau et son sous-préfet* (Fontenay-le-Comte,
1937), 35, 54. (Reports of conversations with him.)

a frustrated affection, showed his preoccupation with human conflict and the little hope he placed in harmony or in love.[1] That is why he was the right man to lead France to victory in 1917. He knew how to fight, not how to yield. But his choice as prime minister in 1906 was less happy.

Clemenceau's nickname was The Tiger. This conveyed his wild destructiveness but it should not mislead into suggesting that he was a mass of strength. He was a small man and after middle age fat as well as short, undistinguished. He was extremely nervous and given to the most profound depression, which he relieved by violent outbursts of rage. Like Bismarck (another mythical man of iron, who spoke with a squeaky voice) Clemenceau was no thunderer. He suffered from an asthmatic condition which compelled him to avoid forcing his tone, so as to prevent fits of coughing. His speech was sharp, short, jerky; Anatole France called him 'the most nervous orator of his time'. He made few gestures, and indeed often spoke with his hands in his pockets. He was more at home in the Vendée than in Paris. He loved the solitary sports of riding and shooting. In old age he started doing gymnastics, for he took great care of his health. He consumed a lot of medicine, frequently consulted doctors and went regularly to Vichy and Carlsbad. In 1906 he was already an old man—sixty-five and out of date, for he stood on the left from cussedness rather than conviction. He was impulsive, impatient, obstinate; he could not do things by halves; he was more a bull than a tiger. Jaurès called him an 'evil man'.[2] They were certainly exact opposites.

Clemenceau derived his influence from his energy. He was an unsuppressable, eternal duellist (in deed, as well as in speech). He had few friends in parliament but he was a deadly opponent. His biting invective seldom missed its mark. He could manipulate his anger with precision. He could display 'now an aggressive and contemptuous ill temper, now an easy manner at once bantering, familiar and abrupt. He spoke like a man who would brook no restraint.'[3] His enmities were fiery and implac-

---

[1] G. Clemenceau, *Les Plus Forts* (1898). Cf. Edmond Gosse, 'The Writings of M. Clemenceau', *Edinburgh Review*, 229 (Apr. 1919), 253–70.

[2] Daniel Ligon, 'Jaurès au Parlement', in *Jean Jaurès présenté par V. Auriol* (1962), 144, and L. Blum, *Jean Jaurès* (1937), 18.

[3] A French contributor, 'M. Jaurès and M. Clemenceau', in *The Dublin Review* (Apr. 1906), 311–17.

able. He was a man not of steel, but of fire. In the country he aroused extreme opinions. He had some difficulty in keeping his seat, lost it twice and in the end retired to the safer senate. His constituents, though proud of his notoriety, complained that he seldom visited them and never got them jobs or favours. When he came, his speeches were great oratorical successes. His opponents aimed not at refuting him, but only at stopping him from speaking. Ernest Judet, editor of *Le Petit Journal* (with a circulation of a million), one of his bitterest enemies, vowed in 1893 that he would lose him his seat. He spent considerable sums hiring Piedmontese hecklers from Marseille to follow him around on his electoral campaign, shouting 'Aoh yes', meaning he was sold to England. A forgery was published showing he was an English spy. Thousands of free copies of *Le Petit Journal* were distributed with a cartoon of him juggling with sacks of sterling. A league of his enemies was formed against him. He was narrowly defeated. This shows the nature of the feelings he roused.[1]

His private life, as recently revealed by his grandson, helps to explain the bitterness of his politics.[2] He had a gay time with women, he was fond of actresses, but he would not tolerate any liberty in his wife. He obtained his divorce from her by taking a policeman with him to catch her in a compromising situation. He had her convicted to fifteen days imprisonment for adultery, and then expelled from the country like a common criminal. He destroyed the bust, the photographs and drawings he and his three children had of her. All the children had marriages as unhappy as his own, with a quite exceptional record of divorces. His son, Michel, after being expelled from various schools, finally completed his education in Zurich, and was then discreetly sent to work in Hungary. In 1905, he returned to France and prospered as a businessman on government contracts—which ended in a scandal. He was exiled to the Vendée; Clemenceau refused to speak to him for several years, but relented when he joined up in the war. Later he prospered again as the agent in France for Vickers-Armstrong armaments.

[1] Yves Malartie, 'Comment Clemenceau fut battu aux élections législatives à Draguignan en 1893', in *Provence historique* (1962), 112–38.
[2] Georges Gatineau-Clemenceau, *Des pattes du tigre aux griffes du destin* (1961).

He divorced his Hungarian wife to marry a secretary thirty years younger than himself; after another divorce he married the widow of a Californian oil magnate. Both of Michel's sons became millionaires: one married the daughter of a Jewish diamond merchant and the other (after a divorce with a descendant of Sarah Bernhardt) the heiress of the New Orleans Grunewald fortune. His direct descendants are Americans. Clemenceau's two daughters had unhappy lives. The husband of one shot himself after finding her committing adultery and, to the fury of Clemenceau, he left a will appointing Poincaré, the latter's rival, as guardian of his son (whose marriage also ended in divorce). The second daughter was deserted by her husband. Clemenceau was severe and tyrannical towards his family. Though he was capable of joviality and kindness, these moods alternated rapidly and inexplicably with ones which inspired terror. He took good care to see his comfort was not spoilt by anyone. He lived in some style, like the petty aristocrat he was. He was looked after in his fashionable Passy flat by two servants cowed into obedience. He wore English clothes and bought his furniture from Maples. He was very definitely a member of the upper class. His brother Paul, an engineer, made such a considerable fortune from dynamite as to become one of the 'Two Hundred' wealthiest men in France. His brother Albert was a successful barrister—and counsel for Stavisky.[1]

Clemenceau passed only one of the seventeen reforms he promised—the nationalisation of the Western Railway[2]— and this he carried through the senate by only three votes, after posing a vote of confidence. Some suggested that the measure was allowed through not from any reforming zeal but in the hope that the inevitably discouraging results of buying a railway in deficit would save the other companies from nationalisation. It smelt of corruption because the shareholders were grossly over-compensated, after having allowed the track to fall into serious disrepair. There was a definite political gain for the radicals, nevertheless, for they acquired

[1] David Watson of the University of Dundee is writing a biography of Clemenceau. Meanwhile see his articles in *The News Letter*, 6, part 1 (1970), 13–19, and *The Historical Journal* (1971), 201–4.

[2] For the list of promised reforms and Clemenceau's 'ministerial declaration' on taking office, see *Revue politique et parlementaire* (Dec. 1906), 604–8.

a very considerable amount of new patronage in the west, where their influence was weakest.[1]

Clemenceau turned out to be so stern an upholder of the rights of the state that his social policy consisted principally in the savage repression of strikes; and in him the state revealed itself an even greater enemy of the workers than the employers. He became minister of the interior a few days after a terrible explosion in the mines at Courrières when over 1,100 men were killed. In the strike which followed Clemenceau quickly showed how tactless and brutal he was. He went to Lens to address the miners, but he spoke to the Broutchoux extreme union—thus discrediting the more moderate union of Basly. He promised not to send troops, but soon after filled the area with no fewer than 20,000 soldiers—one for every two strikers. A month later, he arrested Griffuelhes and Monatte on the eve of the 1 May demonstrations of the C.G.T. and concentrated 40,000 soldiers in Paris, as though in preparation for a siege. He openly declared war on the C.G.T. 'You are behind a barricade, I am in front of it. Your method is disorder. My duty is to preserve order. My role is to oppose your efforts.'[2] Opposition, rather than negotiation or compromise was indeed his tactic. His use of troops inevitably led to bloodshed. In at least five strikes there was loss of life and on one occasion, at Villeneuve-Saint-Georges, the troops apparently charged the strikers without provocation, killing several in the process. In July 1908, the C.G.T. leaders were again arrested. Labour unrest reached unprecedented heights not because there was so much more of it in total, but because a political issue was made of it and it became a struggle against the government. It even seems that Clemenceau or his subordinates used *agents provocateurs* to stimulate some of this violence. It was argued that he was glad to have enemies on the left to keep the support of the right. In any case, the old days when the republic knew no enemies on the left were clearly over.

When the post-office workers went on strike, Clemenceau at once dismissed 300 of them; when the primary teachers

[1] André Dejean, 'La crise de transports et le matériel roulant des chemins de fer', *Revue politique et parlementaire* (Mar. 1907), 542–64.

[2] Jacques Julliard, *Clemenceau, briseur de grèves* (1965), 23. Deals mainly with the affair of Draveil Villeneuve-Saint-Georges (1908), but generally very instructive on Clemenceau's social policy.

protested their right to form a union, they were treated in the same way. To the objections in parliament, Clemenceau replied that these men were civil servants who had 'put themselves in a state of revolt against the French republic'. The restiveness of the civil servants was indeed a sign that the traditional view of their role, which Clemenceau held, was no longer acceptable to them. They were refusing to be considered any longer as simply instruments of the government, required to be politically loyal, subject to favouritism, nepotism and arbitrary dismissal. Their numbers had increased enormously over the last fifty years; and they claimed, with a flourish of exaggeration, that they formed 10 per cent of the electorate.[1] They were demanding to give up their role of election agents, to be admitted and promoted on merit only, by examination, to have a statute guaranteeing their careers. The radicals had placed in their programme the passing of such a statute, but they were disagreed on its details; they argued inconclusively and were unable to undertake any constructive reform. Clemenceau's policy of obstinacy and repression was clearly a failure: he merely made the C.G.T. revolutionaries into martyrs and won for them the sympathy of more moderate workers who normally did not accept their leadership. Briand and Viviani, the two former socialists in his government, lamented Clemenceau's ruthlessness and shortly before his fall began a new policy of using greater tact. Griffuelhes was released. The election of the more moderate Jouhaux to the leadership of the C.G.T. was the reward of their patience.

Although these dramatic strikes by revolutionary workers created an atmosphere of social crisis, the rebellion of the wine-growers in the south in 1907 was perhaps even more serious. It involved larger numbers and it showed that another pillar of the old 'republic of peasants' was tottering. As has been seen, after the replanting of the south with American roots to replace the vines destroyed by phylloxera, there had been a great expansion of the area devoted to vines. The new plant could be grown on the plains as well as the slopes; it spread further north and it produced higher yields. The land planted with vines in the Aude, for example, increased almost threefold between 1863 and 1900. In the latter year, so great was the over-production of *vin ordinaire* that prices tumbled to a fifth of the normal.

[1] Georges Deherme, *La Crise sociale* (1910), 149.

In a dozen years, land values in Béziers fell by between 30 and 60 per cent. In some villages of Roussillon, such was the poverty that men put on masks and went begging. It was impossible to borrow or sell; labourers were dismissed, tradesmen ruined. The blame was put on the merchants who falsified wine, and on the government which allowed them. Marcelin Albert, a small owner who had been agitating for some years in protest against this crisis, suddenly acquired a tremendous popularity. His mass meetings on Sundays attracted, it is said, a quarter and even half a million people. He was compared to the Biblical Apostles, to the Mahdi. Committees to support him sprang up in every village. Placards declared: 'Death to Clemenceau'. Royalists and socialists secretly fanned the agitation. *Curés* announced the movement would bring the end of the republic. The pressure of the agitators stopped people paying taxes, for fear of mob violence if they did. There were mass resignations of municipalities: one-third of the communes of the Aude, Hérault and Pyrénées-Orientales were left without an administration. Crowds besieged the sub-prefecture of Narbonne and the prefecture of Perpignan, and attempted to burn them down. Troops sent to disperse the crowds mutinied. Clemenceau is usually given credit for his handling of Albert. Albert, terrified by a movement he could no longer control, and by the prospect of arrest, fled to Paris and surrendered to Clemenceau personally. Clemenceau chided him paternally, contemptuously gave him his fare home and told him to make amends by restoring peace. The movement suddenly collapsed. It was not just the train fare, however, that destroyed Albert's popularity overnight. He had lost his nerve before that. His followers were tired of the revolt and the interruption of ordinary life was becoming inconvenient. Parliament rapidly passed a law on falsification to assuage the insurgents (it was soon revealed to be inadequate). Clemenceau sent the mutinous soldiers to a distant outpost in Tunisia. But no fundamental reform was undertaken to remedy the economic problems raised by monoculture in this region; nothing was done to reconcile the interests of the growers and the merchants. Was solidarity just talk?[1]

[1] Maurice Le Blond, *La Crise du Midi* (1907), the fullest study; Paul Hamelle, 'La crise viticole', in *Annales des sciences politiques* (1908), 625–61; André Avignon, 'Marcelin Albert et la presse régionale' (Montpellier D.E.S. mémoire, unpublished, 1964).

The measures avowedly designed to put it into practice were so watered down by reservations and by considerations of economy that they had very little practical effect. Clemenceau's minister of labour, Viviani, tried at first to apply the law of 1906 establishing a six-day week, but yielding to pressure, he soon issued so many circulars granting exceptions as to greatly reduce its value.[1] The workers themselves were hostile to it, because they were not paid for their day off. The application of the law of 14 July 1905, providing assistance to the old and incurable, was likewise, as has been seen, a disappointment. This had been inadequate to begin with: the senate had passed it on condition that aid should be given only to those over seventy who could prove that they were incapable of working, and in order not to discourage thrift, savings should be taken into account before the feeble allocation—of a maximum of 20 francs a month—was given. Few people knew how to claim or how much was due to them: such was the chaos that in 1907 the government abolished the means test. Briand in 1909 tried to clarify the procedure for applying but it still remained complicated and the distribution of aid arbitrary.[2]

Again, the minister of labour, Viviani, got a workers' pensions bill through the chamber, but it was only in 1910, in the ministry of Briand, that he passed it through the senate; and it was even less successful. Its *rapporteur* said it represented 'not only the greatest financial effort but the greatest and finest reform of the Third Republic'.[3] But there once again the senate had limited its scope, raising the pension age from 60 to 65, and reducing the benefits: those at present aged between 60 and 70 (after which they had a right to assistance under the 1905 law) would get a pension straightaway, even though they had paid no contributions, but the maximum they could receive was only

---

[1] René Wallier, *Le Vingtième Siècle politique: année 1907* (1908), 260–1.

[2] *Recueil des lois, décrets, circulaires etc.* (1908), 42–52 gives the text of the law; p. 32 gives the modifying article 36 of the budget for 1908; ibid. (1909), 258–61, circular of 3 August 1909 on its application. Henri Ripert, 'L'assistance aux vieillards infirmes et incurables et la loi du 14 juillet 1905', *Annales des sciences politiques* (15 May 1906), 289–316, gives a history of the law's passage; Léon de Seilhac, *Revue politique et parlementaire* (Feb. 1907), has some interesting comments on it; L. Bonnevay in P. Astier *et al.*, *L'Œuvre sociale de la Troisième République* (1912), 153–72, has a good chapter on insurance and pensions.

[3] René Samuel and Georges Bonnet-Maury, *Annuaire du Parlement* (for 1910–11), 9 (1911), 114.

100 francs. Amendments became necessary almost at once and an additional law of 1912 reduced the pension age to 60. This could be done because it soon became clear that the scheme would not be fully implemented and its financial implications need not be taken too seriously. The workers objected to paying contributions at all. Ignorance and suspicion of the law resulted in only one-third of those eligible actually paying anything, and they paid less than they were supposed to. The administrative machinery for the law was inadequate and there were long delays before small sums trickled out to pay some of the pensions due.[1]

The first volume of a new *Code du Travail* (first suggested in 1896) was promulgated in 1910, a second in 1912, but this turned out to be a mere compilation of the existing legislation, and contained nothing new. It showed how inadequate the law on labour was, how much of the influence of the *ancien régime*'s compendium of law, Pothier, remained and how the rights of man, propounded in the Civil Code, ignored the rights of workers. A bill for a minimum wage was spurned; the inspection of factories remained a farce; the problem of accidents at work produced only a long parliamentary report but no action.[2]

The most urgently needed reform was that of taxation. Without it, no social programme could be undertaken. Between 1899 and 1909 government expenditure had increased by 18 per cent, but this was only partially met by the increased yield of existing taxation from economic expansion. In 1907 the budget was just balanced, but in the two following years there were deficits. Parliament, dominated by a fear of offending the electorate, voted only one-third of the new taxes that were needed.[3] Increasing use was made of loans. The achievement of the Third Republic was to give France the largest national debt in the world.[4] Now, quite apart from social reform, increased military expenditure on an unprecedented scale

[1] Louis Béjard, *L'Application de la loi sur les retraites ouvrières et paysannes* (Lyon, 1914)—one of the few studies of the practical application of a law, rather than a theoretical juridical thesis.
[2] Georges Renard, *Le Parlement et la législation du travail* (1913), 28.
[3] E. Pelleray, *L'Œuvre financière du parlement de 1906 à 1910* (1910), viii and 8.
[4] Raphaël-Georges Lévy, 'Comparaison des budgets anglais, allemand, russe, ottoman avec le budget français' in *La Politique budgétaire en Europe*, lectures at the École Libre des Sciences Politiques (1910), 257–307; A. Landry and B. Nogaro, *La Crise des finances publiques en France, en Angleterre et en Allemagne* (1914), 121, 241.

made drastic changes in the financial system essential. French taxes were still basically those of the *ancien régime*: the Revolution had done little more than give them new names. The *taille* became the *impôt foncier*, the *capitation* became the *personnelle-mobilière*, the *droits de jurande* were transformed into the *patente*. The stamp duties of the Years III and VII re-established those of 1671. Finally, a law of 1816, reproducing Colbert's ordinances of 1681, revived most of the old indirect taxes. The only innovation with which the Revolution could be credited was the tax on doors and windows, borrowed from England or possibly from Ancient Rome.

The principal reason for the survival of the old taxation system was that it affected things and not men: the freedom of the individual from the inquisitions of the administration was safeguarded, his style of living, not his income, determined what taxes he paid; and these taxes, being clear and definite, gave rise to very little litigation. But they had two overridingly serious defects: they were very unequally distributed and they were inelastic. The amount of land tax paid depended on where one lived, since the amount to be raised was divided among the departments, partly on an estimate of their prosperity made at the time of the Revolution and partly on surviving privileges of the *ancien régime*: the old *pays d'élection* and the *pays d'état* still paid different rates. Corsica, favoured by Napoleon, paid a derisively small amount in land tax; so did the Landes, once poor but far richer since the Second Empire. The whole system survived because periodically adjustments were made to render it tolerable—usually by reducing the taxes of decaying rural departments. But it was a system incapable of meeting sudden emergencies. In 1848, the imposition of 45 *centimes additionnels*—a small increase—was impossible to apply. The war of 1870 produced another crisis, but once again serious reform was avoided. Loans were used to deal with the immediate problem, but when this was seen to be inadequate, a tax of 3 per cent (increased to 4 per cent in 1890) was imposed on stocks and shares. But state bonds were exempted, preferential treatment was given for foreign bonds and no one was required to declare his income. Later, protection was used to raise further revenue. This, however, was the only reform carried out in the nineteenth century, despite the transformation of the country by industrialisation. New sources of wealth remained virtually untapped.

Between 1872 and 1907 no fewer than sixty-five bills were moved to introduce some form of income tax.[1] They had all come to nothing. Clemenceau had promised that the income tax would be the great achievement of his period in office. He appointed Caillaux, a former inspector of finance and the most authoritative advocate of the income tax, to be his finance minister. But he took little interest in the matter himself and the chamber dealt with it very slowly. It was not until 1913, when military service was increased to three years and vast expenditure on armaments made it inevitable, that Caillaux got a section of his proposals through the senate; it was only in 1917, through the inescapable pressure of war, that the income tax as a whole was passed and then it was passed only with numerous limitations. The long struggle to achieve this reform showed how vested interests had come to dominate the republic and how the radicals, far from representing justice, were in fact the greatest coalition of these vested interests. The details of the debates are interesting because they cast light upon archaic prejudice and privilege, hidden fears and profound conservatism over which the self-advertising political programmes glossed quietly. Different sections of the community thought they had a special claim to a lower rate of tax. This was particularly the case of the peasantry, which because of its massive vote, had long been given tax rebates; now, because the senate was its special representative, it was altogether exempted. Caillaux proposed taxation on different types of income (at different rates), for example, income from property (land, houses, shares) at 4 per cent, on profits from industry, commerce and agriculture which involved reward both for work and interest on capital, $3\frac{1}{2}$ per cent, wages and salaries 3 per cent.[2] This simple arrangement, however, hit too many people. Profits from agriculture had until then been untouched by the land tax (in compensation the new income tax on land was in fact lower than the old land tax). Wages had been

---

[1] J. Caillaux, *Les Impôts en France* (1896–1904), preface; cf. id., *Mes Mémoires* (1942–7).
[2] Marcel Rouffie, 'Le nouveau projet d'impôt sur le revenu', *Revue politique et parlementaire* (Mar. 1907), 495–532.

untaxed too. State bonds (the *rente*) had been exempt and it was claimed that to tax them was the equivalent of declaring national bankruptcy. The great problem was how to discover people's incomes. It was immediately assumed that nobody, if left to himself, would declare his income honestly. The idea that the profits of industry should be made public was attacked as spelling immediate ruin for it: secrecy was its tradition. The bourgeoisie were horrified by the prospect of having their affairs and their fortunes placed at the mercy of petty civil servants who owed their jobs to political intrigue. They were even more incensed by the second part of Caillaux's scheme. In addition to these taxes, levied at a standard rate whatever a man's income, he also proposed a super tax at a progressive rate payable by those with total incomes exceeding 5,000 francs, reaching a maximum of 4 per cent on incomes over 25,000 francs. Statistics were produced claiming that two-fifths of French wealth was owned by 124,000 people, and that about 539,000 people had over 50,000 francs capital each.[1] These would be the victims. The super tax was denounced for dividing the nation, as a tax of the class struggle. The threat to the bourgeoisie brought to light a large number of organisations formed by them: twenty-seven committees and associations of industrialists and merchants (and including the 'association for the defence of the middle classes') now combined to form a Central Committee for Fiscal Study and Defence (Comité central d'études et de défense fiscal) which was a powerful pressure group in parliament.[2] When the chamber of deputies eventually passed the bill, many members did so knowing that it had little chance of getting through the senate.

Even if the tax system had been reformed more rapidly, it is not certain that this would have been enough. An inquiry into a succession of serious naval accidents revealed a staggering amount of waste and inefficiency in the naval department, inadequate supplies of artillery, munitions of bad quality, mistakes in the construction of new vessels, long delays in the

---

[1] Bernard Vandeginste, 'Le Sénat et l'impôt sur le revenu 1909–1917' (unpublished Sorbonne thesis, 1966), i. 68, 168. Very informative, and broader than the title suggests.

[2] Pierre Callet, 'La bataille de l'impôt sur le revenu: fiscalité moderne et réactions bourgeoises (1906–1917)', *Cahiers d'histoire*, 7 (Grenoble, 1962), 465–92. Interesting especially on the bourgeoisie of Lyon.

arsenals.[1] Large credits were needed to bring the navy even
up to the standard at which it stood on paper. This issue
provided the occasion for the overthrow of Clemenceau, but
his position had long been weak. His long tenure of power did
not mean that the radicals had a stable majority. The sterility
of this period was the result of a deep malaise, so that men
began talking of the crisis of radicalism and indeed of the crisis
of the parliamentary regime.[2] A very interesting inquiry was
organised by *La Revue* in 1908, taking as its text a phrase from
Waldeck-Rousseau's *Testament politique* (1905) to the effect that
the pace of reform had slowed down greatly in the last ten
years. 'Public opinion', it said, 'is tired of the increasingly false
promises of the demagogues. General dissatisfaction is extreme.
All faith in parliament has been lost.' So it asked famous men
to explain why. Some, including Poincaré, placed the blame
on the domination of deputies by electoral considerations, by
local committees of politicians and local issues: the remedy was
to replace the *scrutin d'arrondissement* by a *scrutin de liste* and proportional representation. This became one of the major controversies of this period and a lot of time was spent discussing it;
but it would be a reform at the expense of the radicals; so
nothing was done till 1919.[3] Others blamed the indecisiveness
of the government. Paul Leroy-Beaulieu, the conservative
economist, rightly pointed out that the trouble with parliament
was not that it did not pass enough laws but that it passed too
many which were incoherent and inapplicable. (Certainly it
should not be thought that Clemenceau's period in office was
barren of legislation simply because he did not fulfil his programme of reforms. Numerous laws were passed but not ones
of fundamental importance, and they were seldom effective.
For example, one established special houses of correction for
prostitutes under eighteen, but in the following year another

---

[1] Achille Viallate, *La Vie politique dans les deux mondes*, vol. 3 (1908–9): a useful
annual.
[2] Camille Pelletan, 'La crise du parti radical', *La Revue*, 80 (15 May 1909),
145–64; Georges Deherme, *La Crise sociale* (1910); 'L'impuissance parlementaire,
enquête', *La Revue*, 73 (15 April 1908); Henri Chantavoine, *En province: lettres au
directeur du Journal des Débats* (1910); André Cheradame, *La Crise française* (1912);
J. L. de Lanessan, *La Crise de la République* (1914).
[3] Cf. P. G. La Chesnais, 'Les radicaux et la représentation proportionnelle',
Revue politique et parlementaire (Oct. 1906), 50–78; Armand Charpentier, *Le Parti
radical et radical socialiste à travers ses congrès 1901–1911* (1913), 118–88.

postponed its application for two years. There were a large
number of laws amending laws which, despite the long time
they took to get through parliament, turned out to be inadequate. The law of 1909 establishing the inalienable family home
appeared to be a belated triumph for the ideas of Le Play, but
it turned out to be too complicated for many to bother to
make use of it.)[1] Anatole France complained that the members
of the government were too bound up with the institutions they
were supposed to be reforming: the minister of war was a
soldier, the minister of finance was a company director, the
minister of the navy had connections with Le Creusot, the armaments factory. Victor Margueritte thought that only the
abandonment of widespread attitudes could improve matters:
the love of bureaucracy, the fear of risks, the enslavement to
routine and petty interests which was characterising French
life. Durkheim, the sociologist, thought there was no hope at all.
'The evil . . . is profound. It derives above all from the disarray
of consciences and the extreme confusion of ideas. The most
diverse and the most contradictory conceptions clash in men's
minds and hold each other in check. How should the legislature
not be powerless when the country is so uncertain as not to
know what it wants?'[2]

The radical party was much divided within itself, to the
point of finding positive action very difficult, and yet it was to
be the largest single party from 1902 to 1936. Its weakness was
that it was essentially negative. Herriot once said that if they
wanted to know what to do, they had only to see what the right
was doing and follow the opposite course. The radicals who
summoned the congress of 1901 at which the party was founded
had no wish to create anything new. They wrote: 'The deliberations will not be concerned with the establishment of a new
programme. Our programme is known. It was fixed by our
fathers.' The radicals indeed looked back to the Revolution (and
perhaps far forward to a philosophical utopia) rather than to
the present. They had a profound sense of history. They wished
to implement the principles of the Great Revolution. But their
ideas on it were deliberately vague. Clemenceau declared 'the

---

[1] *Recueil des lois, décrets, circulaires etc.* (1908), 335; (1909), 241, 209.
[2] *La Revue*, 73 (15 Apr. 1908), 397.

RADICALISM 715

Revolution is a bloc' and this denial of the variety and contradictions of its ideals showed how imprecise these worshippers of reason were. They remained loyal to the programmes of their historical heroes with almost the same devotion as their Catholic enemies upheld their ancient dogmas. Gambetta's manifesto of 1869, issued at Belleville, summarised most of what they wanted. They had frequently repeated it and could still do so forty years later because they implemented very little of it. It was in fact difficult for them to assume the reins of power and carry out reforms because they were essentially the enemies of power and of authority. Their devotion to reason came from a critical rather than a constructive temperament. They knew who the enemies of the people were. They found it easier to be *against* things than for them. The very first conclusion of their inaugural congress in 1901 was 'the need for union *against* the common enemy'. Alain, the principal philosopher of radicalism[1] held that all power was evil, with an inevitable tendency to tyranny. Freedom was to be found only in individuals; 'thought is revolutionary'; the duty of the citizen was to hold his government in check. 'What matters is not the origin of power, but the continual and efficacious control of the government by the governed.'[2] This was a democratic principle with prophetic importance for the coming age of fascism, but it made a radical government almost self-contradictory. The gradual withering away of the state was a radical principle;[3] and one of the characteristics of the radical party was the consistent hostility and suspicion of the party members towards the *élus*, deputies and councillors.

The conclusion of radicalism was not so much to carry out a programme as to fill the administration with loyal supporters, to evict and destroy the enemy. The radicals ruled for their friends, against their enemies.[4] It is not surprising therefore that they were keener on obtaining ministries which carried patronage and the gift of practical advantages for their clientele rather than the mere show of power. Between 1900 and 1939 no radical was ever president of the republic, and there was a

[1] Émile Chartier, alias Alain, *Éléments d'une doctrine radicale* (1925).
[2] Claude Nicolet, *Le Radicalisme* (1957), 39.
[3] Jules Simon, *La Politique radicale* (1869).
[4] Armand Charpentier, *Le Parti radical et radical socialiste à travers ses congrès, 1901–1911* (1913), 366–70.

radical prime minister for only a quarter of this period. But the ministries of the interior, of education and of agriculture were held by the radicals for 23, 21 and 23 years respectively; indeed the ministry of the interior was theirs for 31 out of 39 years if one also counts periods when a politician favourable to them held it. In 1896 the radicals in parliament vigorously demanded a purge of the civil service when they formed their own ministry for the first time, saying, 'It is above all by the attitude of the civil servants that the country perceives the tendencies of the government.'[1]

The radicals could never work up a fighting enthusiasm for social reform. In 1908 and 1909 three major reports were presented to the party, one on *laissez-faire*, one on property and the class struggle and above all one by Debierre on the social ideas and programme of radicalism; and in 1909 a long social programme was adopted by their congress, involving national-isation of mines and railways, municipalisation of public services of local importance, death-duties, income tax, pensions, insurance assistance, equal pay. But this programme was passed quickly and unanimously and the congress showed quite clearly it did not find it very interesting. Speakers on social questions in the congress were frequently urged to finish, so that in 1911, in the debate on the cost of living, the president protested: 'You would not wish it said that the radical party concerns itself with purely political issues and that economic ones do not interest it.'

The debates which aroused real passion were those on religion and this was still the predominant obsession of the party. It should not be forgotten that Combes remained the party's president until 1913. The party bulletin which published the proceedings of local radical committees had very little on social matters, and far more on religion and education. A volume describing the party congresses between 1901 and 1911 devoted the first 200 of its 450 pages to education, the Church and electoral reform, in that order; it then dealt with finance, the army and the law; and this traditional hierarchy accurately

<hr />

[1] Jacques Kayser, 'Le radicalisme des radicaux', in *Tendences politiques dans la vie française depuis 1789*, edited by Guy Michaud (1960), 75–6. Jacques Kayser's book, *Les Grandes Batailles du radicalisme des origines aux portes du pouvoir 1820–1901* (1962), was unfortunately never continued.

reflected their priorities. Certainly, in education they remained
pioneers: they placed more emphasis on it than anybody else;
and their leading expert Buisson (once Ferry's director of
primary education) got them to adopt resolutions in favour
of absolute equality of opportunity, scholarships for those who
could not afford secondary education, more technical and
vocational training, syllabuses drawn up by the teachers themselves. But though he argued that the *lycées* must stop forming
an élite, he still placed great emphasis on examinations which
ensured, he thought, 'the democratic rule which makes the
winning of social advantages dependent on merit'.[1]

They were not levellers. They represented, said Buisson,
'at least a part of the middle classes animated by a spirit which
hitherto they have never had'. Formerly these middle classes
had been conservative. 'Today—one cannot say how, or why,
or since when—the middle classes no longer think as before;
and they do not vote as before. Have they become less egoist or
more clear sighted? Have they understood their duties or their
interests or the force of circumstances better? In any case,
henceforth, instead of taking up a position against the masses,
they are tending to make common cause with them . . . So
there has entered into the mechanism of our government a vital
part which has hitherto been missing: a majority which is
perfectly sensible, balanced, reasonable and prudent but which
nevertheless decidedly wants reforms.' They had taken up the
'programme of their fathers, the democratic and social republic . . . The petty bourgeois, small employers, small tradesmen,
small landowners, small employees, small civil servants have
discovered that they are nearer the working class than the great
bankers, the great capitalists and the great ones privileged by
wealth.' They have therefore adopted the doctrine of solidarity
—though there was still need to stimulate the feeling of solidarity. The radicals, Buisson concluded, 'are a bourgeois party
which has the soul of a people's party. They paradoxically
reconcile in themselves the two opposites of the social antinomy.
They are, a rare thing in the history of democracies, a class
which aspires to confound itself with the nation. They are a
class of proprietors who work and of workers who have property,
a group of small men who are not parvenus, a sort of family

[1] A. Charpentier, 53.

founded on a marriage of reason, uniting good-will coming
from different sources but heading in the same direction.'[1]
This pregnant definition of radicalism shows clearly enough
why social reform was not its prime aim. The party's frail unity
had been achieved in 1901 in the heat of the Dreyfus affair,
based on a desire to win victory in the religious struggle. Its
immediate and natural result had been the separation of
Church and state: after this victory the radicals were somewhat
at a loss. They could not voluntarily weaken themselves now
by expelling the moderates whose interests were not in social
reform. They had originally won their successes in large cities,
but their main support now came from small towns and above
all rural districts. They gave more attention therefore to the
reform of taxation (always the peasants' principal concern)
than to the improvement of the conditions of the factory worker.
Having achieved power, they were already on the defensive,
they could not throw off the idea that they were somehow
oppressed. The idea that they were building a new society fell
into the background and was taken over by the socialists. Their
social conscience degenerated into a defence of the *small man*,
of whose virtues they now made a myth.[2]

There was a great deal of variety within the party. The
religious issue, which still excited them more than anything,
was interpreted in different ways. The separation of Church and
state, at the level of legislation, was made as moderate as
possible and dissociated from any idea of religious persecution.
But the laws were applied in different ways at a local level.
Many ardent municipalities now fought 'the war of the priest's
house', pulling it down, or turning it into a post-office or other
public use. The executive committee of the party published
a pamphlet to guide radical municipalities in this matter,
which provided the main excitement of local politics in these
years. The question of church schools continued to be debated
ardently too—and the party was divided on the question of
whether education should be a complete state monopoly or not.

[1] F. Buisson, 'La politique radicale socialiste', in *Revue hebdomadaire* (12 Feb.
1910), 159–81.
[2] For an interesting study of radicalism on a local scale, see R. Vandenbusche,
'Aspects de l'histoire politique du radicalisme dans le département du Nord,
1870–1905', *Revue du Nord* (Apr.–June 1965), 223–68. But the problems of this
department were rather special.

It found itself at war with the primary-school masters and the junior civil servants—hitherto its most important representatives in the village. These now wanted to form trade unions, with the right to strike against the state—even the radical state. Could the radicals refuse this elementary right of all men to a single section of the community? They were aghast that the *instituteurs* could turn against their makers. In 1912 they thought of a compromise: the civil servants would be allowed to form unions but these would be forbidden to join the revolutionary C.G.T. They were in a cleft stick and inevitably they lost many of these civil servants to the socialists. Having captured the jobs, these local politicians still wished to remain *against* the state even though it now fed them. Pelletan begged the radical congress not to 'reject [these] small men who were and are still the pioneers of the republic' but there was nothing to be done. The business of reconciling divergent interests (and justice at the same time) presented many difficulties. The radicals solved some of the problems with clever verbal compromises, as in foreign policy, where they declared themselves ardently patriotic but also resolutely in favour of peace and international arbitration, honouring military service but also wishing to transform its character. This was harder to do with electoral reform, since they got 42 per cent of the seats with only 33 per cent of the votes; in 1910 it took an average of 14,000 votes to elect a socialist deputy but only 11,200 to elect a radical. The *scrutin de liste* disagreed with their love of independence; but such was the pressure of public opinion against the 'stagnant pools', as Briand described the single-member constituencies, that they adopted resolutions to reform the system, though without any real intention of doing so.

The radical party was not organised for action. Though founded in 1901, until 1928 it could barely be called a party, and as one of its leaders said, its formation 'preceded what some have defined as the invasion of the masses'.[1] As a party, it did not accept individual enrolments (unlike the S.F.I.O.). Joining it was essentially a local matter, and the only real unit was the local committee. All committees which had a minimum of ten members were considered equal, paying the same subscription (13 francs p.a.) to the central fund and sending the same

[1] Daniel Bardonnet, *L'Évolution de la structure du parti radical* (1960), 9.

number of delegates to the congresses. Such was the looseness
of the movement, however, that there were also many radical
committees which did not join the party, so as to avoid paying
the subscription, minute though it was. In 1910 there were 836
committees adhering to the party and perhaps 600 to 800 outside it: altogether this meant there were probably between about
80,000 and 150,000 members of radical committees. (Compare
the socialists' 54,000 members in 1910, and 90,000 in 1914.)
The local committees met between six and twelve times a year,
and concerned themselves mainly with elections. Attempts were
made to organise them into federations, but by 1910 only twenty-
three departments had a federation, and in any case these had
very little life of their own. The main exception was the Federation of the Seine, run by J. L. Bonnet, the principal advocate
of a centralised party. There were also a few regional federations,
the most active of which was that of the south-east, run by
Estier, but though these held congresses, and helped with
propaganda, they had no powers. The sovereign body in the
party was the national congress, which met annually in October,
and which was attended by all radical deputies, *conseillers
généraux*, delegates of municipal councils, delegates of committees, leagues, unions, clubs, Freemason lodges and newspapers
which accepted the party programme. Local committees could
send as many delegates as they pleased provided they paid the
appropriate fee (10 francs for the first, and 5 for every other).
Some 800 people usually attended these congresses. For about
four days they had a very enjoyable time in passionate debate
and wild outbursts of enthusiasm: they interrupted unpopular
orators mercilessly, sometimes invaded the tribune, and sessions
not infrequently had to be suspended. The congress elected an
executive committee of no fewer than 680 members (including
all members of parliament) which met once a month (though
no more than 100 ever attended any one meeting). It also
elected a *bureau* of 33 (half of them members of parliament)
which met once a week. But neither of these had any real
power; and all efforts to strengthen the central organisation
were rejected by the congresses, which spurned the interference
of Parisians who, as one member said, 'could not speak the
local dialect' and would meddle with matters 'which did not
concern them'.

The result of this was that there was very little discipline in elections and no control of the candidates who stood as radicals. A single constituency could have more than one radical candidate—this was particularly noticeable in 1910. The label itself meant very little. Royalists who thought their chances would be improved by calling themselves radical did so, especially in the south. The radical party in parliament therefore consisted of real members of the party paying their subscriptions, and giving up 200 francs of their salary to the party funds, but also of deputies who had been elected under the radical label but who had not accepted its programme, or who had not paid their subscriptions (in 1910 there were about 80 out of 250 of these). The situation was further confused by there being two radical parties in parliament—the radicals and the radical-socialists—despite the unification of 1901. The radicals had been kept in being partly in order to recruit more deputies to support Combes's religious policy. But the division between these two groups did not coincide with the division between 'true' and 'false' radicals. Moreover, the party had no control over the behaviour of its deputies. These could vote as they pleased, and when they were ministers they could follow what policy they pleased. In 1913 Barthou's ministry, based on the right, was condemned by the radical party, but the vice-president of its executive committee, Dumont, nevertheless became a member of it.

Clemenceau's position as prime minister can now be better understood. He was not the leader of the party—there was no such person, or at least the president was purely honorific. Clemenceau seemed the right man because he had adopted a liberal attitude towards the separation—saying that it was not worth losing lives in order to inventory a few chandeliers—and so he was acceptable to the moderate radicals who held a key position. These moderates, however, were hostile to social reform; strikes and social unrest increased their conservatism. In 1908 when the government demanded the prolongation of the parliamentary session in order to get the income tax bill through, 140 radicals voted with the right to defeat it. On the other hand, Clemenceau's policy of repression alienated the left wing of the party. His harsh treatment of the civil servants led over 100 radicals to vote against him in 1909. The extreme right-wing radicals were virtually indistinguishable from the conservatives: the extreme left often voted with the socialists. It is surprising Clemenceau lasted so long. Already in 1907 Pelletan complained bitterly against his government: 'It must be told that it is time to return to the path of radical policy.' Clemenceau defiantly replied: 'I do not wish to be strangled by the silent seraglio . . . Messieurs les radicaux, je vous attends!' The struggle over the income tax and fear of the social agitation held party and government together for a while but in May 1909, three months before he fell, the executive committee of the party passed a resolution regretting 'that by its improvidence as much as by its successive and contradictory policies the government of M. Clemenceau has deceived the hopes of republican democracy and aggravated the misunderstandings between the various parts; the radical and radical-socialist party rejects all solidarity with a cabinet whose methods of government are contrary to the traditions of the party.'

So, despite their parliamentary majority, the radicals were unable to control the conduct of the ministers. The election of 1910 increased the confusion. On paper the results were more or less the same for them as in 1906, but the radical deputies now included a considerably larger number of men elected with the support of the right and not 'genuine' radicals. Beneath the surface there was a change in the nature of the majority, which was given more and more to outbursts of indignation at the government for not giving it what it wanted, though it did not quite know what it did want. It thus lost the initiative in politics. Clemenceau was succeeded by Briand, an independent socialist favouring appeasement and symbolising the union of the extremes against the radical centre. The radicals complained of his 'reactionary compromises' and overthrew him. But they had no leader with whom to replace him. Pelletan, a radical of the old generation and formerly Clemenceau's lieutenant, was the idol of the constituencies: he believed in favouritism and patronage but his application of these principles when he was minister of the navy created such administrative chaos that it was generally agreed he was too whimsical and demagogic for office. Berteaux, a wealthy stockbroker, was very popular among the radicals in parliament, partly because of his affability and good humour, partly because he lent money freely, so that it was said no less than 100 deputies were his debtors. But he was killed in an accident in 1912. Monis, whom the radicals put in to succeed Briand, was a figurehead; and he was injured in this same accident. Caillaux who succeeded him, though not a radical, pleased them because his policy was at once authoritarian and advanced. But his foreign policy, too conciliatory towards Germany, led to his fall. The radicals could provide no alternative and the chief posts of the republic went to moderates. Poincaré became prime minister and then president; Deschanel, even more moderate, became president of the chamber of deputies. Briand followed as premier once again, and then finally Barthou with a ministry avowedly relying on right-wing support and with only three lone radicals in it. The decline of their influence was seen when the navy was ordered to fly its flags at half mast on Good Friday; when pupils of a public school were forbidden to attend a celebration of the bicentenary of Diderot, on the ground that neutrality should be observed in these matters. Social reforms, the income tax, anticlericalism were forgotten; the only bill of importance brought forward was to increase military service to three years.

In the face of this continued and frightening advance by their opponents, the radicals attempted to rally in 1913. They adopted, first, a programme more practical and up to date than their traditional utopia. They stopped talking, for example, about the election of judges and ceased to add the farcical comment that 'if this cannot be achieved soon', less radical reforms of the judiciary should be undertaken.[1] They produced something much shorter than the Belleville programme and Clemenceau's seventeen points. Two-year military service, a progressive income tax, anticlericalism in education and social insurance became their policy. Church questions no longer occupied first place. Cutting down the army and taxing the rich was a popular cry and in addition could win them support from the socialists. Secondly, an attempt was made to form a single radical group in parliament. This failed in the senate and was only partially successful in the chamber, where splinter groups persisted on both right and left. Despite the party's policy on the army, thirty-eight radicals voted for

[1] F. Buisson, *La Politique radicale, études sur les doctrines du parti radical et radical-socialiste* (1908), 167.

three-year military service. Nevertheless a little more discipline was introduced; some 'false radicals' were unmasked; those who had served in Barthou's ministry were expelled from the party. The executive committee became more active and undertook more propaganda. The subscription was increased to 25 centimes per member. Efforts were made to reduce multiple radical candidatures in the same constituency, again not always successfully—in two constituencies of Creuse, for example, there were nine radical candidates in 1914—but on the whole there was progress. As a result the party emerged from this election a little more disciplined—smaller but less amorphous. Thirdly, they found themselves a new leader, brought in from outside. Caillaux, having broken with the moderates from whom he originated but whom he frightened with his income tax, was in bitter rivalry against all other parliamentary leaders. So he joined the radicals in 1913 and was at once elected president. Though cold and distant, he seemed to be the only man capable of reviving them. Certainly he led them successfully for a while, and a ministry under him and Jaurès should have followed. But once again the radicals had bad luck. Caillaux was the victim of a scandal occasioned by his divorced wife. She shot dead the editor of the *Figaro* who had published letters between her and her husband. His complacency towards Germany made him unacceptable in the new patriotic atmosphere occasioned by the war. So in 1914 the radicals were still a party without a clear sense of direction, unable to take advantage of their popular support.[1]

---

[1] The best guide to this subject is M. Fournier, 'Le parti radical de 1906 à 1914' (unpublished thesis, Fondation Nationale des Sciences Politiques, 1960). For further details on party structure see G. Fabius de Champville, *Le Comité exécutif du parti républicain radical et radical-socialiste de 1897 à 1907* (1908), and Pierre Andréani, 'La formation du parti radical-socialiste', *Revue politique et parlementaire*, 206 (1952), 33–41.

23. Socialism

HISTORIES of socialism in France normally begin in 1870, and have as their principal thread the spread of Marxist doctrine. It is perfectly true that an organised socialist party developed only in the late nineteenth century and that its Marxism had little in common with the socialism of the early utopians. It is impossible, however, to understand the rapid success of the socialist party without going back to 1848. During the Second Republic, the vagueness and moderation of early socialist thought meant that a very large number of people could sympathise with it, and the severe economic crisis made many look to it for the solution of their difficulties. It was in the years 1849–51 that substantial sections of the peasantry were won to socialism, principally in the backward regions of the centre and south-east. It took some forty years for the profound consequences of this event to be appreciated. The socialist party of 1900 could become a major force in politics while France was still hardly industrialised and while there was still only a small minority of industrial workers—the obvious subjects of their propaganda—because these rural areas gave it mass support. By going back to 1848 one sees why the majority of the socialist vote in the early twentieth century came from certain backward rural areas. One sees also why its programme could not be a clear-cut Marxist one. Its peasant backers had been won over to a brand of socialism current in 1848, and to a large extent this is what they still voted for in 1900. The mark of the Second Republic was thus powerfully imprinted upon the movement.

In 1848 the socialists were diverse, individualistic, dispersed, organised at most into tiny societies but without links between each other. The followers of the utopian thinkers did not form active political groups with mass support, let alone one party. The secret societies of revolutionaries in Paris involved only a couple of thousand men; those in the provinces—usually not revolutionary but rather expressing traditional animosities and

the relics of old antagonisms, such as the White Terror of 1815
—were isolated and parochial in outlook. This situation did
not change in the early months of the republic. The socialists
could not stand as a party in the elections of 1848. Only in
Paris were they sufficiently numerous or self-conscious to act
independently. Louis Blanc, in co-operation with socialist
clubs, put up a list of candidates which included twenty
workers. All but one were defeated. The leading socialist
celebrities indeed were generally defeated in Paris, except when
supported by the moderates. They had better luck in the provinces; and altogether some 55 out of the 880 deputies to the
constituent assembly were in some way socialist, or at least
partisans of a 'democratic and social republic'. Already socialism
revealed itself as having an appeal beyond the hothouse of the
capital, but the lines between parties were still too undefined to
make it possible to distinguish at all clearly between them.
Men were often elected on this occasion as individuals, or as
expressing peculiar local conditions, more than for the precise
nature of their opinions. So the socialist deputies included both
Blanquists like Martin Bernard, a compositor with long
experience of conspiracy, who criticised the workers for wanting
to become bourgeois, but also the mason Totain who, while
seeking the improvement of the lot of the masses, wished to
'lengthen the jackets without shortening the frock-coats'.[1]
They were at first isolated. They formed a separate group
in the Assembly—the Société des représentants républicains.
Ledru-Rollin and his followers (essentially Jacobins, looking
back to the revolution of 1793) went to some pains to dis-
sociate themselves from them. Their impetuous involvement in
demonstrations and insurrections led to numerous arrests
among them. One famous trial, at Bourges, was even more
damaging because it revealed their divisions, mutual hostilities
and even treachery.

However, in the course of the Second Republic, the socialists
grew into something like a national movement, for three
reasons. First, the indiscriminate persecuting of the left-wing
republicans which became increasingly intense after the June
days, led the party of Ledru-Rollin and the socialists to unite.

---

[1] *Biographie des 900 représentants à la Constituante*, published by Victor Lecou
(1849), 406; G. Weill, *Histoire du parti républicain en France* (1928), 129 n.

The national leadership remained in the hands of the Jacobins, but they took up a large part of the programme of their new allies. The socialist following thus suddenly swelled. Secondly, vigorous propaganda on a regional or a national scale, in which the Jacobins had grown adept, was now put to the service of socialism, and was directed with unprecedented effectiveness at the poor peasantry. Innumerable pamphlets, almanacs, engravings, songs—all written with the rural constituencies in mind—flooded the countryside despite the censorship, often being recopied by hand over and over again as they were passed around. Banquets, at which political leaders spoke and started a local organisation, became very frequent. In certain areas almost every commune came to have a left-wing secret society. The Solidarité républicaine, a national society founded in Paris to assist Ledru-Rollin's presidential campaign with the Blanquist Martin Bernard as president and the Jacobin Charles Delescluze as secretary, and modelled on the Société des Droits de l'Homme (which had done so much to organise the revolution of 1830), spread branches everywhere.[1] Active leaders got small secret societies to correspond with each other; Alphonse Gent, for example, in this way established a formidable regional organisation in the south-east. Thirdly, the movement spread rapidly not only because its propaganda was highly relevant to the peasantry's immediate needs, but because its methods were grafted on to traditional peasant institutions. The secret societies cannot be explained as a sudden birth. They were a transformation and adaptation of the old *chambrées*, drinking clubs, Freemason lodges, *carbonari* groups, workers' unions and friendly societies; they revived traditional hates against royalists, landlords, enclosers and money-lenders. In certain parts of the country the number of these societies was astonishingly large. In some communes almost every inhabitant was enlisted. In the department of Vaucluse, with 80,000 electors, there were about 12,000 members of left-wing societies, and 6,000 of legitimist ones. In the presidential election of 1848, Ledru-Rollin polled only 370,119 votes, while Raspail standing as a pure socialist won 36,920. After their union, in the legislative elections of 1849, the left made very substantial gains and obtained 40–50 per cent of the votes in

[1] Marcel Dessal, *Charles Delescluze 1809–71* (1952), 93–120.

twenty-three departments. Socialism was in this stage a branch of republicanism and appeared all the more formidable because it could not be readily differentiated from it.[1]

It is no wonder that the bourgeoisie were terrified by the 'Red Menace',[2] and all the more so because the Reds were purposely lying low until the election of 1852. It is true the divisions among the Reds were so great that they would not have known what to do with power if they won it. Some preached the union of classes, but some a revolt of the *petits* against the *gros*. This did not imply a class struggle, however. There was no bitter animosity among the peasantry against large landowners or rich men as such. Their principal enemies were their creditors—who were men of all classes. Socialist propaganda was particularly successful among indebted peasants. It used the economic distress effectively to win them— whether small proprietors, farmers or daily labourers—from traditional attitudes of respect, but it did not go beyond preaching fraternity, credit, a reform of taxes, the ending of poverty. The real leaders of the left-wing societies were principally bourgeois themselves—barristers, notaries, doctors, schoolmasters, landowners, with artisans usually taking the lead only at village level.

The *coup d'état* of 1851 showed the strength of the movement and also destroyed it. In the Drôme 15,000 to 20,000 men took up arms (nearly a quarter of the electorate), in the Basses-Alpes 15,000 out of 45,000 electors. Thirty-two departments were placed in a state of siege.[3] In a few small towns the rebels were able to seize power until troops arrived: their first decree was to 'abolish usury', and debts, and indirect taxation, to proclaim free education and promise the division of common lands among the masses.[4] The large number involved points to the effectiveness of the secret societies; but the almost total absence of pillage or murder shows that it was not total revolution that they planned. 26,000 men were arrested, out of whom about 10,000 were transported out of France. The more prominent leaders who escaped took refuge in exile. More than a dozen

[1] Jacques Bouillon, 'Les démocrates-socialistes aux élections de 1849', *Revue française de science politique*, 6 (Jan.–Mar. 1956), 70–95.
[2] A. Romieu, *Le Spectre rouge en 1852* (1851).
[3] Eugène Tenot, *Étude historique sur le coup d'État* (1877–80).
[4] Philippe Vigier, *La Seconde République dans la région alpine* (1963), 2. 332.

years elapsed before the socialists recovered from this repression. The early successes of Louis Napoleon, it might be added, turned many of them into Bonapartists—for the two parties, to a certain extent, *promised* much the same. The failure of the Second Republic discredited the utopian socialists. It produced a profound intellectual crisis of depression and self-doubt among their followers. 'After the hammer-blow of 2 December', wrote Vallès, 'some went mad, some died . . . Some see and hear still, but their misfortune has withered, wrinkled and emptied them. . . . Still these men were less unhappy than we were. Those who in 1845 were around twenty years old, discovered what it was like to live. We have hardly known it, we who left school in 1850. In 1851 we were already beaten.'[1] However, socialist ideals were not fundamentally modified. Apart from Proudhon (whose ideas did change, as has been seen, on a number of points), there was little new socialist thought during the Second Empire.[2] The socialist movement as such virtually disappeared. The majority adhered to the republican party, which was wide enough to absorb as great a variety of opinion as the party of 1849. In the eyes of the general public socialism, often appearing to be dead for a dozen years, came to be identified with the First International. Socialism in the 1860s is thus very different from that of the 1840s. It was almost entirely an urban and working-class movement.

The French section of the workers' International owes its origin to a rebellion by a small group of workers against the domination of the republican movement by the bourgeoisie, in the belief that the workers could effectively win their emancipation only by their own efforts. The Manifesto of Sixty Workers in 1864 was the first expression of this view and as such is a landmark in French history. But the bronze worker Tolain who, in pursuance of this manifesto, stood for parliament in 1864, obtained only 395 votes.[3] His party, and the International which he helped to found in London, was at first suspect to the socialists because of Tolain's friendly relations with the radical Prince Napoleon. Certainly the government

[1] Jules Vallès, 'Un chapitre de l'histoire du 2 décembre', in *Courrier de l'Intérieur* (8 Sept. 1868), quoted by J. Tchernof, *Le Parti républicain au coup d'État* (1906), 166.
[2] T. N. Bernard, *Le Socialisme d'hier et celui d'aujourd'hui* (1870), 274.
[3] Against 14,444 votes for Garnier-Pagès, the republican candidate, and 6,530 for Frédéric Lévy, the conservative.

tolerated the International, and made no protest when it deposited its statutes. Its working-class character did not prevent a number of bourgeois politicians from joining it, like Jules Simon, Ferdinand Buisson, Henri Martin, which shows how moderate it was. Its founders were keen that it should be a *société d'étude* not a new version of the Carbonari; they were anxious to avoid falling into the old errors of the secret *compagnonnage*, and refused to be a secret society. They were hostile to strikes and at first used their energies to prevent them (as with the builders in 1865–7). Their hostility to revolutionary methods won them the fervent enmity of the Blanquists. They concerned themselves mainly with discussing how workers' societies, co-operatives for production, consumption and credit could be organised. They feared that if they won higher wages, their employers would import foreign labour, so international solidarity was important to them. But they aimed only at reforming capitalist society and obtaining equality for the worker in it, not at overthrowing it. Tolain's purpose was to enable men to exercise their individual initiative; his dream was to 'make every man a property owner'; it was only frustration, through inability to exercise their initiative, that made workers communists which, he said, 'they are neither by belief nor by instinct'.[1]

The International obtained a small office in the rue des Gravilliers which for a year contained only a broken stove, a white wood table and two stools (in the day time Fribourg, one of the founders, used it for his job as a decorator). Only later were four chairs added. The International sent out 20,000 copies of its programme; this was paid for by Edouard Blot, a printer, for they had no money themselves. After seven months they still had recruited only 500 members. Their plans to establish Proudhonian exchange and credit centres could not be put into effect; the practical advantages they offered their members in return for their subscription of 10 centimes a week, in the form of insurance and mutual assurance, were illusory, because their funds were inadequate. They contented themselves with planning to enable workers to buy their own tools and to support them against capitalist competition until they were established. The International began as little more than a friendly society;

[1] *Enquête parlementaire sur l'insurrection du 18 mars 1871* (1872), Tolain's evidence, 425.

it became revolutionary under the pressure of events in the space of a few years.[1]

There was a take-over bid first of all from the republicans.[2] Henri Lefort (whose father, a legitimist convert to Orleanism, had died in 1832 defending the monarchy of Louis-Philippe against a republican rising) was a bourgeois journalist who had himself taken up the ideas of Proudhon, Victor Hugo and the Rochdale pioneers. He tried to effect a union between the A.I.T. and 'republican radicalism'. He claimed he would swell the A.I.T.'s ranks with 10,000 men loyal to him in the co-operative societies he had formed. But the A.I.T. leaders wished neither to be absorbed in this way, nor to involve themselves with the political opposition to Napoleon III, which would only make their existence even more precarious. As a result they expelled Lefort and laid it down that they would admit manual workers only. This was the first of a series of disagreements between the French and other nations in the International (which had non-worker members like Marx). The International at first accepted the moderate mutualism of the French, and their hope of improving existing society rather than destroying it. But in 1868 widespread nationalisation was adopted as the A.I.T.'s programme and in 1869 Proudhonian doctrines were finally defeated in it. The character of the French section changed rapidly. The hostility to strikes disappeared. In February 1867 the strike of bronze workers was supported by the A.I.T. (in which they were strongly represented), and a few thousand francs aid was even obtained from the English section. Rumours spread that millions were being sent across the Channel. The employers gave way in panic. The prestige of the A.I.T. rocketed. Trade unions all over the country began joining it in hope of receiving similar aid. The industrial agitation of the years 1868–70 added an unexpected fillip to its growth. It was widely believed that the A.I.T. was fomenting the numerous strikes: in fact it was the strikes which brought it recruits: joining it became a symbol of the strikers' determination to fight to the end. Notions of the A.I.T.'s power became grossly inflated. The government believed in 1870 that it had 250,000

[1] E. E. Fribourg, *L'Association internationale des travailleurs* (1871), 92–8.
[2] Cf. Charles M. Limousin, 'Coup d'œil historique sur l'Internationale', *Journal des économistes*, 38 (1875), 68–87.

members; the public talked of a million. In fact it probably had only between 20,000 and 40,000 and most of these were affiliated through their unions in a very loose way, for the purpose of benefiting temporarily during a strike.[1] 'People join the A.I.T.', it was said, 'in the same way as they offer and accept a glass of wine.' It had branches in the principal industrial areas of France (it was entirely urban) but these branches were often the creations of a few individuals and rather precarious.[2] Where traditions of political opposition were strong, as in Lyon, the A.I.T. made slow headway.[3]

Involvement in strikes changed the character of the A.I.T. It was no longer able, as its founders had intended, to study economic problems and leave politics aside. It found itself forced to retaliate every time troops were used to suppress strikes, by attacking the government and the bourgeoisie. 'It is impossible for us to live', they wrote in 1869, 'under a social regime in which capital replies with fusillades to demonstrations which are sometimes turbulent but always just.'[4] Arrests and persecution completed the transformation. In the first trial of the leaders of the A.I.T. in 1868 they were very moderate during the defence, and with no hint of any revolutionary intentions. Later, in their appeal against conviction, they were far more independent and further trials accentuated their hostility. The arrest of these moderate leaders led to the election of new leaders to replace them, who marked a further step to the left. By 1869 the original French section of the A.I.T. had virtually disintegrated.

A new leadership now transformed it.[5] It concentrated its efforts on organising the workers into unions, and became avowedly socialist and revolutionary. Varlin in Paris formed a vigorously aggressive federation of workers' societies in December 1869, which was scarcely distinguishable from the A.I.T. In Lyon Richard, in Marseille Bastelica showed the

---

[1] J. Rougerie, 'Sur l'histoire de la Première Internationale', *Le Mouvement social*, 51 (1965), 31 and n.

[2] J. Maitron and G. M. Thomas, 'L'Internationale et la Commune à Brest', *Le Mouvement social*, 41 (1962), 48–53.

[3] J. Rougerie, 'La Première Internationale à Lyon', *Annali dell'Istituto G. Feltrinelli* (1961), 126–93, esp. 145.

[4] Jacques Freymond, *La Première Internationale* (1962), 1. xiv.

[5] Jeannine Verdes, 'Les délégués français aux conférences et congrès de l'A.I.T.', *Cahiers de I.S.E.A.* (Aug. 1964), 83–176.

flirtation with the ideas of Bakunin. The A.I.T. became the new 'red spectre' haunting France and indeed Europe. But the menace was of course superficial, far more so than in 1851. Repression was easy, as soon as it was resolutely decided on. The arrests and trial of its leaders in June 1870, followed by efficient repression in the provinces, destroyed it as effectively as the *coup* of 1851 had destroyed the first socialist party. The war completed its disarray. By the time of the Commune it had virtually ceased to exist.

In England, the A.I.T. was principally backed by artisan unions in declining or traditional industries.[1] In France this was true to a certain extent, but they were far from being its only supporters. France differed from England in having fewer members of the A.I.T. but dispersed over a wider range of occupations and social types. The doctrinal beliefs of the French were also more varied. The view that they were basically Proudhonists is too simple. They may have begun as such but in practice the force of circumstances soon made them give up their hostility to political action, to strikes or to violence. They ignored the precepts of Proudhon in standing for parliament in 1863 and in 1869 (agitating in favour of Poland and Italy). Later the new leaders, even if they were influenced by Bakunin, insisted on political action for all his opposition to it. They were perhaps Marxists without knowing it—but not by any influence. The A.I.T. was composed essentially of practical men, not of theorists.[2]

The history of a couple of workers' leaders, reputed to be leading Proudhonists, is interesting in this connection. Henri Tolain (1828–97) holds a place in working-class history comparable to that of Pelloutier. He was the engraver who did most to organise the workers' delegation to the London Exhibition of 1862, the first workers' parliamentary candidatures in 1863 and the Workers' International in 1864. He was regarded as the leader of the Proudhonist section of the International. But, like Griffuelhes, Tolain was essentially a practical organiser, not a theorist. 'The people', he wrote of Proudhon's abstentionist

---

[1] H. Collins and C. Abramsky, *K. Marx and the British Labour Movement. Years of the First International* (1965), 70.

[2] J. Rougerie, 'Sur l'histoire de la Première Internationale', *Le Mouvement social*, 51 (1965), 40–3.

programme in 1863, 'do not often let themselves be led by a theory, whatever its value may be. The abstract deductions of metaphysics have little hold on them. Almost always at decisive times, they follow the impulse of sentiment much more readily than pure reason.'[1] Their aim, he believed, was above all to obtain 'a liberty equivalent to that which 1789 gave the capitalist and agricultural proprietor'. In 1848 they had been unable to formulate their aspirations clearly, and 'it was more by intuition than by reasoning that the workers adopted this or that social doctrine'. Gradually, in the silence of the early years of the Second Empire, their leaders put aside exaggerated views and impracticable utopias, and sought feasible reforms. Tolain was no revolutionary; and he was even hostile to strikes (not because he was a Proudhonist, but because he saw their practical inconveniences). He quoted with approval from Louis Napoleon's *Extinction of Pauperism*: 'The working class is like a people of helots in the midst of a people of sybarites . . . Poverty will cease to be seditious when opulence ceases to be oppressive.' He hoped for the emancipation of the workers through education, through trade unions (of both workers and employers), 'the mother institution of all future progress', and through the conscious limitation of industrialisation. The snag, to him, about the development of machines was that 'without capital, it was impossible to show one's individual initiative'. So he thought France should not try to compete with England, but concentrate on producing high-class goods, so that 'French taste and artistic sentiment [should not be] extinguished by the discipline of the factory hierarchy'. Tolain soon left the International and he did not support the Commune. Just as the mass of the workers had not followed Proudhon in 1863, so they did not accept the extremism of the International. Tolain, accurately reflecting their moderation, expected to obtain more from within the bourgeois system than by trying to topple it over. He became a deputy in 1871 and a senator in 1876. He spoke with some contempt of workers who accepted communism because it was the simplest idea, 'being as it were self-explanatory'.

The limitations of Proudhon's influence can be seen in a different way in the case of Eugène Varlin (1839–71) who is

[1] H. Tolain, *Quelques Vérités sur les élections de Paris* (1863), 23.

the second great figure in working-class politics of this period. The son of an agricultural labourer (who also owned a tiny plot of land) he was apprenticed to an uncle as a bookbinder in Paris at the age of 13. At 18 he was a founder member of the Bookbinders' Friendly Society; he helped to organise their strikes in 1864 and 1865, in which latter year he joined the International. He placed faith for the emancipation of the workers in trade unions and co-operatives which led him, as his biographer puts it, 'to work in keeping with the theories of Proudhon before he really knew the works of the philosopher of Besançon . . . His own observations have guided him and not any philosophical system.'[1] His independence was shown in his rejection of Proudhon's advocacy of keeping women in the home and leaving education to the control of parents. He decried the 'Proudhoniens enragés', who preached abstention in the election of 1869: he was anxious to have workers opposing candidates of all parties to mark 'the break of the masses with the bourgeoisie'.[2] Though he soon broke away from the mutualists in the International, he did not become a Marxist, for he retained a profound dislike of the state and of authoritarianism. Though he had much in common with Bakunin, he drew his ideas essentially from his own experience as a union organiser, in which he showed exceptional talent. Unlike Tolain, he was not personally ambitious, but dedicated, ascetic, seldom laughing, always active; it was symbolic that one of his last acts was to disallow the expenses incurred by a general of the Commune who sent in a bill for a new uniform, of the finest cloth, made for him by the deposed emperor's tailor. But for his early death, he might have played a major role in the social history of his country.[3]

The Commune

The Commune was not a socialist government. It has a place in the history of socialism, however, because many contemporaries believed it to be socialist. Marx misinterpreted it completely.

[1] Maurice Foulon, *Eugène Varlin, relieur et membre de la Commune* (Clermont-Ferrand, 1934), 45.   [2] Ibid., 108.
[3] On Benoist Malon in these years see Gerald Hoeffel, 'Some Aspects of Reformist Socialism in France' (Oxford D.Phil. thesis, 1973), which is the first part of what will be a major study of this influential figure; see also below, pp. 774–5.

He celebrated it as 'the glorious harbinger of a new society', believing, quite wrongly, that it was 'essentially a working-class government, the result of the struggle of the producing against the appropriating class', establishing the dictatorship of the proletariat, intending to abolish property, so popular with the masses that if it had 'three months free communication with the provinces', it would have brought about 'a general rising of the peasants'.[1] Marx's mythical views had an important influence on Lenin, but in French history the Commune has a totally different significance.

It was first of all not the result of any revolution. Two attempts to start an insurrection by the revolutionaries in the city—chiefly Blanquists—on 31 October 1870 and 22 January 1871, were complete fiascos, raising virtually no support.

The Commune was the product of more subtle causes, some of long standing and some more immediately connected with the Franco-Prussian war. Paris had since 1789 been the principal asylum of advanced republican ideas in France and a faithful source of strength for every opposition. It had made and overthrown governments time and again. Its whims had had to be accepted as commands by the provinces. But though it had mastered the country, it was not free itself. The state had had its revenge by depriving it of self-governing institutions. It was administratively the most backward commune in France. It had no mayor and no municipal independence. The prefect of police watched over it with an army of spies and hated Corsican *agents*. The hostility between town and country reached its highest pitch here. As a rapidly growing city full of recent immigrants, of *arrivistes*, of many lost illusions and few successes, it was immeasurably attractive, hateful and competitive. It contained the strongest contrasts of wealth in the country. The animal degradation of its poor, on the border-lines of starvation and crime, appeared as a constant menace to bourgeois society. Comparing them to savages and barbarians, Buret in his *De la misère et des classes laborieuses en Angleterre et en France* (1840) wondered already whether 'they are perhaps meditating an invasion'.[2]

---

[1] K. Marx, *Civil War in France* (first published 1871; London 1933 edition with an introduction by Engels), 19, 43, 47, 63.

[2] L. Chevalier, *Classes laborieuses et classes dangereuses* (1958), 452–3.

The June days of 1848 and the rising after the *coup d'état* in December 1851, showed just how dangerous Paris could be. The war of 1870–1 exacerbated these old antagonisms: the siege of Paris accentuated the separation of the capital from the rest of the country and filled the inhabitants with an almost hysterical hate of the incompetent government which had lost the war. The National Assembly of 1871, with a monarchist majority, showed the completeness of their isolation, and even more so when it symbolically moved its meetings to Versailles. Paris wanted to preserve the republic and to pursue the war. The overthrow of the conservative government became vital to it when the war-time moratorium on commercial debts was ended, so threatening many small artisans and shopkeepers with bankruptcy. It was not an upsurge of socialism or of any new force that produced the Commune. Paris did not rebel. Rather the Commune was brought about by the conservatives wishing to end the old problem of Parisian insubordination. Thiers had an old score to settle with the city which had overthrown him in 1848. When the Parisians refused to surrender their artillery, he withdrew all troops from the city, and made military preparations to retake it by force, as he believed Louis-Philippe should have done twenty-three years before. He determined not only to obtain the submission of the Parisians but to exterminate once and for all their intransigent radical opposition, the perpetual threat to all stability. It was this withdrawal of the government that created the Commune and made Paris autonomous for 73 days (18 March–28 May 1871).

Suddenly the ministries, the barracks, the police stations, town halls, courts and post-offices were empty. All signs of bourgeois government disappeared. There was no revolution of joy, as in 1848. Gloom, uncertainty, surprise at Thiers's extreme action and his refusal to parley, indignation and hate of the state created a sombre, anxious atmosphere. On the other hand, Paris could now 'live its own life' in conformity with its temperament and its ideas.[1] As a result—and this is perhaps what makes the Commune so fascinating and important to the historian—it is possible now to see Paris naked, for its conventional clothes were suddenly removed. One can see

[1] Arthur Arnould, *Histoire populaire et parlementaire de la Commune de Paris* (Brussels, 1878), 1. 114, 3. 45. (By a participant, very good for atmosphere.)

just where the government and the economic system were repressive—where the clothes had been too tight—but also where masses would continue to behave as they had always done even when official obligations and sanctions were withdrawn. The extent to which popular ideas had changed or remained static since 1848 or indeed since 1789, is revealed first by what the Commune did and secondly by the records of the criminal proceedings which followed it. Almost 40,000 people were arrested after March and files for 15,000 of these survive, in which ordinary men speak in their own words. This is a unique source for making contact with those who normally leave no written trace in history.[1]

In 1871 Paris was not to any great extent socialist or revolutionary. In the elections of that year only four of the forty-three candidates supported by the International were elected; and these were successful partly because they received support from other parties; Blanqui obtained only 50,000 votes. The first thing Paris did on finding itself independent was to hold elections for a municipal council—which then assumed the name of Commune. Twenty-five manual workers (artisans) were returned, and this gave the Commune a uniquely proletarian flavour—but the sixty-five other members were bourgeois—doctors, teachers, lawyers, journalists.[2] About one-third of the population of Paris had left during the war or after the siege, including most of the upper classes: the leadership of the city significantly devolved to the petty bourgeoisie, when the top layer—social and governmental—was removed. Two-thirds of these ninety members of the Commune were Jacobins, inspired not by a vision of a socialist future, but by memories of the Revolution of 1789, seeing the Commune as a continuation of that of 1793, capturing power in the interests of the people and using the authority of the state to destroy its enemies. Only one-third were in some way socialists and these were divided between Proudhonists, seeking the abolition of the state, and Blanquist revolutionaries. The acts of the Commune were generally the work of the Jacobins, but the manifestos and justifications of these actions were written by the more theoreti-

[1] J. Rougerie, *Le Procès des communards* (1964); id., *Paris Libre* (1971).

[2] H. P. O. Lissagaray, *Histoire de la Commune de 1871* (first published 1876, new ed. with an introduction by Amédée Dunois 1947), 135–6.

SOCIALISM 739

cal Proudhonists. So the aims of the Commune are, not surprisingly difficult to discover, and all the more so because even this division between Jacobins, Proudhonists and Blanquists is too simple. The Jacobins were not necessarily antisocialist for some were members of the International. Most social reforms were voted unanimously. The Blanquists had much in common with the Jacobins. There was no coherent socialist minority group, which only existed, if at all, at the very end of the Commune, when they had got to know each other. In any case very few acted consistently according to any one doctrine.

Within the parties there were representatives of several generations with very different outlooks. Beslay had begun as a Bonapartist under the Restoration, and had been in turn a liberal and a republican before becoming a Proudhonian socialist. He was a well-to-do manufacturer, who had unsuccessfully experimented with schemes for sharing profits with his workmen.[1] Delescluze was a journalist, a prefect in 1848, one of Ledru-Rollin's principal supporters. He was a passionate admirer of the men of the great Revolution and particularly of the 'martyrs of Thermidor', whom he regarded as 'infallible oracles'. He had attacked the socialism of both Louis Blanc and Proudhon, as likely to turn France into a 'convent or a barracks'; Robespierre's Declaration of Rights and a revival of the Committee of Public Safety were his programme. But during the Second Empire he had shown much sympathy for the efforts of the workers to establish the International and for practical attempts to win their emancipation by association; though leader of the Jacobins, and accused of being ignorant of social questions, he retained the respect and even won the admiration of the socialists.[2]

The bookbinder Varlin (aged only 32) talked of class struggles; but Vermorel, who also called himself a socialist, spoke of social harmony: already well known as a journalist at 30, he was highly eclectic, as influenced by Delescluze as by Proudhon.[3] Tridon, the wealthy son of a speculator in national lands, was a Blanquist: he devoted himself to restoring the

[1] Charles Beslay, Mes Souvenirs (Neuchâtel and Brussels, 1874).

[2] Marcel Dessal, Charles Delescluze 1809–1871 (1952), 421–6 and passim; B. Malon, La Troisième Défaite du prolétariat français (Neuchâtel, 1871), 141; A. Arnould, 2. 89.

[3] A. Vermorel, Le Parti socialiste (1870), v and passim; Jean Vermorel, Un Enfant du Beaujolais: Auguste Vermorel, 1841–1871 (Lyon and Paris, 1911), 131.

reputation of the revolutionary Hébert, but, though a Blanquist, he sided with the socialists during the Commune. Gustave Flourens, son of an Academician and professor at the Collège de France, himself a professor of some reputation and of brilliant promise, heir to an income of 30,000 francs, had an overwhelming longing for swashbuckling romance and he gave everything up to be a mob leader. Babick, a perfumer, was a religious mystic (a 'fusionist'); and Régère, a veterinary surgeon, was actually a clerical. Allix had invented a lunatic telegraph system using 'sympathetic snails' and as mayor of the eighth *arrondissement* organised gymnasia for women. Assi was a mechanic who had served under Garibaldi and organised strikes at Le Creusot, but Rigault, the youngest member of the Commune (only 24) was the son of a sub-prefect of the Second Empire. He had made himself an expert about the secret service of that regime: he got to know the police spies of Paris by following them after their appearances in court; he compiled a long list of them, just as they had a list of the opposition.[1] These examples are enough to show how varied the composition of the Commune was and how complex the motives of its members were. One of them once said to another: 'The best day of my life will be that on which I shall arrest you.'[2]

The Commune's main preoccupation was to feed and defend itself against the government of Versailles. It had no time to institute, let alone to try out, any far-reaching reforms. The atmosphere of war and siege was not conducive to careful planning: one member recorded that he undressed and went to bed fewer than ten times in these two months. However, the decrees which the Commune passed are highly significant. There was very little in them that was anti-capitalist. The Commune did indeed attempt to establish a few workers' production associations and to give some large firms this form of organisation, but only after promising compensation to the owners. A few trade unions did run factories established in this way, though they were deeply disappointing, inefficient and a prey to endless squabbling. But these experiments represented

[1] Jules Clère, *Les Hommes de la Commune. Biographie complète de tous ses membres* (1871), 16–17, 146; Jean Allemane, *Mémoires d'un communard* (n.d.), 72–3; Charles Rihs, *La Commune de Paris, sa structure et ses doctrines* (Geneva, 1955), 76–94, 143–78.
[2] A. Arnould, 3. 31.

a return to the ideals of 1848, not an implementation of Proudhon's theories. A demand for state intervention continued, which was very much against the ideas of Proudhon. When the Commune abolished night work in bakeries, the Proudhonists objected that though the reform was desirable it was the bakers themselves, not the government, who should have effected it. The Commune indeed failed to become the anarchist non-state: it ended by instituting a Jacobin Committee of Public Safety, to the protests of a sizeable minority. Though it contained so many journalists, it instituted censorship of the press. Rigault, its head of police, was even more arbitrary than the Napoleonic police he had once attacked.

The Commune's most interesting reforms were relatively minor practical ones.[1] The abolition of fines in workshops clearly reflected a popular demand. The granting of pensions to widows of men killed in the fighting—whether legally married or not—was a striking recognition that many workers were not married, and a great blow for the emancipation of women, who, with the wage-earner, were considered the most oppressed sections of the community. Dr. Vaillant, at the head of the Education Committee, ordered the establishment of two experimental technical schools, one for boys and one for girls, in which Fourierist 'integral education, the true basis of social equality' would be given. He also attempted to laicize church schools, but here again the actual changes were very slight. At the Lycée St. Louis, prayers still continued to be said twice a day: all that was different was that the two almoners put on civilian clothing and bowler hats and let their beards grow, to the considerable puzzlement of the children.[2] It was difficult to transform the educational system quickly; but even in the sphere of justice, where this might have been possible, little that was radical was attempted. Protot, who was placed in charge of Justice, was the son of a peasant; he had risen to be a barrister, become an admirer of Blanqui, participated in politics and defended prosecuted socialists. He decreed the election of magistrates, but, fearing the results, in fact appointed

---

[1] *Procès-verbaux de la Commune de 1871*, edited by Georges Bourgin and Gabriel Herriot (1924 and 1945, 2 vols.), i. 159, 187, 282–4.

[2] Maurice Dommanget, *L'Enseignement, l'enfance et la culture sous la Commune* (1964), 54, 57.

new ones himself, most of them bourgeois. He abolished the venality of the offices of notary and court officials, but kept those offices in being, merely bringing them into the civil service. No fundamental reform of the law was undertaken or envisaged.[1] The finances of the Commune, placed in the hands of a methodical and honest book-keeper from a department store, Jourde, were scrupulously conservative. The Bank of France was left unmolested, and money only borrowed from it; there was no mention even of the idea of nationalising it. The traditional taxes continued to be levied, no attempt to reform them—a particularly surprising fact. Church and state were declared separated, the property of religious houses confiscated, but in fact—apart from numerous arrests of priests, and the holding of public meetings in churches, transformed into club-houses—little was done to put these decrees into practice. The Commune's hesitation in social reform was shown by the appointment of a procrastinating commission, to which the public were invited to make suggestions. The very idea of social legislation was suspect to some, who preferred to leave it to the workers to make their own arrangements with their employers, on the grounds that they were now powerful enough to get satisfactory terms. Minimum wages were fixed for public workers, but competition was fully accepted provided it was not at the expense of wages or quality. In its manifesto to the peasantry appealing for support, the Commune offered them not nationalisation of land, but ownership of a house and plot for each one and no taxation for any but the rich.[2]

The Commune would have gone much further had it paid attention to the numerous proposals and delegations sent to it by the political clubs. These multiplied quickly after 18 March, aspiring to a new role, as participants in the construction of a new order rather than as organs of opposition. For their meetings they frequently took over churches, and their debates were published in the equally numerous newspapers. A central club attempted to act as a link between the clubs, to serve as 'a thermometer of public opinion', without imposing its

[1] Georges Laronze, *Histoire de la Commune de 1871 d'après des documents et des souvenirs médits: la justice* (1928), 197, 673–9.

[2] Malon, 169–71; Jean Bruhat, Jean Dautry, and Émile Tersen, *La Commune de 1871* (1960), 191–217; cf. E. Schulkind (ed.), *The Paris Commune of 1871* (1972), for a good analysis of left-wing interpretations.

own views. Popular interest in public affairs reached a degree unprecedented since 1848. The wild and extreme views advocated in these clubs had, however, little practical effect and represented the views of a minority. The majority, as revealed by the files of those arrested after May, was much more conservative. The average man in the street wanted self-government for the capital: the abolition of the prefecture of police, the right to elect its municipal council and the officers of its national guard. He wanted popular sovereignty: the theory of direct government of the people, involving representatives elected for short periods and constantly revocable, was particularly favoured. Some looked on this as giving them an opportunity to hold public office, to obtain state jobs. To more, however, it was just a persistence in the ideal of 1793. Social antagonisms were distinctly vague. Though most of those arrested were wage-earners, and though they spoke vaguely against the rich, the bourgeoisie and the idle, they were not rebels against their employers, and there are practically no instances of class hostility against these. On the contrary, many got their employers to testify in their favour at their trials: the employer was an enemy only when he had fled from Paris. On the whole, the people seemed to hate the clergy more than any other class; after that, their landlord, and then their *concierge*. The only capitalist against whom they aired a particularly strong grievance was the forestaller who raised prices—a traditional pre-revolutionary enemy. All this should not be surprising. Paris in 1871 was economically nearer 1789 than 1940. Most men still spent their lives either in small workshops or on their own, rather than in factories; and even when they had moved into factories, they largely retained the undisciplined traditions of the old artisan. They were not even townsmen: three-quarters of those arrested had been born in the provinces. Nor should the Commune be considered a sudden, unexpected rising against the law: 21 per cent of those arrested, and 29 per cent of those found guilty, had previous convictions.[1]

Historically, the suppression of the Commune was perhaps more important than the regime itself. The army from Versailles, when it finally invaded the city, took a week of bloodshed

[1] Jacques Rougerie, *Le Procès des communards* (1964), based on the archives of the ministry of war, which contain the court-martial files.

to capture it. The resistance by the people was spontaneous, unorganised, based on a 'chauvinisme de quartier', for as soon as the Versailles army penetrated, the Communards rushed back pell-mell each to defend his own street, instead of trying to halt the enemy at the gates. The slaughter by the army, 130,000 strong, was without parallel in the century, far out-stripping the June days of 1848. Between 20,000 and 25,000 people were summarily executed or killed. 38,578 were arrested, after almost ten times as many denunciations had been received. It took two years to try their cases, during which they rotted in atrocious prisons. 10,137 were convicted and nearly half of these deported to New Caledonia. Paris after the Commune was a different city. Bereavement, hunger, empty workshops, gloom, exile. 'The soldiers themselves are silent. Victorious, they are sad; they do not drink or sing. Paris has the atmosphere of a city taken by dumb men.'[1] Outside, the myth spread that the Communards had behaved like savages: the press demanded they should be slaughtered like beasts; at the very mention of an amnesty the peasants outside were terrified and clamoured for merciless punishment.[2] This myth caused a breach between the bourgeoisie and the masses, much more profound than that created in June 1848. It made numerous writers speak with contempt and horror of the poor. The lesson Renan drew from it was that democracy was the cause of all France's ills.[3] It made Taine write his antirevolutionary *Origin of Contemporary France*. It stimulated Albert de Mun to found his Catholic Workers' Clubs in an attempt to cure the masses of their dangerous ideas: had not the pope himself talked of the Communards as 'men escaped from Hell who spread fire through Paris'?[4] The Commune made many bourgeois more conservative, and less sympathetic to the workers than they would otherwise have been. At the same time it made the workers more extremist. 'Since [the bourgeoisie] does not wish to receive us fraternally into the human city', concluded Malon, a member of the Commune and one of its best historians, 'we

---

[1] Catulle Mendès, *Les 73 Jours de la Commune* (1871), 326.
[2] Georges Tersen, 'L'opinion publique et la Commune de Paris (1871–79)', in *Bulletin de la Société d'études historiques, géographiques et scientifiques de la région parisienne* (1960 and 1962, 4 articles).
[3] E. Renan, *La Réforme intellectuelle et morale de la France* (1871).
[4] A. Dansette, *Histoire religieuse de la France contemporaine* (1948), 144.

shall get into it through the breaches.'[1] After all the slaughter, it was difficult for the socialists to be moderate, or more particularly to compromise with their executioners, on pain of seeming to deny their dead. The growth of the moderate trade union movement of the 1860s, was cut short, and the opportunity was given for more violent elements to come to the fore. Old socialist leaders like Louis Blanc and Tolain opposed the Commune from Versailles, and the Commune shot as a hostage Gustave Chaudey, Proudhon's testamentary executor: it thus created a breach among the socialists themselves. After the amnesty of 1879, the leaders who returned from exile brought back a heavy load of bitterness with their memories.[2]

The Guesdists

Marxism was introduced into the socialist movement principally by the efforts of Jules Guesde, who is important also for creating the first centralised and organised political party in France. His name means little to most people today, for he was a far less magnificent or attractive figure than either Jaurès or Blum; but in his own day he incarnated those aspects of socialism which terrified the bourgeoisie most. He was very tall and very thin: he had often nearly starved from sheer poverty. His hair grew to his shoulders; his face had a sickly pallor (from almost constant illness) accentuated by the blackness of his flowing beard. Fiery eyes shone from behind metal-framed glasses. When he spoke, even about ordinary things, his lips seemed to quiver with rage. He talked fast, with passion; his voice was grating, sharp, bitter; his irony was always acrid, his insults violent. He was appropriately nicknamed Pope Guesde or the Red Jesuit. He had a dour, authoritarian temperament and was quite ruthless in his methods; he was not loved and his personal following was always small, so that it is not surprising that he has been forgotten. But he was an outstandingly persuasive, enthusiastic and impressive orator, a vigorous, unsuppressible journalist, a tireless organiser. He exerted enormous influence and left a profound mark on the country.

[1] B. Malon, 532.
[2] For the parliamentary debates leading to the amnesty see J. T. Joughin, *The Paris Commune in French Politics 1871–1880* (Baltimore, Md., 1955).

Born in 1845, the son of a schoolmaster, he had to abandon his studies for lack of money. At nineteen he became a translator in Baron Haussmann's prefecture in Paris, but soon gave up the job to become a journalist. Victor Hugo's *Châtiments* (from which he could still recite long passages in old age) made him a republican as a boy; the eighteenth-century philosophers made him an atheist. He was first a follower of Gambetta, then a sympathiser with the Commune; in 1871 he was sentenced to five years' imprisonment for this. He escaped to Italy where he came under the influence of the anarchists. In 1876 he read Marx, was converted, and henceforth he was the principal populariser of Marxism in France.[1] It was his newspaper, *l'Égalité* (1877), with a circulation of about 5,000, which spread the new vocabulary. It was he who determined to capture the trade union movement for Marxism and turn it into a political party. In collaboration with Marx he prepared a programme and passed it through the Marseille Third Trade Union Congress of 1879 which he filled with his rapidly won supporters. Thus was founded the Parti des Travailleurs Socialistes, later the Parti Ouvrier français, which, standing at once in the elections of 1881, won about 50,000 votes. But Guesde never really captured the trade union movement, for this first victory was due to his swamping its congress with unrepresentative delegates. The trade unions soon expelled him and although he tried to form a rival National Federation of Unions, this failed to win much support. From an early stage he was thus beset by a dilemma which worried the socialists ever after. His aim was to establish a working-class party, in conformity with Marxist dogma, but the party created turned out to be something different. His preoccupation with politics alienated the workers: he took little part in strikes and gave little attention to the organisation of unions; he never participated in industrial life. He simply wished to use the workers for political purposes.

Only the textile workers of the Nord and Pas-de-Calais,

[1] For his youth see Jules Guesde, *Textes choisis 1867–1882*, ed. by Claude Willard (1959), introduction. For a contemporary portrait, Mermeix, *La France socialiste* (1886), 60. A. Compère-Morel, *Jules Guesde, le socialisme fait homme 1845–1922* (1937), is dull but useful. Marx's *Capital* was first translated into French by Jules Roy and published in instalments 1872–5. Gabriel Deville published an abridged version in 1876, which was more influential.

were genuinely won over by him. They soon gave him massive support and made him a power to be reckoned with. The reason for this was that his party penetrated the local life of the textile towns to an extraordinary degree, and used traditional festivals and recreational societies for the service of the party. It organised balls, concerts, country fêtes, competitions, billiard and card-games, dramatic societies and shooting clubs, and in this way gave a new revolutionary content to traditional social activities. It was not just poverty that made men join Guesde's party. The textile weavers of eastern France gave him few votes; the wretched conditions of their employment were not by themselves enough to turn them into extremists. Likewise the miners of the north found that their particular corporate interests were better served by other, more moderate leaders, and Guesde made little headway among them: in this sector he obtained support only from workers in small mines and small ironworks, as at Commentry and Montluçon. From the beginning therefore socialism did not appeal automatically to all industrial workers and Guesde made recruits not where certain economic conditions prevailed, but where a combination of many circumstances, and particularly the activities of an able disciple, organised support for him.

A wide variety of social types entered the party; artisans as well as factory workers, even small shopkeepers (17 per cent of the party, nearly half of them publicans) and peasants (7 per cent of the party, one-third of them proprietors). Guesde's success was confined to three regions, which were very different: the north, the east centre (particularly Allier) and the Mediterranean west. The north was the most solid basis of his power, providing him with one-third of his votes. He was successful here partly because the textile workers had no strong political traditions which clashed with his theories (as they did in Paris for example, where he had few followers), and partly because of the indefatigable propaganda of Gustave Delory (1857–1925). A textile worker, sacked for his union activities, Delory set up as a perambulating newspaper merchant, walking twenty-five miles a day to spread the party teaching; he next opened a wine-shop, and then a printing works, both essential political tools. He became mayor of Lille in 1896 and its deputy in 1902. Likewise a watchmaker, Pedron (1849–1931) was principally responsible for the party's success in the Aube, where his news-paper, his speeches, and his practical organisations of trade unions for the bonnet makers of Troyes and Romilly, no less than the lively *soirées familiales* arranged by them, made many converts.[1] In the centre of France, the Guesdist party grew out of the secret society, *La Marianne*, active in 1850–1 and 1872–7, and itself continuing the traditions of the Charbonnerie. The first socialist mayor of France, Christophe Thivrier (1841–95) of Commentry and Jean Dormoy (1851–98), mayor of Mont-luçon, who between them led the party in the Allier, were both originally members of this society. Thivrier had gone down the mines at the age of ten; he had refused to become a foreman, saying 'he did not want to boss his friends'; seeking indepen-dence, he set up on his own as a baker and later as a brick maker, wine merchant and builder; with his savings he built his own house. In 1872 the *Marianne* secret society first met in his attic; when it outgrew it, it met in fields at night, in a different place each time. Its members had an elaborate secret language: on entering a café they would say 'it is a fine day' in a special way; they clinked their glasses first by the stem and then by the lip; they had a special handshake, and sent out their summonses to meetings concealed in handkerchiefs in the form of a letter from a girl summoning her lover to a rendez-vous. These practices appealed to the miners, so that when Guesde visited Commentry and converted Thivrier to his cause, the party that was built up developed as much as a sort of club as an ideological movement. Thivrier's popularity was due above all to his being a very likeable man. 'He was not proud.' He became nationally famous for wearing a worker's blouse (over his frock-coat) when he got into parliament, a gesture, like Keir Hardie's cap, which signified that he was not abandoning his class origins. On one occasion he was expelled from the chamber and carried out bodily for shouting 'Vive la Commune' and refusing to withdraw. But his socialism was far from being that of an orthodox Marxist. His municipality, for example, demanded the abolition of the mine-workers' co-operative because this was ruining the small shopkeepers. His party absorbed some of the radical leaders—like Deslinières,

---

[1] Henri Millet (1865–1902, bonnet maker, later mayor of Romilly), *L'Évolution socialiste à Romilly-sur-Seine* (Troyes, 1896), 25.

the founder of a Freemason lodge—but not without being somewhat diluted.[1] He himself indeed ended by leaving the Guesdist party. His seat in parliament, it is interesting, was inherited by his son.

His rivalry with the other principal Guesdist leader of the region, Jean Dormoy, stresses the diversity of the party even within a small area. Jean Dormoy had been a metalworker since the age of thirteen. Active in republican politics after 1870, he organised an invitation to Guesde to lecture in Montluçon in 1880 and this converted him to Marxism. In consequence, he lost his job, and instead became a perambulating pedlar. He improved his knowledge of Marxism by spending six months in jail together with Guesde and Lafargue (Marx's son-in-law), after a conviction for incitement to the murder of employers and to pillage. He specialised in union organisation, and introduced the 1 May demonstrations into France. When he died at forty-seven such was his personal popularity that 30,000 people are said to have marched in his funeral procession. However, he was never able to establish anything like the disciplined and organised party structure characteristic of the Guesdists in the Nord and in the Aube.

In the Allier, Guesdism recalled much more the Montagne of 1849.[2] In the south of France, Guesdism was taken up by dissatisfied radicals who saw in it a new form of extremism, but who were not at all interested in its Marxism. Its leaders here were largely of the petty or middle bourgeoisie. The most famous, Dr. Ferroul, mayor of Narbonne from 1892 till his death in 1921, had been in turn a Freemason, a radical, and Boulangist: his popularity came from his genius at defending local interests.

The Guesdist party, therefore, turned out very different from what its founder had intended. Karl Marx was exasperated by it. It became the largest single socialist party in France in the late nineteenth century. By 1898 it had 16,000 members; in the elections of that year it had put up 96 candidates, and won 13 seats with 294,000 votes (2·7 per cent of the electorate). It

[1] Ernest Montusès [1880–1927, editor of Le Socialiste, later Le Combat of Allier], 'Le député en blouse' [a biography of Thivrier], in Les Cahiers du Centre, 52 and 53 (Moulins, May–June, 1913).
[2] Georges Rougeron, Le Mouvement socialiste en Bourbonnais 1875–1944 (Moulins, 1946).

captured control of many municipalities.[1] But in the process it quite ceased to be the vigilant guardian of Marxist orthodoxy, or indeed a party with a coherent policy at all. It won its success frequently by alliances which diluted its doctrines with a variety of the socialisms as well as with radicalism and nationalism. After 1892, it rallied to the defence of the republic, it supported Bourgeois's radical ministry in 1895 and, abandoning its view that capitalism was not worth improving, it adopted reformism. It now said that the municipalities it won could not only serve as a useful preparation for the socialist future but also improve immediately the lot of the masses. Guesde expected to gain power very soon. 'We are on the eve of victory', he said in 1893. 'The new century will be the beginning of the new era', he said in 1897. 'The Revolution is at hand', he repeated again and again. He was determined therefore to win all the seats he could (he hoped to have 115 or 120 deputies in 1898); and he was willing to seek votes by all means. The party's agrarian programme wooed the peasantry with the promise of less taxation and the nationalisation of only the very large properties, leaving the small owner 'in quiet possession of the plot he cultivates with his sweat'. They talked less and less of class struggles and revolution. To get rid of their nickname of 'Prussians' (after Marx), they became patriots, indeed chauvinists. However, these changes did not benefit them. The elections of 1898 were a profound disappointment and after them the Guesdists reverted to their old revolutionary policy. One might speculate that had they been more successful at the polls, they would have become increasingly moderate, and developed into mild radicals, in the tradition of Gambetta. In fact neither moderate nor revolutionary tactics availed them much. They appear to have reached the limit of their expansion by the turn of the century. Their Marxism was somewhat irrelevant to French conditions and they made little effort to adapt it to the changing times. They preached that wages were bound to fall even though in France they were quite clearly rising. They made no study of French capitalism or industry though they claimed their doctrines were scientific. Their stress on theory

[1] Claude Willard, *Le Mouvement socialiste en France 1893–1905: les guesdistes* (1965), 316, 348. This very detailed and informative thesis is the basis for any study of Guesdism and a model of its kind.

degenerated into a facile repetition of inert dogmas. Refusing to be utopians, they did not paint any picture of the society for which they were working—and indeed they had no clear view of the future. The regimented, centralised party Guesde tried to establish was unique at a time when other political groups were extremely loose, but it alienated much support. There seemed to be little room in it for able men who aspired to more than local eminence: when Guesde talked of unity to other socialists, they understood by unity only his dictatorship. Guesde's control of his party was in fact deceptive. The hierarchic organisation of sections and federations was only effectively established in the north; elsewhere there was much more variety and informality. The attempt at national centralisation was inefficient; it only stimulated conflicts, especially when Guesde was ill, as he frequently was. Local parties, particularly in the south, were able to pursue an independent policy of alliances regardless. The Guesdists had little money, and only one paid propagandist (Zévaès). Their newspapers were inadequate: they had 130 between 1890 and 1905, mainly weeklies, but over half of these lasted less than a year and only a fifth more than two years. Only six of them had a circulation of over 5,000; most of them were mediocre and uninspiring. The lack of daily newspapers (except in the north) was a considerable handicap. The party, at the same time, became something of a racket, specialising in finding jobs for its members. 22 out of 36 municipal councillors of Roubaix were licensed tavern keepers. Only two of the party deputies in 1898 were in any case real workers.[1]

Guesde did not have the qualities either to create a truly national party or to unite the various sects behind him. He was too tactless, impatient, authoritarian. He was over-anxious for immediate results in his own lifetime and failed to understand the gradual evolution of political opinion in the Third Republic. His opportunism was unsuccessful. He did not give enough emphasis to the immediate improvement of the lot of the poor and he was unable to win the leadership of the trade unions. He attacked both Boulanger and the bourgeois republicans, and so failed to profit from the crisis. He did

[1] Claude Willard, 'Contribution au portrait du militant guesdiste dans les dix dernières années du xixe siècle', in Le Mouvement social (Oct. 1960 and Mar. 1961).

not take part in the Dreyfus affair, unlike Jaurès and Clemenceau who both profited greatly from doing so. He too puristically ignored anticlericalism, even though it was the most potent prejudice of his time. By the turn of the century he had reached the limit of his achievement.[1] His contribution to the socialist movement was, however, of lasting importance. He continued to be influential in the united party congresses till the war; but, even more, he left behind him a strong tradition of Marxist socialism which is one of the major strands in the party's history after that. The conflict between it and the more humane tradition linked with the name of Jaurès and Blum is one of the principal problems of French socialism. Guesde's tradition lives on to this day, strongest in the north, where he had won most adepts. The triumph of Guy Mollet after the Liberation of 1944 marked the revival and the revenge of Guesdism. The idea that the party should be exclusively the representative of the workers, engaged in a class struggle against the rest of society, once again became the official doctrine, in opposition to Blum's desire to broaden the party's appeal, and to rethink its role in French society. Mollet's defeat in 1965 of Defferre's candidature for the presidential election showed how Guesdism still held sway.[2]

The Possibilists

Guesde's authoritarianism soon brought divisions among the socialists. Dr. Paul Brousse, as early as 1881–2, created a rival party which advocated a very different kind of socialism. Brousse blamed the failure of the socialists at elections on Guesde's rigid dogmatism and he demanded that each constituency party should have the right to decide its own programme, appropriate to local conditions. He argued that Guesde's programme—so esteemed by its supporters for its precision and clarity—was impractical and utopian: it sought to obtain everything at the same time, with the result that it obtained nothing at all. In a phrase that (unconsciously no

[1] See the interesting assessments of Guesde by Marcel Cachin, 'Le centenaire de Guesde', in *La Pensée, revue du rationalisme moderne* (11 Nov. 1945), 5. 19–28, and Samuel Bernstein, 'Jules Guesde, Pioneer of Marxism in France' in *Science and Society* (1940), 29–56.
[2] On neo-Guesdism see B. D. Graham, *The French Socialists and Tripartism 1944–47* (Canberra, 1965), and Club Jean Moulin, *Une Parti pour la gauche* (1965).

doubt) echoed Gambetta, Brousse wrote: 'The ideal should be divided into several practical stages; our aims should, as it were, be *immediatised* so as to render them *possible*.' Guesde contemptuously labelled Brousse and his followers *possibilists*, a new type of opportunist. They accepted the name gladly, saying the alternative was to be, like the Guesdists, *impossibilists*. Thus there occurred within the socialist party much the same development as only a short while before had taken place among the republicans and radicals.

The Broussists differed from the Guesdists in three ways. First, they allowed a great deal of autonomy to local groups: they did not seek doctrinal uniformity but a union of all exploited workers, in which there would be room for different opinions in tactics and doctrines. They called themselves the Federation of Socialist Workers, but each local group had the right to add a sub-title, indicating its special views. Secondly, they abandoned the idea of revolution as a means of achieving their ends. They insisted that experience was needed to run a state; the Commune had failed because it lacked it. 'One cannot suddenly turn oneself into a director of a great public service, simply with the qualification of having made a good speech.' So, thirdly, they concentrated on winning power on a municipal scale, for which Brousse (basing himself on the Belgian socialist César de Paepe) developed an alternative to Marxism, the 'theory of public services'. He argued that there was no problem about whether the bourgeoisie ought or ought not to be expropriated. Economic forces would determine their fate. The inevitable development of capitalism was towards the formation of monopolies. It was logical that these should then be transformed into public corporations or services. Socialism would thus be achieved gradually, at different speeds in different sectors, as economic growth led up to it. Finally, when public services were used to their utmost extent, the cost of administration would be greater than it was worth, and they would become free. This might happen first of all in the post-office. When all services became free, communism would be established. Meanwhile Brousse wished to work for a practical municipal socialism.[1] This political programme was in some ways almost

---

[1] Paul Brousse, *La Propriété collective et les services publics* (first published 1883, reprinted with a preface 1910).

indistinguishable from that of the radicals; the tone of his social programme, in its attitude to the class struggle, recalled the moderation of 1848. He was quite willing to support bourgeois governments if they gave practical benefits to the poor. But the bulk of his programme was concerned with local affairs and the municipalisation of transport, water, gas, etc.—which would be either free or sold at cost price. He obviously met a need—parallel to that which Gambetta had satisfied—for he won considerable popularity and in the 1880s it was his party which made the most rapid progress. One of his supporters was the first socialist to be elected to the municipal council of Paris; by 1887 they had nine members of it; in 1889 they won two seats in parliament and about 50,000 votes. They had two daily newspapers, three provincial weeklies, one monthly journal. Their strength was largely confined to Paris, but they also had some thirty odd groups in the west.[1]

There was never much chance, however, that this would lead to any large movement. Brousse was quite incapable of organising on a national scale. He was a fairly rich doctor (with, it is said, an income of 60,000 francs—£2,800). His grandfather had been a well-to-do grain merchant; his father was a professor of medicine, and he was related to a bishop. It is not clear how far he got away from this respectable world, or indeed whether he tried to at all after his youthful escapades, and little is known about his strange marriage with Natalie Landsberg who, for her part, was the rebel daughter of a Russian prefect of police. Brousse represented a form of bourgeois nonconformity. He had got to know Guesde in Montpellier when he was a student; he had been sentenced to three months' imprisonment for a press offence, had fled to Spain, and joined the International. He then deserted Marx for Bakunin, less for doctrinal reasons than because he objected to any strict orthodoxy.[2] When he eventually settled down in Paris, he built up a very influential position for himself in the seventeenth *arrondissement*, particularly in the quartier des Épinettes, of which he was for long a municipal councillor. He organised a socialist club there and a general trade union of small tradesmen, workers and clerks.

[1] Sylvain Humbert, *Les Possibilistes* (1911), 48 ff.
[2] Paul Brousse, *Le Suffrage universel et le problème de la souveraineté du peuple* (Geneva, 1874), shows him in this phase.

He took great trouble to help his electors in their practical concerns, holding what was perhaps the first political 'surgery' twice a week, and showing himself always very friendly and obliging.[1]

The paradoxical aspect of Brousse's life was that he spent some ten years of it arguing about anarchist and socialist theory, engaging in vituperative disputations in international congresses, when he had a deep distrust of all theory. Because of these early activities, he earned something of a reputation as a dangerous agitator: he had been exiled by France and Switzerland in turn. But he was not made to be a sectary. Both as an anarchist in the Jura Federation and later as one of the founders of the French Socialist Party, he had urged the abandonment of metaphysical debates about doctrine. As an anarchist, he had urged 'propaganda by deed', by which he had meant not assassination and terrorism, whose failure had been conclusively demonstrated, but simply municipal socialism.

The starting-point of Brousse's thinking was that in France there was no chance of a general strike. It was totally unrealistic to expect one when the workers had barely begun to organise and when their political activity was in a pitifully embryonic and chaotic state. The masses did not read books and it was no use trying to convert them with turgid works of theory, or even with newspapers. The only way to make an impact on their ignorance and their prejudices was to show them that socialism worked, in a practical, visible form. Rather, therefore, than try to overthrow the whole bourgeois state, it would be more sensible to obtain control of a few municipalities and reorganise them on socialist lines. This would fit into the tradition of the Paris Commune. But each commune should be allowed to go its own way. Anyone who knew French conditions had to accept the fact that large areas of the country were thoroughly under the influence of the nobles, the clergy or the bourgeoisie. France was an extremely varied amalgam of regions with very different historical traditions. No party had succeeded in winning an outright majority in parliament. The socialists should not therefore expect all communes to be socialist. They must wait until, in due course, the contrast between the happiness of the socialist ones and the misery of the clerical ones

[1] Léon de Seilhac, *Le Monde socialiste* (1904), 37.

became so great that the masses would voluntarily renounce the domination of their traditional rulers.

Brousse did not propose to destroy the state immediately he obtained municipal office. He planned only to transform the commune gradually, so that *public service* should replace government. This meant the elimination of the authoritarianism and the hierarchical character which government inevitably possessed. He attacked the Marxists with vigour, dismissing them as 'revolutionaries by taste, neurotics, fanatics, romantics of insurrection'.

Brousse's aim was to start a Labour Party in France. This was the title he wished to give his organisation, implying a broad, undoctrinaire appeal. He was keen on maintaining contacts with the English trade unions, in contrast with other French socialists who condemned them as reactionary. Brousse co-operated with the radicals in defending the republic when General Boulanger appeared to threaten its existence, and he was a founder member of the Society of the Rights of Man, though his followers soon forced him to withdraw from it. This society was a predecessor of the league which was to be a force in French politics for a generation. Brousse's work survived also, without his name being generally associated with it, in the ministerial socialism of men like Millerand, for whose newspaper, *La Petite République*, Brousse frequently wrote. His absorption into the republic may be seen in the way, when he lost his parliamentary seat in 1910, he was pensioned off with a directorship of a state mental hospital, one of the republic's favourite sinecures.[1]

Just as the socialists had split into Broussists and Guesdists in 1882, so in 1890 the Broussists split in their turn. The leader of the revolt was Jean Allemane (1843–1935), a typographer, trade unionist and member of the Commune sentenced to hard labour in New Caledonia for his participation in it. Allemane represented the protest against the increasing opportunism of Brousse, against association with the radicals, to the extent of becoming scarcely distinguishable from them in the common pursuit of office. Allemane had got involved in a personal rivalry with Brousse, each of them having a daily newspaper of his own. In 1890 he broke away and founded his own group,

[1] David Stafford, *From Anarchism to Reformism* (1971).

the Allemanists. He wanted his party to be genuinely a workers' party, which would unite the merits of Guesdism and Broussism. He was interested in municipalism and immediate reforms but made it clear that they represented the first stage only. He supported the idea of a general strike, but insisted that the workers should first be organised in unions and that the strike should be international. He objected to all hero worship within the party—of which he declared Brousse and Guesde equally guilty—and was indeed hostile to all politicians, because they too easily lost contact with their electors. The Allemanist candidates in elections were strictly subordinate to the local constituency parties, they had to sign an undated letter of resignation, which the party could use if it ever wished to, and they were required to pay their salaries to the party funds, from which they drew a smaller allowance. Allemanism represented a reiteration of the determination of the workers to win their own emancipation by their own efforts; its stress was on egalitarianism, and a distrust of the bourgeoisie. But at the same time it was revolutionary only in principle and it was unable to discover a method of bringing about practical reforms without polluting itself in the mire of the existing system. Allemane himself had been able to do this. His popularity came precisely from his having through the vicissitudes of his career remained always a worker in his habits and his hopes; he never gave the impression that he was a leader on the make. His anarchist ideal of politics without politicians could not, however, work. His party secured five seats in parliament in 1893, outdoing the Broussists and spreading their influence outside Paris. But these deputies soon found their subordination to their constituency parties intolerable, they refused to give up their salaries; in 1896 they resigned from the party and joined the Blanquists. The Allemanists thus in their turn were split; the surviving remnant later joined the independent socialists (showing how the party stood uncertainly between reformism and revolution). This movement too was thus abortive.[1]

Jaurès

Jaurès is, with Gambetta, perhaps the most venerated politician of the Third Republic. He may not be admired by such a broad

[1] Maurice Charnay, *Les Allemanistes* (1912).

variety of parties, but he is admired for a greater variety of qualities, as something more than a politician. Romain Rolland wrote of him: 'Jaurès is a model, almost unique in modern times, of a great political orator who is at the same time a great thinker, uniting enormous culture with penetrating observation, moral elevation with energy for action. One needs to go back to Antiquity to find anything similar. He could raise the masses and enchant the élite at the same time.'[1] Blum said, 'I have never met any man—except perhaps Albert Einstein—on whom the seal of genius was so obviously and so evidently imprinted.'[2] The English socialist, Max Beer, who knew most of the politicians of this generation, wrote that of all the men he had met Lenin and Jaurès impressed him most.[3] More biographies have probably been written of him than of any other French politician of this period; but the materials for a proper assessment of his achievements are still lacking. His complete works comprise only about a tenth of his writings; their publication was abandoned after volume 9; it was estimated that 90 tomes of 400 pages would have been needed to make them comprehensive. Fewer than a hundred of his letters have been published, so that one has to rely almost entirely on his public pronouncements. Only recently have a few researchers embarked on a really detailed examination of his life and in 1960 a Society of Jaurès Studies was founded.[4] The historian must be very conscious of the many questions about Jaurès which remain unanswered. His problem is to see his way through the legend, to assess and explain the unstinted praise Jaurès received, which seems at first sight too exaggerated to obtain credence outside the charmed circle.

Jaurès's political importance is that he created a unified socialist party out of the numerous sects, that he saved it both from the dogmatism and utopianism which had characterised them, and gave it a wide appeal within the framework of the republic and of French life. He came on to the scene at an opportune moment, when the socialists were longing for unity,

[1] *Journal de Genève* (2 Aug. 1915), quoted in *Europe* (Oct.–Nov. 1958), 3.
[2] L. Blum, *Jean Jaurès* (1937), 8.
[3] J. Hampden Jackson, *Jean Jaurès* (1943), 11.
[4] See its *Bulletin de la Société d'études jaurésiennes*. The leading and most thorough biography is by Harvey Goldberg, *The Life of Jean Jaurès* (Madison, Wis., 1962).

but this does not diminish his achievement, for Millerand failed to do what Jaurès did. Jaurès was particularly well suited for his task by his origins, his education and his temperament. He was a bourgeois by birth, from a fairly well-off clan of Castres (Tarn), which had included merchants and barristers, two admirals and a bishop, but his father, though he married the daughter of a cloth manufacturer, was the poorest and least successful of the family; he failed in business several times and ended up with a small farm of fifteen acres. Jaurès thus grew up quite poor. He owed his early education to the generosity of an uncle; but he won all the first prizes at school, and so obtained a scholarship to Paris and to the École Normale Supérieure. He did brilliantly there and passed out third in merit (Bergson was second and a forgotten schoolmaster first). After a period as a sixth-form master at Albi, he became a lecturer and soon after a professor of philosophy at Toulouse University. But as a philosopher he was not the advocate of any particular doctrine: he sought to reconcile logic and common sense, to produce a synthesis of realism and idealism. As a teacher, he treated his pupils as personal friends. For Jaurès was not a typical professor, nor indeed typical of anything.

On first acquaintance he gave a rather uncertain impression. Eulogies of him are so common that it is perhaps worth balancing them by the pretty realistic description given of him by Jules Renard: 'Jaurès looks like a junior secondary schoolmaster who will never get his higher degree (*agrégation*) and who will not take enough exercise, or he looks like a fat merchant who eats well. He is of medium height and square. His head is fairly regular, neither ugly, nor beautiful, neither unusual nor common. Hirsute . . . A nervous tic of the right eyelid . . . A very cultivated intelligence. He does not even allow me to finish my quotations. He is perpetually referring to history or cosmogony. An orator's memory, very full, astonishing. Frequently spits into his handkerchief. I do not sense a strong personality. He gives me the impression rather of a man whose file could say: good health in every respect. At one of his jokes, he laughed too much, with a laugh that climbed down the stairs and didn't stop till the ground. His speech is slow, thick, slightly hesitating, without nuances. In religious matters he appears rather timid. He is embarrassed when this subject is raised. He gets out of it by "I assure you it is more complicated than you think." [1]

Jaurès was a bourgeois but also a peasant—he called himself 'a cultured peasant'.[2] He belonged to the intellectual élite, he was a small proprietor, but in appearance he could be mistaken for a worker on holiday. He wore the bourgeois uniform of a black frock-coat, but so untidily, dirtily and inelegantly—with his trousers always too short, revealing socks falling over his shoes, his pockets crammed full of papers and books—that he did not clearly belong to any class. This was the secret of his charm. He was 'essentially a human—not a professional man, not a member of a class or of a party, or the supporter of an idea, but a complete, harmonious, free man'. He had an extraordinary gift for sympathising with every type of person. He was neither proud, nor competitive, nor self-assertive. He combined his undoubted intellectual gifts with a childish naïveté and perfect plainness. He was thus readily acceptable as a leader, all the more because he had a dislike of deliberately offending anybody. 'He was by nature a pacificator' and his affability was honest.[3]

He was, and this clinched his success as a politician, a spell-binding orator. His technique was not impressive: he could not compare for fluency and perfection of style with Viviani, who had taken lessons at the Comédie Française and who used to re-enact the great speeches of the past for practice. His gestures were banal and repetitive: he used to raise a half-clenched fist and bring it down rapidly to his waist, he would point at the sky or at the audience, occasionally he would raise both arms high above his head in a manner which the experts judged 'heavy'. Yet he was considered to be the equal of Bossuet.[4] He was allowed to go on in parliament for two or three hours in ordinary debates and in important ones for two whole days. He was captivating because his speeches reflected his character but he had an uncanny feeling for the reactions of his audience. He always began hesitatingly until he could sense his way. What

[1] M. Auclair, La Vie de Jean Jaurès (1954), 258.
[2] To Vincent Auriol, Jean Jaurès (1962).
[3] Augustin Hamon, 'Souvenirs sur Jaurès', La Grande Revue, 88 (July 1915), 107–12.
[4] By Bracke, p. 26, in Michel Lannay, 'L'éloquence de Jaurès', Europe (Oct.–Nov. 1958), 23–39.

distinguished him from other speakers was his gift for expressing the feelings of a crowd, for making himself the interpreter of a mass, even though the link between them disintegrated when he had stopped. As soon as he had found the metaphor which combined the ideas he wished to express, he was off, on dazzling verbal flights, whose poetic phrasing and rich imagery were as intoxicating to the audience as to himself. Something said by him or by an interrupter would evoke a whole series of ideas. Blum used to speak as a Parisian intellectual, carefully giving all the arguments for and against, using his speech to satisfy an inner demand of conscience; but Jaurès always reflected the feeling of the moment—'He would then take all those who were listening pell-mell by the hair and unite them round an idea, whether they wished it or not.' His genius, said the Guesdist Bracke (at first an opponent and later an admirer) was 'to formulate the ideas which were common to those who were around him . . . to seek to unite them . . . to draw together bits of ideas and fragments of humanity'.[1] As an orator, he was not just a great tenor, but an attractive personality. Trotsky wrote of him: 'For Jaurès, oratory had no intrinsic value . . . Though the most powerful speaker of his time and perhaps of all times, he was beyond oratory; he was always superior to his speeches, as the artisan is to his tools.'[2]

Jaurès took to politics naturally. He made a brilliant impromptu speech in a public meeting held by a Bonapartist, at which he defended the educational reforms of Jules Ferry. His oratory was compared to that of the youthful Gambetta. He was invited to stand for parliament on the republican opportunist (Ferry) list and was triumphantly elected. He was then only twenty-five and the youngest deputy in parliament. But in Paris he was disappointing. He spoke hardly at all; he felt ill at ease; it took him some time to find his way. In later years he claimed he had always been a socialist, even though he sat in the centre in this parliament, but his consistency was in fact of a different kind. The characteristic of his political opinions was that they were always evolving. Though he made so many speeches, he never said the same thing twice. However, he differed from most other politicians of the Third Republic, who

[1] Bracke, ibid.
[2] Harvey Goldberg, *The Life of Jean Jaurès* (Madison, Wis., 1962), 188.

gradually became more conservative. Jaurès on the contrary came to appreciate the left-wing and also a large number of other points of view. His horizons were constantly widening. It has been well said that he was not converted to socialism: he understood it. He did so because he had an exceptionally open mind. 'The idea that needs to be safeguarded above all', he said in 1895, 'is the idea that no power, no dogma should limit the perpetual effort, the perpetual search of the human race—humanity sits like a great commission of inquiry with unlimited powers. It is the idea that every truth that does not come from us is a lie; it is the idea that in every agreement our critical spirit must nevertheless remain awake.'[1] He respected opposite opinions and abhorred only intolerance. Though forward looking, he also as he himself said, 'worshipped the past. It is not in vain that all the hearths of human generations have burned.'[2] He combined his liberalism with a passion for unity. When he read Cardinal Newman describing how men were being divided by the gulf of damnation, he had nightmares. He applied himself more than anything to bridging this abyss of incomprehension between men. 'The need for unity', he believed, 'is the most profound and the most noble of human needs.'[3] He had a passion for the reconciliation of apparently contradictory ideas. In his philosophical thesis on *The Reality of the Perceptible World* (1891) he expressed the hope of 'bringing about, on the basis of metaphysics and science, the great dream of union.'[4] Now when Jaurès entered politics the very idea of a separate socialist party displeased him. He believed in the union of all republicans. He was a supporter of Jules Ferry, whose colonial policy he thought was helping Frenchmen to forget their petty differences in the accomplishment of national expansion: he talked even of the 'touching union of the family of France'.[5] He was horrified by class antagonisms, by the

---

[1] Speech of 11 Feb. 1895, quoted in M. Jaurès and M. Clemenceau, by a French Contributor, in *The Dublin Review* (Apr. 1906), 310 n.

[2] Romain Rolland, op. cit.

[3] Quoted by Charles Rappoport, *Jean Jaurès, l'homme, le penseur, le socialiste* (1915), 104. A still useful book, particularly for Jaurès's ideas.

[4] Quoted by Félicien Challaye, *Jaurès* (n.d.), 115. This valuable study of Jaurès's philosophy is part of a series in which the other subjects are Socrates, Plato, Descartes, Kant, etc., showing the esteem Frenchmen had for him.

[5] Jean Jaurès, *Textes choisis*, vol. 1, *Contre la guerre et la politique coloniale*, ed. by Madeleine Rebérioux (1959), 13. A good introduction.

bitterness of labour disputes. He wrote in 1889: 'It is not by the violent and exclusive agitation of this or that social faction, but from a sort of national movement that justice must emerge . . . The masses and the working bourgeoisie must unite to abolish capitalist privileges and abuses.'[1] He hoped that the republicans would see the need for bringing about social justice; he himself introduced a bill on workers' pensions, in a premature anticipation of solidarism. But Ferry was not interested in the social question in the same way and failed to provide enough scope for Jaurès's idealism. After Jaurès lost his seat in 1889, therefore, his political method changed. Contact with trade union leaders in Toulouse and in the mining town of Carmaux gave him a new respect for the socialists, whom he no longer considered factious. He began borrowing books from the public library on socialism, and wrote a subsidiary thesis on *The Origins of German Socialism* (1891).[2] His work on the Toulouse municipal council made him take a more practical view of the possibilities of obtaining reforms. So when in 1892 the miners of Carmaux invited him to stand as their socialist candidate for parliament, believing he was specially suited to rallying the peasants in the rural part of the constituency as well, he agreed, and he accepted their condition that he should declare his approval of the P.O.F. programme.[3]

He did not, however, join the party and he sat as an independent socialist. Jaurès was not a Marxist. He accepted some Marxist doctrines but, like Malon, he combined them with other—contradictory—ones. He paid homage to Marx and seldom criticised him openly, but he liked to reconcile idealism with materialism, and he had much in common with Bernstein's revisionism. Just as Bernstein believed that economic forces cease to be supreme in capitalism, so Jaurès argued that when capitalism reaches the stage of monopoly, its great magnates realise the need to satisfy the workers. It is their conscience

---

[1] Rolande Trempé, 'Jaurès, député de Carmaux' in *Jaurès présenté par V. Auriol* (1962), 86–119, quoted p. 90.

[2] For the influence of the librarian of the École Normale Supérieure see Charles Andler, *La Vie de Lucien Herr* (1932).

[3] Madeleine Rebérioux, 'Jaurès et Toulouse 1890–1892', in *Annales du Midi* (1963), 295–310; Rolande Trempé, 'Jaurès et Carmaux', in *Europe* (Oct.–Nov. 1958), 64–73; J. Jaurès, *Discours parlementaires* (1904), introduction by him on 'Le socialisme et le radicalisme en 1885', an important piece of autobiography.

which will change their attitude; a system of morals common to both bourgeoisie and the workers was thus possible and in consequence so was the collaboration of classes. Jaurès believed that capitalism could be penetrated gradually by socialism, and that its violent overthrow was unnecessary. He held that taxation and the development of companies with increasing numbers of shareholders was introducing socialism into the bourgeois state. Capitalism was not worsening the lot of the poor. It was not moving towards crisis, for it had passed the stage of anarchy into one of regulated cartels. It had the elements of progress in it. Jaurès complained that 'Marx had not sufficiently recognised the part of human good faith, of sincere moral and social enthusiasm which at certain times sustained and roused the bourgeoisie'; he praised the bourgeoisie's 'fanaticism for human progress' and in particular he admired 'those great individuals who by their brains, their technical ability, their genius, their courage, create new sources of wealth'. With a Saint-Simonian faith in the great international industrialists and financiers Jaurès believed they could prevent economic crises. The class struggle he considered to be unnecessary in a democracy like France where it was replaced by a political struggle. Parliament represented the general will for him; and socialism would eventually be established by the vote of legislature.[1] He did not accept the Guesdist hostility to colonies as such, but simply demanded a more humane and liberal colonial policy. In the first years of the twentieth century he saw the formation of the Ententes and Alliances as pacific developments, the beginnings of a European federation. He did not wish to destroy the idea of *Patrie*, but to socialise it. Though one kind of capitalism was chauvinist, another was capable of organising peace, under the leadership of the great banks: he could thus remain optimistically pacifist.[2] Like the Saint-Simonians too, he was hostile to the clergy and the military, but not to religion itself. He believed in immortality, and in God, though probably of a pantheistic rather than a personal kind; he laid stress on the importance of ideas and of religion in men's

---

[1] J. Klément, *Jaurès réformiste* (1931), and J. Jaurès, *L'Armée nouvelle* (1910), especially chapter 10, and *Études socialistes* (reprinted in vol. 1 of his *Complete Works*); Edward Claris, 'Du capitalisme au socialisme d'après Jaurès', in *L'Actualité de l'histoire* (Apr.–June 1959), 22–3.

[2] Madeleine Rebérioux, Introduction to *Jean Jaurès, textes choisis* (1959).

lives.[1] Socialism was thus for him, as Blum said, 'the point of convergence, the inheritance of all that humanity, since the obscure beginnings of civilisation, had produced in wealth, virtue and beauty'.[2] And his view of civilisation was constantly broadening. In his last years, he regretted having read too much German and not enough of the English writers: he began reading Newman and Shakespeare. Hume's *Dialogues on Natural Religion* was one of the last books he read and it gave him 'one of his greatest intellectual joys'.[3]

Jaurès's theoretical passion for unity was matched by exceptional skill as a practical politician in achieving it. He was brilliant at drafting resolutions which all sides could accept, at the very moment when their disagreements seemed to have reached a deadlock. His combined gifts as a parliamentarian, a journalist, an intellectual and a speaker at party congresses and at public meetings made him highly influential; and his amiability and self-effacement rendered this influence widely acceptable, so that he ultimately emerged as the leader of the party. His contribution to the growth of the party was very considerable. He was, after Millerand, a prime influence in urging socialist support of bourgeois governments whenever they showed themselves willing to carry out reforms. He backed the radical ministry of Bourgeois in 1895 (which proposed to introduce an income tax), the Waldeck-Rousseau ministry of republican defence (1899–1902), and he was the organiser of the Bloc des Gauches which enabled Combes to separate Church and state. In electoral terms this policy produced very large rewards. Alliances with the radicals made possible most of the socialist victories at the polls, which they could never have achieved if they had remained an isolated, anti-republican party. In the short term, Jaurès's determined desire to collaborate with other republicans accentuated the breach between his followers and those of Guesde, so that in 1900, when an attempt was made to unite the various socialist factions, agreement was impossible, and two separate parties were formed, one under Jaurès and one under Guesde. Guesde sought the help of the

[1] J. Jaurès, *La Question religieuse et le socialisme* (1959); Claude Tresmontant, 'La religion de Jaurès', in *Esprit* (1960), 2038–51.
[2] L. Blum, *J. Jaurès* (1937), 37.
[3] J. Jaurès, *La Question religieuse et le socialisme* (1959), 17.

International, and in 1904 obtained from its Congress of Amsterdam a condemnation of Jaurès's policy of collaboration. It was now that Jaurès showed his magnanimity and his acumen. He accepted this decision; he withdrew from the Bloc des Gauches, he acquiesced in the socialists becoming a revolutionary party. It was in this way that in 1905 a united socialist party was at last formed, as the S.F.I.O. (French Section of the Workers' International).[1] But once unity was achieved, Jaurès gradually influenced it back to his own reformist policy, while at the same time satisfying the revolutionaries. He drafted the declaration of principles issued by the party's congress at Toulouse in 1908, which ingeniously reconciled the conflicting aims by arranging them into a chronological order. The *ultimate* aim of the party was, to please the Guesdists, declared to be the total conquest of power by the revolutionary establishment of collectivism. To please the Blanquists and Allemanists, the party declared that it would, *when opportunity arose*, use insurrection and the general strike. But its *immediate* method was to be electoral campaigning, parliamentary and municipal action, the spread of trade unions, co-operatives and education.[2]

The limitations of Jaurès's achievement must not, however, be overlooked. A unitary, as opposed to a federal, structure was adopted for the S.F.I.O., which issued its own cards to members in return for a subscription paid direct to central funds. The congress was made the sovereign body of the party; it was based on the numerical representation of members; the deputies and federations were kept firmly subordinated to it. Between 1905 and 1914 party membership doubled, to reach 90,725 by the war. But this was trifling compared to the German Social Democrats, who in 1912 had over a million members. The rule of the congress, moreover, was unacceptable to many of the socialist deputies. Twenty-four independents remained outside the party in 1906, and though the S.F.I.O. forbade its supporters to vote for them in elections, even when there was no other socialist candidate, about thirty independents were elected in 1910, forming the *Parti socialiste républicain*. This was

[1] A. Noland, *The Founding of the French Socialist Party 1893–1905* (Cambridge, Mass., 1956).

[2] The text of the Motion de Toulouse is in Georges Lefranc, *Le Mouvement socialiste sous la Troisième République* (1963), 397–8.

numerous enough not to be eclipsed by Jaurès's S.F.I.O., and its able members—notably Briand, Viviani and Millerand— repeatedly held ministerial office uncontrolled by him. It was small consolation to argue that their ambition made them unsuitable for collective action and that they were best outside, for Jaurès would certainly have liked more influence on governments. His nostalgia for the Bloc des Gauches remained; it was only in 1914, when it was too late, that he was able to revive it, finding at last in Caillaux a continuator of Combes. Jaurès was not a man of the opposition. 'The only real and pure joy of public life', he said, 'is to be associated, in all independence, without chicanery, in substantial works of political organisation and of democratic and social progress. All the joys of criticism and combat are noble, no doubt, but they are bitter.'[1] The question of whether he would have accepted power had he not been assassinated just before the outbreak of the war must remain unanswered; but it might well be asked whether he used his talents fully in the years 1905–14.

The unification of the socialists was very far from bringing to an end their doctrinal disputes: on the contrary, it increased them, because all the old battles, which had been settled by separation, now had to be fought again. The duel of Jaurès and Guesde was one of the major events of the congresses. The leaders of the old factions continued to advocate their viewpoint, and in addition new attitudes also emerged. Alexandre Varenne, following Bernstein, demanded that the party should become openly reformist, and bring its proclamations of doctrine into line with its acts. At the other extreme Gustave Hervé led a highly embarrassing campaign for insurrection and total antimilitarism. On the one hand Albert Thomas strongly urged co-operation with the radicals, while on the other Charles Andler expressed contempt for the parliamentary system, and, opposing Jaurès's view that socialism was the logical conclusion of democracy, argued that it was something essentially different.[2] Divisions persisted on the party's attitude to war, on its precise view of nationalisation and municipal socialism. Its newspaper,

---

[1] Quoted by Marcel Prélot, *L'Évolution politique du socialisme français 1789–1934* (1939), 201.

[2] A. Thomas, *La Politique socialiste* (1913); B. W. Schaper, *Albert Thomas* (Assen, Netherlands, 1959); Charles Andler, *Le Civilisation socialiste* (1912).

L'Humanité, founded by Jaurès in 1904 with no fewer than seventeen *agrégés* on its staff, at last became a daily in 1913, but it never enjoyed a mass circulation. The party's finances made really active propaganda impossible; there were only six paid officials; one half of its income came from contributions by the deputies who had to surrender part of their parliamentary salaries.[1]

Above all the party failed to win either the trade unions or the peasantry. The Guesdists were anxious to maintain the primacy of political over economic action. Jaurès succeeded in carrying an acceptance of trade unions and co-operatives as legitimate forms of preparation for socialism, and personally he established good relations with some of the C.G.T.'s leaders. Jouhaux declared at his funeral that Jaurès had 'by the justice and clarity of his mind, succeeded in reducing the disagreements between' their two doctrines; 'he was the link between our two factions',[2] but all the same the trade union movement remained separate. On the question of the peasantry, Jaurès had from an early stage been regarded as an expert, both in parliament and in his party. He continued the policy, which even the Guesdists had adopted, of promising to exempt small peasant proprietors from nationalisation. 'Your property is sacred', he wrote; 'if you are in debt, I shall help you out of your mortgage . . . I shall supply you with machines. To non-owning peasants I say: I shall help you to become proprietors, taking precautions only that you do not become in your turn exploiters of labour.'[3] The Marxist idea that the socialists should appeal only to agricultural labourers was clearly worthless, since the countryside was rapidly being drained of them as they migrated to the towns. There was a strong temptation to become in rural areas a peasant party, rather than a socialist party. In 1906 the Limoges congress decided to 'pursue the realisation of the demands of the peasantry'. It appointed a commission to discover what these were: 20,000 questionnaires were sent out, but very few returned. The report in 1908 showed that these demands were essentially practical, like help

---

[1] Hubert Rouger, *La France socialiste* (1912), 149–52.
[2] Georges Guy-Grand, 'Jaurès, ou le Conciliateur', in *La Grande Revue*, 97 (July 1918), 1–20, quoted p. 10.
[3] G. E. Prévot, *Le Socialisme aux champs* (Toulouse, 1905), preface by Jaurès, 6–8.

with mortgages, reduction in the price of fertilisers, and higher prices for their products. After inconclusive attempts to reconcile this with Marxism—for Compère-Morel, the most active proselytiser of the peasantry, was a Guesdist—and a further inquiry, the party adopted, in 1910, a programme which differed very little from that of the radicals and which remained on the socialist platform till 1919. The conversion of the peasantry to socialism was thus in practice abandoned: and this failure to win the peasants over—as opposed to merely securing some of their votes from reasons of expediency—was to produce a major weakness in the party.[1]

The Independent Socialists

There were still other types of men whom these various forms of socialism did not suit and whose socialism was of a different kind: those who were interested in practical achievement rather than precise doctrine and those who, like the politicians of all other parties, could not accept the idea of being a member of an organised and regimented sect. In 1885 a group of independent socialists was formed in the chamber of deputies by socialists who were not members of any socialist party. They were an anti-party and they long remained simply a group of deputies without any organization in the country. Only a few of them were elected as socialists; the majority were radicals especially interested in social reform. Their programme, though it talked of gradual nationalisation, was couched in very vague terms. Jaurès, elected as a republican in this same year and in search of more definite ideas, thought of joining, and asked one of them what they would do if they got power; he got a very noncommittal answer, that it would depend on the circumstances. The group included some interesting men, whose careers illustrate the changes taking place in the left wing within the republican system. Antide Boyer, who was one of the principal organisers of the group, was the son of an earthenware dealer: he began life as a tiler, became a railway worker, then a

[1] Maurice Lait, *Le Socialisme et l'agriculture française* (1922), 35–41; J. Bourdeau, 'Revue du mouvement socialiste' in *Revue politique et parlementaire* (Sept. 1910), 569–78; A. Compère-Morel, *La Question agraire en France* (1908); id., *La Question agraire et le socialisme en France* (1912); Michel Angé-Laribé, *Grande ou petite propriété* (Montpellier, 1902); Ernest Tarbouriech, 'La propagande agraire du parti socialiste', in *Revue socialiste* (Mar. 1910), 252–76.

book-keeper and finally a socialist journalist and politician. He was one of the leaders of the socialist party in Marseille and entered the chamber in 1885 with radical support. Brialou was first a weaver, then a gas-fitter at Lyon: he was elected on Clemenceau's list. Camelinat, originally a vine labourer, then a factory worker, had been a member of the First International and of the Commune: he too was supported by both radicals and socialists. Numa Gilly, a cooper who after a time had set up on his own, had been elected mayor of Nîmes by a coalition of the extreme left and right, anxious to overthrow the opportunist: he called himself a radical-socialist. Planteau was a porcelain painter of Limoges who had migrated to Paris, learnt foreign languages and become a professional translator: at forty-three he started studying law, in which he got a degree. He had been active in radical, not socialist, politics. A few were old republicans like Daumas, a mechanic who had been imprisoned for his politics for eight years by the Second Empire and had then set up as a brewer in Toulon: he had been a deputy since 1871 and was to end up as a radical senator. There was the Provençal poet Clovis Hugues, who had been elected as a radical in 1881, had joined the Guesdists in the following year, then quarrelled with them because he insisted on attending Louis Blanc's funeral, and so he had returned to the radical benches. He was a colourful character, who had killed a Bonapartist in a duel over his wife, who in turn a few years later shot another man dead for pestering her: both of them had stood trial for these murders and been acquitted. By no means all the independents were workers: there were also doctors and barristers among them. But they called themselves the Socialist Workers' Group. They were really a wing of the radical party, to which some of them continued to belong at the same time. Quite a few of them became Boulangists: their division on this issue destroyed their cohesion, which was slight enough.[1]

After the crisis, Alexandre Millerand (1859–1943), one of the few men to remain neutral over Boulanger, attempted to recreate the group and develop it into a broad-based 'reformist socialist' party. His efforts are highly instructive because they make it possible to understand more easily the relationship of the socialists to the radicals and to appreciate more accurately

[1] Albert Orry, *Les Socialistes indépendants* (1911).

the nature of the achievement of Jaurès, who was to succeed where Millerand failed. Millerand ended his career as a right-wing president of the republic (1920-4) and for this reason he has seldom received his due in histories of socialism, but he should not be dismissed as an ambitious unprincipled renegade. He was certainly very keen on winning office and he became the first socialist minister of the Third Republic. He was an extremely hard and methodical worker, who enjoyed administration. He was uncultured, cold, bovine, with a 'square face, square shoulders, square obstinacy', myopic to the point of being unable to recognise his own family in the street. Born the son of a modest draper, he was a barrister but interested in politics from early youth, he began writing for Clemenceau's *Justice* almost as soon as he had qualified. When still only twenty-five he was elected, on the latter's radical list, to the Paris municipal council and, a year later, to parliament. He was the youngest deputy after Jaurès. He showed considerable independence as a radical, joined the Socialist Workers' Group, and broke with Clemenceau, whom he regarded as being too obsessed by anticlerical questions. In November 1891 he joined René Goblet, the founder of the radical-socialist party, and some other radicals, in issuing an appeal for a new policy, with the stress on economic rather than political reform, to be backed by republicans and socialists alike. A year later, he succeeded Goblet as editor of *La Petite République* and used it to lead a vigorous 'independent socialist' campaign in the elections of 1893. Nine of the men he supported were elected in Paris and a dozen radical deputies from the provinces soon joined them, making the 'Independents' the most numerous socialists in parliament. Millerand tried hard to widen the appeal of this group, to attract as many more radicals as he could, while at the same time drawing in the socialist sects. In a celebrated speech at Saint-Mandé (30 May 1896)[1] he defined his socialism as the gradual substitution of social property for capitalist property (i.e. the nationalisation of monopolies, and the municipalisation of public services, but leaving small proprietors alone). His method was political action directed towards winning a parliamentary majority. He favoured international co-operation with other socialists, though remaining

[1] Printed in A. Millerand, *Le Socialisme réformiste français* (1903), 19-35.

in the tradition of the French Revolution, patriotic at the same time as internationalist. This threefold 'minimum programme' of Saint-Mandé, as it came to be called, provided the basis for unified action by the socialists in parliament, though significantly its approval by the deputies was combined with a proviso that this approval would in no way limit their independence. In the legislature of 1893–8 Millerand was the effective leader of a campaign for practical reforms for the working class. The logical conclusion of his work was that he should accept office as minister of commerce and industry when offered it by Waldeck-Rousseau in 1899. Here he saw the chance to carry through the legislation they had been pressing for, as well as to defend the republic against the reactionary challenge of the anti-Dreyfusards. Unfortunately for him, the minister of war in this cabinet was Gallifet—remembered all too bitterly by the socialists for his repression of the Commune. This was carrying reconciliation too far. The issue of participation in bourgeois governments was thus confused. Millerand was disowned, Jaurès almost alone speaking for him. His career as a socialist leader was cut short. In 1904 he was expelled. In the same year the Guesdists obtained from the International Congress at Amsterdam a condemnation of the policy of co-operating with bourgeois governments. In revulsion against his too rapid triumphs, for which he had failed to prepare them, the socialists rejected his policy.[1]

Millerand shows socialism developing out of radicalism and his career illustrates the attitudes which caused so many radical constituencies to elect socialist deputies. It should not be forgotten that it was on this radical foundation that socialism was largely built, from the point of view of parliamentary representation. Millerand's socialism was a development of the doctrine of solidarity. He had apparently never read Marx, at least not properly. If he talked of the class struggle it was only to regret it and to look forward to its rapid disappearance. He accepted the republic and had no use for talk of violence or revolution. He soon found his ideal in the 'great reformist republican party' which Waldeck-Rousseau's ministry sought to create, and in the practical social reforms it introduced. He saw it in contrast to the mere radicals who only talked of reform; but he placed

[1] L. Derfler, 'Le cas Millerand', *Revue d'histoire moderne et contemporaine* (1965).

himself in the tradition of Gambetta, who had laid down the principle that reform should be divided up into manageable stages and carried through gradually 'treating with tact not only old habits but even prejudices'.[1] Like Gambetta, he was concerned above all with obtaining national support: but what he lacked was Gambetta's skill at keeping his friends happy at the same time. He insisted he did not wish to 'build a church for a sect'.[2] 'One should concern oneself less with one's friends and one's partisans', he said, 'than with one's adversaries, and above all one should consider that indifferent mass which is nearly always the majority. One must know how to draw it to one little by little; above all one should never, by imprudence or by exaggeration—which is both dangerous and useless—turn it away from one or against one.'[3]

He said of himself: 'I was and I remain a timid man.'[4] At this period the country found this timidity more congenial than the wildness of the socialist party. Millerand, however, possessed considerable abilities as an administrator which were not allowed to go to waste. His achievements as minister of commerce in 1899–1902 and as minister of public works in 1909–10 were substantial: his new label for his ideas was 'la politique de réalisations'. He cut down red tape in the post-office, for which he planned a forward-looking modernisation. He instituted the Office du Tourisme. Above all he advocated—and introduced in the public services under his control—consultation between management and workers. He hoped this would at the same time reduce the influence of the revolutionary trade unions (as would compulsory arbitration, his other pet scheme). It is not surprising that he dropped out of the socialist movement. His departure set the pattern for other important defections, of which Briand's and Viviani's were the most famous. As a result of the Millerand case and of its condemnation by the Congress of Amsterdam, ambitious socialists who had parliamentary and administrative gifts could not find scope for their talents within the party and left it. It was in the tradition of Millerand, and

[1] Speech on 'La politique sociale de la République', 28 Feb. 1909, printed in A. Millerand, *Politique de réalisations* (1911), 6.
[2] A. Millerand, *Le Socialisme réformiste français* (1908), 8.
[3] Speech to the Société d'Histoire de la Révolution de 1848, ibid., 348.
[4] Quoted from his unpublished memoirs by J. Magnien, 'Alexandre Millerand' (D.E.S., 1962), 4.

of the radical traditions he continued, that the independent socialists survived as a separate group—as will be seen—after the unification of 1905 had brought all the other socialists together under Jaurès.[1]

The variety and vagueness shown by the independent socialists was given a theoretical justification by a rather remarkable man, who can in some ways be regarded as a second Proudhon. Benoist Malon (1841–93), the son of agricultural labourers in the Forez, grew up in the almost incredible poverty which he later described in an extremely moving fragment of memoirs.[2] Working at first as a shepherd, he learnt to read only at the age of twenty, during a long convalescence spent at the house of his elder brother, a primary-school master. For the rest of his life he was a voracious reader, so that there was scarcely any important book on politics or economics he did not know. He found virtues in practically all of them, for his ideal was as broad as could be. Malon was essentially an amiable, warm-hearted and generous man and he showed this equally in his attitude to ideas and in his relations with men. He spotted a forebear of socialism in almost every author he read, starting with Plato and going on to Cardinal Manning.[3] In Paris, where he took a humble job in a dye works, he quickly became a leading organiser of unions, co-operatives and the First International; he was elected a deputy in 1871, resigned to take part in the Commune, spent his subsequent exile in Italy organising the workers there and then returned to help Guesde found the Parti Ouvrier Français.[4] But Guesde's narrow sectarianism was alien to him, and in 1885 Malon founded La Revue socialiste, a journal to which he invited socialists of every variety and radical fellow-travellers to contribute with a view to bringing about

---

[1] Raoul Persil, *Alexandre Millerand* (1949), 11–13; Jean Magnien, 'Alexandre Millerand' (unpublished D.E.S. mémoire, Paris Faculty of Law, 1962), very useful using Millerand's unpublished memoirs; A. Lavy, *L'Œuvre de Millerand: un ministre socialiste* (1902), for Millerand's work 1899–1902; A. Millerand, *Politique de réalisations* (1911), introduction of 92 pages, signed P. L. G. on his work 1909–10; A. Millerand, *Travail et travailleurs* (1908), his speeches as minister, 1899–1902; A. Millerand, *Le Socialisme réformiste français* (1908), speeches 1896–1902, with an important preface defining reformism; Vincent Badie, *M. Alexandre Millerand, socialiste réformiste. Son œuvre social* (Montpellier, 1931), an interesting apology.

[2] B. Malon, 'Fragment de mémoires', *Revue socialiste* (Jan.–July 1907) (five articles).   [3] B. Malon, *Histoire du socialisme* (1879).

[4] B. Malon, *Le Nouveau Parti* (1881): François Simon, *Une Belle Figure du peuple, Benoît Malon, sa vie, son œuvre* (Courbevoie, 1926).

mutual understanding. This became the organ of a new non-sectarian kind of socialism, of which the independents were the parliamentary representatives. Malon had a passion for reconciliation, and a gift for seeing the common links between apparently different men and theories; his critical abilities were as limited as his sympathies were wide, and so he developed what he called integral socialism. Socialism, he argued, should be the synthesis of 'all the progressive activities of humanity'; Marx, though he paid him due homage, saw things only from one viewpoint. Progress could not be explained simply in economic terms: political, religious and economic factors all contribute to it: 'Innovators should not content themselves with appealing to the class interests of the proletariat, they should also voice all the sentimental and moral forces to be found in the human soul.' So they must seek not only economic change but all types of reform—educational, social, political, civil, the emancipation of women and the 'softening of manners'. He agreed there was a struggle of classes, but regarded this as a tragedy. There was no need to wait till capitalism pauperised the proletariat and proletarianised the bourgeoisie. A start could be made at once, and preferably by peaceful means. Malon is important for drawing into the socialist movement the traditional French concern for humanity, the respect for individuality, the wide idealism. 'No struggle simply concerned with material interests', he wrote, 'has ever drawn the masses.' He provides the link between the ideas of 1848 and those of Jaurès, who was considerably influenced by him.[1]

The Anarchists

The anarchists were important rivals of the socialists. For some time, particularly in the 1890s, they retarded the recruitment of the socialists by providing an alternative revolutionary

[1] B. Malon, *Le Socialisme intégral* (1890-1), 1, 13, 16, 178, 190, 212-14, 443 and *passim*; A. Veber, 'La mort de Benoît Malon', *Revue socialiste*, no. 106, vol. 18 (Oct. 1893), 386-443; Eugène Fournière, 'Benoît Malon et le marxisme', ibid. (Nov. 1893), 541-3; Eugène Spuller, *Figures disparues*, 3rd series (1894), 233-51. Malon's successors as editor were Georges Renard, Gustave Rouanet, and then Eugène Fournière. The last of these is particularly interesting—a self-educated jeweller, he wrote about fifty books. See Justinien Raymond, 'Eugène Fournière', in *L'Actualité de l'histoire*, 25 (Oct.–Dec. 1958). Renard and Rouanet would also repay study.

movement which appealed to many who disliked the regimentation and dogmatism of the socialists. In the following decade, they were influential in many trade unions, with the result that these remained independent of the socialists. Socialism would thus no doubt have been far more successful but for them. There was competition between the two because they were not entirely different. The ultimate ideal of both was a classless communism, in which the state would have withered away. Proudhon, who was the founding father of French anarchism, also inspired some sections of the socialists. Both movements wished to destroy the bourgeois order. But there were fundamental differences between them. The anarchists placed much more emphasis on liberty than on equality. Unlike the Marxists who were willing to use the state for a long time before its ultimate abolition, they considered it to be an instrument of oppression at all times. They wished to abolish it immediately, not to capture it. The principal evil of existing society, according to the socialists, came from the abuses of private property, but the anarchists saw authority as the greatest enemy and they hoped to end it simultaneously in its triple manifestation of the state, the Church and capital. The methods they envisaged were also different. They had no use for electoral agitation and they did not try to get into parliament. They believed in direct action, 'propaganda by deed', 'permanent revolt', living freely, individually, ignoring the legal order, rather than setting up organisations to replace it. By definition they could hardly be a party. There were probably never more than 1,000 active anarchist militants, distributed in about fifty groups, most of them in Paris and Lyon. None of their newspapers ever sold more than about 7,000 copies. But they may well have had 100,000 people sympathetic to them and some of their attitudes infiltrated, often unacknowledged, into the minds of a far larger proportion of the country.[1]

Anarchism passed through several stages in France. In its Proudhonist variety, it was influential in the First Inter-

[1] Figures in Jean Maitron, *Histoire du mouvement anarchiste en France 1880–1914* (1951), 114–15, 128, 432. This is the standard history, with a comprehensive bibliography. For more recent works see the supplementary bibliography in J. Maitron, 'L'anarchisme français 1945–1965', in *Le Mouvement social*, 150 (Jan.–Mar. 1965), 97–110. But there has been far less research on the anarchists than on the socialists.

national, until about 1873, when Bakunin's influence replaced mutualism by anti-state collectivism. Bakunin came to Lyon in September 1870 and on the 28th proclaimed the abolition of the state. The state replied by sending two companies of national guardsmen; and he at once fled to Geneva. This failure turned his interests to other countries, and his expulsion also meant that Switzerland became the headquarters of the movement. There several victims of the repression of the Commune, like Élisée Reclus (the author of the nineteen volumes of the *Nouvelle Géographie universelle*) and Paul Brousse (later the leader of the possibilists) were converted to it. As a result, because of its proximity to Switzerland, it was principally in Lyon that anarchism flourished at first, but in 1883 sixty-six anarchists were arrested and put on trial there. After that the leadership passed to Paris, where several newspapers won some success. Their first paper, *La Révolution Sociale* (1880), started with funds provided by the prefect of police through an *agent provocateur*, was perhaps too serious and dull to attract recruits.[1] (Much later Grave used the fortune of the English-woman he married in 1909, Miss Mabel Holland Thomas, to keep his *Temps Nouveaux* going.)[2] Emile Pouget (who has been mentioned in the chapter on trade unions) ran a very lively *Père Peinard*, scurrilous, witty and slangy, which won some success. Other newspapers caused a stir by raising funds through lotteries in which pistols and daggers were offered as prizes.

After the early optimism, a realisation arose that the struggle for freedom would be a long one. Anarchism now entered a new phase, in which direct acts of violence were its principal method. This phase reached its climax in 1892–4, when terrorism, explosions, robberies and murders, culminating in the assassination of Carnot, president of the republic, turned anarchism into a major threat to bourgeois order. This violence with which anarchism is usually identified in the popular mind, was, however, the work of only a few individuals, acting on their own initiative, and it did not have wide support in the movement, even though the leaders seldom condemned it. Its effect nevertheless was to produce drastic repression by the *lois scélérates* (1894). The anarchists therefore moved on to trying other

[1] L. Andrieux, *Souvenirs d'un préfet de police* (1885), 1. 339.
[2] Maitron, *Histoire*, 434.

methods. They attempted to win the workers through the trade unions, in which they soon obtained highly influential positions. Pelloutier, Yvetot, Delassalle and Pouget made revolutionary syndicalism—anarchism acting through unions rather than individual efforts—a considerable force in French politics. It provided the workers with a doctrine which enabled them to do without the bourgeois state—though too much should not be made of the doctrinal aspect. The workers could call themselves revolutionary syndicalists or anarchists because it justified to them what some of them had long wanted—independence. It was only in 1913, finally, that a party was formed: the Fédération Communiste Révolutionnaire Anarchiste, with antiparliamentarianism, antimilitarism and trade union action as its creed. It condemned individualist violence and terrorism, but it also declared its respect for the independence of individuals within the groups of the party and of the groups within the Fédération. Twenty-five groups from widely dispersed provincial towns joined it; but it did nothing to stimulate any growth of a political movement, and after the war organised anarchism was only a small sect.

The most famous names of anarchism are perhaps found in art. Courbet—friend of Proudhon and member of the Commune—probably applied its ideas to painting most directly.[1] The two Pissarros, Paul Signac and Steinlen contributed illustrations to the anarchist newspapers; Vlaminck regularly supported the cause with the proceeds from the sale of a painting every year from about 1900 to 1939.[2] Grave's paper, *La Révolte*, was read by Anatole France, Stéphane Mallarmé, Leconte de Lisle, J. K. Huysmans. André Gide's *L'Immoraliste* and *Les Caves du Vatican* perpetuate the memory of individual anarchism. The educational experiments of Sébastien Faure and others were pioneering examples of progressive schooling and active methods. Paul Robin, director of the orphanage at Cempuis and a leading advocate of eugenics, published a monthly journal from 1890 to 1905 significantly called *L'Éducation intégrale*; Armand advocated co-education to the extent of not objecting to sexual intercourse between children.[3]

[1] See James Joll's excellent study, *The Anarchists* (1964), 164–70.
[2] J. P. Crespelle, *The Fauves* (English translation by Anita Brookner, 1962), 23.
[3] Maitron, 324–35.

In 1905 *La Science sociale*, the journal of the Le Play school of sociology, published a study of an anarchist, based on a long series of interviews. The man concerned was of no importance at all, an ordinary rank-and-file adherent, and this makes the detailed account of his life all the more illuminating and valuable. The interviewer first met Lebrun in 1897. Lebrun had been working in a cardboard-making factory for twenty-two years, without ever having been unemployed; his wife had worked there for the same period. They had never had a strike, and no dismissals when work was slack; only occasionally had they had a shorter working week. Lebrun expressed esteem and friendship for his boss, who treated them well, insured them against accidents and gave three weeks' maternity benefit. He worked eleven hours a day, earning 5 francs 25 on piece rates. His wife worked ten hours; as a mother she was allowed to arrive half an hour late and to stay away during school holidays. She only earned 3 francs 90 a day. But together their income totalled 70 francs 20 a week. He had a rented flat of three rooms, with no running water. 'I am only an anarchist theoretician', he said. 'I know that society as it exists at present is bad, but personally I have not too much to complain about, since I and my family have pretty well all we need.' It was true his work was no longer skilled, as it had been before machines were introduced, but in compensation, as he philosophically observed, 'it leaves the mind free'.

Lebrun's father had been a practising Catholic, but he read the republican *Siècle* newspaper (which he bought second-hand from a subscriber the day after it was published) and he supported the revolutions of 1830 and 1848. He was also a cardboard maker—he made cartons for porcelain and his hope had been that his son should become a commercial traveller in porcelain. Lebrun's mother had inherited 40,000 francs [£1,600] from her father—a former Chouan—but had lost it all in unsuccessful trade and had become a cardboard maker too. She sent him to a seminary in the hope that he would become a priest, but he was expelled for biting a monk. He then tried his hand at various jobs—as a sculptor of umbrella handles, a maker of artificial flowers (or rather, since this last industry was highly specialised, he made only the leaves while others made the flowers and others still the fruit), and a

gas-fitter. He had then settled down to his present job. Thanks
to his wife's earnings, he was living quite comfortably. They
could afford to send their babies to nurses in the country, at
27 francs a month.

Lebrun had originally been a Gambettist, until 1879 when
he had read some pamphlets published by the Guesdists, which
said that the introduction of machines would produce unemployment: soon after eighteen workers were dismissed for
this very reason. He was greatly impressed and became interested in socialism. A workmate took him to a group called
L'Union Socialiste and so he became a member of the P.O.F.
He read Jules Vallès's paper *Le Cri du Peuple*. Then one day he
read in a conservative paper *La France* an attack by the liberal
Francisque Sarcey on Kropotkin's *Paroles d'un révolté*, giving
extracts and expressing surprise that such an advanced revolutionary could be an honest man. These extracts made Lebrun
want to read the book. He bought it, read it—being particularly struck by the chapter entitled 'Aux jeunes gens'. He
became an anarchist. He left the P.O.F., stopped participating
in electoral agitation and ceased to vote; but he did not join
any anarchist group, though he contributed funds to one of
which he approved. The trouble with it was that it did not
have a library. So instead he formed a club with some anarchist
friends to create a library. They all bought books themselves
and used their subscriptions to buy more; they met weekly for
discussion; and they once published a pamphlet, entitled 'The
Workers of the towns to the workers of the countryside', which
was revised by Malato, who, though not a member, frequently
came to their meetings. But the police dissolved them. So
Lebrun joined the socialist library of the 19th *arrondissement*,
where, for 50 centimes a month, he had access to a thousand
volumes. On Sundays he used to go to anarchist meetings but
less often now that he was getting older. He spent 20 sous a
month on anarchist newspapers and pamphlets; he particularly
liked the *Temps Nouveaux* because it was a serious paper discussing social theories; but he also read S. Faure and Pouget.
He had a passion for reading. His great aim was to become more
educated, though there was no one subject he specially wished
to study. Before he had become a socialist, he had read Rousseau: the *Social Contract*, he said, had made him very discon-

tented and had shown him many defects in society. Voltaire had made him sceptical about God. Darwin, Spencer and Lanessan's *Le Transformisme* had made him an atheist. He had a large collection of books.[1] But he had no savings: the expense of bringing up his family left him little to spare. Still, he led a full life. His wife's great interest was the theatre, and for the first ten or twelve years of their married life they had gone to the theatre twice a week (her brother made shoes for actors and got them tickets at reduced prices); now they were going only once in two months. They ate well—meat every day—buying their food from the co-operative. They had begun their married life with a single bed and one trunk but their flat was now reasonably well furnished. The only outward sign that Lebrun was an anarchist was—apart perhaps from his books—his dress. Fifteen years before he had been a member of a choral society and had bought a frock-coat and top hat for 70 francs, which he had worn on Sundays. 'I was growing into a bourgeois', he recalled laughing. But when he became an anarchist, he found his dress 'insufficiently simple', so he had not worn it since, and instead had an ordinary suit costing 21 francs. He then decided an overcoat was also not sufficiently simple, and he now wore a long hooded cloak, costing only 10 francs 75.

Eight years later, the sociologist interviewer paid him another visit. As a result of Millerand's law, Lebrun was working only 10 hours a day, and his wages were therefore lower, but his wife, now that the children had grown up, was also working 10 hours, so that together their earnings were a little higher, 75 francs a

[1] Henri Martin, *Histoire de France*, 7 vols.; L. Blanc on the Revolution and *Histoire de dix ans*, Regnault on 1840–8, Lavetelle on the eighteenth century, Gordon de Grenouillac, *Paris à travers les siècles*, 5 vols., Challamel, *La France à travers les siècles*, 4 vols.; A. Guilbert, *Histoire des villes de France*; Augustin Thierry, *Histoire de la conquête de l'Angleterre, Récits du temps mérovingien, Histoire du tiers état*; Malte-Brun, *La France illustrée* (bought for 100 francs, and then bound), Alex de Laborde, *Itinéraire de l'Espagne*, 5 vols.; *Histoire pittoresque des grands voyages*. Fourteen volumes of popular science by Camille Flammarion, L. Huard, *La Science pratique*, *Le Monde industriel*; Alexis Clerc, five volumes on physics, chemistry and medicine. Littré's Dictionary. Homer, Plato's *Republic*. Eight volumes of Greek and Roman classics. The complete works of Racine, Molière, Boileau, Mme de Sévigné, Goethe; almost all of V. Hugo, D. Defoe's *Crusoe*, six volumes of Lamartine, Musset, E. Augier, G. Sand, E. Sue, Maupassant. Scott's *Midlothian*, Turgenev, F. Cooper, 5 vols., J. Verne. 200 volumes of La Bibliothèque nationale; twenty volumes of Flammarion's Petite Bibliothèque universelle. Renan's *Jésus*; the Koran; Lamennais's Rousseau, 3 vols., Montesquieu, 3 vols., J. Simon, Dupanloup, Cabet, Mazzini, Blanqui, Kropotkin, H. Spencer. Many pamphlets. But no Proudhon.

week. His son was doing well as a locksmith, and his daughter as a corset maker, though their second daughter had died. He could now save. Despite his anarchist theories, he was growing into a petty bourgeois. In 1899 he had founded a workers' club which invested subscriptions of 1 franc a week in premium bonds—but it never won anything. In 1900 he founded another aiming at the purchase of land for its members. Two years later he found a piece of land—400 square metres—for 1,200 francs. He bought it, paying in instalments. In 1903 he bought another plot, again on instalments. On the one plot he grew vegetables in accordance with the principles of Georges Ville, a writer on intensive agriculture frequently cited by the anarchists; the other he lent to a friend to cultivate, free of charge. He had built himself a shack on his plot, but a storm had destroyed it; he was now building something more solid. His repayments came to 10 francs a week (one-seventh of his income); he was economising to such an extent that he hardly bought books any more. In four years' time, he calculated, his house would be built and both plots paid for. His wife would then give up work to rear chickens and rabbits. He would take a season ticket to his job in Paris. He had lost his faith in his local co-op, where dividends had fallen. He had resigned from his friendly society. He had just joined a trade union of labourers (this is what he called himself, without illusions) but it was only in order to be able to use the library of the Bourse du Travail which had 8,000 volumes. Though still an anarchist, he seemed to hope less from the natural goodness of man. In his own life, certainly, he was turning himself into a petty capitalist. His life story illustrates the triumph of the ideal of property and thrift.[1]

The Progress of Socialism

In the elections of 1906 the united socialists obtained 54 seats in the chamber, in 1910 they got 76 seats and in 1914 103 seats.[2] The regional distribution of these was very unequal. The

[1] Dr. J. Bailhache, 'Un type d'ouvrier anarchiste. Monographie d'une famille d'ouvriers parisiens', *La Science sociale*, 14 (May 1905).
[2] These figures are approximate, because of some individual desertions etc. See E. Fournière, 'Les socialistes à la Chambre', *Revue socialiste*, 44 (Aug. 1906), 205–12. They exclude the independent socialists.

party was particularly successful in the Mediterranean south, in the east and centre, and in the Nord and in Paris. It did not even try to put up candidates in certain departments of the west. In 1910 it obtained, in the first ballot, 1,125,877 votes, i.e. 13 per cent of votes cast, but in the Var it won 42 per cent, in Nord 31 per cent, in Seine 27 per cent; in 23 other departments it won more than 13 per cent but in 7 departments it obtained less than 1 per cent of the votes cast.[1] These regional contrasts make it easier to understand the nature of the support it received, though this is a subject on which a great deal of research is still needed.

Enough has been said of the particular circumstances of Paris and the Guesdist Nord. Most of the other socialist constituencies were rural. But this did not necessarily mean that the peasants there voted socialist. First, many of these deputies got in as a result of an alliance with the radicals. The example of Draguignan (Var) in 1898 shows how a mere third of the votes was enough to secure victory. In the first ballot the conservative candidate obtained 5,821 votes, the socialist 4,554 and the radical 4,131. The radical withdrew in favour of the socialist, who therefore won in the second ballot.[2] Alliance with the radicals sometimes meant that the socialist victor was not really free to press his socialist opinions in practice. In Isère, the alliance was formed in 1906 to expel the opportunists who had been dominant for a long time. In that year Vienne got a socialist mayor, thanks to this alliance. Joseph Brenier had been a weaver in a factory and had risen to be its principal foreman, but having been dismissed for his political activities, he set up a small workshop of his own, which prospered, so that he became an employer though 'loyal to the class of his origins'. His socialism was very mild, for he was more interested really in anticlericalism; and even on this question he was not above bargaining with the Catholics for their votes, in return for which he showed himself benevolent to their Eucharistic Congress in 1912.[3] Such arrangements were by no means unusual

[1] Charles Duffart, 'La poussée socialiste en France d'après les élections générales de 1910', in *Revue socialiste*, 52 (July–Dec. 1910), 37–51, 147–54.

[2] H. Rouger, *Les Fédérations socialistes* (1913), 3. 25–48, has a useful article on Var.

[3] P. Barral, *Le Département de l'Isère sous la Troisième République 1870–1940* (1962), 526–32.

and it was not only with the radicals that the socialists allied. Compère-Morel, the Guesdist, won his seat in Gard thanks to the support of the extreme right wing. Electoral considerations were certainly one factor in keeping the socialists moderate and behind Jaurès. Secondly, in rural constituencies, it was frequently the artisans rather than the peasants who were the chief propagators of socialism. The main nuclei of socialism in rural Var turn out to be very sizeable villages like Flayosc (population 2,500) which had numerous small factories producing shoes, oil, tiles, and Vidauban (population 2,650) which had cork, brick and even machine factories.[1] Often too, peasants were part-time artisans, who migrated to neighbouring towns or to Paris, sometimes for part of the year and sometimes for a considerable portion of their working lives: they returned bringing urban ideas into the countryside.[2] Thus one of the first constituencies to go socialist in the isolated Creuse was Bourganeuf, which exported large numbers of masons and which in 1849 had elected a mason, Martin Nadaud, to parliament.[3] Likewise Ussel in Corrèze was an exporter of coachmen and taxi-drivers; Saint-Sulpice-les-Feuilles in Haute-Vienne exported navvies. Though surrounded by conservative country, they were early converts to socialism. The influence of a socialist town like Limoges, which drew its workers from the surrounding area, was also important, for these workers kept their links with their native villages and the ideas they acquired there travelled home eventually.[4] Once again, however, the nature of this socialism varied. The woodcutters of Allier, Cher and Nièvre, who started one of the most vigorous rural agitations in the 1900s, gave a false impression of socialism, for though they elected socialist deputies, they were principally

[1] Yves Malartic, 'Comment Clemenceau fut battu aux élections législatives à Draguignan en 1893', in *Provence historique* (1962), 112–38, especially 115; Paul Joanne, *Dictionnaire géographique et administratif de la France* (1894–1905), 1498, 5258.
[2] Paul Bois, *Paysans de l'ouest* (1960), is the most brilliant study of this subject.
[3] Gérard Walter, *Histoire des paysans de France* (1963), 409–10, 417; Martin Nadaud, *Mémoires*.
[4] A. Perrier, 'Esquisse d'une sociologie du mouvement socialiste dans la Haute-Vienne et en Limousin', *Actes du 87ème Congrès national des sociétés savantes, Poitiers 1962, section d'histoire moderne et contemporaine* (1963), 377–98. Cf. R. Baubirot, 'Remarques sur la condition au 18 et 19 siècles des communautés des paysans du nord de l'actuel département de la Haute-Vienne', ibid., 905–33.

concerned with the redress of their immediate grievances about
methods of payment for their work. The sharecroppers of
Allier likewise elected a socialist but all he demanded was
detailed reforms of the particular abuses to which sharecroppers were subject in this region.[1] The revolts of the winegrowers in the south in 1907 and in Champagne in 1911 (when
70,000 bottles were destroyed in a wholesaler's cellars by an
angry mob)[2] were not socialist at all.

The force of tradition was important. The leader of the
socialists in Vaucluse said it was not surprising that 'advanced
opinions' were to be found there: 'We are a department of the
south, a department which had the honour to rise against the
coup d'état of 2 December.'[3] Where such traditions were strongest,
Marxism was often weakest, and personal rivalries vigorous. In
Vaucluse, by his own admission, the struggle for socialism was
closely bound up with the desire to evict 'the petty tyrants of
the communes'. Neither economic nor sociological explanations
of the socialist vote are adequate.[4] One can see the importance
of personal factors if one looks at the way a few individuals
were actually converted. Paul Faure was the son of a republican
councillor general of Dordogne and grew up with 'advanced
ideas' but it was a Périgueux journalist who gave him Guesde's
and Lafargue's writings to read, which made him a socialist. At
twenty-five he was elected mayor of his commune—but not
because he was a socialist. When he said he was a socialist, his
supporters replied: 'That is of no importance.' They simply
wanted a new mayor. Arthur Groussier, an engineer, the son
of a left-wing grocer, got involved through trade unionism. He
discussed politics with the workers in his factory who invited
him to join their mechanics' union even though he was not a
worker. They then asked him to act as their delegate to the
Federation of Socialist Workers. He replied he was not a
socialist: they said it did not matter. But in this federation he

---

[1] Simone Derruan-Boniol, 'Le socialisme dans l'Allier de 1848 à 1914' in *Cahiers
d'histoire*, 2 (Grenoble, 1957), 115–61.

[2] P. Koukharski, 'Le Mouvement paysan en France en 1911' in *Questions
d'histoire* (1952), 160–77; P. Monette, 'L'éveil des paysans: La révolte des vignerons
champenois' in *La Vie ouvrière* (Feb.–Apr. 1911), 4 articles.

[3] Alexandre Blanc, *Le Parti radical et le parti socialiste dans Vaucluse* (Cavaillon,
1904), 11–12.

[4] H. Primbault, *Le Socialisme dans les campagnes* (Arras, 1902).

got to know one of the leaders who persuaded him to join the party. It was purely an interest in the practical improvement of the lot of the members of his union, not any doctrinal conviction, that determined his actions. J. B. Severac, the son of the republican deputy mayor of Montpellier, was converted at eighteen while a student at the university there by reading Malon's *Integral Socialism* and Zola's *Germinal* and by talking to his two socialist professors of philosophy there, Gaston Milhaud and Célestin Bouglé. Rather paradoxically for him socialism was never 'a game of ideas; it is a working-class thing. That is why I have never liked canvassing among the bourgeoisie.' Being a bourgeois and an intellectual himself, his conversion to socialism meant breaking with his class and keeping himself free of the contamination of capitalism and the state. 'What is seductive in socialism for me is that it creates true equality between men, it will end personal servitudes.' Vincent Auriol was likewise first introduced to socialism by his philosophy schoolteacher. Among industrial workers socialism was sometimes inherited: J. B. Lebas at fourteen was taken to hear Guesde speak by his father, a textile worker who was a member of the first socialist group of Roubaix; he joined the party at eighteen. At that same age, he wrote to ask Lafargue his opinion of Stuart Mill's book on positivism, which he had just read: Lafargue replied in a letter of four pages, excusing himself for not giving a complete criticism. Unlike Groussier, Lebas's study of Marx was serious, and he used to attend earnest discussions of it at a factory club.[1] These individual instances stress the rich variety of socialism in France, which was both more and less than what it claimed to be.

It might well be asked whether the differences between the socialists and their opponents were greater than the differences within the socialist party itself. It depends on what one stresses. If one is primarily studying institutions, the unification and growth of the party is a clear enough theme. But this traditional perspective has led to the neglect of the values which the socialists shared with other parties, and of the irrational elements in their lives, which were never expressed in official programmes. There is room for a re-classification of politicians on lines other than those which they themselves adopted. The

[1] Louis Lévy, *Comment ils sont devenus socialistes* (1932).

second volume of this work will make some suggestions on this subject.

The conclusion that seems to emerge from the studies in this volume is that the ambitions and frustrations it has revealed cannot be explained without investigating at least three further aspects of the lives of Frenchmen. A constant theme in these pages has been the wide regional variations which complicated and sometimes transformed every movement and every change. The limits of national unity, provincialism, the relations of town and country, and the attitudes of Frenchmen to foreigners need to be understood in order to appreciate the forces with which central politics had to contend. The extent to which, and the way in which, Britanny, Alsace, Provence and Paris were parts of the same country is a question which has too often been avoided in national histories. A second theme of this book has been the clash of innovation and prejudice. Two elements behind this can be disentangled: on the one hand the survival of superstition and traditional modes of thought, and on the other the changes introduced principally through the medium of the schools. To what extent and in what way did the advocates of modernisation alter the approach and mentality of the people they sought to influence? This raises the third problem, of the crucial role played, both in subduing disunity and in attacking traditionalism, by the intellectuals, the flower of this age of education. Their history deserves to be written, not just in terms of the theoretical interest of their work, nor of its literary merit, but also from the point of view of their relations with their public. These three problems represent three levels of national or popular consciousness, which the next volume will attempt to penetrate.

INDEX

Abortion: 'uterine vacuum cleaners', 27; doctors involved in, 33; law of 1920 on, 359; estimates of numbers of, 359.
About, Edmond F. V. (1828–85), 355.
Académie de cuisine, 231.
Académie de médecine, 304.
Académie des sciences morales et politiques, 303, 372, 654.
Académie Française, 56, 76, 288, 294, 297, 302, 325, 328, 421, 551, 602, 607.
Accountants, 101.
Aciéries: de St. Etienne, 56; de Longwy, 74.
Action Committee for Republican Reform, 686.
Action Française, 28, 393, 404, 426–7, 465, 573.
Acton, Lord (1834–1902), 6.
Adolescence: new attitudes towards, 333–5; Jules Romains on, 340.
Adultery, 303, 307; and the theatre, 311; penalties for, 343; Napoleon on divorce and, 357; and the law of 1904, 358; Proudhon on, 460.
Advertising, 110, 195.
Africa, the French in, 630.
Agathon (pseud. of H. Massis and H. Tardieu), 333, 353.
Agen, 41.
Agoult, comtesse d' (1805–76), alias Daniel Stern, 470.
Agricultural Society, of Senlis, 153; of Meaux, 154.
Agriculture: nobles in, 59, 401, 405; statistics on population in, 105–6, 151, 171–4; wages in, 117; methods and varieties of, 136–94; women and children in, 185, 351; opinions on the role of, 190–1, 389, 444, 448, 471, 493–4, 497, 545; unions in, 207, 257–8; in the Sarthe, 376; Méline and, 649, 651–2; also 14, 40, 62, 64, 98, 186–9, 196, 202, 206, 265–6, 440, 555.
Aiguilles, 149, 150.
Aisne, 183.
A.I.T., see First International.
Aix, 157.
Ajaccio, 536.

Alain (pseud. of Émile Auguste Chartier, 1868–1951), 329–31, 353, 715.
Alary, printer, 218.
Albert, Marcelin, 707.
Albi, 759.
Algeria, 73, 81, 104, 167, 177, 254, 421, 427, 438, 510, 515, 520.
Allain-Targé, François-Henri-René (1832–1902), prefect of Angers 1870, deputy 1876–89, minister 1881–2 and 1885–6, 570.
Allemane, Jean (1843–1935), printer, member of the Commune, detained in New Caledonia 1871–9, deputy for Seine 1901–2, 1906–10, 218, 258, 756–7.
Allemanism, 757, 766.
Alliance Républicaine, 242.
Allier, 34, 149 n., 747, 784–5.
Allix, Jules (1818–97), inventor and Communard, leader of Ligue des femmes, 740.
Alpes-Maritimes, 149 n.
Alpine region, the, 381.
Alsace, 33, 65, 67, 69, 79, 141, 219, 474–5, 540, 631, 787.
Ambition: views on, 87–112, 122; peasants and, 170–3; artisans and, 216; and the family, 285, 294, 297, 309, 332, 362; workers and, 265, 269; politicians and, 585, 589, 603, 614, 626, 645, 649.
Amboise, 597.
America, 14, 35, 39, 55, 93, 174, 178, 185, 324, 405, 500; children, 326, 332, 341–2; Civil War, 545–6.
Amiens, 82.
Amigues, Jules M. E. L. (1829–83), Bonapartist journalist, 561–2.
Anarchism, 232, 233, 235, 237, 246, 248, 279, 400, 463, 465, 755, 775–82.
Ancel of Lyon, Bishop, 20.
Andler, Charles (1866–1933), 767.
André, P. M. (b. 1870), 238.
Angers, 28, 47, 251.
Angoulême, 254.
Anjou, 371.
Annonay, 256.
Anticlericalism: doctors and, 37; aroused by clergy, 42; and dancing, 180; Yvetot on, 236; Pelloutier on, 246–7; and the family, 292; Maria

Anticlericalism (*cont.*):
Deraismes on, 348; Louis Blanc's obsession with, 449; Proudhon and, 464; and republicans, 424, 646–7, 449; Bonapartism and, 505, 506; of Jerome Napoleon, 566–7; of Combes, 597, 685; Gambetta and, 616; some explanations of, 628; parish priests and, 648; Méline and abandonment of, 653; and separation of Church and State, *688–98*; in education and the radicals, 723; of Brenier, 783.

Anti-militarism: of Yvetot, 236; Pelloutier's abandonment of, 250; and Federation of B.D.T., 252; in provincial unions, 259; in 1914, 274; Jaurès and, 764; Hervé on, 767; of revolutionary syndicalists, 778.

Anti-semitism, 77, 242, 256, 643, 679, 681.

Anzin, 81, 204, 223, 224, 264, 474, 556, 607.

Anzin Mining Company, 81, 204, 223, 264, 474, 556, 607.

Arago, François (1786–1853), scientist and politician, 26, 489.

Arambourou, R., 377.

Ardèche, 256, 379, 557.

Ariège, 14, 116.

Ariès, Philippe, on children, 315–16.

Aristocracy: and the Revolution, 11; and the bourgeoisie, 16–19; and medicine, 38–9; and marriage, 78, 287, 405; in industry, 99; in the civil service, 127; numbers, 402; false nobles, 403; wealth of, 404–5; recreations of, 406; disputes with their children, 406; politics of, 406–12, 420–2, 429, 451; in 1848, 489; surviving power of, 541–2; Gambetta on, 613, 615; *also* 74–5, 80, 197, 290, 434, 467, 507, 522, 532, 541–2, 645.

Armagnac region, the, 545.

Armainvilliers, 154.

Armand-Rueff commission, 47.

Armentières, 69.

Army: aristocrats in, 17, 542; health in, 28, 304; pay in, 117; pensions in, 121; use against strikers of, 259, 475, 732; syphilis in, 305; brothels in, 309; politics, 390; level of literacy, 478; conscription, 493; role in the state, 508, 518–20; law of 1872, 515; Corsicans in, 535; Bonapartists' courting of, 561; comte de Chambord on, 565; Thiers on, 610; Gambetta on, 615, 638; Freycinet on, 638; Boulanger and, 641; Méline on, 652; and Dreyfus Affair, 679–82; Combes

and, 687–8; and radicals, 716; suppression of Commune by, 743–4. *See also* Military service, Anti-militarism.

Arras, 224, 447.

Artisans: Méline on, 98; tax evasion by, 108; and peasants, 150–1, 172–3, 376–7; numbers of, 179, 210, 351; and the *livret*, 198; as employers, 201; compagnonnage, 212–16; wages of, 226, 258; politics of, 376–7, 379, 389, 409, 475, 478–9, 492, 512, 738, 747, 784; Proudhon and, 458, 463; corporations, 485, 487; and industry, 555–6. *See also* 11, 14–16, 18, 44, 46, 69, 80, 138, 156.

Artists: Charton on, 90; part-time, 129; denigration of bourgeois by, 132.

Artois, 138.

Arts: doctors and the, 42; industrialists and the, 67; as a career, 92, 93; engineers and, 96; patronage of, 110, 514, 551; Museum of Popular Arts and Traditions, 179; and morals, 311–12; in the Liberal Empire, 551.

Assi, Adolphe Alphonse (1840–86), member of the Commune, 740.

Assistance Publique, 142.

Association: Amicale, 227; pour la défense du travail national, 204; for the defence of the middle classes, 712; of the Friends of Order, 409; Gambettiste, 676; libre typographique, 218; nationale républicaine, 676; for the Protection of Workers, National, 312; for the Rights of Women, 347; des Travailleurs des Chemins du Fer Français, 227.

— Considérant on, 443; laws of 1884 and 1901 on, 573; Gambetta on, 616; Waldeck-Rousseau on, 673–4.

Assumptionist Order, and the *ralliement*, 648, 677–8.

Ateliers de la Loire, 77.

Attitudes: of Frenchmen, 2; bourgeois, 11; to life, 23; to doctors, 30; to money, 31, 49, 60–2, 66, 87, 93, 95, 125, 264, 462; to success, 88; to civil service, 114; of peasants, 136, 138, 140, 181, 189–90, 194; to dancing, 180; of workers and unions, 228–9, 233–68, 275; to authorities, 246; to war, 274; to marriage, 289; of clergy to sex, 297; to children's place in society, 317–18; of emancipated women, 354; to innovations and capitalism, 377; of immigrants to cities, 381; towards politics, d'Avenel on, 387; to politics after 1830, 420; encouraged by the utopians, 466.

Aube, 748, 749.
Auclert, Hubertine (1848–1914), 348.
Aude, 112, 116, 706, 707.
Audiffred, Jean-Honoré (1840–1917), president of *Association nationale républicaine*, deputy 1879–1904, senator 1904–17 for Loire, 676.
Augier, Émile (1820–89), 289, 355.
Aumale, duc d' (1822–97), fourth son of King Louis-Philippe, 421.
Auriol, Vincent (1884–1966), socialist, minister 1936–8, 1944, president of the republic 1947–54, 786.
Austria, 62, 174, 422, 545, 588.
Authority: paternal, 48, 89, 299, 319; children and parental, 287, 302, 320–5, 328, 333, 361, 391; of family and teachers, 339; shopkeepers and, 109; peasants and, 134, 162; in 1848, breakdown of, 140; workers and, 237, 244–6, 260, 261, 262; Third Republic and, 394, 494; royalists on, 400, 407; utopians on, 428, 447, 463; Bonapartists on, 504; anarchists and, 776.
Autofinance, 65, 74, 81.
Autun, 308.
Avenel, Vicomte George d' (1855–1939), 387–8.
Avesnes, 582.
Aveyron, 579.
Avignon, 216, 402.
Aynard, Edouard (1837–1913), Lyon banker, deputy 1889–1913, art collector, 56.
Azam, Dr. Eugène (1822–99), professor of pathology in Bordeaux, art collector and president of the Bordeaux archeological society, author on hypnotism, etc., 326.

Babeuf, François-Noel *dit* Gracchus (1760–97), 450.
Babick, Jules-Nicolas (*c.* 1823–1902), tailor, nurse, perfumier, member of the Commune, 740.
Babies: doctors' treatments for, *Monsieur, Madame et Bébé*, 295, 328; death rate of, 361 n.
Baccalauréat, numbers awarded, 480.
Bachoni, Dr., 25.
Bakers, 95, 97, 214, 741.
Bakunin, Mikhail Alexandrovitch (1814–76), 465, 466, 733, 754, 777.
Balzac, Honoré de (1799–1850), 30, 47, 97, 131–2, 481.
Bank of France, 50, 53, 55, 60, 81, 154, 204, 449, 473, 676, 742. *See also* 77–86.

Bankruptcy: notaries and, 45–7; the family and, 65; small businesses and, 108; the south and, 167; and the dowry, 290; in the crisis of 1848, 473–4; of railway companies, 553.
Banks, 56, 77–86, 90, 101, 164, 356, 471, 489, 543, 577, 582; aristocrats in, 17, 405; and peasants, 181, 191; national savings, 181, 240, 629; married women and, 356.
Banque: Franco-Serbe, 77; de Paris et des Pays-Bas, 79, 85; Dupont, 84; Nationale pour le Commerce et l'Industrie, 84.
Barbès, Sigmund Auguste *Armand* (1809–70), socialist, deputy for Aude 1848–9, 432, 488.
Barbey d'Aurevilly, Jules (1808–89), 356.
Barbot, J. P., 40.
Barcelonnette, 574.
Baroche, P. Jules (1802–70), barrister, deputy 1847–51, then senator, minister of Napoleon III, 516.
Barras, Dr. J. P. T., 25.
Barrès, Maurice (1862–1923), 334.
Barristers, republicanism and, 483–4; in parliament under Third Republic, 577; Waldeck-Rousseau as a, 671; in left-wing societies, 728.
Barrot, Odilon (1791–1873), deputy 1830–51, prime minister 1848–9, 493.
Barthou, Louis (1862–1934), deputy for Oloron (Basses-Pyrénées) 1888–1922, senator 1922–4, prime minister 1913, frequently minister, member of the Académie française, 486, 589, 721, 723.
Basly, Émile Joseph (1854–1928), leader of the miners' union, deputy for Seine 1885–9, for Pas-de-Calais 1881–1928, 223–5, 705.
Basse-Provence, 157.
Basses-Alpes, 149 n., 150, 728.
Bastelica, André Augustin alias Louis Lejeune (1845–84), 732.
Bastide, Jules (1800–79), editor of *Le National* 1836–46, minister of foreign affairs 1848, 455.
Baudelaire, Charles (1821–67), 304.
Baudin, Pierre (1863–1917), president of the Paris municipal council 1896, minister 1899–1902 and 1913, 678.
Bazard, Armand (1791–1832), 436.
Bazille, Gaston (1819–94), 166.
B.D.T., *see* Bourses du Travail.
Béarn, 156.
Beauce, the, 189.
Beau de Lomenie, E., 404.

Beaujolais, 166.
Beauvais, 597.
Beauvoir, Simone de (b. 1908), 354.
Béchard, J. J. M. Ferdinand (1799–1870), barrister of Nîmes, deputy 1837–46, 1848–51, writer on decentralisation, 397.
Becquerel, Dr. L. A. (1814–62), 25.
Belgium, 171, 545, 587, 641, 689, 753.
Belliol, Dr. Jean-Alexis, 25.
Benard, Jules, 154.
Bérenger, Henry (b. 1867), 334.
Bergeret, Dr. Louis F. E. (d'Arbois), 92.
Berl, Emmanuel (b. 1892), founder, with Drieu la Rochelle, of *Derniers jours* (1925), editor of *Marianne* (1933–7), and of *Pavés de Paris* (1937–9), 382.
Bernard, Martin (1808–83), printer, colleague of Barbès and Blanqui, commissaire-général 1848, deputy 1848, 1849, and 1871–5, exiled 1849–59, 432, 726–7.
Bernstein, Édouard (1850–1932), 763.
Berri, duchesse de, 394.
Berryer, Pierre-Antoine (1790–1868), deputy 1830–51, 1863–8, legitimist leader, 395, 397, 413.
Bert, Paul (1833–86), professor of physiology, successor of Claude Bernard at the Sorbonne 1869, deputy 1872–86 for Yonne, minister of education 1881–2, 613, 616, 628.
Berteaux, H. Maurice (1852–1911), deputy for Versailles 1893–1910, radical, stockbroker, 722–3.
Berthelot, Philippe (1866–1937), secretary general of the Foreign Ministry 1920–33, son of Marcellin B. (1827–1907), the chemist and minister of foreign affairs in 1895–6, brother of André B. (1862–1938), industrialist, deputy 1898–1902, senator 1920–7, 127.
Besançon, 43, 241, 458, 735.
Best-sellers: a manual of self-medication, 24; on how to succeed in life, 93; on love in marriage, 295; *Eve*, a woman's magazine, 354; political, 388.
Beslay, Charles Victor (1795–1878), 739.
Béziers, 707.
Bichat, Dr. Marie François Xavier (1771–1802), 435.
Bicycles, 180.
Bietry, Pierre (1872–1918), deputy for Finistère 1906–10, 254–6.
Binet, Alfred (1857–1911), 324–5.

Birth-rate, and law of 1920, 359.
Bischoffsheim, Raphaël-Louis (1823–1906), banker, engineer, philanthropist, archeologist, deputy for Nice 1881–5, 1889–1906, 581.
Bismarck, Otto Édouard Léopold, prince von (1815–98), 631, 702.
Blacas, comte de, 399.
Blanche, Dr. Esprit-Sylvestre, 25.
Blanc, Louis (1811–82): socialist, minister of labour in 1848, deputy 1848, 1871–82, 432; life and ideas of, *447–9*, 452, 456–7, 463, 488, 510, 726, 739, 745, 770.
Blanqui, Adolphe (1798–1854), brother of Auguste, economist, deputy for Gironde 1846–8, 111, 131.
Blanqui, Auguste (1805–81), revolutionary, 234, 547, *738–40*.
Blanquists, 736, *738–40*, 757, 766.
Blaumont, 158.
Bloc des Gauches, 765–7.
Blot, Edouard, 730.
Blum, Léon (1872–1950), socialist leader, deputy for Seine 1919–28, for Aude 1929–42, prime minister 1936–7, 1938, president of the provisional government 1946–7, 13, 302, 359, 582, 592, 752, 758, 761, 765.
Boigne, Mme de, 33.
Bois, Paul, 374–7.
Boissarie, Dr. Prosper Gustave, 30.
Boittelle, Symphorien Casimir Joseph (1813–97), army officer 1833–41, prefect 1852–8, prefect of police 1858–66, 517.
Bonaparte, Prince Victor (1862–1926), 567.
Bonapartism: and Orleanism, 420, 421, 424, 506–8; and republicanism (1848), 499–500, 508, 534, 547; intellectuals' hostility to, 504; interpretations of, 505–7; Napoleon III's contribution to, 509 ff.; Saint-Simonianism and, 510, 553; contradictions of, 509–17; and the police state, 517–18; and militarism, 518–20; varieties of, in parliament, 520–1; and centralisation, 521–44; and peasants, 522, 557; and legitimism, 532–4, 543–4, 564; and notables, 530–5, 541; and decentralisation, 537–8; in the towns, 538–41, 553–4; press, 539, 568; and liberty, 544–52; and free trade, 545–6; and trade unions, 547; liberal empire, 548–52; Thiers' attitude to, 549–50; Émile Ollivier's role in, 550–2; and prosperity, 552–8; and the Church,

557; foreign policy, 558–60; workers and, 539–40, 553–4; organisation and policy after 1870, 560–9; *also* 51, 72, 126, 153, 254, 384, 441, 609, 617, 643, 687, 729. *See also* Napoleon III.
Boni de Castellane, comte, 405.
Bonnard, Abel (1883–1968), 334.
Bonnet, J. L. (1856–1925), first secretary-general of the radical party (1901), deputy for Seine 1921–5, 720.
Bonnin, Pascal, 204.
Bookworkers, 237, 242.
Bordeaux, 38–9, 82, 84, 115, 165, 215, 290, 476, 621.
Bordelais, 169.
Bossuet, J. Bénigne (1627–1704), 685, 760.
Bottin Mondain, 404.
Bouchard, Charles (1837–1915), Professor at Paris 1879–1912, 29.
Bouches-du-Rhône, 591.
Boucicaut, Aristide (1810–77), founder of the Bon Marché, 109.
Boudet, Maurice, 20.
Bouglé, Célestin (1870–1940), 786.
Boulanger, Général Georges Ernest Jean Marie (1837–91), minister of war 1886, deputy 1888–9, 242, 261, 393, 425, 568, 583, 641–5, 681, 756, 770.
Boulanger, Lili (1893–1918), 359.
Boulogne, 549.
Bourbonnais, 162, 193.
Bourdeaux, 150.
Bourdet, Dr. Eugène, 326.
Bourganeuf, 784.
Bourgeoisie: power and character of, 2, 11–22, 42, 113, 130, 211, 241; pastimes of, 41; and music, 133; property of, 144; as producers and consumers of wine, 165–6; and the peasantry, 139, 165, 171, 173, 193, 478–9; Guizot's theory on, 200, 416; and the general strike, 225; and the workers, 231–3, 237–48, 270, 273, 453, 463–4, 735; language of, 16, 235; workers' attitudes to, 272–4, 489; criticism of workers, 260–5, 271; anti-militarism and, 274; and the family, 285, 327, 481; and marriage, 287, 291; syphilis among, 304; and the theatre, 311; and feminism, 348–50; and legitimism, 396–7; ennoblement of, 402; and nobles, 407; Louis-Philippe and, 415; Considérant on, 443; Fourier on, 447; Leroux on, 453; Louis Blanc on, 448; Buchez on, 455; newspapers, 455–6, 539; in 1848, 470–1; bankruptcy

among, 473; influence in provinces, 478–9; dissident 'bohemians', 479; Michelet on, 483; Marie on, 502; military service and, 519; Thiers on, 607; Gambetta on, 613–15; Hanotaux on, 659; and income tax, 712; and the 'Red Menace', 728; and the Commune, 738, 744; Brousse on, 753–4; Jaurès on, 763–5; Malon on, 775; *also* 74, 147, 150, 199, 252, 273, 351, 376, 379, 403, 415, 439, 451, 513, 562, 577, 620, 622, 685, 688, 757.
Bourgeois, Léon (1851–1925), deputy 1888–1905, senator 1905–25 for Marne, prime minister 1895–6, president of the chamber of deputies 1902–4, president of the senate 1920–3, 245, 592, 655–7, 685, 765.
Bourges, 726.
Bourses du Travail, 236, 243–53, 254, 276.
Boussac, Marcel (b. 1891), 70.
Bouttain, 581.
Boyer, Antoine, known as Antide (1850–1918), deputy 1885–1909 and senator 1909–12 for Bouches-du-Rhône, 769.
Bracke (Alexandre-Marie Desrousseaux 1861–1955, known as), deputy for Seine 1912–24 and for Nord 1928–36, professor of Greek philosophy at the École des Hautes Études, 761.
Brazza, P. P. F. C. de (1852–1905), 630.
Brenier, Joseph (1876–1943), deputy 1910–19, senator 1924–33 for Isère, mayor of Vienne, socialist textile manufacturer, 783.
Brest, 255.
Brialou, Georges (b. 1833), weaver and gas-worker of Lyon, deputy 1883–9, 770.
Briand, Aristide (1862–1932): deputy for Loire 1902–19, and for Loire Inférieure 1919–32, eleven times prime minister, 55, 247, 250, 261–2, 589, 594, 597, 598, 600; on separation of Church and state, 690–4, 706, 708, 719, 722, 723, 767, 773.
Brierre de Boismont, Dr. A. J. F. (1797–1881), 25.
Briey region, the, 73.
Brincard, Baron Louis Charles Georges (1871–1953), President of Crédit Lyonnais, 54.
Brisson, Henri (1835–1912), deputy 1871–1912, president of the chamber of deputies 1881–5, 1894–8, 1904–5, 1906–12, prime minister 1885–6, 1898, 602.

Brittany, 21, 28, 44, 138, 145, 169, 172-3, 176-8, 181, 193, 371, 373, 393, 395, 787.
Brocq, Dr. Louis (1856-1928), 41.
Broglie, Albert, duc de (1821-1901), ambassador in London 1872, prime minister May 1873-May 1874 and May to November 1877, 155, 419, 421, 563, 578; cf. 405.
Brougham, Lord (1778-1868), on the revolution of 1848, 469.
Broussais, F. J. V. (1772-1838), 24.
Brousse, Dr. Paul L. M. (1844-1912), socialist, deputy for Paris 1906-10, 752-7, 777.
Broussists, 753.
Broutchoux, 225.
Brunetière, Ferdinand (1849-1906), 336.
Brunschwicg, Cécile, 349.
Buchez, P. B. J. (1796-1865), president of Constituent Assembly in 1848, 432, 454-8, 499.
Buck, Father de, 331.
Bugeaud, Marshal T. R. (1784-1849), 133.
Building industry, 210, 229-30, 239, 240, 253, 269, 277, 473, 475, 643.
Buisson, Ferdinand (1841-1932), pacifist, educationist and radical, founder of Les États-Unis d'Europe (journal 1867), director of primary education 1878-96, professor of pedagogy at the Sorbonne 1896, president of the League of the Rights of Man, Nobel Peace Prize 1926, deputy for Paris 1902-14 and 1919-24, 579, 627, 690, 717, 730.
Buloz, François (1804-77), editor of Revue des Deux Mondes, 295.
Bunau-Varilla, M., 57.
Bureau, Paul (1865-1923), professor at the Catholic Institute, 291.
Bureaucracy, see Civil Servants and Centralisation.
Bureau du Roi, 412.
Bureaux d'assistance, 666.
Bureaux de bienfaisance, 665.
Burke, Edmund (1728-97), 395.
Business: aristocrats in, 17; notaries and, 43, 44, 48, 51-2; attitudes towards, 63, 64, 265; family, 65-6; secrecy in, 70; small, 81; as a career, 92-3; women's legal rights in, 343-4; also 13, 18, 84, 87, 98, 101-2, 108, 111, 124, 127, 287, 389-90, 443, 552, 583.
Businessmen: conservatism of, 63; use of banks by, 80, 83; in parliament,

196, 675-6; as conseillers généraux, 542; and the Grand Cercle républicain, 676.

Cabanis, Georges (1757-1808), author of Traité du physique et du moral de l'homme (1802), 435.
Cabarets, 557, 562.
Cabet, Étienne (1788-1856), 445, 449-52, 460, 488.
Caen, 47.
Cahors, 611.
Caillaux, Joseph (1863-1944), deputy 1898-1919, senator 1925-44 for Sarthe, minister of finance 1899-1902, 1906-9, 1911, 1913-14, 1925, 1926, 1935, prime minister 1911-12, 592, 597, 678, 711, 723-4, 767.
Caire du Cheylade, 141.
Caisse d'Épargne, 85-6.
Caisse des Dépôts, 85-6.
Cambacérès, Jean Jacques Régis, duc de (1753-1824), 313.
Cambrai, 696.
Camélinat, Zéphirin (1840-1932), 770.
Canals, 128, 177.
Cannes, 582.
Cantal, 141, 189.
Capitalism, attitudes towards, 181, 190, 232, 237, 259, 263, 268, 278, 281, 282, 377, 441, 520, 623, 629, 740-1, 753, 763-4.
Carbonari, 450, 453, 454, 457, 492, 727.
Carcassonne, 185.
Careers: see The Ambitions of Ordinary Men, 87-112; in public service, 114; open to talent, 116, 505, 512; learned, 117; with large companies, 124; sought in the cities, 173; marriage as a, 295; women and, 344.
Carmaux, 260, 265-7, 668, 763.
Carnegie, Andrew (1835-1919), 93, 99.
Carnot, Lazare Hippolyte (1801-88), deputy 1839-52, 1857-75, senator 1875-88, minister of education 1848, 227, 432, 495, 497.
Carnot, Sadi (1837-94), son of Hippolyte, engineer of the Ponts et Chaussées, deputy 1871-88 for Côte d'Or, president of the republic 1887-94, 595, 661, 777.
Caron, Dr. Alfred Charles, 324.
Carrel, Armand (1800-36), 499-500.
Carrel, Dr. M. J. A. C. B. dit Alexis (1873-1944), 29.
Cars, Amédée François Régis, duc des (1790-1868), 394, 412.
Cassagnac, Bernard Adolphe Granier de (1806-80), deputy for Gers 1852-70, 1876-80, 469.

Cassagnac, Paul de (1843–1904), Bonapartist deputy for Gers 1876–93, 1898–1902, journalist, 568–9.

Castellane, E. V. E. B. comte de (1788–1862), peer of France and senator of the second empire, 474.

Castelnau, Édouard de Curières de, General (b. 1851), 299.

Castres, 759.

Catholic: unions, 253; reaction of the 1900s, 353; press, 380; universities, suppression of, 626.

Catholicism: and the bourgeoisie, 17; and the Crédit Lyonnais, 56; among the textile families, 66; in the civil service, 125; and sex, 297; and children, 318, 356; and discipline, 330–1; and politics, 383–4, 386, 397, 414, 432, 454, 501, 646–8; and education under Ferry, 626–7; and separation of Church and State, 688–98.

Catholic Workers Clubs, Albert de Mun and, 744.

Caux, 138, 169.

Cavaignac, Louis Eugène (1802–57), General, 'head of the executive' 1848, deputy 1848–51, 1852, 1857, 438, 491, 492, 496–8, 513, 519.

Cavaillon, 185.

Cazot, Théodore Jules Joseph (1821–1912), barrister of Nîmes, secretary-general of ministry of the interior 1870, deputy 1871–5, senator 1875–1912, premier président de la cour de Cassation 1881–4, minister 1881, 1884, 627, 676.

Cempius, 778.

Central heating, 331.

Centralisation, 3, 89, 121, 131, 285, 521–44; workers and, 232; nobles and, 406; Proudhon and, 463–4; Lamartine on, 486; theory of, 536–7; Napoleon III and, 551; Thiers and, 609; Ferry and, 628.

Centre of France, the: sharecroppers in, 151, 160; woodcutters of, 193; unions in workshops of, 282; support for the left in, 367; socialism in, 725, 728, 783.

C.G.T., see Confédération Générale du Travail.

C.G.T.U. (Confédération Générale du Travail Unitaire), 276.

Chain-stores, 107.

Chalais-Perigord, prince de, 405.

Chalençon-Polignac, prince de, 406.

Challemel-Lacour, Paul Armand (1827–96), prefect of Rhône, deputy

1872–5, senator 1875–96, foreign minister 1882–3, 612.

Chalons, 158–9.

Chambord, H. C. F. M. D., comte de (1820–83), 398–400, 410, 413, 419–22, 423, 424, 564–6.

Chambrées, 478, 492, 562, 727.

Chambres Consultatives des Arts et Métiers, 203.

Chambrun, J. D. A. P., comte de (1821–99), founder of Musée Social, 72, 404.

Champagne, 158, 785.

Changarnier, General N. A. T. (1793–1877), 519.

Chantilly, 154.

Chanzeaux, 183.

Characterology, 326.

Charente-Inférieure, 149 n., 557, 567.

Charente-Maritime, 191.

Charente, 183, 188, 545, 562, 636, 684.

Charles X (1757–1836), King of France 1824–30, 246, 398, 414, 485.

Charton, Édouard T. (1807–90), 31, 88, 108, 114.

Charton, Jules J. (1840–1921), 96.

Chasseloup-Laubat, Prosper, marquis de (1805–73), minister under Napoleon III, 515.

Chateaubriand, F. R., vicomte de (1768–1848), 319.

Chauchard, H. A. (1821–1909), 109, 661.

Chaudey, A. Gustave (1817–71), 745.

Chaumié, Joseph (1849–1919), senator of Lot-et-Garonne 1897–1919, minister 1902–5, 1905–6, 695.

Chaumont, 240.

Cheese, 187.

Chemicals: employees in, 102; industry, unionisation in, 280.

Chemists, careers for, 96, 99–100.

Cher, 160, 170, 241, 784.

Cherbourg, 107, 178.

Chéron, Henry Frédéric (1867–1936), deputy 1906–13, senator 1913–36 for Calvados, mayor of Lisieux, minister 1913–34 (with intervals), 589.

Chevalier, Louis, 480.

Chevreau, Henri (1823–1903), prefect of Ardèche 1849–51, of Lyon 1864–70, of Seine 1870, head of personnel in ministry of the interior, 1851–64, deputy for Ardèche 1885, 560.

Cheysson, J. J. Émile (1836–1910), engineer, colleague of Le Play, director of Le Creusot, director of the Ponts et Chaussées, 579.

Children: education of, 15, 66, 154, 189, 440–1, 481, 696, 778; relations of parents and, 49, 89, 164, 343, 355, 361; career prospects and ambitions, 90–1, 99, 266, 269, 273; orphaned and abandoned, 142; division of land among, 143–6, 158; illegitimate, 145, 262; marriage and, 286–301; theories about changing attitudes to, 315–16, 318, 324–5; treatment of babies, 317; affection and, 316, 317, 328, 329, 335; Catholic attitudes to, 298, 318; obedience, 319, 327; contrast of French and American, 321, 326, 332, 339, 341; and sex, 321; spoiling of, 322–3, 327, 329; rights of, 323; psychology of, 323–5; Michelet on, 327; Janet on, 327; Alain on, 329; Durkheim on, 330; Vallès on, 335; J. Renard on, 337; Les Copains, 340; peer groups, 339; 'honour your parents', 338; Les Enfants terribles, 329; adolescence, 333; women's legal rights over their, 344, 357; redefinition of role of, 362; at work, 143 n., 668, 668 n., 669; of aristocracy, 406; also 66, 68, 75, 155–7, 173, 185, 270, 272, 311, 390, 391, 406, 661.

Choisy-le-Roi, 347.

Cholet, 378.

Cholvy, Gérard, 380.

Chombart de Lauwe, P., 270.

Christian democracy, 193–4.

Church, the, 11, 21, 47, 66, 80, 105, 138, 257, 401; bourgeoisie versus, 12, 16; textile manufacturers and, 67; expropriation in Revolution of, 143; schools, 154, 314, 381, 557, 688–9, 697, 718, 741; and the peasants, 165, 190, 193, 377; winegrowers and, 169; declining attendance at, 180; freemasonry versus, 212; view of marriage, 298; opposition to sex education, 299; women and, 343, 345, 348, 352, 360; voting habits and power of, 370; hostility or indifference to, 381; and state, separation of, 385, 643, 645–53, 688–98; and legitimism in the west, 397; and the nobility, 406–7; employees in Society of St Vincent de Paul, 409; and the republicans, 426, 499; and the philosophes, 432; Proudhon's hostility to, 464; in Lille in crisis of 1848, 474; Napoleon III and, 509, 557–8; Gambetta and, 616; Ferry and, 625–7, 631; Waldeck-Rousseau and, 677; and Dreyfus Affair, 679–82; Combes and, 683, 685, 687; and the radicals, 716, 718; in the Commune, 742; and the anarchists, 776. See also Clergy, Clericals and Anticlericalism.

Cinema, 180, 273, 311.

Cities: migration to, 89, 172–3; houses in, 186; romanticism in, 286; rootlessness in, 287. See also Towns.

Citroën family, 55.

Civil Code, 109, 142–6, 164, 199, 200, 290, 357, 657, 670.

Civil Servants: numbers of, 113–14, 122; and social mobility, 115 ff., 124–5; geographical origins of, 116, 535; salaries, 68, 116, 122; examinations and favouritism, 118–20; security and pensions, 121–2; prestige, 87, 101, 124; power, 102, 127–9, 269, 365–6, 504, 577, 585, 601, 603, 692, 687; and the bourgeoisie, 13, 18; and the aristocracy, 17, 402, 407; doctors as, 32, 36; share of national expenditure on, 55; savings accounts of, 85, 562; careers, 114–22, 269; changing role of, 124, 127, 706; women, 347, 359; and Catholics, 371; and the unions, 279–80; unionisation of, 19, 207, 277–80; and dowries, 290; newspapers bought by, 380; Saint-Simonian, 437; politics of, 126, 390; and Bonapartism, 504, 507, 516, 517; Corsican, 535–6; peasants and, 535; radicals and, 716, 721; in the chamber of deputies, 577; in the senate, 591; Duguit on, 670. See also Centralisation.

Cladel, Léon A. (1834–92), 132.

Class: views of, 14, 15, 130, 200, 434, 437, 613–14, 716; and education, 18, 98, 102, 104, 114, 264–74; conflicts, 19, 42, 130, 134, 155, 189, 210, 213, 219, 231–3, 240, 255, 262, 266, 269, 272, 277, 337, 660, 772, 775; consciousness, 266, 269, 274–5, 282, 287, 313, 716–17, 764; conciliation of, 512, 550, 625, 764.

Claude, Nicolas (1821–88), deputy 1871–6, senator 1876–88 for Vosges, 650.

Clemenceau, Georges (1841–1929), deputy for Seine 1871–85, for Var 1885–93, senator for Var 1902–20, prime minister 1906–9, 1917–20, 39, 57, 569, 583, 590, 593, 594, 597–9, 626, 691, 698–714, 721–3, 771.

Clergy: position in society, 21, 32, 42, 43, 115, 298, 371, 407, 481–2, 528; politics of, 373, 407, 524–5, 557, 648, 677, 688–98; and women, 292, 297; on sex, 306; and peasants, 192, 661;

Waldeck-Rousseau on, 677; separation of church and state, 688–98; *also* 121, 132, 192, 376, 743, 764. See also Clericals, Anticlericalism, Church.

Clericals, 514, 516, 539, 548, 582, 679–82.

Clients, *see* Patronage.

Clubs: workers', 270–1; *chambrées*, drinking, 478–9, 492, 727; numbers of, 485; in Paris, 487; closing of the, 490; Bonapartists' creation of, 561; Waldeck-Rousseau's, 676; Catholic workers', 744.

Coal: merchants, 81; concessions, 222; price of, 444; protectionist tariffs on, 553; increases in production of, 555.

Cobblers, radicalism of, 214.

Coburg family, Thiers on, 607.

Cochin-China, 515.

Code du Travail, 709.

Coffee, 180.

Cognac region, the, 545.

Cognacq, T. E. (1839–1928), 109.

Coire, François, 195.

Colbert, Jean-Baptiste (1619–83), 58, 390, 710.

Collective bargaining, 276.

Collectivism, 664, 766, 777.

Collège de France, 437, 446, 482, 624, 740.

Collin, G., 325.

Colonies: careers in, 98; decorations, 104; recruitment of civil servants, 119; parliament and, 127; imports from, 204; brothels in, 309; republican policy towards, 424; Napoleon III on, 509; Ferry and, 630–1, 762; Clemenceau and, 701; Jaurès and, 764. *See also* vol. 2.

Colson, René (1913–51), 194.

Combes, Edgar (1864–1907), 602, 687.

Combes, Émile (1835–1921), senator for Charente Inférieure 1885–1921, prime minister 1902–5, 31, 57, 119, 486, 536, 590, 597, 602, 679, *682–91*, 716.

Combisme, 686; and Bonapartism, 687.

Comédie Française, 39, 310, 338, 760.

Comité: central, 204; de l'Afrique Française, 119; des Forges, 71–3, 76, 204, 349; Mascuraud, or *comité républicain du commerce et de l'industrie*, 56, 676; central d'études et de défense fiscal, 712.

Commentry, 225, 747, 748.

Commerce, *95–112*; attitude of bourgeoisie to, 17; as a career, 93–102; place in the economy, 105–6, 109;

salaries in, 117; and peasant organisations, 192; Conseils de Prud'-hommes for, 202; Chambres de, 203; National Conseil Général du, 203; Tribunal de, 204; and union law, 206; attitudes in, 260; Paris Chamber of Export, 263; women in, 351; social effects of, 378; Fourier on, 439; Hennequin on, 444; in Cabet's ideal state, 451; in 1845–7, 471; crisis of 1848 in, 474. *See also* Co-operatives, Retail Trade.

Comminges, Marie Bernard Élie, comte de (1831–94), 408.

Commissions, parliamentary, 586.

Common Market, 70, 545.

Commune, the (18 March–28 May 1871), 206, 336, 449, 454, 465–6, 469, 606, 609, 631, 679, *735–45*, 748, 756, 772, 774, 777, 778.

Communes: taxation in, 522–3; administration of, 523–9; prefects and, 530–1; centralisation and, 538; representation of, 591; mutual benefit societies in, 661; *bureaux de bienfaisances* in, 665; *bureaux d'assistance* in, 666; and upkeep of churches, 694; of Paris, 736; Brousse on, 755–6.

Communism, 71, 299, 374, 385, 477; workers and, 169–70; peasants and, 190; and the unions, 280–1; and the vote for women, 360; in the south and centre, 367; Cabet on, 450–2; in the Third Republic, 575; Brousse on, 753. *See also* vol. 2.

Communist Party, 279–80, 350, 386–7.

Compagnie de la Loire, 221.

Compagnie Générale de Navigation, 56.

Compagnie Transatlantique, 55, 82.

Compagnonnage, *212–17*, 219.

Compat, 239.

Compayré, J. Gabriel (1843–1913), 324.

Compère-Morel, A. (1872–1941), 769, 784.

Competition: attitudes towards, 44, 45, 48, 65, 67, 73, 155, 167, 257, 263; types of, 120, 155, 167; economic, 171, 186; American, 185; female, 460; Fourier on, 439, 441; Louis Blanc on, 448; Napoleon III on, 545; Gambetta on, 616.

Comptoir de Longwy, 71.

Comptoir National d'Escompte, 84.

Comtat, the, 382.

Comte, Auguste (1798–1857): and women, 345, 353; and politics, 390, 547; Gambetta on, 620; Ferry on, 624, 630; and solidarism, 658.

Concentration: in textile industry, 65, 78; in cotton industry, 69; in iron and steel industry, 70, 72–3, 210; in banks, 78.

Condorcet, J. A. N. de C., marquis de (1743–94), 345, 501, 626, 659.

Confédération Générale du Travail (C.G.T.), 225, 228, 230, 231, 233–7, 239, 249–50, 252, 257, 272, *274–82*, 346, 705, 706, 719, 768.

Conscription, *see* Military service.

Conseil d'État, 120, 515–17, 524, 542, 571 n., 581, 668, 670, 678, 694, 695.

Conseil Général des Manufactures, 203–4.

Conseil Général du Commerce, 203.

Conseil National des Femmes Françaises, 350.

Conseil supérieur du travail, 220, 668.

Conseillers généraux, 410, *541–3*, 720.

Conseils de Prud'hommes, 200–2, 222, 261, 667.

Conseils du travail, 71, 668.

Conservatism: of bourgeoisie, 13, 15; of doctors, 29; of civil servants, 125–6; of peasantry, 133–6, 142, 192; of Parti agraire et paysan Français, 194; of English unions, 207; of the compagnonnage, 214; of working-class movement, 218; of northern engine drivers, 228; of employers, 260; of Proudhon, 386, 459, 462; of teachers, 482–3; of Thiers, 609–10; of the army, 610; and sex, 297; and child rearing, 318; and feminism, 345, 353; in the west, 366, 384; in lower Normandy, 373; in the Sarthe, 374, 376; of the east of France, 384; royalist, 389, 397, 415, 419, 423–4; under Napoleon III, 513, 517, 548; in Third Republic, 78, 563–4, 567, 592, 617, 642, 646, 659, 722, 737, 783.

Considérant, Victor (1808–93), 345, 432, 442–4. 446.

Constans, Jean A. E. (1833–1913), governor of Indo-China 1886–8, minister of the interior 1880–1, 1889–92, deputy and senator, 644.

Constant de Rebecque, Benjamin (1767–1830), 548, 551.

Constituent Assembly (1848), 147, 432, 496, 502.

Constitution: of Second Republic, 498–9; of Second Empire, 513–14, 550–1; of Third Republic, 571–604; deputies in, 571–87; interpellations, 585; parliamentary commissions, 586; ministers, 587–90; prime minister, 588,

593; senate, 591–3; president of the republic, 593–601; civil service, 601–4.

Constitutional Right (Jacques Piou), 646–7.

Contraception: Church opposition to, 298; organisation against, 299; ailments caused by, 303; law of 1920 on, 359.

Cooper, Fenimore (1789–1851), 132.

Co-operatives: members of, 107; milk, 142; of tenant farmers, 155; of small proprietors, 155, 169; of nut-growers, 180, peasant members of, 181; politicians and, 191–2; agricultural unions as, 207; printing, 218; Anzin Company's, 223; as instruments of capitalism, 224; unions on, 229, 231, 253; glass-making, 247; Pelloutier on, 250; independent unions and, 253; Bietry on, 256; Fourier on, 441; Louis Blanc on factory, 447–9; Cabet on, 452; Buchez's production, 455; *L'Atelier* and production, 457; republicans on, 497; Méline on, 651; and the First International, 730; Varlin and the, 735; Jaurès and, 766, 768; and Malon, 774.

Corbon, C. Anthime (1808–91), 455, 457.

Cordier, Rieul, 251.

Cormenin, L. de (1788–1868), 522.

Corporations: abolition of, 198; artisan, 485, 487.

Corporatism, 70, 384.

Correspondance Mansard, 561.

Correspondance St Chéron, 413.

Corrèze, 116, 784.

Corsica, 116, 140, 149 n., 450, 535–6, 710.

Cossè, Brissac, 54.

Côte-d'Or, 188, 294.

Cotentin, the, 178.

Côtes du Nord, 145, 191.

Cotton industry, 63–76, 81, 242, 546.

Coty, René (1882–1962), deputy 1923–35, senator 1935–40 for Le Havre, president of the republic 1953–8, 582.

Coup d'état (2 December 1851), 490, 515, 728.

Courbet, Gustave (1819–77), 133, 778.

Courcel, A. C., Baron de (1835–1919), ambassador in Berlin 1881–6, senator 1892–1919, 630.

Courrières, 264, 705.

Court of Cassation, 52, 143, 199, 537, 207–9, 361.

Cousinet, Roger, 340.

Crédit Agricole, 85.

Crédit du Nord, 79.
Crédit Foncier de France, 55, 82, 557.
Crédit Industriel et Commercial, 84.
Crédit Lyonnais, 20, 54, 56, 79, 83–4.
Crédit Mobilier, 82, 84, 554.
Crédit National, 85.
Crédit Populaire, 85.
Crémieux, Adolphe (1796–1880), minister of justice in 1848 and 1870, 358.
Crémieux, Albert, historian, 471–2.
Creuse, 183, 221, 724, 784.
Creusot, Le, 72–3, 75, 80–1, 210, 254, 259, 437, 540.
Crime: rate of notaries, 46; in strikes, 203; and the cinema, 311; juvenile, 334; repression of, 518.
Crimean War, 516.
Croiset, Alfred (1845–1923), professor of Greek eloquence at the Sorbonne 1885, dean 1898, 658.
Croisset, Francis Wiener de (1877–1937), 403.
Crublet, abbé, 193.
Culerre, Dr. A., 92.
Culture: 'culture générale', 16, 42; and class, 18; and careers in industry, 99; moral, 127; of winegrowers, urban, 169; and peasants, 189; workingclass, 264–74; patois and French, 378; abroad, writers and French, 429.
Curel, François de (1854–1928), 75.
Cusenier, Eugène (1832–94), 689.
Cuvelette, Ernest (1869–1936), managing director of Mines de Lens 1919–35, 54.
Cuypers family, 154.

Daladier, Édouard (1884–1970), professor of history, deputy for Vaucluse 1919–40, 1946–58, prime minister 1933, 1934, 1938–40, 53.
Dampierre, Marquis Élie de (1813–96), 190.
Dancing, 180.
Danielou, Madeleine (1880–1956), 356.
Darracq, lorry manufacturers, 56.
Darwin, Charles (1809–82), 656, 781.
Daumas, A. H. (1826–96), political prisoner 1851–9, deputy 1871–89, senator 1889–91 for Var, 770.
Dauphiné, 178.
Da Vinci, Leonardo (1452–1519), 96.
Debierre, Charles (1853–1932), professor of medicine at Lille, senator for Nord 1911–32, president of the executive committee of the radical party 1917, and of the Grand Orient 1918, 716.

Debré, Michel (b. 1912), in Conseil d'État 1934–9, attached to Paul Reynaud 1938–9, resistance leader 1943–4, subsequently prime minister, 390.
Debt, 51, 60, 80, 136, 147, 156, 163, 164, 167, 168, 175, 198, 356, 498, 582.
Decazes, duc, 405, 561.
Decentralisation: royalist views on, 394, 397, 400–1, 407; Orleanists on, 418; Bonapartists and, 537–8; republicans and, 537; 1849 commission on, 538; Ferry and, 628; Waldeck-Rousseau and, 675; Programme of Nancy (1865), 537; also 80, 646.
Declaration of the Rights of Man, 12, 571 n., 655.
Declaration of the Rights of Women, 347.
Decrais, Pierre Louis Albert (1838–1915), prefect 1871–9, ambassador 1880–94, deputy 1897–1903, senator 1903–15, minister for colonies 1899–1902, 678.
Decroly, Ovide (1871–1932), Belgian educational psychologist, 325.
Défense Paysanne, 194.
Defferre, Gaston (b. 1910), mayor of Marseille, 752.
Degas, Edgar (1834–1917), 41.
Delaisi, Francis (1873–1947), 55.
Delamaire, Mgr. (1848–1913), 696.
Delassalle, Paul (1870–1948), 778.
Delcassé, Théophile (1852–1923), 589–90, 597, 612.
Delcourt-Haillot, 253.
Délégation des gauches, 686–7.
Delescluze, Charles (1809–71), 727, 739.
Delore, Dr. Xavier (1869–1940), surgeon in Lyon, 30.
Delory, Gustave (1857–1925), 747.
Democracy: royalists and, 13, 426; oligarchy and, 53, 57; industrialists and, 70; peasants and, 131, 148–9, 190, 196, 370; Christian, 193; Troplong on, 199; workers and, 232; utopians and, 438, 443, 449, 451, 453, 464; Marie on, 502–3; Napoleon III on, 504, 511; the administration and, 521, 522; Third Republic and, 570, 574; Gambetta on, 614, 620; Ferry on, 625, 629; Clemenceau on, 701; Renan on, 744; Jaurès on, 767.
Democratic: careers, 107; education, 115; recruitment in civil service, 118; France, Michelet on, 143; socialism, 447, 487, 490, 491; reforms, Carnot on, 495; Bonapartism seen as, 521; Bonapartists and Gambetta, 567.

Demolins, Edmond (1852–1907), 388.

Denain, 223.

Denmark, 186–8.

Dentists, 35, 90.

Department stores, 101, 107, 109, 235.

Deputies, in the Third Republic, 574–91, 601–4, 619, 642, 646, 647, 652, 675, 678, 686, 720, 721, 757, 768, 769, 770, 771, 772, 783.

Deraismes, Maria (1828–94), 348.

Deroin, Jeanne F. (1805–94), 347.

Deroisin, Hippolyte-Philémon (1825–1910), positivist, mayor of Versailles 1879–92, 624.

Deroulède, Paul (1846–1914), 672.

Desbordes, Jean (1906–44), 334.

Desessartz, J. L. C. (1729–1811), author of Traité de l'éducation corporelle des enfants en bas âge (1760), 317.

Deschanel, Paul (1856–1922), deputy 1885–1920, senator 1921–2 for Eure-et-Loir, president of the republic Jan.–Sept. 1920, 143, 599, 660, 676, 723.

Descuret, Dr. J. B. F. (1795–1872), 91.

Deslinières, Lucien (1857–1937), 748.

Deux-Sèvres, 524.

Devinck, F. J. (1802–78), 262.

Dezamy, Théodore (d. 1850), 452.

Diderot, Denis (1713–84), 428, 723.

Dijon, 165, 450.

Dior, Christian (1905–57), 70.

Directors, company, 57.

Discipline: in factories, 270–2; of children, 319, 327.

Disease, 23–42; venereal, 25, 304–5, 611; gynaecological, 303.

Divorce: law, 291, 296, 357–8; attitudes to, 307, 311, 352, 567, 592, 612; statistics, 358.

Dockers, 242, 252, 261, 277.

Doctors, 23–42; numbers of, 34–7, 189; incomes of, 31, 33, 684; specialisation, 37; advice on ambition, 88, 91–2, 265; on sex, 296, 305; on child-rearing, 317, 331; on sun-bathing, 321; on genius, 431; in politics, 23, 37, 259, 478, 483, 492, 577, 728, 738; in welfare state, 664; also 138, 157, 190, 402.

Dolfuss, 65.

Donzère, 150.

Dordogne, 170, 785.

Dorgères, see d'Halluin.

Dorizon, Louis, director-general of Société Générale, 84.

Dormoy, Jean (1851–98), mayor of Montluçon, 748–9.

Doubs, 254–5, 262, 581.

Doumer, Paul (1857–1932), deputy for Aisne 1888–9, 1902–10, for Yonne 1891–6, senator for Corsica 1912–31, minister 1896, 1917, 1921–2, 1925–6, president of the republic June 1931–May 1932, 55, 600.

Doumergue, Gaston (1863–1937), deputy 1893–1910, senator 1910–24 for Gard, prime minister 1913–14, 1934, president of the republic 1924–31, 55, 598, 600, 695.

Dowries, 16, 18, 33, 65, 83, 152, 156, 157, 163, 266, 287–91, 302.

Draguignan, 783.

Dreux-Brézé, Henri Simon Charles, marquis de (1826–1904), 412.

Dreyfus Affair, 57, 383, 597, 640, 652, 679–82, 691, 701, 718.

Drôme, 149, 150, 597 n., 728.

Drouyn de Lhuys, E. (1805–81), deputy 1842–51, senator under Napoleon III, foreign minister 1848–9, 1851, 1852–5, 1862–5, 190, 558.

Droz, A. Gustave (1832–95), on the family, 295–6, 328.

Droz, Joseph F. X. (1773–1850), author of the Essay on the Art of being Happy, 288, 294, 295, 319.

Duchêne, Georges (1824–76), 54, 534.

Duclos, Jacques (b. 1896), communist deputy 1926–32, 36–40, 44–58, senator since 1959, for Seine, 505.

Duez, Edmond (b. 1858), 689.

Dugard, Marie (b. 1862), novelist and writer on education and the U.S.A., 332.

Duguit, Léon (1859–1928), 143, 670.

Dumas, Alexandre (1802–70), 234.

Dumas, Alexandre (fils) (1824–95), 289, 355.

Dumont, Charles Émile Étienne (1867–1939), deputy 1898–1924, senator 1924–39 for Jura, minister 1911, 1913, 1930, 1832, 721.

Dumont, René, 184, 186.

Dupanloup, Bishop F. A. P. (1802–78), on marriage, 299; on children, 322–4; on the doting mother, 332.

Dupont de Bussac, Jacques François (1800–73), 501.

Dupuy, Charles Alexander (1851–1923), professor of philosophy, inspector of the Academy, deputy 1885–1900, senator 1900–23 for the Haute Loire, minister of education 1892–3, prime

minister 1893, 1894–5, 1898–9, 76, 245.
Dupuy, Jean (1844–1919), owner of *Le Petit Parisien*, senator for Hautes-Pyrénées 1891–1919, minister 1899–1902, 1909–11, 1912–13, 1914, and 1917, 57.
Durkheim, Émile (1858–1917), 330, 340, 714.
Duruy, J. Victor (1811–94), 324, 344, 515.
Duty, in the family, 286, 293, 295, 298, 299, 320.
Duval, Raoul (1832–87), deputy for Seine-Inférieure 1871–6, for Eure 1876–7, 84–7, founder of *La Nation*, 646.
Duverger, Maurice, 548.
Duvernois, Clément A. J. B. (1836–79), 561.

East of France, the, 160, 204, 229, 239, 384, 506, 747, 783.
École: des Beaux Arts, 295, 553; Centrale, 75, 94, 102, 104; Centrale des Arts et Métiers, 95, 102; Coloniale, 119; Libre des Sciences Politiques, 118; Normale, 40, 436, 483, 612, 759; Polytechnique, 94, 96, 102, 103, 104, 442, 553, 600, 633; Supérieure de Commerce de Paris, 111.
Ecommoy, 374.
Economic: role of bourgeoisie, 22, 44, 49, 53, 72, 74, 80; development, 63–4, 80, 86, 87, 95; policy of Second Empire, 82, 512, 515, 540, 545–7, 552–9; role of peasantry, 135–6, 141, 154, 175; crisis of 1847–9, 159, 189, 382, 472–3; republican policy, 175, 497, 623, 631, 635–8, 650–4, 655, 661, 674, 675, 705, 709–13; views of workers, 206, 224, 238, 247–8, 263–7, 277, 301.
Education: primary, 127–8, 134, 175, 344, 626–7; secondary, 12, 15, 193, 344; technical, 175; 231, 551; higher, 193; peasants and, 132, 134, 175, 178, 266; workers and, 233, 244, 247–8, 250, 273, 734; bourgeoisie and, 16–18, 31, 46–9, 113, 118; women and, 66, 292–3, 295, 343–5, 347, 353, 355, 626; and the church, 424, 509, 557; free, 452, 626–7, 658, 728; salaries in, 111; sex, 299, 323–4, 338; scientific, 103; local control, 523; civic, 615–16, 625–7; radicals on, 716–18, 723; anarchists on, 778; Proudhon on, 460, 463–4; in the

Commune, 741; *also* 26, 29, 33, 39–40, 87, 89, 98, 104, 114–15, 132, 289, 352, 390, 408, 417, 450, 478, 483–4, 766, 775.
Egypt, 104, 595.
Eichtal, Adolphe d' (1805–95), banker, deputy 1846–8, 78.
Eichtal, Eugène d' (1854–1936), son of Gustave, vice-president of the Midi Railway and director of the École des Sciences politiques, 579.
Eichtal, Gustave d' (1804–86), brother of Adolphe, Saint-Simonian and advocate of Greek as a universal language, 436, 438.
Eisenhower, Dwight, 427.
Elbeuf, 218, 546.
Elections: significance of, 372–91; money in, 580–3; mayors' influence in, 529; abstentions in, 388; of 1848, 464, 486, 488, 491, 496, 726–7; of 1849, 727; of 1863, 464; of 1869, 549; of 1871, 738; of 1876, 563; of 1877, 578; of 1881, 567, 746; of 1885, 424; of 1889, 196, 580, 644; of 1893, 771; of 1898, 647, 677, 681, 750; of 1902, 254; of 1906, 698, 782; of 1910, 579, 722, 782–3; of 1936, 194; *also* 71, 397, 409, 411, 448, 451, 578–82, 608, 721.
Electoral geography, Gambetta on, 618.
Electoral sociology, 365–80.
Electricity, workers and unions, 236–7.
Elven, 186.
Employers: organisations, 70–1, 73, 203–5, 220, 236, 668; relations with workers, 155, 198–201, 203, 205–9, 213, 218–21, 226–30, 234, 237–8, 242–3, 251, 253, 259–64, 266–8, 272, 276–7, 279–81, 435, 444, 474, 489, 551, 556, 667, 669; *also* 69, 78, 211, 270, 456, 651, 674–6, 743.
Enfantin, Prosper (1796–1864), 436–7, 442, 453–4, 510, 551.
Engineers: careers, 94–105; in civil service, 117, 123, 128; in railwaymen's unions, 227; and Saint-Simonianism, 436, 437; and June rising of 1848, 489; in Parliament under Third Republic, 577.
England, 14, 35, 64, 68, 72, 80, 112, 114, 143, 148, 171, 174, 178, 185–7, 208, 237, 259, 303, 306, 346, 373, 417, 509–10, 536, 545, 547, 549, 559, 582, 666, 733.
English, the, 35, 39, 207, 225, 227, 243, 261, 272, 353, 406, 662, 672, 756.
Ententes, Jaurès and the, 764.

Entrepreneurs, 63 ff., 623.
Equality: for women, 345, 347–8, 352; in education, 717, 741; Droz on, 319; Chambord on, 401; Saint-Simon on 435; Fourier on, 441; L. Blanc on, 448; Cabet on, 450; P. Leroux on, 453; Proudhon on, 460–3; Bonapartists on, 505; Gambetta on, 615; Ferry on, 625; Waldeck-Rousseau on, 673; anarchists on, 776; also 302, 571 n., 605.
Eschassériaux, René François Eugène (1823–1906), deputy for Charente-Inférieure 1849–93, 560–2.
Esquiros, Adèle (1819–86), 293, 301.
Etchegoyen, d', family, property of the, 405.
Étienne, Eugène N. (1844–1921), under Gambetta, 612.
Étival, 242.
Eugénie, Empress (1826–1920), 324, 505, 552, 558, 566.
Evans, Thomas W., dentist, 35.

Fabre, Lucien A. (1852–1920), on peasants, 136.
Factories: workers in, 18, 199, 210, 247, 257–8, 265–6, 269, 271–2, 275, 278, 281–2, 351, 409, 475, 747; laws on, 361, 668–9; also 64–5, 71, 75, 101, 104, 166, 201, 438, 445, 447, 556, 709.
Fallières, C. Armand (1841–1931), president of the republic 1906–13, deputy 1876–90, senator 1890–1906 for Lot-et-Garonne, 312, 590, 597.
Falloux, Frédéric Alfred Pierre, comte de (1811–85), royalist leader, deputy 1846–51 for Maine et Loire, minister of education 1848–9, 395, 469, 533.
Family: 2, 285–6, 299, 362; and social mobility, 21, 41, 287, 289; peasant, 135, 141, 145–6, 152–7, 159, 163; working class, 270–2; bourgeois, 16–17; the '200' families, 13, 53, 57, 63, 70; noble, 402, 404–6; women in, 301, 344, 347, 356, 357; children in, 315–42, 361; notary and, 43, 49; and politics, 336, 390–1, 479, 497; church and, 290, 297; family firms, 63, 65–7, 70, 75, 78–9, 87, 97, 101, 103, 124–5, 266; also 32, 40, 54, 69, 89, 104, 293, 299, 378, 461, 626, 656. See also dowry, women, children, husbands, wives, parents, girls.
Faure, Félix (1841–99), president of the republic 1895–9, deputy for Seine-Inférieure 1881–95, minister of navy 1894, 596–7.

Faure, Paul (1878–1960), editor of Le Populaire du Centre 1904–14, and then of Le Populaire of Paris (jointly with L. Blum) till 1940, secretary-general of the S.F.I.O., deputy 1924–32, 1938–42, minister 1936–8, 785.
Faure, Sébastien (1858–1942), 778, 780.
Favre, Jules (1809–80), deputy 1848–51, 1858–80, foreign minister 1870–1, 221.
Feminism, 345–54.
Fénelon, François de Salignac de la Mothe (1651–1715), 322, 458.
Fermel, 207.
Ferroul, Dr. Ernest (1853–1921), 749.
Ferry, Jules (1832–93), deputy 1869–89, senator 1891–3, prime minister 1880–1, 1883–5, 590, 592, 594, 621–32, 642, 644, 650, 653, 685, 689, 691, 701, 761–3.
Ferté, family, 153, 154.
Filene's Store, Boston, 111.
Finance, Isidore, 220.
Financial: magnates, 13, 56, 77, 82, 83, 110; press, 56, 60, 61; scandals, 128, 583, 635; crises, 141, 473–4; ignorance, 82; professions, 99; administration, 50, 54, 117, 118; element in marriage, 288, 289, 291; support for railway building, 637.
Finistère, 145.
First International, the, 218, 258, 465, 552, 688, 729–35, 738, 754, 766, 774, 776–7.
Flanders, 154.
Flaubert, Gustave (1821–80), 304, 305, 311.
Flayosc, 784.
Fleurant (alias Agricola), 194.
Flexner, Abraham, on prostitution, 308.
Floquet, Charles T. (1828–96), 644.
Flourens, Gustave P. (1838–71), 740.
Folgoët, 371.
Folies Bergères, 310.
Folklore societies, 133.
Fondation Nationale des Sciences Politiques, 373.
Fontaine, Arthur, Office du Travail, 220.
Foreigners, in France, 35, 155, 173.
Foreign policy: study of, 8; of Lamartine, 486; of Ledru-Rollin, 493; of Napoleon III, 548, 558–60; of Poincaré, 598; of Gambetta, 619; of the radicals, 719.
Foremen, 19, 67, 87, 94, 96, 102, 151, 201–2, 261, 272, 489.
Forests, 80, 477.
Forez, 106, 774.

Fortier-Bernoville, Dr., author of *Comment se guérir par l'homoeopathie* (1929), 29.

Fould, family and bank, 54, 406.

Fould, Achille M. (1800–67), deputy 1842–51, senator 1852–67, minister of finance 1849–52, 1861–7, minister of state 1852–61, 78, 515.

Foucault, Dr., 326.

Fourier, Charles (1772–1837), 294, 345, 431, 438–42, 443–8, 453, 458, 460, 470.

Fournier, Alfred (1832–1914), professor, 305.

Fournol, Étienne M. (1871–1940), 579.

France, Anatole (1844–1924), 701–2, 714, 778.

Franche-Comté, 241, 461.

Franco-Prussian War (1870), 552, *558–9*, 617, 710.

Freemasons, 125, 212, 347–8, 409, 650, 687–8, 720, 727, 749. *See also* vol. 2.

Free Trade Treaty of 1860, 166.

Frères de la Doctrine Chrétienne, 236.

Freud, Sigmund (1856–1939), 29, 321, 325, 331, 333.

Freycinet, Charles de (1828–1923), Senator for Seine 1876–1920, prime minister 1879–80, 1882, 1886, 1890–2, 589, 590, 595, 627, 631, 632–8, 646.

Fribourg, Ernest Édouard, 730.

Funerals, 14, 696.

Gaillard, Felix (b. 1919), inspector of finances, prime minister 1957–8, deputy for Charente since 1946, 403.

Galliera, duchesse de (1811–88), 423, 474.

Gallifet, Général de (1830–1909), 679, 772.

Gambetta, Léon Michel (1838–82), deputy 1869–82, prime minister Nov. 1881–Jan. 1882, minister of the interior in the provisional government of 1870–1, 19, 191, 227, 246, 304, 390, 465, 491, 536, 543, 565, 567, 586, 590, 594, 596, 610–21, 632, 633, 647, 652, 671–5, 688, 715, 773.

Gard, 784.

Garnier, Madame E., 355.

Garnier-Pagès, L. A. (1803–78), mayor of Paris and minister of finance 1848, deputy 1848 and 1864–70, member of the provisional government of 1870, 200, 455, 468, 493, 497, 729 n.

Garon, miners' leader, 221.

Garonne, 176–8, 181, 189.

Gascony, 534.

Gasparin, A. E. P., comte de (1783–1857), 162.

Gaule, printer, 220.

Gaulle, General Charles de (1890–1970), 360, 366, 384, 390, 505.

Gaullism, 385.

Gavarni, Paul (1804–66), 329.

Geffriaud, abbé, 193.

General Strike: miners on, 221, 225; Guérard on, 228, 232; of 1 May 1906, 238, 239; Guesde and Briand on, 247, 249; Lagailse and, 249; Pelloutier and, 250; Bietry and, 254; Treich and, 258; C.G.T. on, 274; of 1920, 278; Brousse on, 755; Allemanists and, 757, 766.

Generations, conflict of, 335. *See also* Family *and* Politics.

Genoude, abbé, Antoine Eugène Genoud (1792–1849), later known as, 396.

Gent, Alphonse (1813–94), deputy 1848–9, 1871–82, senator 1882–94 for Vanclure, 727.

Gérault-Richard, A. L. (1860–1911), 596.

Germain, Henri (1824–1905), of Crédit Lyonnais, 20, 54, 83–4.

Germany, 64, 72–3, 106, 171, 174, 188, 237, 241, 463, 545, 582, 587, 609, 610, 651, 659, 679, 693, 723.

Gers, 160.

Gide, André (1869–1951), 313, 334–5, 778.

Gide, Charles (1847–1932), 446, 664.

Gilland, J. P., 457.

Gilly, Numa (1834–95), 770.

Girardin, Émile de (1802–81), 549.

Giraudeau St Gervais, Dr. Jean, 26.

Giraudeau, Fernand, Bonapartist journalist, 561.

Girls: peasant, 145; and dancing, 180; upbringing, 287; education of, 292, 344; and pre-marital sex, 306; and adultery, 307; and facts of life, 322; appearance of *la jeune fille moderne*, 352. *See also* Women.

Gironde, 377.

Goblet, René M. (1828–1905), prime minister 1886–7, minister 1882, 1885–6, 1888–9, deputy 1871–89, 1893–8, senator 1891–3, 652, 771.

Goblot, Edmond (1858–1935), professor of philosophy, 15.

Godin (1817–88), 445.

Goethe, Johann von (1749–1832), 372.

Gold, hoarding of, 62.

Goncourt, Edmond (1822–96) and Jules (1830–70) de, 352.

Gossez, Rémy, 489.

Gouges, Olympe de (1748–93), the first woman feminist, 346.

Graduates: careers for, 97, *99–104*; of Harvard Business School, 111; in industry and business, 124; of National Agronomic Institute, 175; Saint-Simonian, 436; of Polytechnic, 96, 102, 104, 442, 633; politics of, 480; of the *Ponts et Chaussées*, 600.

Gramophones, 331.

Grand Cercle républicain, 676.

Grave, Jean (1854–1939), 777–8.

Gréard, Octave (1828–1904), 127.

Grenoble, 47, 79, 240–1, 309, 379, 562.

Grévy, Jules (1807–91), president of the republic 1879–87, deputy for Jura 1848–51, 1868–79, 594–5, 619.

Griffuelhes, Victor (1874–1922), secretary-general of C.G.T., 234–5, 241, 705, 706.

Grimaud, Abbé, 297.

Groussier, Arthur Jules Hippolyte (b. 1863), deputy for Seine 1893–1902, 1906–24, secretary of Fédération nationale des metallurgistes 1891–3, 785.

Gruyère, 142, 192.

Guérard, Eugène, 227, 229, 239.

Guéroult, Adolphe (1810–72), editor of *L'Opinion Nationale* 1859–72, deputy for Seine 1863–9, 347.

Guesde, Jules (1845–1922), 231–2, 247, *745–54*, 765–7, 774.

Guesdism, 249, *745–53*, 757, 772.

Guilds, 212–13, 257.

Guillain, Antoine Florent (1844–1915), industrialist, *censeur* of the Bank of France, deputy for Nord 1898–1910, minister for the colonies 1898–9, 76.

Guillaumin, Émile (1873–1951), 133, 163.

Guillerey, 30.

Guise, Jean d'Orléans, duc de (1874–1940), 427.

Guizot, François (1787–1874), 200, 343, 355, 414, *416–17*, 469, 482, 504.

Hahnemann, Samuel (1755–1843), 29.

Halbwachs, Maurice (1877–1945), 190.

Hallé, Jean (1868–1951), 41.

Halles, les, construction of, 553.

Halluin, Henri d', alias Dorgères, 194–5.

Hanotaux, Gabriel (1853–1944), 98, 107, 596, 622, 659.

Happiness: in relation to social rank, 90; Joseph Droz on, 288, 294; in marriage, 289; Esquiros on, 293;

Gustave Droz on, 295; George Sand on, 352; Gambetta on society and, 617; Condorcet on, 626; Waldeck-Rousseau on boredom and, 672.

Harvard Business School, 111.

Haussmann, Baron G. E. (1809–91), 515, 553–4, 622.

Haussonville, Joseph de Cléron, comte d' (1809–84), 155, 654.

Haut-Rhin, 472, 621.

Haute-Garonne, 116, 408, 534.

Haute-Loire, 221, 531.

Haute-Marne, 185, 194.

Hautes-Alpes, 140, 149, 184.

Hautes-Pyrénées, 116, 139, 149 n., 156.

Haute-Saône, 34, 145.

Haute-Vienne, 784.

Havre, Le, 77, 227, 259, 553, 596.

Hawthorne, Nathaniel, 446.

H.B.M. (Habitations à bon marché), 85.

Hébert, Jacques (1757–94), 740.

Heine, bank, 54, 78, 406.

Helvétius, Claude Adrien (1715–71), 345.

Hennequin, Victor (1816–54), Fourierist, deputy 1850–1, 444.

Henry V, *see* Comte de Chambord.

Hérard, Hippolyte (1819–1913), president of Academy of Medicine, 41.

Hérault, 112, 116, 189, 380, 707.

Herbette, Jules (1839–1901), 579.

Heredity: and illness, 26; and the republic, 394; and the nobility, 406, 507; Comte de Paris on, 423.

Herriot, Édouard (1872–1957), 592, 602, 714.

Hertz, Cornelius, 583.

Hervé, Gustave (1871–1944), 767.

Hervieu, Paul (1857–1915), 357.

Hieron, Brother, 253.

Holidays: workers', 19, 272; attitudes to, 93; children's, 320–1.

Holland, 186, 545, 766, 772.

Homberg, Octave, 582.

Homosexuality, 313–14; Dupanloup on, 323; Gide and, 334.

Hottinguer, Baron, 154.

Housing: investment in land and, 59–62; standards of, 188–9; miners', 265–6; workers', 271.

Hugo, Victor (1802–85), 347, 633, 731, 746.

Hugues, Clovis H. (1851–1907), deputy 1881–9, 1889–1906, 770.

Humbert, Charles (1866–1927), deputy 1906–8 and senator 1908–20 for Meuse, 56.

Hume, David (1711–76), 765.

Hunt, David, Professor, 316.
Huntley and Palmer, biscuit factory, 281.
Huret, Jules (1864–1915), 260.
Husbands: and wives, relations, 49, 66, 78, 110, 285–314; Alain on role of, 329; legal rights, 352, 356–7.
Huysmans, J. K. (1848–1907), 778.
Ille-et-Vilaine, 183.
Imperial Guard, the, under Napoleon III, 519.
Impressionism, 235.
Imprimerie Nationale, 220.
Incomes, 14, 58; of doctors, 32–4, 39; of notaries, 46; of industrialists, 69, 74; in industry, 94; of bankers, 83; in commerce, 100–1, 110; of civil servants, 116–18; of nobles, 404–5, 542; in agriculture, 153, 156–9, 163, 169; total agricultural, 173, 188; of winegrowers, 473; during Second Empire, 555–6; also 141, 150, 290; see also Pensions.
Indépendants, see Société de l'Union.
India, 65.
Individualism, 340.
Indo-China, 104, 256, 630, 644.
Indre, 149 n.
Industrialisation: rate of, 82; of other countries, 104; peasants and, 188; in Second Empire, 210; and unionisation, 241; in Limoges, 257; politics, 377–8, 381, 384; Proudhon on, 463; Bonapartists on, 539; and solidarism, 641, 645; Méline on, 650–1; Waldeck-Rousseau on, 673; Tolain on, 734; Thiers on, 608.
Industrialists, 63–76, 16, 33, 86, 94, 101, 103, 153, 154, 166, 204, 255, 263, 290, 396, 435, 504, 510, 543, 553, 577, 582, 614, 620, 675–6.
Industry: financing of, 49, 52, 53, 61, 80–4, 113; growth of, 84, 96, 101, 106, 112, 555; careers in, 87, 94–104, 114; population engaged in, 105–6, 209–11; graduates in, 124; employers in, 155, 262, 270, 405; peasants and, 157, 172–3, 175, 188; discipline in, 272; women in, 351; views on, 438, 444, 493–4, 510, 545–7, 608, 649–52. See also 203, 269, 277–8, 378; and under different branches, e.g. Iron and Steel, Textiles, Silk.
Indy, Vincent d' (1851–1931), 133.
Inflation, 61–2.
Inheritance: statistics of, 58; and the peasantry, 144–7, 266; Saint-Simon on abolition of, 434–6; Olinde

Rodrigues on, 438; also 14, 34, 43, 51, 406.
Institut de France, 124, 125, 438, 579.
Instituteurs (primary school teachers), 120, 122, 125, 180, 193, 257, 273, 380–1, 483, 526, 602–3, 705, 719.
Insurance, 17, 71, 83, 102, 253, 265, 371, 629, 658, 730; companies, 33, 55, 77, 82, 304, 405, 444, 449, 562; social (medical, accident, illness, old age, etc.), 37, 85, 204, 208, 248, 275–6, 667, 716, 723; societies, 180, 478, 660, 661 n., 663.
Intellectuals, 1, 42, 427–33, 435, 787; women, 292, 298; politics of, 383, 480–2, 489, 509, 620, 622, 701; and Dreyfus affair, 680–2; students and, 481; also 52, 340, 389, 406, 492, 624. See also vol. 2.
International, the First, see First International.
Investment, patterns of, 552–62; agricultural, 188.
Ireland, 187.
Iron and steel: industrialists, 70–6; upper management in, 102; conseils de Prud'hommes in, 201; employers' associations in, 204; concentration in, 210; workers and, 210, 239–40, 253, 269; unions in, 275–80, 473; wages of women workers in, 359; in Second Empire, 545–6; slump in, 643.
Isère, 150, 783.
Isolation: of different groups within society, 22; of lower grades of civil service, 124–6; of peasants, 173, 377; of village, 179; of the proletariat, 273; of children, escape from, 339; of early feminists, 346; of teachers, 482.
Italy, 106, 174, 322, 463, 545, 551, 557–9, 587, 647, 733, 746, 774.
Izoulet, Jean (b. 1854), professor of social philosophy at the Collège de France, 659.

Jacobins, the, 727, 738–9.
Jacquemart, Paul, Inspector-General of Technical Education, 96–7.
Janet, Paul (1823–99), professor at the Sorbonne 1864 ff., 322, 327.
Janvier de la Motte, Eugène (1823–84), prefect, 544.
Japy, Henri, 255–6, 262, 264.
Jauréguiberry, Admiral Jean Bernardin (1815–87), deputy 1871–5, senator 1879–87, minister 1879–83, 627.

Jaurès, Jean (1859–1914), deputy for Tarn, 1885–9, 1893–8, 1902–14, 209, 274, 596, 644, 687, 700, 702, 771, 757–69, 772, 774–5, 784.

Jeanne, Dr. Hippolyte-Amédée, author of *Projet de tarif des honoraires médicaux* (1897), 34.

Jerome Bonaparte, King (1784–1860), 566.

Jerome-Napoleon, Prince, *alias* Prince Napoleon, or Plon-Plon (1822–91), cousin of Napoleon III, 558, 566–8.

Jesuits, 648, 678.

Jeunesse Catholique, 194.

Jews: in the banking world, 56, 77–8, 82; investments, 154; workers and, 242; Bietry's hostility to, 256; comte de Chambord and, 399; Saint-Simonian, 436; and Boulanger, 643; Dreyfus Affair, 679–82.

Jèze, Gaston (1869–1953), professor, 603.

Jolibois, Eugène (1819–96), barrister and Bonapartist, deputy for Charente Inférieure 1876–93, 567, 684.

Jouhaux, Léon (1879–1954), 274, 465, 706, 768.

Jourde, François (or Francis) (1843–93), 742.

Journalists: careers, 92; worker-, 457; Proudhon as a, 459, 464; republican, 492, 496; in parliament, 577; in Paris Commune, 738. *See also* Press, Newspapers, and vol. 2.

Juan-les-Pins, 255.

Judet, Ernest (1851–1943), editor of *Le Petit Journal*, 703.

July Monarchy, the (1830–48), 34, 70, 75, 77, 88, 116, 215, 444, 450, 469, 481–2, 487, 527, 530, 541, 553, 606, 660.

Jura, 142, 755.

Jura Federation, the, 755.

Kaës, René, 273.

Kahan-Rebecque, Madame, 474.

Keufer, Auguste (1851–1924), 219–20, 228, 238.

Kropotkin, Piotr Alexeïevitch, prince (1842–1921), 780.

Laboulaye, E. R. (1811–83), 462.

Labourers, 59, 147, 151–2, 155–8, 162–3, 170, 190; emigration, 172–3, 178; unions, 193, 195; child, 270; marriage, 289; politics, 389; in agricultural crisis, 472–3.

Labour exchanges, 243.

Labour Party, 237, 756.

Lacroix de Vimeur de Rochambeau, Achille, 404.

Lacroix, Jean, 333.

Lafargue, Jules (1860–87), 334.

Lafargue, Paul (1843–1911), 749, 786.

La Fayette, marquis de, 155.

Laffitte, Jacques (1767–1844), 82.

Laffitte, Pierre (1823–1903), 219, 624.

La Frette, 150.

Lagailse, A., secretary of C.G.T., 249.

Laigné, 374.

Laisser-faire, 655.

Lamartine, Alphonse de (1790–1869), 413, 428, 453, 484–6, 488, 550, 599, 673, 685.

Lamber, Juliette, Madame Adam (1836–1936), 347.

Lambert, Baron Tristan (1846–1929), 568.

Lamennais, Jean-Marie Félicité Robert de (1782–1854), 216, 536.

Lamoricière, General Christophe Léon Louis Jechault de (1806–65), 579.

Lamy, Étienne (1845–1919), 647.

Land: investment in, 59–62, 113; Méline on return to the, 98; and the peasantry, 133–4, 138–58, 160–1, 165, 168, 171–4, 176–8, 184–6, 191, 265–6; Paul Bois on, 374–6; nobles and, 404–5, 407–8; price of, 174, 186, 643.

Landes, 149 n., 160, 710.

Landes, David, professor, family firm theory of, 63–4.

Landlords: relations with, 136, 163, 186, 200, 490, 727, 743; and politics, 370, 374, 461, 490.

Landsberg, Natalie, 754.

Language, different kinds spoken, 16, 235, 378, 478.

Languedoc, 169.

Lanoir, Paul, of Orléans Railway Co., 254, 255.

Laon, 155.

La Réole, 377.

Larmor, 21.

La Rochefoucauld, duc de Doudeauville, 405, 408.

La Rochefoucauld, Duchesse de, 349.

La Rochejacquelin, H. A. G. du Vergier, marquis de (1805–67), 396.

Laroche-Joubert, Jean Edgard (1843–1913), deputy for Charente 1884–1906, 254–5.

Lattre de Tassigny, Laurent de, 403.

Laval, Pierre (1883–1945), prime minister 1931–2, 1935–6, minister 1925, 1926, 1930, 1932, 1934–5, 1940, deputy 1914–19 and 1924–7, senator 1927–44, 592.

Lavedan, 156.
L'Averdy, François de (1723–93), 429.
Lavergne, Léonce de (1809–80), 186.
Lavigerie, Charles, Cardinal (1825–92), 647.
Law, John (1671–1729), 82.
Laws: on charlatans, 27, 35; on doctors, 34; on dentists, 35; on the notaries, 49; on deposit safes, 50; on shop-keepers, 109; on property, 140, 142, 144, 200, 714; on taxation, 160, 523, 710; on *métayers*, 164, 186; on wine, 167–8; Méline's tariff, 174; encouraging agricultural credit societies, 175; on improvement of dwellings, 186; on peasant organisations, 191, 195; on the *livret*, 199; on Conseils des Prud'hommes, 201–2; on workers and unions, 203, 205, 206, 208, 209, 243, 245, 251, 259, 265, 275–6, 357, 517, 546, 573, 667, 668, 669, 688, 708; on nourrisson system, 361 n.; on factories, 361, 668–9; on pensions, 121, 228, 667, 709; on fares, 229; on insurance, 275–6, 667; on marriage, 289; on obscenity, 311–12; on women, 343–4, 352, 356–9, 361; on adultery, 358; on divorce, 358, 592; and the birth-rate, 359; on parental authority, 361; on criminals' children, 361; on wet-nurses, 361; on titles, 403; Army, 515; on the communes, 538; on mayors, 538; on censorship, 539, 881, 596; in Third Republic's constitution, 572; on meetings, 573, 693; on libel, 573; on secrecy in polling booths, 582–3; on nationality, 357, 592; on criminals, 592; on friendly societies, 654, 661, 663; on public assistance, 666, 708 and n.; on congregations, 678; on separation of Church and State, 692–5; attitudes to, 670.
Lawyers: republican, 492; in the *conseils généraux*, 542; in parliament of 1852, 543; in Paris Commune, 738; new ideas of (Duguit), 670.
Lazard, banking family, 54.
League: for Public Morality, 312; for the Rights of Women, 347; for the Emancipation and Well-Being of Women, 349.
Lebas, J. B. (1878–1944), deputy for Nord 1919–28, 1932–42, minister 1937–8, 786.
Lebaudy, Marie Paul Jules (1858–1937) (son of Gustave, 1827–89, deputy 1876–85), deputy for Seine-et-Oise 1890–1910, 54, 580.

Lebœuf, Joseph, secretary of Conseil Général des Manufactures, 204.
Lebrun, 779–82.
Lebrun, Albert F. (1871–1950), president of the republic 1932–40, deputy 1900–20, senator 1920–32 for Meurthe-et-Moselle, minister 1911–14, 1917–19, 55, 600.
Leconte de Lisle, C. M. (1818–94), 778.
Lederlin, Paul (b. 1868), senator for Vosges 1920–7, and for Corsica 1930–45, industrialist and philanthropist, 54.
Ledru-Rollin, A. A. (1807–74), deputy 1841–9, minister of the interior 1848, 444, 452, 488, 491–4, 497, 547, 726–7, 739.
Lefort, Henri, 731.
Legion of Honour, 39, 104, 110, 220, 338.
Legislative Assembly (1849), 547.
Legitimism: three types of leaders, 394–6; further divisions among local supporters, 396–7; Comte de Chambord, pretender to the throne, 397–401, 420–2; programme, 400–1; nobility in legitimist party, 402–11; organisation of party, 412; press, 413, 539; finances, 413; in 1848, 413; in 1852, 543; in 1870–3, 420–2; survival of, 423–4, 426–7; and Napoleon III, 513, 514, 531, 543, 563; influence of, 534, 537; and centralisation, 537, 540.
Legouvé, Ernest (1807–1903), 328–9.
Leisure, 92, 134, 189, 192, 270–2, 389, 747. *See also* cabarets, clubs, dancing, songs, societies, *and* vol. 2.
Lejeune, Louis, *see* Bastelica.
Le Langon, 139.
Le Leuch, secretary, Railwaymen's T.U., 239.
Lelut, Dr. Louis-Françisque, 431.
Lemaître, Jules (1853–1914), 355.
Lenglé, P. E. (b. 1836), 567.
Lens, 223, 264, 705.
Lépine, Louis J. B. (1846–1933), prefect of police 1897–1912, deputy 1913–14, 308.
Le Play, Frédéric (1806–82), 72, 145, 156, 249, 714, 779.
Le Puy, 696.
Leroux, Pierre (1797–1871), 345, 432, 452–4, 499, 658.
Le Roy, Eugène (1836–1907), 133.
Leroy-Beaulieu, Paul (1843–1916), 61, 579, 581, 713.
Le Royer, Philippe Élie (1816–97), 627.

Lesaché, Senator Victor (1860–1938), 53.
Lesneven, 371.
Leuret, Dr. François, 25.
Le Vert-Chotard, Madame, 349 n.
Levis, G. F. C., duc de (1794–1863), 399, 412.
Lévy, Frédéric, 204, 262, 729 n.
Leygues, Georges (1857–1933), 110, 580, 589, 599.
Liard, Louis (1846–1917), 29, 127.
Liberal, 384, 418, 453, 506–7, 603, 647, 660.
Liberal empire, the, 199, 515–16, 538, 544–52.
Liberal professions, as a career, 92, 96–7, 99, 101; numbers in, 106, 157; women in, 351, 359–60; also 60, 87, 108, 114, 270, 273, 389, 481, 542, 577.
Liberty: Napoleon III on, 511–12; in Second Empire, 545; in the Third Republic, 573, 603, 624–5, 647, 655, 656, 657, 670, 679, 681, 690, 734, 776.
Ligne, prince de, 405.
Lille, 202, 260, 270–1, 474, 580, 696, 747.
Limoges, 79, 210, 257–8, 768, 770, 784.
Limousin, Charles Mathieu (1840–1909), 218.
Limousin, 162.
Liszt, Franz (1811–86), 470.
Littré, Émile (1801–81), 311, 620, 624.
livret, the, 198–9, 551, 669.
Local government, 521–44.
Loichot, 208.
Loire, 210, 221, 224.
Loir-et-Cher, 149 n., 405, 473.
Longwy, 74.
Lons-le-Saulnier, 219.
Lorraine, 71, 73, 395, 600.
Lot, 116, 528.
Lot-et-Garonne, 116, 156, 170, 580.
Loubet, Émile (1838–1929), President of the Republic 1899–1906, 254, 597, 654.
Loucheur, Louis A. J. (1872–1931), deputy for Nord 1919–31 and frequently minister, 582.
Louis, Joseph Dominique, Baron (1755–1837), 610.
Louis-Dreyfus, Louis (1867–1940), 194.
Louis Napoleon, see Napoleon III.
Louis XIII (1601–43), 316.
Louis XIV (1638–1715), 390, 399, 403, 415, 567.
Louis XVI (1754–93), 395, 399.
Louis XVIII (1755–1824), 398–9.
Louis-Philippe, King (1773–1850), 12, 14, 52, 59–60, 71, 78, 82, 88, 203,
215–16, 221, 230, 381, 383, 387, 394, 404, 413–14, 416–17, 419, 421, 443, 450, 459, 467–70, 475, 478–9, 485, 491, 493, 495, 498–9, 507, 518, 531, 547, 549, 550, 607.
Louis-Philippe II, comte de Paris did not take title of, 423.
Lourdes, 30.
Louvre Museum, pictures bequeathed to, 110.
Loüys, Pierre (1870–1925), 305.
Lozère, 35, 39, 40, 116.
Lur-Saluces, comte de, 426.
Lycées: class connotations, 18, 154; teaching in, 19, 481; Duruy's law, 344; girls, 292; Buisson on, 717; St. Louis, 741; homosexuality in, 314.
Lyon, 15, 81, 83, 84, 165, 201, 217, 241, 254 n., 260, 282, 344, 397, 475, 545, 553–4, 696, 732, 770, 776–7.
Lyonnais, André, 259.

Mably, Gabriel Bonnot de (1709–85), on executive power and the legislature, 584.
MacClellan, General G. B. (1826–85), 422.
MacMahon, Marshal M. E. P. M. de (1808–93), 563, 594, 596.
Mackau, Anne Frédéric Armand, Baron or Comte de (1832–1918), deputy 1866–70, 76–1918, for Orne, 72, 154, 425, 646.
Mâcon, 166.
Madagascar, 630.
Magne, Pierre (1806–79), minister of finance under Napoleon III, 515.
Maine, 371.
Maistre, Comte Joseph de (1753–1821), 345, 551.
Maistre, Comte Xavier de (1763–1852), 356.
Malato, Charles, 780.
Mallarmé, Stéphane (1842–98), 778.
Mallet, Charles, 77.
Malon, Benoist (1841–93), 674, 744, 763, 774–5, 786.
Mame, Catholic publishers, 54, 219.
Managers, 94–103.
Mancel, abbé, 193.
Manet, Edouard (1832–83), 551.
Mangematin, 254.
Manning, Cardinal Henry Edward (1808–92), 774.
Mansard, journalist, 561.
Marczewski, Jan, 64.
Margérie, Amédie de, 300.
Margueritte, Victor (1866–1942), 338, 714.

Marie, Alexandre-Thomas (1795–1870), 502.

Market gardeners: in Cavaillon, 185; of Roussillon, 189.

Marne, 158.

Marriage: role of doctors in arrangement of, 32 n.; and family firms, 65, 67, 101; and the peasantry, 132, 145, 152, 156, 159, 163; and morals, 285–314; statistics on length of, 315, 358; as the aim of a girl's life, 332; Alain on children in, 329; property rights in, 343; reform, Fourier on, 345; feminists on, 353–4; in Cabet's ideal state, 451; Proudhon on, 460; also 33, 38, 40, 43, 48, 124, 405–6, 696, 741.

Marsanne, 597 n.

Marseille, 35, 79, 157, 219, 232, 241, 261, 282, 309, 356, 397, 517, 524, 540, 550, 553, 591, 732, 746, 770.

Martin, B. L. Henri (1810–83), 730.

Marx, Karl (1818–83), 77, 130, 131, 460, 466, 471, 473, 540, 731, 735–6, 763–4, 775, 786.

Marxism, 745–52, 756, 785–6.

Mascuraud, Alfred (1848–1926), senator 1905–26, 56, 676.

Massif Central, 138, 181.

Matignon Agreement, 276.

Mauchamps, Madame Herbinot de, 347.

Maupassant, Guy de (1850–93), 309.

Maurange, Dr. Gabriel, 38–9.

Maurras, Charles (1868–1952), 387, 454.

Mayenne, 37, 145, 183.

Mayors: position of, 139, 527–9, 530, 539; notaries as, 43; tenant farmers as, 154; newspaper, 179; nobles' acceptance as, 190; and the livret, 199; during factory occupations (1936), 281; re-election after 1848 of, 419, 491; appointment of, 609, 530, 532, 538; Bonapartism and, 541; in elections, 580; and prefects, relations of, 602; and mutual benefit societies, 661; and bureaux de bienfaisance, 665; and curés, relations of, 695.

Meat, 187.

Meaux, 154.

Medals, 662.

Medical services: and mutual societies, 660, 664; and public assistance office, 665–6.

Medicine: Academy of, 304; manuals of, 317. See also Doctors.

Méjan, L., 690.

Méline, Jules (1838–1925), 98, 174–5, 190, 254, 649–54, 676, 681.

Melouga, family, 157.

Melun, 308.

Mende, 39, 40.

Mendras, Henri, 621.

Merchants, 19, 81–2, 105, 156, 165, 168–9, 203–4, 211, 212, 290, 620; École Supérieure de Commerce de Paris founded for, 111–12; and peasant organisations, 192–3; political importance of, 377–8; Saint-Simon on role of, 434; in parliament, 543, 577.

Mercier, Ernest (1878–1955), 54.

Mercier, L. S. (1740–1814), 429.

Meritocracy: Saint-Simon on, 434; students and, 481.

Merrheim, Alphonse (1871–1923), 236, 267.

Métayers, see Sharecroppers.

Meurthe-et-Moselle, 206.

Mexican War, and Napoleon III, 559.

Meyer, Arthur (1844–1924), 425.

Michelet, Jules (1798–1874), 4, 143, 148, 292–3, 326–7, 345, 481–3, 614, 658, 685.

Mickiewicz, Adam (1798–1855), 482.

Midi, the, 185, 579, 633.

Milhaud, 240.

Milhaud, Gaston (1858–1918), 786.

Militarism, Bonapartists, republicans and, 519–20.

Military service, 163, 254, 379, 519–20, 610, 638, 643, 711, 719, 723–4.

Mill, John Stuart (1806–73), 536, 625, 786.

Miller, 55.

Millerand, Alexandre (1859–1943), 71, 119, 228, 233, 245, 254, 258, 338, 589, 599, 654, 669, 674, 689, 767, 770–3.

Milne-Edwards, Alphonse (1835–1900), professor of zoology, 656.

Mimerel, Auguste (1786–1871), president of Conseil Général des Manufactures, 204.

Miners: unionisation, 220–6, 240, 253–4, 276–8; and eight-hour day, 222, 669; politics of, 223, 239; wages, conditions and prospects of, 264–9, 556; recreations, 270–1; and economic crisis of 1848, 473; in 1851, 474; industrial action by, 475; law on insurance for, 667; strike at Carmaux, 668; at Courrières, 705; and Waldeck-Rousseau, 674; and Guesde, 747; of Carmaux and Jaurès, 763.

Mines and mining, 17, 71, 77, 96, 438, 441, 449; upper management in, 102; and the Conseils de Prud'-hommes, 202; Anzin, 81, 204, 223,

Mines and mining (*cont.*):
264, 474, 556, 607; numbers of employers and workers in, 210; Courrières, 264, 704–5; Carmaux, 265–7, 668.
Minimum wage, 669.
Mirabeau, A. B. L. Riqueti, vicomte de (1754–92), 319.
Mirès, Jules (1809–71), financier, 406.
Modena, duke of, 399.
Molinari, Gustave de (1819–1912), 243.
Mollet, Guy (b. 1905), 752.
Monarchists: and democracy, 13; in the west of Sarthe, 374, 377; in the Comtat, 382; *see* Kings and Aristocrats, *393–427*; under the Third Republic, 469, 496, 505–6, 533, 543, 563–4, 568, 576, 582, 593, 609, 617, 641, 643, 646–8, 653–4, 707, 721, 727. *See also* Legitimism *and* Orleanism.
Monasteries, *688–9*, 691.
Monatte, Pierre (1881–1960), 705.
Monet, Claude (1840–1926), 41.
Money: attitudes to, 31, 49, 60–2, 66, 87, 93, 95, 125, 264, 462; left at death, 58–9; the Rule of, 77; and the banks, 80, 83, 181; travelling, 240, 248, 251; in marriage, 286–8, 290–1; in elections, use of, 580–3.
Monis, Ernest (1846–1929), prime minister in 1911, 723.
Monmousseau, Gaston (1883–1960), 279.
Monnet plan, 71.
Monnet-Sully, of the Comédie Française, 39.
Monnier, Dr., 30.
Montalembert, Charles Forbes, comte de (1810–70), 551.
Montauban, 397.
Montbéliard, 208.
Montceau, 225, 254.
Montélimar, 597.
Montesquieu, Charles de S., baron de (1689–1755), 313, 345, 429–30, 620.
Montessori, Maria (1870–1952), 325.
Montherlant, Henry de (1896–1972), 321, 334.
Montluçon, 747, 748, 749.
Montmorency, duchesse de, 405.
Monod, Henri, and public assistance, 665.
Monod, Sarah, president of National Council of French Women, 348.
Montpellier, 24, 27, 397, 754, 786.
Montreuil, 581.
Morality: bourgeois, 16, 99; of the worker, 262; and money-making, 264; Siegfried on, 372; of Catholics

and radicals, 386; comte de Chambord on, 400; in Cabet's ideal state, 451; Henri Marion on, 655; Durkheim on a new, 656; *see* Marriage and Morals, *285–314*.
Morbihan, 28, 145, 186.
Moreau de Tours, Dr. Jacques-Joseph (b. 1804), 431.
Moreau, J. N. (1717–1803), 429.
Morny, C. A. L. J., duc de (1811–65), 506, 514–15, 517, 543, 549.
Mortgages, 147, 156, 164. *See also* Debt.
Moselle, the, 271.
Motor car, 179, 188.
Motte, textile family, 65, 66.
Motte, Fernand (1886–1942), 67.
'Mountain', the, 367, 374; *see* Republicanism.
M.R.P., 360, 384.
Muiron, Just, 442.
Mulhouse, 65, 210.
Mun, Albert, comte de (1841–1914), and founding of a Catholic Party, 646–7; and founding of Catholic Workers' Clubs, 744.
Museum of Popular Arts and Traditions, 179.
Mutualism, 660–4, 667.

Nadaud, Martin (1815–98), 199, 784.
Nancy, 309.
Nancy, programme of (1865), 537.
Nantes, 45, 81, 185, 251, 533.
Napoleon I, Emperor (1769–1821), 64, 123, 178, 198–200, 357, 390, 394, 402, 418, 499, 504–5, 507, 510–11, 535, 542, 609–10.
Napoleon III, Emperor (1808–73): interpretations of, 504–9; contradictions of, 509–10; opportunism of, 510–11; political ideas of, 511–12; and peasants, 512; and legitimists, 513; power of, 513; and the police, 517–18; and army, 518–20; and the notaries, 44, 52; economic activity under, 82; prefects under, 121; and popular poetry, 133; and Conseils de Prud'hommes, 201; and employers organisations, 204; free trade policy of, 204; and strike legislation, 205–6; electoral abstentions under, 388; comte de Chambord on, 401; on the use of titles, 403; and Society of St Vincent de Paul, 409; on public relations, 412; plots against, 420; and Saint-Simonians, 438; Proudhon and, 459; and Lamartine, 486; *see* Bonapartism, *504–69*; and Thiers, 606, 608; and mutual benefit societies,

660–1; *also* 12, 24, 35, 60, 78, 109, 210, 218, 221, 222, 366, 389, 396, 408, 417 n., 418, 419, 442, 469, 483, 490–2, 495, 499, 503, 728, 734.

Napoleon, Eugène-Louis Jean Joseph, Prince Imperial (1856–79), son of Napoleon III, 565–6.

Napoleonic Code, 289, 313, 361, 460, 573.

Naquet, Alfred (1834–1916), 358.

Narbonne, 707, 749.

National Agronomic Institute, 175, 190; Assembly, 226, 420, 537, 542, 560, 591, 617, 737; Association for the Protection of Workers, 312; Council for French Women, 348–9; Economic Council, 276; Federation of Printers, 219, 239; Federation of Unions, 246, 249, 746; Guard, 40, 476, 489, 518–19; League of Mutuality, 661; League against the Venereal Peril, 305; Library, 553; Miners' Federation, 222, 225; School of Administration, 437; Socialist Party, 255; Society for the Encouragement of Agriculture, 191; Union for Women's Suffrage, 349; Union for the Women's Vote, 349; Workshops, 448, 502.

National: identity, 3, 8, 624, 787; glory, Thiers on, 609; debt, 610, 709; unity, 615, 623.

Nationalisation: fears of notaries about, 44; iron and steel and, 71–2; and the banks, 85–6; C.G.T. on, 277; and the insurance companies, 405; of railways, 256, 635–6, 704, 716; of mines, 716; A.I.T. on, 731; Guesde on, 750; Jaurès and, 768; and the independent socialists, 769; Millerand on, 771.

Nationalism: workers', 245; in Paris, 254; royalist, 426; Bonapartist, 548, 550, 558–9; Ferry's, 630; Boulanger's, 643; Waldeck-Rousseau's, 679; in Dreyfus affair, 679–82; *also* 366, 384.

Navel, Georges, 272.

Navy: pay in the, 117; pensions in the, 121; minor role of French, 493; inefficiency in the, 712–13.

Necker, Jacques (1732–1804), 346.

Nérac, 597.

Netter, Yvonne, 349.

Nevers, 81.

Newman, Cardinal John Henry (1801–90), 761, 765.

Newspapers and periodicals: *L'Atelier*, 455–7, 489, 510; *L'Aurore*, 57; *L'Avant-Garde, Journal des Écoles*, 482; *L'Avenir de l'Épargne*, 661; *La Bataille*

Syndicaliste, 230; *Commerce et Industrie*, 93; *Le Concours Médical*, 33; *Le Courrier Royal*, 427; *Le Crédit*, 438; *Le Cri du Peuple*, 780; *Le démocrate de l'ouest*, 247; *La démocratie pacifique*, 443; *La démocratie rurale*, 176; *Le Droit des Femmes*, 347; *L'Écho de la Mutualité*, 661; *L'Éducation intégrale*, 778; *L'Égalité*, 746; *L'Estafette*, 631 n., *Ève*, 354; *La Femme de l'Avenir*, 347; *La Femme Libre*, 347; *La Femme Nouvelle*, 347; *La France*, 780; *La France prévoyante*, 661; *La Gazette des Femmes*, 347; *Le Gaulois*, 426, 560–1; *La Gazette de France*, 396, 408; *Le Globe*, 453; *L'Humanité*, 768; *L'Illustration*, 88; *Le Journal des Débats*, 452, 579; *Journal des Femmes*, 347; *Journal de Médecine*, 40; *Le Journal Officiel*, 539, 584; *Le Petit Journal*, 57, 703; *Lanterne*, 55; *La Lanterne du Quartier Latin*, 482; *Magasin Pittoresque*, 88; *Marie-Claire*, 354; *Le Matin*, 56; *Le Petit Méridional*, 27; *Le Moniteur*, 566; *Le Moniteur Industriel*, 204; *Le Mutualiste*, 661; *La Mutualité*, 661; *Le Napoléon*, 567; *Le National*, 455–6, 499; *L'Ordre*, 561; *L'Ouest-Clair*, 193; *L'Ouvrier des Deux Mondes*, 249; *Le Pays*, 561; *Le Père Duchesne*, 235; *Le Père Peinard*, 235, 777; *La Politique des Femmes*, 347; *Le Populaire*, 450; *La Réforme*, 493, 499; *Le Républicain de Seine-et-Oise*, 348; *La République Française*, 618, 652; *La Petite République*, 619, 756, 771; *La Révolte*, 778; *La Révolution Sociale*, 235, 777; *La Revue*, 713; *La Revue des Deux Mondes*, 295, 551; *La Revue de Famille*, 299; *La Revue des institutions de prévoyance*, 661; *La Revue Socialiste*, 774; *La Science Sociale*, 779; *Le Siècle*, 779; *Le Temps*, 76, 310–11, 622; *Les Temps Nouveaux*, 777, 780; *Le Tour du Monde*, 88; *La Voix du Peuple*, 235; *Le Voltaire*, 619. *See also* 60, 180, 194, 215, 242, 246, 253, 288, 380, 389, 413, 424, 442, 451, 484, 488, 539, 551, 568, 582–3, 648, 720, 751, 754, 756, 776, 778.

New Zealand, 373.

Niel, 237.

Nièvre, 145, 149 n., 784.

Nîmes, 397, 580, 770.

Nobles, *see* Aristocracy.

Noetzlin, banker, 85.

Nord, 35, 45, 65, 183, 220–1, 223–4, 226–7, 253, 397, 474, 484, 783.

Normandy, 68, 69, 145, 186, 188–9, 371, 373, 506, 544, 656.

North of France, the, 116, 137–8, 144, 151, 160, 167, 183, 194, 224, 282, 289–90, 384, 476, 747.

Notables: 36, 39–40, 43, 401, 555, 645, 661, 676; and universal suffrage, 381, 522; Orleanist, 418; republicans and, 467, 487, 491–2, 494, 496; Napoleon I and, 507; Napoleon III and, 509, 514; prefects and, 531–4; Bonapartism and, 541, 544; in conseils généraux, 542.

Notaries, the, 21, 40, 43–52, 80, 117, 155, 157, 180, 347, 478; as money lenders, 81–2; and the peasants, 136, 145; on the dowry, 288, 290; and marriage contracts, 290–1; and mortgages, 557; in parliament under Third Republic, 577; in left-wing societies, 728.

Nouvelles couches sociales, 19, 613, 615, 620, 621, 649, 658.

Odier, Antoine (1766–1853), peer of France, 204.

Office du Tourisme, 773.

Office du travail, 668.

Ollivier, Émile (1825–1913), 205–6, 486, 495, 505, 517, 547, 550–2, 569, 631, 673.

Opéra, the, 553.

Opéra Comique, 111, 310.

Opportunism: Thiers, 606–10; Gambetta, 610–21; Ferry, 621–32; Freycinet, 632–8; political factors, 634; and taxation, 635; stalemate results, 640–5; philosophical basis, 620, 624; defined, 634; and army, 610, 615, 638; foreign policy, 617, 619, 630; and education, 615, 620, 625–6; and class, 612–15, 617, 623–5; and social questions, 616, 629–30; and happiness, 617; press, 618–19, 631; divisions, 619; and parliament, 619; and peasants, 623, 629; and religion, 616, 624, 627, 645–8; and morals, 625; and women, 625; and Protestantism, 627–8; and the state, 628–9; and capitalism, 629–30, 636–7; colonial policy, 630; also 510, 590, 642–4, 646–7, 761, 783. See also Republicanism and Progressists.

Ordinaire, Dionys (1826–96), agrégé des lettres, editor of La Petite République, deputy for Doubs 1880–96, 613.

Ordre Moral, Broglie's, 259.

Orleanism: political ideas of, 414; Louis-Philippe's ideas, 414–16; Guizot's doctrine, 416–17; varieties of, 417–19; attitude to legitimists, 419–

22; comte de Paris, 422–6; Thiers, 606–10; also 384, 394, 499, 506–8, 548.

Orleanists, 13, 51, 413–14, 419–25, 476, 514–15, 519, 531, 534, 537, 539, 543, 607.

Orléans, duc d' (1869–1926): father of comte de Paris, 422; as pretender, 426.

Orléans, 47, 166, 254.

Oudot, C. F. Chevalier (1755–1841), 294.

Owen, Robert (1771–1858), 439, 445, 450, 453.

Paepe, César de (1842–90), 753.

Panama Canal, 442, 510.

Panama scandal, the (1892–3), use of money in politics, 583, 640.

Pankhurst, Mrs. E. (1858–1928), on French feminism, 346.

Parents, relations with children, 66, 89–90, 146, 287, 297, 299, 318–42, 355–6, 361, 696.

Paris, 14, 24, 33, 35, 37–40, 45–6, 60, 72, 77, 79, 82, 85, 97, 102–3, 107, 109–11, 115, 122, 132, 152, 154, 165–6, 183, 193, 199, 204, 207, 214, 216, 218, 219, 222, 226–7, 230–1, 234–6, 243–6, 252–4, 258–9, 262–3, 269–71, 282, 288, 291, 305, 307–11, 344, 347, 352–3, 358–9, 394, 397, 401, 405, 415, 439, 443, 447, 452, 454–5, 464, 468, 473–4, 476, 479, 480–91, 502, 515, 517, 519, 527, 536, 539–40, 542, 551, 553–4, 556, 561, 574, 576, 578, 583, 591, 596, 602, 603, 605, 609, 612, 622, 623, 631, 632, 640, 643, 660–1, 665, 672, 674–6, 675, 678, 684, 696, 702, 726, 732, 736–45, 746, 747, 754, 755, 757, 759, 761, 770, 771, 774, 776–7, 783, 784, 787. See also Sorbonne.

Paris, comte de (1838–94), 421, 422–6.

Paris, Henri, comte de (b. 1908), 427.

Paris Omnibus Co., 61, 72, 82.

Parliament: notables in, 49, 56, 75, 114; peasants in, 196; workers in, 231–2; legitimists in, 395; Orleanists and, 414–16, 424; L. Blanc on, 448; Lamartine on, 486; Napoleon III and, 513, 520, 531, 543; Liberal Empire and, 551; Third Republic and, 391, 572, 574, 577, 584–7, 593, 596; Thiers on, 608; Gambetta on, 619; Waldeck-Rousseau on, 675; délégation des gauches, 686; Jaurès on, 764; also 365–93, 570–605.

Parti: agraire et paysan français, 194; Propriétiste Anti-Étatiste, 255; Socialiste républicain, 766; des Travailleurs Socialistes, 746.
Parti Ouvrier Français, 246, 746, 763, 774, 780.
Pas de Calais, 73, 223, 225, 240, 266, 581, 746.
Pasteur, Louis (1822–95), 390.
Pataud, electrician, 236.
Patois, see Language.
Patriotism, 242, 247, 274, 285, 353, 390, 499, 521, 559, 615, 631; see also Nationalism.
Patronage: in the medical profession, 38, 40; in banking, 78; in jobs, 89, 97, 99; in politics, 114; in the civil service, 119; among workers, 261; of nobles, 408; among writers, 429; revolt against, 467; also 479, 497, 529–30; and see vol. 2.
Pauchet, Dr. Victor, 325.
Pauvert, Odette, 359.
Peasant Front, 195.
Peasants: power of, 131; image of, 131–5; conflicts among, 135–9, 147–8; debts, 136, 147; common rights, 139–43; property, 143–9, 151; savings, 147, 181; variations among small proprietors, 149–51; forms of tenure, 151; social hierarchy, 152–70; rich tenant farmers, 152–6; budgets, 156–60; sharecroppers, 160–5; winegrowers, 165–70; labourers, 170; proportion of population, 171; emigration, 172; relations with towns, 172–3; and protection, 174; and modernisation, 175, 176–84; and education, 132, 134, 175, 178, 266, 338, 417; and the state, 175; taxation, 133, 136, 176, 491, 512, 635, 711, 750; standard of living, 188–9; class consciousness, 189; politics, 190–1, 193–7, 370, 372, 374, 382; Christian democracy and, 193–4; Défense paysanne, 194; Parti agraire et paysan, 194; Jeunesse catholique, 194; size of farms, 184; unions and co-operatives, 190–4, 207, 252; and the church, 193; and Napoleon III, 504, 552, 557; as miners, 221; proletarianisation, 265–6; housing, 266; and the dowry, 287; and the feminist movement, 350; in Sarthe, 376–7; and the 'république paysanne', 381; and legitimism, 397, 408, 410; comte de Chambord on, 401; and nobles, 408; Louis Blanc and, 449; Proudhon on, 461–3; and republicans, 477–9, 487, 490–2; and

military service, 519; and universal suffrage, 522; prosperity under second empire, 557; in parliament, 577; Gambetta's view of, 615, 621; Ferry on, 623, 629; economic problems, 643; Méline and, 652; in mutual societies, 664; and pension insurance, 667; Waldeck-Rousseau and, 674; and entry into the Church, 684; under Clemenceau, 706; and socialism, 725, 727–8, 784; and the Commune manifesto, 742; and Guesdism, 747, 750; and Jaurès, 768–9; also 11, 14, 18, 259, 287, 379–80, 439. See also Sharecroppers and Debt.
Pécaut, Félix (1828–98), 627.
Pedron, Étienne (1849–1931), 747.
Pelletan, Charles Camille (1846–1915), 719, 722.
Pelloutier, Fernand (1868–1901), 194, 233, 236, 246–8, 465, 778.
Pensions: army, 121; clergy, 121, 692, 697; workers', 122, 208, 222, 226–8, 265, 666, 708, 741, 763; cooks', 230; leather workers', 257; watchmakers', 262; 1928 law on, 276; authors', 429; Fourier on, 441; Hennequin on, 444; Louis Blanc on, 447; of Third Republic deputies, 577; and solidarist benefit societies, 660, 663; and the incurable old, 666, 688, 708, 708 n.; in 1910, 708–9; radicals on, 716.
Perdiguier, Agricol (1805–75), 216.
Péreire, Émile (1800–75), 54, 82.
Péreire, Eugène (b. 1831), engineer, deputy for Tarn 1863–9, director of Compagnie generale des omnibus, Crédit mobilier espagnol, etc., 55.
Péreire, Isaac (1806–80), 82.
Péreire family, 83, 154.
Perez, Bernard, 323.
Périer, Casimir (1777–1832), 204.
Périer, Jean Casimir (1847–1907), grandson of Louis Philippe's minister, deputy 1876–94 for Aube, prime minister 1893–4, president of the republic 1894–5, 596.
Perier, Joseph, 204.
Périgueux, 785.
Periodicals, see Newspapers.
Pernot, 242.
Perpignan, 707.
Persigny, V. F. de, duc de (1808–72), 506, 514, 531, 541.
Pétain, Philippe, marshal (1856–1951), 195–6, 389.
Petosse, 139.
Petrol, employees in, 102.

Peyrat, Alphonse (1812–91), 537.
Pharmacists, 90.
Philippe VII, *see* comte de Paris.
Philosophes, 429, 430, 432, 435, 470, 584.
Picardy, 138.
Pichon, Stephen (1857–1933), 599.
Pietri, Joseph-Marie (1820–1902), prefect of police 1866–70, senator for Corsica 1879–85, 534, 560.
Pinel, Dr. Philippe (1745–1826), 433.
Pinot, Robert, 72, 404.
Piorry, Dr. P. A. (1794–1879), 25.
Piou, Jacques (1838–1932), 646.
Pissarros, the, 41, 235, 778.
Pitt-Rivers, Julian, 378.
Pitts, Jesse, 339–40.
Pius X, Pope (1835–1914), 693.
Plancy, marquis de, 406.
Planteau, François Edouard (b. 1836), translator, journalist and deputy for Haute-Vienne 1885–9, 770.
Plebiscites, 505, 551–2.
Plibou, 524–6.
Poincaré, Raymond (1860–1934), deputy 1887–1903, senator 1903–13, 1920–9, president of the republic 1913–20, minister of finances prime minister 1913, 1922–4, 1926–8, 56, 576, 589, 597–9, 659, 676, 704, 713, 723.
P.O.F., *see* Parti Ouvrier Français.
Poitiers, 403.
Poland, 733.
Police: and workers, 199, 203, 206, 245, 275; and homosexuals, 314; in 1848, 468, 490; in Second Empire, *517–18*, 740; in the Commune, 523, 741; Corsicans in, 535; methods, 552, 573; politics, 561; and peasants, 623; in Paris, 736; *also* 780.
Politics: attitudes to, 33, 111, 155, 365–92, 466, 570–95; and industry, 43, 53, 69, 78; workers and, 206, 237, 239, 247, 250, 253, 255, 268, 282, 237, 281; peasants and, 190, 196, 266; nobles and, 191; children's interest in, 339; prestige of, 388, 758.
Polytechnique, École: engineers and the, 94, 103; graduates of the, 96, 102, 104, 442, 600, 633; prestige of the, 102; construction of the, 553.
Poncet de La Grave, Guillaume, on celibacy (1801), 310.
Pons, 684.
Pont-à-Mousson, 76, 272.
Poor, the, 14, 15, 31–2, 40, 59, 200, 349, 381, 510, 665–6, 671, 736, 751, 754, 764; problems of rich and, 58, 140–1, 618, 657.

Pope Leo XIII (1810–1903), 426, 647.
Popular Front, the, 13, 164, 172, 280, 600; *also* vol. 2.
Population: agricultural, industrial and commercial, 105; peasant, 131; wine-growing, 169; industrial, 169, 209–10; decline in the, 171; in agriculture, 171–3; in relation to roads and railways, 178.
Pornography, 310–12.
Portugal, 545.
Positivism: Keufer and, 219–20; and prostitution, 291; republican converts to, 501; Gambetta and, 620; Ferry and, 624, 685; and 1789 Revolution, 655; Combes and, 685; *also* vol. 2.
Possibilists, 258, *752–7*.
Pothier, 709.
Pouget, Émile (1860–1931), 235, *777–8*, 780.
Poujade, Pierre (b. 1920), president of the Union de défense des commerçants et artisans, 195.
Poulot, Denis (b. 1832), 272.
Poultry, 187.
Pouyer-Quertier, Auguste (1820–91), 69.
Power: theories on, 16, 53, 241, 715; administrative, 121, 127, 530–4, 548, 552; political, 365–93, 548, 552, 587–8, 698; economic, 53, 72, 155, 261; local, 527–9; ecclesiastical, 292; social, 408, 507; intellectual, 429–31; paternal, 361, 460; police, 518.
Prefects: status and power, 117, 179, 530–4, 538, 544, 601–4; of the Second Empire, 121, 153, 530–4, 560; of the Third Republic, 601–4; and workers, 540; and elections, 578, 580; under Thiers, 609; under Gambetta, 619; and mutual societies, 661; and Combes, 687.
Presidents of the Third Republic, 593–601.
Press: control of, 13, 53, 56; financial, 60; censorship, 57, 429, 469, 484, 503, 548, 565, 569, 573, 596; in 1848, 484; in politics, 380, 396, 412, 438, 498, 539, 561. *See also* Journalists, Newspapers, *and* vol. 2.
Prestige: of technical knowledge, 42; of notaries, 52; of landownership, 59; and industrial expansion, 101; of state offices, 113; and the peasant, 134–5; of the Military Medal, 195; as a parent, 315; sports and adolescent, 334; feminine, 353; of France abroad, 366, 610; of literature and science over politics, 389; of the

scientist, 430; of the prefects, 530–1; of financiers and industrialists, 553; of the self-made man, 609.

Pretenders to the Throne, 397–8, 425–7.

Priestley, Joseph (1733–1804), 501.

Primogeniture, abolition of, 316, 343.

Prince, Mrs., of Boston, 111.

Printers: unionisation, 218–19, 239–40, 278; National and International Federations of, 239.

Profits, 67, 74, 83, 112, 183, 264.

Progressists: and notion of left and right, 383; and opportunists, 646–7; and Waldeck-Rousseau, 679.

Property: views on, 18, 169, 231, 255–6, 259, 358, 400, 434, 441, 443, 448, 449, 452, 456, 461–2, 462, 494, 512, 565, 608, 614, 657, 659, 674, 716, 730, 768, 776; distribution of, 53–63, 106, 139–52; law on, 200, 290; of unions, 207; and politics, 370–7; marriage and, 287–91, 302; women's, 343–4; church, 688, 692–3; also 60, 151, 155, 247, 252, 266, 370, 489, 577, 614, 747, 768, 771.

Prostitution, 291, 295, 303, 305–14, 345, 349, 360, 713.

Protection: Méline's tariff law, 174–5, 649, 653; textile industry and, 204; Napoleon III and, 509; Thiers on, 608; Ferry on, 629; also 71, 646.

Protestants: textile manufacturers, 67; banks and bankers, 77, 154; Orleanist, 414; legitimists and, 397; comte de Paris and, 423; and republicanism, 501, 628; under Ferry, 627–8; and Dreyfus Affair, 680; and separation of Church and State, 690.

Protot, L. C. Eugène (1839–1921), 741.

Proudhon, P. J. (1809–65), on women, 345–6; politics and, 386, 388; popularity of, 431–2; ideas and influence of, 458–66; also 60, 233, 247, 347, 444, 457, 551, 620, 650, 729, 730–1, 733–5, 738–9, 741, 776, 778.

Proust, Marcel (1871–1922), 294, 313.

Provence, 770, 787.

Provincial: doctors, 33, 38–9; notaries, 47–8; investment, 60; banks, 79; towns, 79, 124; factories, 103; nobles, 191; socialists, 218, 241, 246, 726; prostitution, 308; divorce, 358; politics, 366, 394, 409, 419, 476–9, 485, 674; press, 539; stability, 543; poor, 665; also 84, 85, 144, 543; and see vol. 2.

Prud'hommes, see Conseils de Prud'-hommes.

Psephology, 372.

Psychology: of business, 24–5, 63, 65, 70, 78–9, 87, 97, 101, 103, 266; of success, 87–113; of children, 323–5, 331, 355.

Public assistance, 474, 527, 665, 666.

Puisieux, 155.

Puy-de-Dôme, 221.

Pyrénées, 188, 189.

Pyrénées-Orientales, 116, 145, 149 n., 183, 707.

Quénot, editor of L'Atelier, 457.

Queille, Dr. Henry (b. 1884), radical minister 1924–38 (with intervals), prime minister 1948–9, 1950, 1951, deputy 1914–35, 1946–58, senator for Corrèze 1935–40, 589.

Queyras, 185.

Quinet, Edgar (1803–75), 319, 334, 481, 482.

Racialism, 501.

Radicalism: of winegrowers, 169; of cobblers, 214; republican, 396, 482, 506; of the small man, 494; in the south-west, 534; also 683–724.

Radical party, 714–24; philosophy of, 714–15, 717; membership figures, 720; policy, 718–20; congresses, 716; internal conflicts, 721–4.

Radicals: and the shopkeeper, 109; and women, 349; politics of, 383, 682–744; on morals, 386; under Louis-Philippe, 495; also 536, 575, 583, 590, 626–7, 629, 637–8, 642, 644, 646, 652–3, 674–6, 679, 749, 756, 765, 767, 769–72, 774, 783.

Radiguet, Raymond (1903–23), 334.

Railways: cost of, 44, 128; P.L.M., 56, 72, 77; engines and smoke nuisance, 143; and expansion of markets, 166; in Brittany and Vendée, 178, 394; workers strikes and unions, 226–9, 238–9, 254, 278–9; nationalisation of, 256, 704; Catholics in, 371; nobles in, 405; Enfantin on, 438; Saint-Simonians on, 438; Hennequin on, 444; L. Blanc on, 449; and economic crisis of 1848, 473; workshops and the June rising 1848, 489; attacks after 1848 on, 491; and the prefects, 530, 532; peasants and jobs on, 535; in the second empire, 545, 553–5, 557; in the July Monarchy, 553; Paul de Cassagnac on, 569; Thiers' attitude to, 553, 608; Freycinet and expansion of, 633, 635–7; also 17, 61, 74, 82, 96, 217, 301.

Ralliement, 426, 645–7, 677.

Rambouillet, 596.
Ranc, Arthur (1831–1908), 536.
Raspail, François V. (1794–1878), 24, 727.
Recamier, Dr., 33.
Reclus, Élisée (1830–1905), 777.
Recreation, see Leisure.
Recurt, Adrien Barnabé Athanase (1798–1872), 455.
Red Cross, American, 324.
Red Cross, French, 190.
'Reds', the, 382, 479, 487, 490, 492, 728.
Régère, Dominique Théophile (1816–93), 740.
Regional variations: economic, 21, 78, 84, 111–12, 169; agricultural, 21, 140, 148–54, 160, 165–6, 176, 190–2, 195, 366; political, 136, 256, 366, 370–1, 506, 513; population, 171; wealth, 181; workers, 220, 230, 240, 258, 269, 282, 285; general, 369, 755.
Reims, 69, 107, 158–9.
Reinach, Joseph (1856–1921), chef de cabinet to Gambetta, deputy 1889–98, 1906–14 for Basses-Alpes, 56.
Religion: among upper classes and civil servants, 126; and the peasantry, 190; and the unions, 253, 259; in the home, 292; women and, 301; Alfred Naquet on, 358; and right-wing voting, 373; Siegfried on influence of, 379; comte de Chambord on, 400–1, 565; aristocracy's return to, 407; Orleanists on, 414; comte de Paris on, 426; utopians on, 431–3; Saint-Simonianism and, 436; Cabet and, 452; of humanity, Pierre Leroux's, 454; Proudhon on, 458; republicans of 1848 and, 499, 502, 648; Gambetta on, 616; Ferry on, 624–8; in schools, 646; Méline on, 650; Durkheim on, 656; Allard on, 690; indifference of the young towards, 691; Briand as minister for, 693; and the radicals, 716; Jaurés and, 764. See also vol. 2.
Remiremont, 649.
Renan, Ernest (1823–90), 744.
Renard, Jules (1864–1910), 133, 337.
Renard, Victor (1864–1914), 239.
Renault, Léon Charles (b. 1839) prefect of police, 1871–6, 561.
Rennes, 193, 194.
Renouvier, Charles B. (1815–1903), 628, 658, 659.
Rentiers, 58–62; number of, 106; income of, 55, 85; loans by, 60; dowry among, 290; Thiers on, 610.

Republican League of Small Property, 143.
Republicanism: and centralisation, 125, 268, 537; sources of, 374, 377, 384; and parliamentary government, 424–5; theories about why it succeeded in 1848, 467 ff.; class relations in, 477–9; organisation, 479; students and, 480–2; teachers and, 483; lawyers and, 484; three types in 1848, 485 ff.; utopian, 485–7; Red, 487; moderate, 502–3; Paris workers and, 487–9; peasants and, 490 ff.; republican notables, 494–7, 501, 502; and monarchy, 495; numbers in Constituent Assembly, 496; ideological origins of, 500–1; élitism in, 501; Protestantism and, 501–2; and Bonapartism, 508–9, 522, 533, 535–6; four levels of, after 1870, 605; contradictions in, 606. See also Opportunism, Radicalism, and under names of leading politicians.
Restoration, the (1815–30), 51, 77, 204, 215, 396, 419–24, 482, 506–7.
Retail trade, 87–100, 105–12, 268.
Retirement: aim of early, 95; and living off one's capital, 108; to villages, 139; from factories, 157; from farming, 158; attitude of industrialists to, 263.
Revolution, French (1789), views of, 487, 504, 505, 604, 617, 654, 655, 701, 714, 715.
Revolution: industrial, 112, 510; and peasantry, 133, 136, 140, 185, 196; of 1830, 215, 416, 422, 507, 727; of 1848, 230, 347, 388, 413, 417, 464, 468–90, 658, 660; trade unions and, 231–3, 237–8, 250, 274; B.D.T. and, 248; Keufer on, 219; Navel on, 272; Chambord on, 400; Saint-Simon on, 434; L. Blanc on, 447–9; republicans on, 494; E. Ollivier on, 550; Gambetta on, 616; Solidarists on, 655; Guesde on, 750; Brousse on, 753; Russian, 279; American, 500.
Révolution Sociale, La, 235.
Revue politique et parlementaire, 676.
Rey de Jougla, Dr., 27.
Reybaud, Louis (1799–1879), 80.
Reynaud, Jean (1806–63), 454.
Rhône, 149 n.
Ribot, Alexandre F. J. (1842–1923), 261, 593.
Ricard, Philippe (1800–89), 24.
Rich, the: class connotations, 15; and doctors, 31; the '200 families', 53–7; statistics of, 57–62, 86; in July monarchy, 77; 'idle rich', 59; in civil

service, 117; and peasants, 139, 141, 150, 165; marriage of, 289, 290; Saint-Simon on, 434; taxation of, 498, 712; republicans and, 617, 657, 671; in Bordeaux, 620.
Richard, Albert Marie (1846–1918), 732.
Richard, Cardinal F. M. B. (1819–1908), 696.
Richer, Léon (1824–1911), 347–8.
Rigault, Raoul G. A. (1846–71), 740–1.
Roads: administration of, 128; in Brittany, 177–8; expenditure on, 526; and prefects, 530, 532; in Second Empire, 555; also 569.
Robespierre, M. F. I. de (1758–94), 390, 494, 739.
Robin, Albert (1847–1928), professor of clinical therapeutics, Paris (1906), 41.
Robin, Dr. Gilbert, 331–2.
Robin, Paul, on education, 778.
Roche-Aymond, comte de la, 405.
Rochefort, Henri (1831–1913), 104.
Rochefort, Octave de, 104.
Rochefort, Robert, 319.
Rocheouart-Mortemart, 406.
Rockefeller, John D. (1839–1937), 68.
Rodrigues, Olinde (1794–1851), 82, 436, 438.
Rolland, Romain (1866–1944), 334, 758.
Rollet, Joseph, of Lyon (1824–94), 25.
Romains, Jules (1885–1972), 340.
Romilly, 748.
Rondet, Michel (1841–1908), 221–4.
Roqueredonde, 380.
Rothschild, Alphonse de (1827–1905), 78.
Rothschilds, the, 54, 77–8, 81, 154, 405, 580.
Roubaix, 45, 65, 66, 69, 236, 240, 546, 751, 786.
Rouen, 35, 69, 524, 546.
Rougé, Comte Arthur de, 413.
Rouher, Eugène (1814–84), 516, 538, 560, 563.
Rouillier, E. L. H. C. Edouard (1830–1903), 465.
Rousseau, Jean-Jacques (1712–78), 203, 317–18, 322–4, 345, 431, 463, 501, 511, 620, 780.
Roussillon, 189, 707.
Rouvier, P. Maurice (1842–1911), 583, 590.
Royalism, see Monarchism.
Rural: development, 49; banks, 80–1; population, 131; innovation, 134; community, 143; social structure,

173; trade unions, 252, 258; romanticism, 286; dowries, 290; courtship, 302; strife, 377; see peasants, 131–97.
Russia, 62, 64, 174, 279, 446.

Sables, 533.
Sahara desert, 442.
Saint-Affrique, 579.
Saint-Chaffrey, 184.
Sainte-Barbe school, 483.
Sainte Croix, Avril de, president of National Council of French Women, 349.
Saint-Hilaire-des-Landes, 185.
Saint-Julien-en-Quint, 149.
Saint-Mandé, 771–2.
Saint-Mars, 374.
Saint-Nazaire, 247.
Saint-Priest, E. L. M. G. vicomte de, general (1789–1881), legitimist leader, deputy for Hérault 1849–51, 42.
Saint-Simon, C. H., comte de (1760–1825), 82, 88, 345–7, 388, 390, 430–8, 445, 447–8, 453, 460, 470, 499, 510, 553.
Saint-Simonianism, 436–8, 454, 463, 551; and Bonapartism, 509–10.
Saint-Sulpice-les-Feuilles, 784.
Salesmen: travelling, 97; schools for, 111.
Salleron, Louis, 195.
Sand, George (1804–76), 133, 216, 352, 457.
Saône-et-Loire, 73, 170, 183, 490.
Sarcey, Francisque (1827–90), 780.
Sarraut, Albert M. (1872–1962), 589.
Sarrien, Jean-Marie Ferdinand (1840–1915), 686.
Sarthe, 374–6, 493.
Sartre, Jean-Paul (b. 1905), 354.
Sauternes region, the, 545.
Savings: and workers, 62; and the peasantry, 181.
Savoie, 139.
Say, Léon (1826–96), 61, 119, 579, 627.
Scheurer-Kestner, Auguste (1833–99), 628.
Schnaebele incident, the (1887), 595.
Schneider, Eugène (1805–75), 16, 54, 75.
Schoelcher, Victor (1804–93), 348.
School of Political Science, 68
School of Puericulture, 324.
School of Waters and Forests, 80.
Schools: doctors and, 36; of nurses, 38; for surgeons, 39; technical, 96; engineering, 99, 102; chemists, 100; for salesmen, 111; primary, 154, 175,

Schools (cont.):
483, 626, 646–8, 685, 689, 695;
church, 154, 314, 381, 557, 688–9,
697, 718, 741; secondary, 189, 689,
344; newspaper, 246; workers' attitudes to, 273; sex education in the,
299, 323–4, 338; masturbation and
the, 306; homosexuality in the, 314;
G. Collin on, 325; Alain on, 330;
Durkheim on, 330; Vallès on, 336;
and sociability, 339–40; family attitudes to, 341; girls', 344; lay and
ecclesiastical, 380–1; nobility and the,
406; comprehensive, 441; republicans' plans for, 497; state subsidies
for, 523, 525–6; Ferry and lay, 626–7;
under Waldeck-Rousseau, 678;
changes in the, 787.
Schoolmaster, see Teachers and Instituteurs.
Scotland, 187.
Science: Academy of, 28; respect for,
30, 42, 389; School of Political, 68;
as a career, 87; as an academic subject, 94; aversion of industrialists for
men of, 94; characterology as a, 326;
of anatomy, 326; republicans' lip-
service to, 487; Gambetta and, 616,
620; Méline's attitude to, 651; and
solidarism, 656, 658; and the Dreyfus
Affair, 681; Combes and, 685;
Clemenceau on, 699–700.
Scientific jargon and doctors' remedies,
26; study of traditional and empiric
practices, 30; education, prejudice
against, 103; methods avoided by
peasantry, 135; study of children,
324–5.
Scribe, A. Eugène (1791–1861), 355.
Scrutin d'arrondissement, 574, 713.
Scrutin de liste, 575, 618, 713, 719.
Second Empire, the: property division
in, 144; countryside in, 171; prosperity in, 173–4; industrial population in, 209–10; unions in, 218, 230;
clubs and societies in, 271; prostitution in, 308; homosexuality in,
313; theatre in, 355; industry in, 438;
teachers in, 729; police force and
army in, 517–18; elections in, 580;
taxation in, 610; also 83, 107, 155,
166, 204, 257, 264, 288, 418, 426,
446, 504, 505, 521–2, 528, 530–1,
534, 535, 537–8, 541–5, 552–9, 518,
628, 636, 662. See also Napoleon III
and Bonapartism.
Second Republic, the, 201–2, 243, 246,
438, 448, 475–6, 483, 492, 527, 543,
624, 725–6, 729.

Sée, Camille (1827–1919), 344.
Seine, 37, 149 n., 348, 515, 591, 720,
783.
Seine-et-Marne, 152–3.
Seine-et-Oise, 580.
Senate, the, 591–3.
Senlis, 153.
Servants: fall in numbers of, 14; of
merchants, 19; and the Civil Code,
200; and marriage contracts, 289;
statistics of domestic, 351.
Severac, J. B., 786.
Séverine, pseud. of Caroline Rémy,
Madame Guebhard (1855–1929),
355.
Sèvres, 258.
Sex: marriage and morals, 285–314;
children and, 316–17, 321–3, 335,
778; education, 299, 323–4, 338;
Simone de Beauvoir's The Second Sex,
354; Fourier's ideas on, 441–2; Considérant on, 443; Proudhon on, 460.
S.F.I.O., French section of the Workers'
International, 719, 766–7.
Shakespeare, William (1564–1616),
765.
Sharecroppers, 160–4; Guillaumin as a,
134; indebtedness of, 136; acquired
tenancies, 147; other employment,
150; proprietors and non-proprietors
as, 151; in south-west and centre,
151; social status of, 152; and law of
1946, 186; and other farmers, 190;
of Bourbonnais, 193; as proprietors,
259; socialism and the, 785.
Sheep, 186.
Shopkeepers: mentality of, 11, 19, 105,
110; notaries' wives as, 44; place
in society, 108–9, 614; prosperity
among, 112; peasants' indebtedness
to, 136; and agricultural trade
unions, 207; and strikes, 224; union
of, 253; and co-operatives, 256;
children of, 270; attitudes to feminism, 350; in the Society of St Vincent
de Paul, 409; and economic crisis of
1848, 473; and June rising 1848,
489–90; and mutualism, 664; and
Guesdists, 747.
Shops, 107–11, 138, 166, 179, 211, 235,
261, 273, 669.
Siegfried, André (1875–1959), 68, 367–
74, 379, 381, 382, 505.
Siegfried, Jacques (1840–1909), brother
of Jules, 263.
Siegfried, Jules (1837–1922), 68.
Siegfried, Madame Jules (1848–1922),
president of National Council of
French Women, 349.

Sieyès, Emmanuel Joseph, abbé (1748–1836), 670.

Signac, Paul (1863–1935), 235, 778.

Silk: merchants, 81; manufacturer, 83; industry, 201, 545; merchants' associations, 204.

Simmons College, Boston, 111.

Simon, Jules (1814–96), 21, 299, 483, 499, 580, 626, 730.

Singer, Miss, 405.

Sisley, Alfred (1839–99), 41.

Socialists and Socialism: origins of (1848–51), 725–9; under Napoleon III, 729–35; Commune and, 735–45; Guesdist, 745–51; possibilist, 752–7; Allemanist, 756–7; Jaurès and, 757–69; independent, 241, 722, 757, 763, 766, 769–75; anarchists and, 775–82; Millerandist, 770–3; integral, 774–5; electoral successes of, 750, 754, 757, 782; numbers of supporters, 749, 766, 782–6; press, 751, 768; S.F.I.O., 766; P.O.F., 746; and peasants, 750, 768.

— national, 255; utopian, 431, 449–66, 729; democratic, 447, 487, 490–1; municipal, 524, 753, 755, 767; Christian, 659; 'radical', 686, 700, 721–2, 770–1; 'anti-collectivist', 383; Proudhonian, 739; Marxist, 752; integral, 775; united, 782.

— and Bourses du Travail, 245, 250; views on, 255 (Bietry); 260 (Resseguier); 426 (republicans); 441, 446 (Fourier); 443–4 (Considérant); 452 (Cabet); 454–5 (Buchez); 455–8 (Buchez's followers); 458–66 (Proudhon); 608 (Thiers); 641 (opportunists); 645–6, 660 (solidarists); 652–3 (Méline); 657 (Bourgeois);

— and the 'faceless plutocracy', 61; and the workers, 169, 170, 231, 242; and peasants, 190; and printers, 218; and miners, 224; and capitalists, 232; and unions, 237, 240; and feminists, 345–6; and Orleanists, 419; and civil servants, 719; and the radicals, 722; in the Constituent Assembly, 496; in 1851–2, 548; and the Boulangists, 643–4; and the solidarists, 654–9; and the co-operative movement, 664; and Waldeck-Rousseau, 674, 676, 679; and Dreyfus Affair, 681; and Combes, 686–8; Vallès as a, 336; comte de Paris as a, 423; Clemenceau as a, 700, 707.

Social life, 43, 126, 169, 299, 339–40.

Social mobility: 90, 92, 109, 115, 125, 126, 186, 273, 274, 287, 335–6; *les*

nouvelles couches sociales, 19, 613–14, 620, 621, 649, 658.

Social questions, interest in, 72, 99, 105, 136, 230, 233, 243, 244, 248, 272, 324, 341, 349, 474, 509, 512, 616, 640, 657, 660–4, 665–73, 716, 723, 763.

Social security, 32, 109, 136.

Social status, 14, 17, 30, 32, 36, 59, 89, 90, 113, 124–5, 135, 155, 156, 189, 266, 272–3, 276, 280, 294, 346, 429, 466, 481.

Société générale, 56, 84.

Societies: bourgeois defence, 20; mutual benefit and insurance, 32, 72, 180, 409, 487, 629, 660–3; painting, 41; folklore, 133; agricultural credit, 175; milk-yield recording, 188; restrictions on, 205; friendly, 215, 218, 222, 227, 231, 257, 271, 478, 561, 654, 735; Compagnonnage, 213; to fight venereal disease, 305; antipornographic, 311; puritan, 312; provincial learned, 324; secret, 358, 409, 492, 725, 727, 748; musical, 478; philanthropico-harmonic, 478.

Society: for encouragement of Agriculture, National, 191; Agricultural, of Senlis, 153; Agricultural, of Meaux, 154; Les Amis de Proudhon, 465; Bookbinders Friendly, 735; of Civil Engineers, 104; of French Farmers, 190–1; Hatters', 458; of Jaurès Studies, 758; against Licence in the Streets, 312; of the Rights of Man, 756; for Sanitary and Moral Prophylaxis, 304; of St Vincent de Paul, 409, 672.

Soissonnais, 153, 186.

Solicitors, in parliament under Third Republic, 577.

Solidarism, 446, 640–81, 707.

Songs, politics in, 432.

Sorbonne, the, 126, 324, 344, 428, 446, 483.

Sorel, Georges (1847–1922), 446.

Soulié de Morant, Georges (1878–1955), 29.

South of France, the, 46, 116, 137–8, 144, 149, 151, 160, 165, 167, 169, 177, 179, 186, 190, 193, 282, 289–90, 308–9, 367, 390, 397, 409, 477–8, 491–2, 506, 532–5, 725, 749, 751, 783, 785.

South America, 104, 167, 373.

Spain, 82, 104, 381, 545.

Speculators, 60.

Sports, adolescents and the cult of, 334.

Spuller, Eugène (1835–96), deputy 1876–92, Senator 1892–6, under-secretary 1881–2, minister 1887 and 1889, editor of *La République française*, 612, 613, 645.

St Chéron, M. de, 413.

St Cyr, graduates of, 19.

Steeg, Jules (1836–98), Protestant pastor, deputy for Bordeaux 1881–90, inspector general of education and director of the musée pedagogique 1890–6, director of the école normale de Fontenay 1896–8, 627.

Steel, *see* Iron and steel.

Steele, Henry, English worker in France, 272.

Steinlen, T. A., 778.

Stendhal (Henri Beyle) (1783–1842), 77, 430.

Stern, Daniel, pseudonym of comtesse d'Agoult, *q.v.*

St Étienne, 56, 106, 222, 270–1, 308.

St Gobain, 55–6, 190.

Stopes, Marie (1880–1958), on female right to orgasm, 295.

Strasbourg, 309.

Strikes: legislation on, 205, 208–9, 490, 546–7, 673–4; peasants and, 136, 171, 195; woodcutters, 193; miners, 209, 222–4, 668, 705; artisans, 213, 218; printers, 219; railway, 227–8, 279; various, *227–43*; women's, 258; troops used in, 259, 475, 732; employers and, 260, 267; C.G.T. and, 276, 279–81; Bourses du Travail and, 249–51; occupation of factories, 281; students and, 482; in Paris, 487; Clemenceau and, 705; and the First International, 730–2; Guesde and, 746; *also* 221, 465–6, 475, 493, 540.

Students: and fall of Louis-Philippe, 468; in politics, 480–2, 489; sex life, 310; hair styles, 481; mission of, according to Michelet, 482–3; middle aged, 613.

Sue, Eugène (1804–57), 446.

Suez Canal, 190, 442, 510.

Superstition, 27, 132, 562, 787.

Sweden, 174.

Switzerland, 72, 77, 107, 174, 465, 545, 755, 777.

Syndicalism, *231–41*; revolutionary, 274, 465, 778; anarcho-, 279.

Syphilis, *304–6*; national expert on, 24; Joseph Rollet on, 25; doctors and, 32 n.; Flaubert on, 304.

Taine, Hippolyte A. (1828–93), on strength of traditions, 355; on the rebuilding of Paris, 554; *Origins of Contemporary France*, 744.

Talleyrand, 319, 514.

Talleyrand-Perigord, Charles de (1754–1838), duc de Dino, 405.

Tarde, Gabriel de (1843–1904), 660.

Tardieu, André (1876–1945), 586, 592.

Tarentaise, Bishop of, after the separation, 696.

Tarn, 265, 684, 759.

Tarn-et-Garonne, 132, 149 n.

Taxation: and the notaries, 44, 48, 50, 52; and shopkeepers, 107–8; frauds and, 108, 117; on inheritance, 147; and the peasants, 133, 136, 176, 491, 512, 635, 711, 750; on dogs, 160; on wine, 166, 168, 193; local taxation, 523; and married women, 356; on land, 148, 461, 711; in Corsica, 535, 710; income, 176, 592, 610, 614, 643, 657, 675, 711–12, 716, 721–4, 765; Thiers' conservatism on, 610; ecclesiastical, 696; *also* 55, 61, 80, 113, 126, 128, 204, 239, 400, 404, 477, 493, 497, 498, 522–5, 530, 556, 567, 569, 635, 643, 646, 651, 658, 675, 718, 728, 742, 764.

Teachers: workers' attitude to, 30; university and secondary, 120; unionisation and, 280; Alfred Binet on, 325; and peer groups at school, 339; lack of trained, 344; women, 292, 359, 626, 695; social background and status of, 481; and republicanism, 482, 492; as leaders of student agitation, 482; persecution of, 483; appointment by prefect of, 523; power in the villages, 528–9; Combes' salary as a, 684; in left-wing societies, 728; in the Paris Commune, 738; *also* 123, 129, 175, 194, 338. *See also* Education, Instituteurs.

Telegraph, 553.

Telephone, 180.

Tenant farmers, 152–60; indebtedness of, 136; protection of, 143 n.; politics, 374; Proudhon on, 461–2; in the agricultural crisis, 472.

Terny, 154.

Teste, vice-president of federation of employers' unions, 260.

Textile industry, 64–70; employees in, 102, 179, 239, 746–7; industrialists, 153; regions, 169; conseils de Prud'-hommes and, 201; protection of, 204; concentration in, 210; unions in, 240, 242; and the counter-revolution, 378; and the crisis of 1848, 473.

Theatre: and prostitution, 310; receipts of the, 311; sex in the, 311; portrayals of women in the, 355; in the villages, 478.
Thiérache, 138.
Thiers, Adolphe (1797–1877), 69, 81, 199, 414, 419, 423, 449, 469, 500, 519–20, 549–50, 553, 563, *606–10*, 618, 650, 737.
Thiery, de Bercegol du Moulin, 403.
Thivrier, Christophe (1841–95), 577, 748.
Thomas, Albert (1878–1932), 767.
Thouvenel, Edouard Antoine (1818–66), 558.
Thureau-Dangin, Paul (1837–1913), 56.
Tilly, Charles, on politics in the Vendée, 378.
Tocqueville, Alexis Clérel de (1805–59), 368, 389, 468, 505, 521, 536, 655.
Tolain, Henri (1828–97), 247, 263–4, 729–30; life of, *733–4*, 745.
Tonkin, 631.
Toryism, radical, 396.
Totain, Nicolas (b. 1782), 726.
Toulon, 479, 770.
Toulouse, 397, 696, 759, 763.
Touraine, Alain, on workers' ambitions, 268–9.
Tourists, 157, 773.
Tours, 35.
Toussenel, Alphonse (1803–85), Fourierist, anti-semite and writer on birds, animals and hunting, 77.
Towns: notaries in, 44–6, 48, 51; industrialists in, 65; banks in, 79; shopkeepers in, 109; civil servants in small, 116; and country conflicts, 131, 134, 377–8; migration to, 136, 145, 171–3; wine tax in, 166; peasants and, 169, 190, 195; wages in, 170; slums in, 170; food for, 177, 185; doctors in, 189; conciliation tribunals in, 201–2; Chambres de Commerce in, 203; artisans in, 212, 215, 377; workers and unions in, 243, 356, 269; social class in large, 282; romanticism in small, 286; prostitution in, 308; politics in, 366, 372, 377, 397, 409, 410, 491; Ledru-Rollin on, 494; and railway development, 533; representation of, 591.
Trade, free, 68, 69, 204, 509, 545–6, 567, 649.
Trade Unions:
— notaries, 52; civil service, 120, 125, 278; semi-skilled, 278; agricultural, 180, 191, 193–4, 196, 252; employers',

203–5; printers', 218–20, 241–2; miners', 220–6, 267, 277; Yellow, 243, 253–6; metal workers', 279; railwaymen's, 226–9, 278; building workers', 213–14, 229–30, 277; cooks', 230–1; leather workers', 257; porcelain workers', 258; corsetmakers', 259; teachers', 706.
— conciliation, 202, 668; growth of, 203–5, 212–15, *217–43*; legislation on, 203–9, 546; court decisions on, 207–9; finances of, 207, 239–41; guilds', 212; membership figures, 222, 227, 229, 254, 257, 278–80; leaders, 264–5; after 1914, 274–82.
— and employers, 70, 243, 253 ff., 260–4, 267, 276; and government, 191; and revolution, 231 ff.; and Bourses du Travail, 243–5; and women, 258, 357; writers on, 455, 465, 490, 493; politicians and, 493, 623, 674, 720; socialists and, 734–5, 746, 749, 751, 754, 763, 766, 768, 773, 774; anarchists and, 776–8.
— Confédération Générale du Travail, 233–41, 249–50, 252, 257, 272, 274, 275–82, 346; provincial, 256–60; in Ardèche, 256–7; in Limoges, 257–8; in Le Creusot, 259; and England, 259, 261–2, 423.
Transport, 106, 128, 180, 202, 263, 277, 545, 553, 651, 635–8, 651, 754.
Trégorrois, 373.
Treich, leader of trade union movement in Limoges, 258.
Trélazé, 258.
Trempé, Rolande, *Les Mineurs de Carmaux*, 267.
Tribunal de Commerce, 204.
Tridon, E. M. Gustave (1841–71), 739.
Trochu, Abbé, ran *L'Ouest-Eclair*, 193.
Tronchin, Dr. Théodore (1709–81), 24.
Troplong, Raymond Théodore (1795–1869), First President of Cour de Cassation, 199, 537.
Trotsky, Leo (1879–1940), on Jaurès, 761.
Troyes, 748.
Tsar of Russia, consultant to the, 41.
Tunis, 630.
Turgot, Anne Robert Jacques (1727–81), 396, 501.

Unemployment, 227, 243, 248, 252, 254, 268, 276, 359, 470, 472–4, 489, 497, 651, 658.
Union: Conservatrice, 424, 425; Fédérale, 225; Federation of, 232; Française pour le suffrage des femmes, 350;

Union (*cont.*):
Nationale des Chambres Syndicales, 204; of Ouvriers Megissiers Palisonneurs, 257; des Phalanstériens, 442; Républicaine, 537; Sacrée, 275; Socialiste, 780; Société de l', 215; Le Soleil, 257; des Syndicats Sainte-Barbe, 253; des Travailleurs, 257; Universelle pour le progrès de l'art culinaire, 231; Vosges Bookworkers', 242.

Universal suffrage: peasants and, 131, 491; Pelloutier and, 250; notables and, 381, 396, 408, 496, 531; Guizot on, 416; Bonapartists and, 419, 507, 508, 511, 521–2, 562, 568; comte de Paris on, 424; Louis Blanc and, 447–9; Proudhon on, 464; Lamartine and, 486; Church and, 499; Marie on, 502; Thiers on, 608; Gambetta and, 613, 614, 618; Ferry on, 623.

Universities: role in Third Republic, 12, 603; teachers in, 120; statistics of men and women at, 344, 480; women professors at, 359; and claims of nobility, 402; Olinde Rodrigues on role of, 438; and the Second Empire, 551; suppression of Catholic, 626; Ferry's lay, 630.

Urbanisation, 377, 378, 381, 384. *See also* Towns, Provincial, Villages.

U.S.A., 14, 35, 64, 68, 93, 104, 107, 188, 303, 305–6, 321, 346, 373, 387, 391, 422, 446, 452, 583, 624, 643.

Ussel, 784.

Usury, 80, 164, 532, *See also* Debt.

Utopians: role of, 428–33, 466; Saint-Simon, 433–5; Saint-Simonians, 436–8, their influence, 438; Fourier, 438–42; Fourierists, 442–6; Louis Blanc, 447–9; Cabet, 449–51; 'communists', 452; Pierre Leroux, 452–4; Buchez, 454–6; L'Atelier, 446–7; Proudhon, 458–65; *also* 294, 487, 510.

Uzès, Marie-Clémentine de Rochechouart-Mortemart, duchesse d' (1847–1933), 425.

Vacherot, Etienne (1809–97), 483, 501.

Vaillant, Dr. Edouard (1840–1915), 741.

Valensole, 150.

Valéry, Paul (1871–1945), 294.

Vallès, Jules (1832–85), 335–7, 729, 780.

Var, 112, 149 n., 160, 183, 472, 477, 783–4.

Varenne, Alexandre, 767.

Varlin, Eugène (1839–71), 732, *734–5* 739.

Vaucluse, the, 112, 181, 185, 409, 727, 785.

Vaussay, comte de, 399.

Vendée, the, 27, 138–9, 373, 378, 395, 533, 699, 702, 703.

Venette, Dr. Nicolas (1633–98), 296.

Verbalism, 340, 342.

Vermorel, Auguste (1841–71), 739.

Versailles, 415, 563, 737, 740, 743–5.

Vibraye, marquis de, 405.

Vichy, 308, 702.

Vichy Régime, 8, 36, 195–6, 285, 359, 465.

Vickers-Armstrong, armaments firm, 703.

Vidauban, 784.

Vieillard, Narcisse (1791–1857), artillery officer, tutor to Napoleon III, deputy 1848–51, senator 1852–7 republican-Bonapartist, 510.

Vienne, 170, 783.

Vigier, Philippe, 149, 381–2.

Villages: types of, 134, 137–9, 141, 142, 150, 189, 378–9; notaries in, 44; in Corsica, 140; commons, 157; winegrowing, 169; emigration, 172; history of Morette, 178–80; modernisation in, 183–6; unions in, 193, 195–6; politics in, 366, 370, 382, 390, 409, 477–9; conscription in, 379; power in, 407, 522, 529; clubs, 409, 478–9; police in, 517; administration of, 522–7; history of Plibou, 524–7; Bonapartism and, 540–1; clergy and, 695.

Ville, Georges (1824–97), 782.

Villejuif, 602.

Villèle, Jean Baptiste, comte de (1773–1854), minister 1822–8, 315.

Villeneuve-Saint-Georges, 705.

Violence, 214–15, 341.

Viollet, Jean, 321–2.

Viollet le Duc, Eugène Emmanuel (1814–79), 129.

Viollette, Maurice (1870–1960), socialist deputy 1902–30, minister 1917, 1936–8, governor of Algeria 1925, senator 1930–9, 71, 73.

Viviani, René (1863–1925), 348, 360, 598, 663, 695, 706, 708, 760, 767, 773.

Vlaminck, Maurice de (1876–1958), 778.

Voguë, C. J. Melchior, marquis de (1829–1916), 56, 190.

Voguë, family, 54.

Voltaire, F. M. Arouet de (1694–1778), 4, 24, 429–30, 500, 685, 781.

Vosges, the, 81, 158, 169, 183, 204, 241, 242, 650.

Waddington, William Henry (1826–94), 627.
Wages, 198, 200–2, 218, 244, 265, 267, 268, 488; textile workers', 242; miners, 264, 556, women's, 346, 356, 359; and insurance, 275; collective bargaining on, 276; utopians and, 445, 452, 455, 456; solidarists on, 658, 669; Commune and, 742.
Waldeck-Rousseau, René (1846–1904), 55, 57, 222, 245, 254, 486, 590, 594, 671–9, 685, 686–8, 713, 765, 772.
Walewski, Alexandre Colonna, Comte (1810–68), son of Napoleon I, ambassador, foreign minister 1855–60, minister of state 1860–3, president of the legislature 1865–7, father of a son by the actress Rachel, 558.
Wassy, 185.
Watt, James (1736–1819), 96.
Watchmakers, 72, 241, 254, 262, 747.
Weavers, 210, 214, 218, 241, 475, 477, 491, 747; politics of, 376–7.
Weiss, Louise (b. 1893), agrégée, editor of l'Europe nouvelle 1918–34, and Nouvelle république 1942–4, president of La Femme nouvelle, for equal rights, 1934–9, 350.
Wendel family, 55, 70, 75, 76, 81.
Wendel, François de (1) (1778–1824), 75.
Wendel François de (2) (1874–1949), 76.
Wendel, Ignace de (1741–95), 75.
West of France, the, 137–8, 190, 194, 282, 366, 390, 396, 409–10, 475–7, 506, 532, 747.
Wheat production, 174, 182.
Wilkinson, William (d. 1808), 75.
William II, Emperor of Germany, 659.
Wilson, Daniel (1840–1902), 583, 643.
Wine: history of production and consumption of, 165–7; politics and mentality of growers, 168–9; income from, 174; taxation of, 166, 545; also 77, 176, 185, 189, 192, 193, 473, 706, 785.
Witt-Schlumberger, Madame de, 349 n.
Wives: of bourgeoisie and workers, 18; of officers, 19; as shopkeepers, 44, 179, 261; relations with husbands, 49; rich, 78; and husbands working together, 110; of peasants, 132, 157, 162; 285–362; Monsieur, Madame et

bébé, 328; Alain on, 329. See also Women and Husbands.
Wolfenstein, Martha, 342.
Women: in marriage, 18, 21, 66, 169, 285–314, 318, 343–62; at work, 59, 143 n., 185, 199, 668, 695; and fashion, 180; and politics, 202, 389, 488, 490, 345–9, 354, 592; magazines for, 322; women's liberation, 338, 343–62, 436, 437, 438, 440, 460, 625–6, 775; legal inferiority of, 343, 356–7; educational handicaps for, 344; writers for and against, 345; feminist movement, 345–50; 1914–18 war and, 351; conservatism, 353–4; divorce, 357–8; abortion, 359; wages, 359; in professions, 359; vote, 360.
Wool, 546.
Workers: legal restraints on, 198–209, 709; numbers of, 209–10; divisions among, 210–12; earnings of, 59, 100, 170, 211; pensions, 666–7; savings, 62, 85, 556; mutual insurance, 664, 708–9, 741, 763; accident insurance, 667; and unions, 203–82; and eight-hour day, 669; utopians and, 435, 437, 438, 445, 447, 455–7, 462–5; and republicanism, 479, 487, 488–90, 493, 615, 623; and Bonapartism, 512, 539, 540, 551, 555–6; and socialism, 746, 751, 753, 755, 757, 763–4, 773; and anarchism, 778; and Boulangism, 646; and employers, 253–74; and eight-hour day, 669; and bourgeoisie, 18–19, 272–3; and peasants, 158, 190, 265; women, 155, 302, 306, 350; and Workers International, 729–30; and the Commune, 744; and culture, 264–74; drinking, 165, 166; voting, 169; education, 247.
Worms et Cie, 81.
Wortley, Violet Stuart, 346.
Writers: status of, 428–9; and Saint-Simonianism, 436.
Wylie, Lawrence, 183, 325, 332.

Young, Arthur, 443.
Yver, Colette, Mme Huzard de Bergevin (1874–1953), on women, 354.
Yvetot, Georges (1868–1942), secretary of Bourses section of the C.G.T. 236; successor to Pelloutier, 252; and revolutionary syndicalism, 778.

Zévaès, Alexandre, the Guesdist propagandist, 751.
Zola, Émile (1840–1902), 132, 134, 325, 446, 786.